Instructor's Annotated Edition

Second Edition

À votre tour!

Instructor's Annotated Edition

Second Edition

À votre tour!

Jean-Paul Valette
Rebecca M. Valette
Boston College

Houghton Mifflin Company
Boston New York

Publisher: Rolando Hernández
Sponsoring Editor: Viki Kellar
Associate Editor: Caitlin McIntyre
Editorial Assistant: Erin Beasley
Project Editor: Andrea Dodge
Editorial Assistant: Carrie Parker
Art and Design Manager: Gary Crespo
Senior Photo Editor: Jennifer Meyer Dare
Composition Buyer: Chuck Dutton
Senior Manufacturing Buyer: Karen B. Fawcett
Executive Marketing Director: Eileen Bernadette Moran
Marketing Assistant: Lorreen Ruth Pelletier

Cover photo: "Peniscola" by Andre Duret/Private Collection/Bridgeman Art Library. © 2005 Artists Rights Society (ARS), New York.

Printed in the U.S.A.

Library of Congress Control Number: 2006925034

Instructor's Annotated Edition
ISBN-10: 0-618-69316-5
ISBN-13: 978-0-618-69316-0

For orders, use student text ISBNs
ISBN-10: 0-618-69315-7
ISBN-13: 978-0-618-69315-3

3456789-CRK-10 09 08 07

Preface

À votre tour! is an integrated intermediate college program for students who need an in-depth review of the basic patterns and structures of French. It is particularly appropriate for students who have had two or three years of secondary school French followed by a hiatus of a couple of years during which time they have lost contact with the language. **À votre tour!** is designed to give such students the opportunity to reactivate their prior knowledge and to expand upon that base so that they can learn to communicate with confidence, using the French language creatively in conversational exchanges. The program also introduces students to a broad range of intermediate-level reading materials: magazine articles, informational texts, short stories, and literary selections.

As we were planning the development of **À votre tour!**, we wanted to construct a text that would reflect the style and manner in which intermediate French courses are generally taught. At this level, the teaching of French is no longer linear, and instructors have considerable flexibility in choosing the material they want to present and the skills they want to emphasize. What instructors told us they wanted was a single textbook that could be used as a base for further expansion in the directions of their choice, whether this be communication, vocabulary building, cultural awareness, reading, or grammar. Our aim was, therefore, to create a book that would give instructors a maximum of flexibility by offering different strands to build upon: vocabulary, language, daily-life culture as well as French and francophone civilization.

While the units of **À votre tour!** follow a logical progression in terms of increasing complexity, the text is not meant to be "taught" in a linear manner, beginning with the first page and continuing sequentially to the last page. Rather, each college instructor or course coordinator is encouraged to establish a syllabus on the basis of the skills or outcomes he or she wishes to emphasize. Perhaps this will mean concentrating on certain sections and skipping others or occasionally referring ahead or going back to specific information that is presented in other parts of the text. An instructor who wants to stress oral communication in daily-life situations may wish, for example, to concentrate primarily on the *Français pratique* sections. Another instructor, interested in French civilization and the multi-cultural and mutli-ethnic aspects of the French-speaking world, may allocate much more classroom time to the *Interludes culturels*. Still another instructor, preferring to focus on control of structure and building the reading skill, will spend more time with the *Langue et communication* sections and the *Lectures* and will refer as needed to the information contained in the *Interuludes culturels* to elucidate specific points of French and francophone cultural background. Again, the key consideration is FLEXIBILITY.

Another important point that we would like to mention is that **À votre tour!** is not simply a textbook but an integrated program whose components can be used to develop further the communicative skills and cultural awareness emphasized in the text. *The Written Activities* section of the **Student Activities Manual** reinforces both reading and writing skills. This is where students will find ample opportunity to review and practice the structures and vocabulary presented in the text. The **Audio Program** in conjunction with the *Listening Activities* portion of the **Student Activities Manual** builds the listening skill. The **Video/DVD Program** provides a *vidéo-drame* for each unit, using that unit's vocabulary in context. In addition to these program components, we highly recommend the classroom use of authentic French films. To this effect, we have selected three movies that are particularly appropriate for their general appeal as well as for their very different cultural content. Introductions to these three movies, **Cyrano, Rue Cases-nègres** and **Au revior, les Enfants,** are presented in the *Interludes culturels*.

Finally, the most important aspect of **À votre tour!**, that aspect which distinguishes the text from other intermediate programs, is its ACCESSIBILITY. The program welcomes students where they are, recognizing that they may have forgotten much of what they once knew, and gradually lets them rebuild their language skills and improve their proficiency while discovering the variety and the richness of the francophone world.

Although for many students the completion of intermediate French marks the end of their French studies, we hope that **À votre tour!** will stimulate their interest in both the French language and the culture of those who speak that language, so that they will want to maintain their language skills by taking further courses and perhaps even by traveling, studying or working abroad. Whether they simply enjoy seeing a French film from time to time or whether they become truly bilingual, it is our hope that French will become a meaningful part of their lives.

Jean-Paul Valette Rebecca M. Valette

We would like to thank the following persons for helping us acquire a better insight into their area of the French-speaking world:

Thierry Gustave
Martinique

Yasmina Hacien-Bey
Algeria

Kouadio Konan
Ivory Coast

Ourida Mostefai
Algeria

Introducing À VOTRE TOUR!

À votre tour! immerses students in authentic cultural contexts and language designed to develop and expand effective communication in French.

À votre tour! is a flexible, integrated skills approach to Intermediate French. It provides extensive reading opportunities; varied writing practice; continuing thematic vocabulary and language development; and a wide range of communication activities.

Key Objectives

- Build and reinforce active communication skills
- Develop reading skills and cultural awareness
- Build a strong linguistic base
- Stimulate students' interest in French language and culture so that they will want to continue their study beyond the intermediate level

Key Features

- **Integrated Video/DVD Program** immerses students in authentic language and supports vocabulary development.
- **Cultural Connections** are developed through presentation of the culture of France and the French-speaking world.
- An emphasis on **daily-life themes** develops and expands effective communication.
- Abundant use of **authentic realia** and illustrative material in support of the text provides cultural context and extends learning opportunities.
- A **flexible program** that allows teachers to teach according to their own style and objectives
- A strong **reading strand** that includes reading for pleasure, reading for content and reading fiction
- Abundant **writing practice** in a variety of formats
- **Introduction to literature** is provided through short stories, poems, and brief introductions to important works by French and francophone authors.

Organization of À VOTRE TOUR!

The Student Text contains

- brief review section, **Reprise**
- ten basic units
- ten cultural sections, **Interludes culturels**

Reprise

À votre tour! begins with a short review of basic communicative structures. Students have the opportunity to identify their own strong and weak points, and design their own individualized review.

The Basic Units

The ten units of the text introduce expanded thematic vocabulary and more complex language functions.

Info Magazine Consists of flexible reading sections that introduce and expand the unit theme in a magazine format. The personalized style reflects the viewpoints, attitudes, and accomplishments of young people. Articles and short interviews are illustrated with authentic realia materials, photos and art.

Le Français pratique Presents and activates conversational patterns and useful vocabulary. Students actively participate in a wide variety of oral and written activities for communication practice and self-expression on daily-life topics.

Langue et communication Presents and activates the linguistic goals for each section with a focus on functional language use.

Lecture Offers a short story or fictional piece accompanied by a variety of pre-reading and post-reading activities.

Interludes culturels These cultural interludes provide basic information on the culture, history, art and literature of France and other parts of the French-speaking world: North Africa, West Africa, the Antilles, and North America.

Organization of a Unit

Each unit has a main theme which is developed across its different sections. A unit consists of two (and sometimes three) parts, each introduced by an **Info Magazine** section. Each part of a unit consists of two integrated sections: **Le Français pratique** and **Langue et communication**. The unit ends with a **Lecture**. Units are linked to each other with an **Interlude Culturel**.

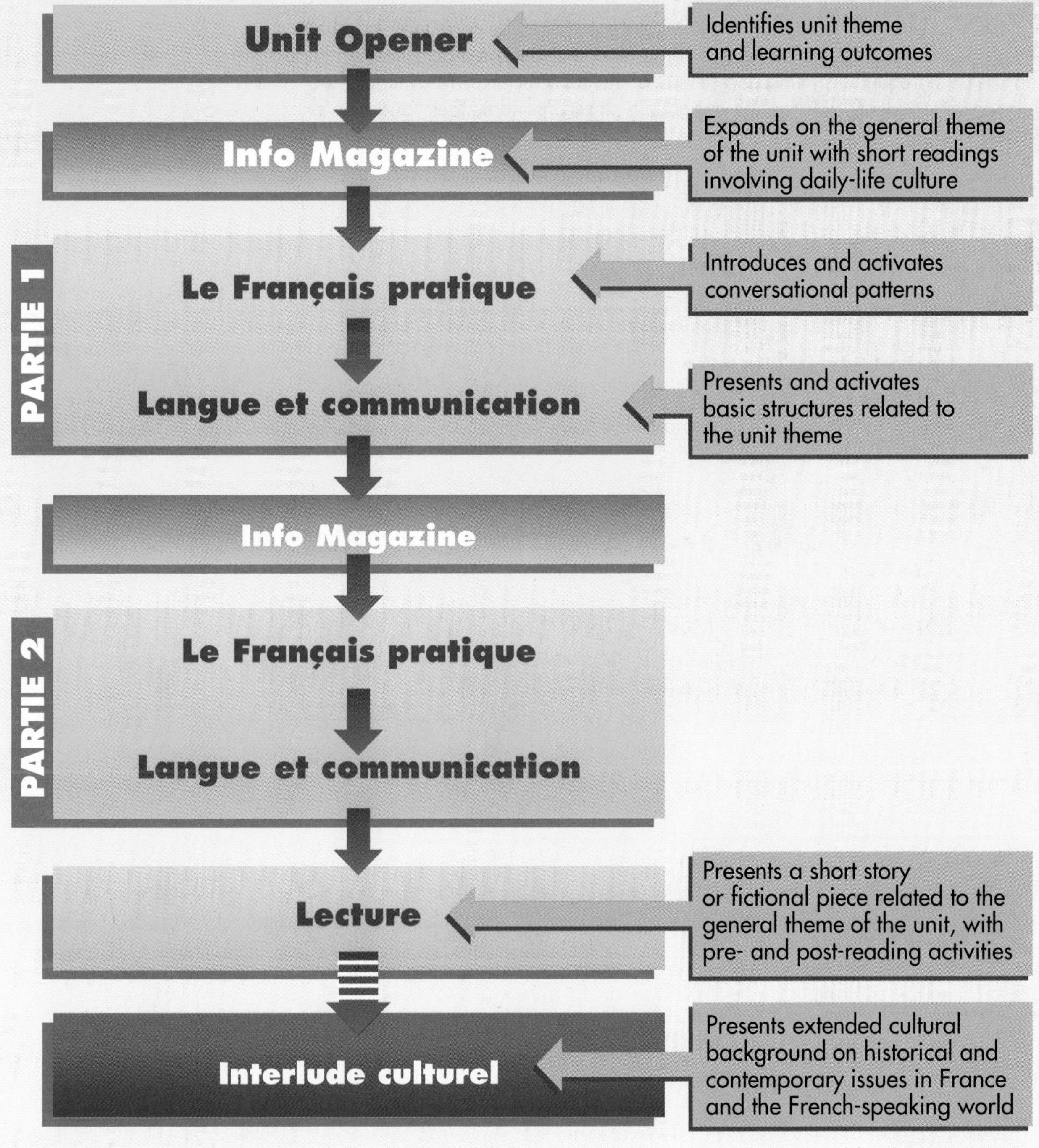

Unit Opener
Identifies unit theme and learning outcomes
Info Magazine
Expands on the general theme of the unit with short readings involving daily-life culture
PARTIE 1
Le Français pratique
Introduces and activates conversational patterns
Langue et communication
Presents and activates basic structures related to the unit theme
Info Magazine
PARTIE 2
Le Français pratique
Langue et communication
Lecture
Presents a short story or fictional piece related to the general theme of the unit, with pre- and post-reading activities
Interlude culturel
Presents extended cultural background on historical and contemporary issues in France and the French-speaking world

Planning the Syllabus

With the *Reprise* chapter and its correlated review charts in Appendix A, students can quickly consolidate the French they once knew. The interpersonal activities during these first days of the academic year give students the opportunity to meet one another as they practice the basic structures in a variety of communicative formats. By taking the time to establish a firm linguistic base at the outset of the course, instructors will find that their students acquire a renewed confidence in their French skills and that the subsequent units will proceed more smoothly. It should be noted that the amount of time spent on the Reprise will depend on the background of the class.

After the *Reprise*, classes will typically spend about two weeks on each of the core units. In courses that meet only three hours a week students will not be able to do all of the suggested activities. An important feature of the program is the regular recycling and reentry of the key structures. This means that, whatever the pace of the course, students will have the opportunity to reconsolidate their language skills as the program progresses.

Sample Syllabi

The following sample show how **À votre tour!** can be scheduled for various configurations of classes on both the semester and the quarter system. Obviously, instructors whose courses meet more frequently will have greater flexibility in their scheduling. Instructors whose courses meet less frequently might find it more appropriate to complete only nine units.

In all of the sample syllabi, we have allowed two class periods for the viewing of the three films that are presented in the Interludes culturels. You will note that in Syllabus E, Units 2 and 1 have been reversed. This flexibility is also possible in other configurations.

A. Two semesters (courses meeting 5 times a week, 15 weeks): ca. 63 days

First semester		Second semester	
Reprise	9 days 1 day: test	**Warmup/review**	2 days
Unit 1	9 days 1 day: test	**Unit 6** film	10 days 1 day: test 2 days
Unit 2	9 days 1 day: test	**Unit 7**	10 days 1 day: test
Unit 3 (film)	9 days 1 day: test 2 days	**Unit 8** (film)	10 days 1 day: test 2 days
Unit 4	9 days 1 day: test	**Unit 9**	10 days 1 day: test
Unit 5	9 days 1 day: test	**Unit 10**	10 days 1 day: test
Review	1 day	**Review**	2 days

B. Two semesters (courses meeting 4 times a week, 15 weeks): ca. 54 days

First semester		Second semester	
Reprise	7 days 1 day: test	**Warmup/review**	2 days
Unit 1	8 days 1 day: test	**Unit 6** (film)	8 days 1 day: test 2 days
Unit 2	8 days 1 day: test	**Unit 7**	8 days 1 day: test
Unit 3 (film)	8 days 1 day: test 2 days	**Unit 8** (film)	8 days 1 day: test 2 days
Unit 4	7 days 1 day: test	**Unit 9**	8 days 1 day: test
Unit 5	7 days 1 day: test	**Unit 10**	8 days 1 day: test
Review	2 days	**Review**	2 days

C. Two semesters (courses meeting 3 times a week, 15 weeks): ca. 41 days

First semester		Second semester	
Reprise	8 days 1 day: test	**Warmup/review**	1 day
Unit 1	6 days 1 day: test	**Unit 5**	6 days 1 day: test
Unit 2	6 days 1 day: test	**Unit 6** (film)	6 days 1 day: test 2 days
Unit 3 (film)	7 days 1 day: test 2 days	**Unit 7**	6 days 1 day: test
Unit 4	6 days 1 day: test	**Unit 8** (film)	6 days 1 day: test 2 days
Review	1 day 1 day: test	**Unit 9**	6 days
		Review	1 day

D. Two quarters (courses meeting 5 times a week, 10 weeks): ca. 45 days

First quarter		Second quarter	
Reprise	8 days 1 day: test	**Warmup/review**	1 day
Unit 1	6 days 1 day: test	**Unit 5, pt. 2**	3 days
Unit 2	6 days 1 day: test	**Unit 6** (film)	6 days 1 day: test 2 days
Unit 3 (film)	6 days 1 day: test 2 days	**Unit 7**	6 days 1 day: test
Unit 4	6 days 1 day: test	**Unit 8** (film)	6 days 1 day: test 2 days
Unit 5, pt .1	3 days	**Unit 9**	6 days 1 day: test
Review	2 days	**Unit 10**	6 days 1 day: test
		Review	2 days

E. Three quarters (courses meeting 3 times a week, 10 weeks): ca. 28 days

First quarter		Second quarter		Third quarter	
Reprise	6 days 1 day: test	**Warmup/ review**	1 day	**Warmup/ review**	1 day
Unit 2	6 days 1 day: test	**Unit 4**	6 days 1 day: test	**Unit 7, pt. 2**	3 days 1 day: test
Unit 1	6 days 1 day: test	**Unit 5**	6 days 1 day: test	**Unit 8** (film)	6 days 1 day: test 2 days
Unit 3	6 days	**Unit 6** (film)	6 days 1 day: test 2 days	**Unit 9**	6 days 1 day: test
Review	1 day	**Unit 7, pt. 1**	3 days	**Unit 10**	6 days
		Review	1 day	**Review**	1 day

Scope and Sequence

The following charts present the scope and sequence of À votre tour!, according to the two main objectives of the Student Text:

- Development and reinforcement of the communication skills
- Development of reading skills and cultural awareness

Reprise

OBJECTIVE Light review of basic patterns and structures of French

BASIC REVIEW	
	Structures
A. La vie courante	■ *Describing the present* • Present of regular verbs • **Être, avoir, aller, faire, venir** and expressions used with these verbs • Other common irregular verbs • Use of present with **depuis** • Regular and irregular adjectives • Use of the partitive article
B. Hier et avant	■ *Describing the past* • Passé composé with **avoir** and **être** • Imperfect and its basic uses
C. Nous et les autres	■ *Referring to people, things, and places* • Object pronouns • Negative expressions • **Connaître** and **savoir** • Other irregular verbs

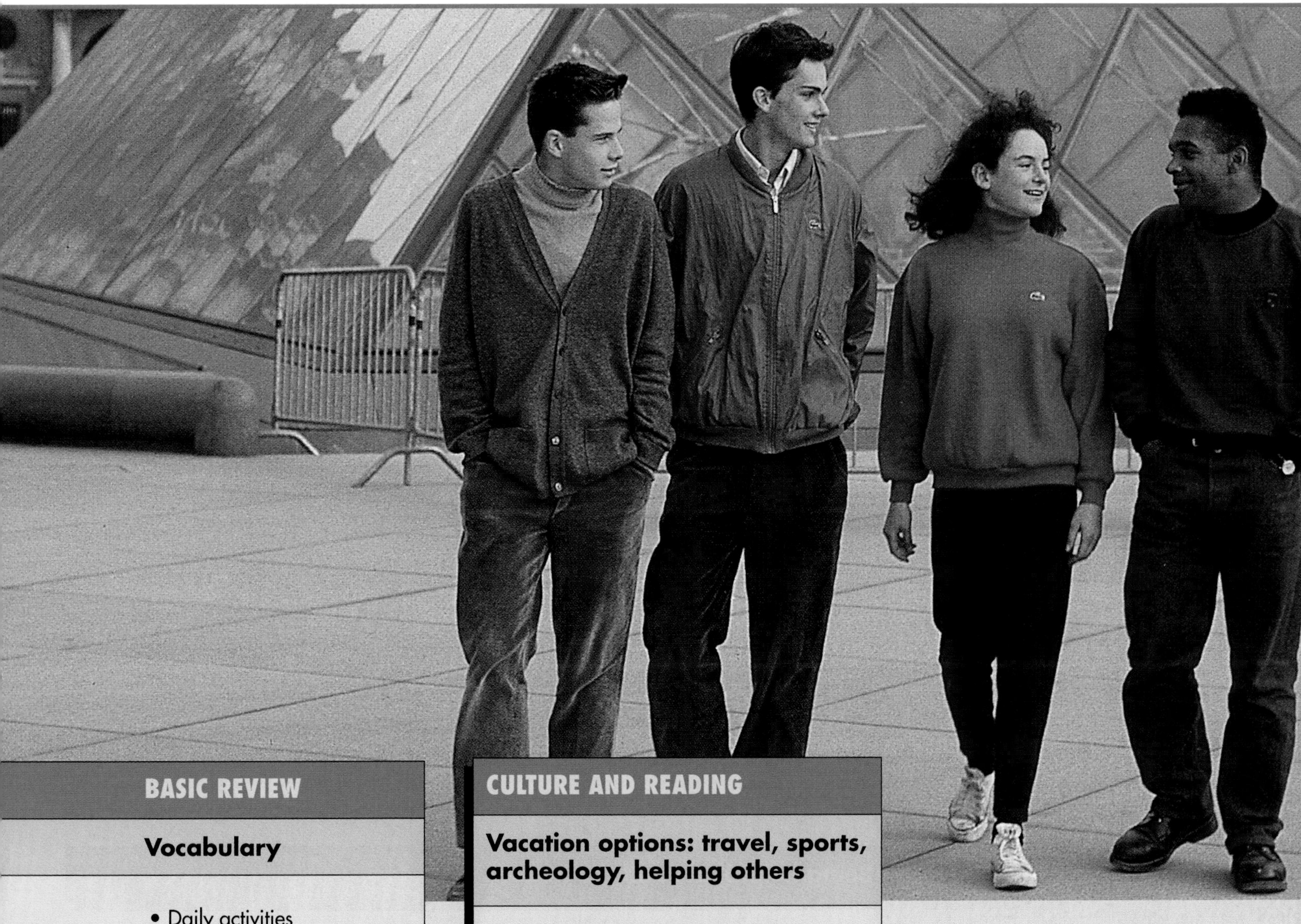

BASIC REVIEW	CULTURE AND READING
Vocabulary	**Vacation options: travel, sports, archeology, helping others**
• Daily activities • Food and beverages	***The French-speaking world:*** Its people
• Clothes	***The French-speaking world:*** Cultural background
	Lecture: *Les trois bagues*

Unité 1 Au jour le jour

MAIN THEME Looking good; one's daily routine

COMMUNICATION OBJECTIVES

COMMUNICATION FUNCTIONS AND CONTEXTS *(Le Français pratique)*	**LINGUISTIC GOALS** *(Langue et communication)*
■ *Describing people* • their physical appearance ■ *Caring for one's appearance* • personal care and hygiene • looking good ■ *Describing the various aspects of one's daily routine* ■ *Expressing how one feels and inquiring about other people*	■ *Describing people and their ailments* • the use of the definite article ■ *Describing what people do for themselves* • reflexive verbs ■ *Explaining one's daily activities* • reflexive verbs: different tenses and uses ■ *Expressing feelings and changes of mood* • reflexive verbs: idiomatic expressions

Unité 2 Soyons utiles!

MAIN THEME Being helpful around the house

COMMUNICATION OBJECTIVES

COMMUNICATION FUNCTIONS AND CONTEXTS *(Le Français pratique)*	**LINGUISTIC GOALS** *(Langue et communication)*
■ *Working around the house* • in the house itself • outside ■ *Asking for help and offering to help* • accepting or refusing help • thanking people for their help ■ *Describing an object* • shape, weight, length, consistency, appearance, etc. • the material it is made of	■ *Explaining what has to be done* • **il faut que** + subjunctive ■ *Telling people what you would like them to do* • **vouloir que** + subjunctive ■ *Expressing opinions about situations and events*

READING AND CULTURAL OBJECTIVES	
DAILY LIFE *(Info Magazine)*	**READING** *(Lecture)*
■ ***How artists have expressed their concept of beauty*** • the importance of *le look* • clothing and personal style ■ ***How important personal appearance is for French young people and what they do to enhance it*** ■ ***How people begin their daily routine***	**Ionesco**, *Conte pour enfants de moins de trois ans*

INTERLUDE CULTUREL 1
Le monde des arts

GENERAL CULTURAL BACKGROUND

French modern art
- **Impressionism** and impressionist artists: **Monet, Degas, Renoir, Manet, B. Morisot**
- Artists of the **post-impressionist** era: **Van Gogh, Gauguin, Matisse, Rousseau, Toulouse-Lautrec**
- **Surrealism** as an artistic and literary movement: **Magritte**

Poems
- **Desnos,** ***La fourmi***
- **Prévert,** ***Pour faire le portrait d'un oiseau***

READING AND CULTURAL OBJECTIVES	
DAILY LIFE *(Info Magazine)*	**READING** *(Lecture)*
■ ***Why do French people enjoy do-it-yourself activities?*** • What is **bricolage**? • What is **jardinage**? ■ ***How should you take care of your plants?*** ■ ***How do French young people earn money?***	*La Couverture* (Une fable médiévale)

INTERLUDE CULTUREL 2
Les grands moments de l'histoire de France (jusqu'en 1453)

GENERAL CULTURAL BACKGROUND

Early French history
- Important events
  - The Roman conquest
  - The Holy Roman Empire
  - The Norman Conquest of England
  - The Hundred Years War
- Important people
  - **Vercingétorix**
  - **Charlemagne**
  - **Guillaume le Conquérant**
  - **Aliénor d'Aquitaine**
  - **Jeanne d'Arc**

Literature:
La Chanson de Roland

Unité 3 Vive la nature!

MAIN THEMES Vacation and outdoor activities; the environment and its protection

COMMUNICATION OBJECTIVES

COMMUNICATION FUNCTIONS AND CONTEXTS *(Le Français pratique)*	LINGUISTIC GOALS *(Langue et communication)*
■ ***Talking about outdoor activities*** • what to do • what not to do ■ ***Describing the natural environment and how to protect it*** ■ ***Talking about the weather and natural phenomena*** ■ ***Relating a sequence of past events***	■ ***Talking about the past*** • the passé composé • the imperfect • contrastive uses of the passé composé and the imperfect ■ ***Narrating past events*** • differentiating between specific actions (passé composé) and the circumstances under which they occurred (imperfect) • providing background information (imperfect) ■ ***Reading literary accounts of past events*** • the passé simple

Unité 4 Aspects de la vie quotidienne

MAIN THEME Going shopping and asking for services

COMMUNICATION OBJECTIVES

COMMUNICATION FUNCTIONS AND CONTEXTS *(Le Français pratique)*	LINGUISTIC GOALS *(Langue et communication)*
■ ***Shopping for various items*** • in a stationery store • in a pharmacy • in a convenience store ■ ***Buying stamps and mailing items at the post office*** ■ ***Having items fixed or cleaned*** ■ ***Having one's hair cut*** ■ ***Asking for a variety of services*** • at the cleaners • at the shoe repair shop • at the photo shop	■ ***Answering questions and referring to people, things, and places using pronouns*** • the pronoun **y** • object pronouns • two-pronoun sequence ■ ***Talking about quantities*** • the pronoun **en** • indefinite expressions of quantity ■ ***Describing services that you have done by other people*** • the construction **faire** + infinitive

READING AND CULTURAL OBJECTIVES

DAILY LIFE *(Info Magazine)*	READING *(Lecture)*
■ ***How the French feel about nature and their land*** • What is **le tourisme vert**? • What is an **éco-musée**? ■ ***How do the French protect their environment?*** • What rules to observe on camping trips • What young people do to protect the environment • Who is **Jacques-Yves Cousteau**? ■ ***Why the French people love the sun***	**Sempé/Goscinny,** *King*

INTERLUDE CULTUREL 3
Les grands moments de l'histoire de France (1453–1715)

GENERAL CULTURAL BACKGROUND

The classical period of French history

- Important periods: **la Renaissance, le Grand Siècle**
- Important people: **François Ier, Louis XIV**
- French castles, as witnesses of French history

Literature:

La Fontaine, *Le Corbeau et le renard*
Prévert, *Soyons polis*

Film:

Rostand, *Cyrano de Bergerac*

READING AND CULTURAL OBJECTIVES

DAILY LIFE *(Info Magazine)*	READING *(Lecture)*
■ ***How certain aspects of daily life are different in France*** • Shopping in a supermarket • Services at the post office • When to tip and not to tip	*Histoire de cheveux*

INTERLUDE CULTUREL 4
Vive la musique!

GENERAL CULTURAL BACKGROUND

The musical landscape of France and the French-speaking world

- Classical musicians: **Lully, Chopin, Bizet, Debussy**
- Historical overview of French songs
- Famous French singers of yesterday and today
- The multicultural aspect of music from the francophone world: **zouk** (Antilles); **raï** (North Africa); **cajun, zydéco** (Louisiana)

Song:

Vigneault, *Mon pays*

Opera:

Bizet, *Carmen*

Unité 5 Bon voyage!

MAIN THEME Travel

COMMUNICATION OBJECTIVES	
COMMUNICATION FUNCTIONS AND CONTEXTS *(Le Français pratique)*	**LINGUISTIC GOALS** *(Langue et communication)*
■ *Planning a trip abroad* ■ *Going through customs* ■ *Making travel arrangements* • Purchasing tickets ■ *Travel in France* • at the travel agency • at the train station • at the airport	■ *Making negative statements* • affirmative and negative expressions • the expression **ne...que** ■ *Describing future plans* • future tense • use of future with **si**-clauses • use of future after **quand** ■ *Hypothesizing about what one would do* • introduction to the conditional

Unité 6 Séjour en France

MAIN THEME Hotels and other places to stay when traveling

COMMUNICATION OBJECTIVES	
COMMUNICATION FUNCTIONS AND CONTEXTS *(Le Français pratique)*	**LINGUISTIC GOALS** *(Langue et communication)*
■ *Deciding where to stay when traveling* ■ *Reserving a room in a hotel* ■ *Asking for services in a hotel*	■ *Comparing people, things, places and situations* • the comparative • the superlative ■ *Asking for an alternative* • the interrogative pronoun **lequel**? ■ *Pointing out people or things* • the demonstrative pronoun **celui** ■ *Indicating possession* • the possessive pronoun **le mien**

READING AND CULTURAL OBJECTIVES	
DAILY LIFE *(Info Magazine)*	**READING** *(Lecture)*
■ ***What are the advantages of visiting France by train?*** • the **TGV** • the **Eurotunnel** ■ ***Why do French people like to travel abroad and what do they do on their vacations?*** • impressions of young people visiting the United States	*Le mystérieux homme en bleu*

INTERLUDE CULTUREL 5
Les grands moments de l'histoire de France (1715–1870)

GENERAL CULTURAL BACKGROUND

The historical foundation of modern France

- Important periods
  - the **French Revolution**
  - the **Napoleonic era**
- Important contemporary French institutions
- Important people
  - **Louis XVI et Marie-Antoinette**
  - **Napoléon**

Song:

Rouget de Lisle, *La Marseillaise*

Literature:

Victor Hugo, *Les Misérables*

READING AND CULTURAL OBJECTIVES	
DAILY LIFE *(Info Magazine)*	**READING** *(Lecture)*
■ ***What inexpensive accommodations are available to students*** • **Auberges de jeunesse** • **Séjour à la ferme** ■ ***How to use the Guide Michelin when traveling in France*** • to find a hotel • to choose a restaurant	*Une étrange aventure*

INTERLUDE CULTUREL 6
Les grands moments de l'histoire de France (1870 au présent)

GENERAL CULTURAL BACKGROUND

France in the 20th century

- Important events
  - the two World Wars
  - the economic union of Europe
- Important people
  - **Marie Curie**
  - **Charles de Gaulle**
  - **Simone Veil**

Literature

Éluard, *Liberté*

Film

L. Malle, *Au revoir, les Enfants*

Unité 7 La forme et la santé

MAIN THEMES Health and medical care

COMMUNICATION OBJECTIVES

COMMUNICATION FUNCTIONS AND CONTEXTS *(Le Français pratique)*	LINGUISTIC GOALS *(Langue et communication)*
■ ***Going to the doctor's office*** • describing your symptoms • explaining what is wrong • giving information about your medical history • understanding the doctor's prescriptions ■ ***Going to the dentist*** ■ ***Going to the emergency ward***	■ ***Expressing how you and others feel about certain facts or events*** • the subjunctive • use of the subjunctive after expressions of emotion ■ ***Expressing fear, doubt or disbelief*** • the verbs **croire** and **craindre** • use of the subjunctive after expressions of doubt and uncertainty ■ ***Expressing feelings or attitudes about past actions and events*** • the past subjunctive

Unité 8 En ville

MAIN THEME Cities and city life

COMMUNICATION OBJECTIVES

COMMUNICATION FUNCTIONS AND CONTEXTS *(Le Français pratique)*	LINGUISTIC GOALS *(Langue et communication)*
■ ***Making a date and fixing the time and place*** ■ ***Explaining where one lives and how to get there*** ■ ***Discussing the advantages and disadvantages of city life*** ■ ***Describing your neighborhood***	■ ***Making wishes or suggestions*** • **si** + imperfect ■ ***Narrating past actions in sequence*** • the pluperfect ■ ***Formulating polite requests*** • the conditional ■ ***Hypothesizing about what one would do under certain circumstances*** • the conditional in **si**-clauses • the conditional and its uses • the past conditional • sequence of tenses in **si**-clauses

READING AND CULTURAL OBJECTIVES

DAILY LIFE *(Info Magazine)*	READING *(Lecture)*
■ ***How the French take care of their health*** • how does the French health system work? • what is the **Sécurité sociale**? • why do the French consume so much mineral water? • what is **thermalisme**? ■ ***How French doctors participate in humanitarian missions around the world*** • what is **Médecins sans frontières**?	**Maupassant,** *En voyage*

INTERLUDE CULTUREL 7
Les Français d'aujourd'hui

GENERAL CULTURAL BACKGROUND

Modern France as a multi-ethnic and multi-cultural society

- The French as citizens of Europe
- The new French mosaic: the impact of immigration on French society
- The **Maghrébins** — their culture and their religion
- **SOS Racisme**
- Two French humanitarians: **L'abbé Pierre** and **Coluche**

Song:
Éthiopie

INTERLUDE CULTUREL 8
Les Antilles francophones

GENERAL CULTURAL BACKGROUND

The French-speaking Caribbean islands

- Historical background
- Important people
  Toussaint Louverture
  Joséphine de Beauharnais
  Aimé Césaire
- Haitian art as an expression of life

Literature:
Césaire, *Pour saluer le Tiers-Monde*

Film:
Palcy: *Rue Cases-nègres*

READING AND CULTURAL OBJECTIVES

DAILY LIFE *(Info Magazine)*	READING *(Lecture)*
■ ***What a typical French city looks like*** • its historical development • its various neighborhoods • its buildings • the ***villes nouvelles*** ■ ***Why French people love to stroll in the streets*** • various street shows • sculpture to view while walking in Paris	**Theuriet,** *Les Pêches*

Unité 9 Les relations personnelles

MAIN THEME Personal relationships, friendships, and family life

COMMUNICATION OBJECTIVES

COMMUNICATION FUNCTIONS AND CONTEXTS *(Le Français pratique)*	LINGUISTIC GOALS *(Langue et communication)*
■ *Describing degrees of friendship* ■ *Expressing different feelings towards other people* ■ *Discussing the state of one's relationship with other people* ■ *Congratulating, comforting, and expressing sympathy for other people* ■ *Describing the various phases of a person's life*	■ *Describing how people interact* • reciprocal use of reflexive verbs ■ *Describing people and things in complex sentences* • the relative pronouns **qui** and **que** • relative clauses • the relative pronoun **dont** • relative pronouns • the relative pronouns **ce qui, ce que,** and **ce dont**

Unité 10 Vers la vie active

MAIN THEME University studies and careers

COMMUNICATION OBJECTIVES

COMMUNICATION FUNCTIONS AND CONTEXTS *(Le Français pratique)*	LINGUISTIC GOALS *(Langue et communication)*
■ *Deciding on a college major* • university courses ■ *Planning for a career* • professions • the work environment • different types of industries ■ *Looking for a job* • preparing a résumé • describing one's qualifications at a job interview	■ *Describing simultaneous actions* • the present participle ■ *Explaining the purpose of an action* • **pour** + infinitive • **pour que** + subjunctive ■ *Explaining the timing, conditions, and constraints of an action* • the use of the infinitive or the subjunctive after certain prepositions and conjunctions ■ *Expressing how your actions may depend on what others do* ■ *Describing how your actions affect others*

INTERLUDE CULTUREL 9
L'Afrique dans la communauté francophone

GENERAL CULTURAL BACKGROUND
The place of Western and Central Africa in the francophone world • Historical periods and events: prehistory, the **African empires**, colonization and independence • Basic facts about Western Africa language and culture religions and traditions • **African art** and its influence on European art ***African Fable:*** *La Gélinotte et la Tortue* ***Literature:*** **D. Diop,** *Afrique* **Dadié,** *La légende baoulé*

READING AND CULTURAL OBJECTIVES

DAILY LIFE *(Info Magazine)*	**READING** *(Lecture)*
■ ***How important are friends and family to French people?*** • the meaning of friendship • family relationships ■ ***How socially concerned are French young people and what type of social outreach do they do?*** ■ ***What is a typical French wedding like?*** • where French spouses meet one another • planning the wedding • a French wedding ceremony	**M. Maurois,** *Le Bracelet*

INTERLUDE CULTUREL 10
La France et le Nouveau Monde

GENERAL CULTURAL BACKGROUND
The French presence in North America • historical background The French in Canada and Louisiana • important people **Jacques Cartier, Jeanne Mance, Cavelier de La Salle** • why certain American cities have French names ***Song:*** **Richard,** *Réveille* ***Literature:*** **La Fayette,** *Lettre à sa femme*

READING AND CULTURAL OBJECTIVES

DAILY LIFE *(Info Magazine)*	**READING** *(Lecture)*
■ ***How important academic success is to French young people*** • the French school system: high schools and universities • **Le bac:** its history and its importance ■ ***What to do after graduation*** • choosing a profession • **Le service militaire** ■ ***Interviewing for a job*** • how to prepare for the interview • how to write a résumé in French	**Thériault,** *Le Portrait*

Introduction to French Literature

Beginning with the intermediate level, the teaching of literature becomes a significant objective in the curriculum of many French courses. Because most authentic French literary pieces are linguistically very complex, it is important that the introduction to French literature be done in a ***progressive*** manner so as to correspond to the linguistic abilities of the students. It should also be done in an ***interesting*** and ***stimulating*** way and include a variety of texts that students can relate to easily.

If the initial introduction to literature is successful, students are more likely to develop an interest in the richness of French literature and breadth of francophone culture. Many will be encouraged to continue their study of French, and perhaps make plans to travel or study in a French-speaking part of the world.

The literature-related contents of À VOTRE TOUR! have been selected to meet the following objectives:

- To ***present integral literary pieces that are linguistically accessible*** to intermediate students. All the twentieth-century texts are presented as written with only minor occasional abridgments. Because of their lexical complexity, however, the short stories of the nineteenth century have been somewhat adapted.
- To show how ***poetry can be used to convey powerful political messages.*** Students tend to dismiss poetry as boring and uninteresting. Here they will discover how Paul Éluard's *Liberté* became a call to resistance in World War II, how David Diop and Aimé Césaire used poetry to promote African independence, and how Zachary Richard uses song lyrics to plead for the maintenance of Cajun culture in Louisiana.
- To ***introduce longer significant literary works*** via summaries and synopses. By encountering some major works of literature through brief summaries, students will broaden their awareness of the breadth of the French cultural heritage and develop a growing interest in French literature.
- To bring students into direct contact with ***the variety of the literature of the French-speaking world,*** by including authors from France, Africa, the Caribbean and North America. Genres include short stories, fables, legends, letters, poetry, as well as introductions to novels and plays.

The breadth of the literary content of À VOTRE TOUR! is shown in the following chart on page T25.

Documents: Le corbeau et le renard

Le corbeau et le renard

À l'école, tous les jeunes Français apprennent par coeur les fables de La Fontaine. Leur auteur est l'un des écrivains les plus célèbres du siècle de Louis XIV. À travers° ses portraits d'animaux, **Jean de La Fontaine** (1621-1695) voulait critiquer les défauts de ses contemporains. La morale de ses fables est en réalité éternelle.

La fameuse fable *Le corbeau et le renard*° s'adresse aux gens qui ont besoin d'être admirés.

Le corbeau et le renard

Maître Corbeau, sur un arbre perché,
Tenait° en son bec un fromage.
Maître Renard, par l'odeur alléché,°
Lui tint à peu près ce langage:°
«Hé! bonjour, Monsieur du Corbeau,
Que vous êtes joli! que vous me semblez beau!
Sans mentir,° si votre ramage°
Se rapporte° à votre plumage
Vous êtes le phénix° des hôtes de ces bois.
À ces mots, le Corbeau ne se sent pas de joie;°
Et pour montrer sa belle voix,
Il ouvre un large bec, laisse tomber° sa proie.°
Le Renard s'en saisit,° et dit: «Mon bon Monsieur,
Apprenez que tout flatteur
Vit° aux dépens° de celui qui l'écoute:
Cette leçon vaut° bien un fromage, sans doute.»

■ *L'histoire de France à travers ses châteaux*

Carcassonne
Comme beaucoup de villes médiévales, Carcassonne était entourée de hauts remparts qui la protégeaient contre d'éventuels envahisseurs.° Elle résista aux Anglais pendant la Guerre de Cent Ans.

Chenonceaux
Le château de Chenonceaux est de pur style Renaissance. Sur ses murs on peut y lire encore des graffiti (en anglais) laissés par les gardes écossais° du roi Henri II.

Angers
Angers était la capitale des Plantagenêts, ducs d'Anjou et futurs rois d'Angleterre. Avec ses grosses tours rondes, le château est un bel exemple d'architecture féodale.

Fontainebleau
Maintes fois transformé, Fontainebleau a servi de résidence à plus de 20 rois de France, parmi lesquels François Ier et Louis XIII, père de Louis XIV. C'est ici que Napoléon a fait ses adieux avant de partir en exil.

Château-Gaillard
Construit en 1196 par Richard Coeur de Lion, Château-Gaillard dominait la Seine et barrait la route entre Paris et Rouen. Dix ans plus tard, le château tomba dans les mains des Français et il n'en reste aujourd'hui que d'imposantes ruines.

Vaux-le-Vicomte
Le château de Vaux-le-Vicomte a été construit par Nicolas Fouquet, surintendant des finances du royaume de France. Un jour, Fouquet eut la mauvaise idée d'y inviter le jeune roi Louis XIV. Celui-ci, jaloux de la richesse de son ministre, le fit emprisonner.

Versailles

Literature Selections in **À votre tour!**

New !

Integrated video/DVD Program for ***À votre tour!***

Each unit of ***À votre tour!*** is accompanied by a *Vidéo-drame* using the unit vocabulary in context.

Filmed on location in Provence:

- Appealing characters and humorous situations make the language come alive for students.
- Available on videocassette and DVD. The DVD version provides teachers with the option of Closed Captioning.
- Among the characters introduced are Mélanie, her boyfriend Guillaume, her brother Nicolas and his best friend Malik.

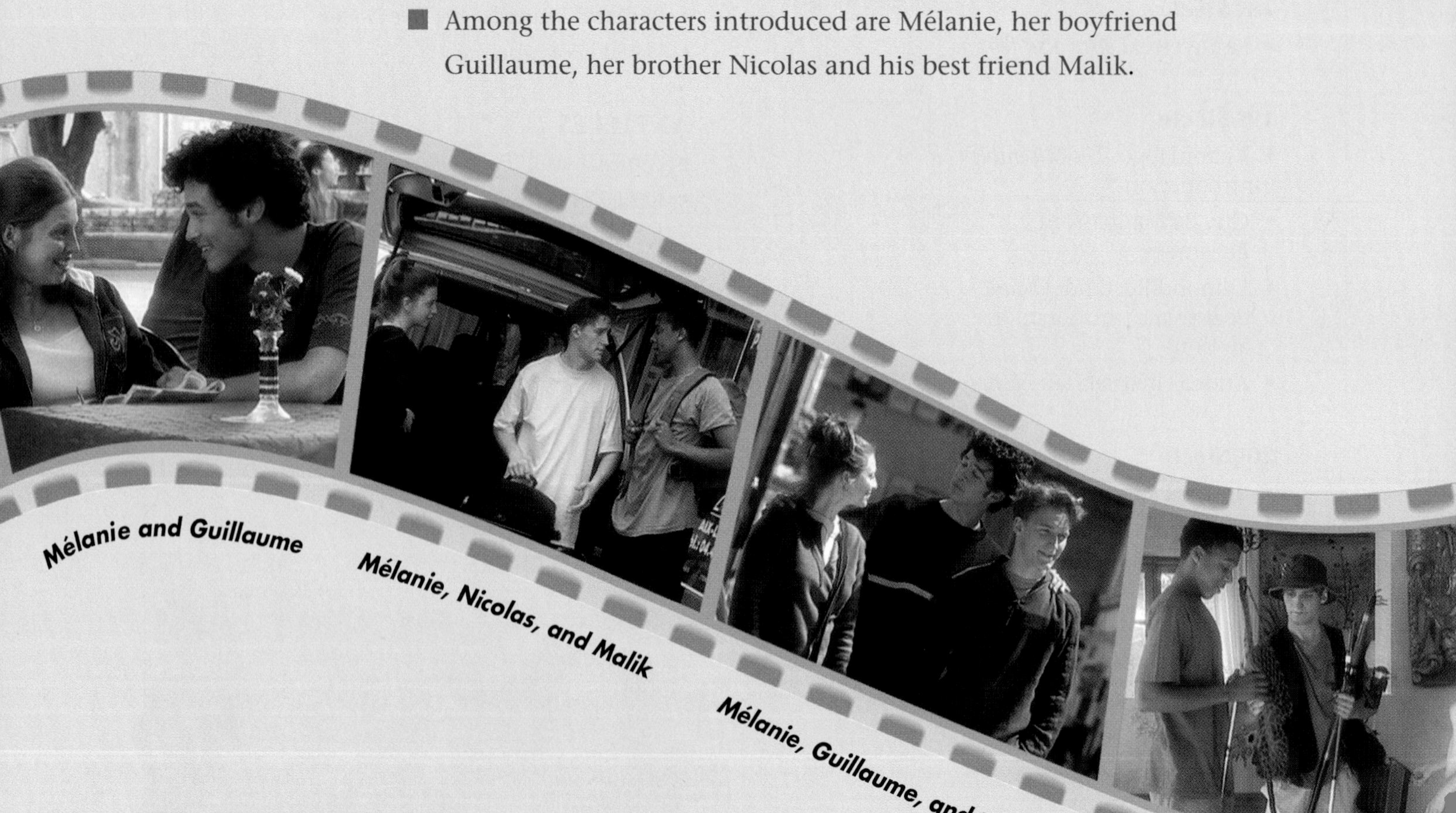

Mélanie and Guillaume

Mélanie, Nicolas, and Malik

Mélanie, Guillaume, and Nicolas

Malik, Nicolas, and Mélanie

Second Edition

À votre tour!

Second Edition

À votre tour!

Jean-Paul Valette
Rebecca M. Valette
Boston College

Houghton Mifflin Company
Boston New York

Publisher: Rolando Hernández
Sponsoring Editor: Viki Kellar
Associate Editor: Caitlin McIntyre
Editorial Assistant: Erin Beasley
Project Editor: Andrea Dodge
Editorial Assistant: Carrie Parker
Art and Design Manager: Gary Crespo
Senior Photo Editor: Jennifer Meyer Dare
Composition Buyer: Chuck Dutton
Senior Manufacturing Buyer: Karen B. Fawcett
Executive Marketing Director: Eileen Bernadette Moran
Marketing Assistant: Lorreen Ruth Pelletier

Cover photo: "Peniscola" by Andre Duret/Private Collection/Bridgeman Art Library. © 2005 Artists Rights Society (ARS), New York.

Printed in the U.S.A.

Library of Congress Control Number: 2006925034

Instructor's Annotated Edition
ISBN-10: 0-618-69316-5
ISBN-13: 978-0-618-69316-0

For orders, use student text ISBNs
ISBN-10: 0-618-69315-7
ISBN-13: 978-0-618-69315-3

123456789-CRK-10 09 08 07 06

CONTENTS

Reprise

UNITÉ 1 Au jour le jour

UNITÉ 2 Soyons utiles!

UNITÉ 3 Vive la nature!

Aspects de la vie quotidienne

Bon voyage!

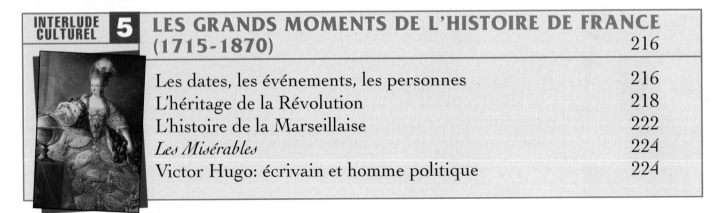

Séjour en France

UNITÉ 7 La forme et la santé

En ville

Les relations personnelles

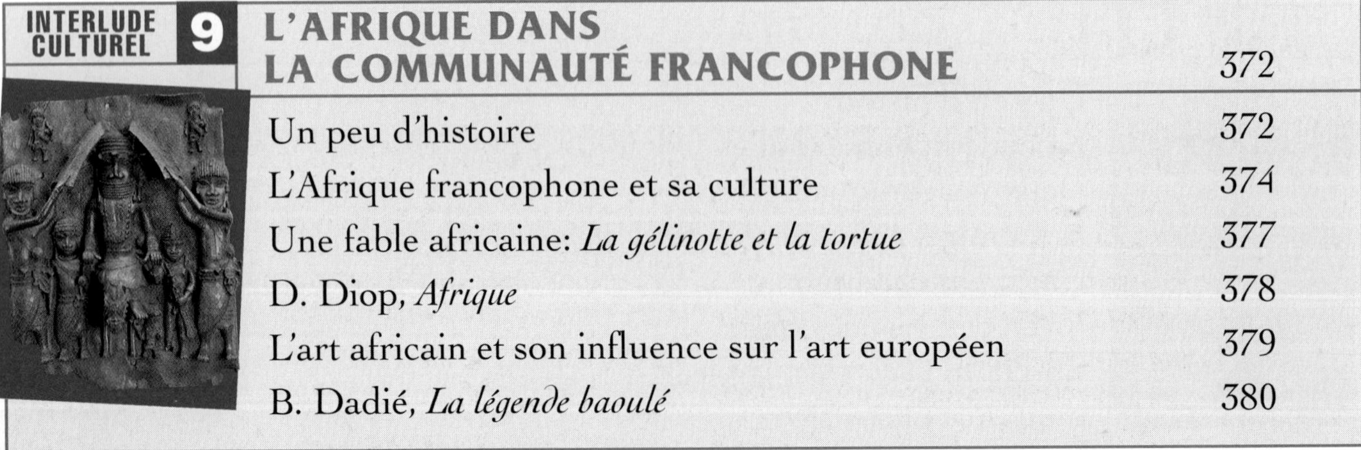

UNITÉ 10 Vers la vie active

REPRISE

MAIN THEME

Everyday life (review)

Communication Function/Contexts
- Introducing and describing
- Ordering in a café or restaurant
- Accepting and refusing invitations
- Talking about daily life activities
- Describing vacation activities
- Talking about events in the past
- Asking for help
- Describing what you do for others

Linguistic Goals

Review/Re-entry:
- Regular and irregular adjectives
- **Avoir, faire,** and expressions
- Regular and irregular verbs, especially **aller, être, venir, prendre, connaître, savoir, voir, écrire**
- Formation and use of the **passé composé** and **imparfait**
- Direct and indirect objects

Online Study Center

Online Teaching Center

Reprise

Retour de vacances!

TEACHING RESOURCES

ANCILLARIES

Student Activities Manual

Chansons Audio CD

HM ClassPrep CD

Transparency Masters

Presentations, Reprise

Assessment

Answer Key

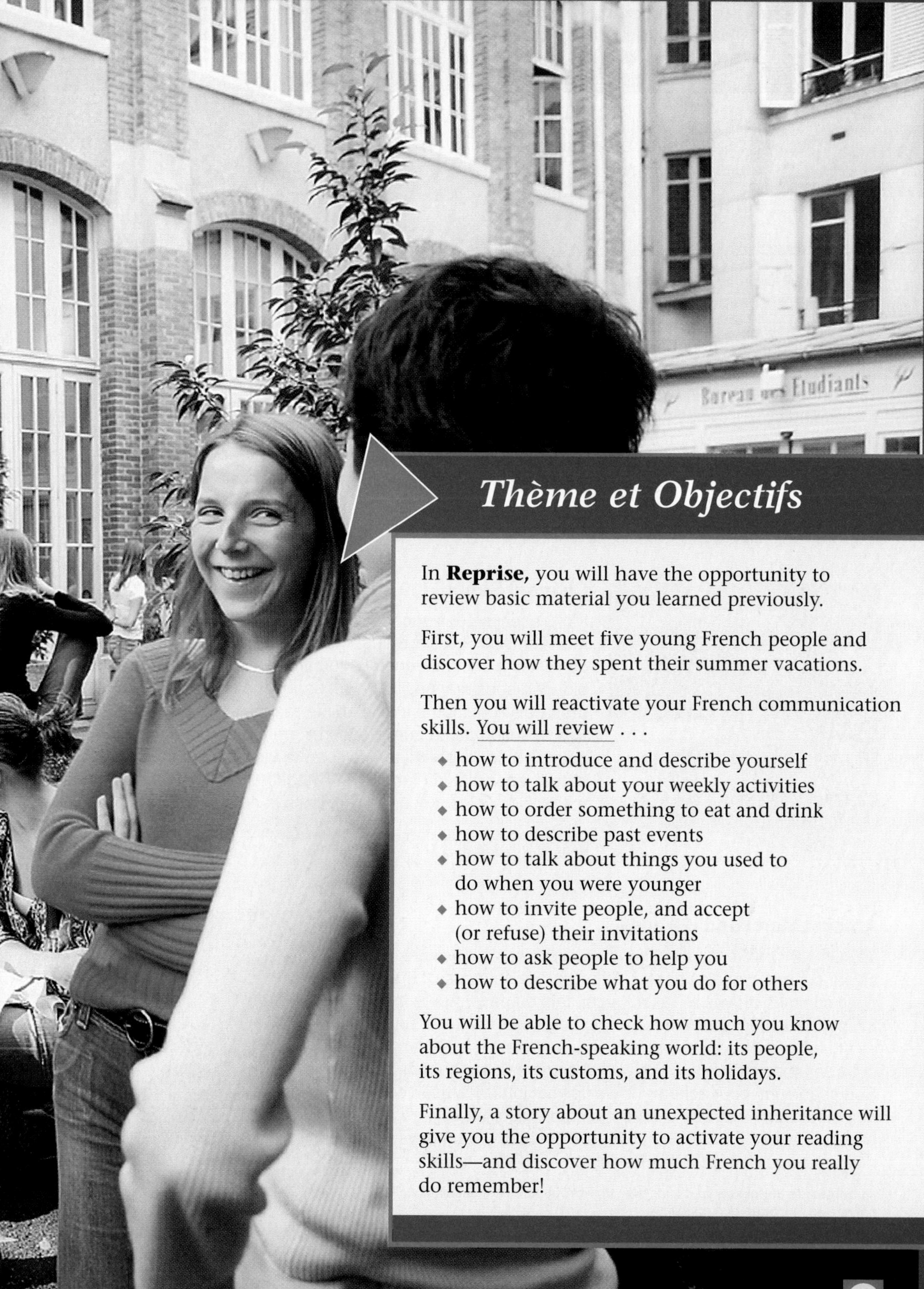

Thème et Objectifs

In **Reprise,** you will have the opportunity to review basic material you learned previously.

First, you will meet five young French people and discover how they spent their summer vacations.

Then you will reactivate your French communication skills. You will review . . .

- how to introduce and describe yourself
- how to talk about your weekly activities
- how to order something to eat and drink
- how to describe past events
- how to talk about things you used to do when you were younger
- how to invite people, and accept (or refuse) their invitations
- how to ask people to help you
- how to describe what you do for others

You will be able to check how much you know about the French-speaking world: its people, its regions, its customs, and its holidays.

Finally, a story about an unexpected inheritance will give you the opportunity to activate your reading skills—and discover how much French you really do remember!

1

Note culturelles

- French students are on vacation during July and August. Most French workers have five weeks of paid vacation per year. They generally take four weeks off in July or August, and one week in the winter. The most popular vacation destination is the seashore, in areas such as Brittany, the Atlantic coast, and the south of France.

Retour de vacances

C'est la rentrée à l'université. Cinq étudiants français parlent de ce qu'ils ont fait pendant l'été.

■ **Teaching Strategy**
Have students locate the areas mentioned on the map on pp. R36–R37 or in an atlas.

Élodie Blanchet (19 ans)

Je suis allée à Beijing avec un programme d'échanges organisé par l'école de commerce où je suis étudiante. Dans notre groupe, nous étions quatre. D'abord nous avons fait un stage° de trois semaines dans une banque internationale. Le travail n'était pas particulièrement intéressant: copier et classer° des documents. Par contre,° le contact avec nos collègues chinois a été extraordinaire. J'ai beaucoup apprécié leur gentillesse et leur curiosité intellectuelle. Après le stage, nous avons fait un voyage de dix jours dans le sud de la Chine. Le pays est en pleine expansion économique. Vraiment, je suis très contente d'avoir assisté au «miracle chinois.»

stage *internship* **classer** *to file* **Par contre** *on the other hand*

Clément Simon (19 ans)

Moi, j'ai passé des vacances sportives! Cet été, j'ai travaillé deux mois au Club Soleil à Sainte-Marie à la Martinique. Mon travail consistait à accompagner les touristes qui désiraient faire de la plongée-sous marine.° Il y avait beaucoup de travail. Le matin, je préparais l'équipement et le soir je rangeais° tout. Il fallait° faire très attention parce que la sécurité était notre préoccupation principale. Quand j'avais du temps libre, je faisais de la yole.° C'est un bateau spécial à la Martinique. Chaque année, il y a une grande course° de yoles autour de l'île, mais je ne suis pas prêt pour cela.

plongée sous marine *deep-sea diving* **rangeais** *put away* **Il fallait** *one had to* **yole** *yawl* **course** *race*

Antoine Marchand (20 ans)

Je suis parti au Sénégal avec ma sœur Claire. Nous avons fait un séjour culturel organisé par les Auberges de Jeunesse.° D'abord, nous sommes arrivés à Dakar, la capitale du pays. Après, nous avons fait un voyage organisé en taxi-brousse.° À Saint-Louis, il y avait un festival de musique et nous avons dansé le Sabar. Quand nous sommes rentrés à Dakar, nous sommes allés au marché de Soumbédioune pour acheter de petites sculptures africaines. Une nuit, nous sommes allés à la pêche en pirogue,° mais il n'y avait pas de poisson! Pendant ce voyage, j'ai découvert un pays magnifique et une vie culturelle très riche.

Auberges de Jeunesse *youth hostels* **taxi-brousse** = taxi africain pour 10 passagers **pirogue** *dug out canoe*

Teaching Strategy: Warm-Up

Hand out a 5 x 5 grid. Each square of the grid should have a different verb and sentence fragment (e.g., **visiter un pays européen**). Have students stand up, circulate and ask questions (in **passé composé**) to find out who did the suggested activities during the summer. Record the initials of each student in the appropriate activity box. The winner is the student who fills in a different student's initials in every box. **Extra practice:** Ask the winning student to name who did each activity. Then ask the student whether or not they did it. Everyone must answer in complete sentences.

Ali Hachani (21 ans)

J'ai fait un stage avec les «Chantiers° Histoire et Architecture Médiévales.» C'est une organisation qui recrute des volontaires pour restaurer les monuments anciens. Le projet de mon groupe était de restaurer le château de Morimont en Alsace. Au 12e siècle,° le château était une forteresse. D'abord, nous avons reconstruit° un mur° qui tombait en ruines. Puis, nous avons travaillé dans le souterrain.° Le travail était dur, c'est vrai, mais il y avait beaucoup d'avantages. J'ai appris beaucoup de choses sur le Moyen Âge° et j'ai rencontré des jeunes d'autres pays d'Europe. Dans notre groupe, il y avait des Allemands, des Belges, des Hollandais, des Anglais... et Giuseppina, une Italienne avec qui je fais maintenant des chats sur Internet.

chantiers *worksites* **un siècle** = 100 ans **reconstruit** *rebuilt* **mur** *wall* **souterrain** = *tunnel* **Moyen Âge** *Middle Ages*

Émilie Nguyen (20 ans)

Cet été, j'ai travaillé dans un centre pour jeunes handicapés mentaux en Haute Savoie. Nous étions une équipe° de quatre personnes pour vingt jeunes. Chaque jour, on faisait une promenade en montagne. Pendant les haltes, on étudiait la faune et la flore locale. Nous devions être bien préparés parce que nos jeunes amis voulaient tout savoir sur les animaux et les plantes. Le soir, nous organisions des jeux et des activités. Par exemple, nous avons fait une chasse au trésor° dans le jardin. Nous avons aussi formé une chorale et les jeunes ont donné un récital. Pour moi, c'était une expérience très enrichissante. J'étudie pour être éducatrice spécialisée° et ce job m'a appris beaucoup de choses.

équipe *team* **chasse au trésor** *treasure hunt* **éducatrice spécialisée** *special ed teacher*

À votre avis *(In your opinion)*

Avec un(e) ou plusieurs partenaires, discutez des questions suivantes.

- Qui a fait la chose la plus intéressante? Expliquez pourquoi.
- Qui a fait la chose la plus utile? Expliquez pourquoi.
- Vous avez la possibilité de passer les vacances comme ces cinq jeunes Français. Quel est votre choix? Pourquoi?
- Quelle région ou quel pays mentionné(e) par ces jeunes Français désirez-vous visiter? Pourquoi?

À votre tour!

Maintenant, parlez de vos vacances.

1. Qu'est-ce que vous avez fait pendant vos vacances?
2. Si vous avez travaillé, quel travail avez-vous fait? Où était votre travail? Quelles étaient vos responsabilités principales?
3. Si vous avez voyagé, où êtes-vous allé(e)? Avec qui? Combien de temps êtes-vous resté(e) là-bas? Qu'est-ce que vous avez vu?
4. Qu'est-ce que vous avez fait d'intéressant? Qu'est-ce que vous avez fait d'utile?

Note culturelles

- **«Chefs d'oeuvre en péril»** was a French television program structured as a **concours** *(competition)* to safeguard and protect historical monuments. There are several organizations that recruit young people to work on architectural restoration sites. They include: **R.E.M.P.A.R.T.S., Jeunesse et Reconstruction, and Club du vieux manoir**, all located in Paris.

Compréhension

1. Où est allée Élodie avec son programme d'échange?
2. Qu'est-ce qu'elle a aimé particulièrement?
3. Pendant combien de temps Clément a-t-il travaillé?
4. En quoi son travail consistait-il?
5. Avec qui Antoine a-t-il passé ses vacances?
6. Qu'est-ce qu'il a acheté au marché?
7. Sur quel projet Ali a-t-il travaillé?
8. Est-ce que c'était facile? Pourquoi?
9. Dans quelle sorte de centre Émilie a-t-elle travaillé?
10. Qu'est-ce qu'elle faisait pendant la journée? pendant la soirée?

Teaching Strategy: Pair Practice

Divide class into pairs and have each pair write a dialog of 10–12 lines between two of the French students on pages 2–3. They should ask and answer questions based on information given, as well as invent possible answers.

Reprise A

La vie courante

Rappel 1

TEACHING RESOURCES

Student Activities Manual, pp. 3–5

Note culturelle
La Touraine is a region of France, south-west of Paris, around the Loire river.

Teaching Notes
You may have students do their poll first, and then compare their answers with those of the Canadian students.

Reprise A *La vie courante*

Rappel  Bonjour!

1 À l'Institut de Touraine

L'Institut de Touraine est une école où beaucoup d'étudiants viennent apprendre le français en été. Vous allez passer un mois à l'Institut de Touraine.

Donnez oralement les renseignements demandés.

INSTITUT D'ÉTUDES FRANÇAISES
DE TOURAINE
1, rue de la Grandière, 37000 TOURS

BULLETIN D'INSCRIPTION

Prénoms et Nom...
Né(e) le...
à...
Nationalité:...
Profession:...
Adresse (dans le pays d'origine):...
École ou université d'origine:...
Nombre d'années d'étude du français:...

2 Les parents idéaux

Quelles sont les qualités les plus importantes pour la mère idéale ou le père idéal? Un magazine québécois, le *Bulletin Pacijou*, a posé cette question à des étudiants de l'Université Laval. Voici les résultats de cette enquête.

LA MÈRE IDÉALE: QUALITÉS ESSENTIELLES

selon les filles		selon les garçons	
compréhensive	29%	gentille	39%
gentille	29%	compréhensive	17%
attentive	15%	joyeuse	17%
confiante°	11%	généreuse	11%
tolérante	9%	patiente	8%
patiente	7%	confiante	8%

LE PÈRE IDÉAL: QUALITÉS ESSENTIELLES

selon les filles		selon les garçons	
gentil	31%	gentil	31%
compréhensif	30%	compréhensif	31%
tolérant	23%	riche et généreux	21%
affectueux	16%	drôle	17%

confiant(e) *trusting*

Maintenant faites une enquête dans votre classe:
- Quelles sont les qualités essentielles pour être la mère idéale?
- Quelles sont les qualités essentielles pour être le père idéal?

Les adjectifs réguliers et irréguliers
Révision ▶ p. R7
Pratique ▶ p. 3

Teaching Strategies

Pair Practice

Review: Question words. Have students look at the form on p. 4 and figure out what questions need to be asked to get the requested information. Divide the class into pairs and have them ask each other these questions and fill in a copy of the form with their partner's information.

Warm-Up

Give each student (orally or on a slip of paper) an **avoir** expression to act out. Then, have each student give a complete sample sentence (e.g., **Quand j'ai faim, je vais au restaurant**).

3 Notre personnalité

Nous avons tous des qualités, mais nous avons aussi des petits défauts. Choisissez une des personnes suivantes (ou une autre personne de votre choix). Décrivez deux qualités—au moins—et un petit défaut de cette personne.

- moi
- mon copain
- ma copine
- mon cousin
- ma cousine
- mes profs
- mes parents
- mes voisins
- les élèves de cette classe
- ??

En général . . .

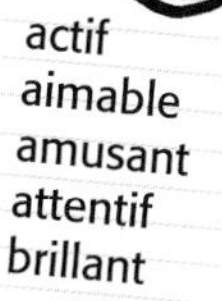

QUALITÉS

actif, aimable, amusant, attentif, brillant, compréhensif, consciencieux, courageux, discret, drôle, dynamique, énergique, gentil, généreux, honnête, imaginatif, intéressant, joyeux, optimiste, organisé, patient, poli, ouvert, sensible *(sensitive)*, sérieux, spirituel *(witty)*, spontané, sympathique, tolérant, ??

mais de temps en temps . . .

DÉFAUTS

bête, distant, égoïste, ennuyeux, impoli, inactif, incompréhensif, indifférent, indiscret, indiscipliné, méchant, paresseux, pénible, pessimiste, prétentieux, renfermé *(uncommunicative)*, sévère, stupide, timide, triste, vaniteux *(vain)*, ??

▶ **En général, ma cousine Élisabeth est très gentille. Elle est aussi drôle et optimiste. De temps en temps, elle est un peu prétentieuse.**

Avoir et les expressions avec **avoir**

Révision ▶ p. R3

Pratique ▶ p. 4

4 Que faire?

Choisissez une expression de la colonne A et décrivez votre situation à votre partenaire. Votre partenaire va vous dire ce qu'il faut faire, en utilisant les suggestions de la colonne B.

▶

J'ai chaud!
Eh bien, tu peux ouvrir la fenêtre!

A. Votre situation
- faim
- soif
- chaud
- froid
- sommeil
- besoin d'un livre
- envie de voir un film
- besoin de ??
- envie de ??

B. Conseils
- mettre un pull
- ouvrir la fenêtre
- aller au ciné
- passer à la bibliothèque
- manger un sandwich
- boire un soda
- dormir
- prendre un café
- ??

RAPPEL!

TO DESCRIBE . . .	USE . . .	
• what you ARE GOING TO DO	**aller** + infinitive	**Je vais sortir.**
• what you ARE DOING RIGHT NOW	**être en train de** + infinitive	**Je suis en train de téléphoner.**
• what you HAVE JUST DONE	**venir de** + infinitive	**Je viens de dîner.**

Il va dîner. Il est en train de dîner. Il vient de dîner.

Aller, être, venir

Révision ▶ p. R3

Pratique ▶ p. 4

Supplementary vocabulary

coléreux *quick tempered*
fier *proud*
jaloux *jealous*
maladroit *clumsy*
moqueur *mocking*
têtu *stubborn*
franc *frank*
indépendant *independent*
indulgent *lenient*
intelligent *smart*
talentueux *talented*
travailleur *hard-working*

Language Note

A familiar form for "annoying, bothersome" is **embêtant(e).**

Expansion

Have students write a list of 10 adjectives, being as creative as possible. Make a list of three–four people/groups of people to be described by the students' adjectives (e.g., **Ma meilleure amie/mon ami idéal/le prof idéal/les frères et les soeurs**).

Ask students to volunteer their adjectives and copy them onto the board. Finally, have students create negative or affirmative sentences about each of the people/groups of people using the adjectives listed (e.g., **Ma meilleure amie n'est pas méchante**).

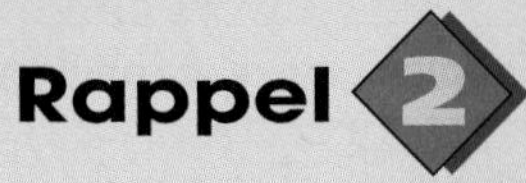

Rappel 2

TEACHING RESOURCES

Student Activities Manual, pp. 5–7

Rappel  Le temps libre

Bonjour,

Je m'appelle Valérie Dussart. J'ai 20 ans et j'habite à Lyon. Je suis étudiante de deuxième année à la fac° de Sciences.

J'ai beaucoup de travail, mais je ne travaille pas tout le temps. Le samedi, par exemple, est un jour que je me réserve entièrement. L'après-midi je vais en ville et je fais du shopping. Quand il y a une bonne exposition, je vais au musée. Le soir, je sors en bande°. (J'ai beaucoup de copains et de copines, mais je n'ai pas de « copain » en particulier.) En général, on va voir un film. De temps en temps, on va danser dans une « boîte° ».

J'ai d'autres loisirs. Je fais du théâtre depuis un an à la Maison des Jeunes. En juin, nous allons présenter « La leçon » une pièce de l'écrivain° Ionesco dans laquelle° je joue le rôle de l'Élève... Je suis° aussi des cours de danse africaine. C'est excellent pour la forme!

Pendant l'année, je n'ai pas l'occasion de faire beaucoup de sport, mais en été je me rattrape°. Ma passion, c'est la planche à voile. Il y a d'autres sports que j'aimerais faire, comme le parapente. Malheureusement, mes parents ne sont pas d'accord!

Et vous, quels sont vos loisirs préférés?

Valérie

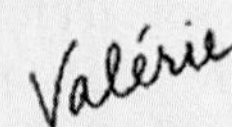

Moi, avec mes amies.

la fac *college* **en bande** = en groupe **une boîte** *club, nightspot* **un écrivain** = une personne qui écrit **laquelle** *which* **suivre** *to take [a class]* **se rattraper** *to catch up with*

RAPPEL!

To describe what you have been doing for or since some time, you use:

present + **depuis** + time

Depuis

Pratique ▶  p. 5

Teaching Strategy: Challenge

Once students have taken turns reading the letter from Valérie, have them go back to the beginning of the letter and imagine that a friend is asking who the letter is from and what it says. Have students make all the changes necessary to put the letter into the third person in order to tell their curious friend about Valérie and her friends.

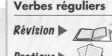

RAPPEL!

- In French, there are three groups of regular verbs: **-er, -ir, -re**.
- **Vouloir, pouvoir, devoir** and verbs like **sortir** are irregular.
- **Faire**, an irregular verb, is used in many expressions.

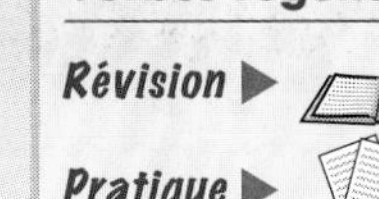

Verbes réguliers
Révision ▶ p. R2
Pratique ▶ p. 6

Quelques verbes irréguliers
Révision ▶ p. R2
Pratique ▶ p. 6

Faire et expressions avec faire
Révision ▶ p. R3
Pratique ▶ p. 7

1 Et vous?

Répondez au questionnaire suivant. Si vous voulez, comparez vos réponses avec les réponses de votre partenaire ou de votre groupe.

1. À la maison, quand j'ai du temps libre *(free time)*, je préfère . . .
   - regarder la télé
   - écouter de la musique
   - lire un bon livre
   - ??
2. Quand je suis en ville, je préfère . . .
   - faire du shopping
   - faire du lèche-vitrine *(window-shopping)*
   - voir une exposition
   - ??
3. Avec mon argent, je préfère . . .
   - aller au cinéma
   - acheter des vêtements
   - acheter des CD
   - ??
4. Le samedi soir, je préfère . . .
   - sortir seul(e) *(by myself)*
   - sortir avec mes copains
   - regarder un DVD à la maison
   - ??
5. Quand je sors avec mes copains, je préfère . . .
   - assister à un concert
   - voir un film
   - aller au restaurant
   - ??
6. Pour rester en forme, je préfère . . .
   - courir
   - faire du vélo
   - faire des exercices de gymnastique
   - ??
7. L'après-midi, quand il fait beau, je préfère . . .
   - faire du jogging
   - faire du roller *(roller blades)*
   - jouer au basket
   - ??
8. Quand je suis à la plage, je préfère . . .
   - nager
   - jouer au volley
   - prendre des bains de soleil
   - ??
9. Pendant les vacances, je préfère . . .
   - faire un voyage
   - rendre visite à des amis ou à des parents
   - travailler et gagner de l'argent
   - ??
10. Je voudrais apprendre à . . .
    - jouer de la clarinette
    - faire du parapente
    - piloter un avion
    - ??

2 Une lettre à Valérie

Écrivez une lettre à Valérie où vous expliquez . . .

- qui vous êtes
- à quelle école vous allez
- ce que vous faites le samedi
- quels sont vos loisirs
- quels sports vous pratiquez
- ce que vous faites en été

Puis comparez votre lettre avec celle de votre partenaire.

■ Expansion: Activity 1

1. jouer aux jeux d'ordinateur, lire des magazines, téléphoner à mes copains
2. aller dans un café, faire une promenade à pied
3. louer des cassettes vidéo, aller au restaurant
4. téléphoner à des amis, faire du baby-sitting
5. assister à un match de baseball, aller danser dans une boîte
6. faire de l'aérobic, nager
7. jouer au football, faire du patin à roulettes, faire de la planche à roulettes
8. jouer au frisbee, faire un pique-nique
9. suivre des cours d'été
10. parler japonais, faire du bateau à voile, faire du ski nautique

Rappel 3

TEACHING RESOURCES

Student Activities Manual,
pp. 8–10

■ Note linguistique

la langouste = *crawfish*
le homard = *lobster*

Notes culturelles

- **Le traiteur** is a specialty shop that sells prepared foods, and caters to special events such as wedding banquets (**la réception de mariage**), or parties.
- **La bouillabaisse** is a specialty from the south of France. It is a fish soup seasoned with garlic, saffron, and olive oil.
- **30 euros s.c.** means that the tip is included in the price. **s.c.= service compris**

Rappel 3 Bon appétit!

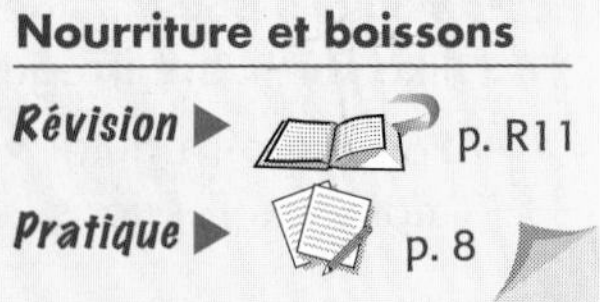

1 Le bon choix

Regardez les illustrations pour compléter les phrases avec l'option qui convient. Soyez logique.

Le Grenier de Notre Dame
RESTAURANT VÉGÉTARIEN
18, rue de la Bûcherie
75005 PARIS ☎ 01 43 29 98 29 +
Métro St. Michel NATURESTO

On va dans ce restaurant si on aime . . .
- ■ les légumes
- ■ la viande de porc
- ■ la cuisine chinoise

La Langouste
Poissons - Fruits de mer - Langouste - Homard - Bouillabaisse
FORMULE HOMARD 30 euros s.c. + CARTE (ouvert dimanche)
Place des Ternes (1, av. des Ternes) - Tél. 01 43 80 15 83

Dans ce restaurant, on peut commander . . .
- ■ du saumon grillé
- ■ du poulet rôti
- ■ une omelette aux champignons

IZRAEL
L'ÉPICERIE DU MONDE
PRODUITS DES AMÉRIQUES DES INDES ET DE LA MEDITERRANÉE
Fermé en Août
30, rue François Miron - Paris 4e
01 42 72 66 23

On va dans ce magasin si on veut acheter . . .
- ■ des côtelettes de veau
- ■ du poivre
- ■ des croissants

Au Prince Gourmand
pâtisserie - traiteur - réception
magasins:
122, rue Saint-Dominique 75007 PARIS - 01 45 51 68 64
2, impasse des Noisetiers-Chamblean 28500 Garnay - 02 37 42 14 93

On va dans ce magasin si on veut acheter . . .
- ■ une tarte aux fraises
- ■ des pommes de terre
- ■ une douzaine d'oeufs

RAPPEL!

- To refer to things you like in general, use: **le (l'), la (l'), les.**
  J'aime le poulet, la salade, les frites.
- To refer to a CERTAIN, UNDEFINED QUANTITY or AMOUNT of something, use: **du (de l'), de la (de l'), des.**
  Je voudrais du poulet, de la salade, des frites.

  Note: In negative sentences: **du, de la, des → de**
  Je ne vais pas prendre de fromage.

Les articles définis et partitifs
Révision ▶ p. R6
Pratique ▶ p. 9

Teaching Strategy: Groups

Divide students into groups of 2 or 3. Have them pick a restaurant from p. 8, or make up their own, and develop a menu for it. Give students 5 minutes to brainstorm on ideas for the menu, and 10 minutes to begin to develop a dialog between waiter and customer(s). Groups of three should also create a part of the dialog between the two customers about their likes and dislikes before the arrival of the waiter.

2 Et vous?

Répondez au questionnaire suivant. Si vous voulez, comparez vos réponses avec celles de votre partenaire ou de votre groupe.

Prendre *(to take, to have)*, **boire** *(to drink)*

Révision ▶ p. R2; pp. R24-R29
Pratique ▶ p. 10

1. Mon repas préféré est . . .
   - le petit déjeuner
   - le déjeuner
   - le dîner
2. Au petit déjeuner, je prends généralement . . .
   - des céréales
   - des oeufs
   - du pain avec du beurre et de la confiture
   - ??
3. Avec ça, je bois . . .
   - du lait
   - du chocolat chaud
   - du jus d'orange
   - ??
4. Je préfère les sandwichs avec . . .
   - du jambon
   - du fromage
   - du beurre de cacahuète *(peanut)*
   - ??
5. Quand je dîne au restaurant, je commande généralement . . .
   - de la viande
   - du poisson
   - des spaghetti
   - ??
6. En général, sur mes hamburgers, je mets . . .
   - du ketchup
   - de la moutarde
   - de la mayonnaise
   - ??
7. Mon plat favori est . . .
   - le steak-frites
   - le poulet rôti
   - le filet de sole
   - ??
8. Il y a certaines choses que je n'aime pas, par exemple, . . .
   - les brocolis
   - les carottes
   - les épinards *(spinach)*
   - ??
9. Comme dessert, je préfère manger . . .
   - de la glace
   - du gâteau au chocolat
   - de la tarte aux pommes
   - ??
10. Ma cuisine favorite est . . .
    - la cuisine italienne
    - la cuisine chinoise
    - la cuisine mexicaine
    - ??

3 À Monoprix

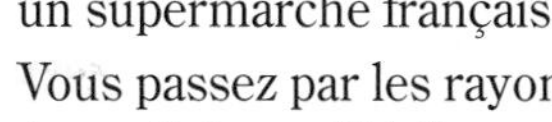

Votre partenaire et vous, vous faites les courses à Monoprix, un supermarché français.

Vous passez par les rayons suivants. Chacun va faire une liste des articles qu'il/elle va acheter.

Achetez deux (2) articles par rayon. Puis comparez vos listes:

- Quels produits identiques avez-vous achetés?
- Quels produits différents avez-vous choisis?

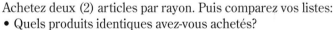

MONOPRIX

← BOISSONS | PRODUITS LAITIERS →

BOUCHERIE
CHARCUTERIE
FRUITS
↓
BOULANGERIE
PÂTISSERIE
LÉGUMES

TU VEUX DU LAIT?
OUI, J'EN VEUX!

RAPPEL!

- **Y** replaces a NAME OF A PLACE introduced by **à**, **dans**, **chez** . . .

  Je vais <u>au restaurant</u>. → J'<u>y</u> vais.
  Je ne vais pas <u>chez Paul</u>. → Je n'<u>y</u> vais pas.
- **En** replaces **de, du, de la, des** + NOUN.

  Je mange <u>du pain</u>. → J'<u>en</u> mange.
  Je ne bois pas <u>de limonade</u> → Je n'<u>en</u> bois pas.

■ **Expansion: Activity 2**

3. du café, du thé
4. de la salade de thon, du rosbif, de la dinde *(turkey)*
6. des oignons, des tomates, du fromage, de la laitue, des cornichons *(pickles)*, du sel, du poivre
7. les pâtes *(pasta)*, les légumes
8. le foie *(liver)*, les rognons *(kidneys)*, les petits pois *(peas)*, les choux de Bruxelles *(Brussel sprouts)*
9. des fraises, des framboises
10. la cuisine thaïlandaise, vietnamienne, française

■ **Teaching Note**

The pronouns **y** and **en** are reviewed here for recognition only. They are actively re-entered in Unit 4.

À votre tour!

À votre tour!

SITUATIONS

Imagine you are in the following situations. Your partner will take the role of the other person in the dialogue and answer your questions.

1 While on an errand, you see a friend waiting at the bus stop.

Ask your friend . . .
- where he/she is going
- what he/she is going to do there
- how long he/she has been waiting for the bus.

2 At a party last weekend, your friend met a French-speaking girl named Juliette. You want to know more about Juliette.

Ask your friend . . .
- how old Juliette is
- if she is French or Canadian
- what she is doing in the United States.

3 You are new in town and you would like some information.

Ask your friend . . .
- to which supermarket he/she goes shopping
- where he/she buys his/her clothes
- what sports one can do in the summer.

4 You are visiting Quebec City with your friend. It is about one o'clock.

Ask your friend . . .
- if he/she is hungry
- if he/she feels like going to a French restaurant
- what he/she feels like eating.

5 You are making weekend plans with your friend.

Ask your friend . . .
- if he/she is going to go out
- what he/she is going to do
- if he/she feels like going to the movies on Sunday.

6 You have invited your friend for dinner next Saturday and want to find out if your friend has any special food preferences.

Ask your friend . . .
- if he/she eats meat
- what desserts he/she likes
- what he/she does not eat.

7 You have been invited to spend a week at the home of your French friend. You are asking about meals.

Ask your friend . . .
- at what time they have breakfast
- what they eat
- what they drink.

Teaching Note
Situation 7
Remind students if necessary *to have breakfast* = **prendre le petit déjeuner.**

Rappel Culturel

Utilisez vos connaissances du monde francophone pour compléter les portraits suivants.

1 Virginie habite à la Martinique. En classe elle parle français, mais avec ses copains elle parle souvent . . .

a. créole
b. italien
c. espagnol
d. alsacien

2 Nathalie est née à Bruxelles. Elle parle français, mais elle n'est pas française. Elle est de nationalité . . .

a. belge
b. suisse
c. allemande
d. luxembourgeoise

3 Aya parle français. Elle est d'Abidjan, une grande ville de 2,5 millions d'habitants. Son pays est . . .

a. l'Algérie
b. le Nigéria
c. le Sénégal
d. la Côte d'Ivoire

4 Albert Bilodeau est un homme de 70 ans. Il habite dans la paroisse d'Iberville où ses ancêtres sont venus il y a plus de deux cents ans. Albert Bilodeau comprend le français et il le parle un peu. Il adore aller aux festivals de musique «cajun» de la région. Albert Bilodeau habite . . .

a. en Floride
b. en Louisiane
c. en Nouvelle-Angleterre
d. dans la province de Québec

5 Yasmina habite en France avec sa famille. Ses parents qui sont immigrés sont d'origine algérienne. Ils pratiquent la religion de leur pays qui est la religion . . .

a. catholique
b. protestante
c. bouddhiste
d. musulmane

6 Jean-Philippe habite à Boston, mais il n'est pas américain. Il comprend le français mais il n'est pas français. Il vient d'un pays qui est une ancienne colonie française et qui est devenu indépendant en 1804. Jean-Philippe est . . .

a. haïtien
b. martiniquais
c. portoricain
d. cubain

7 Gilles habite à Montana dans une région très montagneuse. En hiver, il est moniteur de ski. Là où il habite, on parle français. À l'est, on parle un dialecte allemand. Plus à l'est, on parle italien. Gilles est . . .

a. canadien
b. américain
c. suisse
d. français

8 Mai Van Lee vient d'un pays d'Asie où beaucoup de gens parlaient *(used to speak)* français. Il est . . .

a. coréen
b. vietnamien
c. thaïlandais
d. japonais

Answers: 1-a; 2-a; 3-d; 4-b; 5-d; 6-a; 7-c; 8-b

Rappel Culturel

■ Teaching Note

You may want to have students use the maps in Appendix D, pp. R34–R37 to locate the places mentioned.

Notes culturelles

- French and Dutch (**le néerlandais**) are the official languages of Belgium.
- Vietnam was under French rule between 1859 and 1954. In 1887, Cochin China, Annam, and Tonkin merged with Cambodia to become **l'Indochine,** a French protectorate.
- **Montana-Vermala** is a ski resort in the Swiss canton of Valais. The French-speaking area of Switzerland is in the western part of the country.

Rappel 

TEACHING RESOURCES

Student Activities Manual, pp. 11–12

Realia Notes

- A ticket is **oblitéré** when it is stamped so that it cannot be used again.
- **Les Nouvelles Galeries** is a large supermarket chain that sells clothing as well as food. It is known for its high quality and low prices.
- Jean-Paul Belmondo is a famous French movie actor known particulary for his roles in adventure films and comedies. Three of his best-known movies are *À bout de souffle, Pierrot le fou,* and *The Siren of Mississippi.*

Looking Ahead

The **passé composé** with **être** is reviewed in Rappel 5.

Reprise B *Hier et avant*

Rappel  Le week-end

1 Êtes-vous bon(ne) détective?

Le week-end dernier, vous avez trouvé un portefeuille dans la rue. Dans ce portefeuille il n'y a pas d'argent, mais il y a les choses suivantes. Regardez bien ces choses. Pouvez-vous décrire ce qu'a fait la personne qui a perdu le portefeuille?

** NOUVELLES GALERIES **
COMPACT 18€
LIVRE 9€
TOTAL 27€
CB 5201001190741190
000000002809717 VIV
****
MERCI

- **Où est-ce que cette personne est allée?**
- **Qu'est-ce qu'elle a acheté?**
- **Combien a-t-elle payé chaque objet?**

Chez Jacqueline
CAFÉ - RESTAURANT
21, RUE BERTHELOT
01-47-05-69-34

Table n° 4	
1 steak-frites	6€
1 salade mixte	3€
1 eau minérale	2€
Total	11€

- **Où est-ce que cette personne a déjeuné?**
- **Qu'est-ce qu'elle a mangé?**
- **Qu'est-ce qu'elle a bu?**
- **Combien est-ce qu'elle a dépensé pour le déjeuner?**

CINE-VOX
Festival Belmondo
Les films de la semaine
lundi-vendredi
CARTOUCHE
samedi-dimanche
L'HOMME DE RIO
Séances à 14h30 et 17h

CINE-VOX
ENTREE
7€
350717

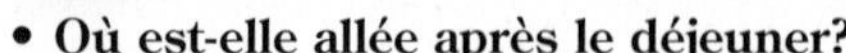

- **Où est-elle allée après le déjeuner?**
- **Qu'est-ce qu'elle a vu?**
- **À quelle heure est-ce que le film a commencé?**

RAPPEL!

To describe what people DID in the past, use the PASSE COMPOSE.

- For most verbs,
  passé composé = **avoir** + PAST PARTICIPLE
  Tu as étudié hier. Je n'ai pas étudié.
- For a few verbs like **aller,**
  passé composé = **être** + PAST PARTICIPLE
  Je suis allé(e) au cinéma.

Le passé composé des verbes réguliers avec avoir

Révision ▶ p. R4
Pratique ▶ p. 11

Teaching Strategy: Warm-Up

Have the class write a group story. Each student will contribute at least one sentence. Give them an amusing subject that lends itself to creativity and to action sentences for **passé composé** practice. Students can take turns copying the story onto the board as it is being developed. Be sure that what is being written is carefully verified for grammatical mistakes by both you and the other students.

2 Oui ou non?

Décrivez deux choses que vous avez faites et une chose que vous n'avez pas faite le week-end dernier. Utilisez les activités suggérées ou d'autres activités de votre choix.

- dormir
- ranger ma chambre
- travailler dans le jardin
- acheter des vêtements
- déjeuner dans un restaurant
- visiter un musée
- assister à un concert
- rendre visite à des copains
- lire un livre
- voir un film
- faire des achats
- avoir un rendez-vous
- faire une promenade à la campagne
- faire du camping
- prendre des photos
- ??

Les participes passés irréguliers

Révision ▶ p. R4
Pratique ▶ p. 12

3 Un week-end à la campagne

Ces personnes ont passé le week-end à la campagne. Dites ce qu'elles ont fait.

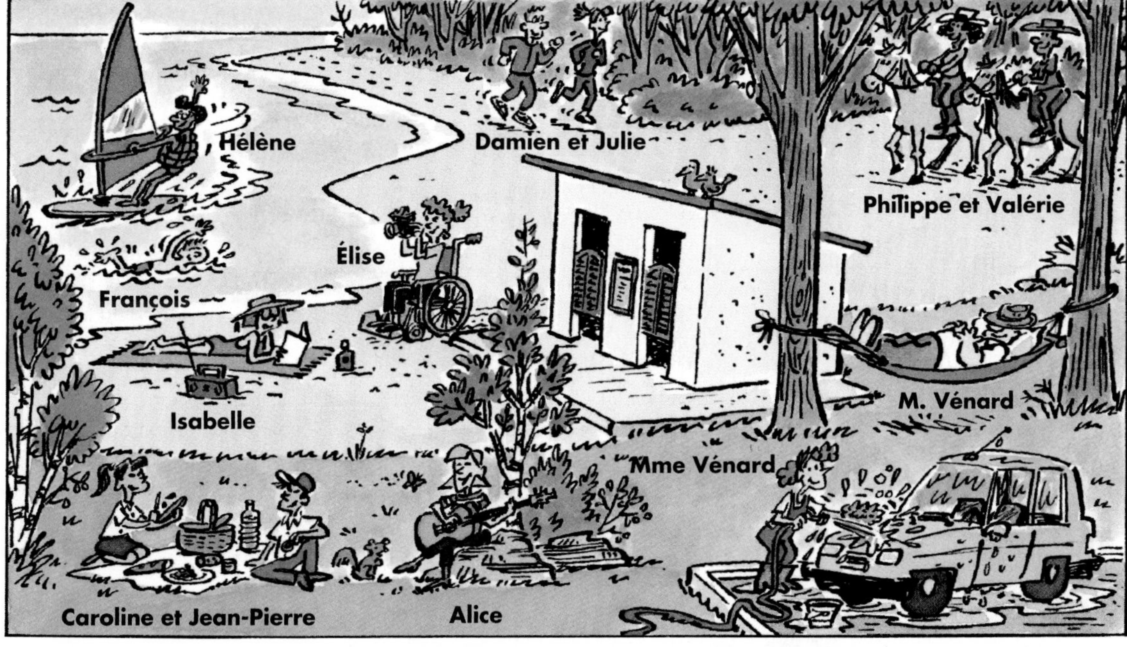

RAPPEL!

To express HOW LONG AGO you did something, use:
il y a + time

J'AI ACHETÉ MA VOITURE IL Y A 70 ANS!

Il y a

Pratique ▶ p. 12

Supplementary vocabulary

aller à la gym *to go to the gym*
aller danser *to go dancing*
cuisiner *to cook*
faire du baby-sitting *to babysit*
louer une vidéo *to rent a (video)tape*
participer à une compétition sportive *to participate in a competition*
regarder la télévision *to watch TV*
surfer sur l'Internet *to surf the Internet*
utiliser un ordinateur *to use a computer*

Teaching Strategy: Extra Practice

Using **Transparency 10**, have students in pairs make lists of every activity they see in 15 minutes.

Variation: Show the transparency for only 20–30 seconds, and have students list as many activities as they remember. Note: This activity may also be done as an A/B activity.

Rappel 5

TEACHING RESOURCES

Student Activities Manual, p. 13

Realia Notes

- **une Kasbah** une citadelle d'un souverain dans les pays arabes.
- **Fès-el-Boli:** la plus ancienne agglomération de Fès, le centre religieux et économique du Maroc.
- **la Médine:** ville sainte pour les musulmans et qui a servi de refuge à Mahomet en 622.
- **Une mosquée** est un temple musulman.
- **Un souk** est un marché, une boutique arabe.

Teaching Strategy: Expansion

Bring in travel brochures and catalogs. Have students (in pairs) prepare brief oral presentations on their "vacations."

Rappel 5 En vacances

1 Un voyage au Maroc

L'été dernier, Gabrielle a fait un voyage au Maroc avec un voyage organisé. Voici le programme de ce voyage. Regardez bien ce programme et répondez aux questions.

- Comment est-elle allée au Maroc?
- Quel jour est-elle partie?
- À quelle heure est-elle arrivée à Rabat?
- Qu'est-ce qu'elle a visité dans cette ville?
- Dans quelle ville est-elle allée ensuite?
- Qu'est-ce qu'elle a fait dans cette ville?
- Quelle est la dernière ville qu'elle a visitée?
- Qu'est-ce qu'elle a vu dans cette ville?
- Quel jour est-elle rentrée en France?
- À quelle heure a-t-elle pris son avion?
- À quelle heure est-elle arrivée à Paris?

Agence Maroc-Tours

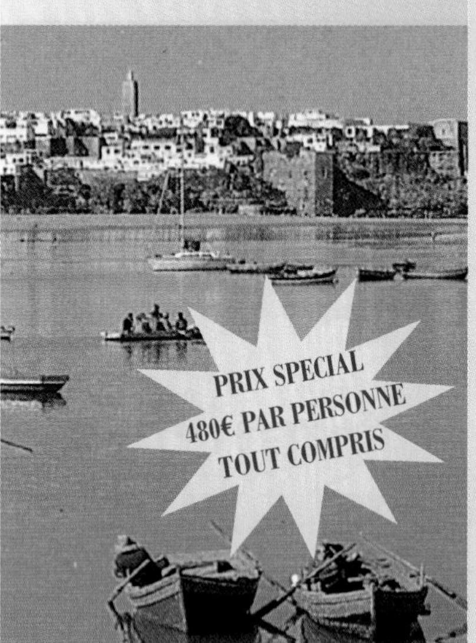

5 jours au Maroc

PROGRAMME DU VOYAGE

VENDREDI, 10 JUIN

matin	Départ de Paris, vol Air Maroc 104, 8h35 Arrivée à Rabat, 11h18
après-midi	Tour de Rabat en autocar

SAMEDI, 11 JUIN

matin	Visite de la Kasbah Musée des Arts marocains
après-midi	Libre

DIMANCHE, 12 JUIN

matin	Départ pour Fès en autobus, 8h00
après-midi	Libre

LUNDI, 13 JUIN

matin	Visite guidée de Fès-el-Boli (vieille ville)
après-midi	Départ pour Marrakech en avion, 18h35

MARDI, 14 JUIN

matin	Marrakech, visite de la Médina Mosquée de la Koutoubia
après-midi	Visite des souks: shopping

MERCREDI, 15 JUIN

matin	Libre
après-midi	Départ pour Paris, vol Air Maroc 121, 12h35 Arrivée à Paris, 15h21

FLASH d'information

Le Maroc est un pays de 30 millions d'habitants situé au nord-ouest de l'Afrique. La majorité des Marocains sont arabes et pratiquent la religion musulmane.

La capitale du Maroc est Rabat, mais la plus grande ville est Casablanca. Marrakech et Fès sont des villes traditionnelles avec des monuments anciens.

Ancien protectorat français, le Maroc est devenu indépendant en 1956. C'est une monarchie constitutionnelle avec un roi, le Roi Mohammed VI.

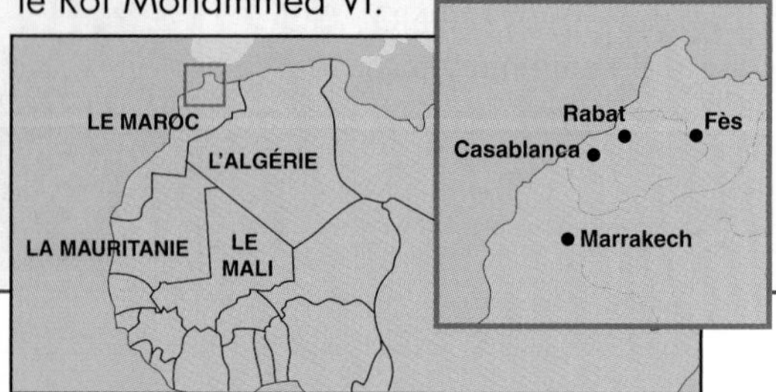

Teaching Strategy: Oral/Aural Practice

Before class, prepare a simple story of about ten negative and affirmative sentences in the **passé composé**. Tell it to the students twice. Ask them to retell the story sentence by sentence in chronological order.

Note: If the story is told in the first person, the students will have the added practice of transforming it into the second person formal since they will now be telling you what you did. You might want to make a transparency of the story (as they will be telling it) so that, as the students come up with the sentences, you can give them the written reinforcement.

RAPPEL!

When the passé composé of a verb is formed with **être**, the past participle AGREES WITH THE SUBJECT.

Julien est arrivé ce matin.
Pauline et Claire sont arrivées hier soir.

Le passé composé

Révision ▶ p. R4
Pratique ▶ p. 13

2 Dialogues

Avec votre partenaire, composez et jouez l'un des dialogues suivants.

▶ **— Tu as étudié hier soir?**
— Non, je suis allé(e) au ciné.
— Qu'est-ce que tu as vu?
— Un film policier.

1. • rester chez toi ce week-end
   • aller à la campagne
   • faire
   • une promenade à vélo

2. • sortir avec ton copain samedi
   • faire des achats
   • acheter
   • un blouson

3. • rentrer chez toi à midi
   • déjeuner au restaurant
   • manger
   • ??

4. • venir à la boum dimanche
   • aller au théâtre
   • voir
   • ??

3 Pendant les vacances

Pendant les vacances, ces personnes ont fait des choses différentes. Avec un(e) partenaire, choisissez une des illustrations et décrivez-la ensemble. Faites trois ou quatre phrases et utilisez votre imagination.

Où sont allées les personnes? Qu'est-ce qu'elles ont fait?

Paul et Robert

Juliette

Monsieur Ramirez

Alice et Julien

Caroline

Cécile et Sophie

Thomas

Olivier

■ Expansion: Activity 3

1. un touriste, prendre des photos de la tour Eiffel
2. prendre un avion, préparer des valises
3. monter sur un chameau, visiter les pyramides de Gizeh (l'Égypte)
4. faire du vélo, faire un pique-nique (du camping)
5. mettre une échelle, monter dans un arbre, jouer dans une cabane
6. descendre dans une caverne, prendre une lampe de poche
7. monter dans un arbre, perdre son équilibre, sauver un chat, tomber
8. un film d'horreur, avoir peur

Rappel 6

TEACHING RESOURCES

Student Activities Manual, pp. 13–14

■ Notes Linguistiques

- Point out the name of the character to the students. **M. Léveillé** = Mr. "Awakened."
- **Plus de peur que de mal** means "more frightened than harmed."

Teaching Strategy

Use **Transparency 11** as an introduction to the story before students read. Make copies of the pictures and have students discuss the sequence.

Rappel  Qu'est-ce qui se passe?

1 Plus de peur que de mal

En général, Monsieur Léveillé dort très bien, mais la nuit dernière, il n'a pas bien dormi. Expliquez pourquoi. Avec votre partenaire, décrivez l'histoire en répondant aux questions correspondant à chaque illustration.

Scène A

1. **Quelle heure était-il?**
   - **Il était onze heures.**
   - **Il était minuit.**
   - **Il était une heure du matin.**
2. **Où était Monsieur Léveillé?**
   - **Il était au salon.**
   - **Il était dans la salle à manger.**
   - **Il était dans sa chambre.**
3. **Qu'est-ce qu'il faisait?**
   - **Il dormait.**
   - **Il lisait le journal.**
   - **Il écoutait son baladeur.**

Scène B

4. **Pourquoi est-ce que Monsieur Léveillé s'est réveillé?**
   - **Il avait chaud.**
   - **Il avait mal à la tête.**
   - **Il a entendu un bruit.**

Scène C

5. **Qu'est-ce qu'il a fait?**
   - **Il est resté au lit.**
   - **Il est descendu.**
   - **Il a téléphoné à la police.**
6. **Qu'est-ce qu'il avait à la main?**
   - **Il avait un revolver.**
   - **Il avait une batte de baseball.**
   - **Il avait une raquette de tennis.**

Teaching Strategy: Expansion

Divide students into pairs and have them draw their own stick figure cartoon with six different scenes. As in the cartoon on pp. 16–17, there should be captions in the **imparfait** and in the **passé composé**.

Have students write captions to their cartoon on six separate pieces of paper. When cartoon and captions are completed, two pairs should exchange their cartoons and captions and try to put the captions to the appropriate pictures. Have both pairs get together afterwards and compare notes.

Note: As with any creative activity, the teacher should circulate constantly in order to verify that vocabulary and structure are correct.

Scène D

7. Qu'est-ce qu'il a vu?
   - Il a vu un homme armé.
   - Il a vu une ombre *(shadow)* dans le jardin.
   - Il a vu des traces sur le sol.

Scène E

8. Qu'est-ce qu'il y avait dans la cuisine?
   - Il y avait un fantôme.
   - Il y avait un cambrioleur *(burglar)*.
   - Il y avait des ratons laveurs *(raccoons)*.
9. Qu'est-ce qu'ils faisaient là?
   - Ils dormaient.
   - Ils jouaient avec le chat.
   - Ils mangeaient la nourriture du chat.
10. Où était le chat?
   - Il était sur la table.
   - Il était sous la table.
   - Il mangeait avec les ratons laveurs.

Scène F

Maintenant racontez la fin de l'histoire.
- Qu'a fait Monsieur Léveillé?
- Et les ratons laveurs?
- Et le chat?

Note culturelle
Raccoons are found in Canada and the United States. They are rare in France.

Teaching Strategy
Have students work on the conclusion in pairs.

RAPPEL!

To describe what you USED TO DO, what you WERE DOING, or to describe the CIRCUMSTANCES of an event, use the **imperfect** tense.

J'allais au ciné.	*I used to go to the movies.* *I was going to the movies.*
Il était six heures.	*It was 6 o'clock.*

→ You will learn more about the use of the imperfect in Unit 3.

L'imparfait
Révision ▶ p. R5
Pratique ▶ p. 13

2 Dialogue

Avec votre partenaire, composez et jouez l'un des dialogues suivants.

▶ — **Où étais-tu hier soir?**
— **J'étais dans ma chambre.**
— **Qu'est-ce que tu faisais?**
— **Je lisais un livre.**
— **Et qu'est-ce que tu as fait après?**
— **J'ai fini mes devoirs.**

1. • cet après-midi
   • au café
   • attendre un copain
   • aller au ciné
2. • à deux heures
   • à la bibliothèque
   • étudier
   • rentrer chez moi
3. • samedi matin
   • au centre commercial
   • faire du shopping
   • ??
4. • samedi après-midi
   • dans le jardin
   • aider mon père
   • ??

Teaching Strategy: Pair Practice

Divide students into pairs. One student will be a police officer and one will be an accused criminal. Have them create a dialog in which the police officer questions the accused and he/she gives an alibi: "What were you doing at 10:00 when the victim died?"

3 Au café

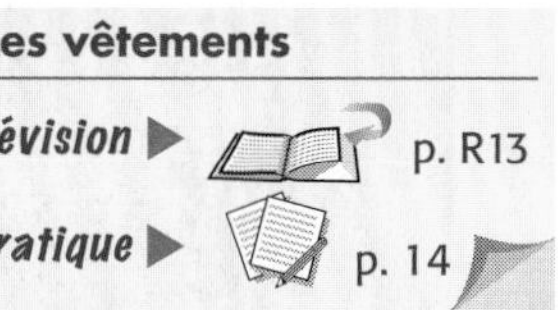

Vous avez passé l'après-midi à la terrasse d'un café. Vous avez vu les personnes suivantes passer dans la rue. Décrivez chacune de ces personnes.

- Il était (quelle heure?)
- J'ai vu (un homme? une dame? . . . ?)
- Il/elle était (jeune? grand(e)? . . . ?)
- Il/elle portait (quels vêtements?)
- Il/elle avait aussi (quoi?)
- Il/elle allait (où?)
- Il/elle allait faire (quoi?)

4 Photos de vacances

Vous avez passé les vacances en France avec votre partenaire. Pendant votre voyage, vous avez pris les photos suivantes. Choisissez deux photos et décrivez ce qui se passait *(what was going on)* quand vous avez pris ces photos. Utilisez l'imparfait.

■ Vocabulary Notes

Terms students may find useful for Act. 3:

1. se promener
2. porter des lunettes
3. avoir une raquette à la main
4. avoir un sac; porter une casquette
5. une personne âgée; faire les courses
6. aller à la pêche

Terms students may find useful for Act. 4:

1. un orchestre; jouer du rock; danser; boire dans un café
2. une course à vélo; des vaches; regarder les coureurs; acheter des glaces
3. jouer au volley; faire du ski nautique; prendre un bain de soleil; faire de la planche à voile
4. la fête de la musique; danser dans la rue; faire un film

Notes culturelles

- July 14 is the national holiday of France. Street dances **(les bals populaires)** are traditionally organized that day as well as parades and fireworks.
- **La fête de la musique** is an international event, usually celebrated on the first night of summer.

Teaching Strategy: Expansion

Have students bring in four pictures of themselves on vacation, at a party, etc. For each picture, students should write a 4–5 sentence description of the scene using **imparfait** and/or **passé composé**: (e.g., how old they were, what season it was, who took the picture, etc.).

À votre tour!

SITUATIONS

Imagine you are in the following situations. Your partner will take the role of the other person in the dialogue and answer your questions.

1 Your friend just told you that he/she saw a great movie last Saturday.

Ask your friend . . .
- with whom he/she went to the movies
- what movie they saw
- what they did afterwards.

2 For his/her birthday, your friend was invited to a French restaurant.

Ask your friend . . .
- if he/she went to this restaurant for lunch or dinner
- what he/she ate
- what he/she drank.

3 You are phoning your French friend Valérie. Her brother/sister answers the phone and says that Valérie is not at home.

Ask Valérie's brother/sister . . .
- what time Valérie left
- where she went
- when she is coming back home.

4 Your friend came back from spring vacation with a tan and looks great.

Ask your friend . . .
- where he/she went
- what he/she did there
- when he/she came back.

5 Last summer your friend traveled through France with his/her family. You want to know more about their trip.

Ask your friend . . .
- how long they stayed in France
- if they traveled by *(en)* car or by train
- what cities they visited.

6 Last night your friend went to a concert by a French rock group.

Ask your friend . . .
- if the group *(le groupe)* sang in French or in English
- what clothes they were wearing
- how many people there were at the concert.

7 After supper last night you called your friend but nobody answered the phone.

Ask your friend . . .
- where he/she was
- what he/she was doing
- what his/her family was doing.

8 You and your friend are talking about your childhood — when you were eight years old.

Ask your friend . . .
- where he/she used to live
- to which school he/she used to go
- what programs *(quelles émissions)* he/she used to watch on TV.

Teaching Strategy
Have students work in pairs or small groups to find the answers to these questions.

Rappel Culturel

A. FAITS CULTURELS

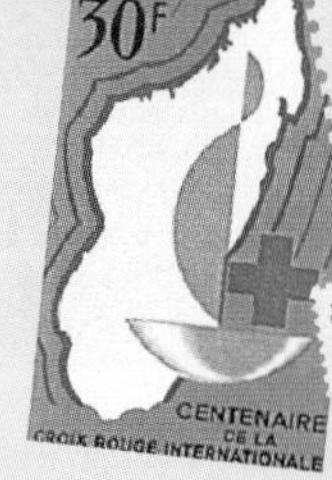

1. La devise *(motto)* de la France est . . .
   a. Paix et Prospérité
   b. Liberté, Égalité, Fraternité
   c. Je me souviens

2. La France métropolitaine est divisée administrativement en 96 . . .
   a. cantons
   b. départements
   c. provinces

3. Le TGV est . . .
   a. un avion supersonique
   b. une voiture électrique
   c. un train très rapide

4. Si on veut faire du ski en hiver, on peut aller . . .
   a. à Monaco
   b. en Normandie
   c. en Savoie

5. La «Belle Province» est le nom que l'on donne à . . .
   a. la Touraine
   b. la Louisiane
   c. la province de Québec

6. La Polynésie française est un groupe d'îles qui font partie de la France d'outre-mer. La plus grande de ces îles est . . .
   a. Tahiti
   b. la Martinique
   c. Madagascar

7. En 1803, la France a vendu aux États-Unis un vaste territoire pour la somme de 15 millions de dollars. Ce territoire était . . .
   a. la Louisiane
   b. la Caroline du Sud
   c. l'Alaska

8. Ce Français est un héros de la Révolution américaine. Il s'appelle . . .
   a. Cavelier de la Salle
   b. Champlain
   c. La Fayette

9. Le continent où il y a le plus grand nombre de pays qui utilisent le français comme langue officielle est . . .
   a. l'Europe
   b. l'Afrique
   c. l'Amérique du Sud

10. L'Algérie est une ancienne colonie française. Ce pays est situé . . .
    a. en Asie
    b. en Afrique noire
    c. en Afrique du Nord

11. En Afrique, les masques sont considérés comme des objets . . .
    a. religieux
    b. de collection
    c. de la vie courante

12. Au Sénégal, la religion principale est . . .
    a. la religion musulmane
    b. la religion catholique
    c. la religion protestante

13. La population de la France est de . . .
    a. 40 millions d'habitants
    b. 60 millions d'habitants
    c. 100 millions d'habitants

14. La «Nouvelle France» est le nom . . .
    a. d'un grand magasin à Paris
    b. d'un satellite français
    c. de l'ancien empire français en Amérique du Nord

Answers: 1-b; 2-b; 3-c; 4-c; 5-c; 6-a; 7-a; 8-c; 9-b; 10-c; 11-a; 12-a; 13-b; 14-c

NOTES CULTURELLES

- **Je me souviens** is the motto of the Canadian province of Quebec.
- **Cavelier de La Salle** (1643–1687) explored the Mississippi region and Louisiana.
- **Samuel de Champlain** (1567–1635) founded the city of Quebec in 1608.
- **La Fayette** (1757–1834) was a French general who took an active part in the American Revolution.

B. SITUATIONS CULTURELLES

1. Les Smith, des touristes anglais, ont visité la France en voiture. À Paris, ils ont vu Notre-Dame. En Normandie, ils ont vu le Mont-Saint-Michel. En Provence, ils ont vu le Pont du Gard. *Qu'est-ce qu'ils ont vu en Alsace?*

- **a.** *Le Futuroscope.*
- **b.** *Le château de Chambord.*
- **c.** *La cathédrale de Strasbourg.*

2. Patrick et Jérôme ont passé leurs vacances dans les Alpes. Un jour, ils ont assisté à un grand événement sportif. Pour voir cet événement, ils sont allés sur une route de montagne et là ils ont attendu patiemment avec des milliers d'autres personnes. Enfin, ils ont vu des voitures, des motos, et finalement les coureurs parmi lesquels ils ont reconnu le «maillot jaune».
À quel événement sportif ont-ils assisté?

- **a.** *Le Grand Prix de Monaco.*
- **b.** *Les 24 Heures du Mans.*
- **c.** *Le Tour de France.*

3. Catherine est une étudiante française. À Noël, elle va généralement faire du ski, mais cette année elle n'a pas fait de ski. Elle a fait un grand voyage, mais elle n'est pas allée à l'étranger. Là où elle est allée, elle a fait de la planche à voile et du ski nautique. Elle est rentrée chez elle très bronzée.
Où est-elle allée?

- **a.** *En Savoie.*
- **b.** *En Normandie.*
- **c.** *À la Guadeloupe.*

4. Chaque année Claire attend patiemment la période de Carnaval. Finalement le Carnaval est arrivé. Le premier jour, Claire a assisté au couronnement de la reine par «Bonhomme». Les jours suivants, Claire a assisté à la course des canoës sur le Saint-Laurent et elle a admiré les sculptures de glace et de neige.
Où habite Claire?

- **a.** *À Québec.*
- **b.** *À Nice.*
- **c.** *En Guyane française.*

5. Hier c'était un jour férié *(holiday)*. Le matin, Julien est allé sur les Champs-Élysées où il a assisté au défilé militaire. L'après-midi, il est sorti avec sa copine Véronique. Le soir, les deux amis ont vu les feux d'artifice *(fireworks)*. Ensuite, ils ont dansé dans les rues comme des millions de Français.
Quelle fête est-ce qu'on célébrait hier?

- **a.** *La fête du Travail.*
- **b.** *La fête nationale.*
- **c.** *La fête de Mardi Gras.*

6. Philippe montre les photos qu'il a prises pendant les vacances. Il explique: «Cet arbre géant est un baobab . . . Le vêtement que porte cette jeune fille s'appelle un boubou . . . Cet homme qui raconte une histoire est un griot.» *Où Philippe est-il allé pendant les vacances?*

- **a.** *Au Sénégal.*
- **b.** *En Algérie.*
- **c.** *À Tahiti.*

7. Il y a environ deux cents ans, Jean-Baptiste Point du Sable, un Français d'ascendance africaine, arrivait dans la région des Grands Lacs. Il a construit la première maison d'un petit village qui allait devenir l'une des plus grandes villes du continent américain.
Quelle est cette ville?

- **a.** *Détroit.*
- **b.** *Chicago.*
- **c.** *Montréal.*

8. Monsieur Dutour est ingénieur pour une compagnie de prospection pétrolière. Dans sa profession, il voyage beaucoup. La semaine dernière, il est allé dans un pays d'Afrique du Nord qui produit beaucoup de pétrole et de gaz naturel.
Où est allé Monsieur Dutour?

- **a.** *Au Congo.*
- **b.** *En Algérie.*
- **c.** *En République Centrafricaine.*

Answers: 1-c; 2-c; 3-c; 4-a; 5-b; 6-a; 7-b; 8-b

NOTES CULTURELLES

- **Le Futuroscope** is a theme park near **Poitiers**. It presents new and future technologies through attractions like 3-D and IMAX movies.
- **Le Grand Prix de Monaco** and **Les 24 heures du Mans** are famous international car races.
- **Le griot** is a traditional African storyteller. **Griots** are poets and musicians who go from village to village, carrying on the oral traditions and folklore.

Nous et les autres

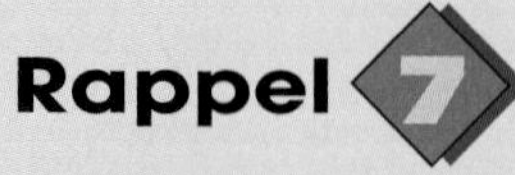

TEACHING RESOURCES

Student Activities Manual, pp. 15–16

Reprise C *Nous et les autres*

Rappel  Vive l'amitié!

Dans la vie, l'amitié est peut-être la chose la plus importante. Mais attention, il y a toutes sortes d'amis! Par exemple . . .

RAPPEL!

When we ask someone to do something for us, we often use OBJECT PRONOUNS:

Téléphone-**moi** ce soir. Prête-**moi** dix dollars.

Note also the constructions:

Tu **me** donnes ton numéro de téléphone?	Tu **nous** invites?
Je **te** donne aussi mon adresse.	Je **vous** invite à ma boum.

- **me, te → m', t'** before a vowel sound.
  Tu **m'**invites? Oui, je **t'**invite.

Les pronoms compléments

Révision ▶ p. R8-R9
Pratique ▶ p. 15

Teaching Strategy: Grammar Drill

Read these questions orally and have students replace the d.o. or the i.o. in their answers:

1. Est-ce que ton ami t'écrit souvent?
2. Tu regardes la télé?
3. Tu achètes tes livres à la librairie ou tu les empruntes à la bibliothèque?
4. Est-ce que ton prof de maths aide tes amis et toi avec les devoirs?
5. Tes parents te prêtent de l'argent?
6. Est-ce que le prof de français vous donne beaucoup de devoirs?
7. Est-ce que le président nous connaît personnellement?

1 S'il te plaît

Vous venez d'arriver en France. Demandez à votre copain français (copine française) trois services et expliquez-lui pourquoi.

▶ **— S'il te plaît, présente-moi à tes copains.**
— Pourquoi?
— Je voudrais rencontrer des jeunes Français.

QUELS SERVICES?
- amener dans une boutique de vêtements
- amener à la banque
- présenter à tes copains
- prêter ton plan *(map)* de la ville
- prêter ton appareil-photo
- donner l'adresse d'un bon restaurant
- montrer où est la poste
- ??

POURQUOI?
- envoyer une lettre
- changer de l'argent
- dîner en ville
- faire une promenade
- prendre des photos
- rencontrer des jeunes Français
- acheter un blouson
- ??

2 Échanges

Demandez certains services à votre partenaire. Il/elle va proposer un échange. Acceptez ou refusez.

▶ **— Dis, Éric, prête-moi ton VTT.**
— D'accord! Je te prête mon VTT si tu me prêtes tes rollers.
— D'accord!
(Non, merci!)

prêter . . .	tes notes tes CD ton VTT *(mountain bike)*
inviter . . .	chez toi à ta fête d'anniversaire
aider . . .	avec le devoir de français avec le devoir de maths
présenter . . .	à ton copain à ta copine
montrer . . .	tes photos tes magazines

TU CONNAIS QUELQU'UN ICI?
NON, JE NE CONNAIS PERSONNE. JE NE SAIS PAS OÙ NOUS SOMMES.

RAPPEL!

Although **connaître** and **savoir** both mean *to know*, they are used differently:
Nous **connaissons** Yasmina.
Nous **savons** où elle habite.

Connaître et savoir
Révision ▶ p. R8-R9
Pratique ▶ p. 16

RAPPEL!

quelqu'un *(someone)*	Je vois **quelqu'un.**	**ne . . . personne** *(no one)*	Je **ne** vois **personne.**
quelque chose *(something)*	Je vois **quelque chose.**	**ne . . . rien** *(nothing)*	Je **ne** vois **rien.**

Note culturelle

Le VTT (= vélo tout terrain) has been popular in France since being imported from the U.S. in 1983.

Expansion: Activity 2

Students ask their partner why he/she wants to borrow the item. The partner answers.
— Dis, Éric, prête-moi ton VTT.
— D'accord, je te prête mon VTT si tu me prêtes tes rollers.
— Pourquoi?
— Parce que je ne veux pas marcher!

Supplementary vocabulary

(Illustration)
l'espace *space*
l'extraterrestre *alien*
le martien *Martian*
l'OVNI (Objet Volant Non Identifié) *UFO*
la planète *planet*
la soucoupe volante *flying saucer*

Expansion: Rappel

Have students invent a story based on the illustration. What just happened? What is the people's reaction? What do the aliens want? What will happen next?

8. Tu téléphones souvent à tes amis?
9. Est-ce que tu m'aimes bien?
10. Est-ce que je vous invite régulièrement au restaurant?

Note: Answers to these questions could be put on a transparency ahead of time to give written reinforcement of the correct answers; students could also write out answers on the board.

TEACHING RESOURCES

Student Activities Manual, pp. 17–18

Notes culturelles

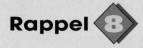

- This type of photo-illustrated story is called **un roman-photo** in France. **Les romans-photos** are mostly published in romance magazines such as **Nous Deux** or **Intimité**.

Rappel  Un jeune homme timide

Dans le cours d'espagnol, il y a une nouvelle étudiante. Elle s'appelle Catherine. Pierre la trouve sympathique, mais il est trop timide pour lui parler.

Après le cours, Pierre et Catherine attendent le bus . . .

Chez lui, Pierre pense toujours à Catherine. Il prend le guide et regarde le programme des films de la semaine.

Mais Pierre ne téléphone pas à Catherine.

Pierre met sa veste et il va seul au cinéma.

Pendant ce temps, Catherine regarde aussi le journal.

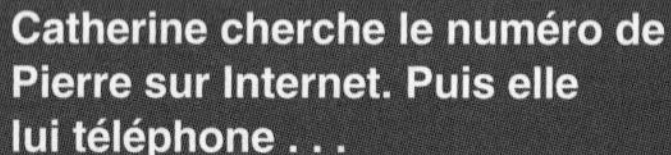

Catherine cherche le numéro de Pierre sur Internet. Puis elle lui téléphone . . .

. . . mais chez Pierre, personne ne répond au téléphone.

Teaching Strategy: Direct Object Pronouns

On a transparency, photocopy or on the board, write a story which repeats the same direct object over and over and read it aloud to the students. Ask them to identify what is wrong with the story. Once they realize the same word is repeated many times, ask them to fix the problem. This is a fairly quick group activity that clearly demonstrates the importance of the direct object pronouns (e.g., **J'ai une nouvelle voiture. J'adore ma voiture. J'ai acheté ma voiture chez Renault. Je vais laver ma voiture tous les jours et je vais garder ma voiture dans le garage...**).

Le lendemain après la classe.
Pierre, il y a un bon film au Rex. Est-ce que tu l'as vu?
Euh oui . . . je l'ai vu. C'est un film vraiment super!

Est-ce que tu veux le revoir avec moi ce soir?
Mais oui, avec plaisir.

Et maintenant, avec votre partenaire, imaginez la suite de l'histoire. Par exemple . . .

- **Quand est-ce que Pierre et Catherine sont allés au cinéma?**
- **Qu'est-ce qu'il lui a dit?**
- **Qu'est-ce qu'elle lui a dit?**
- **Est-ce qu'ils ont eu d'autres rendez-vous?**

RAPPEL!

To refer to people previously mentioned, use:

le / la / les		lui / leur	
Je regarde **Marc**.	Je **le** regarde.	Je téléphone **à Marc**.	Je **lui** téléphone.
Tu connais **Claire**.	Tu **la** connais.	Tu parles **à Claire**.	Tu **lui** parles.
J'invite **mes** amis.	Je **les** invite.	J'écris **à mes amis.**	Je **leur** écris.

- **le/la/les** may also refer to things.
  Je regarde **la photo.** Je **la** regarde.
- **le/la → l'** before a vowel sound
  Nous écoutons **le CD**. Nous **l'**écoutons.

Les compléments d'objet direct et indirect

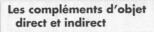

Révision ▶ p. R8-R9
Pratique ▶ p. 17

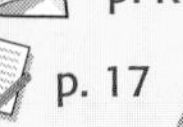

Voir *(to see)*, **écrire** *(to write)*

Révision ▶ pp. R26, R30
Pratique ▶ p. 18

1 Relations personnelles

Demandez à votre partenaire de décrire ses relations avec l'une des personnes indiquées.

▶ **— Tu as une cousine?**
— Oui, bien sûr.
— Tu la vois souvent?
— Oui, je la vois de temps en temps.
— Tu lui écris?
— Non, je ne lui écris jamais.

QUI?	QUOI?	QUAND?
un copain	voir	souvent
des copines	inviter	de temps en temps
une tante	téléphoner (à)	rarement
des cousins	écrire (à)	jamais
une cousine	aider	toujours
des voisins	rendre visite (à)	
	donner des cadeaux (à)	
	donner des conseils *(advice)* (à)	
	demander des conseils (à)	

2 La boum

Vous préparez une boum. Demandez à votre partenaire s'il (si elle) peut vous aider avec les choses suivantes. Votre partenaire va accepter ou refuser.

▶ **— Tu peux préparer les sandwichs?**
— Oui, d'accord, je vais les préparer. (Je suis désolé(e) mais je ne peux pas les préparer.)

- faire les courses
- acheter les boissons
- laver les verres
- ranger la cuisine
- mettre la table
- préparer les sandwichs
- décorer le salon
- apporter ta mini-chaîne
- choisir la musique
- inviter nos amis
- téléphoner aux voisins

Teaching Note

Before doing Activity 1, you may want to review the placement of the object pronoun in front of the infinitive.

Expansion: Activity 2

In case the request for help is refused, students should be encouraged to invent an excuse, e.g.:
Je n'ai pas le temps.
Je dois aider ma mère, etc.

Note: In writing the story, be sure to include sentences in the future, **passé composé**, and negative tenses, etc.

Indirect Object Pronouns
Use the same technique to repeat the same indirect object over and over (e.g., **Ma meilleure amie s'appelle Pauline. Pauline est très sympa. Je téléphone souvent à Pauline. L'autre jour, j'ai téléphoné à Pauline et j'ai demandé à Pauline si elle voulait aller au cirque...**).

À votre tour!

Teaching Notes

- In France, a university cafeteria is called a «restaurant universitaire.» **Une cafétéria** is a self-service restaurant open to everyone.
- You may want to point out again the false cognate:
  la librairie = bookstore
  la bibliothèque = library

À votre tour!

SITUATIONS

Imagine you are in the following situations. Your partner will take the role of the other person in the dialogue and answer your questions.

1 You are an exchange student in France. It is your first day of class and you need help.

Ask another student (who, of course, is willing to help you) . . .
- to loan you a notebook
- to give you a pencil
- to show you where the cafeteria is
- to take you *(amener)* to the library.

2 You are spending two weeks at the home of your French cousin who lives in Paris.

Ask your cousin (who will accept or refuse) . . .
- to introduce you to his/her friends
- to loan you something you need
- to show you a place in Paris you would like to visit
- to take you to a show or an event that you are interested in.

3 Your friend has a Belgian neighbor named Béatrice. You would like to know more about their relationship.

Ask your friend . . .
- how long he/she has known Béatrice
- if he/she knows her parents
- if he/she invites her often
- what he/she is going to give Béatrice for her birthday.

4 Your friend has a Canadian penpal, Jean, who is coming to visit next weekend. You want to know what your friend has planned for Jean's visit.

Ask your friend . . .
- to what restaurant he/she is going to invite Jean
- what places *(quels endroits)* he/she is going to show him
- what gift *(un cadeau)* he/she is going to give him.

5 You are the manager of a tourist shop in Montreal. You are hiring students for the summer and are interviewing one of the candidates.

Ask the candidate . . .
- if he/she knows how to speak French well
- what other languages he/she knows how to speak
- if he/she knows how to answer the phone in French
- what other things he/she knows how to do.

6 You and your friend are planning a party for next Friday night. You are checking if your friend has done his/her share of the work.

Ask your friend . . .
- if he/she sent the invitations
- if he/she called the neighbors
- if he/she chose the music
- if he/she bought the beverages *(les boissons)*.

7 You are visiting Paris with your friend. It is your first trip but your friend has visited Paris before.

Ask your friend . . .
- what monuments he/she knows
- if he/she knows how to get to the Eiffel Tower
- if he/she knows if the Louvre is open *(ouvert)* this afternoon
- if he/she knows a good restaurant.

Les trois bagues

Reading fiction

AVANT DE LIRE

Quand on lit une histoire, il est utile d'anticiper ce qui va se passer d'après les éléments que l'on connaît déjà. Lisez d'abord la **Note culturelle** et **Une annonce.** D'après vous, pourquoi est-ce que les neveux vont aller chez le notaire?

- pour assister à un mariage
- pour vendre la maison familiale
- pour recevoir une somme d'argent
- pour régler *(to settle)* une dispute

Maintenant, continuez votre lecture pour vérifier votre réponse.

NOTE CULTURELLE

Le notaire

Le notaire joue un rôle important dans la vie des familles françaises. Son rôle est d'officialiser un grand nombre d'actes et de contrats de la vie civile (contrat de mariage, testaments,° ventes° de biens immobiliers,° etc.). Un notaire a le titre de **Maître,** Maître Durand, par exemple. Son bureau° s'appelle **une étude.**

testament *will* **vente** *sale*
biens immobiliers *real estate*
bureau *office*

Teaching Note

The purpose of this reading is to review and reactivate some important items and structures in the context of a short and simple self-contained narrative.

In particular, the text exemplifies the contrast between the imperfect and the **passé composé**. It can be used here, or postponed until Unit 3, which focuses on the narration of past events.

Note linguistique

Officier is used to mean "to officiate." **Officialiser** means "to make official."

LES TROIS BAGUES

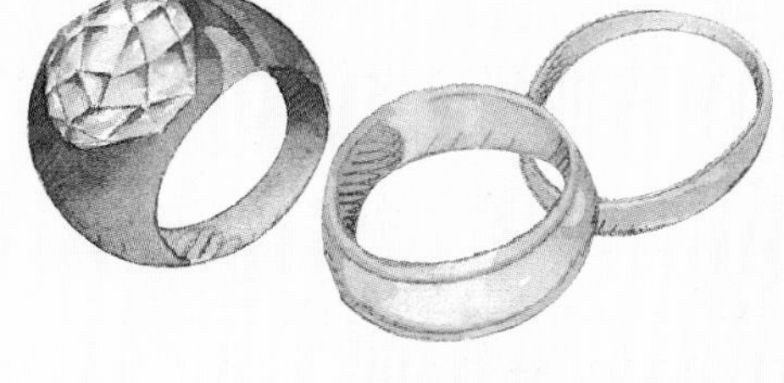

Une annonce

Un jour l'annonce suivante a paru dans *La Nouvelle République* de Tours.

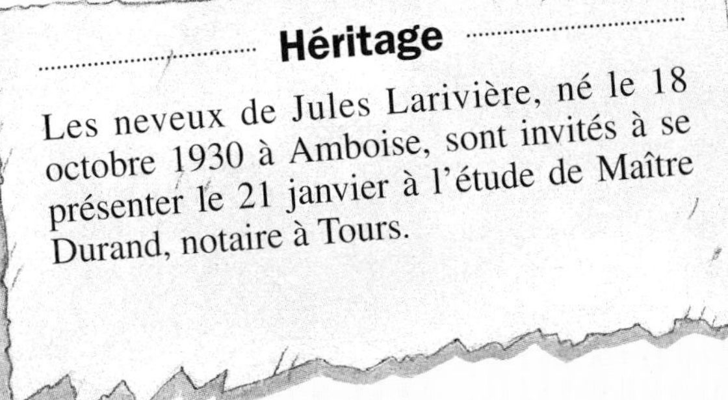

Héritage

Les neveux de Jules Larivière, né le 18 octobre 1930 à Amboise, sont invités à se présenter le 21 janvier à l'étude de Maître Durand, notaire à Tours.

Mots utiles

un neveu	*nephew*
un propriétaire	*owner*
un ouvrier	*worker*
gagner sa vie	*to earn one's living*

NOTES CULTURELLES

- **Tours** is a city on the Loire southwest of Paris. The inhabitants of Tours are called **les Tourangeaux.**
- **Amboise** is another city on the Loire, famous for its Renaissance castle, and the **Manoir du Clos-Lucé** where the artist **Leonardo da Vinci (Léonard de Vinci)** died in 1519.

Teaching Note

Since the action of this story takes place in Touraine, you may want to remind students about that region of France: Tours, the Loire valley, and châteaux such as Amboise and Chenonceaux (*Interlude 3*, p. 147).

Supplementary vocabulary

le neveu ≠ la nièce
l'oncle ≠ la tante
célibataire ≠ marié
le décès ≠ la naissance
l'aîné ≠ le cadet (la cadette)

Les trois neveux

Le 21 janvier, trois hommes se sont présentés° à l'étude de Maître Durand. Neveux de Jules Larivière, ils étaient cousins, mais de condition sociale très différente.

Le premier neveu, Roland Larivière, avait 45 ans et était célibataire.° Propriétaire d'un grand hôtel dans le centre de Tours, il était président de la Chambre de Commerce de la ville. C'était un homme riche et influent.

Le second neveu, Henri Larivière, 38 ans, exerçait la profession de pharmacien et gagnait bien sa vie. Marié, mais sans enfants, il habitait avec sa femme dans une jolie maison située en banlieue.°

Le troisième neveu, Jean-Marc Larivière, 28 ans, était un simple ouvrier agricole. Il habitait dans une petite ferme à la campagne° avec sa femme et ses trois enfants.

La secrétaire de Maître Durand a pris le nom, la profession et l'adresse des trois neveux, puis elle les a introduits° dans le bureau du notaire.

se sont présentés = sont venus **célibataire** = non-marié **banlieue** *suburbs* **campagne** *country* **les a introduits** *led, introduced them*

Avez-vous compris?

1. Quand et pourquoi les trois neveux vont-ils chez le notaire?
2. Qui est le plus riche des trois neveux? le moins riche?
3. À votre avis, lequel des trois neveux exerce la profession la plus intéressante? Pourquoi?
4. À vos yeux, lequel est le plus sympathique? Pourquoi?

Anticipons un peu!

D'après vous, qu'est-ce qui va se passer à la fin de l'histoire?

- Les trois neveux vont recevoir la même somme d'argent.
- Le neveu le plus riche va donner sa part *(share)* à ses cousins.
- Le neveu le moins riche va recevoir plus d'argent que ses cousins.
- Autre possibilité? Expliquez votre opinion.

Maintenant, finissez l'histoire et vérifiez si vous aviez raison.

Avez-vous compris?

(Sample answers)

1. Ils vont chez le notaire le 21 janvier, parce qu'ils ont lu l'annonce mise dans le journal par le notaire.
2. Le plus riche est Roland, propriétaire d'un hôtel. Le moins riche est Jean-Marc, ouvrier agricole.
3. *Answers will vary.*
4. *Answers will vary.*

Teaching Strategy: Expansion

Divide the class into groups and assign a group leader and a recorder. First, have students identify each person in the illustration. On what do they base their answer?

Next, have students decide which ring would they choose and why. The recorder should note student answers so that groups can compare and discuss.

Le Testament

Maître Durand a serré la main des° trois neveux et puis il a commencé à parler.

Me Durand	J'ai le regret de vous annoncer le décès° de votre oncle Jules Larivière. Il est mort le 12 décembre dernier au Mexique dans la ville de Cuernavaca où il habitait depuis son départ de France, il y a quinze ans. Il n'avait pas d'enfants. Vous êtes, par conséquent, ses héritiers.
Roland L.	Qu'est-ce qu'il nous a laissé?
Me Durand	Il vous a laissé trois bagues.
Roland L.	Trois bagues? C'est tout?!
Me Durand	Non, il vous a laissé aussi une très belle photo de lui.
Roland L.	Est-ce qu'on peut voir les bagues?
Me Durand	Oui, bien sûr.

Maître Durand a pris une grande enveloppe dans laquelle il y avait les trois bagues. Il les a mises sur une table et il a continué . . .

Me Durand	Voilà les trois bagues. Comme vous pouvez voir, ces bagues sont très différentes. Il y a une bague de diamant, une bague en or et une bague en argent . . .
Roland L.	Mais ces bagues n'ont pas la même valeur.° Le partage° est impossible.
Me Durand	Au contraire! Le testament de votre oncle est très explicite. Il stipule que c'est à l'aîné de ses neveux de choisir d'abord.
Roland L.	Alors là, mon oncle a eu une bonne idée!
Me Durand	Monsieur Roland Larivière, vous êtes l'aîné! Quelle bague voulez-vous?
Roland L.	Eh bien, c'est facile! Je prends la bague de diamant! Quel merveilleux souvenir de mon oncle!
Me Durand	Voulez-vous aussi la photo de votre oncle?
Roland L.	Euh, non. Je crois que je me souviendrai° mieux de mon oncle avec la bague. Et puis, j'ai assez de vieilles choses chez moi.

Maître Durand s'est tourné° ensuite vers Henri Larivière.

Me Durand	Monsieur Henri Larivière, vous êtes le second neveu. C'est votre tour maintenant.
Henri L.	Eh bien, moi, je proteste! Je ne suis peut-être pas l'aîné, mais c'était moi le neveu préféré de mon oncle. Pourquoi est-ce qu'il ne m'a pas donné la bague de diamant? Oui, je proteste!
Me Durand	Choisissez, s'il vous plaît! La bague en or ou la bague en argent?
Henri L.	Bon, je prends la bague en or, mais . . .
Me Durand	Voulez-vous la photo de votre oncle?
Henri L.	Ah ça, certainement pas! Mon oncle a été trop injuste avec moi!

Mots utiles

un testament	*will*
un héritier	*heir*
laisser	*to leave*
une bague	*ring*
l'or	*gold*
l'argent	*silver*
l'aîné	= le plus âgé
une clé	*key*
un coffre	*safe*
juste ≠ injuste	*fair ≠ unfair*

a serré la main de *shook hands with* **décès** *death* **valeur** *value* **le partage =** la division
je me souviendrai *I will remember* **s'est tourné** *turned*

Supplementary vocabulary

Dans le bureau du notaire, on trouve:
les dossiers *(m.) documents, files*
la plante verte *potted plant*
le tableau *painting*
le classeur *filing cabinet*
le bureau *desk*
le fauteuil *armchair*

■ Variation

What do the other two nephews tell Jean-Marc Larivière after Maître Durand gives him the good news? Do they congratulate him? Imagine their conversation.

Teaching Strategy: Expansion

Ask students:
What would you do first if you received a large sum of money?

Teaching Strategy: Groups

Divide the class into groups and have each student choose a character role. Students respond in character to questions posed by others. Continue until everyone has had a turn.

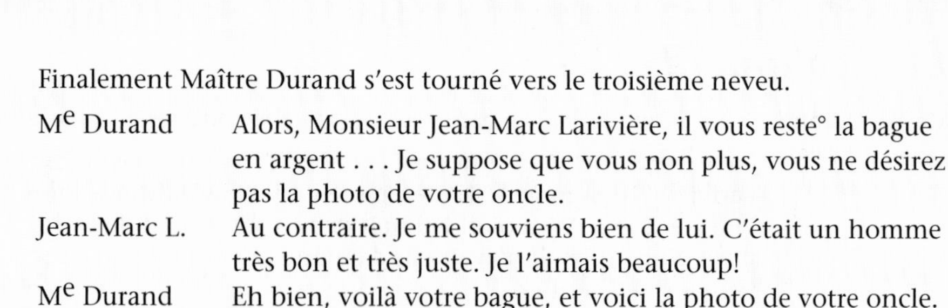

Finalement Maître Durand s'est tourné vers le troisième neveu.

Me Durand	Alors, Monsieur Jean-Marc Larivière, il vous reste° la bague en argent . . . Je suppose que vous non plus, vous ne désirez pas la photo de votre oncle.
Jean-Marc L.	Au contraire. Je me souviens bien de lui. C'était un homme très bon et très juste. Je l'aimais beaucoup!
Me Durand	Eh bien, voilà votre bague, et voici la photo de votre oncle.

Anticipons un peu!

D'après vous, qu'est-ce qui va se passer à la fin?

Maître Durand s'est levé,° puis il a serré très fort° la main de Jean-Marc Larivière.

Me Durand	Félicitations, vous êtes maintenant un homme très riche!
Jean-Marc L.	Mais non, je suis seulement un pauvre ouvrier agricole . . .
Me Durand	Oui, mais vous avez la photo.
Jean-Marc L.	La photo?
Me Durand	Retournez-la . . . Il y a la clé du coffre de votre oncle. Quand il était au Mexique, votre oncle a fait des investissements très profitables. Il est mort multi-millionnaire et c'est vous qui héritez de sa fortune!

il vous reste = vous avez **s'est levé** got up **très fort** = avec beaucoup de force

Avez-vous compris?

1. Pourquoi les neveux de Jules Larivière étaient-ils ses héritiers?
2. Quels objets est-ce que Jules Larivière a laissés à ses neveux?
3. En quoi ces bagues étaient-elles différentes?
4. Pourquoi est-ce que les deux premiers neveux n'ont pas pris la photo de leur oncle?
5. Pourquoi est-ce que le troisième neveu a pris la photo?
6. Comment est-ce qu'il a été récompensé *(rewarded)*?

30 Reprise

EXPRESSION ORALE

Discussion

Voici plusieurs morales possibles pour l'histoire que vous avez lue. Avec votre partenaire, déterminez quelle est la meilleure morale et expliquez pourquoi. (Si vous préférez, vous pouvez suggérer une autre morale.)

- Il y a toujours une justice.
- L'avarice *(greed)* ne paie pas.
- Les riches ont souvent tort.
- L'argent ne fait pas le bonheur.

Dramatisation

Avec vos camarades de classe, jouez la scène du **Testament**. Chaque personne va adopter la personnalité correspondant à son rôle et jouer ce rôle avec beaucoup d'expression.

Situations

Avec votre partenaire, choisissez l'une des situations suivantes. Composez le dialogue correspondant et jouez-le en classe.

1 La bonne nouvelle

Jean-Marc Larivière rentre chez lui et annonce la bonne nouvelle à sa femme qui veut des détails.

Rôles: Jean-Marc Larivière, sa femme

2 Au café

Roland Larivière va au café où il rencontre un(e) ami(e). Il lui raconte l'histoire du testament.

Rôles: Roland Larivière, un(e) ami(e)

3 Un procès

Henri Larivière, très mécontent de ce qui s'est passé, va voir un(e) avocat(e) *(lawyer)*, dans l'intention de faire un procès *(suit)* à son cousin Jean-Marc. Il explique l'injustice de la situation à l'avocat(e) qui veut des détails.

Rôles: Henri Larivière, l'avocat(e)

EXPRESSION ECRITE

L'héritage

Dans un petit paragraphe, décrivez ce que Jean-Marc Larivière va faire avec l'argent de l'héritage.

Les trois neveux

Sur la base de l'histoire que vous avez lue, faites le portrait des trois neveux (leurs qualités, leurs défauts, ce qu'ils aiment, ce qu'ils n'aiment pas, etc.).

Jules Larivière

Écrivez une courte biographie de Jules Larivière. Utilisez votre imagination. Vous pouvez considérer les questions suivantes:

- Que faisait Jules Larivière avant d'aller au Mexique?
- Pourquoi a-t-il quitté la France?
- Qu'est-ce qu'il a fait à Cuernavaca?

Le testament

Choisissez l'un des personnages suivants:
Maître Durand, Roland Larivière, Henri Larivière, Jean-Marc Larivière

Écrivez une lettre dans laquelle vous décrivez l'histoire du point de vue de la personne que vous avez choisie. Comparez votre lettre avec celles que vos camarades ont écrites.

UNITÉ 1

MAIN THEME

Personal appearance
Daily routine

Communication Functions/Contexts

- Describing people
- Caring for one's appearance
- Describing aspects of daily routine
- Expressing how one feels and inquiring about other people

Linguistic Goals

- Describing people and their ailments
- Expressing feelings and changes of mood
- Describing what people do for themselves
- Explaining one's daily activities

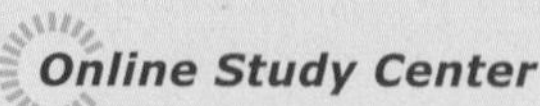

Online Study Center

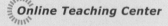

Online Teaching Center

Teaching Strategy: Info Magazine

These readings can be done:
- in class or as homework
- at the beginning of the unit or as a wrap-up activity

Have students look at the realia and photos and guess the theme of the article. Have them skim, looking for cognates, then giving the main idea.

UNITÉ 1

Au jour le jour

Thème et Objectifs

Culture

In this unit, you will discover . . .
- how different artists have expressed the concept of beauty
- what French people call "le look"
- how the French take care of their personal appearance
- what constitutes the daily routine for different French people

Communication

You will learn how . . .
- to describe what a person looks like
- to explain what you do to make yourself look good
- to talk about your daily activities
- to describe how you feel in different circumstances

Langue

You will learn how . . .
- to describe what people do for themselves
- to describe certain aspects of your daily routine
- to express feelings and changes of mood

TEACHING RESOURCES

ANCILLARIES

Student Activities Manual
Audio Program, Unit 1
Video/DVD Program, Unit 1
***Chansons* Audio CD**
Answer Key, Unit 1

HM CLASSPREP CD

Presentations, Unit 1
Audioscript, Unit 1
Videoscript, Unit 1
Assessment, Unit 1

Les visages de la beauté

La recherche de la beauté est universelle, mais la conception de la beauté varie avec les âges. Voici comment ces artistes ont conçu° la beauté...

La beauté, c'est . . .

Pour Léonard de Vinci (1452-1519)

. . . un visage tranquille
. . . des traits° réguliers
. . . un sourire° énigmatique
. . . la discrétion et le mystère

Pour ce sculpteur du Moyen Âge

. . . un visage ovale
. . . des cheveux bouclés
. . . un sourire d'ange
. . . la douceur° et la discrétion

Pour Pierre Auguste Renoir (1841-1919)

. . . un visage rond
. . . des joues° pleines°
. . . un teint° frais
. . . la joie de vivre

Pour Amedeo Modigliani (1884-1920)

. . . un visage ovale
. . . un nez long et fin
. . . des traits symétriques
. . . la délicatesse

Pour Paul Gauguin (1848-1903)

. . . un visage rond
. . . des cheveux abondants
. . . une bouche pleine
. . . la bonté° et la générosité

Pour Pablo Picasso (1881-1973)

. . . un regard profond
. . . des traits marqués
. . . une attitude fière
. . . la personnalité

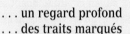

et vous?

- Parmi les six visages représentés, lesquels correspondent le mieux à votre idéal de la beauté? Expliquez pourquoi.
- Apportez en classe des photos ou des portraits de personnes que vous considérez être belles. Décrivez ces portraits.

Et ça!
C'est le contraire de la beauté!

conçu *conceived* **traits** *features* **sourire** *smile* **douceur** *kindness* **joues** *cheeks* **pleines** *full* **teint** *complexion* **bonté** *goodness*

INFO MAGAZINE

Theme: Personal style

Reading Strategy:
Browsing; reading for cultural information

Notes culturelles

- **Léonard de Vinci** was a Renaissance artist known especially for his paintings The Mona Lisa *(la Joconde)* and The Last Supper *(la Cène)*. He was also a designer, sculptor, writer, architect, scientist, musician, and engineer.
- For more information on **Renoir** and **Gauguin**, see pp. 61 and 64 in *Interlude 1*.
- In the Middle Ages (9th–15th centuries) many great churches and cathedrals were built in Europe. The facades often contained statues of saints and other biblical figures.
- **Amedeo Modigliani** was an Italian painter whose portraits were characterized by elongated forms and warm colors.
- **Pablo Picasso** was a Spanish painter who lived for many years in France. His works can be divided into several periods: Blue Period (1901–1904), Pink Period (1905–1907), Cubism (*Les Demoiselles d'Avignon*, 1907), Surrealism and abstraction (1926–1936), Expressionism (*Guernica*, 1937), etc.
- The gutters of Notre-Dame Cathedral are decorated with statues of fantastic monsters known as gargoyles (**des gargouilles**).

Les fringues (*f.*) is a popular slang term for "clothes," almost always used in the plural form. Also frequently used are: **fringuer = habiller, se fringuer = s'habiller.**

un sweat /swit/
levis /lewis/

LE «LOOK»

Le look, c'est une façon de personnaliser son apparence physique, de se créer un style. S'il est difficile de modifier son corps,° on peut facilement changer son look. Il suffit° de choisir les vêtements, les accessoires, la coupe de cheveux° correspondant à l'impression qu'on veut donner. Chaque° génération veut avoir un style différent.

Voici, par ordre d'importance, les éléments du look pour les jeunes Français.

"C'est la première impression qui compte"

Les vêtements

Avec le choix de ses vêtements, on détermine son style général: sport, classique, romantique, etc. À l'université, le style est simple et généralement décontracté:° jean, blouson et chaussures de sport pour les garçons, pantalon, pull ou tee-shirt et tennis pour les filles.

Comme les étudiants sont sensibles° à la mode et à la publicité,° celles-ci° influencent leurs choix de couleurs et de marques° de vêtements ou de chaussures.

La coiffure

La coiffure fait partie° intégrale du look. C'est aussi une façon de manifester ses opinions. Les cheveux longs des années 1970 ou le style "punk" des années 1980 marquaient le refus de s'intégrer à la société des adultes.

Les jeunes aujourd'hui sont retournés à un style assez classique de coiffure avec des cheveux ni° trop longs, ni trop courts. Courts ou longs, frisés, bouclés° ou souples, l'important c'est que les cheveux soient propres et faciles à entretenir.

corps *body* **suffit** = *il est suffisant* **coupe de cheveux** *haircut* **chaque** *each* **décontracté** *relaxed* **sensibles** *sensitive* **publicité** *advertising* **celles-ci** *the latter* **marques** *designer brand names* **fait partie** *is a component* **ni...ni** *neither...nor* **bouclés** *wavy*

Les accessoires

Colliers, bracelets, boucles d'oreille, bijoux, chapeaux, foulards° permettent aux étudiantes de se créer un look ou d'en changer rapidement. Pour leur look, les étudiants utilisent casquettes,° ceintures ou bretelles.°

Les lunettes sont aussi un élément du look. Elles peuvent être rondes, ovales ou rectangulaires. Suivant leur forme et leur couleur, on peut adopter un look sérieux, intelligent, drôle, rétro . . .

Le maquillage et les produits de beauté

Aujourd'hui, les jeunes Françaises préfèrent un style naturel. Leur maquillage° et aussi leur parfum restent généralement discrets. Les jeunes Français, de leur côté, utilisent de plus en plus° de produits de beauté: eaux de toilette, crèmes et lotions pour les mains, gels pour les cheveux. Quant° aux tatouages et aux piercings, ils font rarement partie du look des étudiants français.

... ET LE RELOOKING

Parfois on doit faire "bonne impression," par exemple, quand on va à une entrevue professionnelle. Alors, le relooking° est nécessaire. La veste et la cravate deviennent obligatoires pour les jeunes gens et le tailleur° pour les jeunes filles. Pas de cheveux en désordre, pas de décolletés° trop profonds, pas de maquillages trop lourds, pas de parfums trop violents. Et il est prudent, si c'est le cas, de cacher ses tatouages et d'enlever ses piercings.

et vous?

LE LOOK ET VOUS

D'après vous, quelles sont les trois choses les plus importantes pour le look d'un garçon et le look d'une fille?

	POUR UN GARÇON	POUR UNE FILLE
• avoir beaucoup de vêtements différents	☐	☐
• avoir des vêtements qui vous vont bien	☐	☐
• avoir une coiffure originale	☐	☐
• porter des accessoires exotiques	☐	☐
• porter des couleurs vives°	☐	☐
• avoir un tatouage	☐	☐
• avoir un piercing	☐	☐
• être naturel(le)	☐	☐
• avoir l'air décontracté°	☐	☐
• se sentir° bien physiquement	☐	☐

foulards *silk scarves* **casquettes** *caps* **bretelles** *suspenders* **maquillage** *makeup* **de plus en plus** *more and more* **quant à** *as for* **relooking** *makeover* **tailleur** *woman's suit* **décolletés** *low necklines* **cacher** *to hide* **enlever** *take out* **vives** *bright* **avoir l'air décontracté** *to look relaxed* **se sentir** *to feel*

Supplementary vocabulary

Les styles de mode *fashion styles*
le grunge: la chemise à carreaux, le jean déchiré et les godillots *checkered shirt, torn jeans, and [military] boots*
le BCBG (Bon Chic Bon Genre): le tailleur ou le costume, les chaussures de cuir, les accessoires chics (carré Hermès, collier de perles, montre en or) *Upscale style: women's or men's suit, leather shoes, "chic" accessories (Hermès scarf, pearl necklace, gold watch)*
le style rappeur: le pantalon large, la casquette à l'envers, les baskets *large pants, cap "the wrong way," sneakers*
le style techno: la pantalon large, le tee-shirt aux couleurs fluo, les tennis *large pants, brightly colored tee-shirt, tennis shoes*
le style skater (pour les amateurs de skateboard ou de surf): les jeans larges, les tennis et les tee-shirts avec des logos détournés *wide jeans, tennis shoes, and tee-shirts with rewritten logos*
Rétro usually designates the fashions of the 1920s–1970s

Teaching Strategy: Warm-Up

Once students have read the cultural information on pages 34–35, ask them to talk about how they would characterize **le look** for themselves, using each category **(les vêtements, la coiffure...)**. After this open-ended discussion, compare and contrast French and American attitudes on style. On the board, rate each category as **plus important pour les Français...aussi important pour les Français que pour les Américains... plus important pour les Américains.**

Note: Are there other important categories that contribute to **"le look"** that are not mentioned in the article?

LE FRANÇAIS PRATIQUE

TEACHING RESOURCES

Student Activities Manual, pp. 107–108

Tête-à-Tête Pair Activity, La rentrée, p. PA2

Audio Program, CD 1, Tracks 1–3

HM ClassPrep CD, Audioscript, Unit 1

■ Note linguistique

Note that the following types of adjectives are invariable:

- colors derived from nouns: **marron** *(a chestnut)* **châtain, orange**
- colors modified by an adjective: **bleu clair** (light blue), **vert foncé** (dark green)

■ Teaching note

1 k = 2.2 lb
1 lb = .45 k
1 m = 3.28 ft
1 ft = .30 m
1 in = 2.54 cm
Par exemple:
5′ = 1 mètre 50
5′ 5″ = 1 mètre 63
6′ = 1 mètre 80
100 lb = 45 k
120 lb = 54 k
160 lb = 72 k
180 lb = 81 k

LE FRANÇAIS PRATIQUE

La description physique

	Un garçon / une fille . . .		
LES CHEVEUX	est **brun(e)**	ou	**blond(e)** **roux (rousse)** *(redhead)*
	a les cheveux bruns	ou	**blonds** / **noirs** / **roux** — **châtain** *(chestnut)*, **châtain clair** *(gold)*, **châtain foncé** *(brown)*
	a les cheveux longs	ou	**courts** *(short)*
	lisses *(straight)*	ou	**frisés** *(curly, frizzy)* **bouclés** *(curly, wavy)*
LES YEUX	**a les yeux noirs**	ou	**bleus**, **gris**, **verts**, **marron** *(brown)*
LE VISAGE (LA FIGURE)	**a le visage ovale**	ou	**rond**, **carré** *(square)*, **rectangulaire**
LA TAILLE	**est grand(e)**	ou	**petit(e)** **de taille moyenne** *(average)*
L'APPARENCE GÉNÉRALE	est **mince** *(thin)* **maigre** *(skinny)*	ou	**gros(se)** *(heavyset, fat)*
	est **athlétique** **fort(e)** *(strong)* **costaud(e)** *(solid, well-built)*	ou	**faible** *(weak)*
LES SIGNES PARTICULIERS	**porte des lunettes**	ou	**des verres de contact** **des lentilles** *(lenses)* **de contact**

À noter

la taille *(height)*	**Je mesure** 1 mètre 75.	*I am 5 feet 10 inches tall.*
le poids *(weight)*	**Je pèse** 65 kilos.	*I weigh 143 pounds (65 kilos).*

Teaching Strategy: Warm-Up

Before class, cut out pictures from magazines of different types of people. Hold them up in front of the class and have students give complete sentence descriptions of each one. In order to touch on all aspects of descriptions, you can also ask questions such as **«Est-ce qu'elle est blonde?» «Non, elle est brune.»**

Alternate: With the class in a circle, have students describe the person to their left in three to five sentences.

Ce monsieur. . . **est chauve** | **est barbu; a une barbe** | **a une moustache** | **a une cicatrice** *(scar)*

Ce garçon . . .
Cette fille . . . **a les cheveux en brosse** *(crew-cut)* | **a une queue de cheval** *(ponytail)* | **a des taches de rousseur** *(freckles)* | **a un grain de beauté** *(beauty mark)* sur le menton

1 Dix ans après

Dix ans séparent ces deux photos. Entre temps, les élèves du lycée Descartes ont beaucoup changé. Choisissez un(e) élève sur la photo de l'école et décrivez-le(la). Votre partenaire va décrire cette personne maintenant.

2 Autoportrait

Faites votre autoportrait en donnant le maximum de détails sur votre aspect physique.

Conversations libres

Avec votre partenaire, choisissez l'une des situations suivantes. Composez le dialogue correspondant et jouez-le en classe.

1 Rendez-vous

Votre partenaire vous propose d'aller au cinéma avec un(e) jeune Français(e) qu'il/elle a rencontré(e) récemment. Vous voulez avoir des détails sur cette personne.

2 Un(e) enfant perdu(e)

Vous faites du shopping aux Galeries Lafayette avec votre petit(e) cousin(e). Pendant que vous êtes au rayon des jouets *(toys)*, votre cousin(e) disparaît *(disappears)*. Faites une description de votre cousin(e) au détective du magasin (votre partenaire). Il va vous demander des détails.

Expansion

For extra practice and cultural development, bring to class reproductions of portraits by famous artists and have the students describe the people portrayed. You might select works by the following artists, explaining briefly who they are:

Modigliani (1884–1920)
Picasso (1881–1973)
Renoir (1841–1919)
Matisse (1869–1954)
Van Gogh (1853–1890)
Manet (1832–1883)

Note culturelle

René Descartes (1596–1650) was a French mathematician, physicist, and philosopher. He is the author of the famous statement: **«Je pense, donc je suis.»** (I think, therefore I am.)

Teaching Strategy

Have students work in pairs to describe each other.
Variation Have students bring in photos of family members or friends to describe.

Teaching Strategy: Game

Have each student write down two people for whom they could create a description. Then demonstrate by beginning the game with someone you have picked out (e.g., Arnold Schwartzenegger). Students have ten questions **(oui/non)** in order to guess the person chosen.

LANGUE ET COMMUNICATION

TEACHING RESOURCES

Student Activities Manual, pp. 19–21, 109

Audio Program, CD 1, Track 4

HM ClassPrep CD, Audioscript, Unit 1

A. L'usage de l'article avec les parties du corps

Catherine a **les yeux** bleus. — *Catherine has blue eyes. (=* ***Her eyes*** *are blue.)*
Qu'est-ce que tu as dans **la main**? — *What do you have in* ***your hand?***
J'ai une cicatrice sur **le menton**. — *I have a scar on* ***my chin.***

In French the DEFINITE ARTICLE **(le, la, l', les)** is generally used with parts of the body. (In English, we use possessive adjectives.)

1 Monsieur et Madame Dupont

Monsieur et Madame Dupont sont des touristes français. Complétez la description de Monsieur Dupont et ensuite faites la description de Madame Dupont.

Monsieur Dupont a . . . frisés.

Il porte un chapeau sur . . .
Il a une pipe dans . . .
Il a un foulard autour (de) . . .
Il porte son appareil-photo sur . . .
Il a un magazine (à) . . .
Il porte des sandales (à) . . .

Madame Dupont a . . .

la bouche
les cheveux
le cou
l'épaule
la main
les pieds
la tête

■ **Photo Note**
In two of the pictures, you can see **la Tour Eiffel** and **le Sacré-Coeur,** in Paris.

RAPPEL!

à + le → au **de + le → du**
à + les → aux **de + les → des**

Avoir mal à + les parties du corps

Révision ▶ p. R3; p. R12

2 Dommage!

Aujourd'hui ça ne va pas! Choisissez une chose que vous ne pouvez pas faire et expliquez pourquoi.

▶ **— Je ne peux pas travailler dans le jardin.**
— Mon/ma pauvre! Qu'est-ce que tu as?
— J'ai mal au dos (aux pieds).
— Dommage!

QUELLE ACTIVITÉ?	POURQUOI?
parler	le genou
sortir avec toi	les pieds
dîner avec toi	la main
faire du jogging	le dos
jouer au foot	*la gorge (throat)*
jouer au ping-pong	les jambes
manger des bonbons	le ventre
transporter cette table	les dents
écouter ce CD de rap	la tête
travailler dans le jardin	les oreilles
??	??

3 Enrichissez votre vocabulaire!

Voici certaines expressions que vous pouvez utiliser avec vos amis. Faites correspondre ces expressions avec leurs équivalents anglais.

1. Ne fais pas la tête!
2. Ne mets pas les pieds dans le plat!
3. Tu as un poil *(hair)* dans la main!
4. Tu as les yeux plus gros que le ventre!
5. Tu as le coeur sur la main!
6. Tu coupes les cheveux en quatre.
7. J'ai l'estomac dans les talons *(heels)*.

a. I am very hungry.
b. You are too greedy. (Your eyes are bigger than your stomach.)
c. You are really lazy.
d. Don't look so upset.
e. Don't put your foot in your mouth.
f. You are very finicky. (You are splitting hairs.)
g. You are a very generous person. (You wear your heart on your sleeve.)

ALLONS PLUS LOIN: Autres usages de l'article défini

The definite article is used . . .

- with dates
  le 18 juin **le samedi 3 avril**
- with days of the week (or parts of the day) to refer to a repeated or habitual action
  Compare:
  Que fais-tu **le samedi**? *What do you do **on Saturdays?***
  Que fais-tu **samedi**? *What are you doing **on (this) Saturday?***
- with geographical names (countries, states, rivers, mountains, etc.), except cities
  le Canada **les États-Unis** but **Israël, Cuba, Tahiti, Haïti**
  la Virginie **le Mississippi** **les Alpes**
- with names of languages, colors, and school subjects
  J'étudie **le français** et **les maths**.
  Mes couleurs préférées sont **le bleu** et **le rouge**.
- with certain titles
  le docteur Mercat **la princesse** Diane **la reine** Élizabeth
- with nouns indicating a weight, measure, or quantity
  L'essence coûte un euro **le litre**. *Gas costs one euro **a liter.***

Usages de l'article défini

Pratique ▶  p. 19

Réponses: Activité 3

1. d
2. e
3. c (= you use your hands so little that hair is growing on your palms)
4. b
5. g
6. f
7. a

Supplementary vocabulary

avoir le coeur gros *to be sad*
être tête en l'air *to be forgetful, to have one's head in the clouds*
casser les pieds (de quelqu'un) *to annoy, to be a pain*
avoir bon pied bon oeil *to be still in great shape*
donner un coup de main *to lend a hand, to help*
demander la main (d'une jeune fille) *to propose (marriage)*
mettre le nez dehors *to go out*
prêter l'oreille *to listen carefully; "lend an ear"*

Teaching note

You may wish to review years:
1998 dix-neuf cent quatre-vingt-dix-huit
2000 deux mille
2001 deux mille un
2003 deux mille trois

Full dates are expressed as follows:
14/7/1789 le quatorze juillet dix-sept cent quatre-vingt-neuf

Teaching Strategy: Extra Practice

Divide the class into groups. Give situations and have students use a complete sentence to describe where they have pain.

1. Après le marathon de Boston, qu'est-ce qu'on a?
2. Après un concert de rock très fort, qu'est-ce qu'on a?
3. Après avoir mangé de la viande verte, qu'est-ce qu'on a?
4. Après avoir crié pendant 5 heures au match de football, qu'est-ce qu'on a?
5. Après un rendez-vous chez le dentiste, qu'est-ce qu'on a?
6. Après avoir lu 200 pages d'un livre sans lunettes, qu'est-ce qu'on a?

Forum-campus

■ **Teaching Note**
Have students locate where writers are from on the map on p. R34 or in an atlas.

Forum-Campus Je n'ai pas le look . . .

Ces jours-ci, Juliette n'est pas très heureuse. Elle a décidé de partager° ses problèmes avec d'autres étudiants dans le forum de discussion "Forum-Campus."

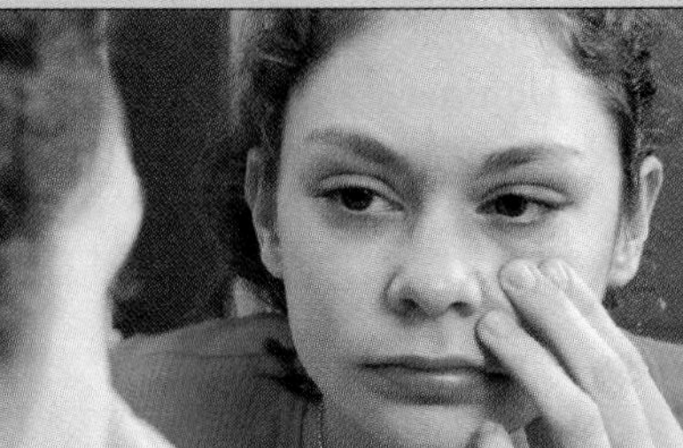
Juliette, 19 ans *(Strasbourg)*

Je viens de changer d'université et j'ai beaucoup de difficultés à m'adapter. Je ne connais personne dans cette ville et dans mes cours personne ne fait attention à moi. C'est peut-être que je n'ai pas le look ou que je ne suis pas assez belle . . . ? Est-ce que vous avez des suggestions?

Juliette

Plusieurs étudiants ont répondu à son message.

Mélanie, 20 ans *(Strasbourg)*

L'année dernière j'étais dans la même situation que toi. Alors, j'ai fait du relooking. Avant, j'étais une petite brune avec de longs cheveux lisses et des lunettes rondes. Maintenant je suis une rousse aux cheveux courts et je porte des verres de contact . . . Tous les samedis je sors avec une bande de copains très sympa. Et j'ai aussi mon petit copain . . .

Tu peux faire comme moi. Ce n'est pas difficile.

Mélanie

partager *to share* **relooking** *makeover*

Clément, 20 ans
(Dijon)

Le problème, ce n'est pas ton look. C'est ton moral. Il faut que tu sois plus positive. Et pour cela, il faut que tu sois plus active. Pour cela, tu peux commencer par faire du sport. Il y a certainement un club de sport dans le quartier où tu habites. Inscris-toi.° Dans 15 jours, tu seras en meilleure forme et tu connaîtras des tas de gens.

Clément

Vincent, 21 ans
(Nice)

La beauté et le look sont des choses importantes, mais ce n'est pas tout. Ce qui compte aussi, c'est le charme et la personnalité. Quand j'invite une fille, ce n'est pas parce qu'elle est super-jolie ou super-intelligente, mais parce qu'elle est sympa, drôle, et qu'elle aime rire!° Alors, change d'attitude. Sois moins sérieuse et cultive ton sens de l'humour. Tu trouveras facilement des amis!

Vincent

Amélie, 22 ans
(Lyon)

Tu sais, je ne suis pas très belle et pourtant j'ai des tas° de copains et de copines. La clé° du succès, c'est de se sentir° bien dans sa peau.° La vraie beauté n'est pas physique. Elle dépend de tes qualités personnelles. Mets les tiennes° en valeur. Et n'oublie pas que la beauté ne fait pas nécessairement le bonheur.° Regarde donc Marilyn Monroe!

Amélie

Et vous?

Expression orale
D'après vous, quelle lettre offre les meilleurs conseils à Juliette? Expliquez pourquoi.

Expression écrite
Écrivez votre propre *(own)* réponse à la lettre de Juliette.

Inscris-toi *sign up* **rire** *to laugh* **des tas =** *des quantités* **clé** *key* **se sentir** *to feel* **peau** *skin* **les tiennes** *yours* **bonheur** *happiness*

■ Teaching Strategy: Additional Activities

- Donnez trois qualités très importantes. Pourquoi sont-elles importantes?
- Donnez un défaut. Pourquoi est-ce un problème?
- Quelle est votre qualité principale?
- Regardez les photos. Qui est le/la plus sympathique? Le plus beau/la plus belle?

Proverbe

«La beauté ne fait pas le bonheur» is a play on the proverb **«L'argent ne fait pas le bonheur.»**

■ Irregular Verbs

(see Appendix C)
rire

Teaching Strategy: Extra Practice

Pose the following question to students and have them discuss in groups, or write short responses if they prefer:

Vincent dit «. . .**cultive ton sens de l'humour et tu auras toujours des amis.**» L'humour est-il une qualité importante ou pas? Pourquoi?

LE FRANÇAIS

PRATIQUE

La toilette et les soins personnels

TEACHING RESOURCES

■ **Note linguistique**

Compare and contrast:
essuyer *to wipe*
s'essuyer *to dry [one's hands] with a towel*
sécher *to dry (out)*
se sécher *to dry [one's hair] with a dryer*

■ **Pronunciation**

Eye-liner is pronounced as in English: /ajlajnœr/

■ **Note culturelle**

Un gant de toilette is a washcloth that resembles a pocket with a slit for one's hand.

LE FRANÇAIS PRATIQUE

La toilette et les soins personnels

Olivier utilise . . .	pour . . .
le rasoir	**se raser**
le savon	**se laver la figure**
la brosse à dents	**se brosser les dents**
la serviette	**s'essuyer les mains**
les ciseaux	**se couper les ongles** *(nails)*

se raser *to shave*

se brosser *to brush*
s'essuyer *to (wipe) dry*
se couper *to cut*

Charlotte utilise . . .	pour . . .
le shampooing	**se laver les cheveux**
le séchoir	**se sécher les cheveux**
le peigne	**se peigner**
le rouge à lèvres	**se maquiller**
l'eye-liner	**se maquiller les yeux**

se sécher *to dry*
se peigner *to comb one's hair*
se maquiller *to apply makeup*

Quelques autres articles de toilette et produits de beauté

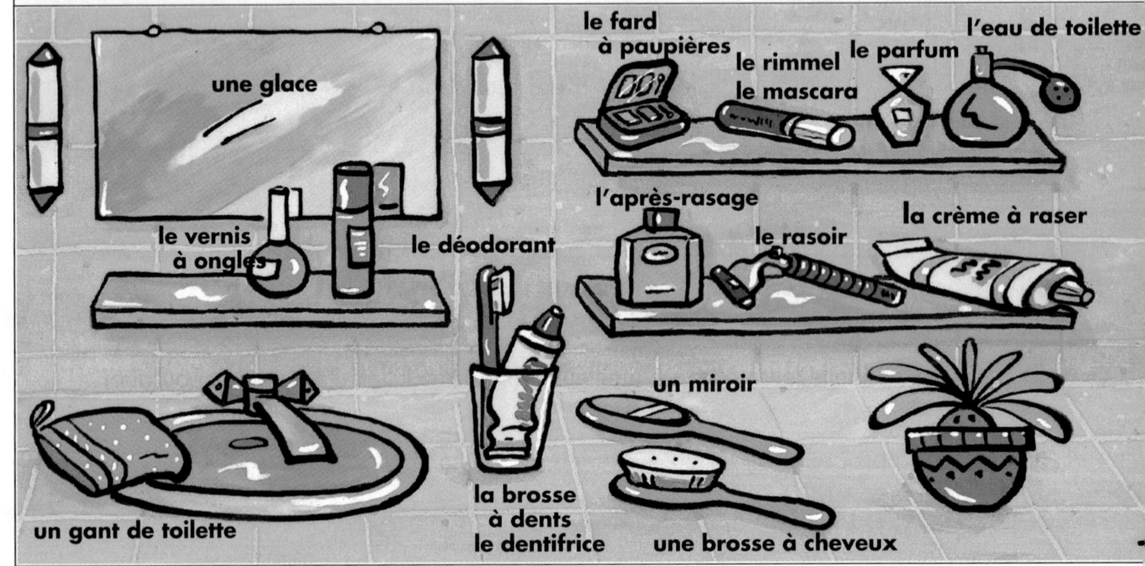

1 La trousse de toilette *(toiletry kit)*

Ce week-end vous n'allez pas rester chez vous. Mentionnez cinq articles—ou plus—que vous allez mettre dans votre trousse de toilette . . .

- si vous allez faire du camping
- si vous allez passer le week-end chez vos cousins.

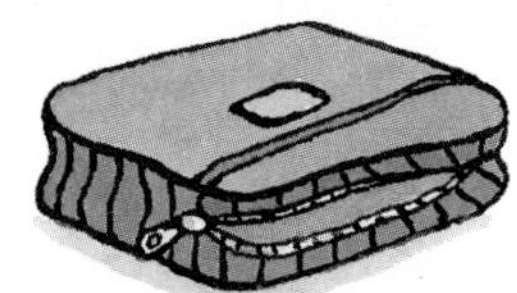

Maintenant imaginez que vous allez en France cet été. Faites une liste de dix articles ou produits que vous allez emporter *(take along)* avec vous.

Comparez vos listes avec celles de votre partenaire. Combien de choses identiques avez-vous prises? Combien de choses différentes?

2 Qu'est-ce qu'ils vont faire?

Lisez les descriptions suivantes. Puis mentionnez deux ou trois choses que chaque personne va faire.

▶ **Philippe vient de jouer au foot. Il va dans la douche du stade.**
Il va prendre une douche.
Il va se laver les cheveux.
Ensuite, il va se sécher et se mettre du déodorant.

1. Il est sept heures du matin. Monsieur Lebot, président de la Banque Industrielle, se lève et va dans la salle de bains.
2. Il est onze heures du soir. Jérôme va se coucher. D'abord il va dans la salle de bains.
3. Ce soir, la fameuse chanteuse d'opéra va jouer le rôle de Carmen. Elle est dans sa loge *(dressing room)* où elle se prépare pour la représentation *(performance)*.
4. Caroline va dîner avec Vincent, son nouveau copain, dans un restaurant très élégant. Elle se prépare pour l'occasion.

3 En voyage

Vous êtes en voyage avec un groupe. Demandez à votre partenaire l'un des objets suivants et expliquez pourquoi vous en avez besoin.

▶ **—Tu as du shampooing?**
—Oui, pourquoi?
—Je voudrais me laver les cheveux.

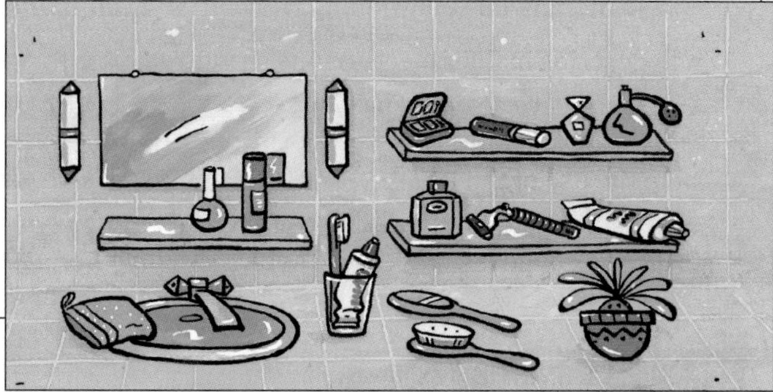

■ Teaching Note

For Activity 3, present supplementary expressions as necessary, e.g.: **se faire les ongles, se mettre du déodorant, se mettre du parfum, se regarder,** etc.

Supplementary vocabulary

une lame de rasoir *razor blade*
l'après-shampooing *conditioner*
le shampooing colorant *coloring shampoo*
la laque à cheveux *hair spray*
le gel coiffant *styling gel*
la crème *lotion*
le fond de teint *foundation*
la poudre *powder*
le sourcil /surci/ *eyebrow*
le cil /cil/ *eyelash*
la paupière *eyelid*
la lèvre *lip*
la peau *skin*

LANGUE ET COMMUNICATION

TEACHING RESOURCES

Student Activities Manual, pp. 21–22; 111

Audio Program, CD 1, Tracks 8–9

HM ClassPrep CD, Audioscript, Unit 1

Teaching Strategy: Extra Practice

(Reflexive verbs: Imperative)
Have students form groups of 2 or 3 and come up with sentences for the following situations using reflexive verbs in the imperative:

1. Give 5 suggestions to a friend who's going for an interview at a trendy fashion magazine.
2. Give 5 suggestions to your friends of things the three of you should/shouldn't do before going out dancing.

As students volunteer their answers, write them on the board in two separate columns in order to assist the visual learners.

Teaching Strategy: Extra Practice

(Reflexive verbs: Future)
Tell students that they have just been asked out by a famous male/female star. Have each student say what he/she is going to do in order to prepare for the date. What are students not going to do? Each student should give one answer.

A. Les verbes réfléchis

REFLEXIVE VERBS are formed with a REFLEXIVE PRONOUN that represents the same person as the subject.

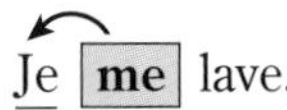

Je **me** lave. Monsieur Martin **se** rase.

FORMS

Review the forms of **se laver** in the present and the imperative.

	PRESENT
AFFIRMATIVE	je **me lave** tu **te laves** il/elle/on **se lave** nous **nous lavons** vous **vous lavez** ils/elles **se lavent**
NEGATIVE	**je ne me lave pas**
INTERROGATIVE	**est-ce que tu te laves?** **te laves-tu?**

IMPERATIVE AFFIRMATIVE	IMPERATIVE NEGATIVE
lave-toi!	**ne te lave pas!**
lavons-nous!	**ne nous lavons pas!**
lavez-vous!	**ne vous lavez pas!**

INFINITIVE CONSTRUCTIONS

Je vais **me** laver. Nous allons **nous** brosser les dents.	Je **ne** vais **pas me** laver les cheveux. Vous **n'**allez **pas vous** raser.

➡ In an infinitive construction, the reflexive pronoun comes immediately before the verb and represents the same person as the subject.

USES

Reflexive verbs are very common in French. They are used:

- to describe actions that the subject is performing on or for himself/herself.
  - Catherine **se regarde** dans la glace. *Catherine **is looking at herself** in the mirror.*
  - Je **me fais** un sandwich. *I **am fixing myself** a sandwich.*
- to describe many aspects of one's DAILY ROUTINE.
  - Je **me lève** à sept heures. *I get up at seven.*

➡ Note the use of the DEFINITE ARTICLE after reflexive verbs.

Tu te brosses **les** dents. *You are brushing **your** teeth.*
Alice se coupe **les** ongles. *Alice is cutting **her** nails.*

DIS, CHRISTOPHE, EST-CE QUE TU TE LAVES ?
NON, JE NE M
LAVE PAS.
JE LAVE LE CHIEN.

Teaching Strategy: Warm-Up

Pass out slips of paper with reflexive or non-reflexive verbs on them to each student in the class. Ask students to act out their verb so that the class can guess. As the verbs are guessed, write two columns on the board—one with reflexives and one with non-reflexives. At the end, ask students if they can explain the difference between the two columns and give the counterpart to each reflexive or non-reflexive verb. (e.g., if **laver** is in the non-reflexive column, have students come up with the verb **se laver** and give a sentence for each of them.)

Le présent des verbes

Révision ▶ p. R2

comme préférer: se sécher pp. R20-21

comme payer: s'essuyer pp. R20-21

Pratique ▶ p. 21

4 Le matin

Choisissez une personne et dites ce qu'elle fait et ce qu'elle va faire après. Soyez logique!

QUI?	
moi	Jean-Philippe
toi	Madame Lescure
nous	Monsieur Dupont
vous	Éric et Thomas
Alice	Sylvie et Catherine

QUOI?	
• se laver	• se brosser les dents
• se raser	• se laver la figure
• se maquiller	• se laver les mains
• se peigner	• se laver les cheveux
• s'essuyer	• se couper les ongles
• se regarder dans la glace	• se brosser les cheveux
	• se sécher les cheveux

▶ **Tu te sèches les cheveux. Après, tu vas te peigner.**

5 Publicité

Composez des slogans publicitaires pour les produits suivants.

dio-Symphonie	se raser
avon SAMBON	se laver
entifrice SOURIRE	se laver les cheveux
u de toilette VÉSUVE	se maquiller
hampooing CAPILLO	se couper les ongles
échoir SAHARA	se couper les cheveux
asoir BLIP	se brosser les dents
ciseaux CLIP	se parfumer
rosse à dents BRIL	se sécher les cheveux
ard CLÉOPÂTRE	se réveiller en musique

▶ **Mesdemoiselles, maquillez-vous avec le fard Cléopâtre!**

6 Baby-sitting

Vous faites du baby-sitting pour l'enfant de vos voisins français. Dites-lui de faire les choses suivantes. L'enfant (votre partenaire) va vous répondre qu'il/elle ne peut pas. Puis, il/elle va vous donner une excuse.

ACTIONS
- se peigner
- se laver les mains
- se laver les cheveux
- s'essuyer les mains
- se brosser les dents
- se sécher les cheveux

EXCUSES POSSIBLES

Je ne trouve pas . . .
Je ne sais pas où est . . .
Je ne peux pas trouver . . .
J'ai perdu . . .

▶ **— Brosse-toi les dents!**
— Je ne peux pas me brosser les dents!
— Et pourquoi donc?
— J'ai perdu ma brosse à dents.
(Je ne trouve pas le dentifrice.)

ALLONS PLUS LOIN

To express what you or other people can do by themselves, use the construction:

STRESS PRONOUN + **même(s)**

J'ai réparé mon vélo **moi-même.** *I fixed my bike* **by myself.**

→ **Même** is also used to reinforce a stress pronoun referring to the subject.

Jérôme parle toujours **de lui-même**. *Jérôme always talks* **about himself.**

Moi-même, toi-même, etc.

Pratique ▶ p. 22

Variation

Have one student give the first sentence, and then call on another student to provide the second sentence.

Allons plus loin

If you decide to assign further practice, you may want to present the complete chart: **moi-même, toi-même, lui-même,** etc.

Variation: Activity 6

Give the following instructions: Demandez à votre partenaire s'il/elle fait les choses suivantes. Il/Elle répond négativement et donne une raison. Exemple:

—Est-ce que tu te brosses les dents?
—Non, je ne me brosse pas les dents.
—Pourquoi?
—Parce que j'ai perdu ma brosse à dents!

Verb Drill

Using specific hand motions which should remain constant throughout the year, drill the class to practice reflexive conjugations. Example: SE LAVER

Point one finger to yourself:	say **je me lave**	Point two fingers (two hands) to yourself:	say **nous nous lavons**
To the class:	say **tu te laves**	to the class:	say **vous vous lavez**
To the right:	say **il se lave**	to the right:	say **ils se lavent**
To the left:	say **elle se lave**	to the left:	say **elles se lavent**

For the negative, use the same motions but shake your head. Also: switch the order of the conjugations, speed up the pace, or put students in pairs. This is a fast and efficient drill.

INFO MAGAZINE

Theme: Daily activities

Teaching Strategy
These readings should be an interesting "break" in the teaching sequence and provide both enjoyment and practice for students.

Notes linguistiques

- Generally, **une résidence** is a group of homes (houses or apartments). **Une résidence secondaire** is a country home.
- **Un(e) banlieusard(e)** is a person who lives in the Paris **banlieue**.

À LA RÉSIDENCE BON REPOS

Aujourd'hui, les gens des villes habitent généralement dan des immeubles.° Ces immeubles ont beaucoup d'avanta . . . et quelques petits inconvénients.

Un jour comme un autre à la résidence° «Bon Repos» dans la banlieue° parisienne. Il est six heures du matin. Tout est calme. . . Tout d'un coup°. . .

SIXIÈME ÉTAGE

Drin. . . Drin . . . Un réveil° sonne° chez Monsieur Léveillé. Drin. . .Drin. . . Monsi Léveillé se réveille en sursaut°. . . Puis il se lève, met sa robe de chambre° et dans la salle de bains. Il se regarde dans la glace, se brosse les dents. Ensu il branche° son rasoir électrique et commence à se raser. Zzz. . . Zzz. . .

CINQUIÈME ÉTAGE

Le bruit° du rasoir électrique de Monsieur Léveillé réveille Madame Dumou Elle ouvre un oeil, puis l'autre, et attend deux ou trois minutes. Finaleme elle se lève et va dans la cuisine pour se préparer une tasse de café. Elle branc son nouveau moulin° électrique. Grr. . . Grr. . .

QUATRIÈME ÉTAGE

Le moulin à café de Madame Dumoulin réveille Mademoiselle Lasouples Elle se lève, enfile° un maillot,° met une cassette vidéo gymnastique et commence ses exercices. Une, deux. . . une, deux. une, deux . . .

TROISIÈME ÉTAGE

Quand il entend Mademoiselle Lasouplesse faire sa gymnastique, Monsi Trémolo se réveille. Il va dans la salle de bains et prend une douche. Qua il se lave, Monsieur Trémolo adore chanter ses airs d'opéra favoris: «Toréad toréador. . .»*

* «Toréador» is a well-known aria from Bizet's **Carmen**.

DEUXIÈME ÉTAGE

La belle voix de Monsieur Trémolo réveille Madame Bellamy. Elle se lè prend un bain, et se lave les cheveux. Puis, elle s'habille, se peigne se maquille. . .

À huit heures et demie, tous les locataires° de la résidence «Bon Repo sont partis pour leurs occupations de la journée. . . Tous sauf° C'est Monsieur Morphée, le locataire du premier étage. Il travaille com portier° de nuit dans un grand hôtel. À l'heure où les autres locatai se rendent° à leur travail, lui, il rentre chez lui. Là, il se déshabille et pre un bon bain. «Quelle chance d'habiter dans une résidence si calm pense-t-il. Puis, il va dans sa chambre, met son pyjama, se couche s'endort° d'un profond sommeil.

Une journée comme les autres vient de commencer.

immeubles *apartment buildings* **résidence** = l'immeuble **banlieue** *suburbs* **Tout d'un coup** *all of a sudd* **réveil** *alarm clock* **sonne** *rings* **en sursaut** *with a start* **robe de chamber** *bathrobe* **branche** *plugs in* **bruit** *noise* **moulin à café** *coffee grinder* **enfile** = met **maillot** *body suit* **locataires** *tenants* **sauf** = ex **portier** *doorman* **se rendent** = vont **s'endort** *falls asleep*

NOTES CULTURELLES

- In Greek mythology, **Morpheus (Morphée)** is the god of sleep. You may want to explain this term and others to students.
- Remind students that in France, the first floor corresponds to the second floor in an American building. The ground floor is called **le rez-de-chaussée.**
- **Georges Bizet** (1838–1875) wrote ***Carmen*** in 1875. For more information on Bizet, go to p. 185.

et vous?

À VOTRE TOUR

- Dites à quelle heure vous vous levez d'habitude et ce que vous faites après.
- Dites comment vous trouvez l'histoire que vous avez lue: réaliste? amusante? triste? exagérée? Expliquez pourquoi.

EXPRESSION ÉCRITE

Décrivez des habitudes d'une personne que vous connaissez bien (par exemple, votre camarade de chambre, votre soeur ou votre frère). Dites à quelle heure chaque personne se lève et ce qu'elle fait ensuite. (Votre description peut être réaliste ou imaginaire.)

Follow-Up

In groups of 4 or 5, have students describe their own routine and create an "apartment" story.

Teaching Strategy: Expansion Questions

1. Qui se réveille en premier?	M. Léveillé
2. Qu'est-ce qui réveille Mlle Lasouplesse?	Le moulin à café de Mme Dumoulin
3. Qu'est-ce que Mme Dumoulin se prépare?	Elle se prépare une tasse de café.
4. Qu'est ce que M. Léveillé fait avant de se brosser les dents?	Il se regarde dans la glace.
5. Est-ce que M. Morphée se réveille à 8h30?	Non, il se couche.
6. Est-ce que M. Trémolo prend un bain?	Non, il prend une douche.
7. Que fait Mlle Lasouplesse quand elle se réveille?	Elle fait sa gymnastique.
8. Qu'est-ce qui réveille Mme Bellamy?	La belle voix de M. Trémolo.

LE FRANÇAIS PRATIQUE

TEACHING RESOURCES

Student Activities Manual,
pp. 23, 112, 175–177

Audio Program,
CD 1, Tracks 10–11

HM ClassPrep CD,
Audioscript, Unit 1

Video/DVD Program,
Unit 1

LE FRANÇAIS PRATIQUE — *La routine quotidienne*

Il y a beaucoup de choses qu'on fait tous les jours. Ces choses font partie de la routine quotidienne *(daily)*. Ici Stéphanie explique sa routine quotidienne:

Le matin . . .
Je me réveille à 7 heures et quart.
Je me lève.
Je me lave.
Je prends **un bain** *(bath)* ou **une douche** *(shower)*.
Je m'habille.

> **se réveiller** *to wake up*
> **se lever** *to get up*
> **se laver** *to wash*
> **s'habiller** *to get dressed*

Après le petit déjeuner . . .
Je me prépare.
Puis, **je me rends** à l'école.
Je me dépêche pour être à l'heure.
(Si je suis en retard, **je m'excuse.)**

> **se préparer** *to get ready*
> **se rendre à** *to go to*
> **se dépêcher** *to hurry*
> **s'excuser** *to apologize*

En classe . . .
J'étudie.
À midi, **je m'amuse** avec mes copains.

> **s'amuser** *to have fun*

L'après-midi, après les cours . . .
Je me promène en ville.
Je m'arrête parfois chez le marchand de glaces, et **je m'achète** une glace.
Je rentre et **je me repose** un peu.

> **se promener** *to take a walk*
> **s'arrêter** *to stop*
> **s'acheter** *to buy (oneself)*
> **se reposer** *to rest*

À sept heures et demie . . .
Je me mets à table et je dîne avec ma famille.
Puis je fais mes devoirs.

> **se mettre à table** *to sit down to eat*

Le soir, **vers** *(at about)* onze heures . . .
Je me déshabille.
Je me couche.
Et finalement **je m'endors.**

> **se déshabiller** *to get undressed*
> **se coucher** *to go to bed*
> **s'endormir** *to go to sleep*

Teaching Suggestion: Video/DVD Program

The *Vidéo-drame: Bonjour, Monsieur Pasquier* in Unit 1 focuses on the daily routine of the Pasquier family. Note that the verbs in these expressions are reflexive. You may want to list some of the verbs that students should listen for, such as **s'habiller, se laver,** and **se dépêcher** before playing the video.

Verbes comme acheter se lever, se promener

Révision ▶ pp. R20-21
Pratique ▶ p. 23

Et vous?

Décrivez certains aspects de votre vie. Comparez vos réponses avec celles de votre partenaire.

1. En semaine, je me réveille . . .
   - avant sept heures
   - à sept heures
   - ??
2. Je me rends à l'école . . .
   - à pied
   - en bus
   - à vélo
   - ??
3. Le soir, je me couche . . .
   - avant dix heures
   - après onze heures
   - ??
4. Généralement, je m'endors . . .
   - vite *(fast)*
   - assez vite
   - difficilement
   - ??
5. Le dimanche, je ne me lève jamais . . .
   - avant huit heures
   - avant neuf heures
   - ??
6. Quand j'ai du temps libre, je préfère . . .
   - me reposer
   - me promener en ville
   - me rendre chez mes amis
   - ??
7. Quand je me promène en ville, j'aime mieux m'arrêter . . .
   - dans les magasins
   - dans un fast-food
   - ??
8. Avec mon argent, je préfère m'acheter . . .
   - des cassettes
   - des vêtements
   - des magazines
   - ??
9. Je me dépêche le plus pour aller . . .
   - à l'école
   - à un rendez-vous
   - à un concert
   - ??
10. En général, je m'excuse quand . . .
    - j'ai tort
    - je suis en retard
    - ??

Conversations libres

Avec votre partenaire, choisissez l'une des situations suivantes. Composez le dialogue correspondant et jouez-le en classe.

1 Camarade de chambre

Vous êtes étudiant(e) à l'université de Montréal. Vous cherchez un(e) camarade de chambre pour le trimestre prochain. Expliquez votre routine quotidienne à un(e) autre étudiant(e) (votre partenaire). Ensuite, posez-lui des questions sur sa routine.

2 Activités du dimanche

Vous avez invité un(e) camarade français(e) (votre partenaire) à passer le week-end chez vous. Expliquez-lui ce que vous faites le dimanche. Demandez-lui s'il/si elle fait les mêmes choses.

Supplementary vocabulary

s'allonger *to lie down*
s'entraîner *to train, practice (a sport)*
s'étirer *to stretch*
se changer *to change (clothes)*
se démaquiller *to take off one's makeup*
se doucher *to take a shower*
se relaxer *to relax*

■ Verb Forms You may have students review the forms of **mettre** (p. R2) and **s'endormir** (like **sortir**, p. R2).

Variation: A/B Pair Activity

Votre partenaire répond à la question, puis vous demande si vous faites la même chose.
Exemple:
—**(Je me réveille avant sept heures.) Et toi? Est-ce que tu te réveilles avant sept heures en semaine?**
—**Oui, je me réveille avant sept heures./Non, je ne me réveille pas avant sept heures, je me réveille à huit heures.**

Teaching Note

You may want to review the formation of information questions:
À quelle heure est-ce que tu te lèves?

Teaching Strategy: Warm-Up

Put the verbs from p. 48 on the board or on a transparency. Have students write a story about what twin sisters, Annique and Hélène, do every day from morning until bedtime. The following class, have students rewrite their story in the past tense.

A. Le passé composé des verbes réfléchis

The PASSÉ COMPOSÉ of reflexive verbs is formed with **être.**

AFFIRMATIVE	je **me suis** **lavé** tu **t'es** **lavé** il/on **s'est** **lavé** nous **nous sommes** **lavés** vous **vous êtes** **lavé(s)** ils **se sont** **lavés**	je **me suis** **lavée** tu **t'es** **lavée** elle **s'est** **lavée** nous **nous sommes** **lavées** vous **vous êtes** **lavée(s)** elles **se sont** **lavées**
NEGATIVE	**je ne me suis pas** **lavé**	**je ne me suis pas** **lavée**
INTERROGATIVE	**est-ce que tu t'es** **lavé?** **t'es-tu** **lavé?**	**est-ce que tu t'es** **lavée?** **t'es-tu** **lavée?**

Usually, but not always, the past participle agrees with the subject.

Éric s'est promené. **Anne et Claire se sont promenées** avec lui.

➡ There is no agreement when the reflexive verb is directly followed by a NOUN. Compare:

Stéphanie **s'est lavée.** Elle **s'est lavé** les mains.

Note also:

Catherine et Sophie **se sont acheté** des vêtements.

1 Samedi dernier

Demandez à votre partenaire s'il/si elle a fait les choses suivantes samedi dernier. Votre partenaire peut donner des précisions correspondant aux questions.

▶ se lever tard (à quelle heure?)

— Est-ce que tu t'es levé(e) tard samedi dernier?
— Non, je ne me suis pas levé(e) tard. Je me suis levé(e) à 8 heures.

1. se promener (où?)
2. s'acheter des vêtements (quels vêtements?)
3. s'acheter autre chose (quoi?)
4. s'amuser (comment?)
5. se reposer (quand?)
6. se coucher tard (à quelle heure?)

LANGUE ET COMMUNICATION

TEACHING RESOURCES

Student Activities Manual, pp. 23–24, 113

Audio Program, CD 1, Track 12

HM ClassPrep CD, Audioscript, Unit 1

Teaching Note

The agreement of the past participle depends on whether the reflexive pronoun functions as a direct or indirect object pronoun.

- DIRECT object = AGREEMENT
  Catherine **s'est lavée.**
  She washed herself.
  Nous **nous sommes amusés.**
  We amused ourselves.
- INDIRECT object = NO AGREEMENT
  Catherine **s'est lavé** les mains.
  She washed the hands (belonging to herself).
  Nous **nous sommes acheté** des vêtements.
  We bought clothes for ourselves.

Since the agreement of the past participle requires sophisticated grammatical analysis, you may want to present the above explanation only to advanced students.

Teaching Strategy: Warm-Up

Put the story about Annique and Hélène (see page 49) on a transparency before class. Tell students that this is not what they do every day but simply what they did yesterday. Have the students put the story into the **passé composé** sentence by sentence.

2 Qu'est-ce qu'ils ont fait?

Informez-vous sur les personnes suivantes et dites ce qu'elles ont fait. Pour cela, utilisez les verbes suggérés.

▶ Monsieur Marty a pris son rasoir. **Il s'est rasé.**

1. Caroline a pris le dentifrice.
2. Tu as pris tes vêtements.
3. Nous avons entendu le réveil *(alarm clock)*.
4. À minuit, tu es allé dans ta chambre.
5. Vous avez pris une semaine de vacances.
6. Nous sommes allées à la campagne.
7. Marc et Philippe ont vu un film très drôle.
8. Dans le bus, j'ai marché *(stepped)* sur les pieds de quelqu'un.
9. Le chauffeur de bus a vu le feu rouge *(red light)*.
10. Tu as pris les ciseaux.
11. Vous avez voulu être à l'heure au rendez-vous.

s'amuser
s'arrêter
se brosser les dents
se coucher
se couper les ongles
se dépêcher
s'excuser
s'habiller
se promener
se raser
se reposer
se réveiller

3 La journée d'un mannequin

Christine est mannequin *(model)* pour un magazine de mode. Lisez comment elle décrit sa journée:

Je me réveille à huit heures. Je ne me lève pas immédiatement. J'attends dix minutes. Ensuite, je me lève et je vais dans la salle de bains. Là, je prends une douche et je me lave les cheveux. Ensuite, je me maquille et je m'habille. Vers neuf heures, je descends dans la cuisine et je me prépare un petit déjeuner très léger *(light)*. Après, je regarde le journal. Je téléphone à mon magazine pour faire mes rendez-vous. Je réponds à mon courrier *(mail)*.

Vers dix heures et demie, je sors et je fais les courses. Je rentre chez moi, mais je ne déjeune pas. À une heure, je prends un taxi. Je vais directement au magazine pour les séances *(sessions)* de photo. Je travaille tout l'après-midi.

À sept heures, je rentre chez moi et je dîne. Ensuite, je regarde un film à la télé. À onze heures je me couche et je m'endors.

Chaque jour, Christine suit la même routine. Décrivez ce qu'elle a fait hier.

▶ **Hier, Christine s'est réveillée à huit heures . . .**

4 Ma routine personnelle

Décrivez votre routine personnelle. Pour cela, composez un petit paragraphe où vous racontez ce que vous avez fait hier. (Si nécessaire, utilisez votre imagination!) Ensuite, comparez votre journée avec celle de votre partenaire.

▶ **Hier, c'était samedi [dimanche]. Je me suis réveillé(e) à . . .**

Conjugation Drill

Give students the verb to be drilled: SE MAQUILLER. See p. 45 for Verb drill.

■ Note linguistique

Un mannequin (model) is always used in the masculine form. **Un mannequin** also means "mannequin."

■ Teaching Strategy: Variation

Activity 3 may be presented as a **dictée** or cloze activity.

Teaching Strategy: Variation

Do Activity 4 as an A/B activity.

LE FRANÇAIS

PRATIQUE

La condition physique et les sentiments

TEACHING RESOURCES

Student Activities Manual, pp. 113–114

Audio Program, CD 1, Tracks 13–15

HM ClassPrep CD, Audioscript, Unit 1

Supplementary vocabulary

Also: **en bonne/mauvaise santé**
Ça sent bon/mauvais.
avoir l'air ...
soucieux(se) *worried*
détendu ≠ **agité**
tranquille ≠ **irrité**

■ Note linguistique

avoir l'air + ADJECTIVE
The adjective can:
- remain masculine (to agree with **air**)
  Pauline a l'air **fatigué.**
- agree with the subject
  Pauline a l'air **fatiguée.**

LE FRANÇAIS PRATIQUE

La condition physique et les sentiments

— Comment te sens-tu?
— Je me sens bien.

COMMENT DEMANDER DES NOUVELLES À UN(E) AMI(E)

Ça va?
Comment te sens-tu? *How do you feel?*
Qu'est-ce que tu as? *What's the matter?*
Qu'est-ce qu'il y a? *What's wrong?*

se sentir *to feel*

COMMENT RÉPONDRE

Ça va. 

Je me sens **bien.**
en forme *(in shape)*
décontracté(e) *(relaxed)*

Je suis **heureux (heureuse).**
content(e)
de bonne humeur *(in a good mood)*

Ça ne va pas. 

Je me sens **mal.**
malade
fatigué(e) *(tired)*
tendu(e) *(tense, uptight)*

Je suis **malheureux (malheureuse).**
triste *(sad)*
de mauvaise humeur *(in a bad mood)*
énervé(e) *(upset)*
furieux (furieuse)
en colère *(angry)*

COMMENT DÉCRIRE QUELQU'UN

Ton ami(e) **semble** / **a l'air** **calme.**

Il/Elle **semble** / **a l'air** **perplexe.**
préoccupé(e) *(worried)*
inquiet (inquiète) *(worried)*
déçu(e) *(disappointed)*

sembler *to seem*
avoir l'air *to look, appear*

À noter

Sentir is conjugated like **dormir**.

sentir	*to smell*	Est-ce que **tu sens** cette bonne odeur?
se sentir (+ adjective or expression)	*to feel*	Est-ce que **tu te sens** fatigué? **Je me sens** en forme.
ressentir (+ noun)	*to feel (a pain or an emotion)*	**Je ressens** beaucoup d'admiration pour cette personne.

Teaching Strategy: Dialog Development

Have students in pairs develop and present two 10-line dialogs:
- One dialog asking about each other and how things are going
- One dialog asking about a mutual friend who seems mad, sad, upset, angry...

1 Ça va?

Choisissez trois des situations suivantes. Décrivez votre condition ou vos sentiments dans chacun des cas.

- Vous êtes en vacances.
- Vous avez un examen.
- Vous avez un rendez-vous.
- Vous faites du sport.
- Vous mangez trop.
- Vous étudiez trop.
- Vous avez une bonne note à un examen.
- Vous étudiez beaucoup mais vous avez une mauvaise note.
- Vous vous disputez avec votre copain (copine).
- Votre copain (copine) n'est pas à l'heure à un rendez-vous.
- Votre frère (soeur) oublie votre anniversaire.
- Le professeur est malade.
- Votre cousin(e) vous téléphone à une heure du matin.
- Vos professeurs sont contents de vous.
- Vos amis vous critiquent.

▶ **Quand j'ai un examen, je me sens malade (je me sens tendu(e), décontracté(e) . . .)**

2 Qu'est-ce qu'ils ont?

Décrivez les personnes suivantes. Avec votre partenaire, trouvez deux raisons pour cette situation.

▶ **— Monsieur Moreau a l'air en colère.**
— C'est parce qu'il a eu un accident de voiture.
— Non, je ne suis pas d'accord. C'est parce que son fils est rentré à deux heures du matin.

3 Créa-dialogue

C'est lundi matin. D'habitude votre partenaire est toujours de bonne humeur. Mais aujourd'hui il/elle est de mauvaise humeur. Vous voulez savoir pourquoi.

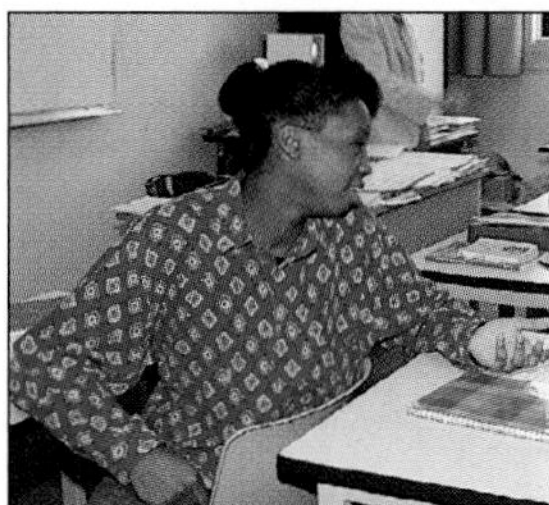

— Ça va?
— Non, ça ne va pas.
— Qu'est-ce que tu as?
— Je suis triste.
— Et pourquoi donc?
— Mon copain a oublié la date de mon anniversaire.

- *Use another expression.*
- *Express another feeling: anger, disappointment, worry . . .*
- *Give an original and appropriate reason.*

LANGUE ET COMMUNICATION

TEACHING RESOURCES

Student Activities Manual, pp. 25–26, 114

Audio Program, CD 1, Track 16

HM ClassPrep CD, Audioscript, Unit 1

Notes linguistiques

- Sometimes a reflexive construction in French corresponds to a passive construction in English. Compare:
  Cela **ne se fait pas.**
  That ***is not done.***
  La fête nationale **se célèbre** le 14 juillet.
  The national holiday ***is celebrated*** *on July 14.*
- Some reflexive verbs are considered idiomatic because their English equivalents do not express a reflexive action. However, in many of these verbs a reflexive meaning is implied (i.e., the subject is acting on itself):
  Elle **se rend** au bureau.
  She ***brings herself*** *to the office.*
  Il **s'impatiente.**
  He ***makes himself*** *impatient.*
  Tu **t'excuses.**
  You ***excuse yourself.***

Verbs

s'asseoir
s'inquiéter (*see* **préférer**)
se taire

A. L'usage idiomatique des verbes réfléchis

NE T'INQUIÈTE PAS!

Reflexive verbs are used:

- to describe certain MOVEMENTS
  se rendre à — *to go to* — Mme Meunier **se rend à** son bureau.
- to describe FEELINGS or changes in feelings
  s'impatienter — *to get impatient* — Pourquoi est-ce que tu **t'impatientes?**
- to describe certain other actions and situations
  s'excuser — *to apologize* — Tu as tort! **Excuse-toi!**
  se trouver — *to be (located)* — Où **se trouve** la pharmacie?

Vocabulaire: Quelques verbes réfléchis

MOVEMENT

s'asseoir	*to sit down*	**s'approcher (de)**	*to come closer*
se lever	*to stand up*	**s'arrêter**	*to stop*
		s'en aller	*to go away*

FEELINGS

s'amuser	*to have fun*	**s'inquiéter**	*to worry*
s'embêter	*to get bored*	**se mettre en colère**	*to get angry*
s'impatienter	*to get impatient*	**se sentir (triste . . .)**	*to feel (sad)*
s'énerver	*to get upset*		

OTHER MEANINGS

s'appeler	*to be called, named*	**se rappeler**	*to remember; to recall*
se trouver	*to be (located)*	**se souvenir (de)**	*to remember*
s'intéresser à	*to be interested in*	**se tromper**	*to make a mistake*
s'occuper de	*to be busy with; to take care of*	**se taire**	*to be quiet; to shut up*

➡ The verb **se souvenir** is conjugated like **venir.**

PRESENT: **je me souviens** **nous nous souvenons** **elles se souviennent**
PASSÉ COMPOSÉ: **je me suis souvenu(e)**

Transports Québec
Je me souviens

➡ The following irregular verbs are commonly used in the imperative:

s'en aller	se taire	s'asseoir
Va-t'en!	Tais-toi!	Assieds-toi!
Allez-vous-en!	Taisez-vous!	Asseyez-vous!

Le présent des verbes s'appeler, se rappeler (comme appeler)
Révision ▶ pp. R20-21
Pratique ▶ p. 25

ALLONS PLUS LOIN

Reflexive verbs are also used to express a reciprocal action, that is, an action in which two or more people interact with one another.

Philippe et Claire **se téléphonent.** — *Philippe and Claire* ***phone each other.***
Marc et moi, **nous nous voyons** souvent. — *Marc and I often* ***see each other.***
Où est-ce que vous allez **vous retrouver?** — *Where are you going* ***to meet (each other)?***

1 Une question de personnalité

Analysez la personnalité des personnes suivantes et dites si oui ou non elles font les choses entre parenthèses.

▶ Tu es toujours calme. (s'inquiéter?)
Tu ne t'inquiètes pas.

1. Tu as une excellente mémoire. (se souvenir de tout?)
2. Vous n'aimez pas attendre. (s'impatienter?)
3. Alice est optimiste. (se sentir triste?)
4. Philippe est très irritable. (se mettre souvent en colère?)
5. Nous sommes curieux. (s'intéresser à tout?)
6. J'aime étudier. (s'embêter en classe?)
7. Tu es très patient. (s'énerver?)
8. Nous avons toujours raison. (se tromper?)

Supplementary vocabulary

s'éloigner *to go away*
se déplacer *to move (over)*
se calmer *to get calm*
se réjouir *to be happy*
s'ennuyer *to be/get bored*
se rendre compte *to realize*
s'apercevoir *to notice*

2 Que dire?

Qu'est-ce que vous allez dire à votre ami français dans les circonstances suivantes? Utilisez l'impératif affirmatif ou négatif des verbes de la liste. Soyez logique dans votre choix!

▶ Votre ami est furieux. **Ne te mets pas en colère!**
▶ Il a tort. **Excuse-toi!**

- Il parle trop.
- Il attend sa copine depuis une heure.
- Il est insupportable *(unbearable)* avec vous.
- Il a un problème avec ses parents.
- Il va à une boum.
- Il a un examen de maths.
- Il est fatigué.
- Il a une entrevue professionnelle dans une semaine.

s'amuser
s'asseoir sur cette chaise
s'en aller
s'excuser
s'impatienter
s'inquiéter
se mettre en colère
se souvenir de la date
se taire
se tromper dans les calculs

3 Et vous?

Complétez les phrases suivantes avec une expression personnelle. Ensuite, comparez vos réponses avec celles de votre partenaire.

1. Je m'intéresse à . . .
2. Je me souviens toujours de . . .
3. Je m'amuse quand . . .
4. Je m'embête quand . . .
5. Je m'inquiète quand . . .
6. Je me sens triste quand . . .
7. Je me sens heureux (heureuse) quand . . .
8. Je me mets en colère quand . . .
9. Je me sens fatigué(e) quand . . .
10. Je ne me tais pas quand . . .

4 Zut alors!

Aujourd'hui les personnes suivantes ont eu des problèmes. Expliquez leurs problèmes. Attention: les phrases peuvent être affirmatives ou négatives!

▶ Philippe / s'amuser à la boum
Philippe ne s'est pas amusé à la boum.

1. vous / s'énerver pendant l'examen
2. moi / se souvenir de mon rendez-vous
3. les élèves / se tromper dans l'exercice
4. Alice / se mettre en colère
5. nous / s'impatienter
6. toi / s'embêter pendant la classe
7. Pierre et Robert / se sentir malades au restaurant
8. Isabelle / se sentir en forme

Reading STRATEGY

Reading fiction

Note culturelle

Le Théâtre de l'Absurde also includes novels and essays, sometimes called **la littérature de dérision.** Some of its authors are Beckett, Obaldia, and Marguerite Duras.

■ Additional Information

Ionesco wrote the following plays: **La Leçon, La Cantatrice chauve, Les Chaises, Rhinocéros.**

LECTURE

Conte pour enfants de moins de trois ans

Eugène Ionesco

Eugène Ionesco (1912-1994) est né en Roumanie. Il fait des études de français à l'université de Bucarest, et devient lui-même professeur de français. En 1938, il quitte son pays menacé par le nazisme et vient s'installer en France. Il commence alors une brillante carrière littéraire qui lui vaudra d'être nommé à l'Académie française.

Ionesco est l'auteur de 33 pièces de théâtre. Dans ses pièces, il dénonce la banalité ou l'angoisse de l'existence avec une arme très puissante: l'humour. Combattant l'absurde par l'absurde, Ionesco a créé un théâtre entièrement nouveau que ses critiques ont justement appelé «Le Théâtre de l'Absurde».

AVANT DE LIRE

Dans ce conte, Ionesco met en scène un père et sa petite fille, âgée de deux ans et demi, dans une situation ordinaire de l'existence. Un matin, papa et sa fille se trouvent seuls à la maison. Pour une raison inexpliquée, la maman est partie chez sa mère. (Il y a peut-être eu une dispute dans le couple.) La petite fille, inquiète° de l'absence de sa mère, veut rester tout près de son père, mais celui-ci, qui veut se laver, n'a pas besoin d'elle. Pour être seul, il joue sur la psychologie des enfants: ce qui est absurde ou illogique pour un adulte peut sembler tout à fait° naturel et logique pour un enfant.

Pour mieux comprendre une histoire, il est utile de savoir quel genre° d'histoire c'est. À votre avis, d'après le titre, les illustrations et la note biographique sur Ionesco, quel genre d'histoire allez-vous lire?

- une histoire réaliste?
- une histoire humoristique?
- un drame psychologique?
- un conte fantastique?
- un récit d'aventures?

inquiète *worried* **tout à fait** = complètement **genre** = sorte

NOTE CULTURELLE

L'Académie française

Créée en 1635, l'Académie française a pour but° de préserver la langue française. Cette prestigieuse institution a 40 membres, appelés les «Immortels». Ce sont généralement des écrivains français très connus. Eugène Ionesco est l'un des rares Académiciens d'origine étrangère.

but = objectif

Mots utiles

avoir mal à l'estomac	*to have an upset stomach*
avoir mal à la tête	*to have a headache*
empêcher de	*to stop, keep from (doing)*
frapper	*to knock*
pleurer	*to cry*
profiter de	*to take advantage of*

56 Unité 1

NOTE CULTURELLE

Les membres de l'Académie française sont élus à vie. On les appelle «Immortels» car quand un Académicien meurt, ses collègues élisent un successeur. Parmi les Académiciens d'origine étrangère: Julien Green (américain), Léopold Senghor (sénégalais), Marguerite Yourcenar (belge).

Conte pour enfants de moins de trois ans

Ce matin, comme d'habitude,° Josette frappe à la porte de la chambre à coucher de ses parents. Papa n'a pas très bien dormi. Maman est partie à la campagne* pour quelques jours. Alors papa a profité de cette absence pour manger beaucoup de saucisson, pour boire de la bière, pour manger du pâté de cochon,** et beaucoup d'autres choses que maman l'empêche de manger parce que c'est pas bon pour la santé.° Alors, voilà, papa a mal au foie,** il a mal à l'estomac, il a mal à la tête, et ne voudrait pas se réveiller. Mais Josette frappe toujours° à la porte. Alors papa lui dit d'entrer. Elle entre, elle va chez son papa. Il n'y a pas maman. Josette demande:

— Où elle est maman?

Papa répond: «Ta maman est allée se reposer à la campagne chez sa maman à elle.»

Josette répond: «Chez Mémée?»°

Papa répond: «Oui, chez Mémée.»

— Écris à maman, dit Josette. Téléphone à maman, dit Josette.

Papa dit: «Faut pas téléphoner.»

Josette dit: «Raconte une histoire avec maman et toi, et moi.»

— Non, dit papa, je vais aller au travail. Je me lève, je vais m'habiller.

Et papa se lève. Il met sa robe de chambre° rouge, par-dessus° son pyjama, il met dans les pieds ses *poutouffles.*° Il va dans la salle de bains. Il ferme la porte de la salle de bains. Josette est à la porte de la salle de bains. Elle frappe avec ses petits poings,° elle pleure.

Josette dit: «Ouvre-moi la porte.»

Papa répond: «Je ne peux pas. Je suis tout nu,° je me lave, après je me rase.»

Josette dit: «Tu laves ta figure, tu laves tes épaules,° tu laves tes bras, tu laves ton dos, tu laves ton *dérère,*° tu laves tes pieds.

— Je rase ma barbe, dit papa.

— Tu rases ta barbe avec du savon, dit Josette. Je veux entrer. Je veux voir.

* **La campagne.** In French, the term **la campagne** (the country) is used to refer to any area outside **la ville** (the city).

** **Mal au foie.** The French believe that eating too many fatty foods, such as **saucisson** (sausage) and **pâté de cochon** (a type of meatloaf made of ground pork and served cold), and drinking too much wine or beer leads to **mal au foie** (abdominal pain indicating liver trouble).

comme d'habitude *as usual* **santé** *health* **toujours** = sans arrêter **Mémée** = grand-mère **robe de chambre** *bathrobe* **par-dessus** = sur **poutouffles** = pantoufles *slippers* **poings** *fists* **nu** *naked, nude* **épaules** *shoulders* **dérère** = derrière *behind, rear end*

Avez-vous compris?

1. Comment le papa de Josette se sent-il ce matin-là? Pourquoi?
2. Qu'est-ce que Josette demande d'abord à son père?
3. Selon vous, pourquoi est-ce que Josette veut rester près de son père?

Anticipons un peu!

Imaginez que vous êtes dans une situation semblable à celle du papa. Vous êtes dans la salle de bains où vous vous habillez pour aller à un rendez-vous. Vous vous dépêchez parce que vous avez peur d'être en retard . . . Votre petit(e) frère (soeur) veut entrer dans la salle de bains. Il/elle pleure, mais vous savez que ce n'est pas trop grave. Qu'est-ce que vous allez faire?

- fermer la porte à clé?
- dire à votre petit(e) frère (soeur) de se taire?
- ouvrir la porte et lui donner une sucette *(lollypop)*?
- sortir de la salle de bains pour lui raconter une histoire?
- trouver une autre solution plus originale? laquelle?

Maintenant, lisez la deuxième partie pour voir ce que le papa de Josette a fait.

Teaching Strategy:

Have students read along as you read the Ionesco short story aloud. Have individual students repeat a line after you and answer a short comprehension question: e.g., **Maman, où est-elle allée? Pourquoi?** (Variation: Have student formulate a question after he or she repeats a line.)

Teaching Strategy

The language used by Ionesco to represent Josette is purposely childish and ungrammatical. You may want to present the corresponding correct forms.

For example:

C'est pas bon pour la santé.
Ce n'est pas bon pour la santé.

Faut pas téléphoner.
Il ne faut pas téléphoner.

Il met dans les pieds ses poutouffles.
Il met ses pantoufles.

Tu laves ta figure.
Tu te laves la figure.

Tu rases ta barbe.
Tu te rases la barbe.

Où tu es?
Où es-tu?

Où elle est maman?
Où est maman?

Note linguistique

Mémée is the affectionate term used by children for their grandmother. **Mamy** is another one. The grandfather is called **Pépé** or **Papy.**

Avez-vous compris?

(Sample answers)

1. Il ne se sent pas bien, parce qu'il a trop mangé et trop bu.
2. Elle demande où est sa mère.
3. Elle veut rester près de son père parce que sa mère est partie, et les enfants n'aiment pas rester seuls.

■ **Irregular Verbs**
(see Appendix C)

courir
revenir (*see* **venir**)

■ **Note linguistique**

Un buffet is used to put away dishes and silverware. **Une armoire** is used for linens or clothing.

un canapé

un buffet

les casseroles

le four

le paillasson

II

Papa dit: «Tu ne peux pas me voir, parce que je ne suis plus dans la salle de bains.»

Josette dit (derrière la porte): «Alors, où tu es?»

Papa répond: «Je ne sais pas, va voir. Je suis peut-être dans la salle à manger, va me chercher.»

Josette court dans la salle à manger, et papa commence sa toilette. Josette court avec ses petites jambes, elle va dans la salle à manger. Papa est tranquille, mais pas longtemps. Josette arrive de nouveau devant la porte de la salle de bains, elle crie à travers la porte:

Josette: «Je t'ai cherché. Tu n'es pas dans la salle à manger.»

Papa dit: «Tu n'as pas bien cherché. Regarde sous la table.»

Josette retourne dans la salle à manger. Elle revient.

Elle dit: «Tu n'es pas sous la table.»

Papa dit: «Alors va voir dans le salon. Regarde bien si je suis sur le fauteuil, sur le canapé, derrière les livres, à la fenêtre.»

Josette s'en va. Papa est tranquille, mais pas pour longtemps. Josette revient.

Elle dit: «Non, tu n'es pas dans le fauteuil, tu n'es pas à la fenêtre, tu n'es pas sur le canapé, tu n'es pas derrière les livres, tu n'es pas dans la télévision, tu n'es pas dans le salon.»

Papa dit: «Alors, va voir si je suis dans la cuisine.»

Josette dit: «Je vais te chercher dans la cuisine.»

Josette court à la cuisine. Papa est tranquille, mais pas pour longtemps. Josette revient.

Elle dit: «Tu n'es pas dans la cuisine.»

Papa dit: «Regarde bien, sous la table de la cuisine, regarde bien si je suis dans le buffet, regarde bien si je suis dans les casseroles, regarde bien si je suis dans le four avec le poulet.»

Josette va et vient. Papa n'est pas dans le four, papa n'est pas dans les casseroles, papa n'est pas dans le buffet, papa n'est pas sous le paillasson, papa n'est pas dans la poche de son pantalon. Dans la poche du pantalon, il y a seulement le mouchoir.

Josette revient devant la porte de la salle de bains.

Josette dit: «J'ai cherché partout. Je ne t'ai pas trouvé. Où tu es?»

Mots utiles

aller voir	*to go look*
courir*	*to run*
crier	*to yell, shout*
embrasser	*to kiss*
être tranquille	*to be alone, undisturbed*
revenir*	*to come back*
sauter	*to jump*
à travers	*across, through*
de nouveau	*again*
ne . . . plus	*no longer, not anymore*

la poche, le mouchoir

une armoire

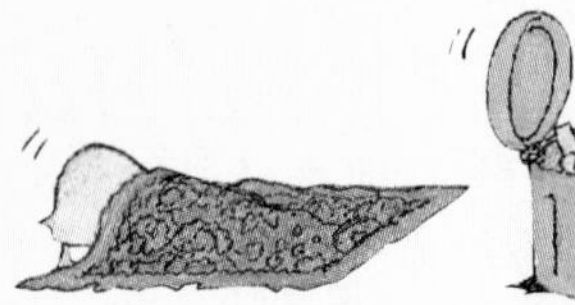

un tapis

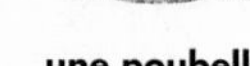

une poubelle

Papa dit: «Je suis là.» Et papa, qui a eu le temps de faire sa toilette, qui s'est rasé, qui s'est habillé, ouvre la porte.

Il dit: «Je suis là.» Il prend Josette dans ses bras, et voilà aussi la porte de la maison qui s'ouvre, au fond du couloir,° et c'est maman qui arrive. Josette saute° des bras de son papa, elle se jette° dans les bras de sa maman, elle l'embrasse, elle dit:

— Maman, j'ai cherché papa sous la table, dans l'armoire, sous le tapis, derrière la glace, dans la cuisine, dans la poubelle, il n'était pas là.

Papa dit à maman: «Je suis content que tu sois revenue. Il faisait beau à la campagne? Comment va ta mère?»

Josette dit: «Et Mémée, elle va bien? On va chez elle?»

au fond du couloir *at the end of the hall* **saute** *jump* **se jette** *throws herself*

Avez-vous compris?

1. Quel stratagème est-ce que le père utilise pour être tranquille?
2. Est-ce que ce stratagème réussit? Pourquoi, selon vous?
3. Comment se termine l'histoire?

APRÈS LA LECTURE

EXPRESSION ORALE

■ Situation

Avec votre partenaire, composez un dialogue correspondant à la situation suivante. Utilisez votre imagination.

u bureau

e papa de Josette parle de son week-end avec un(e) collègue e bureau qui veut des détails. Il décrit . . .

- pourquoi sa femme n'était pas là (il ne dit pas la vérité), et où elle était
- ce qu'il a bu et mangé
- ce qu'il a fait avec sa petite fille
- ce qu'il a fait d'autre

ôles: le papa, le/la collègue

■ Théâtre

Avec votre partenaire, composez une scène semblable au conte que vous avez lu sur le thème suivant: Stéphanie (18 ans) fait du baby-sitting pour Dominique (3 ans). Elle veut téléphoner à son copain, mais Dominique ne la laisse pas tranquille. Pour se libérer, Stéphanie utilise un stratagème semblable à celui de l'histoire. (Variation: c'est Stéphane qui fait du baby-sitting, et il veut téléphoner à sa copine.)

EXPRESSION ÉCRITE

■ Un peu d'humour

Décrivez brièvement les éléments de l'histoire que vous avez trouvés drôles.

■ Une lettre

Imaginez que vous êtes la mère de Josette. Vous écrivez à votre cousine pour lui expliquer les événements du week-end. Vous pouvez mentionner. . .

- la raison de votre dispute avec votre mari (Inventez!)
- où vous êtes allée et ce que vous avez fait (Inventez!)
- quand vous êtes rentrée chez vous et pourquoi vous étiez heureuse de rentrer

■ *Avez-vous compris?*

(Sample answers)

1. Il dit à Josette de le chercher dans toutes les pièces de la maison.
2. Le stratagème réussit, parce que les enfants très jeunes ne savent pas que les parents ne disent pas toujours la vérité.
3. L'histoire se termine bien: le père est habillé et la mère revient à la maison.

Teaching Strategy: Expansion

Assign the following activity to students:

Finissez l'histoire. Josette dit: «Et Mémée, elle va bien? On va chez elle?» Que répond Maman? Vont-ils aller chez Mémée? Quand? Que va dire Josette à Mémée?

INTERLUDE CULTUREL

TEACHING RESOURCES

Student Activities Manual, pp. 178–180

Video/DVD Program, Unit 1, *Vignette culturelle*

General Synopsis of Interlude 1

French Modern Art

- *Impressionism:* Monet, Degas, Renoir, Manet, B. Morisot
- *Post-Impressionism:* Van Gogh, Gauguin, Matisse, Rousseau, Toulouse-Lautrec
- *Surrealism* as an artistic and literary movement: Magritte

Poems

- Desnos, *La Fourmi*
- Prévert, *Pour faire le portrait d'un oiseau*

■ Note linguistique

Les nymphéas = water lilies (Monet's painting, top of page)

Teaching Strategy

The material presented in the *Interlude* should remain enjoyable for students and not overwhelming. Ask students to scan the entire *Interlude*, looking at the illustrations, noting familiar and unfamiliar items, and making a list of names they recognize. Ask them to suggest the theme of the *Interlude*.

INTERLUDE CULTUREL

Monet «Les Nymphéas»

▪ *La Révolution impressionniste* ▪

L'art moderne est né en France dans les années 1870. C'est à cette époque, en effet, qu'un groupe d'artistes, nommés «les **Impressionnistes**», a présenté au monde une nouvelle façon° de concevoir la peinture.° Avant eux, la peinture était très traditionnelle. Les artistes essayaient d'imiter la réalité en reproduisant de façon très exacte et avec beaucoup de détails les sujets qu'ils peignaient. Ils apprenaient leur métier° dans des «académies», c'est-à-dire dans des écoles où ils copiaient minutieusement des modèles sous la direction de maîtres sans grande imagination. Pour ces artistes, l'essentiel dans la peinture était la forme.

Au lieu de° s'intéresser à la forme, les Impressionnistes se sont intéressés à la couleur, et surtout aux effets de la lumière° sur les objets qu'ils représentaient. Au lieu de peindre des scènes de bataille ou des héros de l'Antiquité, ils ont peint des scènes de la vie courante,° des portraits d'amis, et surtout la nature. Au lieu de travailler dans des ateliers,° ils ont travaillé en plein air.° Cette façon simple et naturelle de peindre a révolutionné le monde des arts.

À l'origine, cependant, les Impressionnistes n'ont eu aucun° succès. C'est par dérision° qu'un journaliste leur a donné le nom d'«impressionnistes». Ces peintres ne pouvaient même pas exposer leurs toiles° dans les salons officiels patronnés par le gouvernement. Ils ont donc organisé leurs propres° expositions chez des amis. Il y a eu huit expositions impressionnistes entre 1874 et 1886, mais ces expositions ont été des échecs.° La peinture impressionniste choquait trop le sens esthétique de l'époque!

Peu à peu, les critiques d'art ont finalement compris l'importance de la «révolution» impressionniste. Les collectionneurs ont commencé à acheter les tableaux° de ces peintres. Aujourd'hui, ces tableaux valent° des fortunes. On peut les admirer dans les plus grands musées du monde: à Paris, à New York, à Londres, à Chicago, à Boston, à Saint Pétersbourg.

Les peintres impressionnistes sont considérés parmi° les plus grands artistes de tous les temps: **Monet**, **Manet**, **Cézanne**, **Renoir**, **Degas** . . . Parmi ces artistes, il y avait des femmes: **Berthe Morisot** et une Américaine, **Mary Cassatt**. Mary Cassatt, fille d'un riche banquier de Philadelphie, était venue étudier l'art à Paris. En faisant connaître° l'impressionnisme aux États-Unis, elle en a assuré le triomphe dans le monde.

façon *manner* **peinture** *painting* **métier** *trade* **au lieu de** *instead of* **lumière** *light* **vie courante** *daily life* **ateliers** *studios* **en plein air** *outdoors* **aucun** *no* **dérision** *mockery* **toiles** *paintings (canvases)* **propres** *own* **échecs** *failures* **tableaux** *paintings* **valent** *are worth* **parmi** *among* **en faisant connaître** *by making known*

Teaching Suggestion: Video/DVD Program

Use the Unit 1 *Vignette culturelle* video segment on *l'impressionnisme* to help students understand the Impressionist movement and to identify some of the French artists associated with it. The video will include such artists as Monet, Degas, Renoir and Morisot. Before showing the video to students, brainstorm a list of French Impressionists and write their names on the board.

Quelques peintres impressionnistes

Degas *«Répétition d'un ballet»*

Edgar Degas (1834-1917)

Degas était le fils d'un banquier. Sa mère était issue d'une riche famille de La Nouvelle-Orléans. Degas a étudié le droit°, mais il a abandonné ses études pour se consacrer à la peinture. C'était aussi un sculpteur. Ses sujets préférés étaient les danseuses de l'Opéra, les scènes de café et les chevaux.

Renoir *«La Danse à Bougival»* Photograph © 2007 Museum of Fine Arts, Boston. Dance at Bougival by Renoir.

Manet *«Le fifre»*

Édouard Manet (1832-1883)

Manet voulait être officier de marine, mais après un voyage au Brésil, il a décidé de se consacrer à la peinture. Ses premiers tableaux, de couleurs violentes, ont provoqué l'hostilité du public et des critiques, mais l'admiration de jeunes peintres alors inconnus: Monet, Renoir, Cézanne. C'est ainsi qu'il est devenu le chef d'un nouveau mouvement qui allait être l'impressionnisme. Manet a peint toutes sortes de sujets: portraits de ses amis, scènes de la vie courante et familière, paysages° divers.

Pierre-Auguste Renoir (1841-1919)

Renoir a commencé par peindre des devantures° de café, puis il est allé à l'École des Beaux-Arts. Ce peintre aimait les couleurs chaudes. Ses sujets principaux sont les enfants, les jeunes filles, les femmes, les fleurs, les scènes de café et les bals populaires.

Berthe Morisot (1841-1895)

Berthe Morisot était la belle-soeur d'Édouard Manet. Elle s'est intéressée très jeune à la peinture. Comme beaucoup d'artistes de l'époque, elle a commencé à copier les tableaux du musée du Louvre. C'est là qu'elle a fait la connaissance de Manet. Elle a alors rejoint le groupe des peintres impressionnistes. Elle a peint avec eux et elle a participé à leurs expositions. Berthe Morisot aimait utiliser les couleurs claires.° Ses sujets principaux sont les fleurs, les paysages, les scènes de la vie champêtre° et les portraits de jeunes filles.

Berthe Morisot *«La lecture»* 1888. Oil on Canvas. 29¼ X 56½ in. Museum of Fine Arts, St. Petersburg, FL. Museum purchase in memory of Margaret Acheson Stuart. 1981.2.

droit *law* **devantures** *store fronts* **paysages** *landscapes* **claires** *light* **champêtre** = rurale

Notes culturelles

- When Degas visited the US in 1872, he stayed in New Orleans.
- **Le fifre** is a small flute or the player of this flute. This painting represents an army boy **(un enfant de troupe)** of the Imperial Army **(la garde impériale)** under Napoléon III (1808–1873). **Le Fifre** was rejected by the jury of the 1866 Salon. This rejection prompted an article by Émile Zola, in which he praised the beauty and simplicity of Manet's work. Zola concluded his article with this prophetic line: **«La place de Manet est marquée au Louvre.»**
- Renoir's son, Jean Renoir (1894–1979), became an acclaimed filmmaker. Among his works are the classics **La Grande illusion** and **La Règle du jeu.**
- Manet made several portraits of Berthe Morisot. She is also represented in his painting called **Le Balcon.**
- **Les Beaux-Arts** is a famous art school in Paris where Delacroix, Matisse, and Braque studied.

■ **Contexte historique: 19th century in France**

1815: Fall of the Emperor Napoléon 1er.

1830: Louis Philippe becomes king after a revolution.

1830–1848: Beginning of the Industrial Revolution in France. Romanticism prevails in all arts.

1838: Beginning of photography, with the **daguerréotypes** invented by Jacques Daguerre.

1852–1870: Napoléon III, nephew of Napoléon 1er, reigns as the emperor of France. Haussman landscapes Paris, widening its streets, and creating large avenues as well as the Parc du Bois de Boulogne. The railroad system is put into place.

1870–1871: Third Republic. After a war with Germany (1870), France loses the eastern regions of Alsace and Lorraine.

1871: A socialist revolution, called **La Commune de Paris,** is violently repressed.

1880: Elementary school becomes mandatory and free in France.

1889: The new Eiffel Tower is the talk of the Paris Exhibition.

1894–1899: The Dreyfus Affair divides public opinion and becomes a great scandal.

1895: The **Brothers Lumière,** Louis Jean and Auguste, show the first movie in Paris.

■ *Claude Monet: le peintre de la lumière*

C'est un tableau de **Monet** intitulé **«Impression, soleil levant»**° qui a donné son nom à l'impressionnisme. Monet (1840-1926) était fasciné par les effets de la lumière. Il pensait qu'on pouvait reconstituer les reflets de la lumière sur les objets en décomposant celle-ci° en ses couleurs fondamentales. Il a donc inventé une technique qui consistait à peindre par petites taches° de couleur: du jaune, du rouge, du bleu, du vert, de l'orange et aussi du blanc et du noir.

Monet *«Impression, soleil levant»*

Monet *«Gare Saint-Lazare. Le Train de Normandie»* Claude Monet, Arrival of the Normandy train, Gare Saint-Lazare, 1877.

Claude Monet *(1840-1926)*

Monet aimait peindre et repeindre les mêmes scènes sous des lumières différentes: à midi, très tôt le matin, le soir, au printemps, en plein été, sous la neige. Il a ainsi exécuté des séries entières d'un seul° sujet peint à différents moments de la journée ou de l'année. Monet a peint surtout des paysages, mais il a peint aussi des scènes urbaines très célèbres: **la cathédrale de Rouen, la Gare Saint Lazare** à Paris, **la Tamise**° à Londres.

Pendant de longues années, Monet est resté très pauvre, mais avec le succès de l'impressionnisme, il a finalement connu la célébrité, la gloire et la fortune. Après des années de misère, il est devenu un véritable héros national.

Monet *«La cathédrale de Rouen»*

soleil levant *rising sun* **celle-ci** = la lumière **taches** *spots* **un seul** *only one* **la Tamise** *Thames (River)*

Monet a vécu° longtemps dans une maison de campagne située à **Giverny**, à 60 kilomètres de Paris. Devant cette maison, il avait créé un superbe jardin avec une très grande variété de fleurs qui changeait de couleur avec les saisons. C'est ce jardin aux couleurs chaudes et variées que Monet a peint dans de nombreux tableaux. À Giverny, Monet aimait recevoir ses amis et aussi beaucoup de jeunes peintres qui venaient écouter ses conseils.° Parmi ces peintres, il y avait une colonie d'artistes américains qui s'étaient installés dans un hôtel près de la maison de l'artiste. Vers° la fin° de sa vie, malheureusement, ce grand artiste de la lumière était devenu aveugle,° et ne pouvait plus peindre.

Après la mort de Monet, la maison de Giverny et son jardin ont été abandonnés. Heureusement, grâce à° la générosité d'une riche Américaine, cette maison a été récemment restaurée et le jardin recréé dans sa splendeur originale. Aujourd'hui, des centaines de milliers de visiteurs venus du monde entier viennent chaque année à Giverny saluer la mémoire du grand artiste français et admirer son merveilleux jardin.

Renoir «*Monet peignant dans son jardin à Argenteuil*» Monet painting in His Garden at Argenteuil by Renoir

Monet «Le bassin aux nymphéas» Claude Monet, 1840–1926 *Waterlilies and Japanese Bridge.* Oil on Canvas; 90.5 X 89.7c. Princeton University Art Museum. From the Collection of William Church Osborn, Class of 1883, Trustee of Princeton University (1914-1951), President of the Metropolitan Museum of Art (1941–1947); given by his Family. Photo Credit: Bruce M. White. y1972–15

Le jardin de Monet à Giverny

La maison de Monet à Giverny

vécu *lived* **conseils** *advice* **vers** *towards* **fin** *end* **aveugle** *blind* **grâce à** *thanks to*

NOTE CULTURELLE

Giverny is a small town (547 inhabitants) in Normandy. Rouen, the city where Joan of Arc was executed in 1431, is also in Normandy.

In 1892, Monet painted the cathedral of Rouen forty times, each painting done at a different time of day and thus in a different light.

■ Anecdote

On December 24, 1888, Van Gogh assaulted Gauguin and tried to kill him. To beg his forgiveness, Van Gogh cut off part of his ear and sent it to Gauguin.

Note culturelle

L'archipel des Marquises is a group of ten volcanic islands, and belongs to French Polynesia.

▪ Après l'Impressionnisme ▪

Une conséquence importante de l'impressionnisme a été de libérer l'art des normes esthétiques traditionnelles. Ce mouvement a donc ouvert° des voies° nouvelles à d'autres artistes qui ont pu exercer librement° leur imagination et leur créativité. Après l'impressionnisme, d'autres mouvements artistiques sont nés en France. Vers 1900, Paris était devenu la capitale universelle des arts, attirant° des artistes de tous les pays du monde.

Van Gogh *«La nuit étoilée»*

■ Vincent Van Gogh (1853-1890): Le génie de la folie

Van Gogh était hollandais, mais c'est en France qu'il a peint ses tableaux les plus célèbres. Comme les Impressionnistes, il avait un sens profond de la lumière et des couleurs brillantes, mais il est allé plus loin qu'eux. Van Gogh voulait non seulement peindre ce qu'il voyait, mais cherchait aussi à exprimer les sensations° étranges qu'il éprouvait.° Pour cela, il exagérait l'intensité des couleurs et il donnait un mouvement aux choses inanimées. Ses représentations de la lune° et des étoiles° tournant dans le ciel° sont particulièrement hallucinantes.

Gauguin *«Femmes de Tahiti»*

■ Paul Gauguin (1848-1903): Le peintre de l'exotisme

Gauguin travaillait dans une banque où il gagnait bien sa vie. Un jour, à l'âge de 35 ans, il a décidé de tout abandonner, travail, famille, enfants, vie confortable, pour se consacrer totalement à la peinture. Il a rejoint les peintres impressionnistes, mais c'est dans l'exotisme qu'il a cherché son inspiration. Il est allé à Panama, à la Martinique, à Tahiti et, finalement, dans une petite île des Marquises.* Là, loin de la civilisation et en compagnie de gens simples, mais nobles et généreux, il a peint ses plus belles toiles.

* Les Marquises: a group of islands in the South Pacific

Rousseau *«La bohémienne endormie»*

■ Henri Rousseau (1844-1910): Le douanier inspiré

Pendant la semaine, **Henri Rousseau** était un bureaucrate dont° le travail consistait à contrôler le trafic des marchandises à l'entrée de Paris (d'où son surnom de «douanier»).° Le dimanche, cet employé modèle quittait la ville avec sa boîte de peintures pour aller peindre en plein air. Comme il n'avait jamais étudié dans une école d'art, Rousseau utilisait une technique très rudimentaire où la perspective n'existait pas. Si son style était simple, «naïf», son imagination était débordante.° Ses tableaux les plus célèbres représentent des paysages irréels peuplés° d'animaux exotiques.

ouvert *opened* **voies** *ways* **librement** *freely* **attirant** *attracting* **sensations** *feelings* **éprouvait** *experienced, felt*
lune *moon* **étoiles** *stars* **ciel** *sky* **dont** *whose* **douanier** *customs officer* **débordante** *overflowing* **peuplés** *populated*

Toulouse-Lautrec *«Jane Avril au Jardin de Paris»*

■ **Henri de Toulouse-Lautrec** (1864-1901): **Le peintre de la vie parisienne**

Henri de Toulouse-Lautrec est né dans une famille aristocratique très illustre et très ancienne. À l'âge de 14 ans, il a eu un accident de cheval qui l'a rendu infirme° pour le reste de sa vie. Encouragé par sa mère, il a décidé de devenir artiste et il est allé étudier à l'École des Beaux Arts à Paris. Toulouse-Lautrec aimait fréquenter° les cafés, les cabarets et les music-halls, comme le Moulin Rouge pour lequel° il a dessiné des affiches célèbres.

Dans ses tableaux, il a surtout représenté les scènes de spectacle auxquels il assistait: théâtre, music-hall, cirque, vélodrome°. . . Il a immortalisé les artistes de ces spectacles, comme Jane Avril, dans de nombreux portraits.

■ **Henri Matisse** (1869-1954): **Le grand Fauve**

C'est au lit que **Matisse** a découvert la peinture. Jeune homme, il étudiait le droit pour être avocat. Les complications d'une appendicite l'ont obligé à rester dans sa chambre pendant plusieurs mois. Un jour, pour le distraire°, sa mère lui a offert des pinceaux° et une boîte de couleurs.° Tout d'un coup, Matisse a eu la révélation de sa véritable° vocation. Après sa maladie, il a abandonné ses études de droit pour se consacrer uniquement et entièrement à la peinture.

Matisse est l'un des plus grands artistes du vingtième siècle. Durant sa vie, Matisse a peint dans des styles très différents. Vers 1905, il a fondé avec quelques amis un nouveau mouvement artistique, le «Fauvisme». (On appelle ces artistes les «Fauves»° non seulement parce qu'ils utilisaient des couleurs violentes — rouge, brun, orange — mais aussi parce que leurs ateliers ressemblaient àdes tanières° de bêtes sauvages!)

Matisse *«La desserte rouge» © 2007 Succession H. Matisse, Paris/ Artists Rights Society (ARS), New York. Photo: © Bridgeman-Giraudon/Art Resource, NY*

Plus tard, Matisse a utilisé des couleurs plus claires et plus délicates pour peindre des fruits, des fleurs, des jeunes femmes d'une façon très décorative. Il s'est exprimé dans des médias divers: il a dessiné, sculpté, illustré des livres, fait des collages avec du papier découpé.° Vers la fin de sa vie, il a décoré la petite Chapelle de Vence, près de Nice, dans le Sud de la France.

Matisse *«Icarus, Jazz» © 2007 Succession H. Matisse, Paris/ Artists Rights Society (ARS), New York. Photo: © Archives Matisse, Paris*

■ **Camille Claudel** (1864-1943): **L'élève, égale au maître**

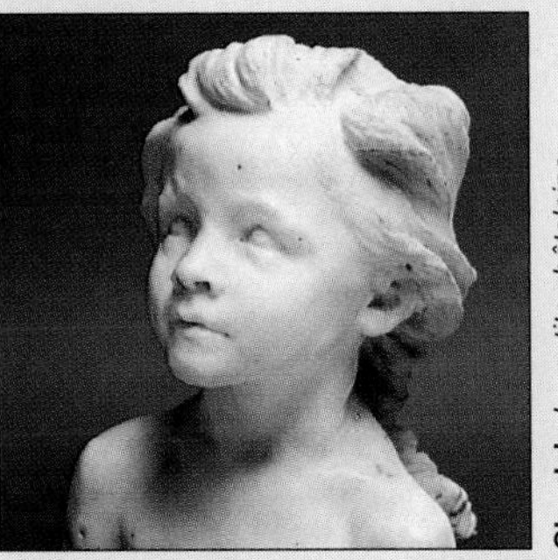

Claudel *«La petite châtelaine»*

Comme beaucoup de jeunes filles de son époque, **Camille Claudel** voulait être artiste. Comme elle s'intéressait à la sculpture, elle a décidé d'aller à Paris pour étudier sous la direction d'Auguste Rodin, le plus grand sculpteur d'alors. D'élève, Camille Claudel est devenue l'assistante et l'inspiratrice du maître. Son influence est présente dans un grand nombre de sculptures de Rodin.

Camille Claudel était elle-même un grand sculpteur, mais ses oeuvres,° produites dans l'ombre° d'un homme que l'on considérait comme l'un des grands génies de son temps, sont longtemps restées ignorées. Un film sur sa vie tragique a fait redécouvrir le talent de cette artiste méconnue.°

infirme *crippled* **fréquenter** = visiter **lequel** *which* **vélodrome** *bicycle racetrack* **distraire** *to amuse* **pinceaux** *brushes* **boîte de couleurs** *paintbox* **véritable** *true* **Fauves** *wild beasts* **tanières** *lairs* **découpé** *cut out* **avant-bras** *forearms* **oeuvres** *works* **ombre** *shadow* **méconnue** *unrecognized*

Additional Information

Matisse traveled to Morocco, Italy, Spain, Germany, Tahiti, and Russia. In 1950, Matisse decorated the interior of the chapel of Saint-Paul-de-Vence, a town in the south of France.

NOTE CULTURELLE

- Dans le film *Camille Claudel* (1988), réalisé par Brunot Nuytten, **Isabelle Adjani** joue le rôle principal de Camille Claudel.
- **Auguste Rodin** (1840–1917) est surtout connu pour sa sculpture *Le Penseur*.

■ Additional Information

- René Magritte was born in Lessines, Belgium, in 1898. He died in Brussels in 1967.
- The first surrealist exhibit took place in 1924, showing works from Chirico, Arp, Ernst, and Miró.

▪ *Le surréalisme* ▪

■ *Peinture . . .*

Regardez bien ce tableau. Il représente un homme avec un chapeau sur la tête et une pomme verte. La juxtaposition de cette personne réelle avec un objet réel constitue une situation qui n'est pas réelle. C'est une situation surréelle ou **«surréaliste»**.

L'artiste qui a peint ce tableau est l'un des plus grands peintres surréalistes. Il était belge et s'appelait **René Magritte**. Magritte ressemblait beaucoup à l'homme du tableau. Il portait souvent une cravate, un manteau et un chapeau, même° quand il peignait. Il n'avait pas de studio. Il peignait ses tableaux dans sa cuisine ou dans son salon. Quand il ne travaillait pas, il aimait faire les courses ou promener son chien Loulou, comme les gens du quartier où il habitait. Cet homme à l'apparence très ordinaire faisait des tableaux absolument extraordinaires.

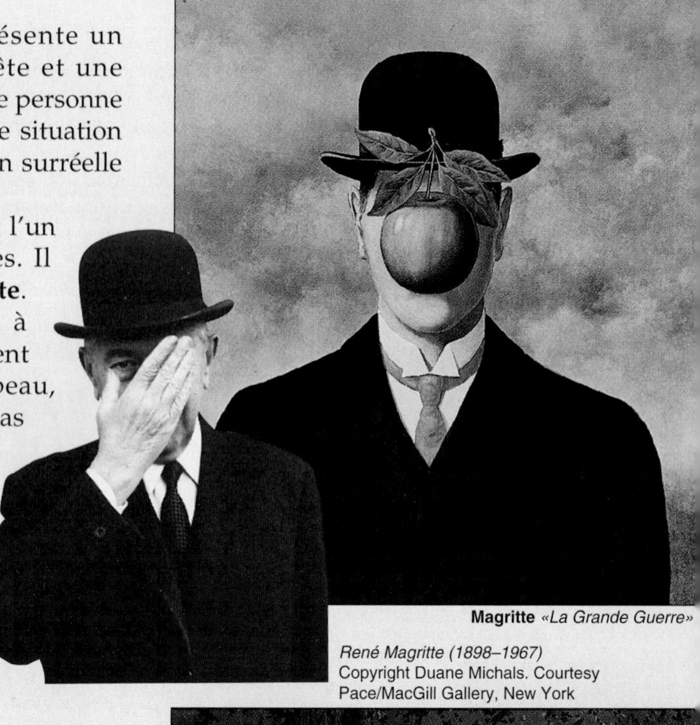

Magritte *«La Grande Guerre»*

René Magritte (1898–1967)
Copyright Duane Michals. Courtesy Pace/MacGill Gallery, New York

Les peintres surréalistes comme Magritte voulaient choquer le public en créant° des scènes bizarres à partir° d'éléments étrangement réels. Quand on regarde un tableau surréaliste, on reste perplexe et on veut savoir ce que veut représenter l'artiste. Quelle est la signification° des scènes qui apparemment n'ont pas de sens? La réponse est donnée par Magritte lui-même. Quand les gens lui demandaient d'expliquer ses tableaux, il répondait: «C'est simple! L'explication, c'est qu'il n'y a pas d'explication!»

Magritte *«Le blanc-seing»*

même *even* **en créant** *by creating* **à partir de** *from* **signification** *meaning*

■ . . . et littérature

Le surréalisme est un mouvement à la fois° artistique et littéraire. Ce mouvement est né en Belgique et en France vers 1920, quelques années après la première guerre mondiale.* Les artistes et les écrivains surréalistes se sont révoltés contre tous les aspects de la société d'alors, responsable, selon eux, de cette terrible guerre.

Pour les surréalistes, le monde tel qu'on le connaît° est une création artificielle. La véritable réalité vient du subconscient qu'on peut atteindre° par le rêve.° Le surréalisme rejette la raison et la logique. La seule° source d'inspiration est l'imagination, mais celle-ci° doit être libre de tout contrôle et de toute convention. Comme les enfants, et comme dans les rêves, les surréalistes ont construit un monde imaginaire où tout est possible.

* La première guerre mondiale *(World War I)*: 1914-1918.

à la fois *at the same time* **tel qu'on le connaît** *as we know it* **atteindre** *to reach* **rêve** *dream* **seule** *only* **celle-ci** = l'imagination

Documents: La fourmi

LA FOURMI

Une fourmi de dix-huit mètres
Avec un chapeau sur la tête,
Ça n'existe pas, ça n'existe pas.

Une fourmi traînant un char
Plein de pingouins et de canards,
Ça n'existe pas, ça n'existe pas.

Une fourmi parlant français,
Parlant latin et javanais,
Ça n'existe pas, ça n'existe pas.

Eh! Pourquoi pas?

Robert Desnos (1900-1945)

Robert Desnos est l'un des fondateurs du surréalisme. Pendant la deuxième guerre mondiale, il a participé à la Résistance contre les Allemands. Fait prisonnier, il est mort dans un camp en Tchécoslovaquie.

Dans ce petit poème très simple, Desnos pose la question fondamentale du surréalisme: **Où est la réalité? Dans ce que nous voyons ou dans ce que nous imaginons?**

Bonjour!
Ave!
Bavonjavour!

Pour en savoir plus
For more information on World War II and the Resistance, see *Interlude 6*, pp. 252–259.

■ Teaching Note
18 mètres = 59 feet

■ Note linguistique
Javanais is the Indonesian dialect of the island of Java. However, for those of Desnos's generation, **javanais** was a coded French slang, similar to Pig Latin, in which the syllables **av** or **va** are inserted after each consonant sound. For example, in **javanais, bonjour** becomes **bavonjavour.**

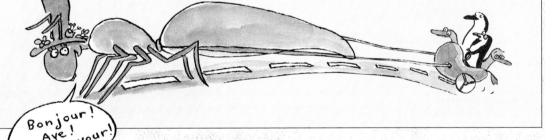

■ Pour en savoir plus

Oeuvres: **Paroles** (1946), **Spectacle** (1951), **La Pluie et le Beau Temps** (1955), **Fatras** (1966)

Films: **Drôle de drame, Les Visiteurs du soir, Les Enfants du paradis** (de Carné); **Remorques, Lumière d'été** (de Grémillon)

■ Note linguistique

la bête = animal

Teaching Strategy

Have students try to guess the meanings of the words marked with (°) by looking at the illustrations; if they are not sure, they can refer to the glosses to verify their guesses.

Pour faire le portrait d'un oiseau

Jacques Prévert (1900-1977)

Jacques Prévert (1900-1977) est un autre poète surréaliste. Il a aussi écrit des chansons et des scénarios° de films. Dans ce poème, il explique de façon humoristique comment peindre° un oiseau.

Peindre d'abord une cage
avec une porte ouverte
peindre ensuite
quelque chose de joli
quelque chose de simple
quelque chose de beau
quelque chose d'utile
pour l'oiseau

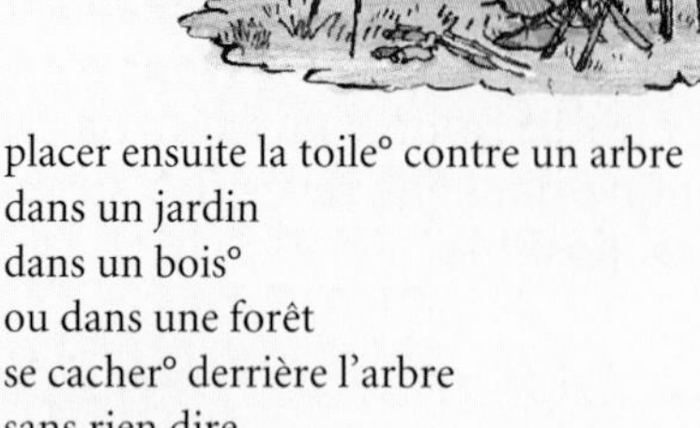

placer ensuite la toile° contre un arbre
dans un jardin
dans un bois°
ou dans une forêt
se cacher° derrière l'arbre
sans rien dire
sans bouger°. . .

Parfois l'oiseau arrive vite
mais il peut aussi bien mettre de
longues années
avant de se décider

Ne pas se décourager
attendre
attendre s'il le faut pendant des
années
la vitesse° ou la lenteur° de l'arrivée
de l'oiseau n'ayant aucun rapport°
avec la réussite du tableau

Quand l'oiseau arrive
s'il arrive
observer le plus profond silence
attendre que l'oiseau entre dans
la cage et quand il est entré
fermer doucement° la porte avec
le pinceau°
puis
effacer° un à un tous les barreaux
en ayant soin de ne toucher aucune
des plumes de l'oiseau

Faire ensuite le portrait de l'arbre
en choisissant la plus belle de ses branches
pour l'oiseau
peindre aussi le vert feuillage° et la fraîcheur° du vent
la poussière° du soleil
et le bruit des bêtes de l'herbe dans la chaleur° de l'été
et puis attendre que l'oiseau se décide de chanter
Si l'oiseau ne chante pas
c'est mauvais signe
signe que le tableau est mauvais
mais s'il chante c'est bon signe
signe que vous pouvez signer
alors vous arrachez° tout doucement
une des plumes de l'oiseau
et vous écrivez votre nom dans un coin° du tableau

scénarios *scripts* **peindre** *to paint* **toile** *canvas* **bois** *woods* **se cacher** *hide* **sans bouger** *without moving* **vitesse** *speed* **lenteur** *slowness* **aucun rapport** *no relationship* **doucement** *gently* **pinceau** *brush* **effacer** *erase* **feuillage** *leaves* **fraîcheur** *coolness* **poussière** *dust (visible in the rays of sunlight)* **chaleur** *warmth* **arracher** *pull out* **coin** *corner*

■ *L'art dans la rue*

Quand on veut voir les oeuvres° des grands artistes, on va dans les musées. À Paris, on va au Louvre pour admirer les chefs-d'oeuvres° classiques, au Musée d'Orsay pour regarder les peintures des Impressionnistes et des grands artistes du 19e siècle, et au Centre Pompidou si on veut voir des tableaux modernes. Si on s'intéresse à l'art moderne, on peut aussi se promener dans la rue.

Cette sculpture mobile flottante se trouve° près du **Centre Pompidou**. C'est la création de **Niki de Saint-Phalle**, une artiste qui a aussi créé des bijoux très originaux.

Cette sculpture, intitulée «Hommage à Picasso», représente un centaure, créature imaginaire, mi-homme,° mi-cheval. C'est l'oeuvre du sculpteur **César Baldaccini**. Dans ses sculptures, César utilise toutes sortes de matériaux. Il est connu en particulier pour ses sculptures faites avec des voitures compressées.

Cette sculpture est l'oeuvre du peintre et sculpteur **Jean Dubuffet**. Elle est typique de son style, caractérisé par l'utilisation de lignes parallèles ou concentriques bleues et rouges sur un fond° blanc.

Cette sculpture, oeuvre du sculpteur **Arman,** se trouve près de la **Gare Saint-Lazare**. Intitulée «Heure de tous», elle rappelle° peut-être aux voyageurs l'importance d'arriver à l'heure.

oeuvres *works* **chefs-d'oeuvres** *masterpieces* **se trouve** *is located* **mi-homme** *half man* **fond** *background* **rappelle** *reminds*

NOTES CULTURELLES

Niki de Saint Phalle (1930–2002), peintre et sculpteur français, membre du groupe des Nouveaux Réalistes des années 60.

Jean Dubuffet (1901–1985), peintre, sculpteur et écrivain français, s'est d'abord inspiré des graffiti et des dessins d'enfants. En 1962 il a commencé à faire des sculptures en matière plastique peinte, comme celle de l'Hôtel de la Monnaie.

César Baldaccini (1921–1999), sculpteur français, apparenté aux Nouveaux Réalistes. Il a surtout travaillé les métaux et les matières plastiques.

UNITÉ 2

MAIN THEME

Household tasks

Communication Function/Contexts
- Working around the house
- Asking for help and offering to help
- Describing objects

Linguistic Goals
- Exploring what has to be done
- Telling people what you would like them to do
- Expressing opinions about situations and events

Online Study Center

Online Teaching Center

Photo Note
The young people pictured are packing **des boîtes de conserve** *(cans)* and **des tubes de dentifrice** *(toothpaste)*

Teaching Strategy: Expansion
Ask students what they think the young people in the picture are doing and why. Why are they wearing name tags?

UNITÉ 2

Soyons utiles!

Thème et Objectifs

Culture
In this unit, you will discover . . .
- what the French call "bricolage"
- what types of creative activities they engage in at home
- how French students earn spending money

Communication
You will learn how . . .
- to talk about various chores and activities around the home
- to ask others to help you, and to give excuses if you cannot be of service to them
- to describe objects: their shape, dimensions, weight, and construction

Langue
You will learn how . . .
- to describe what you have to do
- to ask others to do certain things for you
- to express opinions about situations and events

ANCILLARIES
Student Activities Manual, Unit 2
Audio Program, Unit 2
Video-DVD Program, Unit 2
Chansons Audio CD

HM ClassPrep CD
Presentations, Unit 2
Audioscript, Unit 2
Videoscript, Unit 2
Assessment, Unit 2
Answer Key, Unit 2

LES PASSE-TEMPS ACTIFS

Le samedi, Catherine, 15 ans, sort rarement avec ses copains. Avec sa soeur Mélanie, 16 ans, elle préfère passer son temps à perfectionner Gustave, un robot de leur invention qui peut se déplacer° sur simple commande vocale. Et quand il y a quelque chose à réparer à la maison, un meuble, un appareil électrique ou même° la voiture de Papa, c'est Catherine ou Mélanie qui s'en charge.° «Nous nous amusons et nous apprenons en même temps» déclare Catherine pour expliquer son goût° pour les travaux manuels.

Le cas de Catherine et de Mélanie n'est pas unique. En France il y a des milliers de jeunes qui préfèrent les passe-temps actifs aux passe-temps passifs comme la télévision et la lecture. Voici deux passe-temps qui sont à la fois créatifs et récréatifs:° le bricolage° et le jardinage.°

■ Le bricolage est une des occupations favorites des Français de tout âge.

Le bricolage

Bricoler, c'est faire toutes sortes de petits travaux manuels. Quand on est un peu créatif et pas trop maladroit,° il y a beaucoup de choses qu'on peut faire chez soi.° On peut peindre° sa chambre, construire° des étagères,° installer un système hi-fi ou un système d'alarme, réparer la télé ou la machine à laver, ... Mais attention, quand on démonte° quelque chose, il faut aussi savoir le remonter.° Et surtout, il ne faut pas le casser!°

Le bricolage est une des occupations favorites des Français de tout âge. Et cette occupation n'est pas l'exclusivité des hommes. Aujourd'hui, 75% des Françaises bricolent (et 85% des Français). Pour subvenir° aux besoins des bricoleurs, tous les grands magasins et beaucoup de supermarchés ont un rayon «bricolage» où on trouve l'équipement et les outils° nécessaires. Pour les spécialistes, il y a aussi des magazines comme *Bricolage-Service*. Et pour les passionnés,° il y a à Paris chaque année un Salon° du Bricolage qui attire° des milliers de visiteurs.

se déplacer *move around* **même** *even* **s'en charge** = s'en occupe **goût** *taste* **récréatifs** *recreational* **le bricolage** *fixing and building things*
le jardinage *gardening* **maladroit** *clumsy* **chez soi** = à la maison **peindre** ❄ *to paint* **construire** ❄ *to build* **étagères** *shelves*
démonte *takes apart* **remonter** *to put back together* **casser** *break* **subvenir** ❄ *to meet* **les outils** *tools* **les passionnés** *real devotees*
un Salon *show* **attire** *attracts*

INFO MAGAZINE

Theme: Favorite French pastimes

Reading Strategy:
Reading for pleasure; browsing

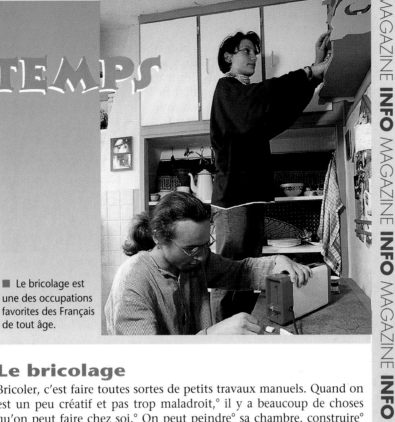

Teaching Strategy

These readings can be done:

- in class or as homework
- at the beginning of the unit or as a wrap-up activity

Encourage "discovery reading," having students identify cognates and read for the main idea in a relaxed way.

■ Notes linguistiques

- **Le grille-pain** (toaster) is invariable: **les grille-pain.**
- Also **une bricole** = a trinket, an insignificant matter

Notes culturelles

- Castorama and **Mr Bricolage** are two store chains catering to the needs of **les bricoleurs**.
- Interior decorating is the favorite occupation of people who love **le bricolage**. It includes such activities as putting up new wallpaper, or assembling a piece of furniture bought in a kit.

■ Irregular Verbs

(see Appendix C)
peindre
construire (*see* **conduire**)
subvenir* (*see* **venir**)
* Note that **subvenir** has **avoir** as an auxiliary.

Le jardinage

Quand on voyage en France au printemps ou en été, on peut admirer les fleurs de toutes les couleurs qui ornent° les parcs publics, les jardins privés et les balcons des maisons. Les Français adorent les fleurs et 60% d'entre° eux pratiquent le jardinage.

Ce n'est pas surprenant° dans un pays où la majorité des gens habitent une maison individuelle et disposent° d'un jardin où ils peuvent planter des fleurs et faire pousser° des légumes. Le jardinage n'est pas seulement une activité manuelle. C'est un loisir écologique qui nous rapproche de la nature et qui est aussi esthétique ... et nutritif. Quoi de plus beau qu'un bouquet de fleurs et quoi de meilleur qu'un plat de tomates qui viennent de son jardin!

et vous?

DÉFINITIONS

Définissez les mots et les expressions suivants. Quand c'est possible, illustrez avec un exemple.

- un robot
- le bricolage
- les travaux manuels
- le jardinage
- un passe-temps
- un loisir écologique

EXPRESSION PERSONNELLE

- Faites-vous des petits travaux manuels chez vous? Qu'est-ce que vous aimez faire et qu'est-ce que vous n'aimez pas faire?
- À votre avis, quel est le passe-temps le plus intéressant: le jardinage ou le bricolage? Expliquez pourquoi.
- Connaissez-vous une personne qui aime bricoler comme Catherine et Mélanie? Décrivez ce que cette personne a fait.

Supplementary vocabulary

les plantes vertes *potted plants*
l'engrais *(m.) fertilizer*
la feuille *leaf*
le pot *pot*
la terre *soil*
la tige *stem*
le géranium *geranium*
le lierre *ivy*
la fougère *fern*

Soyez bon pour les plantes

Les Français aiment beaucoup les plantes. Dans chaque maison française, il y a, en moyenne,° sept plantes.

Les plantes ont beaucoup d'avantages:
— Elles décorent votre chambre.
— Elles purifient l'air que vous respirez.°
— Elles demandent° une attention minime.
— Elles sont propres.°

Les plantes sont des êtres° vivants.° Comme nous, elles ont besoin qu'on s'occupe un peu d'elles. Alors, si vous avez une plante, soyez bon pour elle.

Voici quelques conseils élémentaires:

- Arrosez°-la régulièrement. Mais attention: certaines plantes ont très soif. D'autres ont besoin seulement d'un petit peu d'eau.
- Si elle aime le soleil,° mettez-la près de la fenêtre. Si elle préfère l'obscurité, ne l'exposez pas à la lumière.°
- De temps en temps, mettez-lui de la musique. Les plantes adorent la musique douce.° Elles aiment la musique classique, mais elles détestent le rock et le rap.
- Parlez-lui souvent. Chaque jour, dites-lui bonjour et bonsoir.
- Ne la maltraitez pas.
- Ne l'insultez pas.
- Soyez toujours poli et attentif avec elle.
- Dites-lui souvent «Je t'aime.»

Le magazine préféré de votre jardin
l'Ami des Jardins et de la maison
LES SECRETS D'UN JARDIN ANGLAIS
LES MEUBLES DE LA RENTRÉE
TOUTES LES PLANTES DU
Pour jardiner comme un PRO

et vous?

- Est-ce qu'il y a des plantes chez vous? Quelles plantes? Dans quelles pièces sont-elles?
- Avez-vous des plantes ou des fleurs dans votre chambre? Qu'est-ce que vous faites pour elles?
- Pensez-vous que les plantes sont des êtres sensibles *(that have feelings)*? Expliquez votre position.

ornent = embellissent **d'entre** *among* **surprenant** *surprising* **disposent** = ont **pousser** *to grow* **en moyenne** *on the average* **respirez** *breathe* **demandent** = nécessitent **propres** *clean* **êtres** *beings* **vivants** *living* **arrosez** *water* **le soleil** *sun* **la lumière** *light* **douce** *soft*

General Teaching Strategy: Info Magazines

Although the *Info Magazine* is presented as a light, pleasurable introduction and expansion of the unit theme, some teachers like to check comprehension with a few short questions using the *Info Magazine* quizzes. These quizzes may also be used as a basis for class discussion.

The *Et vous?* activities may be used to encourage class discussion, or as the basis for out-of-class writing assignments.

Ça, c'est la JUSTICE!

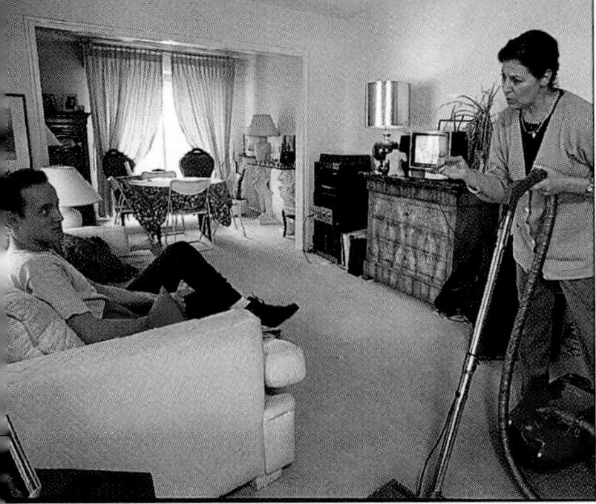

Aujourd'hui, Madame Chauvat a beaucoup de travail. Elle demande à ses enfants Victor et Stéphanie de l'aider, mais ce n'est pas facile de les convaincre.° Elle s'adresse° d'abord à Victor qui regarde la télé au salon.

— Dis, Victor, qu'est-ce que tu fais?
— Tu vois, je regarde la télé.
— C'est bien, mais moi, j'ai besoin de toi.
— Pourquoi donc?
— Pour passer l'aspirateur.°
— Alors ça, c'est pas juste!°
— Comment ça?
— C'est pas juste parce que c'est moi qui ai passé l'aspirateur samedi dernier. Alors, cette fois-ci, c'est pas mon tour.° C'est le tour de Stéphanie. Elle ne fait jamais rien!
— Ah oui, c'est vrai, j'ai oublié! Je vais demander à ta soeur.

Victor pousse un soupir de soulagement° pendant que sa mère monte chercher Stéphanie. Celle-ci° est dans sa chambre en train de jouer à un jeu électronique.

— Dis donc, Stéphanie. Je voudrais que tu passes l'aspirateur au salon…
— Ah non, maman. Ça, c'est pas juste… C'est moi qui fais tout dans cette maison!
— Qu'est-ce que tu as fait récemment?
— Eh bien, par exemple, j'ai fait la vaisselle hier.
— Ah oui, c'est vrai… Bon, je te laisse° le choix: la vaisselle ou l'aspirateur.

Stéphanie réfléchit° un instant.

— Mais dis, il y a beaucoup de casseroles° à laver?
— Oui, y en a plein l'évier.°
— Alors, dans ce cas, je suis d'accord pour passer l'aspirateur.

Madame Chauvat redescend au salon.

— Dis, Victor, est-ce que tu peux éteindre° la télé et faire la vaisselle?
— La vaisselle? Mais pourquoi, maman?
— Parce que c'est ton tour.

Et ça, c'est la justice!

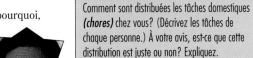

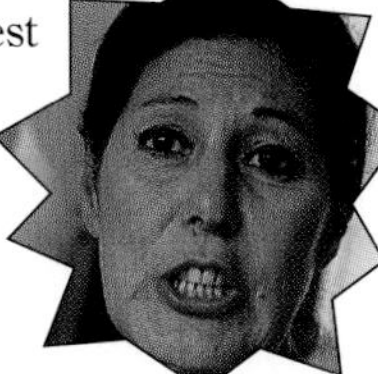

EXPRESSION ORALE

Comment sont distribuées les tâches domestiques *(chores)* chez vous? (Décrivez les tâches de chaque personne.) À votre avis, est-ce que cette distribution est juste ou non? Expliquez.

EXPRESSION ÉCRITE

Imaginez que vous êtes Victor ou Stéphanie. Dans une lettre à un copain (une copine) vous décrivez ce qui est arrivé aujourd'hui.

convaincre ❊ *to convince* **s'adresse** = parle **l'aspirateur** *vacuum cleaner* **juste** *fair* **tour** *turn* **un soupir de soulagement** *breathes a sigh of relief* **celle-ci** = Stéphanie **laisse** *leave* **réfléchit** = pense **casseroles** *pots* **y en a plein l'évier** *the sink is full (of pots)* **éteindre** ❊ *to turn off*

Teaching Strategy

Divide the class into pairs.
- Have students identify all vocabulary that represents a chore.
- Have students identify the expressions that are excuses.
- Have students prepare short dialogs and present them to the class.

■ Irregular Verbs

(see Appendix C)
convaincre
éteindre (*see* **peindre**)

Teaching Strategy: Challenge

Have students notice the differences between *casual* French usage, and *standard* French usage:

CASUAL FRENCH	STANDARD FRENCH
Pourquoi donc?	**Pourquoi?**
C'est pas juste.	**Ce n'est pas juste.**
Comment ça?	**Pourquoi?**
Y en a plein l'évier.	**Il y a en a plein l'évier.** **L'évier en est plein.**

LE FRANÇAIS PRATIQUE

TEACHING RESOURCES

Student Activities Manual, pp. 115–116
Audio Program, CD 2, Tracks 1–3
HM ClassPrep CD, Audioscript, Unit 2

PARTIE 1

LE FRANÇAIS PRATIQUE — *Les travaux domestiques*

Est-ce que . . .
la chambre est **propre** *(clean)* ou **sale** *(dirty)*?
le salon est **rangé** *(picked up)* ou **en désordre**?
Oh là là, j'ai beaucoup de **travail** aujourd'hui.

> **le travail** *work*
> **les travaux domestiques** *household chores*

Dans la chambre et la salle de bains, je dois . . .
faire le ménage *(to clean up)*
faire le lit
ranger les vêtements
nettoyer le lavabo *(sink)*

> **ranger** *to put away*
> **nettoyer** *to clean*

Dans le salon, je dois . . .
ranger les magazines
passer l'aspirateur *(to vacuum)*
nettoyer les vitres *(windows)*
vider la corbeille *(wastepaper basket)*

> **vider** *to empty*

Dans la salle à manger, je dois . . .
mettre la table
mettre le couvert *(silverware)*
débarrasser la table

> **débarrasser** *to clear*

Dans la cuisine, je dois . . .
couper le pain
laver les légumes
éplucher les carottes
faire la vaisselle
ranger la vaisselle
essuyer les verres
essuyer la table
balayer le sol *(floor)*
vider les ordures *(garbage)*
sortir la poubelle *(trash can)*

> **couper** *to cut*
> **laver** *to wash*
> **éplucher** *to peel*
> **essuyer** *to wipe, dry*
> **balayer** *to sweep*
> **sortir** *to take out*

Dans **la lingerie** *(laundry room)*, je dois . . .
laver le linge *(laundry)*
repasser les chemises

> **repasser** *to iron*

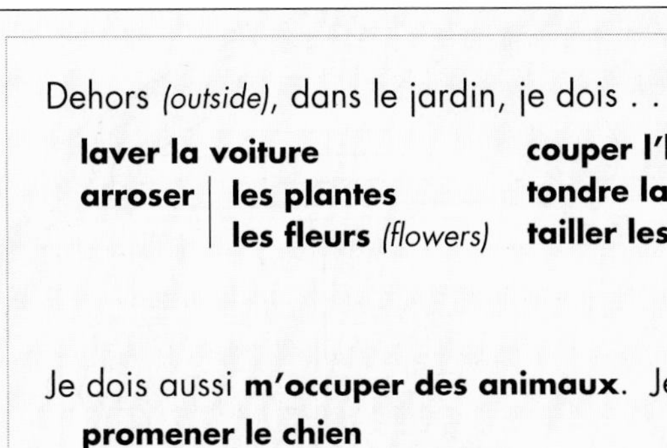

Dehors *(outside)*, dans le jardin, je dois . . .

laver la voiture
arroser | **les plantes**
| **les fleurs** *(flowers)*
couper l'herbe *(grass)*
tondre la pelouse *(lawn)*
tailler les arbustes *(shrubs)*

arroser *to water*
tailler *to prune*
tondre *to mow, to cut very short*

Je dois aussi **m'occuper des animaux**. Je dois . . .

promener le chien
donner à manger | **au chat**
| **au lapin**
vider | **l'aquarium**
remplir |
nettoyer la cage | **de l'oiseau**
| **de la perruche** *(parakeet)*

s'occuper de *to take care of*

donner à manger à *to feed*

remplir *to fill*

Verbes en –ger *(ranger)*

Révision ▶ p.R21

1 Et vous?

Indiquez comment vous participez aux travaux domestiques quand vous êtes chez vos parents pendant les vacances. Comparez vos réponses avec celles de votre partenaire.

1. En général, ma chambre est . . .
   - propre
   - rangée
   - en désordre
   - ??
2. Je fais mon lit . . .
   - le matin
   - le soir
   - jamais
   - ??
3. Je range ma chambre . . .
   - tous les jours
   - toutes les semaines
   - une fois par mois
   - ??
4. Quand j'aide à faire le ménage, je préfère . . .
   - passer l'aspirateur
   - vider les corbeilles
   - nettoyer les vitres
   - ??
5. Quand je travaille dans la cuisine, je préfère . . .
   - éplucher les légumes
   - essuyer les assiettes
   - nettoyer l'évier *(kitchen sink)*
   - ??
6. Pour les repas, je préfère . . .
   - mettre le couvert
   - débarrasser la table
   - faire la vaisselle
   - ??
7. Quand je travaille dans le jardin, je préfère . . .
   - tondre la pelouse
   - arroser les plantes
   - tailler les arbustes
   - ??
8. Le travail que je déteste le plus est de . . .
   - balayer le garage
   - sortir les poubelles
   - vider les ordures
   - ??

Supplementary vocabulary

épousseter *to dust*
enlever la poussière *to dust*
astiquer les meubles *to polish the furniture*
polir l'argenterie *to polish the silverware*
faire la lessive *to do the laundry*

Notes linguistiques

- **Le couvert = le couteau, la fourchette, la cuillère (à soupe et à café)**
- Compare:
  une fenêtre *window*
  une vitre *window pane*
- Note the forms of the **passé composé**:
  sortir *to go out*
  Alice **est sortie** hier.
  sortir *to take out*
  Alice **a sorti** la poubelle.
- The expression **éplucher un texte/un article** means to read a text/an article carefully in order to find a mistake.

Supplementary vocabulary

Quelques animaux domestiques
un cochon d'Inde *guinea pig*
un hamster
un perroquet *parrot*
un poisson rouge *goldfish*
un serin *canary*
une souris *(mouse)* **blanche**

Irregular Verbs

Remind students that **nettoyer, balayer,** and **essuyer** are conjugated like **payer.** *(See Appendix C.)*

Variation

Sample paired dialog:
—**Moi, je préfère faire la vaisselle. Et toi?**
—**Moi aussi. (Moi, je préfère mettre le couvert.)**

TEACHING RESOURCES

Tête-à-tête Pair Activities,
Travaux domestiques, p. PA3

Audio Program,
CD 2, Tracks 1–3

Variation

PAIRED FORMAT

Vous cherchez l'une des personnes de l'illustration. Demandez à votre partenaire où est cette personne et ce qu'elle fait.

— Où est le grand-père?
— Il est dans le jardin.
— Qu'est-ce qu'il fait?
— Il taille les arbustes.

CONVERSATION FORMAT

— Qu'est-ce que tu vas faire cet été?
— Je vais travailler ...
— Ah bon? Qu'est-ce que tu vas faire?
— Je vais ...
— Et toi, qu'est-ce que tu vas faire cet été?
— Je vais travailler ... *(etc.)*

Note linguistique

Remind students that **un boulot** is also a familiar form of "work."

2 La famille Duboulot

Aujourd'hui, tout le monde est très occupé chez les Duboulot. Choisissez deux personnes et dites où sont ces personnes et ce qu'elles font.

3 Jobs d'été

Votre partenaire et vous, vous allez travailler cet été. Choisissez un job de la colonne A. Votre partenaire va choisir un job de la colonne B. Expliquez ce que vous allez faire. Donnez deux ou trois exemples.

▶ **— Moi, je vais travailler dans la cuisine d'un restaurant. Je vais éplucher les légumes et faire la vaisselle. Je vais aussi . . .**
— Et moi, je vais travailler dans un zoo. Je vais . . .

A. Vous

- travailler dans la cuisine d'un restaurant
- travailler pour les jardins publics de la ville
- travailler pour une entreprise de nettoyage *(cleaning)* de bureaux
- travailler chez un marchand d'animaux domestiques *(pets)*
- être garçon d'étage (femme de chambre) dans un hôtel

B. Votre partenaire

- travailler dans la salle *(dining room)* d'un restaurant
- travailler dans un zoo
- travailler comme jardinier *(gardener)* dans un hôtel
- être concierge dans un immeuble *(building superintendent)*
- travailler dans une blanchisserie *(laundry)*
- travailler pour les voisins

Quelques objets utiles

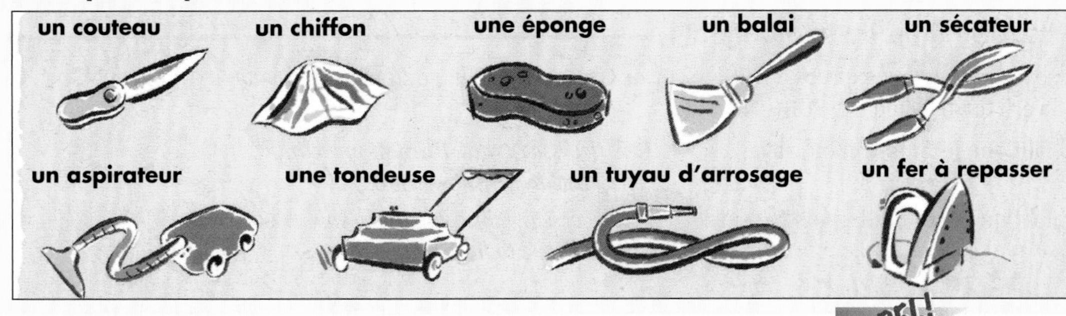

4 Le bon objet

Choisissez un objet de la liste et dites pourquoi vous avez besoin de cet objet.

RAPPEL!
de + le → du
J'ai besoin du couteau.

J'ai besoin de . . .

- l'aspirateur
- le balai
- le fer
- la tondeuse
- le sécateur
- le tuyau d'arrosage
- un chiffon
- un couteau
- une éponge

pour . . .

- essuyer la table
- nettoyer la chambre
- laver la voiture
- éplucher les carottes
- repasser cette chemise
- tondre la pelouse
- nettoyer le lavabo
- tailler le rosier *(rose bush)*
- balayer le garage

5 Le chalet des Laurentides

Vous passez l'été dans la région des Laurentides. Il y a beaucoup de travail dans le chalet que vous avez loué avec vos cousins. Malheureusement, vos cousins ne sont pas très coopératifs. Quand vous leur demandez de faire quelque chose, ils trouvent une excuse. Jouez les dialogues avec votre partenaire.

▶ **— Dis, Annie, est-ce que tu peux essuyer la table?**
— Je voudrais bien, mais j'ai un problème.
— Quoi?
— Je ne trouve pas l'éponge.

TRAVAUX

- tondre la pelouse
- arroser les fleurs
- tailler les arbustes
- essuyer la table
- essuyer les assiettes
- éplucher les pommes de terre
- balayer la terrasse
- repasser les serviettes *(napkins)*
- nettoyer le salon
- ??

EXCUSES

- Le chiffon est sale.
- L'aspirateur est cassé *(broken)*.
- Le fer ne fonctionne pas.
- La tondeuse ne marche pas.
- Je ne trouve pas l'éponge.
- J'ai perdu le sécateur.
- Je n'ai pas de couteau.
- Je ne sais pas où est le balai.
- Il y a un trou *(hole)* dans le tuyau.
- ??

NOTE CULTURELLE

Située dans la province de Québec, la région des **Laurentides** est populaire à la fois pour ses stations de ski en hiver et pour ses stations d'été.

Supplementary vocabulary

la balayette *small broom*
la cire *wax*
la lessive *detergent*
le plumeau *feather duster*
la poudre à récurer *cleanser*
le ramasse-poussière *dustpan*
la corde à linge *clothes line*
l'épingle *(f.)* **à linge/la pince à linge** *clothespin*
la planche à repasser *ironing board*

Teaching Strategy: Activity 5

Call on pairs to check for accuracy.

Teaching Strategy: Connections

Jobs d'été

Ask students to prepare three sentences about their own summer work.

Prepare a chart listing the jobs mentioned and ask students to compile totals, list the most popular jobs, the most unusual jobs, etc. You may wish to have students scan the *Info Magazine* on pp. 82–83 as an extension.

LANGUE ET COMMUNICATION

TEACHING RESOURCES

Student Activities Manual, p. 27

■ **Looking Ahead**

Unit 2 presents the formation of the present subjunctive and focuses on its two main uses: to express NECESSITY and to express EMOTION.

The difference between the SUBJUNCTIVE and the INDICATIVE will be developed in Unit 7.

■ **Note linguistique**

You may point out to students that with **-er** verbs, the present tense and the subjunctive forms are the same for **je, tu, il,** and **ils.**

Je travaille.
Il faut que je travaille. etc.

A. La formation du subjonctif (1)

The sentences below express a NECESSITY or OBLIGATION. In sentences of this type, the French use a verb form called the SUBJUNCTIVE.

Il faut que **je finisse** mon travail.	*It is necessary that **I finish** my work. (I have to finish my work.)*
Il faut que **vous aidiez** vos parents.	*It is necessary that **you help** your parents. (You have to help your parents.)*

The SUBJUNCTIVE is a verb form that occurs frequently in French. It is used after certain verbs and expressions in the construction:

VERB OR EXPRESSION +	**que** +	SUBJECT +	SUBJUNCTIVE VERB . . .
Il faut	**que**	Marc	**tonde** la pelouse

➡ The subjunctive is almost always introduced by **que**.

FORMS

For all regular verbs and many irregular verbs, the subjunctive is formed as follows:

SUBJUNCTIVE STEM +	SUBJUNCTIVE ENDINGS
ils-form of present minus **-ent**	**-e, -es, -e, -ions, -iez, -ent**

Note the subjunctive forms of the regular verbs **parler**, **finir**, **vendre**, and the irregular verb **dire**.

INFINITIVE		**parler**	**finir**	**vendre**	**dire**	SUBJUNCTIVE ENDINGS
PRESENT STEM	ils	**parlent**	**finissent**	**vendent**	**disent**	
		parl-	**finiss-**	**vend-**	**dis-**	
SUBJUNCTIVE	que je	**parle**	**finisse**	**vende**	**dise**	**-e**
	que tu	**parles**	**finisses**	**vendes**	**dises**	**-es**
	qu'il/elle/on	**parle**	**finisse**	**vende**	**dise**	**-e**
	que nous	**parlions**	**finissions**	**vendions**	**disions**	**-ions**
	que vous	**parliez**	**finissiez**	**vendiez**	**disiez**	**-iez**
	qu'ils/elles	**parlent**	**finissent**	**vendent**	**disent**	**-ent**

Dire, lire, écrire

Révision ▶ pp. R26-27
Pratique ▶ p. 28

1 Le subjonctif, s'il vous plaît!

Pour chaque verbe du tableau, donnez la forme **ils** du présent. Ensuite, complétez les phrases avec le subjonctif de ces verbes.

INFINITIF	PRÉSENT	SUBJONCTIF
▶ laver	ils lavent	Il faut que (nous) lavions la voiture.
1. aider	ils . . .	Il faut que (tu, nous, vous) . . . les voisins.
2. réussir	ils . . .	Il faut que (je, vous, les élèves) . . . à l'examen.
3. répondre	ils . . .	Il faut que (je, Pauline, nous) . . . à cette lettre.
4. attendre	ils . . .	Il faut que (nous, tu, les voyageurs) . . . le train.
5. lire	ils . . .	Il faut que (je, Charlotte, vous) . . . cet article.
6. écrire	ils . . .	Il faut que (tu, nous, mes copains) . . . à Philippe.
7. partir	ils . . .	Il faut que (je, Olivier, nous) . . . à six heures.
8. mettre	ils . . .	Il faut que (je, tu, vous) . . . la table.
9. se laver	ils . . .	Il faut que (tu, vous, ce garçon) . . . les cheveux.
10. se dépêcher	ils . . .	Il faut que (Pierre, nous, vos amis) . . .

2 Avant de partir ce week-end

Expliquez ce que chacun doit faire avant de partir ce week-end.

▶ Claire **Il faut que Claire range sa chambre. Et puis, il faut qu'elle . . .**

Claire
- ranger sa chambre
- laver son linge
- passer l'aspirateur

moi
- finir mes devoirs
- écrire une lettre
- téléphoner à mon copain

toi
- laver la cage du lapin
- remplir l'aquarium
- donner à manger au chat

Éric et Vincent
- tailler les arbustes
- tondre la pelouse
- arroser les fleurs

vous
- finir la vaisselle
- vider les ordures
- sortir la poubelle

nous
- regarder la carte *(map)*
- choisir notre itinéraire
- préparer la voiture

3 Après la fête

Votre partenaire et vous, vous avez organisé une fête chez vous. Maintenant vous devez ranger. Vous vous distribuez les tâches. Choisissez une tâche de la colonne A pour votre partenaire. Il/elle va choisir une tâche de la colonne B pour vous.

▶ **—Dis, Bernard, il faut que tu lave les verres.**
—Bon, je vais laver les verres, mais toi, il faut que tu ranges la cuisine.
—D'accord!

A
- ranger le salon
- laver les assiettes
- laver les verres
- débarrasser la table
- vider les ordures
- ??

B
- ranger la cuisine
- passer l'aspirateur
- laver les casseroles *(pots)*
- mettre les chaises à leur place
- sortir la poubelle
- ??

■ Teaching Note

Before doing items 9 and 10 in Activity 1, you may want to present the complete conjugation pattern of a reflexive verb:

Il faut que je me lave.
Il faut que tu te laves.
etc.

B. Comment exprimer une obligation personnelle: l'usage du subjonctif après **il faut que**

Note the use of the subjunctive in the following sentences:

Il faut que je **parte**. *I have to (I must)* ***leave***.
Il faut que vous **travailliez**. *You have to (you must)* ***work***.

To express what people HAVE TO or MUST DO, use the construction:

il faut que + SUBJUNCTIVE

➡ Personal obligations can also be expressed with **devoir** + INFINITIVE.

Je dois **partir**. *I have to* ***leave***.

➡ Note that **il faut** + INFINITIVE is used to express a GENERAL obligation.

Il faut **étudier**. *One has to (one should)* ***study***. *You [people in general] have to* ***study***.

➡ The negative **il ne faut pas que** + SUBJUNCTIVE expresses a PROHIBITION or INTERDICTION.

Il ne faut pas que tu **dormes** en classe. *You should not* ***sleep*** *in class.*

ALLONS PLUS LOIN

The following expressions are used to express the LACK OF OBLIGATION:

Il n'est pas nécessaire que tu partes.
Tu n'es pas obligé(e) de partir.
Tu n'as pas besoin de partir.
Tu n'as pas à partir.
} ***You don't have*** *to leave.*

TEACHING RESOURCES

Student Activities Manual, pp. 28–30, 116
Audio Program, CD 2, Tracks 4–5
HM ClassPrep CD, Audioscript, Unit 2

■ Note linguistique

You may wish to contrast:
Il faut **travailler**.
You [people in general] have to work.
Il faut **que tu travailles**.
You [a specific person] have to work.

4 Obligations?

Voici certains travaux domestiques. Faites une liste des cinq principaux travaux que vous devez faire. Classez-les par ordre d'importance. Puis comparez votre liste avec celle de votre partenaire.

- ranger le salon
- laver la vaisselle
- débarrasser la table
- laver le linge
- sortir la poubelle
- arroser les plantes
- tondre la pelouse
- passer l'aspirateur
- mettre le couvert
- ranger ma chambre
- vider les ordures
- donner à manger au chien/chat
- ??

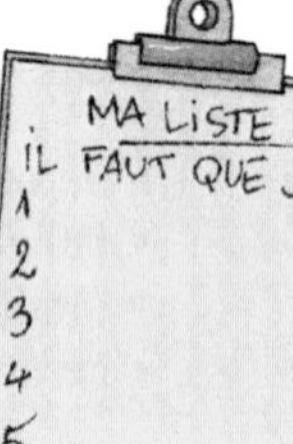

MA LISTE
IL FAUT QUE JE...
1
2
3
4
5

Variation

PAIR WORK
Student A describes the message conveyed by one of the signs.
Student B identifies which sign is being described (or draws a copy of the appropriate sign).

■ Note linguistique

The one-way sign is called **un sens interdit**. It indicates **une rue à sens unique** *(one-way street).*

5 C'est interdit

Vous êtes en France avec des copains. Vous voyez les panneaux *(signs)* suivants. Expliquez ce que vous ne devez pas faire.

INTERDICTION DE . . .

fumer

marcher sur la pelouse

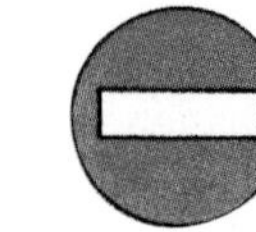
entrer ici

tourner à gauche

déposer des ordures

écrire sur les murs

▶ — **Il ne faut pas que nous . . .**

C. La formation du subjonctif (2)

Boire, prendre, apprendre, voir

Révision ▶ pp. R24-31

Some verbs like **venir** have different stems in the **ils**- and **nous**-forms of the present. Verbs of this type have TWO STEMS in the subjunctive. (Note that the following verbs all have regular subjunctive endings.)

INFINITIVE	venir	
PRESENT	ils	**viennent**
	nous	**venons**
SUBJUNCTIVE	que je	**vienn**e
	que tu	**vienn**es
	qu'il/elle/on	**vienn**e
	qu'ils/elles	**vienn**ent
	que nous	**ven**ions
	que vous	**ven**iez

Il faut que . . .		
acheter	j'**achète**	nous **achetions**
espérer	j'**espère**	nous **espérions**
appeler	j'**appelle**	nous **appelions**
payer	je **paie**	nous **payions**
boire	je **boive**	nous **buvions**
voir	je **voie**	nous **voyions**
prendre	je **prenne**	nous **prenions**

6 Chez le médecin

Vous êtes médecin. Donnez des conseils à un patient, Monsieur Grosjean, qui n'est pas en forme. Commencez vos phrases par **il faut que vous . . .**
ou
il ne faut pas que vous . . .

▶ boire trop de café
Il ne faut pas que vous buviez trop de café.

- boire beaucoup d'eau minérale?
- se lever tôt?
- se lever tard?
- dormir bien?
- acheter un vélo?
- apprendre à nager?
- prendre des vitamines?
- s'inquiéter trop?
- payer ma note *(bill)*?
- revenir dans un mois?

7 La meilleure solution

Avec votre partenaire, choisissez une des situations et décidez ensemble des choses que les personnes doivent faire **(il faut que . . .)** ou ne pas faire **(il ne faut pas que . . .)**.

1. Philippe veut rentrer chez lui, mais il n'a pas la clé.
   - attendre sa mère?
   - casser *(break)* une fenêtre?
   - retourner à l'école?
   - ??
2. Valérie a dîné au restaurant. Elle a oublié son portefeuille.
   - partir sans payer?
   - téléphoner à son copain?
   - travailler dans la cuisine?
   - ??
3. Les touristes sont à l'hôtel. Ils voient de la fumée *(smoke)*.
   - sortir par la porte?
   - sauter *(jump)* par la fenêtre?
   - attendre l'arrivée des pompiers?
   - ??

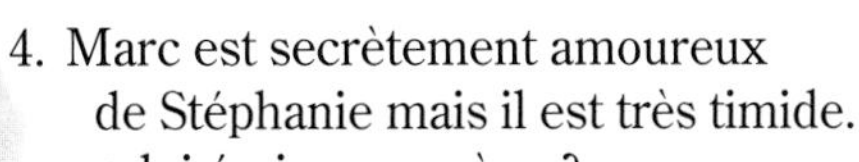

4. Marc est secrètement amoureux de Stéphanie mais il est très timide.
   - lui écrire un poème?
   - lui envoyer une lettre d'amour anonyme?
   - prendre des leçons de danse et inviter Stéphanie dans une discothèque?
   - ??
5. Hélène et Catherine ont eu un accident avec la voiture de leur mère.
   - dire la vérité à leur mère?
   - voir un garagiste?
   - payer la réparation?
   - ??
6. Thomas et Julien ont trouvé un portefeuille dans la rue.
   - apporter le portefeuille à la police?
   - mettre une annonce dans un journal?
   - garder *(keep)* le portefeuille?
   - ??

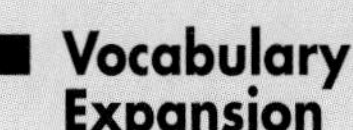

■ Vocabulary Expansion

Also:
croire
que **je croie**
que **nous croyions**
recevoir
que **je reçoive**
que **nous recevions**

■ Note linguistique

Verbs ending in **-ger** and **-cer** have only one subjunctive stem:
ranger (nous rangeons)
que **je range**
que **nous rangions**
commencer (nous commençons)
que **je commence**
que **nous commencions**

Teaching Strategy: Challenge

As homework or as a written assignment, students can create new situations and suggest additional possible solutions.

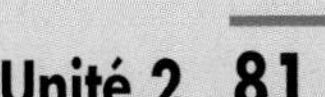

INFO MAGAZINE

Theme: French college students and their jobs.

Teaching Strategy

These readings can be done:
- in class or as homework
- at the beginning of the unit or as a wrap-up activity

As *optional* material, you may wish to use them as practice in reading for pleasure, or as the basis for class discussion.

To verify comprehension, you may ask students to write two sentences (using the subjunctive) which best summarize, advertise, and/or explain each of the jobs.

Irregular Verbs

(see Appendix C)
découvrir (*see* **ouvrir**)

Le travail, ça paie!

En France comme aux États-Unis, beaucoup de jeunes étudiants travaillent pour gagner un peu d'argent. Voici le cas de cinq jeunes Français qui ont découvert° que le travail, ça paie!

Camille, 20 ans, a finit sa 2ème année à l'université. Elle a trouvé un poste° d'un an comme assistante de français dans une école en Écosse.° Elle dit:

« Je suis professeur de français à Dumfries, en Écosse. Je donne dix heures de cours par semaine. Mes élèves ont entre 13 et 15 ans. Ils sont très gentils, mais il faut que je les motive à parler français! Je suis très occupée° parce qu'il faut que je prépare les leçons. Demain, par exemple, je vais faire un cours sur l'environnement. Il faut que je cherche sur Internet un article en français sur ce sujet. Il faut aussi que j'ai des questions intéressantes à poser à mes élèves. J'adore être professeur. C'est super d'aider les jeunes à apprendre des choses nouvelles. Bientôt, je vais rentrer en France pour finir mes études. Je veux être professeur d'anglais. »

Karim, 19 ans, aime l'aventure et il est très sportif. Il a trouvé un job où il peut utiliser ses capacités physiques. Il explique:

« Je fais un stage pour devenir pompier° volontaire. Je dois suivre un entraînement° sportif très rigoureux. Il faut, par exemple, que je monte à une échelle° avec un tuyau d'incendie° très lourd. J'apprends aussi à donner les premiers soins.°

J'ai déjà participé à plusieurs opérations. Il y a parfois des situations amusantes. Un jour il fallait que je cherche un cheval° qui s'était échappé° d'une ferme. Je l'ai trouvé dans le parc. Il mangeait les fleurs!

Je n'ai pas de salaire, mais je suis payé quand je participe à une opération. Et en plus, je suis heureux de rendre service° à la communauté. »

Aïcha, 22 ans, étudie pour être ingénieur.° Pendant l'année scolaire, elle donne des cours de maths. Pendant l'été, elle est très occupée. Elle raconte:

« Moi, je travaille quand les gens sont en vacances! Chaque été en effet, je m'occupe d'une vingtaine de jardins. Je tonds les pelouses, je taille les arbustes, j'arrose les plantes... Vingt jardins, c'est beaucoup de travail. Quand j'ai trop à faire, je recrute de l'aide. J'ai beaucoup d'amis étudiants qui sont toujours prêts à° gagner un peu d'argent. Alors, on travaille en équipe.° C'est une bonne pratique pour ma profession future. »

ont découvert *discovered* **poste** *position* **Écosse** *Scotland* **occupée** *busy* **pompier** *firefighter*
suivre un entraînement *undergo a training* **échelle** *ladder* **tuyau d'incendie** *fire hose* **premiers soins** *first aid* **cheval** *horse*
s'était échappé *had escaped* **rendre service =** *aider* **ingénieur** *engineer* **prêts à** *ready to* **en équipe** *as a team*

Roberto, 22 ans, passe les vacances en Bretagne dans sa famille. Cet été il a trouvé un job à la base navale de Lann-Bihoue. Il décrit son job:

« *J'ai trouvé un job d'animateur° de loisirs à la base navale. Il faut que j'organise des voyages, des promenades et des soirées pour les militaires et leurs familles. Je suis très occupé. Il faut que je trouve des thèmes intéressants et que je prépare tout. Pour célébrer la fête nationale, j'ai créé un spectacle son et lumière° sur le port avec des militaires comme acteurs volontaires. Cela a été un grand succès! Mon patron m'a demandé si je voulais un travail à temps complet.° J'ai répondu: Il faut que je réfléchisse°...* »

Danièle, 20 ans, a créé sa propre° compagnie: Étudiants-Services. Danièle explique:

« *Aujourd'hui, les gens travaillent énormément. Quand ils rentrent le soir, ils sont trop fatigués pour passer l'aspirateur et faire le ménage. Et le week-end, ils veulent se reposer.° Alors, mon frère et moi, nous avons décidé d'aider ces gens dans leurs tâches domestiques.*

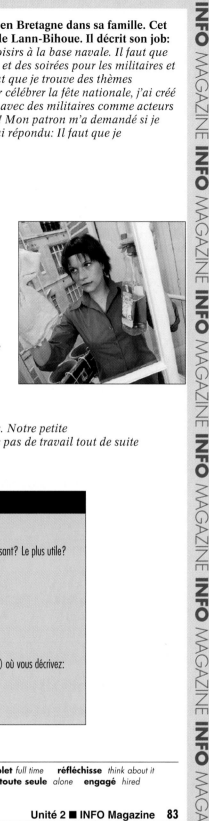

Un jour, j'ai mis une annonce° dans un supermarché pour offrir mes services. J'ai attendu trois semaines avant de recevoir mon premier coup de téléphone.° Ma première cliente m'a recommandée à une amie qui m'a recommandée à une voisine... Bientôt, j'ai eu trop de travail pour moi toute seule.° Alors j'ai engagé° mon frère Vincent qui avait besoin d'argent pour payer ses vacances. Maintenant nous travaillons en équipe. Je range le salon, je passe l'aspirateur dans les chambres. Vincent, lui, s'occupe° de la cuisine. Il fait la vaisselle, range les assiettes, lave le sol° et sort les poubelles.

Un jour nous avons eu l'idée de créer une compagnie: Étudiants-Services. Notre petite entreprise marche très bien. Nous refusons même des clients. Si je ne trouve pas de travail tout de suite après ma licence,° je sais ce que je vais faire! »

et vous?

EXPRESSION ORALE

1. Des jeunes Français décrits dans le texte qui, selon vous, a le job le plus intéressant? Le plus utile? Expliquez pourquoi.
2. Avez-vous un job maintenant? Décrivez ce job.
   - où et quand
   - vos fonctions
   - les avantages et les inconvénients de ce job

EXPRESSION ÉCRITE

Vous avez un job (réel ou imaginaire). Écrivez une lettre á votre ami(e) français(e) où vous décrivez:

- comment vous avez trouvé ce job
- ce que vous faites
- les avantages et les inconvénients de ce job

animateur *organizer* **un spectacle son et lumière** *sound and light show* **à temps complet** *full time* **réfléchisse** *think about it* **propre** *own* **se reposer** *rest* **annonce** *notice, ad* **coup de téléphone** *phone call* **toute seule** *alone* **engagé** *hired* **s'occupe de** *takes care of* **sol** *floor* **licence** *B.A. degree*

Teaching Strategy: Expansion

EXPRESSION ORALE

- Imaginez que vous êtes l'un des jeunes Français décrits dans le texte. Expliquez à un(e) ami(e) (votre partenaire) les avantages et les inconvénients de votre job.

LE FRANÇAIS PRATIQUE

TEACHING RESOURCES

Student Activities Manual, p. 117, 182–184

Audio Program, CD 2, Tracks 6–8

HM ClassPrep CD, Audioscript, Unit 2

Video/DVD Program, Unit 2

LE FRANÇAIS PRATIQUE

Pour rendre service

COMMENT DEMANDER DE L'AIDE

Est-ce que tu peux
- **m'aider?**
- **m'aider à** nettoyer le salon?
- **me donner un coup de main** *(give me a hand)*?
- **me rendre service** *(do me a favor)*?

COMMENT ACCEPTER

Oui,
- **bien sûr.**
- **d'accord.**
- **je veux bien.** *(I'd love to)*

Volontiers! *(With pleasure)*
Avec plaisir!

COMMENT REFUSER . . . ET DONNER UNE EXCUSE

Non, vraiment je ne peux pas.

Écoute,
- j'aimerais bien, mais . . .
- je voudrais bien, mais . . .
- je suis **désolé(e)**, mais . . .
- **je m'excuse**, mais . . .
- **je regrette**, mais. . .

- je suis **occupé(e)** *(busy)*.
- je ne suis pas **libre** *(free)*.
- je n'ai pas **le temps** *(time)*.
- j'ai **d'autres choses à faire.**
- je dois sortir/étudier.

COMMENT REMERCIER . . . ET RÉPONDRE À QUELQU'UN QUI VOUS REMERCIE

C'est **gentil!** / **sympa!**
Merci **beaucoup.** / **mille fois.**
Je te remercie.

De rien. *(You're welcome)*
Il n'y a pas de quoi.
Je t'en prie.

Teaching Suggestion: Video/DVD Program

In this section, *Vidéo-drame: Nicolas a du travail* in Unit 2, students will concentrate on expressions used in requesting help, accepting or rejecting an invitation, and showing gratitude. Take note of the varied responses one can use to get the same idea across.

1 Créa-dialogue

C'est samedi aujourd'hui et vous passez l'après-midi chez votre cousin(e) français(e). Il/elle vous demande de l'aider. Avec votre partenaire, composez un dialogue et jouez-le en classe. Votre partenaire va jouer le rôle de votre cousin(e).

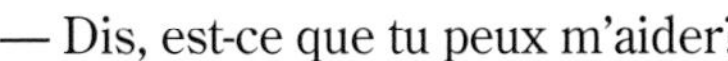

— Dis, est-ce que tu peux m'aider?	• *Use another expression.*
— Oui, bien sûr. Où es-tu?	• *Use another expression.*
— Je suis au salon.	• *Name another part of the house or yard.*
— Qu'est-ce que je peux faire pour toi?	
— Est-ce que tu peux nettoyer les vitres?	• *Mention a chore that needs to be done there.*
— Je voudrais bien, mais je n'ai pas de chiffon.	• *Accept or refuse. If you refuse, give an explanation. If you accept, your partner will thank you.*

Conversations libres

Avec votre partenaire, choisissez l'une des situations suivantes. Composez ensemble un dialogue correspondant à cette situation et jouez ce dialogue en classe.

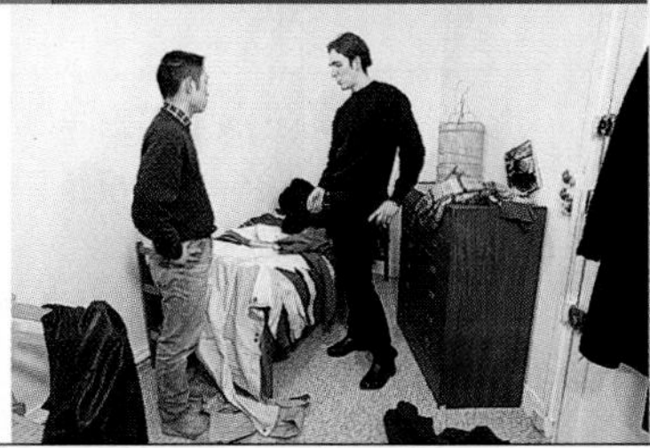

1 À l'université

Jean-Jacques et Christophe sont camarades de chambre à l'université. Jean-Jacques aime l'ordre. Christophe, au contraire, est un garçon très désordonné. Chacun critique les habitudes de l'autre.

Rôles: Jean-Jacques, Christophe

2 Après la soirée

Thomas et Isabelle ont organisé une soirée chez eux. La soirée est finie et Thomas et Isabelle doivent ranger l'appartement qui est vraiment en désordre. Ils discutent de la répartition *(distribution)* des tâches, mais ils ne sont pas d'accord!

Rôles: Thomas, Isabelle

3 Argent de poche

ean-Philippe veut gagner de l'argent e poche cet été. Il va voir ses voisins our leur offrir ses services. Madame runet répond et veut savoir ce que ean-Philippe sait faire.

ôles: Mme Brunet, Jean-Philippe

Le robot

exposition de l'Électro-ménager *usehold appliances)*, un vendeur sente la nouvelle invention de ompagnie: un robot qui fait tes sortes de travaux domestiques. émontre le robot à une cliente qui st pas convaincue *(convinced)*.

s: Le vendeur, la cliente

5 La visite des grands-parents

Les grands-parents de Catherine et de Jean-François vont venir passer le week-end à la maison. Madame Thibault demande à ses enfants de l'aider pour préparer la maison et le jardin. Catherine a d'autres projets et Jean-François est un garçon paresseux.

Rôles: Mme Thibault, Catherine, Jean-François

6 «Le bistrot»

Monsieur Labouffe est propriétaire du restaurant «Le bistrot». Chaque été, il recrute des étudiants pour travailler dans la cuisine et la salle du restaurant. Il explique le travail à deux jeunes employés, Mélanie et Philippe. Ceux-ci demandent des précisions.

Rôles: M. Labouffe, Mélanie, Philippe

7 Drôles de vacances

Robert passe ses vacances chez sa tante Amélie qui a une ferme à la campagne. En réalité, ce ne sont pas de véritables vacances parce que Tante Amélie a toujours des projets pour Robert. Aujourd'hui, Tante Amélie a préparé une longue liste de choses à faire. Robert a décidé de refuser de travailler. Pour chaque chose, il a une excuse.

Rôles: Tante Amélie, Robert

Teaching Strategy: Expansion

La villa à la mer
Charlotte, Juliette et leurs cousins Laurent et David ont loué une villa à la mer pendant les vacances. Ils discutent de la répartition *(distribution)* des travaux domestiques.

Rôles: Charlotte, Juliette, Laurent, David

Supplementary vocabulary

Je te demande pardon, mais ... *I'm sorry, but*
C'est dommage, mais ... *It's too bad, but*
Je suis déjà pris(e). *(busy)*
Je ne peux pas me le permettre. *I can't afford it.*
C'est impossible. Je suis débordé(e)! *I'm swamped!*

Teaching Strategy: Pairs

Divide the class into pairs; have each pair develop a 20-line dialog between a parent and child. The parent asks to have chores done. The student makes up an excuse, using vocabulary from pp. 74–75 and p. 84. The dialog should include at least two sentences in the subjunctive.

Teaching Strategy
The subjunctive forms of **savoir, vouloir, pouvoir,** and **devoir** are not active. You may, however, wish to introduce them here.

que **je veuille**
que **nous voulions**
que **je doive**
que **je puisse**
que **je sache**

Note linguistique
tant pis ≠ tant mieux
too bad ≠ so much the better

Variation: Activity 3
PAIR WORK
Avec votre partenaire, discutez des choses que vous devez faire pour une des périodes suivantes. Ensuite, écrivez ce que chacun doit faire. Commencez vos phrases par **il faut que ...**

A. Le subjonctif: formation irrégulière

The subjunctive forms of **être**, **avoir**, **aller**, and **faire** are irregular.

	être	avoir	aller	faire
que je (j')	**sois**	**aie**	**aille**	**fasse**
que tu	**sois**	**aies**	**ailles**	**fasses**
qu'il/elle/on	**soit**	**ait**	**aille**	**fasse**
que nous	**soyons**	**ayons**	**allions**	**fassions**
que vous	**soyez**	**ayez**	**alliez**	**fassiez**
qu'ils/elles	**soient**	**aient**	**aillent**	**fassent**

1 Tant pis! *(Too bad!)*
Invitez votre partenaire à faire certaines choses avec vous. Il/elle va refuser en donnant une excuse.

▶ **— Tu veux déjeuner avec moi?**
— Je m'excuse, mais il faut que je sois chez moi à midi.
— Tant pis!

INVITATIONS
- sortir
- jouer au volley
- déjeuner
- aller au ciné
- venir chez moi
- faire une promenade
- ??

EXCUSES
- faire mes devoirs
- faire des achats
- aller au supermarché
- aller chez un copain
- être chez moi à midi
- être à un rendez-vous
- ??

2 Que faire?
Lisez ce que les personnes suivantes vont faire et dites ce qu'elles doivent faire.

▶ Tu vas ranger la cuisine. (faire la vaisselle)
Il faut que tu fasses la vaisselle.

1. Je vais voir un film. (aller au ciné / être à l'heure)
2. Tu vas organiser un pique-nique. (aller au supermarché / faire les courses)
3. Nous sommes invités à dîner. (avoir un cadeau / être polis)
4. Vous allez prendre l'avion. (faire vos valises / aller à l'aéroport)
5. Mélanie va faire du parapente. (faire attention / avoir du courage)
6. Anne et Thomas vont participer à un marathon. (être en bonne forme/ faire du jogging régulièrement)

3 Choses à faire
Choisissez une période de temps et nommez deux ou trois choses que vous devez faire en utilisant
il faut que je . . .

- ce soir
- avant le week-end
- ce week-end
- la semaine prochaine
- avant les vacances
- cet été

Teaching Strategy: Warm-Up
Brainstorm a short series of situations in which the subjunctive would be used. Then help students to recognize the subjunctive forms of verbs in sentences.

B. L'usage du subjonctif après certaines expressions impersonnelles

Note the use of the subjunctive in the following sentences.

Il est important **que nous soyons** à l'heure. *It is important **that we be** on time.*
Il est bon **que vous fassiez** du sport. *It is good **that you do** sports.*
Il est dommage **que tu partes**. *It is too bad **that you are leaving.***

In French, the subjunctive is used after certain impersonal expressions of OPINION when they are referring to specific people.

➡ When the expression of opinion is used in a GENERAL sense, it is followed by **de** + INFINITIVE. Compare:

Il est utile **de parler** français. *It is useful (in general) **to speak** French.*
Il est utile **que Marc parle** français. *It is useful **that Marc speaks** French.*

Vocabulaire: Quelques expressions d'opinion		
il est bon que	**il est utile que**	**il est dommage que**
il est important que	**il est naturel que**	**il vaut mieux** *(it is better)* **que**
il est essentiel que	**il est normal que**	
il est indispensable que	**il est juste** *(fair)* **que**	

■ **Note linguistique**

When **il vaut mieux** is used in the general sense, it is followed directly by the infinitive:

Il vaut mieux être à l'heure.

4 D'accord ou non?

Exprimez votre opinion sur l'un des sujets suivants. Votre partenaire va être d'accord ou pas d'accord avec vous. (Ajoutez d'autres sujets à la liste si vous voulez.)

▶ **— Il est important (utile, indispensable) que j'aille à l'université.**
— Je suis d'accord avec toi. Il est important que nous allions à l'université.
(Je ne suis pas d'accord avec toi. Il n'est pas important que nous allions à l'université.)

- aller à l'université
- être en bonne santé *(health)*
- aider mes parents
- être ponctuel en classe
- avoir beaucoup d'amis
- être riche
- réussir aux examens
- faire des progrès en français
- aller en France
- trouver un job cet été
- avoir mon diplôme
- ??

5 Pour rester en forme

Votre partenaire veut commencer un programme pour rester en forme. Il/elle hésite entre plusieurs options. Donnez-lui votre opinion en commençant votre suggestion par **il vaut mieux que . . .**

▶ jouer au volley ou au basket?

— Je voudrais rester en forme. Je ne sais pas si je dois jouer au volley ou au basket.
— Il vaut mieux que tu joues au volley.

1. manger des fruits ou de la viande?
2. boire du thé ou de l'eau minérale?
3. faire du jogging ou de la musculation?
4. aller à la piscine ou au club de sport?
5. acheter un vélo ou des haltères *(weights)*?
6. faire du golf ou du tennis?

C. L'usage du subjonctif après **vouloir que**

Note the use of the subjunctive in the sentences below.

Je **voudrais que tu viennes** chez moi.	***I would like you to come*** *to my house.*
Éric **veut que je sorte** avec lui.	*Éric* ***wants me to go out*** *with him.*
Mon frère **ne veut pas que je prenne** sa voiture.	*My brother* ***does not want me to take*** *his car.*

▌ In French, the SUBJUNCTIVE is used after **vouloir que** to express a WISH.

➡ Note that the wish must concern someone or something OTHER THAN THE SUBJECT.
When the wish concerns the SUBJECT, the INFINITIVE is used.
Contrast:

The wish concerns the subject: INFINITIVE	The wish concerns someone else: SUBJUNCTIVE
Je veux **sortir**. **Mon père** veut **prendre** sa voiture.	**Je** veux que **tu sortes** avec moi. **Mon père** ne veut pas que **je prenne** sa voiture.

➡ The subjunctive is also used after **je veux bien (que)**.

— Est-ce que je peux sortir?	*Can I go out?*
— Oui, **je veux bien que tu sortes**.	*Sure,* ***it's OK with me if you go out.***

QUELQUES EXPRESSIONS DE DÉSIR ET DE VOLONTÉ
(par ordre d'intensité)

je préfère que . . .
je souhaite que . . . *(I wish)*
je désire que . . . *(I wish)*
je voudrais que . . .
j'aimerais que . . .
je veux que . . .
j'insiste pour que . . .
j'exige que . . . *(I demand)*

6 Chez vous

Votre camarade français(e) (votre partenaire) est chez vous.
Il/elle vous demande la permission de faire certaines choses.
Acceptez ou refusez.

▶ regarder tes photos

— Est-ce que je peux regarder tes photos?
— Oui, je veux bien que tu regardes mes photos.
(Pas question! Je ne veux pas que tu regardes mes photos!)

1. mettre un CD?
2. faire un sandwich?
3. lire ton journal *(diary)*?
4. téléphoner à un copain en France?
5. emprunter ton vélo?
6. aller dans la chambre de tes parents?
7. aider avec la vaisselle?
8. promener ton chien?
9. donner à manger à ton chat?

TEACHING RESOURCES

Student Activities Manual, pp. 32–33, 118

Audio Program, CD 2, Tracks 9–10

HM ClassPrep CD, Audioscript, Unit 2

Teaching Strategy: Challenge

PAS D'ACCORD!
Julien voudrait faire certaines choses mais sa mère n'est pas d'accord. Jouez les deux rôles avec votre partenaire.

▶ **sortir ce soir**
JULIEN: **Je voudrais sortir ce soir.**
SA MÈRE: **Eh bien, moi, je ne veux pas que tu sortes ce soir!**

1. prendre la voiture
2. acheter une moto
3. faire du karaté
4. apprendre à faire du deltaplane *(hang-gliding)*
5. avoir un boa dans ma chambre
6. être cascadeur *(stuntman)*

Teaching Strategy: Warm-Up

Write out all the different expressions of *wish* or *desire* from p. 88, both with and without **que**, on separate pieces of paper. Distribute to the class, and ask each student to make a sentence with his/her expression.

Put two columns on the board, one for the expressions with **que** and one for the expressions without **que**. Have the students write their sentences on the board in the appropriate column. When completed, ask students to identify the difference between the two columns.

7 Oui ou non?

Décrivez les souhaits *(wishes)* des personnes suivantes. Utilisez **vouloir que** affirmativement ou négativement. Et soyez logique!

▶ le professeur / les élèves (étudier? dormir en classe?)

Le professeur veut que les élèves étudient.
Il ne veut pas qu'ils dorment en classe.

1. nous / le professeur (être très strict? donner de bonnes notes?)
2. le médecin / ses patients (faire du sport? fumer?)
3. Caroline / son copain (être loyal? sortir avec une autre fille?)
4. tu / ton frère (lire ton journal *[diary]*? casser *[to break]* ta chaîne hi-fi?)
5. je / mes amis (dire des mensonges *[lies]*? être patients avec moi?)
6. mes parents / je (avoir de bonnes notes? être impoli?)

8 D'accord, mais . . .

Nathalie demande à son père de faire certaines choses. Il accepte, mais avec certaines conditions. Jouez les deux rôles avec votre partenaire.

▶ **— Dis, Papa, je voudrais sortir.**
— Écoute, je veux bien que tu sortes, mais à une condition!
— Quelle condition?
— Il faut que tu rentres avant onze heures.
— D'accord, Papa.

1. prendre la voiture
   mettre ta ceinture *(seatbelt)*
2. aller au ciné
   finir tes devoirs
3. inviter des copains
   ranger le salon
4. organiser une boum
   faire la vaisselle
5. faire du parapente
   être très prudente
6. acheter une moto
   porter un casque *(helmet)*

9 C'est vous le patron (la patronne)! *(You're the boss!)*

Choisissez l'une des situations suivantes. Donnez à un(e) jeune employé(e) deux ou trois tâches à faire. Vous pouvez utiliser les expressions du Français pratique à la page 74/75.

Vous êtes . . .
- le chef d'un restaurant
- le directeur (la directrice) d'un zoo
- le chef jardinier du parc municipal
- le directeur (la directrice) d'une campagne de nettoyage *(clean-up campaign)*
- le patron (la patronne) d'une teinturerie *(dry-cleaner's)*

▶ **Je voudrais que tu . . . J'aimerais aussi que tu . . .**

10 Expression personnelle

Choisissez une personne et exprimez certains souhaits pour cette personne.

je { souhaite / désire / voudrais } que
- mes parents . . .
- le professeur. . .
- mon copain . . .
- ma cousine . . .
- les voisins . . .

11 Exigences

Expliquez les exigences *(demands)* d'une des personnes suivantes à votre égard.

mon père / ma mère / mes profs / mon meilleur ami / ma meilleure amie

{ exiger / insister pour / ne pas vouloir } que je . . .

Teaching Notes
- Before doing Activity 7, you may want to quickly review the present of **vouloir**.
- Students may also use **désirer, souhaiter.**

Expansion: Activity 8
Encourage students to invent their own "conditions."

See if students can then transform the sentences so they could be placed in the opposite column. Remind students that the meaning of their sentence will change (e.g., **Je voudrais que tu viennes chez moi ce soir.** would become **Je voudrais venir chez toi ce soir.**)

LE FRANÇAIS PRATIQUE

Comment décrire un objet

TEACHING RESOURCES

Student Activities Manual, pp. 33–34, 118–120

Audio Program, CD 2, Tracks 11–14

HM ClassPrep CD, Audioscript, Unit 2

■ Teaching Note

This section is optional, for vocabulary expansion and enrichment.

■ Notes linguistiques

- **Gros** *(big, fat)* is used when referring to the volume, width, or general size of something.
- **Grand** *(tall, big)* refers more to the height of a person or thing: **Le Saint-Bernard est un gros chien. La tour Eiffel est une grande tour.**
- **poli** comes from **polir** *(to polish)*
  poli also means *polite* *(= in a polished manner)*

LE FRANÇAIS PRATIQUE

Comment décrire un objet

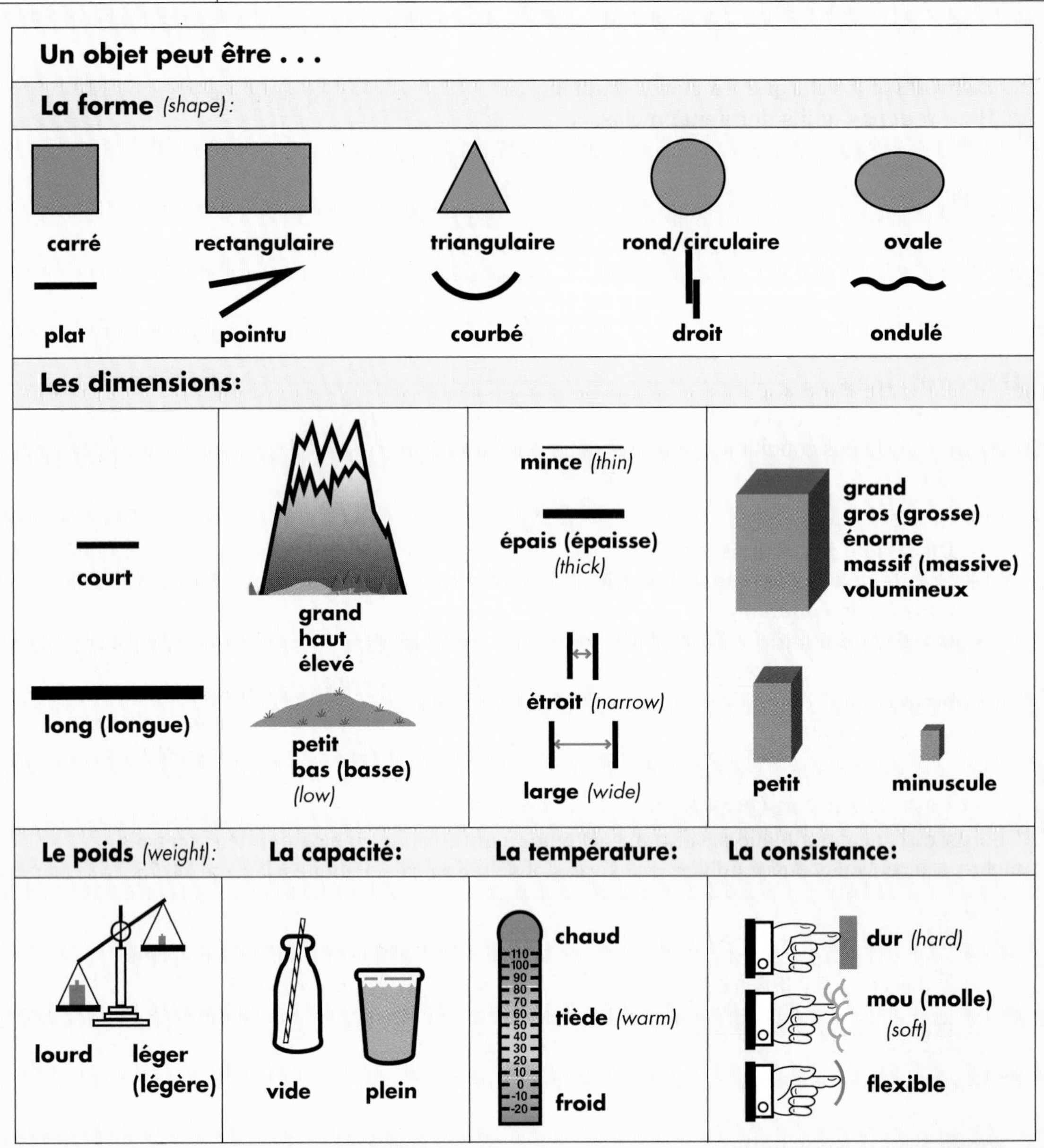

L'état, l'apparence, la condition:

solide	≠	**fragile**
sec (sèche) *(dry)*	≠	**mouillé** *(wet)*, **humide**
lisse *(smooth)*, **poli** *(polished)*	≠	**rugueux (rugueuse)** *(rough, uneven)*
brillant *(shiny)*	≠	**terne** *(dull)*
neuf (neuve) *(new)*	≠	**vieux (vieille), ancien (ancienne)**
		d'occasion *(secondhand, used)*
		usagé *(worn)*

Comment décrire un objet
Pratique ▶ p. 33

Teaching Strategy: Warm-Up

The vocabulary in this section is for enrichment. It can be presented (and practiced) with classroom objects or things which you can bring to class:

une montre	**un ballon de foot**
une bague	**une fenêtre**
un bâton de craie	**une porte**
une balle de ping-pong	**un sac**

You may also mention an adjective and ask students to name objects that exhibit that feature:

chaud → **le thé, le café**
froid → **la glace, le thé glacé**

La matière:

—En quoi est cet objet?
Il est **en plastique**.

le papier
le carton *(cardboard)*
l'étoffe *(fabric)*
le caoutchouc *(rubber)*
le plastique
la matière synthétique

le bois *(wood)*
la pierre *(stone)*
la brique *(brick)*
le verre *(glass)*

le métal (les métaux)
l'acier *(steel)*
le fer *(iron)*
le cuivre *(copper)*
le plomb *(lead)*
l'aluminium

1 Qui suis-je?

Faites correspondre chaque monument avec sa description.

1. la Tour Eiffel

2. La Statue de la Liberté

3. le bâtiment des Nations Unies

4. L'Arche de Saint Louis

(a) Je suis en métal. Je suis mince, plate et assez étroite. À l'intérieur, je suis vide. Je ne suis ni pointue, ni droite, ni ondulée. Ma caractéristique principale est que je suis courbe.

(b) Je suis élevé et droit. Je suis rectangulaire et plat. Le matin et l'après-midi, je suis plein, mais la nuit, je suis généralement vide. Je ne suis pas entièrement en métal. Je ne suis pas en pierre non plus.

(c) Mon socle *(pedestal)* est en pierre, mais je suis en métal. Je suis verte parce que je suis en cuivre. Je suis grande, mais je ne suis pas très épaisse. Ma figure n'est pas carrée. Ma couronne *(crown)* est circulaire.

(d) Je suis très haute—j'ai 300 mètres de hauteur—mais je ne suis pas grosse. Je suis plutôt mince. Je suis lourde parce que je pèse 7300 tonnes, mais je suis relativement légère. Je ne suis pas en verre. Je suis en fer.

2 Qu'est-ce que c'est?

Choisissez un de ces objets. Puis décrivez cet objet sans mentionner son nom. Votre partenaire va deviner ce que c'est.

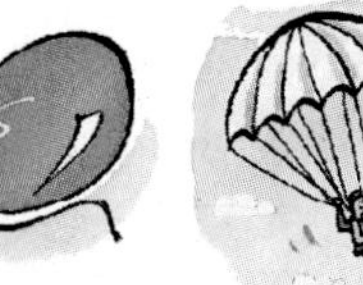

un clou **un fer à repasser** **une bouteille** **une scie** **un ballon** **un parachute** **un réfrigérateur**

Supplementary vocabulary

acéré *sharp*
émoussé *blunt*
compact *compact*
dense *dense*
le papier émeri *emery paper*
le marbre *marble*
le nickel
le cuir *(leather)*

■ Pronunciation

caoutchouc /kautʃu/

■ Réponses: Activité 1

1-d, 2-c, 3-b, 4-a

Reading **STRATEGY**

Reading fiction

Teaching Strategy
- For a broader historical context, you may first have students read *Interlude 2*, pp. 98–107.
- Ask students:
  - What is a fable?
  - What can be expected to happen in a fable?
  - Who are the characters in a fable?
  - Is there a moral?

LECTURE

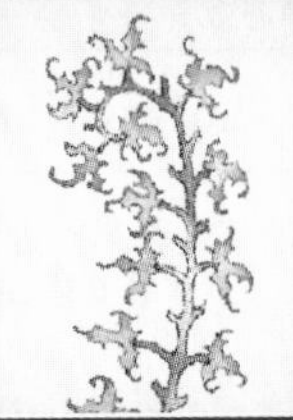

La Couverture

fable du Moyen Âge

AVANT DE LIRE

Le texte que vous allez lire est basé sur une fable très ancienne, puisqu'elle a été écrite au 13e siècle par un certain Bernier. Au Moyen Âge°, les fables ou **fabliaux** étaient très populaires en France, surtout dans la région du Nord. La fable est une histoire, généralement assez courte, qui a pour objet d'illustrer une vérité morale importante pour les gens de l'époque. Les personnages de fables peuvent être réels ou imaginaires. Dans *La Couverture*, les personnages sont intéressants parce qu'ils sont réels et qu'ils représentent assez bien la vie et la société au Moyen Âge.

le Moyen Âge *Middle Ages*

Anticipons un peu!

Dans la première partie de la fable, un père, qui est commerçant, apprend que son fils veut se marier avec une fille d'une classe sociale plus élevée. Malheureusement, ce fils, qui vient de terminer ses études, n'a ni argent ni maison. Que doit faire le père?

- Conseiller à son fils de trouver une femme qui soit de la même classe sociale que lui.
- Donner sa maison au jeune couple et acheter pour lui une maison plus petite, tout en continuant son commerce.
- Vendre son commerce et en donner les profits ainsi que sa maison au jeune couple.

Maintenant, lisez la première partie de la fable pour voir quelle décision le père a prise.

NOTE CULTURELLE

La noblesse

Avant la Révolution de 1789, la société française était divisée en trois groupes qui n'avaient pas les mêmes droits: **la noblesse** (militaire), **le clergé** (religieux) et **le peuple**. En général, les gens nobles ne se mariaient pas avec les gens du peuple.

Dans ce texte, la différence de classe sociale entre le marchand et le noble est reflétée dans le langage que chacun utilise pour parler à l'autre:

- **Brave homme** *(my good man)* est une expression condescendante.
- **Messire** (dérivé de **monsire** et **monseigneur**) était le terme utilisé au Moyen Âge pour parler à une personne noble. (C'est la forme ancienne de **monsieur**, qui aujourd'hui n'exprime pas la supériorité sociale.)

NOTES CULTURELLES

- The most famous French fabulist is **Jean de La Fontaine** (1621–1695). In his fables, animals personify personalities of his time such as the king and his courtesans. Among his 230 fables are **Le Renard et le Corbeau** (The Fox and the Raven), and **La Cigale et la Fourmi** (The Cricket and the Ant).
- The university of **La Sorbonne** was founded in 1257 in Paris. At the time, it offered three degrees: **la déterminance, le baccalauréat, and la licence.**

LA COUVERTURE

I

À Abbeville* vivait autrefois° un homme heureux. C'était un marchand qui avait un commerce de tissus.° Il avait peu de biens, mais, grâce à son travail, il gagnait honnêtement sa vie. Cet homme était marié à une femme qu'il adorait. Ils avaient un fils unique. Ce garçon était beau, fort, intelligent et respectueux de ses parents. Chaque jour, le marchand et sa femme rendaient grâce à Dieu° de leur bonheur. Ce bonheur, malheureusement, n'a pas duré éternellement. Un jour, la femme du marchand est tombée malade d'une fièvre subite°. Une semaine plus tard, elle était morte . . . Inconsolable, notre marchand continua° à travailler dur et à s'occuper de l'éducation de son fils. Quand celui-ci eut° dix-huit ans, il l'envoya° à Paris faire des études de droit.

Après deux ans d'études, le jeune homme revient à Abbeville pour travailler comme clerc de notaire. Un dimanche, pendant la messe,° il remarque une très belle jeune fille qui est assise au premier rang° de l'église. Il s'enquiert° de l'identité de celle-ci. On lui dit qu'elle est orpheline et qu'elle vient d'une famille très noble mais sans fortune.

Les dimanches suivants, le jeune homme revoit la jeune fille qui lui sourit°. Il tombe éperdument amoureux° d'elle. Finalement il se décide à lui parler et il se rend compte que la jeune fille l'aime aussi. Alors, un jour il lui demande: «Voulez-vous m'épouser?» La jeune fille lui répond: «Je voudrais bien vous épouser, mais vous n'êtes pas noble. Il faut donc que votre père aille voir mon frère aîné et obtienne le consentement de celui-ci.»

Le jeune homme va trouver son père pour lui expliquer la situation. Le marchand, qui veut faire le bonheur de son fils, va chez le frère de la jeune fille. Celui-ci écoute sa requête, hésite et finalement dit:

— Brave homme, je veux bien que ma soeur épouse votre fils, mais à deux conditions.

— Quelles sont ces conditions, messire?

— D'abord, je veux que vous donniez votre maison à votre fils pour que ma soeur soit chez elle et non chez vous.

*Abbeville. Abbeville est une petite ville de Picardie, une province située dans le Nord de la France. Au Moyen Âge, cette ville avait une industrie textile très importante.

autrefois = dans le passé **tissus** *fabrics*
rendaient grâce à Dieu *gave thanks to God* **subite** *sudden*
continua = a continué **eut** = a eu **envoya** = a envoyé
la messe *(Catholic) Mass* **rang** *row*
s'enquiert de = pose des questions concernant
sourit *smiles* **éperdument amoureux** *hopelessly in love*

Mots utiles

les biens	*wealth*
le bonheur	*happiness*
une couverture	*blanket*
un marchand	*merchant*
appartenir à	*to belong to*
avoir lieu	*to take place*
durer	*to last*
épouser	*to marry*
remarquer	*to notice*
se rendre compte	*to realize*
celui-ci, celle-ci	*the latter*
grâce à	*thanks to*

■ Notes linguistiques

- This introduction to the fable is written in the past. The second paragraph contains three examples of the **passé simple:**
  il continua
  celui-ci eut 18 ans
  il l'envoya
  The **passé simple** is formally introduced in Unit 3, p. 133.
- The remainder of the fable is written in the historical present.

■ Irregular Verbs

- **s'enquérir** *(to ask for information)* is conjugated like **acquérir** *(to acquire):*
  je m'enquiers
  il s'enquiert
  nous nous enquérons
  ils s'enquièrent
- **appartenir** (*see* **tenir**) *(see Appendix C)*

- In the 13th century, universities were privately owned and autonomous. Most were located in Paris, in the **Quartier Latin**, so named because all scholars spoke Latin.
- The main objective of the **French Revolution** was to establish equality among all people, and, therefore, to abolish the privileges enjoyed by the nobility and the clergy. This is reflected in the second term of the French motto: **Liberté**, **Égalité**, **Fraternité**. (For more information on the French Revolution, you may want to refer students to *Interlude 5,* pp. 216–225.)

— C'est facile! Tout ce qui m'appartient appartiendra à mon fils. Je lui donnerai ma maison la veille° même de son mariage. Et la seconde condition, messire?

— Je veux que vous me donniez 10.000 écus d'or.**

— Mais, c'est impossible, messire. Je n'ai pas cette somme sous la main.°

— Que faites-vous dans la vie, brave homme?

— Je suis marchand de tissu.

— Eh bien, il faut que vous vendiez votre commerce et que vous m'apportiez le produit de cette vente°.

— Je ferai tout ce que vous voulez pour assurer le bonheur de mon fils.

Comme convenu°, le marchand vend son commerce et donne sa maison à son fils. Le mariage a lieu. Les jeunes époux viennent habiter chez l'ancien marchand qui leur laisse sa chambre, la plus belle pièce de la maison.

Au début, tout se passe bien. Le jeune couple est heureux. L'ancien marchand, qui n'exerce plus sa profession, aide son fils et sa belle-fille dans tous les petits travaux de la vie domestique. Il bricole, répare les ustensiles de cuisine, coupe du bois pour le chauffage° de la maison, nourrit° les animaux, s'occupe du jardin. Quand le premier enfant du couple naît, il cède° sa chambre au bébé et va habiter dans une chambre plus petite. C'est lui qui s'occupe de son petit-fils. Il joue avec l'enfant, il le promène, il lui apprend à marcher et à parler.

****10 000 écus d'or.** **L'écu** était une pièce de monnaie utilisée en France jusqu'à la Révolution en 1789. Dix mille écus d'or représentaient une somme considérable.

la veille = le jour avant **sous la main** *at hand, available* **vente** *sale* **comme convenu** *as agreed* **vente** *sale* **chauffage** *heating* **nourrit** = donne à manger à **cède** = donne

Avez-vous compris?

1. Pourquoi est-ce que le marchand était un homme heureux?
2. Quels sont les sentiments du jeune homme et de la jeune fille? Quel est l'obstacle à leur mariage?
3. Pour le marchand, laquelle des deux conditions émises *(expressed)* par le noble est la plus difficile à réaliser? Pourquoi?
4. Que fait le marchand après le mariage de son fils? Décrivez sa vie.

Anticipons un peu!

Dans la deuxième partie de la fable, le grand-père, qui est maintenant âgé et très infirme, habite encore chez son fils. Malheureusement, la femme trouve de plus en plus difficile de s'occuper du grand-père malade. Que doit faire le fils?

- Engager une infirmière pour s'occuper du vieillard.
- Garder *(keep)* le grand-père à la maison et demander à toute la famille de faire le sacrifice nécessaire pour s'en occuper.
- Envoyer le grand-père dans un hospice pour gens âgés.
- Autre solution?

■ Avez-vous compris?

(Sample answers)

1. Il était heureux parce qu'il avait une femme qu'il adorait, un bon fils, et il gagnait bien sa vie.
2. Ils s'aiment, mais la jeune fille est noble, et le jeune homme ne l'est pas.
3. Les 10 000 écus d'or sont la condition la plus difficile, parce qu'il ne les a pas.
4. Il donne sa maison à son fils et sa belle-fille. Il habite avec eux et il les aide beaucoup: il coupe le bois, nourrit les animaux, il répare les outils de cuisine.

NOTES CULTURELLES

- You may point out to the students the many different household chores that were necessary in the past. These included chopping wood (which was used not only for heating, but also for cooking), taking care of the animals raised for food (chickens, ducks, geese, rabbits), and tending the vegetable garden and the orchard.

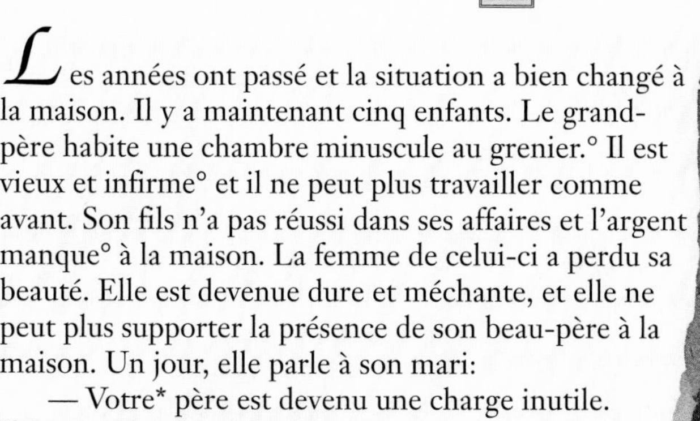

II

Les années ont passé et la situation a bien changé à la maison. Il y a maintenant cinq enfants. Le grand-père habite une chambre minuscule au grenier.° Il est vieux et infirme° et il ne peut plus travailler comme avant. Son fils n'a pas réussi dans ses affaires et l'argent manque° à la maison. La femme de celui-ci a perdu sa beauté. Elle est devenue dure et méchante, et elle ne peut plus supporter la présence de son beau-père à la maison. Un jour, elle parle à son mari:

— Votre* père est devenu une charge inutile. Il faut qu'il quitte la maison.

— Mais, mon amie . . .

—Oubliez-vous qui vous avez épousé? Il faut que vous choisissiez: votre père ou moi!

Le fils est morfondu.° Il va trouver son père et essaie de trouver une excuse.

— Père, il faut que vous* quittiez votre chambre.

— Mais, mon fils, pourquoi veux-tu que je la quitte?

— Père, nous avons besoin d'argent. Il faut que nous louions cette chambre.

— Écoute, mon fils, je veux bien aller loger dans l'étable avec les chevaux...

— Père, c'est impossible!

— Et pourquoi donc me chasses-tu?

Embarrassé, le fils doit avouer la vérité: «Père, ma femme exige que vous partiez.»

Le vieillard, consterné, regarde son fils. «Et où veux-tu que je loge?»

—Vous irez à l'hospice des vieillards.° Ils vous recevront.°

— Mais, il fait froid là-bas.

Le fils appelle son fils aîné, un garçon de quatorze ans, celui-là même que son grand-père avait élevé quand il était petit.

— Fils, va dans ma chambre. Dans l'armoire, tu trouveras une grande couverture de laine.° Prends-la et donne-la à ton grand-père.

Mots utiles

les affaires	*business*
une charge	*burden*
un couteau	*knife*
la moitié	*half*
dur	*hard-hearted*
méchant	*mean, nasty*
allumer un feu	*to light a fire*
avouer	*to admit, avow*
élever	*to raise (children)*
exiger	*to insist*
expliquer	*to explain*
garder	*to keep*
loger	*to live, lodge*
supporter	*to bear, stand*

***L'usage de *vous*.** Autrefois, l'usage de **vous** (au lieu de **tu**) était beaucoup plus courant que maintenant. C'était une marque de respect utilisée par les enfants pour parler à leurs parents, et par les époux quand ils se parlaient entre eux.

grenier *attic* **infirme** = invalide **l'argent manque** = il n'y a pas d'argent **morfondu** *upset* **vieillards** = personnes âgées **vous recevront** = vont vous prendre **laine** *wool*

Teaching Strategy: Expansion

Le fils a besoin d'argent. Il veut louer la chambre de son père. Que pourrait-il faire d'autre pour gagner de l'argent?

- Country houses generally had stables **(des étables)**, since horses were needed for transportation as well as for farm work.
- In the Middle Ages, many towns had shelters **(des hospices)** for indigent old people, but the living conditions they offered were very rudimentary.

Teaching Strategy

Ask students to identify uses of the **passé composé** and the subjunctive in the story.

■ Avez-vous compris?

(Sample answers)

1. Le père est vieux et infirme. L'argent manque.
2. Il dit qu'il a besoin d'argent. Il veut louer la chambre.
3. Il doit prendre une couverture de laine. Il coupe la couverture en deux.
4. Il explique que son père aura besoin de l'autre moitié un jour.
5. L'histoire finit bien. Le père va rester à la maison.

Teaching Strategy: Expansion

Ask students:

- D'après vous, comment est le petit-fils? Quelles sont ses qualités?
- Pensez-vous que le petit-fils va envoyer son père à l'hospice plus tard? Pourquoi?

Le garçon monte dans la chambre de ses parents, ouvre l'armoire et prend la couverture. Puis, il prend son couteau et coupe la couverture en deux. Il descend dans la cour° et donne la moitié de la couverture à son grand-père.

Son père, surpris, lui demande:

— Fils, pourquoi as-tu coupé la couverture en deux? Et pourquoi n'en donnes-tu que la moitié à ton grand-père?

— Parce qu'un jour, vous aurez besoin de l'autre moitié.

L'homme regarde son fils sans comprendre.

—Il faut que tu t'expliques! Quand donc aurai-je besoin de cette couverture?

—Quand vous serez devenu vieux et quand, à mon tour, je vous enverrai à l'hospice des vieillards.

L'homme finalement comprend son ingratitude. Il s'excuse et va embrasser son père qui fond en larmes.° Puis, il va trouver sa femme pour lui dire qu'il a décidé de garder son père à la maison. Celle-ci, qui a vu toute la scène de sa fenêtre, a aussi compris. Elle monte dans la chambre de son beau-père pour allumer un bon feu de cheminée,° puis elle va préparer un grand repas. Une nouvelle vie familiale commence . . .

cour *courtyard* **fond en larmes** *breaks into tears* **cheminée** *fireplace*

Avez-vous compris?

1. Qu'est-ce qui a changé à la maison du marchand? Décrivez un ou deux de ces changements.
2. Quelle excuse est-ce que le fils donne à son père quand il lui demande de quitter sa chambre?
3. Qu'est-ce que le petit-fils doit faire dans la chambre de son père? Qu'est-ce qu'il fait en plus?
4. Qu'est-ce que le garçon explique à son père?
5. Comment finit l'histoire?

NOTE CULTURELLE

Until 30 or 40 years ago, most French children carried a pocket knife **(un couteau de poche** or **un canif)**, especially in the rural areas. They used these knives for all sorts of purposes: slicing bread, eating at the table, sharpening pencils, making whistles, whittling wood, etc.

Would this have been true in rural areas in the United States also? Ask students to compare/contrast.

96 Unité 2

APRÈS LA LECTURE

EXPRESSION ORALE

■ Dramatisation
Avec votre partenaire, choisissez une scène de la fable que vous avez trouvée intéressante et jouez-la en classe.

■ Situations
Avec votre partenaire, choisissez l'une des situations suivantes. Composez le dialogue correspondant et jouez-le en classe.

1 Rencontre

Après sa visite au noble, le marchand rencontre un(e) ami(e) qui est marchand(e) aussi. Il explique sa décision de vendre son commerce. L'autre marchand(e) essaie de le dissuader.

Rôles: le marchand de tissus, un ami(e)

2 Explication

Après la scène de la couverture, le petit-fils explique à un(e) jeune frère (soeur) ce qui s'est passé. Celui-ci (celle-ci) veut des détails.

Rôles: le petit-fils, un frère (une soeur)

■ Discussion: La morale de l'histoire
Comme nous l'avons vu, l'objet d'une fable est généralement d'illustrer un certain principe moral.

A. Voici plusieurs morales possibles pour la fable que vous avez lue.
   - Les gens riches ne sont jamais heureux.
   - Il ne faut pas se marier avec une personne d'une autre classe sociale.
   - Les jeunes sont charitables; les adultes sont égoïstes.
   - Tout est bien qui finit bien.
   - On ne peut pas compter sur ses enfants. Pour cela, toute personne raisonnable doit garder ses biens jusqu'à sa mort.
   - Il ne faut pas faire aux autres personnes ce qu'on ne voudrait pas qu'elles nous fassent à nous.

   Choisissez la morale qui, selon vous, correspond le mieux au récit de *La Couverture*. (Ou, si vous voulez, trouvez une autre morale.) Expliquez votre choix à votre partenaire.

B. D'après vous, quelle était la morale de cette histoire au Moyen Âge? (Pour connaître cette réponse, allez au bas de la page.)

EXPRESSION ÉCRITE

■ D'un autre point de vue
Imaginez que vous êtes le petit-fils ou la petite-fille du marchand de tissu. Dans une lettre à un(e) ami(e), vous racontez de votre point de vue la scène de la couverture.

■ En famille
Décrivez la vie de la famille <u>après</u> l'incident. Pour cela, composez un texte où vous décrivez ce que chacun fait à la maison pour aider les autres.

■ Fable moderne
Transformez *La Couverture* en fable moderne. Pour cela, composez une nouvelle fable que vous situerez à l'époque actuelle en gardant la morale générale de l'histoire.

■ D'un oeil critique
Expliquez pourquoi *La Couverture* est une fable très ancienne. Pour cela, faites une liste de tous les détails qui indiquent que l'action de cette fable se passe autrefois plutôt que maintenant.

LA MORALE DE L'HISTOIRE
L'auteur du Moyen Âge qui a écrit cette fable voulait conseiller aux parents de garder leurs biens et leurs ressources pour leurs vieux jour

■ Note linguistique
The original text, transcribed in modern French, reads: **«Mirez-vous dans ce miroir, vous qui avez des enfants à marier. Ne suivez pas l'exemple du vieillard. Si vous êtes en avant, ne vous mettez pas en arrière. Méfiez-vous: les enfants sont sans pitié. Ils en ont assez de leurs pères quand ceux-ci ne sont plus bons à rien. Se mettre à la merci d'autrui, c'est s'exposer à grande affliction.»**

Expansion
Students may wish to compare *La Couverture* to Shakespeare's *King Lear*.

INTERLUDE CULTUREL

■ **Note linguistique**
In 1987, the **Académie française** announced that the word **événement** could also be written **évènement** (with a grave accent on the second "e"). You may allow your students to use either spelling.

■ **Notes historiques**
- **La Gaule** was renamed **Francia Occidentalis** (Franks from the West) after a treaty signed in Verdun, in 843.
- The name "France" comes from the Franks, one of the Germanic tribes that invaded Gaul in the fifth century.

Notes culturelles
- **Nîmes** and **Arles** are two cities in the south of France where one can admire great Roman ruins, such as arenas.
- The battle of Azincourt is the main scene in Shakespeare's play *Henry V*.

INTERLUDE CULTUREL

■ *Les dates*

Période gallo-romaine
- 200 av. J.-C.
- 151 *Provincia Romana*
- 52 ***Vercingétorix à Gergovie***
- 0
- 450 apr. J.-C.
- 508 *Clovis, roi des Francs*

Empire de Charlemagne
- 778 *Roland à Roncevaux*
- 800 ***Sacre de Charlemagne***
- 1066 *Guillaume le Conquérant: Bataille de Hastings*
- 1152 *Aliénor d'Aquitaine épouse Henri Plantagenêt*

Guerre de Cent Ans
- 1337
- 1429 ***Jeanne d'Arc délivre la ville d'Orléans***
- 1453

■ *Les événements*

La période romaine (200 av. J.-C. - 450 apr. J.-C.)

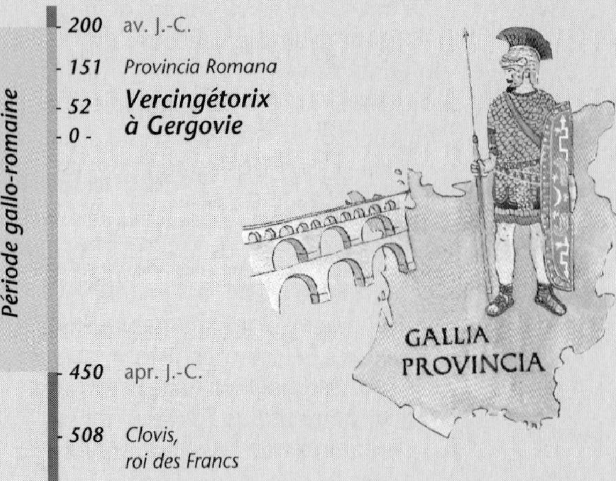

Les premières légions romaines arrivent dans le suc de **la Gaule** (l'ancien nom de la France) au deux-ième siècle avant Jésus-Christ. En 151 av. J.-C., Rome annexe cette région qui devient «Provincia Romana» ou Provence. En 58 av. J.-C., **Jules Césa** arrive en Gaule pour conquérir le reste du pays Ses troupes sont victorieuses, malgré la résistance héroïque du chef gaulois, **Vercingétorix**.

Les Romains construisent de nombreux monuments, visibles encore aujourd'hui: arènes amphithéâtres, arcs de triomphe, temples . . . Ils apportent aussi leur langue, le latin, qui es la base du français moderne.

À partir de 400, une série d'invasions met fin à la civilisation gallo-romaine. Les Francs, tribu d'origine germanique, conquièrent la Gaule. En 508, **Clovis**, leur roi choisit Paris comme capitale. La Gaule va devenir la France.

L'Empire de Charlemagne (800-814)

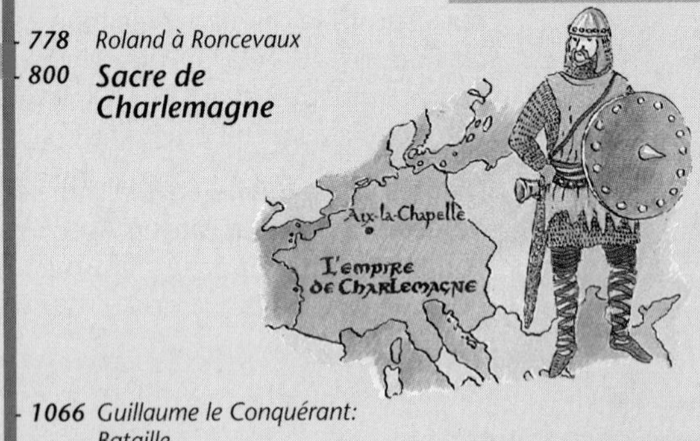

En 800, **Charlemagne**, ou Charles le Grand, ro des Francs, est sacré empereur de l'Occident Son empire est immense: il comprend la France l'Allemagne, la Belgique, la Hollande, l'Itali du Nord et le nord de l'Espagne. Ave Charlemagne, l'unification de l'Europe est pou la première fois réalisée.

La Guerre de Cent Ans (1337-1453)

Cette guerre représente plus de 100 an de conflits franco-anglais. Ell commence en 1337 quand **Édouard II** roi d'Angleterre, veut devenir ro de France. Les armées anglaises débar quent en France et remporten de brillantes victoires à **Crécy** (1346) à **Poitiers** (1356) et à **Azincourt** (1415) Les Anglais occupent une grande partie du territoire français e dévastent le pays.

Finalement la chance tourne. En 1429, **Jeanne d'Arc**, une jeun fille de 19 ans, rallie l'armée française, qui va peu à peu libérer la France

Teaching Strategy

This *Interlude* may be used in a wide variety of ways, but the presentation should remain enjoyable and not overwhelming. You may wish to begin by showing students segments of a film on Joan of Arc, reminding them of **Astérix** cartoons (p.100), or comparing historical events in other parts of the world.

The *Interlude* quizzes may be used to assess comprehension rather than as a grading tool. Research projects may also be assigned, or creative writings where students imagine what it would have been like to live in this period.

Les personnes

Vercingétorix: un général de 20 ans

Vercingétorix (72- 46 av. J.-C.) est le premier héros national français. En gaulois, son nom signifie «chef suprême des combattants». En 52 av. J.-C., il a vingt ans. Jeune et courageux, il décide de se révolter contre l'occupant romain. Il rallie les tribus gauloises, devient leur chef et attaque les légions romaines. **César** contre-attaque. Malgré la supériorité des Romains, Vercingétorix est victorieux à **Gergovie**. Mais le combat est inégal et finalement, quelques mois plus tard, Vercingétorix est capturé. Enchaîné, il est emmené à Rome où il figure au triomphe de César, puis il est exécuté.

Pour les Français, Vercingétorix symbolise le courage, le patriotisme, l'esprit d'indépendance et la résistance contre l'ennemi.

Vercingétorix (72 - 46 av. J-C) le premier héros national français

Charlemagne: Empereur de l'Occident

Charlemagne (747-814) est un grand conquérant et un grand administrateur. Pour gouverner son très vaste empire, il établit sa capitale à **Aix-la-Chapelle** au centre de cet empire et crée une administration centralisée.

Charlemagne (742 - 814), Empereur de l'Occident

Charlemagne fonde aussi un grand nombre d'écoles, les «écoles du palais». C'est un homme cultivé qui parle latin et grec et s'intéresse aux sciences. Il encourage la littérature, la philosophie, les sciences, la médecine, les arts, l'architecture. Dans sa capitale, il fonde une Académie où viennent les plus grands savants° du monde.

Jeanne d'Arc: héroïne et martyre

On trouve la statue de **Jeanne d'Arc** (1412-1431) dans toutes les églises de France. C'est non seulement une sainte de l'église catholique, mais aussi la grande héroïne française. Jeanne a seulement 17 ans quand le roi de France lui donne le commandement de son armée. Elle rallie les troupes démoralisées par de nombreuses défaites. Puis, elle délivre **Orléans**, assiégée par les Anglais, et va de victoire en victoire. Elle est finalement capturée par des soldats bourguignons° qui la vendent à leurs alliés anglais. Elle est jugée, accusée de sorcellerie° et condamnée à être brûlée.° La mort héroïque de Jeanne d'Arc, à l'âge de 19 ans, ne profite pas aux Anglais qui sont définitivement chassés de France quelques années plus tard.

Jeanne d'Arc (1412 -1431), grande héroïne française

savants *scientists* **bourguignons** = de Bourgogne *(Burgundy)* **sorcellerie** *witchcraft* **brûlée** *burned at the stake*

Supplementary vocabulary

l'armure *(f.) armor*
le bouclier *shield*
le casque *helmet*
le chevalier *knight*
la cotte de maille *coat of mail*
l'épée *(f.) sword*
l'étendard *(m.) banner*

■ Notes linguistiques

To enhance the humor in the *Astérix* series, the authors invented names based on phonetic versions of contemporary French words and expressions.

- Gallic names end in the suffix **-ix** (as in the name **Vercingétorix**):
  Astérix (astérisque, *asterisk)*
  Obélix (obélisque, *obelisk)*
  Idéfix (idée fixe, *fixed idea, obsession)*
  Panoramix (panoramique, *panoramic)*
- Roman names end in the suffix **-us** or **-um**
  Babaorum (baba au rhum, *a sponge cake soaked with rum)*
  Petibonum (petit bonhomme, *little man)*
  Marchéopus (marché aux puces, *flea market)*

▪ *Astérix et sa bande* ▪

Tous les Français connaissent **Astérix le Gaulois**. C'est un petit homme blond avec de grandes moustaches. Il est très petit, mais il est très musclé, très intelligent et très courageux. Il a un copain, **Obélix**, qui est très loyal, très fort, mais pas très intelligent.

Astérix est d'une force° exceptionnelle. Son secret est une potion magique préparée par le druide **Panoramix**. Quand Astérix boit un peu de cette potion, ses forces sont multipliées par cent.

Bien sûr, Astérix n'est pas une personne réelle. C'est le héros d'une bande dessinée très populaire en France.

Les aventures d'Astérix ont lieu vers 50 avant Jésus-Christ. À cette époque, la Gaule entière est occupée par les Romains. Il y a un seul° village qui résiste, le village où habitent Astérix et ses copains. Astérix étant° Gaulois, les Romains sont évidemment ses ennemis mortels . . .

Une légion romaine est signalée près de son village. Notre héros prend un peu de potion magique et avec Obélix il va à l'attaque de l'ennemi. Crac! Boum! Zap! En une minute la légion romaine est décimée. Tous les Romains sont prisonniers.

Astérix connaît d'autres aventures. Toujours avec Obélix, il va à Rome où il rencontre **Jules César**. Il va en Égypte où il rencontre **Cléopâtre**. Il va en Belgique, en Angleterre, en Allemagne, en Suisse . . . Chaque aventure est le sujet d'un nouvel album et chaque album a un succès phénoménal.

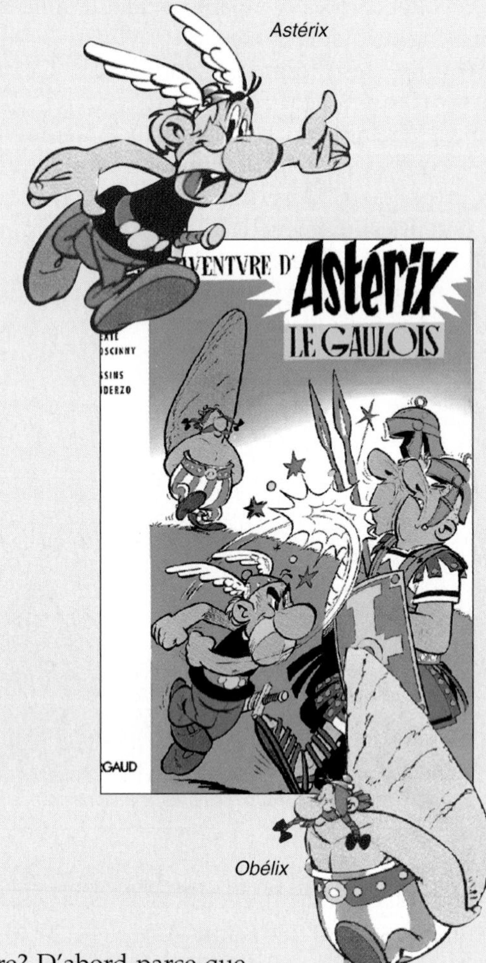

Pourquoi Astérix est-il si populaire? D'abord parce que ce petit homme moustachu symbolise l'esprit de la France en lutte° contre ses ennemis. Et aussi parce qu'il représente assez bien le caractère national français. Il est aventureux, brave, astucieux.° Il est aussi irritable, impatient, agressif et vaniteux.° Avant tout, il est indépendant. Astérix correspond à l'image que les Français ont d'eux-mêmes. Il a leurs qualités . . . et leurs défauts!°

force *strength* **un seul** *only one* **étant** *being* **en lutte** *struggling* **astucieux** *smart* **vaniteux** *boastful* **défauts** *faults, failings*

NOTES CULTURELLES

- Albert Uderzo published his thirtieth **Astérix** album in October 1996. Entitled **La Galère d'Obélix** *(Obelix's Galley)*, it features a runaway slave named Spartikis who is drawn to look like Kirk Douglas (who played the part of Spartacus in the movies).
- In France, you can visit the **Parc Astérix**, a theme park based on the comic strip. Located in Plailly, north of Paris, the park offers many rides and attractions such as water slides and a typical Gallic village.

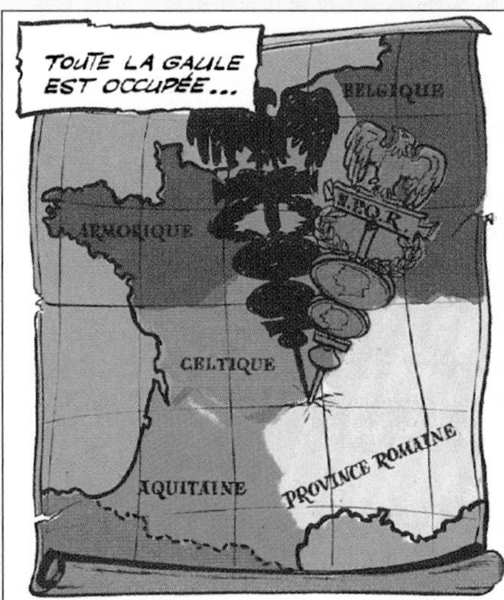

Une Aventure d'Astérix le Gaulois, Goscinny / Uderzo, Dargaud, S.A., p.5

Teaching Note

- The character of Obélix is often seen carrying a huge stone because he is supposed to be a maker of menhirs. **Menhirs** are megalithic monuments erected during prehistoric times. There are several sites in Brittany where menhirs still stand, notably by the city of Carnac.

Notes linguistiques

- The Roman characters in *Astérix* often use proverbial Latin phrases to express themselves. Most of these Latin expressions are still in use in France, such as:
  ipso facto = par le fait même (as an inevitable consequence)
  sic = ainsi (often used after a quote to indicate it is reproduced as said, errors included)
  vae victis = malheur aux vaincus (woe to the vanquished)
- To express physical pain, the French use the expression **aïe!** [aj] or **ouille!** [uj], the approximate equivalent of *ouch!*

■ Teaching Note

Les Pyrénées are the mountains that separate France from Spain, forming a natural frontier. Have students locate them on the map on p. R34.

▪ *Roland, l'homme et la légende* ▪

Roland est à la fois un personnage historique et le héros d'une des plus grandes légendes françaises.

■ L'histoire

Nous sommes en l'an 778. **Charlemagne** est en Espagne où il fait la guerre° à des princes arabes. Une insurrection éclate° dans son royaume.° Charlemagne retourne précipitamment en France avec ses meilleures troupes, mais il ne peut pas emmener ses bagages, qui sont trop lourds.° Il confie° leur transport à **Roland**, l'un de ses officiers.

Dans les Pyrénées, le convoi de bagages est attaqué par une bande de pillards° qui capturent le butin° et tuent° Roland.

■ La légende

La légende embellit les faits historiques et le rôle de Roland. Dans la légende, Roland est le neveu préféré de Charlemagne. C'est aussi le plus noble et le plus brave de ses chevaliers.° Il accompagne l'empereur dans toutes ses expéditions militaires. Il est avec lui en Espagne où les Francs combattent les Sarrasins,* ennemis de la chrétienté.°

Comme dans l'histoire, Charlemagne doit rentrer à la hâte en France. C'est à Roland qu'il confie son arrière-garde°. Roland est trahi° par l'infâme **Ganelon**, son beau-père. À **Roncevaux**, son armée de 20 000 hommes tombe dans une embuscade° tendue par 400 000 Sarrasins. Quand **Olivier**, le loyal compagnon de Roland, voit l'arrivée des ennemis, il demande à Roland de sonner° son oliphant (un cor° en ivoire d'éléphant) pour appeler Charlemagne. Homme d'honneur, Roland refuse: il préfère se battre.°

Roland sonne son oliphant

Les Francs et les Sarrasins en combat.

L'infâme Ganelon

Charlemagne et son neveu préféré, Roland

Notes culturelles

- **Un troubadour** was a poet-musician in the 12th and 13th centuries.
- **Charlemagne** reigned over a vast empire. His favorite capital city was **Aix-la-Chapelle**, now a German city called **Aachen**.

* **Sarrasins**: nom donné aux conquérants arabes venus en Europe au 8e siècle.

guerre *war* **éclate** *breaks out* **royaume** *kingdom* **lourds** *heavy* **confie** *entrusts* **pillards** *looters* **butin** *booty* **tuent** *kill* **chevaliers** *knights* **chrétienté** *Christendom* **arrière-garde** *rear guard* **trahi** *betrayed* **embuscade** *ambush* **sonner** *to blow* **cor** *horn* **se battre** *to fight*

Roland avec son épée Durendal

Charlemagne revint avec ses troupes . . . .

La belle Aude

Toute la journée, les Francs, avec Roland et Olivier à leur tête, repoussent les ennemis. Ils multiplient les actes de courage, mais à un contre vingt le combat est inégal. Peu à peu, tous les compagnons de Roland sont massacrés. Roland voit que la bataille est perdue. Avant de mourir, il sonne son «oliphant» pour que Charlemagne vienne venger° ses compagnons. Roland essaie de briser° son épée° **Durendal** contre un rocher. Il frappe° dix fois, mais l'épée ne se brise pas.

Charlemagne revient sur ses pas.° Il détruit l'armée sarrasine, enterre° ses morts et, rempli° de tristesse, rentre dans sa capitale. Là, il donne l'épée de Roland à la fiancée de celui-ci, la belle **Aude**. La jeune fille meurt en apprenant la disparition de son bien-aimé.°

La Chanson de Roland

Au 12e siècle, c'est-à-dire plus de 300 ans après les faits historiques, un moine° anonyme écrit *La Chanson de Roland*. C'est un long poème épique de 4 000 vers qui relate en détail la légende. *La Chanson de Roland* est la première grande oeuvre littéraire écrite en langue française. Elle a un succès immédiat dans tout le monde occidental.° Pour certains historiens, les raisons de ce succès sont politiques. Au 12e siècle, en effet, les chevaliers chrétiens partent en croisade pour délivrer Jérusalem prise par les Turcs. Ils sont inspirés par *La Chanson de Roland* qui représente un épisode de la guerre sainte des Chrétiens contre les Musulmans.

Troubadours

venger *to avenge* **briser** *to break* **épée** *sword* **frappe** *strikes* **pas** *steps* **enterre** *buries* **rempli** *filled* **bien-aimé** *beloved* **moine** *monk* **occidental** *western*

💡 **Teaching Strategy**

Have students note the following:

- **Guillaume** = William
- **Richard Coeur de Lion** = Richard the Lionhearted
- Some English words that are the legacy of William the Conqueror: mutton (**mouton**), veal (**veau**), and beef (**boeuf**).

Quand les rois d'Angleterre étaient français

Guillaume le Conquérant et la conquête de l'Angleterre (1066)

Les ancêtres de **Guillaume le Conquérant** (1028-1087) sont scandinaves. Ce sont ces terribles **«Normands»** (homme du Nord) qui, venus de Norvège° et du Danemark sur leurs **drakkars**, ont attaqué et dévasté l'ouest de la France au 9e siècle. Ils ont pris et brûlé° Orléans, Tours et Paris. Pour avoir la paix,° le roi de France a donné à leur chef le duché de Normandie . . . et la main de sa fille. Les Normands sont devenus de bons et loyaux vassaux° du roi de France.

«Drakkar» scandinave

Guillaume est le fils de Robert Ier, duc de Normandie. Il a seulement huit ans quand son père meurt. Il devient alors lui-même duc de Normandie. Jeune homme, il fait un voyage en Angleterre pour rendre visite à son cousin, le roi **Édouard**. Celui-ci lui promet la couronne d'Angleterre à sa mort. Mais il y a un autre prétendant: **Harold le Saxon**. Un jour, Harold vient en Normandie où il est immédiatement fait prisonnier. Guillaume lui propose un échange: la liberté contre la promesse de renoncer à la couronne° d'Angleterre. Harold accepte l'échange, retourne en Angleterre, et là il oublie sa promesse.

Quand Édouard meurt en 1066, Harold se fait nommer° roi. Guillaume apprend cette trahison.° Furieux, il décide de punir Harold et de conquérir l'Angleterre par la force. Pour cela, il organise une formidable expédition. Le 23 septembre, ses bateaux chargés° de soldats arrivent en Angleterre. Le 14 octobre, il défait l'armée d'Harold à **la bataille de Hastings**. Le jour de Noël, il est couronné à Londres roi d'Angleterre sous le nom de **Guillaume Ier**.

Une conséquence de la conquête est que le français va devenir pendant plusieurs siècles la langue de la cour d'Angleterre.

L'histoire de la conquête de l'Angleterre par Guillaume est représentée graphiquement dans une très belle tapisserie° de 70 mètres de long, la tapisserie de Bayeux. C'est, en quelque sorte, la première «bande dessinée» de l'histoire.

Scène de la tapisserie de Bayeux, la première «bande dessinée»

Norvège *Norway* **brûlé** *burned* **paix** *peace* **vassaux** = sujets **couronne** *crown* **se fait nommer** *has himself named* **trahison** *betrayal* **chargés** *loaded* **tapisserie** tapestry

NOTE CULTURELLE

The tapestry of Bayeux was said to have been stitched by Queen Mathilde, the wife of William the Conqueror. In fact, it was ordered by the Bishop of Bayeux from Saxon embroiderers. The tapestry features 626 characters in 72 different scenes.

This scene of the Battle of Hastings shows the English foot soldiers of King Harold (on the right) forming a wall with their shields to defend themselves against the attack of the mounted knights of William the Conqueror.

Aliénor d'Aquitaine: Reine de France et Reine d'Angleterre

Elle a été reine° de France, puis reine d'Angleterre. C'est aussi la mère de deux rois d'Angleterre.

Fille et héritière° du duc d'Aquitaine, **Aliénor** (1122-1204) est une princesse d'une grande beauté. À l'âge de quinze ans, elle épouse° le roi de France, **Louis VII**, avec qui elle part en croisade contre les Turcs. Après leur retour de Terre Sainte,° Aliénor et Louis ont deux filles, mais le roi, qui veut des fils, fait annuler le mariage.

Quelques semaines plus tard, Aliénor se remarie avec **Henri Plantagenêt**, duc de Normandie, qui devient roi d'Angleterre en 1153. À leur tour, leurs fils, **Richard Coeur de Lion** et **Jean sans Terre** vont aussi être rois d'Angleterre. À cette époque, les rois d'Angleterre possèdent de vastes territoires en France: la Normandie, l'Anjou, l'Aquitaine. Cette situation est une des causes principales de la **Guerre de Cent Ans**.

Aliénor d'Aquitaine est très belle, très intelligente et très cultivée. En France et en Angleterre, elle crée une cour brillante où elle protège les poètes et les artistes. Princesse libérale, elle donne beaucoup de libertés aux habitants des villes qu'elle possède. À la fin° de sa vie, elle se retire en France, dans son abbaye de Fontevrault, où sont enterrés° deux rois d'Angleterre, son mari et son fils, Richard.

À la cour d'Aliénor d'Aquitaine

reine *queen* **héritière** *heiress* **épouse** *marries* **Terre Sainte** *Holy Land* **à la fin** *towards the end* **enterrés** *buried*

Notes historiques

ALIÉNOR D'AQUITAINE ET SA FAMILLE:

- **Louis VII** (1120–1180)
- **Henri II Plantagenêt** (né au Mans 1133, mort à Chinon 1189)
- **Richard Ier Coeur de Lion** (né à Oxford 1157, mort à Châlus 1199)
- **Jean sans Terre** (né à Oxford 1167, mort en Nottinghamshire 1216). En 1215, il a été contraint à accepter la **Grande Charte** (*Magna Carta*). C'est contre le roi Jean que luttait **Robin des Bois** *(Robin Hood)*.

Teaching Strategy: Expansion

Ask students:

- Quel âge avait Aliénor d'Aquitaine quand elle a épousé Henri Plantagenêt?
- Quel âge avait-elle à la naissance de son fils Richard? de son fils Jean?
- À quel âge est-elle morte?

Jeanne d'Arc à Chinon

Le château de Chinon

Un jour, Jeanne a entendu des voix.

Jeanne d'Arc est née en 1412 à Domrémy un petit village de Lorraine. À cette époque la France était occupée par les Anglais. Un jour Jeanne a entendu des voix. Elle a reconnu Sainte Catherine, Sainte Marguerite et Saint Michel Ces voix lui ont dit: «Jeanne, c'est toi qui vas délivrer le pays!»

«Moi? Mais je suis une paysanne° qui sait à peine° lire et écrire,» a répondu Jeanne.

Mais les voix ont insisté: «Jeanne, va chez le roi et dis-lui que c'est Dieu° qui t'envoie.»

Jeanne et le sire de Baudricourt.

Jeanne a accepté la mission, mais maintenant elle est inquiète°. «Aller chez le roi? Oui, mais comment? Le roi habite si loin et les routes sont pleines° de brigands.»°

Jeanne va trouver un seigneur° local, le sire de Baudricourt.

— Messire, donnez-moi une escorte. Je veux aller chez le roi de France.

— Et qui t'envoie?

— Le Roi du Ciel.°

Baudricourt se moque de° Jeanne et la renvoie chez elle. Jeanne revient. Elle insiste et finalement elle obtient une escorte. C'est avec cette escorte de six hommes qu'elle arrive devant le château de Chinon où réside Charles, roi de France, avec sa cour. Immédiatement elle demande d'être présentée au roi.

Jeanne et son escorte arrivent au château de Chinon.

paysanne *peasant girl* **à peine** *hardly* **Dieu** *God* **inquiète** *worried* **pleines** *full* **brigands** = bandits **seigneur** *lord* **Messire** = Monsieur **Roi du Ciel** *King of Heaven* **se moque de** *makes fun of*

NOTES CULTURELLES

- Chinon is a city in Touraine, on the Vienne river. Its fortress, built between the 10th and 15th centuries, still stands, comprised of three castles, including the one where Joan of Arc met the king.
- **La fleur de lys** has been the symbol of the French monarchy since the 8th century. This flower represents holiness and purity.
- Charles VII was crowned in Reims on July 17, 1429.
- Reims became the traditional crowning site for the French kings after King Clovis was baptized there in 496.

Jeanne a reconnu le vrai roi malgré ses humbles apparences.

Le roi Charles est un roi sans royaume.° Il a perdu sa capitale. Paris est occupé par les Anglais, qui ont choisi un autre roi de France, un roi anglais, bien sûr. Charles est un jeune homme timide et sans énergie. Il ne croit plus en la victoire et certainement pas aux miracles. «Qui est cette Jeanne et qu'est-ce qu'elle veut de moi?»

Un courtisan, Bernard de Chissay, suggère au roi de jouer un bon tour° à Jeanne. «Déguisons-nous! Je vais mettre vos vêtements et vous, vous allez vous déguiser en simple courtisan. Nous allons voir si cette petite paysanne va reconnaître le vrai roi.» Bernard de Chissay met les vêtements du roi alors que° Charles met un simple vêtement noir. Jeanne entre dans la grande salle° du château. Il y a plusieurs centaines de dames et de chevaliers. Bernard de Chissay, magnifiquement habillé, reçoit les hommages des courtisans. Charles, le vrai roi, est au fond° de la salle, mais c'est vers lui que Jeanne s'avance.

— Gentil roi de France, le Roi du Ciel m'envoie vers vous.

— Mais ce n'est pas moi, le roi. Le roi est là-bas.

— C'est vous le roi, et pas un autre . . .

Oui, Jeanne a reconnu le vrai roi malgré° ses humbles apparences. Charles est très impressionné. Il décide d'écouter Jeanne. Jeanne et Charles ont une longue conversation secrète. Charles est maintenant convaincu.° Jeanne est l'envoyée° de Dieu.

Jeanne devant la ville d'Orléans.

Charles est couronné roi de France.

Le roi lui donne une armée. Jeanne d'Arc, qui a seulement 17 ans, prend le commandement des troupes royales. Elle part délivrer Orléans, assiégée par les Anglais. Arrivée devant la ville, elle exhorte ses compagnons d'armes: «Entrez hardiment° parmi° les Anglais!» Surpris par le courage de cette jeune fille, les soldats attaquent. Le lendemain, Orléans est délivrée!

La libération de la France vient de commencer. Jeanne d'Arc gagne d'autres batailles. Son grand triomphe a lieu quelques mois après l'entrevue de Chinon quand Charles est solennellement couronné roi de France dans la cathédrale de Reims.

sans royaume *without a kingdom* **tour** *trick* **alors que** *whereas* **salle** *hall* **au fond** *in the back* **malgré** *in spite of* **convaincu** *convinced* **l'envoyée** = la messagère **hardiment** *boldly* **parmi** *among*

Note historique

Jeanne d'Arc assiste au sacre de Charles VII à Reims le 17 juillet 1429, mais peu après, son armée échoue devant Paris. En mai 1430, elle est faite prisonnière. Les Anglais la font juger comme sorcière devant un tribunal ecclésiastique à Rouen. Déclarée hérétique, elle fut brûlée le 30 mai 1431.

Teaching Strategy: Game

Prepare **"Jeopardy"**-style answers for the material in the *Interlude*.

Group students in three teams. The teams compete by supplying questions to the answers previously prepared.

UNITÉ 3

MAIN THEME

Vacation, outdoor activities
The environment

Communication Function/Contexts
- Talking about outdoor activities
- Describing the natural environment and how to protect it
- Talking about weather, natural phenomena
- Relating a seqence of past events
- Describing habitual past actions

Linguistic Goals
- Talking about the past
- Narrating past events
- Reading literacy accounts of past events

Online Study Center

Online Teaching Center

UNITÉ 3

Vive la nature

Thème et Objectifs

Culture
In this unit, you will discover . . .
- why the French people feel close to their roots
- how the French incorporate «tourisme écologique» into their vacation plans
- how the French people feel about their environment
- why Jacques Cousteau is so well known and what important work he did
- what the «culte du soleil» represents for French people

Communication
You will learn how . . .
- to talk about vacation activities
- to tell people who are on vacation that they should take certain precautions and avoid dangers
- to describe weather conditions and natural phenomenon

Langue
You will learn how . . .
- to narrate a sequence of past events
- to describe the setting of these past events
- to read literary accounts of past events

TEACHING RESOURCES

ANCILLARIES
Student Activities Manual, Unit 3
Audio Program, Unit 3
Video-DVD Program, Unit 3
***Chansons* Audio CD**

HM ClassPrep CD
Presentations, Unit 3
Audioscript, Unit 3
Videoscript, Unit 3
Assessment, Unit 3
Answer Key, Unit 3

OUI à la nature!

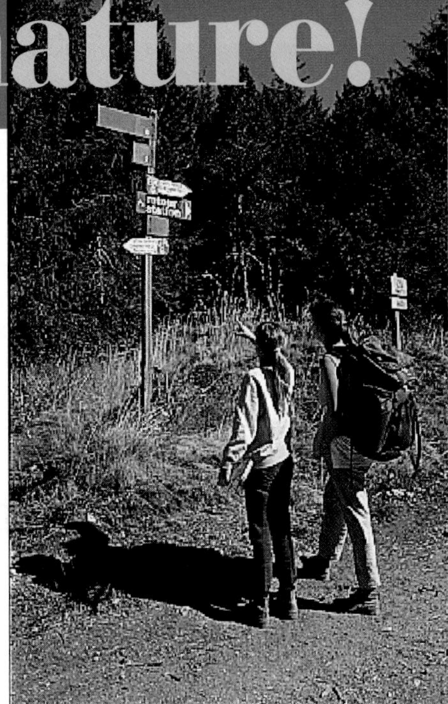

■ Deux adeptes de la randonnée pédestre

Les racines°

Cécile Pécoul, 25 ans, est infirmière. Elle habite et travaille à Paris, mais c'est à la campagne qu'elle se sent vraiment bien. Elle explique: «J'ai besoin d'air pur.° Alors, le week-end, je pars souvent en Normandie* avec mes copains. Parfois je vais faire de l'escalade° dans la forêt de Fontainebleau.** Et en été, je passe les vacances dans la ferme de mes grands-parents en Auvergne.*** C'est là d'où vient ma famille. C'est donc là où je suis vraiment chez moi, parce que c'est là où sont mes racines.»

Aujourd'hui, la majorité des Français habitent dans des grandes villes mais, comme Cécile, ils restent très attachés à leur province d'origine. Ils y retournent à l'occasion des vacances, pour retrouver leurs racines, mais surtout pour établir un contact avec la nature. Cet amour de la terre° et de la nature explique le succès du tourisme «vert» ou du tourisme «écologique».

Notre planète, ça nous concerne

■ L'escalade en montagne

Le tourisme vert

Il y a différentes façons de pratiquer le tourisme écologique. La forme la plus simple est évidemment la marche à pied.° Si on aime celle-ci,° on peut faire de la «randonnée pédestre°» le long° des milliers de kilomètres de sentiers° ruraux. On part le matin, sac au dos.° On marche pendant 35 à 40 kilomètres. On s'arrête le soir dans un gîte° rural où on passe la nuit. En dix jours, on peut ainsi visiter toute une région «de l'intérieur», sans rencontrer beaucoup de gens. Un avantage de la randonnée pédestre est qu'on peut la pratiquer à tout âge. C'est une activité très populaire en France. La Fédération Française de Randonnée Pédestre compte plus de 300.000 membres.

Quand on passe les vacances à la montagne, celle-ci offre une grande variété d'activités qui nous mettent en contact direct avec notre milieu naturel. En plus° de la randonnée pédestre, on peut faire du VTT, du ski sur l'herbe,° de l'escalade, de l'alpinisme° et, si on aime les sensations fortes, du delta-plane et du parapente.°

*Normandie une région à l'ouest de Paris **Fontainebleau une forêt au sud de Paris où il y a des rochers ***Auvergne une province au centre de la France

racines *roots* **pur** *fresh* **l'escalade** *rock climbing* **la terre** *land* **la marche à pied** *walking* **celle-ci** *the latter* **la randonnée pédestre** *hiking* **le long** *along* **sentiers** *trails* **sac au dos** *with a back pack* **un gîte** *simple lodging* **En plus** *In addition* **l'herbe** *grass* **l'alpinisme** *mountain climbing* **parapente** *parasailing*

INFO MAGAZINE

Theme: Outdoor activities; the environment

Reading Strategy: Reading for pleasure; browsing; scanning for information

■ Notes linguistiques

- **35 à 40 km** = 21.7 to 24.8 miles
- **VTT** = **Vélo Tout Terrain** (mountain bike)
- **la Terre** = Earth, soil, land
- **pratiquer** is a false cognate. **pratiquer un sport** = to play a sport; **s'entraîner, s'exercer** = to practice

Notes culturelles

- **L'Auvergne** is a region of extinct volcanoes located in the **Massif Central**. It is renowned for its many spas and springs, such as **Vichy** and **Volvic.**
- The role of the **Ministère de l'Environnement** is to control and prevent all pollution, protect water resources, and do research.

Teaching Strategy

Divide the class into groups and assign each group to prepare a definition of the key words in the *Et vous?* activity:

Définitions

- Nos **racines,** c'est là d'où vient notre famille.
- On fait du **tourisme écologique** quand on passe ses vacances en contact avec la nature, par exemple en faisant de la randonnée pédestre.
- La **randonnée pédestre,** c'est quand on marche sur des sentiers spéciaux à la campagne.
- On peut explorer toute une région en marchant sur ces sentiers spéciaux, qui s'appellent des **sentiers ruraux.**
- Un **gîte rural** est une sorte d'auberge très simple, sans luxe, qu'on trouve à la campagne et où on peut passer la nuit quand on fait une randonnée pédestre.
- Un **parc national** est une réserve naturelle pour protéger les plantes et les animaux. On ne peut pas y camper, et il ne faut pas toucher les plantes et les animaux.
- On appelle la **faune** les animaux qui vivent dans un endroit naturel.
- Dans un **éco-musée,** on peut voir comment on vivait à la campagne autrefois.

La protection de la nature

Quand on aime la nature, il faut la protéger. À cet effet, le gouvernement français a créé des réserves naturelles et de grands parcs nationaux. Ces parcs sont situés principalement dans les zones de montagne (Alpes, Pyrénées, Massif Central). Là, tout est fait pour préserver la faune° et la flore° typiques de la région, et en particulier les espèces en danger. Il est interdit de camper, de faire du feu,° de toucher à la végétation et de déranger° les animaux.

Évidemment, la protection de la nature n'est pas seulement l'affaire° du gouvernement. C'est l'affaire de tout le monde. Pour 80% des Français, l'environnement est «un problème immédiat et urgent.» Cette préoccupation explique sans doute le succès des partis° écologiques. Aux élections, les «écolos» ou les «verts» obtiennent généralement 10% ou 12% des voix. Ce n'est pas beaucoup, mais c'est assez pour avoir une action politique efficace. Cette action se porte° sur beaucoup de domaines: protection de l'environnement, lutte° contre la pollution, limitation et contrôle de l'énergie nucléaire, aide et subventions° pour le développement de l'énergie solaire. Si on veut préserver la qualité de la vie de demain, c'est aujourd'hui qu'il faut agir!°

Les éco-musées

Une autre forme de tourisme écologique consiste à visiter les «éco-musées». Le but de ces musées est de préserver la vie rurale d'autrefois quand la majorité des Français habitaient à la campagne. Ces musées sont souvent des reconstructions de fermes et de villages anciens où l'on peut voir les outils,° les instruments, les ustensiles qu'on utilisait à l'époque.

et vous?

DÉFINITIONS

Définissez en français les mots et expressions suivantes:

- les racines
- le tourisme écologique
- la randonnée pédestre
- un sentier rural
- un gîte rural
- un parc national
- la faune
- un éco-musée

EXPRESSION ORALE

- À votre avis, est-ce que les Américains ont «l'amour de la terre»? Expliquez.
- Avez-vous jamais fait du camping ou de la randonnée pédestre? Décrivez cette expérience.
- Avec votre partenaire, discutez des différentes façons de protéger l'environnement. Préparez un rapport.

EXPRESSION ÉCRITE

Dans une lettre à un(e) ami(e) français(e), vous expliquez comment on peut faire du «tourisme écologique» dans la région ou l'état où vous habitez.

la faune *wildlife* **la flore** *plant life* **feu** *fire* **déranger** *bother* **l'affaire** *business* **des partis** = partis politiques **se porte** = concerne **lutte** *fight* **subventions** *subsidies* **agir** *to act* **outils** *tools*

NOTES CULTURELLES

- **Le Jour de la Terre** (Earth Day) has been celebrated in France since 1990.
- **Les Verts** and **Génération Écologie** are two French political parties with a platform based entirely on the protection of the environment.

Ask students if they are familiar with any local, national, or international organizations for the protection of the environment.

Les sept commandements du campeur

Chaque année, des millions de Français font du camping. Si vous venez un jour en France, vous aurez peut-être l'occasion d'en faire aussi. Voici quelques consignes° à observer.

1. Respectez les règlements.°

En France le camping est en principe libre° sur le territoire public . . . sauf° là où il est interdit. Le camping est interdit sur les plages de mer, dans les réserves naturelles, près des points d'eau utilisés pour la consommation, près des monuments historiques. Et si vous campez sur un terrain privé, n'oubliez pas de demander l'autorisation au propriétaire.°

2. Faites attention au feu.

L'incendie est la plus grande menace qui existe pour la forêt. Chaque année, des milliers d'hectares de forêts sont détruits° par des incendies° causés par des campeurs imprudents.°

3. Préservez l'environnement.

La nature est fragile et a besoin de notre protection. Alors, préservez la végétation au lieu de° la détruire. Ne cassez° pas les branches des arbres. N'arrachez° pas les plantes. Ne cueillez° pas les fleurs, qui ne sont pas pour vous seulement, mais pour tout le monde.

4. Ne dérangez pas les animaux.

Les animaux sont chez eux et vous, vous êtes sur leur territoire. Ce sont vos hôtes. Agissez° avec eux en invité° respectueux, et non pas en barbare.

5. Ne contaminez pas l'eau.

L'eau est une ressource précieuse non seulement pour les humains, mais aussi pour tous les habitants de la nature. Pensez aux animaux qui viennent boire tous les jours dans les rivières et les lacs.

6. Ne laissez pas de déchets.°

Emportez° vos déchets avec vous. Déposez-les dans les réceptacles spéciaux que vous trouverez sur les routes. Surtout, ne laissez pas d'objets en plastique. Le plastique n'est pas biodégradable et il peut provoquer la mort° des animaux qui le mangent.

7. Ne faites pas de bruit.

Si vous avez décidé de faire du camping, c'est pour profiter du calme de la nature et non pas pour écouter de la musique. Alors, laissez votre radio chez vous et n'oubliez pas que le bruit est une forme de pollution.

D'après vous, quels sont les trois commandements les plus importants? Expliquez pourquoi.

consignes *rules* **règlements** *rules* **libre** = autorisé **sauf** = excepté **propriétaire** *owner* **détruire** ❊ *to destroy* **incendies** *fires* **imprudents** = qui ne font pas attention **au lieu de** *instead of* **casser** *to break* **arracher** *pull up* **cueillir** *to pick* **agir** *to act* **invité** *guest* **déchets** *trash* **emporter** *to take along* **la mort** *death*

Supplementary vocabulary

la caravane *trailer*
le feu de camp *campfire*
le matelas pneumatique *air mattress*
le réchaud *(portable) stove*
le sac de couchage *sleeping bag*
la tente *tent*
le terrain de camping *campground*

Realia Note

La Camargue is a region in the south of France, not far from Marseille, famous for its swamps and ponds and herds of horses and bulls. The town of **Saintes-Maries-de-la-Mer** is host to a large gypsy pilgrimage in May. Part of the region is a natural park.

■ Irregular Verb

(see Appendix C)
détruire *(see* **conduire***)*

LE FRANÇAIS
PRATIQUE

TEACHING RESOURCES

Student Activities Manual, pp. 121–122

Audio Program, CD 3, Tracks 1–4

HM ClassPrep CD, Audioscript, Unit 3

PARTIE 1

LE FRANÇAIS PRATIQUE

Les vacances: Plaisirs et problèmes

Quand on est en vacances, on peut faire beaucoup de choses.
Mais il faut aussi **éviter** certains dangers et faire attention!

éviter *to avoid*

Au bord de la mer, on peut . . .

- **nager**
- **se baigner**
- **bronzer**
- **prendre un bain de soleil** *(sunbath)*
- **faire une promenade en bateau** *(boat)*
- **faire de la planche à voile**
- **faire de la plongée sous-marine** *(scuba diving)*

Mais attention! Il ne faut pas . . .

- **se noyer**
- **attraper un coup de soleil** *(sunburn)*
- **avoir le mal de mer**
- **tomber dans l'eau**
- **perdre l'équilibre**

se baigner *to go swimming*
se noyer *to drown*
bronzer *to get tan*
attraper *to catch, get*
avoir le mal de mer *to be seasick*
perdre l'équilibre *to lose one's balance*

À la campagne, on peut . . .

- **se promener**
- **faire un tour** *(walk)*
  - **dans les champs** *(fields)*
  - **dans la forêt**
  - **dans les bois** *(woods)*
- **faire un pique-nique sur l'herbe**
- **faire du camping**
- **observer les animaux**

Mais attention! Il ne faut pas . . .

- **se perdre**
- **être piqué par des moustiques** *(mosquitos)*
- **mettre le feu**
- **marcher sur un serpent**

se perdre *to get lost*

piquer *to sting*
mettre le feu *to set a fire*
marcher sur *to step on*

À la montagne, on peut . . .

- **faire de l'escalade** *(rock climbing)*
- **faire de l'alpinisme** *(mountain climbing)*
- **aller à la pêche** *(fishing)*

Mais attention! Il ne faut pas . . .

- **glisser**
- **tomber**
- **se blesser**
- **se casser la jambe**

glisser *to slip*
se faire mal *to get hurt*
se blesser *to injure oneself*
se casser *to break (a leg)*

Et dans tous les cas, il faut . . .

- **respecter** | **protéger** — **la nature** | **l'environnement**

Il ne faut pas . . .

- **polluer**
- **laisser** | **jeter** — **des déchets** *(refuse)* | **des vieux papiers**
- **détruire la végétation**
- **casser les branches des arbres**
- **faire peur aux animaux**

polluer *to pollute*
protéger *to protect*
laisser *to leave*
jeter *to throw*
détruire* *to destroy*
casser *to break*
faire peur à *to scare*

Les formes des verbes: jeter, détruire
Révision et Expansion ▶ pp. R20-23

1 Et vous?

Complétez les phrases en exprimant votre opinion personnelle.
Comparez vos réponses avec celles de votre partenaire.

1. Je préfère passer les vacances . . .
   - à la mer
   - à la montagne
   - à la campagne
   - ??
2. Quand je suis à la plage, je préfère . . .
   - me baigner
   - prendre des bains de soleil
   - faire de la planche à voile
   - ??
3. Pour me protéger contre les coups de soleil . . .
   - je porte un chapeau
   - je garde *(keep on)* mon tee-shirt
   - je mets de la crème solaire
   - ??
4. Quand je vais à la campagne, je préfère . . .
   - me promener dans les champs
   - faire un tour dans les bois
   - faire de l'escalade
   - ??
5. Quand on se perd à la campagne, l'objet le plus utile est . . .
   - une boussole *(compass)*
   - une carte de la région
   - une lampe de poche
   - ??
6. Ce que je déteste le plus est de (d') . . .
   - attraper un coup de soleil
   - être piqué(e) par les moustiques
   - me baigner dans l'eau froide
   - ??
7. Quand on fait un tour dans une forêt, la chose la plus stupide est de . . .
   - laisser des vieux papiers
   - casser les branches des arbres
   - faire peur aux animaux
   - ??
8. Quand on fait du camping, la chose la plus stupide est de . . .
   - détruire la végétation
   - jeter des déchets
   - mettre le feu à la forêt
   - ??

Conversations libres

Avec votre partenaire, choisissez l'une des situations suivantes. Composez le dialogue correspondant et jouez-le en classe.

1 Deux week-ends différents

Samedi dernier, Catherine est allée à la campagne où elle a passé une journée très agréable. Son cousin Guillaume est allé à la plage où il a passé une très mauvaise journée. Catherine et Guillaume se téléphonent pour décrire leur week-end respectif.

Rôles: Catherine, Guillaume

2 Escalade

[Ca]role, une jeune fille très sportive, adore faire [de] l'escalade. Elle veut enseigner *(to teach)* ce [sp]ort à son copain Bertrand. Bertrand, qui [n'e]st pas très courageux, refuse absolument, [ex]pliquant les dangers de ce sport.

[Rô]les: Carole, Bertrand

3 Camping dans la forêt

Florence est monitrice dans une colonie de vacances. Elle organise un week-end de camping dans la forêt. Maintenant elle explique aux jeunes ce qu'ils doivent faire et ce qu'ils ne doivent pas faire. Ils veulent savoir pourquoi. Florence répond.

Rôles: Florence, une campeuse

Notes linguistiques

- The term **plongée sous-marine** is used both for scuba diving and snorkeling, although technically, **faire de la plongée sous-marine autonome** = scuba diving.
- **un homme-grenouille** = scuba diver *(frogman)*
- **le tuba** = snorkel
  le masque = mask
  les palmes *(f.)* = flippers
- **l'alpinisme** comes from the adjective **alpin**, meaning "from the Alps." Another related word is: **un(e) alpiniste** (mountain climber).
- **escalader** = to climb (rocks, mountains). **Les alpinistes escaladent l'Everest.**

Supplementary vocabulary

Il ne faut pas marcher dans ...
- **les orties** *nettles*
- **l'herbe à puce** *poison ivy (Canadian expression)*

On peut être piqué par...
- **un insecte**
- **une abeille** *bee*
- **une guêpe** *wasp*
- **une fourmi** *ant*

Quelques animaux qu'on peut voir à la campagne:
- **un cerf** /sɛr/ *stag*
- **un chevreuil** *deer*
- **un corbeau** *crow*
- **un coyote** /kɔjɔt/ *coyote*
- **un écureuil** *squirrel*
- **un élan** *elk*
- **un lapin** *rabbit*
- **un loup** *wolf*
- **un ours** /urs/ *bear*
- **un raton laveur** *raccoon*
- **un renard** *fox*
- **une grenouille** *frog*
- **une loutre** *otter*
- **une marmotte** *groundhog, woodchuck*
- **une tortue** *turtle*

À la montagne, il ne faut pas ...
- **déraper** *to slip, slide down*

LANGUE ET COMMUNICATION

TEACHING RESOURCES

Student Activities Manual, pp. 35–36, 123

Audio Program, CD 3, Tracks 5–7

HM ClassPrep CD, Audioscript, Unit 3

Révision

Optional, for reference and quick review.

Notes linguistiques

- Also: **jamais** *(ever)*
  Est-ce que tu as **jamais** visité Paris?
- Other adverbs usually come after the past participle, but may come before, depending on emphasis or the rhythm of the sentence.
  Il a couru **rapidement**.
  Il a **rapidement** compris la question.

Allons plus loin

The same distinction exists with **rentrer** *(to go home, to take in)* and **retourner** *(to return, to turn over)*.

Pierrre **est rentré** chez lui.
Il **a rentré** son vélo au garage.
Corinne **est retournée** au salon. Elle **a retourné** le tapis.

LANGUE ET COMMUNICATION

Les participes passés irrég... verbes conjugués avec ê...

Révision ▶ pp. R4
(participes passés) p. R4 pp. R2...
(verbes / être) p. R4

A. Révision: Le passé composé

The PASSÉ COMPOSÉ is used to describe what people DID, what HAPPENED.

Je **suis allé** au cinéma. **J'ai vu** une comédie. Après, je **me suis promené.**

Review the forms of the passé composé:

voyager	aller	s'amuser
j'**ai voyagé** tu **as voyagé** il/elle/on **a voyagé** nous **avons voyagé** vous **avez voyagé** ils/elles **ont voyagé**	je **suis allé(e)** tu **es allé(e)** il/elle/on **est allé(e)** nous **sommes allé(e)s** vous **êtes allé(e)(s)** ils/elles **sont allé(e)s**	je me **suis amusé(e)** tu t'**es amusé(e)** il/elle/on s'**est amusé(e)** nous nous **sommes amusé(e)s** vous vous **êtes amusé(e)(s)** ils/elles se **sont amusé(e)s**
je n'**ai** pas **voyagé**	je ne **suis** pas **allé(e)**	je ne me **suis** pas **amusé(e)**
est-ce que tu **as voyagé?** **as**-tu voyagé?	est-ce que tu **es allé(e)?** **es**-tu **allé(e)?**	est-ce que tu t'**es amusé(e)?** t'**es**-tu **amusé(e)?**

➡ Review the following expressions:

déjà	*ever*	Est-ce que tu as **déjà** visité Paris?
ne . . . jamais	*never*	Non, je **n'ai jamais** visité Paris.
déjà	*yet, already*	Est-ce que vous avez **déjà** vu ce film?
ne . . . pas encore	*not yet*	Non, je **n'ai pas encore** vu ce film.

➡ Note the position of the following ADVERBS in the passé composé.

AFTER the past participle: Je me suis levé **tôt.**	**tôt** *(early)*, **tard** *(late)* Éric s'est couché **tard**.
BEFORE the past participle: Sophie a **beaucoup** aimé ce film.	**bien, mal, souvent, beaucoup, trop, assez** Nous nous sommes **bien** amusés.

1 Oui ou non?

Il y a beaucoup de choses qu'on peut faire en vacances. Demandez à votre partenaire s'il (si elle) a fait une des choses suivantes. En cas de réponse affirmative, demandez des précisions: où? quand? à quelle occasion? avec qui?

▶ faire du ski nautique?

— **Est-ce que tu as déjà fait du ski nautique?**
— **Oui, j'ai déjà fait du ski nautique.**
— **Ah bon? Où ça?**
— **Dans le Michigan.**
(Non, je n'ai jamais fait de ski nautique.)

- visiter la Floride?
- aller en Suisse?
- faire de l'alpinisme?
- voir un ours *(bear)*?
- monter dans un hélicoptère?
- descendre dans un sous-marin *(submarine)*?
- faire une promenade à cheval?
- se promener à dos de chameau *(camel)*?
- faire de la plongée sous-marine?
- avoir le mal de mer?
- attraper un coup de soleil?
- se perdre dans une forêt?
- se casser la jambe?

Teaching Strategy: Dialog Development

Divide students into pairs and have them write a twenty-line dialog in which the students compare notes concerning their ideal winter vacation. They should be sure to use as much vocabulary from p. 112 as possible, using the **passé composé.**

2 Créa-dialogue: Pas de chance!

Avec votre partenaire, composez un dialogue où vous décrivez un problème.

— Où es-tu allé(e) ce week-end?	*Choose another time.*
— Je suis allé(e) à la montagne avec ma cousine.	*Choose another place: beach, city . . . Choose another person.*
— Ah bon? Qu'est-ce que vous avez fait?	
— Nous avons fait de l'alpinisme.	*Choose an appropriate activity.*
— Vous vous êtes amusé(e)s?	
— Oui, mais il y a eu un problème.	
— Ah bon? Quoi?	
— Ma cousine a glissé et elle s'est cassé le bras.	*Describe another problem corresponding to the situation.*
— C'est vraiment pas de chance!	

3 Une lettre de Paris

Amélie, une jeune Canadienne, vient d'arriver à Paris avec son frère Pascal. Elle écrit une lettre à son amie Gabrielle. Complétez la lettre d'Amélie avec le passé composé des verbes entre parenthèses.

> Ma chère Gabrielle,
>
> Eh bien, voilà! Je suis à Paris depuis deux jours avec mon frère Pascal. Nous ________ (arriver) avant-hier mais nous ________ (déjà faire) beaucoup de choses.
>
> Hier matin, nous ________ (se lever tôt) et nous ________ (se promener) dans le quartier Latin. Nous ________ (prendre) le petit déjeuner dans un café où nous ________ (rencontrer) un groupe de jeunes Français. Pascal, qui ne perd pas de temps, ________ (donner) rendez-vous à une jeune fille très sympathique.
>
> Après, nous ________ (s'arrêter) dans une boutique où j' ________ (acheter) des cartes postales. À midi, nous ________ (déjeuner) dans un restaurant algérien. J'________(manger) un couscous et j' ________ (boire) du thé à la menthe. C'était délicieux!
>
> L'après-midi, nous________ (faire) une promenade en bateau sur la Seine et ensuite nous ________(monter) à la Tour Eiffel. Du sommet on a une vue splendide sur Paris. Évidemment, j'________ (prendre) beaucoup de photos. Quand nous ________ (descendre), Pascal ________ (vouloir) téléphoner à sa nouvelle amie. Il ________ (chercher) son portefeuille, mais il ________ (ne pas le trouver). Alors, il ________ (remonter) au sommet et heureusement il ________ (trouver) son portefeuille!
>
> Le soir, Pascal ________ (sortir) avec la jeune fille. Moi, je________ (ne pas sortir) avec eux. Je ________ (rester) à l'hôtel et j'________ (écrire) des lettres. À onze heures, je ________ (se coucher) et j'________(dormir). Ce matin, je ________ (se réveiller) à huit heures. Pascal, qui ________(rentrer) très tard hier soir, dort encore!
>
> Je t'embrasse, *Amélie*

4 Et vous?

Écrivez une lettre où vous décrivez une journée que vous avez passée dans une grande ville au cours *(during)* d'un voyage (réel ou imaginaire).

■Réponses: Activité 3

...nous *sommes arrivés*
...nous *avons déjà fait*
...nous *nous sommes levés tôt*
...nous *nous sommes promenés*
...Nous *avons pris*
...nous *avons rencontré*
...Pascal...*a donné*
...nous *sommes arrêtés*
...*j'ai acheté* des cartes
...nous *avons déjeuné*
...*J'ai mangé*
...*j'ai bu*
...nous *avons fait*
...nous *sommes montés*
...*j'ai pris*
...nous *sommes descendus*
...Pascal *a voulu* téléphoner
...Il *a cherché*
...il *ne l'a pas trouvé*
...il *est remonté*
...il *a trouvé*
...Pascal *est sorti*
...je *ne suis pas sortie*
...Je *suis restée*
...*j'ai écrit*
...je *me suis couchée* et *j'ai dormi.*
...je *me suis réveillée*
...qui *est rentré*

Notes culturelles

- **Le couscous** is a North African specialty made of semolina grain served with vegetables and meat (lamb or chicken) in a spicy sauce.
- You can tour the Seine River in Paris on a **bateau-mouche,** a sight-seeing boat.

TEACHING RESOURCES

Student Activities Manual, p. 37

Révision

1. You may have students review other imperfect stems in the verb appendix.
2. You may point out the imperfect forms of verbs ending in **-ger, -cer**:
   manger: nous mangeons
   je mangeais,
   tu mangeais,
   il mangeait,
   ils mangeaient
   BUT: **nous mangions,**
   vous mangiez
   commencer:
   nous commençons
   je commençais
   tu commençais
   il commençait
   ils commençaient
   BUT: **nous commencions**
   vous commenciez
3. In Act. 6, make sure your students repeat the subject before each verb.

▶ **Après, je me lavais et je prenais mon petit déjeuner.**

Vocabulary Expansion

Also:
pleuvoir → **il pleuvait**
falloir → **il fallait**

B. Révision: L'imparfait

The IMPERFECT is used to describe:

- what people USED TO DO, what USED TO BE
  Quand j'**étais** petit, — *When I **was** little,*
  je **jouais** au Monopoly. — ***I used to play** Monopoly.*
- what people WERE DOING, what WAS GOING ON, what WAS HAPPENING
  Hier soir, je **n'étais pas** chez moi. — *Last night I **was not** home.*
  Je **dînais** avec un copain. — ***I was having** dinner with a friend.*

IMPERFECT STEMS	
visiter	je **visitais**
finir	je **finissais**
vendre	je **vendais**
avoir	j'**avais**
faire	je **faisais**
aller	j'**allais**
être	j'**étais**
venir	je **venais**
sortir	je **sortais**
mettre	je **mettais**
vivre	je **vivais**
savoir	je **savais**
recevoir	je **recevais**
prendre	je **prenais**
boire	je **buvais**
lire	je **lisais**
dire	je **disais**
écrire	j'**écrivais**
voir	je **voyais**
connaître	je **connais**[illegible]

Review the formation of the imperfect.

dîner nous **dînons**	**faire** nous **faisons**	**se promener** nous **nous promenons**	ENDINGS
je **dînais**	je **faisais**	je **me promenais**	**-ais**
tu **dînais**	tu **faisais**	tu **te promenais**	**-ais**
il/elle/on **dînait**	il/elle/on **faisait**	il/elle/on **se promenait**	**-ait**
nous **dînions**	nous **faisions**	nous **nous promenions**	**-ions**
vous **dîniez**	vous **faisiez**	vous **vous promeniez**	**-iez**
ils/elles **dînaient**	ils/elles **faisaient**	ils/elles **se promenaient**	**-aient**

➡ The imperfect stem is formed as follows:

nous-form of the present minus **-ons**

➡ **Être** is the only verb with an irregular imperfect stem: **ét-** → **j'étais** **nous étions**

5 En 1900

Imaginez la vie en 1900. Dites ce qu'on faisait et ce qu'on ne faisait pas.

▶ on / utiliser des ordinateurs? **On n'utilisait pas d'ordinateurs.**

1. tout le monde / avoir des voitures?
2. les gens / voyager en train?
3. on / travailler beaucoup?
4. les gens / respecter l'environnement?
5. on / consommer beaucoup d'essence (*gas*)?
6. beaucoup de gens / habiter à la campagne?
7. les jeunes/ faire de la planche à voile?
8. on / être plus heureux qu'aujourd'hui?

6 En colonie de vacances

Marc est allé en colonie de vacances cet été. Il décrit ce qu'il faisait.

▶ En général, nous (se lever à 6 heures et demie) **En général, nous nous levions à 6 heures et demi**[illegible]

1. Après, je (me laver et prendre mon petit déjeuner)
2. Le matin, on (aller à la plage et se baigner)
3. De temps en temps, mes copains (faire une promenade en bateau)
4. D'habitude, on (déjeuner à midi et après faire la sieste)
5. Après la sieste, nous (nous promener dans les bois et observer les animaux)
6. Parfois, on (faire une promenade dans la montagne et faire de l'escalade)
7. Le week-end, nous (prendre nos tentes et faire du camping)
8. D'habitude, tout le monde (se coucher à 10 heures et dormir très bien)

Si vous avez été en colonie de vacances, racontez votre propre expérience en décrivant votre routine quotidienne.

Teaching Strategy: Warm-Up

Have each student give two sentences that describe themselves and/or their families and what they do in the *present tense.* Then, ask them to tell you how this person was or what they used to do 10 years ago.
(e.g. **Aujourd'hui ma mère est blonde et elle a 40 ans.**
Il y a 10 ans, ma mère était brune et elle avait 30 ans.)
This drill should be done quickly so that the idea of the imperfect as the tense of description in the past is confirmed.

7 Souvenirs d'enfance

Posez des questions à votre partenaire sur son enfance. Il/elle va vous poser les mêmes questions.

▶ où / habiter?

— Où est-ce que tu habitais?
— J'habitais à Charleston. Et toi?
— Moi, j'habitais à Savannah.

1. à quelle école / aller?
2. comment / aller à l'école?
3. à quelle heure / se lever?
4. à quelle heure / se coucher?
5. à quels jeux *(games)* / jouer?
6. quels sports / faire?
7. quelles émissions / regarder?
8. qui / être ton acteur favori?
9. qui / être ta chanteuse favorite?
10. quels objets / collectionner?
11. où / passer les vacances?
12. quel animal domestique / avoir?

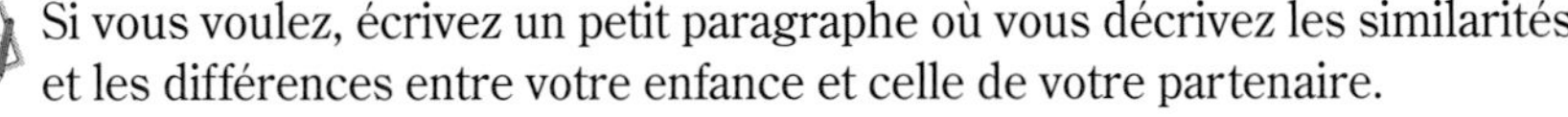

Si vous voulez, écrivez un petit paragraphe où vous décrivez les similarités et les différences entre votre enfance et celle de votre partenaire.

8 Pourquoi personne n'a répondu . . . ?

Hier après-midi vers deux heures, Pierre a voulu téléphoner à ses copains. Personne n'a répondu. Expliquez pourquoi en disant où chacun était et ce qu'il faisait. Soyez logique!

Qui?	Où?	Quoi?
moi	à la plage	déjeuner
toi	à la piscine	lire un livre
nous	à la campagne	jouer au basket
vous	au restaurant	tondre la pelouse
Béatrice	dans le jardin	faire des achats
Jean-Paul	en ville	faire un pique-nique
Philippe et Claire	au club de sport	faire de la plongée sous-marine
Marc et Alice	à la bibliothèque	prendre un bain de soleil
Jérôme et Stéphanie	dans les bois	se baigner
		se promener

▶ **Moi, j'étais à la plage. Je me baignais.**

9 Tout change!

Tout change avec le temps. Avec votre partenaire comparez les photos et décrivez les différences entre aujourd'hui et autrefois.

Maintenant, Monsieur Lescroc est riche. Il est assez gros et . . .

Maintenant, Valérie . . .

Maintenant Madame Leblanc . . .

Autrefois, il était jeune. Il était grand et mince . . .

Autrefois, elle . . .

Autrefois, . . .

Teaching Strategy: Expansion

Ask students to respond to the following, either orally or in written form:

Et vous? Dites ce que vous faites et comment vous êtes maintenant. Puis, dites ce que vous faisiez et comment vous étiez autrefois.

Teaching Strategy: Writing Practice

Have the class write a group story. Each student will contribute at least one sentence. Give them an amusing subject that lends itself to creativity and to action sentences for **passé composé** practice.
(e.g. Describe Julia Roberts as a little girl and tell about a vacation that she took at the beach when she was 15 years old. Remind the students that this should be fictitious. It is not necessary for them to have facts.)

Students can take turns copying the story onto the board as it is being developed.

TEACHING RESOURCES

Student Activities Manual, p. 38

■ Note linguistique

Note that English does not always make the same distinctions that French does.

Pierre **avait peur**.
*Pierre **was scared**.*

Pierre **a eu peur** quand il a vu le fantôme.
*Pierre **was (got) scared** when he saw the ghost.*

C. L'usage du passé composé et de l'imparfait

In talking about the past, the French use the IMPERFECT and the PASSÉ COMPOSÉ. The choice of tenses reflects the type of action or events that are being described.

IMPERFECT	PASSÉ COMPOSÉ
• HABITUAL OR REPEATED ACTIONS *(what people **used to do**)*	• SPECIFIC ACTIONS *(what people **did**)*
Le samedi soir, nous **allions** au ciné.	Samedi dernier, je **suis allé** à un concert.
D'habitude, on **faisait** de la planche à voile.	Un jour, on **a fait** de la plongée sous-marine.
• PROGRESSIVE ACTIONS *(what **was going on**)*	
Je **me promenais** sur la plage.	J'**ai rencontré** un copain.
Nous **faisions** du camping.	Nous **avons vu** un ours *(bear)*.

➡ Depending on how the speaker interprets the action, the passé composé or the imperfect may be used.

Hier à 9 heures, nous **dînions**.	*Yesterday at nine we **were eating dinner**.*
Hier nous **avons dîné** à 9 heures.	*Yesterday we **ate dinner** at nine.*
Tous les jours, j'**allais** à la plage.	*Every day I **used to go** to the beach.*
Tous les jours, je **suis allée** à la plage.	*Every day I **went** to the beach.*

10 Une explosion

Tout le monde parle de l'explosion qui a eu lieu hier soir dans le quartier Saint-Victor. Dites ce que chaque personne faisait au moment de l'explosion et ce qu'elle a fait immédiatement après.

▶ Monsieur Duval (travailler dans le jardin / rentrer chez lui)
Monsieur Duval travaillait dans le jardin. Il est rentré chez lui.

1. nous (dîner / regarder par la fenêtre)
2. vous (faire la vaisselle / téléphoner à la police)
3. moi (me promener / aller sur la scène de l'incident)
4. toi (rentrer chez toi / prendre des photos)
5. mes parents (regarder la télé / sortir sur le balcon)
6. mon grand-père (dormir / se réveiller)

11 Allô!

Téléphonez à votre partenaire pour lui demander ce qu'il/elle faisait à certains moments. Il/elle va répondre avec les réponses suggérées ou des réponses de son choix.

▶ **— Où étais-tu hier soir?**
— J'étais chez moi.
— Qu'est-ce que tu faisais?
— J'étudiais.
— Et après, qu'est-ce que tu as fait?
— J'ai regardé un film à la télé.

1. • ce matin • dans le jardin • tondre la pelouse • se promener
2. • cet après-midi • à la plage • bronzer • se baigner
3. • après le pique-nique • dans la forêt • observer les animaux • prendre des photos
4. • avant le dîner • chez un copain • regarder ses photos • rentrer chez moi

Teaching Strategy: Extra Practice

Find or prepare a story that uses verbs in both the **passé composé** and in the **imparfait**. Tell this story to the class orally *twice*. As you tell the story the second time, write one key word per sentence on the board as a means for students to remember the sentence. Once you have repeated the story twice and written the words on the board, ask the students to tell you the story as you told it.

For written practice, have students write the sentence on the board next to the appropriate key word.

12 L'été dernier

Décrivez ce que les personnes ont fait ou faisaient l'été dernier. Utilisez le passé composé ou l'imparfait.

1. tous les jours / nous / aller à la plage
2. un jour où il faisait très chaud / Julien / attraper un coup de soleil
3. le samedi / mes copains / faire une promenade en bateau
4. pendant la promenade / Pierre / tomber dans l'eau
5. le 14 juillet / Catherine et Pauline / assister aux feux d'artifice *(fireworks)*
6. le week-end / vous / faire du camping
7. pendant la nuit / toi / être piqué par un moustique
8. nous / rentrer chez nous / à la fin de juillet

13 Souvenir de vacances

Monsieur Mercier raconte un souvenir de vacances. Complétez son histoire en mettant les verbes au passé. Utilisez l'imparfait ou le passé composé.

Quand j'__________ (être) étudiant, je __________ (passer) mes vacances à Annecy. En général, je __________ (ne pas me lever) avant dix heures du matin. L'après-midi, je/j' __________ (aller) à la piscine où je __________ (prendre) des bains de soleil. Parfois, je/j' __________ (faire) de la planche à voile sur le lac. Le soir, je__________ (sortir) avec mes copains et je __________ (rentrer) tard chez moi.

Un jour, un copain m' __________ (inviter) à faire de l'escalade avec lui. Le lendemain, je __________ (me lever) tôt et je __________ (partir) avec mon copain. Malheureusement, pendant l'escalade, je/j' __________ (glisser) et je __________ (me casser) la jambe. À l'hôpital où je/j' __________ (aller), je/j' __________ (rencontrer) une jeune infirmière très sympathique. Un jour, je lui __________ (demander) si elle voulait se marier avec moi. Elle __________ (accepter) et aujourd'hui, c'est ma femme!

■ **Réponses: Activité 13**

...j'étais /...je passais /...je ne me levais pas /...j'allais / ...je prenais /...je faisais / ...je sortais /...je rentrais / ...m'a invité /...je me suis levé / ...je suis parti /...j'ai glissé / ...je me suis cassé /...je suis allé, j'ai rencontré /...je lui ai demandé /...Elle a accepté

Note culturelle

The city of Annecy is located on the Swiss border in the French Alps. The **lac d'Annecy** is a popular tourist attraction.

14 Photos de vacances

Pendant vos vacances en France, vous avez pris des photos de vos amis français.

Pour chaque photo, dites:

- où vous étiez
- ce que chaque personne faisait au moment de l'incident
- ce que ces personnes ont fait après

Utilisez votre imagination.

Pierre et Caroline | **Juliette et Jérôme** | **Christine et Jean-Pierre**

Teaching Strategy

Give a list of verbs that can be used to describe habitual or progressive actions, and have students place them in the **imparfait.** Give a list of verbs that could be used to describe specific actions, and have students put them in the **passé composé.** Ask them to then order the sentences to create a logical sequence.

INFO MAGAZINE

Theme: Ecology

Teaching Strategy

- Begin by asking students to look at the photographs, then ask them to remember what they know about Jacques-Yves Cousteau. Then have them skim the article and summarize.
- Next, have students compose short descriptive paragraphs or oral presentations on Cousteau's work.
- You may wish to mention that Jacques-Yves Cousteau passed away on June 25, 1997. He was born June 11, 1910.

■ Additional Information

For more information on **l'Académie française**, see p. 56.

■ Irregular Verbs

entreprendre (*see* **prendre**)
élire (*see* **lire**)

JACQUES-YVES COUSTEAU champion de l'écologie marine

Jacques-Yves Cousteau (1910-1997) était un homme universel. À la fois° scientifique, explorateur, inventeur, écrivain, cinéaste, il a mis ses innombrables talents au service d'une seule° cause: la protection des océans. Aujourd'hui, son nom reste associé à la protection de l'écologie marine.

■ Jacques-Yves Cousteau

Cousteau a d'abord été officier dans la Marine française. C'est à cette époque qu'il a inventé le scaphandre autonome (ou SCUBA* en anglais), permettant l'exploration des espaces sous-marins. Au cours de° ses expéditions sur ses fameux bateaux, la Calypso, l'Alcyone, la Calypso II, Cousteau a exploré les fonds° marins un peu partout dans le monde, en France, en Grèce, en Égypte, au Brésil, à Madagascar, dans l'Atlantique, le Pacifique et l'Océan Indien. De ces expéditions, il a rapporté° de nombreux films documentaires. Ces films, comme *Le monde du silence* et *Le monde sans soleil,* et plus tard ses séries télévisées *Découvertes du monde,* ont fait connaître° au grand public l'univers merveilleux de la mer.

■ Le commandant Cousteau à bord de la Calypso.

«Il faut sauver les océans! Il faut sauver notre planète, la Terre!»

Mais Cousteau ne s'est pas contenté° d'être l'un des grands explorateurs de ce siècle. Il a aussi entrepris° une croisade mondiale pour la protection de l'environnement. Son message est simple: À long terme,° l'avenir° de l'humanité dépend de la préservation de notre environnement naturel et, en particulier, du monde marin. Aujourd'hui, celui-ci° est menacé non seulement par la pollution, mais aussi par une exploitation économique incontrôlée. Il faut donc le protéger. Il faut sauver les océans! Il faut sauver notre planète, la Terre! Cousteau s'est engagé° totalement dans cette croisade. Pour cela, il a créé une fondation internationale, la Fondation Cousteau, et aussi la «Cousteau Society» qui a 200.000 membres aux États-Unis. Dans son travail, il était secondé par son fils, Jean-Michel Cousteau, qui habite en Californie.

■ Jean-Michel Cousteau

Jacques-Yves Cousteau faisait aussi partie° de l'élite littéraire. Pour son oeuvre°, il a été élu° membre de l'Académie française, le plus prestigieux groupe d'écrivains français.

à la fois *at the same time* **d'une seule** *only one* **au cours de** = durant **les fonds** *depths* **rapporté** *brought back* **faire connaître** *made known* **contenté** = limité **entreprendre** ❊ *to undertake* **À long terme** *In the long run* **l'avenir** *future* **celui-ci** = le monde marin **engagé** *committed himself* **faisait partie** = était membre **oeuvre** *work* **élire** ❊ *to elect*

*Un acronyme pour Self-Contained Underwater Breathing Apparatus.

NOTE CULTURELLE

Madagascar is a French-speaking island to the west of the coast of Mozambique, Africa. Deforestation is the greatest problem on the island, depriving Madagascar's unique fauna of its natural habitat. Madagascar is the only place in the world where lemurs live.

L'Écologie à la maison

Préserver l'environnement, ce n'est pas difficile. Il suffit d'y penser.° L'écologie commence à la maison. Des jeunes Français expliquent comment ils pratiquent l'écologie chez eux.

Stéphanie:

« Je recycle le verre. Ce n'est pas compliqué. Il suffit de séparer les bouteilles et de les déposer dans les réceptacles spéciaux qu'on trouve partout dans les villes, et même à la campagne. »

Danièle:

« J'ai demandé à ma mère de n'acheter que° des produits favorables à l'environnement. J'ai un argument convaincant:° Je refuse de faire la vaisselle ou de laver le linge° avec des produits qui contiennent des phosphates, nocifs° à l'environnement. »

Xavier:

« J'essaie de conserver l'eau au maximum. Par exemple, au lieu de° prendre des bains, je prends des douches qui utilisent moins d'eau. Quand je me lave les mains, je ferme l'évier.° Quand je me brosse les dents, je ferme le robinet.° J'économise un peu d'eau chaque fois et, à la longue,° ça compte! »

Vincent:

« Quand j'achète quelque chose, je fais attention aux produits qu'il contient.° En général, je donne la préférence aux produits recyclables ou recyclés. Et j'utilise toujours des emballages° en papier, jamais en plastique. »

Zoé:

« Je n'utilise plus d'aérosols, parce que les CFC (chlorofluorocarbures) qu'ils contiennent détruisent l'ozone de l'atmosphère. Et les savons, les shampooings, les dentifrices et les produits de beauté que j'utilise sont toujours à base de produits naturels. »

et vous?

Faites une liste des choses que vous faites pour pratiquer l'écologie chez vous.

Il suffit d'y penser. *You just have to think about it.* **que** *only* **convaincant** *convincing* **linge** *laundry* **nocifs** *harmful* **au lieu de** *instead of* **l'évier** *sink* **robinet** *faucet* **à la longue** *in the long run* **contenir** ❊ *to contain* **emballages** *packaging*

Realia Note

In almost every French city you will find large green hexagonal bins for recycling glass and plastic containers.

Notes linguistiques

- The term **la lessive** *(laundry detergent)* is more commonly used than **la poudre à laver.** **La lessive** also designates the clothes to be washed.
- **l'essuie-tout** *(m.)* = paper towels, from **essuyer** *(to wipe)* and **tout** *(everything).*

Irregular Verb

(see Appendix C)
contenir (*see* **tenir**)

Teaching Strategy: Expansion

After reading the different ways in which the five French students contribute to the preservation of the environment, have students prepare a list of different things that can be done to be "environment-friendly."

Le soleil, notre bonne étoile

Chaque jour, le soleil nous donne sa lumière,° sa chaleur° et son énergie. Il est source de toute vie.° Sans lui, il n'y aurait pas° de plantes, pas de fleurs, pas d'arbres, pas d'animaux et, évidemment, pas de vie humaine. C'est lui qui cause la pluie, le vent, les différences de climat et les changements de saison. Grâce à° lui, les rivières coulent° et les plantes poussent.° Le soleil est vraiment notre bonne étoile!°

À cause de ses innombrables bienfaits,° les civilisations anciennes ont créé un culte du soleil. Pour les Égyptiens, Amon-Râ, le soleil, était le dieu° suprême. En Amérique, les Incas et les Aztèques adoraient aussi le soleil.

Aujourd'hui, le culte du soleil existe toujours, mais il a pris une forme nouvelle. Chaque année, par exemple, des millions de Français vont sur les plages de l'Atlantique et de la Méditerranée pour se baigner, mais surtout et avant tout pour bronzer au soleil. On peut aussi bronzer à la piscine, à la montagne, dans son jardin, ou même sur son balcon. En moyenne, les Français bronzent 2 heures 15 minutes par jour pendant les vacances.

Il y a différentes raisons pour lesquelles° les Français s'exposent au soleil. Selon une enquête,° 50% des personnes interrogées° trouvent que c'est agréable, 22% pensent que c'est bon pour la santé,° 18% déclarent qu'être bronzé, c'est à la mode. Le bronzage fait en effet partie du «look». Aujourd'hui la majorité des femmes déclarent préférer les hommes bronzés et, alternativement, la majorité des hommes préfèrent les femmes qui ont un joli bronzage.

Si le soleil est indispensable au succès des vacances, il peut aussi créer des problèmes pour les personnes imprudentes.° La lumière solaire contient, en effet, des rayons ultra-violets (UV). Quand ces rayons sont trop intenses, ils sont dangereux pour la peau° et pour les yeux. Si on ne fait pas attention, on peut attraper un coup de soleil ou, chose plus grave, être victime d'une insolation.° À long terme, le soleil contribue au vieillissement° de la peau. Pour les personnes qui ont une peau délicate, le soleil est aussi un facteur de risque important du cancer cutané.°

lumière *light* **chaleur** *heat* **vie** *life* **il n'y aurait pas** *there wouldn't be* **Grâce à** *Thanks to* **coulent** *flow* **poussent** *grow* **étoile** *star*
bienfaits *benefits, blessings* **le dieu** *god, deity* **lesquelles** *which* **enquête** *survey* **interrogées** *asked* **santé** *health*
imprudentes *who are not careful* **peau** *skin* **insolation** *sunstroke* **vieillissement** *aging* **cutané** *of the skin*

NOTES CULTURELLES

- **Amon-Râ**, or **Rê**, was the Egyptian sun-god. He was often represented as a man with the head of a falcon.
- The Aztecs dominated Mexico until Cortés led the Spanish conquest in 1521. The Aztec sun-god was called Huitzilopochtli.
- The Incas ruled Peru until Pizzarro's arrival in the 16th century. The Inca religion was based on the worship of the sun, which they called Uiracocha. The emperor, or Inca, was also the religious leader and was considered to be **le fils du Soleil.**

Avant de s'exposer au soleil, il est donc important de prendre quelques précautions élémentaires. Voici certains conseils:

- Bronzez progressivement et modérément. Le premier jour, restez seulement cinq minutes au soleil, puis augmentez° de quelques minutes par jour la durée° de vos bains de soleil. N'oubliez pas qu'un bronzage même progressif n'est pas une protection naturelle contre les effets du soleil.
- Évitez° de vous mettre au soleil entre 11 heures du matin et 2 heures de l'après-midi. C'est à ce moment que les rayons ultra-violets sont les plus intenses.

- Protégez-vous la tête avec un chapeau à large bord° et les yeux avec de bonnes lunettes de soleil qui les recouvrent entièrement.
- Utilisez une bonne crème solaire. Les crèmes solaires filtrent les rayons ultra-violets. Choisissez une crème solaire adaptée à votre peau.
- N'utilisez pas de produits qui contiennent des substances photo-sensibilisantes, comme l'eau de cologne ou certains parfums. Ces substances sont à l'origine de réactions cutanées anormales.
- Soyez vigilants en hiver aussi bien qu'en été. La neige reflète les rayons ultra-violets plus que le sable.° Si la lumière est intense, portez des lunettes de soleil.

et vous?

DÉBAT: LE SOLEIL: AMI OU ENNEMI?

Prenez une position sur ce sujet et débattez-le avec votre partenaire (qui prendra la position contraire). Présentez vos arguments par ordre d'importance.

EXPRESSION ÉCRITE

Êtes-vous un(e) «adorateur(trice) du soleil»? Composez un paragraphe où vous allez expliquer ...

- pourquoi vous aimez le soleil
- où et quand vous bronzez
- quelles précautions vous prenez

Jacques Prévert (1900-1977) est un écrivain et aussi l'auteur de chansons populaires et de plusieurs scénarios de films. Dans ses poèmes, il décrit avec humour et fantaisie les thèmes simples de l'existence: la nature, l'amour, l'amitié, l'enfance, la réalité de tous les jours.

Dans cet extrait, Prévert explique:

- pourquoi il faut être poli avec la terre et le soleil
- les relations personnelles qui existent entre la terre, le soleil et la lune

SOYEZ POLIS

Le soleil est amoureux de la terre
La terre est amoureuse du soleil
Ça les regarde
C'est leur affaire
Et quand il y a des éclipses
Il n'est pas prudent ni discret de les regarder
Au travers de sales petits morceaux de verre fumé
Ils se disputent
C'est des histoires personnelles
Mieux vaut ne pas s'en mêler
Parce que
Si on s'en mêle on risque d'être changé
En pomme de terre gelée
Ou en fer à friser

Le soleil aime la terre
La terre aime le soleil
C'est comme ça
Le reste ne nous regarde pas
La terre aime le soleil
Et elle tourne
Pour se faire admirer
Et le soleil la trouve belle
Et il brille sur elle
Et quand il est fatigué
Il va se coucher

Et la lune se lève
La lune c'est l'ancienne amoureuse du soleil
Mais elle a été jalouse
Et elle a été punie
Elle est devenue toute froide
Et elle sort seulement la nuit
Il faut aussi être très poli avec la lune
Ou sans ça elle peut vous rendre un peu fou
Et elle peut aussi
Si elle veut
Vous changer en bonhomme de neige
En réverbère
Ou en bougie

Prévert, Histoires (Paris: Gallimard, 1963, pp. 66-69)

augmentez *increase* **durée** = le temps **nocifs** *harmful* **Évitez** *Avoid* **bord** *brim* **sable** *sand*

Additional Information

Jacques Prévert wrote the classic French movies: *Les Visiteurs du soir* and *Les Enfants du paradis.*

Notes linguistiques

le verre fumé = tinted glass
le fer à friser = curling iron
Ça ne nous regarde pas = It's none of our business.
le réverbère = street light

Irregular Verbs

Point out that **contenir** is conjugated like **tenir**. Remind students of the irregular imperative forms of **être: sois, soyons, soyez.**

Teaching Strategy: Additional Activities

- Votre partenaire et vous, vous passez les vacances de printemps à la Martinique. C'est votre premier jour là-bas. Votre partenaire a décidé d'aller à la plage. Faites-lui au moins cinq recommandations importantes.
- Faites une enquête dans votre classe. Déterminez:
  - combien de temps par jour vos camarades bronzent en été
  - pourquoi ils aiment bronzer
  - les précautions qu'ils doivent prendre en ce qui concerne leur santé

  Comparez les résultats avec ceux de l'enquête faite en France.

PARTIE 2

LE FRANÇAIS PRATIQUE

TEACHING RESOURCES

Student Activities Manual, pp. 124–126

Audio Program, CD 3, Tracks 8–12

HM ClassPrep CD, Audioscript, Unit 3

Video/DVD Program, Unit 3

■ **Note linguistique**
In 1987, the **Académie française** announced that the word **événement** could also be written **évènement** (with a grave accent on the second "e"). You may allow your students to use either spelling.

Supplementary vocabulary

Quelques événements
une altercation *dispute*
une bonne action *good deed*
une catastrophe *catastrophe*
une collision *collision, crash*
un défilé *parade*
un vol *robbery*
un vol a l'étalage *shoplifting*
un vol à la tire *purse snatching*

LE FRANÇAIS PRATIQUE — *Quoi de neuf?*

COMMENT DÉCRIRE UN ÉVÉNEMENT, COMMENT RACONTER UNE HISTOIRE

— **Quoi de neuf?** *(What's new?)*
Devine!

deviner *to guess*

— Je ne sais pas!
Qu'est-ce qui est arrivé? **Qu'est-ce qui a eu lieu?**
Qu'est-ce qui s'est passé? **Qu'est-ce qu'il y a eu?**

arriver *to happen*
se passer *to happen*
avoir lieu *to take place*
qu'est-ce qu'il y a *what's happening*
assister à to be present at, *to see*
être témoin de *to witness*

J'ai **assisté à** / J'ai **été témoin de** / J'ai vu } quelque chose de bizarre.

— Ah bon? Quand?
C'est arrivé / **Ça s'est passé** / **Ça a eu lieu** } **hier** / **hier soir** / **avant-hier** — **lundi dernier** / **la semaine dernière** / **le mois dernier** — **il y a** deux heures / **il y a** dix jours

— Où étais-tu?
J'étais / **Je me trouvais** } **dehors** *(outside)* / en ville — dans un magasin / chez un copain

se trouver *to be*

— Alors, raconte! Qu'est-ce que tu as fait?
Eh bien, **d'abord** *(first)*, j'ai téléphoné à . . .
puis *(then)* . . .
ensuite *(next)* . . .
après *(after, afterwards)* . . .
enfin *(at last)* . . .
finalement *(finally)* . . .

raconter *to tell (what happened)*

Quelques événements	
un accident	**un événement** *(event)*
un incendie *(fire)*	**un fait** *(fact)*
un cambriolage *(burglary)*	**un fait divers** *(minor news item)*

Teaching Suggestion: Video/DVD Program

In the Unit 3 *Vidéo-drame: Un accident*, students will learn expressions that will help them tell a story or describe an event. This section focuses on Malik and Nicolas explaining the accident that took place on their fishing excursion. You may want to point out to students the use of the **passé composé** versus the imperfect when posing and answering the question **Qu'est-ce qui s'est passé?**

Comment exprimer la surprise

Vraiment?	*Really?*	**C'est incroyable!**	*That's unbelievable!*
Pas possible!	*That's not possible!*	**Ce n'est pas croyable!**	*That's not for real!*
Mon Dieu!	*My goodness!*	**Tu plaisantes!**	*You're kidding!*

1 Journalisme

Vous êtes journaliste pour le magazine RADAR. Dites quand et où les événements de la colonne A ont eu lieu en choisissant un élément des colonnes B et C. Soyez logique.

A: QUOI?	B: QUAND?	C: OÙ?
un cambriolage	ce matin	à l'église St. Charles
un accident	à deux heures cet après-midi	sur l'autoroute A4
un incendie	hier soir	dans une galerie d'art
un violent orage *(storm)*	vendredi dernier	dans la région de Toulouse
une avalanche	le week-end dernier	dans la forêt d'Amboise
un ouragan *(hurricane)*	la semaine dernière	dans les Alpes
le mariage de l'acteur Georges Belhomme	l'hiver dernier	à la Martinique
	en avril dernier	au zoo de Vincennes

▶ **Un accident a eu lieu ce matin (à deux heures cet après-midi) sur l'autoroute A4 (dans la forêt d'Amboise).**

2 Créa-dialogue

Avec votre partenaire, choisissez un événement au bas de la page (ou imaginez un événement original). Composez le dialogue où vous racontez cet événement.

— Quoi de neuf?
— Devine!
— Je ne sais pas! Qu'est-ce qui est arrivé? • *Use another expression.*
— J'ai rencontré le président! • *Imagine a different event.*
— Tu plaisantes! Quand? • *Use another expression of surprise.*
— Ce matin. • *Mention another time.*
— Où étais-tu?
— Je me trouvais à l'aéroport. • *Mention another place.*
— Qu'est-ce que tu as fait alors?
— J'ai pris une photo et j'ai demandé un autographe. • *Mention two things you did.*
— C'est incroyable! • *Use another expression of surprise.*

Événements
- J'ai rencontré Oprah Winfrey.
- J'ai vu un OVNI *(UFO)*.
- J'ai été témoin d'un cambriolage.
- J'ai assisté à un accident spectaculaire.
- J'ai assisté au mariage de . . .(?)
- J'ai découvert un trésor.

Teaching Strategies: Warm-Up

- Divide the class into groups of three and have each group write an original dialog using EVERY vocabulary word/expression from pp. 124–125. When there are synonymous expressions, they should still incorporate each of them logically into the dialog. Encourage students to be creative.

Note culturelle

All French super highways are designated by the letter **A** **(A = Autoroute principale)** followed by a number. The A4 (**l'A4**) links Paris to Metz in the east.

LE FRANÇAIS PRATIQUE

Comment parler de la pluie et du beau temps

Supplementary vocabulary

une étoile filante *shooting star*
il fait gris *it's a cloudy day*
une éclaircie *bright interval of sun*
la tornade *tornado*
l'ouragan *(m.) hurricane*
une averse *shower*

Note linguistique

La météo is the abbreviation of **la météorologie** (meteorology, weather forecasting).

Teaching Strategy: Vocabulary Building

- Why is an umbrella called **un parapluie?** It protects *"against-the-rain."*
- Similarly: **un parachute (une chute** *fall)* Also *lightning rod:* **un paratonnerre**
- What is **un gratte-ciel? (gratter** *to scratch)*

LE FRANÇAIS PRATIQUE — Comment parler de la pluie et du beau temps

prédire *to predict*

Pour le week-end, **la météo** *(weather forecast)* **a prédit:**

du beau temps
- **du soleil** *(sun)*
- **un ciel** *(sky)* **bleu**

du mauvais temps
- **de la pluie** *(rain)*
- **du vent** *(wind)*

de la neige *(snow)*
une tempête de neige

des nuages *(clouds)*
de la brume *(mist)*
du brouillard *(fog)*

un orage *(thunderstorm)*
une tempête *(storm)*
un ouragan *(hurricane)*

du verglas *(sheet ice)*

Quand il fait beau . . .

Le soleil **brille.**
Le ciel est bleu.

Quand il fait mauvais . . .

Le ciel est **couvert** *(overcast).*
La pluie tombe.

Quand il y a un orage . . .

Le vent **souffle.**
On voit **des éclairs** *(lightning).*
On entend **le tonnerre** *(thunder).*

Quand il fait nuit ...

Il fait noir.
On voit **la lune** *(moon).*
et **les étoiles** *(stars).*

Quand il fait froid . . .

La neige **tombe.**
Il y a **de la glace** *(ice).*
Le lac est **gelé** *(frozen).*

briller *to shine*
souffler *to blow*
il fait noir *it is d*

AUJOURD'HUI	HIER		DEMAIN
il pleut **il neige** **il y a un orage**	**il pleuvait** **il neigeait** **il y avait un orage**	**il a plu** le matin **il a neigé** à midi **il y a eu un orage** dans la nuit	**il va pleuvoir** **il va neiger** **il va y avoir un orage**

Teaching Strategy: Warm-Up

Use the Unit 3 *Presentation* slides to introduce the weather. Then have students develop short weather dialogs in which they phone a friend living in another part of the country that has weather conditions that are very different from their own.

3 Une question de temps

Complétez les phrases en décrivant le temps (ou le moment de la journée).

1. Je mets mes lunettes de soleil quand . . .
2. Je mets mon imperméable quand . . .
3. On peut faire du ski quand . . .
4. On peut voir des éclairs quand . . .
5. On ne voit pas le soleil quand . . .
6. On voit des étoiles quand . . .
7. La visibilité sur la route est mauvaise quand . . .
8. On peut faire du patinage *(go skating)* sur un lac quand . . .

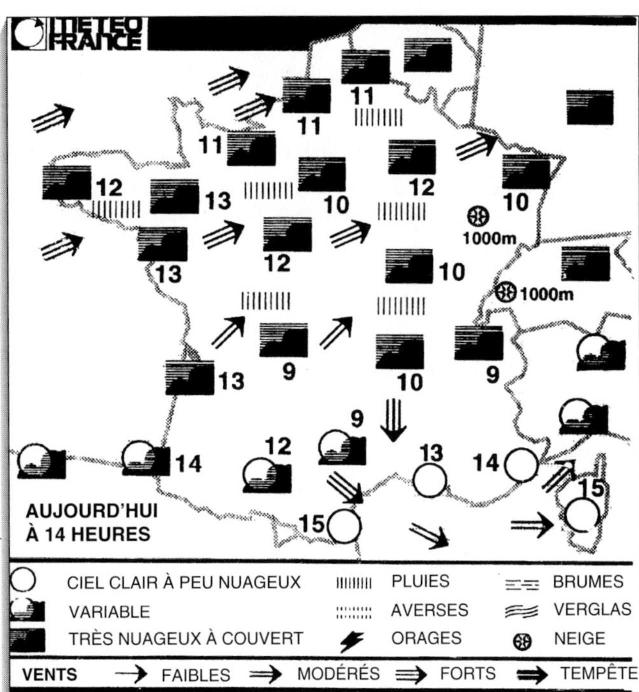

Conversations libres

Avec votre partenaire, choisissez l'un des sujets suivants. Composez le dialogue correspondant à la situation et jouez-le en classe.

1 Les vacances de printemps

Béatrice passe les vacances de printemps à la Martinique où il fait très, très beau. Xavier les passe au Québec où il fait très, très froid. Les deux cousins se téléphonent et parlent du temps.

Rôles: Béatrice, Xavier

2 Un ouragan

Nous sommes en septembre. Carole, une étudiante française, visite la Floride. Aujourd'hui, il y a un terrible ouragan. Elle téléphone à son père qui veut avoir des détails.

Rôles: Carole, son père

3 Week-end

Votre partenaire et vous, vous avez décidé de passer la journée de samedi ensemble. La météo a prédit un temps incertain. Discutez de ce que vous allez faire suivant le temps.

Rôles: vous, votre partenaire

■ Réponses: Activité 3

Encourage students to find several completions for each sentence. Sample answers might include:

1. Je mets mes lunettes de soleil quand il fait beau (quand le soleil brille).
2. Je mets mon imperméable quand il pleut (quand le ciel est couvert).
3. On peut faire du ski quand il a neigé (quand il neige).
4. On peut voir des éclairs quand il y a un orage.
5. On ne voit pas le soleil quand le ciel est couvert (quand il fait nuit).
6. On voit des étoiles quand il fait nuit (quand il fait noir).
7. La visibilité sur la route est mauvaise quand la neige tombe (quand il fait noir, quand il y a du brouillard).
8. On peut faire du patinage sur un lac quand le lac est gelé.

Expansion: Les proverbes

Give several examples of French proverbs:

- **Après la pluie, le beau temps.** (Joy comes after sadness.)
- **Autant en emporte le vent.** (Gone with the wind.)
- **Le soleil luit pour tout le monde.** (The sun shines on everyone.)

Ask students to come up with their own new proverbs—these may be serious or silly!

LANGUE ET COMMUNICATION

LANGUE ET COMMUNICATION

TEACHING RESOURCES

Student Activities Manual, pp. 39, 126

Tête-à-tête Activity, Cambriolage, p. PA4

Audio Program, CD 3, Tracks 13–14

HM ClassPrep CD, Audioscript, Unit 3

A. La description d'un événement: le passé composé et l'imparfait

The following sentences tell about an accident.
The sentences on the left give the main facts.
The sentences on the right describe the scene and the background.

MAIN EVENTS	BACKGROUND AND DESCRIPTION
J'**ai vu** un accident.	C'**était** samedi soir. Il **était** 8 heures. Il **pleuvait**. La visibilité **était** mauvaise. J'**allais** à un rendez-vous. Je **voulais** être à l'heure.
Une voiture **est rentrée** dans un arbre.	C'**était** une voiture de sport. Le conducteur **était** un jeune homme blond.
J'**ai téléphoné** à la police qui **est arrivée** immédiatement.	Le jeune homme ne **portait** pas de ceinture de sécurité. Il **était** légèrement blessé.

The PASSÉ COMPOSÉ tells WHAT HAPPENED and narrates the ACTION	The IMPERFECT sets the SCENE and gives the BACKGROUND
It is used to describe: • SPECIFIC EVENTS • the ACTIONS which constitute the STORY LINE	It is used to describe: • EXTERNAL CONDITIONS date weather time scenery • DESCRIPTIONS OF THE CHARACTERS age physical traits health attitudes appearance clothing feelings intentions • BACKGROUND ACTIVITIES what people were doing what was going on

1 Une question de temps

Expliquez logiquement les actions suivantes en décrivant le temps qu'il faisait.

CE QUI EST ARRIVÉ	QUEL TEMPS?
• J'ai glissé.	Il pleut.
• Stéphanie a bien bronzé.	Il fait noir.
• Nous avons fait du ski.	Il est gelé.
• Vous avez pris vos imperméables.	Il y a du verglas.
• Patrick a pris sa lampe de poche *(flashlight)*.	Il y a de la neige.
• On n'a pas vu le sommet de la montagne.	Il y a des nuages.
• Nous avons fait du patin à glace sur le lac.	Il y a de la brume.
• J'ai entendu l'avion mais je ne l'ai pas vu.	Il y a beaucoup de soleil.

▶ **J'ai glissé parce qu'il y avait du verglas.**

Teaching Strategy: Warm-Up

Passé Composé/Imparfait
Ask students:
- What they were doing at 8:00 last night
- What they did this past weekend
- What they ate for dinner yesterday
- What they used to do with their friends after a day at grammar school
- Where they were yesterday afternoon at 3:00
- When they began college
- What they looked like when they were ten years old
- Where they went on vacation last year

2 Un mauvais témoin

Monsieur Loiseau a été témoin d'un cambriolage samedi dernier. Malheureusement il n'a pas bonne mémoire. Lisez son témoignage *(account)* et rectifiez-le.

Monsieur Loiseau:

«Il était une heure et demie de l'après-midi. Il faisait beau. Il n'y avait pas de voitures dans la rue. Le bandit est sorti par la porte. C'était un homme petit et assez gros. Il avait une barbe noire. Il portait un masque de ski. Il portait un pull. Sa complice l'attendait derrière la banque. C'était une jeune fille brune. Elle avait les cheveux courts et frisés. Elle portait un collier autour du cou. Elle n'avait pas de lunettes. Le bandit et sa complice sont partis en voiture.»

▶ **Mais non! C'est faux! Il n'était pas une heure et demie. Il était trois heures! . . .**

Variation: Activity 2

Have students work in pairs. One looks at the picture while the other reads the text. The student looking at the picture corrects the mistakes as his/her partner reads.

3 Pourquoi?

Demandez à votre partenaire pourquoi il/elle a fait les choses suivantes. Il/elle va répondre avec l'explication suggérée (ou une autre explication de son choix).

▶ aller au café (j'ai soif)
— **Pourquoi est-ce que tu es allé(e) au café?**
— **Parce que j'avais soif.**
(Parce que je voulais rencontrer mes copains, . . .)

1. aller au restaurant (j'ai faim)
2. aller à la plage (il fait beau)
3. mettre de la crème solaire (il y a du soleil)
4. aller à la disco (j'ai envie de danser)
5. rentrer chez toi (il est minuit)
6. se dépêcher (je veux être à l'heure)
7. téléphoner à ta cousine (c'est son anniversaire)
8. prendre de la dramamine (j'ai le mal de mer)

Variation: Activity 3

Demandez à votre partenaire pourquoi il/elle n'a pas fait les choses suivantes. Il/Elle vous répond en utilisant l'explication suggérée ou une explication de son choix.
Exemple:
- Pourquoi n'es-tu pas allé(e) au café?
- Parce que je n'avais pas soif. (Parce que je ne voulais pas rencontrer mes copains,...)

Write some of the answers on the board in two separate columns—**passé composé** and **imparfait.** Ask students to explain why the sentences belong in each category.

4 Une promenade romantique?

Pierre habite à Annecy. L'été dernier, il s'est acheté un bateau. Voilà ce qui lui est arrivé un jour.

C'est samedi. Il est sept heures du soir. Il fait beau. Pierre est chez lui. Il a envie de sortir. Il téléphone à Armelle, sa nouvelle copine. Il lui propose de faire une promenade en bateau sur le lac d'Annecy. Armelle accepte. Pierre prend sa moto et il va chercher Armelle. Il arrive chez elle. Armelle l'attend. Elle porte une belle robe rouge à fleurs et ses nouvelles chaussures.

Pierre et Armelle arrivent au lac. Ils montent dans le bateau de Pierre. Pierre prend sa guitare. Il chante des chansons romantiques. Le ciel est clair. La lune et les étoiles brillent dans le ciel. Armelle écoute Pierre. Elle est très contente.

Tout d'un coup° Pierre fait un mouvement brusque. Il tombe dans l'eau. Armelle perd l'équilibre et tombe dans l'eau aussi. L'eau est très, très froide. Pierre et Armelle nagent jusqu'à la plage. Armelle est trempée° . . . et furieuse. Sa robe et ses nouvelles chaussures sont fichues°. Elle demande à Pierre de la raccompagner chez elle. Pauvre Pierre, il n'a pas de chance!

tout d'un coup *(all of a sudden)* **trempée** *(soaked)* **fichues** *(ruined)*

▶ Maintenant, mettez l'histoire au passé.
C'était un samedi pendant les vacances. . . .

5 Faits divers

Vous avez été témoin des faits divers suivants. Votre partenaire va choisir un de ces faits et vous poser des questions comme:

- C'était quand?
- Où étais-tu?
- Qu'est-ce que tu faisais?
- Qu'est-ce qui s'est passé?
- Qu'est-ce que tu as vu?
- Qu'est-ce que tu as fait?

Répondez à ses questions en utilisant votre imagination.

INCENDIE

Un incendie a eu lieu dans la nuit du 5 février aux établissements Dumoulin. Cet incendie, provoqué,° semble-t-il, par un court-circuit, a détruit l'atelier° de constructions mécaniques et a fait un million d'euros de dégâts.°

provoqué *caused*
atelier *workshop*
dégâts *damages*

ACCIDENT

Un accident de la circulation a eu lieu hier après-midi vers trois heures à l'intersection de la rue Victor Hugo et l'avenue de la République. Une voiture de tourisme, conduite par Monsieur Picard, professeur au lycée Descartes, est entrée en collision avec un camion de l'armée. L'accident, provoqué par la neige, n'a pas fait de victime.

CAMBRIOLAGE

Un cambriolage a eu lieu le week-end dernier dans un magasin d'antiquités de la rue de la Paix. D'après les déclarations de Madame Durand, la propriétaire, les cambrioleurs ont emporté° quelques statues sans valeur mais ont laissé une collection de monnaies° anciennes estimée à deux cent mille euros.

emporter *to carry off, steal*
monnaies *coins*

MARIAGE PRINCI

Le mariage de la princ Sophie a été célébré le 15 dans la chapelle du châtea Rambucourt. La prince vêtue de satin blanc, a accompagnée à l'autel° pa père, l'archiduc Ferdinand

autel *altar*

6 À votre tour

Racontez un événement de votre vie. Décrivez la scène et les événements principaux. Vous pouvez décrire, par exemple . . .

- un accident
- un anniversaire
- un mariage
- une fête familiale
- un événement sportif auquel vous avez participé
- un concert ou un spectacle

TEACHING RESOURCES

Student Activities Manual, pp. 40–41

■ **Vocabulary Expansion**

les pompiers *firefighters*

Teaching Strategy: Expansion

Have the students draw or cut out from magazines or newspapers a picture that they could then describe using ten sentences in both the **passé composé** and the **imparfait**. Their sentences should include a description of the background scene and background information as well as an explanation of the specific action that is taking place in the picture. The next day in class they should show their pictures to the class and present their description without reading the prepared sentences.

B. L'imparfait et le passé composé dans la même phrase

In describing a past event, we may use both the PASSÉ COMPOSÉ and the IMPERFECT in the same sentence.

SPECIFIC ACTION *(what people did)*	ON-GOING OR PROGRESSIVE ACTION *(what was happening)*
J'**ai vu** un accident . . .	pendant que j'**attendais** le bus.
Le cambrioleur **est entré** . . .	pendant que les voisins **dormaient**.
Quand tu **as téléphoné**, . . .	je **regardais** la télé.
Quand l'orage **a commencé**, . . .	nous **nous promenions**.
J'**ai observé** un oiseau . . .	qui **chantait** dans un arbre.
Tu **as pris** une photo de ton cousin . . .	qui **faisait** de la planche à voile.

The relationship between events and the corresponding choice of the passé composé or the imperfect can be illustrated as follows:

SPECIFIC ACTION — J'**ai vu** un accident / Quand tu **as téléphoné** / J'**ai observé** un oiseau

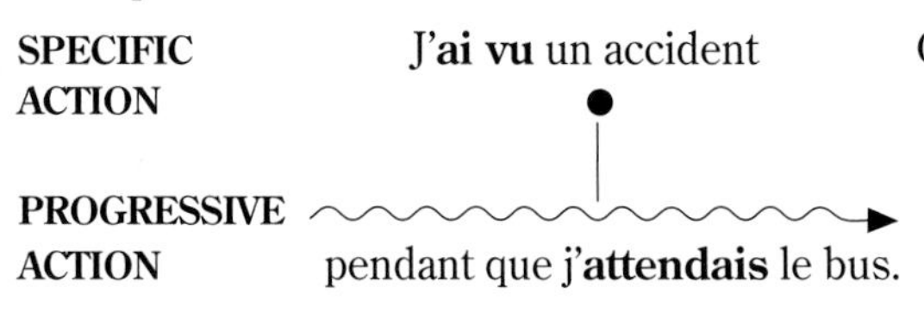
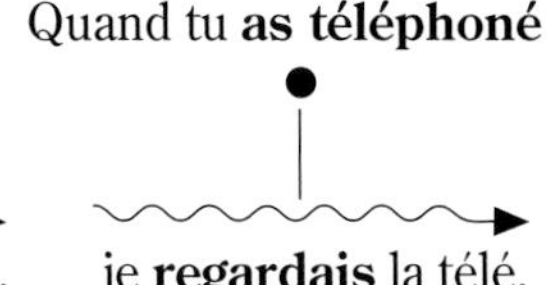
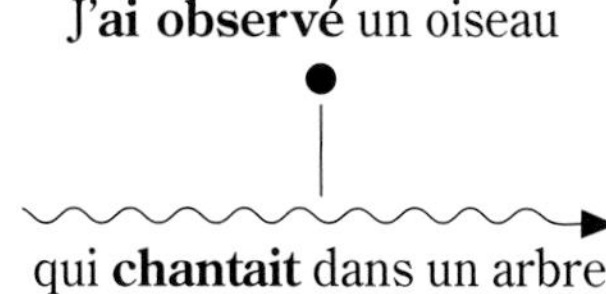

PROGRESSIVE ACTION — pendant que j'**attendais** le bus. / je **regardais** la télé. / qui **chantait** dans un arbre.

➡ Depending on what action is being described, either the PASSÉ COMPOSÉ or the IMPERFECT may be used after **quand.**

J'ai téléphoné **quand tu regardais** la télé. — *I called **when you were watching** television.*
Je téléphonais **quand tu es parti.** — *I was talking on the phone **when you left.***

Les expressions de temps

PREPOSITION (+ noun)		
pendant	*during*	Qu'est-ce que tu as fait **pendant** les vacances?
CONJUNCTION		
pendant que	*while*	Qu'est-ce que tu as fait **pendant que** je jouais au golf?
lorsque	*when*	J'ai rencontré Paul **lorsqu'**il travaillait à Paris.
au moment où	*just as*	Je suis arrivé à la gare **au moment où** le train partait.

7 Où étais-tu?

Demandez à votre partenaire où il/elle était quand certaines choses sont arrivées. Il/elle va répondre en utilisant l'expression suggérée ou une expression de son choix.

▶ **—Où étais-tu quand j'ai téléphoné?**
—J'étais dans ma chambre.
—Qu'est-ce que tu faisais?
—Je dormais.

1. • je suis passé(e) • au jardin • tondre la pelouse
2. • tu as vu l'incendie • dans la rue • me promener
3. • tu t'es cassé la jambe • à la montagne • faire de l'alpinisme
4. • tu as vu l'ours *(bear)* • à la campagne • faire du camping
5. • le cambrioleur est entré • dans la salle de bains • se laver les cheveux
6. • l'homme s'est noyé • à la plage • prendre un bain de soleil

■ **Note linguistique**

It is also possible for two specific actions or two progressive actions to occur in the same sentence.

Je **suis parti**

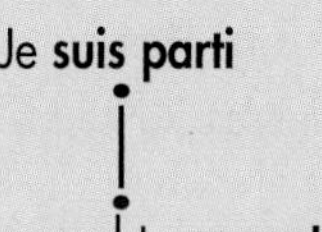

quand tu **es rentré**.

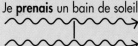

Je **prenais** un bain de soleil

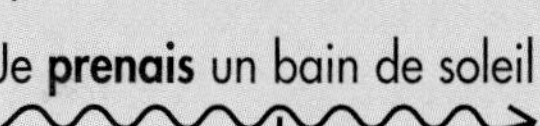
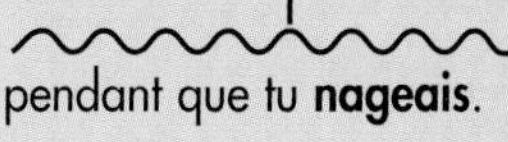

pendant que tu **nageais**.

TEACHING RESOURCES

Student Activities Manual,
pp. 41–44

■ **Teaching Note**
120 kilomètres à l'heure =
74.5 mph

8 Rencontres de vacances

Décrivez les rencontres suivantes.

▶ à la plage / Thomas / parler à une fille / prendre un bain de soleil
À la plage, Thomas a parlé à une fille qui prenait un bain de soleil.

1. à la montagne / nous / voir des gens / faire de l'escalade
2. pendant l'excursion / Philippe / rencontrer un camarade / se promener dans les bois
3. à la mer / tu / prendre des photos d'un ami / faire de la planche à voile
4. au café / nous / écouter un étudiant / jouer de la guitare
5. au musée / vous / parler à des touristes / visiter la ville
6. dans la rue / Sophie / rencontrer des copains / aller au cinéma

9 Zut alors!

Certaines choses arrivent toujours au mauvais moment. Décrivez ce que les personnes faisaient quand certaines choses sont arrivées.

▶ Je visite la Guadeloupe / quand / il y a un ouragan
Je visitais la Guadeloupe quand il y a eu un ouragan.

1. Philippe regarde les filles / quand / il tombe dans l'eau
2. Mon cousin va à 120 à l'heure / lorsque / la police l'arrête
3. Nous faisons une promenade à pied / quand / l'orage commence
4. Thomas écrit à sa copine / au moment où / le professeur lui pose une question
5. Marc gagne le match de tennis / lorsque / il glisse et se casse le bras
6. Jérôme embrasse *(kisses)* Alice / au moment où / le père d'Alice entre

10 D'autres mésaventures

Décrivez les mésaventures *(mishaps)* suivantes au passé.

1. Nous montons à la Tour Eiffel. Pendant que nous sommes dans l'ascenseur, il y a une panne d'électricité.
2. Caroline et Sandrine font du camping. Pendant qu'elles dorment, un raton laveur *(raccoon)* mange leurs provisions.
3. Monsieur Malchance monte sur le toit pour réparer l'antenne de télévision. Pendant qu'il la répare, un vent fort souffle et l'échelle *(ladder)* tombe. Monsieur Malchance reste toute la nuit sur le toit.
4. Roméo va sous le balcon de Juliette et lui chante une chanson d'amour. Pendant qu'il chante, le père de Juliette lui jette un seau *(bucket)* d'eau sur la tête.

C. Le passé simple

Like the PASSÉ COMPOSÉ, the PASSÉ SIMPLE is used to describe what people DID, what HAPPENED.

Although you do not need to learn how to write the passé simple, you should be able to recognize its forms since the tense is often used in written narration and literary texts.

Passé simple

Expansion ▶ pp. R32-33

Note the passé simple of regular verbs:

INFINITIVE		parler	finir	répondre
PASSÉ SIMPLE	je	parl**ai**	fin**is**	répond**is**
	tu	parl**as**	fin**is**	répond**is**
	il/elle/on	parl**a**	fin**it**	répond**it**
	nous	parl**âmes**	fin**îmes**	répond**îmes**
	vous	parl**âtes**	fin**îtes**	répond**îtes**
	ils/elles	parl**èrent**	fin**irent**	répond**irent**

➡ For most irregular verbs, the stem of the passé simple is similar to the past participle:

aller (**allé**) → il **alla** ils **allèrent** prendre (**pris**) → il **prit** ils **prirent**
avoir (**eu**) → il **eut** ils **eurent** recevoir (**reçu**) → il **reçut** ils **reçurent**

Note the following common irregular forms:

être → il **fut** ils **furent** venir → il **vint** ils **vinrent**
faire → il **fit** ils **firent** voir → il **vit** ils **virent**

1 Un peu d'histoire

Lisez l'histoire d'une exploration importante. Puis, racontez cette histoire à votre partenaire en remplaçant le passé simple par le passé composé.

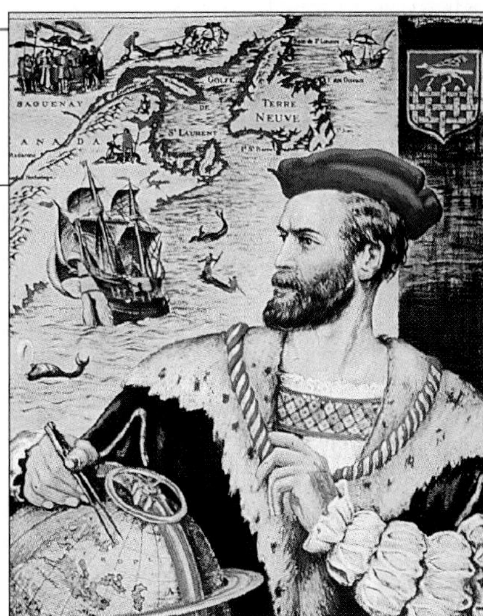

Jacques Cartier (1491–1557) est l'un des grands explorateurs français. Il naquit à Saint-Malo en 1491. Dans sa jeunesse, il alla au Portugal, au Brésil et probablement dans la région de Terre-Neuve.° En 1534, le roi de France lui donna la mission d'explorer les côtes° de l'Amérique du Nord. Cartier et ses hommes partirent de Saint-Malo le 20 avril et arrivèrent dans la région de Gaspé au Canada le 25 juillet. Cartier descendit à terre, planta une croix dans le sol et prit possession de la région au nom du roi de France. L'expédition revint en France où elle fut reçue en triomphe. Jacques Cartier fit un second voyage en 1535 avec la mission cette fois de chercher de l'or et des pierres précieuses. Il ne trouva pas d'or mais il découvrit un immense fleuve qu'il nomma Saint-Laurent. Cartier remonta le fleuve jusqu'au site d'un village indien, Hochelaga, aujourd'hui Montréal. Les premiers colons français s'installèrent au Canada 70 ans plus tard. C'est ainsi que le Canada devint un territoire français.

Terre-Neuve *(Newfoundland)* **les côtes** *(coast)*

Note culturelle
Jacques Cartier died in Saint-Malo, France, after having made another trip to Canada.

Teaching Strategy: Extra Practice

For additional recognition practice, have students identify the infinitives of the following **passé simple** forms:

il crut (croire) **il dit** (dire)
il but (boire) **il lut** (lire)
il partit (partir) **il mit** (mettre)

Have students guess:

il écrivit (écrire)
il découvrit (découvrir)
il construisit (construire)
il mourut (mourir)

LECTURE

Reading STRATEGY

Reading fiction

■ **Additional Information**
Other books featuring Petit Nicolas are: **Le petit Nicolas**, and **Le petit Nicolas et les copains.**

■ **Note linguistique**
La récré is the popular abbreviated form of **la récréation** *(recess).*

■ **Pour en savoir plus**
For more information on *Astérix,* refer students to *Interlude 2,* pp. 100–101.

LECTURE

King

Sempé et Goscinny

AVANT DE LIRE

L'histoire suivante est extraite d'un album humoristique intitulé **Les Récrés du petit Nicolas**. Le petit Nicolas est un peu l'équivalent français de «Denis la Menace». C'est un garçon de 6 ou 7 ans. Il est généreux, affectueux, vif d'esprit,° parfois turbulent, mais sans méchanceté.° Il adore ses parents, aime les animaux, et il a toute une bande de copains. Comme à tous les enfants de son âge, il lui arrive parfois de° «faire des bêtises»,° ou bien, très innocemment, de créer des situations plus ou moins embarrassantes pour ses parents, ses voisins ou ses professeurs.

Notez que dans ce récit, c'est le petit Nicolas qui parle. Les impressions présentées et le style utilisé sont, par conséquent, ceux d'un jeune enfant français.

Les divers albums relatant les aventures du *Petit Nicolas* sont le produit de la collaboration d'un illustrateur et d'un écrivain. **Jean-Jacques Sempé** (né en 1932), l'illustrateur, a collaboré à de nombreux magazines. Il est aussi le père d'un fils qui s'appelle ... Nicolas. **René Goscinny** (1926-1977), l'écrivain, a créé d'autres personnages très célèbres en France comme *Astérix* et le cow-boy *Lucky Luke.*

NOTE CULTURELLE

Le jardin public

Les villes françaises ont généralement un **jardin** ou **parc public** où les petits enfants viennent jouer, les personnes âgées se reposer, et les gens de tout âge se promener. Ces jardins publics sont généralement très bien entretenus° et très bien équipés. On y trouve généralement des massifs de fleurs,° des pelouses de gazon,° une pièce d'eau° avec une fontaine, des jeux pour les petits enfants, et des bancs.° Pour maintenir le bon usage de ces jardins, un grand nombre d'activités sont interdites.° Il est interdit, par exemple, de faire de la bicyclette dans les allées, de marcher sur les pelouses, de jouer au frisbee ou au volley, de faire des pique-niques et d'aller à la pêche dans les pièces d'eau.

Les jardins publics sont généralement placés sous la surveillance d'un gardien. Le gardien est souvent un homme âgé (un ancien militaire, par exemple). Il porte un uniforme et une casquette, del et, pour maintenir l'ordre, il utilise un sifflet.

Anticipons un peu

Pour mieux comprendre une histoire, il est parfois utile de participer indirectement à cette histoire en prenant la place d'un observateur et en essayant d'anticiper ce qui va arriver. Imaginez, par exemple, que vous êtes le frère aîné ou la soeur aînée du petit Nicolas. Vous avez appris que celui-ci est parti faire une promenade avec ses copains dans un endroit où il y a un étang.° Connaissant bien votre petit frère, vous vous doutez bien° qu'il va rapporter quelque créature vivante de cette promenade. Avant de lire l'histoire, essayez de deviner°...

- quel animal le petit Nicolas va rapporter de l'étang
- qu'est-ce qu'il a l'intention de faire avec cet animal
- comment vos parents vont réagir°

vif d'esprit *alert* **méchanceté** = malice **il lui arrive parfois de** *it sometimes happens that he* **bêtises** = choses pas très intelligentes **entretenus** *maintained* **massifs de fleurs** *flower beds* **gazon** *grass* **pièce d'eau** *pool* **banc** *bench* **interdites** *forbidden* **étang** *pond* **vous vous doutez bien** = vous êtes assez sûr **deviner** *guess* **réagir** *to react*

Teaching Strategy

This story uses a variety of verb forms: the *present,* the *passé composé,* the *imperfect,* the *pluperfect,* the *subjunctive,* and also the *future* and *conditional*. With respect to the future and conditional forms in the text, you may ...

- simply treat them as vocabulary items;
- BRIEFLY review the basic forms of the future;
- BRIEFLY present the future and conditional as anticipatory structures (cf. Unit 5, pp. 201, 204, 207).

King 1.

Mes copains et moi, nous avons décidé d'aller à la pêche!

Il y a un square° où nous allons jouer souvent, et dans le square il y a un chouette étang. Et dans l'étang il y a des têtards, et c'est ça que nous avons décidé de pêcher. Les têtards, ce sont de petites bêtes qui grandissent et qui deviennent des grenouilles.

À la maison, j'ai pris un bocal à confitures° vide et je suis allé dans le square, en faisant bien attention que le gardien ne me voie pas. Le gardien du square a une grosse moustache, une canne, et un sifflet à roulette comme celui du papa de Raoul, qui est agent de police.° Le gardien nous gronde° souvent, parce qu'il y a des tas de choses qui sont défendues dans le square: il ne faut pas marcher sur l'herbe, monter aux arbres, arracher les fleurs, faire du vélo, jouer au football, jeter des papiers par terre, et se battre.° Mais on s'amuse bien quand même!

Édouard, Raoul, et Clotaire étaient déjà au bord de l'étang avec leur bocaux. Alceste est arrivé le dernier—il nous a expliqué qu'il n'avait pas trouvé de bocal vide et qu'il avait dû en vider un. Il avait encore plein de° confiture sur la figure, Alceste.

Comme le gardien n'était pas là, on s'est tout de suite mis à pêcher.

C'est très difficile de pêcher des têtards! Il faut se mettre à plat ventre° sur le bord° de l'étang, plonger le bocal dans l'eau, et essayer d'attraper les têtards qui bougent et qui n'ont pas du tout envie d'entrer dans les bocaux. Le premier qui a eu un têtard, c'était Clotaire, et il était tout fier, parce qu'il n'est pas habitué° à être le premier en quoi que ce soit.°

Et puis, à la fin, nous avons tous eu notre têtard. C'est-à-dire qu'Alceste n'a pas réussi à en pêcher un, mais Raoul, qui est un pêcheur formidable, en avait deux dans son bocal, et il a donné le plus petit à Alceste.

— Et qu'est-ce qu'on va faire avec nos têtards? a demandé Clotaire.

square = jardin public **confitures** *jam* **un agent de police** *policeman* **gronde** *scolds* **se battre** *to fight* **plein de** = beaucoup de **se mettre à plat ventre** *lie down on your stomach* **bord** *edge* **habitué à** *accustomed, used to* **quoi que ce soit** *whatever it is*

Mots utiles

un têtard	
une grenouille	
un étang	
un bocal	
un sifflet à roulette	
aller à la pêche	*to go fishing*
emmener	*to bring*
grandir	*to grow (in size)*
se mettre à *	= commencer à
pêcher	*to fish*
plonger	*to plunge*
vider	*to empty*
défendu	*forbidden*
fier (fière)	*proud*
vide	*empty*
quand même	*anyhow*

Langage familier

une bête = un animal
chouette = super
rigolo = amusant
des tas de = beaucoup de

■ Note linguistique

Le square is a small public park, generally fenced.

■ Irregular Verb

(see Appendix C)
mettre

If you prefer, you may hold this reading until after Unit 5 where the future and conditional are formally introduced.

— Ben, a répondu Raoul, on va les emmener chez nous, on va attendre qu'ils grandissent et qu'ils deviennent des grenouilles, et on va faire des courses. Ce sera rigolo.

— Et puis, a dit Édouard, les grenouilles, c'est pratique, ça monte sur une petite échelle et ça vous dit le temps qu'il fera!

— Et puis, a dit Alceste, les cuisses de grenouilles, avec de l'ail, c'est très, très bon!

Et Alceste a regardé son têtard, en se passant la langue° sur les lèvres.

langue *tongue*

NOTE CULTURELLE

Les grenouilles sont des animaux très communs en France. On les trouve un peu partout: dans les étangs, dans les lacs, dans les rivières. Les grenouilles font partie du folklore français.

- **Les grenouilles et la météo.** D'après le folklore, on peut prédire le temps en observant les grenouilles. Si les grenouilles restent dans l'eau, il va faire beau. Si les grenouilles sortent de leur étang pour chercher un terrain sec,° il va pleuvoir. Autrefois, on mettait une grenouille dans un grand bocal avec de l'eau et une petite échelle. Si la grenouille montait à l'échelle, c'était un signe d'orage.
- **La course de grenouilles.** Traditionnellement, à la campagne, les enfants attrapaient des grenouilles et organisaient des courses pour voir laquelle irait le plus vite.

- **Les cuisses de grenouilles.** Contrairement à ce que pensent beaucoup d'Américains, les cuisses de grenouilles ne sont pas un plat typiquement français. En fait, pratiquement aucun° restaurant français ne sert ce plat.

sec *dry* **aucun** *no*

Avez-vous compris?

1. Qu'est-ce que c'est qu'un têtard?
2. En quoi consiste le travail du gardien du square?
3. Comment Nicolas et ses copains ont-ils attrapé les têtards?
4. Qu'est-ce qu'Alceste a fait pour obtenir un bocal vide?
5. Comment Alceste a-t-il eu un têtard?
6. Qu'est-ce que les enfants veulent faire avec leurs têtards?

Anticipons un peu

Quelle va être la réaction de la mère du pe Nicolas quand elle va voir le têtard?

- Elle va être heureuse que son fils s'intéres à la nature.
- Elle va acheter un aquarium pour le têtard.
- Elle va demander à son fils de se débarrc er de *(to get rid of)* cet animal immédiatement.
- Elle va se débarrasser elle-même de l'animal.
- Autre possibilité?

Avez-vous compris?

(Sample answers)

1. Un têtard, c'est un petit animal qui devient une grenouille plus tard.
2. Le gardien du square surveille les gens qui viennent dans le square. S'ils font des choses défendues, il utilise son sifflet.
3. Ils ont attrapé les têtards dans des bocaux de confiture vides.
4. Pour obtenir un bocal vide, Alceste a mangé toute la confiture!
5. Il n'a pas attrapé de têtard, mais Raoul lui en a donné un.
6. Ils veulent les emmener chez eux et attendre qu'ils deviennent des grenouilles.

NOTE CULTURELLE

French children are very familiar with frog stories, such as those in the fables of La Fontaine: **La grenouille qui voulait se faire plus grosse que le boeuf** and **Les grenouilles qui voulaient un roi.**

Ask students if they know any frog stories in English. (Students will know Kermit, from Sesame Street, of course!)

2.

Et puis nous sommes partis en courant parce que nous avons vu le gardien du square qui arrivait. Dans la rue, en marchant, je voyais mon têtard dans le bocal, et il était très chouette. Il bougeait° beaucoup, et j'étais sûr qu'il deviendrait une grenouille formidable, qui allait gagner toutes les courses. J'ai décidé de l'appeler King; c'est le nom d'un cheval blanc que j'ai vu jeudi dernier dans un film de cow-boys. C'était un cheval qui courait très vite et qui venait quand son cow-boy le sifflait. Moi, je lui apprendrai à faire des tours, à mon têtard, et quand il sera grenouille, il viendra quand je le sifflerai.

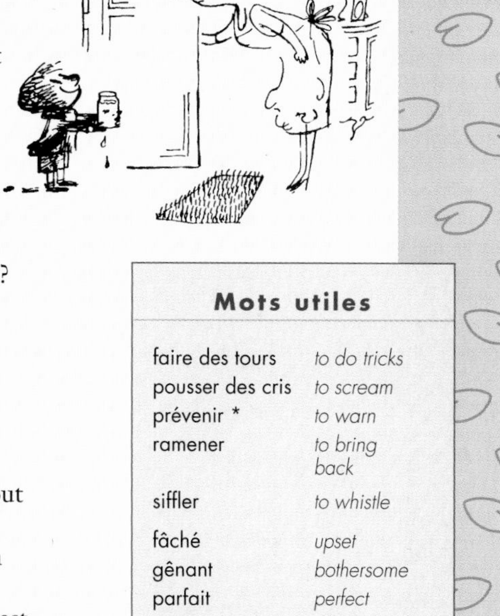

Quand je suis entré dans la maison. Maman m'a regardé et elle s'est mise à pousser des cris: «Mais regarde-moi dans quel état tu t'es mis! Tu as de la boue° partout, tu es trempé comme une soupe! Qu'est-ce que tu as encore fabriqué?»

C'est vrai que je n'étais pas très propre, surtout que j'avais oublié de rouler° les manches° de ma chemise quand j'avais mis mes bras dans l'étang.

— Et ce bocal? a demandé Maman, qu'est-ce qu'il y a dans ce bocal?

— C'est King, j'ai dit à Maman en lui montrant mon têtard. Il va devenir grenouille, il viendra quand je le sifflerai, il nous dira le temps qu'il fait, et il va gagner des courses!

Maman a fait une tête avec le nez tout chiffonné.°

— Quelle horreur! a crié Maman. Combien de fois faut-il que je te dise de ne pas apporter des saletés° dans la maison?

— Ce n'est pas des saletés, j'ai dit, c'est propre comme tout, c'est tout le temps° dans l'eau, et je vais lui apprendre à faire des tours!

— Eh bien, voilà ton père, a dit Maman; nous allons voir ce qu'il en dit!

Et quand Papa a vu le bocal, il a dit: «Tiens! C'est un têtard.» Et il est allé s'asseoir dans le fauteuil pour lire son journal. Maman était toute fâchée.

— C'est tout ce que tu trouves à dire? elle a demandé à Papa. Je ne veux pas que cet enfant ramène toutes sortes de sales bêtes à la maison!

— Bah! a dit Papa, un têtard, ce n'est pas bien gênant...

Mots utiles

faire des tours	*to do tricks*
pousser des cris	*to scream*
prévenir *	*to warn*
ramener	*to bring back*
siffler	*to whistle*
fâché	*upset*
gênant	*bothersome*
parfait	*perfect*
propre ≠ sale	*clean ≠ dirty, nasty*
trempé	*soaking wet*
partout	*everywhere*
puisque	*since*

bougeait *was moving around* **boue** *mud* **rouler** *to roll up* **manches** *sleeves* **chiffonné** *wrinkled* **une saleté** *something gross, dirty* **tout le temps** = toujours

Langage familier

fabriquer = faire

Avez-vous compris?

1. Pourquoi les enfants ont-ils quitté l'étang en courant?
2. Quel nom le petit Nicolas a-t-il donné à son têtard et pourquoi?
3. Dans quel état le petit Nicolas est-il rentré chez lui?
4. Quelle a été la réaction de sa mère quand elle a vu le bocal?
5. Quelle a été la réaction de son père?

Anticipons un peu

D'après vous, que va faire le père du petit Nicolas pour résoudre le conflit?

■ Irregular Verb

(see Appendix C)
prévenir (*see* **venir**)

■ *Avez-vous compris?*

(Sample answers)

1. Ils ont quitté l'étang en courant parce que le gardien arrivait, et c'est interdit de pêcher dans l'étang.
2. Il l'a appelé King, le nom d'un cheval qui courait très vite dans un film de cowboy, un nom de champion!
3. Il est rentré très sale et trempé.
4. Sa mère n'a pas été contente. Elle a dit que c'était une saleté.
5. Il a dit: «Tiens! C'est un têtard.» et il a commencé à lire son journal.

Teaching Strategy

Point out some familiar French expressions from the text. Have students infer their meaning:

- **Il était très chouette.** (It was really great. **chouette** = owl)
- **pousser des cris** (to scream)
- **être trempé comme une soupe** (to be soaking wet)
- **C'est propre comme tout.** (It's very clean.)

3.

Eh bien, parfait, a dit Maman, parfait! Puisque je ne compte pas, je ne dis plus rien. Mais je vous préviens, c'est le têtard ou moi!

Et Maman est partie dans la cuisine.

Papa a poussé un gros soupir° et il a plié son journal.

— Je crois que nous n'avons pas le choix, Nicolas, il m'a dit. Il va falloir se débarrasser de cette bestiole.°

Moi, je me suis mis à pleurer. J'ai dit que je ne voulais pas qu'on fasse du mal à King, et que nous étions déjà copains tous les deux. Papa m'a pris dans ses bras.

— Écoute, mon petit bonhomme,° il m'a dit. Tu sais que ce petit têtard a une maman grenouille. Et la maman grenouille doit avoir beaucoup de peine d'avoir perdu son enfant. Maman ne serait pas contente si on t'emmenait dans un bocal. Pour les grenouilles, c'est la même chose. Alors, tu sais ce qu'on va faire? Nous allons partir tous les deux et nous allons remettre le têtard où tu l'as pris, et puis tous les dimanches tu pourras aller le voir. Et en revenant à la maison, je t'achèterai une tablette° de chocolat.

Moi, j'ai réfléchi un moment, et j'ai dit: «Bon, d'accord.»

Alors, Papa est allé dans la cuisine et il a dit à Maman, en riant, que nous avions décidé de la garder, et de nous débarrasser du têtard.

Maman a ri aussi. Elle m'a embrassé et elle a dit que pour ce soir elle ferait un gâteau. J'étais très consolé.

Quand nous sommes arrivés dans le jardin, j'ai conduit Papa, qui tenait le bocal, vers le bord de l'étang. J'ai dit: «C'est là.» Alors, j'ai dit au revoir à King, et Papa a versé dans l'étang tout ce qu'il y avait dans le bocal.

Et puis nous nous sommes retournés pour partir et nous avons vu le gardien du square qui sortait de derrière un arbre avec des yeux ronds.

— Je ne sais pas si vous êtes tous fous, ou si c'est moi qui le deviens, a dit le gardien, mais vous êtes le septième bonhomme, y compris° un agent de police, qui vient aujourd'hui jeter le contenu d'un bocal d'eau à cet endroit précis° de l'étang.

a poussé un gros soupir *let out a large sigh* **une bestiole** = une petite bête
bonhomme = homme **tablette** *bar* **y compris** *including* **cet endroit précis** *this very spot*

Mots utiles

avoir de la peine	= être triste
conduire *	*to lead*
se débarrasser	*to get rid of*
faire du mal à	*to hurt*
plier	*to fold (up)*
réfléchir	*to think things over*
rire *	*to laugh*
tenir *	*to hold*
verser	*to pour*
fou (folle)	*crazy*
vers	*toward*

Avez-vous compris?

1. Qu'est-ce que le père du petit Nicolas explique à son fils?
2. Quelle est la première réaction du petit Nicolas?
3. Quels arguments le père utilise-t-il pour convaincre son fils de remettre le têtard dans l'étang?
4. Que fait la mère lorsqu'elle apprend la bonne nouvelle?
5. Qu'est-ce que le gardien du square a vu? Pourquoi pense-t-il que ces gens sont fous?

■ *Avez-vous compris?*

(Sample answers)

1. Il lui explique qu'il ne peut pas garder le têtard à la maison.
2. Il se met à pleurer.
3. Il dit que la maman grenouille est triste parce que le têtard est parti.
4. Elle rit, et elle dit qu'elle va faire un gâteau.
5. Il a vu sept hommes qui ont jeté le contenu de bocaux dans l'étang. Il pense qu'ils sont fous parce qu'il ne sait pas qu'il y a des têtards dans les bocaux.

■ Irregular Verbs

(see Appendix C)
conduire
rire
tenir

Teaching Strategy: Expansion

Divide the class into groups. Have students brainstorm an expansion on the story by imagining an additional scene. After each group has come up with a scenario, have them present it to the class.

Scenario: Le lendemain, Petit Nicolas rencontre son ami Alceste. Ils racontent et comparent ce qui s'est passé quand ils sont rentrés chez eux et ont montré le têtard à leurs parents.

Rôles: Petit Nicolas, Alceste

EXPRESSION ORALE

Expérience personnelle
Quand vous étiez petit(e), avez-vous trouvé un jour un animal que vous avez voulu apporter à la maison? Décrivez ce qui est arrivé. Par exemple . . .

- Quel animal était-ce?
- Où l'avez-vous trouvé?
- Quelle a été la réaction de votre père/mère?
- Qu'est-ce que vous avez fait de l'animal? Est-ce que vous l'avez gardé? Sinon, qu'est-ce que vous avez fait de lui?

Situations
Avec votre partenaire, choisissez l'une des situations suivantes. Composez le dialogue correspondant et jouez-le en classe.

1 Au marché

Au marché, la mère du petit Nicolas rencontre la mère d'Alceste. Elles parlent de ce que leurs enfants ont fait hier et quelles ont été leurs réactions.

Rôles: la mère de Nicolas, la mère d'Alceste

2 Au café

Le père du petit Nicolas et le père de Raoul se rencontrent au café et parlent de ce qui s'est passé. Ils décrivent...

- ce que leurs enfants ont fait
- comment leurs épouses ont réagi *(reacted)*
- comment le problème a été résolu *(solved)*

Rôles: le père de Nicolas, le père de Raoul

EXPRESSION ÉCRITE

Le sens de l'humour
Les Récrés du petit Nicolas est un livre humoristique. Décrivez deux ou trois scènes ou situations qui vous paraissent humoristiques dans le récit que vous avez lu et expliquez pourquoi vous les trouvez drôles.

Une lettre
La mère du petit Nicolas écrit une lettre à sa soeur. Elle lui explique ce qui s'est passé hier.

Le rapport du gardien
Le gardien écrit un rapport sur ce qu'il a vu hier dans le square. Il décrit . . .

- où il était
- ce qu'il faisait
- ce qu'il a vu
- pourquoi c'était bizarre

—> **Hier, j'ai été témoin de quelque chose de bizarre. . . .**

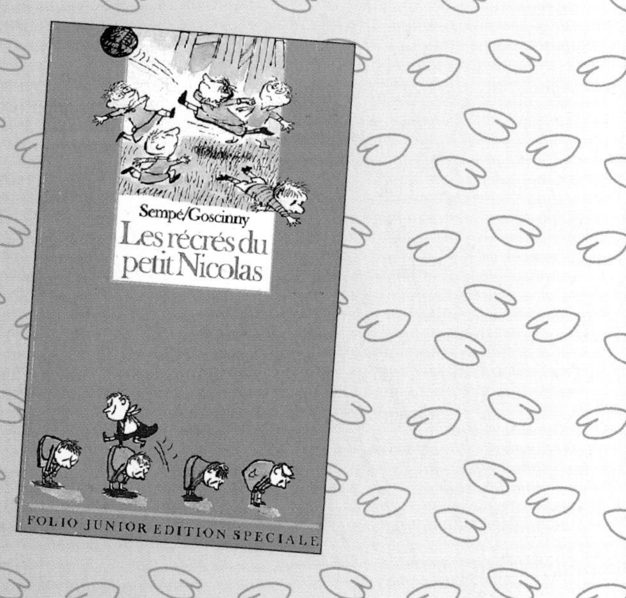

Sempé/Goscinny
Les récrés du petit Nicolas
FOLIO JUNIOR EDITION SPECIALE

Expansion

Expérience personnelle

Suggestions:
un oiseau blessé *(injured)*
une salamandre
un petit écureuil
une tortue
un lapin
une souris
une grenouille
un serpent
un petit chat

Le sens de l'humour

Exemples de situations comiques:

- comment Alceste a trouvé/obtenu un bocal vide
- ce que les enfants projettent de faire avec leurs têtards
- comment le petit Nicolas essaie de convaincre sa mère
- comment le père essaie de convaincre son fils
- pourquoi le gardien du square est surpris

Realia Note

Sur la couverture du livre **Les Récrés du petit Nicolas**, on voit les enfants jouer au football et jouer à saute-moutons *(to play leapfrog)*.

INTERLUDE CULTUREL

■ **Looking Ahead**
The **châteaux** of France are featured on p. 147 of this *Interlude*.

INTERLUDE CULTUREL

■ *Les dates*

La Renaissance

- *1453* Fin de la Guerre de Cent Ans
- *1515*
- ***Règne de François Ier***
- *1547*
- *1589*
- Règne d'Henri IV
- *1610*
- Règne de Louis XIII

Le Grand Siècle

- *1643*
- ***Règne de Louis XIV***
- *1715* Mort de Louis XIV

■ *Les événements*

La Renaissance (1500-1570)

La cour de François Ier

Après la Guerre de Cent Ans et la reconquête de son territoire, la France est finalement en paix. La période qui commence s'appelle la «**Renaissance**», c'est-à-dire le renouvellement. C'est une période de grande activité artistique et culturelle. C'est à cette époque que les rois de France ont habité en Touraine où ils ont construit de magnifiques châteaux: **Chenonceaux, Amboise, Chambord.**

Le château de Chambord est immense, avec plus de 400 pièces et 365 cheminées.

Le Grand Siècle (1643-1715)

Le Grand Siècle, c'est le siècle de **Louis XIV**, ou **«Roi-Soleil»**. C'est aussi la période la plus brillante de l'histoire de France. Louis XIV est devenu roi à l'âge de cinq ans et il a régné sur la France pendant 72 ans. Pendant son règne, il a encouragé les arts et les sciences. Il a créé des académies de peinture, de sculpture, de sciences, d'architecture. Avec Louis XIV, le prestige de la culture française s'est répandu° dans toute l'Europe. Mais Louis XIV était aussi un roi autoritaire et ambitieux. De son château de **Versailles** il exerçait un pouvoir absolu sur le reste du pays. C'est lui qui a dit: «L'État, c'est moi!» Louis XIV a engagé la France dans de nombreuses guerres qui ont fini par ruiner le pays.

Louis XIV à la guerre

s'est répandu *spread*

Les personnes

François Ier et Mona Lisa

Jean Clouet *«François Ier»*

Le roi **François Ier** (1494-1547) était très grand, très beau et très athlétique. Il aimait tous les sports de son époque, et en particulier le jeu de paume, l'ancêtre du tennis actuel. Sa grande passion était la chasse° qu'il pratiquait dans les forêts de ses châteaux de **Chambord** et **d'Amboise.**

C'était aussi un esprit fin° et cultivé qui aimait la musique, les arts et les lettres. Il a fait venir° dans son château d'Amboise le grand artiste italien **Léonard de Vinci** à qui il a acheté la **«Joconde»** ou «Mona Lisa», aujourd'hui le portrait le plus célèbre du monde.

Léonard de Vinci *la «Joconde»*

La vie de cour sous François Ier

Louis XIV et sa cour

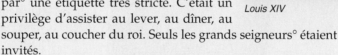

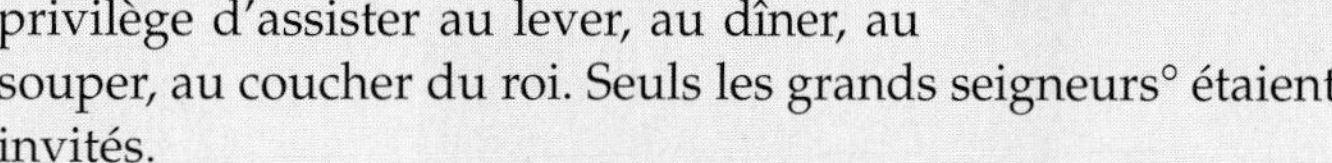

Louis XIV (1638-1715) a longtemps vécu au château de **Versailles.** Il a construit ce château non seulement pour son plaisir, mais pour attirer les nobles du pays. C'était une façon de les contrôler et de les empêcher° de se révolter contre lui. Trois mille personnes vivaient au château de Versailles.

À la cour de Louis XIV, tout était organisé autour de la personne du roi. Les événements de sa vie quotidienne° étaient des cérémonies officielles, réglées par° une étiquette très stricte. C'était un privilège d'assister au lever, au dîner, au souper, au coucher du roi. Seuls les grands seigneurs° étaient invités.

Louis XIV

Patron des arts et des lettres, Louis XIV s'intéressait personnellement à la musique, au théâtre et surtout au ballet. Parfois, il participait lui-même aux représentations. Un jour, il a paru sur scène déguisé en soleil, d'où son nom de **«Roi-Soleil»**. Ce nom est avant tout° symbolique. Louis XIV brillait sur sa cour, sur la France et sur le monde. Il se considérait vraiment comme le centre de l'univers.

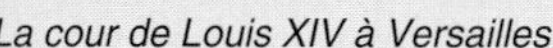

La cour de Louis XIV à Versailles

a chasse *hunting* **fin** *refined* **fait venir** *brought* **empêcher** *to prevent* **quotidienne** *daily*
églées par *structured according to* **seigneurs** = nobles **avant tout** *above all*

Notes historiques

- C'est au nom de François 1er que Jacques Cartier prit possession du Canada en 1534.
- En 1682, Cavelier de La Salle prit possession d'un vaste territoire en Amérique du Nord qu'il appella Louisiane en l'honneur de son roi, Louis XIV.
- Louis XIV a survécu à son fils et à son petit-fils. À sa mort, ce fut son *arrière-petit-fils* qui a pris sa succession sous le nom de Louis XV.

Notes culturelles

- Léonard de Vinci a peint le tableau *La Joconde* vers 1499–1512. François 1er l'a acheté en 1517 pour un prix de 4000 florins d'or, soit 15 kilos *(33 lbs)* d'or. Léonard de Vinci est mort en France, en 1519, près de la ville d'Amboise. *La Joconde* est aujourd'hui l'attraction principale du musée du Louvre à Paris.
- Le château de Versailles était un modeste pavillon de chasse du roi Louis XIII. Le palais devint un musée de l'histoire de France en 1887. En 1783, la France reconnaît l'indépendance des treize colonies américaines et signe le traité de Paris au château de Versailles.

Teaching Note

Students should be encouraged to see Rappeneau's movie version of *Cyrano de Bergerac*, which is available on videocassette. <u>If the film is used in class, you will want to focus on those scenes where the dialog is clear and understandable, and view rapidly (or skip) those passages which are well above the students' linguistic level.</u>

Notes culturelles

- Edmond Rostand (1868–1918) was a member of the **Académie française**. He wrote **Cyrano de Bergerac** in 1897.
- **Savinien de Cyrano de Bergerac** (1619–1655) wrote several plays as well as imaginary travel logs such as **Histoire comique des États et Empires de la lune**, and **Histoire comique des États et Empires du soleil.**
- Jose Ferrer won the Oscar for Best Actor for his interpretation of the title role in the 1950 movie *Cyrano de Bergerac*.

Teaching Strategy: Expansion

Have students look at the movie poster and give their opinion. What do they think the movie is about? Does the poster make them feel like going to see this movie? Why or why not?

Cyrano de Bergerac

Cyrano de Bergerac a vraiment existé. Il a vécu à l'époque de **Louis XIV**. C'était un soldat et un écrivain qui a laissé° un curieux roman de science-fiction où il décrit un voyage dans la lune. Ce personnage historique serait cependant resté dans une tranquille obscurité s'il n'avait pas été transformé en héros de légende et immortalisé dans une comédie célèbre du 19e siècle.

Cette comédie, intitulée *Cyrano de Bergerac*, écrite il y a cent ans par Edmond Rostand, a connu un très grand succès à son époque. Depuis, elle a été mise en musique, adaptée à l'écran,° et maintes° fois transformée et parodiée.* Le dernier film en date, dans lequel l'acteur Gérard Depardieu joue le rôle principal, est une reproduction assez fidèle° de la pièce originale.

Cyrano de Bergerac est essentiellement une histoire d'amour, basée sur un gigantesque quiproquo° tragico-comique. **Cyrano** aime **Roxane** qui aime un autre homme, **Christian**. Mais si Roxane a d'abord été attirée° par la beauté physique de Christian, c'est pour la beauté de sa poésie qu'elle l'aime vraiment. Or, cette poésie n'est pas celle de Christian, mais celle de l'infortuné Cyrano.

* Une parodie classique est le film américain *Roxanne* où Steve Martin joue le rôle d'un pompier *(fireman)* amoureux.

Cyrano, le héros de l'histoire, est un vaillant soldat du régiment des Cadets de Gascogne. Il est brave, courageux, téméraire° à l'extrême. C'est aussi un poète à l'âme tendre.° Il est bon, loyal, généreux, intelligent, spirituel,° sensible et il écrit de magnifiques vers. Il a toutes les qualités possibles sauf une: il n'est pas beau.

Cyrano est en effet affligé d'une infirmité incurable: Il a un nez monstrueusement long. Cette infirmité le rend très susceptible° auprès des° hommes, et très timide auprès des femmes. Personne en sa présence ne peut mentionner le mot «nez». Cyrano est secrètement amoureux de sa cousine Roxane, mais il sait qu'il n'a aucune chance, précisément à cause de cet immense nez qui le défigure. . .

Documents: «Cyrano de Bergerac»

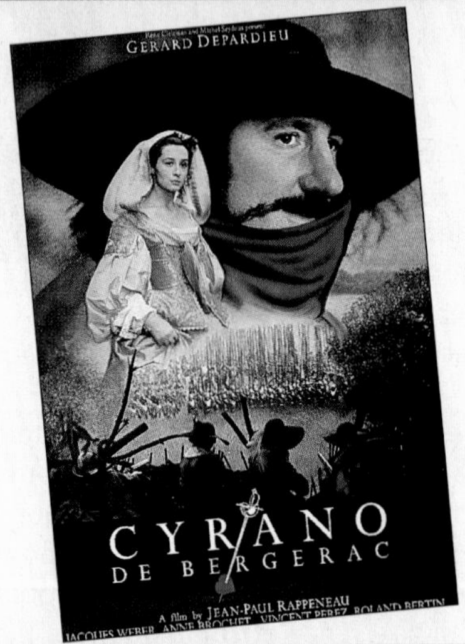

Le film Cyrano de Bergerac (1990) reproduit fidèlement la pièce de théâtre.

L'action de la pièce se passe dans la France du 17e siècle. Dans la première scène, une foule° se presse° pour assister à un spectacle de **Montfleury**, comédien en vogue, mais ennemi de Cyrano. Dans cette foule, on reconnaît tous les personnages principaux de l'histoire, et d'abord **Roxane**.
1 Elle est belle, coquette, romanesque et éprise° de poésie. Tous les hommes sont amoureux d'elle. Ce jour-là, elle est accompagnée de **de Guiche**, un seigneur noble et puissant° qui lui fait la cour.°

laissé *left* **écran** *screen* **maintes** = plusieurs **fidèle** *faithful* **quiproquo** *misunderstanding* **attirée** *attracted* **téméraire** *bold* **à l'âme tendre** *with a soft heart* **spirituel** *witty* **susceptible** *touchy* **auprès de** = avec **foule** *crowd* **se presse** *hurries* **éprise** *enamoured* **puissant** *powerful* **lui fait la cour** *is courting her*

Mais Roxane pense secrètement à un jeune homme qu'elle a aperçu un jour et dont elle est tombée secrètement amoureuse. C'est le beau
2 **Christian**, qui, lui aussi, est dans la foule à la recherche de Roxane. Le public s'impatiente.

On attend Montfleury, mais on attend aussi
3 **Cyrano** qui a promis de lancer un défi° à Montfleury. Montfleury entre en scène. Est-ce que Cyrano viendra? Oui, il arrive! D'une voix éclatante,° il ridiculise Montfleury et le chasse de scène.

Tous les spectateurs ne sont pas contents de l'interruption du spectacle, en particulier de Guiche et son neveu Valvert. Celui-ci va défier Cyrano en lui disant «Monsieur, vous avez un grand nez». Stimulé par cette insulte suprême, Cyrano se lance alors dans la fameuse tirade où il fait l'éloge de son appendice nasal. Puis, il traite Valvert de sot° et engage celui-ci dans un duel, tout en composant des vers. Tout cela se passe sous les yeux de la
4 belle Roxane, très fière de la bravoure et de l'intelligence de son cousin.

Après le duel, Cyrano va accompagner un ami chez lui. Il tombe dans une embuscade° d'où il sort victorieux à un contre cent. L'histoire de cet exploit fait le tour° de la ville et Cyrano devient le héros du jour. Entre-temps°, Roxane lui a envoyé sa dame de compagnie° pour lui demander un rendez-vous.

Intimidé, mais reprenant espoir,° Cyrano va au rendez-vous. Après un long préambule où elle évoque leur enfance passée ensemble et leur longue amitié, Roxane déclare son amour pour . . . Le visage de Cyrano s'illumine.° Pour lui? Hélas, non! Ce n'est pas lui que Roxane aime, mais le beau Christian. Oui, c'est lui qu'elle aime et si elle est venue voir Cyrano, c'est pour lui demander de prendre Christian sous sa protection. Celui-ci va, en effet, entrer au régiment des Cadets de Gascogne, le régiment de Cyrano.

3 *Le spectacle a commencé et Cyrano vient d'arriver. En présence de sa cousine Roxane, Cyrano s'adresse à son ennemi, le comédien Montfleury, et le ridiculise.*

4 *La querelle oratoire entre Valvert et Cyrano s'est transformée en duel. Pendant le duel, Cyrano se moque de son adversaire, tout en composant des vers.*

lancer un défi *to challenge* **éclatante** *very loud* **sot** = stupide **embuscade** *ambush* **fait le tour** *goes around* **entre-temps** = pendant ce temps **dame de compagnie** *lady-in-waiting* **espoir** *hope* **s'illumine** *brightens*

■ Teaching Note

The video version of *Cyrano,* accompanied by Lesson Plans, is available from
FilmArobics, Inc.,
9 Birmingham Place,
Vernon Hills, IL 60061
1-800-832-2448.

■ Notes linguistiques

- In the 17th century, **un cadet** was a young nobleman who served in the army to begin his military career.
- **La Gascogne** is an area between the French regions of Aquitaine and Midi-Pyrénées. Have students locate it using the map on p. R34.

Cyrano promet de protéger Christian, mais c'est déçu° et triste qu'il va rejoindre ses compagnons d'armes. Tout le monde le salue en héros. Cyrano, trop peiné,° ne fait pas attention. Soudain, Christian, la nouvelle recrue du régiment, entre dans la salle d'armes.° Ne connaissant pas Cyrano, il se moque de lui, répétant sans cesse le mot «nez». L'assistance° est pétrifiée! Que va-t-il se passer? Est-ce que Cyrano va
5 tuer° Christian? Non! Fidèle° à la promesse faite à Roxane, Cyrano traite son rival en ami et en frère.

6 Dès lors,° Cyrano va assister Christian dans toutes ses démarches amoureuses° auprès de Roxane. Christian avoue° qu'il est sot, qu'il n'a pas d'éloquence, qu'il ne sait pas parler aux femmes. Que cela ne tienne!° C'est Cyrano qui sera sa voix, son porte-parole.° C'est lui qui écrira à Roxane les lettres d'amour que Christian ne sait pas écrire. L'inspiration lui est facile puisque,° lui aussi, il aime éperdument° Roxane.

Les lettres de Cyrano, signées Christian, enflamment de plus en plus le coeur de Roxane qui consent à accorder° un rendez-vous au beau Christian. Celui-ci va seul au rendez-vous, mais sans l'éloquence de Cyrano, il ne dit que des banalités. Roxane, qui s'attendait° à des torrents de déclamations lyriques, est déçue et renvoie° le jeune homme.

Christian obtient un nouveau rendez-vous, mais
7 cette fois, avec l'assistance de Cyrano, qui lui souffle° chaque mot de sa déclaration d'amour, il réussit à conquérir Roxane dans la célèbre scène du balcon. Au cours de° cette scène, Christian monte au balcon de Roxane, entre chez elle où les deux amants sont mariés par un prêtre envoyé par de Guiche, toujours° amoureux de Roxane.

De Guiche arrive lui-même chez Roxane où il apprend le mariage. Furieux et jaloux, il annonce qu'il vient d'être nommé commandant de l'armée française chargée de déloger les Espagnols de la ville d'Arras. Il décide d'y envoyer sur le champ° le régiment des Cadets de Gascogne, séparant ainsi Christian de sa nouvelle femme.

L'action change de lieu.° Nous sommes maintenant . Arras où le régiment de Christian et de Cyrano es cantonné.° La guerre a mal tourné pour les Français Assiégés par les Espagnols, les fougueux° soldats d Gascogne meurent de faim.° Cyrano veut tenir l promesse qu'il a faite à Roxane. Chaque jour, elle reçoi une lettre de Christian. En réalité, c'est toujours Cyran qui lui écrit, évidemment à l'insu de° son ami, de billets° d'un lyrisme magnifique.

Dans le camp français, la situation est maintenan désespérée. Sur les ordres de de Guiche, le régiment d Gascogne doit être sacrifié. Cyrano écrit à Roxane un dernière lettre d'adieu, toujours signée du nom d Christian. Entre-temps, émue° par l'intensité de
8 lettres poétiques de son mari, Roxane décide de tou risquer pour le rejoindre à Arras. Elle traverse° le lignes espagnoles et arrive dans le camp quelque heures avant la bataille finale. En présence de Cyrano elle avoue à Christian que ce n'est plus pour sa beaut qu'elle l'aime, mais pour sa poésie, et qu'elle l'aimerai même s'il était laid.° Déconcerté par cet aveu, Christian part à l'assaut. Au cours de l'engagement,° est blessé.° Il meurt, réconforté par l'amour de Roxan et l'amitié de Cyrano. La bataille finale a lieu. Pendan cette bataille, Cyrano et de Guiche combatten
9 héroïquement. Christian est mort, mais sa femme e ses amis sont sauvés.

Quinze ans ont passé. Roxane a pris le deuil de Christian et s'est retirée dans un couvent. Là, ell reçoit régulièrement la visite de ses deux amis, d Guiche, devenu duc et maréchal de France, et Cyranc pauvre, mais toujours aussi fier.° Un jour, celui-ci arriv
10 en retard au rendez-vous. Il a été blessé dans un embuscade tendue par ses ennemis et il va mourir.

Ce jour-là, Roxane comprend enfin que c'est bie lui l'auteur des merveilleuses lettres d'amour qu'ell recevait de Christian. Cyrano meurt dans ses bras finalement aimé par celle qu'il avait aimée toute sa vie

Note culturelle

Arras is a city in northern France that fell under Spanish rule in 1492. It was reconquered by Louis XIII in 1640.

■ Note linguistique

L'expression **à l'insu de** vient du participe passé de **savoir (su)** et du préfixe **in- (sans)**. Autre usage: **à mon/votre insu** *(without my/your knowledge)*.

déçu *disappointed* **peiné** *in pain* **salle d'armes** *fencing hall* **l'assistance** = les personnes dans la salle **tuer** *to kill* **fidèle** *faithful* **dès lors** *from then on* **démarches amoureuses** *steps in his courtship* **avoue** = admet **que cela ne tienne** *that won't matter* **porte-parole** *spokesperson* **puisque** *since* **éperdument** *madly* **accorder** *to grant* **s'attendait à** *was expecting* **renvoie** *sends away* **souffle** *prompts* **au cours de** = pendant **toujours** *still* **sur le champ** = immédiatement **lieu** *location* **cantonné** *quartered* **fougueux** = braves **meurent de faim** *dying of starvation* **à l'insu de** *without the knowledge of* **billets** = lettres **émue** *moved* **traverse** *crosses* **laid** *ugly* **aveu** *admissio* **au cours de l'engagement** = pendant la bataille **blessé** *wounded* **a pris le deuil de** *is in mourning for* **fier** *proud*

Teaching Strategy: Expansion

Make copies of the film scenes (pp. 143, 145), covering the captions. Ask students to write their own dialog or caption for each scene. Alternately, copy the existing captions and separate them from the accompanying scene. In groups, have students match the correct scenes and captions.

5 Dans la salle d'armes du régiment, Cyrano fait connaissance de son rival Christian qu'il a promis de protéger.

6 Cyrano et Christian deviennent amis. Malgré lui, Cyrano va aider Christian à gagner le coeur de Roxane.

7 Émue par la poésie des lettres signées Christian, mais écrites en réalité par Cyrano, Roxane a donné rendez-vous à Christian sous son balcon. C'est Christian qui parle, mais c'est Cyrano qui exprime son amour pour elle.

8 Roxane arrive devant Arras avec un chariot de vivres (food) pour les Français assiégés. Elle traverse les lignes espagnoles avec Christian et Cyrano.

9 Christian est mort héroïquement. Ses amis Cyrano et Ragueneau emmènent sa femme loin du champ de bataille.

10 Bien des années ont passé. Un jour, Cyrano arrive en retard à son rendez-vous habituel avec Roxane. Blessé, il va mourir, mais avant, Roxane apprendra enfin son secret.

Teaching Strategy: Challenge

Ask students if they like the ending of the movie. What could the other possible endings be? Which one would they prefer and why?

Give students the following assignment:

Faites la critique de ce film. Jugez si, d'après vous, c'est un bon film ou non et expliquez pourquoi. Allez-vous recommander ce film? Combien d'étoiles lui donnez-vous?
(cinq étoiles = super; aucune étoile = nul)

■ Notes linguistiques

- **Maître** est aujourd'hui le titre honorifique des avocats et des notaires; au 17e siècle, ce titre était donné aux gens de condition moyenne.
- **Monsieur du Corbeau** est un titre cérémonieux de noblesse.
- **Le phénix** est un oiseau fabuleux de la mythologie qui, d'après la légende, renaît de ses propres cendres.

Teaching Strategy: Expansion

Expliquez: «Tout flatteur vit aux dépens de celui qui l'écoute.» Êtes-vous d'accord? Pourquoi ou pourquoi pas?

Le corbeau et le renard

À l'école, tous les jeunes Français apprennent par coeur les fables de La Fontaine. Leur auteur est l'un des écrivains les plus célèbres du siècle de Louis XIV. À travers° ses portraits d'animaux, **Jean de La Fontaine** (1621-1695) voulait critiquer les défauts de ses contemporains. La morale de ses fables est en réalité éternelle.

La fameuse fable *Le corbeau et le renard*° s'adresse aux gens qui ont besoin d'être admirés.

Le corbeau et le renard

Maître Corbeau, sur un arbre perché,
Tenait° en son bec un fromage.
Maître Renard, par l'odeur alléché,°
Lui tint à peu près ce langage:°
«Hé! bonjour, Monsieur du Corbeau,
Que vous êtes joli! que vous me semblez beau!
Sans mentir,° si votre ramage°
Se rapporte° à votre plumage
Vous êtes le phénix° des hôtes de ces bois.
À ces mots, le Corbeau ne se sent pas de joie;°
Et pour montrer sa belle voix,
Il ouvre un large bec, laisse tomber° sa proie.°
Le Renard s'en saisit,° et dit: «Mon bon Monsieur,
Apprenez que tout flatteur
Vit° aux dépens° de celui qui l'écoute:
Cette leçon vaut° bien un fromage, sans doute.»
Le Corbeau, honteux° et confus,°
Jura,° mais un peu tard, qu'on ne l'y prendrait plus.°

(*Fables choisies*, Livre I, 1688)

à travers = avec **le corbeau et le renard** *the crow and the fox* **tenait** = avait **alléché** = attiré **lui tint à peu près ce langage** = lui parla ainsi **sans mentir** = en vérité **ramage** = chant **se rapporte** = est égal **le phénix** = l'oiseau le plus fabuleux **ne se sent pas de joie** = est transporté de joi **laisse tomber** *drops* **proie** = le fromage qu'il a trouvé **s'en saisit** = la prend **vit** *lives* **aux dépens** *at the expense* **vaut** *is worth* **honteux** *ashamed* **confus** *upset* **jura** *swore* **on ne l'y prendrait plus** *he wouldn't be taken in again*

NOTES CULTURELLES

- Quelques châteaux de la Loire célèbres construits sous François 1er: Amboise (en photo), Blois, Azay-le-Rideau, Chambord, Chenonceaux (en photo).
- Nicolas Fouquet (1615–1680), Vicomte de Vaux, devint le surintendant des finances en 1653. Grand amateur d'art, il protégea de nombreux artistes dont Molière, La Fontaine et Poussin. À la suite d'une fête grandiose dans son château de Vaux, Louis XIV devint jaloux de sa fortune. Il accusa Fouquet de fraude et de rébellion puis le condamna à l'exil, avant de changer cette condamnation en une peine de prison. Fouquet fut enfermé sous des conditions rigoureuses au fort de Pignerol où il mourut.

L'histoire de France à travers ses châteaux

Carcassonne

Comme beaucoup de villes médiévales, Carcassonne était entourée de hauts remparts qui la protégeaient contre d'éventuels envahisseurs.° Elle résista aux Anglais pendant la Guerre de Cent Ans.

Angers

Angers était la capitale des Plantagenêts, ducs d'Anjou et futurs rois d'Angleterre. Avec ses grosses tours rondes, le château est un bel exemple d'architecture féodale.

Château-Gaillard

Construit en 1196 par Richard Coeur de Lion, Château-Gaillard dominait la Seine et barrait la route entre Paris et Rouen. Dix ans plus tard, le château tomba dans les mains des Français et il n'en reste aujourd'hui que d'imposantes ruines.

Amboise

Le château d'Amboise est situé sur un rocher qui domine la Loire. Sa grosse tour ronde permettait aux cavaliers° et aux carrosses° d'accéder directement au château. C'est au château d'Amboise que le roi François Ier recevait Léonard de Vinci.

Chenonceaux

Le château de Chenonceaux est de pur style Renaissance. Sur ses murs on peut y lire encore des graffiti (en anglais) laissés par les gardes écossais° du roi Henri II.

Fontainebleau

Maintes fois transformé, Fontainebleau a servi de résidence à plus de 20 rois de France, parmi lesquels François Ier et Louis XIII, père de Louis XIV. C'est ici que Napoléon a fait ses adieux avant de partir en exil.

Vaux-le-Vicomte

Le château de Vaux-le-Vicomte a été construit par Nicolas Fouquet, surintendant des finances du royaume de France. Un jour, Fouquet eut la mauvaise idée d'y inviter le jeune roi Louis XIV. Celui-ci, jaloux de la richesse de son ministre, le fit emprisonner.

Versailles

Toute la majesté de Louis XIV et la puissance de la France sont exprimées dans la splendeur du château de Versailles et de ses magnifiques jardins. C'est ici que vivait le roi, entouré de milliers de courtisans.

envahisseurs *invaders* **cavaliers** *horsemen* **carrosses** *horse-drawn carriages* **écossais** *Scottish*

Anecdote

En 1814, Napoléon est vaincu et Louis XVIII accède au trône. Napoléon est à Fontainebleau où il essaie de s'empoisonner. Le poison étant trop vieux, il n'agit pas et Napoléon doit faire ses adieux à sa garde avant de partir en exil pour l'île d'Elbe.

Note culturelle

In the 17th century, food and drinks were usually served cold in Versailles because the kitchens were too far away from the dining rooms.

Teaching Note

Ask students:
Regardez les photos des châteaux. Lequel préférez-vous et pourquoi?

UNITÉ

4

MAIN THEME

Shopping
Asking for services

Communication Functions/Contexts

- Shopping in a stationery store, pharmacy, and convenience store
- Buying stamps/mailing at the post office
- Having items fixed or cleaned
- Having one's hair cut
- Asking for services at photo and shoe repair shops, cleaners, etc.

Linguistic Goals

- Answering questions; using pronouns
- Talking about quantities
- Describing services done by others

■ **Photo Note**

The word **la maroquinerie** (leather goods, leather goods store) comes from **maroquin**, a type of sheep or goat leather that used to be made in **Maroc** (Morocco).

Online Study Center

Online Teaching Center

UNITÉ 4

Aspects de la vie quotidienne

Thème et Objectifs

Culture

In this unit, you will discover . . .

- where to buy various items and obtain various services
- how shopping habits differ in France and the United States

Communication

You will learn how . . .

- to buy stamps and mail letters
- to purchase small items you might need
- to have items fixed or cleaned
- to get a haircut
- to ask for various services

Langue

You will learn how . . .

- to answer questions using one or more pronouns
- to talk about numbers of people and things without specifying exact quantities
- to describe actions that people have others do for them

TEACHING RESOURCES

ANCILLARIES

Student Activities Manual, Unit 4
Audio Program, Unit 4
Video-DVD Program, Unit 4
Chansons Audio CD

HM ClassPrep CD

Presentations, Unit 4
Audioscript, Unit 4
Videoscript, Unit 4
Assessment, Unit 4
Answer Key, Unit 4

EN FRANCE, FAITES COMME les

Il y a beaucoup d'endroits où nous devons aller régulièrement pour répondre aux besoins de la vie quotidienne.° Nous allons au centre commercial pour faire nos achats, au supermarché pour faire les courses, à la poste pour acheter des timbres,° à la banque pour déposer ou retirer° de l'argent. Et de temps en temps, nous allons chez le coiffeur pour nous faire couper les cheveux.° Si les Français font les mêmes choses que les Américains, ils les font parfois un peu différemment.

Un jour vous irez peut-être en France. Voilà quelques conseils pour vivre° «à la française».°

■ Avant de faire votre shopping, surfez sur Internet. Avec Internet, vous trouverez les magasins qui vendent ce que vous cherchez. Vous pourrez étudier les catalogues, comparer les prix, et vous découvrirez peut-être des soldes° extraordinaires. Si vous ne voulez pas vous déplacer,° vous pourrez passer° votre commande° directement sur Internet.

■ Si vous allez au supermarché, n'oubliez pas de prendre de la monnaie.° Pour obtenir° un chariot,° vous devrez, en effet, déposer une pièce d'un euro. Quand vous passerez à la caisse,° ne vous attendez pas° à ce que la caissière empaquette° vos achats. Vous devrez faire cela vous même. Et si vous voulez récupérer l'euro que vous avez déposé pour votre chariot, n'oubliez pas de rapporter votre chariot à l'endroit où vous l'avez pris.

■ Si vous préférez un service plus personnalisé, allez chez les petits commerçants du quartier où vous habitez. Là, les prix sont plus élevés,° mais la qualité est souvent meilleure. Et vous pouvez faire la connaissance des gens de votre quartier. Évidemment n'oubliez pas de dire bonjour et au revoir à la marchande et aux clients qui se trouvent dans la boutique. Sinon, vous serez considéré comme une per-

quotidienne *daily* **timbres** *stamps* **retirer** *to withdraw* **faire couper les cheveux** *to get a haircut* **vivre** *to live* **«à la française»** = comme les Français
soldes *sales* **(ne voulez pas) vous déplacer** = quitter votre maison **passer** = donner **commande** *order* **monnaie** *change* **obtenir** *to get*
chariot *cart* **caisse** *check-out* **ne vous attendez pas** *don't expect* **empaquette** *bag* **élevés** *high* **mal élevée** = impolie

INFO MAGAZINE

Theme: Shopping in France

Reading Strategy: Skimming, browsing

Supplementary vocabulary

À la banque
l'argent liquide *cash*
le distributeur automatique de billets *ATM*
la carte bancaire *bank card*
le chéquier *checkbook*
le compte-chèques *checking account*
le retrait *withdrawal*

■ Notes linguistiques

- **Les soldes** is a masculine noun, almost exclusively used in the plural form.
- **Le pressing** *(dry cleaner's)* is actually an anglicism, from the English verb "to press."
- **La teinturerie** offers more services than **le pressing**, for example the dyeing of clothes. (**la teinture** = dyeing, dye).

■ Photo Note

(Opposite page)
The green cross with even branches (also called a Greek cross) is an emblem found on every French pharmacy.

■ Irregular Verbs

(see Appendix C)
obtenir (*see* **tenir**)
empaqueter is conjugated like **jeter:**
j'empaquette
nous empaquetons
ils empaquettent

Teaching Strategy

Ask students to create their own cartoons illustrating cultural «faux pas.»

■ Si vous allez chez le coiffeur, n'oubliez pas de donner un pourboire° à la personne qui vous a coupé les cheveux, même si vous n'êtes pas très satisfait du résultat. Mais au café et au restaurant, vous n'êtes pas obligé de laisser de pourboire. Il est compris° dans l'addition.

■ Si vous avez besoin d'une photo d'identité, ne perdez pas votre temps à chercher un photographe. Allez dans un grand magasin. Là vous trouverez un «Photomaton» où vous aurez votre photo en cinq minutes. Dans ce même magasin, vous trouverez aussi d'autres services très pratiques: une photocopieuse, un service de réparation de chaussures, un service de reproduction de clés.°

pourboire *tip* compris = inclus clés *keys*
bureau de tabac *tobacco shop* cabine *booth*

■ Si vous avez besoin de timbres un jour où la poste est fermée, allez alors dans un bureau de tabac.° Là, vous pourrez acheter des timbres ordinaires, et aussi des télécartes, indispensables si vous voulez téléphoner d'une cabine° publique.

Maintenant vous savez comment vivre en France. C'est simple. Faites comme les Français!

DÉFINITIONS

Donnez une définition des mots et expressions suivantes.

- un centre commercial
- une poste
- une banque
- des soldes
- un supermarché
- un chariot
- la caisse
- une télécarte
- un coiffeur
- un pourboire
- l'addition

SITUATIONS

1. Vous habitez en France. Vous faites les courses avec un(e) ami(e) américain(e) qui vous rend visite. Expliquez à votre ami(e) — votre partenaire — les différences entre un supermarché en France et aux États-Unis.
2. Un(e) ami(e) français(e) vous rend visite. Expliquez à votre ami(e) — votre partenaire — dans quelles circonstances on donne un pourboire aux États-Unis.
3. Imaginez que vous allez passer deux ou trois mois en France. Est-ce que vous pourrez vous adapter facilement à la vie quotidienne décrite dans le texte?
   - Quels aspects vous semblent pratiques et intéressants?
   - Avec quels aspects auriez-vous des difficultés?

NOTES CULTURELLES

- Although a tip is always included on the bill in France, it is customary to leave additional extra change on the table of the café or restaurant upon leaving.
- **Le photomaton** is the name of the machine (booth) that takes pictures automatically. The same word is also used for photographs taken by such a machine.
- **La carte à puce** was invented by a Frenchman, Roland Moréno, in 1974. It has been in use since 1985.

Scènes de la vie courante

Au supermarché

Si on veut utiliser un chariot, il faut payer une caution.° Pour cela, on introduit une pièce dans un petit réceptacle qui se trouve sur le chariot. Celui-ci se débloque° automatiquement. Quand on a fini ses courses, on rapporte le chariot à l'endroit où on l'a trouvé et on récupère son argent.

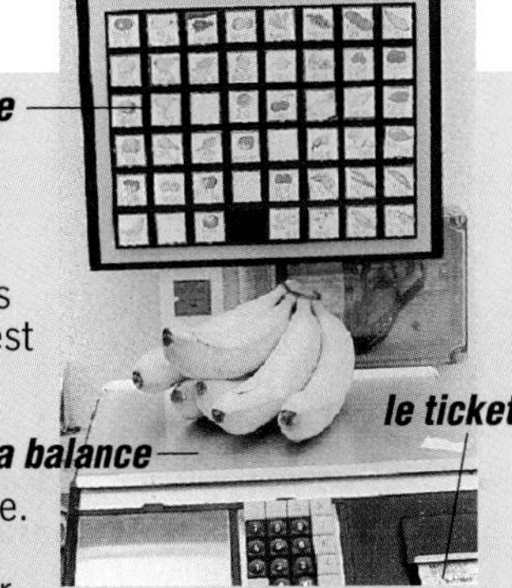

Au rayon des fruits et légumes, tout est «self-service». Le client doit peser° les différentes choses qu'il achète. Pour cela, on met chaque produit sur une balance° automatique et on appuie° sur la touche correspondant à ce produit. La balance imprime° un ticket qu'on colle° sur le produit.

Chez les petits commerçants

Chez les petits commerçants, le service est plus personnel. En parlant avec les gens, on y apprend les nouvelles du quartier où on habite.

Au café

Partout° en France, il y a des cafés. On va au café non seulement pour prendre une boisson ou un sandwich, mais aussi pour bavarder.°

Pour téléphoner

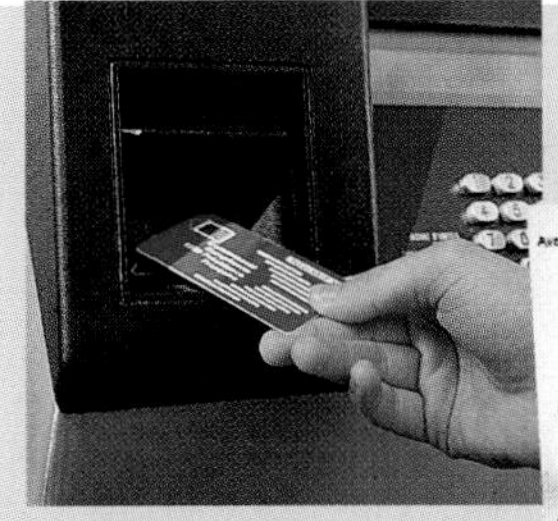

télécarte, (carte à puce)

Si on veut téléphoner d'une cabine téléphonique, on doit avoir une télécarte. Les télécartes sont des «cartes à puce»° qui permettent de téléphoner pendant un certain nombre de minutes. Créées il y a vingt ans seulement, les télécartes sont devenues des objets de collection, comme les timbres.

L'usage des télécartes est très simple! On décroche° le récepteur,° on introduit la télécarte dans l'appareil, et on compose° le numéro. Quand on a terminé son appel, on reprend la carte. Les télécartes s'achètent dans les postes ou dans les bureaux de tabac.

caution *deposit* **se débloque** *unlocks* **peser** *to weigh* **balance** *scale* **appuie** *pushes* **imprime** *prints* **colle** *sticks* **partout** *everywhere* **bavarder** *to chat* **puce** *microchip* **décroche** *picks up* **récepteur** *receiver* **compose** *dials*

Photo Culture Note

On the French telephone pad, you can notice these two keys:
(la touche) bis = redial (key)
(la touche) R = (key) reserved for special future services (message waiting,...)

Supplementary vocabulary

la touche *mute (key)*
la fonction mains libres *"hands-off": speaker-phone function*
le signal d'appel *call waiting*

LE FRANÇAIS

PRATIQUE

Comment faire des achats

TEACHING RESOURCES

Student Activities Manual,
pp. 127–128

Audio Program,
CD 4, Tracks 1–4

Video/DVD Program,
Unit 4

Supplementary vocabulary

<u>À la papeterie</u>
le (stylo-) feutre *felt-tip pen*
la cartouche (d'encre) *ink cartridge*
<u>À la poste</u>
faire la queue *to wait in line*
affranchir (une lettre) *to stamp (a letter)*
le chronopost *express-mail delivery*

Teaching Note

Contrast:
avoir besoin de + NOUN
J'ai besoin de papier à lettres.
il me faut + PARTITIVE + NOUN
Il me faut du papier à lettres.

PARTIE 1

LE FRANÇAIS PRATIQUE — *Comment faire des achats*

À la papeterie

— Vous désirez?

Je voudrais	
Pouvez-vous me donner	**du papier à lettres.**
S'il vous plaît, donnez-moi	

— Vous désirez **quelque chose d'autre** *(something else)*? / **autre chose?**

Oui, **donnez-moi aussi** / **j'ai besoin d'** / **il me faut** *(I need)* **un stylo à bille.**

— Et avec ça?
C'est tout, merci!
Ça fait combien?
Combien est-ce que je vous dois?
— Ça fait 6 euros cinquante.
Voici 10 euros.
— Et voici **votre monnaie** *(change).*
Merci.

devoir *to owe*

À la poste

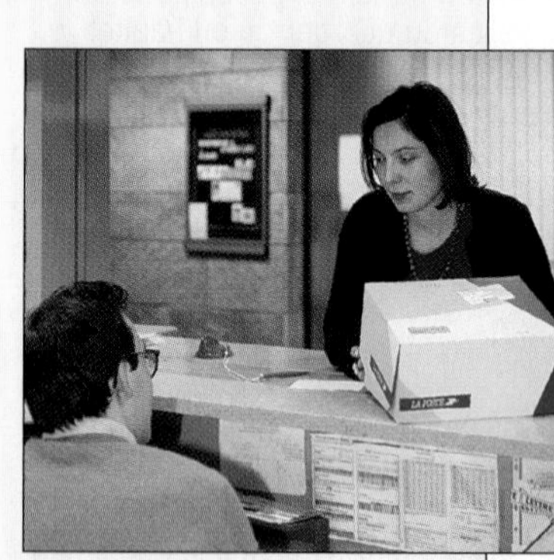

— C'est votre tour *(it's your turn)*, Mademoiselle.
Je voudrais **des timbres** *(stamps)* à 67 centimes.
— Combien en voulez-vous?
Donnez-m'en dix, s'il vous plaît.
— Voilà. C'est tout?
Non, je voudrais aussi . . .

envoyer **cette lettre**. / **cette carte postale**. / **ce colis** *(package)*. / **ce paquet** *(package)*.
faire **des photocopies**.
prendre **mon courrier** *(mail)* **à la poste restante** *(general delivery)*.

Teaching Suggestion: Video/DVD Program

In the Unit 4 *Vidéo-drame: Mélanie fait les courses,* students will have a chance to go shopping with Mélanie for some typical items for the home. This section is rich in useful expressions for shopping and dealing with money. As you watch the video, have students write down the new expressions they hear. During this time, you may also ask them comprehension questions like:

Qu'est-ce que Mélanie achète chez le photographe?; Où est-ce que Mélanie va pour acheter des articles comme le shampooing et le dentifrice?

Quelle boutique? Quel rayon *(department)*?	Quels articles *(items)*?	Quelles quantités?
À la papeterie Au rayon «Papeterie»	**un carnet** *(notebook)* **un crayon** **un stylo à bille** *(ballpoint pen)* **du papier, du papier à lettres** **des enveloppes** **de la colle** *(glue)* **du scotch** *(scotch tape)* **un trombone** *(paper clip)* **un élastique** *(rubber band)*	**un bloc** de papier **un paquet** d'enveloppes **un tube** de colle **un rouleau** de scotch **une boîte** | de trombones | d'élastiques
Chez le photographe Au rayon «Photo»	**une pellicule** *(film)* **en noir et blanc** **une pellicule-couleurs** **des diapos** *(slides)* **une pile** *(battery)*	**un rouleau** de diapos
À la pharmacie Chez le pharmacien Chez la pharmacienne Au rayon «Produits d'hygiène»	**du dentifrice** **de l'aspirine, des vitamines** **du shampooing** **de l'eau de toilette** **un coton-tige** *(cotton swab)* **un mouchoir en papier** *(tissue)* **de l'ouate** *(cotton)* **un pansement adhésif** *(Band-aid)*	**un tube** | de dentifrice | d'aspirine **une bouteille** | de shampooing | d'eau de toilette | de parfum **une boîte** | de coton-tiges | de mouchoirs **un paquet** | d'ouate | de pansements
À la supérette Au rayon «Produits d'entretien» «Produits de maison»	**du savon** **de la lessive** *(detergent)* **du papier hygiénique** *(toilet paper)* **du Sopalin** *(paper towels)* **de la ficelle** *(string)* **une allumette** *(match)* **une épingle** *(pin)* **une épingle de sûreté** *(safety pin)*	**un paquet** de lessive **un rouleau** | de papier hygiénique | de Sopalin **une pelote** *(ball)* de ficelle **une boîte** | d'allumettes | d'épingles

Note linguistique

Paquet is the general term for *package.* **Colis** usually refers to a package which is sent by mail.

Notes culturelles

- In France, the post office also functions as a bank. Many French people have a **compte-chèques postal** (also called **le CCP**). All related banking transactions are done at the post office.

Anecdote

In 1962, Jacques Marette, Minister of the PTT, decreed that all letters sent to Santa Claus should be answered by a postcard. Since then, children from any country who write a letter to Santa in the care of the French post office receive a card. Each year, **la Poste** sends about 500,000 cards to children.

Notes linguistiques

- **Une diapo** is the shortened form of **une diapositive.**
- To ask for a roll of film with a certain number of exposures, one asks for **une pellicule de [24] poses.**
- **Sopalin** est le nom d'une marque *(brand)* de papier absorbant. Maintenant on utilise ce nom d'une manière générique.

Supplementary vocabulary

À la pharmacie

le démêlant *conditioner*
le démaquillant *makeup remover*
un flacon *(small bottle, flask)* **d'eau de cologne / de parfum**
du fil *thread*
une aiguille *needle*
un bouton *button*

NOTES CULTURELLES

- **Le chronopost** (note: no **e** at the end) is an express-mail delivery system set up by the French post office in 1986.
- In 1991, the Ministry of **Postes et Télécommunications** (also known by its former logo **PTT** or **Poste, Télégraphe et Téléphone**) was split into two independent Government-controlled entities: **La Poste** (for mail service, as well as money orders and postal savings accounts) and **France Télécom** (for phone services). In 1997, France Télécom was partially privatized, with its capital open to individual investors.

TEACHING RESOURCES

Tête-à-tête Pair Activity,
Les courses, p. PA5

1 Votre liste

Vous allez passer les vacances de printemps à la Martinique avec votre partenaire. Chacun va faire une liste de dix articles qu'il va emporter *(take along)* avec lui. Utilisez le tableau qui figure à la page 153.
Puis comparez vos listes:

- Qu'est-ce que vous avez pris de semblable *(similar)*?
- Qu'est-ce que vous avez pris de différent?

2 À la Samaritaine

Vous êtes allé(e) à la Samaritaine, un grand magasin à Paris. Là, vous avez acheté l'un des articles suivants. Dites . . .

- à quel rayon vous êtes passé(e)
- ce que vous avez acheté (nommez l'article)
- deux autres choses que vous avez achetées à ce rayon.

▶ **Je suis passé(e) au rayon «Papeterie». J'ai acheté une boîte de trombones. J'ai aussi acheté . . .**

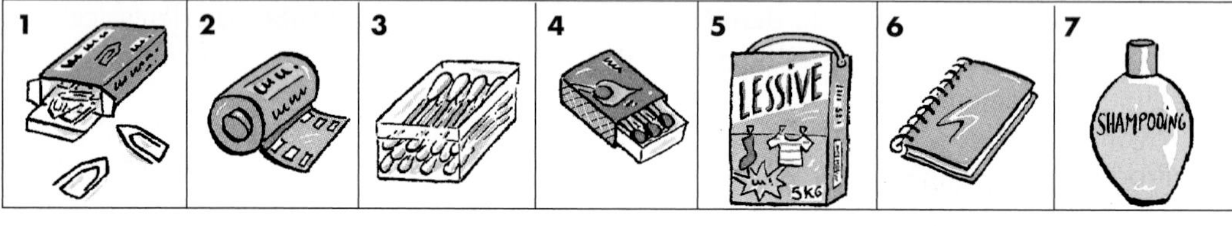

3 Achats

Un groupe d'étudiants américains visite la France. Ces étudiants passent dans un grand magasin. Déterminez les besoins de chacun. Dites à quel rayon il passe et ce qu'il achète.

▶ Betty veut prendre des photos du groupe.
Elle passe au rayon «Photo» où elle achète une pellicule-couleurs (un rouleau de diapos).

1. John veut écrire à ses parents.
2. Jim veut laver ses chemises.
3. Elizabeth a perdu sa trousse de toilette *(toiletry kit)*.
4. Anne a mal à la tête.
5. Jacqueline a des ampoules *(blisters)* aux pieds.
6. Cindy éternue *(sneezes)* constamment.
7. Alice veut se laver les cheveux.
8. Robert veut faire un paquet qu'il va envoyer à ses parents.

■ Variation: Activity 3

Dites dans quel magasin ces jeunes Français doivent aller et ce qu'ils doivent y acheter pour pouvoir faire les choses suivantes.

- Lucas veut écrire à ses amis pour les inviter à son anniversaire. [à la papeterie: un bloc de papier à lettres, un paquet d'enveloppes, un stylo à bille)
- Samantha veut laver son vélo. [à la supérette: un paquet de lessive, un rouleau de Sopalin]
- Amélie veut prendre des photos au mariage de sa soeur dimanche prochain. [chez le photographe: un rouleau de diapos, une pellicule-couleurs, des piles]
- Stéphane veut fabriquer une marionnette en papier. [à la papeterie: un tube de colle, un rouleau de scotch, du papier]
- Ahmed vient de tomber en faisant du roller. Son genou est égratigné *(scratched)*. [à la pharmacie: un paquet de pansements, un paquet d'ouate]

Teaching Strategy: Warm-Up

Divide the class into groups of three. Each group will prepare two short dialogs based on the following situations (or original scenarios if preferred).

- You need supplies for a first aid kit for a camping trip.
- A friend is leaving for college and needs supplies.
- You have a new penpal in Senegal and you are going to the post office to send a letter.
- You are making a collage of photos with captions for a friend's birthday.

4 À la poste

C'est votre première semaine à Paris. Vous allez à la poste pour certaines choses. Composez le dialogue suivant avec votre partenaire qui va jouer le rôle de l'employé(e) de poste.

Employé(e): *Say hello.*
Client(e): Say hello and ask for stamps at 50 centimes.
Employé(e): *Ask how many stamps the client wants.*
Client(e): Mention a number.
Employé(e): *Ask if that is all.*
Client(e): Say that you have something to mail (mention the item: a letter? a postcard? a package?).
Employé(e): *Determine the price of the items requested and ask the client for the money.*
Client(e): Pay the postal clerk the sum requested.

5 Créa-dialogue

C'est samedi aujourd'hui et vous avez beaucoup d'achats à faire. Choisissez une boutique où vous allez faire quelques achats. Avec votre partenaire, composez un dialogue pour cette boutique et jouez-le en classe. Votre partenaire va jouer le rôle du vendeur (de la vendeuse).

▶ — Vous désirez, mademoiselle?
— Je voudrais un tube de dentifrice.
— Et avec ça?
— J'ai besoin aussi d'une bouteille de shampooing.
— Voici le dentifrice et le shampooing.
— Merci. C'est combien, s'il vous plaît?
— 11 euros cinquante centimes.
— Voici vingt euros.
— Et voici votre monnaie: 8 euros et cinquante centimes.

- *Use appropriate greeting.*
- *Mention another product.*
- *Use another expression.*
- *Use another expression and name another product.*
- *Give client the items requested.*
- *Use another expression.*
- *Give a price under 100 euros.*
- *Give a bill to cover the amount.*
- *Return the correct change.*

Conversations libres

Avec votre partenaire, choisissez l'une des situations suivantes. Composez le dialogue correspondant et jouez-le en classe.

1 Shopping

Vous êtes un(e) étudiant(e) français(e). Vous venez d'arriver à cette école avec un programme d'échange. Faites une liste de trois ou quatre choses dont vous avez besoin et demandez à votre partenaire où vous pouvez les acheter.

2 Une erreur

Vous êtes allé(e) dans un grand magasin où vous avez acheté plusieurs articles. Quand vous rentrez chez vous, vous vous rendez compte *(realize)* que vous avez pris le sac d'une autre personne. Téléphonez au magasin pour expliquer la situation. L'employé(e) va vous demander ce que vous avez acheté et ce qu'il y a dans le sac que vous avez ramené chez vous.

3 Camping

Ce week-end vous allez faire du camping avec votre partenaire. Pour la préparation de cette expédition, votre partenaire veut acheter toutes sortes d'articles. Vous dites que ce n'est pas nécessaire et vous donnez des raisons *(reasons)*.

- You have a summer job in an office and have been asked to pick up some essential desk supplies.
- Your sister or brother has just moved into a new apartment and needs to shop for kitchen and bathroom supplies.

■ Note linguistique

le postier/la postière = l'employé(e) de la poste

■ Additional Information

Some popular French brands:
Toothpaste: **Fluocaril**
Shampoo: **L'Oréal, Klorane,**
Beauty products: **Nivea, Lancôme, Vichy**

■ Note culturelle

French **parfums** and **eaux de toilette** are known all over the world. The perfume industry developed in the 18th century around the city of **Grasse** in Provence, with the cultivation of large fields of flowers used in the manufacture of essence extracts.

Students may be familiar with the following names of French companies which make perfumes and colognes.
Cacharel (Anaïs)
Chanel (Chanel No. 5)
Dior (Miss Dior, Eau Sauvage)
Givenchy (Ysatis, Le De)
Lancôme (Ô, Ô oui, Poème, Trésor)
Guy Laroche (Fidji)
Rochas (Homme)

LANGUE ET COMMUNICATION

TEACHING RESOURCES

Student Activities Manual, pp. 45–47, 129

Audio Program, CD 4, Tracks 5–6

HM ClassPrep CD, Audioscript, Unit 4

■ Notes linguistiques

- The pronoun **y** is commonly used with verbs indicating movement or location:
  - **aller (à, chez)**
  - **entrer (à, dans)**
  - **monter (à, sur)**
  - **partir (à)**
  - **se rendre (à, chez)**
  - **rentrer (à)**
  - **retourner (à)**
  - **se trouver (à, dans, sous)**
- To refer to people, the construction **à** + STRESS PRONOUN is used.
  Je pense **à mon copain.**
  Je pense **à lui.**
  Je pense **à mon travail.**
  J'**y** pense.
- To refer to people, the construction **de** + STRESS PRONOUN is used.
  Je parle **de mon prof d'anglais.**
  Je parle **de lui.**
- Other verbs with **à:**
  - **répondre à (une lettre)**
  - **s'intéresser à**
- Other verbs with **de:**
  - **sortir de**
  - **se souvenir de**
  - **s'approcher de**
  - **s'occuper de**

Proverbe

Qui s'y frotte, s'y pique.
Gather thistles, expect prickles.

A. Révision: Le pronom y

The object pronoun **y** replaces a noun or noun phrases introduced by a preposition of place **(à, en, dans, chez, sur, sous,** etc.**)**. It is the equivalent of *there.*

Tu vas **au supermarché**?	Oui, j'**y** vais.
Tu es passé **chez le pharmacien**?	Non, je n'**y** suis pas passé.

➡ **Y** is also used to replace **à** + NOUN referring to a THING.

Tu vas participer **au championnat**?	Oui, je vais **y** participer.

Verbs used with **à**

jouer à
participer à
croire à
penser à
assister à
faire attention à

B. Révision: Le pronom en

The object pronoun **en** replaces **du**, **de la**, **de l'**, **des**, **de** + NOUN.
It is the equivalent of *some, any.*

Tu prends **des vitamines**?	Non, je n'**en** prends pas.
Tu as acheté **du dentifrice**?	Oui, j'**en** ai acheté.

➡ **En** is also used to replace:

- the preposition **de** + NOUN

Tu viens **de la pharmacie**?	Oui, j'**en** viens.
Tu as besoin **de ton stylo à bille**?	Non, je n'**en** ai pas besoin.

- a noun introduced by **un** or **une**

Tu as **une guitare**?	Oui, j'**en** ai **une**.

- a noun introduced by a NUMBER

Marc a acheté **deux cartes postales**.	Moi, j'**en** ai acheté **trois**.

- **de** + NOUN after an expression of quantity

Tu as **beaucoup d'argent**?	Non, je n'**en** ai pas **beaucoup**.
Vous voulez **deux kilos d'oranges**?	Oui, j'**en** veux **deux kilos**.
Combien de rouleaux de diapos as-tu pris?	J'**en** ai pris **un rouleau**.

Verbs used with **de**

venir de
parler de
avoir besoin de
avoir envie de
avoir peur de

➡ Note the use of **en** with **il y a** and **donnez-moi**.

Il y a une papeterie dans mon quartier.	Il y **en** a une.
Donnez-moi deux blocs de papier.	Donnez-m'**en** deux.

RAPPEL!

The pronouns **y** and **en** come BEFORE the verb, except in affirmative commands. Compare:

Tu vas à la papeterie?	Tu **y** vas?	Vas-**y**.
Tu achètes des enveloppes?	Tu **en** achètes?	Achètes-**en**.

Teaching Strategy: Expansion

In affirmative commands, have the students note the liaison /z/ sound and the addition of an "s" in the affirmative imperative before **y** and **en**.

Va à la boulangerie. **Vas-y.**
Achète des croissants. **Achètes-en.**

1 La vie de star

Vous interviewez un(e) star de cinéma français(e) sur sa vie. Votre partenaire va vous répondre affirmativement en donnant des précisions et en utilisant **y** ou **en**.

▶ aller souvent au concert? (avec mes amis)

— Vous allez souvent au concert?
— Oui, j'y vais souvent avec mes amis.

1. aller au cinéma? (de temps en temps)
2. jouer au tennis? (pendant les vacances)
3. faire du jogging? (tous les matins)
4. faire attention à votre santé? (tout le temps)
5. boire de l'eau minérale? (à tous les repas)
6. manger des fruits? (beaucoup)
7. donner des interviews? (de temps en temps)
8. participer au festival de Cannes? (tous les ans)
9. avoir une voiture de sport? (une)
10. avoir des admirateurs? (beaucoup)
11. avoir besoin d'encouragement? (souvent)

2 Les courses

Vous passez les vacances dans un petit village de Normandie. Votre partenaire a fait les courses ce matin. Demandez-lui ce qu'il/elle a acheté.

▶ **— Tu es allé(e) à la papeterie?**
— Oui, j'y suis allé(e).
— Tu as acheté des enveloppes?
— Oui, j'en ai acheté un paquet.

1. • à la poste • des timbres • vingt
2. • chez le photographe • des diapos • deux rouleaux
3. • à la pharmacie • du shampooing • une bouteille
4. • au marché • des tomates • deux kilos
5. • chez le crémier • des oeufs • une douzaine
6. • à la boulangerie • des croissants • six

3 Camping

Maintenant vous allez faire du camping. Votre partenaire vous demande ce qu'il/elle doit prendre. Répondez-lui en lui donnant des quantités. Soyez logique!

▶ **— Je prends des allumettes?**
— Oui, prends-en une boite. (deux boîtes)

QUOI?
du dentifrice
de la lessive
du shampooing
des coton-tiges
de la ficelle
de l'ouate
des pansements
du Sopalin
des allumettes
du papier hygiénique

QUELLE QUANTITÉ?
un paquet
un tube
une boîte
une bouteille
une pelote
un rouleau

■ Teaching Note: Activity 1

You may encourage your more creative students to expand the dialog by giving original answers.

Note culturelle

Le festival de Cannes is an international film festival started in 1946. It takes place every May and is attended by movie makers and actors from all over the world. The best movie wins **la Palme d'or**.

TEACHING RESOURCES

Student Activities Manual, pp. 47–48

C. Expressions indéfinies de quantité

Indefinite expressions of quantity refer to an undetermined number of people or things.

ADJECTIVE (+ NOUN)		PRONOUN	
quelques . . .	*some, a few*	**quelques-uns** **quelques-unes**	*some, a few*
un(e) autre . . . **d'autres . . .**	*another* *other, some other*	**un(e) autre** **d'autres**	*another one* *others, some others, other ones*
plusieurs . . .	*several*	**plusieurs**	*several*
certain(e)s . . .	*some, several*	**certain(e)s**	*some, certain ones*
la plupart de . . .	*most of*	**la plupart**	*most (of them)*

The above expressions of quantity can be used either as subjects or as objects.

ADJECTIVE	PRONOUN
SUBJECT	
Quelques amies sont venues.	**Quelques-unes** sont venues.
Plusieurs lettres sont arrivées ce matin.	**Plusieurs** sont arrivées ce matin.
OBJECT	
J'ai invité **quelques** amis.	J'en ai invité **quelques-uns**.
Nous avons visité **plusieurs** monuments.	Nous en avons visité **plusieurs**.

➡ Note that **en** is used with the indefinite pronouns of quantity when these expressions are the direct object of the verb.

4 S'il te plaît!

Vous êtes chez votre partenaire. Il/elle vous offre à nouveau certaines choses. Acceptez-les (ou refusez, en expliquant pourquoi).

▶ une limonade
— Tu veux une limonade?
— Oui, donne-m'en une autre, s'il te plaît.
(Non, merci, je n'ai pas soif.)

1. un hamburger
2. un jus d'orange
3. une part de pizza
4. un sandwich
5. une tasse de café
6. un thé glacé

Teaching Strategy: Challenge

Give students a sentence which includes an indefinite adjective. Ask them to restate the sentence using **en** and an indefinite pronoun. (Give them one or two examples since this concept can be difficult for some students.)

5 Un après-midi à Montréal

Vous êtes à Montréal avec votre partenaire. Cet après-midi, vous êtes resté(e) à votre hôtel, mais votre partenaire est sorti(e). Demandez-lui ce qu'il/elle a fait.

▶ acheter des souvenirs (quelques-uns)

— Tu as acheté des souvenirs?
— Oui, j'en ai acheté quelques-uns.

1. prendre des photos (quelques-unes)
2. écrire des lettres (quelques-unes)
3. envoyer des cartes postales (plusieurs)
4. acheter un guide de la ville (un autre)
5. acheter des CD (plusieurs)
6. rencontrer des jeunes Canadiens (quelques-uns)

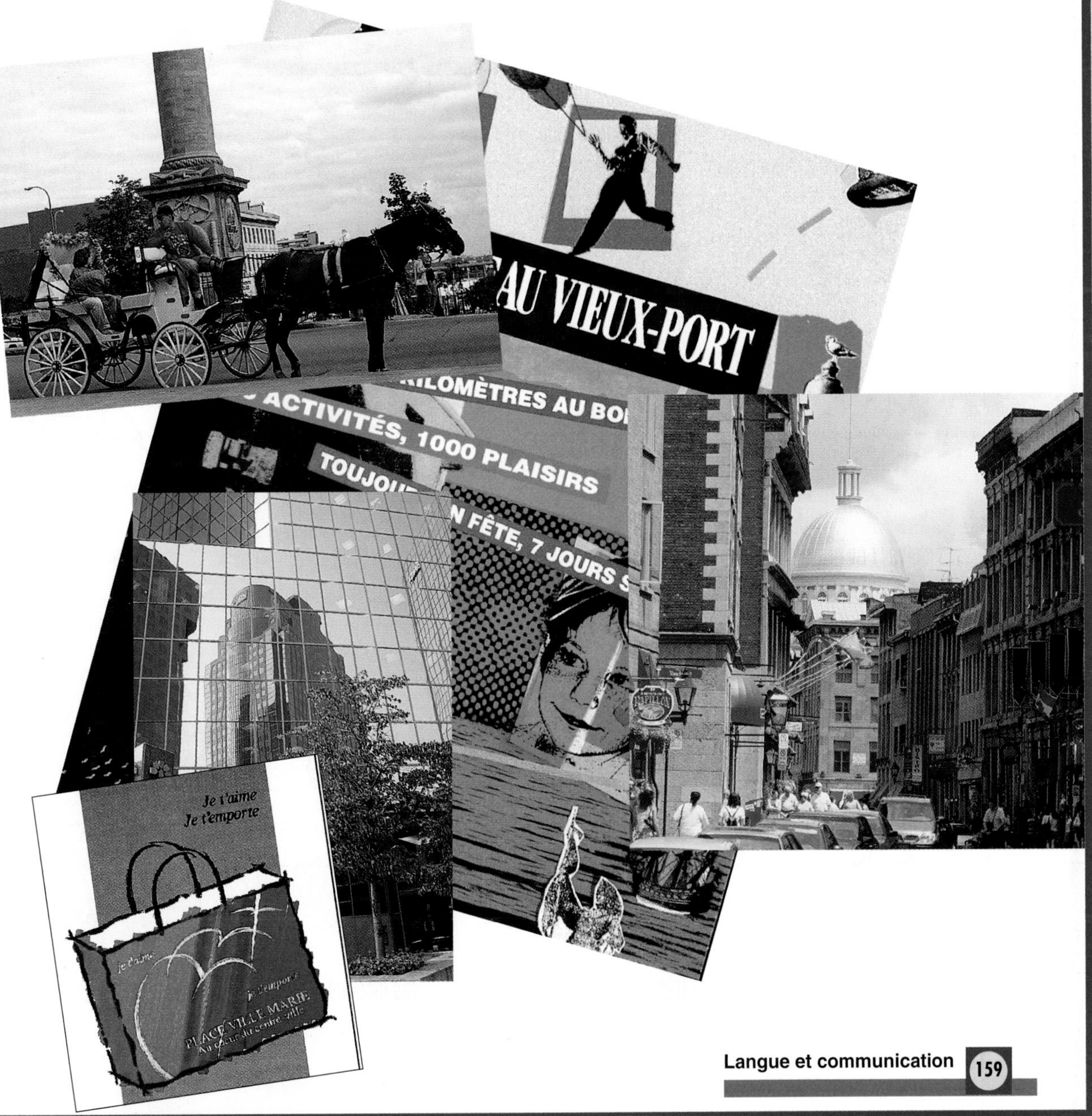

■ **Realia Note**
2 km = 1.2 miles

NOTES CULTURELLES

- **Montréal** started as a small colony called **Ville-Marie de Montréal**. It was founded in 1642 by **Paul de Chomedey, sieur de Maisonneuve**.
- The **Vieux-Port** is a popular tourist attraction, offering many sights and activities. For example, you can shop at a flea-market, visit the replica of a 1693 tall ship, cruise the harbor, or rent a bicycle. Carriage rides are also a popular way to discover **la vieille ville.**

INFO MAGAZINE

Theme: Personal style

■ **Note linguistique**

Un(e) visagiste is a hairstylist who enhances the natural characteristics of a face by choosing an appropriate hairstyle.

■ **Teaching Note**

For a review of related vocabulary, see Unité 1, p. 36.

À chacun son

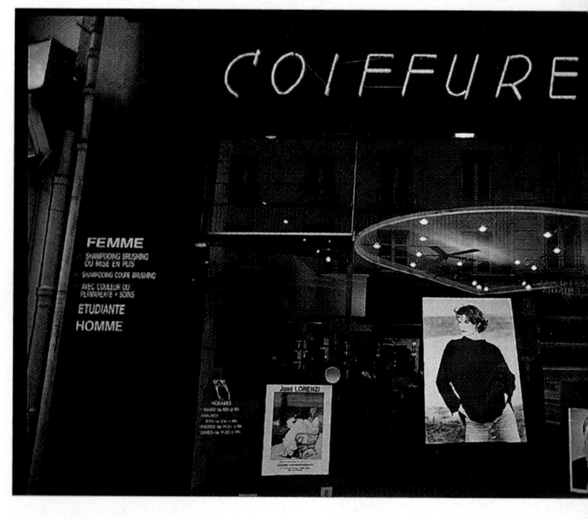

Dans notre apparence personnelle, nous sommes tous un peu différents. Chacun peut choisir son style de vêtements, son style de chaussures et son style de coiffure.

Quel style de coiffure demanderiez-vous à votre coiffeur si vous étiez en France? Aimeriez-vous avoir . . . ?

les cheveux en brosse

les cheveux au carré

une raie sur le côté

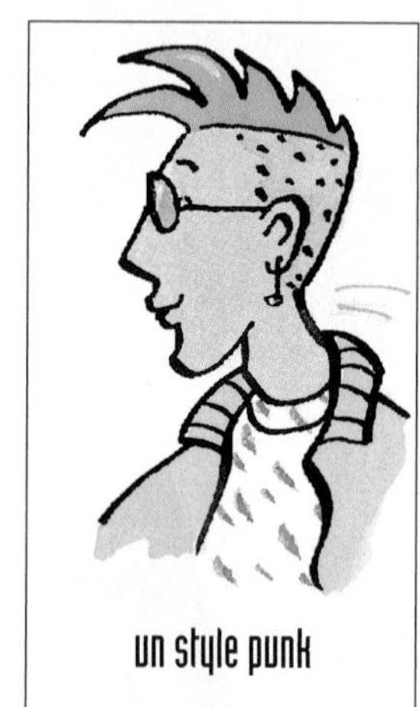

un style punk

une frange

des tresses très serrées

des mèches

une permanente

Teaching Strategy: Expansion

You may wish to use this short optional article to personalize the practical situational vocabulary presented on p. 161.

Ask students to look at the pictures and choose the hairstyle that is closest to their own. Have students imagine they are in a hair salon in France and ask them to prepare short dialogs.

LE FRANÇAIS PRATIQUE

Au salon de coiffure

JORDI COIFFURE

JORDI COIFFURE
Coiffure Hommes et Dames
Spécialiste des Enfants
Garçons et Filles
20 av de Breteuil
75007 Paris ______01 45 51 47 05

ZINZIUS ALAIN

ALAIN ZINZIUS
Haute Coiffure Création
Visagiste Ouvrier de France 1982
108 av Gambetta
75020 Paris __________01 40 30 55 57
1 r Paris (face au RER)
94340 Joinville le Pont_____01 42 83 86 15

— **C'est votre tour**, monsieur (mademoiselle).
Pouvez-vous **me couper les cheveux**?

Est-ce que vous pouvez me faire
- **une coupe de cheveux** *(haircut)*?
- **une coupe-brushing** *(haircut and blow-dry)*?
- **un shampooing?**
- **une permanente?**
- **une mise en pli** *(set)*?

— Comment est-ce que je vous coupe les cheveux?

Dégagez-les	**sur les côtés** *(on the sides)*.
Coupez-les-moi courts	**sur le devant** *(in front)*.
Laissez-les-moi longs	**sur le dessus** *(on top)*.
Ne me les coupez pas trop courts	**derrière** *(in back)*.

dégager *to cut back, shorten (hair)*
laisser *to leave*

1 Chez le coiffeur *(At the hairdresser)*

Vous êtes dans un salon de coiffure. Votre partenaire va jouer le rôle du coiffeur (de la coiffeuse). Inventez votre dialogue.

Coiffeur(se): *Tell the client that it is his/her turn.*
Client(e): Ask for a haircut.
Coiffeur(se): *Ask if the client wants something else (for example, a shampoo).*
Client(e): Accept or refuse politely.
Coiffeur(se): *Ask how the client wants his/her hair cut.*
Client(e): Tell the hairdresser how to cut your hair.

LE FRANÇAIS PRATIQUE

TEACHING RESOURCES

Student Activities Manual, p. 130
Audio Program, CD 4, Tracks 7–9
HM ClassPrep CD, Audioscript, Unit 4

Supplementary vocabulary

mettre un après-shampooing *to condition, to use a conditioner*
faire une décoloration *to bleach (one's hair)*
faire des mèches *to streak (one's hair)*
colorer les cheveux *to color one's hair*

Also:
Faites-moi
- **une raie** *part*
- **une frange** *bangs*
- **des boucles** *curls*
- **des nattes, des tresses** *braids*

Tressez-moi les cheveux *braid my hair*

LANGUE ET COMMUNICATION

TEACHING RESOURCES

Student Activities Manual, pp. 49, 131

Audio Program, CD 4, Tracks 10–11

HM ClassPrep CD, Audioscript, Unit 4

■ Teaching Notes

You may review the forms of the object pronouns very quickly. The focus in this section is on the contrast between these pronouns and **y** and **en**. The next section practices word order in sentences with two object pronouns.

LE, LA, LES

- You may remind students that direct objects answer the questions *whom? what?*
- Remind students that **le** and **la** become **l'** before a vowel sound:
  Cécile: Je **la** connais. Je l'invite au concert.
  Vincent: Je ne **le** connais pas. Je ne **l'**invite pas à la boum.
- In French, the past participle agrees with a preceding direct object.
  Quelle veste as-tu achetée?
  Où est la veste **que** tu as achetée?

LUI, LEUR

- You may remind students that indirect objects answer the question *to whom?*
- The following verbs are frequently used with indirect objects:

dire à	**promettre à**
écrire à	**rendre visite à**
parler à	**répondre à**
permettre à	**téléphoner à**
obéir à	**désobéir à**
donner à	**demander à**
montrer à	**envoyer à**

- Remind students that there is no agreement of the past participle with **lui, leur**.

A. Révision: les pronoms le, la, les et lui, leur

LE, LA, LES

Le, la, les are direct-object pronouns.
They replace PEOPLE or THINGS.

Tu vois **cette fille** là-bas?	Oui, je **la** vois.
Tu vois **ces maisons**?	Oui, je **les** vois.

➡ Compare the use of **en** and **le, la, les.**

Tu achètes **le journal**?	Oui, je **l'**achète.
Tu achètes **du pain**?	Oui, j'**en** achète.

➡ In the passé composé, the past participle agrees with **le, la, les,** but not with **en.**

Tu as pris **la carte postale**?	Oui, je **l'**ai **prise.**
Tu as pris **mes photos**?	Oui, je **les** ai **prises**.
BUT: Tu as pris **des photos**?	Non, je n'**en** ai pas **pris.**

L'accord du participe passé

Pratique ▶ p.49

LUI, LEUR

Lui and **leur** are indirect-object pronouns.
They replace **à** + NOUN designating PEOPLE.

Tu as écrit **à tes cousins**?	Non, je ne **leur** ai pas écrit.

➡ Compare the use of **y** and **lui, leur.**

Tu as répondu **à Pauline**?	Oui, je **lui** ai répondu.
Tu as répondu **à cette lettre**?	Oui, j'**y** ai répondu.

➡ Note that **lui, leur** are not used with **penser.**

Tu penses **à tes amis**?	Oui, je pense **à eux.**

RAPPEL!

Object pronouns always come BEFORE the verb, except in affirmative commands.
Compare:

Je prends ces magazines?	Ne **les** prends pas.	Oui, prends-**les**.
Je téléphone à Christine?	Ne **lui** téléphone pas.	Oui, téléphone-**lui**.

1 Au revoir!

Vous avez visité Genève avec vos amis. C'est bientôt *(soon)* le départ. Dites que vos amis ont fait les choses suivantes en répondant affirmativement aux questions. Utilisez le pronom qui convient **(l', les, lui, leur, en, y)**.

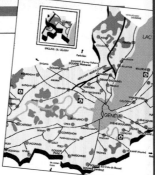

▶ Catherine a acheté du parfum? **Oui, elle en a acheté.**

1. Julien a fait ses valises?
2. Pauline a téléphoné à sa mère?
3. Pierre est allé à l'agence de voyages?
4. Marc et Éric ont acheté leurs billets?
5. Claire a trouvé son passeport?
6. Thomas a pris des photos?
7. Isabelle a acheté des souvenirs?
8. Antoine a dit au revoir à ses amis?
9. Alice a acheté un foulard?
10. Véronique a écrit plusieurs cartes postales?

2 Le week-end dernier

Demandez à votre partenaire s'il/si elle a fait l'une des choses suivantes le week-end dernier. Il/elle va répondre affirmativement ou négativement en utilisant le pronom qui convient **(l', les, lui, leur, en)**.

▶ **— Est-ce que tu as écouté de la musique classique le week-end dernier?**
— Oui, j'en ai écouté. (Non, je n'en ai pas écouté.)

- lire le journal du dimanche?
- regarder les bandes dessinées?
- acheter des vêtements?
- voir un film?
- voir tes voisins?
- téléphoner à ton copain/ta copine?
- ranger ta chambre?
- écouter de la musique classique?
- écouter du rap?
- faire du jogging?
- écrire à ta cousine?
- rendre visite à tes grands-parents?
- aider tes parents?
- ??

3 Pourquoi pas?

Demandez à votre partenaire s'il/si elle a fait les choses suivantes. Il/elle vous répond que non. Demandez pourquoi. Il/elle va vous répondre avec l'excuse suggérée ou une autre excuse.

▶ inviter Pauline
(elle est trop snob)

— Tu as invité Pauline?
— Non, je ne l'ai pas invitée.
— Mais pourquoi est-ce que tu ne l'as pas invitée?
— Elle est trop snob.

1. téléphoner à tes copains
(ils ne sont pas chez eux)
2. laver ta voiture
(elle n'était pas sale)
3. acheter de la limonade
(je n'avais pas soif)
4. faire les courses
(j'ai dîné au restaurant)
5. écrire à Catherine
(j'ai perdu son adresse)
6. prendre des photos
(je n'avais pas mon appareil)
7. tondre la pelouse
(la tondeuse est cassée)
8. aller à la pharmacie
(elle est fermée aujourd'hui)

4 L'assistant(e)

Vous êtes l'assistant(e) du président (de la présidente) d'une compagnie française. Demandez-lui si vous devez faire les choses suivantes. Votre partenaire va répondre affirmativement ou négativement.

▶ téléphoner à Madame Simon (oui)
— Je téléphone à Madame Simon?
— Oui, téléphonez-lui!

1. téléphoner à Monsieur Lamy (non)
2. répondre à ces clients (oui)
3. copier ces documents (oui)
4. répondre à cette lettre (non)
5. écrire à Madame Susuki (oui)
6. inviter Monsieur Schmidt (non)
7. passer à la poste (oui)
8. envoyer ce chèque (non)
9. aller à la papeterie (oui)
10. commander du papier à lettres (oui)
11. acheter des enveloppes (non)
12. acheter votre billet d'avion (oui)
13. réserver une chambre d'hôtel (oui)
14. confirmer la réservation (non)

■ Teaching Note

These activities practice and contrast the use of the various pronouns reviewed: **y, en, le, la, les, lui, leur.**

■ Expansion: Activity 2

Encourage students to continue their conversation, e.g.:
Quelles bandes dessinées est-ce que tu as lues?
J'ai lu ...
Est-ce que tu les as trouvées drôles? etc.

Teaching Strategy: Personalization

In Activity 3, encourage students to invent original excuses.

■ Expansion: Activity 4

Also:
faire attention à
Nous faisons attention **à eux.**
s'intéresser à
Paul s'intéresse **à eux.**

NOTES CULTURELLES

- The south shore of the **Lac Léman** is French. The north shore is Swiss. The part of the lake nearest the city of **Genève** is also called **le lac de Genève**.
- **Berne** is the capital of Switzerland.
- Ask students to use the map in their text to locate Switzerland, or use **Presentation Maps** to point out **Lac Léman**.

B. L'ordre des pronoms

Sometimes a sentence may contain two object pronouns. Note the sequence of these pronouns in the following sentences:

DIRECT- AND INDIRECT-OBJECT PRONOUNS

le **la** **les**	before	**lui** **leur**	Je prête **mon vélo à Alice.** Tu envoies **cette carte à tes cousins.** Nous montrons **nos diapos à Éric.**	Je **le lui** prête. Tu **la leur** envoies. Nous **les lui** montrons.

➡ This order is also used in affirmative commands.

Montre **la photo à Catherine.** Montre-**la-lui.**

me **te** **nous** **vous**	before	**le** **la** **les**	Vous **me** donnez **le journal**. Le coiffeur **te** coupe **les cheveux**. Paul **nous** vend **sa chaîne-stéréo**. Sylvie **vous** prête **ses CD**.	Vous **me le** donnez. Il **te les** coupe. Paul **nous la** vend. Elle **vous les** prête.

➡ Note the order in affirmative commands:

le **la** **les**	before	**moi** **nous**	Donne-**moi ton adresse.** Montre-**nous ces photos.**	Donne-**la-moi.** Montre-**les-nous.**

OBJECT PRONOUNS AND **Y, EN**

le/la/les **lui/leur** **me/te/nous/vous**	before	**y** **en**	J'amène **mes amis au concert**. Je donne **des conseils à Marc**. Alice **me** prête **de l'argent**. L'employé **nous** vend **des timbres**.	Je **les y** amène. Je **lui en** donne. Elle **m'en** prête. Il **nous en** vend.

➡ This order is also used in affirmative commands.

Donne **des timbres à Catherine**. Donne-**lui-en**.
Donne-**moi du papier à lettres**. Donne-**m'en**.

ALLONS PLUS LOIN

When two pronouns are used with a reflexive verb, the reflexive pronoun always comes first.

Je m'achète des vêtements. Je **m'en** achète.
Alice s'est coupé les cheveux. Elle **se les** est coupés.

Comment est ce
je vous les coupe

TEACHING RESOURCES

Student Activities Manual, pp. 50–51

■ Note linguistique

The past participle always agrees with a preceding direct object, even in sentences where there are two object pronouns.

J'ai prêté **mes piles** à Paul.
Je **les** lui ai **prêtées**.

5 Conversation

Demandez à votre partenaire s'il/si elle fait les choses suivantes. Il/elle va répondre affirmativement ou négativement.

▶ prêter ton portable à ton copain?

— Est-ce que tu prêtes ton portable à ton copain?
— Oui, je le lui prête. (Non, je ne le lui prête pas.)

1. prêter de l'argent à tes copains?
2. montrer ton journal *(diary)* à ta copine?
3. montrer tes notes *(grades)* à tes parents?
4. emprunter la tondeuse à tes voisins?
5. demander des conseils à ton prof?
6. donner de l'argent aux pauvres?
7. dire la vérité à tes amis?
8. couper les cheveux à ton petit frère?

6 Échanges

Votre partenaire va vous demander de lui prêter une des choses suivantes. Négociez un échange avec lui/elle. Votre partenaire va accepter ou refuser.

▶ **— Dis, prête-moi ton baladeur.**
— D'accord, je vais te le prêter si tu me prêtes ta bicyclette.
— Bon, je vais te la prêter.
(Non, je ne veux pas te la prêter.)

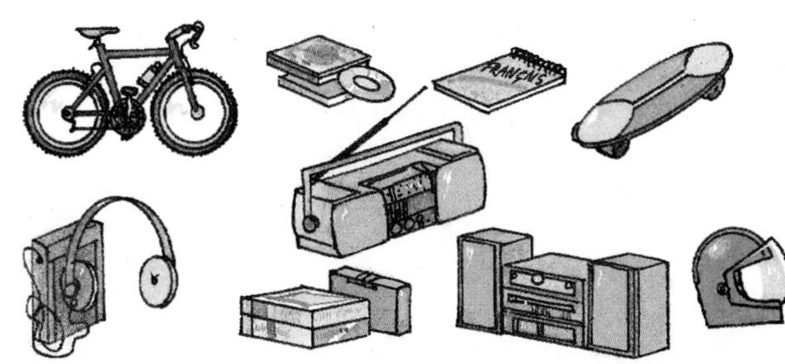

7 Oui ou non?

Répondez aux questions suivantes, affirmativement ou négativement. Utilisez les pronoms **lui/leur** et **en**. Soyez logique!

▶ Est-ce qu'on donne de l'aspirine à un malade?
Oui, on lui en donne.

1. Est-ce qu'on donne des allumettes aux enfants?
2. Est-ce qu'on parle de ses problèmes à ses amis?
3. Est-ce qu'on offre du chocolat à une personne qui est au régime *(on a diet)*?
4. Est-ce qu'on demande des conseils à ses parents?
5. Est-ce qu'on raconte des histoires de fantômes à une personne impressionnable?
6. Est-ce qu'on envoie des cartes de voeux *(season's greetings)* à ses amis?
7. Est-ce qu'on donne un bon pourboire à un serveur désagréable?
8. Est-ce qu'on sert de la viande à un végétarien?
9. Est-ce qu'on écrit des poèmes à une personne qu'on aime?

8 À Paris

Vous travaillez à Paris dans l'un des endroits suivants. Offrez certains services à votre partenaire, qui va accepter. (S'il/si elle refuse, votre partenaire va vous donner une explication.)

▶ **— Je vous apporte le menu?**
— Oui, apportez-le-moi, s'il vous plaît.
(Non, pas maintenant! Je vais attendre un peu.)

AU RESTAURANT	CHEZ LE COIFFEUR
▶ • apporter le menu • décrire le plat du jour • donner du pain • servir du café	• faire un shampooing • couper les cheveux très courts • mettre du gel
DANS UN MAGASIN DE DISQUES	**À L'HÔTEL**
• montrer nos nouveaux CD • faire un paquet • donner un sac en plastique	• montrer votre chambre • monter vos bagages • préparer votre note *(bill)* • commander un taxi

LE FRANÇAIS PRATIQUE

Services

TEACHING RESOURCES

Student Activities Manual, pp. 131–132

Audio Program, CD 4, Tracks 12–14

HM ClassPrep CD, Audioscript, Unit 4

Supplementary vocabulary

coudre (recoudre) ce bouton *to sew this button (back on)*

réparer la fermeture éclair *to fix the zipper*

■ Notes linguistiques

- **La cordonnerie** est la boutique du cordonnier.
- **La teinturerie** est la boutique du teinturier. On porte des vêtements chez le teinturier/à la teinturerie.

LE FRANÇAIS PRATIQUE

Services

Chez le cordonnier

(At the shoe repair shop)

— Est-ce que vous pouvez | **réparer** ces chaussures?
| **changer les talons** *(heels)*?

réparer *to fix*

— Quand est-ce que **ce sera prêt** *(when will it be ready)*?

Tout à l'heure! *(In a little while!)*
Dans deux jours.
D'ici une semaine. *(A week from now.)*

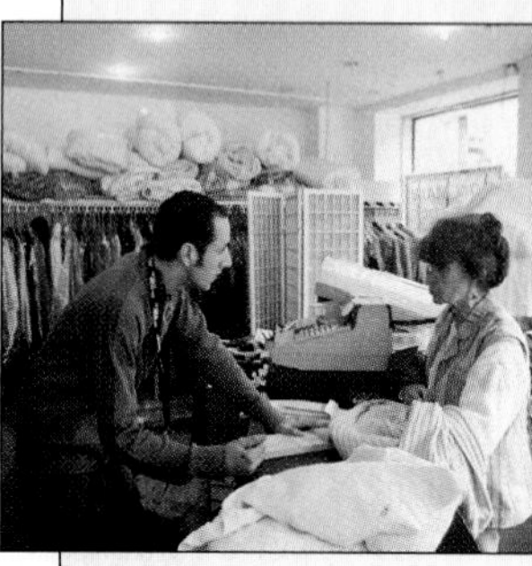

Chez le teinturier *(At the cleaners)*

— Est-ce que vous pouvez | **nettoyer** cette veste?
| **laver** ces chemises?
| **repasser** ce pantalon?
| **enlever cette tache** *(spot, stain)*?

repasser *to iron*
enlever *to remove*

Chez le photographe

— Est-ce que vous pouvez **développer ces photos**?
Est-ce que vous pouvez aussi **réparer mon appareil-photo**?

Oui, quel est le problème?
Qu'est-ce qu'il y a?
Qu'est-ce qui ne marche pas?

marcher *to work, to function*

Le flash | **est cassé.**
| **ne fonctionne pas.**
| **ne marche pas.**

La pile est **usée** *(worn out)*.

1 Réparations

Vous avez un objet à réparer et vous allez chez un spécialiste. Avec votre partenaire, choisissez un des objets suivants et composez le dialogue correspondant.

▶ **— S'il vous plaît, est-ce que vous pouvez réparer ma montre?**
— Oui, bien sûr. Quel est le problème?
— Elle ne marche pas. C'est peut-être la pile qui est usée.
— Bon, je vais voir ça.

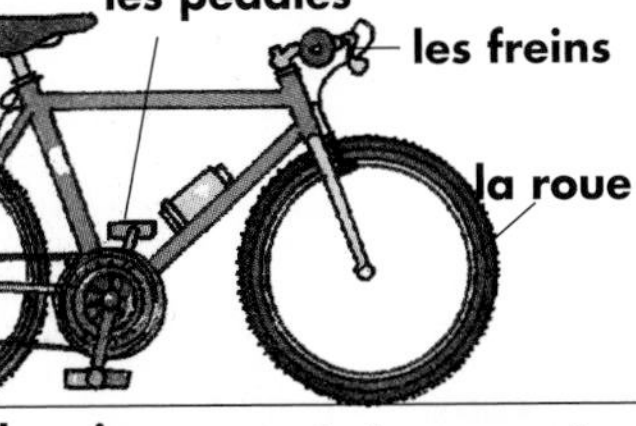

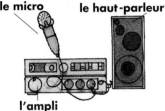

le micro
le haut-parleur
l'ampli

- **mon appareil-photo**
  le flash? la pile? le téléobjectif?
- **ma chaîne stéréo**
  le micro? l'ampli?
  le haut-parleur?
- **mon aspirateur?**
  la brosse? le tuyau?
  la prise?
- **mon vélo**
  les freins? la roue?

2 Créa-dialogue

Lisez le dialogue «Chez l'électricien». Puis, avec votre partenaire, choisissez une autre boutique et préparez un nouveau dialogue. Par exemple, vous allez chez le teinturier, chez le photographe ou chez le cordonnier.

«CHEZ L'ÉLECTRICIEN»

— Bonjour, madame. Est-ce que vous pouvez changer cette prise *(plug)*?	• *Use the appropriate form of address.* • *Ask for a service available at the shop.*
— Bien sûr, monsieur. Ce sera tout?	• *Use the appropriate form of address.*
— Non, est-ce que vous pouvez aussi réparer cette lampe?	• *Ask for another service.*
— D'accord, je vais faire ça.	
— Quand est-ce que ce sera prêt?	
— D'ici dix jours.	• *Give the number of days from now.*
— Ce n'est pas possible avant?	
— Si, peut-être. Revenez lundi prochain.	• *Give another day closer in time.*

■ Variation: Activity 1

- mon ordinateur
  le lecteur de CD-ROM? le modem? le lecteur de CD?
- mes rollers *(rollerblades)*
  les roues? les freins?
  la chaussure?
- mon caméscope *(camcorder)*
  le zoom? l'objectif? la prise de son? *(sound recorder)*

LANGUE ET COMMUNICATION

TEACHING RESOURCES

Student Activities Manual, pp. 51–54, 132

Audio Program, CD 4, Track 15

HM ClassPrep CD, Audioscript, Unit 4

Supplementary vocabulary

faire savoir *to let (someone) know*
Faites-le moi savoir dès que possible.

faire faire *to have done, made*
Je me suis fait faire une robe.

faire construire *to have built (a house)*
Ils ont fait construire (la maison) l'année dernière.

Teaching Strategy: Challenge

Ask students to look at the following sentence and notice that there is no agreement of the past participle:
[ma montre] Je l'ai fait réparer.
There is no agreement of the past participle in the **faire** + INFINITIVE construction. This is because the pronoun **le/la/les** is not the direct object of **faire**, but rather the direct object of the infinitive.

The reflexive pronoun is generally omitted before an infinitive introduced by **faire:**
Je l'ai fait asseoir.
Elle s'était levée, mais le docteur l'a fait coucher.

A. La construction **faire** + infinitif

Note the use of the construction **faire** + INFINITIVE.

Je **fais développer** les photos.	*I **am having** the pictures **developed**.*
Tu **as fait réparer** ton vélo.	*You **had** your bicycle **fixed**.*
Nous allons **faire laver** notre voiture.	*We are going **to have** our car **washed**.*

The construction **faire** + INFINITIVE is used to describe actions that people have done by someone else.

➡ In this construction, it is the verb **faire** that is used:
- in the negative
  Je fais réparer ma télé. — Je **ne fais pas** réparer mon portable.
- with pronouns
  Ma montre était cassée. — Je **l'**ai fait réparer.
  Ta voiture est sale. — Fais-**la** laver.

Faire + infinitif
Pratique ▶ p.51

The construction **faire** + INFINITIVE is also used to describe actions that we make or have other people do.

Le professeur **fait étudier** les élèves. — *The teacher **makes** the students **study.***

ALLONS PLUS LOIN

- The construction **faire** + INFINITIVE is used in certain expressions:
  faire cuire *to cook* **faire frire** *to fry* **faire bouillir** *to boil*
  Also: **faire marcher** *to operate (equipment)* **faire voir** *to show*
- Note the use of **se faire** + INFINITIVE to describe actions that people are having done for themselves.
  Je vais **me faire couper les cheveux.** — *I am going **to have my hair cut.***

1 Services

Demandez à votre partenaire pourquoi il va à certains endroits. Il/elle va répondre logiquement.

▶ **— Tu vas à la teinturerie?**
— Oui, je vais faire nettoyer mon blazer.

OÙ?

- à la station-service
- chez le mécanicien
- à la teinturerie
- chez le photographe
- à la laverie *(laundry)*
- à la boutique d'appareils électriques
- chez le serrurier *(locksmith)*
- chez le vétérinaire

POURQUOI?

- réparer mon vélo
- réparer mon séchoir
- changer cette serrure *(lock)*
- nettoyer mon blazer
- laver mon linge
- laver ma voiture
- vacciner mon chien
- développer mes diapos

2 Que faire?

Votre partenaire vous explique certains problèmes. Dites-lui ce qu'il/elle doit faire.

▶ **— Ma montre est cassée.**
— Fais-la réparer.

PROBLÈMES

- Ma montre est cassée.
- Ma veste a une tache *(spot)*.
- Mes cheveux sont trop longs.
- Mon baladeur ne marche pas.
- Les piles de ma radio cassette sont usées *(worn out)*.
- Mon chien n'a pas eu ses vaccins *(shots)*.

QUE FAIRE?

changer . . .
couper . . .
nettoyer . . .
réparer . . .
vacciner . . .

«Ma montre est cassée.»

«Mes cheveux sont trop longs.»

«Mon baladeur ne marche pas.»

«Les piles de ma radio cassette sont usées.»

«Ma veste a une tache.»

«Mon chien n'a pas eu ses vaccins.»

LECTURE

Une histoire de cheveux

Comédie en 4 scènes

Reading STRATEGY

Reading fiction

Realia Notes

- **UV** means that the place offers a tanning booth.
- **Le hammam** is a place to have a steam bath. **Hammam** is a turkish/arabic word meaning "hot bath."
- **Le cireur** = shoeshiner (**cirer:** to wax, to polish; **la cire** wax, shoe polish)
- **Le voiturier** = car service

AVANT DE LIRE

Le titre et le sous-titre de ce texte indiquent qu'il s'agit d'° une histoire plutôt humoristique avec pour sujet un événement assez ordinaire de la vie quotidienne: une coupe de cheveux.

Pour vous mettre dans l'esprit de cette histoire, répondez aux questions suivantes.

- Est-ce que vous attachez beaucoup d'importance à votre coiffure? Pourquoi ou pourquoi pas?
- Quel style de coiffure préférez-vous?
- Est-ce que vos parents sont toujours d'accord avec ce style? (Si non, pourquoi pas?)
- Quel coiffeur vous coupe les cheveux habituellement? Combien de fois par an (ou par mois) y allez-vous?
- Si votre coiffeur était indisponible° un jour, est-ce que vous permettriez à quelqu'un d'autre (un copain ou une copine, votre sœur ou votre frère, votre mère ou votre père...) de vous couper les cheveux? Pourquoi ou pourquoi pas?

il s'agit de *it is about* **indisponible** *unavailable*

Alain
MAITRE BARBIER COIFFEUR
"SALON MUSEE"
DU MARDI AU SAMEDI DE 9H15 A 19H
8 rue St Saint-Claude
75003 Paris 01 42 77 55 80
Une histoire de cheveux
Comédie en 4 scènes
MARC DELACRE
Coiffure et Soins Esthétiques
Pour Hommes
Soins Cheveux Corps Visage
Manucure Pédicure Médicale
UV, Sauna, Hammam
Restaurant, Cireur, Voiturier
17 av George V
75008 Paris 01 40 99 77 70

Teaching Strategy

Use the *Avant de lire* questions to focus student interest on the theme of the story and generate a pre-reading discussion.

As a follow-up, students may write their own **Histoire de cheveux**. Personalizing the reading can help students to pay closer attention to the storyline and develop their reading skills.

Scène 1

Patrick, 15 ans, a un problème commun à tous les jeunes de son âge. Il n'a jamais assez d'argent. Alors, de temps en temps, il en demande à son père. Malheureusement, aujourd'hui, celui-ci n'est pas d'humeur généreuse.

—Dis, Papa, tu peux me donner un peu d'argent?

—Mais, je t'ai donné vingt euros la semaine dernière.

—S'il te plaît, papa, c'est la dernière fois que je t'en demande.

—N'insiste pas, Patrick, la dernière fois, c'était la dernière fois…

Le père de Patrick examine son fils de plus près.

—Dis donc, Patrick, tourne-toi un peu.

Patrick se retourne.

— Tu as les cheveux drôlement longs.

— Mais Papa, c'est la mode.

— Eh bien, moi, je n'aime pas tellement la mode des cheveux longs… Il faut absolument que tu ailles chez le coiffeur.

— Tu oublies que je n'ai pas d'argent.

— Ah oui, c'est vrai. Combien est-ce que ça coûte, une coupe de cheveux?

— Dans les° quinze euros.

— Bon. Eh bien, voilà. Je te donne vingt euros, mais je ne veux plus voir cette horrible tignasse!

— Merci, papa, à ce soir!

dans les = approximativement

Mots utiles	
l'humeur	*mood*
se tourner	*to turn around*
de près	*closely, from close up*
de temps en temps	*from time to time*

Langage familier
drôlement = vraiment
tellement = beaucoup

une tignasse

Avez-vous compris?

1. Qu'est-ce que Patrick demande à son père?
2. Pourquoi est-ce que le père refuse?
3. Qu'est-ce qu'il remarque quand il examine Patrick de près?
4. Qu'est-ce qu'il demande à son fils de faire?
5. Combien d'argent lui donne-t-il?

Anticipons un peu!

Selon vous, est-ce que Patrick va aller chez le coiffeur ou non? Expliquez pourquoi.

■ *Avez-vous compris?*

(Sample answers)

1. Il lui demande de l'argent.
2. Il refuse parce qu'il lui a donné vingt euros la semaine dernière.
3. Il remarque que Patrick a les cheveux longs.
4. Il lui demande d'aller chez le coiffeur.
5. Il lui donne vingt euros.

Teaching Strategy

Ask students to discuss the following questions:

- Quelle coupe de cheveux est à la mode en ce moment? Décrivez-la.
- Aimez-vous cette coupe?
- La prochaine fois que vous allez chez le coiffeur, quel type de coupe allez-vous choisir?

Scène 2

Patrick prend le billet de vingt euros que son père a sorti de son portefeuille, puis il met son blouson et quitte la maison. En route, il rencontre Béatrice, une nouvelle élève du lycée où il va. C'est une grande fille brune avec de merveilleux yeux bleus. Patrick la trouve très sympa et très mignonne, mais jusqu'ici, il n'a pas eu vraiment l'occasion de lui parler.

— Salut, Béatrice! Ça va?

— Oui, ça va.

— Dis donc, où est-ce que tu vas comme ça?

— Je vais au ciné.

— Qu'est-ce que tu vas voir?

— Le dernier film de Depardieu. Il paraît que° c'est génial... Si tu veux, on peut y aller ensemble.

Patrick voudrait bien accepter la proposition de Béatrice. Malheureusement, il y a cette maudite° coupe de cheveux.

— Euh, c'est que je dois aller chez le coiffeur.

— Mais, pourquoi? Je t'aime bien comme ça avec tes cheveux longs...

Patrick rougit.

— Malheureusement, j'ai un père qui préférerait me voir avec les cheveux courts.

— Ah bon, je comprends... Écoute, j'ai une idée!

— Quoi donc?

— On peut aller au ciné, et puis après, on peut aller chez moi. Mon père est coiffeur. Il va te faire une coupe super... Et, en plus, tu économiseras ton argent.

— Ben, oui, c'est une idée! Tu es bien sûre que ton père sera chez toi tout à l'heure?

— Absolument! C'est son jour de congé aujourd'hui.

— Alors, dans ce cas, j'accepte!

il paraît que = on dit que **maudite** *darned*

Mots utiles

un jour de congé	*day off*
rougir	*to blush*
jusqu'ici	*until now*
tout à l'heure	*in a while*

Avez-vous compris?

1. Qui est Béatrice et qu'est-ce que Patrick pense d'elle?
2. Pourquoi Patrick n'accepte-t-il pas immédiatement la proposition de Béatrice?
3. Selon vous, pourquoi Patrick rougit-il?
4. Quelle solution Béatrice propose-t-elle à Patrick?

Anticipons un peu!

Selon vous, qu'est-ce qui va se passer après le film?

Notes linguistiques

- **Un congé** is a short period of time taken off from work, such as a national holiday, or a weekend. **Les vacances** implies a longer period of time off.
- **se rendre compte** = to realize (**Rappel: réaliser** = to achieve)

■ *Avez-vous compris?*

(Sample answers)

1. Béatrice est une nouvelle élève du lycée. Patrick la trouve très sympa et mignonne.
2. Il n'accepte pas immédiatement la proposition de Béatrice parce qu'il doit aller chez le coiffeur.
3. Il rougit parce que Béatrice lui dit des choses gentilles et il est un peu amoureux d'elle.
4. Elle propose que son père, qui est coiffeur, coupe les cheveux de Patrick après le cinéma.

Teaching Strategy: Expansion

Expansion linguistique

Remind students of the difference between forms in written and spoken French. Ask students if similar differences exist in spoken and written English; ask for examples.

Then point out the abbreviations used in spoken French which appear in this story:

sympa (sympathique)
le ciné (le cinéma)
Et aussi: **T'en fais pas** (**ne t'en fais pas s'en faire** = to worry *fam.*),
c'est pas si mal (ce n'est pas si mal).

Scène 3

Patrick et Béatrice sont allés au cinéma. Après le film, Patrick a invité Béatrice dans un petit restaurant italien où ils ont mangé une pizza. Ensuite, ils sont allés chez Béatrice. Là, ils ont une mauvaise surprise: il n'y a personne à la maison. Patrick s'inquiète.

— Où est ton père?

— Je ne sais pas! Il a dû faire un tour en ville avec ma mère. Ne t'inquiète pas. Je suis sûre qu'ils rentreront bientôt.

Mots utiles

un côté	*side*
un désastre	= une catastrophe
la lumière	*light*
arriver à	*to manage to*
sonner	*to ring*

Une heure passe, et toujours personne. Finalement, le téléphone sonne. C'est la mère de Béatrice qui lui dit de ne pas l'attendre. Elle et son mari sont invités à dîner chez des amis. Ils ne vont pas rentrer avant onze heures. Béatrice se rend compte du problème.

Langage familier

t'en fais pas = ne t'inquiète pas

— Dis, Patrick, mes parents ne vont pas rentrer ce soir.

— Et ma coupe de cheveux?

— T'en fais pas! C'est moi qui vais te les couper.

— Comment? Tu sais couper les cheveux, toi?

— Ben oui, tu sais, j'ai souvent regardé mon père.

Patrick n'est pas très rassuré, mais il n'a pas le choix. Il est bien obligé d'accepter l'offre de Béatrice.

Béatrice va chercher les ciseaux de son père. Elle demande à Patrick de s'asseoir sur un tabouret. Puis, elle commence à lui couper les cheveux. Clic, une mèche par ci! Clac, une mèche par là. Clic! Clac! Clic! Clic! Il est bien évident que Béatrice n'a jamais coupé de cheveux de sa vie et le résultat est un véritable désastre. Elle a beau° passer° de l'eau et du gel fixatif sur les cheveux de Patrick, elle n'arrive pas à masquer les échelles qu'elle a faites de tous les côtés.

un tabouret

une mèche

des échelles

Patrick se regarde dans la glace. Il comprend alors l'ampleur° de la catastrophe.

— Mon Dieu, qu'est-ce que je vais faire?

Béatrice essaie de le rassurer.

— Écoute, c'est pas si mal que ça! Mets-toi un peu dans l'obscurité°... Non, ce n'est pas trop mal. Un conseil: quand tu seras chez toi, ne te mets pas trop près de la lumière, et personne ne verra rien.

Mais Patrick n'écoute pas. Il prend son blouson et sort de chez Béatrice, très inquiet...

elle a beau = c'est en vain qu'elle essaie de
passer = mettre
ampleur *extent*
l'obscurité = un endroit où il fait noir

Avez-vous compris?

1. Pourquoi est-ce que Patrick s'inquiète?
2. Qu'est-ce que la mère de Béatrice annonce à sa fille quand elle lui téléphone?
3. Qu'est-ce que Béatrice fait pour résoudre le problème de Patrick?
4. Comment réussit-elle dans ce projet? Expliquez.
5. Qu'est-ce qu'elle conseille à Patrick de faire pour ne pas être trop visible?

Anticipons un peu!

Selon vous, quelle va être la réaction du père de Patrick quand il va voir son fils? Est-ce qu'il va être heureux? furieux? perplexe? Expliquez pourquoi.

■ *Avez-vous compris?*

(Sample answers)

1. Il s'inquiète parce que les parents de Béatrice ne sont pas chez eux.
2. Elle lui dit qu'elle et son père rentreront tard.
3. Béatrice coupe elle-même les cheveux de Patrick.
4. C'est une catastrophe! Elle coupe trop, et mal, elle fait des échelles de tous les côtés.
5. Elle lui dit de ne pas se mettre près de la lumière.

■ Verb

s'inquiéter is conjugated like **espérer:**

je m'inquiète
nous nous inquiétons
ils s'inquiètent

Teaching Strategy: Expansion

Ask students:
Pourquoi Patrick est-il obligé d'accepter de se faire couper les cheveux par Béatrice?

Scène 4

Vingt minutes après, Patrick arrive chez lui. Il a l'air vraiment pitoyable. Sa mère ne peut pas s'empêcher de rire.

— Mon pauvre Patrick! Tu as l'air d'un chat qui est tombé dans l'eau... Qui est-ce qui t'a coupé les cheveux? Allez, dis-moi la vérité.

Patrick hésite un peu. Puis, il raconte à sa mère ce qui s'est passé. Celle-ci essaie de le consoler.

—Tu as de la chance! Ton père n'est pas encore rentré! En attendant qu'il rentre, je vais essayer d'arranger cela!

Elle va dans la salle de bains chercher la tondeuse qu'elle utilisait quand Patrick était petit. Puis elle commence l'opération... En cinq minutes, elle a complètement tondu le crâne de Patrick.

— C'est un peu court, mais au moins ça peut passer...

Puis elle va ranger la tondeuse pendant que Patrick va se regarder dans la glace.

— J'ai la boule à zéro! Qu'est-ce que mes copains vont penser de moi?

— Ils vont trouver ça très bien. Je suis sûre que tu vas lancer une nouvelle mode... Tiens, voilà ton père.

Le père de Patrick vient en effet de rentrer. Il regarde Patrick avec surprise.

— Bravo, mon garçon! Tu as beaucoup de courage... Je te félicite! Tiens, pour te récompenser, je vais t'emmener au cinéma ce soir. Est-ce que tu veux aller voir le dernier film de Depardieu? Il paraît que c'est très bon!

— Merci, Papa, ...mais j'ai des devoirs à faire!

— Comme tu veux! Et excuse-moi d'avoir été un peu brusque avec toi cet après-midi.

la tondeuse

le crâne

avoir la boule à zéro

Mots utiles

arranger	*to fix*
s'empêcher de	*to stop, prevent oneself from*
lancer	*to launch*
récompenser	*to reward*
rire *	*to laugh*
tondre	*to clip very short*
pitoyable	*pitiful*

Avez-vous compris?

1. Quelle est la réaction de la mère de Patrick quand elle voit son fils?
2. Qu'est-ce qu'elle fait pour aider Patrick?
3. Quel est le résultat de cette action?
4. Quelle est la réaction du père de Patrick?
5. Qu'est-ce qu'il propose à son fils?
6. Qu'est-ce que Patrick répond à l'invitation de son père? Quelle est la véritable raison de son refus?

■ Teaching Note

For an overview of a Gérard Depardieu movie, see **Cyrano de Bergerac**, pp. 142–145.

■ Verb

Convaincre is conjugated like **vaincre**:
je convaincs
il convainc
nous convainquons
ils convainquent

■ *Avez-vous compris?*

(Sample answers)

1. Elle rit.
2. Elle utilise la tondeuse.
3. Il a le crâne complètement tondu, «la boule à zéro».
4. Il est surpris et fier de son fils. Il admire son courage.
5. Il lui propose d'aller voir le dernier film de Depardieu avec lui.
6. Patrick répond qu'il ne peut pas parce qu'il a des devoirs. Mais la vraie raison, c'est qu'il vient de voir ce film avec Béatrice.

■ Irregular Verb

(see Appendix C)
rire

APRÈS LA LECTURE

EXPRESSION ORALE

■ Dramatisation

En petits groupes, préparez une lecture dramatique de cette histoire. Chaque groupe présentera une scène.

- D'abord, choisissez un narrateur et distribuez les autres rôles.
- Pendant les parties «narratives», les acteurs feront les gestes et montreront les émotions indiquées.
- Pendant les dialogues, chaque acteur lira son texte avec beaucoup d'expression.

■ Situations

Avec votre partenaire, choisissez l'une des situations suivantes. Composez le dialogue correspondant et jouez-le en classe.

1. Au téléphone

Le soir, après le dîner, Béatrice téléphone à Patrick pour lui demander ce qui est arrivé quand il est rentré chez lui. Patrick le lui explique.

Les rôles: Béatrice, Patrick

2. En classe

Le lendemain, un(e) camarade de classe de Patrick est très étonné(e) de voir son ami avec «la boule à zéro». Il/Elle lui demande ce qui s'est passé. Patrick lui répond. (Patrick peut lui dire la vérité ou bien il peut inventer une histoire complètement différente.)

Les rôles: le/la camarade de classe, Patrick

3. La nouvelle mode

Maintenant, Patrick est très fier de sa nouvelle coiffure. Il explique à un autre copain les avantages d'avoir «la boule à zéro» et il essaie de le convaincre de faire la même chose. Le copain n'est pas tellement convaincu.

Les rôles: Patrick, le copain

EXPRESSION ÉCRITE

■ Imaginons un peu

Quelle va être la réaction des copains de Patrick quand celui-ci ira au lycée demain matin? Qu'est-ce que Patrick va leur dire? À vous d'écrire la Scène 5.

■ Page de journal

Imaginez que vous êtes Patrick ou Béatrice. Écrivez une page ou deux dans votre journal intime (diary) où vous ferez un résumé des événements de la journée.

■ Teaching Notes

- You may wish to use the short **Lecture** quiz as a comprehension check or as an assessment option.

  Use the **Transparency Masters** to expand/retell the story.

Teaching Strategy: Expansion

Pose this problem scenario to students:

Votre meilleur(e) ami(e) arrive à la fac avec la boule à zéro. Quelle est votre réaction? Que lui dites-vous? Imaginez votre dialogue.

Rôles: Vous, votre ami(e)

INTERLUDE CULTUREL

Pour en savoir plus
Much of the historical material mentioned in this text is developed in other *Interludes culturels:*
- la Chanson de Roland, pp. 102–103
- le Moyen Âge, p. 98
- Louis XIV, p. 140–141
- la Révolution française, p. 216
- la Résistance et la guerre de 1940, pp. 252–256

Use the **Transparency Masters** to help students situate the various musical periods within a larger historical context.

Teaching Note
Play the *Chansons* Audio CD to introduce students to such hits as *Les Passants* by Georges Brassens, *Les Grands Boulevards* by Yves Montand, and *Quelque chose de Tennessee* by Johnny Hallyday.

Histoire de la chanson française

Un proverbe français dit que «tout finit par des chansons». On pourrait° dire aussi que tout a commencé par une chanson. L'histoire de la chanson française est en effet un peu l'histoire de France. La première grande oeuvre° littéraire française date du douzième siècle.° C'était une chanson: *La Chanson de Roland*.

Troubadour du Moyen Âge

Au Moyen Âge,° les **«troubadours»** allaient de cour° en cour en chantant des poèmes qu'ils composaient. Sous **Louis XIV**, les soldats allaient à la guerre en chantant des chansons comme «Malbrough s'en va-t-en guerre»° ou «Auprès de° ma blonde». En 1789, les Français ont fait la Révolution en chantant «Ça ira!»° Pendant la guerre de 1940, le «Chant des partisans» était le cri de ralliement° de la Résistance contre les troupes allemandes.

Mais la chanson n'est pas seulement un phénomène historique. C'est aussi un art populaire et un spectacle. Les premiers chanteurs populaires chantaient dans la rue. Ils recevaient un peu d'argent si leurs chansons étaient bonnes . . . et parfois un seau° d'eau sur la tête si leurs chansons étaient mauvaises.

Plus tard, la chanson a fait son entrée dans les **«cabarets»**. Le cabaret le plus célèbre était un cabaret de Montmartre qui s'appelait le «Chat noir». C'était un cabaret artistique où se réunissaient° les peintres, les musiciens, les poètes, les étudiants pour écouter les «chansonniers» de l'époque. Ces chansonniers chantaient surtout des chansons politiques, des chansons satiriques et parfois des chansons comiques.

Picasso *«Femme à la Mandoline»*

Le «Chat Noir», cabaret artistique à Montmartre.

pourrait *could* **oeuvre** *work* **siècle** *century* **au Moyen Âge** *in the Middle Ages* **cour** *court* **s'en va-t-en guerre** *goes off to war* **auprès de** *next to* **ça ira** *things will go well* **cri de ralliement** *rallying cry* **seau** *bucket* **se réunissaient** *used to get together*

Teaching Strategy: Cultural Connection

You may wish to begin the presentation of this *Interlude culturel* by bringing in recordings of French songs to class. The songs listed under *Leurs grands succès* are appropriate, but you may want to introduce other songs that you particularly like. The recordings may be from any of the periods or artists mentioned. Students should scan the information in the *Interlude* while listening to the music.

Leurs grands succès

Édith Piaf:
La vie en rose
Mon légionnaire
Milord Non, je ne regrette rien

Yves Montand:
Les feuilles mortes
Les grands boulevards
À Paris
Mon manège à moi

Georges Brassens:
Chanson pour l'Auvergnat
Une jolie fleur
Auprès de mon arbre
Les croquants

Jacques Brel:
Ne me quitte pas
Amsterdam
Le plat pays

Charles Aznavour:
La Mamma
Il faut savoir
Tu te laisses aller

Le grand public, lui, allait au «café-concert» ou au «music-hall». Dans les années 1930, la grande vedette° était **Joséphine Baker**, une danseuse noire américaine que tout le monde applaudissait quand elle chantait «J'ai deux amours: mon pays et Paris». Peu après, les Français ont découvert **Édith Piaf**, célèbre pour ses robes noires et sa voix terriblement poignante. Dans les années 1960, avec le développement de l'amplificateur et le succès de la guitare électrique, une nouvelle forme de chanson est apparue en France. C'était la chanson «yé-yé». Ce qui comptait,° ce n'était plus° le texte de la chanson, mais son rythme et surtout les contorsions du chanteur ou de la chanteuse sur scène° . . . La vedette de l'époque était **Johnny Hallyday** qui en quelques mois est devenu l'idole des jeunes Français. La chanson personnelle n'a cependant pas disparu. Elle est restée vivante° et variée avec **Georges Brassens**, l'anarchiste sympa, **Yves Montand**, le gentleman romantique, **Jacques Brel**, le poète venu du pays des brumes,° et **Charles Aznavour**, le petit bonhomme° à la voix grêle.°

Yves Montand

Georges Brassens

Jacques Brel

Charles Aznavour

Les vedettes d'hier . . .

Édith Piaf (1915-1963)

Édith Piaf a disparu il y a plus de quarante ans, mais sa voix est restée immortelle. Pour les millions de gens qui ont écouté cette voix vibrante d'émotion, elle est toujours la plus grande des chanteuses françaises. Édith Piaf a eu une enfance° misérable. Elle est née dans la rue et c'est dans la rue qu'elle a commencé à chanter pour gagner quelques pièces d'argent.° Un jour, alors qu'°elle chantait au coin° du boulevard MacMahon à Paris, le directeur d'un cabaret célèbre l'a entendue. Ému° par sa voix poignante, il l'a immédiatement engagée.° La phénoménale carrière de Piaf venait de commencer.

Le succès de ses chansons est facile à expliquer. Édith Piaf a chanté passionnément sa vie passionnée. Cette vie a été faite de moments heureux et surtout de moments tragiques. C'est donc avec une extraordinaire sincérité qu'Édith Piaf pouvait chanter le bonheur et le malheur, la fatalité et l'espoir,° l'amour merveilleux et l'amour désespéré. Quand Édith Piaf était sur scène, le public ne pouvait pas faire la différence entre sa vie et ses chansons.

vedette *star* **ce qui comptait** *what counted* **plus** *no longer* **sur scène** *on the stage* **vivante** *alive* **brumes** *fog, mist*
bonhomme = homme **grêle** *frail* **enfance** *childhood* **pièces d'argent** *coins* **alors que** *while* **au coin** *on the corner*
Ému *moved* **engagée** *hired* **espoir** *hope*

Notes linguistiques

- **Le café-théâtre** is a café where people can watch new plays or performance artists.
- **Le music-hall** generally presents variety and vaudeville acts, reviews, and singers.

Notes culturelles

- Up to 1914, French people could go to le **café-concert** (or **le caf'conc'**) to watch vaudeville acts.
- **Jacques Brel** was born in Bruxelles in 1929. The quality and poignancy of his lyrics made him one of the best French songwriters. He spent his last years living on the Marquesas Islands (**les îles Marquises**) before dying in France in 1978.
- **Georges Brassens** (1921–1981) sang his poems accompanying himself on an acoustic guitar. He was able to play with and manipulate the French language into witty lyrics, expressing gentle mockery and nonconformism.
- **Yves Montand** was born in Italy in 1921. He made his career in France as a singer and actor, playing leads in such movies as **Le Salaire de la peur** *(Wages of Fear)*. He died in 1991.
- **Charles Aznavour** is a singer and actor. He was born in Armenia in 1924.

■ Anecdote
Jean-Claude Baker, one of Joséphine Baker's adopted sons, runs a French restaurant in New York City called **Chez Joséphine**.

Joséphine Baker (1906–1975)

Joséphine Baker sur scène

Joséphine Baker était une artiste de music-hall. Pour des millions de Français, elle a aussi été une grande héroïne nationale. Pourtant Joséphine Baker n'était pas d'origine française, mais américaine. Elle est née dans une famille pauvre de la ville de Saint Louis dans le Missouri. À seize ans, elle est partie à New York pour faire une carrière dans le théâtre. Mais là, victime de la discrimination et du chômage,° elle n'a pas trouvé de travail.

Heureusement, un jour, la chance° lui a souri.° Un imprésario français l'a embauchée° pour faire une tournée° en France avec un groupe d'artistes noirs américains. Joséphine a fait ses débuts au Théâtre des Champs-Élysées en octobre 1925. Chacune° de ses entrées en scène était un triomphe. Pendant cette tournée, Joséphine Baker est tombée amoureuse de° Paris et Paris est tombé amoureux de «l'oiseau des îles». Joséphine Baker était la grande star du spectacle. Tous les soirs, elle donnait aux Français des leçons de danse. Bientôt, toute la France s'est mise à° danser le charleston. En quelques semaines, Joséphine Baker est devenue la reine° de Paris. Elle avait tout juste vingt ans.

Joséphine Baker a fait de nombreuses tournées à travers° l'Europe, mais c'est en France qu'elle se sentait chez elle.° En 1937, elle a décidé d'adopter la nationalité française. Pendant la guerre, fidèle° à son nouveau pays, elle a travaillé dans la Résistance. Pour ses services, elle a reçu les deux plus hautes décorations françaises: la Légion d'honneur et la Médaille de la Résistance. Pour la cérémonie, Joséphine Baker portait son uniforme de lieutenant de l'Armée de l'Air Française.

Après la guerre, Joséphine Baker a voyagé aux États-Unis. En butte à° nouveau à la discrimination, elle a décidé de se fixer° définitivement en France et de consacrer sa vie et sa fortune aux oeuvres° de charité. Elle a acheté un château pour accueillir° une douzaine d'orphelins de différentes races qu'elle avait adoptés et sauvés de la faim° et de la misère. C'était sa «tribu arc-en-ciel».° Ses ressources financières n'étant plus° suffisantes, elle est remontée sur scène à l'âge de 69 ans pour subvenir aux besoins° de sa famille d'adoption. À nouveau elle a connu le succès et c'est en plein triomphe qu'elle est morte en 1975.

Le jour de son enterrement,° la France entière a pris le deuil.° À Paris, une foule° immense a suivi le cortège funèbre.° Vingt et un coups de canon° ont été tirés° en son honneur: le plus grand adieu° français réservé à une femme américaine!

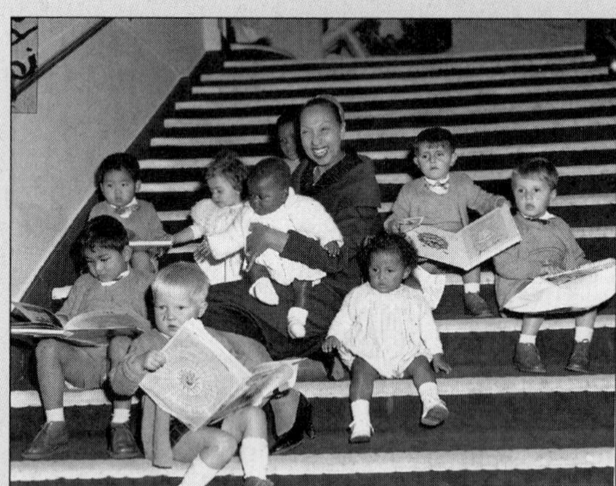

Joséphine Baker et sa «tribu arc-en-ciel»

chômage *unemployment* **chance** *luck* **souri** *smiled* **embauchée** *hired* **tournée** *tour* **chacune** *each one* **tombée amoureuse de** *fell in love with* **s'est mise à** *began to* **reine** *queen* **à travers** *across* **se sentait chez elle** *felt at home* **fidèle** = loyale **en butte à** *faced with* **se fixer** *to settle* **oeuvres** *works* **accueillir** *to provide shelter* **faim** *hunger* **arc-en-ciel** *rainbow* **n'étant plus** *no longer being* **subvenir aux besoins** *meet the needs* **enterrement** *funeral* **pris le deuil** *went into mourning* **foule** *crowd* **cortège funèbre** *funeral procession* **vingt et un coups de canon** *21-gun salute* **tirés** *fired* **adieu** *farewell*

. . . et vedettes d'aujourd'hui

Johnny Hallyday

Johnny Hallyday, le roi° du rock'n roll français, est entré en scène dans les années 1960. Comme° il avait un nom anglais, on pensait qu'il était américain. En réalité, il s'appelait Jean-Philippe Smet, était belge et ne parlait pas un mot d'anglais. Il portait un blouson de cuir, roulait° en grosse moto, jouait de la guitare et chantait «Je suis l'idole des jeunes».

Quarante ans plus tard, Johnny Hallyday n'a pas quitté la scène. Il est toujours° l'idole des jeunes . . . et des moins jeunes. Et quand il donne un grand concert public, 200 000 spectateurs viennent l'applaudir. Un record pour un chanteur français!

Jean-Jacques Goldman

Jean-Jacques Goldman est l'un des représentants du rock français moderne. Il compose lui-même ses chansons et les interprète à la guitare électrique. Il a commencé sa carrière avec un grand succès, «Quand la musique est bonne», et depuis vingt ans ses chansons sont généralement en tête du hit-parade français. Il a composé la musique du film **Astérix.**

Simple et généreux, Jean-Jacques Goldman participe souvent aux concerts organisés pour soutenir° les grandes causes humanitaires.

Lara Fabian

Lara Fabian a commencé sa carrière à quatorze ans, dans son pays natal, la Belgique. Elle est maintenant canadienne, et ses albums connaissent un vrai succès au Canada et en Europe. Elle interprète le personnage d'Esmeralda dans le film de Walt Disney, *Le Bossu° de Notre-Dame.*

Liane Foly

Liane Foly, lyonnaise, écrit elle-même beaucoup de ses chansons. Elle compose aussi une bonne partie des mélodies, et sa voix est à l'aise° dans une variété de styles: jazz, blues, music-hall. Elle incorpore aussi parfois le soul et le *rhythm 'n blues* à sa musique.

Pascal Obispo

Fils d'un joueur de football professionnel, Pascal Obispo préférait la musique et le sport à ses études quand il était au lycée. Devenu chanteur et compositeur, c'est aujourd'hui le grand représentant de la chanson romantique française moderne. En 2000, il a écrit une comédie musicale, *Les dix Commandements,* qui a connu un succès phénoménal.

roi *king* **comme** *since* **roulait** *drove* **toujours** *still* **soutenir** *to support* **Le Bossu** *Hunchback* **à l'aise** *comfortable*

Supplementary vocabulary

le CD *CD, compact disc*
la compilation (la compil) *compilation*
le compositeur *composer*
le disque d'or/de platine *gold/platinum record*
le single *single (record)*
le tube *(fam.) hit*
la vedette *star*

Teaching Note

The *Chansons* CD has songs by Johnny Hallyday and other contemporary artists.

Note linguistique

Le hit-parade (*pl.* **les hit-parades**) lists the top singers, songs, actors, or movies of the moment. The French government recommends the use of **le palmarès** instead of **le hit-parade.**

La musique des jeunes

«De la musique avant toute chose» a dit un poète français.* Aujourd'hui, la musique fait partie de la vie de tout le monde, et en particulier des jeunes. À la maison, on peut écouter des CD sur sa chaîne hi-fi et télécharger de la musique sur son ordinateur. En voiture, on peut écouter la radio ou des cassettes. Quand on se promène dans la rue ou quand on fait du jogging, on peut écouter son baladeur.

Pour exprimer leur amour de la musique, les Français organisent chaque année une grande fête nationale appelée «la Fête de la Musique». Cette fête a lieu le 2 juin. Dans toutes les villes de France, il y a des concerts publics gratuits.° Ce jour-là, tous les Français sont dans la rue. Ils dansent, chantent, ou bien, ils écoutent la musique des orchestres° qui jouent un peu partout° dans les villes. Le slogan du jour est: «Pour la Fête de la Musique, faites de la musique.»

Quelle musique écoute-t-on en France quan on est jeune? En tête° du hit-parade, vienner les grandes vedettes de la chanson français **Jean-Jacques Goldman, Lara Fabian, Liane Jol Pascal Obispo**.... Mais à côté° de cette musiqu relativement traditionnelle existe une autr musique très populaire chez les jeunes. Cett musique reflète la réalité multiculturelle de l France d'aujourd'hui. La France est, en effet, un mosaïque de gens d'origines très différentes. À côté des Français de souche,° il y a aussi le immigrés venus d'autres pays européens, d Maghreb,** d'Afrique Noire, d'Asie... Chaqu groupe a apporté sa culture et, en particulier, s musique.

La musique française s'est enrichie de ce apports° et aussi des influences d'autre musiques populaires dans le monde: musique américaine, anglaise, espagnole. . . . Elle est ains devenue une musique originale et variée.

L'influence américaine: le rap

Le rap est né aux États-Unis dans les années 1980 et depuis il a fait le tour du monde. En France, il est représenté par **MC Solaar**. Ce «Monsieur Rap» est un Français d'origine tchadienne.*** Dans ses chansons, il exprime des messages sociaux positifs où il met en garde° les jeunes contre la violence et la délinquance.

MC Solaar, «Monsieur Rap»

L'influence antillaise: le zouk

Le groupe Malavoi

Le zouk vient des **Antille françaises (Martinique** e **Guadeloupe**). Pour le Antillais, «zouk» signifi «fête». Le zouk est don une musique de fête o s'expriment la joie, l'humou et la fierté° d'être ce qu'o est.

La musique de zou est typiquement antillaise Expression de la culture martiniquaise et guadeloupéenne, ell représente la fusion d'éléments caraïbes, africains, français e espagnols. Dans un orchestre de zouk, le chanteur chante e créole. L'instrument principal est le tambour° ou la batterie qui donne un rythme fort. Les autres instruments sont l synthétiseur, la basse, la guitare et parfois le piano.

Né il y a dix ans, le zouk est très populaire chez les jeune Français. Il est représenté par des groupes comme *Kassa* (Martinique et Guadeloupe) et *Malavoi* (Martinique). Ce groupes ont fait connaître° le zouk en dehors° de la France et en particulier, sur la côte est des États-Unis. Aujourd'hui, l zouk a un succès international.

* Paul Verlaine (1844-1896)

** Le Maghreb: l'Algérie, le Maroc, la Tunisie. Ces pays, en majorité arabes et musulmans, sont d'anciennes colonies ou protectorats français.

*** le Tchad: un pays d'Afrique

gratuits *free* **orchestres** *bands* **partout** *everywhere* **en tête** *on top* **à côté** *besides* **de souche** *native born* **les apports** *contributions* **met en garde** *warns* **la fierté** *pride* **le tambour** *drum* **la batterie** *drums* **fait connaître** *made known* **en dehors** *outside*

Supplementary vocabulary

le clip *video clip*
le hip-hop *hip-hop music*
rapper *to sing/play rap music*
le rapper *rap artist*
la tournée *tour*

Notes culturelles

- **MC Solaar** is the stage name of **Claude M'Barali**. He pronounces MC as in English: "emcee."
- **Ménélik** is a French rap artist, originally from Cameroon. His album **O.Q.P.** is available in the US as is MC Solaar's album **Le tour de la question**.
- Since January 1, 1996, at least 40% of the songs played on French radio stations must be in French. This new law has boosted French rap sales and widened its audience by giving it more air time.
- Other French-speaking African artists whose albums are sold in the US: **Ismael Lo** was dubbed the Bob Dylan of Senegal. Album: **Iso** (Mango records). **Salif Keita**, from Mali, has worked on the music of Disney's Lion King *(Le Roi Lion)*. Album: *Folon* (**"le passé,"** Mango Islands records).

L'influence arabe: le raï

Le raï vient d'**Afrique du Nord** et plus particulièrement d'**Algérie**. Il exprime la mélancolie mais aussi la joie et l'espoir° des jeunes **Maghrébins**. C'est un peu leur «soul music». Le chanteur de raï chante en arabe et parfois en français ou même en anglais. Il est accompagné d'instruments traditionnels et aussi de guitare et de synthétiseur. Les grands représentants du raï, **Khaled, Faudel** et **Cheb Mami,** sont Algériens ou d'origine algérienne.

Khaled

L'influence africaine: le rythme

Depuis une vingtaine d'années, **la musique africaine** a beaucoup de succès en France. Très variée, elle est représentée par un grand nombre de musiciens et de groupes qui viennent des différents pays de l'Afrique francophone.

1. **Touré Kunda** vient du **Sénégal** et chante en wolof,* sa langue maternelle,° et en français. Sa musique est traditionnelle et raffinée.
2. **Youssou N'Dour** vient aussi du **Sénégal**. Ses disques ont été produits aux États-Unis par le cinéaste américain, Spike Lee.
3. Le groupe **Soukous Stars** vient du **Zaïre** et joue de la musique africaine très rythmée avec beaucoup de tambour.
4. Les chanteuses du groupe **Zap Mama** sont d'origine européenne (belge) et africaine (zaïroise). Elles reprennent les chants traditionnels des peuples d'Afrique centrale. Dans d'autres chansons, elles mélangent° le français, l'espagnol, l'arabe et les langues africaines.

Manu Chao

MANU CHAO

Né en France de parents espagnols, Manu Chao a passé son enfance° dans la banlieue° parisienne. Influencé par le rock anglais, il a fondé° Mano Negra, un groupe de rock alternatif très populaire. Il a quitté ce groupe pour voyager en Espagne, en Amérique latine et en Afrique de l'Ouest. Là, il a enregistré les musiques locales sur un studio portable. Riche de ses expériences, il a décidé de chanter en solo.

Manu Chao écrit et chante en plusieurs langues (français, espagnol, anglais...). Ses chansons parlent de l'état du monde, des immigrants, de solidarité entre les peuples et de la lutte pour la vie.° Quelle que soit° la langue dans laquelle° il est exprimé°, ce message est universellement compris.

* la principale langue du Sénégal

espoir *hope* **la langue maternelle** *native language* **mélangent** *mix* **enfance** *childhood* **banlieue** *suburbs* **a fondé** *founded* **la lutte pour la vie** *struggle for survival* **quelle que soit** *whatever* **laquelle** *which* **exprimé** *expressed*

Notes culturelles

- **Raï** is an Arab word that means "opinion." Raï takes its roots in the music of the Bedouins, the nomadic people of the desert. In the Maghreb, raï was a poetic improvisation sung by its author who used this medium to share his vision of the world. Today, raï reflects the diverse influences of new rhythms, such as pop, reggae, and soul music.
- En mai 1997, le président Laurent Kabila a changé le nom du Zaïre en République démocratique du Congo (le Congo démocratique).

Teaching Strategy: Community Connections

Ask students if they are familiar with any of the musicians or groups mentioned. If so, they may be able to bring in recordings to share with the class. Local music stores or libraries may also have copies available. While playing music, ask students to compare the music from the francophone world to music they listen to at home. Do they see similarities? What differences can they point out? Have each student discuss his/her personal reaction.

Notes culturelles

- **Céline Dion**, born into a French-speaking Quebec family, now sings in English as well as French. She became internationally known for singing the title songs of popular movies such as *Beauty and the Beast* (**La Belle et la Bête**) and *Titanic*.
- **Gilles Vigneault** was born in Natashquan, Quebec, in 1928.
- **Laissez les bons temps rouler**, the literal translation of "Let the good times roll," is the unofficial motto of New Orleans.

Notes linguistiques

- Notez qu'en Louisiane, on prononce **les haricots** avec liaison: /lezarico/.
- Certains attribuent une origine plus ancienne au mot **zydéco** qui pourrait être un terme africain.
- Le terme **la-la** est encore utilisé par les francophones d'origine africaine. Il désigne une musique de danse, voisine du zydéco, ou la danse elle-même.
- En pays cajun, particulièrement dans les zones rurales, il y avait de nombreuses familles d'origine africaine dont la langue maternelle était le français. Certains de leurs descendants parlent encore français.

La musique francophone en Amérique

La chanson québécoise

Au Québec, chanter c'est affirmer son identité et sa culture, c'est exprimer sa fierté° d'être différent, c'est manifester° sa joie de vivre. Les interprètes de la chanson québécoise sont nombreux: **Gilles Vigneault**, le «poète de la chanson» qui chante son pays, **Isabelle Boulay**, **Garou** (de son vrai nom, **Pierre Garand**) et **Céline Dion**, qui est devenue une grande vedette° aux États-Unis.

Il faut également° mentionner les chanteurs acadiens du Nouveau Brunswick comme **Roch Voisine**, devenu une «idole» en France.

Céline Dion

La musique cajun

En pays cajun, on travaille dur,° mais on aime aussi la nourriture, la fête, la musique et la danse. Il n'est donc pas surprenant° que le grand événement de l'année soit le festival de musique cajun qui a lieu au mois de septembre à Lafayette.

Un orchestre joue du zydéco au festival

On vient de toute la région pour écouter l musique et danser aux sons° des orchestres d musique cajun et de zydéco.

La musique cajun est une musique de fête très rythmée, où les musiciens utilisent de instruments traditionnels comme le violon l'accordéon et la guitare, et où le chanteu mélange° l'anglais, le vieux français et le françai moderne. Cette musique descend directement d la musique acadienne d'autrefois, mais au cours des siècles et au contact de groupes ethnique différents, elle s'est enrichie d'éléments anglais espagnols, indiens et africains. Aujourd'hui grâce à° ses interprètes comme **Zachary Richar** et le groupe **Beausoleil,** la musique cajun connaî un regain° de popularité non seulement e Louisiane, mais dans tout le monde francophone.

Le zydéco

Le **zydéco** tire son nom du mot français «les haricots» et plus précisément du titre d'une chanson célèbre «Les haricots sont pas salés» composée par le légendaire **Clifton Chénier** (1925-1987). Le zydéco est né en Louisiane dans la région de Lafayette. C'est la forme moderne du **la-la**, musique de danse traditionnelle des Louisianais francophones d'origine africaine.

Clifton Chénier

Le zydéco est une variété de musique cajun, encore plus rythmée avec des accents de rock et de blues. Le chanteur chante en français ou en anglais et s'accompagne toujours d'un accordéon qui est l'instrument caractéristique du zydéco.

la fierté *pride* **manifester** = montrer **vedette** *star* **également** = aussi **dur** *hard* **surprenant** *surprising* **les sons** *beat* **mélange** *mixes* **au cours** *across* **grâce à** *thanks to* **regain** *renewal*

Teaching Strategy: Challenge

Ask students to compare the Canadian and French phrases. Are there particular usages (such as the importation of English words) that seem more frequent in one than the other?

Quelques expressions canadiennes:	Expressions françaises correspondantes:
faire du magasinage	faire du shopping/des achats
la fin de semaine	le week-end
séraphin *(adj.)*	avare
la gang	la bande d'amis/de copains
le fun	l'amusement
le char	la voiture

Une chanson: Mon pays

Mon pays ce n'est pas un pays c'est l'hiver
Mon jardin ce n'est pas un jardin c'est la plaine
Mon chemin ce n'est pas un chemin c'est la neige°
Mon pays ce n'est pas un pays c'est l'hiver

Dans la blanche cérémonie
Où la neige au vent° se marie
Dans ce pays de poudrerie°
Mon père a fait bâtir° maison
Et je m'en vais être fidèle°
À sa manière à son modèle
La chambre d'amis sera telle°
Qu'on viendra des autres saisons
Pour se bâtir à côté d'°elle

Mon pays ce n'est pas un pays c'est l'hiver
Mon refrain ce n'est pas un refrain c'est rafale°
Ma maison ce n'est pas une maison c'est froidure°
Mon pays ce n'est pas un pays c'est l'hiver

De mon grand pays solitaire
Je crie° avant que de me taire
À tous les hommes de la terre
Ma maison c'est votre maison
Entre mes quatre murs de glace°
Je mets mon temps et mon espace
À préparer le feu° la place
Pour les humains de l'horizon
Et les humains sont de ma race

Mon pays ce n'est pas un pays c'est l'envers°
D'un pays qui n'était ni pays ni patrie°
Ma chanson ce n'est pas ma chanson c'est ma vie
C'est pour toi que je veux posséder mes hivers

Gilles Vigneault

Dans les chansons qu'il compose, Gilles Vigneault exprime l'amour, l'amitié, la joie, l'attachement à son pays. Voici l'une des ses chansons les plus connues: *Mon pays.*

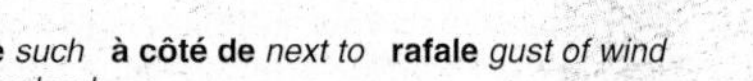

la neige *snow* **le vent** *wind* **la poudrerie** *powdery snow* **bâtir** = construire **fidèle** *faithful* **telle** *such* **à côté de** *next to* **rafale** *gust of wind*
la froidure *cold weather* **crie** *scream* **la glace** *ice* **le feu** *fire* **l'envers** *reverse* **la patrie** *motherland*

Teaching Strategy: Expansion

There are many excellent recordings of *Mon pays* which may be played for students. If any of the students play an instrument or sing, perhaps they might perform the song, giving their own interpretation.

Et la musique classique?

Quand on pense à la musique classique, on pense généralement aux grands compositeurs allemands (Mozart, Beethoven . . .) ou italiens (Vivaldi, Verdi . . .). À tort,° on a tendance à oublier la musique classique française. Pourtant, au cours° des siècles, la France a produit de grands musiciens dont° les oeuvres° sont toujours au répertoire des plus grands orchestres du monde.

Aujourd'hui, la musique classique connaît un regain° de popularité chez les Français de tout âge et de toute condition sociale. Pour un quart d'entre° eux, c'est la musique qu'ils écoutent le plus souvent. Et, contrairement à ce qu'on peut penser, les jeunes ne lui sont pas hostiles. En fait, la musique classique vient au cinquième rang de leurs préférences musicales, après le rock et les chansons bien sûr, mais avant le jazz et la musique populaire.

Lully et le ballet

Le ballet est né en Italie, mais c'est en France qu'il s'est développé à l'époque de **Louis XIV** (1638-1715). Ce roi était un grand patron des arts et il aimait particulièrement la musique et la danse. Pour mettre en musique les comédies-ballets dans lesquelles° il jouait parfois lui-même, il a fait appel° à **Jean-Baptiste Lully** (1632-1687), un musicien d'origine italienne. Celui-ci a composé un grand nombre de ballets et d'opéras. C'est sous son influence que le ballet s'est codifié et a acquis sa technique classique. Le ballet était alors un spectacle à la fois grandiose et formel où les danseurs entraient en scène masqués et habillés des magnifiques costumes de l'époque.

Un ballet de Lully présenté à la cour de Louis XIV

Chopin: le poète du piano

T. Kwiatkouski *«La polonaise de Chopin»*

Frédéric Chopin (1810-1849) est né en Pologne d'un père français et d'une mère polonaise. Enfan prodige, il compose et donne son premier concert l'âge de neuf ans. À vingt ans, il quitte son pay emportant dans une urne un peu de la terre° natal qu'il ne reverra jamais.°

Chopin s'établit° à Paris où il rencontre le artistes et les écrivains les plus célèbres de so époque. Parmi ceux-ci, il y a une jeune femme **George Sand**, pour qui il va éprouver° une grand passion. Inspiré par l'amour et plus tard par l tristesse de la séparation, il compose pour le pian des oeuvres d'une grande intensité émotionnelle études, ballades, nocturnes, fantaisies, préludes impromptus, sonates et aussi polonaises e mazurkas en l'honneur de son pays natal. De santé délicate et miné° par la tuberculose, il meurt à Pari à l'âge de 39 ans.

À tort *wrongly* **au cours** *across* **dont** *whose* **les oeuvres** *works* **un regain** *renewal* **d'entre** *of* **lesquelles** *which* **a fait appel** *asked*
Pologne *Poland* **la terre** *soil* **ne reverra jamais** *will never see* **s'établit** *settles* **éprouver** *feel* **la santé** *health* **miné** *weakened*

Note historique
The introduction of the "tutu" dates to 1830 and the Romantic ballets of that period. In the late 19th century, what we know as classical ballet was perfected in Russia, maintaining French terminology and basic French steps.

NOTES CULTURELLES

- **George Sand** was the pseudonym of Aurore Dupin (1804–1876). She wrote many books, including **La Mare au diable, La Petite Fadette, François le Champi.**
- **Chopin** was a leader of a new musical movement called **la musique romantique**. In this genre, music becomes descriptive and tries to express the feelings of its composer. At 19, Chopin was the best pianist in Poland. He left on November 1, 1830 to study abroad, but never returned to his homeland. He composed 14 **polonaises**, and 20 **nocturnes**.

«Carmen» présenté à New York (Metropolitan Opera)

Bizet et l'opéra romantique

Tous les amateurs d'opéra connaissent l'air° célèbre «Toréador, en garde, Toréador! Toréador!» Cet air est tiré de° l'opéra *Carmen*, oeuvre du compositeur **Georges Bizet**.

Bizet (1838-1875) était un prodige musical. Il est entré au Conservatoire de Paris à l'âge de neuf ans et il en est sorti à dix-huit ans avec le premier Grand Prix de Rome, distinction réservée aux meilleurs jeunes musiciens de l'époque. De ses nombreuses compositions, la plus connue reste *Carmen*, opéra romantique plein° de passion, d'émotions intenses et d'action dramatique. Jugé immoral, cet opéra n'a pas eu de succès à l'époque de sa création. Très affecté par cet échec,° Bizet est mort trois mois après la première représentation° de son chef-d'oeuvre.°

Aujourd'hui, *Carmen* est le plus populaire des opéras français. Modernisé, il a été adapté pour le cinéma dans plusieurs versions.

Une affiche: «Carmen» vers 1900

L'action se passe à Séville dans l'Espagne romantique du dix-neuvième siècle. L'héroïne est Carmen, une gitane° belle, fière, passionnée, mais d'humeur changeante . . . Carmen travaille dans une manufacture de tabac. Un jour, elle blesse° une de ses collègues d'un coup de couteau à la joue. Le brigadier Don José vient l'arrêter. Pendant qu'elle est sous sa garde, Don José tombe éperdument amoureux de la belle gitane et il la laisse s'échapper. Il déserte lui-même et s'enfuit avec Carmen dans les montagnes où ils rejoignent une bande de contrebandiers.° Don José devient alors contrebandier.

Un jour, Micaela, une jeune fille du village où il habitait vient annoncer à Don José que sa mère est sur le point° de mourir. Celui-ci retourne dans son village pour voir sa mère. Pendant ce temps, Carmen va à Séville avec ses amies pour assister à une corrida. Là, elle n'a d'yeux que pour le héros de la corrida, le toréador Escamillo, qui est son nouvel amour. Don José revient pour chercher Carmen. Il la trouve à la corrida et il la tue° dans une crise° de jalousie. Puis, il se livre° à la police.

Debussy et la musique impressionniste

On considère **Claude Debussy** (1862-1918) comme l'un des fondateurs de la musique moderne. Élève au Conservatoire de Paris, il étudie les oeuvres des grands compositeurs, mais il refuse absolument d'imiter leur style ou leur technique. Il se révolte en particulier contre la musique romantique dominée par l'intensité dramatique et l'émotion.

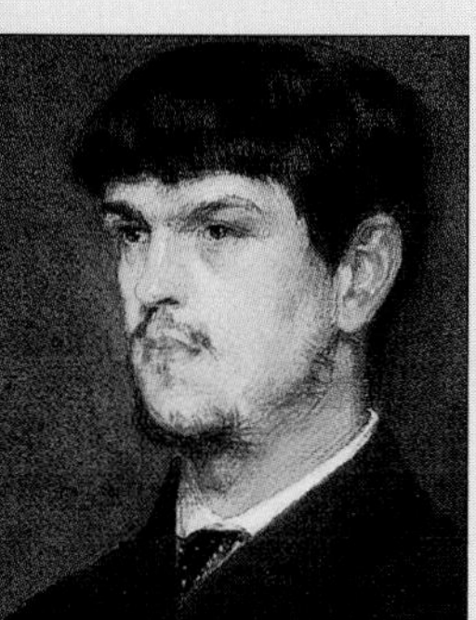
Claude Debussy (1862-1918)

Comme l'ont fait les peintres impressionnistes pour la peinture, Debussy veut libérer la musique de tout principe, de toute convention, de toute tradition. En rejetant, par exemple, la règle des accords° progressifs et en utilisant les dissonances et les silences, il donne à la musique des sonorités nouvelles qui ont pu sembler étranges aux gens de son époque. La musique de Debussy, exemplifiée par son célèbre poème symphonique «La Mer», est une musique fluide, délicate, toute en nuances, où l'impression produite remplace l'émotion.

l'air *aria* **tiré de** = vient **plein** *full* **un échec** *failure* **la représentation** *performance* **le chef-d'oeuvre** *masterpiece* **gitane** *gypsy* **blesse** *wounds* **contrebandiers** *smugglers* **sur le point** *is going* **tue** *kills* **une crise** *fit* **il se livre** *gives himself up* **accords** *chords*

- **Debussy** was a composer of **musique impressionniste**, a music written in small **touches** as if to capture colors. (For more on the Impressionist movement, see pp. 60–63.)
- **Lully** was a composer of **musique baroque**, an ornate style of music developed in Italy.
- Some other famous French composers are:
  Hector Berlioz (1803–1869): *Symphonie Fantastique*
  Charles Gounod (1813–1893): *Faust*
  Paul Dukas (1865–1935): *L'Apprenti Sorcier*
  Maurice Ravel (1875–1937): *Boléro*

UNITÉ 5

MAIN THEME

Travel

Communication Functions/Contexts

- Planning a trip abroad
- Going through customs
- Making travel arrangements
- Travel in France

Linguistic Goals

- Making negative statements
- Describing future plans and events
- Hypothesizing about what one would do

Proverbe

Les voyages forment la jeunesse.

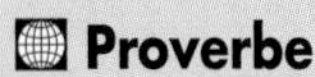

Online Study Center

Online Teaching Center

UNITÉ 5

Bon voyage!

Thème et Objectifs

Culture

In this unit, you will discover . . .

- what French young people do when they travel abroad and where they go
- why the train is the most popular means of transportation in France
- how the Eurotunnel has linked Great Britain to France and the rest of Europe

Communication

You will learn how . . .

- to make travel plans and purchase tickets
- to go through passport control and customs
- to travel by plane and by train

Langue

You will learn how . . .

- to discuss future plans
- to talk about future events
- to describe what you would do under certain conditions

TEACHING RESOURCES

ANCILLARIES

Student Activities Manual, Unit 5
Audio Program, Unit 5
Video-DVD Program, Unit 5
Chansons Audio CD

HM ClassPrep CD

Presentations, Unit 5
Audioscript, Unit 5
Videoscript, Unit 5
Assessment, Unit 5
Answer Key, Unit 5

La Passion des voyages

■ Pour ces jeunes voyageurs, «vacances» est synonyme de «voyage»!

Pour les jeunes Français, le terme «vacances» est synonyme de «voyage.» Ceux qui restent en France vont bronzer sur les plages de l'Atlantique et de la Méditerranée ou faire de la marche à pied dans les Alpes et les Pyrénées. Mais aujourd'hui, ceux qui vont à l'étranger sont de plus en plus nombreux. Aller dans un pays où la langue, les gens, et les coutumes sont différents, ça, c'est l'aventure!

Suivant° leurs objectifs, on peut classer ces jeunes voyageurs en différentes catégories.

Les «linguistes»

Les «séjours linguistiques» représentent la majorité des voyages à l'étranger. La formule classique consiste à passer deux ou trois semaines dans une famille en Angleterre (l'anglais étant° la langue la plus étudiée dans les lycées français).

Aujourd'hui, avec le développement des transports aériens et la diminution° du prix des voyages, les jeunes Français vont de plus en plus loin pour perfectionner° leur anglais. Patrick, par exemple, a passé le mois d'août dans une famille de Denver. Le haut point de son voyage a été la dernière semaine où la famille est allée faire du rafting dans le Colorado. Charlotte, elle, est allée en Australie dans une famille de ranchers. Là, elle a participé à toutes les activités, y compris la tonte des moutons.°

Les «actifs»

Ce sont ceux qui ont un projet particulier. Certains font un «stage» payé ou non payé dans une entreprise. Catherine a ainsi passé un mois en Allemagne à mélanger des colorants° dans une compagnie de produits chimiques. Là, elle a appris les dangers de la pollution et les moyens° de contrôler celle-ci.

Pour d'autres, leur projet a un objectif humanitaire. Jean-Baptiste, un étudiant de 22 ans, est allé au Sénégal avec une bande de copains. Il explique: «Notre but° n'était pas de faire du tourisme, mais d'accomplir quelque chose d'utile. Nous avons participé à la construction d'un système d'irrigation dans un petit village. Pendant notre séjour, nous avons travaillé très dur, mais aussi nous avons découvert un mode° de vie tout à fait° différent et nous avons fait connaissance de gens absolument extraordinaires. Pendant ces trois semaines, nous avons appris plus que pendant deux ans à l'université!»

suivant *according to* **étant** *being* **diminution** *decrease* **perfectionner** *improve* **tonte des moutons** *sheep shearing*
mélanger des colorants *to mix dyes* **moyens** *means* **but** = objectif **mode** *way* **tout à fait** *quite*

INFO MAGAZINE

Theme: Travel

Reading Strategy:
Browsing, reading for pleasure, scanning

■ Teaching Strategy

These optional readings can be done:

- in class or as homework
- at the beginning of the unit or as a wrap-up activity

■ Note linguistique

la marche à pied = hiking
le rafting = whitewater rafting
le stage = training course, work placement

Notes culturelles

- On distingue les langues vivantes *(modern languages)* et les langues mortes *(dead languages)*.
- Les langues les plus étudiées par les étudiants français sont (dans l'ordre): l'anglais, l'espagnol, l'allemand, l'italien, le russe, le portugais, l'hébreu moderne et le chinois.
- Les étudiants français sont obligés d'étudier au moins une langue étrangère.
- L'apprentissage d'une langue est obligatoire à partir de la sixième (1e année de collège).
- Les étudiants peuvent ensuite choisir d'apprendre le latin à partir de la 4e.
- Le basque, le breton, le corse, l'alsacien, le catalan et l'occitan sont des langues régionales enseignées dans certains lycées français.

Teaching Note

In Activity 1, p. 190, students list countries that they would like to visit. You may want to compare those lists to the one on this page.

Realia Notes

(Stamps)

- **La Gorée** is an island off the coast of Senegal where people were held before being transported to other countries as slaves. There is now an historical museum on the island. The doll on the stamp represents **la marchande** *(the vendor)*.
- **Le Dahomey** is an African country now called **le Bénin**. French is the official language of this former colony. The Nagos (pictured on the stamp) are one of the many tribes of Benin.
- **L'artocarpus** is a tree most commonly known as **l'arbre à pain** (breadfruit tree). Its fruits generally need to be cooked before eating.

■ Note linguistique

Le trekking (or **le trek**) is a difficult hike high up in the mountains.

■ Irregular Verb

(see Appendix C)
parcourir (*see* **courir**)

Leurs destinations préférées

AMÉRIQUE DU NORD
AMÉRIQUE CENTRALE
AMÉRIQUE DU SUD
EUROPE
ASIE
AFRIQUE
OCÉAN ATLANTIQUE
OCÉAN INDIEN
OCÉAN PACIFIQUE
AUSTRALIE
□ = 1 semaine
○ = 1-2 mois

Dans quel pays ou quelle région du monde aimeriez-vous passer vos vacances? Évidemment votre choix dépendra du temps que vous aurez à votre disposition. Voici, dans l'ordre, les destinations préférées des Français.

VACANCES D'UNE SEMAINE	VACANCES D'UN OU DEUX MOIS
1. l'Espagne, le Portugal	1. la Martinique, la Guadeloupe
2. l'Angleterre	2. les États-Unis
3. l'Italie	3. le Canada
4. la Grèce	4. les pays d'Amérique latine**
5. la Martinique, la Guadeloupe	5. la Grèce
6. les pays scandinaves*	6. le Mexique
7. l'Allemagne	7. l'Espagne, le Portugal
8. les États-Unis	8. les pays scandinaves*
9. la France	9. les pays d'Afrique noire***
10. l'Algérie, le Maroc, la Tunisie	10. l'Italie

* le Danemark, la Suède, la Norvège
** le Pérou, l'Argentine, le Brésil, l'Equateur, le Costa Rica, etc.
*** le Sénégal, la Côte d'Ivoire, le Cameroun, etc.

Les «explorateurs»

Ceux-là renouvellent la tradition des explorateurs français d'autrefois. Ils partent à l'aventure, sac au dos,° sans but précis pour des destinations mystérieuses. Julien, un étudiant en médecine, a parcouru° les hauts plateaux du Pérou en bus et en autostop. Marthe et Véronique, deux étudiantes d'une école de commerce, ont fait du trekking dans l'Himalaya. Elles sont parties du Népal et sont allées à pied par des sentiers° de haute montagne jusqu'au Tibet.

Pendant des semaines, les parents de ces voyageurs intrépides n'entendent pas parler° d'eux et s'inquiètent.° Mais finalement, ils reviennent, bronzés, heureux et avec plein° d'anecdotes sur les dangers qu'ils ont évités° et les rencontres qu'ils ont faites pendant leur fabuleux voyage. ■

DISCUSSION
Avec votre partenaire, imaginez que vous allez visiter la France (ou un autre pays francophone) cet été. Est-ce que vous voyagerez plutôt comme «linguiste,» comme «actif,» ou comme «explorateur»? Expliquez vos projets.

COMPOSITION
Décrivez des vacances «actives» que vous avez passées.

sac au dos *with a backpack* **parcourir** ✻ *to travel through* **sentiers** *trails* **n'entendent pas parler** *do not hear* **s'inquiètent** *worry* **plein** = beaucoup **évités** *avoided*

Teaching Strategy: Cultural Comparisons

Put two categories on the board:
VACANCES DE DEUX SEMAINES
VACANCES DE DEUX MOIS

Ask students to indicate their preferred destinations in each category, then compare with the ones chosen by French students. Are the kinds of activities and destinations similar or quite different? Ask students to suggest reasons for differences (Ex: geographically closer etc.). Have students do a survey of other French classes and compile the results.

Impressions d'Amérique

Les États-Unis ont toujours fasciné les jeunes Français. Nous avons demandé à quelques jeunes Français qui sont allés aux États-Unis de nous donner leurs impressions sur ce pays. Voici ce qu'ils disent.

Alioune "Les États-Unis sont un pays vraiment gigantesque. Là-bas, tout est grand: les maisons, les voitures, les gens, les distances. C'est aussi un pays magnifique. L'été dernier, j'ai voyagé en voiture en Arizona et au Texas. J'ai visité le Grand Canyon, un site unique au monde. J'ai aussi vu le désert, des cactus géants et même une ville fantôme.° C'était fabuleux. J'ai pris des tonnes° de photos pour montrer à ma famille et à tous mes copains."

Sarah "Ce qui m'a intéressée, c'est la variété ethnique des Américains. Ce qui est formidable, c'est que tous les groupes ethniques de la terre° y sont représentés. À New York, où j'ai fait un séjour linguistique, j'ai pu parler français avec des Haïtiens et des Canadiens. J'ai aussi parlé espagnol avec des Portoricains et avec une famille qui venait du Pérou. Ils m'ont parlé de leur culture et de leurs traditions. Tous ont choisi de venir habiter aux États-Unis pour avoir une vie meilleure. Ça, c'est super!"

Christophe "J'ai fait un stage de six mois dans une firme américaine. Quand je suis arrivé, j'avais un peu peur parce que je ne connaissais personne. Je me suis vite relaxé! Aux États-Unis, il est très facile de lier conversation° avec des gens qu'on ne connaît pas. En France, c'est quasi-impossible. Au travail, les relations entre les collègues sont cordiales et très égales. Dans les réunions,° par exemple, chacun° peut exprimer° son opinion, même si on est un jeune de 22 ans comme moi!"

Léa "J'ai travaillé comme jeune fille au pair en Californie. Avant de partir, je pensais que les Américains mangeaient mal et mangeaient trop. C'est vrai que l'obésité est un problème, mais la bouffe° n'est pas si mauvaise que ça! Bien sûr, il ne faut pas manger des hamburgers tout le temps. Ce n'est pas difficile, car il y a beaucoup de choix. On trouve des tas° de restaurants chinois, thaïlandais, indiens, mexicains, italiens où on mange des choses délicieuses.

Mehdi "Les Américains sont des gens dynamiques et superactifs. Malheureusement, ils sont trop stressés par le travail. Je suis resté chez ma tante qui est mariée avec un Américain. Ils travaillent tous les deux. Ils ont des jobs importants et ils rentrent très tard à la maison. Et leur fils de quinze ans travaille dans un supermarché le week-end. La vie de famille est donc° limitée. Le soir, en général, chacun prépare et mange son repas séparément. Il n'y a pas souvent de repas en commun. En France, on mange en famille. Je préfère cela, parce que c'est plus convivial et c'est très agréable de discuter ensemble des choses de la journée."

Sonia "J'ai passé un an dans une université américaine pour mon diplôme d'anglais. Les États-Unis sont un pays très intéressant. Il y a un mélange° de cultures très riche. Mais certains aspects de la culture me déplaisent.° Il y a une certaine fascination de l'argent et aussi de la violence. Les films et les jeux vidéos, par exemple, sont très violents. Dans la ville où j'étais, le journal et la chaîne° locale à la télévision reportaient des crimes tous les jours. J'avais peur de sortir seule le soir. Finalement, je n'ai jamais eu de problème. Mais je suis contente d'être à nouveau dans ma petite ville tranquille."

1. Avec votre partenaire, choisissez deux des jeunes Français. Dites si vous êtes entièrement, partiellement, ou pas du tout d'accord avec leurs impressions d'Amérique. Expliquez votre opinion.
2. Avez-vous voyagé à l'étranger ou dans une autre région? Qu'est-ce qui vous a impressionné(e)? Qu'est-ce que vous avez aimé? Qu'est-ce que vous n'avez pas aimé?

ville fantôme *ghost town* **tonnes** *tons* **terre** *earth* **lier conversation** = *parler* **réunions** *meetings*
chacun *each person* **exprimer** *express* **bouffe** *food (slang)* **des tas** *a lot* **donc** *therefore* **mélange** *mix*
me déplaisent *don't please me* **chaîne** *station*

INFO MAGAZINE INFO MAGAZINE INFO MAGAZINE INFO MAGAZINE INFO MAGAZI

■ Notes linguistiques

- Le nom des États américains en français:
  le Nouveau-Mexique,
  la Caroline du Nord/du Sud,
  la Floride, la Louisiane,
  la Géorgie, la Californie,
  la Pennsylvanie, la Virginie.
  (All other state names remain the same in French as in English.)
- The expression **la bouffe** comes from the verb **bouffer** *(to puff up)* by analogy, since the cheeks of someone who eats are puffed up with food. Consequently **bouffer** also means *to eat.*

■ Sujets de discussion

- Décrivez une région des États-Unis que vous avez visitée. Comment avez-vous trouvé le pays? les gens? la nourriture? Quelles autres impressions avez-vous de cette région?
- Un jour, vous visiterez peut-être la France. Avec votre partenaire, discutez des impressions que vous avez déjà sur ce pays. Vous pouvez donner vos impressions sur:
  - le pays
  - les gens
  - la nourriture
- Quand on visite un pays étranger, on découvre des similarités et des différences avec son propre *(own)* pays. Choisissez un pays que vous aimeriez visiter. Quelles similarités et quelles différences pensez-vous rencontrer? Expliquez votre opinion. Vous pouvez considérer les éléments suivants:
  - le pays
  - la nourriture
  - les voitures
  - les villes
  - les gens
  - le confort

PARTIE 1

LE FRANÇAIS
PRATIQUE
Les voyages

TEACHING RESOURCES

Student Activities Manual, pp. 133–135

Audio Program, CD 5, Tracks 1–5

HM ClassPrep CD Audioscript, Unit 5

■ **Pronunciation**
un pays /pei/

Note culturelle
The name **Sénégal** comes from the Wolof expression: **Sunu Gaal**, which means "our **pirogue** *(canoe)*." (**Wolof** is one of the main tribal languages of Senegal.)

■ **Realia Notes**
- **composter** = to stamp
- Uri, Schwyz, and Obwalden are Swiss cantons (districts). There are 20 cantons in Switzerland. The country takes its name from one of the original cantons: Schwytz.

LE FRANÇAIS PRATIQUE — Les voyages

Les voyages

— Où vas-tu aller cet été?

Je vais **voyager** / **faire un voyage** / **faire un séjour** | **à l'étranger** *(abroad)*.

faire un séjour *to spend some time*

— Ah bon? Dans quels **pays** *(countries)*?

Je vais visiter . . .
le Portugal.
la Grèce.
les Canaries.

Je vais aller . . .
au Mexique.
en Russie.
aux États-Unis.

Les pays

Révision ▶  pp. R14-R15

1 Voyages à l'étranger

Faites une liste de dix (10) pays que vous aimeriez visiter. Classez les pays par ordre de préférence. Comparez votre liste avec celle de votre partenaire.

- Quels sont les pays qui sont sur les deux listes?
- Quels sont les pays qui sont seulement *(only)* sur votre liste?

Maintenant expliquez pourquoi vous aimeriez aller dans les trois premiers pays de votre liste.

▶ **J'aimerais visiter le Sénégal parce que je voudrais mieux connaître l'Afrique . . .**

Au contrôle des passeports

— Vous avez **une pièce d'identité** *(ID document)*?

Oui, j'ai | **un passeport.**
une carte d'identité.
un permis de conduire *(driver's license).*

À la douane *(customs)*

— Vous avez des **bagages** *(luggage)*?

Oui, j'ai | **une valise** *(suitcase).* **un bagage à main** *(carry-on bag).*
un sac. **un sac à dos** *(backpack).*

— Est-ce que vous avez **quelque chose à déclarer?**

Non, je n'ai **rien à déclarer.**

NOTE CULTURELLE

Les Américains qui vont en France ont besoin d'un passeport (et aussi d'un visa, s'ils veulent faire un long séjour).

Les citoyens *(citizens)* des pays de l'Union européenne ont besoin seulement d'une pièce d'identité.

Arrivée en France

Cet été, vous faites un grand voyage autour du monde *(around the world)*. Vous arrivez en France, après avoir visité plusieurs pays. Vous passez au contrôle des passeports et à la douane. Composez et jouez le dialogue avec votre partenaire.

— Bonjour, monsieur/mademoiselle. Avez-vous une pièce d'identité?
— *(Present an ID document.)*
— Quels pays avez-vous visités avant de venir en France?
— *(Name a few countries.)*
— Avez-vous des bagages?
— *(Indicate the luggage that you are carrying.)*
— Avez-vous quelque chose à déclarer?
— *(Answer negatively.)*
— Où avez-vous acheté . . . ? *(customs officer names two or three things in your luggage, such as items of clothing, perfume, souvenirs)*
— *(For each item, mention a different country where you purchased it.)*
— Merci, monsieur/mademoiselle, et bon séjour en France.

■ Note Culturelle

The European Community (now known as the European Union) is composed of 25 European countries that have united to form a political and economic whole. The countries are: France, Germany, Italy, Belgium, the Netherlands, Great Britain, Ireland, Denmark, Greece, Spain, Luxembourg, Portugal, Austria, Finland, Sweden, Cyprus, Czech Republic, Estonia, Hungary, Latvia, Lithuania, Malta, Poland, Slovakia, and Slovenia. Although citizens of these countries use a European passport to travel outside of Europe, they need none to travel within the continent.

■ Teaching Strategy

Have each student choose a French-speaking country and draw a map with labels in French. Next, have students prepare a two-minute explanation of the country's attractions and a discussion of what they would need to bring and how long they would plan to stay. All students will make presentations to the class.

■ Additional Information

The French passport is valid for five years. Young people under 15 can have their own passport or be registered on a parent's passport.

A. Les expressions négatives

Note the following negative expressions and their use in the present and the passé composé.

AFFIRMATIVE	NEGATIVE	
quelqu'un *(someone, somebody)*	**ne . . . personne** *(no one, nobody)*	Je **ne** connais **personne** ici. Je **n'**ai rencontré **personne**.
quelque chose *(something)*	**ne . . . rien** *(nothing)*	Je **n'**ai **rien** à déclarer. Je **n'**ai **rien** acheté.
quelque part *(somewhere)*	**ne . . . nulle part** *(nowhere)*	Je **ne** me promène **nulle part**. Je **ne** suis allé **nulle part.**
quelque(s) *(some)*	**ne . . . aucun(e)** *(no, not any)*	Je **n'**ai **aucune** idée. Je **n'**ai acheté **aucun** cadeau.
et / ou *(and/or)*	**ne . . . ni . . . ni** *(neither . . . nor)*	Je **ne** vais **ni** au ciné **ni** au théâtre. Je **n'**ai visité **ni** Paris **ni** Québec.

➡ In the passé composé, negative expressions come AFTER the past participle, except **rien** which comes before.

Nous **n'**avons vu **personne**. BUT: Nous **n'**avons **rien** vu.

➡ **Personne** and **rien** can be used as subjects.

Personne n'a téléphoné. **Rien n'**est impossible.

ALLONS PLUS LOIN

Note the following constructions:

quelqu'un, quelque chose personne, rien	+ **de** + masculine adjective	J'ai rencontré **quelqu'un d'intéressant.**
quelqu'un, quelque chose personne, rien	+ **à** + infinitive	Nous **n'**avons **rien à déclarer.**

B. L'expression ne . . . que

The expression **ne . . . que** is not a negative expression. It is a limiting expression that means *only.* Its equivalent is **seulement**. Note its use in the following sentences.

Je parle français.	
Je **ne** parle **que** français.	*I speak* ***only*** *French.*
Je **ne** parle français **qu'**en France.	*I speak French* ***only*** *in France.*
Je **ne** parle français en France **qu'**avec mes amis.	*I speak French in France* ***only*** *with my friends.*

➡ Note the word order with **ne . . . que:**
- **ne** comes before the verb
- **que** comes before the word or phrase to which the restriction applies.

➡ Since **ne . . . que** is not a negative expression, the indefinite and partitive articles do not change after the verb.

Je mange **des légumes.** Je **ne** mange **que des légumes.**

LANGUE ET COMMUNICATION

TEACHING RESOURCES

Student Activities Manual, pp. 55, 135

Audio Program, CD 5, Tracks 6–7

HM ClassPrep CD, Audioscript, Unit 5

Notes linguistiques

- **Personne** and **rien** may also be used after a preposition.
  Je **n'**ai parlé **à personne.**
- The expressions **aucun** and **ni ... ni** may introduce the subject.
  Aucun invité n'est venu.
  Ni Pierre **ni** Marc **n'**est venu.
- They may also be used with prepositions. Note the word order:
  Je **n'**ai parlé à **aucun** invité.
  Je **n'**ai parlé **ni** à Pierre **ni** à Marc.

Teaching Note

Have students note in the **passé composé:**

Je **n'**ai **rien** fait **d'intéressant.**

Teaching Strategy: Challenge

You may also want to present the construction **ne faire que:**

Je ne fais que travailler.
The only thing I do is work.
Tu ne fais que te plaindre.
The only thing you do is complain.

1 C'est évident!

Informez-vous sur les personnes suivantes et dites ce qu'elles ne font pas. Utilisez les verbes entre parenthèses et une expression négative: **ne . . . personne, ne . . . rien, ne . . . nulle part**.

▶ Jean-Pierre est timide. (parler à)
Il ne parle à personne.

1. Carole se repose. (faire)
2. Pauline est très malade. (manger)
3. Marc n'est pas sociable. (inviter)
4. Thomas reste chez lui. (aller)
5. Antoine n'a pas soif. (boire)
6. Philippe ne voyage pas cet été. (partir)
7. Bernard est un nouvel élève. (connaître)
8. Catherine n'a pas d'argent. (acheter)

2 Une mauvaise surprise

Quand Brigitte est rentrée du concert, elle a trouvé la porte et les fenêtres de son appartement grandes ouvertes *(wide open)* et les lumières allumées *(turned on)*. Elle appelle un inspecteur de police qui lui pose les questions suivantes. Brigitte répond négativement. Jouez le rôle de Brigitte.

▶ L'inspecteur: Avez-vous entendu quelque chose?
Brigitte: **Non, je n'ai rien entendu.**

1. Avez-vous vu quelqu'un quand vous êtes rentrée?
2. Avez-vous observé quelque chose d'anormal?
3. Avez-vous remarqué quelqu'un de suspect?
4. Est-ce que vous avez donné votre adresse à quelqu'un récemment?
5. Est-ce que vous avez fait quelque chose de spécial hier soir?
6. Est-ce que vous avez invité quelqu'un chez vous la semaine dernière?
7. Est-ce que quelqu'un vous a téléphoné dans l'après-midi?
8. Est-ce que quelque chose d'important a disparu *(disappeared)*?
9. Est-ce que quelqu'un est venu réparer l'électricité récemment?
10. Est-ce qu'il y avait quelque chose de grande valeur *(value)* dans votre appartement?

3 À la douane

Vous arrivez à l'aéroport de Dorval à Montréal. Le douanier (joué par votre partenaire) vous pose certaines questions. Répondez-lui en choisissant une expression entre parenthèses.

▶ **—Vous avez des bagages?**
—Je n'ai qu'un bagage à main.
(Je n'ai que deux valises.)

QUESTIONS	RÉPONSES
Vous avez des bagages?	(deux valises / un sac à dos / un bagage à main)
Vous avez une pièce d'identité?	(mon passeport / mon permis de conduire / une carte d'étudiant)
Vous avez des cadeaux?	(du parfum / des chocolats / des tee-shirts)
Vous avez de l'argent?	(des dollars / des travellers chèques / une carte de crédit)
À part l'anglais, vous parlez d'autres langues?	(espagnol / allemand / français)
Vous allez rester longtemps?	(3 jours / 2 semaines / un mois)
Vous allez visiter plusieurs villes?	(Québec / Montréal / Toronto)

■ Réponses: Activité 1

1. Elle ne fait rien.
2. Elle ne mange rien.
3. Il n'invite personne.
4. Il ne va nulle part (Il ne va chez personne).
5. Il ne boit rien.
6. Il ne part nulle part.
7. Il ne connaît personne.
8. Elle n'achète rien.

Theme: Train travel

Teaching Strategy
Ask students to look at the illustrations, scan for cognates, and guess the theme of the article before reading.

Note culturelle
Each year, French students get two weeks off around the time of Mardi Gras (February/ March). These vacations are also called **les vacances d'hiver**. Many French people use this time to go skiing.

La France en train

■ Le train: c'est plus rapide, plus pratique et plus sûr!

Pour les vacances de Mardi Gras, Marie-Hélène, une étudiante parisienne, est allée chez sa grand-mère qui habite à Marseille. Elle aurait pu° prendre l'avion ou conduire° sa voiture, mais elle a choisi d'y aller en train. Pourquoi? Parce que c'est plus rapide, plus pratique et plus sûr. Avec le TGV (Train à Grande Vitesse), on peut aller de Paris à Marseille (750 kilomètres) en 3 heures. Il n'y a pas d'embouteillage,° pas de péage° à payer, et on arrive à sa destination frais et dispos.°

Le TGV, produit de la technologie française, est ce train super rapide qui circule sur un système spécial de rails et peut rouler° à une vitesse de 300 kilomètres à l'heure. La première ligne (Paris-Lyon) a été inaugurée en 1981, mais aujourd'hui le TGV dessert° presque° toutes les grandes villes françaises. Il y a un TGV Sud-est (orange), un TGV Atlantique (bleu) et un TGV Nord... En fait, 50% du service voyageurs est assuré par le TGV. Les autres trains sont peut-être un peu moins rapides, mais ils sont aussi confortables et aussi pratiques.

Les Français sont très fiers° de leurs trains et ceci pour de bonnes raisons:

■ Les trains français sont toujours à l'heure. Ils partent à l'heure indiquée et arrivent à l'heure indiquée. Avec le train, on n'est jamais en retard.

■ Les trains sont propres et confortables. Si on a faim, on peut prendre un repas au wagon-restaurant.° Sur les grandes distances, on peut voyager en wagon-lit.°

■ Le train est bon marché et très flexible. Il y a des réductions de prix pour les jeunes, pour les familles, pour les personnes âgées, pour les personnes qui voyagent souvent. Pour toutes ces personnes, les prix des billets varient selon l'époque où on voyage. Ils sont plus élevés° en période rouge (vacances) ou blanche (week-ends), et moins élevés en période bleue (le reste du temps).

Pour les touristes, il y a d'autres services intéressants. Avec «train + vélo» et «train + auto,» on peut voyager en train et louer un vélo ou une voiture quand on arrive à sa destination. Avec «train + hôtel,» on trouve toujours une chambre d'hôtel.

Les jeunes Américains peuvent acheter un Eurailpass. Cette carte leur permet de sillonner° l'Europe pendant plusieurs semaines pour un prix relativement modique°. Pour beaucoup de jeunes qui utilisent ce système, le train est non seulement un moyen° de transport mais c'est aussi un hôtel, un restaurant, une cafétéria et un lieu où ils peuvent rencontrer d'autres jeunes qui, comme eux, viennent découvrir le vieux continent. ■

Paris à Marseille

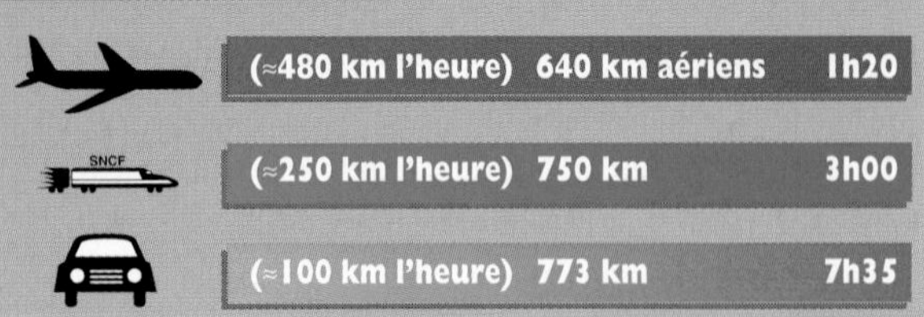

(≈480 km l'heure)	640 km aériens	1h20
(≈250 km l'heure)	750 km	3h00
(≈100 km l'heure)	773 km	7h35

et vous?

DISCUSSION
Vous allez visiter la France avec votre partenaire. Il/Elle voudrait voyager en avion, mais vous préférez voyager en train. Expliquez-lui les avantages du train. Votre partenaire va poser des questions.

COMPOSITION: UNE LETTRE
Alice, une copine française, va visiter les États-Unis cet été. Elle ne sait pas si elle va voyager en train ou en bus, et elle vous demande votre avis (opinion). Dites-lui quel système vous préférez et expliquez-lui les avantages et les inconvénients de ce système.

aurait pu *could have* **conduire** ✻ *to drive* **embouteillage** *traffic jam* **péage** *toll* **frais et dispos** *fresh and rested* **rouler** = aller **dessert** *services* **presque** *almost* **fiers** *proud* **wagon-restaurant** *dining car* **wagon-lit** *sleeping car* **plus élevés** *higher* **sillonner** = voyager à travers **modique** *low* **moyen** *means*

L'EUROTUNNEL

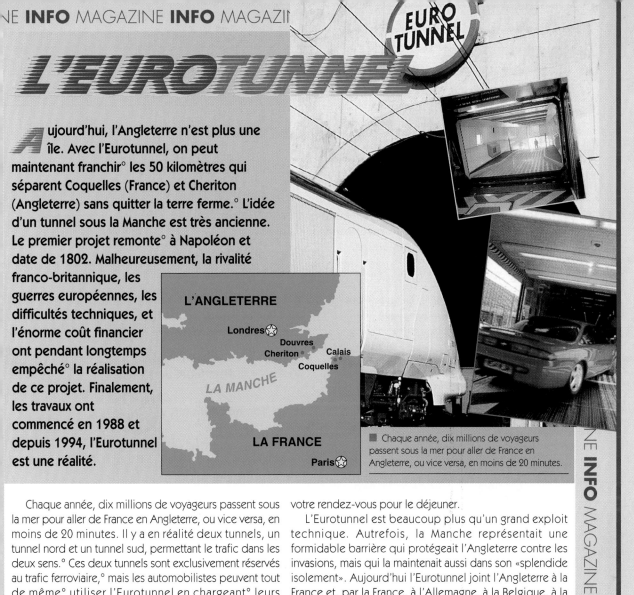

Aujourd'hui, l'Angleterre n'est plus une île. Avec l'Eurotunnel, on peut maintenant franchir° les 50 kilomètres qui séparent Coquelles (France) et Cheriton (Angleterre) sans quitter la terre ferme.° L'idée d'un tunnel sous la Manche est très ancienne. Le premier projet remonte° à Napoléon et date de 1802. Malheureusement, la rivalité franco-britannique, les guerres européennes, les difficultés techniques, et l'énorme coût financier ont pendant longtemps empêché° la réalisation de ce projet. Finalement, les travaux ont commencé en 1988 et depuis 1994, l'Eurotunnel est une réalité.

■ Chaque année, dix millions de voyageurs passent sous la mer pour aller de France en Angleterre, ou vice versa, en moins de 20 minutes.

Chaque année, dix millions de voyageurs passent sous la mer pour aller de France en Angleterre, ou vice versa, en moins de 20 minutes. Il y a en réalité deux tunnels, un tunnel nord et un tunnel sud, permettant le trafic dans les deux sens.° Ces deux tunnels sont exclusivement réservés au trafic ferroviaire,° mais les automobilistes peuvent tout de même° utiliser l'Eurotunnel en chargeant° leurs voitures sur des trains spéciaux.

Imaginez, par exemple, que vous habitez à Paris et que vous voulez déjeuner avec votre copain qui habite à Londres. C'est simple. Si vous préférez le train, vous prendrez l'Eurostar à 10 heures et vous arriverez à Londres à midi. Si, au contraire, vous préférez conduire, vous devez partir à sept heures. Vous prendrez l'autoroute° qui va de Paris jusqu'à l'accès de l'Eurotunnel. Là, vous monterez avec votre voiture sur une navette° spéciale qui vous amènera jusqu'au° terminal britannique. De là vous continuerez votre route. S'il n'y a pas trop d'embouteillages° dans Londres, vous serez à votre rendez-vous pour le déjeuner.

L'Eurotunnel est beaucoup plus qu'un grand exploit technique. Autrefois, la Manche représentait une formidable barrière qui protégeait l'Angleterre contre les invasions, mais qui la maintenait aussi dans son «splendide isolement». Aujourd'hui l'Eurotunnel joint l'Angleterre à la France et, par la France, à l'Allemagne, à la Belgique, à la Hollande et à tout le continent européen. C'est le symbole de la Nouvelle Europe, unie et en paix° avec elle-même. ■

QUESTIONS

1. Comment peut-on aller de Paris à Londres par la terre ferme?
2. Quels ont été les obstacles à la construction de l'Eurotunnel?
3. Pourquoi l'Eurotunnel est-il un grand exploit technique?
4. Quel est le symbole politique de l'Eurotunnel?

franchir = traverser **terre ferme** *ground* **remonte** *goes back* **empêché** *prevented* **sens** = directions **ferroviaire** *railroad* **tout de même** *nevertheless*
chargeant *loading* **l'autoroute** *turnpike* **navette** *shuttle train* **jusqu'au** *up to* **embouteillages** *traffic jams* **paix** *peace*

NE INFO MAGAZINE INFO MAGAZI

Teaching Strategy: Challenge

Initiate a discussion on the different modes of transportation used in the United States, and how and why these differ from those most commonly used in France. (*e.g.*: Do we use the train or the plane more in the United States? What about France? Why the difference? Do we have anything like the TGV or the EuroTunnel here in the U.S.?)

■ Note culturelle

Le TGV qui relie Paris et Londres s'appelle l'Eurostar.

NOTES CULTURELLES

- It is as fast to take the TGV from Paris to London via the Eurotunnel as to fly the same distance and then take a taxi or a train to London. Both trips take about three hours.
- Eurostar (or **TGV Transmanche**) is the name of the high-speed train that travels between Paris and London.
- A total of 139 plans have been made since 1802 to build an underwater connection between France and Great Britain. The first project (1802) called for a stone-paved road in an underground passageway under the Channel. The second project (1803) called for a tunnel made of metal tubes.

LE FRANÇAIS PRATIQUE

TEACHING RESOURCES

Student Activities Manual, pp. 136–137

Tête-à-tête Pair Activity, À l'agence de voyage, p. PA6

Audio Program, CD 5, Tracks 8–12

HM ClassPrep CD, Audioscript, Unit 5

Video/DVD Program, Unit 5

LE FRANÇAIS PRATIQUE

Partons en voyage

À l'agence de voyages

—Je voudrais | **acheter un billet** *(ticket)*.
réserver une place *(seat)*.
confirmer ma réservation.
annuler ma réservation.
louer une voiture.

annuler *to cancel*
louer *to rent*

POUR ACHETER UN BILLET DE TRAIN OU D'AVION

— Quelle sorte de billet désirez-vous?
Un aller simple *(one way)*. **Un aller et retour** *(round trip)*.

—En quelle classe?
En **première classe.** | En **deuxième classe** [en train].
En **classe affaires** *(business)* | En **classe économique** [en avion].

—En quelle section?
En section **fumeur.**

En section **non-fumeur.**

— Quel siège *(seat)* | préférez-vous?
— Quelle place
Un siège | près de la fenêtre.
Une place | près du **couloir** *(aisle)*.

—Voici | votre billet.
votre **carte d'embarquement** *(boarding pass)*.

POUR OBTENIR DES RENSEIGNEMENTS *(information)*

—Est-ce que | **le vol** *(flight)* pour Nice / le train pour Marseille | est **direct**?
Non, il y a | **une escale** *(stop, stopover [of the plane])* / **une correspondance** *(change of plane, train)* | à Lyon.

—Est-ce que le vol/le train est **à l'heure** *(on time)*?
Non, il est | **en avance** *(early)*. Il a **dix minutes d'avance.**
en retard *(late)*. Il a **une heure de retard.**

Le vol numéro 23 à destination de Londres est **annulé.**

—Est-ce que le vol/le train est **complet** *(full)*?
Non, il y a **de la place** *(room)*.

—Est-ce que ce siège/cette place est **libre** *(free)*?
Non, il/elle est **occupé(e).**

Teaching Suggestion: Video/DVD Program

In the Unit 5 *Vidéo-drame: Nicolas fait un voyage,* students will learn about traveling in France. They will become familiar with making reservations and preparing for a trip, as well as useful phrases such as **réserver une place** and **confirmer ma réservation**. As you play the video, listen carefully to Nicolas and Malik as they make a plane reservation. As students watch the video, ask: **Qu'est-ce qu'il faut faire avant de monter dans le train? Où est-ce que Nicolas va pour prendre le train?**

Les passagers doivent . . .

AU DÉPART	**présenter** leur billet. **obtenir** leur carte d'embarquement. **enregistrer** leurs bagages. **se présenter** à la porte de départ. **embarquer.**
PENDANT LE VOL	mettre leur bagage à main sous le siège. **attacher** leur **ceinture de sécurité** *(seat belt).*
À L'ARRIVÉE	**débarquer.** **chercher** leurs bagages. **passer par** la douane.

L'avion va **décoller** / **atterrir** dans 10 minutes.

obtenir *to get*
enregistrer *to check [luggage]*
embarquer *to board [a plane]*

attacher *to fasten*

débarquer *to deplane*
passer par *to go through*

décoller *to take off*
atterrir *to land*

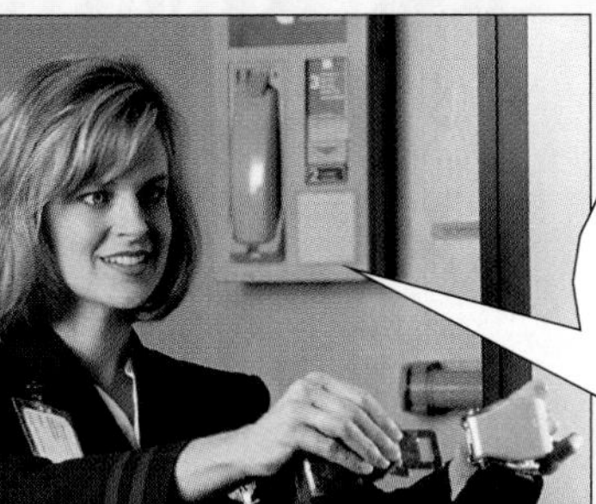

Mesdames et messieurs, bonjour.
Le capitaine Pascal et son équipage vous souhaitent la bienvenue à bord du vol Air France numéro 346 à destination de Montréal.
La durée du vol sera approximativement de 7 heures et 25 minutes et notre arrivée à Montréal est prévue pour 17h45 heure locale.
En prévision du départ, veuillez attacher votre ceinture de sécurité.

Note culturelle

Air France is France's major airline. There are also many regional airlines, such as Air Guadeloupe, Air Guyane, or Air Transport Pyrénées.

Teaching Note

You might want to remind students that all schedules in France are posted in the 24-hour time system.

Teaching Strategy: Group Practice

Divide students into groups of 4 or 5. One person from each group will be the travel agent working behind the counter at the airport/train station. The other 3 or 4 people will be travelers in need of information. The travel agent should ask at least one question of each person and answer all of their questions. Each person should ask at least two questions of the travel agent. In the dialogs, the students should attempt to be as original as possible and use as much vocabulary from the text as possible.

Irregular Verb

(See Appendix C.)
obtenir is conjugated like **tenir**.

Language Note

l'équipage *(m.)* = crew

Photo Note

Orlyval is the subway line that connects Orly airport to Paris.

Teaching Strategy: Expansion

Have students draw a map or illustration of an airport and train station, adding the following labels:

À L'AÉROPORT	**la piste de décollage/d'atterrissage** *(take off/landing) runway* **la tour de contrôle** *control tower* **la boutique hors-taxe** *duty-free shop*
EN VOITURE	**la voiture de location** *rental car* **le kilométrage illimité** *unlimited mileage*
EN AVION	**le stand-by** *stand-by* **la classe affaires** *business class* **la soute à bagages** *cargo bay*
EN TRAIN	**la couchette** *berth* **le compartiment** *compartment* **le wagon** *(train) car*

Notes culturelles

- In every French station, you will find **un composteur** on your way to the platforms. It is an orange-colored machine (see illustration and photo) in which the traveler inserts his train ticket to have it automatically stamped with the time and date.
- **Lille** is the main city in the north of France. It is located just below the Belgian frontier.

Note linguistique

Un **haut-parleur** *(loudspeaker)* est utilisé pour annoncer les départs et les arrivées *(voir photo).*

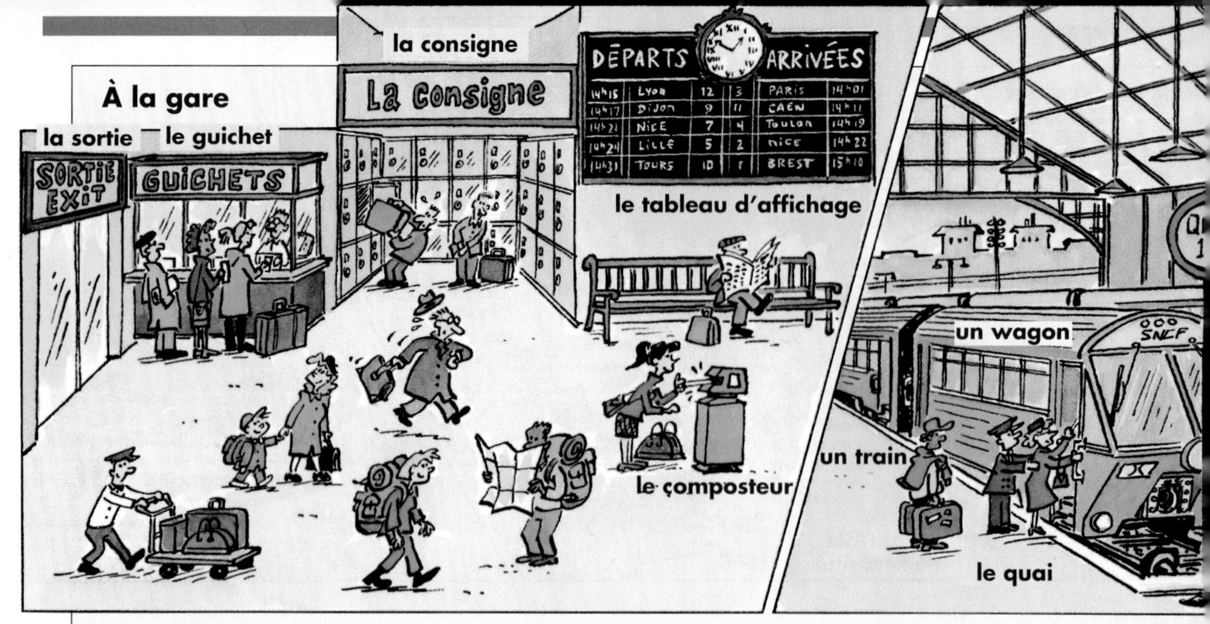

Les passagers doivent . . .

acheter un billet.
composter le billet.
monter dans leur train.
descendre de leur train à l'arrivée.

composter *to punch [a ticket]*
monter (dans) *to get on [a train]*
descendre (de) *to get off [a train]*

Mais attention, il ne faut pas **rater** le train.
Si on rate le train, il faut **prendre** **le prochain train.** / **attendre** **le train suivant.**

rater *to miss*

NOTE CULTURELLE

Avant de monter dans le train, les voyageurs doivent composter leurs billets. Le composteur indique l'heure et la date à laquelle le billet a été composté. Pendant le voyage, le contrôleur *(conductor)* passe dans les wagons pour contrôler les billets. Si on n'a pas composté son billet, on reçoit une amende *(fine)*.

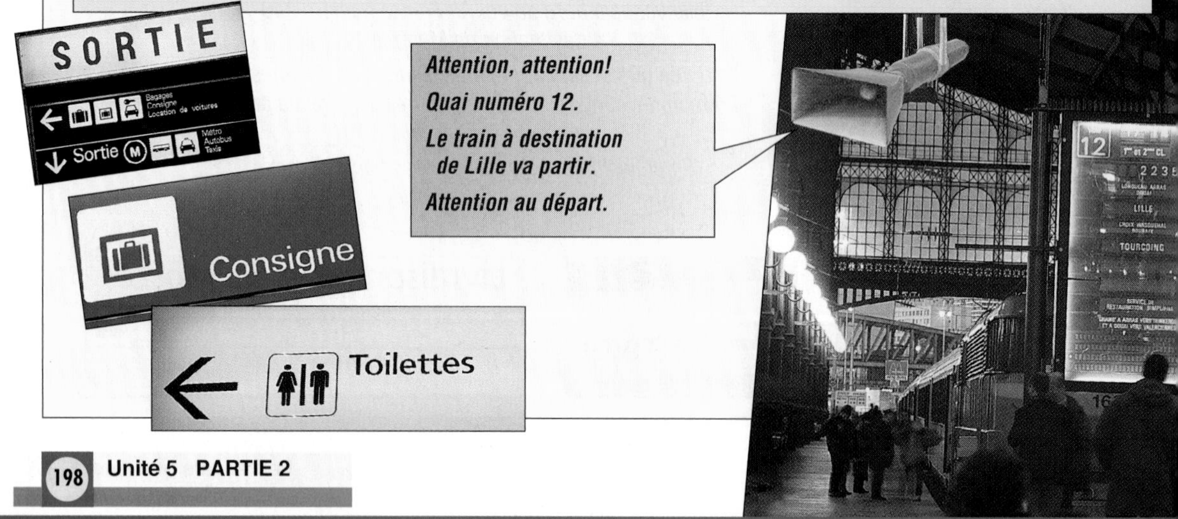

SORTIE
Sortie
Consigne
Toilettes
Attention, attention!
Quai numéro 12.
Le train à destination de Lille va partir.
Attention au départ.

Un voyage en avion

Vous êtes à Genève avec votre partenaire. Demain, vous avez l'intention d'aller à Nice en avion. Décrivez toutes les étapes *(steps, stages)* de ce voyage en avion en mettant les activités suivantes dans l'ordre chronologique.

- attacher nos ceintures de sécurité
- aller à l'aéroport
- débarquer
- embarquer
- dormir un peu
- passer par la douane
- aller à la porte 18
- chercher nos places dans l'avion
- passer le contrôle de sécurité
- aller au comptoir d'Air France
- montrer notre carte d'embarquement à l'hôtesse
- enregistrer nos bagages
- réserver deux places pour Nice
- sortir de l'aéroport
- téléphoner à l'agence de voyages
- chercher nos valises à la livraison des bagages

▶ **D'abord, nous allons téléphoner à l'agence de voyages. Nous allons . . .**

Un voyage en train

Maintenant vous allez de Nice à Cannes en train. Avec votre partenaire, décrivez ce que vous allez faire pendant ce voyage, dans l'ordre chronologique.

À l'Agence Tours-Soleil

L'Agence Tours-Soleil organise des voyages très bon marché. Choisissez un voyage et une date de départ. Avec votre partenaire, complétez le dialogue correspondant et jouez-le en classe. (Votre partenaire va jouer le rôle de l'agent de voyages.)

L'AGENT: Où désirez-vous aller, monsieur/ mademoiselle?
VOUS: – – –
L'AGENT: Quel jour désirez-vous partir?
VOUS: – – –
L'AGENT: Désirez-vous un aller simple?
VOUS: – – –
L'AGENT: En quelle classe?
VOUS: – – –
L'AGENT: Quelle place préférez-vous?
VOUS: – – –
L'AGENT: Désirez-vous louer une voiture? (Quelle voiture?)
VOUS: – – –

VOYAGES TOURS-SOLEIL

DESTINATIONS	DÉPARTS	
Dakar	3 juin	4 juillet
Casablanca	10 avril	5 septembre
Tahiti	8 juillet	2 août
Hong Kong	1er août	3 septembre
Moscou	6 mai	4 juin
Tel Aviv	12 juin	10 août
Fort-de-France	1er juillet	10 septembre

HONG KONG

MARTINIQU

■ **Note linguistique**

In Canada, **un guichet automatique** is an ATM machine. It is called **le distributeur de billets** or the **guichet automatique de banque (GAB)** in France. **Le guichetier/la guichetière** is the person who works behind the counter in a train station, a bank, or a post office.

Teaching Strategy: Challenge

Ask students: À votre avis, pourquoi l'agence de voyages s'appelle-t-elle Tours Soleil? (Parce que la majorité des destinations proposées sont vers des pays chauds et tropicaux.)

Note culturelle

Dakar is the capital of Senegal. **Casablanca** is the largest city in Morocco. **Fort-de-France** is the main city of Martinique.

Teaching Strategy: Groups

Divide the class into groups. Ask students: Regardez les symboles (pictogrammes) à la page 198. Pouvez-vous deviner *(guess)* ce qu'ils représentent sans lire l'explication? Quels autres symboles de ce type connaissez-vous? Décrivez-les en français. *(fork and knife: restaurant; bed: hotel; tent: campground; gas pump: gas station.)*

TEACHING RESOURCES

Student Activities Manual, pp. 57–58, 138

Audio Program, CD 5, Tracks 13–15

HM ClassPrep CD, Audioscript, Unit 5

Teaching Strategy: Expansion, Activity 5

Have students do the same activity comparing:
la voiture/le train;
le bateau/l'avion;
le bus/le train.

Additional Situations

Pas de chance!
Jacques Lachance n'a pas de chance. Ce soir, il doit prendre l'avion de Montréal. Quand il arrive au comptoir, il ne peut pas trouver son billet.
Rôles: Jacques Lachance / l'employé(e)

Le passager nerveux
Sur le vol Paris–Athènes, il y a un passager très, très nerveux. L'hôtesse de l'air essaie de le calmer.
Rôles: l'hôtesse / le passager nerveux

4 Pas de chance

Il y a des voyageurs qui n'ont pas de chance. Avec votre partenaire, complétez les échanges suivants.

1. «Est-ce que cette place est libre?»
   «Non, – – – .»
2. «Est-ce que le train est à l'heure?»
   «Non, – – – .»
3. «Est-ce que le vol à destination de Toronto a été confirmé?»
   «Non, – – – .»
4. «Est-ce que le vol est direct?»
   «Non, – – – à Genève.»
5. «Est-ce que le train pour Tours est direct?»
   «Non, – – – à Saint-Pierre.»
6. «Est-ce qu'il y a de la place sur le prochain vol?»
   «Non, – – – .»

5 Train ou avion?

Vous voulez visiter l'Europe avec votre partenaire. Vous n'êtes pas d'accord sur le mode de transport que vous allez utiliser pendant le voyage: train ou avion?

Chacun va choisir un mode de transport (train ou avion) et essayer de convaincre *(to convince)* son partenaire. Présentez vos arguments par ordre de préférence. Qui va gagner le débat? Voici quelques idées:

TRAIN 

- C'est moins cher.
- On peut mieux voir le paysage.
- On peut faire connaissance de plus de personnes.
- On peut se déplacer *(to get around)* plus facilement.
- ??

AVION 

- C'est plus rapide.
- C'est plus confortable.
- On est moins fatigué.
- On a plus de temps pour visiter le pays.
- ??

6 *Conversations libres*

Avec votre partenaire, choisissez l'une des situations suivantes. Composez le dialogue correspondant et jouez-le en classe.

1 Un voyage à Genève

Madame D'Argent est une femme d'affaires très occupée. Demain matin, elle a un rendez-vous à Genève. Elle téléphone à son agence de voyage qui lui annonce que malheureusement il n'y a plus de place sur l'avion Paris-Genève. L'employé(e) propose d'autres solutions, par exemple, le train, le vol Paris-Zurich/Zurich-Genève, etc.
Rôles: Madame D'Argent / l'employé(e)

2 Un voyage en avion

Caroline va aller à la Martinique avec son petit frère Julien, 8 ans. C'est la première fois que Julien prend l'avion. Il pose beaucoup de questions à sa soeur qui lui explique comment va se passer le voyage.
Rôles: Caroline / Julien

3 Trop tard!

Aujourd'hui vous partez en France. Malheureusement vous arrivez à l'aéroport avec cinq minutes de retard. Votre avion vient juste de partir. Allez au comptoir d'Air France et expliquez la situation à l'employé(e). (Donnez des précisions sur le vol que vous avez raté.) Demandez-lui de vous trouver une place sur le vol suivant.
Rôles: vous / l'employé(e) d'Air France

4 Contrôle de billets

Vous êtes dans le train Paris-Strasbourg. Vous avez acheté u billet de 2e classe. Vous n'avez fait attention et vous êtes allé(e dans un wagon de 1re classe. Le contrôleur *(conductor)* arrive. Il vous demande de payer un sup plément. Vous n'avez pas assez d'argent. Expliquez-lui la situati
Rôles: vous / le contrôleur

Unité 5 PARTIE 2

A. Le futur

The FUTURE tense is used to describe what people WILL DO, what WILL HAPPEN. The verbs in the following sentences are in the future tense.

L'avion **partira** dans dix minutes.	*The plane **will leave** in ten minutes.*
Nous **irons** en France cet été.	*We **will go** to France this summer.*

The future tense is a SIMPLE tense. It is formed as follows:

FUTURE STEM + FUTURE ENDINGS

INFINITIVE		parler	finir	vendre	FUTURE ENDINGS
FUTURE STEM		parler-	finir-	vendr-	
FUTURE	je	**parlerai**	**finirai**	**vendrai**	**-ai**
	tu	**parleras**	**finiras**	**vendras**	**-as**
	il/elle/on	**parlera**	**finira**	**vendra**	**-a**
	nous	**parlerons**	**finirons**	**vendrons**	**-ons**
	vous	**parlerez**	**finirez**	**vendrez**	**-ez**
	ils/elles	**parleront**	**finiront**	**vendront**	**-ont**
NEGATIVE	je **ne**	**parlerai pas**			
INTERROGATIVE	**est-ce que tu**	**parleras?**			
		parleras-tu?			

The stem of the future always ends in **-r.**

➡ For most verbs,

FUTURE STEM = INFINITIVE *(minus* **-e**, *if any)*

partir → je **partir**ai   **écrire** → j'**écrir**ai

ARRIVÉE
La prochaine fois, je partirai à temps, je ne m'arrêterai pas en route, et j'arriverai le premier.

➡ Some verbs have irregular future stems.

INFINITIVE	FUTURE STEM	
acheter	**achèter-**	**j'achèterai**
appeler	**appeller-**	**j'appellerai**
payer	**paier-**	**je paierai**
avoir	**aur-**	**j'aurai**
être	**ser-**	**je serai**
aller	**ir-**	**j'irai**
faire	**fer-**	**je ferai**
venir	**viendr-**	**je viendrai**

INFINITIVE	FUTURE STEM	
devoir	**devr-**	**je devrai**
pouvoir	**pourr-**	**je pourrai**
vouloir	**voudr-**	**je voudrai**
envoyer	**enverr-**	**j'enverrai**
recevoir	**recevr-**	**je recevrai**
savoir	**saur-**	**je saurai**
voir	**verr-**	**je verrai**

Also: il y a → **il y aura**   il pleut → **il pleuvra**

Le futur
Pratique p. 57

NOTE CULTURELLE

Le Lièvre et la Tortue is a famous fable by French author Jean de La Fontaine (see pp. 136 and 146 for more information). It is the story of how a hare lost a race to a turtle. The hare was so sure of his speed that he took a rest along the way. When he finally realized that the turtle would win the race, it was too late for him to catch up. The moral of the fable is: **Rien ne sert de courir, il faut partir à point** *(on time)*.

1 Cet été

Demandez à votre partenaire s'il/si elle fera les choses suivantes cet été.
Si votre partenaire répond affirmativement, essayez de continuer la conversation.

▶ travailler?

— Tu travailleras cet été?
— Oui, je travaillerai.
— Ah bon, qu'est-ce que tu feras?
— Je serai serveur/serveuse dans un restaurant.
(Non, je ne travaillerai pas.)

- gagner de l'argent?
- rester chez toi?
- écrire à tes copains?
- être chez toi en août?
- avoir un job?
- faire du sport?
- faire du camping?
- aller à la mer?
- avoir l'occasion de voyager
- aller à l'étranger?
- voir tes grands-parents?
- rendre visite à tes cousins?

■ Notes linguistiques
épicé = spicy, hot
une épice = spice
épicer = to spice

2 Des vacances différentes

Cet été vous allez faire les choses de la colonne A. Votre partenaire a des projets différents (des projets de la colonne B ou d'autres projets). Chacun expliquera ses projets à l'autre.

A	B
aller à la Martinique	aller au Canada
prendre l'avion	prendre le train
louer une voiture	louer un vélo
aller à l'hôtel	faire du camping
manger des plats épicés	manger du homard *(lobster)*
faire de la planche à voile	visiter les Parcs Nationaux
assister aux spectacles folkloriques	voir les matchs de baseball
voir mes copains	rendre visite à mon oncle
se reposer	être très actif/active
??	??

▶ **— Moi, j'irai à la Martinique. Je prendrai l'avion.**
— Eh bien, moi, je n'irai pas à la Martinique. J'irai au Canada. Je . . .

Teaching Note
Activity 3 reviews object pronouns.

3 Procrastination

Vous faites un voyage avec un(e) camarade qui ne fait jamais immédiatement ce qu'il/elle doit faire. Votre partenaire va répondre à vos questions en utilisant un pronom complément.

▶ visiter le musée (samedi)
— Quand est-ce que tu visiteras le musée?
— Je le visiterai samedi.

1. écrire à tes parents (demain)
2. téléphoner à ta copine (samedi)
3. envoyer ces lettres (ce soir)
4. acheter ton billet (la semaine prochaine)
5. confirmer ta réservation (dans une semaine)
6. acheter des cadeaux (le jour du départ)
7. prendre des photos (pendant le week-end)
8. voir ce monument (dimanche)

NOTES CULTURELLES

- In a typical restaurant in Quebec, you will be served **la poutine**, a dish consisting of french fries topped with melted white cheese and brown gravy. (Even McDonald's in Montreal serves this typical side dish.)
- Two Canadian baseball teams are the Toronto Blue Jays and the Montreal Expos.

ALLONS PLUS LOIN

Note the different uses of **quitter** and **partir:**

quitter + NOUN	*to leave (a place)*	Nous **quitterons** l'hôtel à 6 heures.
	to take leave of, to leave (a person)	**J'ai quitté** mon cousin à la gare.
partir	*to leave*	Je **partirai** demain matin.
partir de	*to leave from (a place)*	Nous **partirons de** New York.
partir à (en, pour)	*to leave for (a destination)*	Nous **partons en** France.

4 Un voyage à Québec

Vous allez visiter Québec avec un voyage organisé. Demandez à votre guide (votre partenaire) des détails sur ce voyage. Il/elle va vous répondre sur la base du programme.

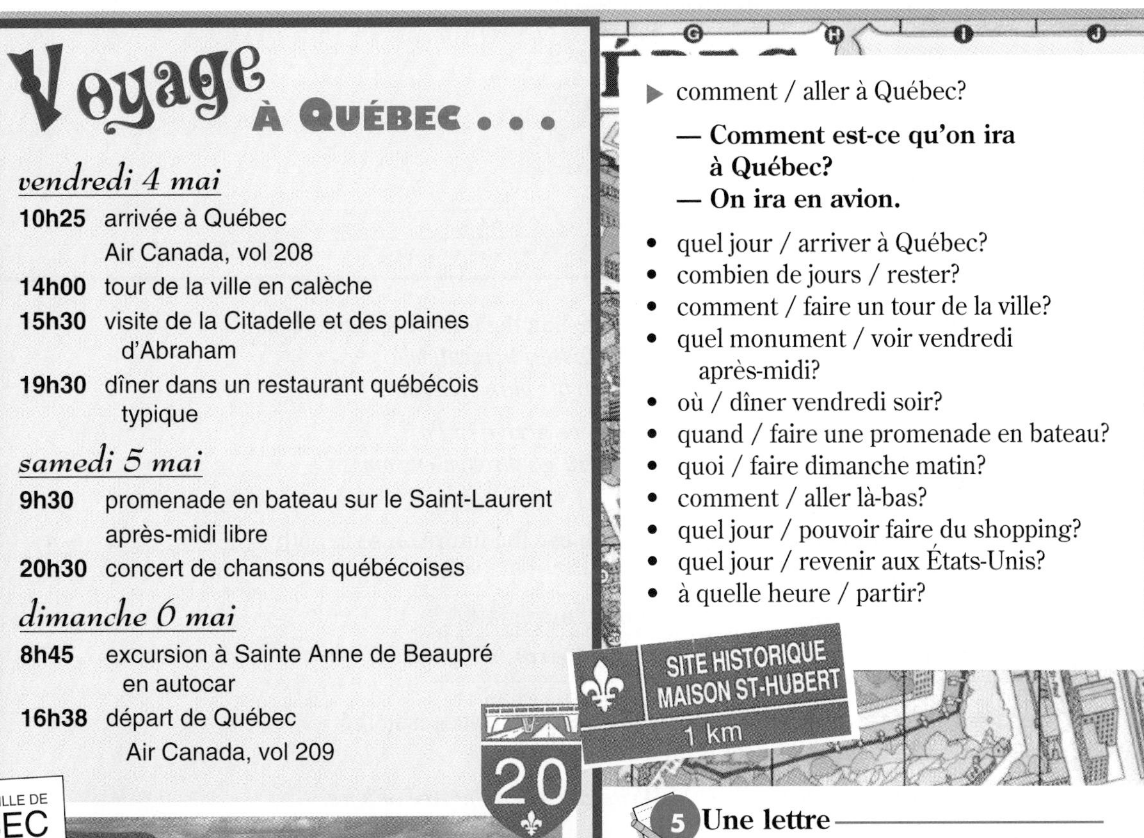

Voyage à Québec . . .

vendredi 4 mai

10h25 arrivée à Québec Air Canada, vol 208
14h00 tour de la ville en calèche
15h30 visite de la Citadelle et des plaines d'Abraham
19h30 dîner dans un restaurant québécois typique

samedi 5 mai

9h30 promenade en bateau sur le Saint-Laurent après-midi libre
20h30 concert de chansons québécoises

dimanche 6 mai

8h45 excursion à Sainte Anne de Beaupré en autocar
16h38 départ de Québec Air Canada, vol 209

▶ comment / aller à Québec?

— **Comment est-ce qu'on ira à Québec?**
— **On ira en avion.**

- quel jour / arriver à Québec?
- combien de jours / rester?
- comment / faire un tour de la ville?
- quel monument / voir vendredi après-midi?
- où / dîner vendredi soir?
- quand / faire une promenade en bateau?
- quoi / faire dimanche matin?
- comment / aller là-bas?
- quel jour / pouvoir faire du shopping?
- quel jour / revenir aux États-Unis?
- à quelle heure / partir?

5 Une lettre

Maintenant écrivez une lettre à votre cousin Patrick. Dans cette lettre, décrivez le voyage que vous allez faire.

> Mon cher Patrick,
> Voici le programme de notre voyage organisé à Québec. Nous partirons le 4 mai. Nous voyagerons en avion...

Langue et communication 203

■ Notes linguistiques

le voyage organisé = package tour
1 km = 0.6214 mile
la calèche = carriage

NOTES CULTURELLES

- The British built **la Citadelle** in 1759 after the battle between the French and the British. Its purpose was to protect Quebec City from further attack. Visitors can see the changing of the guard **(la relève de la garde)** by the Royal 22nd Regiment.
- The Quebec National Battlefields Park **(le Parc des Champs de bataille)** is located on **les plaines d'Abraham**, commemorating the battle of 1759. It is now a favorite spot for strollers, joggers, picnickers, and tourists.
- **Sainte-Anne de Beaupré:** Pilgrims have come to this church since the 17th century to pay their respects to Saint-Anne, the mother of the Virgin Mary.

TEACHING RESOURCES

Student Activities Manual, pp. 58–60

Teaching Strategy: Expansions linguistiques

- You may point out that, depending on emphasis, the **si**-clause may come in first or second position.
  Je passerai chez toi si j'ai le temps.
- The **quand**-clause may come before or after the main clause.

Teaching Strategy: Expansions

Si, used as a conjunction, is different from both **si** used as an adverb of degree, and **si** used to replace **oui** in answering a negative question. Examples:

- CONJUNCTION
  Si je n'ai plus mal aux dents, j'irai au restaurant avec vous.
- ADVERB
  J'ai si mal aux dents que je ne peux rien manger.
- REPLACES OUI
  Tu n'as plus mal aux dents? Si! (phrase word)

B. L'usage du futur dans les phrases avec si

Note the use of the future in the following sentences.

Si le bus **n'arrive pas,** nous **prendrons** le train.	*If the bus **does not come,** we **will take** the train.*
Si je **passe** par l'agence de voyages, j'**achèterai** les billets.	***If I go** by the travel agency, I **will** buy the tickets.*

The above sentences express what WILL HAPPEN *if* a certain condition is met. They consist of two parts:

- the **si** *(if)* clause, which expresses the condition
- the result clause, which tells what WILL HAPPEN

In French, as in English, the pattern of tenses is:

si-clause: PRESENT	result clause: FUTURE
Si j'**ai** de l'argent,	je **voyagerai**.

C. L'usage du futur après quand

Compare the use of tenses in French and English in the following sentences.

J'**attacherai** ma ceinture **quand** l'avion **partira.**	*I **will fasten** my seat belt **when** the plane **leaves.***
Quand nous **arriverons** à Paris, nous **passerons** par la douane.	***When** we **arrive** in Paris, we **will go** through customs.*

When referring to future events, the French use the future tense in both the **quand** *(when)* clause and the main clause. The pattern is:

quand-clause: FUTURE	result clause: FUTURE
Quand j'**aurai** de l'argent,	je **voyagerai**.

➡ The future is also used after **quand** when the main clause is in the IMPERATIVE and a future event is implied.

Écris-moi quand tu **seras** à Nice. ***Write me** when you **are** in Nice.*

Vocabulaire: Quelques conjonctions de temps

lorsque	*when*	**Lorsque** j'aurai mon passeport, je partirai.
dès que	*as soon as*	J'écrirai à Sylvie **dès que** j'aurai son adresse.
aussitôt que	*as soon as*	Nous vous téléphonerons **aussitôt que** nous serons à Nice.

➡ The future is used after these conjunctions, as it is after **quand.**

6 Attention!

Quand on voyage, il faut faire certaines choses sinon on aura un problème. Exprimez cela pour les personnes suivantes.

PERSONNES	CHOSES À FAIRE	PROBLÈMES
vous	arriver à l'heure	rater la correspondance
nous	se dépêcher	rater le train
Béatrice	réserver à l'avance	ne pas trouver de place
les touristes	confirmer la réservation	payer un supplément
M. Duval	composter le billet	avoir une amende *(fine)*
	avoir un passeport	ne pas pouvoir voyager
	présenter la carte d'embarquement	monter dans l'avion
	enregistrer les bagages	devoir les mettre sous le siège

▶ **Si M. Duval ne se dépêche pas, il ratera la correspondance.**

7 Une question de circonstances

Ce que nous faisons dépend des circonstances. Choisissez une question et dites ce que vous ferez suivant les circonstances. Comparez vos réponses avec celles de votre partenaire.

1. Qu'est-ce que tu feras ce week-end . . .
   - s'il pleut?
   - s'il fait beau?
   - si tu restes chez toi?
2. Qu'est-ce que tu feras cet été . . .
   - si tu travailles?
   - si tu as assez d'argent?
   - si tu vas à la mer?

3. Qu'est-ce que tu feras après l'université . . .
   - si tu continues tes études?
   - si tu veux gagner ta vie?
   - si tu ne trouves pas de travail?

4. Qu'est-ce que tu feras plus tard . . .
   - si tu es marié(e)?
   - si tu gagnes beaucoup d'argent?
   - si tu n'aimes pas ton travail?

8 Projets de voyage

Choisissez une personne et dites ce qu'elle fera quand elle sera dans un certain endroit.

nous	aller	(l') Égypte	assister à (une corrida, ??)
vous	être	(la) France	voir (les pyramides, ??)
Pauline	visiter	(le) Canada	aller à (un match de hockey, ??)
mes cousins		(les) États-Unis	visiter (le Grand Canyon, ??)
		(l') Espagne	parler (français, ??)
		(le) Mexique	acheter (du parfum, ??)
		(la) Chine	manger (du poulet frit, ??)

▶ **Quand Pauline sera en Espagne, elle parlera espagnol. Elle mangera . . .**

■ Teaching Strategies

Activité 7

You may wish to suggest the following variations:

1. si tu es malade
2. si tu es en France
3. si tu as ton diplôme
4. si tu habites seul(e)

Activité 8

Autres pays: Israël, le Japon, l'Inde, la Russie, l'Italie, l'Australie.

TEACHING RESOURCES

Student Activities Manual, pp. 60–62

Teaching Strategy

Have students prepare a tourist brochure — with illustrations — inviting French visitors to your city or region. Use the future tense to explain what the tourists will be able to do.

Venez visiter Boston! Vous vous promènerez dans la vieille ville. Vous visiterez Faneuil Hall et King's Chapel. Vous verrez ... *etc.*

9 S'il te plaît!

Votre partenaire vous dit ce qu'il/elle va faire. Demandez-lui de faire les choses suggérées (ou d'autres choses de votre choix).

▶ **— Je vais aller à la poste.**
— Eh bien, quand tu iras à la poste, envoie cette lettre, s'il te plaît.
— D'accord, j'enverrai cette lettre.

1. partir (fermer la porte)
2. faire les courses (acheter du fromage)
3. passer à la bibliothèque (rendre ce livre)
4. aller à la gare (prendre les billets)
5. aller à l'agence de voyages (réserver les places)
6. voir Patrick (l'inviter à la boum)

10 Une visite à Genève

Jean-Philippe, un étudiant belge, va aller à Genève. Il écrit à sa copine Nathalie qui habite dans cette ville. Complétez sa lettre avec le présent ou le futur des verbes indiqués.

Ma chère Nathalie,

Je ___ le vol Swissair 804 qui ___ à Genève le 2 juin à 10h35. (prendre / arriver) Je te ___ dès que je ___ à mon hôtel. (téléphoner / être) Si tu ___ libre, on ___ déjeuner ensemble. Sinon, je ___ un peu, (être / pouvoir / se reposer) et s'il ___ beau, je ___ un tour en ville. (faire / faire)

De toute façon (anyway), on ___ ensemble le soir. (sortir) Si tu ___, on ___ dans un restaurant qu'un copain m'a recommandé. (vouloir / aller) Quand je te ___, je te ___ les photos que j'ai prises l'année dernière. (voir / montrer)

Écris-moi lorsque tu ___ cette lettre. (recevoir)

À bientôt,
Jean-Philippe

11 Bienvenue chez nous!

Votre amie française Frédérique va passer le week-end dans votre ville. Préparez un programme d'activités que vous ferez ensemble et écrivez une lettre à Frédérique où vous expliquez ce programme. Utilisez des verbes comme **aller, voir, visiter, faire, dîner, déjeuner, prendre, se promener, s'arrêter.**

Ma chère Frédérique,
Je suis très content(e) que tu passes le week-end dans ma ville. J'irai te chercher à l'aéroport [à la gare / à la station de bus] vendredi soir. Voici ce que nous ferons lorsque tu seras ici.
Samedi matin, nous ...

D. Le conditionnel

In the sentences below, the verbs in heavy print are in the CONDITIONAL.

Si c'était les vacances, . . .	*If it were summer vacation, . . .*
• je **voyagerais**	• *I **would travel***
• nous **irions** au Sénégal	• *we **would go** to Senegal*
• vous **n'étudieriez pas**	• *you **would not study***

The CONDITIONAL is used to describe what people WOULD DO, what WOULD HAPPEN if a certain condition were to be met.

The CONDITIONAL is a simple tense which is formed as follows:

FUTURE STEM + IMPERFECT ENDINGS

INFINITIVE	parler	finir	vendre	aller	IMPERFECT ENDINGS
FUTURE	je **parler**ai	**finir**ai	**vendr**ai	**ir**ai	
CONDITIONAL	je **parlerais** tu **parlerais** il/elle/on **parlerait** nous **parlerions** vous **parleriez** ils/elles **parleraient**	**finirais** **finirais** **finirait** **finirions** **finiriez** **finiraient**	**vendrais** **vendrais** **vendrait** **vendrions** **vendriez** **vendraient**	**irais** **irais** **irait** **irions** **iriez** **iraient**	**-ais** **-ais** **-ait** **-ions** **-iez** **-aient**
NEGATIVE	**je ne parlerais pas**				
INTERROGATIVE	**est-ce que tu parlerais?** **parlerais-tu?**				

➡ Verbs that have an irregular future stem keep the same stem in the conditional.
avoir **aur-** j'**aur**ais être **ser-** je **ser**ais

12 Vivement les vacances! *(Waiting for summer vacation)*

Les personnes suivantes rêvent des vacances. Dites ce qu'elles feraient et ce qu'elles ne feraient pas. Soyez logique!

▶ Mme Leduc (travailler? se reposer?)
Mme Leduc ne travaillerait pas. Elle se reposerait.

1. nous (préparer l'examen? voyager?)
2. les élèves (aller à la plage? étudier?)
3. vous (rester chez vous? faire du camping?)
4. Marc (être tout le temps à la plage? regarder la télé?)
5. toi (te lever tôt? dormir jusqu'à dix heures?)
6. moi (faire mes devoirs? sortir avec mes copains?)

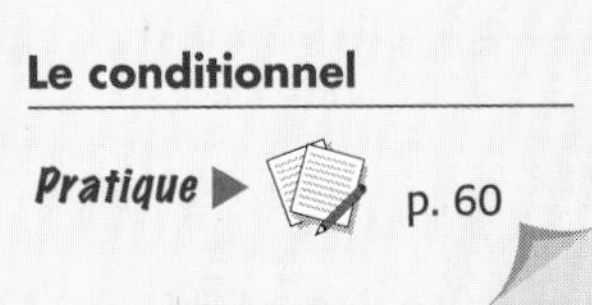

p. 60

Teaching Strategy: Expansion

Ask students:
Que feriez-vous si vous étiez riche? Répondez aux questions affirmativement ou négativement en formant des phrases complètes. **Si j'étais riche,...**

1. acheter des vêtements au marché aux puces? (j'achèterais.../ je n'achèterais pas de...)
2. avoir un ordinateur portable? (j'aurais/je n'aurais pas d'...)
3. être généreux(euse) avec vos amis? (je serais/je ne serais pas...)
4. utiliser une petite voiture? (j'utiliserais/je n'utiliserais pas de...)
5. prendre beaucoup de vacances? (je prendrais/je ne prendrais pas...)
6. sortir tous les soirs? (je sortirais/je ne sortirais pas...)

Teaching Notes

- The conditional is presented here primarily for recognition. The use of the conditional is presented in more detail in Unit 8.
- To review the imperfect tense, see Unité 3, page 116.

LECTURE

Reading STRATEGY

Reading fiction, extended reading

■ Note linguistique

Familles de mots:

l'inspecteur, inspecter, l'inspection *(f.)*
l'espion, espionner, l'espionnage *(m.)*
le voleur, voler, le vol

■ Irregular Verb

(see Appendix C)

disparaître (*see* **connaître**)

LECTURE

Le mystérieux homme en bleu

AVANT DE LIRE

Quand on lit une histoire illustrée, il est important de regarder les illustrations pour comprendre le sens général. Si on peut deviner° plus ou moins ce qui va arriver, il est beaucoup plus facile de comprendre les détails.

Le mystérieux homme en bleu est une histoire policière illustrée. Avec votre partenaire, regardez bien les illustrations pour avoir une idée générale de ce qui se passe. Avant de commencer la lecture de l'histoire à la page suivante, essayez de répondre aux questions suivantes.

1. Qui est le mystérieux homme en bleu?
   - un détective privé
   - un inspecteur de police
   - un espion international
2. Qui est Caroline?
   - une jeune touriste
   - la complice de l'homme en bleu
   - la cousine de l'homme à la mallette jaune
3. Pourquoi est-ce que la chambre de Caroline est en désordre?
   - Des voleurs sont entrés pour voler ses chèques de voyage.
   - La police est venue chercher des documents volés.
   - L'homme à la mallette est venu chercher son passeport.

Maintenant lisez l'histoire et voyez si vous aviez raison.

deviner *to guess*

Mots utiles

LES PERSONNAGES		LES ACTIONS	
un détective privé	*private eye*	récupérer	*to get back, recuperate*
un inspecteur de police	*police detective*	arrêter	*to arrest*
un(e) espion(ne)	*spy*	cacher	*to hide*
un voleur (une voleuse)	*thief*	voler	*to steal*
un(e) complice	*accomplice*	sauver	*to save*
une bande	*gang*	disparaître *	*to disappear, to go away*

QUELQUES OBJETS

une loupe	*magnifying glass*
une mallette	*briefcase*
une plaque d'immatriculation	*license plate*

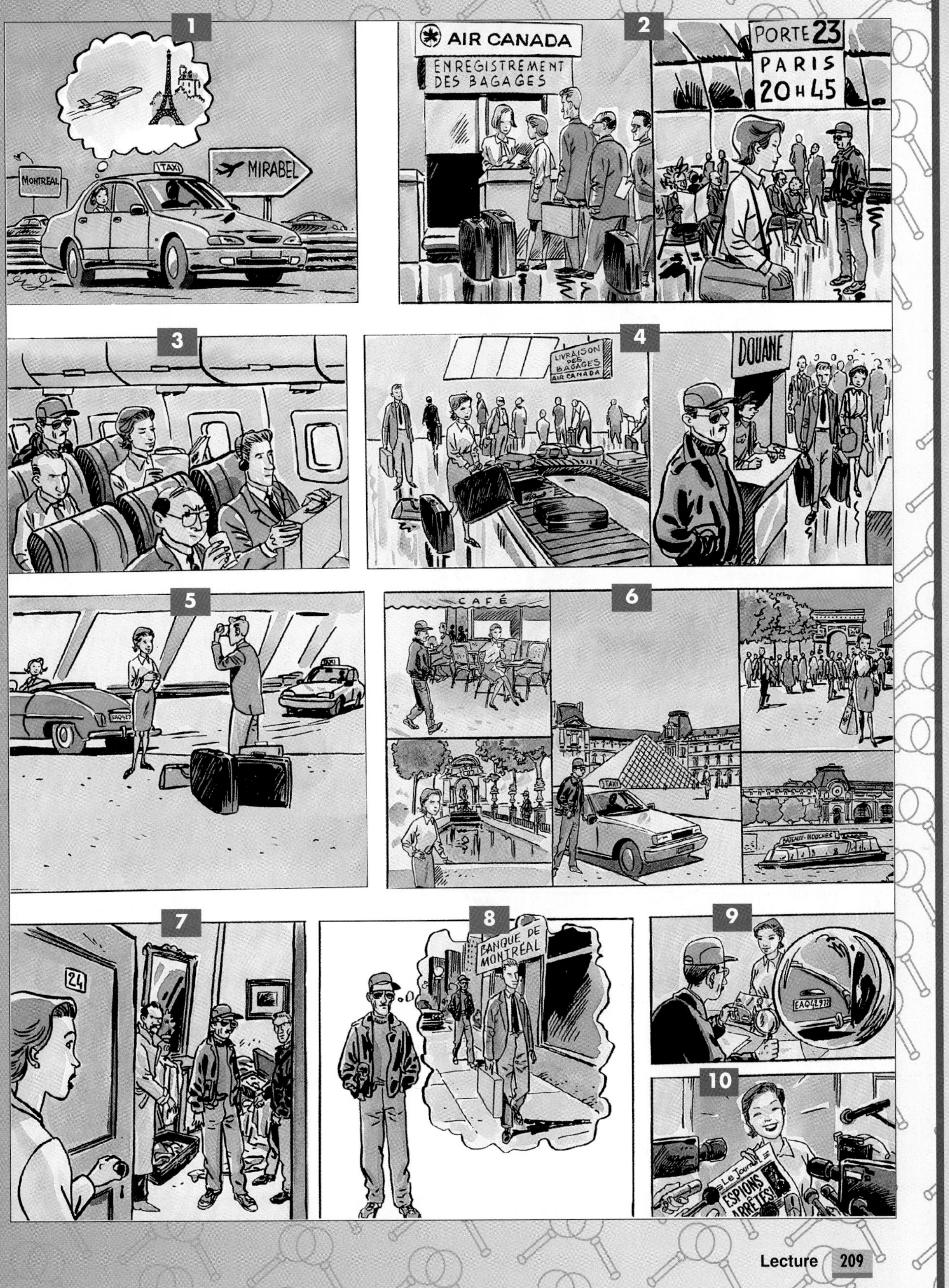

Note culturelle

This story is presented here as a **bande dessinée**, the most popular form of reading material among French teens. Ask students if there are similar formats read by teens in the U.S.

Teaching Strategy: Expansion

Divide the class into groups. Each group is assigned one of the numbered pictures and must then write a description and a corresponding narrative (saying who the character is, what is happening, where the character is going and what he is doing and why). Then gather the material and have groups read their descriptions in the order of the pictures. Ask students:

- Do you have a coherent story?
- Can you develop one from what the group wrote?

Le mystérieux homme en bleu

Première partie

Supplementary vocabulary

Dans l'avion

la cabine *cabin*
le hublot *window*
les écouteurs *(m.) headphones*
le porte-bagages *overhead bin*
le compartiment de rangement *storage bin*

Caroline a fait ses valises. Puis elle a pris son passeport et son billet d'avion et elle a appelé un taxi pour aller à Mirabel, l'aéroport international de Montréal. Dans le taxi, Caroline pense au voyage qu'elle va faire. C'est la première fois qu'elle va en France. Elle passera trois semaines là-bas, avec l'argent qu'elle a économisé pendant l'année. Elle espère faire un excellent voyage. Ce sera peut-être un voyage plein d'aventures extraordinaires. Qui sait?

Caroline est arrivée à l'aéroport une heure avant le départ de l'avion Montréal-Paris. Elle est allée au comptoir d'Air Canada où elle a présenté son billet et son passeport et elle a enregistré ses bagages.

Puis, elle est allée dans la salle d'embarquement. Là, elle a immédiatement remarqué un mystérieux homme vêtu de bleu:° pantalon bleu, pull bleu, blouson bleu, casquette bleue et lunettes de soleil. «Quel homme étrange!» a pensé Caroline.

Bientôt° on a annoncé le départ pour Paris. Caroline et les autres passagers sont montés dans l'avion. L'homme en bleu aussi.

Caroline est allée à sa place. Le mystérieux homme en bleu est venu s'asseoir derrière elle. Pendant le voyage, Caroline a regardé quelques magazines, puis elle a dîné et elle a vu le film. Après le film, elle a dormi un peu. Quand elle s'est réveillée, Caroline a regardé derrière elle. L'homme en bleu n'était plus là... il avait changé de place.

Finalement, après six heures de vol, l'avion est arrivé à Roissy, l'aéroport de Paris.

vêtu de bleu = qui portait des vêtements bleus **bientôt** = dans peu de temps

NOTES CULTURELLES

- **Mirabel** is also the name of a town near the airport. It is located north-west of Montreal. Ask students to locate Montreal on a map. Have any students in the class visited Montreal?
- There are two main airports in Paris: **Roissy-Charles de Gaulle** (north of the city) and **Orly** (south of the city).

Caroline a pris son sac à main et elle est sortie de l'avion. Puis elle est allée chercher ses deux valises. Malheureusement, celles-ci sont très lourdes et Caroline n'est pas très forte. Voyant° l'embarras° de Caroline, un grand jeune homme blond avec une mallette de cuir jaune s'est approché d'elle.

– Est-ce que je peux vous aider avec vos valises?

– Ah oui, s'il vous plaît.

– Tenez, prenez ma mallette et moi, je vais porter vos valises.

Caroline a pris la mallette du jeune homme et le jeune homme a pris les valises de Caroline. Ils sont passés ensemble par la douane, sans problème.

De l'autre côté de° la douane, il y avait l'homme en bleu. Il a regardé longuement Caroline, puis il a disparu. «Ce type° est vraiment bizarre,» a pensé Caroline.

Caroline et son compagnon sont sortis de l'aéroport. Une femme très élégante, dans une petite voiture de sport rouge, attendait le jeune homme. Elle avait l'air un peu irritée de voir Caroline. Le jeune homme a posé les valises de Caroline par terre° et il a appelé un taxi pour elle. Caroline a remercié le jeune homme et elle lui a demandé un petit service.

– J'ai promis à mes amies de leur envoyer des photos de moi à Paris. Voici mon appareil. Est-ce que vous pouvez prendre une ou deux photos?

– Mais, bien sûr! Avec plaisir!

Caroline s'est mise° à côté de la voiture de sport et le jeune homme a pris plusieurs photos.

– Merci beaucoup.

– Bon séjour en France!

Le jeune homme est monté dans la voiture de sport qui est partie très vite. Caroline est montée dans le taxi et elle est allée directement à son hôtel.

voyant = quand il a vu **l'embarras** = la difficulté **de l'autre côte de** = après **ce type** = cette personne
a posé = a mis **par terre** = sur le trottoir (*sidewalk*) **s'est mise** = est allée se placer

Avez-vous compris?

1. À quelle occasion est-ce que Caroline a rencontré l'homme en bleu pour la première fois? Décrivez-le.
2. Qu'est-ce que Caroline a fait dans l'avion Montréal-Paris?
3. À l'arrivée à l'aéroport, que fait le jeune homme blond pour aider Caroline? Qu'est-ce qu'elle fait en échange?
4. Quel service est-ce que Caroline demande au jeune homme à la sortie de l'aéroport?

À votre avis

Pourquoi la femme élégante était-elle irritée de voir Caroline?

- Elle était jalouse de Caroline.
- Elle était très pressée (*in a hurry*) de partir.
- Elle avait une autre raison. Laquelle?

■ **Irregular Verb**

(See Appendix C.)
promettre is conjugated like **mettre**

■ ***Avez-vous compris?***

(Sample answers)

1. Elle l'a vu pour la première fois dans la salle d'embarquement de l'aéroport de Montréal. Il était habillé tout en bleu: pantalon, pull, blouson, casquette, tout était bleu. Il portait des lunettes de soleil.
2. Elle a regardé des magazines, elle a dîné et elle a vu le film.
3. Il porte les valises de Caroline, qui sont très lourdes. En échange, elle porte la mallette du jeune homme.
4. Elle lui demande de prendre des photos d'elle parce qu'elle veut les envoyer à ses amies.

Teaching Strategy: Expansion

Ask students:
Pourquoi Caroline pense-t-elle que l'homme en bleu est mystérieux? Et vous? Auriez-vous remarqué cet homme? Pourquoi?

■ **Illustrations**

Clockwise from bottom left:
- Caroline au jardin du Luxembourg
- Caroline à la terrasse d'un café
- la pyramide dans la cour Napoléon au musée du Louvre
- l'Arc de Triomphe au bout des Champs-Élysées
- le bateau-mouche sur la Seine.

Deuxième partie

À l'hôtel, Caroline a défait ses valises. Elle a changé de vêtements et elle est sortie. Elle est allée d'abord dans un café où elle a commandé un café et des croissants. Quelques minutes après, l'homme en bleu est, lui aussi, entré dans le café.

«Encore lui!° Mais qu'est-ce qu'il fait ici?» a pensé Caroline. Elle a fini son café et ses croissants, et elle est sortie du café en vitesse.°

Caroline est allée au jardin du Luxembourg où elle a fait une promenade. Derrière, il y avait l'homme en bleu. Elle a pris un taxi et elle est allée au musée du Louvre. L'homme en bleu est sorti d'un autre taxi et il est entré au Louvre.

«Zut, zut et zut! Pourquoi est-ce que ce type me suit partout?» Caroline est sortie du musée et elle a pris un bus pour aller aux Champs-Elysées. Elle a regardé derrière elle. Cette fois-ci, l'homme en bleu ne la suivait pas. «Je l'ai finalement perdu… Je suis sauvée!» a-t-elle pensé.

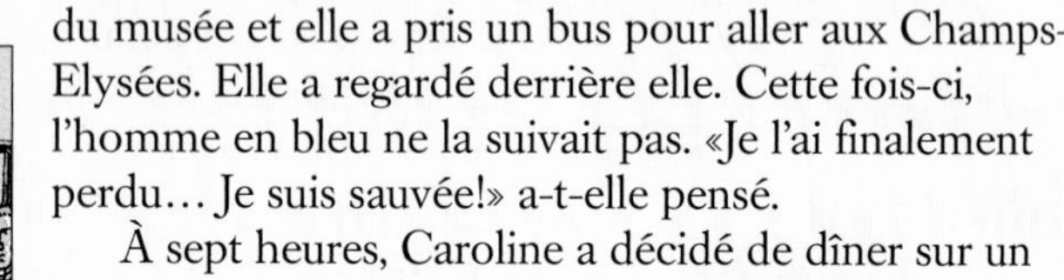

À sept heures, Caroline a décidé de dîner sur un bateau-mouche.* Quelle façon magnifique de passer une première soirée à Paris! Finalement, à onze heures, elle est rentrée à son hôtel. Pas de trace de l'homme en bleu!

Quand Caroline a ouvert la porte de sa chambre, elle a tout de suite° vu que celle-ci° était dans le désordre le plus complet. Et debout,° au milieu de la chambre, était l'homme en bleu accompagné de deux hommes en imperméable beige.

«Qu'est-ce que vous faites dans ma chambre? a crié Caroline. Si vous ne sortez pas immédiatement, j'appellerai la police.»

«Mais, mademoiselle, a répondu l'homme en bleu, nous sommes de la police.» Et il a montré sa carte de police à Caroline.

– Qu'est-ce que vous voulez?

– Nous voulons savoir où est la mallette.

– Quelle mallette?

– La mallette de cuir jaune que votre complice vous a donnée.

– Je ne comprends pas. De quel complice parlez-vous?

– Allons, mademoiselle, ne faites pas l'innocente.°

– Mais je suis innocente!

– Alors, qui est ce jeune homme blond qui est sorti de l'aéroport avec vous ce matin?

– Mais, je ne sais pas! Je ne le connais pas!

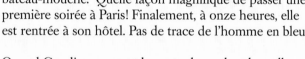

* Les bateaux-mouches sont des bateaux touristiques qui traversent Paris. Le soir, on peut y dîner.

encore lui = toujours la même personne **en vitesse** = rapidement
tout de suite = immédiatement **celle-ci** *the latter* [= sa chambre] **debout** *standing* **ne faites pas l'innocente** *don't act innocent*

NOTES CULTURELLES

- Spacelab, or **le Labo Spatial**, is a European space laboratory which is regularly launched into space and retrieved. Its crew of four performs diverse scientific tests and experiments. Spacelab can remain in orbit for up to 30 days.
- The French space agency is called le **CNES (Centre national d'études spatiales)**. There are three French space centers: Toulouse, Évry, and Kourou in French Guiana. The satellite launch rocket, the **Ariane**, always takes off from Kourou.

L'homme en bleu a compris que Caroline disait la vérité. Alors, il a expliqué:

«Je suis l'inspecteur de police Louis Legrand. Il y a un mois, des documents secrets très importants ont été volés au Ministère des Transports. Ces documents concernent la construction de la station spatiale franco-canadienne. La semaine dernière, un de nos agents a signalé la présence à Montréal du chef de la bande responsable de ce vol. Cette personne, c'est le jeune homme blond avec qui vous étiez ce matin. Samedi dernier, je suis allé à Montréal pour prendre contact avec notre agent. Grâce aux renseignements,° j'ai pu retrouver la trace du jeune homme en question. Je l'ai suivi quand il a pris l'avion Montréal-Paris.

«À Roissy, il vous a donné la mallette dans laquelle sont les documents. J'ai pensé que vous étiez sa complice. En réalité, il a profité de vous pour passer la mallette par la douane sans problème. Je vous ai suivie parce que je pensais que vous aviez toujours° la mallette. J'ai fait erreur et je m'excuse. Évidemment, le problème pour nous, c'est que nous avons perdu la trace de ce dangereux bandit et de la mallette.»

«Je crois que je peux vous aider,» a répondu Caroline.

– Mais comment?

– Attendez demain, et donnez-moi votre adresse.

L'inspecteur Legrand a donné sa carte à Caroline et il a quitté l'hôtel, accompagné de ses deux assistants.

grâce aux renseignements = avec l'information qu'il m'a donnée **toujours** *still*

Avez-vous compris?

1. Où est-ce que Caroline a revu l'homme après être sortie de l'hôtel? Où est-ce qu'elle l'a perdu?
2. Quelle surprise Caroline a-t-elle eue quand elle est rentrée chez elle?
3. Comment est-ce que l'homme en bleu et ses assistants ont justifié leur présence dans la chambre de Caroline?
4. D'après l'homme en bleu, qui est le jeune homme blond? Pourquoi a-t-il pensé que Caroline était sa complice?

Anticipons un peu!

Comment est-ce que Caroline va aider les policiers à retrouver le jeune homme blond?

- Elle a sa photo.
- Elle a son adresse.
- Elle a un autre renseignement. Lequel?

■ **Avez-vous compris?**

(Sample answers)

1. Elle l'a revu dans un café, puis au jardin du Luxembourg et au musée du Louvre. Elle l'a perdu quand elle a pris un bus pour aller aux Champs-Élysées.
2. Quand elle est rentrée à l'hôtel, elle a trouvé l'homme en bleu et deux autres hommes dans sa chambre, qui était dans un grand désordre.
3. Ils ont dit qu'ils étaient de la police.
4. Le jeune homme blond est le chef d'une bande qui a volé des documents très importants. L'homme en bleu a pensé que Caroline était sa complice parce qu'elle portait la mallette.

- In many Parisian cafés, you will find a basket filled with croissants on the table. You may help yourself, but they are not free! The waiter will know how many croissants you have eaten by counting those that are left.

Troisième partie

Le lendemain à deux heures de l'après-midi, Caroline est allée voir l'inspecteur Legrand au quartier général de la police.

– Bonjour, Inspecteur, j'ai une très bonne nouvelle pour vous.

– Ah bon? Quoi?

– Vous allez pouvoir retrouver la trace de vos voleurs de documents.

– Vraiment? Comment?

Caroline a ouvert son sac d'où elle a tiré° les photos prises hier à l'aéroport.

– Regardez bien ces deux photos. Je les ai fait développer ce matin.

– Mais ce sont des photos de vous!

– Oui, bien sûr, mais regardez de plus près la voiture de sport rouge.

– Je vois bien. C'est une Alfa-Roméo.

– C'est aussi la voiture qu'ont prise le jeune homme et sa véritable° complice à l'aéroport. Prenez votre loupe. Vous pourrez lire très nettement son numéro d'immatriculation.

L'inspecteur Legrand a pris sa loupe.

– Vous avez raison, mademoiselle. Je vais alerter immédiatement tous les postes de gendarmerie pour qu'on retrouve cette voiture et ses occupants.

Une semaine après, la police a arrêté le chef de bande et sa complice et les documents secrets ont été récupérés.

L'histoire de Caroline a été publiée en première page de tous les journaux. Caroline a donné plusieurs interviews à la radio et à la télévision. Un studio de cinéma lui a proposé un rôle dans un prochain film et une maison d'édition a pris contact avec elle pour publier le récit° de ses aventures.

a tiré = a sorti **véritable** = réelle **le récit** = l'histoire

Avez-vous compris?

1. Qu'est-ce que Caroline a apporté le lendemain?
2. En quoi est-ce que cela a aidé l'inspecteur?
3. Comment s'est terminée l'histoire pour le jeune homme blond? pour Caroline?

Et vous?

Imaginez que vous êtes Caroline. Qu'est-ce que vous allez faire?

- Accepter l'offre du studio de cinéma?
- Écrire le récit de vos aventures?

Pourquoi avez-vous choisi cette option?

■ Notes linguistiques

- Le numéro d'immatriculation est inscrit sur la plaque d'immatriculation, aussi appelée la plaque minéralogique.
- Un inspecteur de police est un policier en civil *(in civilian clothes)* qui est chargé de mener les enquêtes. Le commissaire de police est chargé des travaux de police administrative. L'agent de police porte un uniforme.

■ *Avez-vous compris?*

(Sample answers)

1. Elle a apporté les photos prises par le jeune homme blond.
2. Sur les photos on voyait la voiture rouge des bandits et on pouvait lire son numéro d'immatriculation.
3. Le jeune homme a été arrêté, et Caroline est devenue célèbre. On lui a proposé un rôle dans un film, et elle va écrire le récit de ses aventures.

APRÈS LA LECTURE

EXPRESSION ORALE

■ Dramatisation

Avec un groupe de camarades, transformez cette histoire en petite pièce de théâtre et jouez-la.

■ Situations

Avec votre partenaire, choisissez l'une des situations suivantes. Composez le dialogue correspondant et jouez-le en classe.

1 Un coup de téléphone

Caroline téléphone à un(e) ami(e) québécois(e) pour lui raconter ses aventures. L'ami(e) interrompt souvent et lui pose beaucoup de questions sur ce qui est arrivé.
(Utilisez la forme **tu**.)

Rôles: Caroline, son ami(e)

2 Une interview

Un(e) journaliste pour Radio-Québec a obtenu une interview avec Caroline et lui pose beaucoup de questions. Il/Elle voudrait savoir ce que Caroline fera si elle accepte la proposition du studio de cinéma ou de la maison d'édition. Caroline est très contente de répondre. (Utilisez la forme vous.)

Rôles: le/la journaliste, Caroline

APRÈS LA LECTURE

EXPRESSION ÉCRITE

L'histoire de «l'homme en bleu» est écrite objectivement, et cependant vous avez pu remarquer que l'auteur décrit les événements du point de vue de Caroline. Utilisez votre imagination pour raconter la même histoire d'un autre point de vue. Voici trois options:

■ Le rapport de l'inspecteur de police

L'inspecteur Louis Legrand, qui vient de recevoir les photos de Caroline, écrit un rapport à son chef. Dans ce rapport, il décrit ce qui est arrivé et aussi comment il arrêtera les voleurs.

■ Journal d'un prisonnier

L'homme à la mallette jaune (vous pouvez lui donner un nom) est maintenant en prison. Dans son journal intime, il décrit les événements qui ont mené à son arrestation.

■ Article de journal

Un(e) journaliste écrit un article où il décrit comment la police a récupéré les documents volés. Il utilise un style très direct.

■ Notes linguistiques

éditer/publier *to publish*
l'édition *publishing*
l'éditeur *publisher*
Note: **le réviseur/ le correcteur** *editor/ proofreader*
le rédacteur *editor (of a magazine)*

INTERLUDE CULTUREL

■ Note linguistique
le moulin à vent = windmill

Note historique
Après sa défaite à Leipzig (Allemagne) en 1814, **Napoléon** est exilé à l'île d'Elbe. Il revient en France en mars 1815 et remonte sur le trône, mais son nouveau règne ne dure que cent jours. Son armée est vaincue à **Waterloo** (Belgique) le 18 juin 1815, et Napoléon est exilé à **Sainte-Hélène** où il passera la fin de sa vie.

■ Irregular Verb
conquérir is conjugated like **acquérir**:
je conquiers
il conquiert
nous conquérons
ils conquièrent

INTERLUDE CULTUREL

■ *Les dates*

- *1715*
- *Règne de Louis XV*
- *1774*
- *Règne de Louis XVI*
- *1789: Prise de la Bastille*
- ***Révolution française***
- *1804*
- ***Premier Empire: Napoléon Ier***
- *1814*
- *1830 Révolution*
- *1852*
- *Second Empire: Napoléon III*
- *1870*

■ *Les événements*

La Révolution française (1789-1799)

La Révolution française est peut-être la période la plus importante de l'histoire de France. Cette révolution a été inspirée par la Révolution américaine. Le 14 juillet 1789, les Français ont pris **la Bastille**, une prison qui était le symbole de l'autorité royale. Le 26 août de la même année, ils ont voté la **Déclaration des Droits de l'Homme et du Citoyen** qui proclamait un principe nouveau: l'égalité et la liberté pour tous les hommes.

Trois ans plus tard, les Français ont aboli la monarchie et ont institué la République. C'est la Révolution qui a donné à la France sa devise:° **«Liberté, Égalité, Fraternité»**.

La Révolution a aussi divisé la France en «départements» et a institué le système métrique.

L'épopée napoléonienne (1799-1815)

Napoléon Bonaparte (1769-1821) était le plus brillant général de la Révolution française. En 1799, à l'âge de 30 ans, il a pris le pouvoir° absolu. Cinq ans plus tard, en 1804, il s'est proclamé empereur des Français sous le nom de **Napoléon Ier**.

À cette époque, la France avait beaucoup d'ennemis: tous les pays d'Europe étaient coalisés° contre elle. Allant de victoire en victoire, «l'Aigle» (c'était le nom que les soldats avaient donné à Napoléon) a battu ses adversaires les uns après les autres. Au passage, Napoléon annexait les pays qu'il venait de conquérir. En dix ans, il a conquis presque toute l'Europe. Mais finalement la chance a tourné et l'armée de Napoléon a été défaite en Russie. Prisonnier des Anglais, Napoléon est mort en exil sur une petite île loin de la France.

Génie militaire, Napoléon a été aussi un grand administrateur. Il a développé l'industrie. Il a encouragé les sciences. Il a ouvert de nombreuses écoles d'ingénieurs. Il a établi une solide administration. Il a institué le **Code Napoléon** qui reste la base du système de justice en France.

devise *motto* **pouvoir** *power* **coalisés** = alliés **chance** *luck*

Teaching Strategies: Expansion

Ask students to prepare a comparative time line showing world events, US events, and overlay the French timeline.

Play recordings of *La Marseillaise* and *Les Misérables* while students scan the *Interlude*.

Les personnes

Marie-Antoinette, Reine de France

Marie-Antoinette (1755-1793) est peut-être la figure la plus tragique de l'histoire de France. C'était une princesse autrichienne,° mais elle avait autant de sang° français que son mari, **Louis XVI**. Elle a épousé° celui-ci à l'âge de 15 ans et est devenue reine° à 19 ans.

Idéaliste et généreuse, elle a pris parti pour la cause des insurgés américains. C'est en partie grâce à° son influence que Louis XVI a envoyé sa marine et ses meilleures troupes aider les Américains pendant la Guerre d'Indépendance.

Romantique, très belle et pleine° de vie, elle aimait les fêtes. Pendant la Révolution, la famille royale a tenté, sans succès, de s'échapper de France. Arrêtée, Marie-Antoinette a été accusée d'avoir aidé les ennemis de la patrie. Elle a été emprisonnée, jugée, condamnée à mort et guillotinée.

Marie-Antoinette (1755-1793)

Napoléon couronné empereur

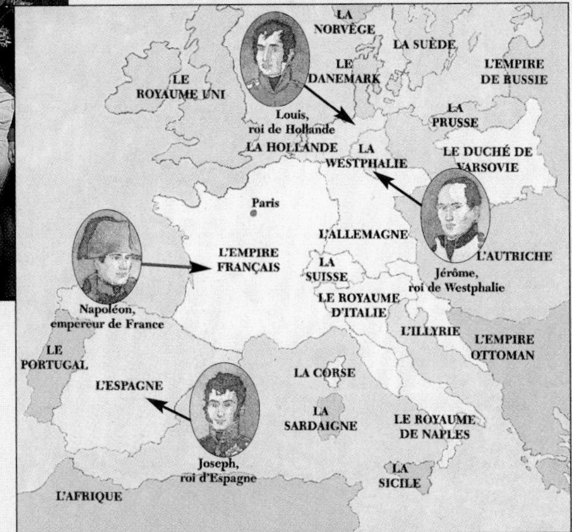

L'Empereur Napoléon et sa famille

Napoléon (1769-1821) est né en Corse,° une petite île au sud de la France. À l'âge de dix ans, il est allé en France faire ses études dans une école militaire. Ses camarades se moquaient de° lui parce qu'il parlait français avec l'accent corse. Napoléon, lui, pensait à sa famille à laquelle il était très attaché.

Vingt-cinq ans plus tard, quand il a été couronné empereur, toute sa famille était présente. Napoléon avait trois frères: **Joseph**, **Louis**, **Jérôme**. Quand il a conquis l'Europe, il a donné à chacun un royaume.° C'est ainsi que Joseph est devenu roi d'Espagne, Louis, roi de Hollande, et Jérôme, roi de Westphalie.

Napoléon avait une famille encore plus grande qui était son armée, la «**Grande Armée**». Il a couvert d'honneurs ses généraux victorieux, et il leur a donné des titres rappelant° leurs victoires ou leurs campagnes. Son meilleur général, **Murat**, était aussi son meilleur ami et le mari de sa soeur, Caroline. Napoléon l'a nommé maréchal, grand amiral, prince d'Empire, grand duc de Berg et finalement roi de Naples.

Napoléon avait un fils, qu'il a nommé Roi de Rome à sa naissance, mais qui n'a pas régné. Son neveu, **Charles Louis Napoléon**, est devenu empereur des Français en 1852, sous le nom de **Napoléon III**.

autrichienne *Austrian* **sang** *blood* **a épousé** *married* **reine** *queen* **grâce à** *thanks to* **pleine** *full*
Corse *Corsica* **se moquaient de** *were laughing at* **royaume** *kingdom* **rappelant** *recalling*

Notes historiques

- **Louis XVI:** fils de Louis XV et d'une princesse polonaise, Louis XVI avait seulement un grand-père français.
- **Marie-Antoinette:** fille de l'impératrice autrichienne Marie-Thérèse et de François, duc de Lorraine, Marie-Antoinette avait une grand-mère et un grand-père français.
- La ville de **Marietta** (Ohio) est nommée en l'honneur de Marie-Antoinette.
- **La guillotine** est une machine servant à exécuter les condamnés à mort. Elle a été inventée pendant la Révolution par un certain docteur Guillotin, qui a été lui-même guillotiné.
- Les autres membres de la famille de Napoléon:
  - **Lucien** Bonaparte, prince de Canino
  - **Elisa** Bonaparte, grande duchesse de Toscane
  - **Pauline** Bonaparte, duchesse de Guastalla
  - **Caroline** Bonaparte, reine de Naples

NOTE: Napoléon III était le fils de Louis Bonaparte.

Photo Note

In his painting called *Le Sacre* (coronation), French artist Louis David recorded the coronation of Napoleon in the Cathedral of Notre-Dame in Paris. Napoleon is shown crowning his wife, Joséphine, after he himself received the crown of emperor.

■ **Additional Information**

Charles Dickens' novel *A Tale of Two Cities* is set during the French Revolution.

▪ L'héritage ▪ de la Révolution

La prise de la Bastille

La **Révolution** est probablement la période la plus importante de l'histoire de France. Elle met fin à° l'**Ancien Régime*** et à ses abus. Elle établit les bases d'un gouvernement démocratique en affirmant l'égalité de tous les citoyens.° Ce fut pendant la Révolution que furent proclamés la République, l'abolition de l'esclavage° et les droits° de l'homme et du citoyen. La Révolution française fut aussi marquée par un énorme effort de centralisation qui unifia la France en donnant un certain nombre d'institutions communes au pays. La plupart de ces institutions subsistent aujourd'hui. Voici quelques institutions françaises qui remontent° à la Révolution.

Documents: Déclaration des Droits de l'Homme

Déclaration des Droits de l'Homme

Article I

«Les hommes naissent et demeurent libres et égaux en droits.»

Article IV

«La liberté consiste à pouvoir faire tout ce qui ne nuit pas à autrui.»

Article IX

«La libre communication des pensées et des opinions est un des droits les plus précieux de l'homme.»

■ La devise de la France: Liberté, égalité, fraternité

Cette devise° rappelle les objectifs politiques et sociaux de la Révolution. Elle fut adoptée en juin 1793. Malgré plusieurs interruptions, la fameuse trilogie est restée la devise officielle de la France. Aujourd'hui elle figure° sur les documents officiels et sur les pièces de monnaie.

* L'Ancien Régime: entre le 15e siècle et 1789, la France était une monarchie et la société française était divisée en trois ordres: le clergé, la noblesse *(nobility)* et le Tiers État *(third estate)*.

met fin à *puts an end to* **citoyen** *citizen* **esclavage** *slavery* **droits** *rights* **remontent** *go back* **devise** *motto* **figure** *is on*

NOTE CULTURELLE

The fortress of the Bastille was built between 1370 and 1382. Originally designed as a citadel to house soldiers and protect the city, it became a jail under Louis XIII (1601–1643). Soon it came to symbolize royal power in its most abusive form. Most prisoners in the Bastille were of noble origins. There were also dissenting writers such as Voltaire. When the Parisians stormed the Bastille, they found only seven prisoners within its walls: four counterfeiters, two insane persons, and one young noble who was in too much debt.

La première fête du 14 juillet en 1790

■ La fête nationale du 14 juillet

La **fête nationale** commémore la prise° de la Bastille par les Parisiens le 14 juillet 1789. Par ce geste symbolique, la population remettait en question° le pouvoir° royal. La Bastille fut démolie et ses pierres servirent à la construction de nombreuses maisons parisiennes. Ce n'est qu'en 1880 que la date du 14 juillet a été adoptée comme fête nationale.

La «Fête nationale» aujourd'hui

■ Le drapeau bleu, blanc, rouge

Avant la Révolution, il n'existait pas de drapeau national mais uniquement des drapeaux militaires dont les couleurs et les motifs variaient de régiment à régiment. (Le seul symbole national était alors la personne du roi.) L'origine du drapeau français remonte à la prise de la Bastille le 14 juillet 1789. Les révolutionnaires qui participèrent à cet événement portaient au chapeau une cocarde bleue et rouge, aux couleurs de la ville de Paris. Quelques jours plus tard, le roi Louis XVI ajouta° cette cocarde° bleue et rouge à la cocarde blanche royale (le blanc était alors le symbole de la monarchie française), créant ainsi la cocarde tricolore.

Ces trois couleurs — bleu, blanc, rouge — firent leur apparition sur les drapeaux et les étendards° des armées révolutionnaires. En 1830, le drapeau tricolore à bandes verticales égales devint de façon définitive l'emblème national.

Marianne

■ Marianne: symbole de la République

Cette femme coiffée du bonnet révolutionnaire est le symbole de la République française. (On attribue le nom «Marianne» à une citoyenne de Colmar, Marie-Anne Reubell.) Cette figure allégorique apparut d'abord sur les pièces de monnaie de la Révolution. Elle réapparut brandissant un drapeau dans le fameux tableau de Delacroix, *La Liberté guidant le peuple.* Depuis 1880, les bustes de Marianne ornent° toutes les mairies de France et son portrait est représenté sur les timbres et les pièces de monnaie.

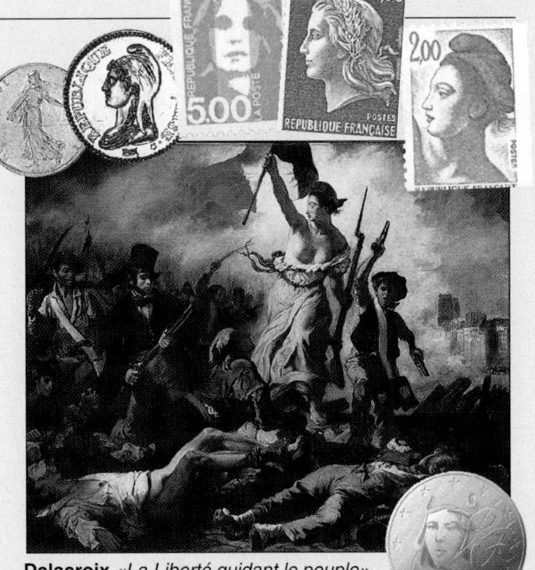

Delacroix «La Liberté guidant le peuple»

prise *taking* **remettait en question** *was questioning* **pouvoir** *power* **ajouta** *added* **cocarde** *cockade* **étendards** *military banners*
ornent = décorent

Note culturelle

Delacroix's painting *La Liberté guidant le peuple* commemorates the July Revolution (**La Révolution de Juillet**) that took place in 1830.

NOTE CULTURELLE

The statues of Marianne are changed regularly, and Marianne takes on a new appearance, generally that of a famous Frenchwoman of the time. Brigitte Bardot, Catherine Deneuve (see 5.00F stamp pictured), and fashion model Inès de la Fressange have been models for Marianne.

■ Additional Information

- Since 1989, the pyramid in front of the Louvre has been the entrance to new underground galleries. It also provides light for the galleries. The pyramid and new galleries were designed by the Chinese-American architect I.M. Pei.

  The Louvre is famous for its extensive collections of Egyptian artifacts, Greek and Roman antiques, as well as the *Mona Lisa* by Da Vinci.
- Martinique, Guyane, Guadeloupe and Réunion are also French **départements**. They are called **les départements d'outre-mer**, or **DOM**. France also governs the following territories: Wallis et Futuna, Nouvelle-Calédonie, Polynésie française, terres australes et antarctiques. They are called **les territoires d'outre-mer (TOM)**. Overseas departments and territories are generally referred to as **les DOM-TOM.**

■ Le musée du Louvre

Situé dans l'ancien palais royal du **Louvre**, le musée du Louvre est une création de la Révolution. Construit au 12ᵉ siècle, le Louvre était à l'origine une forteresse. Embelli et maintes° fois transformé, il a été pendant longtemps la résidence des rois de France. Quand Louis XIV a installé sa cour à Versailles, le Louvre est laissé plus ou moins à l'abandon. En 1793, le gouvernement de la Révolution a décidé d'en faire un grand musée national où le peuple pouvait admirer les collections confisquées aux rois de France.

Sous l'Empire, le Louvre est devenu le Musée Napoléon. Napoléon y apportait les trésors d'art qu'il avait saisis° au cours de ses campagnes à travers° l'Europe. Plus tard, le Louvre s'est enrichi d'antiquités romaines, grecques, égyptiennes et orientales. Aujourd'hui, c'est l'un des plus grands musées du monde.

Le Louvre et la pyramide du Louvre

■ Les départements français

Les **départements** ont remplacé les «généralités» de l'Ancien Régime. Leur création est le résultat d'une réforme proposée peu avant la Révolution et mise en place en 1790. Le découpage° de la France en départements permettait une administration plus facile du pays. (Il était possible à un homme à cheval de parcourir° un département en une journée.) À l'origine, il y avait 83 départements. Aujourd'hui, il y a 96 départements métropolitains.

maintes = beaucoup de **saisis** = pris par force **à travers** *across*
le découpage = la division **parcourir** *to travel across*

■ Le franc et la monnaie française

Avant la Révolution, la monnaie consistait en une multitude de pièces d'or, d'argent et de bronze (écus, louis, sous, deniers, liards**) dont la valeur et le poids° pouvaient varier. La Révolution française uniformisa le système monétaire en adoptant une unité décimale, le **franc**, divisible en décimes et centimes. Le franc est resté la monnaie nationale jusqu'° en 2001.

** **Écus, louis, sous, deniers, liards**: ce sont les noms de ces diverses pièces de monnaie.

■ Le système métrique

Avant la Révolution, on utilisait des unités de distance, de poids et de volume qui variaient de région en région. Ainsi, suivant les provinces, le pied pouvait représenter 10 ou 12 pouces.° Suivant les villes, la livre° pouvait représenter 12, 14 ou 15 onces. . . Le gouvernement révolutionnaire décida de créer un système simple et uniforme. C'est ainsi que fut créé en 1793 le système métrique décimal.

■ L'armée nationale

Avant la Révolution, l'armée était un privilège de la noblesse. Pour être officier, il fallait être noble ou acheter sa charge.° Les soldats étaient des engagés° et des mercenaires étrangers. Les armées de la Révolution incorporèrent les Français de toute condition sociale. À la bataille de Valmy (20 septembre 1792), l'armée française crie pour la première fois: «Vive la Nation!»

La bataille de Valmy, 1792

poids *weight* **jusqu'** *until* **pouces** *inches* **la livre** *pound* **charge** *rank* **engagés** = volontaires

■ Note culturelle

In 2002, the franc was replaced by the euro, which was officially adopted as the currency of France in 1999.

■ Note linguistique

Literally, the word **pouce** means *thumb*. In the old measurement system, **un pied** was the length of a man's foot, and **un pouce** was the length of the last joint of the thumb.

Photo Notes

- **Rivière-Beaudette** and **Saint-Télesphore** are two cities in Quebec, located south of Montreal, by the Ontario border.
- **Montluçon** is a French city located in the central department of **Allier**.

Teaching Note

Rappel:
1 mile = 1.609 kilomètres;
1 pied = 30 centimètres (0.3 mètre);
1 livre = 453 grammes (0.453 kilogramme)

Note historique

The French army regained confidence after its victory against the Prussians at **Valmy**. This battle stopped their advance and prevented the occupation of France by the Prussians.

■ L'histoire de la «Marseillaise»

La **«Marseillaise»** est **l'hymne national** de la France. Elle a été composée pendant la Révolution, mais, malgré° son nom, elle n'est pas d'origine marseillaise. Où donc est née cette célèbre chanson et dans quelles circonstances? Voici son histoire.

Avril 1792. Nous sommes en pleine effervescence révolutionnaire. La France vient de déclarer la guerre à l'Autriche.° Pour protéger la frontière,° une armée, l'armée du Rhin, a été cantonnée° à Strasbourg. Il y a des soldats partout° dans les rues. Le 24 avril, le maire° de Strasbourg offre un grand banquet aux officiers de la garnison. On mange, on boit, on chante, et on crie des slogans: «Vive la patrie!», «À bas° la tyrannie!», «À bas les ennemis de la France!» La ferveur patriotique et révolutionnaire est à son comble.°

Parmi° les officiers, il y a un jeune capitaine. Il s'appelle **Rouget de Lisle**. Militaire, il aime aussi la poésie et il joue du violon. Le maire de Strasbourg s'adresse à lui: «Dites donc, Rouget, vous êtes bien poète et musicien. Alors, pourquoi est-ce que vous ne composez pas quelque chose pour ces braves soldats qui vont défendre la patrie?»°

Rouget de Lisle ne dit rien, mais, rentré chez lui, il prend son violon et joue quelques notes. Puis il prend une plume° et écrit ces mots sur une feuille de papier: **«Allons, enfants de la patrie. . . Le jour de gloire est arrivé. . .»** Toute la nuit, il travaille et retravaille les paroles et la musique d'un puissant° chant de guerre. Au petit matin, il a fini.

À dix heures, il se présente chez le maire. «Monsieur le maire, j'ai votre chanson.» Il se met° au piano et commence: «Allons, enfants de la patrie. . .» Chez le maire, c'est l'enthousiasme général. Rouget joue et rejoue l'air qu'il a intitulé «Chant de guerre pour l'armée du Rhin».

Le lendemain, le texte de cette chanson est imprimé° et distribué. Quelques jours plus tard, la musique de la Garde Nationale joue cet hymne révolutionnaire sur la place d'Armes° de Strasbourg. Dans la foule,° c'est le délire. Tout le monde reprend en choeur «Marchons, marchons. . .»

Bientôt° le «Chant de guerre pour l'armé du Rhin» est dans la bouche de tous les soldats Il passe de garnison en garnison. Partout i enflamme les esprits. En juin 1792, la chanson arriv à Marseille. Là, un régiment de volontaires l'adopt comme son chant de marche. Ces soldats marseillai montent à Paris en chantant la redoutable chanson Le chant de l'armée du Rhin devient le «Chant de Marseillais», puis, plus simplement, la «Marseillaise»

Le 14 juillet 1795, jour anniversaire de la Pris de la Bastille, la Marseillaise devient officiellemen l'hymne national, mais pour quelques année seulement. En 1799, la Révolution est terminée Un peu plus tard, Napoléon devient empereur Général issu de la Révolution, il se méfie maintenant de la révolution en général et des chant révolutionnaires en particulier. Il interdit° de joue la Marseillaise.

La Marseillaise n'est plus l'hymne nationa français, mais elle devient un hymne révolutionnair universel. C'est aux accents° de la Marseillaise qu se font les révolutions du 19e siècle, en Allemagne en Italie, dans le monde entier. . . Finalement la République est rétablie en France et la Marseillaise redevient l'hymne national, mais seulement en 1879.

Depuis 1792, de nouvelles strophes° ont ét ajoutées° au texte de la Marseillaise. Aujourd'hui ce texte est l'objet de controverse. La Marseillais est, en effet, un hymne terriblement guerrier° qu incite à la lutte° sans merci contre les ennemis d la patrie. À l'heure actuelle, la France n'a plu d'ennemis et elle veut la paix dans le monde Pourquoi ne pas transformer la Marseillaise en ur hymne pour la paix en changeant le texte? Beaucoup de Français seraient d'accord, mais beaucoup d'autres préfèrent garder ce texte traditionnel.

---

malgré *in spite of* **Autriche** *Austria* **frontière** *border* **cantonnée** *stationed* **partout** *everywhere* **maire** *mayor* **à bas** *down with* **à son comble** *at its height* **parmi** *among* **patrie** *homeland* **plume** *(quill) pen* **puissant** *powerful* **se met** = s'assied **imprimé** *printed* **place d'Armes** *parade ground* **foule** *crowd* **bientôt** *soon thereafter* **se méfie** *is distrustful* **interdit** *prohibits* **accents** *tune* **strophes** *verses* **ajoutées** *added* **guerrier** *warlike* **lutte** *fight*

■ **Note linguistique**

au petit matin = très tôt le matin
le délire = frenzy, great joy/excitement

Teaching Strategy: Expansion

Ask students:

- À votre avis, est-ce une bonne idée de changer les paroles d'un hymne national?
- Doit-on garder l'hymne national sans y toucher? Pourquoi?
- Connaissez-vous l'hymne de votre pays?
- Souhaiteriez-vous le changer? Pourquoi?

Documents: «La Marseillaise»

MARCHE DES MARSEILLOIS
CHANTÉE SUR DIFERANS THEATRES
Chez Frere Paſsage du Saumon

La Marseillaise

Allons, Enfants de la Patrie,
Le jour de gloire est arrivé!
Contre nous de la tyrannie,
L'étendard sanglant° est levé,
L'étendard sanglant est levé.
Entendez-vous dans les campagnes
Mugir° ces féroces soldats?
Ils viennent jusque dans nos bras
Égorger° nos fils, nos compagnes.
refrain:
Aux armes, Citoyens!
Formez vos bataillons!
Marchons, marchons!
Qu'un sang impur abreuve nos sillons!°

Claude Joseph Rouget de Lisle (1760-1836)

Dans sa vie, le compositeur de la Marseillaise n'a pas eu de chance. Rouget de Lisle était d'origine noble. Quelque temps après avoir composé le célèbre hymne révolutionnaire, il est accusé d'être royaliste et, paradoxalement, d'être un ennemi de la Révolution. Condamné à mort, il échappe in extremis à la guillotine. (C'est la mort du dictateur Robespierre qui le sauve!)

Rouget de Lisle reprend l'uniforme et il est blessé° au combat. Il quitte l'armée et retourne à sa véritable vocation: la poésie et la musique. Il compose des chansons et écrit des pièces de théâtre, mais celles-ci n'ont pas beaucoup de succès. Vers° la fin de la vie, il n'a plus d'argent, mais beaucoup de dettes. Il meurt dans la misère.

blessé *wounded* **vers** *towards* **étendard sanglant** *blood-stained battle flag* **mugir** *roar* **égorger** *to slit the throats of*
qu'un sang impur abreuve nos sillons *may the impure blood [of our enemies] soak the furrows [of our fields].*

Teaching Strategy

Play a recording of the *Marseillaise* for students. Next, play a recording of the *Star-Spangled Banner* and *O Canada.* Ask students to compare and contrast these national anthems, describing similarities, and differences in tone, subject matter, etc.

■ Note linguistique

In extremis is a commonly used adverbial phrase. These latin words literally mean "at the extremity." The expression itself means *at the last minute.*

NOTE CULTURELLE

In 1974, French president Giscard d'Estaing ordered the Marseillaise to be reorchestrated, following the rhythm of an older version. It was reinstated as a military march in 1981.

Before the Revolution, different religious hymns were used as anthems. They were picked according to the circumstances (parades, war...).

■ **Additional Information**

Disney made an animated movie, loosely based on Victor Hugo's novel *Notre-Dame de Paris* called *The Hunchback of Notre-Dame.* Victor Hugo wrote *Les Misérables* in 1862. French artists Alain Boublil and Jean-Michel Schonberg wrote the book and music of the musical **Les Misérables.**

Note culturelle

Victor Hugo est aussi connu pour son roman du Moyen Âge, *Notre-Dame de Paris,* avec Quasimodo, le sonneur de Notre-Dame, et la belle Esmeralda qui se promène à travers Paris avec sa chèvre.

Documents: «Les Misérables»

Chef-d'oeuvre° de la littérature française, *Les Misérables* a été adapté plus de 30 fois au cinéma. Plus récemment, une comédie musicale, tirée du° roman, a connu un succès retentissant° en France, en Angleterre et aux États-Unis.

L'action des *Misérables* se passe en France et se déroule° sur une période d'une vingtaine d'années au début du 19e siècle. Le personnage principal s'appelle **Jean Valjean**. Dans sa jeunesse, il a été arrêté pour avoir volé° un pain, un jour d'hiver. Arrêté pour ce menu° larcin,° il a été condamné au bagne* où il passe dix-neuf ans. Après plusieurs tentatives d'évasion,° il est finalement relâché,° mais il sera poursuivi toute sa vie par un policier implacable nommé **Javert**.

Sans argent, Jean Valjean va demander l'aumône° à la porte d'un évêque.° Celui-ci es un homme bon qui non seulement reçoit Jea Valjean, mais le traite comme un égal, l'invite sa table et lui offre l'hospitalité. La nuit, Jean Valjea quitte la maison de l'évêque en emportant° de plats d'argent. Il est arrêté par la police et recondu chez l'évêque. Au lieu de l'accuser, ce personnag charitable explique aux policiers qu'il a donn les plats d'argent à Jean Valjean et qu'il n'y a pa conséquent aucune raison de l'arrêter.

* **Le bagne:** Lieu où on envoyait les hommes condamnés à des travaux forcés. On appelait ces prisonniers des «bagnards» ou des «forçats».

Victor Hugo, écrivain et homme politique

Victor Hugo (1802-1885), l'auteur des *Misérables*, est l'un des géants de la littérature française. C'est peut-être le plus grand écrivain du 19e siècle. Chef de l'école romantique, il a écrit un grand nombre de poésies, de romans et de pièces de théâtre qui ont fait scandale à l'époque pour leur audacité et leur caractère révolutionnaire.

Victor Hugo a aussi joué un rôle politique important. C'était le fils d'un général de Napoléon. S'il admirait beaucoup cet empereur, il détestait profondément son neveu, Louis-Napoléon, qui avait lui-même pris le pouvoir° par un coup d'État et était devenu empereur sous le nom de Napoléon III. Condamné pour ses idées républicaines, Victor Hugo a été obligé de s'enfuir° en Angleterre où il a passé plusieurs années d'exil.

Victor Hugo est rentré en France après l'abdication de Napoléon, acclamé comme un héros. Devenu sénateur, il a pris le parti des opprimés,° des déshérités, des gens sans protection et sans ressources et il s'est battu° pour la liberté, l'égalité et la justice. C'est cet esprit de compassion pour les petits gens qu'il manifeste dans sa grande oeuvre° *Les Misérables.*

Victor Hugo (1802-1885)

chef-d'oeuvre *masterpiece* **tirée de** = basée sur **retentissant** = très grand **se déroule** *takes place* **volé** *stolen* **menu** = petit **larcin** *theft* **tentatives d'évasion** *escape attempts* **relâché** *released* **l'aumône** = la charité **évêque** *bishop* **emportant** = prenant avec lui **pouvoir** *power* **s'enfuir** *to flee* **opprimés** *oppressed* **s'est battu** *fought* **oeuvre** *work*

NOTE CULTURELLE

When Victor Hugo died, his body lay in state under the Arc de Triomphe in Paris. He was then given a magnificent national funeral before being brought to the Panthéon, where he was laid to rest beside France's greatest figures, such as Voltaire, Rousseau, Bonaparte, and La Fayette.

You may wish to show a picture of the **Panthéon**, or ask students to locate it on a map of Paris.

Cet acte généreux va transformer Jean Valjean. Il prend le nom de **Monsieur Madeleine** et sous ce nom devient un personnage riche et respecté de tous. Élu° maire° de sa ville, il mène° une vie simple et exemplaire. À son tour, il est charitable et généreux avec tout le monde.

Un jour, il apprend qu'un homme vient d'être arrêté pour un vol° que lui, Jean Valjean, a commis autrefois. Pris° de remords, il va se dénoncer à la police. Condamné cette fois à la prison à vie, il arrive à° s'évader,° toujours poursuivi par Javert.

Gavroche, gamin de Paris

Immortalisé par Victor Hugo dans *Les Misérables*, Gavroche est l'éternel «gamin° de Paris». Il a une douzaine d'années. On ne sait où il vit, ni de quoi il vit. Sa vraie famille, c'est le petit peuple du quartier où il passe ses jours et ses nuits. C'est un rebelle, mais il n'est pas révolté. Il siffle,° il chante. . . Il est libre, insouciant,° joyeux. . . Il n'a peur de rien. Quand la révolution éclate, il monte sur les barricades. Frappé° par une balle,° il meurt héroïquement, en chantant une chanson.

Les années ont passé. Jean Valjean habite maintenant à Paris. Il a recueilli° **Cosette**, une petite orpheline dont il a connu la mère autrefois. Cosette est fiancée à **Marius**, un étudiant aux idées révolutionnaires. Un jour la révolution éclate.° Marius prend la tête d'une barricade. Javert est fait prisonnier par les insurgés, mais Jean Valjean intervient en sa faveur et lui sauve la vie.

Marius est blessé lors d'une contre-attaque des forces gouvernementales. Averti° par **Gavroche**, un gamin° de Paris, Jean Valjean arrive. Il prend Marius dans ses bras et le transporte pendant des kilomètres à travers les égouts° de Paris. Javert l'attend. Il reconnaît l'ancien bagnard évadé. Les deux hommes se font face. Javert n'ose° pas arrêter l'homme qui lui a sauvé la vie. Il se suicide. . . Peu après, Marius et Cosette se marient, et Jean Valjean meurt, heureux d'avoir contribué à leur bonheur.

élu *elected* **maire** *mayor* **mène** *leads* **vol** *theft* **pris** *seized de* **arrive à** *manages to* **s'évader** *to escape* **recueilli** = adopté
éclate *breaks out* **averti** *notified* **gamin** *kid* **égouts** *sewers* **ose** *dares* **siffle** *whistles* **insouciant** *carefree*
frappé *hit* **balle** *bullet*

■ Teaching Strategy
Play portions of a recording of *Les Misérables* for students.

Note culturelle
Parts of the sewers of Paris are open to the public. Visitors can even take an underground boat ride!

■ Irregular Verbs
(See Appendix C).
Commettre *(to commit)* is conjugated like **mettre** (See Appendix C).
Intervenir *(to intervene)* is conjugated like **venir**

■ Note historique
This is the revolution of 1830, during which the Parisians deposed King Charles X. (See historical time line on p. 216.)

NOTES CULTURELLES

- Eugène Delacroix (1798–1863) painted *La Liberté guidant le peuple* shortly after the events of July 1830.
- In his depiction of Gavroche, Victor Hugo was probably inspired by the young boy in the Delacroix painting. For a full picture of Delacroix's painting, see p. 219.

MAIN THEME

Places to stay when traveling

Communication Functions/Contexts

- Deciding where to stay
- Reserving a hotel room
- Asking for hotel services

Linguistic Goals

- Comparing people, things, places, situations
- Asking for an alternative
- Pointing out people or things
- Indicating possession

Online Study Center

Online Teaching Center

UNITÉ 6

Séjour en France

Thème et Objectifs

Culture
In this unit, you will discover . . .
- the different places where you can stay while visiting France
- how to use a French guidebook to find a hotel

Communication
You will learn how . . .
- to reserve a hotel room
- to ask for services in a hotel

Langue
You will learn how . . .
- to compare people or things
- to express who or what is the best
- to indicate what belongs to you and what belongs to other people
- to point out specific people or things and ask questions about them

TEACHING RESOURCES

ANCILLARIES
Student Activities Manual
Audio Program, Unit 6
Video-DVD Program, Unit 6
Chansons Audio CD

HM ClassPrep CD
Presentations, Unit 6
Audioscript, Unit 6
Videoscript, Unit 6
Assessment, Unit 6
Answer Key

Les jeunes touristes en France

Chaque année, soixante-quinze millions de touristes étrangers visitent la France. Ces touristes viennent principalement d'Allemagne, d'Angleterre, de Belgique, de Hollande et d'Italie, mais il y a aussi beaucoup de touristes américains, canadiens, japonais .... Pour accueillir° ces millions de touristes, la France dispose° d'un grand nombre d'hôtels de toutes catégories. Il y a des hôtels très simples et des hôtels très luxueux. Le sommet du luxe consiste à passer quelques jours dans un château historique datant du seizième ou du dix-septième siècle. Là, vous serez vraiment traité comme un prince — ou une princesse! Évidemment, tout le monde n'a pas les moyens° financiers de se payer «la vie de château.» Heureusement, pour les jeunes qui préfèrent l'aventure au confort et au luxe, il y a d'autres solutions moins chères et aussi intéressantes. En voici quelques-unes.

Les auberges de jeunesse

Ce sont des hôtels très bon marché réservés aux jeunes touristes qui sont de passage dans une ville. Certaines auberges ont des chambres individuelles, mais généralement on dort dans un dortoir pour 6 à 10 personnes. L'atmosphère des auberges est sympathique et communale: on rencontre d'autres jeunes venus de tous les pays du monde, on fait la cuisine et on mange ensemble. On parle de ses voyages, on raconte des histoires et on rit° beaucoup. Si le confort est élémentaire,° la bonne humeur est toujours présente.

Pour aller dans les auberges de jeunesse, il faut être âgé de 18 ans et posséder une carte de la FUAJ (Fédération Unie des Auberges de Jeunesse) qu'on peut acheter pour 10 euros.

Le camping

Il y a différentes façons de faire du camping. On peut aller dans un terrain de camping aménagé.° En France, il existe des milliers° de terrains de camping équipés d'eau courante, de WC et de douches. Si on préfère la nature ou la solitude, on peut aussi faire du «camping sauvage.» Dans ce cas, on plante sa tente là où on veut: dans une prairie, dans une forêt, près d'une rivière.... Mais attention! Si on est sur une propriété privée, il faut demander et obtenir° l'autorisation du propriétaire.°

Le séjour à la ferme

Si on aime le grand air et si on n'a pas besoin de grand confort, on peut faire un séjour dans une ferme. Pendant les vacances, beaucoup de fermiers louent des «chambres d'hôte»° pour des prix très raisonnables. Le petit déjeuner est généralement compris° dans le prix de la chambre. Si on veut, on peut prendre les autres repas à la ferme aussi. L'ambiance est familiale et les produits de la ferme (souvent des spécialités régionales) sont absolument délicieux!

En été, il y a beaucoup de travail à faire dans les champs. Les fermiers ont souvent besoin de main d'oeuvre.° Ils recrutent parfois des étudiants pour participer à ces travaux. Dans ce cas le logement et la nourriture sont gratuits° et, en plus,° on reçoit° un peu d'argent.

et vous?

DISCUSSION

Avec votre partenaire, discutez le sujet suivant:

- Vous allez faire un voyage en France cet été, mais vous n'avez pas beaucoup d'argent. Quelle solution allez-vous choisir pour votre logement? (faire du camping? aller dans les auberges de jeunesse? prendre une chambre dans une ferme? trouver une autre solution?) Expliquez les avantages et les inconvénients de la solution que vous avez choisie.

accueillir ❊ *to welcome* **dispose** = a **moyens** = les ressources **rire** ❊ *to laugh* **élémentaire** = rudimentaire **aménagé** = équipé **milliers** *thousands* **obtenir** ❊ *to get, obtain* **propriétaire** *owner* **chambres d'hôte** *guest rooms* **compris** = inclus **main d'oeuvre** = travailleurs **gratuits** *free* **en plus** *in addition* **reçoit** = gagner

INFO MAGAZINE

Theme: Student travel in France

Reading Strategy: Scanning, browsing, reading for information

Warm-Up

After having students look at illustrations and compile lists of cognates, ask them to guess the meaning:

- **le tourisme vert** = séjours à la ferme ou dans un petit village, pour redécouvrir la nature et la campagne française
- **le tourisme du souvenir** = visite des champs de bataille et des sites historiques
- **le tourisme industriel** = visite d'usines ou de manufactures locales

Notes culturelles

- The first youth hostel (**auberge de jeunesse**) was created in France in 1929 by Marc Sangnier, an advocate for world peace. Now, there are more than 200 youth hostels in France, and more than 6,000 in 62 countries.
- Some youth hostels organize activity camps, for skiing or handicrafts, etc.
- Since most French people vacation in July or August, reservations must be made as early as January or February for popular tourist spots.

■ Irregular Verbs

(see Appendix C)

accueillir (*see* **cueillir**)
rire (*see* **dire**)
obtenir (*see* **tenir**)
recevoir

Notes culturelles

There are two types of *Michelin* guides:

- the **Guide Rouge** which lists and rates the hotels and restaurants
- the **Guides Verts** which describe the main tourist attractions of a particular area.
- Michelin's logo, the tire man, is called **le bonhomme Michelin**, or **le bibendum Michelin**.

Irregular Verbs

(see Appendix C)
suivre
atteindre (*see* **peindre**)

Language Note

100 km/h = 62 mph

Note linguistique

Le best-seller (pl. **les best-sellers**) is more commonly used in France than its French equivalents **le succès de librairie** or **le livre à gros tirage**.

Le Guide MICHELIN

Quand on voyage, il est utile d'avoir des renseignements° pratiques sur les villes qu'on va visiter. Par exemple: Quelles sont les choses les plus intéressantes à voir? Quel est l'hôtel le plus confortable, ou le moins cher? Où sont les meilleurs restaurants? Pour obtenir ces renseignements, on peut téléphoner au bureau de Tourisme de la ville ou on peut suivre° les recommandations d'un ami, mais le plus simple est d'acheter un guide. Le plus célèbre guide français est *Le Guide Michelin*.

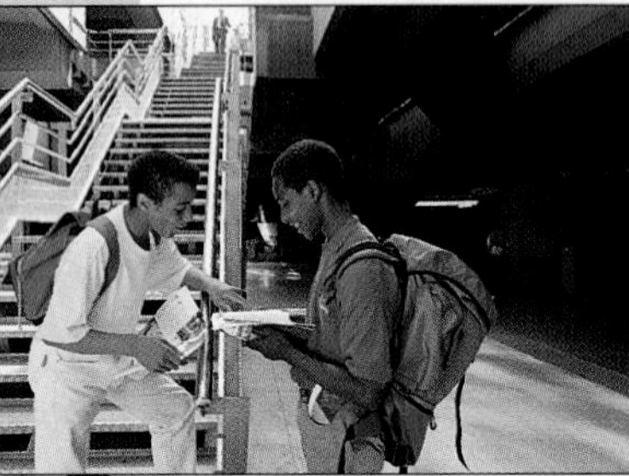

Pour chaque ville, *Le Guide Michelin Rouge* présente une sélection d'hôtels et de restaurants (et, si la ville est assez grande, un plan de la ville). Pour chaque hôtel et chaque restaurant de cette liste, tous les renseignements nécessaires sont donnés: adresse, qualité, prix, etc.... Les touristes peuvent facilement choisir les hôtels et les restaurants qui correspondent à leurs goûts... et à leurs ressources financières.

Le Guide Michelin est publié chaque année. Pour s'assurer de la qualité d'un restaurant ou du confort d'un hôtel, les inspecteurs Michelin visitent régulièrement mais à l'improviste,° ces établissements. Suivant° les résultats de l'enquête, un restaurant ou un hôtel peut monter ou descendre de catégorie. Pour les grands restaurants, la classification dans *Le Guide Michelin* est extrêmement importante. Une étoile signifie le succès, deux étoiles l'honneur, trois étoiles la gloire. Dans toute la France, il y a seulement 22 restaurants «trois étoiles.»

une étoile

deux étoiles

trois étoiles

La société Michelin

Michelin est l'une des plus grandes entreprises françaises. Son activité principale n'est pas la publication de guides touristiques, mais la fabrication des pneus.° Aujourd'hui Michelin est le deuxième producteur de pneus du monde avec 18% de la production mondiale.

Le succès de cette firme remonte° à l'invention en 1891 du pneumatique démontable° avec chambre à air° par deux frères, André et Édouard Michelin. Cette invention a d'abord été appliquée à la bicyclette, puis à la voiture à cheval et finalement à l'automobile. Premier succès: en 1895, une voiture équipée de pneus Michelin a terminé la course Paris-Bordeaux-Paris, faisant ainsi la preuve° qu'on pouvait rouler° sur de l'air. En 1899, grâce au° pneu, une autre automobile, la «Jamais Contente» a atteint° pour la première fois la vitesse° alors inimaginable de 100 kilomètres à l'heure.

Pour encourager la vente des pneus, il fallait encourager le tourisme. Pour cela, les frères Michelin ont eu l'idée géniale de publier des cartes et des guides touristiques (les Cartes et les Guides Michelin). Le Guide Michelin a été créé en 1900. Jusqu'en 1920, il était distribué gratuitement° à tous les automobilistes. Aujourd'hui, c'est le «best seller» français: 1 500 000 exemplaires° du fameux guide rouge sont vendus chaque année dans le monde!

renseignements = informations **suivre** ❊ *to follow* **l'improviste** *unannounced* **suivant** *according to* **pneus** *tires* **remonte** *goes back* **démontable** *which can be removed* **chambre à air** *innertube* **faisant la preuve** = prouvant **rouler** *drive* **grâce à** *thanks to* **atteindre** ❊ *to reach* **vitesse** *speed* **gratuitement** *free of charge* **exemplaires** *copies*

Expansion culturelle

The castle at Amboise was built between 1492 and 1498. Its architecture foreshadows that of the Renaissance, giving for the first time some emphasis on comfort. Its two large towers have spiral staircases with ramps instead of steps so people could climb up on horseback. See p. 147 for a photo and description.

Comment lire le Guide Michelin

Les catégories

 *Grand luxe et tradition*

 *Grand confort*

 *Très confortable*

 *De bon confort*

 *Assez confortable*

Simple mais convenable

L'installation

 *Repas au jardin ou en terrasse*

 *Salle de remise en forme - Tennis*

 *Piscine en plein air / couverte*

Jardin

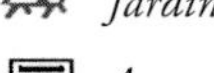 *Ascenseur - Air conditionné*

 *Chambres pour non-fumeurs*

 *Prise Modem dans la chambre*

 *Parking - Parking clos - Garage*

 *Chambres accessibles aux handicapés physiques*

 *Télévision dans la chambre*

Petit déjeuner

Imaginez que vous allez visiter le château d'Amboise, près de Tours. Vous avez réservé une chambre à l'hôtel Belle Vue. Voici la description de cet hôtel:

Un hôtel à Amboise

Amboise est une petite ville très touristique, à cause de son impressionnant château royal. Voici la description d'un hôtel à Amboise, l'hôtel Belle Vue, dans le *Guide Michelin.*

 **Belle Vue** sans rest, 12 quai Ch. Guinot ✆ 02 47 57 02 26, *Fax 02 47 30 51 23* – 🛗 TV. GB.
15 mars-15 nov. – 6 – **32 ch** 46/57.
◆ Hôtel simple en bordure de Loire. Les chambres, assez grandes, sont de bon confort. Sur l'arrière, elles sont plus calmes et offrent une jolie vue sur le château.

1 **la catégorie**
L'hôtel Belle Vue est un hôtel confortable. (C'est un hôtel de bon confort.)

2 **le restaurant**
Cet hôtel n'a pas de restaurant. (Il est sans restaurant.)

3 **l'adresse**
Cet hôtel est situé 12, quai Charles Guinot. Le numéro de téléphone est le 02 47 57 02 26. Le numéro de fax est le 02 47 30 51 23.

4 **l'installation**
Il y a un ascenseur. Les chambres ont la télévision et le téléphone.

5 **le mode de paiement**
On accepte les cartes bancaires: Visa et Mastercard.

6 **la période d'ouverture**
L'hôtel est ouvert du 15 mars au 15 novembre.

7 **le petit déjeuner**
Le petit déjeuner coûte 6 euros.

8 **le nombre et le prix des chambres**
Il y a 32 chambres. Le prix des chambres est de 46 à 57 euros par jour.

1. Selon vous, quels sont les trois éléments les plus importants de l'installation d'un hôtel? Pourquoi?
2. Imaginez que vous allez visiter Amboise (ou une autre ville française.) Avec un(e) camarade, consultez le «Guide Michelin Rouge» sur l'Internet et choisissez un hôtel. Expliquez votre choix.

■ **Additional Information**
Michelin publishes road maps of cities, regions, and countries throughout the world. Its green guides are also published in English.

Teaching Strategy
You may wish to bring in a copy of a **Guide Michelin** if available so that students can see the many different kinds of information listed.

PARTIE 1

LE FRANÇAIS PRATIQUE
À l'hôtel

TEACHING RESOURCES

Student Activities Manual, pp. 139–141

Audio Program, CD 6, Tracks 1–5

HM ClassPrep CD, Audioscript, Unit 6

LE FRANÇAIS PRATIQUE — *À l'hôtel*

Où loger?

On peut	**aller** **loger** **séjourner** **passer la nuit**	dans	**un hôtel de luxe.** **un hôtel bon marché** mais confortable. **une auberge** *(inn)* à la campagne. **une auberge de jeunesse** *(youth hostel).*

loger *to stay*
séjourner *to stay*

À la réception *(reception desk)*

— Bonjour, mademoiselle/monsieur. Vous désirez?
Je voudrais | une chambre.
Je voudrais **réserver** | une chambre.

— **Quel genre** *(type)* de chambre désirez-vous?
J'aimerais une chambre . . .

pour une personne — **pour deux personnes**
à un lit — **à deux lits**

avec
douche
salle de bains
téléphone
télévision
accès internet
WiFi
la climatisation *(air conditioning)*
l'air conditionné
un balcon
une belle vue *(view)*

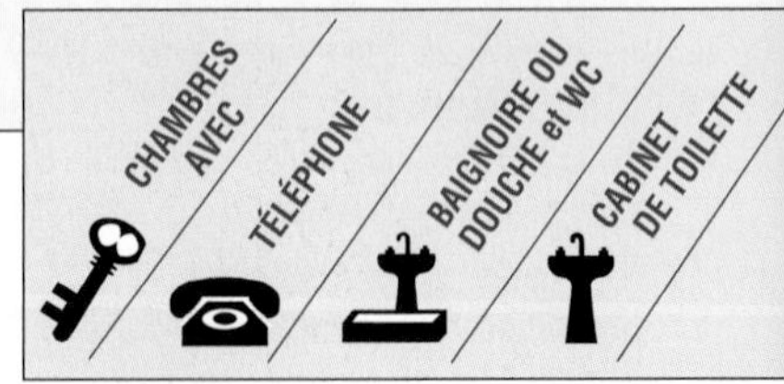

— **Combien de temps** | **comptez**-vous rester?
Jusqu'à *(until)* **quand**

Je compte rester . . .

deux nuits	jusqu'à mardi
une semaine	jusqu'au 12 juillet
	du 2 au 15 juin

compter *to plan, to count on*

— Comment allez-vous payer?
Je vais payer . . .

en espèces *(cash)*	**avec des chèques de voyage**
par chèque	**avec une carte de crédit**

— Vous avez la chambre 315.
Voici votre **clé** *(key)*.

RENSEIGNEMENTS SUPPLÉMENTAIRES

— Est-ce que l'hôtel a . . .
- **une piscine**
- **une salle d'exercices**
- **le service en chambre** *(room service)*
- **un ascenseur**
- **un accès pour personnes handicapées**

— Est-ce que je pourrais avoir une chambre . . .

plus grande	**plus claire**
plus spacieuse	**mieux située**
plus confortable	**moins chère**
plus calme	**moins bruyante**

spacieux *roomy*
clair *sunny*
bien situé *well located*
bruyant *noisy*

— Combien coûte . . .

la chambre	**la pension complète** *(full room and board)*
le petit déjeuner	**la demi-pension** *(room, breakfast and dinner)*

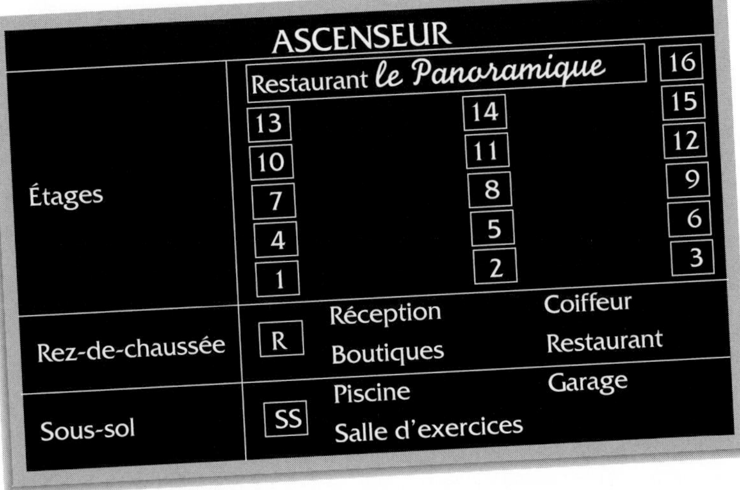

Supplementary vocabulary

payer en liquide *to pay cash*
la suite *suite*
la chambre climatisée *air-conditioned room*
la télévision avec câble *cable T.V.*
le bain à remous *whirlpool bath*
le jacuzzi *jacuzzi*
le forfait *package deal*
un grand lit *double bed*
un lit double
des lits jumeaux *twin beds*
donner sur *to look out on, to have a view over*
une chambre qui donne sur la mer

À NOTER:
l'hôtel particulier *large private house in a city, owned by one family*
l'hôtel de ville *town hall*
l'hôtel-Dieu *city hospital (generally founded in a past century)*

Teaching Strategy: Warm-Up

Divide the class into groups and ask each group to develop a short hotel scenario. Have groups exchange their scenarios. Using the new vocabulary presented on these pages, have students create a dialog appropriate to their scenario. Encourage students to be creative. You may wish to put additional vocabulary on the board or on an overhead transparency for reference. Each group will present to the whole class.

TEACHING RESOURCES

Tête-à-tête activity,
Vacances, p. PA7

■ **Teaching Notes: Activity 1**

The pictograms show the following:
- un climatiseur
- un lavabo
- une bicyclette (un vélo) d'intérieur
- deux flèches
- un téléphone
- une personne handicapée/un fauteuil roulant
- un poste de télévision *(T.V. set)*
- un plongeur/une piscine
- une terrasse/une chaise-longue
- une femme de chambre

The corresponding amenities are *(left to right)*:
- l'air conditionné
- une salle de bains
- une salle d'exercices
- l'ascenseur
- le téléphone dans la chambre
- l'accès pour les personnes handicapées
- la télévision
- la piscine
- une belle vue
- le service en chambre

1 La chose la plus importante

Quand on voyage, il est toujours agréable de séjourner dans des hôtels confortables. Voici certains éléments de confort symbolisés par des illustrations.

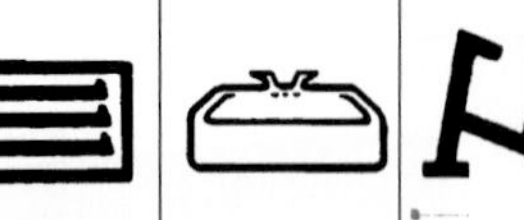

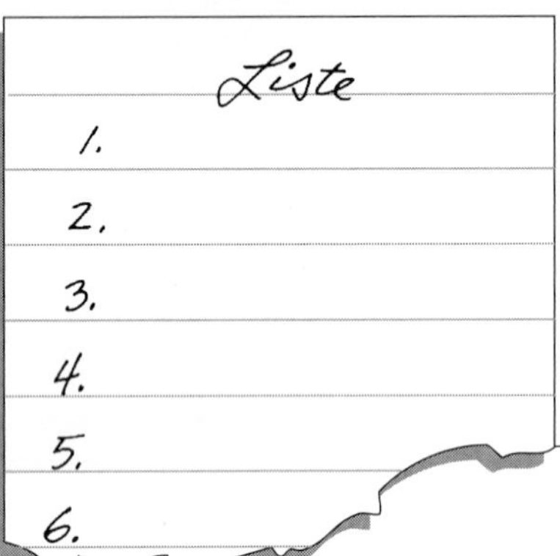

Quels sont les six éléments que vous considérez être les plus importants pour vous?

- Établissez votre liste en écrivant le nom de ces éléments par ordre d'importance.
- Comparez votre liste avec celle de votre partenaire.
- Quels sont les éléments que vous avez en commun avec votre partenaire?

2 Créa-dialogue: À l'hôtel Saint-François

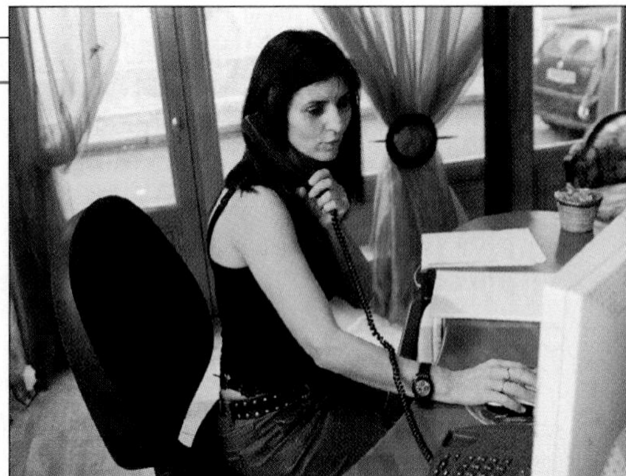

Les touristes suivants veulent réserver une chambre à l'hôtel Saint-François. Choisissez l'un(e) de ces touristes. Avec votre partenaire, composez et jouez le dialogue entre ce/cette touriste (T) et le/la réceptionniste (R) de l'hôtel.

R: Allô, ici Hôtel Saint-François, bonjour!
T: *Say hello and say that you would like to reserve a room.*
R: *Ask what type of room the client would like.*
T: *Describe the room you would like to have, giving as many details as you wish.*
R: *Ask how long the client wants to stay.*
T: *Answer by giving the length of your stay.*
R: Je peux vous réserver une chambre *(give a price between 50 and 200 dollars)*.
T: *Say whether you are going to take the room or not. If not, say thank you and good-bye.*
R: *If the client accepts, ask how he/she is going to pay.*
T: *Indicate your mode of payment.*
R: Parfait! Je vous réserve votre chambre.

TOURISTES
- un(e) étudiant(e) qui n'a pas beaucoup d'argent
- un professeur de français en vacances
- un(e) représentant(e) de commerce *(travelling salesperson)* en voyage d'affaires *(business trip)*
- un(e) journaliste
- un(e) millionnaire avec sa femme/son mari
- un couple de jeunes mariés *(newlyweds)*
- un couple de retraités *(retired couple)*

AMBOISE
Auberge de la ramberge

3 Une lettre de réservation

Vous voulez passer plusieurs jours cet été dans la ville d'Amboise avec votre cousin(e). Écrivez une lettre de réservation à l'Hôtel Belle Vue en consultant le Guide Michelin à la page 229. Suivez le modèle proposé.

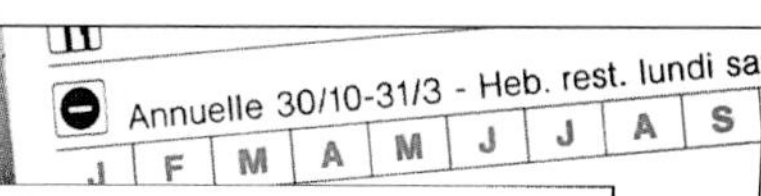

Auberge Saint-Christophe
Caves Médiévales - Dîners aux Chandelles
2, rue de l'Église
95510 Vétheuil
téléphone 01 34 78 11 50 fermé le mercredi

938 Grant Place
Boulder, CO 80302 USA
le 10 avril 200__

Novotel
Route de Chenonceaux
37400 Amboise, France

Monsieur, Madame,

Je voudrais réserver une chambre non-fumeur pour une personne. Je préférerais une chambre avec une vue sur le château. J'arriverai à Amboise le 21 juillet et je partirai le 23.

Dans l'attente de votre confirmation, je vous prie d'agréer, Monsieur, Madame, l'expression de mes sentiments distingués.

Patricia McDougall

Patricia McDougall

Conversations libres

Avec votre partenaire, choisissez l'une des situations suivantes. Composez le dialogue correspondant et jouez-le en classe.

1 Un touriste difficile

Vous êtes réceptionniste dans un hôtel à Québec. Un(e) touriste très difficile veut une chambre. Vous lui montrez plusieurs chambres, mais le/la touriste difficile veut toujours quelque chose de différent. Il/elle n'est jamais satisfait(e).

Rôles: le/la réceptionniste, le/la touriste

2 Une auberge de campagne

Vous voyagez en France avec toute votre famille — 5 personnes au total. Un soir vous arrivez dans une petite auberge de campagne. Vous n'avez pas réservé. L'hôtelier *(innkeeper)* vous informe qu'il y a seulement deux possibilités: une très petite chambre sans confort et un grand appartement très confortable mais très cher. Négociez avec lui.

Rôles: le/la touriste, l'hôtelier

3 Une erreur

Vous avez réservé une chambre bon marché dans un grand hôtel à la Martinique. Quand vous arrivez, on vous donne un magnifique appartement avec plage privée. Vous vous installez. Dix minutes après, la réceptionniste vous téléphone pour vous dire qu'il y a erreur et que vous devez changer de chambre. Négociez avec la réceptionniste pour garder votre appartement.

Rôles: la réceptionniste, le/la touriste

4 Déception

Vous allez passer deux semaines en Normandie avec votre famille. Avant votre départ, votre agence de voyages vous a réservé des chambres dans «une auberge de campagne très pittoresque». En réalité, c'est un vieil hôtel sans confort situé près d'une gare où passent des trains toute la nuit. À votre retour, vous passez chez votre agent de voyages pour vous plaindre *(to complain)*.

Rôles: le/la touriste, l'agent de voyages

5 La note

Vous venez de passer une semaine dans une petite auberge en Touraine. Au moment de payer, vous présentez votre carte de crédit américaine. La propriétaire vous dit que l'hôtel accepte seulement l'argent liquide *(cash)*. Expliquez la situation et négociez une solution.

Rôles: le/la touriste, la propriétaire

Note linguistique

Rappel:
la déception *disappointment*
la fraude/la tromperie *deception*
tromper *to deceive*
décevoir *to disappoint*

Notes culturelles

- You may point out that the French **code postal** (here, 37400) precedes rather than follows the name of the city. The first two digits of the code indicate the **département.**
  - 37 = Indre-et-Loire
  - 37000 = Tours (chef-lieu du département)
  - 37400 = Amboise
- In French, business letters end with a long closing sentence.

LANGUE ET COMMUNICATION

A. Le comparatif

Comparative constructions are used to compare people or things.

Cet hôtel est **aussi moderne que** l'autre. — *This hotel is **as modern as** the other one.*
J'ai **moins d'argent que** vous. — *I have **less money than** you.*

ADJECTIVES AND ADVERBS				
+ **plus** − **moins** = **aussi**	ADJECTIVE (or ADVERB)	**(+ que)**	**plus** moderne **(que)** **moins** moderne **(que)** **aussi** moderne **(que)**	***more*** *modern* ***(than)*** ***less*** *modern* ***(than)*** ***as*** *modern* ***(as)***

➡ STRESS PRONOUNS are used after **que.**

Je suis aussi intelligent **que toi.**

➡ The comparative of the ADJECTIVE **bon/bonne** is **meilleur/meilleure**.
The comparative of the ADVERB **bien** is **mieux.**
Compare:

Je suis **meilleur** en tennis **que** toi. — *I am **better** at tennis **than** you.*
Je joue **mieux**. — *I play **better**.*

NOUNS			
+ **plus de** − **moins de** = **autant de**	NOUN **(+ que)**	**plus d'**argent **(que)** **moins d'**argent **(que)** **autant d'**argent **(que)**	***more*** *money* ***(than)*** ***less*** *money* ***(than)*** ***as much*** *money* ***(as)***

1 Ah, le bon vieux temps!

Monsieur Ladoux a passé toute sa vie dans le même village. Il se souvient du bon temps de sa jeunesse où tout était meilleur qu'aujourd'hui. Jouez le rôle de Monsieur Ladoux. Soyez logique!

▶ air / pur?

1. les rivières / polluées?
2. les produits / artificiels?
3. la nourriture / bonne?
4. les jeunes / sérieux?
5. les gens / préoccupés par l'argent?
6. les relations entre les gens / bonnes?
7. la société / matérialiste?
8. les problèmes de l'existence / compliqués?
9. la vie / simple?

LANGUE ET COMMUNICATION

TEACHING RESOURCES

Student Activities Manual, pp. 63, 141

Audio Program, CD 6, Tracks 6–7

HM ClassPrep CD, Audioscript, Unit 6

■ Notes linguistiques

- **Moindre** is the comparative of **petit.** It is used when **petit** conveys the meaning of inferiority, or something smaller in size or quantity. Examples: **C'est la moindre des choses.** *It's the least I can do.* **Le moindre bruit la réveille.** *The least noise wakes her.*
- In a list of several comparisons, **plus/moins/aussi** must be repeated with each adjective. Example: **Il est plus généreux, plus intelligent, plus gentil et plus patient que son frère aîné.**
- The other forms are regular: **moins bon(ne) que** **aussi bon(ne) que** **moins bien que** **aussi bien que**

Proverbes

- On ne trouve jamais meilleur messager que soi-même.
- Le mieux est l'ennemi du bien.

■ Illustration Note

un break *station wagon*
une enseigne *(store) sign*

Teaching Strategy: Warm-Up

Have the students bring in five pairs of pictures that can be compared to each other. For each picture have them write three comparative sentences using **plus ...que**, **moins ...que** and **aussi ...que**, as well as **meilleur ...que** and/or **mieux ...que** comparing, for example, two famous people.

2 Où loger?

Vos amis et vous, vous voyagez en Touraine. Où allez-vous loger? Dans une auberge de campagne *(country inn)* ou dans un grand hôtel à Tours? Avec votre partenaire (ou votre groupe), faites une liste des avantages que vous désirez et classez-les par ordre d'importance. Faites votre choix sur la base de cette liste.

Auberge de campagne
- C'est moins cher.
- C'est plus calme.
- On s'y repose mieux.
- La nourriture est meilleure.
- On mange plus de produits naturels.
- L'air est plus pur.
- Les chambres sont moins bruyantes.
- Le service est plus personnalisé.
- On dort mieux.
- ??

Grand hôtel en ville
- C'est plus luxueux.
- C'est plus confortable.
- Les chambres sont mieux équipées.
- La piscine est plus grande.
- Le service est mieux organisé.
- On est servi plus rapidement.
- On visite plus facilement la ville.
- Il y a plus de choses à faire.
- Il y a plus de choses intéressantes à faire.
- ??

3 Décisions, décisions

Avec votre partenaire, discutez les choix suivants. Chacun va expliquer son choix et essayer de convaincre l'autre personne. Utilisez les suggestions suivantes ou votre imagination.

▶ Visiter le Canada ou le Mexique?
C'est un pays (intéressant? pittoresque? accueillant *[welcoming]*?. . .)

— Tu vas visiter le Canada ou le Mexique?
— Je vais visiter le Mexique.
— Ah bon? Pourquoi?
— C'est un pays plus accueillant!
— D'accord, mais le Canada est un pays aussi accueillant et plus pittoresque....

1. Visiter San Francisco ou New York? C'est une ville (jolie? grande? intéressante? polluée? . . .)
2. Prendre l'avion ou le train? C'est un transport (cher? rapide? dangereux? polluant? . . .)
3. Étudier le japonais ou l'espagnol? C'est une langue (facile? difficile? utile? . . .)
4. Dîner dans un restaurant italien ou chinois? La nourriture est (bonne? légère? riche en calories? chère? naturelle? . . .)
5. Manger du poulet frit ou de la sole? C'est un plat (bon? naturel? léger? riche en calories? . . .)
6. Apprendre à faire du parapente ou de la voile? C'est un sport (facile? dangereux? . . .)

4 C'est évident!

Comparez les choses ou les personnes suivantes en utilisant l'adjectif entre parenthèses. Faites une autre comparaison en utilisant la phrase qui suit. Soyez logique!

▶ Jacques (+ pauvre) Annie / Il a de l'argent.
Jacques est plus pauvre qu'Annie. Il a moins d'argent.

1. Nathalie (+ sportive) Philippe / Elle fait du sport.
2. Roger (+ économe) Antoine / Il dépense de l'argent.
3. Albert (= brillant) Thérèse / Il a des idées originales.
4. Sandrine (– heureuse) Sophie / Elle a des problèmes.
5. les voitures américaines (= économiques) les voitures japonaises /Elles consomment de l'essence *(gas)*.
6. l'hôtel Méridien (+ grand) l'hôtel Ibis / Il a des chambres.

■ Teaching Strategy: Activity 4

Be sure students do not use articles after **plus/moins/autant de.**

1. Elle fait plus de sport.
2. Il dépense moins d'argent.
3. Il a autant d'idées originales.
4. Elle a plus de problèmes.
5. Elles consomment autant d'essence.
6. Il a plus de chambres.

TEACHING RESOURCES

Student Activities Manual,
pp. 64–65

■ **Note linguistique**

If the adjective normally precedes the noun, the superlative construction may either precede or follow it, depending on the emphasis: **le plus petit hôtel** or **l'hôtel le plus petit.**

With other adjectives, however, the superlative always follows the noun: **la ville la plus intéressante.**

B. Le superlatif

Superlative constructions are used to compare people or things with the rest of a group.

Voici l'hôtel **le plus moderne de** la ville.	*Here is **the most modern** hotel **in** the city.*
Et voilà **le plus petit** hôtel.	*And here is **the smallest** hotel.*

ADJECTIVES		
le/la/les { **plus** / **moins** } + ADJECTIVE (+ **de**)	**le/la/les plus** moderne(s) **(de)**	***the most*** *modern* ***(in)***
	le/la/les moins moderne(s) **(de)**	***the least*** *modern* ***(in)***

➡ After a superlative construction, **de** is used to introduce the reference group.

➡ The superlative of **bon / bonne** is **le meilleur / la meilleure** *(the best).*

Voici **le meilleur** restaurant du quartier.

➡ In a superlative construction, the position of the adjective (before or after the noun) is usually the same as in the regular construction. Note that when the adjective comes AFTER the noun, the article **(le, la, les)** is used twice.

le plus grand musée   **le** musée **le plus** intéressant

➡ A superlative construction may be introduced by a possessive adjective.
Compare: **ma plus belle** veste   **mon** livre **le plus intéressant**

ADVERBS	
le plus / **le moins** } + ADVERB	Qui voyage **le plus souvent?** Qui voyage **le moins vite?**

➡ The superlative of **bien** is **le mieux.**

C'est moi qui joue **le mieux** au volley.

NOUNS	
le plus de / **le moins de** } + NOUN	C'est moi qui ai **le plus d'idées** mais **le moins d'argent.**

5 Compliments

Faites un compliment à votre partenaire. Il/elle va vous faire un compliment aussi.

▶ **— Alice, tu es la fille la plus intelligente de mes amies.**
— Et toi, David, tu es le garçon le plus drôle de mes amis.

• amusant	• intelligent
• sympa	• patient
• gentil	• étonnant *(amazing)*
• drôle	• mignon
• intéressant	• dynamique
• sportif	• ??

Expansion linguistique

When a superlative construction is followed by a relative clause, the verb is usually in the subjunctive if the speaker has used the superlative to express an opinion. Compare:

Paris est **la plus belle ville que je connaisse.**
(This is my opinion, based on cities I am familiar with.)

Paris est **la plus grande ville que j'ai visitée** cet été. *(This is a fact.)*

The superlative may also be used when only two people or things are involved.

Il y a deux hôtels dans le quartier.
There are two hotels in the neighborhood.
Lequel est **le plus moderne?**
*Which one is the **most modern?***

Au Bureau de Tourisme

Vous travaillez au Bureau de Tourisme. Des touristes (vos partenaires) cherchent des hôtels avec l'une des caractéristiques suivantes. Renseignez-les.

▶ **— Je cherche un hôtel.**
— Quelle sorte d'hôtel cherchez-vous?
— Un hôtel calme.
— L'hôtel le plus calme de la ville est l'hôtel Bellevue.

- calme
- grand
- cher
- confortable
- bon marché
- petit

Bureau de Tourisme				
HÔTEL	NOMBRE DE CHAMBRES	CONFORT	CALME	PRIX DES CHAMBRES
Hôtel Ibis	45	✱✱	(1)	60€
Hôtel Napoléon	150	✱✱✱	(2)	120€
Hôtel d'Isly	18	✱	(1)	85€
Hotel Bellevue	30	✱✱✱✱	(3)	125€

Le meilleur choix

Vous voyagez avec votre partenaire. Expliquez-lui pourquoi vous faites certains choix.

▶ aller dans cet hôtel (moderne / la ville)

— Allons dans cet hôtel!
— Pourquoi cet hôtel?
— C'est l'hôtel le plus moderne de la ville.
— Alors, d'accord!

1. visiter ce musée (intéressant / la région)
2. prendre ce train (rapide / la journée)
3. acheter ces souvenirs (bon marché / le magasin)
4. dîner dans ce restaurant (bon / le quartier)
5. choisir ce plat (typique / le menu)

8 Les Oscars

Dites qui, à votre avis, est le/la meilleur(e) dans les catégories suivantes.

- un bon acteur
- une bonne actrice
- un athlète sympathique
- une comédienne amusante
- un bon film de l'année
- une comédie drôle
- une émission *(TV program)* intéressante
- un sport intéressant
- une classe facile
- une bonne équipe de basket

▶ **Quel est le sport le plus intéressant?**
À mon avis, c'est le football.
(C'est le sport le plus spectaculaire.)

Au Syndicat d'Initiative

(At the Chamber of Commerce)

Vous travaillez pour le Syndicat d'Initiative de votre ville. Votre bureau vient de recevoir la lettre suivante d'un(e) touriste français(e). Répondez à sa lettre.

Madame, Monsieur,

Nous pensons visiter votre ville le mois prochain. Pourriez-vous nous indiquer:

un hôtel moderne,
un bon restaurant,
des boutiques intéressantes,
des endroits pittoresques?

En vous remerciant de votre attention, je vous prie de croire, Madame, Monsieur, à l'expression de mes sentiments distingués.

Jacques Delavigne
Jacques Delavigne

OFFICE DE TOURISME
SYNDICAT D'INITIATIVE

Monsieur,

Nous vous remercions de l'intérêt que vous portez à notre ville. Permettez-moi de répondre à vos questions. L'hôtel le plus moderne est . . .

En espérant que les renseignements vous seront utiles, nous vous prions de croire, Monsieur, à l'expression de nos sentiments distingués.

Note culturelle

Rappel: $1 = environ 1€

Expansion: Activity 7

Additional items for Activity 7:

6. acheter ces cartes postales (joli/le magasin)
7. aller voir ce film (bon/la semaine)
8. aller dans ces magasins (grand/le quartier)

Teaching Strategy

Activity 8 may also be conducted as a class poll. Have students make two or three nominations in each category and then vote on the choices. Tally the results on the board or overhead projector. If you have more than one Level Three class, students may be interested in comparing the results between classes.

Teaching Strategy

Divide the class into groups of five. Have each group create five sentences (three comparative and two superlative) about their group. Each student should be mentioned at least once.

Have Group 1 write the five adjectives they used on the board. The other groups will write down the comparisons.

INFO MAGAZINE

Theme: Good and bad hotels

Teaching Strategy

This short anecdote provides an opportunity for students to read for pleasure while practicing new vocabulary. Before reading the text, ask students to look at the illustrations and guess what is happening in each situation.

Note culturelle

Le Finistère is a **département** in the western part of Brittany **(la Bretagne)**. It is known for its rugged coastline.

Language Notes

le grand air *open air*
3 km = 1.86 miles

Notes linguistiques

- **Quant à** is a preposition **(locution prépositionnelle)**, meaning *"as for."*
- **Quant à** comes from the Latin expression *Quantum ad* (**= autant que cela intéresse**). **Quand** comes from the Latin word *quando* (**= quand**).

À l'Hôtel de la Plage

Hôtel de la Plage

Florida et gal
10 Rue Joliot
29138 Lesco
(Finistère)
Tél. 02.98.87

- À l'hôtel, le meilleur accueil est réservé aux heureux voyageurs.
- À l'hôtel, vous profiterez du calme et de la tranquillité absolus.
- Les hôtels de qualité offrent à leurs clients tout le confort de la vie moderne.
- Le grand air de la c… vous permettra de… comme si vou… enfant.
- La nuit person… troubler votre…
- Les hôtels o… complet à c… raisonnables.

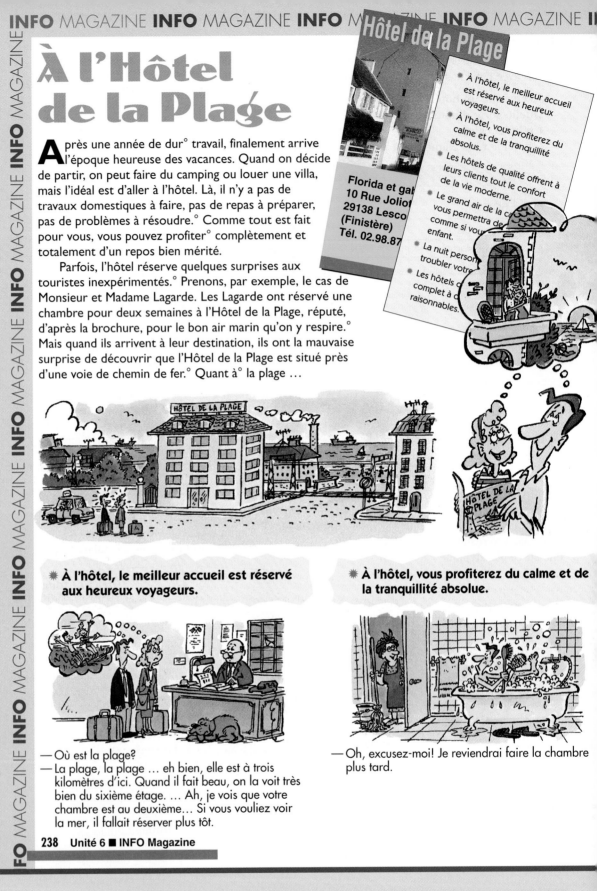

Après une année de dur° travail, finalement arrive l'époque heureuse des vacances. Quand on décide de partir, on peut faire du camping ou louer une villa, mais l'idéal est d'aller à l'hôtel. Là, il n'y a pas de travaux domestiques à faire, pas de repas à préparer, pas de problèmes à résoudre.° Comme tout est fait pour vous, vous pouvez profiter° complètement et totalement d'un repos bien mérité.

Parfois, l'hôtel réserve quelques surprises aux touristes inexpérimentés.° Prenons, par exemple, le cas de Monsieur et Madame Lagarde. Les Lagarde ont réservé une chambre pour deux semaines à l'Hôtel de la Plage, réputé, d'après la brochure, pour le bon air marin qu'on y respire.° Mais quand ils arrivent à leur destination, ils ont la mauvaise surprise de découvrir que l'Hôtel de la Plage est situé près d'une voie de chemin de fer.° Quant à° la plage …

HÔTEL DE LA PLAGE

✸ À l'hôtel, le meilleur accueil est réservé aux heureux voyageurs.

— Où est la plage?
— La plage, la plage … eh bien, elle est à trois kilomètres d'ici. Quand il fait beau, on la voit très bien du sixième étage. … Ah, je vois que votre chambre est au deuxième… Si vous vouliez voir la mer, il fallait réserver plus tôt.

✸ À l'hôtel, vous profiterez du calme et de la tranquillité absolue.

— Oh, excusez-moi! Je reviendrai faire la chambre plus tard.

Les hôtels de qualité offrent à leurs clients tout le confort de la vie moderne.

—Oh là là, chéri!° Quelle chaleur!° Peux-tu vérifier si le climatiseur° fonctionne?
—Oui, il fonctionne, mais c'est de l'air chaud qui sort!

Le grand air de la campagne vous permettra de dormir comme si vous étiez un enfant.

—Je n'arrive pas° à dormir. Qu'est-ce que c'est que ce bruit? Est-ce qu'il y a des souris° ici?
—Mais non, ce sont les voisins d'à côté° qui mangent des chips.

La nuit personne ne viendra troubler votre sommeil.°

—Bonjour, Monsieur Martin. Vous m'avez demandé de vous réveiller à cinq heures et demie. Bonne journée!
—Allô! Quoi! Qu'est-ce que vous dites? Martin? Vous faites erreur! Je suis Monsieur Lagarde!

Les hôtels offrent un service complet à des prix très raisonnables.

—Comment? vingt euros pour le petit déjeuner? Je croyais que tout était compris dans le prix! Et cette taxe locale de 5%! Qu'est-ce que c'est?

et vous?

EXPRESSION ORALE

Vous êtes Monsieur ou Madame Lagarde. Pour chaque épisode, vous téléphonez au directeur de l'hôtel (joué par votre partenaire) pour expliquer le problème. Le directeur essaie de trouver une solution.

EXPRESSION ÉCRITE

- Vous êtes Monsieur ou Madame Lagarde et vous écrivez à un(e) ami(e). Dans votre lettre, vous parlez des problèmes que vous avez eus pendant votre séjour.
- Décrivez un problème (réel ou imaginaire) que vous avez eu pendant un voyage et comment vous avez résolu ce problème.

dur *hard* **résoudre** ❊ *to solve* **profiter** *to enjoy* **inexpérimentés** = sans expérience **respire** *breathes* **chemin de fer** *railroad track* **Quant à** *As for* **accueil** *welcome* **chéri** *darling* **chaleur** *heat* **climatiseur** *air conditioner* **Je n'arrive pas** = je ne peux pas **souris** *mice* **d'à côté** *next door* **sommeil** *sleep*

Note culturelle

The tax in France is called the **T.V.A. (Taxe à Valeur Ajoutée)**. Its rate is generally 18.6%.

■ Irregular Verb

(see Appendix C)
résoudre

LE FRANÇAIS PRATIQUE

Services à l'hôtel

TEACHING RESOURCES

Student Activities Manual, pp. 142–143, 205–208

Audio Program, CD 6, Tracks 8–11

HM ClassPrep CD, Audioscript, Unit 6

Video/DVD Program, Unit 6

Supplementary vocabulary

le directeur de l'hôtel *hotel manager*
le groom *bellboy*
le chasseur *messenger, bellhop*
le portier *doorman*
l'heure d'arrivée/de départ *check-in/out time*
Also: **le caissier/la caissière** *cashier*

Notes linguistiques

- Remind students that **monter** and **descendre**, when used in this sense, are conjugated with **avoir** in the **passé composé.**
  Nous **avons monté/descendu** les bagages.
- Remind students that **servir** is conjugated like **dormir.**

LE FRANÇAIS PRATIQUE

Services à l'hôtel

COMMENT DEMANDER UN SERVICE

Au garçon *(bellboy)*

Pouvez-vous | **monter** / **descendre** | mes bagages?

monter *to bring up, carry up*
descendre *to bring down, carry down*

À la femme de chambre *(chambermaid)*

Pouvez-vous m'apporter
- **une couverture** *(blanket)*?
- **un drap** *(sheet)*?
- **un oreiller** *(pillow)*?
- **une serviette** *(towel)*?
- **un portemanteau** *(hanger)*?
- **un cintre** *(hanger)*?

Pouvez-vous | **mettre** / **augmenter** / **baisser** | **le chauffage** *(heat)*? / **la climatisation**? / **l'air conditionné**?

mettre *to turn on*
augmenter *to turn up, raise*
baisser *to turn down, lower*

Au (à la) réceptionniste

Pouvez-vous | me **servir** le petit déjeuner dans la chambre? / m'**appeler** un taxi?

servir *to serve*
appeler *to call*

Au standard *(operator)*

Pouvez-vous me **réveiller** à six heures et demie?

réveiller *to wake*

Au (à la) gérant(e) *(manager)*

Pouvez-vous préparer ma **note** *(bill)*?

relais-hôtel de Montmirat
MONTMIRAT — 48 - St-Etienne-du-Valdonnez

Doit M
Montmirat, le
Chambre N°

MOIS											TOTAL GÉNÉRAL

Service
TOTAL

Teaching Suggestion: Video/DVD Program

In the Unit 6 *Vidéo-drame: À l'hôtel,* students will concentrate on hotel services and how to ask for what they need. You may want to ask students some comprehension questions based on the vocabulary in this section.

1 Que dire?

Vous voyagez en France et vous êtes à l'hôtel. Qu'est-ce que vous allez demander dans les circonstances suivantes? (Votre partenaire va jouer le rôle du personnel de l'hôtel.)

▶ Vous arrivez à l'hôtel avec deux grosses valises.
— **Est-ce que vous pouvez monter mes bagages, s'il vous plaît?**
— **Oui, mademoiselle (monsieur). Tout de suite.**
— **Merci bien.**

- Vous voulez payer.
- Vous avez un train à 6h30 demain matin.
- Il fait très, très chaud dans votre chambre.
- Vous avez froid.
- Vous voulez rester au lit tard, mais vous voulez prendre votre petit déjeuner.
- Vous avez payé votre note et vous voulez aller à l'aéroport.
- Il va faire froid cette nuit.
- Vous devez quitter l'hôtel mais les bagages dans votre chambre sont très lourds.
- Vous avez beaucoup de vêtements que vous voulez pendre *(to hang up)*.

Teaching Strategy
Bring in as much tourist information on francophone countries as possible from local travel agents, magazines, and newspapers. Ask them to devise an advertisement for a hotel to appeal to different types of travellers (families, students, groups, etc.) The ads may be in any form: music, print, informational statistics, etc. Then ask students to look at the material you brought to class and attempt to categorize the real ads in a similar way.

Teaching Strategy
Ask students:
- Regardez les photos des hôtels à la page 241. Lequel choisiriez-vous si vous alliez en vacances en France? Pourquoi?
- Quels services particuliers offre-t-il?

Realia Note
- **S.V.P.** = s'il vous plaît
- Most kings of France were crowned in **Reims**, a city which is also known for its local wine: **le champagne.**
- **un relais** *post house, inn*

Teaching Strategy: Warm-Up
Have the students think of original questions/comments that they would ask/say to each of the hotel workers listed on p. 240. **(Au standard: Quel est le numéro pour service en chambre?)** Encourage them to use the vocabulary from pp. 230–231. Once they have thought up one question/comment per hotel employee, have them volunteer to read each one so that the class can guess to whom this question/comment would be directed.

LANGUE ET COMMUNICATION

TEACHING RESOURCES

Student Activities Manual, pp. 66, 144

Audio Program, CD 6, Tracks 12–14

HM ClassPrep CD, Audioscript, Unit 6

■ Notes linguistiques

- **Lequel** and its forms can also be used as relative pronouns.
- You may remind students that when a preposition (**à, de, avec,** etc.) is used in a question, it must come at the beginning of the question:
  À qui parles-tu?
  De quoi as-tu besoin?
- You may also wish to remind students that the demonstrative pronouns are a combination of **ce** + the third person stress pronouns:
  ce + lui → **celui**
  ce + elle → **celle**
  ce + eux → **ceux**
  ce + elles → **celles**

A. Le pronom interrogatif **lequel?**

The interrogative pronoun **lequel?** *(which one?)* replaces **quel?** + NOUN.

Quel hôtel préfères-tu? **Lequel** préfères-tu?

Lequel? has the following forms:

	MASCULINE	FEMININE
SINGULAR	**lequel?**	**laquelle?**
PLURAL	**lesquels?**	**lesquelles?**

➡ The pronoun **lequel** consists of two parts, both of which agree with the noun it replaces:

lequel = le + quel

➡ Note how **à** and **de** contract with **lequel** to give the following forms:

à + lequel	→ **auquel**	de + lequel	→ **duquel**
à + lesquels	→ **auxquels**	de + lesquels	→ **desquels**
à + lesquelles	→ **auxquelles**	de + lesquelles	→ **desquelles**

Il y a deux concerts. **Auquel** veux-tu aller? (= **à quel concert**?)
J'ai plusieurs cartes de la région. **Desquelles** as-tu besoin? (= **de quelles cartes**?)

B. Le pronom démonstratif **celui**

The demonstrative pronoun **celui** *(this one, the one)* replaces **ce** or **le** + NOUN.

Celui has the following forms:

	MASCULINE	FEMININE
SINGULAR	**celui**	**celle**
PLURAL	**ceux**	**celles**

Celui is never used alone. It occurs in the following combinations:

- **celui-ci, celui-là** *(this one, that one)*
  — Ta valise, c'est **celle-ci**? *Your suitcase, is it **this one**?*
  — Non, c'est **celle-là**. *No, it's **that one.***

- **celui de** *(that of, the one belonging to)*
  Ce n'est pas mon passeport.
  C'est **celui de Valérie**. *It's **Valérie's.** (= **that of Valérie**)*

  J'ai raté le train de 10 heures.
  Je prendrai **celui de 11 heures.** *I will take **the 11 o'clock.** (= **the one of 11 o'clock**)*

Teaching Strategy

Before class, draw, cut out or bring in two like objects (two hats: one red, one blue). Place the objects at different spots around the room: some next to each other, some under or on top of the desk, etc. Then ask: **Aimez-vous le chapeau?** To answer your question they will have to ask you: **Lequel?** You can then answer: **Celui qui est bleu.** Continue, asking them **Lequel est plus grand?** Students must answer with **Celui qui.../ celui de...** You can also bring in a pen and a pencil and ask the students **Est-ce que vous vous servez des stylos? des crayons?...**

- **celui qui, celui que** *(the one who(m), the one that)*

J'aime les hôtels confortables,
mais je préfère **ceux qui** ont une belle vue. — *I prefer* ***those (the ones) that*** *have a nice view.*

1 Préférences

Vous faites du shopping avec votre partenaire. Vous discutez des choses que vous voyez.

▶ **— Tu aimes cette veste?**
— Non, pas vraiment.
— Alors, laquelle préfères-tu?
— Celle-ci!
— Pourquoi?
— Elle est plus jolie.

1. ces chaussures / plus élégantes
2. ce vélo / plus solide
3. ces livres / plus intéressants
4. cette voiture / plus rapide
5. cet ordinateur / plus moderne
6. ces tee-shirts / plus à la mode

2 Comparaisons

Lisez les descriptions suivantes et comparez ces choses à celles qui sont indiquées entre parenthèses.

▶ Ma maison est grande.
(mon meilleur ami?)

Ma maison est plus (moins / aussi) grande que celle de mon meilleur ami.

1. Notre voiture est grande.
(les voisins?)
2. Ma chambre est spacieuse.
(mes parents?)
3. Mes progrès en français sont rapides.
(les autres étudiants?)
4. La cuisine de ma mère est bonne.
(la cafétéria?)
5. L'air de la campagne est pollué.
(la ville?)
6. Le climat de la Nouvelle-Angleterre est agréable.
(la Floride?)
7. Les monuments de Paris sont beaux.
(New York?)

3 Au choix

Vous voyagez à Paris avec votre partenaire. Vous avez le choix entre deux possibilités. Demandez à votre partenaire de choisir.

▶ deux hôtels (l'un a une grande piscine / l'autre, des chambres confortables)
— Il y a deux hôtels. Auquel veux-tu aller?
— Je préfère aller à celui qui a des chambres confortables. (Je préfère aller à celui qui a une grande piscine.)

1. deux restaurants
(l'un sert des spécialités françaises / l'autre, des spécialités vietnamiennes)
2. deux musées
(l'un a une exposition de photos / l'autre, une exposition d'art moderne)
3. deux piscines
(l'une est au centre-ville / l'autre, dans la banlieue)
4. deux cinémas
(l'un joue une comédie / l'autre, un western)
5. deux boutiques
(l'une vend des jeans / l'autre, des chaussures)

■ **Note linguistique**

Note also the expression **celui où:**
J'aime bien ce restaurant mais je préfère **celui où** nous avons dîné hier.

Teaching Strategy: Expansion

The conversations in Activity 3 could be expanded to a negotiation situation in which the two students come to an agreement.

Duquel vous servez-vous le plus souvent? This will give them further practice using/hearing the contractions with **lequel.** As students use the important expression, write it on the board for visual reinforcement.

TEACHING RESOURCES

Student Activities Manual, pp. 67–68

■ Pronunciation Note
Be sure that students pronounce **nôtre** and **vôtre** with the closed /o/: **nôtre** /notʀ/ and **vôtre** /votʀ/.

C. Le pronom possessif le mien

POSSESSIVE PRONOUNS replace nouns introduced by a possessive adjective. Note the forms of the French possessive adjectives in the following sentences.

Ce n'est pas ta guitare. C'est **la mienne**. *It's **mine**.*
Marc écoute ses CD. Anne écoute **les siens**. *Anne is listening to **hers**.*
Votre chambre est grande. **La nôtre** est confortable. ***Ours** is comfortable.*

	SINGULAR		PLURAL	
	MASCULINE	FEMININE	MASCULINE	FEMININE
mine *yours* *his, hers, its*	**le mien** **le tien** **le sien**	**la mienne** **la tienne** **la sienne**	**les miens** **les tiens** **les siens**	**les miennes** **les tiennes** **les siennes**
ours *yours* *theirs*	**le nôtre** **le vôtre** **le leur**	**la nôtre** **la vôtre** **la leur**	**les nôtres** **les vôtres** **les leurs**	

➡ Possessive pronouns consist of two parts, both of which agree with the noun they replace:

le + POSSESSIVE WORD

➡ Note how **à** and **de** contract with the possessive pronoun:

à + le mien →	**au mien**	de + le mien →	**du mien**
à + les miens →	**aux miens**	de + les miens →	**des miens**
à + les miennes →	**aux miennes**	de + les miennes →	**des miennes**

Pronoms possessifs
Pratique ▶  p. 67

4 Possessions

Insistez sur la propriété des choses suivantes.

▶ Ce sont mes clés.
Ce sont les miennes!

▶ C'est la voiture de mes parents.
C'est la leur!

1. C'est ma serviette.
2. Ce sont tes lunettes de soleil.
3. C'est sa valise.
4. Ce sont ses CD.
5. Ce sont vos bagages.
6. C'est notre sac.
7. C'est l'ordinateur de Paul.
8. C'est le vélo d'Alice.
9. C'est le portable de Jérôme.
10. C'est la maison de tes cousins.
11. Ce sont les valises de Pierre et d'Isabelle.
12. C'est la tondeuse de nos voisins

Expansion linguistique

Possessive pronouns are used less frequently in French than in English.

- The possessive pronoun is not used after **être** when the subject is a noun or a personal pronoun. Instead French uses the construction **être à** + STRESS PRONOUN.
  Ce livre **est à moi**. *That book is **mine**.*

However, possessive pronouns are used after **c'est/ce sont**.
C'est le mien. *It's **mine**.*

- Note the following constructions:
  une de mes amies *a friend of mine*
  des amis à nous *friends of ours*
  un de ses cousins *a cousin of his/hers*
  des cousines à lui *cousins of his*

5 Camping

Vous faites du camping avec votre partenaire. Vous avez oublié certaines choses. Demandez à votre partenaire si vous pouvez prendre les siennes.

▶ mon couteau
— Dis, Daniel, j'ai oublié mon couteau. Est-ce que je peux prendre le tien?
— Le mien? Oui, d'accord!
(Le mien? Ça non, pas question!)

1. ma lampe de poche
2. mon sac de couchage
3. mes jumelles *(f. binoculars)*
4. ma serviette
5. mon savon
6. mon dentifrice
7. ma guitare
8. mes vitamines *(f.)*

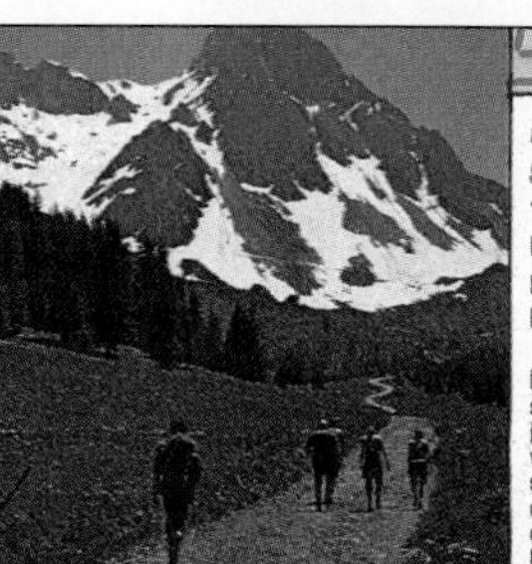

SEJOUR SPORTIF

LA FOUX D'ALLOS (Alpes de Haute-Provence)
SEJOUR SPORTIF EN MONTAGNE
TOUS NIVEAUX : Minimum 11 à 14 ans (maxi)
DUREE : 21 jours formule 1
DATES : 03.7 au 24.7 - 01.8 au 22.8
PRIX : 600€ pension complète

PROGRAMME : Différents sports sont proposés durant ces séjours : planche à voile (5 j.) tennis (10h. de cours et 2h. de jeu libre), équitation (6h.), randonnées à cheval, à pied, découverte de la flore, de la faune, petits torrents et sites grandioses, à proximité du Parc national du Mercantour. En résumé, un stage sportif tout compris pour débutants et confirmés, encadrés par du personnel qualifié, au coeur de la Haute-Provence, là où la nature est encore intacte.

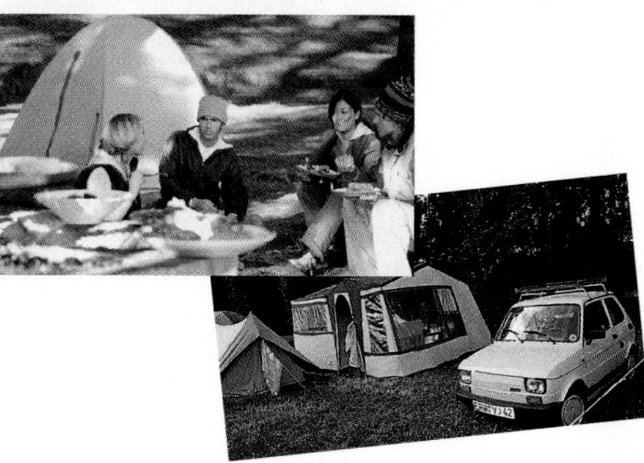

Realia Note

La Foux d'Allos est une station de sports d'hiver près de la ville d'Allos, dans les Alpes de Haute-Provence.

6 À qui est-ce?

Vous faites un voyage au Canada avec votre école. Vous avez trouvé certains objets mais vous ne savez pas à qui ils sont. Votre partenaire va vous aider à identifier le propriétaire.

▶ **— C'est ta serviette?**
— Non!
— Tu es sûr(e)?
— Absolument! La mienne est plus grande.
— Alors, c'est celle de François.
— Oui, c'est probablement la sienne.

1. • ton sac • moins grand • Philippe
2. • ton appareil-photo • plus petit • Isabelle
3. • tes lunettes de soleil • noires • Claire
4. • ta veste • verte • David
5. • ta caméra • moins chère • Éric et Thomas
6. • tes valises • jaunes • Alice et Pauline

7 À l'aéroport

Vous êtes à l'aéroport avec votre partenaire. Il/elle vous dit ce qu'il/elle va faire. Dites-lui que vous allez faire les mêmes choses.

▶ **— Je vais téléphoner à mon copain.**
— Eh bien, moi, je vais téléphoner au mien.

1. Je vais téléphoner à mes cousins.
2. Je vais dire au revoir à ma mère.
3. Je vais prendre une photo de ma soeur.
4. Je vais m'occuper de mon billet.
5. Je vais m'occuper de mes valises.
6. Je vais écrire une carte postale à mon professeur.

- With more advanced students, you may contrast the following constructions:

This is *her* suitcase.	C'est **sa** valise.
It is *hers.*	C'est **la sienne**. (or: **Elle** est **à elle.**)
It is not *Catherine's.*	Ce n'est pas **celle de Catherine**. (or: Elle n'est pas **à Catherine**.)

Reading STRATEGY

Reading fiction

LECTURE

Une étrange aventure

AVANT DE LIRE

Le titre d'une histoire donne parfois aux lecteurs une idée générale du contenu et du ton de l'histoire. Elle leur permet ainsi d'anticiper ce qui va arriver. C'est le cas, par exemple, du titre «Une étrange aventure».

- Vous savez que vous allez lire une **aventure**, c'est-à-dire un récit où l'action joue un rôle important.
- Vous savez aussi qu'au cours du récit quelque chose d'**étrange** va arriver.

En général, les histoires de ce genre commencent de façon très normale, très ordinaire. Puis, un petit problème survient et le mystère commence.

Au début (Partie I)
Déterminez le cadre général de l'histoire.

- Qui sont les protagonistes?
- Qu'est-ce qu'ils vont faire? Où vont-ils?
- Quel problème rencontrent-ils?

Au milieu (Partie II)
À mesure que l'histoire se développe, essayez de déterminer . . .

- les éléments qui vous semblent réels, vrais, ordinaires
- les éléments qui vous semblent étranges, mystérieux, irréels, bizarres

À la fin (Partie III)
Essayez . . .

- d'anticiper ce qui va se passer ensuite
- de trouver une solution au mystère de l'histoire

NOTE CULTURELLE

Les villages en France

Autrefois, la France était un pays rural. La majorité des Français habitaient dans des petits villages de moins de 2 000 habitants. Construits généralement autour d'une église, ces villages étaient reliés° entre eux par des petites routes le long desquelles° se trouvaient des fermes isolées. Les cafés, les boutiques, les petits commerces de toutes sortes, les nombreux ateliers d'artisan° donnaient beaucoup de vie et d'animation aux villages d'autrefois.

Avec l'exode rural et le développement des grandes villes, ces villages ont perdu de leur importance et surtout de leur animation. Aujourd'hui, la vie y est calme et monotone. La nuit, leurs rues sont complètement désertes.

reliés *linked* **le long desquelles** *along which* **ateliers d'artisan** *workshops*

Teaching Strategy

The students will better appreciate the strange ending of this story if they are somewhat familiar with the Nazi occupation of France and the French Resistance in World War II. You may first want to read *Interlude 6,* especially the texts *Les Guerres mondiales* (p. 252) and *Jean Moulin* (p. 253).

Une étrange aventure

I

John et Bob, deux étudiants américains, sont arrivés à Paris à la fin de juin. Là, ils ont acheté un scooter d'occasion avec l'intention de visiter la France pendant l'été. Ils sont partis de Paris le premier juillet dans la matinée.° Ils espèrent être à Clermont-Ferrand dans la soirée. Ils ont un copain là-bas qui les a invités.

Hélas, John et Bob ne savent pas que le premier juillet, c'est le jour des grands départs.* Il y a beaucoup de circulation sur les autoroutes et même sur les routes nationales. Alors, John et Bob décident de prendre des petites routes. Là, il y a moins de circulation, mais le scooter n'avance pas vite.

Il est neuf heures du soir maintenant. La nuit commence à tomber et les deux garçons sont encore loin de leur destination. C'est John qui conduit le scooter. Il demande à Bob: « Tu sais où nous sommes?»

Bob regarde la carte.

— Non, pas exactement. Dis, est-ce que tu as encore de l'essence?

— Euh non! Pas beaucoup.

— Alors, il faut s'arrêter au prochain village. J'espère qu'il y a une station-service.

— . . . Ou un hôtel!

Au prochain village, il y a bien une station-service, mais elle est fermée . . . et il n'y a pas d'hôtel. John demande:

— On continue?

— Oui, on continue . . . on n'a pas le choix.

Il fait maintenant nuit noire.° Pas une voiture sur la route. John aperçoit une toute petite lumière au loin.

— Regarde la lumière là-bas!

— C'est probablement une ferme. Nous avons de la chance!

Les deux garçons arrivent à la ferme. Ils frappent à la porte. Toc, toc, toc . . . Une voix d'homme répond:

— Qui êtes-vous? Et qu'est-ce que vous voulez?

— Nous sommes Américains. Nous sommes perdus.

— Américains? Attendez! Je vous ouvre.

* **Le jour des grands départs:** Le jour où des millions de Français partent en vacances.

la matinée = le matin **il fait . . . nuit noire** *it is pitch black*

Mots utiles

une autoroute	*superhighway*
la circulation	*traffic*
l'essence	*gas*
une ferme	*farm*
une lumière	*light*
apercevoir *	*to notice*
conduire *	*to drive*
au loin	*in the distance*
d'occasion	*second-hand, used*

Avez-vous compris?

1. Qui sont John et Bob?
2. Comment vont-ils voyager en France?
3. Pourquoi est-ce qu'ils décident de prendre des petites routes?
4. Qu'est-ce qu'ils doivent trouver avant la nuit?
5. Qu'est-ce qu'ils font quand ils ne trouvent pas d'hôtel?

■ Notes linguistiques

- **Un artisan** is a craftsman who generally owns his shop, such as a locksmith **(le serrurier)** or a cobbler **(le cordonnier)**.
- **L'exode rural** is the expression used to describe the massive migration of people from the countryside to the big cities, mostly to find work, thus emptying villages and swelling urban areas.

■ *Avez-vous compris?*

(Sample answers)

1. John et Bob sont des étudiants américains en vacances en France.
2. Ils vont voyager en scooter.
3. Ils décident de prendre les petites routes parce qu'il y a trop de circulation sur les autoroutes et les routes nationales.
4. Avant la nuit, ils doivent trouver de l'essence ou un hôtel.
5. Ils continuent leur route et ils arrivent à une ferme.

■ Irregular Verbs

(see Appendix C)
apercevoir (*see* **recevoir**)
conduire

NOTES CULTURELLES

- **Clermont-Ferrand** is a city in **Auvergne**, a central region of France. It is located 388 km (241 miles) south of Paris.
- The speed limit on a French highway varies between 110 and 130 km/h (68-80 mph). On a **route nationale** the speed is limited to 90 km/h (55 mph), and to 50 km/h (30 mph) when crossing a village.

II

La porte de la ferme s'ouvre.

— Entrez vite . . . La nuit, cette route est très dangereuse, surtout pour vous!

John et Bob entrent dans la ferme. À l'intérieur, il y a un homme et une femme, le fermier et la fermière. Ils sont habillés en noir, comme les paysans d'autrefois. C'est la femme qui parle:

— Vous avez certainement faim. Hélas, nous n'avons pas grand-chose.° Je vais vous préparer des pommes de terre avec du lard.° Mon mari va vous chercher une bouteille de cidre à la cave.

John et Bob examinent la salle où ils sont. Les meubles sont rustiques et très anciens. Dans la cheminée, il y a un feu et sur la table il y a des chandelles.

L'homme revient avec la bouteille de cidre. La femme apporte le plat de pommes de terre. John et Bob mangent avec grand appétit.

— Merci, c'est délicieux!

L'homme parle: «Pourquoi merci? Nous sommes tellement heureux de vous recevoir! Mais vous êtes probablement très fatigués . . . Je vais vous montrer votre chambre.»

L'homme prend une chandelle et accompagne les deux garçons jusqu'à leur chambre.

— Excusez-nous, mais nous n'avons plus d'électricité. Je vous laisse la chandelle . . . Bonne nuit!

Puis l'homme descend les escaliers.

Bob dit à John:

— C'est rustique ici!

— Oui, c'est vraiment la campagne. Nous avons de la chance d'avoir trouvé cette ferme.

— Ces gens sont pauvres, mais ils sont vraiment généreux!

Quand Bob et John se réveillent le lendemain, il fait grand jour.°

— Quel jour sommes-nous?

— Nous sommes le deux juillet!

— Au fait, tu as entendu les voitures qui se sont arrêtées devant la ferme pendant la nuit?

— Oh là là, oui! Quel bruit!

— Qu'est-ce que disaient les passagers?

— Je ne sais pas. Ils ne parlaient pas français. Je n'ai pas compris. Mais vraiment ils avaient l'air furieux!

— Je me demande bien qui c'était.

— Dis, il faut partir maintenant.

— C'est vrai! Il est dix heures déjà!

Bob et John descendent dans la salle où ils étaient hier. Mais il n'y a personne.

— Où sont nos hôtes?

— Je ne sais pas. Appelons-les.

— Monsieur? Madame?

Silence. Ils crient plus fort: «Monsieur! Madame!» Personne ne répond.

— Ils sont peut-être partis travailler dans les champs.

Bob et John sortent de la ferme, mais il n'y a personne dans les champs.

— Qu'est-ce qu'on fait?

— Il faut partir. On va laisser un mot sur la table et quand on reviendra à la fin de juillet, on s'arrêtera pour remercier ces gens de leur hospitalité.

— Bonne idée!

grand-chose = beaucoup
du lard salt pork
il fait grand jour the sun is up and shining

Mots utiles

un bruit	*noise*
les champs	*fields*
un paysan	*peasant, far*
apporter	*to bring*
remercier	= dire merci
le lendemain	= le jour suiv
fort	*loudly*

Avez-vous compris?

1. Qui sont les habitants de la ferme? Décrivez-les.
2. Quelle est l'atmosphère générale de la ferme? Décrivez-la.
3. Quelle est l'attitude du fermier et de la fermière envers *(toward)* les jeunes Américains?
4. En quoi consiste le repas?
5. Que font John et Bob après le dîner?
6. Qu'est-ce qu'ils entendent pendant la nuit?
7. Quelle surprise les attend le lendemain?

■ Note linguistique

le lard *bacon*
le bacon *Canadian bacon*
le saindoux/la graisse de porc *lard*

■ *Avez-vous compris?*

(Sample answers)

1. Les habitants de la ferme sont un homme et une femme. Ils sont habillés en noir.
2. L'atmosphère est ancienne: les meubles sont rustiques, et il y a un feu dans la cheminée. Il n'y a pas d'électricité, on utilise des chandelles.
3. Ils sont très gentils envers les jeunes Américains.
4. Le repas consiste en des pommes de terre et du cidre.
5. Après le dîner, John et Bob vont dormir dans une chambre.
6. Ils entendent des voitures, et aussi des gens furieux qui ne parlent pas français.
7. Le lendemain ils ne trouvent personne dans la ferme ou dans les champs.

Expansion linguistique

- **Le cidre** is a drink made with fermented apple juice. It is produced mainly in Normandy **(la Normandie)**, where there are many apple orchards.

III

Bob et John sont partis vers onze heures. Ils ont trouvé une station d'essence au prochain village et ils ont continué leur route . . .

Pendant quatre semaines ils ont parcouru la France en scooter. C'est maintenant la fin des vacances et le retour vers Paris. Bob et John pensent à leur aventure du premier juillet . . . Ils ont acheté des cadeaux pour leurs hôtes: une bouteille de cognac pour le fermier et un joli vase de cristal pour sa femme.

John regarde la carte. Dans dix minutes, ils seront à la ferme. Ils pourront finalement remercier leurs hôtes de leur hospitalité . . .

— Je reconnais bien la route maintenant.

— Moi, aussi.

— Regarde les grands arbres là-bas. La ferme est juste en face.

Le scooter s'est arrêté devant les grands arbres, mais il n'y a pas de ferme.

— Tu es sûr que c'est ici?

— Absolument certain!

À la place de la ferme, il y a une haie d'arbustes et devant cette haie, une stèle avec une inscription.

— Dis, Bob, va voir ce qui est écrit.

Bob descend du scooter et va regarder l'inscription. Il revient vite, très, très pâle.

— Mon Dieu, c'est impossible!

— Qu'est-ce qu'il y a?

— Va voir toi-même!

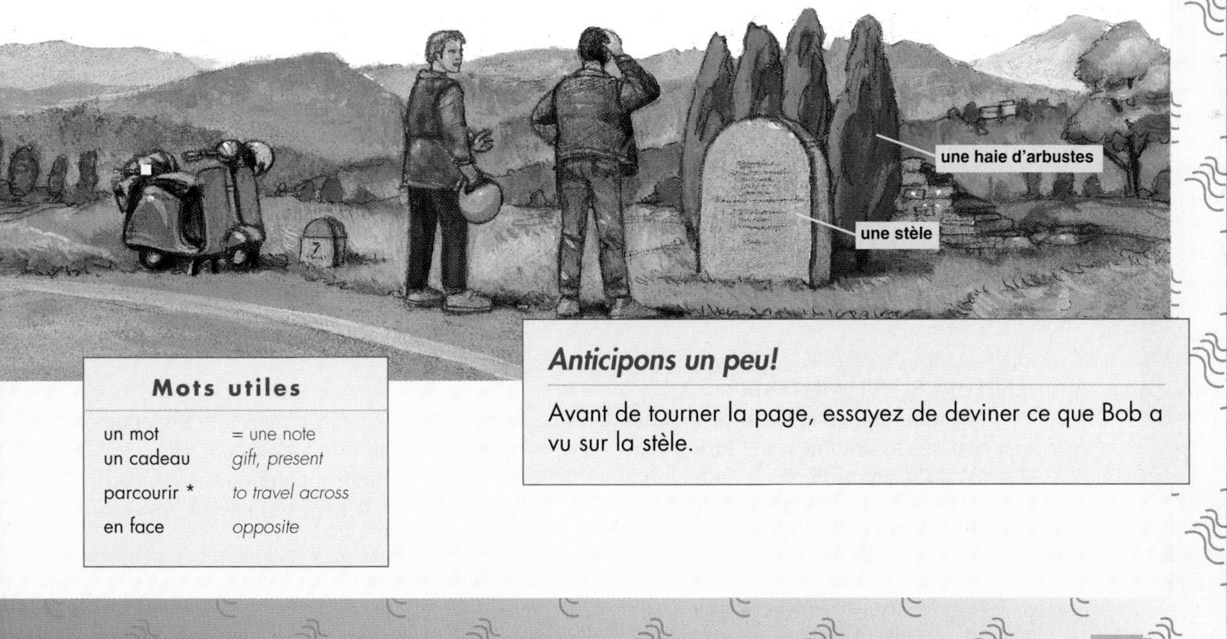

Mots utiles

un mot	= une note
un cadeau	*gift, present*
parcourir *	*to travel across*
en face	*opposite*

Anticipons un peu!

Avant de tourner la page, essayez de deviner ce que Bob a vu sur la stèle.

Note culturelle

Le cognac is a brandy made from wine. It comes from the region around Cognac, in southwestern France.

Irregular Verb

(see Appendix C)
parcourir (*see* **courir**)

John descend à son tour du scooter. Il lit l'inscription suivante:

ICI REPOSENT
EUGÉNIE ET MARCEL DUVILLARD
HÉROS DE LA RÉSISTANCE
FUSILLÉS° PAR LES NAZIS
LE DEUX JUILLET 1944
POUR AVOIR HÉBERGÉ°
DES PARACHUTISTES AMÉRI-
CAINS

À L'EMPLACEMENT°
DE CETTE STÈLE
S'ÉLEVAIT LEUR FERME
QUI FUT INCENDIÉE°
LE LENDEMAIN.
PASSANTS,° PRIEZ° POUR EUX!

fusillés *shot and killed* **pour avoir hébergé** *for having sheltered* **emplacement** = endroit **s'élevait** *stood* **incendiée** *burned to the ground* **passants** = vous qui passez par ici **priez** *to pray*

Avez-vous compris?

1. Que font Bob et John avant de quitter la ferme?
2. À la fin des vacances, pourquoi est-ce qu'ils veulent retourner à la ferme?
3. Quelle surprise les attend?
4. Qu'est-ce qui s'est passé à la ferme au début de juillet 1944?

LECTURE SUPPLÉMENTAIRE

L'histoire que vous avez lue évoque une époque très tourmentée de l'histoire de France: **l'Occupation** par les Allemands (1940-1944), puis la **Libération** par les Alliés (principalement des soldats américains et anglais), et par la **Résistance française**. Voir Interlude 6, pp. 252-255.

Pour découvrir un autre récit concernant cette période, lisez le texte *Au Revoir, les Enfants* (pp.256-259).

■ ***Avez-vous compris?***
(Sample answers)
1. Ils laissent un mot sur la table.
2. Ils veulent retourner à la ferme pour remercier le fermier et la fermière de leur hospitalité. Ils ont acheté des cadeaux pour eux.
3. Il n'y a plus de ferme. Il y a une stèle avec une inscription.
4. Le fermier et la fermière ont été fusillés par les nazis parce qu'ils ont aidé des parachutistes américains, et la ferme a été incendiée.

Teaching Strategies

Ask students:
- À votre avis, quelle est la réaction de John et Bob quand ils lisent l'inscription de la stèle?
- Est-ce qu'ils ont peur? sont curieux?
- Est-ce qu'ils pensent qu'ils rêvent *(dream)*?

APRÈS LA LECTURE

EXPRESSION ORALE

■ Discussion
Selon vous, est-ce que l'histoire que vous avez lue est possible ou impossible? Discutez votre opinion avec un(e) partenaire qui n'a pas la même opinion que vous.

■ Débat
Dans beaucoup de cultures, on peut trouver des «histoires de fantômes» *(ghost stories)* semblables à l'histoire racontée dans **Une étrange aventure**.
Vous-même, croyez-vous aux fantômes ou non? Exprimez votre opinion sur ce sujet et débattez la question avec un(e) partenaire qui n'a pas la même opinion que vous. Si possible, donnez des exemples en support de votre opinion.

■ Situations
Avec votre partenaire, choisissez l'une des situations suivantes. Composez le dialogue correspondant et jouez-le en classe.

1 Devant la stèle.

Bob et John sont devant la stèle. Ils viennent de lire l'inscription et maintenant ils essaient d'interpréter ce qui est arrivé lors de leur passage la nuit du premier juillet, en fonction des événements qui ont eu lieu les 1er et 2 juillet 1944. Par exemple:
- pourquoi le fermier a dit que la route était dangereuse
- selon les fermiers, qui étaient Bob et John et pourquoi ils étaient heureux de les recevoir
- qui étaient les gens qui étaient venus dans la nuit et qu'est-ce qu'ils cherchaient
- pourquoi le fermier et sa femme n'étaient pas là le lendemain matin

Rôles: Bob, John

2 Aux États-Unis.

En rentrant aux États-Unis, John a une conversation avec son grand-père qui lui aussi a été parachuté en France lors de l'invasion en 1944. Au cours de cette conversation, l'ancien soldat raconte ses aventures de guerre, par exemple, comment il a été recueilli *(picked up)* par les Résistants français.

Rôles: John, son grand-père

EXPRESSION ÉCRITE

■ Un peu d'histoire
Écrivez un petit rapport sur l'histoire de France entre 1940 et 1944. Dans ce rapport, expliquez en particulier le rôle . . .
- des Allemands
- des Américains
- de la Résistance française

(Source: Encyclopédies, Manuels d'histoire)

■ Une étrange aventure
Écrivez votre propre «étrange aventure». Commencez par une situation très réaliste. Ensuite, ajoutez un élément mystérieux ou bizarre. Utilisez votre imagination.

■ Teaching Strategies
- DISCUSSION
  As a preliminary step, you may conduct a poll:
  - **Qui croit que cette histoire est possible?**
  - **Qui croit qu'elle n'est pas possible?**

  Group students according to their responses.
- EXPANSION
  Autre dialogue: John raconte son aventure à un(e) ami(e) qui ne le croit pas. John essaie de le/la persuader qu'il a rencontré deux fantômes. L'ami(e) exprime ses doutes et pose des questions à John qui y répond en détail.
  Rôles: John, son ami(e)
- ASSESSMENT
  You may wish to use the *Lecture* quiz as a basis for discussion or as a quick comprehension check.

INTERLUDE CULTUREL

Pre-reading Questions

Pouvez-vous répondre aux questions suivantes?

- Quel pays d'Asie a été colonisé par la France?
- Où est situé Utah Beach?
- Qu'est-ce que le «Marché Commun»?

Notes historiques

- Les événements du 6 juin 1944 (D-Day ou **Jour-J**) ont été immortalisés dans le film *Le jour le plus long*.
- La Cochinchine, l'Annam, le Tonkin, le Cambodge et le Laos formaient l'Indochine française.

Pour en savoir plus

- Les étapes de l'unification européene sont résumées dans *Interlude 7*, p. 292.
- Pour des renseignements sur les mouvements artistiques mentionnés, voir *Interlude 1*, p. 60.

INTERLUDE CULTUREL

Les dates

La Belle Époque

- **1870** *La France devient une république*
- **1914** ***Première Guerre mondiale***
- **1918**
- **1939** ***Deuxième Guerre mondiale***
- **1945**
- **1957** *Marché Commun*
- **1960** *Fin de l'ère coloniale*
- **1979** *Premier Parlement Européen*
- **1993** *Formation de l'Union européenne*
- **2002** *Adoption de l'euro*

Les événements

La Belle Époque (1870-1914)

Paris à la Belle Époque, représenté par le peintre Jean Béraud

C'est une époque de prospérité économique et d'intense création artistique, littéraire et scientifique. D'importants mouvements artistiques **(impressionnisme, fauvisme, cubisme, surréalisme)** naissent en France. Paris devient la capitale mondiale des lettres et des arts.

À l'extérieur, la France s'engage dans des expéditions coloniales et se construit un empire en Afrique occidentale et en Asie (Indochine).

Les guerres mondiales (1914-1918 et 1939-1945)

Soldats américains défilant sur les Champs-Élysées

Ces deux terribles guerres opposent la France et l'Allemagne impériale (Première Guerre mondiale) puis l'Allemagne nazie (Deuxième Guerre mondiale). Dans ces deux guerres, l'intervention américaine est décisive.

En 1940, la France est occupée par les Allemands. Le 6 juin 1944, les troupes alliées commandées par le Général Eisenhower, débarquent sur les plages de Normandie: Utah Beach, Omaha Beach . . . La Libération de la France commence.

La France moderne (1945 - présent)

Le Louvre et sa pyramide, symboles du passé et de l'avenir.

Ruinée par la guerre, la France reconstruit son économie. La construction de la France moderne passe par deux étapes° importantes.

- La décolonisation (1945-1962). Les anciennes colonies françaises d'Afrique du Nord, d'Afrique occidentale et d'Asie deviennent des républiques indépendantes.
- L'intégration à l'Europe (1957 - présent). En 1957, la France devient membre de la **Communauté Économique Européenne** ou **«Marché Commun»**. La création de cette grande zone de libre-échange permet l'expansion commerciale et industrielle de la France. Intégrée à l'Europe, la France est aujourd'hui un pays moderne avec l'un des niveaux de vie° les plus élevés du monde.

étapes *steps, stages* **niveau de vie** *standard of living*

NOTES CULTURELLES

- Parmi les artistes étrangers qui viennent en France et qui ont constitué **l'École de Paris,** on peut mentionner: **Picasso** (Espagne), **Modigliani** (Italie), **Diego Rivera** (Mexique), **Foujita** (Japon), **Soutine** (Lituanie), **Chagall** (Russie).
- Quelques anciennes colonies et protectorats français:
  Afrique du Nord: **Maroc, Algérie, Tunisie**
  Afrique occidentale: **Sénégal, Côte d'Ivoire,** etc.
  Asie: **Vietnam, Cambodge, Laos**

■ *Les personnes*

Marie Curie (1867-1934)

Marie Curie, née Sklodowska, est l'un des grands génies scientifiques des temps modernes. D'origine polonaise, elle vient à Paris en 1891 pour continuer ses études scientifiques. En 1895, elle épouse son professeur, **Pierre Curie**. Ensemble, ils découvrent le radium et le polonium, auquel elle donne le nom de son pays d'origine. En accord avec l'esprit scientifique, les Curie refusent de prendre une patente sur leur découverte et d'en tirer° tout° bénéfice commercial.

En 1898, Pierre et Marie Curie reçoivent le Prix Nobel de Physique pour leurs travaux sur la radioactivité. Après la mort accidentelle de son mari en 1905, Marie Curie continue ses travaux, isole le radium et reçoit le Prix Nobel de Chimie en 1911.

Marie Curie dans son laboratoire.

Jean Moulin, héros de la Résistance

Jean Moulin (1899-1943)

Jean Moulin est le héros de **la Résistance** française pendant la Deuxième Guerre mondiale. En 1940, il se rallie au gouvernement de la France Libre, dirigé à Londres par le **Général de Gaulle**. Parachuté en France, il organise la Résistance contre les Allemands. Il est arrêté et torturé par la Gestapo.* Après sa mort, la Résistance continue. Les résistants, organisés en «maquis»° harcèlent les troupes d'occupation et préparent la **Libération**.

Simone Veil (1927-)

Simone Veil est une championne de l'Europe unie et des droits de la femme. Pendant la Deuxième Guerre mondiale, elle est déportée dans un camp de concentration nazi. Après la guerre, elle fait de brillantes études de droit et de sciences politiques. À l'âge de 20 ans, elle devient attachée auprès du Ministre de la Justice. De 1974 à 1979, elle est nommée Ministre de la Santé. En 1979, elle est élue Député au Parlement européen et elle en est la première présidente.

Simone Veil et le drapeau européen

* La Gestapo (Geheime Staats Polizei = police secrète d'état) était l'instrument le plus dangereux du régime policier nazi.

tirer *to derive* **tout** *any* **maquis** *guerrilla groups*

Notes culturelles

- **Jean Béraud** (1849–1935) was a successful French painter, born in Saint Petersburg. He painted many scenes of daily life, representing people in their homes, on the street, or at the theater.
- **Dwight David Eisenhower** was the 34th president of the United States (1953–1961).
- **Marie Curie** was the first woman to hold a chair at the Sorbonne University in Paris.
- **Irène Joliot-Curie**, daughter of Pierre and Marie Curie, became a scientist herself, and won the Nobel prize for Chemistry in 1935, along with her husband **(Frédéric Joliot-Curie)** for discovering artificial radioactivity.

Notes culturelles

Les endroits suivants sont nommés en l'honneur de Charles de Gaulle:

- l'aéroport Charles de Gaulle (ou Roissy, l'aéroport international de Paris)
- la place Charles de Gaulle (ou Place de l'Étoile, en haut des Champs-Élysées)

Additional Information

General De Gaulle was born in Lille in 1890, and died in Colombey-les-Deux-Églises in 1970.

Charles de Gaulle, homme d'action

Charles de Gaulle est peut-être l'homme qui a eu la plus grande influence sur l'histoire de la France du vingtième siècle. Jeune officier, il est fait prisonnier par les Allemands pendant la Première Guerre mondiale. Plus tard, il préconise° une stratégie militaire basée sur l'utilisation massive des tanks, mais on ne l'écoute pas.

Charles de Gaulle, Président de la République

En 1940, la France capitule et est occupée par l'armée allemande. De Gaulle refuse d'accepter la défaite et part pour l'Angleterre. Le 18 juin 1940, il lance° à la radio de Londres son célèbre appel où il demande à tous les Français de continuer le combat contre l'Allemagne nazie. Pour cet acte de rébellion contre l'autorité officielle, il est condamné à mort par le gouvernement français d'alors. Il organise la Résistance et crée un gouvernement de la «**France Libre**».

Le Général de Gaulle passe en revue les volontaires féminines de la France Libre.

Documents: Appel du 18 juin 1940

Appel du 18 juin 1940

Moi, Général de Gaulle, actuellement à Londres, j'invite les officiers et les soldats français qui se trouvent en territoire britannique ou qui viendraient à s'y trouver, avec leurs armes ou sans leurs armes, j'invite les ingénieurs et les ouvriers spécialistes des industries d'armement qui se trouvent en territoire britannique ou qui viendraient à s'y trouver, à se mettre en rapport avec moi. Quoi qu'il arrive,° la flamme de la résistance française ne doit pas s'éteindre° et ne s'éteindra pas.

Général de Gaulle

préconise *advocates* **lance** *sends out* **quoi qu'il arrive** *whatever happens* **s'éteindre** *to go out, to be extinguished*

En août 1944, le Général de Gaulle rentre dans Paris libéré par les troupes alliées. En 1945, il est élu président provisoire de la République française, mais il démissionne° parce qu'il n'a pas les pouvoirs° de gouverner.

Peu après, la France connaît deux longues et tragiques guerres coloniales, d'abord la guerre d'Indochine, puis la guerre d'Algérie. L'Algérie est alors un territoire français avec une population en majorité musulmane.° Les Algériens musulmans veulent leur indépendance et décident de prendre les armes contre la France. Le gouvernement français ne sait pas comment arrêter cette guerre impopulaire. La France est au bord de° la guerre civile.

Les Français font appel à de Gaulle qui devient Président de la République en 1959. De Gaulle comprend que l'ère coloniale est finie. Il négocie l'indépendance avec l'Algérie, puis avec les colonies françaises d'Afrique Noire qui deviennent des républiques amies de la France.

De Gaulle veut restaurer la grandeur de la France. Il comprend que l'avenir° de la France dépend de son intégration dans une Europe forte et indépendante. Il mène° alors une politique marquée par la réconciliation avec l'Allemagne et une certaine distance vis-à-vis des États-Unis. De Gaulle veut aussi réformer les institutions françaises. Beaucoup de Français n'acceptent pas ses réformes et protestent en organisant de violentes manifestations en mai 1968. Peu après, de Gaulle se retire de la vie publique.

Le Général de Gaulle sur les Champs-Élysées à la Libération de Paris en 1944

Le Général de Gaulle avec un chef d'État africain

Les manifestations à Paris, mai 1968

démissionne *resigns* **pouvoirs** *powers* **musulmane** *Moslem*
au bord de *on the edge of* **l'avenir =** le futur **il mène =** il fait

Realia Notes

La Nouvelle-Calédonie is an island in Melanesia, in the Pacific Ocean. Discovered by Cook in 1774, it became French in 1853, and still remains a French territory. Its inhabitants are called **les néo-calédoniens**.

NOTE CULTURELLE

The revolution of May 1968 **(la Révolution de Mai 68)**, started with demonstrations in high schools and universities in January 1968. In May, students in the Latin Quarter set up barricades and organized demonstrations that became violent. Student leader Daniel Cohn-Bendit was then deported to Germany, his native country. Workers joined the students, and many strikes paralyzed the country. One of the most significant consequences was the reform of the educational system. Universities, which were still operating as they did under Napoleon 1st, became less elitist, more accessible and more affordable.

💡 Pour en savoir plus

- For a description of surrealism, see *Interlude 1*, pp. 66–67.
- **Fernand Léger** (1881–1955) was a French painter. He started as a cubist, then went on to take his inspiration from the dynamism of modern life and industry. He also made stained glass, ceramics and mosaics.

■ Language Notes

- **réaliser** *to produce/ make a movie*
  le réalisateur *film director*
- **Un pupitre** is an old-fashioned school desk, with inclined desktop.

Anecdote

Louis Malle appeared in an episode of the sitcom "Murphy Brown" starring his wife, Candice Bergen.

■ Teaching Strategy

Students might enjoy listening to readings and music of the **Résistance**. A local library or music store may be able to locate *La Résistance: Ses chants et ses poètes.*

■ Liberté, liberté

Pour l'humanité, la liberté est le bien° le plus précieux. C'est le principe fondamental de la démocratie. Dans la *Déclaration d'indépendance* américaine et dans la *Déclaration des droits de l'homme* de la Révolution française, la liberté est un droit inaliénable et imprescriptible.°

Pourtant,° tous les êtres humains ne sont pas libres. Les Français, par exemple, ont perdu leur liberté quand leur pays a été occupé par les troupes allemandes entre 1940 et 1944. Ils rêvaient° alors de cette liberté qu'il fallait reconquérir et beaucoup sont morts pour elle en combattant dans la Résistance.

Paul Éluard

Paul Éluard, auteur du poème *Liberté*, était un poète surréaliste et un membre très actif de la Résistance. Il a publié ce poème pendant l'occupation dans un livre intitulé *Poésie et vérité* 1942. Interdit° par la censure allemande, ce livre était distribué clandestinement et parachuté en milliers d'exemplaires° par l'aviation alliée.

un bien = une possession **imprescriptible** *which cannot be legally taken away*
pourtant *however* **rêvaient** *dreamed* **interdit** *forbidden* **exemplaires** *copies*

Illustrations du poème par l'artiste Fernand L

■ Au Revoir, les Enfants

Au Revoir, les Enfants est un film réalisé par le cinéaste français contemporain **Louis Malle**. C'est un film autobiographique dans lequel Louis Malle évoque un épisode dramatique de sa jeunesse.

Louis Malle, réalisateur du film, avec deux des acteurs principaux

Liberté

Paul Éluard

Sur mes cahiers d'écolier
Sur mon pupitre° et les arbres
Sur le sable° sur la neige
J'écris ton nom

Sur toutes les pages lues
Sur toutes les pages blanches
Pierre sang° papier ou cendre°
J'écris ton nom

Sur les images dorées°
Sur les armes des guerriers°
Sur la couronne° des rois
J'écris ton nom

Sur la jungle et le désert
Sur les nids° sur les genêts*
Sur l'écho de mon enfance
J'écris ton nom

Sur mes refuges détruits
Sur mes phares écroulés°
Sur les murs de mon ennui
J'écris ton nom

Sur l'absence sans désirs
Sur la solitude nue°
Sur les marches° de la mort
J'écris ton nom

Sur la santé revenue
Sur le risque disparu
Sur l'espoir° sans souvenirs
J'écris ton nom

Et par le pouvoir° d'un mot°
Je recommence ma vie
Je suis né pour te connaître
Pour te nommer *Liberté.*

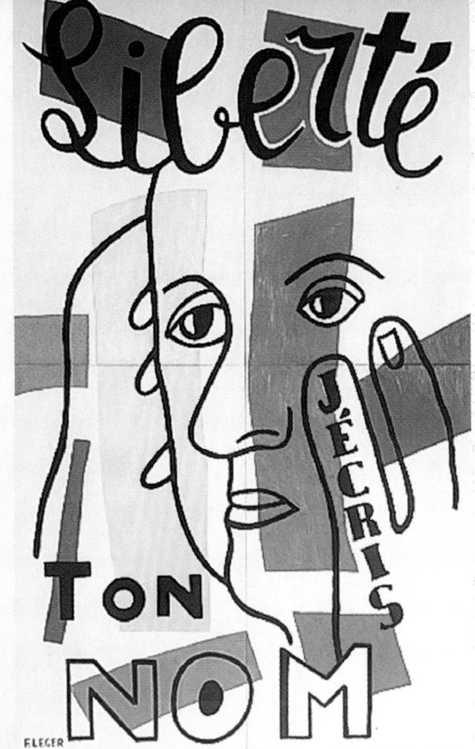

*Genêt or *broom* is a European shrub with bright yellow flowers that grows wild in the woods and uncultivated fields

pupitre *school desk* **sable** *sand* **sang** *blood* **cendre** *ashes* **dorées** *gilded* **guerriers** *warriors* **couronne** *crown* **nids** *nests*
phares écroulés *lighthouses that have collapsed* **nue** *naked* **marches** *steps, stairs* **espoir** *hope* **pouvoir** *power* **mot** *word*

Le film se passe au cours de° l'hiver 1944. À cette époque la France est occupée par les Allemands qui ont imposé la loi° hitlérienne partout. Les Juifs,° en particulier, sont traqués,° et quand ils sont pris, ils sont envoyés dans les camps d'extermination. Les Français qui les aident ou les abritent° sont, eux aussi, passibles de mort.

Parmi les Français, il y a ceux qui résistent aux Allemands, et ceux qui collaborent avec eux, mais la majorité attend passivement l'arrivée des Alliés et la fin de la guerre.

La vie est difficile. Comme la nourriture manque,° le marché noir s'installe partout. De plus en plus fréquemment, la population civile est soumise aux bombardements de l'aviation alliée . . .

au cours de = pendant **loi** *law* **Juifs** *Jews* **traqués** *hunted down* **abritent** *shelter* **manque** *is lacking*

À NOTER:
The middle section of *Liberté* reads as follows:

Sur les merveilles des nuits
Sur le pain blanc des journées
Sur les saisons fiancées
J'écris ton nom

Sur tous mes chiffons d'azur
Sur l'étang soleil moisi
Sur le lac lune vivante
J'écris ton nom

Sur les champs sur l'horizon
Sur les ailes des oiseaux
Et sur le moulin des ombres
J'écris ton nom

Sur chaque bouffée d'aurore
Sur la mer sur les bateaux
Sur la montagne démente
J'écris ton nom

Sur la mousse des nuages
Sur les sueurs de l'orage
Sur la pluie épaisse et fade
J'écris ton nom

Sur les formes scintillantes
Sur les cloches des couleurs
Sur la vérité physique
J'écris ton nom

Sur les sentiers éveillés
Sur les routes déployées
Sur les places qui débordent
J'écris ton nom

Sur la lampe qui s'allume
Sur la lampe qui s'éteint
Sur mes maisons réunies
J'écris ton nom

Sur le fruit coupé en deux
Du miroir et de ma chambre
Sur mon lit coquille vide
J'écris ton nom

Sur mon chien gourmand et tendre
Sur ses oreilles dressées
Sur sa patte maladroite
J'écris ton nom

Sur le tremplin de ma porte
Sur les objets familiers
Sur le flot du feu béni
J'écris ton nom

Sur toute chair accordée
Sur le front de mes amis
Sur chaque main qui se tend
J'écris ton nom

Sur la vitre des surprises
Sur les lèvres attentives
Bien au-dessus du silence
J'écris ton nom

Teaching Strategies

- If students are interested, you might draw their attention to how the poem begins with familiar images of childhood, and then moves to more violent images **(sang, cendre)** and scenes of destruction **(mes refuges détruits),** before ending on a note of hope.
- Special project: Have students select one phrase from the poem and illustrate it in a poster.
- Ask students the following questions:
  – Et vous? Qu'est-ce que la liberté pour vous?
  – Donnez votre définition de la liberté et des exemples.
- Point out that **soumettre** (*p.p.* **soumis**) is conjugated like **mettre**. (See Appendix C.)

■ Additional Information

Louis Malle also made the following films in English:

- *Crackers* (1984), with Sean Penn, a remake of *Big Deal on Madonna Street.*
- *God's Country* (1985) about the life of a small farming town in Minnesota.
- *Alamo Bay* (1985) with Ed Harris and Ho Nguyen, about the conflict between Vietnamese immigrants and Texas fishermen.

Note culturelle

En 1988, *Au Revoir, les Enfants* a gagné le César (l'équivalent français de l'Oscar) pour le meilleur film de l'année.

Documents: Au Revoir, les Enfants

L'action du film a lieu dans une école catholique de garçons dont le directeur, **le père Jean**, est un prêtre° d'une grande intégrité morale. Le héros du film est un jeune garçon d'une douzaine d'années, **Julien Quentin** (c'est, bien sûr, Louis Malle lui-même), qui est pensionnaire° avec son frère aîné François dans cette école.

1 Le film commence à la rentrée des classes après les vacances de Noël. Dans la première scène, Julien est à la gare. Il dit au revoir à sa mère, puis il prend son train. Quand il arrive au collège, il retrouve tous ses copains. Dans la classe, il y a un nouvel élève qui s'appelle
2 **Jean Bonnet**. C'est un garçon timide et réservé qui ne parle jamais de sa famille. C'est aussi un brillant élève, en maths, en français, en musique. Julien, qui était jusqu'alors° le meilleur élève de la classe, sent en lui un rival. Il questionne Jean sur son passé, mais celui-ci lui répond d'une façon évasive.

Louis Malle (1932-1995)

Louis Malle est l'un des grands réalisateurs° du cinéma français moderne. Il a d'abord fait des films documentaires, comme son premier film *Le Monde du silence* réalisé en coopération avec Jacques-Yves Cousteau, l'explorateur du monde marin.°

Dans ses films plus récents, Louis Malle a traité de thèmes personnels comme celui évoqué dans *Au revoir, les Enfants.*

Louis Malle était marié avec l'actrice américaine Candice Bergen et habitait à New York.

1 *Julien dit au revoir à sa mère avant de prendre son train pour rentrer au collège.*

2 *Au collège, il y a un nouvel élève. Il s'appelle Jean Bonnet.*

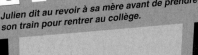

3 *Les deux garçons deviennent amis.*

réalisateur *director* **marin** = de la mer **prêtre** *priest* **pensionnaire** *boarding student* **jusqu'alors** *until then*

IMPORTANT TEACHING NOTE

Although the film *Au Revoir, les Enfants* is rated PG, it contains some language which may be INAPPROPRIATE and OBJECTIONABLE for a class viewing.

Before deciding to show the film in class, you should definitely preview it carefully, paying attention to the dialogs between the boys at the school. If you decide to show the movie, you should be prepared to deal with the objectionable language, or use only selected scenes for class viewing.

4 Le jeune employé est renvoyé pour avoir fait du marché noir.

5 Un soldat allemand entre dans la salle de classe pour arrêter Jean.

6 Le père Jean dit un dernier au revoir aux élèves de l'école.

Un jour, Julien découvre la vérité: Jean Bonnet
s'appelle en réalité Jean Keppelstein et il est juif. Les
prêtres l'ont recueilli° avec deux autres enfants juifs pour le
soustraire à° la police allemande. Au collège, il est en
sécurité tant que° sa véritable identité reste cachée.° Depuis
cette découverte, les relations entre les deux garçons
3 changent et ils deviennent amis.

Un samedi, au cours d'une sortie, ils se perdent dans la
forêt. Julien arrête une voiture de patrouille allemande.
Jean veut s'échapper, mais il est rattrapé.° Les soldats
allemands ramènent les deux garçons à l'école. Cette
fois-ci, il y a plus de peur° que de mal!° Un autre jour, la
famille de Julien invite Jean à déjeuner dans un grand
restaurant. Jean assiste à une scène pénible° où un client
juif, décoré de la Légion d'Honneur,* est insulté par un
milicien, auxiliaire français de la police allemande.

Les jours passent . . . Un employé de l'école est
4 renvoyé° pour avoir fait du marché noir avec les élèves.
Pour se venger, il dénonce la présence d'enfants juifs à
l'école. La police allemande arrive et encercle l'école. Un
soldat entre dans la salle de classe pour arrêter Jean.
5 D'autres soldats fouillent° l'école. Les deux autres élèves
juifs sont découverts et arrêtés ainsi que° le père Jean qui
était membre de la Résistance. Au moment de
quitter l'école, escorté par des soldats allemands, le
6 père Jean dit un dernier au revoir à ses élèves:
«Au revoir, les enfants! À bientôt!»

Personne ne reviendra. Jean et ses deux camarades juifs mourront à Auschwitz. Le père Jean mourra au camp de Mauthausen.

* La Légion d'Honneur: haute distinction donnée aux gens qui ont servi la France.

recueilli *taken in* **soustraire à** *to protect from* **tant que** *as long as* **cachée** *hidden* **rattrapé** *caught*
peur *fright* **mal** *harm* **pénible** *painful* **renvoyé** *fired* **fouillent** *to search* **ainsi que** *as well as*

Teaching Strategy

You may wish to obtain a copy of the film as well as accompanying Lesson Plans from:

Film Aerobics
9 Birmingham Place
Vernon Hills, IL 60061
1-800-832-2448

Note linguistique

Remind students that **le collège** = junior high school.

UNITÉ 7

MAIN THEME

Health and Medical Care

Communication Function/Contexts
- Going to the doctor's office
- Going to the dentist
- Going to the emergency room

Linguistic Goals
- Expressing how you and others feel
- Expressing fear, doubt, disbelief
- Expressing feelings or attitudes about past actions and events

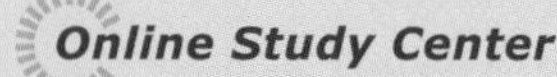
Online Study Center

Online Teaching Center

UNITÉ 7

La forme et la santé

Thème et Objectifs

Culture

In this unit, you will discover . . .
- how the French take care of their health
- why the French drink mineral water
- how the French help provide health care to less fortunate people around the world

Communication

You will learn how . . .
- to see a doctor or dentist and explain what is wrong
- to follow the doctor's instructions

Langue

You will learn how . . .
- to express your doubts and fears
- to affirm your beliefs
- to let people know how you feel about both present and past events

TEACHING RESOURCES

ANCILLARIES

Student Activities Manual, Unit 7
Audio Program, Unit 7
Video-DVD Program, Unit 7
Chansons Audio CD

HM ClassPrep CD

Presentations, Unit 7
Audioscript, Unit 7
Videoscript, Unit 7
Assessment, Unit 7
Answer Key, Unit 7

Les Français et leur santé

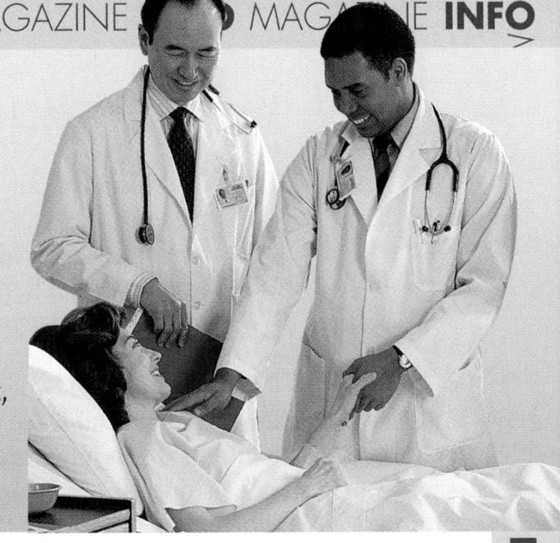

En France comme ailleurs,° la santé et la forme sont la préoccupation de tout le monde. Pour rester en forme, les jeunes Français pratiquent toutes sortes de sports: la natation en été, le ski en hiver, le foot, le basket, le vélo, le jogging, la marche à pied en toute saison. Il arrive° cependant que les personnes en excellente santé tombent malades. Il faut alors aller voir un médecin.

Pour les maladies ordinaires, on va voir un médecin généraliste. Pour les maladies spécifiques, on doit consulter un spécialiste: oculiste pour les yeux, cardiologue pour le coeur, dermatologue pour les maladies de peau,° stomatologue pour la bouche, gastro-entérologue pour l'estomac ... Si on a besoin d'une radio,° on va chez un radiologue.

En cas d'urgence° ou d'accident sérieux, on peut téléphoner au SAMU (Service d'Aide Médicale Urgente). Il suffit de composer le numéro 15. Le SAMU est un service public rattaché à un hôpital. Suivant la gravité du problème, le SAMU envoie un médecin d'urgence, une ambulance de réanimation ou une ambulance ordinaire.

Le système médical français a le grand avantage d'être presque gratuit.° La majorité des Français sont inscrits° à la Sécurité Sociale. Avec la Sécurité Sociale, le gouvernement français prend en charge les dépenses médicales et la santé de ses citoyens.° Les gens qui vont chez le médecin ou chez le dentiste présentent leur carte vitale (carte d'anuré social) qui leur permet° d'être remboursés de 60 à 70% des frais. Et quand ils vont chez le pharmacien, beaucoup de médicaments° sont aussi remboursés.

Les Français aiment se soigner.° Ce sont les plus grands consommateurs de médicaments du monde. En général, les médicaments qu'ils prennent, comme l'aspirine ou les vitamines, sont fabriqués par les grandes compagnies pharmaceutiques. Ils prennent aussi toute une variété de médicaments à base de produits naturels (fruits, fleurs, plantes, herbes sauvages,° feuilles° ou écorce° d'arbre, etc.). Ce sont des infusions pour la digestion, l'insomnie ou la migraine, des pilules° pour le foie,° des pastilles° et des sirops pour la toux,° des crèmes et des pommades° pour la peau, etc.... En pratiquant cette médecine «écologique,» ils redécouvrent° les secrets des remèdes traditionnels.

Les femmes-médecins

Aujourd'hui, il y a beaucoup de femmes-médecins en France. Elles représentent 35% du corps médical. C'est seulement en 1870 que la première femme a reçu son diplôme de médecin de la Faculté de Médecine de Paris. Cette jeune femme n'était d'ailleurs pas française, mais anglaise!

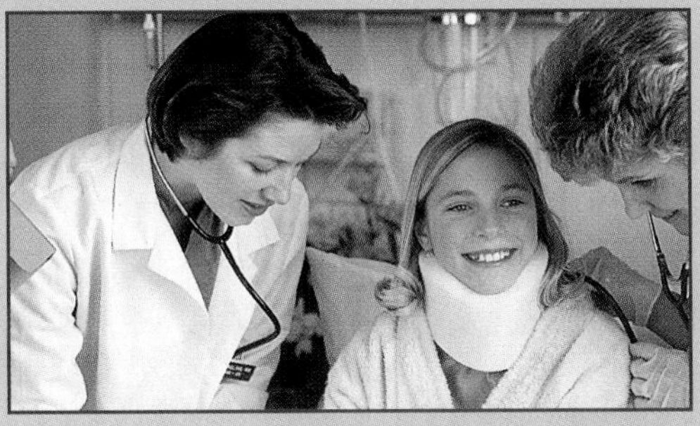

et vous?

DÉBATS

Choisissez un des sujets de débat et prenez une position pour ou contre. Débattez votre position avec votre partenaire. Si possible, utilisez des exemples pour établir votre position.

1. Les Américains consomment trop de médicaments.
2. Le sport est la meilleure prévention contre la maladie.
3. Quand on est malade, il est préférable d'utiliser des médicaments naturels.

ailleurs *elsewhere* **il arrive** *it happens* **peau** *skin* **radio** *x-ray* **cas d'urgence** *emergency* **gratuit** *free of charge*
inscrire ❊ *to register* **citoyens** *citizens* **remplissent** *fill out* **feuille** *form* **permettre** ❊ *to allow* **médicaments** *medicine, drugs*
se soigner *to take care of one's health* **sauvages** *wild* **feuilles** *leaves* **écorce** *bark* **pilules** *pills* **foie** *liver* **des pastilles** *tablets*
la toux *cough* **des pommades** *ointments* **redécouvrir** ❊ *to rediscover*

INFO MAGAZINE

Theme: Health care in France

Reading Strategy: Reading for information

Teaching Strategy

These readings can be done:

- in class or as homework
- at the beginning of the unit or as a wrap-up activity

Have students look at the realia and photos and guess the theme of the article. Have them skim, looking for cognates, then giving the main idea. Short *Info Magazine* quizzes may be used to test for comprehension or as a basis for discussion.

Note culturelle

The **pharmacies de garde** are open at night and on Sundays for people requiring emergency medical attention. (These designated establishments are listed in newspapers as well as on the doors of all **pharmacies.**)

Note linguistique

La parapharmacie is a drugstore that sells non-prescriptions drugs, vitamins, herbs, and beauty products.

Débats

Additional topics for debate or discussion:

- Les compagnies pharmaceutiques s'intéressent plus à leurs profits qu'à la santé de la population.
- En quoi le système médical français est-il différent du système américain?

Irregular Verbs

(see Appendix C)

inscrire (*see* **écrire**)
permettre (*see* **mettre**)
redécouvrir (*see* **ouvrir**)

■ **Additional Information**

Perrier water comes from a spring in Vergèze (Gard). It owes its name to the original owner of the spring: Docteur Louis Perrier. The bottled water is naturally carbonated. Other popular French spring waters sold in American supermarkets are Vichy and Evian.

■ **Notes linguistiques**

Définitions

- **Un minéral:** un élément de la terre
- **Un rhumatisme:** quand on a un rhumatisme, on a mal aux genoux ou aux mains, par exemple
- **Une source thermale:** dans une source thermale, il y a des minéraux bons pour la santé
- **Une cure thermale:** on fait une cure thermale quand on utilise les sources thermales pour se soigner ou se mettre en forme
- **La thalassothérapie:** un traitement par l'eau de mer et l'air marin
- **Un sauna:** un bain de vapeur très chaud
- **Un bain de boue:** pour un bain de boue, on ne se baigne pas dans de l'eau, mais dans de la boue
- **Le stress:** c'est quand on est fatigué parce qu'on a trop travaillé, par exemple, ou parce qu'on a beaucoup de problèmes

L'eau, c'est la santé

Au café ou au restaurant, Stéphanie commande généralement de l'eau minérale. Sandrine en boit un grand verre le matin quand elle se lève, et le soir quand elle se couche. Quant à° Christophe, il ne va jamais au lycée sans emporter° une bouteille d'eau minérale dans son sac. L'eau minérale est la boisson favorite des Français. Ils en boivent en moyenne° 125 litres par personne (hommes, femmes et enfants) et par an. Ce sont les champions du monde de la consommation d'eau minérale.

■ Au café, les jeunes commandent de l'eau minérale.

L'eau a de nombreux avantages. C'est le plus naturel des produits. Elle contient° zéro calorie. Elle facilite l'élimination des toxines et la régénération des cellules de notre corps. (N'oublions pas que le corps° humain est composé de deux tiers° d'eau!)

En outre,° les eaux minérales ont certaines propriétés thérapeutiques qui dépendent des minéraux qu'elles contiennent (magnésium, calcium, potassium, sodium, etc.) Certaines eaux sont bonnes pour la digestion, d'autres pour le foie° ou les reins.° Certaines sont recommandées pour les rhumatismes, d'autres pour les maladies de peau.° En France, il existe des centaines d'eaux minérales différentes. Ces eaux viennent de sources° thermales situées principalement dans les zones montagneuses: Massif Central (Vichy), Alpes (Évian), Vosges (Vittel, Contrexéville), Pyrénées (Amélie-les-Bains).

La façon la plus normale d'utiliser une eau minérale est d'en boire tous les jours. Une autre façon consiste à faire une «cure» dans la région qui produit° une eau particulière. Là, non seulement on boit de grandes quantités d'eau minérale, mais on utilise celle-ci pour prendre des bains et pour se faire faire des massages. Cette tradition remonte° aux Romains qui connaissaient bien les vertus de l'eau et qui ont découvert° un grand nombre de sources thermales en Gaule il y a 2000 ans. Aujourd'hui, des centaines de milliers de Français vont chaque été faire une cure dans les stations thermales spécialisées.

D'autres personnes préfèrent aller à la mer et pratiquer la «thalassothérapie.» Cette méthode consiste à profiter des avantages combinés de l'eau de mer, de l'air et du climat marins. On peut prendre des bains de mer très chauds, des saunas ou des bains de boue.° La thalassothérapie est recommandée pour les personnes qui souffrent° de fatigue ou de stress, pour celles qui veulent se remettre° en forme, et aussi pour les athlètes professionnels.

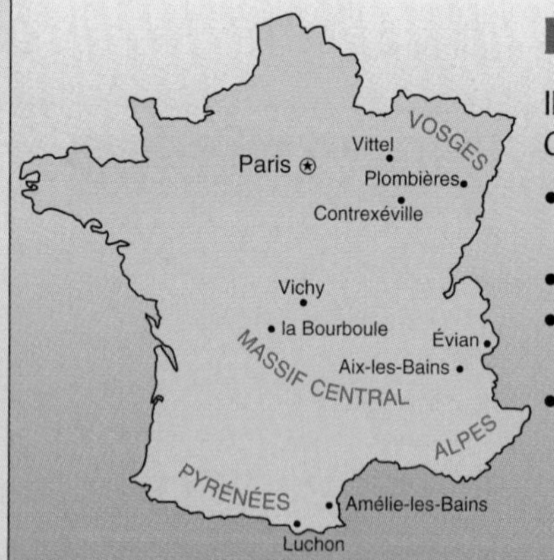

La France des eaux

Il existe plus de 100 stations thermales en France. Chacune a sa spécialité.

- Si vous avez des problèmes de digestion, allez à Vichy, Vittel, Évian ou Contrexéville.
- Si vous avez de l'asthme, allez à Amélie-les-Bains.
- Si vous avez une peau délicate, allez à la Bourboule.
- Si vous avez des rhumatismes, allez à Aix-les-Bains, comme autrefois la reine Victoria, ou à Plombières, comme l'empereur Napoléon III.

PROJET

Allez dans un supermarché et faites une liste des eaux minérales qu'on y vend. Indiquez l'origine géographique de ces eaux minérales.

quant à *as for* **emporter** *to take along* **en moyenne** *on the average* **contenir** ❊ *to contain* **le corps** *body* **deux tiers** *two-thirds* **en outre** = en plus **le foie** *liver* **les reins** *kidneys* **la peau** *skin* **les sources** *springs* **produire** ❊ *to produce* **remonte** *dates back* **découvrir** ❊ *to discover* **boue** *mud* **souffrir** ❊ *to suffer* **se remettre** ❊ *to get back (into shape)*

Teaching Strategy: Warm-Up

As homework, have students read pp. 261–262, and then ask them to prepare five to ten questions per page. Have each student ask one of his/her questions and choose a student to answer. Repeat this until all the questions have been asked and answered.

Le savez-vous?

Que savez-vous de votre santé et de la santé en général? Faites le test suivant. Combien de phrases pouvez-vous compléter? [Pour connaître les réponses, allez au bas de la page.]

1. **Le matin, notre température normale est de ...**
   a. 35 degrés
   b. 37 degrés
   c. 40,2 degrés

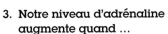

2. **En moyenne, un adolescent de 16 ans a besoin de ... par jour.**
   a. 1.500 calories
   b. 2.800 calories
   c. 3.400 calories

3. **Notre niveau d'adrénaline augmente quand ...**
   a. on a faim
   b. on a la grippe
   c. on se met en colère

4. **La grippe est une maladie causée par ...**
   a. un virus
   b. le froid
   c. la mauvaise hygiène

5. **Un dermatologue est un médecin qu'on peut consulter quand on a ...**
   a. de l'acné
   b. des rhumatismes
   c. mal à la tête

6. **Le calcium est l'élément principal du squelette et des dents. Une excellente source de calcium est ...**
   a. le lait
   b. la viande
   c. le poisson

7. **Il ne faut pas fumer parce que le tabac est un poison qui peut provoquer beaucoup de maladies sérieuses, en particulier ...**
   a. l'anémie
   b. la tuberculose
   c. le cancer du poumon

8. **La pénicilline est un antibiotique. Son rôle est de ...**
   a. faciliter la digestion
   b. éliminer les produits toxiques
   c. détruire les bactéries qui provoquent les infections

9. **Quand on est à la plage, il est prudent de se protéger contre le soleil. À long terme, l'exposition trop longue au soleil peut provoquer ...**
   a. l'insomnie
   b. la polio
   c. le cancer de la peau

10. **Les personnes qui ont un problème avec leur cholestérol doivent éviter** *(avoid)* **de manger ...**
    a. des fruits
    b. des légumes
    c. des oeufs

11. **La mononucléose est une maladie qui affecte ...**
    a. le sang
    b. les muscles
    c. l'estomac

12. **Le jogging, le cyclisme et la gymnastique sont des activités aérobiques. Le résultat principal d'une activité aérobique est ...**
    a. de développer nos muscles
    b. d'augmenter notre rythme cardiaque
    c. d'éliminer les toxines

13. **En cas de transfusion sanguine, il est important de connaître son groupe sanguin. Le groupe sanguin le plus rare est ...**
    a. le groupe A
    b. le groupe B
    c. le groupe O

14. **Quand on est diabétique, il est déconseillé de manger ...**
    a. du pain
    b. du sucre
    c. du fromage

RÉPONSES 1b, 2b, 3c, 4a, 5a, 6a, 7c, 8c, 9c, 10c, 11a, 12b, 13b, 14b

Proverbe

Santé passe richesse. *(Health before wealth.)*

■ Note linguistique

Traditionnellement, au nouvel an en France, on dit «Bonne année, bonne santé» aux membres de sa famille et à ses amis.

■ Language Note

35°C = 95°F; 37°C = 98.6°F; 40,2°C = 104.3°F

Note culturelle

Spa is a city in Belgium, renowned for its **station thermale**. The waters from the seven main springs of Spa are said to help people with rheumatism.

NOTES CULTURELLES

- By 1997, every French person over 16 was issued a **carnet de santé**, a medical record in which doctors write their diagnoses and prescriptions. For privacy, there is no name on the booklet, only a social security number. A patient must bring his **carnet** when going to see a doctor. In 1999, the **carnet** was replaced by the **carte de santé**, with all medical information recorded on its electronic chip.
- The first social security system appeared in France in 1913.

LE FRANÇAIS PRATIQUE

Une visite médicate

TEACHING RESOURCES

Student Activities Manual, pp. 145–146

Audio Program, CD 7, Tracks 1–4

HM ClassPrep CD, Audioscript, Unit 7

Video/DVD Program, Unit 7

Supplementary vocabulary

le médecin généraliste
le neurologue
le pédiatre
le cardiologue
le psychiatre
J'ai bonne mine. *I look good/healthy.*
J'ai mauvaise mine. *I look bad/sick.*

■ Additional Information

Penicillin was dicovered in 1928 by Alexander Fleming, a British physician. Fleming received the Nobel Prize in Medicine in 1945.

LE FRANÇAIS PRATIQUE

Une visite médicale

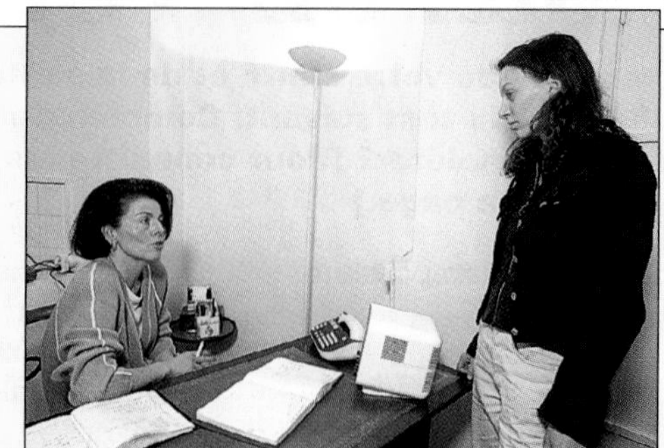

Dans la salle d'attente *(waiting room)*

— Avez-vous **un rendez-vous** *(appointment)*?
Oui, j'ai un rendez-vous avec le docteur Lavie à deux heures.

le médecin	**le/la chirurgien(ne)** *surgeon*
le/la dentiste	**l'infirmier(ère)** *nurse*
le/la spécialiste	**l'oculiste**

FMP (FÉDÉRATION MUTUALISTE PARISIENNE
CENTRES OPTIQUE MÉDICALE
24 r St Victor 75005 P________ 01 40 46 11 37
10-12 av Georges Clémenceau
93139 Noisy le Sec________ 01 48 44 00 32

Dans le cabinet *(office)* du médecin

— Comment allez-vous?
Comment vous sentez-vous?
Ça va, **je me sens bien.**
je me **porte** bien.
je suis **en bonne santé** *(health)*.
je suis **bien portant(e)** *(in good health)*.

se sentir *to feel*
se porter bien *to be in good health*

Ça ne va pas. | **Je ne me sens pas bien.**
Je suis | **malade** *(sick)*.
Je me sens

fatigué	**faible** *weak*
nerveux	**déprimé** *depressed*

— Avez-vous **de la fièvre?**
Oui, j'ai de la fièvre.
J'ai **39 degrés de température.**

Médecins qualifiés: chirurgie générale
• Bougival
NATHAN Georges
2 rte Celle St Cloud________ 01 39 12 28 84
• Celle Saint Cloud(La)
ROMANO Mauro
22 av Jonchère________ 01 30 82 23 48
• Chambourcy
MIRABEL André
1 all résidence________ 01 39 65 32 48

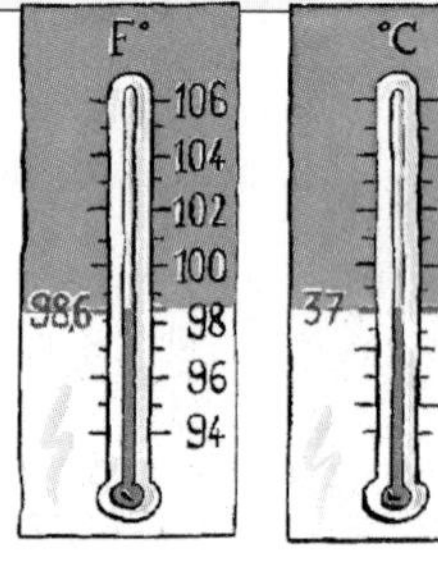

Teaching Suggestion: Video/DVD Program

In the Unit 7 *Vidéo-drame: Nicolas est malade*, students will go with Nicolas to the doctor. They will hear Nicolas identify his symptoms, and see the doctor prescribe the appropriate treatment. After watching the video, have students pair up and re-enact a doctor's visit based on the video. Encourage them to make up different symptoms and treatments.

— Est-ce que **ça vous fait mal**?
Aïe *(Ouch)!* Oui, ça fait mal.
Non, ça ne fait pas mal.

faire mal *to hurt*

— Où **avez-vous mal?**
J'ai mal | **à la tête.**
à la gorge *(throat).*
au ventre *(stomach).*
J'ai mal au coeur *(I feel nauseous).*

Les parties du corps
Révision ▶ p. R12

— **Qu'est-ce qui ne va pas?** *(What's wrong?)*

Je tousse.

tousser *to cough* — **éternuer** *to sneeze*
vomir *to throw up* — **saigner** *(to bleed)* **du nez**

J'ai **un rhume** *(a cold)*. Je suis **enrhumé(e)**.
J'ai **une douleur** *(pain)* dans le dos.

des nausées
de l'eczéma
des vertiges *dizzy spells*
des boutons *a rash*

— Quelles **maladies** *(diseases)* **d'enfance** avez-vous eues?
J'ai eu **la rougeole** *(measles)*.

les oreillons *mumps*
la varicelle *chicken pox*
la rubéole *German measles*
la coqueluche *whooping cough*

VOTRE DOS VOUS FAIT MAL?
Association d'orthopédie du Québec

République Rwandaise
Ministère de la santé Publique et des Affaires Sociales

Programme de Vaccination

Vaccination	Dose	Date
le tétanos		
la tuberculose		
la poliomyélite		
la diphtérie		
la coqueluche		
la rougeole		

Teaching Strategy

Divide the class into pairs and have each pair of students role play the interchanges from the practical vocabulary. Encourage students to use gestures to clarify meaning and to make the dialogs more fun. Ask each pair to choose their most successful and amusing dialog to present to the class. Use **Transparency Master 43** to extend and expand the dialogs.

Supplementary vocabulary

Ouille! /uj/ *ouch!*
transpirer *to sweat*
C'est douloureux. *It's sore.*
Ça gratte. *It's itchy.*
Ça démange. *It's itchy.*
un bleu *bruise*
une égratignure *scratch*
une brûlure *burn*
une ampoule *blister*

Realia Notes

- Point out the pun: **«Comment vous santé vous?» (Comment vous sentez-vous?)**
- **le soulagement** *relief*

NOTES CULTURELLES

- The first inoculation was made in 1796 by British physician Edward Jenner (1749–1823).
- French scientist **Louis Pasteur** (1822–1895) discovered the vaccine against rabies (1885). He also discovered two other vaccines, the process now called **la pasteurisation**, and founded the **Institut Pasteur** in 1888 in Paris. There are many branches of the Institute around the world serving as major research and vaccine production centers.
- Often, a French person will subscribe to **une mutuelle**, private insurance which will supplement the reimbursement of medical care made by the **Sécurité Sociale**.

—Est-ce que vous pouvez **ouvrir la bouche?**

avaler *to swallow*
respirer *to breathe, breathe in*
tousser

—Je vais vous
- **examiner.**
- **prendre la température.**
- **prendre la tension** *(blood pressure).*
- **faire une analyse de sang** *(blood test).*
- **faire une piqûre** *(shot, injection).*
- **faire une radio** *(x-ray).*

—Vous avez **une pneumonie.**

un rhume	**une angine** *strep throat*
de l'asthme	**une bronchite**
la grippe *flu*	**la mononucléose**

—Je vais vous **soigner** *(to treat).*
Voici **une ordonnance** *(prescription).*
Prenez **ce médicament** *(medicine)* . . .
- **le matin et le soir.**
- **deux fois** *(times)* **par jour.**
- **toutes les 4 heures.**

de l'aspirine	**ces comprimés** *pills*
cet antibiotique	**ces cachets** *tablets*
ces vitamines	**ces gouttes** *drops*

—Vous devez
- **vous reposer.**
- **vous soigner.**
- **rester au lit.**
- **prendre rendez-vous** } dans une semaine.
- **revenir** } dans une semaine.

se reposer *to rest*
se soigner *to take care of oneself*

Supplementary vocabulary

faire aah *to say "aah"*
tirer la langue *stick out your tongue*
ausculter *to listen to one's chest (with a stethoscope)*
le sirop *syrup*
le remède *remedy, cure*
le traitement *treatment*
le régime *diet*
l'auscultation *auscultation (sounding)*
la consultation *consultation*
les honoraires *(m.)* *fees*
guérir *to heal, to cure*
à jeun *on an empty stomach*

Obtenez la réponse
LE DIMANCHE
27 FÉVRIER
Prises de tension artérielle
GRATUITES
ENTRÉE 11 H ET 18 H
dans toutes les PJC Jean Coutu

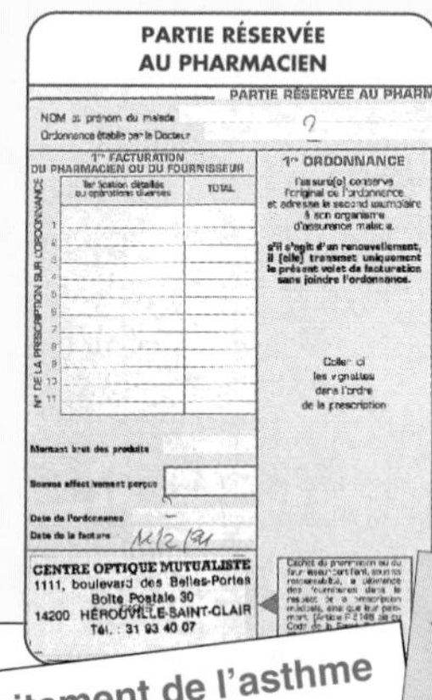

Clinique de traitement de l'asthme
HSC
555, avenue University
Toronto (Ontario) M5G 1X8

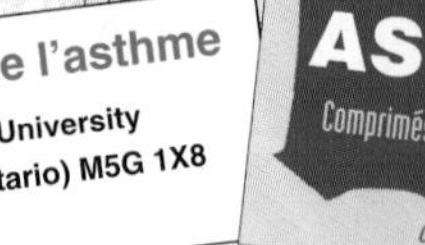

200 COMPRIMÉS
325 CHACUN
ASPIRINE
Comprimés d'Acide Acétylsalicylique
ON PEUT S'Y FIER

1 Qu'est-ce qu'ils ont?

Choisissez l'option **a**, **b** ou **c** qui correspond logiquement à chaque situation.

1. Thomas va chez l'oculiste.
   a. Il va bien.
   b. Il a les oreillons.
   c. Il a mal aux yeux.

2. Roger a 39 degrés de température.
   a. Il est bien portant.
   b. Il a de la fièvre.
   c. Il a froid.

3. J'ai des difficultés à avaler.
   a. J'ai une angine.
   b. J'ai la rubéole.
   c. J'ai une crampe d'estomac.

4. Ma petite soeur tousse tout le temps.
   a. Elle a la varicelle.
   b. Elle a une bronchite.
   c. Elle est déprimée.

5. Thierry a envie de vomir.
   a. Il éternue.
   b. Il a de la tension.
   c. Il a mal au coeur.

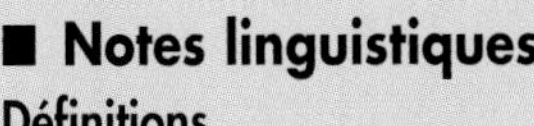

6. Vous avez des boutons.
   a. Vous avez la grippe.
   b. Vous avez la rougeole.
   c. Vous ne respirez pas bien.

7. Je me mets des gouttes dans le nez.
   a. J'ai un rhume.
   b. Je prends des cachets.
   c. J'ai besoin de vitamines.

8. L'infirmière m'a fait une radio.
   a. Je prends des comprimés.
   b. J'ai beaucoup de tension.
   c. Je me suis cassé le bras.

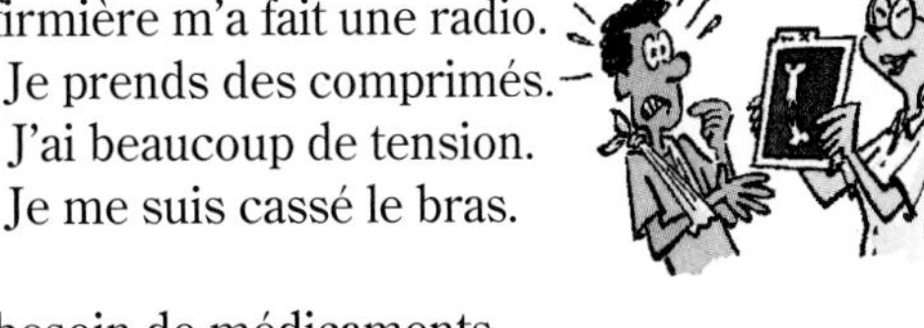

9. J'ai besoin de médicaments.
   a. Je vais à la pharmacie.
   b. Je vois le chirurgien.
   c. Je suis en bonne santé.

10. Je voudrais voir le médecin.
    a. Je me soigne.
    b. Je me sens bien.
    c. Je dois prendre rendez-vous.

2 Créa-dialogue

Aujourd'hui vous ne vous sentez pas bien du tout. Regardez la liste et choisissez une maladie ou un malaise. Décrivez vos symptômes à votre partenaire.

▶ — **Ça va?**
— **Non, je ne me sens pas bien.**
— **Qu'est-ce que tu as?**
— **Je crois que j'ai le rhume des foins.**
— **Tu es sûr(e)?**
— **Oui, j'éternue tout le temps et j'ai mal aux yeux.**

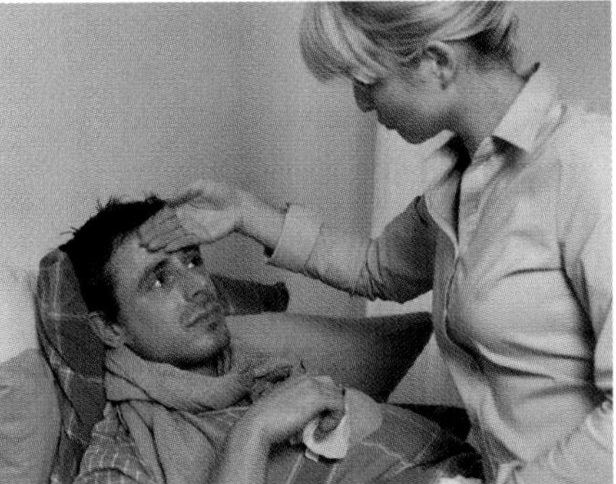

la grippe	**la mononucléose**	**un rhume**	**une bronchite**
une angine	**une indigestion**	**de l'asthme**	**une pneumonie**
le rhume des foins *(hay fever)*		**une allergie**	**??**

■ Notes linguistiques

Définitions

- **Un médecin généraliste:** quelqu'un qui soigne les maladies ordinaires
- **Un médecin spécialiste:** quelqu'un qui soigne des maladies spécifiques
- **Un médecin d'urgence:** quelqu'un qui s'occupe des cas d'urgence, des accidents
- **Le SAMU:** c'est le Service d'Aide Médicale Urgente
- **La Sécurité Sociale:** c'est une assurance qui rembourse les dépenses médicales
- **Une compagnie pharmaceutique:** une compagnie qui fabrique des médicaments
- **La médecine «écologique»:** médecine basée sur des produits naturels (plantes, fruits, etc.) et des remèdes traditionnels

Note culturelle

Quand quelqu'un éternue en France, il est poli de dire «À vos (tes) souhaits!» ou bien: «Santé!»

■ Anecdote

The stethoscope was invented by the French physician **René Laennec** (1781–1826).

3 À la clinique

Un(e) malade va dans une clinique où il/elle a rendez-vous. Avant de voir le médecin, l'infirmier(ère) lui pose des questions. Complétez le dialogue et jouez-le en classe avec votre partenaire.

Infirmier(ère): Vous avez un rendez-vous?
Malade: Answer affirmatively and give the time.
Infirmier(ère): Comment vous sentez-vous?
Malade: Say how you feel.
Infirmier(ère): Avez-vous de la fièvre?
Malade: Give your temperature.
Infirmier(ère): Où avez-vous mal?
Malade: Explain.
Infirmier(ère): Avez-vous d'autres symptômes?
Malade: Give at least two symptoms.
Infirmier(ère): Quelles maladies d'enfance avez-vous eues?
Malade: Mention two.
Infirmier(ère): Est-ce que vous avez été malade cet hiver?
Malade: Answer affirmatively and explain.
Infirmier(ère): Est-ce que vous prenez des médicaments?
Malade: Answer affirmatively and explain.
Infirmier(ère): Merci. Le médecin va vous examiner.

4 C'est vous le médecin!

Vous êtes médecin. Vos malades vous parlent de leurs problèmes. Dites-leur de ne pas s'inquiéter et expliquez-leur ce que vous allez faire. Puis, donnez-leur une ordonnance.

▶ **— Je me sens très faible.**
— Ne vous inquiétez pas.
Je vais vous prendre la tension.
Si c'est nécessaire, je vais vous faire une analyse de sang.
Voici une ordonnance.
Prenez ces cachets deux fois par jour.

- Je tousse tout le temps.
- J'ai de la fièvre.
- J'ai des boutons.
- J'ai des vertiges.
- J'ai des difficultés à respirer.
- J'ai des douleurs dans le dos.
- J'ai été mordu *(bitten)* par un chien.
- J'ai des palpitations *(rapid pulse)*.

Conversations libres

Avec votre partenaire, choisissez l'une des situations suivantes. Composez le dialogue correspondant et jouez-le en classe.

1 Zut alors!

Vous voyagez en France. Un jour vous vous réveillez avec un malaise généralisé et des boutons sur la figure. Vous téléphonez au médecin qui vous demande des détails.

Rôles: le/la touriste, le médecin

2 Un(e) malade imaginaire

Ce matin, il y a un examen de maths très important que vous n'avez pas préparé. Vous allez voir l'infirmier(ère) de l'école. Vous lui expliquez que vous êtes très malade. (Inventez des symptômes pour cette maladie imaginaire.) L'infirmier(ère) a des doutes sur votre maladie.

Rôles: l'élève, l'infirmier(ère)

3 Histoire médicale

Vous êtes infirmier(ère) dans une école française. Vous interviewez un(e) candidat(e) pour l'équipe de foot. Posez-lui des questions sur son état général, par exemple . . .

- s'il (si elle) a des problèmes de santé
- s'il (si elle) a mal quelque part
- quelles maladies d'enfance il(elle) a eues
- s'il (si elle) a été malade cet hiver
- s'il (si elle) prend des médicaments, etc.

Rôles: l'infirmier(ère), l'athlète

4 Une cure miracle

Un charlatan prétend avoir inventé une cure miracle pour toutes sortes de maladies. Un journaliste très incrédule lui pose des questions.

Rôles: le charlatan, le journaliste

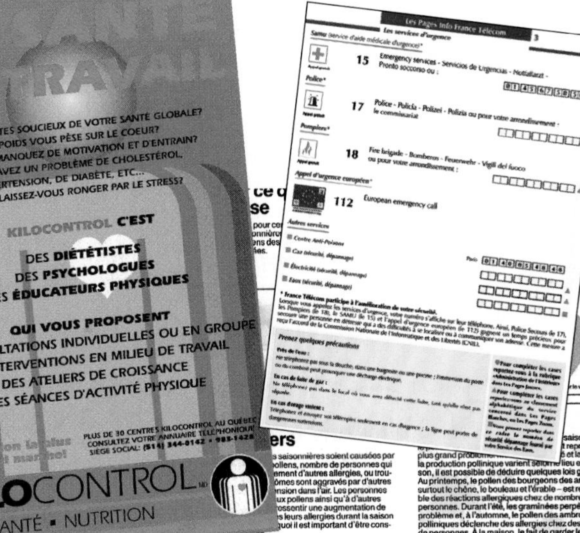

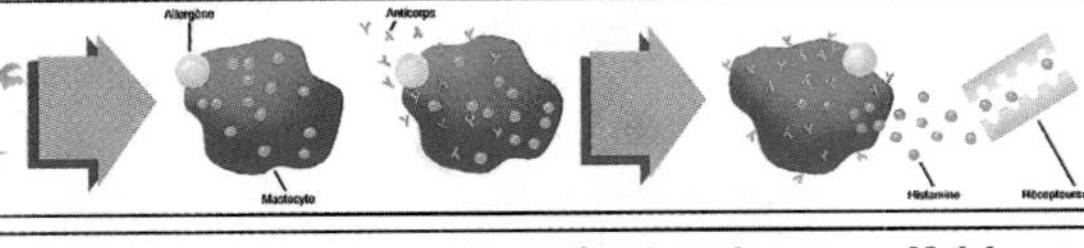

Si vous souffrez d'allergies saisonnières, voici ce que vous devriez savoir...

Animaux

Poussière de maison

Moisissures

■ **Additional Topic**

À L'INFIRMERIE

Vous êtes infirmier(-ère) dans une colonie de vacances. Un matin, un(e) enfant vient vous voir avec des symptômes étranges. Faites-lui un examen complet.

Realia Notes

- **la moisissure** *mould*
- **avoir de l'entrain** *to be full of life*
- **Kirkland** is a city located south of Montréal.
- **Lac Saint-Louis** is a lake south of Montreal.

Note culturelle

Le caducée is the universal symbol of the medical profession. This ancient symbol represents a snake wrapping itself around a staff, topped by "the mirror of Prudence." In mythology, both Hermes and Mercury carried a **caducée**. Today, every French doctor has this symbol on the windshield of his car, as a sign of his profession.

■ **Notes linguistiques**

- **La clinique** is generally a privately owned hospital. **L'hôpital** is public.
- **Le diététiste** (*dietician*—Canada) is called **le diététicien** in France.
- **L'éducateur physique** *physical therapist*

LANGUE ET COMMUNICATION

TEACHING RESOURCES

Student Activities Manual, pp. 69–70, 146–147

Audio Program, CD 7, Tracks 5–8

HM ClassPrep CD, Audioscript, Unit 7

■ Proverbe

Il faut qu'une porte soit ouverte ou fermée. *(There can be no middle ground.)*

A. Le concept du subjonctif: temps et modes

When we use verbs, we use them in a certain TENSE and a certain MOOD.

- The TENSE of a verb indicates when the action takes place.
  The PRESENT, the PASSÉ COMPOSÉ, the IMPERFECT and the FUTURE are tenses.
- The MOOD reflects the attitude of the speaker or the subject toward the action.
  The INDICATIVE and the SUBJUNCTIVE are moods.

The INDICATIVE MOOD is *objective.*
It is used to describe *facts.* It states what is considered to be *certain.*
It is the mood of *what is.*

The SUBJUNCTIVE MOOD is *subjective.*
It is used to express *feelings, judgments,* and *emotions* relating to an action.
It states what is considered to be *desirable, possible, doubtful,* or *uncertain.*
It is the mood of *what may or might be.*

➡ Although the subjunctive is rarely used in English, it is a mood frequently used in French. Compare the moods in the following sentences:

(fact)	Je sais que tu **es** généreux.	*I know that you* **are** *generous.*
(wish)	Je souhaite que tu **sois** plus patient avec moi.	*I wish that you* **were** *more patient with me.*

Both the indicative and the subjunctive may occur in a dependent clause introduced by **que**. The choice between the indicative and the subjunctive depends on what the subject or speaker expresses in the main clause.

MAIN CLAUSE (the subject expresses . . .)	DEPENDENT CLAUSE
• a **fact**, a **belief**	→ INDICATIVE
• a **wish**, a **necessity**, an **obligation** • an **emotion** or **feeling** • a **doubt** or **possibility**	→ SUBJUNCTIVE

Le subjonctif:
formation régulière
formation irrégulière

Révision ▶ pp. R19, R21; R23-31

Je sais que tu as une belle moto.
J'aimerais mieux que tu aies une voiture de sport!
BROM BROM

Chez le médecin

Vous êtes médecin. Choisissez un patient et dites ce qu'il doit faire et ne pas faire.

	PATIENTS	ACTIVITÉS	
il faut que	tu	faire du sport	manger trop
il ne faut pas que	vous	aller à la piscine	manger des produits naturels
	M. Marcoux	être déprimé(e)	boire de l'eau minérale
	Mme Lenoir	être nerveux(se)	prendre ces médicaments
	ces enfants	être optimiste	se coucher tard
	ces malades	avoir trop de tension	se reposer
		avoir peur de la piqûre	se soigner

B. Les verbes **croire** et **craindre**

	croire *(to believe)*		**craindre** *(to fear, to be afraid of)*	
PRÉSENT	je **crois**	nous **croyons**	je **crains**	nous **craignons**
	tu **crois**	vous **croyez**	tu **crains**	vous **craignez**
	il/elle/on **croit**	ils/elles **croient**	il/elle/on **craint**	ils/elles **craignent**
PASSÉ COMPOSÉ	j'**ai cru**		j'**ai craint**	

Verbes conjugués comme **craindre:**

plaindre *(to be sorry for)*
se plaindre de *(to complain about)*
peindre *(to paint)*
éteindre *(to turn off, to extinguish)*

Teaching Notes

This is a review of **croire.** **Craindre** is a new verb. **Atteindre** (*to reach*) is conjugated like **craindre.**

Les alpinistes **atteignent** le sommet de la montagne.

Also conjugated like **craindre: contraindre** *to force (someone to do something)*

2 Vive la différence!

Chacun fait des choses différentes. Exprimez cela en faisant les substitutions suggérées.

1. Jérôme se plaint de sa copine.
(les élèves - le professeur / le professeur - l'administration / toi - tout)
2. Isabelle croit à son horoscope.
(moi - l'avenir [*future*] / vous - l'amitié / Roméo et Juliette - l'amour éternel)
3. Marc peint un tableau *(picture)*.
(vous - la cuisine / moi - mon bureau / ces artistes - des portraits)
4. J'ai peint ma chambre en bleu.
(mes cousins - en jaune / vous - en gris / nous - en rouge)

Teaching Strategy

Give pairs of students the following scenarios:

Vous allez partir camper dans la forêt. Avant de partir, vous demandez à vos compagnons de voyage ce qu'ils craignent. Avec un partenaire, formez les questions et les réponses d'après les suggestions données.

Exemple: tu/les araignées? (non)

Est-ce que tu crains les araignées?
Non, je ne crains pas les araignées.

1. vous/les animaux sauvages (non)
2. Paul/les incendies de forêt (oui)
3. Ashley et Laura/les moustiques (oui)
4. toi/l'isolement (non)
5. vous/les disputes (non)
6. nous/les serpents (oui)

C. L'usage du subjonctif: émotions et sentiments

Note the use of the subjunctive in the following sentences.

Je suis content **que tu sois** en bonne santé.	*I am happy **that you are** in good health.*
Nous sommes tristes **que vous partiez.**	*We are sad **that you are leaving.***
Le médecin craint **que j'aie** les oreillons.	*The doctor fears **that I have** mumps.*

The SUBJUNCTIVE is used after a verb or expression of EMOTION (happiness, sadness, fear, surprise, anger, regret, . . .), when the emotion concerns someone or something *other than the subject.*

➡ When the emotion concerns the subject itself, an infinitive construction is used. Compare:

INFINITIVE	SUBJUNCTIVE
Je suis content d'**aller** en France. Alice a peur d'**être** malade.	Je suis content **que tu ailles** en France. Le médecin a peur **qu'Alice soit** malade.

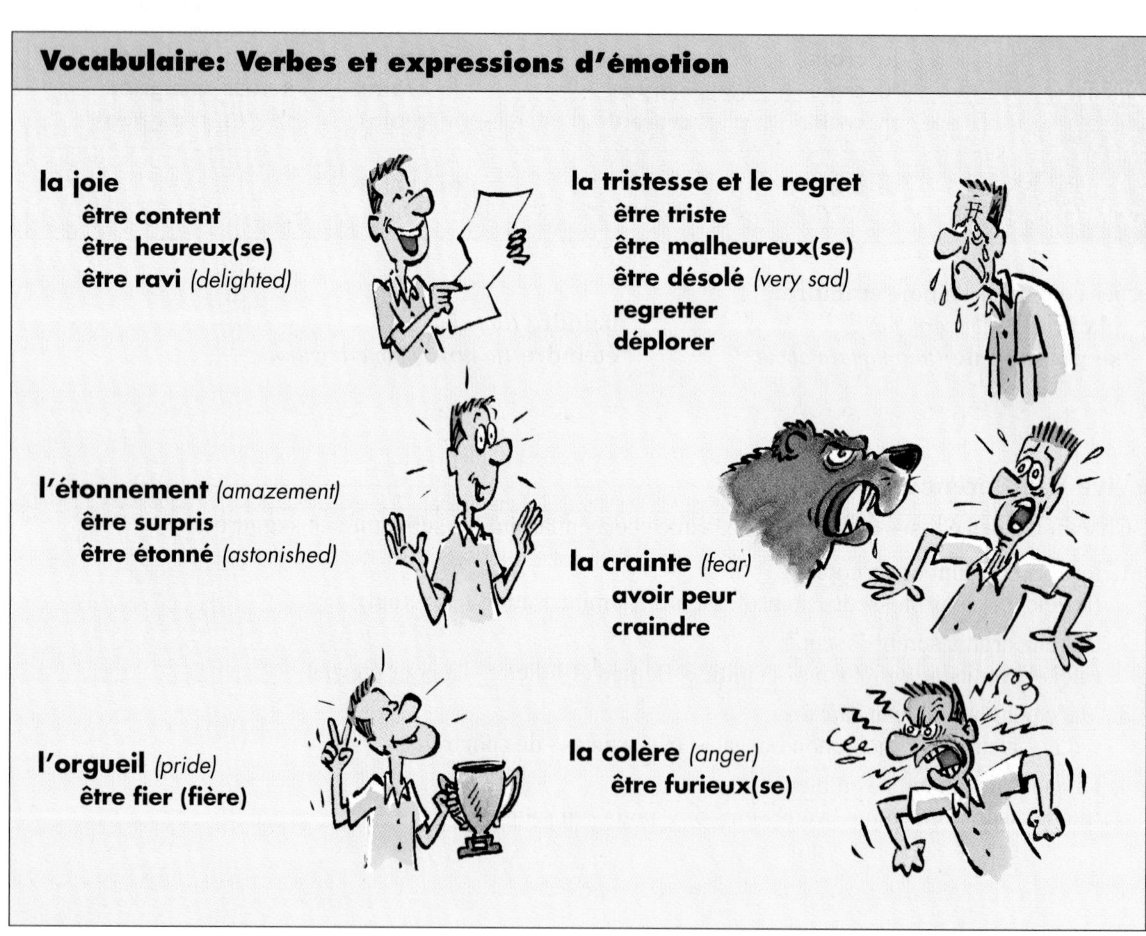

Vocabulaire: Verbes et expressions d'émotion
la joie
être content
être heureux(se)
être ravi (delighted)
la tristesse et le regret
être triste
être malheureux(se)
être désolé (very sad)
regretter
déplorer
l'étonnement (amazement)
être surpris
être étonné (astonished)
la crainte (fear)
avoir peur
craindre
l'orgueil (pride)
être fier (fière)
la colère (anger)
être furieux(se)

TEACHING RESOURCES

Student Activities Manual, pp. 71–72

■ Note linguistique

Some subjunctive forms have become word-phrases in French, e.g. **Soit!** *(So be it!)* or **Vive le roi!** *(Long live the King!).* **Note: vive** comes from the verb **vivre**. Agreement can be made or not, e.g. **Vive les vacances!** or: **Vivent les vacances!** *(Three cheers/ hooray for the holidays!)*

Supplementary vocabulary

le bonheur *(happiness)*
être enchanté
se réjouir

la honte *(shame)*
avoir honte
être gêné *(bothered)*
être embarrassé

la tristesse
être navré *(very sorry)*

l'émotion
être ému *(moved)*

■ Teaching Strategy

Tell students:
Pour chaque illustration de la page 272, exprimez ce qui arrive au personnage en utilisant une des expressions correspondantes et votre imagination! Exemples:
Il est content d'avoir une lettre.
Il est surpris d'entendre la nouvelle.

3 Consultations

Vous êtes médecin. Votre partenaire va décrire un symptôme. Vous allez exprimer votre diagnostic.

▶ **— Je tousse tout le temps.**
— J'ai peur que vous ayez une bronchite.

SYMPTÔMES	DIAGNOSTIC
• éternuer	• une allergie
• avoir mal au ventre	• une indigestion
• avoir très mal à la gorge	• une angine
• tousser tout le temps	• une bronchite
• avoir des boutons	• la grippe
• se sentir très faible	• la mononucléose
• avoir de la fièvre	• le rhume des foins *(hay fever)*
	• ??

4 Mes sentiments

Décrivez vos sentiments dans les circonstances suivantes.
Choisissez une des options entre parenthèses ou une option de votre choix.

▶ (heureux ou triste?) Mes copains vont en France cet été.
Je suis heureux/heureuse que mes copains aillent en France cet été.

1. content ou jaloux? (Mes cousins ont une voiture de sport.)
2. désolé ou surpris? (Mon frère ne dit pas la vérité.)
3. triste ou content? (Le professeur est malade aujourd'hui.)
4. furieux ou étonné? (Ma copine/mon copain ne vient pas au rendez-vous.)
5. content ou désolé? (L'examen de français est annulé.)
6. surpris ou fier? (L'équipe de baseball de l'école gagne le championnat.)

5 Leurs réactions

Décrivez les réactions des personnes suivantes aux situations entre parenthèses.
Utilisez une expression d'émotion du Vocabulaire.

▶ Alice (Son copain sort avec une autre fille.)
Alice est triste (furieuse) que son copain sorte avec une autre fille.

1. Thomas (Sa copine française écrit toutes les semaines.)
2. Le médecin (Monsieur Larose fait des exercices.)
3. Stéphanie (Marc vient à sa boum.)
4. Monsieur Dupont (Sa fille a le premier prix du conservatoire.)
5. Le professeur (Le mauvais élève réussit à l'examen.)
6. Nathalie (Jean-Pierre est en retard au rendez-vous.)
7. Catherine (Sa cousine oublie la date de son anniversaire.)
8. Les supporteurs *(fans)* (Leur équipe perd le match.)
9. Les écologistes (On fait des économies d'énergie.)

■ Notes linguistiques

- **Le conservatoire** est une école spécialisée où on apprend la musique, la danse et le théâtre.
- **Le supporteur**, ou **le supporter**, encourage (supporte) son équipe sportive favorite. **Le fan** est un admirateur enthousiaste de quelqu'un ou quelque chose.

Teaching Strategy

Presenting this mnemonic device is a good point of departure for quick reference on the subjunctive.

W	wishes	**J'aimerais que...Je voudrais que...**
E	emotions	**Je suis triste que...J'ai peur que...**
I	impersonal expressions	**Il faut que...Il est important que...**
R	relative clauses	**Nous cherchons un secrétaire qui sache taper.**
D	doubts	**Je doute que...Je ne pense pas que...**
O	orders	**J'exige que...J'ordonne que...**
S	superlatives	**C'est le meilleur restaurant que je connaisse.**

TEACHING RESOURCES

Student Activities Manual, pp. 73

D. Le subjonctif après les expressions de doute

Compare the use of the INDICATIVE and the SUBJUNCTIVE in the sentences below.

CERTAINTY OR BELIEF (INDICATIVE)	DOUBT, DISBELIEF OR UNCERTAINTY (SUBJUNCTIVE)
Je crois que tu **es** fatigué.	Je doute que tu **sois** malade.
Le médecin pense que **j'ai** la grippe.	Il ne pense pas que **j'aie** la mononucléose.
Il est sûr qu'Alice **est** trop pâle.	Il n'est pas sûr qu'elle **soit** déprimée.
Tu crois que tu **es** très intelligent!	Crois-tu que tu **sois** sympathique?

The INDICATIVE is used after verbs and expressions of CERTAINTY or BELIEF.
The SUBJUNCTIVE is used after verbs and expressions of DOUBT and UNCERTAINTY.

➡ Verbs like **croire, penser, être sûr, être certain,** and expressions like **il est sûr, il est certain,** are used to convey belief, knowledge, or conviction of certain facts.

- When used in the AFFIRMATIVE, they are followed by the INDICATIVE.
- When used in the INTERROGATIVE or the NEGATIVE, however, these verbs and expressions may convey an element of doubt or uncertainty. In this case they are followed by the SUBJUNCTIVE.

ALLONS PLUS LOIN

Depending on the level of certainty or doubt that the speaker wants to convey, certain expressions may be followed by the indicative OR the subjunctive.
Compare:

Il semble que tu **as** raison.	*It seems that you are right.* (This is pretty sure.)
Il semble que tu **aies** raison.	*It would seem that you are right.* (It is much less sure.)

Teaching Strategy

Tell the students about various problems that you or someone you know is having at home, at school, with their children, etc. Ask the students to make suggestions to solve the problems. Each sentence/suggestion should use an expression that necessitates the subjunctive. You may also give situations concerning cruel or kind things that someone did to you and ask them to use the subjunctive expressions to explain their feelings about this person.

Vocabulaire: Verbes et expressions de certitude et de doute

EXPRESSIONS DE CERTITUDE (+ INDICATIF)	EXPRESSIONS DE DOUTE (+ SUBJONCTIF)
je sais que . . . **je dis que . . .**	**je doute que . . .**
je crois que . . .	**je ne crois pas que . . .** **crois-tu que . . . ?**
je pense que . . .	**je ne pense pas que . . .** **penses-tu que . . . ?**
je suis sûr(e) que . . .	**je ne suis pas sûr(e) que . . .** **es-tu sûr(e) que . . . ?**
il est sûr / vrai / certain que . . .	**il n'est pas sûr / vrai / certain que . . .** **est-il sûr / vrai / certain que . . . ?**
il est clair que . . . **il est probable que . . .** **il est évident que . . .**	**il est douteux que . . .** **il est possible que . . .** **il est impossible que . . .**

■ Teaching Note

Autres expressions de certitude:

Je suis convaincu(e)
Je suis persuadé(e).

6 L'optimiste et le pessimiste

L'optimiste voit l'existence sous un aspect positif. Le pessimiste voit l'existence sous un aspect négatif. Avec votre partenaire, jouez le rôle de l'optimiste et du pessimiste.

Je crois que la vie est belle.
Je doute que la vie soit belle.

▶ la vie / être belle

1. les gens / être généreux
2. les jeunes / avoir un idéal
3. les parents / faire le maximum pour aider leurs enfants
4. la situation économique / être excellente
5. on / faire des progrès dans tous les domaines
6. les journalistes / dire la vérité
7. le président / être honnête avec le public
8. le monde / être moins dangereux qu'avant
9. on / découvrir prochainement *(soon)* une cure contre le SIDA *(AIDS)*

■ Note linguistique

Un optimiste voit la vie en rose. Un pessimiste voit tout en noir.

Note culturelle

SIDA is an acronym for **Syndrome Immunodéficitaire Acquis**. If appropriate, you may mention that it was a French scientist, Professor Montagnier of the Institut Pasteur, who was the first to isolate HIV, the virus causing **SIDA** (also: **VIH, virus d'immuno-déficience humaine**).

7 Êtes-vous d'accord?

Voici quelques propositions. Choisissez une proposition et exprimez votre opinion sur ce sujet. Pour cela, utilisez l'une des expressions du vocabulaire. Si possible, illustrez votre opinion en formulant une réflexion personnelle.

▶ la majorité des gens / être superstitieux?
Je ne pense pas que la majorité des gens soient superstitieux. Moi, par exemple, je n'hésite pas à voyager le vendredi 13.

1. l'argent / faire le bonheur?
2. les gens / être fondamentalement honnêtes?
3. les gens idéalistes / être naïfs?
4. la liberté / être un mythe?
5. les femmes / avoir les mêmes responsabilités que les hommes?
6. les extraterrestres / exister?
7. il / être facile de changer son destin?
8. il / être possible d'éliminer la violence dans la société?
9. tout le monde / avoir les mêmes choses?

Teaching Strategy

Using Activity 7 as a base, divide the class into pairs and have each partner express a different opinion. Add the following as expansion scenarios:

- nous/être plus heureux qu'il y a cent ans?
- le président/être concerné par les problèmes des jeunes?
- nous/faire assez d'efforts pour assurer la paix dans le monde?
- le professeur de français/avoir des problèmes avec sa classe?
- toi/vouloir habiter à l'étranger?

INFO MAGAZINE

Theme: Humanitarian aid
Reading Strategy: Reading for information

Notes culturelles

Médecins sans Frontières was awarded the international Nobel Peace Prize in Oslo, Norway on October 15, 1999. This award honors the organization's relief workers who provide medical and humanitarian assistance in more than 80 countries worldwide.

Irregular Verbs
(see Appendix C)
obtenir (*see* **tenir**)
souffrir (*see* **ouvrir**)
vivre

Les médecins et l'action humanitaire

Nathalie, 27 ans, vient d'obtenir° son diplôme de médecin. Dans quelques semaines elle va partir pour l'Afghanistan. Hélène, une infirmière de 35 ans, rentre de Thaïlande où elle a passé dix mois dans les camps de réfugiés. Emmanuel, 25 ans, n'a pas de spécialité médicale, mais il a passé deux ans au Bangladesh avec «Médecins sans frontières.»° Nathalie, Hélène, Emmanuel: trois exemples parmi° des milliers de Français qui ont décidé de faire quelque chose pour les oubliés° de la terre.°

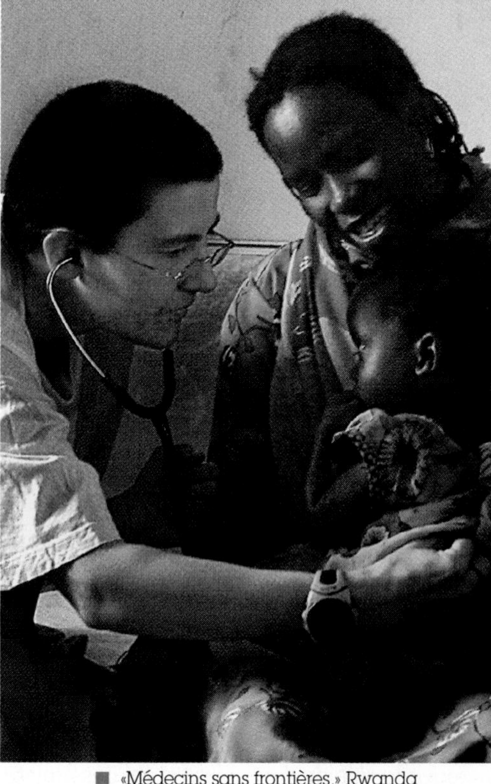

«Médecins sans frontières,» Rwanda

Nathalie explique: «Comme médecins, notre premier rôle est d'aider les gens qui sont dans la détresse. Aujourd'hui, la détresse humaine existe partout° dans le monde, et spécialement dans les pays du tiers-monde° où des centaines de milliers de gens souffrent° de la misère, de la faim et de la maladie. Dans ces pays, les catastrophes naturelles, les épidémies, la guerre° civile font des millions de victimes chaque année. Nous autres° citoyens° des pays dits *civilisés,* nous ne pouvons pas rester insensibles° au sort° de ces êtres° humains qui sont nos frères et nos soeurs. Nous devons agir.° Malheureusement, les besoins sont immenses et nos ressources très limitées. Nous sommes là non seulement pour soigner les gens, mais pour leur redonner° l'envie° de vivre.»°

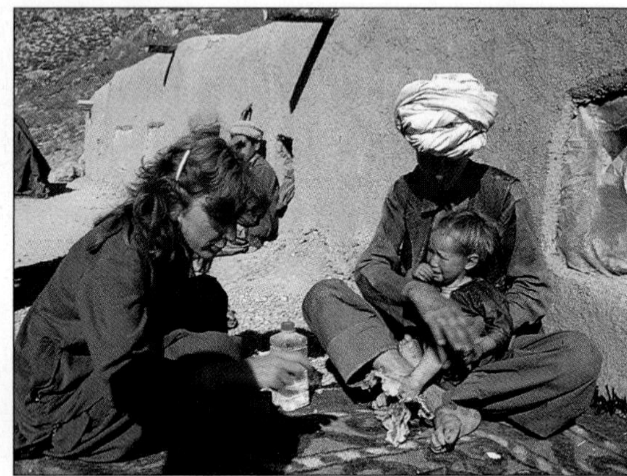

Les organisations comme «Médecins du monde,» «Les Médecins aux pieds nus,» et «Médecins sans frontières» envoient des volontaires dans les régions où il y a une urgence médicale.

Plusieurs organisations ont été créées en France pour répondre aux besoins de santé des pays du tiers-monde. Ces organisations envoient des volontaires dans des régions où il y a une urgence médicale, et plus spécialement dans des pays d'Afrique et d'Asie: en Éthiopie, en Somalie et au Libéria, au Pakistan, au Cambodge, par exemple.

obtenir ❊ *to get, obtain* **frontières** *borders* **parmi** *among* **les oubliés** *forgotten people* **la terre** *earth* **partout** *everywhere* **tiers-monde** *third world* **souffrir** ❊ *to suffer* **la guerre** *war* **autres** *others* **citoyens** *citizens* **insensibles** *insensitive* **au sort** *fate* **êtres** *beings* **agir** *to act* **pour leur redonner** *to give back (to them)* **l'envie** *desire* **vivre** ❊ *to live*

Teaching Strategy

Ask students to scan the article and illustrations and guess the main theme. Then ask each student to list five ways they would *personally* choose to help those less fortunate than themselves.

Pour être volontaire, il n'est pas nécessaire d'être médecin ou infirmier. Il suffit° d'être une personne de bonne volonté° et de croire à la solidarité des peuples de la terre. Les organisations les plus connues sont «Médecins sans frontières» qui intervient° dans plus de 80 pays, «Médecins du monde» qui a 6000 volontaires dans 40 pays, et «Les Médecins aux pieds nus.»° L'originalité de cette dernière organisation est d'utiliser des médicaments d'origine végétale ou animale et les techniques traditionnelles des pays d'intervention, comme par exemple, l'acupuncture dans les pays d'Asie.

DÉFINITIONS

Définissez les mots ou expressions suivants. (Quand c'est possible, donnez des exemples.)

- un(e) volontaire
- la bonne volonté
- une épidémie
- la solidarité
- un(e) réfugié(e)
- l'action humanitaire
- les pays du tiers-monde
- une catastrophe naturelle
- la guerre civile

EXPRESSION ÉCRITE

1. Imaginez que vous voulez être volontaire pour l'une des organisations mentionnées dans le texte. Écrivez une courte lettre où vous expliquez ...
   - pourquoi l'action humanitaire vous intéresse
   - dans quel pays vous voudriez aller et pourquoi
   - ce que vous voulez faire pour aider les gens de ce pays
2. Imaginez que vous collectez des fonds pour "Médecins Sans Frontières." Dans une lettre à un ami, vous décrivez cette organisation.

"Médecins Sans Frontières" — une organisation humanitaire mondiale

Malgré° le progrès scientifique, le monde moderne n'échappe° pas aux catastrophes humaines et naturelles de toutes sortes: guerres,° révolutions, tremblements de terre,° inondations,° famines, épidémies... Ces catastrophes n'ont pas de frontières, mais elles affectent généralement les pays les plus pauvres et créent des urgences médicales pour les populations les plus vulnérables: enfants, femmes et personnes âgées. Pour répondre à ces urgences, il faut agir° rapidement et indépendamment de toute considération politique.

Dans ce but,° un groupe de médecins français a créé en 1971 une organisation qui a pour mission d'envoyer des volontaires partout° où les populations sont en danger. Cette organisation, appelée "Médecins Sans Frontières," est maintenant une organisation internationale. Chaque année, 2500 volontaires—médecins, chirurgiens, infirmiers—partent en mission à travers° le monde. Leur but est non seulement d'apporter une aide médicale à ceux qui en ont besoin, mais aussi de faire respecter la dignité humaine. Présents sur tous les continents, les "Médecins Sans Frontières" sont intervenus en Somalie, en Éthiopie, au Kosovo, au Congo, en Afghanistan, en Palestine... Pour son travail humanitaire, cette organisation a reçu le prix° Nobel de la Paix° en 1999.

il suffit = il est suffisant **volonté** *will* **intervenir** ⁂ *to intervene* **pieds nus** *bare feet* **malgré** *in spite of* **échappe (à)** *escapes (from)* **guerres** *wars* **tremblements de terre** *earthquakes* **inondations** *floods* **agir** *to act* **dans ce but** *to this end* **partout** *everywhere* **à travers** *across* **prix** *prize* **paix** *peace*

INFO MAGAZINE INFO MAGAZINE INFO MAGAZINE INFO MAGAZINE INFO MAGAZI

Teaching Note

The **Définitions** activity encourages students to paraphrase. With open-ended activities of this kind, you may wish to encourage students to consult a monolingual dictionary (e.g., *Le Petit Robert* series). These dictionaries motivate students to "think in French" and serve as a useful vehicle to improve their overall proficiency/fluency.

■ Expansion

Imaginez que vous êtes membre du comité qui décerne le Prix Nobel de la Paix. Votre candidat pour ce prix est le docteur Kouchner. Expliquez aux autres membres du comité (les élèves de la classe) pourquoi vous l'avez choisi.

■ Irregular Verb

(see Appendix C)
intervenir (*see* **venir**)

■ Notes Culturelles

- The doctors of **Médecins sans Frontières** and **Médecins du Monde** are sometimes referred to as "the French doctors" since the French created this type of humanitarian aid.
- It takes about eight years of study in France to become a doctor. Doctors who go on missions with **Médecins sans Frontières** are all volunteers. They may volunteer for three months, six months, or two years, depending on their commitment. After three months, they receive a small stipend.

LE FRANÇAIS PRATIQUE

TEACHING RESOURCES

Student Activities Manual, pp. 148–150

Tête-à-tête Activity, Chez le médecin, p. PA8

Audio Program, CD 7, Tracks 9–13

HM ClassPrep CD, Audioscript, Unit 7

LE FRANÇAIS PRATIQUE

Accidents et soins dentaires

À l'hôpital

Cette personne est **blessée** *(injured, hurt)*.
Elle vient de **se blesser** *(to get hurt)*.
Elle s'est cassé le bras.

se blesser à la tête	**se casser** *(to break)* **la jambe**
se couper *(to cut)* **à la main**	**se fracturer l'épaule**
se brûler *to get burned*	**se fouler** *(to twist)* **la cheville** *ankle*

L'infirmier(ère) va lui **faire une radio** *(x-ray)*.

faire un plâtre *cast*	**faire un pansement** *bandage*
donner des béquilles *crutches*	**mettre des sutures** *stitches*

1 Créa-dialogue: Qu'est-ce qui est arrivé?

Vous rencontrez les personnes suivantes. Avec votre partenaire choisissez l'une des illustrations. Composez le dialogue correspondant et jouez-le en classe. Utilisez votre imagination pour expliquer l'accident!

— Eh Antoine, ça va?
— Hm, comme ci comme ça.
— Pourquoi est-ce que tu as un plâtre?
— Je me suis cassé le bras.
— Comment est-ce que c'est arrivé?
— Eh bien, voilà. Je faisais de l'alpinisme samedi dernier et je suis tombé.

Teaching Strategy: Warm-Up

Have the class write a group story. Each student will contribute at least two sentences. Tell them that the story is to take place in the emergency room of the local hospital. You might want to give them the first sentences: **«L'autre jour, Raoul est allé à l'hôpital. Il est tombé dans l'escalier.»** Have them include dialog in the story, as much vocabulary as possible and a minimum of four verbs in the subjunctive

Chez le dentiste

—Oh là là, j'ai **mal aux dents**.
Vous avez **une carie** *(cavity)*.
Je vais vous | faire **un plombage** *(filling)*.
faire **une piqûre de novocaïne**.
enlever *(to remove)* | **cette dent.**
cette dent de sagesse *(wisdom tooth)*.

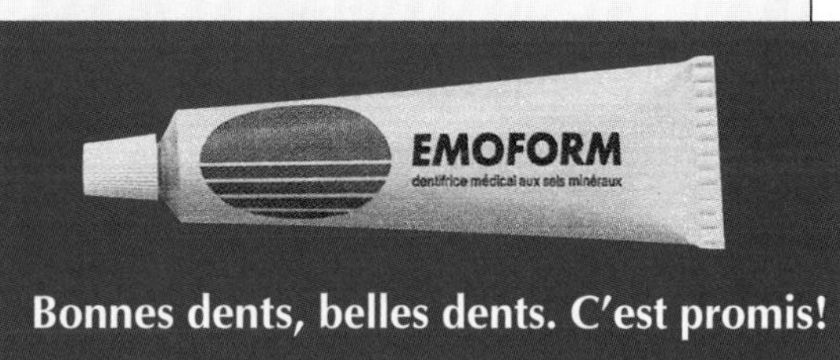

EMOFORM
dentifrice médical aux sels minéraux
Bonnes dents, belles dents. C'est promis!

2 Chez le dentiste

Avec votre partenaire, composez le dialogue suivant entre le/la dentiste et le/la patient(e).

Dentiste: *Ask the patient what's wrong.*
Patient: *Say that you have a toothache.*
Dentiste: *Ask patient to open his/her mouth.*
Say that the patient has a cavity and explain what you are going to do.
Patient: *Ask if it is going to hurt.*
Dentiste: *Say no, and tell your patient that you will give him/her a shot of novocain.*
Patient: *Say that you are not feeling well . . . and then faint.*

Conversations libres

Avec votre partenaire, choisissez l'une des situations suivantes. Composez le dialogue correspondant et jouez-le en classe.

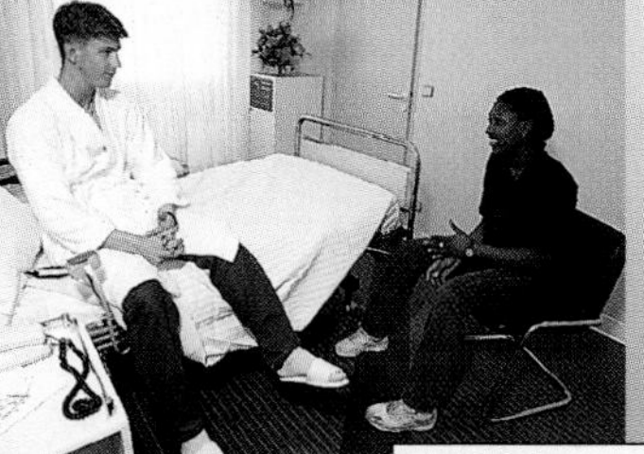

1 Accident de moto

Xavier a eu un accident de moto. Le lendemain, son amie Florence lui rend visite à l'hôpital et lui pose des questions. Xavier explique ce qui est arrivé et ce que le médecin a fait.

Rôles: Xavier, Florence

2 Visite chez le dentiste

Le petit Pierre (6 ans) a mal aux dents. Sa mère pense qu'il a probablement une carie et veut l'emmener chez le dentiste. Pierre a peur, et sa mère essaie de le rassurer en expliquant ce que le dentiste va faire. Pierre n'est pas du tout rassuré.

Rôles: la mère, Pierre

Supplementary vocabulary

se tordre le poignet *to sprain one's wrist*
avoir une entorse *to have a sprain*
boîter *to limp*
le service des urgences *emergency room*
le brancard *stretcher*
le brancardier *stretcher-bearer*

■ Notes linguistiques

- **plâtrer**—Le médecin m'a plâtré le poignet.
- **marcher avec des béquilles**
- **suturer (une plaie)** *to stitch (a cut)*

Supplementary vocabulary

nettoyer les dents *to clean one's teeth*
arracher une dent *to pull a tooth*
mettre un appareil dentaire *to put on braces*
s'évanouir *to faint*

LANGUE ET COMMUNICATION

TEACHING RESOURCES

Student Activities Manual, pp. 74–76, 150

Audio Program, CD 7, Track 14

HM ClassPrep CD, Audioscript, Unit 7

Teaching Strategy

You may want to review the agreement of the past participle:

- Verb conjugated with **avoir** → Agreement with preceding direct object (if any):
  Karine **a fait** du ski.
  La pierre? Elle ne l'**a** pas **vue.**
- Verb conjugated with **être** → Agreement with subject:
  Elle **est tombée.**
- Reflexive verb → Agreement with reflexive pronoun (= subject) when it is a direct object:
  Elle **s'est blessée.**
  Elle **s'est cassé la jambe.**

A. Le passé du subjonctif

FORMS

The past subjunctive is a compound tense formed according to the pattern:

present subjunctive of **avoir** or **être** + past participle

parler	aller	s'amuser
que j'**aie parlé**	que je **sois allé(e)**	que je me **sois amusé(e)**
que tu **aies parlé**	que tu **sois allé(e)**	que tu te **sois amusé(e)**
qu'il **ait parlé**	qu'il **soit allé**	qu'il se **soit amusé**
qu'elle **ait parlé**	qu'elle **soit allée**	qu'elle se **soit amusée**
que nous **ayons parlé**	que nous **soyons allé(e)s**	que nous nous **soyons amusé(e)s**
que vous **ayez parlé**	que vous **soyez allé(e)(s)**	que vous vous **soyez amusé(e)(s)**
qu'ils **aient parlé**	qu'ils **soient allés**	qu'ils se **soient amusés**
qu'elles **aient parlé**	qu'elles **soient allées**	qu'elles se **soient amusées**

➡ The agreement of the past participle in compound tenses also applies to the past subjunctive.

Je suis content que tu **aies téléphoné** à ces filles.

Je suis heureux que tu les **aies invitées** à la boum.

USES

Compare the use of the present and the past subjunctive.

Je doute que Paul **téléphone** ce soir.	*I doubt that Paul* ***will call*** *tonight.*
Je doute qu'il **ait téléphoné** hier.	*I doubt that he* ***called*** *yesterday.*
Je regrette que vous **ne veniez pas** cet après-midi.	*I am sorry that you* ***are not coming*** *this afternoon.*
Je regrette que vous **ne soyez pas venu** samedi.	*I am sorry that you* ***did not come*** *on Saturday.*

The past subjunctive is used instead of the present subjunctive to refer to past events or situations.

1 Drôles d'excuses!

Votre partenaire n'est pas venu(e) à une répétition *(rehearsal)* de la chorale samedi dernier. Il/elle va choisir une (mauvaise!) excuse. Vous êtes le directeur/la directrice et vous avez des doutes.

▶ **— Je ne suis pas venu(e) à la répétition parce que j'ai raté le bus.**
— Ah oui? Écoute, Christophe, je doute que tu aies raté le bus.

EXCUSES

- J'ai eu la grippe.
- Je me suis foulé la cheville.
- Je suis tombé(e) dans les escaliers.
- Je suis allé(e) chez le dentiste.
- J'ai raté *(missed)* le bus.
- Le bus a eu un accident.
- Mon réveil *(alarm clock)* n'a pas sonné.
- Ma cousine s'est mariée.
- Mon arrière-grand-mère est morte.

Teaching Strategy

Tell the students which you will be drilling first: past or present. Then show them the hand signals you'll be using to represent **je.../tu.../il.../elle.../nous.../vous.../ils.../elles...: Je** (point 1 finger at yourself) **Tu** (point 1 finger to the right) **Elle** (point 1 finger to the left) **Nous** (point 2 fingers at yourself) **Vous** (point 2 fingers at them) **Ils** (point 2 fingers to the right) **Elles** (point 2 fingers to the left). Give them a verb, then begin doing the hand signals so that they give you the verb in the present/past subjective for the subject indicated. Start out slowly, with few verb changes, doing the pronouns in order. As they (and you) get better at it, speed up, switch verbs frequently and mix up the order.

Réactions!

Votre partenaire va décrire un événement (imaginaire) qui lui est arrivé. Exprimez votre réaction. Pour cela, choisissez une expression de la page 272.

ÉVÉNEMENTS

- mon oncle / avoir un accident
- ma cousine / se marier
- mon copain / voir un OVNI *(UFO)*
- ma grande soeur / gagner une bourse *(scholarship)* pour l'université
- ma grand-mère / se casser le bras
- ma copine / oublier la date de mon anniversaire
- mes parents / rencontrer le président des États-Unis
- ma tante / m'acheter une voiture de sport

RÉACTIONS

joie?
tristesse?
surprise?
doute?

▶ **—Ma tante m'a acheté une voiture de sport!**
—Ah oui? Écoute, je doute qu'elle t'ait acheté une voiture de sport.
(Eh bien, bravo! Je suis ravi(e) qu'elle t'ait acheté une voiture de sport.)

3 Ce qu'ils pensent

Décrivez ce que pensent les personnes suivantes.

▶ l'infirmière / craindre / tu / te fouler la cheville.
L'infirmière craint que tu te sois foulé la cheville.

1. le médecin / ne pas croire / je / me casser la jambe.
2. je / être content / tu / venir à la boum
3. Pauline / être heureuse / Jérôme / lui écrire une lettre
4. vous / être surpris / l'équipe / gagner le match
5. le guide / avoir peur / les alpinistes *(mountain climbers)* / se perdre dans la montagne
6. le professeur / douter / vous / faire vos devoirs
7. Madame Dumont / être fière / sa fille / réussir à l'examen d'ingénieur

4 Les mystères de l'univers

Beaucoup de mystères n'ont pas été élucidés *(cleared up)*. Avec votre partenaire, choisissez un des sujets suivants et discutez-le. Exprimez votre opinion en utilisant une expression de doute ou de certitude, et le passé du subjonctif ou le passé composé de l'indicatif.

▶ les Vikings / découvrir l'Amérique?
Je doute (je ne crois pas / il est douteux) que les Vikings aient découvert l'Amérique.
ou: **Je suis sûr(e) (il est probable) que les Vikings ont découvert l'Amérique.**

1. les Égyptiens / utiliser l'électricité?
2. Dracula / exister?
3. un écrivain inconnu *(unknown)* / écrire les pièces de Shakespeare?
4. des navigateurs romains / explorer l'Amérique du Sud?
5. des extraterrestres / venir sur la Terre?
6. des ingénieurs russes / inventer la bombe atomique?
7. un agent soviétique / assassiner le président Kennedy?

■ Language Note
OVNI is an acronym for **O**bjet **V**olant **N**on-**I**dentifié.

Teaching Strategy

You may wish to add the following information when using Activity 4 in class:

- Dracula is the main character of a novel created by British author Bram Stoker (1847–1912).
- Some people believe that Francis Bacon (1561–1626), a philosopher and essayist, wrote the plays attributed to Shakespeare.
- The first atomic bomb was designed in the U.S. by a team of American and exiled European scientists led by J. Robert Oppenheimer in 1945. It was called the Manhattan Project.
- President J.F. Kennedy was assassinated on November 22, 1963 in Dallas by Lee Harvey Oswald.

LECTURE

Reading STRATEGY

Reading fiction

LECTURE

En voyage

d'après Guy de Maupassant

AVANT DE LIRE

L'histoire que vous allez lire est racontée par un médecin au cours d'un voyage en train. Les autres passagers du compartiment où il se trouve ont déjà fait le récit d'aventures plus ou moins rocambolesques° dont ils sont évidemment les héros. Ces histoires ont un point commun: elles se passent toutes dans un train.

C'est maintenant le tour du médecin. L'histoire qu'il choisit de raconter est une histoire d'amour, l'amour simple et purement spirituel unissant un homme et une femme qui se sont rencontrés dans un train.

rocambolesques = avec beaucoup d'incidents extraordinaires

NOTE CULTURELLE

Guy de Maupassant (1850-1893) a écrit des romans et des pièces de théâtre, mais il est surtout célèbre pour les centaines de contes et nouvelles qu'il a publiés. Maupassant utilise un style clair, objectif et impersonnel. Il décrit avec précision les faits, laissant au lecteur le souci° de découvrir les sentiments qui animent les personnages de ses contes.

souci *care*

Le contexte historique

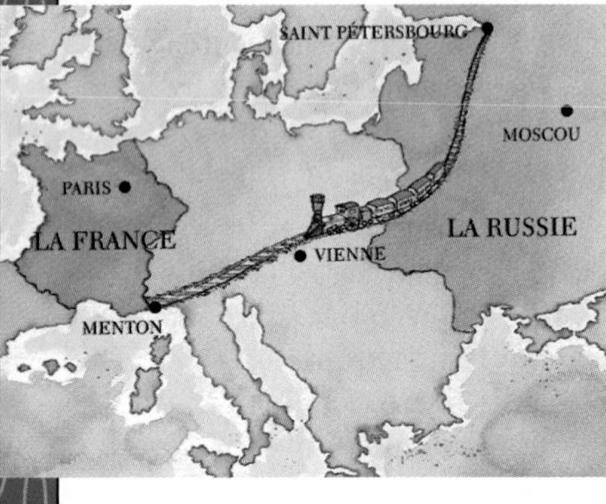

Pour comprendre une histoire, il faut la situer dans son contexte historique. L'action de l'histoire racontée par le médecin se passe à la fin du 19e siècle dans un train qui va de Russie jusqu'à la Côte d'Azur en France. Les voyages de ce genre étaient très longs. Ils étaient relativement sûrs,° mais de temps en temps les trains étaient attaqués par des bandits ou par des révolutionnaires, alors particulièrement actifs dans les pays de l'Europe de l'Est et surtout en Russie.

Parmi° les passagers du train, il y a une jeune femme mariée à un aristocrate russe. Très malade, elle va en France pour se soigner. Comme les gens riches de l'époque, elle est accompagnée de ses serviteurs et elle a réservé un wagon pour elle seule.

sûrs *safe* **parmi** *among*

Anticipons un peu!

Imaginez que vous êtes la jeune femme russe. Au cours du voyage, un homme fait irruption dans le compartiment où vous êtes seule. Il est très pâle, paraît confus et vous remarquez qu'il est blessé. Cet homme vous demande de l'aider.

Qu'est-ce que vous allez faire?
- tirer la sonnette d'alarme
- appeler vos serviteurs
- aider l'homme

À supposer que vous avez décidé d'aider cet homme, qu'est-ce que vous allez demander à cet homme de faire?
- se livrer à la police
- aller à l'hôpital
- ne jamais plus vous parler

Teaching Strategy

This story is longer and linguistically more sophisticated than the prior selections. To read it fluently, students need to be able to understand the **passé simple**. You may want to review this tense in Appendix C (pp. R32–R33).

Use the **Transparency Master L7** to help students retain important elements of the story. Use the *Anticipons un peu* activities to set the stage for the reading.

En Voyage

1

Le médecin commença ainsi son histoire:

«Moi, je n'ai pas d'aventure extraordinaire à vous raconter. Je vais seulement vous parler d'une jeune femme que j'ai connue, une de mes clientes, à qui il arriva la chose la plus singulière° du monde, et aussi la plus mystérieuse et la plus attendrissante.°

C'était une Russe, la comtesse Marie Baranow, une très grande dame, d'une exquise beauté. Vous savez comme les Russes peuvent être belles, avec leur nez fin, leur bouche délicate, leurs yeux d'une indéfinissable couleur, d'un bleu gris, et leur charme à la fois tendre et sévère, que les Français trouvent tellement séduisant.

La comtesse Marie souffrait depuis plusieurs années de tuberculose. Pour la soigner, son médecin, qui la savait très malade, voulait l'envoyer dans le sud de la France, mais elle refusait obstinément de quitter Saint Pétersbourg. Finalement, l'automne dernier, le docteur, réalisant la gravité de l'état° de sa patiente, parla à son mari qui ordonna à sa femme de partir pour Menton.

Résignée, elle prit le train. Elle était seule dans son wagon, ses gens de service° occupant un autre compartiment. Elle restait contre la portière, un peu triste, regardant passer les campagnes et les villages de la Russie. Elle se sentait bien isolée dans la vie, sans enfants, sans parents et avec un mari qui ne l'aimait plus et qui avait décidé de l'exiler à des milliers de kilomètres de son pays.

À chaque station, son serviteur Ivan venait voir si elle avait besoin de quelque chose. C'était un vieux domestique, totalement dévoué, à qui elle pouvait demander n'importe quoi.

singulière = étrange **attendrissante** *touching* **l'état** = la condition **gens de service** = domestiques

Mots utiles

la comtesse	*countess*
la portière	= la porte d'un train
souffrir *	*to suffer*
dévoué	*devoted*
exquis	*exquisite*
séduisant	*attractive*
à la fois	*at the same time*
n'importe quoi	*anything*

Notes culturelles

La tuberculose. La tuberculose est une maladie très grave qui attaque les poumons.° Au 19e siècle, c'était une maladie très commune et, comme il n'y avait pas de vaccin et pas d'antibiotiques, elle était généralement mortelle. Pour se soigner, les gens riches allaient dans les régions où l'air était pur et le climat sain°: dans les Alpes, par exemple, ou sur la Côte d'Azur.

Saint Pétersbourg. Saint Pétersbourg, ou Pétersbourg, était la capitale de la Russie impériale. C'était là que les tsars et les aristocrates russes avaient leurs palais.°

Menton et la Côte d'Azur. Menton est une petite ville très pittoresque située sur la Côte d'Azur ou Riviera française. Aujourd'hui, cette région attire° des millions de touristes chaque année. Au siècle dernier, les seuls visiteurs étaient des familles anglaises et des aristocrates russes qui venaient là à cause du climat. Dans le cimetière de Menton, on peut voir encore aujourd'hui de nombreuses tombes aux inscriptions russes.

poumons *lungs* **sain** *healthy* **palais** *palaces* **attire** *attracts*

Avez-vous compris?

1. Qu'est-ce que le médecin pense des femmes russes?
2. Quelle était la maladie de la comtesse?
3. Qu'est-ce que son docteur en Russie voulait qu'elle fasse?
4. Avec qui a-t-elle fait le voyage?
5. Quels étaient les sentiments de la comtesse quand elle était dans le train?
6. Est-ce qu'elle avait une vie familiale intéressante? Expliquez.

Anticipons un peu!

Quelque chose de dramatique va arriver dans la scène suivante. Selon vous, qu'est-ce qui va se passer?

■ Note linguistique

The adjective **rocambolesque** comes from **Rocambole**. Rocambole was the hero of a popular series of more than thirty novels written by Ponson du Terrail (1829–1871).

■ Additional Information

Other works by Maupassant include:

Boule-de-Suif
Le Horla
Bel-Ami
Contes du jour et de la nuit

■ Irregular Verb

(see Appendix C)
souffrir (*see* **ouvrir**)

Supplementary vocabulary

la locomotive à vapeur *steam engine*

■ *Avez-vous compris?*

(Sample answers)

1. Il pense qu'elles sont très belles.
2. La comtesse avait la tuberculose.
3. Il voulait l'envoyer se soigner dans le sud de la France.
4. Elle a fait le voyage avec des serviteurs.
5. Elle était triste, elle se sentait seule.
6. Elle n'avait pas une vie familiale intéressante: elle n'avait plus de parents, elle n'avait pas d'enfants, et elle pensait que son mari ne l'aimait plus.

Notes culturelles

- Saint Petersburg was renamed Petrograd in 1914 before becoming Leningrad in 1924. Saint Petersburg is 2143 km (1331 miles) away from Paris, France.
- France and Russia became allies in 1881. Russia needed French funds, and France was hoping that, with the help of Russia, it would win back Alsace and Lorraine from Germany.
- Chopin, Musset, Molière, and Kafka died of tuberculosis.

2

La nuit commençait à tomber. Le train allait maintenant très vite. Très énervée,° la comtesse ne pouvait pas dormir. Elle eut alors l'idée de compter l'argent que son mari lui avait donné avant son départ. Elle ouvrit son sac, en vida le contenu sur ses genoux et commença à compter les pièces d'or.

Tout d'un coup, la comtesse Marie sentit un vent froid sur son visage. Elle leva la tête et elle vit un homme qui venait d'entrer dans son wagon. Il était grand, bien habillé, et il était blessé à la main. Il referma la porte, s'assit en face de la comtesse et la regarda de ses grands yeux noirs. Puis, il prit un mouchoir dans sa poche et en enveloppa son poignet pour arrêter le sang qui coulait.

La jeune femme eut très peur. Cet homme certainement l'avait vue compter son or. Il était venu pour la voler, ou, pire encore, pour la tuer. Il la regardait fixement, essoufflé,° le visage convulsé, prêt, sans doute, à l'attaquer.

Il dit brusquement:

— Madame, n'ayez pas peur.

Elle ne répondit rien, incapable d'ouvrir la bouche. Son coeur battait et ses oreilles bourdonnaient.°

L'homme continua:

— Je ne suis pas un malfaiteur°, madame.

Elle ne disait toujours rien, mais ses genoux tremblaient tellement que tout l'or tomba sur le sol° du wagon.

Surpris, l'homme regarda ce flot° de métal, puis il se baissa pour ramasser les pièces.

Prise de panique, la comtesse se leva. Elle courut vers la portière pour sauter du train. L'homme comprit ce qu'elle voulait faire. Il l'attrapa, la saisit dans ses bras, et l'obligea à s'asseoir.

— Écoutez-moi, madame, dit-il. Je ne suis pas un malfaiteur. La preuve° c'est que je vais ramasser cet argent et vous le rendre. Je suis moi-même en grand danger. Si vous ne m'aidez pas à passer la frontière, je suis un homme mort. Dans une heure, nous serons à la dernière station russe. Dans une heure dix, nous serons dans un autre pays. Si vous ne me secourez° pas, je suis condamné. Je ne peux pas vous expliquer pourquoi, mais croyez-moi. Je n'ai pas tué. Je n'ai pas volé, et je n'ai rien fait de mal. Je vous jure que je suis un homme d'honneur, mais je ne peux pas vous en dire plus.

énervée = nerveuse **essoufflé** *out of breath* **bourdonnaient** *were buzzing* **malfaiteur** = criminel **sol** *floor* **flot** *stream, cascade* **preuve** *proof* **secourez** = aidez

Mots utiles

un coin	*corner*
une frontière	*border*
le genou; les genoux	*knee; lap*
un mouchoir	*handkerchief*
une pièce d'or	*gold coin*
le poignet	*wrist*
se baisser	*to stoop, bend down*
battre *	*to beat*
compter	*to count*
couler	*to flow*
envelopper	*to wrap*
jurer	*to swear*
ralentir	*to slow down*
ramasser	*to pick up*
remplir	*to fill*
rouler	*to roll (along); to travel*
sauter	*to jump*
siffler	*to whistle*
tuer	*to kill*
vider	*to empty*
voler	*to steal*
muet (muette)	*silent*
pire	*worse*

■ Note linguistique

Pire is the comparative and superlative of **mauvais**.

■ Irregular Verb

(see Appendix C)
battre

Teaching Strategy: Expansion

Ask students the following questions:

- À votre avis, pourquoi l'homme a-t-il besoin d'aide?
- Que pensez-vous qu'il ait fait?
- Que se passera-t-il à la frontière si elle ne l'aide pas?

Expand by asking students to write a short paragraph giving their opinions and the reasons behind their views.

L'homme se mit à genoux. Comme il l'avait dit, il ramassa toutes les pièces d'or, et en remplit le sac qu'il donna à la comtesse. Puis il alla s'asseoir à l'autre coin du wagon.

La comtesse Marie ne bougeait° pas. Immobile et muette, elle retrouva peu à peu son calme. L'homme ne faisait pas un geste pas un mouvement. Il restait droit,° les yeux fixés devant lui. De temps en temps, elle le regardait rapidement. C'était un homme de trente ans environ.° Il était très beau, avec l'apparence d'un gentilhomme.

Le train continuait à rouler très vite dans la nuit. Puis, il siffla plusieurs fois, ralentit et finalement s'arrêta.

bougeait = changeait de position **droit** *sitting upright* **environ** = approximativement

Avez-vous compris?

1. Qu'est-ce que la comtesse faisait quand l'homme est entré dans le wagon?
2. Quelle était l'apparence physique de cet homme? Décrivez-le.
3. Quelle a été la réaction de la comtesse quand elle a vu cet homme? Pourquoi?
4. Qu'est-ce que l'homme a fait quand l'argent a roulé sur le sol?
5. Qu'est-ce que la comtesse a voulu faire ensuite?
6. Quel service est-ce que l'homme a demandé à la comtesse?

Anticipons un peu!

À votre avis, est-ce que la comtesse va protéger l'inconnu?

- Si oui, comment?
- Si non, qu'est-ce qu'elle va faire?

Note culturelle

La monnaie russe s'appelle le rouble. Il y a cent kopecks dans un rouble.

■ *Avez-vous compris?*

(Sample answers)

1. Elle comptait des pièces d'or.
2. Il était grand, beau, bien habillé. Il avait les yeux noirs. Il était blessé.
3. Elle a eu très peur, parce qu'elle pensait qu'il allait voler son argent ou la tuer.
4. Il l'a ramassé.
5. Elle a voulu sauter du train.
6. Il lui a demandé de l'aider à passer la frontière.

3

Ivan, le vieux serviteur, parut à la portière du wagon pour prendre les ordres de la comtesse. Celle-ci regarda son étrange compagnon, puis elle dit à son serviteur d'une voix brusque:

— Ivan, je n'ai plus besoin de toi. Tu vas retourner à Saint Pétersbourg.

Le serviteur, très surpris, ouvrit des yeux énormes. Tremblant d'émotion, il put à peine dire:

— Mais, madame . . . Je pensais que . . .

D'un ton très assuré, la comtesse répondit:

— J'ai changé d'avis. Tu ne viendras pas avec moi à Menton. Je veux que tu restes en Russie… Tiens, prends cet argent pour payer ton billet de retour. Et donne-moi ton manteau, ta casquette et ton passeport.

Ivan enleva sa casquette et son manteau qu'il lui donna, sans comprendre, à la comtesse. Il lui tendit son passeport et, puis, les larmes aux yeux, descendit du train.

Le train repartit vers la frontière. Alors, la comtesse dit à son voisin:

— Mettez ce manteau et cette casquette. Vous êtes maintenant Ivan, mon serviteur. Je mets une seule condition à ce que je fais pour vous: vous ne me parlerez jamais. Je ne veux pas que vous me disiez un seul mot, même pour me remercier.

L'inconnu s'inclina,° sans prononcer un mot. Bientôt le train s'arrêta de nouveau. Des policiers en uniforme entrèrent dans le wagon. Ils regardaient partout comme s'ils cherchaient quelqu'un. La comtesse leur dit d'un ton impérieux:

— Je suis la comtesse Baranow de Saint Pétersbourg, et voici mon domestique Ivan.

s'inclina *bowed*

Mots utiles

une casquette	*cap*
un inconnu	*stranger*
une larme	*tear*
changer d'avis	*to change one's mind*
enlever	*to take off*
paraître*	*to appear*
rompre	*to break*
tendre	*to hand, give*
à cause de	*because of*
à peine	*hardly, scarcely*
debout	*standing*

■ **Irregular Verb**
(see Appendix C)
paraître (*see* **connaître**)

Teaching Strategy

Divide the class into groups. Have each group discuss the following questions and prepare answers to present to the class:

- À votre avis, pourquoi Ivan pleure-t-il?
- Est-ce parce qu'il est triste de quitter la comtesse ou est-ce parce qu'il est heureux de rentrer en Russie?
- Y a-t-il une autre explication possible? Laquelle?

Puis elle tendit les passeports à un officier qui les lui rendit en saluant. Les hommes sortirent du wagon et continuèrent leur ronde d'inspection. Après une heure d'arrêt, le train se remit en route.

Pendant toute la nuit, l'homme et la femme restèrent en tête-à-tête,° muets tous les deux. Le matin, le train s'arrêta dans une gare allemande. L'inconnu descendit du wagon. Debout, sur le quai, il dit à la comtesse:

— Pardonnez-moi, madame, de rompre ma promesse, mais à cause de moi, vous avez perdu votre domestique. Il est juste que je le remplace. Avez-vous besoin de quelque chose?

Elle répondit froidement:

— Allez chercher ma femme de chambre.

Il y alla, puis il monta dans un autre wagon.

Quand elle descendait à quelque buffet° de gare, elle le voyait de loin qui la regardait . . . Le train arriva finalement à Menton.

en tête-à-tête *face to face* **buffet** *food wagon*

Avez-vous compris?

1. Qu'est-ce que la comtesse demande à Ivan, son vieux serviteur?
2. Comment est-ce que l'inconnu échappe *(escapes)* au contrôle des policiers?
3. Quelle promesse est-ce que la comtesse exige de l'inconnu?
4. Que fait l'inconnu quand le train s'arrête à la gare allemande?

Anticipons un peu!

- D'après vous, est-ce que l'inconnu va tenir *(keep)* sa promesse?
- Comment va se terminer cette histoire?

■ Note linguistique

rompre sa promesse ≠ tenir sa promesse

■ *Avez-vous compris?*

(Sample answers)

1. Elle lui demande de retourner à Saint Pétersbourg.
2. Il échappe au contrôle des policiers parce qu'il a mis la casquette et le manteau d'Ivan.
3. Elle exige qu'il ne lui parle jamais.
4. Il descend du train et monte dans un autre wagon.

■ **Note linguistique**

Point out to your students the following French expressions from the text:

pleurer comme un enfant
suivre comme une ombre
se sauver comme un fou

Can students infer and explain the meanings?

■ **Irregular Verb**

(see Appendix C)
suivre

4

Le docteur toussa, puis il continua son histoire:

Un jour que je recevais mes clients dans mon cabinet, j'eus la visite d'un grand garçon que je n'avais jamais vu. Il me dit:

— Docteur, je viens vous demander des nouvelles de la comtesse Marie Baranow. Elle ne me connaît pas. Je suis un ami de son mari. C'est lui qui m'envoie.

Je répondis:

— La comtesse est très, très malade. Je doute qu'elle rentre un jour en Russie.

À ces mots, cet homme se mit à pleurer comme un enfant. Il se leva et sortit brusquement de mon cabinet.

Ce soir-là, comme d'habitude, je rendis visite à la comtesse dans son hôtel. Je lui dis qu'un étranger était venu m'interroger° sur sa santé. Elle parut émue et me raconta toute l'histoire que je viens de vous dire. Puis elle ajouta:

— Cet homme que je ne connais pas me suit maintenant comme mon ombre. Je le rencontre chaque fois que je sors. Il me regarde d'une étrange façon, mais il ne m'a jamais parlé.

Elle réfléchit, puis ajouta:

— Je parie qu'il est sous mes fenêtres.

interroger = poser des questions

Mots utiles

un baiser	*kiss*
un être	*human being*
un fou	*crazy person*
une ombre	*shadow*
un sourire	*smile*
ajouter	*to add*
deviner	*to guess*
gâter	*to spoil*
parier	*to bet*
pleurer	*to cry*
se retourner	*to turn back*
réfléchir	*to think, reflect on*
suivre *	*to follow*
bouleversé	*overwhelmed*
douloureux	*painful*
ému	*moved, touched*
jusqu'au bout	*to the end*

Teaching Strategy: Expansion

Help your students to develop their active reading skills by asking the following questions:

- À votre avis, la comtesse a-t-elle raison de refuser de parler à l'homme?
- Que se passerait-il s'ils se parlaient?
- Comment agiriez-vous si vous étiez la comtesse?
- Si vous étiez l'homme?

Elle quitta sa chaise longue, alla à la fenêtre et me montra, en effet, l'homme qui était venu dans mon cabinet. Il était assis sur un banc et regardait dans la direction de l'hôtel. Quand il nous vit, il se leva et partit sans se retourner.

J'assistai ainsi à une chose surprenante et douloureuse, à l'amour muet de ces deux êtres qui ne se connaissaient pas.

Il l'aimait passionnément, avec la reconnaissance° et la dévotion d'un animal sauvé de la mort. Chaque jour, il venait me demander «Comment va-t-elle?», comprenant que j'avais deviné leur amour. Et il pleurait affreusement quand il apprenait qu'elle était chaque jour plus faible et plus pâle.

Elle me disait: «Je ne lui ai parlé qu'une seule fois, mais il me semble que je le connais depuis toujours.»

Et quand ils se croisaient° dans la rue, elle lui rendait son salut avec un sourire grave et charmant. Je sentais qu'elle était heureuse, elle qui savait qu'elle était perdue. Oui, je la sentais heureuse d'être aimée ainsi, avec ce respect et cette constance, avec cette poésie exagérée, avec cette dévotion totale et absolue. Et pourtant, elle refusait désespérément de le rencontrer, de connaître son nom, de lui parler . . .

Elle disait: «Non, non, cela me gâterait cette étrange amitié. Il faut que nous restions étrangers l'un à l'autre.»

Lui aussi continua à garder ses distances. Il voulait respecter jusqu'au bout l'absurde promesse de ne jamais lui parler, promesse qu'il avait faite dans le wagon.

Souvent, pendant ses longues heures de faiblesse, elle se levait de sa chaise longue et allait à sa fenêtre pour voir s'il était là. Et quand elle l'avait vu, toujours immobile sur son banc, elle revenait se coucher avec un sourire aux lèvres.

Elle est morte un matin vers dix heures. Comme je sortais de l'hôtel, il vint vers moi, le visage bouleversé. Il savait déjà la nouvelle.

— Je voudrais la voir une seconde seulement, en votre présence, dit-il.

Je lui pris le bras et rentrai dans la maison. Quand il fut devant le lit de la morte, il lui prit la main et l'embrassa d'un interminable baiser. Puis il se sauva° comme un fou. Je ne l'ai jamais revu.

la reconnaissance = la gratitude **se croisaient** = se rencontraient **se sauva** = partit

Le docteur toussa de nouveau, et il dit:

— Voilà certainement la plus singulière aventure de train que je connaisse. Il est vrai que les hommes sont un peu fous.

Une femme dit à mi-voix.°

— Ces deux êtres-là étaient moins fous que vous ne croyez . . . Ils étaient . . . ils étaient . . .

Et elle se mit à pleurer, sans terminer sa phrase. On changea de conversation pour la calmer. Personne n'a su ce qu'elle voulait dire.

à mi-voix *in a low voice*

Avez-vous compris?

1. Sous quel prétexte l'inconnu va-t-il voir le médecin? Quelle est sa réaction quand il apprend la vérité?
2. Qu'est-ce que la comtesse explique au médecin ce soir-là? Où était l'inconnu à ce moment-là?
3. Quel sentiment est-ce que la comtesse éprouve *(feel)* pour l'inconnu? Comment explique-t-elle son refus de lui parler?
4. À votre avis, comment est-ce que l'inconnu a appris la mort de la comtesse? Qu'est-ce qu'il demande au médecin?
5. À votre avis, est-ce que l'inconnu était un fou ou un héros? Expliquez pourquoi?

■ Note linguistique

The adverb **mi-** is used with nouns as a prefix, meaning *half.* **Examples: à mi-chemin** *(halfway),* **à la mi-juillet** *(in mid-July),* **la mi-temps** *(halftime of a game),* **travailler à mi-temps** *(to work part time).*

■ *Avez-vous compris?*

(Sample answers)

1. Il dit qu'il est un ami du mari de la comtesse, et que c'est le mari qui l'envoie demander des nouvelles.
2. Elle explique que l'homme la suit toujours. Il est sur un banc sous la fenêtre de la comtesse.
3. Elle éprouve de l'amitié pour lui. Elle aime son amour platonique. Elle pense que parler changerait les choses.
4. Il a peut-être compris qu'elle était morte parce qu'elle n'est pas venue à la fenêtre ce matin-là. Il demande au médecin s'il peut la voir.
5. *Answers will vary.*

Teaching Strategy: Expansion

Ask students to complete the following activities:

- *Expression écrite:* L'inconnu décrit la scène du train dans son journal. Écrivez cette page.
- Complétez la phrase de la jeune femme à la fin de l'histoire avec votre opinion personnelle.
- Avez-vous aimé cette histoire? Expliquez pourquoi.

These questions may be answered as a group activity if students prefer to debate their answers and opinions.

EXPRESSION ORALE

■ Dramatisation

Avec un(e) partenaire, jouez la scène du train (partie 3 de l'histoire).

■ Sujets de discussion

A. L'inconnu du train

Avec votre partenaire, créez une identité et une personnalité à l'inconnu du train. Imaginez, par exemple:

- qui il est
- d'où il vient
- comment, pourquoi, et dans quelles circonstances il a été blessé?
- comment et pourquoi il est entré dans le wagon où était la comtesse?
- pourquoi il a demandé sa protection?

Rappelez-vous: L'inconnu a dit qu'il était un homme d'honneur, qu'il n'avait pas tué, qu'il n'avait pas volé, et qu'il n'avait rien fait de mal.

B. L'amour platonique

Un amour platonique est un amour purement spirituel, comme l'amour qui unit l'inconnu et la comtesse russe.

- Pensez-vous que cet amour soit réel?
- Pensez-vous qu'un tel amour puisse exister aujourd'hui?

Prenez une position pour ou contre et illustrez-la avec des exemples.

■ Situations

Avec votre partenaire, choisissez l'une des situations suivantes. Composez le dialogue correspondant et jouez-le en classe.

1. Une visite

La comtesse sait qu'elle va mourir. Quelques jours avant sa mort, elle accorde *(grants)* une visite à l'inconnu du train en lui demandant d'expliquer ses actions.

Rôles: la comtesse, l'inconnu

2. Explications

La comtesse vient de mourir. Rentré chez lui, le docteur raconte à sa femme les faits de la journée. La femme du docteur demande des explications.

Rôles: le docteur, sa femme

3. Il y a trente ans . . .

Trente ans ont passé. Au lieu de retourner en Russie, l'inconnu est resté en France. Un jour, il raconte l'histoire à un(e) ami(e) qui demande des détails.

Rôles: l'inconnu, son ami(e)

Teaching Note

L'inconnu du train can also be assigned as a composition.

EXPRESSION ÉCRITE

■ Notice nécrologique *(Obituary)*

Vous êtes journaliste. Écrivez une brève notice nécrologique sur la comtesse Marie Baranow. (Inventez-lui une biographie.)

■ Journal intime

Dans son journal intime, la comtesse décrit la scène du train. Écrivez cette page de journal.

■ Lettre d'adieu

Sachant que la comtesse va mourir, l'inconnu lui écrit une lettre où il avoue ses sentiments. (Évidemment il ne la lui enverra pas, parce qu'il respecte la promesse qu'il a faite.) Écrivez cette lettre d'adieu.

■ Irregular Verb

(See Appendix C)

mourir is an irregular verb:

je meurs
il meurt
nous mourons

INTERLUDE CULTUREL

■ Pour en savoir plus

For more background on **Simone Veil**, see *Interlude 6*, page 253.

■ Anecdote

To prepare for the switch from francs to euros in 2002, the French created a converting machine. This credit-card size calculator is able to convert any amount instantly from francs into euros and vice-versa.

INTERLUDE CULTUREL

▪ *Français et Européens* ▪

Pour les Français d'aujourd'hui, l'Europe est une réalité bien concrète. Ils portent des chemises italiennes et des imperméables anglais. Ils mangent des oranges espagnoles et du fromage hollandais. Au café, ils commandent de la bière belge ou irlandaise. Ils conduisent des voitures allemandes et suédoises. Ils voyagent avec un passeport européen et passent leurs vacances en Grèce, au Portugal ou en Finlande. Là, ils paient leurs dépenses avec une monnaie unique: l'euro. Avec le programme **Erasmus**, les jeunes Français peuvent faire des études universitaires dans une vingtaine de pays différents. Quand ils ont leur diplôme, ils peuvent travailler dans le pays de leur choix sans la nécessité d'un permis de travail.

La construction de l'Europe a commencé après la Deuxième Guerre mondiale,° avec la création du **Marché Commun** qui réunissait la France, l'Allemagne, l'Italie, la Belgique, les Pays-Bas et le Luxembourg. Le but° principal de cette union était de faciliter les échanges commerciaux et d'unifier les institutions de façon à promouvoir° l'expansion économique dans tous les pays membres.

Depuis, l'**Union européenne** s'est agrandie. Elle comprend maintenant 25 pays différents mais unis par les mêmes° intérêts et la même vision du monde. Son objectif est d'assurer le progrès économique et social. Sa mission consiste aussi à formuler une politique européenne commune sur les grandes questions d'aujourd'hui: respect des droits° humains et de la diversité culturelle, promotion de la liberté et de la démocratie, maintien de la paix et de la sécurité, protection de l'environnement, solidarité avec les pays du tiers monde.°

PAYS	POPULATION
Allemagne	82 000 000
Autriche	8 000 000
Belgique	10 000 000
Chypre	170 000
Danemark	5 000 000
Espagne	42 000 000
Estonie	1 000 000
Finlande	5 000 000
France	62 000 000
Grèce	11 000 000
Hongrie	10 000 000
Irlande	4 000 000
Italie	58 000 000
Lettonie	2 000 000
Lituanie	3 000 000
Luxembourg	500 000
Malte	400 000
Pays-Bas	16 000 000
Pologne	38 000 000
Portugal	10 000 000
Slovaquie	5 000 000
République tchèque	10 000 000
Royaume Uni	60 000 000
Slovénie	2 000 000
Suède	9 000 000

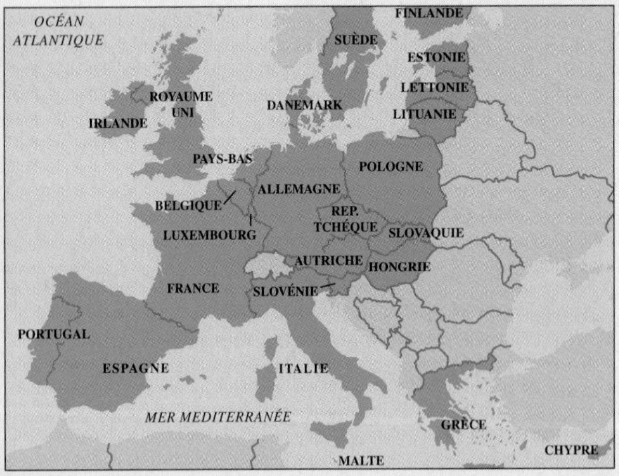

OCÉAN ATLANTIQUE
FINLANDE
SUÈDE
ESTONIE
LETTONIE
LITUANIE
ROYAUME UNI
IRLANDE
DANEMARK
PAYS-BAS
POLOGNE
ALLEMAGNE
BELGIQUE
REP. TCHÈQUE
SLOVAQUIE
LUXEMBOURG
AUTRICHE
HONGRIE
FRANCE
SLOVÉNIE
PORTUGAL
ESPAGNE
ITALIE
MER MEDITERRANÉE
GRÈCE
CHYPRE
MALTE

Deuxième Guerre mondiale *World War II* **but** *objective* **de façon à promouvoir** *in order to promote* **mêmes** *same* **droits** *rights* **tiers monde** *Third World*

NOTES CULTURELLES

- The European **flag** bears 12 stars, regardless of how many member states there may be in the Union. This flag was originally designed for the Council of Europe in 1949.
- Other European countries may eventually join the **European Union.** To qualify, a country must meet certain economic conditions and the people must vote affirmatively in a referendum on the question.
- The four countries which did not adopt the **euro** in 1999 were Denmark, Greece, Great Britain and Sweden.

■ *Oui à l'Europe!*

Les Français sont généralement très favorables à l'Europe. Nous avons demandé à quatre Français d'âges différents d'expliquer pourquoi.

Un lycéen (14 ans)

Pendant les vacances de printemps, je suis allé passer dix jours en Hollande avec les élèves de ma classe. Je ne me suis pas senti dépaysé° du tout. Évidemment, les Hollandais parlent une autre langue, et leur nourriture est différente, mais en général nous avons beaucoup de points communs avec eux. Et je suis sûr que c'est la même chose avec les Allemands, les Anglais et les Italiens. Nous sommes tous européens!

Une étudiante (21 ans)

Je suis étudiante à l'IEP (Institut d'Études politiques) de Strasbourg. Dans ma classe, il y a 25 pourcent d'étudiants étrangers, surtout allemands, anglais et belges. Moi-même, je vais passer l'année prochaine à l'université de Fribourg en Allemagne. Tout ça, grâce au programme *Erasmus*, qui facilite les échanges entre les universités européennes. Avec *Erasmus*, l'Europe est une réalité bien concrète pour nous, étudiants.

Une jeune cadre° (28 ans)

Je suis diplômée d'une école de commerce française, mais maintenant je travaille en Allemagne pour une compagnie anglaise. J'ai un job intéressant et je gagne très bien ma vie. Si un jour je décide de changer d'entreprise, avec mon expérience internationale je n'aurais pas de problèmes à trouver quelque chose d'autre. Si l'Europe n'existait pas, je n'aurais pas ces possibilités!

Un retraité (80 ans)

Autrefois l'histoire européenne, c'était l'histoire des conflits permanents entre la France et l'Allemagne ou l'Angleterre. Je parle en connaissance de cause° parce que j'ai fait la guerre de 40* et que j'ai passé quatre ans en Allemagne dans un camp de prisonniers. Maintenant, avec la nouvelle Europe, la guerre est devenue impossible. Je suis pour l'intégration politique de l'Europe parce que cela signifie paix° et prospérité pour mes petits-enfants . . . et leurs enfants.

* La guerre de 40, c'est la Deuxième Guerre mondiale (1940-1944). Voir à la page 252.

Les symboles de l'Europe

Le drapeau européen

Le drapeau européen représente un cercle de 12 étoiles jaunes sur un fond° bleu. Les douze étoiles représentent les douze pays de la Communauté européenne.

Le passeport européen

Les citoyens des pays de **l'Union européenne** ont un passeport de format unique, le passeport européen. Cependant, ce passeport n'est pas nécessaire pour aller dans les autres pays de la CE: une simple pièce d'identité suffit.°

dépaysé *lost (in a strange place)* **cadre** *executive* **en connaissance de cause** *knowingly* **paix** *peace*
fond *background* **suffit** = est suffisant

Note culturelle

Erasme (1466–1536) était un humaniste hollandais. Pendant la Renaissance (voir page 140), les humanistes étaient des esprits universels qui s'intéressaient à tous les aspects de la connaissance humaine, et plus particulièrement à l'histoire et à la littérature grecque et romaine. Aujourd'hui, Erasme reste le symbole de l'universalité de la connaissance humaine.

Realia Note

Le passeport européen
Although each country issues its own passport, all the information inside the passport is given in each of the languages of the "EU" members.

■ Pour en savoir plus

Pour davantage de renseignements sur la Résistance, voir pages 254–259.

Note culturelle

Emmaüs est un village au nord de Jérusalem. Dans la tradition chrétienne, c'est là où Jésus s'est manifesté à ses disciples incrédules la nuit de sa résurrection.

Supplementary vocabulary

le squatter *squatter*
squatter *to squat (in a building)*
le chômage *unemployment*
la délinquance *delinquency*
le SDF (Sans Domicile Fixe) *homeless person*
la solidarité *solidarity*
un(e) sans-abri *homeless person*

■ Nous, c'est les autres! ■

La France d'aujourd'hui est un pays riche et prospère. Ses habitants ont l'un des niveaux de vie les plus élevés du monde. Pourtant, comme toute société moderne, la société française a ses problèmes et ses victimes.° Il y a les chômeurs,° les sans-abri,° les gens qui ont faim. Que fait-on pour ces déshérités de la société? Certains Français ont répondu à cette question par leurs actions.

L'abbé Pierre et les «Chiffonniers d'Emmaüs»

L'abbé* **Pierre** a 90 ans ou un peu plus. C'est un homme simple qui, depuis 40 ans, porte le même béret et la même pèlerine° noire. C'est aussi l'un des hommes les plus admirés de France. Issu d'une famille riche, l'abbé Pierre a décidé de mettre sa religion en pratique et de devenir l'apôtre° des pauvres.

En réalité, l'abbé Pierre s'appelle Henri Grouès. C'est pendant la Guerre de 1940, quand il travaillait dans la Résistance, qu'il a pris le nom d'Abbé Pierre. Cette guerre, qui a duré° quatre ans, a causé la destruction d'un très grand nombre de maisons et d'immeubles dans toute la France. À la fin de la guerre, il y avait des milliers de «sans-abri». L'abbé Pierre est devenu leur porte-parole° lorsqu'il a été élu° député° à l'Assemblé Nationale** en 1945.

Mais pour l'abbé Pierre, l'activité politique n'était pas suffisante. Devant l'inaction du gouvernement, il a décidé de passer à l'action tout court.° C'est ainsi qu'il a créé les «Chiffonniers° d'Emmaüs», une organisation qui donnait du travail, un logement, et surtout une raison de vivre° à ceux que personne ne voulait employer: les alcooliques, les anciens repris de justice,° et tous les déshérités de la terre. Pour rappeler° aux Français l'existence des sans-abri, l'abbé Pierre a décidé de «squatériser», d'une manière illégale mais non injuste, les immeubles vides° ou abandonnés. Plus récemment, en 1991, il a créé des «boutiques-solidarité» pour aider les gens qui n'ont pas les moyens° de vivre comme tout le monde.

L'abbé Pierre et deux de ses protégés

L'abbé Pierre aujourd'hui

La misère n'a évidemment pas de frontière° et l'action de l'abbé Pierre est devenue internationale. Il y a aujourd'hui plus de 250 centres Emmaüs en France et 600 dans le monde.

* **L'abbé**: un titre religieux donné à certains prêtres catholiques.
** **L'Assemblée Nationale**: Avec le Sénat, chambre parlementaire qui vote les lois *(laws)*. C'est l'équivalent du «House of Representatives» du congrès américain.

victimes *casualties* **chômeurs** *unemployed* **sans-abri** *homeless* **pèlerine** *cape* **apôtre** *apostle, defender* **duré** *lasted* **porte-parole** *spokesperson* **élu** *elected* **député** *congressman* **tout court** = directement **chiffonniers** *ragpickers* **raison de vivre** *aim in life* **anciens repris de justice** *former prison inmates* **rappeler** *remind* **vides** *empty* **moyens** *means* **frontière** *border*

NOTES CULTURELLES

- L'abbé Pierre est né en 1912. Il entre au monastère à l'âge de 19 ans, après avoir distribué sa part d'héritage et fait voeu de pauvreté. À 34 ans, il est élu député de Meurthe-et-Moselle et devient ainsi le porte-parole des pauvres.
- Le film français intitulé *Hiver 54* relate le combat de l'abbé Pierre pour soulager la misère des pauvres gens et pour fonder les Chiffonniers d'Emmaüs.
- L'abbé Pierre s'est retiré dans un monastère italien à Paglia, près de Padoue, en 1996.
- Des sondages récents ont montré que l'abbé Pierre est la personne la plus admirée en France.

Coluche et les «Restos du Coeur»

À son époque, **Coluche**, de son vrai nom Michel Colucci, était le comédien le plus célèbre de France. Son visage bonhomme,° ses manières rustres,° sa salopette° étaient universellement connus. Mais pour Coluche, faire des films, se produire° à la télévision et gagner de l'argent, ne suffisait pas. Coluche était un homme généreux, courageux et juste qui ne pouvait pas tolérer la misère ou les inégalités sociales. Alors, un jour il est passé à l'action et il a créé les «**Restaurants du coeur**». Cette organisation prépare des repas chauds pour les sans-abri, pour les personnes sans ressources, et généralement pour tous ceux qui ont faim et qui n'ont pas d'argent.

En 1986, Coluche s'est tué dans un accident de moto, mais son oeuvre° continue. Aujourd'hui, les 1500 «Restos° du coeur», animés par des milliers de bénévoles,° servent 60 millions de repas gratuits par an.

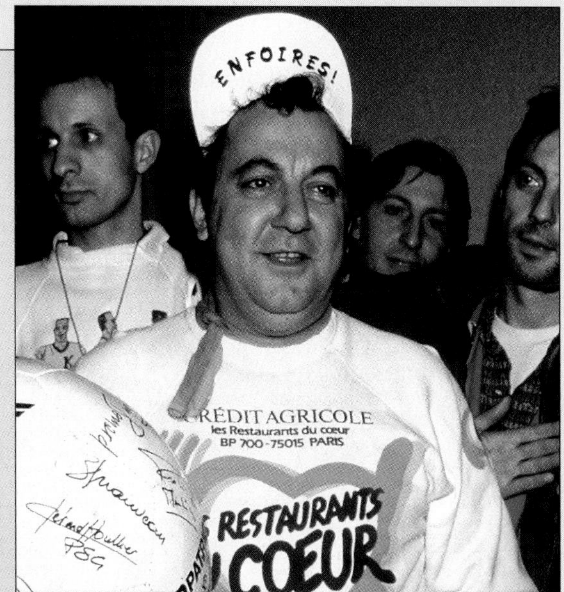

Coluche, le comédien au grand coeur

Jeunes Français, bénévoles qui servent des repas gratuits aux «Restos du coeur»

bonhomme *good-natured* **rustres** *boorish, lacking good manners* **salopette** *overalls* **se produire** = se montrer **oeuvre** *charitable works*
restos = restaurants **bénévoles** = volontaires

Note culturelle

Officially, France closed its borders to permanent workers in 1974, except for people from member states of the EU.

Notes historiques

LES INVASIONS

- The Roman occupation is described in *Interlude 1*, p. 98.
- Among the invading German tribes were the **Franks,** who gave their name to the country.
- The Scandinavians or Vikings came from Norway, Sweden, and Denmark. They were also known as Norsemen or Normans **(les hommes du Nord).** See p. 104.

Supplementary vocabulary

la carte de séjour *visa, green card*
la naturalisation *naturalization*
l'intégration *assimilation*
le travailleur clandestin *illegal worker*
le réfugié (politique) *(political) refugee*
le demandeur d'asile *asylum seeker*
l'autorisation de travail *work permit*

La France, une mosaïque

Les Français d'aujourd'hui ne s'appellent pas seulement Dupont, Moreau, Petit ou Normand. Ils s'appellent aussi Belkacem, Lopez, Nguyen et Meyer. Ils sont blancs, noirs, bruns et jaunes. Ils vont à l'église, à la mosquée, au temple et à la synagogue*. . . Loin d'être un pays homogène, la France est en réalité une mosaïque marquée par l'intégration, la fusion et la cohabitation de cultures différentes.

Historiquement, la France a d'abord été une terre d'invasion. Au cours des° dix premiers siècles,° elle a été occupée par les Romains, les Germains, les Scandinaves . . . Au 19e siècle, elle est devenue une terre d'asile° pour des milliers de réfugiés politiques venus d'Allemagne, de Pologne, de Hongrie et de Russie.

Au 20e siècle, la France est devenue une terre d'immigration pour des millions de travailleurs étrangers. Le développement économique et industriel a en effet créé un énorme besoin de main d'oeuvre.° Pour répondre à ce besoin, le gouvernement français a invité des étrangers à venir travailler en France. Dans les années 20, ces travailleurs venaient principalement d'Italie et de Pologne. Dans les années 50, ils venaient surtout du Portugal et d'Espagne.

Depuis les années 60, la majorité des travailleurs étrangers qui viennent en France ne sont pas européens. Ce sont principalement des Maghrébins (Algériens, Marocains et Tunisiens) venus des pays d'Afrique du Nord. D'autres, moins nombreux, viennent d'Afrique occidentale° (Mali, Sénégal, Cameroun . . .) et d'Asie (Viêt Nam, Laos, Cambodge).

Après les États-Unis, la France est le pays du monde qui a le plus grand nombre d'immigrants. Les 4,5 millions d'étrangers qui habitent en France représentent 8% de la population du pays. Ces étrangers, d'origine européenne, africaine ou asiatique, donnent à la France d'aujourd'hui un visage véritablement multi-culturel et multi-ethnique.

* En France, les **Catholiques** vont **à l'église**, les **Musulmans** *(Moslems)* vont **à la mosquée**, les **Protestants** vont **au temple**, les **Juifs** vont **à la synagogue**.

au cours de = pendant **un siècle** = 100 ans **terre d'asile** *land of asylum* **main d'oeuvre** *labor, manpower* **occidentale** *Western*

Le Maghreb et les Maghrébins

Maghreb est un mot arabe qui signifie *le pays où le soleil se couche*.° Autrefois, le Maghreb représentait l'extrémité occidentale du monde musulman. Le Maghreb désigne les trois pays d'Afrique du Nord: l'**Algérie**, le **Maroc** et la **Tunisie**. Les Maghrébins sont les habitants de ces pays.

La majorité des Maghrébins sont arabes et musulmans. Leur religion est l'**Islam**. Un grand nombre de Maghrébins (environ deux millions) ont émigré en France où ils représentent le groupe le plus important d'étrangers.

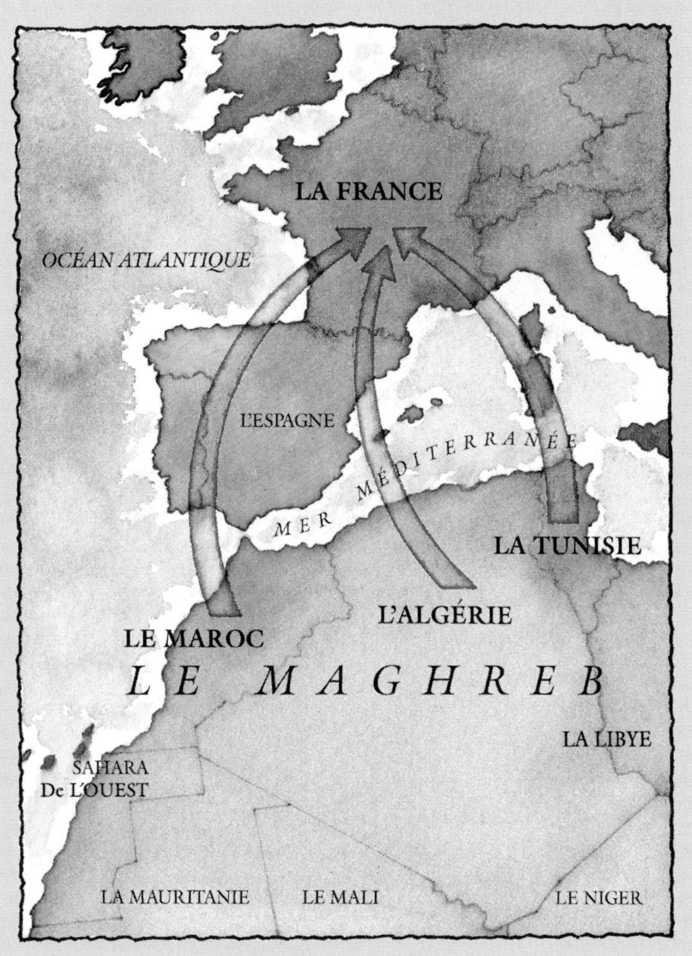

LES ÉTRANGERS EN FRANCE

Algériens	1 250 000	Espagnols	350 000
Marocains	700 000	Tunisiens	350 000
Portugais	600 000	Vietnamiens	250 000
Italiens	400 000	Turcs	180 000

se couche *sets*

Note culturelle

The Arabs of North Africa are the descendants of the conquerors who came from the Arabian peninsula in the 8th century. However, not all those who live in the Maghreb are Arabs. There are also the Berbers whose ancestors were living in the Maghreb centuries before the Arab invasion. Now both Arabs and Berbers are Muslim.

Note linguistique

In French-speaking African countries you might hear the following idioms:

gréver (Sénégal) = faire grève
avoir les dents dehors (Congo) = rire
un payé-cousu (Cameroun) = un vêtement acheté en prêt-à-porter
faire l'avion par terre (Côte d'Ivoire) = se dépêcher, marcher vite

■ Note linguistique

Le mot **beur** est un néologisme dérivé du **verlan** qui est un argot codé dans lequel on inverse les syllabes des mots.

Par exemple:
l'envers → **verlan**
bizarre → **zarbi**
pourri → **ripou**

Le mot **beur** vient d'une double transformation du mot arabe en **verlan:**
arabe → **rabeu**
rabeu → **beur**

La beurette (féminin de beur) est une jeune fille d'origine maghrébine, née en France.

■ Additional Information

L'aïd célèbre la fin du Ramadan.

Note culturelle

Mahomet, le fondateur de l'Islam, considérait les patriarches et les prophètes de la Bible commes ses précurseurs.

■ *Djamila ou le dilemme de l'intégration*

Djamila, 17 ans, est une jeune «beur». Cela signifie qu'elle est fille d'immigrés maghrébins. Ses parents sont venus d'Algérie il y a vingt ans, et elle, elle est née à Marseille. Elle a la nationalité française, parle français, va dans un lycée français où presque tous ses copains sont d'origine française. Après le bac, elle compte aller à l'université et un jour devenir vétérinaire. Est-ce qu'elle se sent vraiment française? Ou bien, est-elle restée algérienne? Djamila explique son dilemme.

«Fondamentalement, je suis française, mais je suis différente parce que ma famille est différente. Mes parents sont arabes et musulmans pratiquants.° Cela ne signifie pas seulement qu'ils célèbrent l'aïd* et qu'ils ne mangent pas de porc et ne boivent pas d'alcool. Cela signifie aussi qu'ils ont une conception différente de la vie. Mon père, par exemple, ne veut pas que je sorte seule avec un garçon, alors que mes copines françaises n'ont pas besoin de demander la permission. C'est parfois une situation difficile mais j'obéis parce que j'ai beaucoup de respect et d'admiration pour mon père. C'est un homme honnête qui a travaillé très dur pour donner un minimum de confort à sa famille.

* **L'aïd:** Cette fête musulmane, aussi appelée «fête du mouton», rappelle le sacrifice d'Abraham et d'Isaac.

■ *L'influence maghrébine en France*

La présence de plus de deux millions de Maghrébins en France a modifié et enrichi la culture française dans beaucoup de domaines. Par exemple:

■ Religion

Aujourd'hui, l'**Islam** est la deuxième religion pratiquée en France, après la religion catholique et avant les religions protestantes et juives. Il y a 6000 mosquées en France et 5 millions de Musulmans.

■ Cuisine

Le **couscous**, plat traditionnel d'Afrique du Nord, est devenu un plat très populaire en France. C'est un plat de semoule° cuit à la vapeur° et servi avec des légumes, de la viande et une sauce très pimentée.° Pour manger un bon couscous, on peut aller dans les restaurants marocains, algériens ou tunisiens. Si on veut manger un couscous chez soi, il suffit d'acheter une boîte de couscous au supermarché.

D'autres spécialités maghrébines sont les gâteaux au miel,° les gâteaux aux amandes° appelés «cornes° de gazelle» et le thé à la menthe.°

■ Vocabulaire

La langue française d'aujourd'hui contient un certain nombre de mots d'origine arabe, comme:

un toubib	*un médecin*
un bled	*un petit village, généralement isolé et sans intérêt*
un méchouï	*une grande fête où on mange généralement du mouton rôti*
avoir la baraka	*avoir de la chance*
c'est kif-kif	*c'est la même chose*

pratiquants = qui observent les préceptes de leur religion **semoule** *semolina* **cuit à la vapeur** *steamed* **pimentée** *hot, spicy* **miel** *honey* **amandes** *almonds* **cornes** *horns* **menthe** *mint*

«Mes parents ont la nostalgie de leur pays. Parfois, ils parlent de rentrer en Algérie et ils voudraient que je vienne avec eux. Je suis allée plusieurs fois en Algérie où nous avons de la famille, mais là-bas, je ne me sens pas chez moi. Chez moi, c'est en France. C'est là où j'habite et c'est là où je vais faire ma vie. Parce que je suis intégrée, je sais que je n'aurai pas de difficulté à trouver un bon emploi. Pourtant, il y a des problèmes. Par exemple, quand je sors avec mes copines beurs et que nous parlons arabe entre nous, j'ai parfois l'impression qu'on nous regarde de travers.° À ce moment-là, je me sens alors algérienne, et fière° d'être différente.»

Quelques prénoms arabes

FILLES

Aïcha	Ourida
Djamila	Sakinna
Farida	Soraya
Leïla	Yasmina
Malika	Zeïna
Nacera	Zohra

GARÇONS

Ahmed	Latif	Omar
Ali	Malek	Rachid
Farid	Malik	Saïd
Hacine	Mohamed	Toufik
Ismaïl	Mouloud	Youssef
Kateb	Mustapha	

La grande mosquée de Paris

Les cinq principes de la religion musulmane

La religion musulmane est l'une des religions les plus importantes du monde. Elle est pratiquée par plus d'un milliard° de personnes, principalement au Moyen Orient, au Pakistan, en Indonésie, en Afrique du Nord et en Afrique occidentale.

La religion musulmane a cinq principes fondamentaux. Ces principes sont assez simples.

- Il y a un seul Dieu,° **Allah**.
- Chaque jour, le Musulman doit faire ses prières° cinq fois, tourné dans la direction de la **Mecque**,° ville natale du prophète Mahomet, et ville sainte° de l'Islam.
- Le Musulman doit être charitable. Chaque année, il doit donner un pourcentage de sa fortune aux pauvres.
- Chaque année, le Musulman doit faire le jeûne° du **Ramadan**. Pendant les 30 jours du Ramadan, il doit s'abstenir totalement de manger et de boire du matin jusqu'au soir.
- Durant sa vie, le Musulman doit aller une fois en pèlerinage° à la Mecque. Ce pèlerinage s'appelle le **hadj**.

Horaires des prières

Al-Fajr	*4 h 27*
Ach-Chrouq	*5 h 58*
Ad-Dohr	*12 h 36*
Al-Asr	*16 h 10*
Al-Maghrib	*19 h 08*
Al-Ichaa	*20 h 37*

de travers = d'une manière étrange **fière** *proud* **un milliard** *one billion* **Dieu** *God* **prières** *prayers* **Mecque** *Mecca (today in Saudi Arabia)* **sainte** *holy* **jeûne** *fast* **pèlerinage** *pilgrimage*

Realia Note

Whereas standard Muslim practice requires five daily prayers, there are often optional prayers. The fundamental prayers, as they appear in this newspaper announcement, are the following:

Al-Fajr: morning (sunrise)
Ad-Dohr: noon
Al-Asr: mid-afternoon
Al-Maghrib: evening
Al-Ichaa: night

On this particular day, **Ach-Chrouq** was listed an additional optional prayer.

NOTES CULTURELLES

- Islam is important in many areas of the French-speaking world: Algeria, Morocco, Tunisia, and several countries of West Africa (see p. 375). It is presented here for general information about the culture of these regions.
- Le prophète **Mahomet** (570–632) a fondé la religion musulmane en 622, l'an zéro du calendrier musulman.
- Le livre sacré des Musulmans s'appelle **le Coran** et est écrit en arabe. Il contient la parole d'Allah telle qu'elle a été transmise à Mahomet par l'archange Gabriel.
- Dans le calendrier musulman, le mois de **Ramadan** est le mois où le Coran a été révélé à Mahomet.

SOS Racisme

Les travailleurs immigrés qui viennent en France apportent avec eux une culture spécifique. Ils ont leurs coutumes, leurs traditions, leur religion, leur langue, leur musique, leur cuisine, leur façon de s'habiller . . . Ces immigrés sont généralement heureux d'habiter en France, même si les conditions de travail et de logement sont souvent difficiles.

De leur côté,° la majorité des Français, les jeunes en particulier, acceptent assez bien les immigrés même si leur culture est différente de la culture traditionnelle française. D'autres, au contraire, ont beaucoup de difficultés à accepter la réalité multi-culturelle de la France d'aujourd'hui. Ils ne comprennent pas que cette réalité est irréversible. Certains pensent que les immigrés sont responsables des problèmes comme le chômage,° la délinquance ou la drogue.° Des extrémistes voudraient même renvoyer° les immigrés dans leur pays d'origine. En France, comme dans d'autres pays européens, le racisme et la discrimination contre les immigrés sont devenus des problèmes importants à résoudre.°

Comment combattre le racisme? Un jour, il y a dix ans, des copains d'origine diverse discutaient justement° de leurs différences. «Nous sommes blancs, noirs, marron, bronzés!° Nous sommes copains depuis des années et nous le resterons, parce que nous disons oui à la solidarité et non au racisme.» Ce jour-là, un grand mouvement, **SOS Racisme**, était né.

De père martiniquais et de mère alsacienne, **Harlem Désir**, le fondateur et premier président de **SOS Racisme**, est bien le symbole même de la France multi-ethnique. «Chez nous, dit-il, on respecte l'individu et on écoute les autres.»

Une manifestation, SOS Racisme

Les activités de **SOS Racisme** sont très nombreuses: aider les immigrés, trouver des avocats pour les victimes de la discrimination, combattre le racisme sous toutes ses formes, et, plus généralement, changer les attitudes et faire accepter le droit° à la différence. Pour mobiliser l'opinion, **SOS Racisme** organise des campagnes, des marches, et surtout de grands concerts publics où les jeunes viennent manifester leur solidarité au mouvement.

L'emblème° de **SOS Racisme** est une main ouverte, bleue, rouge ou orange, avec un slogan «Touche pas à mon pote!»° Ce slogan signifie «Nous sommes différents, mais nous sommes frères et sœurs. Si tu attaques l'un de nous, nous sommes là pour le défendre et le protéger.» Cette petite main symbolique a eu un succès extraordinaire, non seulement en France, mais aussi en Suisse et en Belgique. Des dizaines de milliers de jeunes, surtout des lycéens, portent cet emblème sur leurs vêtements. C'est une façon de dire à tout le monde: «Je suis pour la justice, pour l'intégration et contre le racisme et la discrimination.»

de leur côté *as far as they are concerned* **chômage** *unemployment* **drogue** *drug addition* **renvoyer** *to send back* **résoudre** *to solve* **justement** *as a matter of fact* **bronzés** *light brown* **droit** *right* **emblème** = logo **pote** = copain *(slang)*

Teaching Strategy

Divide the class into pairs. Each pair will role-play an interview between a journalist and **Harlem Désir** twice, allowing each person to play both roles. Students should use their imaginations, asking questions about **S.O.S. Racisme** and its creation, etc.

Éthiopie

La chanson *Éthiopie** est chantée sur la musique universellement connue de *We are the world*. Cette chanson exprime la solidarité du peuple français avec les peuples les moins favorisés de la terre° et en particulier avec le peuple éthiopien, victime de la famine et de la guerre civile. Les chanteurs français les plus célèbres l'ont chantée dans de grands concerts publics organisés pour aider les enfants d'Éthiopie.

PASSEPORT EUROPÉEN CONTRE LE RAC...

"L'homme libre est celui qui aide l'autre à le devenir"

Ils n'ont jamais vu la pluie
Ils ne savent même plus sourire°
Il n'y a même plus de larmes°
Dans leurs yeux si grands

Les enfants d'Éthiopie
Embarqués sur un navire°
Qui n'a plus ni voiles° ni rames°
Attendent le vent.

Loin du coeur et loin des yeux
De nos villes, de nos banlieues
L'Éthiopie meurt peu à peu
Peu à peu

Rien° qu'une chanson pour eux
Pour ne plus fermer les yeux
C'est beaucoup et c'est bien peu
C'est bien peu.

Mais à chaque enfant qui tombe
Qui meurt loin des yeux de l'occident°
Notre ciel devient plus sombre°
Et notre avenir moins grand

Sur cette terre de sécheresse°
Ne fleurissent° que les tombes°
Malgré° toutes nos richesses
Leur soleil nous fait de l'ombre.°

(***refrain***)
Donnons-leur des lendemains°
En échange de rien
Donnons-leur la vie
Seulement la vie

Chez nous, la forêt succombe°
Là-bas, le désert avance°
Plus vite que la colombe°
Dans un ciel d'indifférence

Les enfants du tiers-monde°
N'ont que l'ombre d'une chance
Chaque jour, chaque seconde
Faisons taire° le silence.

* L'Éthiopie est un pays d'Afrique, voisin de la Somalie.

terre *earth* **sourire** *to smile* **larmes** *tears* **navire** = bateau **voiles** *sails* **rames** *oars* **rien que** = seulement **l'occident** *Western world* **sombre** = noir **sécheresse** *drought* **fleurissent** *blossom* **tombes** *tombstones* **malgré** *in spite of* **nous fait de l'ombre** *casts a shadow on us* **lendemains** *tomorrows* **succombe** = meurt **avance** = progresse **colombe** *dove* **tiers-monde** *Third World* **faisons taire** = mettons fin à

Notes culturelles

- **L'Éthiopie** is an East African country. Its official language is Amharic **(l'amharique)**. Many people also speak English. This country has suffered through many droughts and famines.
- *We are the World* was written in 1985 by Michael Jackson and Lionel Richie, and sung by a group of popular artists.

UNITÉ 8

MAIN THEME

Cities and City Life

Communication Function/Contexts
- Making a date
- Explaining where one lives
- Discussing city life
- Describing your neighborhood

Linguistic Goals
- Making wishes or suggestions
- Narrating past actions in sequence
- Formulating polite requests
- Hypothesizing

Online Study Center

Online Teaching Center

UNITÉ 8

En ville

Thème et Objectifs

Culture
In this unit, you will discover . . .
- how French cities developed historically and what they look like
- the advantages and disadvantages of urban life
- what types of street artists you might see in Paris or other large cities

Communication
You will learn how . . .
- to arrange to meet friends
- to explain where people live
- to describe your neighborhood

Langue
You will learn how . . .
- to make wishes or suggestions
- to formulate polite requests
- to narrate past actions in sequence
- to indicate what you would do in certain circumstances

TEACHING RESOURCES

ANCILLARIES
Student Activities Manual, Unit 8
Audio Program, Unit 8
Video-DVD Program, Unit 8
Chansons Audio CD

HM ClassPrep CD
Presentations, Unit 8
Audioscript, Unit 8
Videoscript, Unit 8
Assessment, Unit 8
Answer Key, Unit 8

◆ LES VILLES FRANÇAISES ◆

Les Français sont des citadins.° Aujourd'hui, 90% de la population habite en zone urbaine et presque° la moitié° dans des villes de plus de 100 000 habitants. L'urbanisme est peut-être un phénomène relativement récent, mais les grandes villes françaises sont très anciennes. Marseille et Nice ont été fondées au sixième siècle avant Jésus-Christ par des marins° grecs. Paris, Lyon, Bordeaux, Toulouse, Strasbourg, Rouen et Tours étaient déjà des centres urbains à l'époque romaine, il y a 2000 ans.

STRASBOURG

À l'origine, les villes ont été créées autour d'un point stratégique important: un port naturel, le croisement° de deux routes, le passage d'une rivière . . .

- ◆ Au Moyen Age, on a construit° un château et des remparts pour protéger ces villes.
- ◆ Quand les villes ont grandi° à partir° du XVIIe siècle, les remparts ont été détruits.° Les villes se sont alors développées autour d'un nouveau centre, ou le long de° larges avenues, suivant° un plan d'urbanisme bien établi.
- ◆ Avec la révolution industrielle au XIXe siècle, de vastes banlieues industrielles se sont développées concentriquement autour des villes.
- ◆ Au XXe siècle et particulièrement après 1960, les possibilités de travail ont attiré° des millions d'habitants de la campagne vers les grandes villes. Cet exode rural a nécessité la construction d'énormes quartiers résidentiels dans la banlieue de ces villes.

1300 200.000 HAB

1650 600.000 HAB

1850 1.000.000 HAB

1960 2.800.000 HAB

L'histoire des villes françaises explique leur géographie. *(Suite à la page 310-311)*

et vous?

Faites un bref historique de la ville où vous habitez ou d'une grande ville des États-Unis. Vous pouvez mentionner . . .

- quand cette ville a été fondée: par qui? et pourquoi?
- comment elle s'est développée
- combien d'habitants elle a aujourd'hui et quelles sont ses activités principales

NOM FRANÇAIS	NOM LATIN
Paris	LUTETIA
Lyon	LUGDUNUM
Marseille	MASSILIA
Bordeaux	BURDIGALA
Toulouse	TOLOSA
Nice	NICAEA
Strasbourg	ARGENTORATUM
Rouen	ROTOMAGUS
Tours	CAESARODUNUM

citadins *city people* **presque** *almost* **moitié** *half* **marins** *sailors*
croisement *crossing* **✱ construire** *to build* **grandi** *grew in size*
à partir *beginning in* **✱détruire** *to destroy* **le long de** *along*
suivant *according to* **attiré** *attracted*

INFO MAGAZINE

Theme: French cities

Reading Strategy: Reading for information, scanning

■ Additional Information

- Louis XIV commissioned **Sébastien Vauban** *(1633–1707)*, his favorite engineer, to fortify many French cities. Most of Vauban's fortifications still stand. Dunkerque, Lille, Besançon, Perpignan... all have great walls around their former boundaries. Because fortifications were built for military purposes, the walls have turrets and are surrounded by moats, allowing cities to defend themselves against invading armies.
- Paris started as a small fishing village where the tribe of the Parisii settled on an island on the Seine river. In 52 B.C., the village fell in the hands of the Romans who renamed it Lutaetia **(Lutèce).** The Parisii took their city back during the invasion led by Attila the Hun in 451. **Clovis** *(466–511)* was the first French king to make Paris his capital.

■ **Additional Information**

- Louis XIV commissioned **Sébastien Vauban** *(1633–1707)*, his favorite engineer, to fortify many French cities. Most of Vauban's fortifications still stand. Dunkerque, Lille, Besançon, Perpignan... all have great walls around their former boundaries. Because fortifications were built for military purposes, the walls have turrets and are surrounded by moats, allowing cities to defend themselves against invading armies.
- Paris started as a small fishing village where the tribe of the Parisii settled on an island on the Seine river. In 52 B.C., the village fell in the hands of the Romans who renamed it Lutaetia **(Lutèce).** The Parisii took their city back during the invasion led by Attila the Hun in 451. **Clovis** *(466–511)* was the first French king to make Paris his capital.

VILLE OU CAMPAGNE?

Êtes-vous un(e) citadin(e) ou un(e) villageois(e)? Êtes-vous plutôt fait(e) pour la vie en ville ou pour la vie à la campagne? Pour déterminer cela, évaluez les avantages et les inconvénients des villes. Donnez une note positive de 0 (pas important) à +5 (très important) à chacun des avantages. Donnez une note négative de 0 (pas important) à -5 (très important) à chacun des inconvénients.°

AVANTAGES

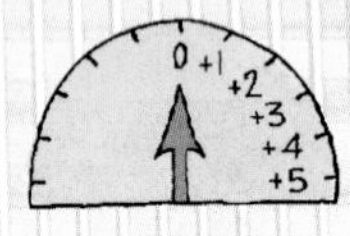

- **Il y a beaucoup d'endroits où on peut aller.**
  On peut aller au ciné, dans les magasins, aux restaurants . . .

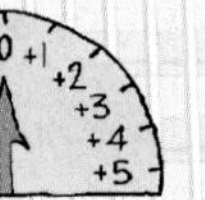

- **Il y a beaucoup de choses intéressantes à faire.**
  On peut voir des expositions, assister à des événements culturels . . .

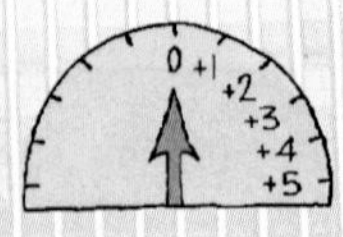

- **On peut faire la connaissance de beaucoup de gens d'origines° différentes.**
  Dans les villes, il y a une grande diversité ethnique, culturelle et sociale.

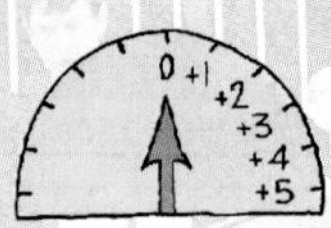

- **Les villes sont généralement animées.**
  On ne s'ennuie° jamais parce qu'il y a toujours de la vie et du mouvement.

INCONVÉNIENTS

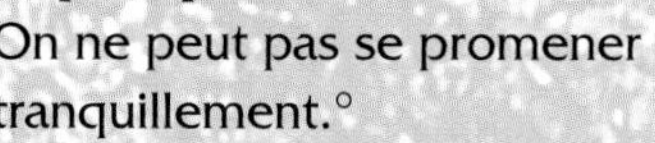

- **Il y a trop de voitures et, par conséquent, trop de bruit et trop de pollution.**
  On ne peut pas se promener tranquillement.°

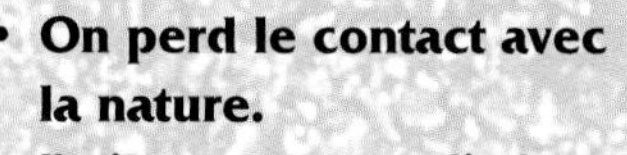

- **On perd le contact avec la nature.**
  Il n'y a pas assez d'arbres, pas assez de plantes, pas assez de fleurs.

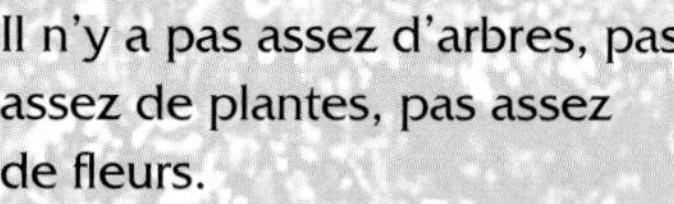

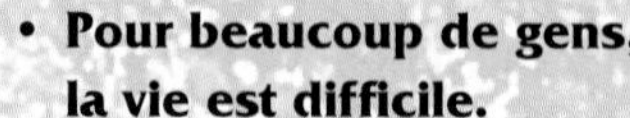

- **Pour beaucoup de gens, la vie est difficile.**
  Pour cela, les gens des villes sont souvent stressés et irritables.

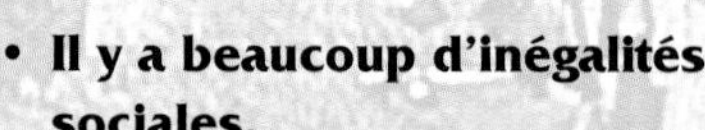

- **Il y a beaucoup d'inégalités sociales.**
  Il y a trop de gens pauvres et sans-abri.°

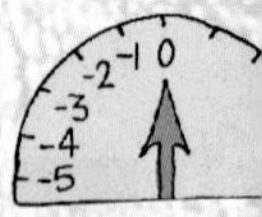

inconvénients *drawbacks* **origines** *backgrounds* **s'ennuie** *gets bored* **tranquillement** *safely* **sans-abri** *homeless*

INTERPRÉTATION

Faites le total des points positifs et négatifs. Quel total obtenez-vous?

de 15 à 20 points
Vous êtes certainement un(e) citadin(e), mais vous ignorez les charmes de la campagne. Un jour, vous devriez y faire un tour.

de 5 à 14 points
Vous êtes une personne optimiste et vous aimez la proximité des gens. Vous appréciez les avantages de la vie en ville. Pour cela, vous en minimisez les inconvénients.

de 4 à -4 points
Vous êtes une personne réaliste. Vous êtes conscient(e) des problèmes des grandes villes, mais vous les tolérez.

de -5 à -14 points
Vous n'aimez pas vivre là où il y a trop de gens. Vous préférez le calme et la tranquillité.

de -15 à -20 points
La ville n'est évidemment pas faite pour vous. Mais ne soyez pas trop idéaliste! La campagne aussi a ses problèmes.

INTERVIEW DANS LA RUE

Nous sommes place de Jaude à Clermont-Ferrand, un samedi après-midi.

Une journaliste de «La Montagne», le journal local, interviewe les gens qui passent. Elle parle maintenant à un homme d'une cinquantaine d'années qui porte un sac à provisions.°

— Bonjour, Monsieur. Vous êtes d'ici?
— Non, je suis de la campagne.
— Qu'est-ce qui vous attire° à Clermont? Le cinéma? les restaurants? les cafés?
— Non, je n'y vais jamais.
— Pouvez-vous me dire alors pourquoi vous venez ici?
— Ben, vous voyez, je viens pour faire mes courses.
— Il n'y a pas de supermarché chez vous?
— Si, mais en ville il y a un plus grand choix.
— Vous venez souvent à Clermont-Ferrand?
— Oui, toutes les semaines.
— Vous aimez cette ville?
— Pas tellement.°
— Pourquoi donc?
— Ben, il y a trop de circulation,° trop de bruit. . . Et puis, les gens sont pressés° et malpolis.°
— Alors, pourquoi est-ce que vous ne restez pas chez vous?
— Parce que chez moi, c'est trop calme. Alors, je viens en ville pour trouver un peu d'animation.

sac à provisions *shopping bag* **attire** *attracts* **pas tellement** *not that much* **circulation** *traffic* **pressés** *in a hurry* **malpolis** = impolis

Notes culturelles

The following U.S. cities have French origins:

- **Detroit,** Michigan, was founded by French explorer **Sieur Antoine de la Mothe Cadillac** in 1701.
- **Chicago,** Illinois, was a fur-trading post founded by **Jean-Baptiste Point du Sable** after the site was visited by French explorer **Robert Cavelier, Sieur de la Salle,** in 1682.
- **Fort Wayne,** Indiana, was a French fort in 1680.
- **Memphis,** Tennessee, was a French fort by 1797.
- **Minneapolis,** Minnesota, started when the site was discovered by the French missionary **Louis Hennepin** in 1680. Hennepin also "discovered" Niagara Falls.
- **Mobile,** Alabama, was settled by the brothers **Pierre** and **Jean-Baptiste Lemoyne** in 1702. It was the capital of French Louisiana between 1710 and 1719.
- **New Orleans,** Louisiana, was founded by **Jean-Baptiste Lemoyne, Sieur de Bienville** in 1718.
- **Saint Louis,** Missouri, was a French fur-trading post in 1764. It became American when bought as part of the Louisiana Purchase in 1803.

PARTIE 1

LE FRANÇAIS

PRATIQUE

TEACHING RESOURCES

Student Activities Manual, pp. 151–152

Tête-à-tête Pair Activity, Rendez-vous parisien, p. PA9

Audio Program, CD 8, Tracks 1–4

HM ClassPrep CD, Audioscript, Unit 8

LE FRANÇAIS PRATIQUE

Un rendez-vous en ville

COMMENT SE DONNER RENDEZ-VOUS

— Qu'est-ce que tu fais samedi?
Je suis libre.

— Est-ce que tu veux | aller au ciné / voir une exposition / **prendre un pot** / faire un tour en ville | avec moi?

prendre un pot *to have something to drink in a café*

— Où est-ce qu'on va **se donner rendez-vous?**
Chez moi.
Au café «Le Bistro».
Devant *(in front of)* le ciné.
À côté de *(next to)* la poste.
En face de *(across from)* la librairie.

— À quelle heure est-ce qu'on va | **se retrouver?** / **se rencontrer?**
À deux heures et demie.

— Alors, | d'accord! / **entendu** *(agreed)*. | **À samedi,** deux heures et demie devant le ciné. *(See you on Saturday . . .)*

1 Créa-dialogue: Une invitation

Il y a un(e) nouvel(le) élève français(e) dans votre classe. Invitez-le/la. Composez le dialogue avec votre partenaire qui va jouer le rôle de l'élève.

— Ask your friend what he/she is doing on a date of your choice.	⇄	*(He/she is free.)*
— Propose something interesting to do.	⇄	*(He/she accepts.)*
— Ask where you can meet.	⇄	*(He/she selects a place close to th[e] activity you proposed.)*
— Ask at what time you are going to meet.	⇄	*(He/she chooses a time.)*
— Say that you will see him/her at the time and place you have agreed on.	→	

306 Unité 8 PARTIE 1

LES RENCONTRES ET LES RENDEZ-VOUS

On peut	**rencontrer** *(meet by chance, run into)* **faire la connaissance de** *(meet for the first time)*	**quelqu'un.**
On peut	**sortir avec** **avoir un rendez-vous avec** **donner rendez-vous à** *(make a date)*	**quelqu'un.**
On peut	**se donner rendez-vous** *(agree to meet)* **se rencontrer** *(meet each other)* **se retrouver** *(meet each other)*	**quelque part** *(somewhere)*.

Conversations libres

Avec votre partenaire, choisissez l'une des situations suivantes. Composez ensemble un dialogue correspondant à cette situation et jouez ce dialogue en classe.

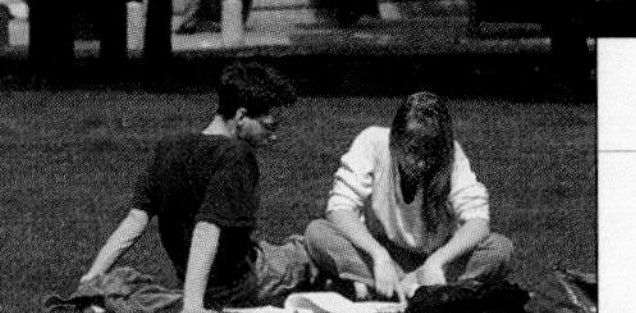

1 Une jeune fille amoureuse

Jérôme veut téléphoner à sa camarade de classe Véronique. C'est Sylvie, la soeur de Véronique, qui répond. Sylvie, qui est secrètement amoureuse de *(in love with)* Jérôme, essaie d'obtenir un rendez-vous avec lui.

Rôles: Jérôme / Sylvie

2 Au Jardin du Luxembourg

Une étudiante américaine est au Jardin du Luxembourg (un parc public à Paris). Un étudiant français engage la conversation. Il veut inviter la jeune Américaine à un concert de rock à la Villette. D'abord la jeune fille refuse poliment. L'étudiant français insiste. Elle finit par accepter l'invitation.

Rôles: l'étudiant français / l'étudiante américaine

3 Rendez-vous

Philippe téléphone à Juliette pour voir une exposition. Juliette a déjà vu cette exposition et propose autre chose.

Rôles: Philippe / Juliette

4 Une amie de passage *(A visiting friend)*

Marc téléphone souvent à sa cousine. Aujourd'hui, elle n'est pas chez elle et c'est une amie de passage qui répond. Marc s'excuse, puis il continue la conversation. Dans cette conversation il essaie de savoir ce que cette jeune fille aime faire. Finalement, il propose un rendez-vous. La jeune fille accepte, puis refuse.

Rôles: Marc / la jeune fille

Teaching Note

To review reflexive verbs, see **Unité 1**, p. 44.

Note linguistique

In France, you might also hear the familiar expressions: **d'acc.!** (instead of **d'accord**) and **O.K.**

Teaching Strategy

Have students write a group story, each person contributing two sentences. The premise of the story should be that students met their friend/friends somewhere. Encourage students to be original and creative, and to use as much vocabulary from pp. 306–307 as possible. At least one of each student's sentences should include a vocabulary word. As the story is created, a secretary will copy it onto the board. Switch secretaries after several sentences.

Supplementary vocabulary

aller boire un verre *to go have a drink*
faire les magasins *to go shopping*
faire du lèche-vitrine *to go window shopping*
(se) présenter à *to introduce (oneself) to*
croiser quelqu'un *to pass by someone*
tomber sur quelqu'un *to come across/meet someone*

Looking Ahead

The reciprocal use of reflexive verbs is reviewed and practiced in Unit 9.

Teaching Strategy

Divide the class into pairs and give them the following scenario:

Un rendez-vous

Votre camarade français(e) et vous, vous avez décidé de sortir ensemble ce week-end.

Décidez …

- d'une activité à faire
- d'un endroit pour le rendez-vous
- d'une heure

Composez et jouez le dialogue correspondant avec votre partenaire qui va jouer le rôle de votre camarade français(e).

LANGUE ET COMMUNICATION

TEACHING RESOURCES

Student Activities Manual, pp. 77–79, 152

Audio Program, CD 8, Tracks 5–6

HM ClassPrep CD, Audioscript, Unit 8

Notes linguistiques

- **Attention: si** becomes **s'** before **il** or **ils** only. **S'il venait. S'ils savaient. Si elle venait. Si elles savaient.**
- The noun **le bifteck** comes from the English expression *beef steak.* The expression **gagner son bifteck** means *to earn a living.*

Formation de l'imparfait

Révision ▶ p. R5

A. La construction si + imparfait

Note the use of the IMPERFECT in the following sentences:

Ah, si j'**étais** riche . . .	*Oh, if only I **were** rich . . .*
Ah, si mon frère me **prêtait** sa voiture . . .	*Oh, if only my brother **would lend me** his car . . .*
Dis, Alain, **si on allait** en ville?	*Hey, Alain, **what about going** downtown?*
Dis, Sophie, **si tu m'aidais?**	*Hey, Sophie, **what about helping me?***

To express a WISH or to make a SUGGESTION, the French often use the construction:

si + IMPERFECT

B. Le plus-que-parfait

As in English, the PLUPERFECT **(le plus-que-parfait)** is used to describe what people HAD DONE or WHAT HAD HAPPENED before another past action or event.

Cet été, j'ai visité Québec.	*This summer I visited Quebec City.*
L'année d'avant, **j'avais visité** Montréal.	*The year before, **I had visited** Montreal.*
Quand nous sommes arrivés à la gare, le train **était parti.**	*When we arrived at the station, the train **had left.***

The PLUPERFECT is formed as follows:

IMPERFECT of **avoir** or **être** + PAST PARTICIPLE

INFINITIVE	voyager	aller	s'amuser
PLUPERFECT	j' **avais voyagé** tu **avais voyagé** il/elle **avait voyagé** nous **avions voyagé** vous **aviez voyagé** ils/elles **avaient voyagé**	j' **étais allé(e)** tu **étais allé(e)** il/elle **était allé(e)** nous **étions allé(e)s** vous **étiez allé(e)(s)** ils/elles **étaient allé(e)s**	je **m'étais amusé(e)** tu **t'étais amusé(e)** il/elle **s'était amusé(e)** nous **nous étions amusé(e)s** vous **vous étiez amusé(e)(s)** ils/elles **s'étaient amusé(e)s**
NEGATIVE	je **n'avais pas voyagé**	je **n'étais pas allé(e)**	je **ne m'étais pas amusé**
INTERROGATIVE	est-ce que tu **avais voyagé?** **avais-tu voyagé?**	tu **étais allé(e)?** **étais-tu allé(e)?**	tu **t'étais amusé(e)?** **t'étais-tu amusé(e)?**

➡ In the pluperfect, the agreement rules for the past participle are the same as in the passé composé.

J'ai vu **Pauline** ce matin. Je **l'**avais vu**e** hier aussi.

J'ai développé **les photos que** j'avais pris**es** cet été.

1 En ville

Vous rencontrez votre partenaire en ville. Suggérez-lui de faire quelque chose avec vous (colonne A). Votre partenaire va refuser et expliquer pourquoi. Il/elle va aussi proposer autre chose (colonne B). Acceptez ou refusez. Continuez le dialogue jusqu'à ce que vous trouviez une chose d'intérêt commun.

▶ **— Dis, Corinne, si on prenait un pot?**
— Hm, je n'ai pas soif. Si on allait plutôt au ciné?
— Bonne idée! Allons au ciné. (Écoutez, j'ai vu tous les films de la semaine. Et si on...)

A : VOUS	B: VOTRE PARTENAIRE
▪ aller dans une pizzeria	▪ aller dans un restaurant chinois
▪ prendre un pot	▪ aller au ciné
▪ faire un tour dans le centre	▪ se promener dans le parc
▪ voir une exposition	▪ jouer aux jeux vidéo
▪ aller dans les magasins	▪ téléphoner à des copains
▪ ??	▪ ??

2 Et avant?

Lisez ce que ces personnes ont fait et dites ce qu'elles avaient fait avant.

▶ Le week-end dernier, Philippe est sorti avec Alice. (le week-end d'avant / avec Karine)
Le week-end d'avant, il était sorti avec Karine.

1. Dimanche, nous sommes allés au ciné. (samedi soir / à un concert)
2. Hier, j'ai pris un pot au Balto. (avant-hier / au Saint Victor)
3. Cet après-midi, tu t'es promené en ville. (ce matin / dans le parc)
4. Hier, tu as donné rendez-vous à Catherine dans un café. (jeudi / devant le musée)
5. Ce week-end, les touristes ont visité le château d'Amboise. (le week-end dernier / le château de Chenonceaux)
6. Cet été, nous sommes allés au Canada. (l'été d'avant / au Mexique)

3 Trop tard!

On fait parfois les choses trop tard. Décrivez ce qui est arrivé aux personnes suivantes.

▶ Jean-Claude arrive à l'aéroport.
L'avion est parti.
Quand Jean-Claude est arrivé à l'aéroport, l'avion était parti.

1. Nous arrivons au théâtre.
   La pièce *(play)* a commencé.
2. Olivier téléphone à Catherine.
   Elle est sortie avec Jean-Paul.
3. La serveuse apporte l'addition.
   Les clients sont partis.
4. Monsieur Renaud entre dans la cuisine.
   Le chien a mangé le bifteck.
5. Vous arrivez à la pâtisserie.
   Le pâtissier a vendu le dernier gâteau.
6. Le lièvre *(hare)* arrive.
   La tortue *(tortoise)* a gagné la course.

4 Pourquoi?

Expliquez pourquoi les choses suivantes sont arrivées. Attention: le verbe peut être affirmatif ou négatif.

▶ Les touristes n'ont pas trouvé de chambre d'hôtel. (réserver?)
Ils n'avaient pas réservé.

1. Monsieur Dupont a raté son avion. (se dépêcher?)
2. Tu n'as pas vu l'éclipse de lune *(moon)*. (se coucher trop tôt?)
3. Vous n'êtes pas allés au concert. (acheter les billets?)
4. Thomas n'a pas vu le film à la télé. (rentrer trop tard chez lui?)
5. Nous avons eu une indigestion. (manger trop?)
6. Les élèves ont eu une mauvaise note à l'examen. (étudier?)

■ **Teaching Note**
For photos of the castles of **Amboise** and **Chenonceaux**, see **Interlude 3**, p. 147.

■ **Réponses: Activité 4**
1. Il ne s'était pas dépêché.
2. Tu t'étais couché(e) trop tôt.
3. Vous n'aviez pas acheté les billets.
4. Il était rentré trop tard chez lui.
5. Nous avions trop mangé.
6. Ils n'avaient pas étudié.

Variation:
Demandez pourquoi les choses suivantes sont arrivées. Attention: le verbe peut être affirmatif ou négatif.
Exemple:
Les touristes n'ont pas trouvé de chambre d'hôtel. (réserver?)
N'avaient-ils pas réservé?/ Est-ce qu'ils n'avaient pas réservé?

INFO MAGAZINE

Theme: French cities

Reading Strategy: Scanning, reading for information

■ **Anecdote**

La plus vieille maison de Paris est située au **51, rue de Montmorency.** Elle a été construite par **Nicolas Flamel,** en 1407.

■ **Irregular Verbs**

(see Appendix C)

se distraire:

je me distrais
tu te distrais
il/elle se distrait,
nous nous distrayons
vous vous distrayez
ils/elles se distraient

s'asseoir

La géographie des villes françaises

L'histoire des villes françaises, décrite brièvement à la page 303, explique leur aspect et leur structure si différents des villes américaines. Une ville française typique comprend° les quartiers suivants:

LA VILLE MÊME

La «vieille ville»

C'est le quartier historique, aujourd'hui très touristique, où l'on trouve les vestiges du passé: la cathédrale, des rues étroites,° des maisons anciennes très pittoresques, parfois un château, des vestiges de remparts et même des ruines romaines. Les maisons anciennes ont souvent été restaurées. Ce sont des résidences très recherchées° par les habitants des villes qui y trouvent à la fois° le confort du présent et le charme du passé.

Le «centre-ville»

C'est l'endroit le plus dynamique, le plus animé et, pour beaucoup de gens, le plus intéressant de la ville. Situé généralement autour d'une place monumentale, on y trouve les bâtiments administratifs (la mairie, le palais de justice, la poste. . .), les grands magasins, les boutiques de luxe, les cinémas, le théâtre municipal, les cafés et les meilleurs restaurants de la ville. Il y a parfois un jardin public avec des fontaines, des parterres de fleurs° et des bancs.° Le week-end les gens viennent au centre-ville pour faire leur shopping et pour se distraire.° Quand il fait beau, ils s'asseyent° à la terrasse des cafés pour voir le spectacle de la rue et aussi pour être vus.

Les quartiers résidentiels

Ils sont situés autour du centre-ville et le long d'avenues transversales. C'est là que les gens habitent. Les immeubles ont un maximum de six étages. Leur rez-de-chaussée est généralement occupé par des boutiques. Le reste est divisé en appartements.

comprend *includes* **étroites** *narrow* **recherchées** *sought after* **à la fois** *at the same time* **parterres de fleurs** *flower beds* **bancs** *benches* **se distraire** *to have fun* ***s'asseoir** *to sit down*

LA BANLIEUE

Les banlieues qui s'étendent° autour des villes sont modernes, mais la vie y est généralement monotone, banale, même ennuyeuse.° Il y a différentes sortes de banlieues. Dans les banlieues «chics», les gens habitent dans des maisons individuelles entourées° de jardins. Dans les banlieues ouvrières,° les gens habitent dans des «grands ensembles».° Ce sont des immeubles de 10, 20 ou 30 étages, à l'architecture simple mais souvent sans grand intérêt. Dans les banlieues les plus défavorisées, les gens habitent dans des logements précaires sans confort et sans hygiène. Pour aider les habitants des banlieues pauvres, le gouvernement français a financé la construction d'HLM (habitation à loyer modéré°) où les gens pourraient avoir l'occasion de louer ou acheter leur appartement à des conditions avantageuses.

Les «villes nouvelles»

Toutes les grandes villes du monde ont un problème commun: la qualité de la vie y est menacée par une expansion trop rapide et souvent anarchique. Pour limiter l'expansion de Paris et de sa banlieue, le gouvernement français a décidé de créer cinq villes entièrement nouvelles dans la région parisienne: Cergy-Pontoise, Saint-Quentin-en-Yvelines, Évry, Melun-Sénart, Marne-la-Vallée. Ces «villes nouvelles» sont de dimension moyenne.° Elles ont de 80 000 à 250 000 habitants. Tout a été planifié° pour assurer à ceux-ci un bon équilibre entre le travail et les loisirs. Ces villes offrent° à leur population non seulement des logements et des emplois, mais aussi des centres commerciaux, des équipements culturels et sportifs, des parcs de loisirs. Et, pour maintenir le contact avec la nature, des espaces verts et des plans d'eau° y ont été aménagés.°

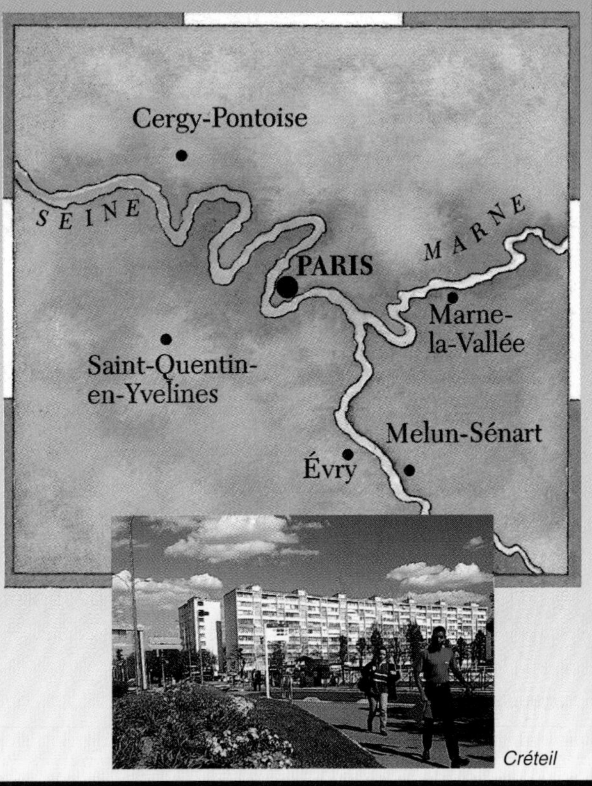

Créteil

et vous?

Imaginez que vous allez passer une année dans une grande ville française. Où préféreriez-vous habiter? dans la vieille ville? dans le centre-ville? dans un quartier résidentiel? dans la banlieue? dans une «ville nouvelle»? Expliquez pourquoi.

s'étendent *extend* **ennuyeuse** *boring* **entourées** *surrounded* **ouvrières** *working class* **grands ensembles** *housing projects* **loyer modéré** *low rent* **moyenne** *average* **planifié** *planned* ***offrir** *to offer* **plans d'eau=** lacs artificiels **aménagés =** développés

■ Notes linguistiques

- The expression **le bidonville** originated in North Africa. A compound of **le bidon** *(can)* and **la ville,** it designates rudimentary shelters made of scraps in the poorest areas.
- The abbreviation **H.L.M.** can be either masculine or feminine: **le H.L.M,** or **la H.L.M.**

■ Teaching Strategy

Assign the following:

- **Photos.** Choisissez une des photos du texte et décrivez ce que vous voyez.
- **Débat**. Votre partenaire et vous, vous allez passer l'été dans une ville française. Vous cherchez un appartement. Votre partenaire voudrait habiter dans un quartier résidentiel moderne. Vous, au contraire, vous préférez habiter dans la vieille ville. Débattez les avantages et les inconvénients de chaque situation.

■ Irregular Verb

(see Appendix C)
offrir *(see* **ouvrir***)*

NOTES CULTURELLES

- **Euro Disney** opened in April 1992 in Marne-la-Vallée. The theme park is about 20 miles from Paris.
- Although they existed before World War II, more **H.L.M.** started being built in 1947 to deal with the housing crisis brought on by war damages.

PARTIE 2

LE FRANÇAIS PRATIQUE

LE FRANÇAIS PRATIQUE — Comment expliquer où on habite

TEACHING RESOURCES

Student Activities Manual, pp. 153–156

Audio Program, CD 9, Tracks 1–5

HM ClassPrep CD, Audioscript, Unit 8

Video/DVD Program, Unit 8

Les nombres

Révision ▶ p. R10

— Où habites-tu?

J'habite | 10, rue de la République. | 25, avenue Victor Hugo. | 120, boulevard Raspail. | 18, place Voltaire. | dans la 35e rue. | dans la 6e avenue.

— Où est-ce exactement?

C'est | dans **le centre-ville.** | dans **la banlieue** *(suburbs).* | dans **le quartier** *(district, area, neighborhood)* Saint-Pierre.

— Dans quel genre de résidence habites-tu?

J'habite dans | **une maison individuelle.** | **un appartement.** | **une tour** *(high rise).* | **un immeuble** *(apartment building)* | **un HLM*** *(low-income housing project)*

— C'est près d'ici?

Oui, c'est | **tout près** *(nearby).* | **à 100 mètres.** | **à dix minutes à pied.**

Non, c'est | **loin.** | **à 3 kilomètres.** | **à vingt minutes en bus.**

— Comment est-ce qu'on peut aller là-bas?

On peut y aller | à pied. | à vélo.

On peut prendre | un bus. | un taxi. | le métro.

* **HLM** = Habitation à Loyer Modéré *(low-rent housing)*

1 Une invitation à dîner

Vous avez invité votre camarade français(e) à dîner chez vous. Votre camarade accepte, mais il/elle a besoin de renseignements pour aller chez vous. Il/elle veut savoir . . .

- votre adresse
- dans quelle partie de la ville vous habitez
- si c'est loin de l'école
- comment aller chez vous

Vous lui expliquez. Composez le dialogue correspondant avec votre partenaire et jouez-le en classe.

Teaching Suggestion: Video/DVD Program

In this section of the Unit 8 video, *Vidéo-drame: Un rendez-vous en ville*, the theme of giving directions to one's house is covered. As you play the video the first time, have students write down some of the directions being given. Next, review the directions by playing the video one more time. After watching the video, have each student explain how to get from one place on campus to another using some of the phrases from the video.

Dans mon quartier, il y a . . .

des boutiques	**un centre sportif**	**un parc**
des commerces *(small businesses)*	**un centre de loisirs** *(recreation center)*	**un jardin public**
un grand centre commercial *(mall)*	**une Maison des Jeunes** *(Youth center)*	**une mairie** *(city hall)*
		une poste *(post office)*
une station-service	**une bibliothèque**	**un poste de police** / **une gendarmerie** *(police station)*
	un musée	
		une caserne de pompiers

FLASH d'information

La police nationale et la gendarmerie sont deux corps de police distincts. Certaines de leurs fonctions sont semblables, mais d'autres sont différentes. L'un des rôles de la gendarmerie est d'assurer la police° des routes. C'est à eux qu'on a affaire° quand on ne respecte pas le code de la route.°

la police *law enforcement*
avoir affaire à *to have to deal with* **code de la route** *traffic regulations*

2 Créa-dialogue: En ville

Votre partenaire, qui est français(e), visite votre ville. Il/elle veut faire l'une des choses suivantes. Dites-lui à quel endroit aller et si c'est loin d'ici.

▶ **— Je voudrais envoyer des lettres.**
— Va à la poste.
— Est-ce que c'est loin d'ici?
— Non, c'est à 500 mètres.
— Comment est-ce que je peux aller là-bas?
— Vas-y à pied.
(Prends le bus.)

- faire réparer ma voiture
- faire une promenade à pied
- jouer au volley
- rencontrer de jeunes Américains
- emprunter un livre
- faire des achats
- déclarer la perte *(loss)* de mon passeport
- interviewer un membre du conseil municipal *(city council)*
- envoyer des lettres
- voir une exposition de photos

Teaching Strategy: Game

Vocabulaire
Give each student an equal number of vocabulary words. Ask them to write definitions or explanations for each word. Each student then reads the definitions aloud and the class tries to guess which vocabulary word matches the definition.

Supplementary vocabulary

une maison jumelée *two-family house*
un grand ensemble *residential area consisting of large blocks of apartments*
un gratte-ciel *skyscraper*
un studio *studio*
un pavillon *single house*
un pied-à-terre *pied-à-terre (secondary or temporary lodging)*
un meublé *furnished apartment*

Note culturelle

The **gendarmes** are part of the military, whereas the **police** are not. The uniforms for each corps used to be different, but now they are quite similar. The only differences are the hat and the stripes on the **épaulettes.** The **police** wear hats similar to those worn by our police force, whereas the **gendarmes** wear the traditional **képi.**

Teaching Note

Some distance equivalences (approximately):

200 feet	60 mètres
500 feet	150 mètres
half a mile	800 mètres
a mile	1 kilomètre et demi

NOTES CULTURELLES

- **Victor Hugo (1802–1885)** was a very influential writer of his time. He was the author of masterpieces such as *Les Misérables* and *Notre-Dame de Paris.* (For more information, see p. 224.)
- **François Raspail (1794–1878)** was a chemist and a political activist who went to jail and was exiled for his democratic ideals. He was elected **député** *(representative)* in 1876.
- **Voltaire (François-Marie Arouet, 1694–1778)** was a writer famous for his sharp wit and ruthless fights against injustice. He was jailed in the Bastille and was exiled for questioning the monarchy. His works include *Candide, Zadig,* and many poems.

LANGUE ET COMMUNICATION

TEACHING RESOURCES

Student Activities Manual, pp. 157

Audio Program, CD 8, Tracks 6–7

HM ClassPrep CD, Audioscript, Unit 8

Teaching Strategy: Variation

- Activity 1 can be done in pairs with partners comparing their choices.
- It can also be done as a class survey: first the students each write out their answers, and then the results are tabulated.

A. Révision: le conditionnel

The CONDITIONAL is used to express what WOULD HAPPEN, what people WOULD DO in certain circumstances.

Formation du conditionnel

Révision ▶ p. R19

Review the formation of the conditional:

FUTURE STEM + IMPERFECT ENDINGS

INFINITIVE		parler	ENDINGS
FUTURE	je	**parler**ai	
CONDITIONAL	je	**parlerais**	**-ais**
	tu	**parlerais**	**-ais**
	il/elle/on	**parlerait**	**-ait**
	nous	**parlerions**	**-ions**
	vous	**parleriez**	**-iez**
	ils/elles	**parleraient**	**-aient**

Verbs with irregular stems:

payer	je **paier**ais	devoir	je **devr**ais
acheter	j'**achèter**ais	pouvoir	je **pourr**ais
		vouloir	je **voudr**ais
appeler	j'**appeller**ais		
être	je **ser**ais		
avoir	j'**aur**ais	envoyer	j'**enverr**ais
aller	j'**ir**ais	recevoir	je **recevr**ais
faire	je **fer**ais	savoir	je **saur**ais
venir	je **viendr**ais	voir	je **verr**ais

1 Au choix

Supposez que vous ayez le choix entre les possibilités suivantes. Que choisiriez-vous? (Si vous voulez, expliquez votre choix.)

▶ habiter en ville ou à la campagne?
J'habiterais à la campagne (parce que j'aime la nature).

1. habiter dans le centre-ville ou en banlieue?
2. travailler dans un restaurant ou dans un supermarché?
3. assister à un concert ou à un match de foot?
4. passer les vacances à la mer ou à la campagne?
5. aller au ciné ou au restaurant?
6. voir une comédie ou un film d'aventures?
7. avoir une moto ou une voiture de sport?
8. faire du ski nautique ou du parapente?
9. être acteur (actrice) de cinéma ou athlète professionnel(le)?

2 Les élections municipales

Vous êtes journaliste pour le journal de votre ville. Vous interviewez votre partenaire qui est candidat(e) à la mairie.

▶ construire des HLM?
— Est-ce que vous construiriez des HLM?
— Oui, je construirais des HLM.
(Non, je ne construirais pas de HLM.)

- développer les transports publics
- fermer le jardin public la nuit
- contrôler la pollution
- taxer les commerces
- créer un centre de loisirs pour les personnes âgées
- construire une nouvelle caserne de pompiers
- fermer la bibliothèque le dimanche
- interdire la circulation dans le centre-ville

3 La meilleure solution

Imaginez que vous êtes dans les situations suivantes. Qu'est-ce que vous feriez? Comparez votre solution avec celle de votre partenaire.

SITUATION A

Vous êtes allé(e) dans le centre-ville en bus. Au moment de rentrer sur le campus, vous vous apercevez *(realize)* que vous avez perdu votre porte-monnaie *(wallet)*.
Que feriez-vous?

- rentrer à pied?
- demander de l'argent à un passant *(passerby)*?
- faire de l'auto-stop *(hitchhiking)*?
- ??

SITUATION B

Pour son anniversaire, vous avez invité votre meilleur(e) ami(e) à dîner chez vous. Au moment de préparer le repas, vous vous apercevez *(realize)* que la cuisinière *(stove)* ne marche pas. Que feriez-vous?

- téléphoner à votre ami(e) et annuler le repas?
- acheter une pizza?
- inviter votre ami(e) au restaurant?
- ??

SITUATION C

Votre frère a une copine. Un jour vous découvrez que cette copine sort avec un autre garçon. Que feriez-vous?

- dire la vérité à votre frère?
- parler à la copine de votre frère?
- envoyer une lettre d'insultes à l'autre garçon?
- ??

SITUATION D

Vous êtes dans un ascenseur quand une panne d'électricité *(power failure)* paralyse tout l'immeuble. Que feriez-vous?

- attendre calmement l'arrivée des pompiers?
- forcer la porte?
- monter sur le toit de l'ascenseur?
- ??

4 Les vacances idéales

Avec votre partenaire, discutez des vacances idéales. Posez-vous les questions suivantes (en français, bien sûr!):

- *where would you go?*
- *how would you travel?*
- *how long would you stay?*
- *in what type of hotel would you stay?*
- *at what time would you get up?*
- *what would you do in the morning?*
- *what would you do in the afternoon?*
- *what would you do to meet people?*
- *what would you do to stay in shape* **(en forme)?**
- *what would you do in the evenings?*

Puis, mettez-vous d'accord et écrivez un petit paragraphe où vous décrivez ce que vous feriez.

▶ **Pour nos vacances idéales, nous irions...**

■ Expansion: Activity 2

Have students continue the conversation by explaining their positions.
— Pourquoi?
— Parce que je veux aider les gens qui n'ont pas beaucoup d'argent.

Teaching Strategy: Activity 4

You may wish to practice the questions before students do the activity in pairs.
Où irais-tu?
Comment voyagerais-tu?
etc.

TEACHING RESOURCES

Student Activities Manual,
pp. 80–81

Proverbe

Avec des *si,* on mettrait Paris en bouteille. *(In theory, anything is possible.)*

Note culturelle

Le Parc de la Villette, in Paris, is a popular attraction. In **la Cité des sciences et de l'industrie** you will find an IMAX theater and a science museum, while in **la Cité de la musique,** you will find a concert hall and a music school.

B. Le conditionnel dans les phrases avec si

Note the use of the conditional in the following sentences.

Si j'avais une voiture, j'**irais** à la campagne.	*If I had a car (but I don't), I **would go** to the country.*
Si nous habitions à Paris, nous **voyagerions** en métro.	*If we were living in Paris (but we aren't), we **would travel** by subway.*

The CONDITIONAL is used to express what WOULD HAPPEN, if certain conditions contrary to reality were met.
In such sentences, the construction is usually:

si-clause: IMPERFECT	result clause: CONDITIONAL
Si je **gagnais** à la loterie,	j'**achèterais** une moto.

➡ In French, the CONDITIONAL is never used in the **si**-clause.

5 Si j'habitais . . .

Pour chaque endroit, décrivez 2 ou 3 choses que vous feriez si vous habitiez là.

▶ à Paris
Si j'habitais à Paris, je parlerais français tout le temps.
Je voyagerais en métro.
Je visiterais de temps en temps le musée d'Orsay.
J'irais parfois écouter des concerts à la Villette . . . .

1. à San Francisco
2. en Floride
3. à la Martinique
4. dans le centre-ville
5. dans un petit village à la campagne
6. dans la banlieue d'une grande ville

6 Rêves *(Dreams)*

Rêver ne coûte rien. Expliquez les rêves des personnes suivantes en utilisant les éléments des colonnes A et B. Soyez logique!

	A	B
nous	• invisible	• savoir tout
vous	• multi-millionnaire	• protéger les innocents
Sandrine	• extra-lucide	• voyager dans l'espace
Philippe	• Superman/Wonder Woman	• habiter dans un château
mes copains	• Robin des Bois *(Robin Hood)*	• avoir une Rolls-Royce
		• aider les pauvres
		• voler comme des oiseaux
		• passer à travers les murs
		• connaître le passé, le présent et l'avenir

▶ **Si Philippe était Robin des Bois, il aiderait les pauvres.**

7 Problèmes et solutions

Votre partenaire va choisir l'un des problèmes suivants. Dites-lui ce que vous feriez à sa place. Donnez-lui 2 ou 3 suggestions (affirmatives ou négatives).

Je grossis.
Si je grossissais, je mangerais moins.
J'irais au centre sportif et je ferais de la gymnastique tous les jours.
Je ne prendrais pas le bus pour aller en ville. J'irais à pied.

- Je n'ai pas d'appétit.
- Je dors trop.
- Je ne me sens pas très bien.
- Je perds mon temps.
- Je ne réussis pas à mes examens.
- J'ai besoin d'argent.
- Je suis déprimé(e) *(depressed)*.
- J'ai un problème avec mon copain (ma copine).
- J'ai des difficultés avec mes parents.
- Mon frère (ma soeur) m'embête tout le temps.

8 Que feriez-vous?

Choisissez l'une des situations suivantes et composez un petit paragraphe où vous décrivez ce que vous feriez (ou ce que vous ne feriez pas) si vous étiez dans cette situation. Utilisez le conditionnel . . . et votre imagination!

1. Pour impressionner Stéphanie, sa nouvelle copine, Raphaël l'a invitée dans un grand restaurant. Au moment de payer, Raphaël s'aperçoit *(realizes)* qu'il a perdu son portefeuille.
   Si j'étais Raphaël, . . .
2. Depuis plusieurs semaines, Caroline reçoit des lettres d'un admirateur inconnu. Elle veut savoir qui est ce mystérieux correspondant.
   Si j'étais Caroline, . . .
3. Jérôme a emprunté la voiture de Cécile. Au moment de rendre la voiture à son amie, il remarque une éraflure *(dent, scratch)* fraîche. Il n'est pas sûr que cette éraflure était là quand il a emprunté la voiture.
   Si j'étais Jérôme, . . .
4. Jean-Claude a passé la soirée dans une petite salle de la bibliothèque municipale. Il est maintenant onze heures. Au moment de sortir, Jean-Claude s'aperçoit qu'il est seul et que toutes les portes sont fermées à clé.
   Si j'étais Jean-Claude, . . .
5. Madame Lescot a invité ses amis à dîner. Au moment de préparer le repas, elle s'aperçoit que sa cuisinière *(stove)* ne marche pas.
   Si j'étais Madame Lescot, . . .
6. Monsieur Rimbaud voyage souvent en avion. Un jour, il prend par erreur une valise qui n'est pas à lui. Chez lui, il ouvre la valise et découvre un million de dollars . . . et l'adresse d'une bande de terroristes.
   Si j'étais Monsieur Rimbaud, . . .

Teaching Strategy: Expansion

Comparez votre paragraphe avec celui de votre partenaire.

9 Qu'est-ce que vous feriez à leur place?

Avec votre partenaire, choisissez une des situations suivantes et dites ce que vous feriez dans ces situations.

A

B

C

Supplementary vocabulary

la barque *small boat*
couler *to sink, drown*
la soucoupe volante *flying saucer*
le martien *martian*
atterrir *to land*
la panne (de voiture) *(car) breakdown*
tomber en panne *to break down*

TEACHING RESOURCES

Student Activities Manual, pp. 82–83

■ Expansion

Also: il faut → **il faudrait**
il vaut mieux → **il vaudrait mieux**

■ Teaching Strategy

You may wish to tell your students that polite requests with **pouvoir** are particularly useful when traveling in French-speaking areas. For example:

Pourriez-vous me dire où se trouve la banque la plus proche?, etc.

The conditional in English is similarly used to express politeness.

■ Note linguistique

In indirect speech, a statement is made using a DECLARATIVE VERB, such as:

dire, déclarer, annoncer, écrire, prédire, promettre, etc.

C. Le conditionnel: autres usages

POLITE REQUESTS

The conditional of verbs such as **vouloir, pouvoir, devoir** is used instead of the present to express a WISH or REQUEST in a MORE POLITE manner. Compare:

Je veux regarder tes photos.	***I want*** *to look at your pictures.*
Je voudrais regarder tes photos.	***I would like*** *to look at your pictures.*
Peux-tu me prêter ton vélo?	***Can you*** *loan me your bike?*
Pourrais-tu me prêter ton vélo?	***Could you*** *loan me your bike?*
Vous devez être à l'heure.	***You must*** *be on time.*
Vous devriez être à l'heure.	***You should*** *be on time.*

INDIRECT SPEECH

The conditional is used to report what people mentioned IN THE PAST about a FUTURE EVENT. It describes what they said they WOULD DO or what WOULD HAPPEN later.
Compare the use of tenses in the following sentences:

Maintenant, Éric **dit** qu'il **ira** au ciné.	*Now Eric* ***says*** *that he* ***will go*** *to the movies.*
Hier, il **a dit** qu'il **irait** au concert.	*Yesterday he* ***said*** *that he* ***would go*** *to the concert.*

After a declarative verb (such as **dire** or **écrire**), future events are expressed according to the following tense sequence:

DECLARATIVE VERB	FUTURE EVENT
present	future
past (imperfect, passé composé, pluperfect)	conditional

Qu'est-ce que la météo a annoncé hier?
Elle a annoncé qu'il ferait beau ce weekend!
HOTEL DE LA PLAGE

Teaching Strategy

Divide the class into pairs and give them the following situation:

Isabelle et Florent sont sortis ensemble pendant quatre ans. Ils se sont fait beaucoup de promesses. Maintenant, Isabelle veut son indépendance alors elle quitte Florent. Florent rappelle à Isabelle toutes ses/leurs promesses. Qu'est-ce que Florent lui dit? (Tu m'as dit que...)

Each pair of students should come up with an original dialog to present to the class.

Soyons polis!

Montrez que vous êtes poli(e). Pour cela, reformulez les phrases suivantes en utilisant le conditionnel.

▶ Est-ce que tu veux un dessert?
Est-ce que tu voudrais un dessert?

1. Je veux te parler.
2. Nous voulons sortir avec vous.
3. Peux-tu m'inviter à ta boum?
4. Pouvons-nous amener nos amis?
5. Pouvez-vous être à l'heure?
6. Tu dois m'aider.
7. Vous devez être plus généreux.
8. Vous ne devez pas mentir *(tell lies)*.

Messages téléphoniques

Votre partenaire a écouté votre répondeur *(answering machine)* et il/elle a noté les messages suivants. Demandez-lui qui a téléphoné et ce que chaque personne a dit.

▶ **— Est-ce qu'il y a eu des messages?**
— Oui, Paul a téléphoné.
— Et qu'est-ce qu'il a dit?
— Il a dit qu'il viendrait demain.

Messages Téléphoniques

- Paul va venir demain.
- Marc et Sophie vont t'attendre à 5 heures au Balto.
- Ta cousine va se marier cet été.
- Sandrine va te retrouver samedi au match de foot.
- Claire et Florence vont aller au concert dimanche.
- Isabelle va voir un film ce soir.
- Tes copains vont rester chez eux ce week-end.

Supplementary vocabulary

(Realia)
le publiphone *phone booth (where you can pay with a card)*
la cabine téléphonique *phone booth*
la télécarte *prepaid phone card*
composer (un numéro) *to dial (a number)*
décrocher (le combiné) *to pick up (the receiver)*
le numéro vert *toll-free number*

Notes culturelles

- Almost all phone booths in France require the use of a phone card instead of change. The **télécarte** is a smart card with a prepaid amount recorded on its electronic chip. These cards are avidly sought after by collectors who seek rare designs and limited editions.
- Like Americans, French people may choose to have an unlisted number **(être sur la liste rouge)**.

Teaching Strategy

Have the students write a story (including dialog) in which they employ all the different uses of the conditional (pp. 314–319). Ideas:

- winning the lottery / promised to share with someone
- eating grapefruit for 3 weeks / friend said he/she lost 20 lbs. doing same

Encourage students to be creative and to use as much vocabulary and as many verbs in the conditional as possible.

INFO MAGAZINE

Theme: Street entertainers in France

Reading Strategy: Reading for pleasure

Note culturelle

The most popular French mime is **Marcel Marceau.** Born in Strasbourg in 1923, Marcel Marceau reinvented the art of mime with his character, a gentle clown called Bip. Marceau opened an international mime school in Paris, and has travelled around the world as Bip, his silent alter-ego.

Additional Information

In Paris, you will always see various artists performing in front of the **Pompidou Center.** In Montreal (Quebec) the **Place Jacques Cartier** in the old town is a favorite stage for performance artists.

Irregular Verbs

(see Appendix C)

vivre

se distraire *(see p. 310)*

plaire

suivre

s'apercevoir (see **recevoir**)

rire

Le spectacle EST DANS LA RUE

Pour les Français, la rue n'est pas seulement un endroit où l'on passe pour aller au travail, à l'école, ou dans des magasins. C'est aussi un endroit où l'on vit.° On y rencontre ses amis. On s'y repose (à la terrasse des cafés). On y dîne (à la terrasse des restaurants). Et surtout, on s'y distrait.°

La rue est en effet un théâtre permanent qui offre toutes sortes de spectacles aux «badauds».° Certains spectacles sont spontanés et gratuits: un accident, une querelle entre deux automobilistes, une manifestation,° le passage d'une personne célèbre,° le tournage° d'un film, etc. Les autres spectacles sont organisés par des «artistes» et laissés° à l'appréciation personnelle des passants. Si vous jugez° que le spectacle est bon, vous laisserez° quelques pièces de monnaie° dans le chapeau que vous tendra° l'artiste. Sinon, vous quitterez les lieux avant la fin° du spectacle.

Autrefois, les «artistes des rues» étaient des jongleurs,° des chanteurs, des montreurs° d'animaux (ours,° singes,° chiens savants,° etc. . .). Les artistes d'aujourd'hui ne sont pas tellement° différents des artistes d'autrefois et leur principe est le même: l'artiste s'installe dans un endroit fréquenté; les «badauds» arrivent; l'artiste commence son spectacle; à la fin du spectacle, il fait la quête.° Il y a plusieurs catégories d'artistes de rue:

◇ LES MUSICIENS

Ce sont les plus nombreux.° Suivant° la clientèle ou le quartier, ils jouent du jazz, du rock, de la musique folklorique, de la musique indienne, des rythmes africains, ou même de la musique classique. L'important° est que la musique soit bonne et que le musicien soit sympathique ou ait l'air exotique. Parce que leur musique plaît,° les jeunes musiciens américains qui jouent en France ont généralement beaucoup de succès!

◇ LES MIMES

Ils opèrent° généralement devant la terrasse d'un café. Leur costume est classique: pantalon noir, gilet° rayé,° chapeau noir. La technique du mime consiste à suivre° un passant et à imiter tous ses gestes avec la plus grande exactitude possible. Le passant ne s'aperçoit° de rien, mais les spectateurs qui sont à la terrasse du café rient° . . . et contribuent!

***vivre** *to live* ***se distraire** *to have fun* **badauds** *onlookers* **manifestation** *demonstration* **célèbre** *famous* **tournage** *making* **laissés** *left* **jugez** = pensez **laisserez** = mettrez **monnaie** *coins* **tendra** = présentera **fin** *end* **jongleurs** *jugglers* **montreurs** *exhibitor* **ours** *bears* **singes** *monkeys* **savants** *trained* **tellement** *that (much)* **fait la quête** *passes the hat* **nombreux** *numerous* **suivant** *according to* **L'important** = la chose importante ***plaire** *to please* **opèrent** = travaillent **gilet** *vest* **rayé** *striped* ***suivre** *to follow* ***s'apercevoir** *to notice* ***rire** *to laugh*

Teaching Strategy

This *Info Magazine* article provides additional cultural information on life in French cities. It is designed to provide easy reading practice. Since these readings are optional, you may allow students to choose whether or not to concentrate heavily on this material. If you wish to use the quizzes as a self-check for comprehension, students may find it useful.

LES AUTOMATES

Ils sont déguisés en personnages d'autrefois. Leur visage couvert de poudre° ne manifeste° aucune expression. Leurs gestes sont complètement mécaniques. Ils tournent la tête à droite, à gauche, ils lèvent° le bras comme des marionnettes. On ne sait vraiment pas s'ils sont réels . . . jusqu'au° moment où ils descendent de leur piédestal et passent le chapeau.

et vous?

DÉFINITIONS

Définissez les mots suivants.

- un badaud
- une manifestation
- un animal savant
- un jongleur
- un mime
- un automate
- une marionnette
- faire la quête

EXPRESSION ÉCRITE

Vous êtes en vacances à Paris. Écrivez une lettre à un(e) ami(e) où vous décrivez un spectacle de rue auquel vous avez assisté. Mentionnez, par exemple:

- le genre de spectacle
- ce que «l'artiste» a fait (donnez des détails)
- comment vous avez trouvé le spectacle
- si vous avez donné de l'argent (pourquoi ou pourquoi pas)

L'automate

C'est une «automate». Nous l'avons rencontrée un jour d'été à Strasbourg devant la cathédrale. Il était sept heures du soir. Elle avait le visage encore° tout blanc, et elle portait un grand chapeau de paille,° à la mode de 1900. Le spectacle était terminé et elle allait partir sur sa grosse moto. Nous lui avons parlé.

— Vous êtes d'ici?

— Non, je suis de la banlieue. Je viens ici parce que ça marche bien.

— Ça a marché aujourd'hui?

— Pas trop mal. J'ai fait 150 euros!

— Quel est votre endroit préféré?

— Ici devant la cathédrale. . . Il y a toujours des cars° pleins° de touristes étrangers.

— Quels sont vos meilleurs clients?

— En général, tout le monde donne quelque chose, mais j'aime beaucoup les Allemands. Ils comprennent l'effort et la qualité du travail.

— Est-ce que votre métier° est dur?°

— Très dur! Il faut se concentrer. . . C'est difficile quand il y a tant° de gens qui passent, le bruit, le vent. . . Et puis il y a la préparation, le maquillage.° Ça prend du temps! Enfin, l'essentiel, c'est que les gens s'amusent. Quand ils s'amusent, comme aujourd'hui, je sais que j'ai bien fait mon travail.

— Merci, et bonne chance.

poudre *powder* **manifeste** = montre **lèvent** *raise* **jusqu'au** *until* **encore** *still* **paille** *straw* **cars** *buses* **pleins** *full*
métier = profession **dur** = difficile **tant** *so many* **maquillage** *make-up*

Supplementary vocabulary

le caricaturiste *caricaturist*
le portraitiste *portrait artist*
la diseuse de bonne aventure *fortune teller*
le magicien *magician*
l'avaleur *(m.)* **de sabres** *sword swallower*
le cracheur de feu *fire eater*

LANGUE ET COMMUNICATION

TEACHING RESOURCES

Student Activities Manual, pp. 84, 158

Audio Program, CD 9, Tracks 8–9

HM ClassPrep CD, Audioscript, Unit 8

PARTIE 3

LANGUE ET COMMUNICATION

A. Le conditionnel passé

The PAST CONDITIONAL is used to express what WOULD HAVE HAPPENED under certain circumstances. Note the forms of the verbs in heavy print:

À ta place, je **n'aurais pas pris** ma voiture.	*In your place (If I had been you),* ***I would not have taken** my car.*
Je **serais allé(e)** en ville en bus.	***I would have gone** downtown by bus.*

FORMS

The PAST CONDITIONAL is formed as follows:

CONDITIONAL of **avoir** or **être** + PAST PARTICIPLE

In the past conditional, the agreement rules for the past participle are the same as in the passé composé.

Tu n'as pas invité **ta copine.** À ta place, je l'aurais invitée.

INFINITIVE		voyager		aller		s'amuser
PAST CONDITIONAL	j'	**aurais voyagé**	je	**serais allé(e)**	je	**me serais amusé(e)**
	tu	**aurais voyagé**	tu	**serais allé(e)**	tu	**te serais amusé(e)**
	il/elle/on	**aurait voyagé**	il/elle/on	**serait allé(e)**	il/elle/on	**se serait amusé(e)**
	nous	**aurions voyagé**	nous	**serions allé(e)s**	nous	**nous serions amusé(e)s**
	vous	**auriez voyagé**	vous	**seriez allé(e)(s)**	vous	**vous seriez amusé(e)(s)**
	ils/elles	**auraient voyagé**	ils/elles	**seraient allé(e)s**	ils/elles	**se seraient amusé(e)s**
NEGATIVE	je	**n'aurais pas voyagé**	je	**ne serais pas allé(e)**	je	**ne me serais pas amusé**
INTERRROGATIVE	est-ce que tu	**aurais voyagé?** **aurais-tu voyagé?**	tu	**serais allé(e)?** **serais-tu allé(e)?**	tu	**te serais amusé(e)?** **te serais-tu amusé(e)?**

USES

The following sentences express what WOULD HAVE HAPPENED **if** certain past conditions HAD BEEN MET.

Note the use of tenses in the sentences below.

Si j'**avais étudié**, j'**aurais réussi** à l'examen.	*If I **had studied**,* *I **would have passed** the exam.*
Si vous **étiez allés** à la boum, vous **vous seriez amusés**.	*If you **had gone** to the party,* *you **would have had fun.***

Hypothetical sentences that refer to the past are usually formed according to the pattern:

si-clause	MAIN or RESULT clause
pluperfect	past conditional

Teaching Strategy

Divide the class into pairs. Have them imagine that they have a very obnoxious friend who enjoys letting them know she/he's always right by saying "I told you so...!" Ask the students to write five sentences, from the point of view of the obnoxious friend, pointing out what you did wrong using the past conditional.

ALLONS PLUS LOIN

Note the English equivalents of the past conditional of **vouloir, pouvoir** and **devoir**.

J'**aurais voulu voir** ce film.	*I **wish I had seen** that movie.* *(I **would have liked to see** that movie.)*
Tu **aurais pu me téléphoner.**	*You **could have called me.***
Vous **auriez dû attendre.**	*You **should have waited.***

1 L'incendie

Sébastien habite au deuxième étage d'un immeuble. Hier, il y a eu un commencement *(beginning)* d'incendie *(fire)* dans cet immeuble. Voici ce qu'il a fait. Dites si oui ou non vous auriez fait les mêmes choses.

▶ Sébastien est resté calme.
Moi aussi, je serais resté(e) calme.
(Moi, je ne serais pas resté(e) calme.)

1. Il a téléphoné aux pompiers.
2. Il a téléphoné à sa copine.
3. Il a fermé la porte de l'appartement à clé.
4. Il a pris sa mini-chaîne.
5. Il a laissé son argent dans un tiroir *(drawer)*.
6. Il est allé dans la salle de bains.
7. Il a mis une serviette mouillée *(wet)* sous la porte.
8. Il a ouvert la fenêtre.
9. Il a attendu dix minutes.
10. Il s'est impatienté.
11. Il a sauté *(jumped)* par la fenêtre.
12. Il s'est cassé la jambe.

2 Vive la différence!

Votre partenaire est allé(e) en ville. Il/elle explique ce qu'il/elle a fait. Dites lui que vous auriez fait quelque chose de différent. (Utilisez le même verbe, mais avec une expression de votre choix.)

▶ aller au musée
— Je suis allé(e) au musée.
— Eh bien moi, à ta place, je ne serais pas allé(e) au musée.
Je serais allé(e) au ciné (au café, dans les magasins, . . .).

1. voir une exposition
2. déjeuner au café
3. manger un sandwich
4. se promener dans le parc
5. passer à la Maison des Jeunes
6. aller au centre commercial
7. acheter des CD
8. rentrer à pied

3 Tant pis pour toi!

Votre partenaire vous décrit certains problèmes qu'il/elle a eus. Dites-lui que c'est de sa faute et expliquez pourquoi.

▶ rater l'examen / étudier
— J'ai raté l'examen.
— Est-ce que tu avais étudié?
— Non, je n'avais pas étudié.
— Tant pis pour toi! Si tu avais étudié, tu n'aurais pas raté l'examen.

1. se perdre en ville / prendre ton plan *(map)*?
2. attendre une heure au restaurant / réserver une table?
3. arriver en retard au rendez-vous / regarder ta montre?
4. attraper un coup de soleil / mettre de la crème solaire?

Note linguistique

- The past conditional is sometimes called the CONDITIONAL PERFECT.
- Stress that the past conditional only occurs in the RESULT clause. It is never used in the **si**-clause, as it is in English.
  Si j'**avais su,** ...
  *If I **would have known***
  *(If I **had known**), ...*
  je ne t'**aurais** pas **écouté**.
  *I **would** not **have listened** to you.*
- The underlying condition may be expressed by a phrase other than a **si**-clause. For example:
  À ta place, je serais parti.
  ***In your place,** I would have left.*
  Avec plus d'argent, j'aurais ...
  ***With more money,** I would have ...*
  acheté une voiture plus grande.
  bought a bigger car.

Note linguistique

Remind students:
The past participle of **devoir** takes a circumflex accent only in the singular masculine form: **dû, due, dus, dues.**

Teaching Strategy: Expansion

Give students the following situations: Avec votre partenaire, choisissez l'une des situations suivantes. Discutez de ce que vous auriez fait et de ce que vous n'auriez pas fait dans cette situation. Si vous voulez, écrivez une composition où vous décrirez les résultats de votre discussion.

1. S'il avait fait très beau (ou très mauvais) le week-end dernier ...
2. S'il y avait eu une panne d'électricité *(power failure)* hier soir ...
3. Si vous étiez allé(e) en France l'été dernier ...
4. Si vous aviez eu plus de temps le mois dernier ...
5. Si vous étiez né(e) dans une famille très riche ...

TEACHING RESOURCES

Student Activities Manual, pp. 85–86

■ Note linguistique

In French, as in English, the sequence of tenses may be modified to reflect the sequence of facts or situations described.

si-clause → result clause

IMPERFECT → PAST CONDITIONAL

Si tu **étais** généreux, tu m'**aurais prêté** ta voiture.

PLUPERFECT → PRESENT CONDITIONAL

Si tu **avais dormi** la nuit dernière, tu **ne serais pas** fatigué maintenant.

4 Dommage!

Les personnes suivantes n'ont pas fait certaines choses. Décrivez ce qui serait arrivé si elles avaient fait ces choses. Attention: le verbe entre parenthèses peut être affirmatif ou négatif.

▶ Jérôme n'a pas fait attention. (tomber dans les escaliers?)
Si Jérôme avait fait attention, il ne serait pas tombé dans les escaliers.

1. Nous ne nous sommes pas dépêchés. (rater le train?)
2. Patrick n'a pas lu les annonces. (trouver un job cet été?)
3. Mes copains n'ont pas acheté de billets. (aller au concert?)
4. Je n'ai pas utilisé ma calculatrice. (se tromper dans le problème?)
5. Les joueurs ne se sont pas entraînés. (gagner le match?)
6. Vous n'avez pas attendu. (voir l'éclipse?)
7. Tu n'as pas mis ton manteau. (attraper une pneumonie?)
8. Les élèves ne se sont pas reposés. (dormir pendant la classe?)
9. Le Petit Chaperon Rouge *(Little Red Riding Hood)* n'a pas écouté sa mère. (rencontrer le loup *[wolf]*?)

B. Résumé: l'usage des temps avec si

Review the sequence of tenses with **si**.

To describe. . .	**si**–clause	main or result clause	
• a possibility (concerning a future event)	PRESENT	FUTURE IMPERATIVE	**Si** je **vais** en ville, j'**achèterai** le journal. **Si** tu **vas** au supermarché, **achète** du pain.
• a hypothetical situation (usually contrary to reality)	IMPERFECT	CONDITIONAL	**Si** j'**avais** un billet, j'**irais** au concert.
• a hypothetical situation in the past	PLUPERFECT	PAST CONDITIONAL	**Si** j'**avais étudié**, je **n'aurais pas raté** l'examen.

5 Vive la différence!

Vous et votre partenaire, vous n'êtes pas d'accord. Votre partenaire vous dit ce qu'il/elle fera. Dites-lui ce que vous feriez si vous étiez dans les mêmes circonstances. (Choisissez une option différente.)

▶ avoir faim / manger quoi?
— Si j'ai faim, je mangerai un sandwich.
— Eh bien, moi, si j'avais faim, je mangerais une pizza.

1. avoir soif / boire quoi?
2. avoir de l'argent / acheter quoi?
3. sortir samedi / aller où ?
4. aller au cinéma / voir quoi?
5. aller à Paris / visiter quoi?
6. aller en Europe / voyager comment?

Et si cela arrivait . . . ?

Avec votre partenaire, choisissez une des situations suivantes et discutez de ce que vous feriez et de ce que vous ne feriez pas si vous étiez dans cette situation. Puis, écrivez un paragraphe d'au moins 5 lignes où vous décrirez les résultats de votre discussion.

1. Vous êtes témoins d'un cambriolage.
2. Vous êtes prisonniers (prisonnières) de dangereux bandits.
3. Vous êtes perdu(e)s dans la jungle tropicale.
4. Vous êtes invité(e)s à la Maison Blanche.
5. Vous assistez au mariage d'un copain français.
6. Un réalisateur *(movie producer)* vous offre un rôle dans son prochain film.
7. Vous découvrez un trésor *(treasure)* dans une maison abandonnée.

■ **Pronunciation**
jungle /ʒœ̃gl/ or /ʒɔ̃gl/

Achats

Complétez les phrases suivantes avec la forme du verbe **acheter** qui convient.

1. Si je vais à la poste, j'___ des timbres.
2. Si nous ___ des billets, nous aurions pu aller au concert samedi soir.
3. S'il avait de l'argent, mon oncle ___ un appartement dans le centre-ville.
4. Qu'est-ce que tu ___ si tu gagnes de l'argent l'été prochain?
5. Si j'étais passé à la boulangerie, j'___ des croissants.
6. Si tu ___ des CD dans ce magasin, tu paieras moins cher.
7. Est-ce que tu ___ cette veste si elle était en solde?
8. Si Paul ____ une moto, il vendrait son vélo.

Un discours électoral

À chaque élection, Monsieur Duroc est candidat à la mairie de Clocheville. Cette année, il se présente à nouveau. Vous êtes son/sa secrétaire. Complétez son discours *(speech)* avec la forme correcte du verbe entre parenthèses.

Mesdames et Messieurs,

J'ai le plaisir d'annoncer pour la sixième fois ma candidature à la mairie de Clocheville. Si vous (voter) pour moi aux dernières élections, vous (voir) les nombreuses améliorations que j'(apporter) à notre bonne ville. Je/j' (construire) une nouvelle gendarmerie, une nouvelle poste et, bien sûr, une nouvelle mairie. J'(éliminer) la pollution et la criminalité. Aujourd'hui, votre ville (être) belle, propre et sans danger.

Malheureusement, aux dernières élections, vous avez voté pour mon adversaire qui est un incapable. Si je/j' (être) à sa place, je/j' (avoir) honte de me présenter à nouveau. Heureusement, vous êtes intelligents. Quand vous (voter) pour moi dimanche prochain, vous (voter) pour quelqu'un de responsable et d'honnête. Si je/j' (être) élu, vous (pouvoir) être fiers à nouveau de votre ville!

Merci!

NOTES CULTURELLES

- In France, a mayor is elected by the city council, called **le conseil municipal.** The council itself is elected by the citizens of the city. The mayor and the council are elected for six years. To run for mayor, you must be at least 21, while you need only be 18 to become a member of the council.
- In France, elections are always held on Sundays. If none of the candidates for a particular position receives an absolute majority (more than 50% of the vote), a run-off election is held.

Reading STRATEGY

Reading fiction

■ **Additional Information**

At the same time he was an author, **André Theuriet** also had a career as a civil servant in the Department of Finance. Some of his other works include:

Le Bleu et le noir,
Amour d'automne,
La Fortune d'Angèle,
Reine des bois.

■ **Note linguistique**

le standing = la position sociale

LECTURE

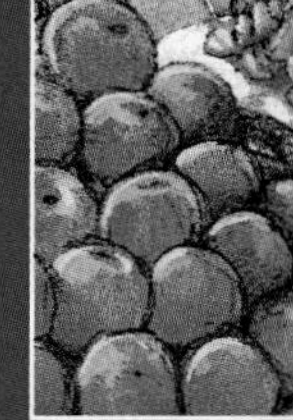

Les pêches

d'après André Theuriet

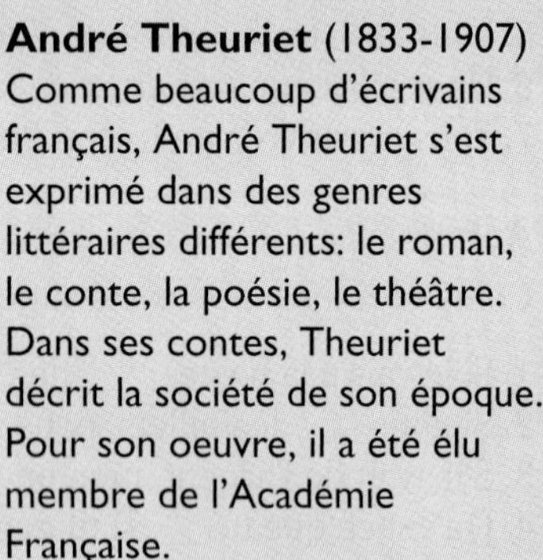

André Theuriet (1833-1907)
Comme beaucoup d'écrivains français, André Theuriet s'est exprimé dans des genres littéraires différents: le roman, le conte, la poésie, le théâtre. Dans ses contes, Theuriet décrit la société de son époque. Pour son oeuvre, il a été élu membre de l'Académie Française.

AVANT DE LIRE

Le contexte historique

Pour bien comprendre une histoire, il faut la placer dans son contexte historique. L'histoire suivante se passe à la «Belle Époque», il y a environ° cent ans. La vie était alors assez différente d'aujourd'hui et deux aspects sont particulièrement importants pour l'histoire que vous allez lire.

- À cette époque, les gens riches organisaient de temps en temps de grandes réceptions° chez eux. Ces fêtes, généralement très formelles, étaient des événements importants de la vie mondaine.° Il était donc essentiel pour son standing social d'y être invité.

- Un autre aspect important pour l'histoire concerne l'alimentation d'alors. Comme les transports étaient très limités (l'automobile et l'avion n'existaient pas encore!), la distribution des produits frais,° et particulièrement des fruits, était très localisée et très saisonnière. Si on voulait manger des fruits frais, il fallait attendre l'été, ou bien, si on avait beaucoup d'argent, il fallait faire venir° spécialement ces produits de Provence, d'Italie ou d'Espagne.

environ = approximativement **réception** = soirée de gala **mondaine** = sociale **frais** *fresh*
faire venir *to have shipped*

Teaching Notes

- This story fits the cultural and linguistic themes of both Units 8 and 10. Depending on your scheduling, you can either present this story now or postpone it until Unit 10.
- For a definition of **la Belle Époque,** refer your students to *Interlude 6,* p. 252.
- Use the *Anticipons un peu* questions to help students read with a critical focus.

Anticipons un peu

Imaginez que vous êtes invité(e) à un très grand mariage. Votre meilleur(e) ami(e), qui est malade, ne peut pas vous accompagner. Vous lui avez promis de lui rapporter un morceau° du gâteau nuptial.

Le gâteau a été servi, mais comme vous êtes un peu timide, vous n'avez pas osé° en demander un second morceau à l'hôtesse. Vous n'avez cependant pas oublié votre promesse.

Vous allez au buffet et, quand personne ne regarde, vous prenez un morceau de gâteau pour votre ami(e). Comment feriez-vous pour le ramener° sans être vu(e)?

- Je le mettrais dans ma poche de pantalon ou de jupe.
- Je le cacherais sous ma veste.
- Je le mettrais dans mon sac.
- Je l'envelopperais dans une serviette.°

morceau *piece* **osé** *dared* **ramener** *to bring back* **serviette** *napkin*

LES PÊCHES

1

C'est au cours d'un dîner organisé par les anciens élèves du lycée de province où j'avais fait mes études que j'ai revu mon copain d'enfance Vital Herbelot. C'est lui qui est venu me saluer° après le café. À vrai dire, je ne l'avais pas reconnu. Vêtu d'un costume de velours côtelé° et d'une chemise à carreaux,° les cheveux en brosse et le visage bronzé, il respirait° la santé et la bonne humeur. Certes, ce n'était pas le grand garçon élégant, distingué, mais un peu timide, que j'avais connu vingt-cinq ans avant. Élève très doué, il était promis à l'avenir le plus brillant. Après le bac, il avait tout de suite trouvé un poste dans la plus grande banque de la ville.

Un peu surpris de le revoir, je lui ai demandé:

— Alors, tu es° toujours dans la banque?

— Oh non, il y a bien longtemps que je l'ai quittée. . . J'habite à la campagne maintenant... Je suis cultivateur!

— Cultivateur, toi?! Mais je croyais que tu t'intéressais à la finance.

— C'est vrai... Et si j'avais continué, j'aurais certainement fait une «brillante carrière», comme on dit . . .Aujourd'hui je serais peut-être le président d'une grande banque nationale ou internationale... Qui sait? Mais tu vois, il m'est arrivé quelque chose°, il y a vingt ans de cela.

— Quoi? Qu'est-ce qui t'est arrivé?

— Oh, une histoire de pêches . . . mais une histoire qui a changé mon existence. Pour le meilleur!

— Tu as dit «une histoire de pêches»?

— Oui, une absurde histoire de pêches.

Voulant satisfaire ma curiosité évidente, Vital Herbelot a commencé à me raconter son histoire.

Mots utiles

un ancien élève	*alumnus*
un cultivateur	*farmer*
une pêche	*peach*
doué	*gifted*
vêtu de	*dressed in*
au cours de	*during, in the course of*
à vrai dire	*to tell the truth*

saluer = dire bonjour **velours côtelé** *corduroy* **à carreaux** *plaid* **respirait** = était l'expression de
tu es = tu travailles **il m'est arrivé quelque chose** *something happened to me*

■ **Pour en savoir plus**
For more information on the history of the **bac,** and the **bac** of today, refer your students to *Info Magazine 1* of Unit 10, pp. 383–385.

Teaching Strategy

You may wish to point out the following homonyms in French:

la pêche *peach*
la pêche *fishing*
le pêcher *peach tree*
le péché *sin*
pêcher *to fish*
pécher *to sin*
le pêcheur *fisherman*
le pécheur *sinner*
(la pêcheuse–*fisherwoman)*
(la pécheresse–*sinner)*

Tu sais que j'étais fils et petit-fils d'employés relativement modestes.° C'est ma mère qui a insisté pour que je fasse des études et que j'obtienne mon bac. Tu te souviens, sans doute, que j'aimais les études et que j'ai obtenu mon bac avec mention.° Aussi, je n'ai pas eu de difficulté à trouver du travail.

Après le bac, j'ai été immédiatement embauché dans une grande banque d'affaires.° Tous mes camarades de classe convoitaient° le poste que je venais d'obtenir. Rappelle-toi comme vous étiez tous un peu jaloux de moi! Comme j'étais très travailleur et très discipliné et que je réussissais bien dans les affaires que je traitais, j'ai vite obtenu plusieurs promotions, et avec celles-ci des augmentations de salaire importantes.

Au bout de trois ans, j'étais devenu l'un des adjoints° principaux du patron de la banque. Je t'assure que je gagnais bien ma vie, mais en contrepartie,° je devais sacrifier tout mon temps aux affaires de la banque. C'est à ce moment-là que je me suis marié avec une jeune fille qui avait toutes les qualités et qui, de plus, était très jolie.

Mots utiles

embaucher	*to hire*
obtenir *	*to get, obtain*
au bout de	*after, at the end of*

Avez-vous compris?

1. À quelle occasion est-ce que le narrateur rencontre Vital Herbelot?
2. Pourquoi est-ce qu'il ne le reconnaît pas?
3. Quelle est la profession de Vital Herbelot maintenant?
4. Quelle était sa profession autrefois?

Anticipons un peu!

Vital Herbelot avait une situation brillante. Maintenant, il est cultivateur.
À votre avis, qu'est-ce qui s'est passé?

- Il a eu un grave accident.
- Il a commis une faute *(mistake)* professionnelle.
- Sa femme est tombée malade.
- Quelque chose d'autre s'est passé. Imaginez quoi!

2

Mon patron était un homme très riche et très mondain.° De temps en temps il organisait de grandes réceptions où il invitait tous les notables° de la ville et quelques-uns de ses employés supérieurs.° Il y avait généralement un repas suivi d'un bal.

Peu de temps après mon mariage, j'ai reçu ma première invitation à l'une de ces réceptions. Malheureusement, quelques jours avant l'événement, ma femme est tombée malade. Je pensais envoyer mes excuses, mais ma femme a insisté pour que j'aille à cette réception.
— Ton patron est un homme généreux, mais très autoritaire. S'il ne te voyait pas à la première réception à laquelle il t'invite, il serait certainement très vexé, et cela nuirait à° ta carrière.

modestes = assez pauvres **avec mention** with honors
une banque d'affaires investment bank **convoitaient** = désiraient secrètement
adjoints = assistants **en contrepartie** in exchange **mondain** of fashionable society
notables = personnes importantes **employés supérieurs** top executives **nuirait à** = ruinerait

■ Irregular Verbs

(See Appendix C)

- **devoir**
- **nuire** is conjugated like **cuire: je nuis, il nuit, nous nuisons, ils nuisent.**
- **obtenir** (*see* **tenir**)

■ *Avez-vous compris?*

(Sample answers)

1. Il le rencontre au cours d'un dîner d'anciens élèves de son lycée.
2. Il ne le reconnaît pas parce qu'avant il était élégant et timide, et maintenant il est moins élégant, bronzé, de bonne humeur.
3. Il est cultivateur.
4. Autrefois, il travaillait dans une banque. Il était adjoint du patron.

Teaching Strategy

- Ask students if they have noticed any differences in the presentation of the story on this page versus page 327. (If they do not notice the change in typeface, indicating a change in narrator, point it out to them.) Why is this device used? Is it successful?
- Ask students the following questions: À votre avis, pourquoi est-il important pour Vital Herbelot d'aller à cette réception? Quelles pourraient être les conséquences de son absence à cette soirée?

Bien sûr, j'aurais préféré rester avec ma femme, mais, convaincu par ses arguments, j'ai finalement accepté l'invitation.

Ce soir-là, je me suis donc habillé pour l'occasion. Alors qu'elle m'aidait à ajuster ma cravate, ma femme m'a dit:
—Je regrette vraiment de ne pas pouvoir t'accompagner.
Il y aura un très beau buffet . . . et j'ai entendu dire que la femme de ton patron a fait venir° spécialement des primeurs* du Midi. Il paraît même qu'il y aura des pêches... Tu sais comme je les aime.
Et pourtant, c'est absolument impossible d'en trouver dans les magasins en cette saison... Oh, ces pêches! Est-ce que tu pourrais m'en rapporter une . . . Une seule . . . S'il te plaît!

Surpris de cette requête inattendue, j'ai essayé d'expliquer à ma femme que c'était difficile. Comment un monsieur en habit noir° pourrait-il prendre une pêche et la mettre dans sa poche sans être vu?

Mais ma femme a insisté: «Rien de plus facile, au contraire . . . Tu profiteras d'un moment où tout le monde sera en train de danser. Tu t'approcheras du buffet et tu prendras une pêche comme si c'était pour toi et tu la dissimuleras° adroitement.° Personne ne te verra... Oh, je sais bien, c'est un caprice,° mais ça me ferait tellement plaisir! Allez, promets-moi . . .»

Comment refuser quelque chose à la femme qu'on aime? J'ai fini par promettre, puis j'ai pris mon manteau et mon chapeau. Au moment où j'allais partir, ma femme m'a regardé de ses grands yeux bleus et m'a dit: «N'oublie pas!»

Mots utiles

un bal	*dance*
un caprice	*whim*
une pêche	*peach*
une requête	*request*
s'approcher de	*to approach*
convaincre *	*to convince*
entendre dire	*to hear (it said)*
faire plaisir à	*to please*
profiter de	*to take advantage of*
inattendu	*unexpected*
alors que	*while*

Avez-vous compris?

1. Pourquoi Madame Herbelot ne va-t-elle pas à la réception?
2. Pourquoi conseille-t-elle à son mari d'y aller?
3. Qu'est-ce qu'elle lui demande de faire?
4. Pourquoi est-ce que son mari hésite?

Anticipons un peu!

À votre avis, comment est-ce que Vital Herbelot va satisfaire la requête de sa femme?

- Il va demander à l'hôtesse de la réception la permission de prendre une pêche.
- Il va prendre une pêche sans demander la permission.
- Il va acheter des pêches chez un marchand.
- Il va rentrer chez lui sans pêche.
- Il va faire autre chose. Imaginez quoi!

3

Ce soir-là, toute la société° de la ville était réunie° chez mon patron. Il y avait le maire, le président du tribunal, le général commandant la garnison et ses officiers supérieurs, et toutes les grandes familles de la ville.

Mon patron avait bien fait les choses. Le dîner était exquis. Après le dîner, les invités passèrent au grand salon et le bal commença. Vers

* **Les primeurs du Midi.** À cause de son climat, le Midi (dans le sud de la France) produit des **primeurs**, c'est-à-dire, des fruits et légumes consommables avant la saison normale.

a fait venir = a commandé **habit noir** formal evening dress **dissimuleras** = cacheras **adroitement** *skillfully* **caprice** *whim* **la société** = la haute société **était réunie** = se trouvait

■ Irregular Verb
(see Appendix C)
convaincre (*see* **vaincre**)

■ Avez-vous compris?
(Sample answers)
1. Elle ne va pas à la réception parce qu'elle est tombée malade.
2. Elle lui conseille d'y aller parce que c'est utile pour sa carrière.
3. Elle lui demande de lui rapporter une pêche.
4. Il hésite parce que ce n'est pas facile de le faire discrètement.

Teaching Note
In episodes 3 and 4, the narrator shifts to the **passé simple** as he begins to narrate the action. If necessary, you may want to review this tense in Appendix C, pp. R32–R33.

■ **Note linguistique**
Le buffet is the table where cold food, pastries, and refreshments are served during a party.

■ **Irregular Verb**
(see Appendix C)
se produire (*see* **conduire**)

■ ***Avez-vous compris?***
(Sample answers)
1. Les pêches sont servies après minuit par le maître d'hôtel, aux personnes indiquées par le patron. Elles sont coupées en deux.
2. Il prend les pêches quand les domestiques sont partis.
3. Il met les pêches dans son chapeau.

minuit, il y eut un temps de repos pendant lequel un buffet fut servi dans une petite pièce à côté du salon. Au milieu de la table trônaient° les fameuses pêches venues° spécialement du Midi. Disposées° en pyramide sur un plateau de faïence,° elles provoquaient l'admiration générale. Oui vraiment, elles étaient superbes! Je pensais alors à la promesse que j'avais faite à ma femme et me demandais comment j'allais la réaliser. Ce n'était pas facile!

Les domestiques préposés° au service montaient une garde vigilante° autour de ces magnifiques et coûteux fruits. De temps en temps, sur un signe de mon patron, le maître d'hôtel prenait délicatement une pêche, la découpait avec un couteau d'argent, et en présentait les deux moitiés à un invité de marque.° Il en restait encore une demi-douzaine quand l'orchestre se remit à° jouer. Les invités se précipitèrent au salon et on recommença à danser.

C'est alors que j'exécutai mon projet. Je pris mon chapeau et mon manteau, comme si j'allais partir. Puis, sous un prétexte quelconque,° je passai dans la petite salle où était dressé° le buffet. Heureusement les domestiques étaient partis. Je me trouvais donc seul. M'assurant que personne ne me regardait, je ne pris non pas une mais deux de ces magnifiques pêches et je les mis discrètement dans mon chapeau. Pressant celui-ci très fort° contre ma poitrine, j'allai saluer° mon hôte et mon hôtesse. Je les remerciai de leur aimable invitation, puis je me dirigeai, digne et fier de moi, vers la sortie.

Mon projet avait parfaitement réussi. Que ma femme serait heureuse quand elle verrait le produit de mon larcin inoffensif! C'est alors que se produisit l'incident . . .

trônaient = occupaient la place d'honneur **venues** *brought* **Disposées** = arrangées **faïence** *glazed pottery* **préposés** *assigned* **montaient une garde vigilante** *kept watchful guard* **de marque** = important **se remit à** = recommença à **un prétexte quelconque** some pretext or other **dressé** = placé **fort** *tightly* **saluer** = dire au revoir à

Mots utiles

un larcin	*small theft*
la moitié	*half*
la poitrine	*chest*
s'assurer	*to make sure*
découper	*to cut (into pieces)*
se demander	*to wonder*
se diriger vers	*to move toward*
se précipiter	*to dash*
se produire	*to happen*
digne	*dignified*
inoffensif	*harmless*
comme si	*as if*
reste . . .	*there is/are . . . left*

Avez-vous compris?

1. À quel moment de la réception sont servies les pêches? Par qui? À qui? Comment?
2. Comment Vital Herbelot réussit-il à prendre deux pêches?
3. Qu'est-ce qu'il fait pour passer inaperçu *(unnoticed)*?

Anticipons un peu!

À votre avis, qu'est-ce qui va se passer ensuite?
- Vital Herbelot va apporter les pêches à sa femme qui sera très contente.
- Il sera dénoncé par un domestique qui l'a vu et il sera arrêté par la police.
- Après être sorti, il fera tomber *(will drop)* les pêches dans la rue et il ne pourra pas les rapporter à sa femme.
- Quelque chose d'autre arrivera. Imaginez quoi.

Teaching Strategy

- Ask students to name a food that would be comparably extravagant today to the peaches in the story. (Exemples: le caviar, le homard, les truffes, le foie gras...)
- Ask students: À votre avis, Vital Herbelot a-t-il commis une faute grave? Expliquez votre opinion.

4

Avant de sortir, il fallait que je traverse le salon où les jeunes gens et les jeunes filles continuaient à valser.° On organisait justement une nouvelle figure: une danseuse est placée au centre des danseurs qui exécutent une ronde° autour d'elle. Elle doit tenir un chapeau à la main et en coiffer° le jeune homme avec qui elle veut danser. C'était justement la fille de mon patron qui devait se placer au centre du groupe. Me voyant avec mon chapeau pressé contre la poitrine, elle s'écria:

— Monsieur Herbelot! Monsieur Herbelot! Nous avons besoin de votre chapeau! S'il vous plaît, prêtez-le-nous pour quelques minutes seulement.

Et sans attendre ma réponse, elle me prit le chapeau des mains d'un mouvement brusque. Les pêches tombèrent et roulèrent sur le sol devant les invités ébahis.°

La musique s'arrêta. Tout le monde riait maintenant, sauf mon patron qui avait l'air absolument furieux. Même les domestiques semblaient se moquer de moi... Alors la fille du patron me donna mon chapeau en me disant d'une voix ironique:

— Eh bien, monsieur Herbelot, ramassez donc vos pêches!

J'aurais voulu être cent pieds sous terre.° Rouge de confusion, je pris mon chapeau, balbutiai° quelques mots d'excuses, et partis comme un fou. Je rentrai chez moi et, la mort dans le coeur, je racontai le désastre à ma femme.

Le lendemain, l'histoire courait° la ville. Quand je suis entré à mon bureau ce matin-là, mes collègues savaient ce qui s'était passé. Les plus malicieux° murmuraient° à mon passage: «Hé, Monsieur Herbelot, ramassez donc vos pêches.» Dans la rue, j'entendais les enfants des écoles dire en me montrant du doigt: «Regardez! C'est le monsieur aux pêches!»

Huit jours après, j'ai quitté la banque et la ville. Ma femme et moi, nous nous sommes installés à la campagne, chez un vieil oncle qui avait une grande ferme. Je ne connaissais rien aux travaux des champs,° mais avec l'aide de mon oncle, j'ai vite appris. Quand celui-ci est mort, j'ai hérité de la ferme. C'est comme ça que je suis devenu cultivateur!

Tiens, si tu es libre dimanche prochain, viens donc me rendre visite. Nous déjeunerons ensemble.

valser = danser la valse *(waltz)* **exécutent une ronde** = dansent dans un cercle **coiffer** = mettre sur la tête **ébahis** *open-mouthed*
sous terre *underground* **balbutiai** *mumbled* **courait** = circulait dans
malicieux *inclined to tease* **murmuraient** *would say in a low voice*
travaux des champs *farm work*

Mots utiles

hériter de	*to inherit*
s'installer	*to settle*
montrer du doigt	*to point at*
se moquer de	*to laugh at, to make fun of*
ramasser	*to pick up*
traverser	*to go across, to cross*
justement	*precisely at that moment*

Avez-vous compris?

1. De quelle façon le larcin de Vital Herbelot a-t-il été découvert?
2. Quelle a été la réaction des autres invités?
3. Quelle a été la réaction de ses collègues le lendemain?
4. Qu'est-ce qu'il a décidé de faire à la suite de l'incident?

Et vous?

Qu'est-ce que vous auriez fait si vous aviez été à la place de Vital Herbelot? Expliquez pourquoi.

- J'aurais présenté mes excuses à mon patron et j'aurais gardé mon poste.
- J'aurais fait un procès *(filed a suit)* à mes collègues de bureau pour harcèlement professionnel.
- J'aurais quitté la ville et j'aurais cherché un travail similaire dans une autre ville.
- J'aurais fait comme Vital Herbelot.
- J'aurais fait quelque chose d'autre. Expliquez quoi.

■ **Irregular Verb**
(See Appendix C)
courir

Teaching Note
Have students note that this is the end of the Herbelot narration.

■ ***Avez-vous compris?***
(Sample answers)

1. Son larcin a été découvert parce qu'une jeune fille lui a demandé son chapeau pour une danse.
2. Les autres invités ont beaucoup ri.
3. Le lendemain, ses collègues ont dit: «Ramassez vos pêches!»
4. Il a décidé de quitter la banque et la ville, et d'aller chez un oncle qui avait une ferme.

Teaching Note
Ask students if they noted that the conclusion is presented by the initial narrator.

■ **Irregular Verbs**
(see Appendix C)
cueillir
sourire (*see* **rire**)

■ **Note linguistique**
The expression **un bureaucrate** is pejorative. It generally refers to a petty civil servant who thinks he is very powerful.

Mots utiles	
un verger	*orchard*
un pêcher	*peach tree*
cueillir *	*to pick*
sourire *	*to smile*
d'ailleurs	*besides*
en souvenir de	*in memory of*

5

Intrigué par l'histoire de mon ancien camarade de lycée j'ai accepté son invitation. Le dimanche suivant, je suis donc allé chez lui. Là, j'ai fait la connaissance de sa femme, toujours jolie à quarante-cinq ans, et de leurs magnifiques enfants. Nous avons fait un excellent déjeuner, accompagné d'un agréable vin blanc que mon ami faisait lui-même.

Après le déjeuner, il m'a proposé de faire un tour de la ferme. Il était particulièrement fier de son verger. Alors que j'admirais particulièrement un pêcher chargé de° fruits splendides, il m'a dit:

— Celui-là, je l'ai planté en souvenir de l'histoire que je t'ai racontée! J'ai eu de la chance. Sans cette histoire absurde, je serais resté un bureaucrate toute ma vie. D'accord, j'aurais peut-être plus d'argent, mais je ne serais pas plus heureux. D'ailleurs, comment être plus heureux? J'ai tout pour moi.

Puis, il a cueilli deux énormes pêches et il me les donna en souriant:

— Tu verras! Ce sera les meilleures pêches que tu aies jamais mangées!

chargé de *laden with*

■ ***Avez-vous compris?***
(Sample answers)
1. À la ferme, l'atmosphère est sympathique.
2. Il est très heureux de son sort.

Avez-vous compris?

1. Quelle est l'atmosphère générale à la ferme de Vital Herbelot?
2. Qu'est-ce que Vital Herbelot pense de son sort *(fate)*?

À votre avis

Est-ce que Vital Herbelot a pris la meilleure décision possible? Expliquez pourquoi.

APRÈS LA LECTURE

EXPRESSION ORALE

■ **La morale de l'histoire**
L'histoire des pêches peut avoir plusieurs morales. Choisissez l'une des morales suivantes (ou bien, créez votre propre morale) et expliquez pourquoi elle correspond le mieux à l'histoire.

- L'argent ne fait pas le bonheur.
- Les petits incidents peuvent avoir des conséquences importantes.
- Il vaut mieux être pauvre que ridicule.
- Le crime ne paie pas.
- Il ne faut jamais écouter les mauvais conseils.
- Le ridicule tue.
- Les gens trop ambitieux sont toujours punis.

Notes linguistiques

- When **ce + être** is followed by a plural noun, **être** generally agrees with the noun. The singular form is, however, commonly used in the spoken language. Here:
  Ce sera les meilleures pêches... (spoken)
  Ce seront les meilleures pêches... (written)
- When **ce + être** is followed by the pronoun **moi, toi, nous,** or **vous,** then **être** is in the 3rd person singular: **C'est moi. / C'est nous qui avons mangé la tarte.**
- When **ce + être** is followed by the pronoun **eux** or **elles,** then **être** is in the 3rd person plural: **Ce sont eux. Ce sont elles**. The singular is commonly used, especially in the negative form: **Ce n'est pas eux. C'est elles.**

■ Débat

Avec votre partenaire, débattez les avantages et les inconvénients de la vie en ville et à la campagne, en fonction de l'histoire que vous avez lue. Chacun va choisir une opinion différente.

■ Situations

Avec votre partenaire, choisissez l'une des situations suivantes. Composez le dialogue correspondant et jouez-le en classe.

1 Détails

Quand elle voit rentrer son mari le soir de la réception, Madame Herbelot comprend que quelque chose d'extraordinaire s'est passé. Elle veut avoir des détails.

Rôles: Monsieur et Madame Herbelot

2 À la fête

Une personne qui a assisté à la fête raconte l'histoire des pêches à un(e) voisin(e). Ce(tte) voisin(e) pose beaucoup de questions. La personne qui a été à la fête a tendance à exagérer un peu pour faire plus d'effet.

Rôles: la personne qui a été à la réception et son(sa) voisin(e)

3 Une décision

Le jour après l'incident, Vital Herbelot explique à sa femme ce qui s'est passé au bureau et dans la rue. Ils discutent de ce qu'ils doivent faire pour éviter *(to avoid)* ces problèmes. Ils prennent une décision.

Rôles: Monsieur et Madame Herbelot

4 Vingt ans après

Vingt ans après l'incident, l'un des enfants de Vital Herbelot apprend que son père a été cadre *(executive)* dans une banque. Il veut connaître le passé de son père.

Rôles: Monsieur Herbelot et son fils (sa fille)

5 Ville ou campagne ?

Après la promenade dans la ferme, le camarade de lycée de Vital Herbelot explique à son ami que la vie en ville a beaucoup d'avantages aussi. Vital Herbelot n'est pas d'accord.

Rôles: Vital Herbelot et son camarade de lycée

EXPRESSION ÉCRITE

■ «La Belle époque»

Relisez le texte et faites une liste des détails qui indiquent que cette histoire se passe il y a cent ans.

■ Lettre à un(e) ami(e)

Imaginez que vous êtes dans la situation de Vital Herbelot. Après avoir terminé vos études, vous avez trouvé un bon poste dans une banque (ou une autre sorte de travail). Vous avez reçu plusieurs promotions et vous gagnez très bien votre vie. Un jour, cependant, vous réalisez que cette existence ne correspond pas à ce que vous voulez vraiment faire.

Écrivez une lettre à un(e) ami(e). Dans cette lettre, informez-le(la) de votre décision de quitter votre travail, expliquez pourquoi et dites ce que vous allez faire.

■ Sujets de composition

1. Une situation embarrassante.
Décrivez une situation embarrassante, réelle ou imaginaire, dans laquelle une personne que vous connaissez s'est trouvée.

2. Un incident
Décrivez une situation, réelle ou imaginaire, dans laquelle un petit incident a eu des conséquences très importantes pour vous ou pour une personne que vous connaissez.

■ Note linguistique

Note the following familiar expressions:

- **avoir la pêche** *to be in great form/spirits*
- **se fendre la pêche** *to laugh*

■ Teaching Note

You may wish to use the short *Lecture* quiz as a comprehension check before students begin the activities in the *Après la lecture* section.

INTERLUDE CULTUREL

Un peu d'histoire

INTERLUDE CULTUREL

Les dates	Les événements
-1492-1502	Christophe Colomb fait plusieurs voyages en Amérique. Au cours de° ces voyages, il «découvre» plusieurs îles qui seront plus tard occupées par les Français: Hispaniola (1492), la Guadeloupe (1493), la Martinique (1502). À l'époque de Christophe Colomb, ces îles étaient habitées depuis des siècles par différents groupes d'«Indiens» — nom donné par Christophe Colomb aux populations caraïbes. Ces Indiens sont rapidement décimés° par les maladies et les mauvais traitements des Européens.
-1635	Les premiers colons° français arrivent à la Martinique et à la Guadeloupe. Peu après, ils font venir° de force des Africains pour travailler comme esclaves° dans leurs plantations.
-vers 1640	L'île de la Tortue,° au nord-ouest d'Hispaniola, sert de base à des pirates de toutes nationalités. Des colons français s'installent à Saint-Domingue, la partie ouest d'Hispaniola.
-1697	Saint-Domingue (Haïti) devient officiellement une colonie française.
-1763	La France perd ses colonies continentales d'Amérique (le Canada, la Louisiane), mais elle garde ses îles des Antilles.
-1791	Les Africains de Saint-Domingue se révoltent contre les Français. Toussaint Louverture devient l'un des chefs de cette révolte.
-1794	La Révolution française déclare l'abolition de l'esclavage dans toutes ses colonies
-1802	L'esclavage est rétabli par Napoléon, ce qui provoque une nouvelle insurrection Haïti. Napoléon envoie ses troupes pour mater° cette insurrection.
-1804	Après la victoire des Africains révoltés sur les troupes françaises, Saint-Domingue devient un pays indépendant et prend le nom d'Haïti. Les Français quittent Haït mais le français reste la langue officielle du pays.
-1848	L'esclavage est définitivement aboli dans les colonies françaises. Les habitants de Martinique et de la Guadeloupe deviennent des citoyens° français à part entière
-1902	L'éruption de la montagne Pelée à la Martinique fait plus de 30 000 morts.
-1946	La Martinique et la Guadeloupe deviennent des départements d'outre-mer.°
-1990	Jean-Bertrand Aristide est élu démocratiquement Président de la République haïtienne. Quelques mois après, un coup d'État militaire l'oblige à s'exiler aux États-
-1994	La démocratie est rétablie avec l'aide du gouvernement américain.
-2002	L'euro devient la monnaie officielle en Martinique et Guadeloupe.

au cours de = pendant **décimés** *killed* **colons** *settlers* **ils font venir** = ils amènent **esclaves** *slaves* **tortue** *turtle* **mater** *to put down* **citoyens** *citizens* **à part entière** = 100% **outre-mer** *overseas*

INTERLUDE CULTUREL

Notes linguistiques

- **Martinique** vient du nom Martin, car l'île fut découverte le onze novembre, date qui correspond à la Saint Martin dans le calendrier catholique.
- **Guadeloupe** vient de Notre-Dame de Guadalupe d'Estremadure. Christophe Colomb choisit ce nom pour remercier Notre-Dame qu'il avait priée lors d'une tempête. Avant cela, les habitants appelaient leur île **Calouacaera**.

Pour en savoir plus

For more information on the events leading up to 1763, see *Interlude 10,* p. 412.

NOTES CULTURELLES

- **Les Antilles** est le nom généralement donné aux îles de la mer Caraïbe. (Les Caraïbes étaient les Indiens qui habitaient ces îles avant l'arrivée de Christophe Colomb.) Les Antilles francophones comprennent les départements français de la Martinique et de la Guadeloupe, et la république d'Haïti.
- La fameuse **Île de la Tortue**, repaire de pirates, était française de 1665 à 1804. Depuis 1804, cette île, connue sous le nom espagnol de Tortuga, fait partie d'Haïti.

La malédiction caraïbe

Nous sommes à la Martinique en 1900. À cette époque, Saint-Pierre est la capitale de l'île. Avec ses distilleries, ses docks, ses magasins, ses banques, c'est un centre économique et commercial très actif. Dans le port, on peut voir des bateaux français, mais aussi des bateaux anglais, des bateaux américains, des bateaux italiens, des bateaux japonais, des bateaux chiliens . . . Sur ces bateaux, les marins chargent° le sucre, le rhum et les produits tropicaux de l'île.

Saint-Pierre est aussi une ville artistique et culturelle. Le dimanche, les gens vont au concert ou au théâtre. Il y a, en effet, un théâtre, le seul théâtre de toutes les Antilles. Saint-Pierre mérite bien son nom de «Paris des Antilles».

En réalité, Saint-Pierre est une ville en danger. La ville est située au pied d'un volcan, la montagne Pelée. Le 8 mai 1902, à sept heures cinquante du matin, la montagne Pelée explose! À huit heures, la ville est totalement dévastée. La cathédrale, le théâtre, le jardin botanique, les monuments, les maisons sont maintenant un immense désert de ruines. En moins de cinq minutes, toute la population de Saint-Pierre a péri.° Il y a 30 000 victimes . . . et un survivant. Ce survivant est un prisonnier. Ironiquement, les murs de la prison l'ont protégé contre la violence de l'explosion.

L'explosion de la montagne Pelée est une des grandes catastrophes dans l'histoire de l'humanité. Cette catastrophe a été annoncée dans une vieille légende caraïbe. Les Indiens caraïbes sont les premiers habitants de la Martinique. Quand les Français arrivent en 1635, ils veulent faire des Caraïbes leurs esclaves. Les Caraïbes résistent, mais ils sont finalement battus.° Courageusement, ils préfèrent la mort à l'esclavage.

Avant de mourir, le dernier chef caraïbe donne sa malédiction° aux Français:

«Aujourd'hui, vous êtes les plus forts,
mais demain
la montagne de feu va nous venger.»°

La «montagne de feu», c'est bien sûr la montagne Pelée. Le 8 mai 1902, la malédiction caraïbe s'est réalisée!

chargent *load* **péri** *perished, died* **battus** *beaten* **malédiction** *curse* **venger** *to avenge*

■ Note historique

Fort-de-France est devenue la capitale (ou **chef-lieu**) de la Martinique après la destruction de Saint-Pierre.

■ Anecdote

The survivor of the eruption of **Mt. Pelée,** a man called **Sipares**, later joined the Barnum and Bailey circus.

■ Additional Information

Guadeloupe is another volcanic island. The volcano **la Soufrière** is the highest point of the island at 1467 meters (4812 feet). It erupted in 1956 and 1976 and is still active today.

■ **Pour en savoir plus**
For historical background on the French Revolution, see *Interlude 5,* pp. 216–225.

Note culturelle
More than 50,000 African slaves were sent to Martinique in 1636 to work in the plantations. They came mostly from Angola, Guinea, and Senegal.

■ **Additional Information**
- Unable to give an heir to Napoleon, **Joséphine** was repudiated in 1809. The civil marriage was annulled on the grounds that one of the witnesses was under age (he was nineteen at the time). Joséphine had two children from her previous marriage with **de Beauharnais.** After the annulment, she kept her imperial title and retired in her castle of **Malmaison** where she died in 1814.
- **La Guyane française,** in South America, is adjacent to Brazil and Suriname. It was used as a penal colony; criminals were sent to the infamous Devil's Island until 1953.

Deux Martiniquais célèbres

L'impératrice Joséphine (1763-1814)

Joséphine Tascher de la Pagerie est née à la Martinique dans la plantation de ses parents. Un jour, quand elle était petite, sa gouvernante° noire lui dit: «Un jour, tu gouverneras la France.» Joséphine évidemment ne croit pas cette prédiction extraordinaire. Elle grandit° et devient une jeune fille très belle et très élégante. À seize ans, elle épouse un jeune officier noble, Alexandre de Beauharnais, mais celui-ci est guillotiné pendant la Révolution. Joséphine elle-même est emprisonnée et échappe de peu° à la mort.

Peu de temps après, Joséphine rencontre Napoléon qui tombe éperdument° amoureux d'elle. Ils se marient en 1796. Quand Napoléon devient empereur en 1804, Joséphine devient impératrice,° réalisant ainsi la prédiction de sa gouvernante. Joséphine et Napoléon n'ont pas d'enfant. Napoléon veut avoir un fils pour assurer la succession de son trône. Il divorce et se remarie avec une princesse autrichienne.° Cependant, Napoléon reste très ami avec Joséphine qui, pour les Français, continue d'être la véritable° impératrice.

L'impératrice Joséphine

Aimé Césaire, poète et homme politique

Aimé Césaire (1913-): Poète et homme politique

Originaire de la Martinique, **Aimé Césaire** va à Paris pour faire ses étud universitaires. Là, il rencontre d'autres étudiants noirs avec qui il fonde u journal intitulé *L'Étudiant noir.* C'est dans ce journal qu'il définit la notion d **négritude**. Pour exprimer la valeur de la personnalité noire, Césaire chois la poésie. En 1939, il écrit un livre de poèmes intitulé *Cahier d'un retour a pays natal.* Césaire est aussi un homme d'action et, pour lui, l'action, c'est politique. Il rentre à la Martinique où il fonde un parti, *le Parti Progressis Martiniquais*. Il devient maire° de Fort-de-France. Élu° député° de Martinique, il défend les intérêts des habitants de son île.

Qu'est-ce que la négritude?

La négritude est un mouvement littéraire, philosophique et politique, né à Paris dans les années 1930. Les fondateurs de ce mouvement étaient des étudiants noirs, venus de différentes colonies françaises: Aimé Césaire (Martinique), Léon Damas (Guyane française), Léopold Senghor (Sénégal).

En quête de° leur identité, ces écrivains redécouvrent leurs racines° africaines qu'ils veulent valoriser.° La négritude est la reconnaissance d'une identité noire spécifique. Les Noirs ont leur personnalité, leur culture, leur système de valeurs, leur façon de percevoir et de comprendre l'univers. Ils doivent préserver et être fiers de cette identité spécifique liée° à l'Afrique, terre° de leurs ancêtres communs.

> *«La négritude est la conscience d'être noir, simple reconnaissance d'un fait, qui implique acceptation, prise en charge de son destin de noir, de son histoire et de sa culture.»*
>
> *— Aimé Césaire*

gouvernante *governess* **grandit** = devient grande **échappe de peu** *narrowly escapes* **éperdument** = passionnément **impératrice** = la femme de l'empereur **autrichienne** *Austrian* **véritable** = réelle **maire** *mayor* **Élu** *elected* **député** *congressman* **en quête de** *in search of* **racines** *roots* **valoriser** *to emphasize the value of* **liée** *linked* **terre** *land*

Pour saluer le Tiers-Monde

Dans ce poème, écrit en 1960, Aimé Césaire, de son île de la Martinique, salue les pays d'Afrique qui viennent de gagner leur indépendance. Ce poème est dédié à son ami, Léopold Senghor, président du Sénégal.

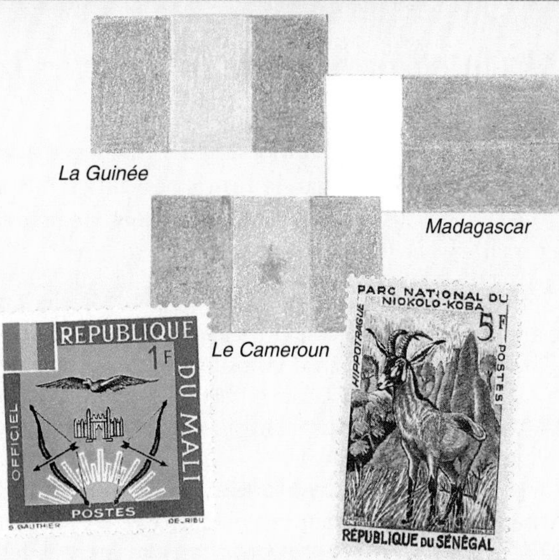

La Guinée
Madagascar
Le Cameroun

Ah!
mon demi-sommeil d'île si trouble
sur la mer!

Et voici de tous les points du péril
l'histoire qui me fait le signe° que
j'attendais.

Je vois pousser° des nations.
Vertes et rouges*, je vous salue,
bannières, gorges° du vent ancien,
Mali, Guinée, Ghana
et je vous vois, hommes,
point maladroits° sous ce soleil nouveau!

Écoutez:
de mon île lointaine°
de mon île veilleuse°
je vous dis Hoo!
Et vos voix me répondent
et ce qu'elles disent signifie:
«Il y fait clair.» Et c'est vrai:
même à travers orage et nuit
pour nous, il y fait clair.

Vois:
l'Afrique n'est plus
au diamant du malheur
un noir coeur qui se strie;°

notre Afrique est une main hors du ceste,°
c'est une main droite, la paume° devant
et les doigts bien serrés;°

c'est une main tuméfiée,°
une blessée-main-ouverte,
tendue,°
brunes, jaunes, blanches,
à toutes mains, à toutes les mains blessées
du monde.

* Les drapeaux des pays africains de Mali, de Guinée et de Ghana ont les couleurs vertes, rouges et jaunes

le signe = le signe de la liberté **pousser** *grow* **gorges** *pride* **point maladroits** *not at all clumsy* **lointaine** = qui est loin (de l'Afrique) **veilleuse** = lente **se strie** *is lacerated [by the diamond of misfortune]* **ceste** *boxing glove* **paume** *palm* **bien serrés** *close together* **tuméfiée** *swollen* **tendue** *stretched out*

Realia Note

F.A.O. = *Food and Agriculture Organization* **(Organisation pour l'Alimentation et l'Agriculture)**
This U.N. agency offers technical assistance to developing countries in order to increase and promote their agricultural revenues and productions.

Teaching Note

Brief interpretation of *Pour saluer le Tiers-Monde:*

verses 1, 2 From his island that is still half asleep, Césaire recognizes the sign of freedom rising from areas where it was in peril.

verse 3 He sees the banners of the new African nations, and he sees the citizens of these countries under a new sun.

verse 4 From his far-away island (which is slow in gaining its independence), he calls out to the people of Africa who respond that light is dawning in their land.

verse 5 Africa is no longer a bleeding heart.

verse 6 It is a strong hand, recovering from its wounds, reaching out to all the hands of the world.

■ Note linguistique

Haïti is the name that had been given to the island by its pre-Columbian inhabitants, the Arawaks. The word means "mountainous island."

■ Additional Information

- **Toussaint Louverture** was jailed in the fort of Joux, France, where he died just before Haiti gained its independence.
- There were many plantations in **Saint-Domingue,** most growing sugar cane, coffee, and indigo.
- U.S. forces occupied **Haiti** between 1915 and 1934 to restore order after political unrest.

▪*Haïti*▪

■ *Un champion de la liberté: Toussaint Louverture (1743-1803)*

Haïti est une nation indépendante depuis près de 200 ans.
Le héros de l'indépendance haïtienne s'appelle Toussaint Louverture.
Voici l'histoire de ce grand champion de la liberté.

Cette histoire commence à la fin du 18ᵉ siècle. La partie occidentale° d'Haïti s'appelait alors Saint-Domingue. C'était une colonie française où il y avait 20 000 Français et 500 000 Africains qui travaillaient très dur comme esclaves dans les plantations des Français.

En 1789, ces esclaves ont eu un grand espoir.° Une révolution libérale venait d'éclater en France. Est-ce que cette révolution allait émanciper les Noirs? En principe, oui. Les révolutionnaires français ont décidé d'abolir l'esclavage dans les colonies. Malheureusement, Saint-Domingue était loin de Paris et les Français de l'île ont refusé de libérer leurs esclaves. Pour les Africains, il y avait une seule° solution: la révolte. En 1791, les Africains de Saint-Domingue sont entrés en rébellion contre leurs maîtres.

Trois ans plus tard, en 1794, les Anglais, qui étaient en guerre contre la France, ont voulu occuper Saint-Domingue. Pour les Français, la situation était extrêmement grave. Le gouverneur de Saint-Domingue a décidé alors de rencontrer le chef des esclaves révoltés. Ce chef était Toussaint Louverture. Il avait 4 000 hommes sous ses ordres. Il a proposé au gouverneur un marché:° «Garantissez la liberté des Noirs et mes troupes vont combattre avec vous contre les Anglais.» Le gouverneur n'avait pas le choix. Il a accepté.

Quelques semaines après, Toussaint Louverture, l'ancien esclave, a été nommé commandant. C'était un brillant stratège. Ses troupes ont chassé les Anglais de Saint-Domingue. En juillet 1795, Toussaint Louverture a été nommé général de brigade et vice-gouverneur de Saint-Domingue. En réalité, c'était maintenant lui le chef de l'île.

Avec l'émancipation des esclaves, Toussaint Louverture avait réalisé sa première ambition. Cependant, il avait une autre ambition: obtenir l'indépendance de Saint-Domingue. Oui, mais comment? Il fallait d'abord organiser le pays. Toussaint Louverture a créé une administration moderne. Il a ouvert des écoles. Il a développé le commerce. S'il a réussi dans ses projets, c'est parce que c'était un homme juste. Il ne faisait pas de distinction entre les anciens maîtres blancs et les anciens esclaves noirs. Ainsi, il a p mobiliser tous les talents. Les résultats de cett politique ont été immédiats. En 1800, Saint Domingue était un pays riche et prospère Économiquement, c'était un pays indépendant.

Toussaint Louverture, un champion de la liberté.

Administrativement, cependant, Saint Domingue était toujours une colonie française. L France, à ce moment-là, était gouvernée pa Napoléon Bonaparte. Napoléon était un généra brillant mais très autoritaire. Il n'aimait pa l'indépendance de Toussaint Louverture. Pire,° a décidé de rétablir l'esclavage à Saint-Domingue Pour cela, il a préparé une formidable expéditior Le premier février 1802, 22 000 soldats françai sont arrivés dans l'île. C'était la guerre! La guerr d'indépendance a mal commencé pour les Noirs Leur chef, Toussaint Louverture a été capturé pa traîtrise.° Déporté en France, il est mort après di mois de captivité.

La mort de Toussaint Louverture a encourag la résistance des Noirs. Ceux-ci ont finalemer battu l'armée française. Le premier janvier 180 Saint-Domingue est devenue une natio indépendante et a pris le nom d'Haïti.

occidentale *western* **espoir** *hope* **une seule** *only one* **un marché** *a deal* **pire** *worse* **traîtrise** *treachery*

NOTE CULTURELLE

Jean-Jacques Dessalines was born in Guinea, Africa, circa 1758. This former slave and lieutenant of Toussaint Louverture took over the fight, leading the country to declare its independence on January 1st, 1804. He then proceeded to make himself emperor, under the name of **Jacques 1ᵉʳ**. A tyrannical ruler, he was assassinated in 1806. Haiti became a republic in 1844 after years of internal fighting and political division.

Pour Haïti

René Depestre est né en Haïti en 1926. À l'âge de vingt ans, il a été exilé de son pays à cause de ses activités politiques. Il habite actuellement° à Paris. Depestre est un poète engagé° qui dénonce l'oppression et l'injustice. Dans ce poème, il évoque sa terre° natale qu'il a quittée il y a longtemps, mais à laquelle il pense sans cesse.°

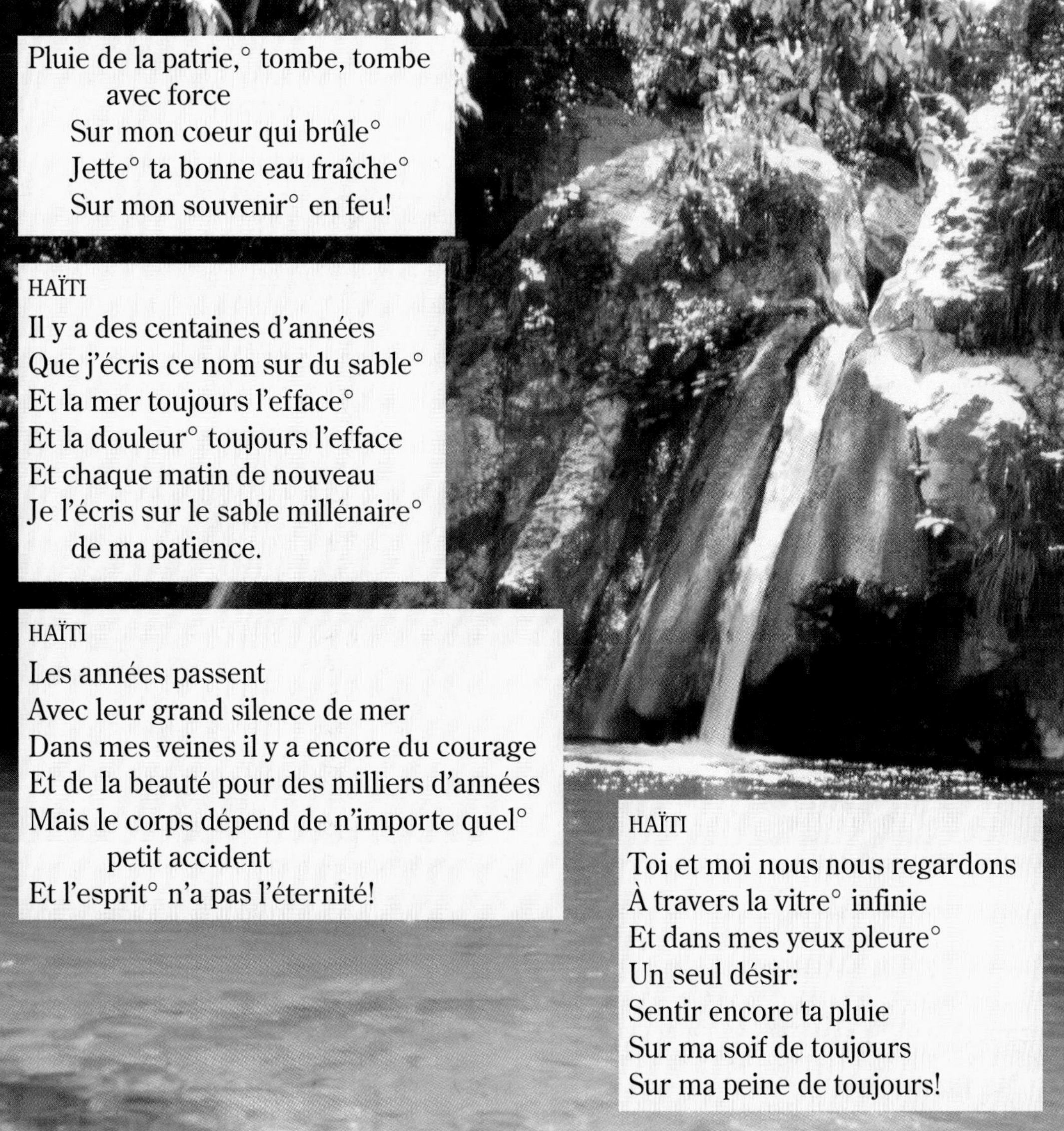

Pluie de la patrie,° tombe, tombe
avec force
Sur mon coeur qui brûle°
Jette° ta bonne eau fraîche°
Sur mon souvenir° en feu!

HAÏTI
Il y a des centaines d'années
Que j'écris ce nom sur du sable°
Et la mer toujours l'efface°
Et la douleur° toujours l'efface
Et chaque matin de nouveau
Je l'écris sur le sable millénaire°
de ma patience.

HAÏTI
Les années passent
Avec leur grand silence de mer
Dans mes veines il y a encore du courage
Et de la beauté pour des milliers d'années
Mais le corps dépend de n'importe quel°
petit accident
Et l'esprit° n'a pas l'éternité!

HAÏTI
Toi et moi nous nous regardons
À travers la vitre° infinie
Et dans mes yeux pleure°
Un seul désir:
Sentir encore ta pluie
Sur ma soif de toujours
Sur ma peine de toujours!

René Depestre, ***Journal d'un animal marin*** *(Paris, Seghers, 1964)*

Teaching Note
Have students compare the second verse of this poem with *Liberté* by Paul Éluard, page 257.

actuellement = à présent **engagé** *politically active* **terre** *land* **sans cesse** *unceasingly* **patrie** *native land (= Haïti)* **brûle** *is burning* **jette** *throw* **fraîche** *cool* **souvenir** *memory* **sable** *sand* **efface** *erases* **douleur** *pain, suffering* **millénaire** = qui a mille ans **n'importe quel** *any* **esprit** *soul, spirit* **vitre** *glass* **pleure** *is crying*

Teaching Note

You might want to have students compare the style of these Haitian paintings with the «naïf» style of Henri Rousseau, p. 64.

Teaching Strategy

Ask the students to look at the paintings for three minutes, jotting down their impressions. Then ask students:
Qu'est-ce que ces tableaux évoquent pour vous? Dites lequel vous préférez et pourquoi.

En Haïti, l'art, c'est la vie

Tous les Haïtiens, ou presque, ont une âme° d'artiste. En Haïti, l'art est partout:° sur les murs, sur les devantures des magasins,° sur les volets° des maisons, dans les églises, sur les autobus, sur les camions° ou sur les voitures. Et maintenant, il se trouve aussi dans les collections privées et dans les musées.

L'art haïtien est avant tout un art populaire: il est issu du peuple et il est fait pour le peuple. À la différence des artistes européens ou américains, les artistes haïtiens n'ont généralement pas reçu de formation technique dans des écoles d'art spécialisées. Ils ont appris eux-mêmes à peindre.° Leur style, souvent appelé «style naïf», est caractérisé par un dessin° relativement simple, l'absence de perspective et l'usage d'une palette aux couleurs chaudes et vibrantes.

Les sources de l'art haïtien sont intérieures et personnelles: c'est l'environnement immédiat de l'artiste, la nature, la culture, la religion et les croyances° d'un peuple aux profondes racines° africaines. Les sujets représentés expriment la vie et l'âme de ce peuple. Ce sont souvent des scènes de la vie quotidienne, la ville avec ses gens aux vêtements multicolores ou la campagne haïtienne avec sa végétation luxuriante, parfois des cérémonies ou des sujets religieux, ou des scènes historiques.

C'est un Américain, DeWitt Peters, qui a fait découvrir au monde les merveilles de l'art haïtien. Peters était venu en Haïti au début° des années 1940 pour enseigner° l'anglais. Lui-même peintre, il a tout de suite° été séduit° par l'art simple et coloré des peintres haïtiens. Avec l'aide des gouvernements haïtien et américain, il a ouvert un Centre d'Art où étaient exposées les oeuvres° des meilleurs peintres haïtiens. L'existence de ce centre a encouragé de nombreuses vocations d'artistes. Autrefois méconnu,° l'art haïtien est aujourd'hui apprécié par un nombre croissant° d'amateurs° un peu partout dans le monde.

J.M. Obin *«La Bataille de Vertières»*

J.M. Obin est spécialiste de scènes historiques. Ce tableau représente la dernière bataille de la guerre d'indépendance haïtienne qui a eu lieu le 13 novembre 1803 à Vertières. Au cours de cette bataille décisive, l'armée des anciens esclaves, commandée par le général Dessalines (au centre), met en fuite l'armée française (à droite). Quelques jours plus tard, l'armistice est déclaré. Le premier janvier 1804, Haïti devient une nation indépendante.

Salnave Philippe-Auguste *«Les crocodiles»*

Avocat de profession, **Salnave Philippe-Auguste** s'est consacré à plein temps à la peinture à l'âge de 51 ans. Dans un style délicat et symbolique, il peint des scènes exotiques remplies d'animaux sauvages. Ici, il a choisi comme sujet des crocodiles qu'on trouve encore dans les régions marécageuses° et reculées° d'Haïti. Ces crocodiles semblent protéger des fleurs aquatiques, symboles de la liberté chèrement acquise par les Haïtiens en 1804.

âme *soul* **partout** *everywhere* **devantures des magasins** *storefronts* **volets** *shutters* **camions** *trucks* **peindre** *to paint* **dessin** *design* **croyances** *beliefs* **racines** *roots* **début** *beginning* **enseigner** *to teach* **tout de suite** = immédiatement **séduit** *attracted, seduced* **oeuvres** *works* **méconnu** = peu connu **croissant** *increasing* **amateurs** *art-lovers* **marécageuses** *swampy* **reculées** *remote*

NOTES CULTURELLES

- À remarquer le drapeau français représenté avec des bandes horizontales plutôt que verticales.
- À la bataille de Vertières, l'armée française était commandée par le général Rochambeau, fils de Rochambeau, héros de l'indépendance américaine. (Voir page 413.)
- Jean-Jacques Dessalines, le général victorieux de la bataille de Vertières, se proclame empereur d'Haïti et prend le nom de Jacques Ier.

Préfète Duffaut *«Village magique»*

Dans ce tableau, **Dieuseul Paul** représente des *loas*, esprits bénéfiques° ou maléfiques° de la religion vaudou. Cette religion populaire d'Haïti a inspiré beaucoup d'autres artistes haïtiens. Originaire du Bénin en Afrique, le vaudou intègre les croyances et rituels des religions animistes* africaines avec certains éléments de la religion catholique. Les pratiquants du vaudou vénèrent un grand nombre de dieux et de loas représentant les forces visibles et invisibles du monde qui nous entoure. Chaque pratiquant a son propre° loa.

Dieuseul Paul *«Loas»*

Préfète Duffaut est l'un des peintres haïtiens les plus célèbres. Il n'avait jamais vu d'oeuvres artistiques quand il a commencé à peindre vers l'âge de 20 ans. Dans un style tout à fait personnel, il aime peindre des villages imaginaires, mais très détaillés, avec des rues en zigzag qui s'accrochent aux flancs des montagnes. La présence de montagnes caractérise les tableaux de Duffaut et rappelle l'origine du nom d'Haïti qui, en langue arawak, signifie «pays de montagnes».

Hector Hyppolite, *«Agoué et son consort»*

Hector Hyppolite, l'un des premiers peintres exposés au Centre d'Art, était aussi un *houngan*, c'est-à-dire un prêtre vaudou. Dans ce tableau, Hyppolite a peint Agoué, loa de la mer, symbolisée ici par une ancre marine, et son consort.

Pauleus Vital *«Paysage de Sables-Cabaret»*

Comme son demi-frère Préfète Duffaut, **Pauleus Vital** aime peindre les paysages de montagnes, mais d'une façon réaliste et précise. Dans ce tableau, l'artiste représente le travail quotidien des gens de la campagne. On peut remarquer la régularité des champs et la luxuriance de la végétation haïtienne, rendue encore plus intense par les couleurs brillantes utilisées par l'artiste.

* Pour une définition de l'animisme, voir page 375.

bénéfiques = qui font du bien **maléfiques** = qui font du mal **propre** *own*

■ Note historique

Les Arawaks étaient le peuple qui habitait Haïti avant l'arrivée de Christophe Colomb.

NOTES CULTURELLES

- **Hector Hyppolite**
  The painter Hector Hyppolite (who died in 1948) was one of the first Haitian painters to be discovered not only by DeWitt Peters but also by the French surrealists. On a visit to Haiti, the French writer André Breton was absolutely fascinated by Hyppolite and bought several of his paintings. Now Hyppolite's works are in collections all over the world.
- **Le houngan**
  À la fois prêtre, prophète, pharmacien, médecin et conseiller de sa communauté, **le houngan** joue encore un rôle important dans la société haïtienne d'aujourd'hui.

Documents: Rue Cases-nègres

Rue Cases-nègres est un film entièrement martiniquais. Réalisé par **Euzhan Palcy**, une cinéaste martiniquaise, d'après l'oeuvre° de l'écrivain martiniquais **Joseph Zobel**, il est joué par des acteurs martiniquais, sur une musique de biguine martiniquaise.

L'action du film se passe en 1930 dans une Martinique bien différente de la Martinique d'aujourd'hui. Les différentes scènes sont reliées° entre elles par la présence d'un jeune garçon d'une douzaine d'années, **José Hassam**, un orphelin° élevé° par sa grand-mère, **M'man-Tine** (Grand-maman Amantine). Tous deux habitent rue Cases-Nègres, une rue pauvre d'un petit village de Martinique.

Les conditions de vie sont difficiles. Tout le monde doit travailler très dur° dans les champs de canne à sucre pour ne gagner presque rien. Pour échapper à° cette misère, il n'y a qu'une solution: l'instruction.°

Le jeune José a plusieurs mentors. D'abord, M'man-Tine, la vieille grand-mère pieuse,° qui va tout faire pour que son petit-fils aille à l'école. Il y a aussi le vieux **Médouze**, en quelque sorte le père spirituel de José. Médouze a passé toute sa vie au travail et maintenant son corps est usé° et brisé.° Il rêve° de l'Afrique lointaine, pays des ancêtres où il voudrait un jour retourner. Il raconte à José l'histoire du peuple: le départ forcé d'Afrique, l'esclavage dans les plantations des «Békés»*, l'émancipation qui en réalité n'a pas changé grand-chose, et le travail, le travail, toujours le travail . . . Émerveillé° et attentif, le jeune José écoute le vieillard° évoquer les éléments de la sagesse° africaine: respect de la nature, respect de la vie . . .

Il y a aussi les professeurs de José. Ils ont remarqué l'intelligence du jeune garçon et en sont d'abord surpris. L'un d'eux accuse même José d'avoir triché° à une composition. José est reçu au certificat d'études** et reçoit une bourse° partielle pour aller étudier à Fort-de-France. Malheureusement, la bourse n'est pas suffisante. M'man-Tine est une femme fière et déterminée. Elle a décidé que son petit-fils continuerait ses études, quoi qu'il lui en coûte° à elle. Malgré° son âge, la vieille femme va s'établir° à Fort-de-France où elle travaille comme lingère° pour gagner l'argent des études. L'administration comprend finalement la situation et accorde° une bourse complète à José.

*Pour son film **Rue Cases Nègres**, la réalisatrice° Euzhan Palcy a reçu le César (Oscar français) du meilleur premier film.*

M'man-Tine peut retourner à son village où elle meurt heureuse d'avoir accompli son rêve.

Cette histoire simple sert de trame° générale au film où se succèdent° une série de petites scènes souvent réalistes, parfois comiques (les rapports entre José et sa tante Madame Léonce), parfois pénibles° (les rapports entre son copain Léopold et le père de celui-ci). Par son décor, le monde qu'Euzhan Palcy nous présente dans son film peut paraître archaïque et lointain.° Les gens qui vivent dans ce monde sont pauvres et simples, mais ils sont honnêtes, droits,° généreux, fiers et avant tout ils sont humains!

* «Békés» est un mot créole qui désigne les descendants des anciens colons blancs venus de France pour établir des plantations dans les Antilles.

** Le certificat d'études = un diplôme de fin des études primaires.

l'oeuvre = le livre **reliées** *linked* **orphelin** = enfant qui a perdu son père et sa mère **élevé** *raised* **dur** *hard* **échapper à** *to escape from* **l'instruction** *education* **pieuse** *pious* **usé** *worn out* **brisé** *broken* **rêve** *dreams* **émerveillé** *amazed* **vieillard** = vieil homme **sagesse** *wisdom* **triché** *cheated* **bourse** *scholarship* **quoi qu'il lui en coûte** *whatever it may cost her* **malgré** *in spite of* **s'établir** *to settle* **lingère** *laundry woman* **accorde** = donne **trame** *plot* **se succèdent** *follow one another* **pénibles** *painful* **lointain** *distant* **droits** *straightforward* **réalisatrice** *director*

Notes culturelles

- **Euzhan Palcy** made her first feature film, *Rue Cases-nègres*, at the age of 27. The film, which was produced on a budget of less than one million dollars, was acclaimed as a masterpiece on its release in 1982. In addition to the César award for the Best First Film, it also was honored with a Silver Lion at the Venice Film Festival. All the actors in the film, except two, were non-professional.

  In a more recent film, *Siméon*, Palcy depicts a group of Zouk musicians from Martinique who go to Paris to get a record contract.
- **Joseph Zobel**, author of the autobiographical novel *La rue Cases-nègres*, makes a brief cameo appearance in the film (as the priest). Born and raised in Martinique in circumstances similar to those of José, Zobel continued his schooling and went to Sénégal to become a teacher.

Teaching Notes

The film **Rue Cases-nègres** *(Sugarcane Alley)* has been rated PG. You will definitely want to preview the movie, however, before deciding whether or not it is appropriate for your classes.

- In the scene at Léopold's house, Léopold's mother plays a record that she has just received from France: we hear Joséphine Baker singing her signature piece: «J'ai deux amours, mon pays et Paris» (cf. *Interlude 4*, p. 178).

Quelques scènes du film

Sur cette photo, on peut voir les personnages principaux du film. Au premier plan, le jeune José Hassam en costume et chapeau blancs. Derrière lui, sa grand-mère M'Man Tine. Derrière M'man Tine, on peut remarquer Euzhan Palcy, la réalisatrice du film.

Dans les champs de canne à sucre, les habitants du village travaillent très dur sous l'oeil vigilant d'un contremaître (foreman) à cheval.

José habite avec M'man Tine dans une case très simple. Pendant que sa grand-mère reprise (darns) les vêtements, José s'adonne (devotes himself) à son passe-temps favori: la lecture.

Tous les jours, José va à l'école avec les enfants du village.

José est l'élève le plus brillant de sa classe. Il répond avec intelligence et imagination aux questions de l'instituteur (teacher), Monsieur Roc.

José vient d'être reçu au certificat d'études. Monsieur Roc est très fier de son élève.

José a reçu une bourse partielle pour continuer ses études au lycée. M'man Tine part avec lui pour Fort-de-France.

Teaching Note

If you would like to purchase a copy of the film, as well as Lesson Plans and activities, contact:

FilmAerobics
9 Birmingham Place
Vernon Hills, IL 60061
1-800-832-2448

NOTE CULTURELLE

In 1882, **Jules Ferry** promulgated a new law, which made schooling mandatory and free for all children between the ages of 7 and 13.

Le certificat d'études used to be awarded to students who finished elementary school and were not going to pursue any higher education. It became obsolete when school became mandatory until the age of 16, since from then on, all children would go on at least to junior high school. The certificate was abrogated in 1989.

UNITÉ 9

MAIN THEME

Personal Relationships, Friendships, Family Life

Communication Function/Contexts
- Describing friendship
- Expressing feelings towards other people
- Discussing relationships
- Congratulating, comforting, expressing sympathy
- Describing life phases

Linguistic Goals
- Describing how people interact
- Describing people and things in complex sentences

Online Study Center

Online Teaching Center

Teaching Strategy

After reading the article, ask students to compare and contrast family life in France and the U.S. For further discussion, ask students: À votre avis, qu'est-ce que «l'esprit de famille»? Donnez une définition et des exemples pour illustrer votre point de vue.

UNITÉ 9

Les relations personnelles

Thème et Objectifs

Culture

In this unit, you will discover . . .
- what friendship and family life mean to the French
- what young people in France do to help the disadvantaged
- what is involved in planning a wedding in France

Communication

You will learn how . . .
- to talk about friends and acquaintances
- to explain how people get along with one another
- how to congratulate people on their success or comfort them when they are feeling down
- to describe the various phases of the life cycle

Langue

You will learn how . . .
- to talk about how people interact with each other
- to describe people and things in a clear and complete manner

TEACHING RESOURCES

ANCILLARIES

Student Activities Manual, Unit 9
Audio Program, Unit 9
Video-DVD Program, Unit 9
Chansons Audio CD

HM ClassPrep CD

Presentations, Unit 9
Audioscript, Unit 9
Videoscript, Unit 9
Assessment, Unit 9
Answer Key, Unit 9

Les amis et la famille

Pour les Français, les rapports humains ont énormément d'importance. L'amitié, par exemple, est considérée comme la valeur la plus importante de l'existence. Elle passe avant le travail, l'argent et même l'amour. Un ami, évidemment, n'est pas n'importe qui.° Ce n'est pas une personne qu'on rencontre un jour et qu'on oublie le lendemain. C'est généralement quelqu'un qu'on connaît depuis très longtemps, souvent depuis l'enfance et avec qui on a beaucoup d'expériences communes.° C'est la personne spéciale à qui on dit tout, avec qui on partage° ses joies et ses peines° et sur qui on peut compter dans les moments les plus difficiles de l'existence. Les vrais amis sont peu nombreux, mais ces amis-là, c'est pour la vie.

Un autre aspect de la vie en France est la solidité des relations familiales. Autrefois, le milieu familial était très vaste et la vie familiale très active. La famille comprenait° non seulement enfants, parents, grands-parents, cousins, tantes et oncles, mais aussi toutes les autres personnes qui avaient une ascendance° commune ou qui étaient alliées par le mariage. On se réunissait assez régulièrement le dimanche, autour d'un grand repas familial, ou plus occasionnellement pour les fêtes de famille: anniversaires, mariages, cérémonies religieuses, etc.

Aujourd'hui, la famille proche se limite au couple, à leurs enfants et aux parents qu'on voit régulièrement. Cette famille est généralement très unie. Parents et enfants s'entendent° bien, même au moment difficile de l'adolescence. D'après une enquête, 77% des adolescents français considèrent que leurs relations avec leurs parents sont excellentes ou très bonnes. De même, 88% des jeunes de 18 à 24 ans déclarent s'entendre bien avec leurs parents.

Si la vie de famille est moins active qu'autrefois, «l'esprit de famille» est resté intact. La solidarité familiale joue beaucoup dans les différentes phases de l'existence. Les parents font énormément d'efforts et de sacrifices pour assurer une bonne éducation à leurs enfants. Après leurs études, ils continuent à les aider moralement et matériellement. À leur tour, les enfants s'occupent de leurs parents au moment de leur vieillesse.

Pour les Français, la famille, c'est sacré!

n'importe qui *just anyone* **communes** *shared, in common* **partage** *shares* **peines** *sorrows* **comprenait** *included* **ascendance** *ancestry* **s'entendent** *get along*

INFO MAGAZINE

Theme: Friends and family

Reading Strategy: Skimming, scanning

Teaching Strategy

These readings can be done:
- in class or as homework
- at the beginning of the unit or as a wrap-up activity

Have students look at the realia and photos and guess the theme of the article. Have them skim, looking for cognates, then give the main idea. Short *Info Magazine* quizzes may be used to test for comprehension or as a basis for discussion.

Supplementary vocabulary

la famille éclatée *extended family*
le beau-père *stepfather/father-in-law*
la belle-mère *stepmother/mother-in-law*
les beaux grands-parents *step-grandparents*
le demi-frère *stepbrother*
la demi-soeur *stepsister*
le demi-oncle *step-uncle*
la demi-tante *step-aunt*
le fils adoptif *adopted son*
la fille adoptive *adopted daughter*
les parents adoptifs *adoptive parents*

Note culturelle

Les cérémonies religieuses qui réunissent les familles peuvent être, pour les catholiques, **le baptême** *(christening)* et **la communion** *(confirmation);* pour les juifs **la bar-mitsva** ou **bat-mitsva.** Les familles se réunissent également pour **un mariage** et lors de **l'enterrement** *(funeral)* d'un proche.

■ **Teaching Note**

For a longer list of characteristics, see *Reprise A, Rappel 1*, p. 5.

Proverbe

Les amis de nos amis sont nos amis.

Les qualités d'un(e) ami(e)

Nous choisissons nos amis parce qu'ils ont beaucoup de qualités. Évidemment, certaines qualités sont plus importantes que d'autres. Parmi les qualités suivantes, choisissez les cinq qui comptent le plus pour vous et classez-les par ordre d'importance.

- **l'intelligence**
- **l'humour**
- **le courage**
- **la patience**
- **la loyauté**
- **l'apparence physique**
- **la bonne humeur**
- **la franchise**
- **la sincérité**
- **l'honnêteté**
- **??**
- **la générosité**
- **la sensibilité**
- **la discrétion**

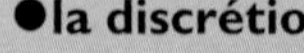

et vous?

Comparez votre liste de qualités avec celles de vos camarades de classe. Vous pouvez aussi établir une liste des préférences de toute la classe.

NOUS ET LES AUTRES

La vie moderne a beaucoup d'avantages. La majorité des gens habitent dans des maisons confortables et modernes, gagnent bien leur vie, et ont des loisirs intéressants. Mais en France, comme ailleurs, il y a aussi beaucoup de gens qui ne profitent pas de ces avantages. Il y a des jeunes qui n'ont pas de travail, des familles qui n'ont pas d'argent et parfois pas d'abri,° des personnes âgées qui sont malades et qui n'ont pas de famille pour s'occuper d'elles. Ces personnes aussi font partie de la société, mais la société a tendance à les oublier.

ACCUEIL TRAVAIL

Nous accueillons des personnes en difficulté, à la recherche d'un hébergement, et qui acceptent par leur travail de participer à la vie de la communauté.

Seule source de revenus, il permet de faire face aux besoins de la communauté. Chaque compagnon est appelé à travailler selon ses capacités et ses moyens. Il est ainsi reconnu et revalorisé.

NE JETEZ PAS VOTRE CŒUR A LA POUBELLE
IL PEUT ENCORE SERVIR.
EMMAÜS

abri *shelter*

Realia Note

Pictured here is a pamphlet for **Les Chiffonniers d'Emmaüs,** a French charity that caters to the needs of the homeless. This organization was founded by **L'abbé Pierre.** For more information, see p. 294.

Teaching Strategy

Ask students to bring in pictures of family members or friends. Ask them to talk about three of these people in front of the class, including information about where they live, when the student sees them and what they generally do/talk about together.

Heureusement, tout le monde n'est pas égoïste. Voici le cas de trois jeunes Français qui ont décidé de «faire quelque chose» pour les autres.

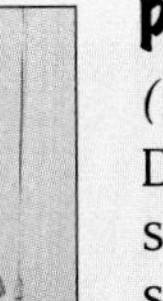

Patrick Esquivel

(15 ans, lycéen)

Dans l'immeuble où j'habite, il y a une vieille dame qui a perdu son mari l'année dernière et qui maintenant vit° toute seule dans son appartement au cinquième étage sans ascenseur. Je fais les courses pour elle une ou deux fois par semaine. Ça l'aide un peu, mais le plus important, c'est quand je passe une heure ou deux à bavarder° avec elle. Je lui parle de ce que je fais au lycée et elle me raconte sa vie. J'apprends des choses fascinantes, et elle ne se sent plus seule.°

Claire Delamotte

(19 ans, étudiante)

Je travaille deux jours par mois aux «Restos° du coeur». C'est une organisation bénévole° qui prépare des repas chauds pour les sans-abri,° les personnes sans ressources et, plus généralement, pour tous ceux qui ont faim. Mon travail varie. Parfois je travaille à la collecte de la nourriture. D'autres fois, je travaille à la cuisine ou bien je sers les repas.

Dans une société qui glorifie l'argent et la réussite, il est important de préserver les vraies valeurs qui n'ont rien à voir° avec celles que nous proposent les médias. Quand je travaille aux «Restos», je suis en contact avec la réalité de la misère humaine et je peux faire quelque chose d'utile. Le problème, c'est que nous avons de plus en plus de clients!

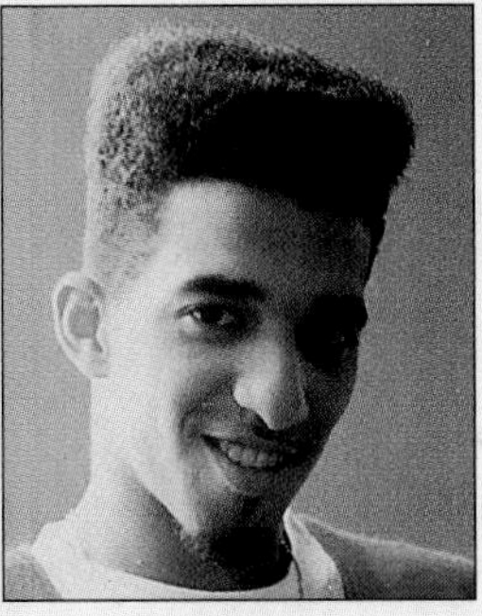

Steevy Gustave

(23 ans, musicien professionnel)

Je suis d'origine martiniquaise, mais maintenant j'habite dans la région parisienne. Dans ma banlieue, il y a beaucoup de problèmes de délinquance juvénile et de drogue. Heureusement, il y a une «Maison des Jeunes» qui attire° pas mal° de monde. J'y travaille souvent comme animateur. Mon but,° c'est de récupérer les jeunes drogués en les intéressant à la musique. Ce n'est pas toujours facile, mais avec de la persévérance et beaucoup d'encouragement, on y arrive.°

- Selon vous, lequel de ces jeunes Français fait la chose la plus utile? Expliquez pourquoi.
- Avez-vous déjà travaillé comme «volontaire»? Décrivez votre expérience.

vit / vivre *to live* **bavarder** *to chat* **seule** *lonely, alone* **Restos** = restaurants **bénévole** *charitable* **sans-abri** *homeless* **rien à voir** = rien à faire **attire** *attracts* **pas mal** = beaucoup **but** = objectif **on y arrive** *one can do it*

Supplementary vocabulary

le bénévolat *volunteer work*
le bénévole *volunteer*
l'entraide *(f.) mutual assistance*
la charité *charity*
la solidarité *solidarity*
le soutien *support*
l'isolement *(m.) isolation*
l'humanisme *(m.) humanism*

Pour en savoir plus

LES RESTOS DU COEUR
For more information on this organization, see *Interlude 7*, p.295.

Note culturelle

Les Maisons des Jeunes et de la Culture (M.J.C.) were created in 1944. They are financed by the cities with the help of the **Ministère de la Jeunesse et des Sports** and offer a wide variety of activities to young people. At the M.J.C. French young people may learn a craft, watch movies, play sports, or even display their own artwork.

■ Irregular Verb

(see Appendix C)
vivre

Teaching Strategy

After the students have read the profiles of the young French people on p. 347, have them write a similar profile of themselves or a friend, imagining that it is going to be included in an English textbook to demonstrate American culture and patterns of community service. Encourage the students to write longer sentences as opposed to simple subject-verb sentences.

PARTIE 1

LE FRANÇAIS
PRATIQUE

TEACHING RESOURCES

Student Activities Manual,
pp. 159–162

Audio Program,
CD 10, Tracks 1–5

HM ClassPrep CD,
Audioscript, Unit 9

Video/DVD Program,
Unit 9

LE FRANÇAIS PRATIQUE

Les amis, les copains et les relations personnelles

— Tiens, voilà Catherine.
— Qui est-ce?
— C'est une copine.
— Tu la connais depuis longtemps?
— Oui, depuis deux ans.
— Est-ce que tu peux me la présenter?
— Oui, volontiers!

LES PERSONNES QU'ON CONNAÎT

un ami **une amie**	est quelqu'un	qu'on connaît depuis longtemps pour qui on a beaucoup d'affection en qui on a **une confiance** *(trust)* absolue
un copain **une copine**	est quelqu'un	qu'on connaît bien qu'on voit souvent avec qui on fait beaucoup de choses
un camarade **une camarade**	est quelqu'un	avec qui on va en classe
une connaissance	est quelqu'un	qu'on connaît assez bien qu'on voit de temps en temps

1 Un(e) ami(e) n'est pas n'importe qui *(A friend is not just anybody)*

Quelle est votre définition d'un ami?
- Considérez la liste suivante et faites une liste des cinq caractéristiques les plus importantes. Vous pouvez aussi mentionner d'autres caractéristiques.
- Comparez votre liste avec celle de votre partenaire.

Faites la même chose pour la définition d'une amie.

Un ami / Une amie | est quelqu'un . . .

- qui est toujours d'accord avec moi
- qui me comprend
- à qui je peux parler de tout
- qui me dit toujours la vérité
- qui m'aide quand j'ai un problème
- en qui j'ai complète confiance
- pour qui j'ai beaucoup d'admiration
- qui ne me critique jamais
- qui me donne des conseils
- qui me prête de l'argent quand j'en ai besoin
- qui est toujours loyal(e)
- que je respecte
- qui me respecte
- qui me pardonne *(forgives)* toujours
- ??

Teaching Suggestion: Video/DVD Program

In the Unit 9 *Vidéo-drame: Dispute et réconciliation*, students will learn about relationships. This section focuses on feelings and relations between people. Before watching the video, you may point out to students the different levels of friendship that exist in France. Next, play the video once without interruption. Then, ask students to explain why Mélanie is upset and what phrases Nicolas uses to console her.

LES SENTIMENTS

On éprouve . . . 

- **de l'amitié** *(friendship)*
- **de l'affection**
- **de la sympathie** *(instinctive liking)*
- **de l'admiration**
- **du respect**

ou au contraire . . . 

- **de l'envie**
- **de la jalousie** *(jealousy)*
- **de l'antipathie**
- **de l'animosité**
- **de l'aversion**

éprouver *to feel*

L'amitié et l'amour

On | **aime bien** quelqu'un.
| **a de l'amitié pour** quelqu'un.

On | **tombe amoureux/amoureuse de** quelqu'un.
| **aime** quelqu'un.
| **a le coup de foudre pour** quelqu'un.

aimer bien *to like*
aimer *to love*
tomber amoureux de *to fall in love with*
avoir le coup de foudre pour *to fall in love with at first sight*

2 Mes sentiments

Choisissez deux des personnes suivantes et décrivez quel(s) sentiment(s) vous éprouvez pour chaque personne. Comparez vos sentiments avec ceux de votre partenaire.

Supplementary vocabulary

un(e) camarade de chambre *roommate*
un pote *(fam.) pal*
un petit ami *boyfriend*
une petite amie *girlfriend*
un inconnu *stranger*
un voisin *neighbor*
On a confiance en quelqu'un/ quelque chose *to have confidence/faith in*
On fait confiance à quelqu'un/ quelque chose *to trust*

Proverbe

Les petits cadeaux entretiennent l'amitié.

Teaching Strategy: Warm-Up

Have students brainstorm for two minutes, listing all the words meaning "friend" in English, recording all suggestions on the board or on a transparency. Next, list the new vocabulary above and ask students to see if the categories of friendship listed are similar in French and English. Then move into Act. 1, dividing the class into groups for discussion.

Supplementary vocabulary

du mépris *scorn*
de la pitié
de la rancune *resentment*
de la haine *hatred*
détester *to dislike*
haïr *to hate*
faire connaissance avec quelqu'un *to become acquainted with someone*
faire la connaissance de quelqu'un *to meet someone*
perdre/reprendre connaissance *to lose/regain consciousness*
prendre connaissance de quelque chose *to study, examine something*

If students ask...

un coup de foudre *lightning bolt (love at first sight)*

LES RELATIONS PERSONNELLES

— Qu'est-ce que tu fais samedi?
— Je sors avec une copine.
— Tu t'entends bien avec elle?
— Oui, en général je m'entends bien avec elle. Parfois on se dispute, mais après on se réconcilie.

Les rapports / Les relations

On peut . . .

avoir de **bons rapports** avec / de **bonnes relations** avec quelqu'un.

s'entendre bien avec *(to get along with)*
être d'accord avec *(to agree with)*
se réconcilier avec *(to make up with)*
avoir confiance en *(to trust)*

avoir de **mauvais rapports** avec / de **mauvaises relations** avec quelqu'un.

s'entendre mal avec
ne pas s'entendre avec
se disputer *(to have an argument)*
avoir une dispute avec
se quereller *(to have a fight)*
se fâcher avec *(to be upset at)*
rompre avec *(to break up with)*

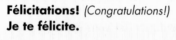

COMMENT FÉLICITER QUELQU'UN

Bravo!
Quelle bonne nouvelle!

Je suis content(e) / **Je me réjouis** pour toi.

Félicitations! *(Congratulations!)*
Je te félicite.

féliciter *to congratulate*
se réjouir *to be happy*

COMMENT PLAINDRE ET CONSOLER QUELQU'UN

plaindre* *to feel sorry for*

Mon pauvre! Ma pauvre!
Quel dommage!
Quelle malchance *(bad luck)***!**
Tu n'as pas de chance.

Je te plains.
Je suis désolé(e) pour toi.
Ne t'en fais pas! *(Don't worry! Don't feel bad!)*
Ça s'arrangera! *(Things will be okay! Everything will work out all right!)*

■ Irregular Verb

(see Appendix C)
Rompre is conjugated like **rendre** except for the 3rd person singular: **il rompt.**

■ Notes linguistiques

To review the forms of **plaindre,** have students refer to page 271.

- **plaindre** *to pity*
  se plaindre *to complain*
- Note the following expressions:
  s'entendre comme les deux doigts de la main *to get along very well*
  s'entendre comme chien et chat *to not get along*

■ Vocabulary Expansion

Also: **Tout s'arrange.**

Teaching Strategy: Warm-Up

Using twenty of the vocabulary words from pp. 348–350, have students write twenty sentences about various books, T.V. shows, movies and/or plays they have read or seen. Have them discuss the relationships between the characters using the vocabulary given; avoid obscure characters.

3 Mon copain et moi

Décrivez vos relations avec votre copain (copine).
Comparez vos réponses avec celles de votre partenaire.

1. J'ai une confiance --- en lui/elle.
    - complète
    - presque totale
    - assez limitée
    - ??
2. En général, je m'entends --- avec lui/elle.
    - parfaitement
    - très bien
    - relativement bien
    - ??
3. Quand nous nous querellons, c'est d'habitude *(usually)* moi qui . . .
    - ai raison
    - gagne
    - cède *(gives in)* le premier/la première
    - ??
4. Quand nous avons une dispute sérieuse, nous nous réconcilions . . .
    - immédiatement
    - au bout *(after)* d'une heure
    - au bout d'une semaine
    - ??
5. Quand nous nous disputons, c'est à cause de . . .
    - ses copains
    - sa famille
    - mes copains
    - ??
6. En ce moment, nos rapports sont . . .
    - excellents
    - relativement bons
    - tendus *(tense)*
    - ??

4 Mes rapports personnels

Choisissez l'une des personnes suivantes et décrivez vos rapports avec cette personne.

mon meilleur ami	mon petit/grand frère	mes voisins
ma meilleure amie	ma petite/grande soeur	mon prof de maths
un(e) autre ami(e)	mes cousins	mon prof d'anglais
	un(e) autre membre de ma famille	un(e) autre adulte

▶ **En général, je m'entends bien avec ma cousine, mais je ne suis pas tout le temps d'accord avec elle. De temps en temps, je me dispute avec elle. . . .**

5 Ça va?

Choisissez d'être l'une des personnes suivantes. Votre partenaire va vous demander si ça va et pourquoi. Décrivez un événement heureux ou malheureux. Il/elle va vous féliciter ou exprimer sa sympathie.

▶ **— Ça va?**
— Non, ça ne va pas.
— Qu'est-ce qui t'est arrivé?
— Je viens de me fâcher avec ma copine.
— Ne t'en fais pas. Ça s'arrangera.

Supplementary vocabulary

complimenter *to compliment*
s'accorder bien *to get along well*
se fréquenter *to go out with, to see*

Teaching Strategy: Expansion

Give students the following assignment:
Choisissez deux personnes:
- l'une avec qui vous vous entendez bien
- l'autre avec qui vous vous entendez mal

Décrivez vos rapports avec ces deux personnes.

LANGUE ET COMMUNICATION

TEACHING RESOURCES

Student Activities Manual, pp. 87, 162

Audio Program, CD 10, Track 6–8

HM ClassPrep CD, Audioscript, Unit 9

■ Notes linguistiques

- In the **passé composé**, the past participle agrees with the reflexive object only if the reflexive pronoun is a direct object. Compare:
  Marc a vu **Valérie**.
  Valérie a vu **Marc**.
  Ils se sont **vus**.
  (direct object: AGREEMENT)
  Anne a téléphoné **à Pierre**.
  Pierre a téléphoné **à Anne**.
  Ils se sont **téléphoné**.
  (indirect object: NO AGREEMENT)
  Examples of verbs where the reflexive pronoun is an indirect object:
  se parler, se téléphoner, s'écrire
- In French, reflexive verbs may be followed by an expression to reinforce the idea of reciprocity, such as: **l'un(e) l'autre; les un(e)s les autres; entre eux; mutuellement.**
  Elles se querellent les unes les autres.
  Ils se battent entre eux.

A. Les verbes réfléchis: sens réciproque

Reflexive verbs may be used to express a RECIPROCAL ACTION. In this case, the reflexive pronouns often correspond to the English expression *each other.* In the examples below, note the form of the verbs in heavy print.

Alain connaît Sophie. Sophie connaît Alain.	Ils **se connaissent.**	*They **know each other.***
J'écris à ma copine. Ma copine m'écrit.	Nous **nous écrivons**.	*We **write each other.***
Tu téléphones à Claire. Claire te téléphone.	Vous **vous téléphonez.**	*You **phone each other.***

Since a reciprocal action involves two or more people, the subject of a reciprocal verb is always plural: **nous, vous, ils, elles.**

➡ The subject may also be **on** used in the plural sense of **nous**.
On se verra demain. — ***We will see each other*** *tomorrow.*

Ils s'entendent bien.
Oui, mais hier, ils se sont disputés.

1 Entre amis

Les personnes suivantes sont des amis. Décrivez leurs relations.

▶ Jérôme et moi / se voir souvent
Nous nous voyons souvent.

1. Marc et Pauline / se téléphoner tous les jours
2. toi et tes amis / s'écrire pendant les vacances
3. Philippe et Cécile / se donner souvent rendez-vous
4. moi et mes copains / se retrouver après les classes
5. toi et François / se rendre visite tous les week-ends
6. toi et tes voisins / s'entendre bien
7. moi et mes cousins / se disputer rarement
8. Caroline et Charlotte / se réconcilier après chaque dispute

2 Relations personnelles

Informez-vous sur les personnes suivantes et décrivez leurs relations en utilisant les verbes entre parenthèses dans des phrases affirmatives ou négatives.

▶ Jérôme et Alice sont fiancés. (s'aimer?)
Ils s'aiment.

1. Marc et François sont de bons copains.
(s'aider? se disputer? se fâcher souvent?)
2. Mes voisins et moi, nous avons de bons rapports.
(s'entendre? s'inviter? se téléphoner?)
3. Jean-Paul et toi, vous êtes amis mais vous n'habitez pas dans la même ville.
(se voir souvent? se téléphoner? s'écrire?)
4. Claire et sa cousine ne sont jamais d'accord.
(se disputer? s'entendre bien? se réconcilier facilement?)
5. Delphine et moi, nous sommes fâchés.
(se parler? s'entendre mal? se quereller?)

3 Courrier du coeur

Complétez les lettres à Zoé avec les formes appropriées des verbes suggérés.

(1) s'entendre *(présent)*
(2) se fâcher *(passé composé)*
(3) ne plus se parler *(présent)*
(4) se disputer *(imparfait)*
(5) ne pas se revoir *(passé composé)*

Chère Zoé,

Je sors avec une fille depuis trois mois. En général, nous —— (1) très bien, mais la semaine dernière, il y a eu un drame.

Nous —— (2) parce que je suis arrivé à un rendez-vous avec vingt minutes de retard. Depuis, nous —— (3). Je ne veux pas rompre, mais j'ai peur de faire le premier pas!

Désolé

Cher désolé,

C'est toi qui étais en retard. Alors, si tu veux te réconcilier avec ta copine, c'est à toi de faire le premier pas.

Zoé

Chère Zoé,

L'été dernier, j'ai fait la connaissance d'un garçon avec qui je suis sortie pendant quelques temps. Un jour, j'ai rompu avec lui parce que nous —— (4) tout le temps. Depuis, nous —— (5).

Samedi dernier, j'ai appris, par hasard, qu'il sortait avec ma cousine. Maintenant, je ne peux plus dormir. Je pense sans cesse à lui et je crois que je l'aime toujours!

Nostalgique

Chère Nostalgique,

Tu n'es pas amoureuse, seulement jalouse! Oublie ton copain et cherche quelqu'un de plus compatible avec toi.

Zoé

4 À votre tour

Maintenant, écrivez une lettre à Zoé. Dans cette lettre, vous décrivez un problème que vous avez avec un(e) ami(e) imaginaire. Votre partenaire jouera le rôle de Zoé et vous donnera un conseil.

■ Proverbe

Les jours se suivent mais ne se ressemblent pas.
(The days follow each other but are not alike.)

B. Révision: Les pronoms relatifs **qui** et **que**

When we want to describe people or things, we often use adjectives. We can also use CLAUSES which refer back or relate to the people and things being described (the ANTECEDENTS). Such clauses are called RELATIVE CLAUSES and are introduced by RELATIVE PRONOUNS. Note how the French relative pronouns **qui** and **que** are used to convert two clauses into a single sentence.

J'ai un ami. **Il** habite à Paris.
→ J'ai un ami **qui** habite à Paris. — *I have a friend* ***who*** *lives in Paris.*

J'ai un ami. Je **l'**invite souvent.
→ J'ai un ami **que** j'invite souvent. — *I have a friend* ***whom (that)*** *I often invite.*

J'ai lu le livre. **Il** était sur la table.
→ J'ai lu le livre **qui** était sur la table. — *I read the book* ***that*** *was on the table.*

J'ai lu le livre. Tu **l'**as apporté.
→ J'ai lu le livre **que** tu as apporté. — *I read the book* ***that*** *you brought.*

Both **qui** and **que** may refer to people, things, or ideas.
The choice between **qui** and **que** is determined by their function in the sentence.

- **Qui** (*who, that, which*) is the SUBJECT of the verb of the relative clause.
- **Que** (*whom, that, which*) is the DIRECT OBJECT of the verb of the relative clause.

➡ The verb that follows **qui** always agrees with the ANTECEDENT of **qui.**

Est-ce que c'est **vous qui avez pris** ces photos?

➡ Although the object pronoun *whom, that, which* may be omitted in English, **que** is always expressed in French.

➡ When the verb that follows **que** is in the passé composé, its past participle agrees with the ANTECEDENT of **que.**

J'ai aimé **le film que** j'ai **vu** hier. J'ai téléphoné **aux filles que** j'ai **vues** au cinéma.

5 Mes amis

Ces personnes sont vos amis. Présentez-les à vos copains, d'après le modèle.

▶ Juliette (Elle habite à Québec.)
Je vous présente Juliette. C'est une fille qui habite à Québec.

▶ Marc (Je l'invite souvent.)
Je vous présente Marc. C'est un garçon que j'invite souvent.

1. Thomas (Je le connais depuis cinq ans.)
2. Nathalie (Elle habite près de chez moi.)
3. Sandrine (Elle va à mon école.)
4. Philippe (Je le vois tous les week-ends.)
5. Claire (Elle est dans ma classe de maths.)
6. Antoine (Il est venu chez moi le week-end dernier.)
7. Bruno (Je l'ai rencontré pendant les vacances.)
8. Delphine (Je l'ai invitée à la boum.)

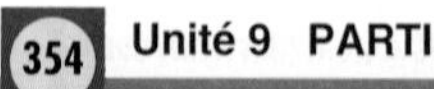

TEACHING RESOURCES

Student Activities Manual, pp. 88–89

Teaching Strategy

As a teaching help, you may want to present the following diagram:

ANTECEDENT + **qui** + VERB
ANTECEDENT + **que** + SUBJECT + VERB

■ Notes linguistiques

- Remind students that **que** becomes **qu'** before a vowel sound:
  Jean-Paul téléphone à la fille **qu'**il a rencontrée ce matin.
- This is another case of the agreement of the past participle with a preceding direct object.

Teaching Strategy

Ask students to bring in photos or pictures from magazines. Have them describe each person in their pictures by using a relative pronoun (either *qui* or *que*). Similarly, cut out pictures of famous people and places before class. Show these to the students and ask them to describe these people/places using both relative pronouns in one sentence.

Picture of Disney World:
C'est un parc qui est très amusant et que j'adore.

Have each student write one sentence on the board.

6 Pauvre Corinne!

Corinne n'a pas de chance. Expliquez pourquoi en complétant les phrases suivantes avec **qui** ou **que (qu')**.

1. Elle a voulu aller dans un magasin _____ était fermé aujourd'hui.
2. Elle a pris un bus _____ est tombé en panne *(broke down)*.
3. Elle a acheté une montre _____ ne marche pas.
4. Elle n'a pas compris les exercices _____ le professeur a donnés.
5. Elle a vu un film _____ elle a trouvé stupide.
6. Elle a invité à dîner une copine _____ n'est pas venue.
7. Elle a perdu le numéro de téléphone d'un garçon _____ elle a rencontré à une boum.
8. Elle a perdu le bracelet _____ son père lui avait donné pour son anniversaire.

7 Compliments . . . et insultes

Votre ami(e) français(e) — votre partenaire — veut avoir votre opinion sur certaines choses qu'il/elle a faites. Faites-lui un compliment . . . ou une insulte.

▶ la veste / acheter
très belle . . . ou moche?

— Qu'est-ce que tu penses de la veste que j'ai achetée?

— Elle est très belle! (Elle est moche!)

1. les copines / inviter
sympathiques . . . ou snobs?
2. l'ami / rencontrer
intelligent . . . ou stupide?
3. le repas / préparer
délicieux . . . ou infect *(disgusting)*?
4. les photos / prendre
jolies . . . ou ratées?
5. le poème / écrire
sublime . . . ou ridicule?
6. l'histoire / raconter
amusante . . . ou idiote?

C. La construction préposition + pronom relatif

In the examples below, the relative clause is introduced by a preposition **(avec)**. Note the forms of the relative pronouns as they refer to people or things.

Philippe a une copine. Il va souvent au cinéma **avec cette copine.**

→ Philippe a une copine **avec qui** il va souvent au cinéma.
*Philippe has a friend **with whom** he often goes to the movies.*

Tu as des idées. Je ne suis pas d'accord **avec ces idées.**

→ Tu as des idées **avec lesquelles** je ne suis pas d'accord.
*You have ideas **with which** I do not agree.*

When relative pronouns are used with prepositions (**avec**, **pour**, **sur**, etc.), the constructions are:

PREPOSITION	+	**qui**	to refer to people
PREPOSITION	+	**lequel**	to refer to things

➡ **Lequel** agrees with the noun it represents. It has the same forms as the corresponding interrogative pronoun:

lequel **laquelle** **lesquels** **lesquelles**

➡ In French, the preposition (**avec, pour,** etc.) always comes before the relative pronoun. (In English, the preposition may come at the end of the sentence.) Compare:

Tu as des idées **avec lesquelles** je ne suis pas d'accord.
*You have ideas **with which** I do not agree.*
*You have ideas **that** I do not agree **with.***

■ Activité

Qui ou que sont-ils? Complétez les phrases avec **qui** ou **que** selon le cas.

1. **La statue de la Liberté.** C'est la statue ___ est dans le port de New York. C'est le cadeau ___ la France a fait aux États-Unis. [*qui, que*]
2. **Le basket de rue.** C'est un sport ___ est à la mode et ___ les jeunes aiment beaucoup. [*qui, que*]
3. **Internet.** C'est un réseau *(network)* ___ permet d'explorer le monde à partir de chez soi et ___ relie toute la planète. [*qui, qui*]
4. **MTV.** C'est la chaîne ___ je préfère et ___ passe les meilleurs clips. [*que, qui*]
5. **La pollution de l'air.** C'est un problème ___ les écologistes considèrent comme très important et ___ il faut résoudre *(to solve)* rapidement. [*que, qu'*]

■ Notes linguistiques

- Although **qui** is preferred with people, **lequel** may also be used:
Qui est la copine **avec qui/avec laquelle** tu es sortie?
- **Lequel** must always be used after the prepositions **entre** *(between)* and **parmi** *(among)*, even when the antecedent is a person.

Teaching Strategy

Using the same pictures from the activity listed on p. 354, ask the students to define the people/places by giving complete sentences which include a preposition before the relative pronoun **qui** or **lequel/laquelle....**

Picture of New York: **C'est une ville dans laquelle je me perds toujours.**

TEACHING RESOURCES

Student Activities Manual, p. 90

■ Note linguistique

Lequel is used with **de** only when **de** is part of a prepositional phrase (**près de, loin de, à cause de, ...**). In all other cases, **dont** is used.

C'est l'hôtel près **duquel** j'habite.

C'est l'hôtel **dont** je t'ai parlé.

Teaching Strategy

You may wish to extend Act. 8 by using the following additional cues:

un aspirateur: nettoyer le salon
un couteau: couper du pain
une brosse à cheveux: se brosser les cheveux
le shampooing: se laver les cheveux
une machine à laver: laver les vêtements
un porte-manteau: ranger sa veste
une éponge: nettoyer la salle de bains

ALLONS PLUS LOIN

The relative pronoun **lequel,** like the interrogative **lequel?,** contracts with **à** and **de.**

Tu as assisté **à ce concert**?	Oui, c'est le concert **auquel** j'ai assisté.
Tu habites **près de ce parc**?	Oui, c'est le parc **près duquel** j'habite.

8 Qu'est-ce qu'on fait avec?

Définissez les choses suivantes en expliquant ce qu'on fait avec.

un ordinateur	• un objet	tondre la pelouse
un sécateur	• une chose	se brosser les dents
une raquette	• un appareil	repasser les chemises
une tondeuse	• une machine	surfer sur l'Internet
un fer	• un produit	couper des fleurs
le dentifrice	• un instrument	jouer au tennis

▶ **Une tondeuse est une machine avec laquelle on tond la pelouse.**

9 Relations personnelles

Décrivez vos relations avec trois personnes de votre choix en utilisant les suggestions suivantes.

☺	quelqu'un	aller souvent chez . . .
	un(e) ami(e)	téléphoner souvent à . . .
	une personne	avoir beaucoup d'admiration pour . . .
	un(e) adulte	pouvoir compter sur . . .
	une personne de ma famille	éprouver du respect pour . . .
	un professeur	éprouver de l'amitié pour . . .
	des gens	avoir confiance en . . .
??	??	s'entendre bien avec . . .
		s'entendre mal avec . . .
		??

▶ **Mon oncle George est une personne de ma famille sur qui je peux compter.**

10 Le job d'Alice

Alice a trouvé un job dans une entreprise d'électronique. Un jour, elle montre à un ami l'endroit où elle travaille. Complétez ses phrases.

▶ Voici la compagnie pour **laquelle je travaille.**

1. Voici le laboratoire dans ______.
2. Voici les collègues avec ______.
3. Voici le projet sur ______.
4. Voici l'ordinateur avec ______.
5. Voici les nouvelles machines avec ______.
6. Voici l'ingénieur pour ______.

D. Le pronom relatif dont

Note how in the examples below, the relative pronoun **dont** replaces a noun introduced by **de**.

Je ne connais pas la fille. Tu parles **de cette fille**.
→ Je ne connais pas la fille **dont** tu parles.
*I don't know the girl **(whom, that)** you are talking **about.***

Je connais le restaurant. Tu parles **de ce restaurant**.
→ Je connais le restaurant **dont** tu parles.
*I know the restaurant **(that)** you are talking **about.***

Marc a trouvé le livre. Il avait besoin **de ce livre**.
→ Marc a trouvé le livre **dont** il avait besoin.
*Marc found the book **(that)** he needed.*

The relative pronoun **dont** replaces

de + NOUN or NOUN PHRASE

Dont is, therefore, often used with verbs and verbal expressions that are followed by **de:**

avoir besoin de	**parler de**
se souvenir de	**faire la connaissance de**
avoir envie de	**discuter de**
s'occuper de	**être amoureux de**

➡ **Dont** may refer to PEOPLE or THINGS.

➡ Note the word order with **dont**:

(antecedent) + **dont** + subject + verb . . .

ALLONS PLUS LOIN

Dont is also used to replace **de** + NOUN in sentences where **de** indicates possession or relationship. In this type of construction, **dont** is the equivalent of *whose*.

Voici l'ami.
La soeur **de cet ami** habite à Paris.

Voici l'ami **dont** la soeur habite à Paris.
*This is the friend **whose** sister lives in Paris.*

Voici l'ami.
Je t'ai donné l'adresse **de cet ami**.

Voici l'ami **dont** je t'ai donné l'adresse.
*This is the friend **whose** address I gave you.*

11 Tant mieux!

Décrivez ce que les personnes suivantes ont fait.

▶ Christophe / trouver les livres (Il avait besoin de ces livres.)
Christophe a trouvé les livres dont il avait besoin.

1. Pauline / acheter les chaussures (Elle avait envie de ces chaussures.)
2. Marc / trouver le magazine (Il avait besoin de ce magazine.)
3. Madame Lavoie / acheter la voiture (Elle avait envie de cette voiture.)
4. Thomas / voir le film (Sa copine lui a parlé de ce film.)
5. Véronique / visiter l'exposition (On a parlé de cette exposition dans le journal.)
6. Bruno / sortir avec la fille (Il a fait la connaissance de cette fille chez Sophie.)
7. Christine / avoir des nouvelles des enfants (Elle s'était occupée de ces enfants pendant les vacances.)
8. Caroline / se marier avec le garçon (Elle était amoureuse de ce garçon.)

12 Et vous?

Mentionnez un exemple d'une chose ou d'une personne correspondant aux définitions suivantes. Comparez vos réponses avec celles de votre partenaire.

▶ un objet dont vous avez besoin tous les jours **Mon stylo (mon peigne, ma brosse à dents, . . .) est un objet dont j'ai besoin tous les jours.**

1. un objet dont vous n'avez pas besoin en ce moment
2. une chose dont vous avez envie
3. un sujet dont vous parlez avec vos amis
4. un sujet dont vous discutez avec vos parents.
5. un événement important dont vous vous souvenez bien
6. une personne dont vous avez fait la connaissance récemment
7. une personne dont vous avez fait la connaissance pendant les vacances

Teaching Strategy: Warm-Up

As a preliminary activity, you may want to practice the use of **dont** with the expression **avoir besoin**. Ask students if they need the following things:

▶ **l'argent**
— As-tu besoin d'argent?
— Oui, c'est une chose **dont** j'ai toujours besoin. (Non, c'est une chose **dont** je n'ai pas souvent besoin.)

- ton livre de français
- l'amitié de tes copains
- la compréhension de tes professeurs

INFO MAGAZINE

Theme: Marriage

Supplementary vocabulary

la liste de mariage *bridal registry*
la demoiselle d'honneur *bridesmaid*
le garçon d'honneur *best man*
le bouquet de la mariée *bridal bouquet*
le contrat de mariage *prenuptial agreement*
la lune de miel *honeymoon*

Note culturelle

Le mariage civil est le seul mariage reconnu légalement. En général, mais pas toujours, le mariage civil et le mariage religieux ont lieu le même jour.

Irregular Verbs

(see Appendix C)

promettre (*see* **mettre**)
offrir (*see* **ouvrir**)
inscrire (*see* **écrire**)

Le mariage EN FRANCE

Un jour, un jeune homme et une jeune fille qui s'aiment, décident de se marier. Ils annoncent la bonne nouvelle° à leurs familles respectives et à leurs amis proches.° Pour célébrer cet événement, il y a parfois une cérémonie assez simple, les fiançailles,° où le jeune homme et la jeune fille promettent° de se marier. Comme symbole de cette promesse, le fiancé offre° une bague — la bague de fiançailles — à sa fiancée.

Le mariage a lieu six mois ou un an plus tard. C'est un événement qui demande beaucoup de préparation. Il faut fixer la date du mariage, organiser la cérémonie, établir la liste des invités, envoyer les invitations, etc.

En principe, pour se marier, les jeunes époux doivent être âgés de 18 ans minimum. En réalité, les Français attendent beaucoup plus longtemps avant de se marier. En moyenne,° les hommes se marient à 28 ans et les femmes à 26 ans. Avant le mariage, les fiancés doivent accomplir un certain nombre de formalités administratives: examen médical, publication des bans° de mariage, etc... S'ils le désirent, ils peuvent aussi établir officiellement un «contrat de mariage» qui détermine la disposition de leurs biens.° Quand ces formalités sont faites, ils peuvent se marier. En général, les gens choisissent de se marier le week-end et en été. (80% des mariages français sont célébrés le samedi. 60% ont lieu de juin à septembre.)

La majorité des Français ont deux mariages: un mariage civil et un mariage religieux. Le mariage civil est obligatoire. Il a lieu à la mairie de la ville où l'on habite. C'est d'habitude une cérémonie assez simple à laquelle assistent seulement le jeune couple, leurs familles proches, leurs témoins° et quelques amis intimes. Pour cette occasion, le maire° porte une écharpe° tricolore,° signe de sa fonction officielle. Il marie les époux,° les félicite° et leur délivre° un document officiel, le «livret° de famille» où seront inscrits° les événements importants de leur vie commune (naissance des enfants, décès°...). Le jeune homme et la jeune fille sont maintenant légalement mariés.

Cinquante-deux pour cent des Français décident d'avoir aussi un mariage religieux. Le mariage religieux a toujours lieu *après* le mariage civil. Il est célébré à l'église (pour les catholiques), au temple (pour les protestants) ou à la synagogue (pour les juifs).

nouvelle *news* **proches** *close* **fiançailles** *engagement* **promettent / promettre** *to promise* **offre / offrir** *to give* **En moyenne** *on the average* **bans** = annonce officielle **biens** *assets* **témoins** *witnesses* **maire** *mayor* **écharpe** *sash* **tricolore** = bleu-blanc-rouge **époux** *spouses* **félicite** *congratulate* **délivre** = donne **livret** *booklet* **inscrits / inscrire** *to inscribe* **décès** *death*

Teaching Strategy

You may wish to limit class discussion or group work if you decide that this article poses sensitivity issues in the class. If so, you may choose to have students read the article on their own and write a short reaction to it. You might also adapt the **sondage** on p. 359 to a U.S. context and ask students how they think the percentages would differ if the questions were asked in their own community.

C'est généralement une grande cérémonie à laquelle assistent toute la famille et un grand nombre d'invités: amis, voisins, relations, etc. Traditionnellement, la mariée porte une longue robe blanche. À la main, elle tient° un bouquet de fleurs d'oranger. Sur la tête, elle porte une couronne.° Un voile de dentelle° lui couvre° le visage. Accompagnée de son père, elle avance vers l'autel° où l'attend son fiancé. Pendant la cérémonie, le jeune homme et la jeune fille échangent leurs alliances° en présence de leurs témoins. Après la cérémonie, les jeunes mariés sortent de l'église accompagnés des garçons d'honneur° et des demoiselles d'honneur.° On prend beaucoup de photos. Puis tout le monde va au repas de noces.°

Comme les Français aiment se marier à la campagne, le repas de noces a souvent lieu dans une petite auberge ou dans la maison de campagne des parents de la mariée. C'est un repas très joyeux. On fait des discours.° On porte des toasts au bonheur des jeunes mariés. On raconte des histoires. On chante des chansons. Et surtout, on mange bien. Au dessert, il y a une «pièce montée», c'est-à-dire un gâteau à l'architecture compliquée, que découpent° les mariés. Après le repas, on danse. Les jeunes mariés restent quelque temps avec les invités, puis ils partent en voyage de noces dans leur voiture décorée de rubans° blancs.

Comment se sont-ils rencontrés?

Autrefois les gens qui se mariaient avaient beaucoup de choses en commun. Ils étaient issus du même milieu social et avaient la même religion. Généralement, ils habitaient dans la même ville ou le même village et souvent ils se connaissaient depuis leur enfance.

Aujourd'hui, le mariage unit de plus en plus de gens qui se sont rencontrés par hasard.° Voici comment les futurs couples se forment:

Sur 100 jeunes mariés, se sont rencontrés ...

▪ au bal	18%
▪ dans un lieu public	14%
▪ au travail	13%
▪ chez des particuliers°	10%
▪ pendant leurs études	9%
▪ dans un club ou une association	8%
▪ au cours d'°une fête chez des amis	7%
▪ à l'occasion d'une sortie ou au spectacle (cinéma, concert, théâtre,. . .)	5%
▪ pendant les vacances	5%
▪ dans une discothèque	4%
▪ par relations de voisinage	3%
▪ dans une fête publique	3%
▪ par annonces°, agence matrimoniale, Internet	1%

THÉÂTRE

et vous?

DÉFINITIONS

Définissez les mots et les expressions suivants.

- les fiançailles
- les bans
- un contrat de mariage
- une alliance
- un mariage civil
- le livret de famille
- le mariage religieux
- la famille proche
- les témoins
- une écharpe tricolore
- les garçons d'honneur
- les demoiselles d'honneur
- le repas de noces
- une «pièce montée»
- un voyage de noces

DISCUSSION

Avec votre partenaire, faites une liste des similarités et des différences entre un mariage français et un mariage américain.

EXPRESSION ORALE

Imaginez que vous allez vous marier. Préférez-vous avoir un mariage simple ou un mariage formel? Expliquez pourquoi.

EXPRESSION ÉCRITE

Décrivez un mariage (réel ou imaginaire) auquel vous avez assisté.

(Qui étaient les mariés? Où a eu lieu la cérémonie? Combien y avait-il d'invités? Comment était habillés le marié et la mariée? les demoiselles et les garçons d'honneur? Comment s'est déroulé la cérémonie? . . .)

tient / tenir *to hold* **couronne** *crown, tiara* **voile de dentelle** *lace veil* **couvre / couvrir** *to cover* **autel** *altar* **alliances** *wedding rings* **garçons d'honneur** *ushers* **demoiselles d'honneur** *bridesmaids* **noces =** mariage **discours** *speeches* **découpent =** coupent **rubans** *ribbons* **par hasard** *by chance* **chez des particuliers** *at the home of friends or acquaintances* **au cours de =** pendant **annonces** *personal ads*

Additional Information

- By law, a French worker may take a four-day paid vacation when he/she gets married.
- Legally, each spouse keeps his/her own name. The wife may take her husband's last name, or husband and wife may adapt both their names by joining them with a hyphen.

■ Irregular Verbs

(see Appendix C)
tenir
couvrir (*see* **ouvrir**)

NOTES CULTURELLES

- In French, the best man and the maid of honor are called **les témoins,** since they sign the official documents at the city hall.
- Generally, engaged couples leave a list of desired gifts in a store of their choice for guests to consult before choosing a present.
- Before the wedding reception, the families may host **un vin d'honneur** to toast the bride and groom with friends and relatives. Wine and snacks are served.

LE FRANÇAIS PRATIQUE

TEACHING RESOURCES

Student Activities Manual, pp. 163–164

Tête-à-tête Pair Activity, Marie Curie, p. PA10

Audio Program, CD 10, Tracks 9–12

HM ClassPrep CD, Audioscript, Unit 9

LE FRANÇAIS PRATIQUE

Les phases de la vie

L'ENFANCE
on **naît**
on **grandit**

LA JEUNESSE
L'ADOLESCENCE
(la vie scolaire)
on **développe** sa personnalité
on **fait des études** élémentaires / secondaires / universitaires

(la vie sociale)
on **fait connaissance** / on **rencontre** d'autres personnes
on **se fait** des amis

L'ÂGE ADULTE
(la vie familiale)
on **rencontre** quelqu'un de spécial
on **tombe amoureux** de cette personne
on décide de **vivre** ensemble / **se fiancer** / **se marier**
ou de rester **célibataire** *(single)*

on **élève** une famille

parfois on **se sépare** / **divorce**
et on **se remarie**

(la vie active)
on **choisit** un métier ou une profession
on **trouve** un job
on **travaille** dur
on **gagne** sa vie
on **obtient** une promotion

LA VIEILLESSE
on **prend** sa retraite
on **s'occupe** de façons diverses
on **vieillit**
parfois on **tombe malade**
on **meurt**

naître* *to be born*
grandir *to grow up*

développer *to develop*

se faire des amis *to make friends*

tomber amoureux de *to fall in love with*
vivre *to live*
se fiancer *to get engaged*
se marier *to get married*

élever *to raise*

se séparer *to separate*
divorcer *to get divorced*
se remarier *to remarry*

gagner sa vie *to earn a living*
obtenir* *to get*

prendre sa retraite *to retire*
s'occuper *to keep busy*
vieillir *to grow old*
tomber malade *to get sick*
mourir* *to die*

RAPPEL!
naître: il/elle est né(e)
mourir: il/elle est mort(e)

Teaching Strategy

Have the students predict their futures and write a one-page description of their lives. Obviously, they should only mention main events but give as much humorous or specific information as possible. Their predictions should include as much vocabulary from p. 360 as possible.

1 Mon avenir

Faites une liste de 5 choses que vous voulez accomplir dans votre vie. Classez-les par ordre d'importance. Comparez votre liste avec celle de votre partenaire.

Cinq choses que je voudrais faire dans ma vie
1.
2.
3.
4.
5.

2 Débat

Vous avez décidé de vous marier. Votre partenaire a décidé de rester célibataire (ou vice versa). Chacun va expliquer les raisons et les avantages (et désavantages) de sa décision.

3 Une vie

Catherine parle de son grand-père. Complétez cette description avec le passé composé des verbes de la liste. Soyez logique!

élever	naître
faire la connaissance	prendre sa retraite
faire ses études	tomber amoureux
ne pas gagner	tomber malade
grandir	travailler dur
se marier	trouver un job
mourir	ne pas vieillir

Mon grand-père ____ dans un petit village de la province de Québec où il ____ et où il ____ secondaires. À l'âge de 17 ans, il a immigré aux États-Unis et il ____ dans une usine de textile.

Un jour, il ____ d'une jeune fille, ma grand-mère dont il ____. Ils ____ peu de temps après et ensemble ils ____ une famille de six enfants.

Durant sa vie, mon grand-père ____, mais il ____ beaucoup d'argent. Il ____ après 50 ans de travail dans la même usine. Malheureusement, mon grand-père et ma grand-mère ____ ensemble. Ma grand-mère, en effet, ____ et elle ____ en 1975. Mon grand-père ____ dix ans après, à l'âge de 85 ans.

4 À votre tour

Composez la biographie d'une personne de votre famille (votre grand-père ou votre grand-mère) ou d'une personne âgée imaginaire.

Supplementary vocabulary

demander en mariage *to propose (marriage)*
fonder un foyer *to set up a household/to get married*
venir au monde *to be born [to come into the world]*
prendre de l'âge *to age*
décéder *to die*
perdre son travail *to lose one's job*
démissionner *to quit (one's job)*
être renvoyé(e) *to be fired*
être mis(e) à la porte *to be fired*
être mis(e) au chômage *to be laid off*

Irregular Verbs

To review the conjugations of **naître, vivre,** and **mourir,** see Appendix C.

Note linguistique

Le troisième âge est une expression qui désigne les personnes qui sont à la retraite et qui ont quitté la vie active. Les clubs du troisième âge organisent des voyages et diverses activités pour les retraités.

Proverbe

Si jeunesse savait, si vieillesse pouvait. *Youth is wasted on the young.*

Réponses: Activité 3

est né/a grandi/a fait ses études/a trouvé un job/a fait la connaissance/est tombé amoureux/se sont mariés/ont élevé/a travaillé dur/n'a pas gagné/a pris sa retraite/n'ont pas vieilli/est tombée malade/est morte/est mort

Note: The verb **mourir** is used twice.

Teaching Strategy

Extend Act. 1 by giving students the following assignment:
Votre passé. Faites une liste de cinq choses que vous avez accomplies dans votre vie. Utilisez des mots et expressions du vocabulaire de la page 360.

Sample answers:
Je suis née dans le Missouri.
J'ai fait des études élémentaires à l'école x.
J'ai fait connaissance de mon amie Gail à Boston.
J'ai travaillé dans un supermarché l'été dernier.
Je suis tombée amoureuse de x au mois d'avril.

LANGUE ET COMMUNICATION

TEACHING RESOURCES

Student Activities Manual, pp. 91, 164

Audio Program, CD 10, Tracks 13–14

HM ClassPrep CD, Audioscript, Unit 9

■ **Note linguistique**

As in English, **où** *(where)* is generally used instead of **dans lequel.**

... le bureau **où** je travaille ...

■ **Teaching Note**

In Activity 1, item 5, it is also possible to use **où** rather than **dans laquelle.**

A. Résumé: les pronoms relatifs

Review the use of the relative pronouns in the chart below.

The relative pronoun functions as . . .	The relative pronoun refers to: PEOPLE	THINGS
SUBJECT	**QUI** l'ami **qui** est arrivé	**QUI** la lettre **qui** est arrivée
DIRECT OBJECT	**QUE** la fille **que** tu connais	**QUE** le café **que** tu connais
OBJECT OF A PREPOSITION (other than **de**)	**QUI** la personne **avec qui** je travaille	**LEQUEL** la machine **avec laquelle** je travaille
OBJECT OF THE PREPOSITION **de**	**DONT** le garçon **dont** je te parle	**DONT** le livre **dont** je te parle

1 Photos de vacances

Catherine montre ses photos de vacances à son frère Marc. Jouez les deux rôles en faisant les substitutions suggérées. (Utilisez les pronoms qui conviennent.)

▶ Mélanie / Nous avons rencontré cette fille à la plage.

— Tu te souviens de Mélanie?
— Non, pas vraiment.
— Mais si! C'est la fille que nous avons rencontrée à la plage!
— Ah, oui. Je me souviens maintenant.

1. Jean-Paul / Tu jouais au tennis avec ce garçon.
2. Pierre et Jérôme / Ces garçons nous ont invités à une boum.
3. Alice / J'ai dîné chez cette fille un jour.
4. Véronique / Tu as fait la connaissance de cette fille dans un café.
5. La Tulipe noire / Nous passions nos soirées dans cette discothèque.

2 Quel pronom?

Complétez les phrases avec le pronom qui convient.

1. Je n'ai pas trouvé le livre . . .
   ___ j'avais besoin.
   ___ était sur la table.
   dans ___ il y a des photos de Paris.
   ___ j'ai acheté ce matin.
2. Ma cousine va se marier avec un jeune homme . . .
   avec ___ elle est fiancée depuis un an.
   ___ elle connaît depuis deux ans.
   ___ elle a fait la connaissance à la Martinique.
   ___ travaille pour une agence de voyage.
3. Nous allons dîner dans le restaurant . . .
   ___ mon frère m'a recommandé.
   ___ sert des spécialités régionales.
   ___ tout le monde parle.
   devant ___ nous sommes passés ce matin.
4. Je suis sorti avec les amis . . .
   ___ je t'ai parlé.
   ___ m'ont téléphoné ce matin.
   avec ___ je suis allé en vacances.
   ___ j'ai vus le week-end dernier.

Teaching Strategy

Divide the class into pairs and have each pair write a dialog between two friends about the relationship of one of the friends with another person/people. Encourage the students to use their imaginations, a wide vocabulary, **ce que, ce qui** (p. 364), and at least four other relative pronouns.

3 La légende de Tristan et Yseult

Complétez le texte suivant avec les formes appropriées des pronoms qui conviennent.

Tristan et Yseult est une très vieille légende __(1)__ date du Moyen Âge et __(2)__ on retrouve dans les littératures anglaise, française et allemande de l'époque.

Cette légende relate la tragique histoire de deux jeunes gens, unis par un amour __(3)__ ils ne peuvent pas contrôler. Dans cette légende, le roi Marc va épouser une jeune fille __(4)__ il ne connaît pas mais __(5)__ ses conseillers lui ont parlé. Il envoie Tristan, son neveu en __(6)__ il a toute confiance, chercher cette jeune fille __(7)__ s'appelle Yseult et __(8)__ habite en Irlande. Tristan trouve Yseult et la ramène en Cornouailles,° le pays du roi Marc. Sur le bateau __(9)__ les transporte, Tristan et Yseult boivent par mégarde° une potion __(10)__ un magicien avait préparée pour assurer l'amour éternel entre Marc et Yseult. Sous l'influence de la potion __(11)__ ils ont bue, Tristan et Yseult tombent éperdument° amoureux l'un de l'autre.

À leur retour, le roi Marc, __(12)__ a découvert la vérité, chasse le pauvre Tristan. Des années passent. Tristan a épousé une autre jeune fille __(13)__ il a fait la connaissance dans son exil. En réalité, il ne cesse de penser à la belle Yseult __(14)__ il est resté amoureux. Un jour, il participe à une bataille au cours de __(15)__ il est très grièvement° blessé! Yseult à __(16)__ on a annoncé la nouvelle veut revoir l'homme __(17)__ elle aime toujours. Malheureusement, quand elle arrive chez Tristan, celui-ci est déjà mort. À son tour, Yseult meurt de désespoir. Les deux amants __(18)__ la vie a séparés sont finalement unis par la mort.

Cornouailles *Cornwall (in southwestern England)* **par mégarde** = par accident **éperdument** *madly*
grièvement = très sérieusement

■ Réponses: Activité 3

1. qui	7. qui	13. dont
2. qu'	8. qui	14. dont
3. qu'	9. qui	15. laquelle
4. qu'	10. qu'	16. qui
5. dont	11. qu'	17. qu'
6. qui	12. qui	18. que

4 Descriptions

Choisissez l'une des situations suivantes et décrivez la chose ou la personne dont il est question. Pour cela, utilisez la construction relative dans au moins trois phrases différentes.

▶ Vous avez perdu votre cahier d'exercices. Décrivez ce cahier.
C'est un cahier qui est assez grand.
C'est le cahier que j'avais avec moi ce matin.
C'est le cahier dans lequel j'ai pris beaucoup de notes.
C'est un cahier dont j'ai absolument besoin.

1. Vous avez perdu la montre que votre oncle vous a donnée pour votre anniversaire. Décrivez cette montre.
2. Vous avez dîné dans un restaurant qu'un ami vous a recommandé. Décrivez ce restaurant.
3. Vous avez trouvé un job pour l'été. Décrivez ce job.
4. Vous avez inventé une machine. Décrivez cette machine.
5. Vos parents ont acheté une nouvelle voiture. Décrivez cette voiture.
6. Vous avez fait la connaissance d'un(e) étudiant(e) francophone très sympathique à la dernière réunion du club français. Décrivez cet(te) étudiant(e).
7. L'été dernier, vous avez rencontré une personne très intéressante. Décrivez cette personne.

NOTES CULTURELLES

- The legend of **Tristan et Yseult** probably originated in Cornwall. Several versions were written by the end of the 12th century. The poets **Thomas d'Angleterre** and **Béroul** are two of its most notable authors. The story of Tristan and Yseult was later incorporated in the Arthurian legends.
- In 1900, French author **Joseph Bédier (1864–1938)** compiled several versions of the story into a new and more complete one.
- *Tristan und Isolde* is an opera by **Richard Wagner**, based on the medieval legend.

TEACHING RESOURCES

Student Activities Manual
pp. 92–94

■ Notes linguistiques

- **Ce** is considered in this case a neutral pronoun that refers to things.
- **Ce que** and **ce qui** are used to form indirect interrogative sentences, e.g.:
  Demande-lui ce qu'il aimerait manger.
  (qu'est-ce qu'il aimerait manger)
  Demande-lui ce qui est intéressant à voir.
  (qu'est-ce qui est intéressant à voir)
- **Ce qui** is followed by a singular verb. It is modified by a masculine singular adjective.

B. Ce qui, ce que et ce dont

Note the use of **ce qui, ce que** and **ce dont** in the following sentences.

Je voudrais savoir **ce qui** t'intéresse.	*I would like to know* ***what*** *interests you.*
Dis-moi **ce qui** est arrivé.	*Tell me* ***what*** *happened.*
Je ne sais pas **ce que** tu fais.	*I don't know* ***what*** *you are doing.*
Montre-moi **ce que** tu as acheté.	*Show me* ***what*** *you bought.*
Dis-moi **ce dont** tu as envie.	*Tell me* ***what*** *you want.*
Je ne comprends pas **ce dont** tu parles.	*I don't understand* ***what*** *you are talking about.*

Ce qui, **ce que**, and **ce dont** correspond to *what*.
- **Ce qui** is equivalent to **la chose/les choses qui . . . .**
  It functions as the SUBJECT of the verb that follows.
- **Ce que** is equivalent to **la chose/les choses que . . . .**
  It functions as the DIRECT OBJECT of the verb that follows.
- **Ce dont** is equivalent to **la chose/les choses dont . . . .**
  It replaces a phrase with **de**.

Je voudrais savoir ce qui t'intéresse.
METRO
Dis-moi ce qui est arrivé!
Montre-moi
tu as ach
Je ne comprends
ce dont tu parl

5 Précisions

Votre partenaire vous explique certaines choses sans préciser. Demandez-lui de préciser en utilisant les expressions entre parenthèses avec **ce qui, ce que** ou **ce dont.**

▶ Quelque chose m'amuse. (Dis-moi . . .)
Dis-moi ce qui t'amuse.

▶ J'ai besoin de quelque chose. (Je voudrais savoir . . .)
Je voudrais savoir ce dont tu as besoin.

1. Quelque chose m'intéresse. (Explique-moi . . .)
2. Je fais quelque chose. (Je voudrais savoir . . .)
3. J'ai envie de quelque chose. (Dis-moi . . .)
4. Quelque chose m'est arrivé. (Raconte-moi . . .)
5. J'ai acheté quelque chose. (Montre-moi . . .)
6. Mon copain m'a parlé de quelque chose. (Dis-moi . . .)

6 Qu'est-ce qu'ils font?

Complétez les phrases avec **ce qui, ce que (ce qu')** ou **ce dont.**

1. Je suis au supermarché. J'achète . . .
   ___ est sur ma liste
   ___ j'ai besoin
   ___ j'ai oublié hier

2. Marc veut faire un cadeau d'anniversaire à Sylvie. Il lui demande . . .
   ___ l'intéresse
   ___ elle a envie
   ___ elle aimerait avoir

3. Christine et Françoise font du shopping. Elles regardent . . .
   ___ est en solde
   ___ elles ont envie
   ___ elles voudraient acheter si elles avaient de l'argent

4. Le professeur aide les élèves. Il explique . . .
   ___ il a parlé la semaine dernière
   ___ est difficile
   ___ ils ne comprennent pas

5. Monsieur Dumont nettoie son appartement. Il range . . .
   ___ est en désordre
   ___ il veut garder
   ___ il n'a pas besoin

6. Madame Moreau a été témoin d'un accident. Elle explique à la police . . .
   ___ elle a vu
   ___ elle se souvient
   ___ est arrivé

LECTURE

Reading STRATEGY

Reading fiction

■ Pour en savoir plus
For more information on the **Académie française,** refer your students to p. 56.

LECTURE

Le bracelet

Michelle Maurois

AVANT DE LIRE

Lisez le titre de cette histoire et puis regardez l'illustration. Décrivez avec le maximum de détails:
- la jeune fille
- la marchande d'antiquités
- le magasin
- le bracelet qui est dans la vitrine

Michelle Maurois (1914–1994) vient d'une famille d'écrivains et d'intellectuels. Son père, André Maurois, était membre de l'Académie française. Connue pour ses contes, Michelle Maurois a aussi écrit des essais et des romans.

Anticipons un peu!

Répondez aux questions suivantes, en expliquant votre opinion.
- Quel genre d'histoire est-ce? une histoire drôle? une histoire policière? une histoire sentimentale?
  Maintenant lisez l'histoire pour voir si vous avez raison.
- Quel est le sujet de cette histoire?
- Est-ce que la marchande vendra le bracelet à la jeune fille? Pourquoi ou pourquoi pas?

Maintenant lisez l'histoire pour voir si vous avez raison.

Le bracelet

Teaching Strategy

Using the *Avant de lire* activities, help students to use critical thinking skills to predict the genre of the story and possible plot points. Before reading, ask students to look at all the illustrations to see if they contain "hints" about the characters and plot. Ask students to imagine why the girl is looking at the bracelet in the shop window. List possible reasons on the board, then have students read the first segment of the story and answer the comprehension questions.

I

—Bonjour Madame, dit Denise, entrant dans le magasin de bric-à-brac.°

—Mademoiselle ... Je ne suis pas encore Madame.

—Excusez-moi, dit la jeune fille déconcertée. Bonjour Mademoiselle.

—Entrez ma belle, dit la marchande sans lâcher° son tricot.

Denise se dirige vers la très vieille femme, vêtue d'une longue robe rouge, assise sur une chaise basse. Son visage est usé,° ses cheveux d'un blanc de neige, mais son regard° reste jeune et souriant.°

—S'il vous plaît, Mademoiselle, quel est le prix du bracelet qui se trouve au milieu de la vitrine?

—Il n'est pas à vendre, dit la vieille, souriant toujours.

—Comment cela?

—Tout est à vendre, sauf le bracelet.

—Mais ... vous l'exposez.

—Oui, mais pas pour qu'on l'achète.

—Ah! dit Denise étonnée.° C'est dommage. Il me plaît. J'aime beaucoup les bijoux anciens.

La marchande se lève. Elle est toute voûtée° et avance à petits pas.° La jeune fille regarde autour d'elle avec curiosité; ces vieux objets excitent son imagination, rappellent des époques disparues, des familles éteintes.° Ici sont mêlés° tasses chinoises, assiettes romantiques,° boîtes marquées du «N» napoléonien,* vases de Venise° plus ou moins cassés, verres de Bohême.°

La marchande prend dans la vitrine le bracelet et revient vers la jeune fille. Ce bracelet est en or, recouvert de° pierres de toutes les couleurs. Chaque pierre a la forme d'un cœur.

—Il est fermé par un saphir de la couleur de mes yeux, dit la vieille femme. Il est joli, n'est-ce pas, mon bracelet?

—Très joli, dit Denise en le prenant dans ses mains.

Quand elle le voit de près, la jeune fille est encore plus tentée. Le travail° est fin, délicat. C'est un charmant bijou qui vient d'être nettoyé et qui brille de mille feux. On le remarque d'autant plus que tout ce que contient le magasin° est recouvert de poussière.

Mots utiles

un bracelet	*bracelet*
des bijoux	*(pieces of) jewelry*
la marchande d'antiquités	*antique dealer*
une pierre	*stone, gem*
la poussière	*dust*
le tricot	*knitting*
une vitrine	*store window*
briller	*to shine*
se diriger vers	*to go toward*
exposer	*to exhibit*
plaire *	*to please*
tenter	*to tempt*
d'autant plus que	*all the more that*
autour de	*around*
sauf	*except*

* **Boîtes marquées du «N» napoléonien.** As presents to his courtiers, Napoleon used to give small boxes decorated with the imperial «N».

bric-à-brac = antiquités bon marché **lâcher** = laisser **usé** = vieux **son regard** = les yeux **souriant** *smiling* **étonnée** *astonished* **voûtée** *bent over* **pas** *steps* **éteintes** = qui n'existent plus **mêlés** *mixed together* **romantiques** = décorées de sujets romantiques **vases de Venise** *Venitian glass vases* **verres de Bohême** *[red] Bohemian glasses* **recouvert de** *covered with* **travail** *workmanship* **ce que contient le magasin** = ce qu'il y a dans le magasin

Avez-vous compris?

1. Pourquoi est-ce que Denise entre dans le magasin?
2. À votre avis, quel âge a la marchande (approximativement)? Expliquez pourquoi vous pensez cela.
3. À votre avis, est-ce qu'elle est mariée? Expliquez comment vous savez cela.
4. En quoi le bracelet est-il différent des autres objets? Décrivez ce bracelet.

Anticipons un peu

À votre avis, pourquoi est-ce que la marchande ne veut pas vendre le bracelet? Expliquez pourquoi vous pensez cela.

- Le bracelet n'est pas à elle.
- C'est un souvenir personnel.
- Elle l'a promis à une personne de sa famille.
- Il coûte trop cher.
- Une autre raison. Imaginez laquelle.

Note culturelle

En France, il est d'usage d'appeler "Mademoiselle" toute femme non mariée, quel que soit son âge.

Note linguistique

L'expression **le bric-à-brac** est invariable **(les bric-à-brac).**

Supplementary vocabulary

Les pierres précieuses

Le saphir est bleu.
L'émeraude est verte.
Le rubis est rouge.
Le diamant est blanc.

Les pierres fines

L'améthyste est violette.
Le grenat est rouge foncé.
La topaze est jaune.
L'aigue-marine est bleu clair.
La turquoise est bleu vert.

Irregular Verb

(see Appendix C)
plaire

Avez-vous compris?

(Sample answers)

1. Elle entre dans le magasin parce qu'elle veut acheter le bracelet qui est dans la vitrine.
2. Elle a peut-être quatre-vingt-dix ans. Je pense cela parce qu'elle est très voûtée et marche très lentement.
3. Non, elle n'est pas mariée. On sait cela parce qu'elle dit qu'elle est «Mademoiselle», pas «Madame».
4. Il est différent des autres objets parce qu'il est très beau, et il brille. Les autres objets sont recouverts de poussière et ont moins de valeur. Le bracelet est en or, avec des pierres de toutes les couleurs, qui ont la forme d'un cœur.

Supplementary vocabulary

Les bijoux
la bague *ring*
la gourmette *chain bracelet*
les clips *(m.)* **d'oreilles** *clip earrings*
les boucles *(f.)* **d'oreilles** *earrings*
le collier *necklace*
le pendentif *pendant*
le tour de cou *choker*
le sautoir *chain (long necklace)*

II

Denise adore les bijoux, elle en possède plusieurs, mais elle n'a pas de bracelet. Elle vient de recevoir son salaire du mois et elle a envie de faire une folie.°

—Mais pourquoi, demande-t-elle, pourquoi ne voulez-vous pas me le céder?°

—Parce qu'il est à moi et parce que j'y tiens plus qu'à tout au monde.

—Mais tout, ici, n'est-il pas à vous?

—Non. Les autres objets, je les ai achetés, tandis que ce bracelet m'a été donné.

—Alors, pourquoi l'exposer?

—C'est un cadeau de mon fiancé.

Denise regarde la marchande et se tait. Le mot «fiancé» dans la bouche de la vieille femme est surprenant.

—Frédéric avait vingt ans ... Frédéric Cottet, c'est le nom de mon fiancé. Un jour il m'a apporté ce bracelet pour me tenir compagnie pendant son absence. Il partait pour un très long voyage ... Il n'est pas revenu.

—Excusez-moi, j'ai été indiscrète. Comme c'est triste!

—Oh non! Je l'attends.

—Vous ... vous l'attendez ...? dit la jeune fille.

—Tous les jours, à toutes les heures. Et comme il ne sait sans doute pas où me trouver, je laisse le bracelet au milieu de la vitrine pour qu'il le reconnaisse: voilà pourquoi il n'est pas à vendre.

—Je comprends, dit Denise lentement.

—Je vais d'ailleurs vite le remettre. Si Frédéric passait juste maintenant ...

«La vieille femme est sûrement folle, se dit Denise en la suivant des yeux, mais touchante, mystérieuse. Peut-être ne finit-on jamais de rêver?»

La marchande prend un verre sur lequel on peut lire en lettres dorées,° un peu effacées,° «souvenir» et le tend° à la jeune fille.

—Je vous le donne parce que vous êtes si jolie.

—Oh! C'est trop gentil,° mais je ne peux pas l'accepter...

—Cela me fait plaisir. Et revenez me voir.

Denise part, le verre serré° dans sa main, le cœur un peu lourd. Cette nuit-là, dans son lit, elle ne réussit pas à s'endormir. Son esprit° ne peut pas se détacher° de la vieille marchande, attendant toute sa vie sans se décourager.

une folie = quelque chose d'extravagant **me le céder** = to let me have it **dorées** = d'or **effacer** *to erase* **tend** = donne **gentil** = généreux **serré** *held tightly* **esprit** *mind* **se détacher** = oublier

Mots utiles

faire plaisir à	*to please*
posséder	*to own, possess*
remettre *	*to put back*
rêver	*to dream*
suivre *	*to follow*
surprendre *	*to surprise*
tenir * à	*to hold dear, to cherish*
tenir *compagnie	*to keep company*
fou (folle)	*crazy*

Avez-vous compris?

1. Qui est Frédéric Cottet?
2. Pourquoi est-ce que la marchande ne veut pas vendre le bracelet?
3. Pourquoi est-ce qu'elle continue à l'exposer dans la vitrine?
4. Qu'est-ce que Denise pense de la marchande?

À votre avis

Exprimez votre opinion sur les sujets suivants et expliquez pourquoi vous avez cette opinion.

- Est-ce que la vieille femme est bizarre, complètement folle ou simplement sentimentale?
- Est-ce que Frédéric Cottet est une personne réelle ou bien est-ce qu'il existe seulement dans l'imagination de la vieille femme?
- Est-ce que Frédéric Cottet va revenir un jour? Si oui, dans quelles circonstances?

■ Irregular Verbs

(see Appendix C)
remettre (*see* **mettre**)
suivre
surprendre (*see* **prendre**)
tenir

■ *Avez-vous compris?*

(Sample answers)

1. Frédéric Cottet était le fiancé de la marchande quand elle était jeune.
2. Elle ne veut pas vendre le bracelet parce que c'est un cadeau de Frédéric.
3. Elle continue à l'exposer dans la vitrine parce qu'elle pense que Frédéric reviendra et reconnaîtra le bracelet dans la vitrine.
4. Elle pense que la marchande est folle mais intéressante.

Teaching Strategy

After students have read the first two segments of the story, divide the class into groups to discuss the *À votre avis* questions. If there are differences of opinion, have students tally the responses. Have each group present their answer to one of the questions to the whole class. Compare with other groups' answers.

You may also wish to add an additional question for all groups:

À votre avis, pourquoi la vieille dame n'est-elle pas partie avec son fiancé? (Utilisez votre imagination pour trouver une explication!)

Discuss the answers in class.

III

Quelques mois plus tard, l'été est venu. Denise en sortant du bureau, rentre un soir par la rue où se trouve le magasin de bric-à-brac. Brillant de tous ses feux, le bracelet est toujours là. La vieille femme est assise sur le trottoir devant la porte, travaillant au même tricot. Elle reconnaît la jeune fille et lui fait un grand sourire.

—Venez vous asseoir avec moi, ma belle, prenez une chaise à l'intérieur.°

La jeune fille s'installe contre le mur de la maison à côté de la marchande.

—Vous avez eu beaucoup de clients aujourd'hui? demande Denise.

—Oh non! Je n'ai eu personne. J'ai été plus tranquille pour penser. Moi, je ne suis jamais seule ... Frédéric est près de moi ... Et vous? Avez-vous un fiancé?

—Non, dit la jeune fille en rougissant.

—Pourquoi?

—Je connais peu de jeunes gens ...

—Quand Frédéric viendra, je lui demanderai de vous présenter un de ses amis.

Denise frissonne; elle est saisie par une sorte d'anxiété.°

—Je dois rentrer, dit-elle. Ma mère m'attend. Il va être l'heure du dîner.

—Je laisse ouvert° le plus longtemps possible. Frédéric termine peut-être tard son travail. Mais je vais fermer dans quelques minutes.

La marchande se dirige vers la vitrine, sort le bracelet que Denise regarde une fois de plus avec admiration et l'attache à son bras.

—Je le mets tous les soirs pour dormir, dit-elle.

—Je reviendrai vous voir, dit la jeune fille.

—Adieu, ma belle. À bientôt.

Mais quelques jours plus tard, Denise tombe malade et reste couchée° près d'un mois. Elle est obligée d'aller se reposer à la montagne. Les soucis causés par sa maladie lui ont fait un peu oublier la vieille dame et son éternellement jeune fiancé.

à l'intérieur = à l'intérieur du magasin **anxiété** = peur **je laisse ouvert** = je garde le magasin ouvert
couchée = au lit

Mots utiles

un souci	*concern, worry*
un sourire	*smile*
un trottoir	*sidewalk*
frissonner	*to shiver, shudder*
saisir	*to seize, take*

Avez-vous compris?

1. Selon vous, est-ce que les choses ont changé quand Denise revient plus tard?
2. Qu'est-ce que la marchande propose à Denise quand elle apprend que celle-ci n'est pas mariée?
3. Quelle est la réaction de Denise?
4. Pourquoi est-ce que Denise ne revient pas voir la marchande?

Anticipons un peu

Selon vous, comment va se terminer l'histoire? Expliquez votre réponse.

- Frédéric Cottet reviendra et il se mariera avec la marchande.
- La marchande apprendra la mort de Frédéric Cottet et finalement vendra le bracelet à Denise.
- Un jour Denise fera la connaissance du petit-fils de Frédéric Cottet et se mariera avec lui.
- Quelque chose d'autre arrivera. Imaginez quoi.

Avez-vous compris?

(Sample answers)

1. Non, les choses n'ont pas changé. C'est l'été, et la vieille femme est assise devant la porte, mais elle attend toujours Frédéric.
2. Elle lui propose que Frédéric lui présente un de ses amis.
3. Elle trouve que c'est trop bizarre. Elle a peur. Elle part.
4. Elle ne revient pas parce qu'elle tombe malade et va se reposer à la montagne. Elle oublie un peu la vieille femme.

IV

À son retour, Denise passe par hasard, un jour, devant le magasin qui lui plaisait tant. De très loin, elle voit que le bracelet n'est plus dans la vitrine. Elle s'aperçoit aussi que quelque chose a changé. Il y a plus d'ordre, tout paraît plus propre qu'autrefois. Surprise, elle ouvre la porte du magasin et voit une femme brune de cinquante ans environ, installée derrière un bureau.

—La vieille dame n'est plus là? demande la jeune fille.

—Non ... elle est morte depuis un mois ...

—Oh! Cela me fait de la peine,° dit Denise. Elle était si charmante.

—Elle est morte brusquement. On l'a trouvée un matin ici, par terre. Vous savez, elle était un peu bizarre ...

—Oui, dit Denise, un peu bizarre ...

—Je ne sais pas ce que je vais faire du magasin ...

—Oh! J'espère que vous le garderez, il a tant de charme.

—Est-ce que vous désirez quelque chose?

—Il y avait dans la vitrine, dit la jeune fille, un bracelet avec des pierres de couleur en forme de cœurs: il me plaisait beaucoup.

—En effet, il était très joli. Ma tante l'avait déjà quand j'étais toute petite° ... Je l'ai vendu quelques jours après sa mort. Un matin, un vieux monsieur, tout voûté, est resté longtemps dans la rue à regarder la vitrine. Puis il est entré. Il était complètement sourd° et nous avons eu beaucoup de mal° à nous comprendre. Je crois qu'il trouvait le bracelet trop cher mais il en avait très envie et, à la fin il l'a acheté.

—Vous ne savez pas comment il s'appelait?

—Je ne me souviens pas, mais il m'a payée par chèque. Cela vous intéresse de savoir son nom?

—Oui. J'attendais d'avoir assez d'argent pour acheter ce bracelet. Je vais essayer de joindre le vieux monsieur et lui demander de me le céder.°

La femme brune ouvre un secrétaire,° cherche dans des papiers.

—Ah voilà le nom: Frédéric Cottet.

me fait de la peine = me rend triste **toute petite** = très jeune
sourd *deaf* **beaucoup de mal** = beaucoup de difficultés
me le céder = me le vendre
un secrétaire = un petit bureau

Mots utiles

s'apercevoir *	*notice*
joindre *	*to contact (someone*
paraître *	*to look, app seem*
environ	*about, approxim*
par hasard	*by chance*
par terre	*on the grour*
tant de	*so much*

Avez-vous compris?

1. Qu'est-ce qui a changé quand Denise retou au magasin?
2. Qui est la nouvelle marchande par rapport à l'ancienne?
3. Qui a finalement acheté le bracelet?

■ Irregular Verbs

(see Appendix C)

s'apercevoir (*see* **recevoir**)
joindre (*see* **peindre**)
paraître (*see* **connaître**)

■ *Avez-vous compris?*

(Sample answers)

1. La vieille marchande est morte. Il y a une nouvelle marchande.
2. La nouvelle marchande est la nièce de l'ancienne.
3. Frédéric Cottet a acheté le bracelet.

Teaching Strategy

Using the illustrations and characters from the story, have students list two adjectives to describe as many elements as possible:

- la vieille dame *(patiente, fidèle...)*
- Denise *(curieuse, sympathique...)*
- l'histoire *(romantique, triste...)*

Then have students write a paragraph about the story using the adjectives they compiled.

EXPRESSION ORALE

■ Débat: L'amour éternel

Selon vous, est-ce que l'amour éternel, tel qu'il est décrit dans l'histoire, est possible? Prenez une position pour ou contre et débattez le sujet avec votre partenaire. Si possible, donnez des exemples.

■ Situations

Avec votre partenaire, choisissez l'une des situations suivantes. Composez le dialogue correspondant et jouez-le en classe.

1 Coups de téléphone

Après chaque visite au magasin, Denise téléphone à un(e) ami(e) pour raconter ce qui s'est passé. L'ami(e) demande des détails.

Rôles: Denise, l'ami(e)

2 Conversation

Denise a réussi à retrouver Frédéric Cottet. Celui-ci lui pose des questions sur sa fiancée d'autrefois.

Rôles: Denise, Frédéric Cottet

EXPRESSION ÉCRITE

■ Frédéric Cottet

Écrivez l'histoire de Frédéric Cottet en inventant des détails. Par exemple:

- Où, quand et comment Frédéric a-t-il rencontré la dame de la boutique?
- À quelle occasion est-ce qu'il lui a offert le bracelet?
- Pourquoi est-il parti à l'âge de vingt ans?
- Où est-il allé et qu'est-ce qu'il a fait là-bas?
- Pourquoi a-t-il mis si longtemps à revenir?
- Pourquoi est-ce qu'il est finalement revenu?
- Quelles étaient ses pensées en revoyant le bracelet dans la vitrine? etc.

■ Une lettre

La vieille dame, avant de mourir, décide d'écrire une lettre à Frédéric Cottet. Dans cette lettre, elle explique ce qu'elle a fait pendant son absence, pourquoi elle l'a attendu si fidèlement *(faithfully)* et comment elle espérait le revoir.

■ Une autre conclusion

Imaginez une autre conclusion moins triste et plus romantique à l'histoire que vous avez lue. Pour cela, réécrivez complètement le quatrième épisode.

INTERLUDE CULTUREL

Note historique

On a découvert les peintures préhistoriques de Tassili dans le sud de l'Algérie en 1956. Ces peintures témoignent de l'évolution de ce peuple africain: c'était d'abord des chasseurs (de 6000 à 4000 av. J.-Chr.), puis des bergers (de 4000 à 1000 av. J.-Chr.).

Additional Information

- **Mali** means "place where the king lives."
- Until 1957, **Ghana** was known as the Gold Coast **(La Côte de l'Or)**.

INTERLUDE CULTUREL

Un peu d'histoire

Les dates

- 6000 *av. J.-C.*
- *Tassili*
- 0
- 670 *Arrivée des Arabes*
- 700 *Empire du Ghana (700-1200)*
- 1200 *Empire du Mali (1200-1500)*
- 1300 *Empire de Songhaï (1350-1600)* *Royaume du Bénin (1350-1900)*
- 1500
- 1600
- 1860
- 1900
- 1960 *Indépendance*
- 2000

Empires africains · *Colonisation* · *Indépendance*

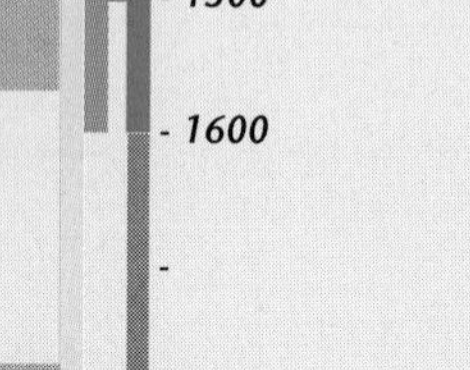

Les événements

La préhistoire en Afrique occidentale

Pendant six mille ans avant Jésus-Christ, le Sahara était une savane habitée par un peuple qui a laissé de remarquables peintures rupestres° dans la région de Tassili.

7e - 8e siècles: Conquête de l'Afrique du Nord par les Arabes

En 670, les Arabes arrivent en Afrique du Nord où ils imposent la religion musulmane. Ils établissent progressivement des relations commerciales avec les populations d'Afrique occidentale. Au contact des Arabes, beaucoup d'Africains adoptent la religion musulmane.

10e - 16e siècles: Période de prospérité et de grande civilisation

De puissants et vastes empires se succèdent en Afrique occidentale: empire du **Ghana**, empire du **Mali**, empire de **Songhaï**. La prospérité de ces empires est basée sur le commerce avec l'Afrique du Nord. Les caravanes chargées de° sel traversent le Sahara. Elles arrivent à Tombouctou, capitale de l'empire du Mali, et repartent avec de l'or et des pierres précieuses. Une civilisation brillante se développe dans toute la région.

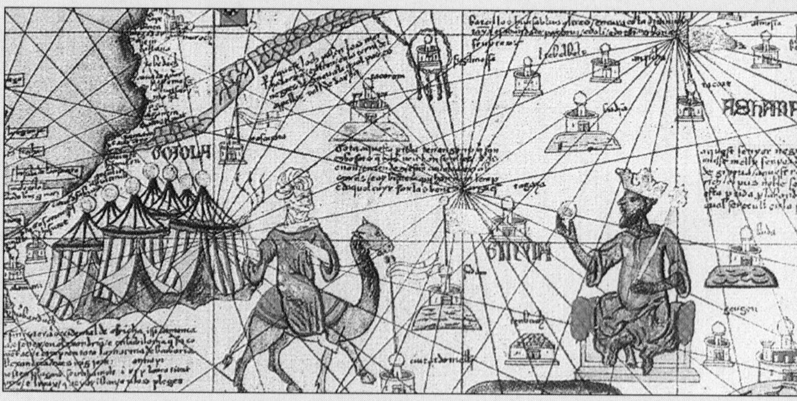

Cette illustration, tirée d'un atlas du 14e siècle, montre un marchand arabe rendant visite au Roi du Mali. Celui-ci tient dans sa main une pépite° d'or.

rupestres *on rock walls* **chargées de** *loaded with* **pépite** *nugget*

NOTES CULTURELLES

- The **Sahara** is the largest desert in the world. It reaches across Africa from the Atlantic Ocean to the Red Sea and beyond as the Arabian desert.
- The discovery of cave paintings representing plants and animals proved that there used to be water in the Sahara in prehistoric times.
- The **Songhaï** empire conquered the empire of Mali in the 15th century. Its dominance lasted until 1591, when it fell to Moroccan soldiers.

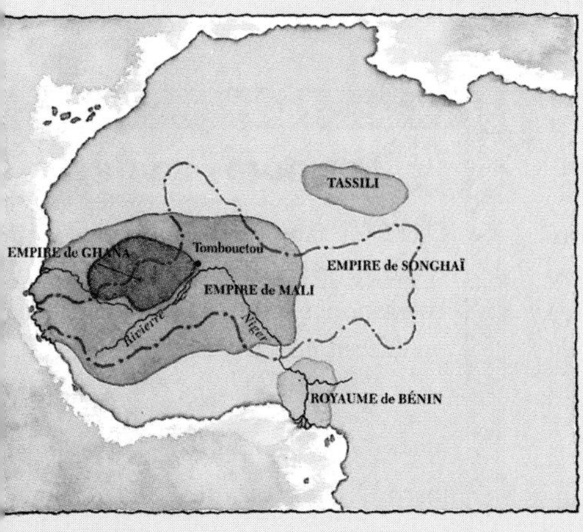

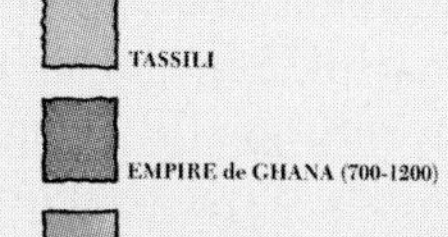

14e - 19e siècles: Le royaume de Bénin

Indépendamment des empires d'Afrique occidentale, le royaume du Bénin se développe dans la région tropicale près du Golfe de Guinée. Le génie de cette civilisation est préservé dans de splendides sculptures de bronze.

*Cette plaque de bronze représente l'**oba** ou roi du Bénin avec sa famille. Ses serviteurs le protègent du soleil.*

17e et 19e siècles: Arrivée des Européens — esclavage et colonisation

À partir du 17e siècle, l'arrivée des Européens provoque le déclin progressif de cette grande civilisation africaine. Les Européens viennent en Afrique chercher des esclaves pour travailler dans leurs plantations des Antilles, de Louisiane, du Brésil . . . Des centaines de milliers d'Africains sont arrachés° de leur terre° ancestrale et déportés en Amérique dans des conditions épouvantables.° Cet odieux trafic d'êtres° humains dure jusqu'au début du 19e siècle.

Dans la seconde moitié du 19e siècle, les Européens, qui ont déjà établi des comptoirs° sur le littoral,° décident de coloniser l'intérieur du continent. C'est ainsi que l'Afrique occidentale et équatoriale est découpée° en colonies anglaises, françaises et belges. Les Européens imposent des structures administratives et économiques qui ne correspondent pas à la culture africaine traditionnelle.

20e siècle: De l'exploitation à l'indépendance

Les pays européens exploitent leurs colonies africaines. Un grand nombre de soldats africains sont recrutés par l'armée française et combattent courageusement en Europe pendant les deux guerres mondiales (1914-1918 et 1939-1945).

Après la Seconde Guerre mondiale, les leaders politiques africains réclament l'indépendance des colonies avec de plus en plus d'insistance. À partir de 1960, ces colonies deviennent des pays indépendants, membres de l'organisation Nations unies.

Notes historiques

- C'est à la suite de la Conférence de Berlin (1884) que les puissances européennes décidèrent de se partager l'Afrique.

France	Afrique de l'ouest
Belgique	région du Congo
Angleterre	Nigeria, Afrique de l'est et du sud
Allemagne	Afrique du sud-ouest et du sud-est
Portugal	Angola, Mozambique

- Depuis l'indépendance, certains pays ont décidé de changer leur nom.

COLONIE		RÉPUBLIQUE
Dahomey	→	Bénin
Haute Volta	→	Burkina
Soudan français	→	Mali

arrachés *torn away* **terre** *land* **épouvantables** *ghastly* **êtres** *beings* **comptoirs** *trading posts* **littoral** *coast* **découpée** *cut up*

Notes culturelles

- L'enseignement du français varie de pays en pays. En Côte d'Ivoire, par exemple, il commence dès l'école maternelle.
- En mai 1997, le président Laurent Kabila a changé le nom du Zaïre en République démocratique du Congo (le Congo démocratique).

Note linguistique

Ces expressions franco-africaines sont typiques des pays mentionnés:

l'essencerie = la station-service [Sénégal]

un gros mot = un mot savant [Bénin]

NOTE: In France, un gros mot = swearword

froidir = se calmer [Côte d'Ivoire]

À NOTER:
Pour plus d'expressions, se référer à la page 297 de ce livre.

Anecdote

In **Congo** (formerly **Zaire**), the expression **avoir l'Apollo** means to suffer from conjunctivitis. This originated in 1969, when an epidemic of conjunctivitis in Africa immediately followed the explosion of an Apollo rocket. People then attributed their red eyes to the fall of the debris.

L'Afrique francophone et sa culture

Qu'est-ce que c'est que l'Afrique francophone?

C'est un groupe d'une douzaine de pays d'Afrique occidentale et équatoriale où le français est la langue officielle. Parmi ces pays, les plus importants sont **le Sénégal, la Côte d'Ivoire, le Mali, la République démocratique du Congo, le Bénin, le Cameroun** . . . Autrefois ces pays étaient des colonies françaises ou belges. Indépendants depuis 1960, ils ont décidé de garder le français comme langue administrative et commerciale. En général, les jeunes apprennent le français à l'école secondaire et parfois dès° l'école primaire.

Les noms baoulés

Dans les familles baoulés, les noms traditionnels donnés aux enfants correspondent aux jours de la semaine où ils sont nés.

	GARÇONS	FILLES
lundi	**Kouassi**	**Akissi**
mardi	**Kouadio**	**Adjoua**
mercredi	**Konan**	**Amelan**
jeudi	**Koffi**	**Affoué**
vendredi	**Yao**	**Aya**
samedi	**Kouakou**	**Ahou**
dimanche	**Kouamé**	**Amoin**

Quelles langues parle-t-on en Afrique?

Il y a un très grand nombre de langues africaines. Au Sénégal, par exemple, on parle **wolof**. En Côte d'Ivoire, on parle **baoulé** et **dioula**. Au Mali, il y a dix langues régionales. Ces langues reflètent la grande diversité ethnique des peuples d'Afrique. En Côte d'Ivoire, par exemple, on compte au moins soixante groupes ethniques différents.

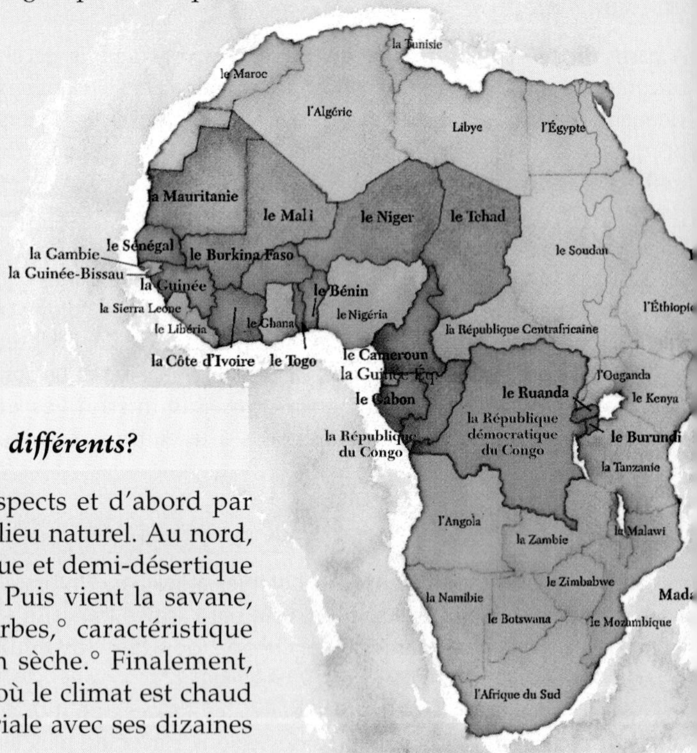

Est-ce que les pays de l'Afrique francophone sont semblables ou différents?

Ils sont différents par beaucoup d'aspects et d'abord par leur climat, leur végétation et leur milieu naturel. Au nord, par exemple, il y a une zone désertique et demi-désertique qui est le prolongement° du Sahara. Puis vient la savane, c'est-à-dire une région de hautes herbes,° caractéristique des régions chaudes à longue saison sèche.° Finalement, plus au sud et le long du littoral,° là où le climat est chaud et humide, on trouve la forêt équatoriale avec ses dizaines d'espèces d'arbres différents.

dès *as of* **prolongement** = extension **herbes** *grass* **sèche** *dry* **littoral** *coast*

■ *Quelles sont les religions de l'Afrique francophone?*

Cela dépend des pays. La religion musulmane est très importante dans les régions de l'ouest et du nord où il y a eu beaucoup de contacts avec les Arabes. C'est le cas, par exemple, au Mali, au Sénégal, et au Niger, où la grande majorité des gens sont musulmans. Au sud et au centre, au contraire, ce sont les religions animistes qui prédominent, par exemple, en Côte d'Ivoire, au Bénin, et au Burkina. Dans tous ces pays, il y a aussi des minorités catholiques. N'oublions pas, par exemple, que la plus grande basilique catholique du monde, la Basilique de Notre Dame de la Paix, se trouve à Yamoussoukro, en Côte d'Ivoire, et qu'elle a été inaugurée en 1989 par le pape Jean-Paul II.

Mosquée de Djemé, Mali

La Basilique de Notre Dame de la Paix à Yamoussoukro

Une mosquée au Niger

■ *Qu'est-ce que l'animisme?*

C'est la religion traditionnelle de l'Afrique noire. L'animisme attribue une âme° aux plantes, aux animaux, aux phénomènes naturels, et plus généralement à toutes les forces de la nature. Les animistes pratiquent ainsi le culte des ancêtres avec qui on peut communiquer et qui peuvent avoir une influence positive ou négative sur les événements de la vie quotidienne.° L'animisme explique l'importance de la nature, des animaux et des génies dans la littérature africaine.

âme *soul* **quotidienne** *daily*

Note historique

Le christianisme a été introduit en Afrique occidentale dans la deuxième moitié du 19e siècle. Les populations chrétiennes se trouvent principalement le long du littoral, là où arrivaient les missionnaires européens.

■ Additional Information

- The basilica of **Notre Dame de la Paix** has 36 stained-glass windows. Designed by an architect from the Ivory Coast, they were hand-blown in France.
- It took only three years to build the basilica, which cost about $300 million.

■ Note linguistique

Le mot **animisme** vient du latin, **anima** *(soul).*

■ Quel est le rôle de la famille dans la société africaine?

Pour les Africains, la famille représente une structure très importante. Tous les membres de la famille s'aident et doivent s'entraider.° La famille africaine est très vaste. Elle comprend° non seulement les grands-parents, les parents et les enfants, mais aussi tous les oncles, tantes, cousins et cousines unis par les liens de sang° et de mariage.

Dans les villages où la polygamie existe, l[a] famille est encore plus grande puisqu'ell[e] comprend aussi les demi-frères et les demi-soeurs. Le père est le chef de famille. Il est respecté et so[n] autorité n'est pas contestée. S'il a plusieur[s] femmes, chacune a sa propre case ou maison o[ù] elle élève° ses enfants.

À côté de la famille visible, il y a aussi l[a] famille invisible, celle des ancêtres qui restent trè[s] présents dans la mémoire des Africains. On peu[t] communiquer avec l'esprit de ses ancêtres e[t] inversement, ils peuvent communiquer avec nou[s] et influencer les événements de notre vi[e] quotidienne.

En Mauritanie, la décoration des maisons est traditionnellement réservée aux femmes. À cause des conditions climatiques, ces maisons doivent souvent être repeintes. Ici, une femme utilise des élements géométriques pour décorer sa maison.

s'entraider *help each other* **comprend** *includes* **liens de sang** *blood ties* **élève** *raises*

■ Additional Information

- **Mauritania** is a desert country, about twice the size of France.

■ Photo Note

The type of house shown is typical of the city of Oualâta, Mauritania. Women use dyes to decorate both the inside and outside of their homes with intricate geometric designs.

Note culturelle

In most African cities, Western fashion coexists with more traditional wear. Women traditionally wear **un boubou,** a long embroidered dress, or a loose top over a wrapped skirt **(le pagne).** Men wear **un grand boubou,** a loose embroidered robe worn over pants.

NOTES CULTURELLES

- La polygamie tend à disparaître, surtout dans les villes. Elle subsiste cependant dans certains villages où la population est musulmane.
- Dans certaines sociétés africaines, chez les Baoulés de la Côte d'Ivoire, par exemple, c'était la mère qui traditionnellement était le chef de la famille. Aujourd'hui, ce matriarcat a disparu, mais la mère est toujours très écoutée et très respectée.

■ *Quelles sont les caractéristiques de la littérature africaine traditionnelle?*

La littérature africaine traditionnelle est très différente de la littérature européenne. C'est avant tout une littérature orale. Son but° principal est d'expliquer et de transmettre de génération en génération les coutumes, les traditions et les valeurs du groupe. Ses thèmes sont variés: la création du monde, l'origine de l'humanité, l'histoire des ancêtres et de la tribu, les relations entre les gens. Ses formes d'expression sont la poésie, la fable, la légende, et surtout le conte.° Il y a toutes sortes de contes: contes moraux, contes humoristiques, contes d'aventures, contes d'amour, contes du merveilleux . . . Dans ces contes, les personnages sont souvent des animaux qui représentent en réalité les humains avec leurs qualités et leurs défauts.

Les conteurs° africains s'appellent des «griots». Dans les villages de l'Afrique traditionnelle, le griot joue un rôle très important. C'est lui qui transmet l'histoire et les traditions de chaque famille du village.

Aujourd'hui, il y a aussi une littérature écrite très abondante. Cette littérature reprend les thèmes de la littérature orale (contes, fables) ou traite les thèmes plus personnels (poésie, romans, récits autobiographiques). L'un des représentants les plus connus de la littérature africaine moderne est l'écrivain sénégalais Léopold Sédar Senghor. Ce poète s'exprime en français sur des thèmes africains ou des thèmes universels, comme la liberté. Considéré comme l'un des plus grands écrivains d'expression française, il a été élu en 1980 membre de l'Académie française.

Léopold Sédar Senghor: Poète et homme d'action

Homme de lettres et brillant intellectuel, Léopold Senghor (1906 - 2001) a aussi joué un rôle politique très mportant dans l'histoire de l'Afrique francophone. Après la Seconde Guerre mondiale, il a milité pour l'indépendance de son pays, le Sénégal. Quand le Sénégal est devenu une république indépendante en 1958, il en est devenu le premier président (1958-1980).

Documents: Une fable africaine

La gélinotte et la tortue

Un jour, une gélinotte° rencontra une tortue qui avançait lentement à travers la plaine. «Pourquoi est-ce que tu ne vas pas plus vite?» demanda-t-elle à la tortue. «Parce que je suis une tortue» répondit la tortue. «Eh bien, moi, je te suis supérieure non seulement parce que je vais plus vite que toi, mais aussi parce que je peux voler.»°

À ce moment des chasseurs passèrent par là. Ils mirent le feu aux herbes de la plaine pour déloger des gazelles qui s'y étaient cachées.° Le cercle de feu se rapprocha des deux animaux exposés à un péril certain. La tortue se cacha dans le trou° laissé par le pied d'un éléphant, et elle survécut. La gélinotte voulait s'envoler, mais elle fut étouffée° par la fumée° et mourut.

N'est pas supérieur celui qui se vante°

but = objectif **conte** *short story* **conteurs** *storytellers* **gélinotte** *grouse* **voler** *to fly*
cachées *hidden* **trou** *hole* **étouffée** *suffocated* **fumée** *smoke* **se vante** *boasts*

Note culturelle

Quand Senghor était étudiant à Paris dans les années 1920, lui et son ami Aimé Césaire ont fondé le journal *L'Étudiant noir* dans lequel ils ont défini le concept de «négritude» (voir à la page 336).

■ Additional Information

- Born in **Joal**, a town near **Dakar** (Senegal), **Léopold Sédar Senghor** became the mayor of **Thiès** (France) before being elected to the French parliament in 1946.

■ Pour en savoir plus

For more information on the **Académie française,** see p. 56.

Afrique

Afrique mon Afrique
Afrique des fiers guerriers° dans les savanes ancestrales
Afrique que chante ma grand-Mère
Au bord° de son fleuve° lointain°
Je ne t'ai jamais connue

Mais mon regard est plein de ton sang
Ton beau sang noir à travers les champs répandu°
Le sang de ta sueur°
La sueur de ton travail
Le travail de l'esclavage
L'esclavage de tes enfants

Afrique dis-moi Afrique
Est-ce donc toi ce dos qui se courbe°
Et se couche° sous le poids° de l'humilité
Ce dos tremblant à zébrures° rouges
Qui dit oui au fouet° sur les routes de midi

Alors gravement une voix me répondit
Fils impétueux cet arbre robuste et jeune
Cet arbre là-bas
Splendidement seul au milieu de fleurs blanches et fanées°
C'est l'Afrique ton Afrique qui repousse°
Qui repousse patiemment obstinément
Et dont les fruits ont peu à peu
L'amère° saveur° de la liberté.

David Diop (1927-1960)

Né en France d'un père sénégalais e d'une mère camerounaise*, Davi Diop est l'un des écrivains les plu militants de la littérature africaine Dans ce poème, publié en 1956, dénonce le colonialisme et entrevoit l'indépendance de l'Afrique. Diop es mort dans un accident d'avion alor qu'°il venait s'établir° définitivemen au Sénégal, devenu° depuis peu° u état indépendant.

* **Le Cameroun** = un pays de l'Afrique francophone

Baobab dans la savane africaine

guerriers *warriors* **au bord** *on the shore* **fleuve** = rivière **lointain** = distant **répandu** *spilled* **sueur** *sweat* **se courbe** *is bent over* **se couche** *is doubled over* **poids** *weight* **zébrures** *stripes (caused by lashing)* **fouet** *whip* **fanées** *withered* **repoussse** *grows back* **amère** *bitter* **saveur** *taste* **entrevoit** = anticipe **alors que** *when* **s'établir** *to settle* **devenu** = qui était devenu **depuis peu** = récemment

Note culturelle

Le nom **baobab** signifie «arbre de mille ans». Ses fruits, de la taille d'une orange, ont le goût un peu amer. Pour Diop, cet arbre majestueux, dont le tronc peut atteindre 23 mètres de circonférence, symbolise le dynamisme et l'avenir de l'Afrique.

Teaching Strategy

You may wish to help students with a brief analysis of *Afrique* if they are having difficulty:

Verse 1 The poet evokes the Africa of noble warriors which he has never known.

Verse 2 What he sees is the blood and sweat of slavery.

Verse 3 He wonders if the Africa that he sees bent over and humiliated is the real Africa.

Verse 4 A voice answers him that the tree he sees growing tall and strong is the symbol of the rebirth of a free Africa.

▪ *L'art africain* ▪
et
son influence sur l'art européen

Parmi les arts africains traditionnels, la forme la plus développée est la sculpture. Les principaux objets sculptés sont des statues et des masques. Pour les Africains, ces objets ne sont pas considérés comme des objets artistiques, mais comme des objets religieux. Dans les cérémonies rituelles, par exemple, les masques sont portés par des danseurs pour honorer l'esprit des ancêtres et demander leur protection.

La majorité des masques africains sont en bois. Ils représentent généralement des figures humaines sous des formes stylisées. On peut noter l'importance des formes géométriques: lignes droites° ou courbes, cercles, ovales, triangles, etc. Cette stylisation transforme le corps et le visage humains et permet l'expression d'émotions très intenses.

Au début du 20e siècle, les Européens ont pris connaissance° de l'art africain grâce à plusieurs expositions coloniales où figuraient masques et statues de l'Afrique noire. L'originalité de cet art a d'abord choqué le public peu habitué° à la représentation non-conventionnelle de l'être humain. Les grands artistes de l'époque, au contraire, ont été très impressionnés par la simplification stylistique de l'art africain. Matisse, Modigliani et surtout Picasso ont incorporé cette simplification dans leurs propres oeuvres.° En particulier, l'usage des formes géométriques, directement inspiré par la sculpture africaine, est à la base du cubisme qui allait révolutionner l'art européen du 20e siècle.

e masque africain a ›partenu au peintre laminck qui l'a montré ses amis artistes. On peut ›ter les ressemblances entre › masque et la sculpture › Modigliani.

Modigliani, *Tête de femme*

À remarquer l'influence des masques africains sur le célèbre tableau de Picasso, *Les Demoiselles d'Avignon.*

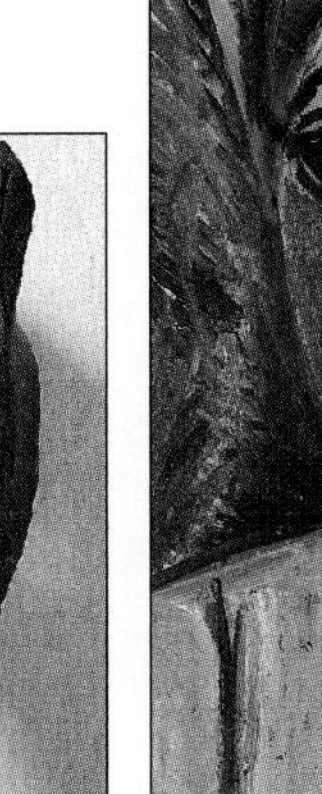

Picasso, *Étude pour les Demoiselles d'Avignon*

droites *straight* **ont pris connaissance** *became aware* **habitué** *accustomed* **oeuvres** *works*

Note culturelle

Le cubisme est un mouvement artistique qui est né à Paris vers 1906. Les fondateurs de ce mouvement sont Georges Braque (1881–1963) et Pablo Picasso (1882–1973). Les artistes cubistes représentent leurs sujets sous des perspectives différentes et les décomposent en formes géométriques fondamentales: cubes, sphères, ovales, un peu à la manière des sculpteurs africains. Dans son tableau révolutionnaire, *Les Demoiselles d'Avignon* (1907), Picasso a peint certains de ses personnages en leur donnant des visages ressemblant d'assez près à des masques

■ Additional Information

- French painter **Maurice de Vlaminck (1876–1958)** was a leader of the fauvism school.
- In Côte d'Ivoire, **le festival des masques** is celebrated every February. It is famous for its mask-wearing performers who dance on stilts.
- In Mali, masks are an essential symbol for the **Dogon** people who use them for funerals and many festivals, including the **Signi,** a ceremony held only once every sixty years.

Documents: La Légende baoulé

Bernard Dadié

Bernard Dadié, né en 1916, est originaire de la Côte d'Ivoire. C'est l'un des écrivains les plus féconds° de la littérature africaine d'expression française. Il a écrit des contes, des poèmes, des romans et des pièces de théâtre. Militant nationaliste, Dadié a été arrêté en 1949 et a passé seize mois en prison pour ses activités politiques. Après l'indépendance de la Côte d'Ivoire, il a été nommé Ministre de la Culture de son pays.

La Légende baoulé est extraite du livre **Légendes africaines**. Dans ce récit, Dadié explique comment son peuple, les Baoulés, ont reçu leur nom grâce au sacrifice de leur reine, la reine Pokou.

Il y a longtemps, très longtemps, vivait au bord d'une lagune calme, une tribu paisible° de nos frères. Ses jeunes hommes étaient nombreux, nobles et courageux, ses femmes étaient belles et joyeuses. Et leur reine, la reine Pokou, était la plus belle parmi les plus belles.

Depuis longtemps, très longtemps, la paix était sur eux et les esclaves mêmes, fils des captifs des temps révolus,° étaient heureux auprès de leurs heureux maîtres.

Un jour, les ennemis vinrent nombreux comme des magnans.° Il fallut quitter les paillotes,° les plantations, la lagune poissonneuse,° laisser les filets,° tout abandonner pour fuir.°

Ils partirent dans la forêt. Ils laissèrent aux épines° leurs pagnes,* puis leur chair.° Il fallait fuir toujours, sans repos, sans trêve,° talonné° par l'ennemi féroce.

Et leur reine, la reine Pokou, marchait la dernière, portant au dos son enfant.

* **Pagne**: a rectangular strip of cloth made of vegetal fibers which is worn as a loincloth or wrapped around the hips to form a short sk

féconds *prolific* **paisible** *peaceful* **révolus** *long past* **magnans** *red ants* **paillotes** *straw huts* **poissonneuse** = avec beaucoup de poissons
filets *nets* **fuir** *to flee* **épines** *thorns* **chair** *flesh* **sans trêve** *unceasingly* **talonné** *followed close on their heels*

 **NOTE** CULTURELLE

Les Baoulés Aujourd'hui les Baoulés représentent l'un des groupes ethniques les plus importants de la Côte d'Ivoire. Autrefois, ce peuple habitait dans la région du Ghana actuel. À une époque lointaine et pour des raisons mystérieuses, les Baoulés ont été chassés de leur territoire et ont dû s'enfuir en Côte d'Ivoire. La légende baoulé décrit l'exil de ce peuple et explique l'origine de son nom.

La reine Pokou Le rôle joué par la reine Pokou dans la légende souligne l'importance de la femme, et particulièrement de la mère dans la société baoulé traditionnelle.

À leur passage l'hyène ricanait,° l'éléphant et
e sanglier° fuyaient, le chimpanzé grognait°
et le lion étonné° s'écartait du chemin.°

Enfin, les broussailles° apparurent, puis la savane et les rôniers° et, encore une fois, a horde entonna° son chant d'exil:

Mi houn Ano, Mi houn Ano, blâ ô
Ebolo nigué, mo ba gnan min —

> *Mon mari Ano, mon mari Ano, viens,*
> *Les génies de la brousse° m'emportent.*

Harassés, exténués,° amaigris,° ils arrivèrent sur le soir au bord d'un grand leuve dont la course° se brisait° sur d'énormes rochers.

Et le fleuve mugissait,° les flots° montaient jusqu'aux cimes° des arbres et retombaient et les fugitifs étaient glacés d'effroi.°

Consternés,° ils se regardaient. Était-ce là l'Eau qui les faisait vivre naguère,° l'Eau, leur grande amie? Il avait fallu qu'un mauvais génie l'excitât contre eux.

Et les conquérants devenaient plus proches.°

Et, pour la première fois, le sorcier° parla: «L'eau est devenue mauvaise, dit-il, et elle ne s'apaisera° que quand nous lui aurons donné ce que nous avons de plus cher.»° Et le chant d'espoir° retentit:°

Ebe nin flê nin bâ
Ebe nin flâ nin nan
Ebe nin flê nin dja
Yapen'sè ni djà wali

> *Quelqu'un appelle son fils*
> *Quelqu'un appelle sa mère*
> *Quelqu'un appelle son père*
> *Les belles filles se marieront.*

Et chacun donna ses bracelets d'or et d'ivoire, et tout ce qu'il avait pu sauver.

Mais le sorcier les repoussa du pied° et montra le jeune prince, le bébé de six mois: «Voilà, dit-il, ce que nous avons de plus précieux.»

Et la mère, effrayée,° serra° son enfant sur son coeur. Mais la mère était aussi la reine et, droite° au bord de l'abîme, elle leva l'enfant souriant° au-dessus de sa tête et le lança dans l'eau mugissante.

Alors des hippopotames, d'énormes hippopotames émergèrent et, se plaçant les uns à la suite° des autres, formèrent un pont° et sur ce pont miraculeux le peuple en fuite° passa en chantant:

Ebe nin flê nin bâ
Ebe nin flâ nin nan
Ebe nin flê nin dja
Yapen'sè ni djà wali

> *Quelqu'un appelle son fils*
> *Quelqu'un appelle sa mère*
> *Quelqu'un appelle son père*
> *Les belles filles se marieront.*

Et la reine Pokou passa la dernière et trouva sur la rive° son peuple prosterné.°

Mais la reine était aussi la mère et elle put dire seulement «baouli», ce qui veut dire: l'enfant est mort.

Et c'était la reine Pokou et le peuple garda le nom de Baoulé.

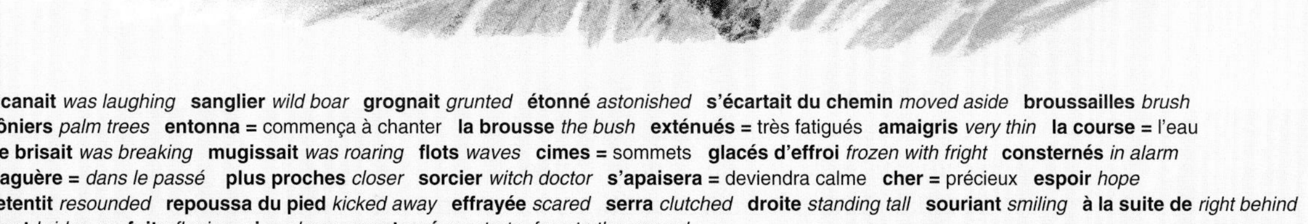

ricanait *was laughing* **sanglier** *wild boar* **grognait** *grunted* **étonné** *astonished* **s'écartait du chemin** *moved aside* **broussailles** *brush*
rôniers *palm trees* **entonna** = commença à chanter **la brousse** *the bush* **exténués** = très fatigués **amaigris** *very thin* **la course** = l'eau
se brisait *was breaking* **mugissait** *was roaring* **flots** *waves* **cimes** = sommets **glacés d'effroi** *frozen with fright* **consternés** *in alarm*
naguère = *dans le passé* **plus proches** *closer* **sorcier** *witch doctor* **s'apaisera** = deviendra calme **cher** = précieux **espoir** *hope*
retentit *resounded* **repoussa du pied** *kicked away* **effrayée** *scared* **serra** *clutched* **droite** *standing tall* **souriant** *smiling* **à la suite de** *right behind*
pont *bridge* **en fuite** *fleeing* **rive** *shore* **prosterné** *prostrate, face to the ground*

■ Teaching Strategy

Ask students:

- Relevez tout ce qui, d'après vous, révèle que l'histoire se passe en Afrique. En quoi ces détails sont-ils significatifs?
- À votre avis, y avait-il une autre solution possible pour traverser le fleuve? Laquelle?
- Connaissez-vous une autre légende? Laquelle? Pouvez-vous la résumer brièvement?

■ Irregular Verb

(See Appendix C)
fuir

■ Note linguistique

Bâ = l'enfant; **ou li** = est mort

UNITÉ 10

MAIN THEME

University studies and careers

Communication Function/Contexts

- Deciding on a college major
- Planning for a career
- Looking for a job

Linguistic Goals

- Describing simultaneous actions
- Explaining the purpose of an action
- Explaining the timing, conditions, and constraints of an action
- Expressing how your actions may depend on what others do
- Describing how your actions affect others

Online Study Center

Online Teaching Center

UNITÉ 10

Vers la vie active

Thème et Objectifs

Culture

In this unit, you will discover . . .

- what the **bac** is all about and why it is so important for French young people
- which are the most popular professions in France
- how to prepare for an interview with a French company

Communication

You will learn how . . .

- to talk about what you plan to study in the future
- to indicate what type of job or profession you would like to have
- to describe your personal qualifications
- to prepare a résumé in French

Langue

You will learn how . . .

- to describe simultaneous actions
- to indicate why you do certain things
- to explain under which conditions or constraints you do certain things
- to express how your actions may depend on what others do
- to describe how your actions have an effect on other people

TEACHING RESOURCES

ANCILLARIES

Student Activities Manual, Unit 10
Audio Program, Unit 10
Video-DVD Program, Unit 10
***Chansons* Audio CD**

HM ClassPrep CD

Presentations, Unit 10
Audioscript, Unit 10
Videoscript, Unit 10
Assessment, Unit 10
Answer Key, Unit 10

CE FAMEUX BAC!

Corinne, 17 ans, et Guillaume, 18 ans, sont en «terminale», c'est-à-dire, en dernière année de leurs études secondaires. Dans quelques semaines, ils vont passer le bac. Corinne est une excellente élève et pourtant elle a le trac.° «J'ai beaucoup étudié, mais on ne sait jamais. Qu'est-ce que je vais faire si je ne suis pas reçue?° Je n'ai vraiment pas envie de redoubler.»° Guillaume, lui, redouble. Il est plus philosophe et plus décontracté° que Corinne. «Si je n'ai pas mon bac cette fois, je vais m'engager dans l'armée. Après, on verra!»

Chaque année, en juin, 645 000 jeunes Français passent le bac. C'est un examen très important qui marque la fin des études secondaires et qui détermine, en grande partie, l'avenir des lycéens. S'ils sont reçus, ils peuvent aller à l'université et continuer leurs études. S'ils ratent le bac, ils peuvent redoubler et se représenter° l'année suivante, ou bien ils peuvent faire des études techniques, ou entrer dans la vie professionnelle. Heureusement, 80% des candidats sont reçus et pour la majorité, ils continuent leurs études.

Il y a plusieurs types (ou "séries") de bac. Ils sont désignés par des lettres. Dans chaque série, l'élève doit choisir une spécialité. Voici les trois séries principales et leurs spécialités:

Ces spécialités sont importantes parce qu'elles déterminent le genre d'études universitaires qu'on peut faire et, par conséquent, sa profession future. Par exemple, si on veut être médecin ou pharmacien, il est conseillé° de faire un bac S, spécialité sciences de la vie et de la terre. Si on pense faire des études de droit° et devenir avocat, il est préférable de faire un bac ES, spécialité sciences économiques et sociales.

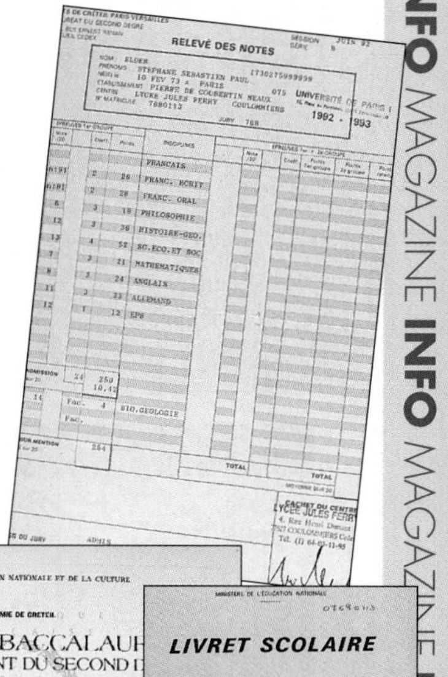

Série littéraire, bac L:
- langues vivantes
- philosophie
- art
- mathématiques

Série économique et sociale, bac ES:
- sciences économiques et sociales
- mathématiques
- langues vivantes

Série scientifique, bac S:
- mathématiques
- physique chimie
- sciences de la vie et de la terre
- technologie industrielle

DIPLÔME DU BACCALAU... DE L'ENSEIGNEMENT DU SECOND D...

LIVRET SCOLAIRE

ELDER

a le trac *is scared, nervous* **si je ne suis pas reçue** = si je ne réussis pas **redoubler** *to repeat a grade* **décontracté** *relaxed* **se représenter** *retake (the exam)* **conseillé** = recommandé **droit** *law*

INFO MAGAZINE

Theme: Education in France

Reading Strategy: Reading for information, skimming, scanning

Note culturelle

The **Bac** series **L**, **ES**, and **F** were implemented in 1995 to allow more flexibility, replacing the old bac A (now **L**), bac B (now **ES**), and bacs C, D, E, and S (now **F**). In each **série** and **spécialité**, students are offered optional courses **(les options)** such as ancient Greek, Latin, science, and art history.

Teaching Strategy

These readings can be done:
- in class or as homework
- at the beginning of the unit or as a wrap-up activity

Have students look at the realia and photos and guess the theme of the article. Have them skim, looking for cognates, then give the main idea. Short *Info Magazine* quizzes may be used to test for comprehension or as a basis for discussion.

Note culturelle

After passing the **baccalauréat**, most French young people continue their studies. Many go to the university (**l'université**, often referred to as **la fac** or **la faculté**, which is a division of the university) where they can study humanities, social sciences, law, science, medicine and pharmacy. Most French universities are government controlled and tuition is minimal. Other students go to professional schools (e.g., business schools, engineering schools) which are private and charge tuition.
- Les classes d'un lycée français sont:
  - **la seconde** (= 11th grade)
  - **la première** (= 12th grade)
  - **la terminale**

Notes culturelles

The **baccalauréat** tests the students on all subjects, including physical education.

Supplementary vocabulary

le programme *curriculum*
la moyenne *average (grade)*
l'orientation *(f.) career choice*
la classe préparatoire *class to prepare students for the entrance exam of "une grande école"*
le manuel scolaire *textbook*

Quelques expressions familières employées par les lycéens français:
- **bachoter** *to cram (for an exam)*
- **sécher** *not to know the answer (lit.: to dry up)*
- **bûcher** *to cram (work hard)*
- **la bourse** *scholarship*
- **le restaurant universitaire (le resto U)** *college cafeteria*
- **la cité universitaire** *dorm*
- **l'association des anciens élèves** *alumni association*
- **les débouchés** *(m.) prospects, openings (career)*

Irregular Verb

(see Appendix C)
obtenir (*see* **tenir**)

Les études universitaires durent au moins deux ans. Aussi, certains jeunes qui ont le bac préfèrent étudier en I.U.T. (Institut Supérieur de Technologie) où ils peuvent obtenir un diplôme universitaire de technologie après deux années d'études. Les "grandes écoles" sont une autre option. Ce sont des écoles spécialisées dans certains domaines: commerce, administration publique, professions d'ingénieur, etc. Pour entrer° dans ces écoles prestigieuses, il faut passer un concours° extrêmement difficile, auquel la plupart des candidats échouent.° Cependant, si on est reçu, et si on obtient° le diplôme d'une de ces écoles, on a toutes les chances de faire une brillante carrière dans le commerce, la finance, l'industrie et même la politique.

Comme on peut le voir, les diplômes ont beaucoup d'importance en France. Un diplôme représente une carte d'entrée dans la vie professionnelle. Voilà pourquoi les parents insistent pour que leurs enfants étudient. Les enfants sont généralement d'accord pour faire l'effort nécessaire. En France, les études, c'est sérieux!

Petite histoire du bac

- Au Moyen Âge, un bachelier* était un jeune gentilhomme qui voulait être chevalier.° Vers 1500, c'était un étudiant qui avait écrit une thèse° de philosophie.
- Le bac moderne date de Napoléon qui l'a institué° en 1808. La première année, il y avait 32 candidats. En 1900, il y en avait 4 000. Aujourd'hui, il y en a 645 000.
- Le bac a d'abord été un examen exclusivement masculin. La première «candidate» se présenta en 1861. (C'était une institutrice° de 37 ans!) Aujourd'hui, 57% des candidats sont en réalité . . . des candidates.
- À l'origine, l'examinateur interrogeait° le candidat sur une liste de questions préparées à l'avance et tirées au sort.° En un an, le candidat devait apprendre la réponse à 500 questions différentes. Ce système donna lieu° à la pratique du «bachotage», selon laquelle l'élève apprend par coeur un grand nombre d'informations sans en connaître nécessairement le sens.°
- Le bac se démocratise.° En 1900, seulement un jeune Français sur cent passait le bac. Aujourd'hui, cette proportion est de 80%.

* De nos jours, un «bachelier» est une personne qui a son baccalauréat.

et vous?

DÉFINITIONS

Définissez les mots ou expressions suivants:
- le «bac»
- la «terminale»
- redoubler
- être reçu à un examen
- l'université
- être prioritaire
- une «grande école»
- un concours

ET VOUS?

Quel genre d'étudiant(e) êtes-vous? Êtes-vous plutôt comme Corinne ou comme Guillaume? Expliquez.

EXPRESSION ORALE
- Avec votre partenaire, discutez les avantages et les inconvénients d'aller à l'université.
- Expliquez à un(e) ami(e) français(e) (votre partenaire) le système d'enseignement aux États-Unis (par exemple, quels sujets on peut choisir à l'école secondaire, comment on obtient son diplôme, ce qu'on doit faire pour aller à l'université, etc.)

EXPRESSION ÉCRITE

Écrivez une lettre à un copain français où vous dites ce que vous allez faire si vous avez votre diplôme d'études secondaires et si vous ne l'avez pas.

entrer = être accepté **concours** *competitive exam* **échouent** = ne réussissent pas **obtient / obtenir** *to obtain, get* **chevalier** *knight* **thèse** = essai **institué** = créé **institutrice** = professeur d'école primaire **interrogeait** = posait des questions **tirées au sort** *chosen at random* **donna lieu** *gave rise* **sens** *meaning* **se démocratise** = devient démocratique

NOTES CULTURELLES

Les études universitaires en France sont divisées en trois cycles. Chaque cycle est sanctionné par un diplôme:
- 1er cycle: **le DEUG** (Diplôme d'Études Universitaires Générales; en 2 ans)
- 2e cycle: **la licence** (BA) et ensuite **la maîtrise**
- 3e cycle: **le DESS** (Diplôme d'Études Supérieures Spécialisées), **le DEA** (Diplôme d'Études Approfondies) et **le doctorat**.
- Les **IUT** furent créés en 1966. Ils font partie de l'université et offrent une formation de technicien supérieur en deux ans (avec 35 heures de cours par semaine).

Il a raté le bac

Mathieu gagne très bien sa vie. Il a une voiture de sport, voyage en première classe et, surtout, il fait ce qu'il aime. Pourtant, il a raté le fameux bac. Il raconte:

« Je ne suis pas fait° pour les études. Au lycée, ça n'allait vraiment pas. J'étais nul° en maths et en sciences, médiocre° dans les autres disciplines. La seule activité que j'aimais, c'était le sport. Là, j'étais vraiment «top», mais évidemment, ça ne suffisait° pas. J'ai raté mon bac une première fois, j'ai redoublé et je l'ai raté à nouveau. Alors, j'ai abandonné mes études. J'ai cherché un job. Tous les jours, je lisais les petites annonces dans les journaux et je téléphonais, mais sans bac je n'avais aucune chance. Alors, j'ai décidé de m'engager° dans l'armée.° J'ai opté pour un engagement° de trois ans. Pendant ce temps, j'ai continué à faire du sport et, surtout, j'ai fait un stage° de parachutisme.

Malheureusement, après mon service, ma situation n'avait pas changé! J'avais pensé être professeur d'éducation physique, mais sans diplôme, ce n'était pas possible. Alors, j'ai fait des petits boulots.° J'ai été chauffeur de taxi. J'ai travaillé dans un fast-food. J'ai été garde du corps° d'un banquier. Tout cela n'était pas ma vocation, et je cherchais désespérément à faire autre chose.

Un jour, finalement, la chance° m'a souri.° On tournait° un film dans le quartier où j'habitais. Je suis allé là pour regarder. Il y avait une scène où l'acteur principal devait sauter° du troisième étage d'une maison en flamme. Ce jour-là, le cascadeur° qui devait le remplacer n'est pas venu. Le metteur en scène° avait l'air désespéré. Alors, j'ai offert mes services. Ça a si bien marché° qu'on m'a embauché° pour le reste du film.

Depuis, je suis cascadeur professionnel. J'ai déjà une vingtaine de films à mon actif.° Évidemment, je ne suis pas la grande vedette,° mais je suis bien payé. Je voyage dans tous les pays du monde. Je connais des tas° d'acteurs et d'actrices et de temps en temps on me demande mon autographe. . . Et surtout, j'ai trouvé ma voie!° »

Les jeunes Français et l'armée

Le service militaire a été longtemps une tradition nationale en France. Symbole de démocratie et d'égalité, il était obligatoire° pour les garçons et volontaire° pour les filles. À 18 ans, les jeunes gens faisaient un service militaire de dix mois. Ce service militaire, aussi appelé «service national,» a été supprimé° en 2002.

Le système traditionnel a été remplacé par un système plus simple. À l'age de 16 ans, tous les jeunes Français, garçons et filles, doivent être recensés° à la mairie.° Avant l'âge de 18 ans, ils doivent suivre une journée° de «Préparation à la défense,» pour laquelle ils reçoivent un certificat de préparation.

Les volontaires° peuvent faire une courte «préparation militaire» ou s'engager° dans l'armée, la police ou chez les pompiers° pour une période plus longue.

Service NATIONAL

Vous et nous, un service à se rendre.

et vous?

- Selon vous, quelle est la «morale» de l'histoire de Mathieu?
- Aimeriez-vous être cascadeur / cascadeuse? Expliquez pourquoi ou pourquoi pas.

EXPRESSION ORALE

- Vous êtes journaliste. Interviewez Mathieu (joué par votre partenaire).
- Connaissez-vous des personnes qui n'étaient pas faites pour les études mais qui ont trouvé un job intéressant? Donnez un ou plusieurs exemples.

ne suis pas fait *cut out* **nul** = zéro **médiocre** *below average* **suffisait** = c'était suffisant **m'engager** *enlist* **l'armée** *the army* **engagement** *service* **stage** *training session* **petits boulots** = jobs **garde du corps** *bodyguard* **chance** *luck* **souri / sourire** *to smile* **tournait** = filmait **sauter** *to jump* **cascadeur** *stuntman* **metteur en scène** *director* **si bien marché** *went so well* **embauché** *hired* **à mon actif** *behind me* **vedette** = star **tas** = beaucoup **voie** *way* **obligatoire** *compulsory* **volontaire** *optional* **supprimé** *abolished* **recensé** *registered* **mairie** *town hall* **journée** *day* **volontaires** *volunteers* **s'engager** *enlist* **pompiers** *firefighters*

■ Notes linguistiques

- Remind your students that **passer un examen** = *to take a test.* **être reçu/réussir à un examen** = *to pass a test*
- **les langues étrangères** = les langues vivantes (≠ les langues mortes)
- **les lettres classiques** = le français, la philosophie, le latin et le grec

■ Additional Information

- In May 1996, President Chirac called for reform of the military service in France, changing it from a mandatory recruitment to a voluntary system.
- Until 1998, conscientious objectors had to serve 20 months (instead of 10) within the administration, or with a humanitarian organization.
- Some French draftees used to do their military service in the United States as technical advisers in French consulates, or as teachers in Canada.

■ Irregular Verb

(see Appendix C)
sourire (*see* **rire**)

- Quelques grandes écoles françaises: **HEC** (Haute École de Commerce); **Polytechnique** (Hautes Études Scientifiques), **l'ENA** (École Nationale d'Administration qui forme les hauts fonctionnaires de l'État).

PARTIE 1

LE FRANÇAIS PRATIQUE

TEACHING RESOURCES

Student Activities Manual, pp. 165–166

Tête-à-tête Pair Activity, Choix professionnels, p. PA11

Audio Program, CD 11, Tracks 1–4

HM ClassPrep CD, Audioscript, Unit 10

LE FRANÇAIS PRATIQUE — *Études ou travail?*

—Qu'est-ce que tu vas faire quand tu auras ton diplôme?

Je vais | continuer mes études | faire une maîtrise (Master's degree) | faire un doctorat (PhD)

chercher | **du travail** | **un emploi** *job*

gagner ma vie

gagner sa vie *to earn a livin*

— Qu'est-ce que tu vas étudier?

Je vais | **étudier** les sciences | **faire des études de** biologie | **me spécialiser en** chimie

se spécialiser en *to major ir*

— Qu'est-ce que tu veux faire plus tard?

Je voudrais être médecin.

LES ÉTUDES

Les études scientifiques et techniques
- la **chimie**
- la **physique**
- les **maths**
- l'**informatique**
- les **études d'ingénieur**

Les études médicales
- la **biologie**
- la **médecine**
- la **pharmacie**
- les **études vétérinaires**

Les sciences humaines
- l'**histoire**
- la **psychologie**
- les **sciences économiques**
- les **sciences politiques**

Les études commerciales
- le **commerce** *business*
- la **gestion** *management*
- le **marketing**
- la **publicité** *advertising*
- la **comptabilité** *accounting*

Les études juridiques
- le **droit** *law*

Les études littéraires et artistiques
- la **philosophie**
- la **littérature**
- les **langues étrangères**
- le **journalisme**
- la **musique**
- le **dessin** *art, design*

1 Mes études

Décrivez les études que vous faites à l'université.
Mentionnez:
- votre spécialité principale *(major)*
- votre spécialité secondaire *(minor)*

Comparez votre choix de spécialités avec le reste de la classe.

QUELQUES PROFESSIONS

La médecine
- un **médecin**
- un(e) **chirurgien(ne)** *surgeon*
- un(e) **dentiste**
- un(e) **pharmacien(ne)**
- un(e) **vétérinaire**
- un(e) **infirmier (-ère)**

Le commerce, les affaires *business*
- un(e) **vendeur (-euse)** *salesperson*
- un(e) **représentant(e)** de commerce
- un(e) **spécialiste de marketing**
- un(e) **homme (femme) d'affaires**

La finance
- un(e) **banquier (-ière)**
- un(e) **agent de change** *stockbroker*

Le droit *law*
- un(e) **avocat(e)** *lawyer*
- un(e) **juge**

La fonction publique *civil service*
- un(e) **fonctionnaire** *civil servant*
- un(e) **diplomate**
- un(e) **assistant(e) social(e)** *social worker*

La technique et les sciences
- un(e) **scientifique**
- un **ingénieur**
- un(e) **chercheur (-euse)** *researcher*
- un(e) **technicien(ne)**
- un(e) **informaticien(ne)**
- un(e) **spécialiste de logiciel** *software*
- un(e) **spécialiste de données** *data*

L'administration
- un(e) **cadre** *executive*
- un(e) **patron(ne)** *boss*
- un(e) **chef** *(head)* **de personnel**
- un(e) **directeur (-trice)** *manager*

Les emplois de bureau *office*
- un(e) **employé(e)** *clerk*
- un(e) **secrétaire**
- un(e) **comptable** *accountant*

Les services
- un **agent immobilier** *real estate agent*
- un **agent d'assurances** *insurance agent*

FLASH d'information

Les professions préférées des Français

Ce qui compte le plus dans le choix d'une profession, ce n'est pas nécessairement la possibilité de gagner beaucoup d'argent, c'est avant tout de faire quelque chose d'intéressant. Voici la liste des dix professions préférées des Francais, par ordre d'intérêt.

1. Chercheur scientifique	16%		6. Acteur	10%
2. Pilote	14%		7. Chef de publicité	7%
3. Médecin	14%		8. Professeur d'université	5%
4. Journaliste	14%		9. Avocat	5%
5. Chef d'entreprise	11%		10. Banquier	4%

2 Choix professionnels

Faites une liste des cinq professions qui sont les plus intéressantes pour vous et des cinq professions qui sont les moins intéressantes. Comparez votre liste avec celle de votre partenaire et expliquez votre choix.

Ma Liste
☺ ☹
1.
2.
3.
4.
5.

3 Après votre diplôme

Vous avez décidé de continuer vos études, mais votre partenaire a décidé de chercher du travail (ou vice versa). Expliquez votre décision respective en donnant des arguments. Considérez, par exemple, les aspects suivants . . .

- gagner sa vie
- être indépendant(e)
- se perfectionner en . . . *(to increase one's skills in)*
- avoir plus d'options plus tard

Teaching Strategy: Warm-Up

Have each student choose a job and describe where it is done (**au bureau, à l'école** etc.). From that information; the class will try to identify the job itself. If the class is unable to guess from the place of work or the name of the company, students should then give a sentence explaining the job, what is worn to work, or some other hint that will help the class identify the job. Continue until someone guesses it correctly. Keep a list and compare with the survey from p. 387.

Supplementary vocabulary

les métiers d'avenir
l'analyste-programmeur *systems analyst*
le concepteur de circuit intégré *integrated circuit designer*
le spécialiste de maintenance informatique *computer maintenance expert*
le cogniticien *engineer specialized in artificial intelligence*
le logisticien *logistics specialist (within a business)*
le juriste d'entreprise *corporate lawyer*
l'analyste de crédit *credit analyst*
ALSO:
un(e) architecte
un(e) décorateur (-trice)
un(e) commerçant(e) *shopkeeper*
un(e) boulanger(-ère) *baker*
un(e) pâtissier(-ère) *pastry cook*
un chef, un(e) cuisinier(-ère) *cook*
un maçon *mason*
un menuisier *cabinet maker*
un plombier *plumber*
un(e) mécanicien(-ienne)
un(e) réparateur(-trice) *repairman*
un(e) ouvrier(-ère) qualifié(e)
un(e) ouvrier(-ère) spécialisé(e)
un contremaître *foreman*
un(e) ouvrier(-ère) agricole *farm worker*

LANGUE ET COMMUNICATION

TEACHING RESOURCES

Student Activities Manual, pp. 95–98, 167

Audio Program, CD 11, Tracks 5–6

HM ClassPrep CD, Audioscript, Unit 10

■ Expansion

The infinitive is also used after:

au lieu de *instead of*
Étudier **au lieu de** t'amuser.

à condition de *on condition that*
Je gagnerai ma vie **à condition de** trouver un job.

afin de *in order to*
Pauline travaille **afin de** s'acheter une voiture.

Note culturelle

Molière popularized this saying of Socrates in *L'Avare:*
«Suivant le dire d'un ancien, il faut manger pour vivre, et non pas vivre pour manger.»

A. La construction préposition + infinitif

Note the use of the infinitive in the following sentences.

Je voudrais aller à l'université **pour me spécialiser** en informatique.	*I would like to go to college **(in order) to major** in computer science.*
Tu ne réussiras pas à ton examen **sans étudier.**	*You will not pass your exam **without studying.***
Donne-moi ton adresse **avant de partir** en vacances.	*Give me your address **before leaving** on vacation.*

In French, the INFINITIVE is used after prepositions such as
pour *(in order to)*
avant de *(before)*
sans *(without)*

Il faut manger pour vivre, et non pas vivre pour manger.

1 À l'université

Chacun a ses raisons pour aller à l'université. Expliquez les raisons des étudiants suivants.

▶ Christine étudie la physique.
Christine va à l'université pour étudier la physique.

1. Nous étudions la biologie.
2. Vous apprenez la comptabilité.
3. Je fais des études de droit.
4. Jean-Paul se spécialise en chimie.
5. Tu continues tes études de musique.
6. Hélène et Alice retrouvent leurs copains de lycée.
7. Marc est avec sa copine.
8. Philippe et Antoine jouent dans l'équipe de football.

2 Ne t'en fais pas! *(Don't worry!)*

Dites à votre partenaire ce qu'il/elle doit faire. Il/elle va suivre vos conseils.

▶ **—sortir / prendre la clé**
—Ne sors pas sans prendre la clé!
—Ne t'en fais pas! Je prendrai la clé avant de sortir.

1. aller chez tes copains / téléphoner
2. organiser une boum / demander la permission à tes p
3. répondre à cette question / réfléchir *(think)*
4. quitter le restaurant / payer l'addition
5. prendre la voiture / faire le plein d'essence
6. partir en vacances / réserver une chambre d'hôtel
7. aller à l'entrevue / préparer ton curriculum vitae

3 Conseils

Votre partenaire va choisir un objectif de la liste ou un objectif de son choix. Expliquez-lui ce qu'il faut faire pour atteindre *(to reach)* cet objectif.

OBJECTIFS

- être interprète
- être avocat
- être ingénieur
- gagner de l'argent
- aller à l'université
- être millionnaire
- devenir professeur
- devenir vétérinaire
- ??

▶ **Pour être ingénieur, il faut faire des études d'ingénieur (être bon en maths, aller dans une univers spécialisée, . . .)**

Teaching Strategy

Have every student write a sentence using each of the prepositions from p. 388. These sentences should be about themselves or about friends or family. Have students choose one of their sentences to put on the board. Have three columns on the board: one for **sans**, one for **avant de**, and one for **pour**. Students should write their sentences in the proper column.

B. L'infinitif passé

The verbs in heavy print are in the PAST INFINITIVE. Note the forms of the past infinitive in the following sentences.

Je suis content d'**avoir trouvé** un emploi.	*I am happy to* ***have found*** *a job.*
Nous ne regrettons pas d'**être allés** à l'université.	*We do not regret* ***to have gone*** *(having gone) to college.*
Alice a étudié après **s'être reposée.**	*Alice studied after* ***having rested.***

FORMS

The PAST INFINITIVE is formed as follows:

avoir or **être** + PAST PARTICIPLE

➡ When the past infinitive is a reflexive verb, the reflexive pronoun represents the same person as the subject of the sentence.

Je ne me souviens pas de **m**'être promené dans ce parc.

USES

The PAST INFINITIVE is used instead of the present infinitive to describe an action that takes place before the action of the main verb. It is always used after **après.**

Qu'est-ce que tu vas faire **après avoir fini** tes études?	*What are you going to do* ***after having finished (after finishing)*** *your studies?*

4 Leurs sentiments

Expliquez les sentiments des personnes suivantes en fonction de ce qu'elles ont fait.

▶ Patrick / être content / trouver un bon job

Patrick est content d'avoir trouvé un bon job.

1. Alice / être heureuse / aller au Canada l'été dernier
2. Thomas / être enchanté / faire la connaissance de ta cousine
3. nous / avoir peur / rater l'examen
4. Bruno / être furieux / se tromper dans le problème de maths
5. vous / s'excuser / arriver en retard au rendez-vous
6. Madame Simon / être fière / créer sa propre *(own)* entreprise.

5 Hier

Demandez à votre partenaire à quelle heure il/elle a fait les choses suivantes hier et ce qu'il/elle a fait après.

▶ te coucher

—À quelle heure est-ce que tu t'es couché?
—À dix heures et demie.
—Et qu'est-ce que tu as fait après t'être couché?
—J'ai lu un livre.
(Je me suis endormi.
J'ai regardé la télé...)

1. te lever
2. prendre le petit déjeuner
3. arriver à l'école
4. déjeuner
5. rentrer chez toi
6. dîner
7. finir tes devoirs

■ Notes linguistiques

■ FORMS

The rules of agreement of the past participle apply to the past infinitive. Note the following examples of agreement of the past infinitive:

(with subject)

Alice s'excuse d'être **arrivée** en retard.

(with preceding direct object)

Je ne me souviens pas de **les** avoir **rencontrés**.

(with reflexive pronoun when it is a direct object)

Nous regrettons de **nous** être **disputés.**

■ USES

In the negative, **pas** may come before the auxiliary or between the auxiliary and the past participle.

Je regrette de ne **pas** avoir appris l'espagnol.

Je regrette de n'avoir **pas** appris l'espagnol.

ALSO:

The past infinitive in French may correspond in English to a past infinitive *(to have done)* or a verb form ending in *-ing (having done).*

C. Le participe présent

FORMS

Note the forms of the PRESENT PARTICIPLE in the following sentences.

Parlant français et anglais, je voudrais travailler pour une firme internationale. — ***Speaking** French and English, I would like to work for an international co*

J'ai rencontré mes copains en **allant** au cinéma. — *I met my friends while **going** to the movies.*

The PRESENT PARTICIPLE always ends in **-ant.** It is formed as follows:

STEM	+	ENDING
nous-form of the present	+	**-ant**

parler:	nous **parl**ons	→ **parlant**	aller:	nous **all**ons	→ **allant**
finir:	nous **finiss**ons	→ **finissant**	faire	nous **fais**ons	→ **faisant**
attendre:	nous **attend**ons	→ **attendant**	sortir:	nous **sort**ons	→ **sortant**
acheter	nous **achet**ons	→ **achetant**	voir:	nous **voy**ons	→ **voyant**
commencer:	nous **commenç**ons	→ **commençant**	lire:	nous **lis**ons	→ **lisant**
manger:	nous **mange**ons	→ **mangeant**	prendre:	nous **pren**ons	→ **prenant**

➡ There are three irregular present participles:
être → **étant** avoir → **ayant** savoir → **sachant**

➡ With reflexive verbs, the reflexive pronoun represents the same person as the subject.
En **me** promenant, **j'**ai rencontré mon professeur d'histoire.

USES

The construction **en** + PRESENT PARTICIPLE is used to express:

- SIMULTANEOUS ACTION *(while, on, upon* doing something)
  Éric écoute la radio **en lavant** sa voiture. — *Éric is listening to the radio **while washing** his car.*
- CAUSE AND EFFECT *(by* doing something)
  Il gagne de l'argent **en lavant** des voitures. — *He earns money **by washing** cars.*

C'est en forgeant qu'on devient forgeron.

6 Études de langues

Pour chaque personne, choisissez une langue et dites comment cette personne apprend cette langue.

moi	l'espagnol
vous	le français
mon copain	l'anglais
Alice et Catherine	

- écouter Radio-France
- étudier à l'Alliance Française
- regarder des westerns à la télé
- écouter des chansons mexicaines
- passer les vacances en Argentine
- surfer sur l'Internet
- sortir avec des amis québécois
- lire des romans d'Hemingway

▶ **Mon copain apprend l'espagnol en écoutant des chansons mexicaines (en passant ses vacances en Argentine).**

TEACHING RESOURCES

Student Activities Manual, pp. 88–89, 167
Audio Program, CD 11, Track 7
HM ClassPrep CD, Audioscript, Unit 10

Teaching Strategy: Additional Practice

You may ask for students to provide the present participles of other irregular verbs:

boire	**buvant**
conduire	**conduisant**
connaître	**connaissant**
croire	**croyant**
devoir	**devant**
dire	**disant**
écrire	**écrivant**
peindre	**peignant**
pouvoir	**pouvant**
recevoir	**recevant**
rire	**riant**
venir	**venant**
vouloir	**voulant**

Notes linguistiques

- La forme **en + participe présent** forme ce que l'on appelle **le gérondif.** En général, le gérondif se rapporte au sujet de la phrase et décrit les circonstances de l'action.
- Expansion:
  forger *to forge*
  le forgeron *blacksmith*
  la forge *forge*
  le fer forgé *wrought iron*

Teaching Notes: Activity 6

- Quelques titres d'Hemingway en français: *Le Soleil se lève aussi; Pour qui sonne le glas; L'Adieu aux armes; Le Vieil Homme et la mer.*
- For more information on **Astérix,** see pp. 100–101.

Teaching Strategy

Give students sentences using **pendant que...** to transform by eliminating **pendant que...** and using the present participle. **Je regarde la télévision pendant que je parle avec ma soeur. = Je regarde la télé en parlant avec ma soeur.**

Next, give students two sentences which explain how one arrives at a goal. Have them rewrite the sentences to explain the process in one logical sentence using the present participle: **Je suis devenu(e) prof de français. J'ai étudié beaucoup. C'est en étudiant beaucoup que je suis devenu(e) prof de français.**

7 C'est simple!

Cet été Céline a travaillé pour gagner de l'argent. Marc lui pose des questions sur son job. Céline lui répond. Avec votre partenaire, jouez les deux rôles.

▶ gagner de l'argent cet été
travailler dans un restaurant

— **Comment as-tu gagné de l'argent cet été?**
— **C'est simple! J'ai gagné de l'argent en travaillant dans un restaurant.**

1. trouver ce job
   lire les annonces
2. contacter le restaurant
   téléphoner à la propriétaire *(owner)*
3. réussir à l'entrevue
   avoir une bonne attitude
4. apprendre ton travail
   regarder les autres employés
5. recevoir tes pourboires *(tips)*
   être attentive et polie avec les clients

8 Zut alors!

Les personnes suivantes ont eu des problèmes. Expliquez quand ou comment c'est arrivé.

▶ Monsieur Lasalle s'est coupé. (Il se rasait.)
Monsieur Lasalle s'est coupé en se rasant.

1. Stéphanie s'est blessée. (Elle faisait de l'alpinisme.)
2. Je suis tombé. (Je descendais les escaliers.)
3. Tu t'es cassé une dent. (Tu mangeais du homard [*lobster*].)
4. Vincent a perdu son portefeuille. (Il allait au cinéma.)
5. Nous nous sommes perdus. (Nous nous promenions à la montagne.)
6. Vous avez eu un accident. (Vous faisiez du parapente.)

9 Comment?

Dites comment les personnes suivantes font certaines choses.

▶ Philippe célèbre son anniversaire. Il organise une boum.
Philippe célèbre son anniversaire en organisant une boum.

1. Catherine reste en forme. Elle nage tous les jours.
2. Isabelle se repose. Elle écoute de la musique classique.
3. Jérôme amuse ses amis. Il imite Jim Carrey.
4. Alice gagne de l'argent. Elle fait du baby-sitting.
5. Thomas aide ses parents. Il passe l'aspirateur.
6. Stéphanie s'informe. Elle lit des magazines.
7. Carole reste en contact avec ses amis. Elle leur écrit pour leur anniversaire.
8. Marc soigne sa grippe. Il boit du thé chaud.
9. Édouard contribue à la protection de l'environnement. Il ramasse *(picks up)* les vieux papiers.
10. Hélène fait des bonnes actions *(deeds)*. Elle aide une famille d'immigrés.

10 Et vous?

Avec votre partenaire, dites comment vous faites les mêmes choses que celles de l'activité 9.

▶ **Moi, je célèbre mon anniversaire en faisant du bowling avec mes copains.**

Teaching Strategy: Variation

The students playing the role of Céline may use object pronouns in their answers:
J'en ai gagné en travaillant dans un restaurant.

1. Je l'ai trouvé ...
2. Je l'ai contacté ...
3. J'y ai réussi ...
4. Je l'ai appris ...
5. Je les ai reçus ...

INFO MAGAZINE

Theme: Job interviews

Teaching Strategy
With your partner, role-play two interviews:

- one goes very well, the candidate answers all questions and is clearly qualified and enthusiastic.
- one goes badly when the candidate makes many mistakes, saying the wrong things, asking the wrong questions.

Rôles: le/la candidat(e), l'interviewer

■ Irregular Verb
(see Appendix C)
interrompre (*see* **rompre**)

COMMENT SE PRÉSENTER À UNE ENTREVU

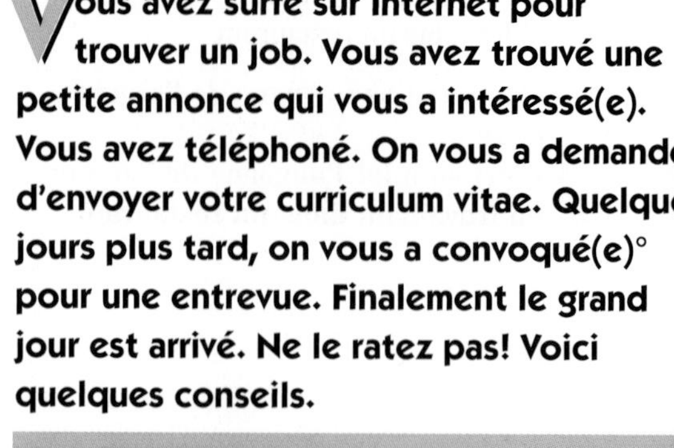

Vous avez surfé sur Internet pour trouver un job. Vous avez trouvé une petite annonce qui vous a intéressé(e). Vous avez téléphoné. On vous a demand d'envoyer votre curriculum vitae. Quelqu jours plus tard, on vous a convoqué(e)° pour une entrevue. Finalement le grand jour est arrivé. Ne le ratez pas! Voici quelques conseils.

Pour l'entrevue

◆ **Habillez-vous correctement.**

La présentation a beaucoup d'importance. Soignez-la!° Pour les jeunes gens, mettez un costume et une cravate. Pour les jeunes filles, mettez un tailleur. Si vous avez le temps, passez chez le coiffeur quelques jours avant l'entrevue. Laissez vos lunettes de soleil chez vous, même s'il fait beau. Évitez les couleurs criardes° et les parfums excessifs. Et pas de coiffure extravagante.

◆ **Arrivez à l'heure ou même un peu avant.**

Soyez poli avec la réceptionniste. Attendez patiemment votre tour, même si la personne avec qui vous avez rendez-vous est en retard.

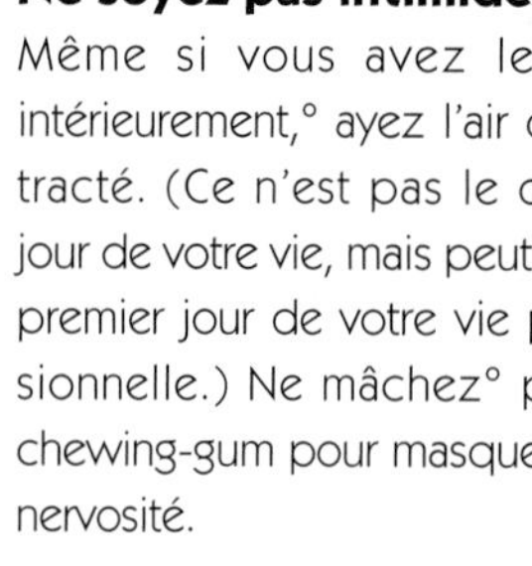

◆ **Ne soyez pas intimidé.**
Même si vous avez le trac° intérieurement,° ayez l'air décontracté. (Ce n'est pas le dernier jour de votre vie, mais peut-être le premier jour de votre vie professionnelle.) Ne mâchez° pas de chewing-gum pour masquer votre nervosité.

Pendant l'entrevue

◆ **Répondez clairement et distinctement au questions de l'interviewer.**
Mettez en valeur° vos talents et vos qualifications, mais sans les exagérer. Surtout, ne vous inventez pas un curriculum vitae extraordinaire. (À votre âge, il est normal que votre expérience professionnelle soit limitée.)

◆ **Soyez attentif et respectueux.**

Ayez l'air intéressé par ce qu'on vous dit. N'interrompez pas l'interviewer quand il vous parle. Posez des questions, mais seulement au bon° moment. À l'occasion, prenez des notes. (Pour cela, n'oubliez pas d'apporter un carnet et un stylo à l'entrevue. Cela fera bonne impression.) Ne regardez jamais votre montre pendant l'entrevue.

◆ **Ne soyez pas trop personnel**
Parlez de votre vie personnel seulement si cela a un rapport° avec vo qualifications pour le job. Ne soyez p familier avec votre interviewer. (P exemple, n'essayez pas de savoir q sont les personnes sur les photos q peuvent être sur son bureau!)

convoqué(e) *called* **Soignez-la!** *pay careful attention to it* **criardes** *loud* **avez le trac** *are scared, nervous* **intérieurement** *inside* **mâchez** *chew* **mettez en valeur** *emphasize* **interrompez / interrompre** *to interrupt* **bon** *right* **rapport** *connection*

- **Ne parlez jamais de salaire.**
  Si vous êtes accepté pour le job, il sera temps d'en discuter à ce moment-là.

Après l'entrevue

- **Soyez persévérant sans être trop insistant.**
  Si possible, écrivez une lettre assez courte dans laquelle vous remerciez l'interviewer de l'entretien qu'il vous a donné. Cela l'aidera à se souvenir de vous. Ne téléphonez pas tous les jours à la compagnie pour connaître les résultats de l'entrevue. En fait, attendez au moins 15 jours avant de vous informer sur votre sort.°

- **Restez optimiste.**
  Même en cas de réponse négative, vous avez acquis° l'expérience de l'entrevue. Cela vous sera utile pour la prochaine fois.

et vous?

Avec votre partenaire, déterminez quels sont les trois (3) conseils les plus utiles et dites pourquoi.

EXPRESSION ÉCRITE

Décrivez une entrevue personnelle que vous avez eue. Mentionnez, par exemple:

- comment vous étiez habillé(e)
- quand vous êtes arrivé(e) à l'entrevue
- comment vous vous sentiez
- qui était l'interviewer
- quelles questions il/elle vous a posées
- comment vous avez répondu
- quels problèmes vous avez eus pendant l'entrevue
- qu'est-ce que vous avez fait après l'entrevue
- quel a été le résultat de cette entrevue

CURRICULUM VITAE

et vous?

Vous voulez travailler pour une compagnie française. Préparez votre propre curriculum vitae sur le modèle indiqué.

CURRICULUM VITAE

Karine PERRAUDIN
125, rue de l'Ermitage
37100 Tours
tél. 02-47-31-22-51
23 ans

ÉTUDES	École Supérieur de Commerce de Tours Bac S, mention assez bien
LANGUES	Anglais (courant°) Allemand Notions d'espagnol
EXPÉRIENCES	été 2006 Stage d'un mois à CANAL + (service marketing) été 2005 Réceptionniste dans un hôtel 3 étoiles à Hambourg été 2004 Animatrice dans une colonie de vacances pour enfants handicapés
POSTE SOUHAITÉ	Emploi dans un service de publicité ou de marketing. Préférence pour compagnie internationale.
SPORTS ET LOISIRS	Tennis, natation, escalade, musique (violon), photo
RÉFÉRENCES	Sur demande.°

sort *fate*
acquis / acquérir* *to acquire*
courant *fluent*
sur demande *on request*

Notes culturelles

- **Le C.V.** est l'abréviation usuelle de **curriculum vitae. Curriculum vitae** est une expression invariable d'origine latine signifiant littéralement "la course de la vie."
- Il est d'usage en France d'inclure son âge et son état civil **(marié[e], célibataire, divorcé[e] ou veuf/veuve)** sur son C.V. De plus, beaucoup de compagnies exigent une lettre d'accompagnement écrite à la main de manière à pouvoir en faire **l'analyse graphologique** avant de décider d'interviewer le candidat ou non.

Irregular Verb

(see Appendix C)
acquérir

Teaching Strategy

Divide the two pages of reading into three parts: **Pour l'entrevue/Pendant l'entrevue/Après l'entrevue.** Divide the class into groups and give each group one of the sections. Have them read each section carefully, prepare an explanation/presentation about it and write three questions about the information to give to the class as a mini-quiz.

LE FRANÇAIS PRATIQUE

TEACHING RESOURCES

Student Activities Manual, pp. 168–171

Audio Program, CD 12, Tracks 1–5

HM ClassPrep CD Audioscript, Unit 10

Video/DVD Program, Unit 10

LE FRANÇAIS PRATIQUE — *La vie professionnelle*

— Où voudrais-tu travailler?

Je voudrais travailler **dans/pour une banque.**

un bureau	**une compagnie internationale**
une usine *factory*	**un cabinet** *(office)* **d'avocat**
une agence de voyages	**un laboratoire de recherches**

— **Dans quelle branche d'activité** voudrais-tu travailler? / **faire carrière?**

J'aimerais travailler dans **la finance**.

le commerce *trade*	**l'informatique**
l'industrie	**la recherche** *(research)* **scientifique**
la communication	**la fonction publique** *civil service*
la publicité *advertising*	**les relations publiques**
les assurances *insurance*	**l'immobilier** *real estate*
les affaires *business*	**l'électronique**

— **Pour quel genre d'entreprise** voudrais-tu travailler?

Je voudrais travailler **pour une** **petite** / **grande** **entreprise.**

une compagnie	**moyenne** *average size*
une firme	**multinationale**
une société	

Je voudrais travailler **à mon compte** *(for myself)*. / **créer ma propre** *(own)* **entreprise**.

— **Qu'est-ce que tu recherches** / **Qu'est-ce qui t'intéresse** / **Qu'est-ce qui compte le plus** dans ce travail?

Je recherche **un bon salaire.**

une bonne ambiance *atmosphere*
de bonnes conditions de travail
la possibilité de promotion
des responsabilités importantes
des avantages sociaux *fringe benefits*

rechercher *to look for, search*

Teaching Suggestion: Video/DVD Program

In the Unit 10 *Vidéo-drame: Guillaume trouve un job,* students will learn new vocabulary dealing with employment. As you play the video, ask students to write down some of the new vocabulary they hear. Then, encourage them to discuss what kind of job they would like to have, what qualifications they would need, etc.

1 Un sondage

Conduisez un sondage dans la classe pour déterminer . . .

- le lieu de travail préféré
- le type d'entreprise préféré
- la branche d'activité préférée
- l'aspect le plus important d'un travail

2 Choix professionnel

Votre partenaire et vous, vous allez choisir une profession qui vous intéresse. (Chacun va choisir une profession différente.) Comparez les avantages de chaque profession sur la base des éléments suivants.

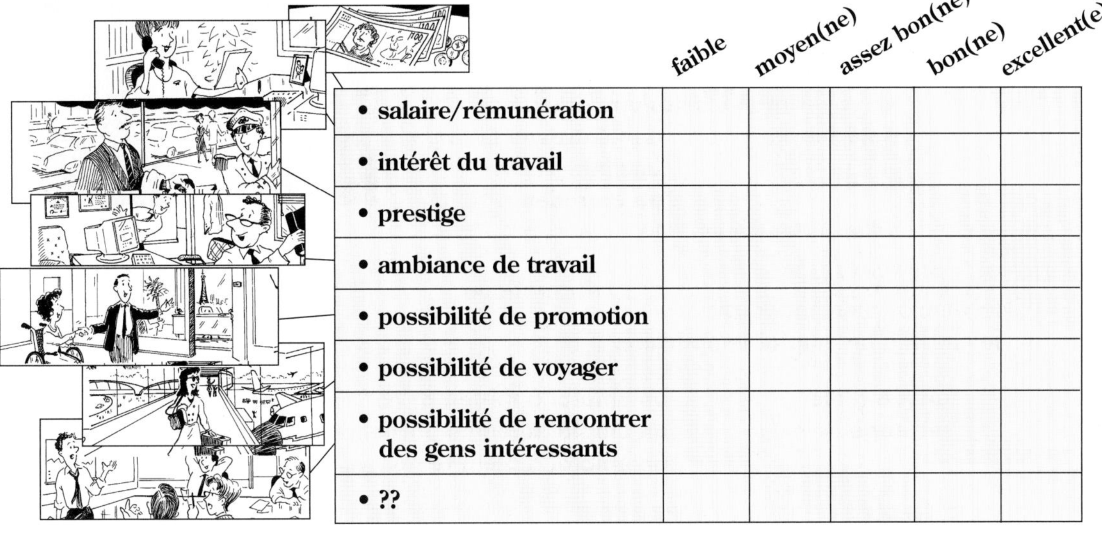

	faible	moyen(ne)	assez bon(ne)	bon(ne)	excellent(e)
• salaire/rémunération					
• intérêt du travail					
• prestige					
• ambiance de travail					
• possibilité de promotion					
• possibilité de voyager					
• possibilité de rencontrer des gens intéressants					
• ??					

3 La meilleure solution

Préféreriez-vous travailler pour une compagnie ou créer votre propre entreprise? Chaque solution a ses avantages, mais aussi ses désavantages. Avec votre partenaire, évaluez ces avantages et ces désavantages.

- Quelle est la meilleure solution pour vous?
- Quelle est la meilleure solution pour votre partenaire?

AVANTAGES		
peu important	important	très important

DÉSAVANTAGES		

Créer sa propre entreprise

- Satisfaction personnelle
- Indépendance
- Heures flexibles
- Possibilité de devenir riche
- ??

- Possibilité d'échec *(failure)*
- Risques financiers
- Travail très dur
- Trop de responsabilités
- ??

Travailler pour une compagnie

- Horaires réguliers
- Salaire régulier
- Avantages sociaux
- Responsabilités limitées
- ??

- Salaire limité
- Hiérarchie pesante *(heavy)*
- Travail monotone
- Pas assez de responsabilités
- ??

Note culturelle

The minimum wage was created in France in 1950. Since July 2005, the minimum hourly wage is 8,03€ (about). The minimum wage is regularly increased.

Note linguistique

Les nouvelles technologies, telles que les ordinateurs personnels et les télécopieurs, permettent à un certain nombre de personnes de travailler chez elles. C'est ce que l'on appelle en France **"le télétravail" (travail à distance).**

Supplementary vocabulary

la flexibilité *flexibility*
les heures supplémentaires *overtime*
le pointage *clocking in/out*
le stress
la vocation *vocation*
le rendement *output, efficiency*
le déplacement business *travel*
un organisme
une organisation
une affaire *business*
la sécurité de l'emploi *job security*

Note linguistique

Note that the verb "to commute" has no direct translation in French.

to commute = **faire la navette (pour se rendre au travail tous les jours)**

commuter = **personne qui fait la navette (pour se rendre au travail tous les jours)**

Attention: the French verb **commuter** means *to switch over; to commute (as in a penalty)*

LE FRANÇAIS

PRATIQUE

À la recherche d'un emploi

■ **Note linguistique**

Entrevue/interview/entretien: These three expressions are synonymous.

Supplementary vocabulary

mettre une annonce
lire les offres d'emploi
j'ai travaillé dans ...
un restaurant
un fast-food

LE FRANÇAIS PRATIQUE

À la recherche d'un emploi

POUR TROUVER DU TRAVAIL

— Qu'est-ce que tu vas faire pour trouver du travail?

Je vais
- **lire les annonces** *classified ads.*
- **répondre à l'annonce.**
- **téléphoner au chef du personnel.**
- **prendre rendez-vous** *to make an appointment.*
- **envoyer mon curriculum vitae** *résumé.*
- **solliciter** *to ask for* | **une entrevue** *interview.* / **une interview.** / **un entretien.**
- **aller à l'entretien.**

PENDANT L'INTERVIEW

— Quel emploi cherchez-vous?

Je cherche **un emploi temporaire.**

un job d'été	**un emploi à mi-temps** *half time*
un stage *internship*	**un emploi à temps partiel** *part time*
	un emploi à plein temps *full time*

— Avez-vous déjà travaillé?

Oui, j'ai travaillé dans
- un hôpital.
- une boutique.
- un supermarché.

Non, je n'ai **pas d'expérience professionnelle.**

— Qu'est-ce que vous savez faire?

Je sais **parler anglais.**

parler français, espagnol, chinois . . .
conduire une voiture
utiliser / **me servir d'** | **un ordinateur**
classer des documents

conduire *to drive*
se servir de *to use*
classer *to file*

— Quelles sont vos qualifications personnelles?

J'ai **l'esprit d'initiative.**

de l'ambition
le sens des contacts humains
le goût (*liking*) **des responsabilités**
une bonne formation (*education*) **générale**
des connaissances (*knowledge*) **techniques**

NOTES CULTURELLES

- One way to find work in France is to use the services of the **ANPE (Agence Nationale Pour l'Emploi)**. This agency, created in 1967, helps French citizens find jobs, and provides training workshops as well as career counseling.

— Quels documents avez-vous apportés?
J'ai **mon curriculum vitae**.

des lettres de recommandation
mes références
mes diplômes

— Merci! **Vous faites l'affaire!** *(You are qualified.)*
Nous allons vous | **offrir** un emploi.
| **embaucher.**

Je suis désolé(e), mais **vous ne faites pas l'affaire**.

offrir *to offer*
embaucher *to hire*

Conversations libres

Avec votre partenaire, choisissez l'un des sujets suivants. Composez et jouez le dialogue correspondant à ce sujet. Votre partenaire va jouer l'autre personne.

1 **Jobs d'été**

Votre camarade et vous, vous habitez en France. Discutez de ce que vous allez faire pour trouver un job cet été.
Rôles: deux étudiants français.

2 **Télémarketing**

Dans le journal, vous avez lu une annonce dans laquelle une firme française de produits cosmétiques cherche des étudiants américains pour vendre ses produits par téléphone. Téléphonez à cette firme pour expliquer vos qualifications.
Rôles: un(e) étudiant(e) américain(e) / le représentant de la firme

3 **Agence de voyages**

Une agence de voyages française cherche un(e) assistant(e). Vous avez obtenu une entrevue avec le chef du personnel. C'est le jour de l'entrevue.
Rôles: un(e) candidat(e) / le chef du personnel

4 **Compagnie internationale**

Vous venez d'obtenir votre diplôme universitaire avec une spécialité en littérature française. Vous répondez à l'annonce d'une compagnie internationale qui recrute des étudiants pour son département de marketing. Vous n'avez pas fait d'études de marketing. Expliquez à l'interviewer pourquoi vous voulez le job et pourquoi vous êtes tout de même *(nevertheless)* qualifié(e).
Rôles: un(e) candidat(e) / l'interviewer

5 **Office de Tourisme**

Vous habitez en France. L'Office de Tourisme de votre ville recrute des étudiants parlant anglais pour développer le tourisme dans la région. Vous avez une entrevue avec la directrice de l'Office du Tourisme.
Rôles: un(e) candidat(e) / la directrice

Supplementary vocabulary

renvoyer *to fire, let go*
mettre à la porte *to fire*
licencier *to dismiss/lay off*
le (la) demandeur(-euse) d'emploi *job seeker*
l'intérimaire *(f. & m.)* *temp (worker)*
les compétences *(f.)* *qualifications*
le dynamisme *dynamism*
le traitement de texte *word processing*
taper *to type*

Note culturelle

- Une façon moderne de trouver un job d'été est de consulter les offres d'emploi sur **Internet**, à la page "jobs on line." Si on n'a pas accès à l'Internet chez soi, on peut aller dans **un cyber-café.**
- Pour répondre à une offre d'emploi, il faut accompagner son C.V. d'une **lettre de motivation.**

TEACHING RESOURCES

Student Activities Manual, pp. 101–104, 172

Audio Program CD 12, Tracks 6-7

HM ClassPrep CD Audioscript, Unit 10

■ **Notes linguistiques**

- The subjunctive is also used after:
  afin que *in order that*
  bien que *although*
  quoi que *although*
  pourvu que *provided that*
- The pleonastic (or redundant) **ne** is optional after **avant que** and **sans que.** It is more frequently used with **à moins que.**
  Je finirai mon travail **avant que** vous **ne** veniez.
  Nous sortirons **à moins qu'**il **ne** fasse mauvais.
- The infinitive is used under the same conditions after:
  à moins de
  à condition de
  afin de

A. La construction conjonction + subjonctif

Note the use of the subjunctive in the following sentences.

Je te prête le journal **pour que tu lises** les petites annonces.	*I am lending you the paper* ***so that you read*** *the ads.*
Téléphone au chef du personnel **avant qu'il parte** en vacances.	*Call the head of personnel* ***before he leaves*** *on vacation.*
Nous vous engagerons **à condition que vous ayez** de bonnes recommandations.	*We will hire you* ***provided that you have*** *good recommendations.*

The SUBJUNCTIVE is used after certain conjunctions which express:

- PURPOSE or INTENT

pour que	*so that*	Le professeur explique **pour que** vous **compreniez**.

- CONDITION or RESTRICTION

à condition que	*provided, on condition that*	Nous ferons une promenade à vélo **à condition qu'**il **fasse** beau.
à moins que	*unless*	J'irai à la plage **à moins qu'**il **fasse** mauvais.
sans que	*without*	Philippe est parti **sans que** tu lui **dises** au revoir.

- TIME LIMITATION

avant que	*before*	Je vous téléphonerai **avant que** vous **partiez.**
jusqu'à ce que	*until*	Nous attendrons **jusqu'à ce que** vous **veniez**.

➡ The INFINITIVE is used after **avant de, pour,** and **sans** when the subject of the main clause and the dependent clause are the same.

Victor est venu . . .	Victor est venu . . .
pour parler de ses projets.	**pour que vous parliez** de vos projets.
avant d'aller en France.	**avant que vous alliez** en vacances.
sans avoir rendez-vous.	**sans que vous ayez** rendez-vous.

➡ Remember that the INDICATIVE is used after conjunctions, such as **parce que, pendant que, depuis que, lorsque.**

Je cherche du travail **parce que** j'**ai** besoin d'argent.

1 Prêts

Vous êtes une personne généreuse qui prête ce qu'elle a. Choisissez une chose et dites à qui vous allez la prêter et pourquoi.

▶ **Je vais prêter dix dollars à mon cousin Christophe (à ma soeur Michelle) pour qu'il/elle aille au cinéma.**

QUOI?	POURQUOI?
mon vélo	s'acheter un livre
mon gant de baseball	faire un tour à la campagne
ma radiocassette	aller au ciné
ma mini-chaîne	prendre des photos
dix dollars	organiser une boum
vingt dollars	écouter ce nouveau CD
??	??

2 Il y a toujours une raison

Expliquez pourquoi les personnes suivantes font certaines choses pour d'autres personnes.

▶ Madame Bertrand / donner de l'argent à sa nièce / s'acheter une mini-chaîne
Madame Bertrand donne de l'argent à sa nièce pour qu'elle s'achète une mini-chaîne.

1. Thomas / prêter son vélo à son copain / faire une promenade à la campagne
2. Monsieur Thibault / payer les études à sa fille / être avocate
3. Madame Rémi / envoyer un chèque à son fils / payer sa scolarité *(tuition)*
4. le professeur / écrire des lettres de recommandation aux élèves / trouver du travail
5. Marc / inviter sa copine à dîner / faire la connaissance de ses parents
6. Madame Lombard / envoyer ses enfants en Angleterre / apprendre l'anglais

3 Dépêchez-vous!

Dites à votre partenaire de se dépêcher de faire certaines choses.

▶ aller à la bibliothèque (elle va fermer)

Va à la bibliothèque avant qu'elle ferme.

1. téléphoner à ta copine (elle va sortir)
2. ranger ta chambre (tes copains vont venir)
3. finir tes devoirs (on va aller au ciné)
4. promener le chien (il va faire noir)
5. acheter cette mini-chaîne (les prix vont augmenter)
6. chercher un job (les vacances vont commencer)
7. demander des lettres de recommandation (tes profs vont partir en vacances)
8. répondre à cette annonce (la compagnie va embaucher quelqu'un d'autre)

4 Conditions

François demande à sa mère s'il peut faire certaines choses. Sa mère accepte mais à certaines conditions. Avec votre partenaire, jouez les deux rôles.

▶ aller à la boum / rentrer avant minuit

FRANÇOIS: **Dis, est-ce que je peux aller à la soirée?**

SA MÈRE: **Je veux bien, mais à condition que tu rentres avant minuit.**

FRANÇOIS: **Bon, d'accord! Je rentrerai avant minuit.**

1. regarder mon nouveau DVD / finir tes devoirs
2. écouter mes CD / ne pas faire de bruit
3. inviter un copain à dîner / mettre la table
4. organiser un pique-nique / faire les courses
5. prendre la voiture / être prudent
6. voyager cet été / réussir à tes examens

5 Négociation

Votre partenaire va vous demander de faire une des choses suivantes pour lui/elle. Négociez un échange.

- prêter ton VTT
- prêter ton portable
- prêter dix dollars
- inviter au café
- inviter à ta boum
- présenter à tes copains
- aider avec le devoir
- aider à ranger ma chambre

▶ **— Dis, est-ce que tu peux me prêter ton VTT?**
— D'accord, mais à condition que tu me prêtes ton appareil-photo (que tu m'aides avec le problème de maths, . . .)

6 Une promenade à vélo

Vous êtes en Touraine avec votre partenaire. Vous organisez une promenade à vélo. Expliquez vos projets à votre partenaire.

▶ Nous ferons une promenade samedi.
(à condition que / il fait beau)
Nous ferons une promenade samedi à condition qu'il fasse beau.

1. Le matin, nous visiterons le château d'Amboise.
(à moins que / il est fermé)
2. Je te prêterai mon appareil-photo.
(pour que / tu prends des photos)
3. Après, nous ferons un pique-nique.
(à moins que / nous trouvons une petite auberge sympathique)
4. Nous irons dans cette auberge.
(à condition que / elle a des spécialités régionales)
5. Ensuite nous continuerons notre promenade.
(jusqu'à ce que / nous sommes fatigués)
6. Nous rentrerons.
(avant que / il fait nuit)

le château d'Amboise

■ Teaching Note
For more information on the castle of **Amboise** see p. 147.

7 Double effet

En général, nos actions nous concernent nous-mêmes. Elles peuvent aussi concerner d'autres personnes. Exprimez cela d'après le modèle.

▶ J'achète le journal pour lire les petites annonces. (tu)
J'achète le journal pour que tu lises les petites annonces.

1. Madame Gustave passe un an au Brésil pour apprendre le portugais. (ses enfants)
2. Monsieur Guyon commande un taxi pour être à l'heure au rendez-vous. (son patron)
3. Nous allons dans ce magasin pour regarder les ordinateurs. (vous)
4. Je rendrai visite à mes cousins avant de partir en vacances. (ils)
5. Nous te téléphonerons avant d'aller en France. (tu)
6. Monsieur Durand ne partira pas sans avoir son passeport. (sa femme)
7. Nous ne quitterons pas Paris sans voir Notre Dame. (nos enfants)
8. Monsieur Thomas achète un nouveau logiciel *(software)* pour faire sa comptabilité *(accounting)*. (sa secrétaire)
9. Je téléphone à la directrice pour avoir une entrevue. (tu)
10. Madame Rimbaud relit la lettre avant de signer. (son patron)
11. Le chef du personnel n'engagera pas ces candidats sans parler au président de la compagnie. (ils)

8 C'est vous le président!

C'est vous le président de votre propre entreprise. Tous les mois, vous réunissez votre personnel. Faites votre présentation en complétant les phrases suivantes.

1. Je vous ai demandé de venir pour que . . . (vous / discuter des progrès de l'entreprise)
2. Nos ventes *(sale)* ont progressé depuis que . . . (je / vous avoir parlé le mois dernier)
3. En particulier, nos exportations vers le Japon ont augmenté depuis que . . . (l'euro / avoir été dévalué)
4. J'ai contacté notre agence de Tokyo pour que . . . (elle / faire de la publicité à la télévision)
5. Nous devons développer de nouveaux produits sans que . . . (nos concurrents / le savoir)
6. Pour financer ces produits, je vais emprunter de l'argent à la Banque Nationale de Paris pendant que . . . (les taux [*rates*] d'intérêt / être favorables)
7. Nous allons réussir à moins que . . . (la situation économique / devenir mauvaise)
8. J'augmenterai vos salaires à condition que . . . (vous / continuer dans vos efforts)
9. Pour ma part, je vais continuer à travailler jusqu'à ce que . . . (cette compagnie / être la première compagnie dans sa spécialité)
10. C'est possible parce que . . . (nos produits / être les meilleurs produits du monde)

Expansion linguistique

- In France, the CEO of a company is referred to as **le PDG (Président-Directeur-Général)**. An executive is **un cadre**.
- Quelques logiciels populaires en France:
  le traitement de texte *word processing*
  le tableur *spreadsheet*
  la gestion/la comptabilité *accounting*

Reading STRATEGY

Reading fiction

Note culturelle

Yves Thériault wrote about the natural beauty of Quebec in *Le Dompteur d'ours.* He became interested in the **inuit** (Eskimos) in his book *Agaguk,* and Native Americans in *Askini.*

LECTURE

Le portrait

Yves Thériault

AVANT DE LIRE

Le but d'un conte est de distraire.° Pour cela, un conte doit contenir un élément qui attirera et maintiendra l'attention du lecteur: humour, intrigue, développement psychologique, etc.

Dans le conte que vous allez lire, Hélène, une jeune fille canadienne, découvre un portrait dans le grenier de la ferme où elle habite avec sa famille. Elle apprend que c'est le portrait d'un oncle mort il y a longtemps et dont personne ne veut parler.

D'après cette courte introduction, quel est, selon vous, l'élément que l'auteur utilisera pour retenir l'attention des lecteurs?

- l'humour?
- le mystère?
- l'intrigue?
- le récit d'aventures?
- le développement psychologique?
- autre élément?

distraire *to entertain*

Yves Thériault (1915-1983) est un auteur québécois. Avant de se consacrer à la littérature, il a fait un peu tous les métiers: conducteur de camion, marchand de fromages, présentateur à la radio, traducteur. . . Écrivain très prolifique, il a écrit des essais, des contes sur des thèmes canadiens, aussi bien qu'une série de romans policiers.

Teaching Strategy

Have students read the material in the *Avant de lire* section and work in groups to discuss the questions. Ask students to summarize the responses from their group and tally the results for the whole class.

1

J'ai trouvé le portrait dans le grenier, un matin de juin. J'y étais allée chercher des pots° pour les confitures de fraises, puisque nous étions au temps de l'année pour ces choses.

Le portrait était derrière un bahut.° J'ai vu la dorure° du cadre. J'ai tiré à moi, et voilà que c'était le portrait.

Celui d'un homme jeune, aux cheveux bruns, à la bouche agréable, et des yeux qui me regardaient. De grands yeux noirs, vivants . . .

J'ai descendu le portrait dans la cuisine.

— Voilà, mère, c'était au grenier.

Elle regarda le portrait d'un air surpris.

— Nous avions donc ça ici, ma fille? Tiens, tiens . . .

J'ai demandé:

— Qui est l'homme? Parce que c'est un bel homme. Il est vêtu° à la mode ancienne, mais c'est un magnifique gaillard . . .°

— Ton oncle, dit-elle, le frère de ton père. Le portrait a été peint alors qu'il était jeune.

— Quel oncle?

Je ne connaissais qu'une vague tante, pâle, anémique, qui vivait à la ville et venait chez nous une fois l'an. C'était, à ma connaissance, la seule parente de mon père.

Je l'ai dit à ma mère.

— Je ne me connais pas d'oncle . . .

— C'était le plus jeune frère de ton père. Ils étaient quatre. Trois garçons, une fille. Il ne reste que ton père et ta tante Valérienne.

— Les autres sont morts?

Elle fit° oui de la tête.

— Même celui-là? dis-je, même ce bel oncle-là?

— Oui.

Mots utiles

le cadre	*frame*
la colère	*anger*
le grenier	*attic*
chercher à	= essayer de
descendre	*to bring down*
pendre	*to hang*
secouer	*to shake*
tirer	*to pull, draw*
ça n'a pas d'importance	*that doesn't matter*
il ne reste que...	*there is/are only . . . left*
mieux vaut	= il vaut mieux

pot *jar* **bahut** *cupboard* **dorure** *gilt* **vêtu** *dressed* **gaillard** *guy* **fit** = dit

■ Note linguistique

In the Middle Ages, **un bahut** was a wooden chest used when traveling. Nowadays, it means a cupboard and is familiar teenage slang for **le lycée (aller au bahut = aller au lycée).**

■ Additional Information

Strawberries are in season in June and July.

■ Irregular Verb

(See Appendix C)
mourir

Teaching Strategy

Ask students to look at the illustrations in the first section of the story without reading the text. Then ask them to write a short caption for each picture that describes what seems to be happening. Then have students read the story and determine whether their predictions based on visual cues were accurate.

■ Note linguistique

Cru est un adjectif dérivé du latin "crudus" (**saignant:** *bleeding*). **Cru** désigne quelque chose de direct, que rien n'atténue au passage: **la lumière crue, une couleur crue.**

— Ce n'est pas juste de mourir quand on est si jeune et si beau . . . Non, ce n'est pas juste . . . Eh bien, oui, j'avais un bel oncle. Dommage qu'il soit mort . . .

Ma mère me regardait curieusement.

—Hélène, tu dis de drôles de choses . . .

Mais je n'écoutais pas ma mère. Je regardais le portrait. Maintenant, à la lumière plus crue° de la cuisine, le portrait me paraissait encore plus beau, encore mieux fait . . . Et j'aimais bien les couleurs.

— Je le pends dans ma chambre, dis-je . . .

— Comme tu voudras, dit ma mère, aujourd'hui, ça n'a plus d'importance.

La remarque n'était pas bien claire, et j'ai voulu savoir.

— Vous ne trouvez pas que c'est d'en dire beaucoup, et bien peu, mère?

— Peut-être. De celui-là, mieux vaut en dire le moins possible . . .

— Comment se nommait-il?°

— Tout simplement Jean . . .

— Et qu'est-ce qu'il faisait, demandai-je, qu'est-ce qu'il faisait dans la vie?

Mais ma mère secoua la tête.

— Pends, dit-elle, ce portrait où tu voudras . . . Ça n'a plus d'importance, mais si tu veux un bon conseil, ne dis rien, ne cherche à rien savoir. Et surtout, ne parle de rien à ton père.

Au fond,° ça n'avait pas d'importance. J'aimais le coup de pinceau° de l'artiste. J'aimais sa façon de tracer, de poser° la couleur, j'aimais les teintes° chaudes . . .

crue *direct* **se nommait-il** = s'appelait-il **au fond** *deep down* **coup de pinceau** *brush stroke*
poser = mettre **teintes** = couleurs

404 Unité 10

Je trouvais l'oncle bien beau, et bien jeune. Mais ça n'était pas si important que je doive encourir° d'inutiles colères. Et quelque chose me disait, quelque chose dans le ton de la voix de ma mère, dans la détermination de son visage, que mon père n'aimerait pas du tout que j'aborde° le sujet de son frère Jean.

encourir *to incur* **aborde** = approche

Avez-vous compris?

1. Comment Hélène a-t-elle découvert le portrait?
2. Qu'est-ce que sa mère lui explique? Qu'est–ce qu'elle ne lui explique pas?
3. Qu'est-ce qu'Hélène pense de son oncle?
4. Qu'est-ce qu'elle veut faire du portrait?

Anticipons un peu!

Hélène a décidé de mettre le portrait dans sa chambre. D'après vous, qu'est-ce qui va se passer dans l'épisode suivant?

- Le portrait va disparaître.
- Le portrait va vouloir communiquer quelque chose à Hélène.
- Hélène va tomber malade et mourir mystérieusement.
- L'oncle Jean va réapparaître dans la maison familiale bien vivant *(alive)*.
- Autre possibilité?

Expliquez votre choix.

■ Irregular Verb
(See Appendix C)
encourir is conjugated like **courir**

Teaching Strategy
Tell students:
Regardez l'illustration qui représente le tableau de l'oncle. Quelle impression vous donne la personne représentée? Pouvez-vous donner deux adjectifs pour décrire cette personne?

■ *Avez-vous compris?*
(Sample answers)

1. Elle a découvert le portrait au grenier, où elle cherchait des pots pour les confitures de fraises.
2. Sa mère lui explique que l'homme du portrait était le frère de son père, et qu'il est mort. Elle ne lui explique pas pourquoi on ne parle jamais de lui.
3. Elle pense qu'il est très beau.
4. Elle veut pendre le portrait dans sa chambre.

■ Notes linguistiques

- **Souffler la lampe:** on souffle sur la flamme d'une lampe à pétrole pour l'éteindre.
- The expression **la bougeotte** comes from the verb **bouger** *(to move).* **Avoir la bougeotte** is a familiar expression meaning *to have itchy feet.*

2

J'ai pendu le portrait au mur de ma chambre.

Je l'ai regardé chaque matin en m'éveillant, et chaque soir avant de souffler la lampe.

Et puis, au bout de deux semaines, une nuit, j'ai senti que quelqu'un me touchait l'épaule.

Je me suis éveillée en sursaut,° j'ai allumé ma lampe de chevet.° J'avais des sueurs froides le long du corps . . . Mais il n'y avait personne dans ma chambre.

Machinalement,° j'ai regardé le portrait, et en le voyant j'ai crié, je crois, pas fort,° mais assez tout de même, et je me suis enfoui° la tête sous l'oreiller.°

Dans le portrait, l'oncle Jean, très habilement° rendu,° regardait droit devant lui... Mais lorsque je me suis éveillée, j'ai vu qu'à cette heure-là de la nuit, il regardait ailleurs. En fait il regardait vers la fenêtre. Il regardait dehors . . .

Le matin, je n'ai rien dit. Je n'ai rien dit non plus les jours suivants, même si, chaque nuit, quelqu'un . . . ou quelque chose m'éveillait en me touchant l'épaule. Et même si chaque nuit, l'oncle Jean regardait par la fenêtre . . .

Naturellement, je me demandais bien ce que ça voulait dire. Plusieurs fois je me suis pincée, très fort,° pour être bien sûre que je ne dormais pas.

Chose certaine, j'étais bien éveillée.

Et quelque chose se passait . . . Mais quoi?

Au sixième matin . . . vous voyez comme je suis patiente . . . j'ai voulu tout savoir de maman.

— L'oncle Jean, qui est-il? Qu'est-ce qu'il faisait? Pourquoi ne faut-il pas en parler devant papa, de cet oncle?

— Tu as toujours le portrait dans ta chambre? dit ma mère.

— Oui.

Elle continua ses occupations pendant quelques minutes, puis elle vint s'asseoir devant moi, à la table.

— Ma fille, me dit-elle, il y a des choses qui sont difficiles à dire. Moi, ton oncle Jean, je l'aimais bien, je le trouvais charmant. Et ça mettait ton père dans tous les états° quand j'osais dire de telles choses.

Je lui ai demandé:

— Mais pourquoi, mère?

— Parce que ton oncle Jean, c'était une sorte de mouton noir dans la famille . . . il a eu des aventures, je t'épargne° les détails. Surtout, il avait la bougeotte.° Il s'est enfui jeune de la maison, on ne l'a revu que plus tard . . .. Puis il est reparti. Un jour, ton père a reçu une lettre. Ton oncle Jean s'était fait tuer,° stupidement, dans un accident aux États-Unis. On a fait transporter son corps ici, pour être enterré dans le lot° familial au cimetière. Il n'aurait pas dû . . . mais . . .

en sursaut *with a start* **de chevet** *bedside* **machinalement** *unconsciously* **pas fort** *not very loud* **enfoui** *buried* **oreiller** *pillow* **habilement** *skillfully* **rendu** = peint **pincée très fort** *pinched hard* **dans tous les états** = en colère **épargne** *spare* **bougeotte** *travelling urge* **s'était fait tuer** *was killed* **lot** *plot*

Mots utiles

l'épaule	*shoulder*
la sueur	*sweat*
un testament	*will*
allumer	*to light*
crier	*to scream*
se demander	*to wonder*
s'enfuir *	*to run awa*
éveiller	*to wake u*
oser	*to dare*
souffler	*to blow ou*
vouloir dire	*to mean*
ailleurs	*elsewhere*
au bout de	= après
tel (telle)	*such*

■ Irregular Verb

(see Appendix C)
s'enfuir (*see* **fuir**)

406 Unité 10

— Pourquoi? ai-je demandé, pourquoi n'aurait-il pas dû?

— Parce que, dans un testament découvert par la suite dans les effets de Jean, celui-ci exigeait d'être enterré n'importe où, mais pas dans le lot° familial . . . Il disait dans cet écrit qu'il n'avait aucunement° le désir de reposer aux côtés de la paisible° et sédentaire famille. Il avait un autre mot pour eux . . . pas très gentil.

Moi je croyais comprendre, maintenant.

— Est-ce que papa l'a fait transporter ailleurs?

— Euh . . . non . . . question° des dépenses que ça signifiait° . . . Jean n'a rien laissé, il est mort pauvre.

lot *plot* **aucunement** = pas du tout **paisible** *quiet* **question des** = à cause des **signifiait** = représentait

Avez-vous compris?

1. Pourquoi est-ce qu'Hélène s'est éveillée en sursaut?
2. En quoi le portrait de son oncle était-il différent à ce moment-là?
3. Que pensait la mère d'Hélène de l'oncle Jean?
4. Quels étaient les rapports entre le père d'Hélène et son frère Jean?
5. Comment est mort l'oncle Jean?
6. Qu'est-ce que son testament stipulait? Est-ce qu'il a été respecté?

Anticipons un peu!

D'après vous, qu'est-ce que l'oncle Jean voulait communiquer à Hélène?

- Qu'elle ouvre la fenêtre.
- Qu'elle sorte *(take out)* le portrait de la maison.
- Qu'elle prie *(pray)* pour lui.
- Qu'elle quitte elle-même la maison familiale et parte à l'aventure.

Expliquez votre choix.

■ Note linguistique

les effets *(m.)* = *personal belongings*

■ *Avez-vous compris?*

(Sample answers)

1. Elle s'est éveillée en sursaut parce qu'elle a senti que quelqu'un lui touchait l'épaule.
2. L'oncle regardait par la fenêtre.
3. Elle pensait qu'il était charmant.
4. Leurs rapports étaient mauvais.
5. Il est mort dans un accident aux États-Unis.
6. Il voulait être enterré n'importe où, mais pas dans le lot familial. On n'a pas respecté son testament.

Teaching Strategy

Divide the class into groups after reading the second section of the story and answering the *Avez-vous compris?* comprehension questions. Ask the group to answer the following questions; if there are differences of opinion, both/all answers should be recorded. Have each group present its answers to the class.

- À votre avis, qui ou quoi touche l'épaule d'Hélène la nuit? Est-ce un fantôme? De qui? Est-ce un insecte? Sa mère? Ou est-ce un rêve *(dream)*? Expliquez votre opinion.
- À votre avis, qu'est-ce que Jean est parti faire aux États-Unis?

Notes linguistiques

Attention à ne pas confondre:

- **soit:** 3ᵉ personne singulier du subjontif du verbe **être**
- **soit...soit:** conjonction *(either...or)*
  Soit Marie, soit Lucie, mais pas Henri.
- **soit:** subjonctif du verbe **être** utilisé pour introduire une supposition *(given [that] a...)*
  Soit un carré dont la surface est de...
- **soit:** adverbe d'affirmation *(so be it)*
  Soit! Allons à Genève demain.

Additional Information

Sigmund Freud (1856-1939) est le père de la psychanalyse. Il a écrit, entre autre, *L'Interprétation des rêves* en 1900.

Avez-vous compris?

(Sample answers)

1. Elle porte le portrait dehors, parce qu'elle pense que l'oncle Jean veut être dehors.
2. Il semble sourire, parce qu'Hélène a compris ce qu'il voulait.
3. Cette nuit-là il l'embrasse, pour la remercier.
4. Le portrait disparaît.
5. Elle n'a pas d'explication. C'est peut-être un rêve, ou peut-être des faits, elle ne sait pas.

3

Ce soir-là, j'ai mieux dormi. J'ai été éveillée vers quatre heures, et toute la scène d'habitude s'est répétée.

— Soit,° ai-je déclaré au portrait de l'oncle Jean . . . Demain, je vais faire quelque chose.

Et le lendemain matin, j'ai pris le portrait, et je l'ai porté dehors, derrière la remise.° Je l'ai appuyé là, face au soleil levant.°

Plusieurs fois dans la journée, je suis allée voir. L'oncle Jean regardait en face, mais j'ai cru voir comme une lueur° amusée dans ses yeux. Je me suis dit que je n'avais pas remarqué ce sourire auparavant.°

Au crépuscule,° le portrait était encore là . . .

Durant la nuit, je fus éveillée de nouveau. Seulement, au lieu d'une main discrète sur mon épaule, ce fut un très gentil baiser sur la joue qui m'éveilla.

Et je vous jure que pendant les quatre ou cinq secondes entre le sommeil profond et l'éveil complet, j'ai bien senti des lèvres tièdes° sur ma joue.

Je me suis rendormie paisiblement. J'avais comme une sensation de bien-être.

Au matin, le portrait n'était plus à sa place.

J'ai demandé à papa s'il l'avait pris, et il m'a dit que non. Maman n'y avait pas touché. Mes petits frères non plus.

Le portrait avait disparu. Et moi j'étais convaincue que sa disparition° coïncidait avec le baiser de reconnaissance si bien donné au cours de la nuit.

Vous voulez une explication? Je n'en ai pas. La chose est arrivée. Elle s'est passée comme ça peut être une suite° de rêves. Freud aurait une explication, je suppose . . . N'empêche que° les faits sont là. Un portrait est disparu, et l'oncle Jean regardait. Pour un homme qui avait toujours eu la bougeotte, c'était tout de même assez significatif . . .

soit *all right, so be it* **remise** *shed* **levant** *rising* **lueur** *gleam* **auparavant** = avant **crépuscule** *dusk* **tièdes** *warm* **disparition** *disappearance* **suite** *series, sequence* **n'empêche que** *nevertheless*

Mots utiles

un baiser	*kiss*
le bien-être	*well-being*
l'éveil	*wakefulness*
la reconnaissance	= *la gratitude*
un rêve	*dream*
le sommeil	*sleep*
appuyer	*to lean*
jurer	*to swear*
se rendormir *	*to go back to sleep*

Avez-vous compris?

1. Qu'est-ce qu'Hélène fait avec le portrait? Pourquoi?
2. Quelle semble être la réaction du portrait? Pourquoi?
3. Qu'est-ce qui se passe cette nuit-là? Pourquoi?
4. Que devient le portrait?
5. Quelle est l'explication d'Hélène?

Et vous?

D'après vous, qu'est-ce qui est arrivé au portrait?

Teaching Strategy

Ask students to think about what they have learned about the character of the uncle while reading the story and develop a list of adjectives to describe him. Then ask students to look at the list and compare themselves to the character. Are there any adjectives that are the same? Have students note similar adjectives and add a second column of adjectives describing themselves.

EXPRESSION ORALE

Situations

Avec votre partenaire, choisissez l'une des situations suivantes. Composez le dialogue correspondant et jouez-le en classe.

1 L'histoire du portrait

Hélène raconte l'histoire du portrait à un(e) copain (copine). Incrédule, celui-ci (celle-ci) veut connaître les détails.

Rôles: Hélène, le copain (la copine)

2 La rupture

Quelques années après, Hélène demande à son père les raisons de la rupture avec son jeune frère Jean. Le père hésite et finalement répond à Hélène qui veut des détails. (Imaginez les raisons de cette rupture.)

Rôles: Hélène, le père

EXPRESSION ÉCRITE

Le journal d'Hélène

Vous êtes Hélène. Dans votre journal, décrivez les événements suivants.

- la découverte du portrait
- ce qui s'est passé la première nuit
- ce qui s'est passé la dernière nuit

La biographie de l'oncle Jean

Un jour Hélène a trouvé dans le grenier le journal de l'oncle Jean dans lequel il décrit sa vie. Avec votre partenaire, imaginez la biographie de l'oncle Jean. Décrivez, par exemple . . .

- où il a passé sa jeunesse
- quelles étaient ses relations avec sa famille (Pourquoi s'est-il disputé avec sa famille?)
- quels problèmes il a eus
- pourquoi il s'est enfui une première fois
- où il est allé et qu'est-ce qu'il a fait
- pourquoi il est revenu
- pourquoi il est reparti une seconde fois
- où il est allé cette fois-là et qu'est-ce qu'il a fait
- comment il est mort

Supplementary vocabulary

le mystère *mystery*
l'énigme *(f.) enigma*
le fantôme *ghost*
l'apparition *(f.) apparition*
l'esprit *(m.) spirit*
hanter *to haunt*
l'au-delà *(m.) afterlife*

INTERLUDE CULTUREL

L'histoire franco-américaine en dix questions

Depuis cinq siècles, l'histoire de la France et celle de l'Amérique du Nord sont étroitement liées.° Voici quelques pages d'histoire franco-américaine.

1. Combien est-ce qu'il y a d'Américains d'origine française?

Aux États-Unis, il y a plus de trois millions et demi de personnes qui se considèrent d'origine française. En outre,° il y a aussi dix millions de personnes qui ont au moins un ancêtre d'origine française. Ces personnes habitent principalement dans les États de la Nouvelle Angleterre et en Louisiane.

Festival en Louisiane

La Nouvelle-Orléans

Une fête française à Bosto

2. Quand est-ce que les premiers Français sont venus sur le continent américain?

L'arrivée de Jacques Cartier à Gaspé (1534).

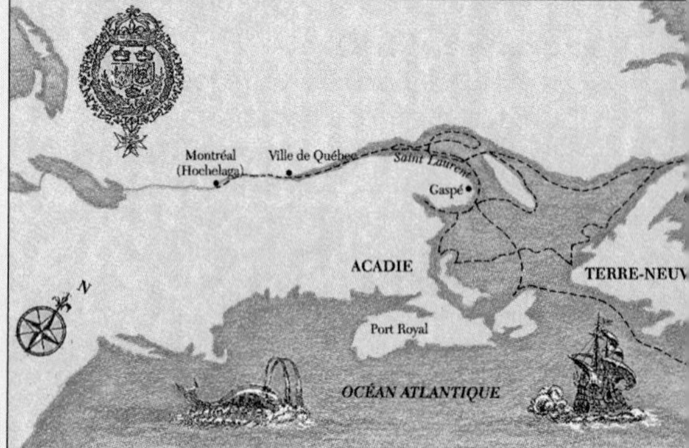

Jacques Cartier, un explorateur français, est arrivé au Canada en 1534. Sa mission était de trouver des mines d'or et de diamants pour le roi de France. Au lieu de découvrir des richesses fabuleuses, il a découvert un immense pays inconnu des Européens: le Canada. Il a débarqué° à Gaspé le 24 juillet 1534. Là, il a planté une croix° dans le sol,° et il a pris possession de la région au nom du roi de France. Au cours d'une seconde expédition l'année suivante, il a découvert l'estuaire d'un grand fleuve° qu'il a appelé le Saint-Laurent (parce que c'était le 10 août, fête de Saint Laurent). Puis il a remonté° ce fleuve jusqu'à un petit village indien appelé Hochelaga, site de la future ville de Montréal.

Les premiers colons français sont arrivés au Canada seulement 70 ans plus tard. Ils se sont d'abord installés° en Acadie (aujourd'hui la Nouvelle Écosse°) où ils ont fondé Port Royal (aujourd'hui Annapolis Royal) en 1605. En 1608, **Samuel de Champlain** a fondé la ville de **Québec**.

liées *interwoven* **en outre** *in addition* **a débarqué** *landed* **croix** *cross* **sol** *ground* **fleuve** = rivière **a remonté** *sailed up* **se sont installés** *settled* **Nouvelle Écosse** *Nova Scotia*

Notes culturelles

- **Mont-Royal,** an extinct volcano, was a site where Iroquois Indians lived as early as 1000 B.C.
- **Jacques Cartier** was the first European to explore in the valley of the Saint Lawrence River.
- In 1775, the American revolutionaries took over the city of Montreal but failed to take Quebec in 1776. Benjamin Franklin had hoped to make Montreal the fourteenth colony. Montrealers refused because they could not have retained their French roots and language.

3. *Quand a été fondé Montréal?*

En 1642, une petite expédition de 50 Français sous le commandement de Paul Chomedey de **Maisonneuve** est arrivée sur le site du village indien d'**Hochelaga**. Le but° de cette expédition était de créer une communauté religieuse pour soigner les malades et convertir les Iroquois. C'est ainsi qu'est née la ville de **Montréal**, appelée alors Ville Marie de Montréal. Parmi les membres de l'expédition, il y avait une jeune femme, **Jeanne Mance**, co-fondatrice de Montréal avec Maisonneuve. En 1644, elle a fondé l'Hôtel-Dieu*, un hôpital qui existe toujours aujourd'hui.

Peu à peu, Montréal a grandi.° C'est devenu un important centre du commerce de la fourrure° et le point de départ d'importantes expéditions vers la région des Grands Lacs et le Mississippi. Avec une population de 3 300 000 d'habitants, en majorité francophones, Montréal est aujourd'hui la seconde ville d'expression française du monde.

Jeanne Mance et Paul Chomedey de Maisonneuve, fondateurs de Montréal

Les «Filles du Roy»

Après la fondation de Québec (1608) et de Montréal (1642), des familles françaises se sont installées au Canada, mais ces familles n'étaient pas nombreuses: quelques dizaines seulement. Le roi Louis XIV, qui voulait établir une grande colonie, a encouragé le départ de centaines de colons. C'étaient des «habitants» qui travaillaient la terre,° des «coureurs des bois»° qui faisaient le commerce de la fourrure° avec les Indiens, et des soldats qui défendaient la colonie contre les attaques des Anglais et de leurs alliés iroquois.

Évidemment, pour assurer la survie° et le développement de cette petite colonie, il fallait que ces hommes se marient et aient des enfants. Oui, mais où trouver des épouses? L'administration royale a eu l'idée de recruter des jeunes filles françaises, volontaires pour partir dans un pays totalement inconnu et y fonder une famille. Pour les encourager, le roi leur donnait une dot° et leur assurait une éducation.

Les «filles du Roy» arrivent au Canada (1665-1675)

C'est ainsi qu'entre 1665 et 1675, plus de mille jeunes Françaises, les «Filles du Roy», ont quitté leur pays pour la grande aventure. Arrivées au Canada, elles étaient accueillies° dans des centres d'apprentissage° fondés par une autre Française, **Marguerite Bourgeoys**. Là, elles apprenaient ce qui était nécessaire pour survivre dans un pays rude° et parfois hostile. Puis, elles se mariaient . . .

Un très grand nombre de familles québécoises d'aujourd'hui descendent directement de ces courageuses pionnières, arrivées au Canada il y a plus de 300 ans.

* **Hôtel-Dieu**: nom donné autrefois à l'hôpital public de la ville.

but = objectif **a grandi** = s'est développé **fourrure** *fur* **terre** *earth* **coureurs des bois** *fur trappers* **survie** *survival* **dot** *dowry*
accueillies *welcomed* **centres d'apprentissage** = écoles **rude** *rough*

Photo Notes

- **Jean-Baptiste Lemoyne de Bienville** was born in Montreal in 1680 and died in Paris in 1768. His father, a French colonist in Montreal, worked as an interpreter with the Huron Indians. Jean-Baptiste moved to Louisiana in 1702, where he acted as governor until 1726 when Louis XIV dismissed him for being a bad manager.
- **Bourbon** is the family name of many French kings, including Louis XIII, Louis XIV, Louis XV and Louis XVI.

Note linguistique

Coureurs des bois: literally, *men who travel through the forests on foot.*

Notes culturelles

- **Marguerite Bourgeoys (1620-1700)** was the daughter of a French factory worker. She was a nun and Maisonneuve hired her to teach the children in Ville-Marie. She established the very first school in Montreal (1653) and founded the Congregation of Notre-Dame where young women were offered a proper education.
- **"Les filles du Roy"** were poor factory workers, widowed or orphaned young women.

4. Qu'est-ce qu'on appelle les «guerres françaises et indiennes» (1689-1763)?

Les Français ont créé une vaste colonie qu'ils ont appelée **la Nouvelle France**. Ce n'était pas les seuls occupants de cette partie de l'Amérique du Nord. Il y avait aussi les Anglais qui s'étaient établis en Nouvelle Angleterre. La rivalité entre ces deux groupes était intense. Chacun avait des alliés indiens. Les alliés des Français étaient les Hurons et les Algonquins. Les alliés des Anglais étaient les Iroquois. De temps en temps, chaque groupe faisait des raids sur le territoire de l'autre.

Finalement en 1756, une guerre générale a éclaté° entre la France et l'Angleterre. Au début, les Français ont été victorieux. Mais l'armée anglaise était bien supérieure en nombre et les forts français sont tombés les uns après les autres. Les Anglais ont pris Québec en 1759 et Montréal en 1760. Au traité de Paris de 1763, la France a dû abandonner toutes ses colonies d'Amérique du Nord. Le Canada et toute la rive est du Mississippi sont passés sous contrôle anglais.

Les «guerres françaises et indiennes»

5. Quand la Louisiane était-elle française?

La Salle prend possession de la Louisiane au nom de la France

Vers le milieu du 17e siècle, des expéditions françaises, parties de Montréal, avaient exploré la région des Grands Lacs. En 1673, le père **Marquette** avait découvert le Mississippi, mais personne ne savait jusqu'où allait ce long fleuve. **Cavelier de La Salle** décida d'entreprendre° cette exploration. En 1681, il organisa une petite expédition et il partit à l'aventure. Après un voyage très difficile, il arriva à l'estuaire du Mississippi le 9 avril 1682.

Au passage, La Salle prit possession des territoires qu'il traversait° au nom de la France. Il nomma cette région **Louisiane** en l'honneur du roi Louis XIV. Plus tard, d'autres Français arrivèrent dans la région. Ils fondèrent **la Nouvelle Orléans** en 1718 et construisirent des forts le long du Mississippi. À cette époque, la Louisiane était un immense territoire puisqu'elle représentait toute la vallée du Mississippi et ses affluents.°

À la suite° de traités, la France dut abandonner la Louisiane. La rive° ouest du Mississippi devint espagnole en 1762 et la rive est devint anglaise en 1763.

En 1800, la France acquit° par traité la partie espagnole. En 1803, Napoléon, qui avait besoin d'argent pour financer ses guerres, la revendit aux États-Unis pour la somme de 15 millions de dollars.

a éclaté *broke out* **entreprendre** *undertake* **traversait** *crossed* **affluents** *tributaries* **à la suite** *as a result* **rive** *shore, bank* **acquit** *acquired*

Additional Information

- **La Nouvelle-Orléans** was founded in 1717-18 by a French engineer named Pauger. The city was named in honor of the Duc d'Orléans.
- In 1756, there were 65,000 French colonists in Canada compared to 1,200,000 British.
- After the **Traité de Paris,** the left side of the Mississippi was given to the British while the rest of Louisiana was given to Spain.

Anecdote

Hochelaga signifie "place du castor" *(beaver)*. Le nom Canada viendrait de l'expression iroquoise "Kanata" qui signifie "village."

NOTES CULTURELLES

- In 1774, **l'Acte de Québec** allowed French Canadians to retain their religion, institutions and language. French-speaking Catholics were then called **les canayens**.
- **Peter Minuit (1580–1638)** was sent to America by the Dutch West India Company. He bought the island of Manhattan with trinkets worth about $24.
- **Paul Revere (1735–1818)** was a silversmith from Massachusetts who became a messenger for the colonists in 1774. On the night of April 18, 1775, he rode to warn Adams and Hancock that a British army was marching on to Concord and Lexington. This heroic ride was immortalized in a poem by Longfellow.

6. *Qui sont les Huguenots français?*

«Huguenot» était le nom que les Français donnaient aux Protestants au 16e siècle. À cette époque, il y avait des guerres de religion entre Protestants et Catholiques. Les Protestants, très inférieurs en nombre, ont été persécutés et chassés° de France. Beaucoup sont allés en Hollande et en Allemagne. Certains ont immigré en Amérique. Des Huguenots français venus de La Rochelle, France, ont fondé la ville de New Rochelle, New York, en 1688.

Parmi les Américains d'origine huguenote: Peter Minuit qui a acheté Manhattan pour 24 dollars, Paul Revere, patriote et héros de la Révolution américaine, John Jay, premier juge de la Cour Suprême, Louis Tiffany, joaillier de réputation internationale.

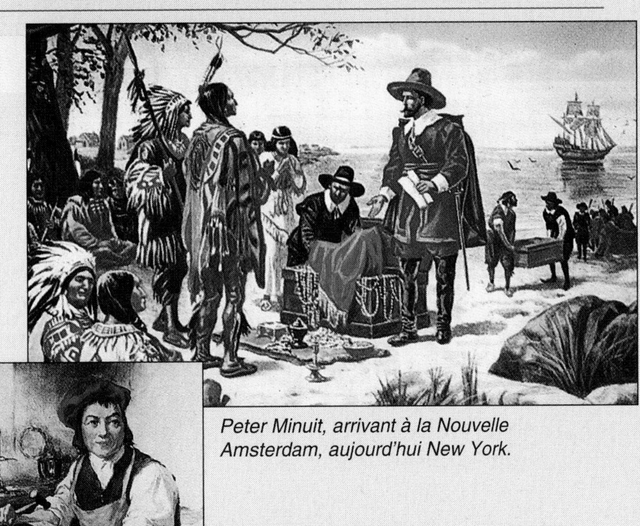

Peter Minuit, arrivant à la Nouvelle Amsterdam, aujourd'hui New York.

Paul Revere, patriote américain d'origine française

7. *Comment les Français ont-ils aidé les Américains pendant la guerre d'Indépendance?*

Quand ils ont déclaré leur indépendance en 1776, les Américains avaient besoin d'aide. Pour obtenir cette aide, ils ont envoyé Benjamin Franklin comme ambassadeur en France. Franklin, qui était très admiré et très respecté des Français, a pleinement réussi dans cette mission. Conseillé par sa femme Marie-Antoinette, le roi de France, Louis XVI, a reconnu° la jeune république des États-Unis en 1778. Mieux, il a décidé d'envoyer sa flotte° et ses meilleures troupes au secours° des «insurgés» américains.

La bataille de Yorktown

La bataille décisive de la guerre d'Indépendance a eu lieu à Yorktown en octobre 1781. D'un côté° il y avait une armée anglaise commandée par Cornwallis. De l'autre côté, il y avait une armée américaine commandée par Washington et une armée française commandée par **Rochambeau.** Pendant que la bataille faisait rage,° la flotte française empêchait° les renforts° anglais d'arriver. Encerclées, les troupes anglaises ont capitulé. Cette victoire franco-américaine a mis fin aux hostilités. Deux ans plus tard, l'Angleterre reconnaissait l'indépendance des États-Unis.

chassés *expelled* **reconnu** *recognized* **flotte** *fleet* **au secours** = pour aider **côté** *side* **faisait rage** *was raging*
empêchait *prevented* **renforts** *reinforcements*

- **John Jay (1745–1829)** helped draft the constitution of New York State. He was governor of New York for two terms (1795–1801).
- **Charles Louis Tiffany (1812–1902)** started to manufacture his own jewelry in 1848. He opened a branch of his store in Paris in 1850.
- **Charles Cornwallis (1735–1805)** led the British army in the Yorktown battle. He later became governor of India and Viceroy of Ireland.
- **Jean Baptiste Donatien de Vimeur, Comte de Rochambeau (1725–1807)** landed in Newport R.I. in 1780 with 6,000 French soldiers. Imprisoned in France after the French Revolution, his rank was later restored to him by Napoleon.

Notes historiques

- La Fayette landed at North Island, near Charleston, South Carolina. From there he went overland to Philadelphia where he received his commission from the Continental Congress on July 31, 1777.
- It was La Fayette who gave the order to destroy the fortress of **La Bastille** in July 1789 after it was attacked by the people of Paris.
- In 1802, La Fayette helped in finalizing the **Louisiana Purchase.** (He had acquired land in Louisiana.) La Fayette refused the post of governor of Louisiana offered to him by the U.S. Congress.
- In 1824, La Fayette returned to the United States where he was greeted as a hero and given land and a pension by the U.S. government.
- **Adrienne de Noailles de La Fayette** was the daughter of the **Duc d'Ayen.** She married La Fayette in 1774.

8. *Qui était La Fayette?*

Une université, de nombreuses écoles, plusieurs villes portent le nom de ce héros de la guerre d'Indépendance américaine. Qui était exactement **La Fayette**?

La Fayette (1757-1834) était un aristocrate français qui appartenait° à l'une des familles les plus illustres du pays. En 1777, il avait seulement vingt ans et il était immensément riche. Un jour, il a entendu parler de° la Révolution américaine. Il a pris contact avec Benjamin Franklin qui était alors l'ambassadeur des États-Unis en France. Après cette entrevue, il a décidé de rejoindre les «insurgés» américains comme volontaire. Malheureusement, le roi de France était tout à fait opposé à cette idée et lui a interdit de partir. Que faire? La Fayette était un jeune homme déterminé avec beaucoup d'imagination ... et beaucoup d'argent. Il a quitté la France en secret. Il est allé en Espagne où il a acheté un bateau qu'il a appelé *La Victoire* et il est parti pour les États-Unis.

Après avoir débarqué° en Caroline du Sud, La Fayette est allé à Philadelphie pour offrir ses services au Congrès américain. Le Congrès, impressionné par ses qualités et son enthousiasme, l'a nommé général auprès de° George Washington. Les deux hommes sont immédiatement devenus de grands amis.* En Octobre 1777, La Fayette a pris part à sa première bataille et il a été blessé à la jambe. Peu de temps après, le Congrès, reconnaissant son courage et ses talents militaires, lui a donné le commandement de la division de Virginie.

En 1779, La Fayette est retourné brièvement en France. Sa mission était de plaider la cause américaine et d'obtenir l'aide de la France. Il est allé voir le roi qui cette fois-ci l'a écouté. Quelques temps après, l'armée française est arrivée aux États-Unis. De retour aux États-Unis, La Fayette a rejoint son poste de commandement. À la bataille décisive de Yorktown, en 1781, il était à la tête d'une division américaine dans l'armée de Washington.

Après la guerre d'Indépendance, La Fayette est rentré en France où il a continué à combattre pour la justice et pour les idées nouvelles de liberté et d'égalité. Quand la Révolution française a éclaté en 1789, c'était l'homme le plus populaire de France. C'est lui qui a proposé la déclaration européenne des *Droits de l'homme et du citoyen* et qui a fait accepter le drapeau tricolore comme drapeau national. La Fayette était aussi un membre très actif du Club des Amis des Noirs, un club politique qui voulait l'abolition de l'esclavage° dans les colonies françaises. À cause du rôle important qu'il a joué aux États-Unis d'abord et en France ensuite, on appelle souvent La Fayette «le héros des deux mondes».

La Fayette, héros de la guerre d'Indépendance américaine.

* Plus tard, La Fayette a nommé son fils George Washington La Fayette.

appartenait *belonged to* **a entendu parler de** *heard about* **débarqué** *landed* **auprès de** *on the staff of* **esclavage** *slavery*

Une lettre du Marquis de La Fayette à Madame de La Fayette

La Fayette est arrivé aux États-Unis le 13 juin 1777. Quelques jours plus tard, il était à Charleston où il a écrit la lettre suivante à sa jeune femme. Dans cette lettre, il décrit ses premières impressions sur le pays et ses habitants.

Adrienne de Noailles de La Fayette

1777, à Charlestown

... Je vais à présent vous parler du pays, mon cher coeur, et de ses habitants. Ils sont aussi aimables que mon enthousiasme avait pu se le figurer.° La simplicité des manières, le désir d'obliger,° l'amour de la patrie° et de la liberté, une douce° égalité, règnent ici parmi tout le monde. L'homme le plus riche et le plus pauvre sont de niveau,° et quoiqu'il y ait° des fortunes immenses dans ce pays, je défie° de trouver la moindre° différence entre leurs manières respectives les uns pour les autres.

J'ai commencé par la vie de campagne, chez le major Huger; à présent, me voici à la ville. Tout y ressemble assez à la façon anglaise, excepté qu'il y a plus de simplicité chez eux qu'en Angleterre. La ville de Charlestown est une des plus jolies, des mieux bâties° et des plus agréablement peuplées que j'aie jamais vues. Les femmes américaines sont fort jolies, fort simples et d'une propreté° charmante...

Ce qui m'enchante ici, c'est que tous les citoyens sont frères. Il n'y a en Amérique ni pauvres, ni même ce qu'on appelle paysans.° Tous les citoyens ont un bien honnête,° et tous, les mêmes droits° que le plus puissant° propriétaire du pays.

Les auberges sont bien plus différentes d'Europe; le maître et la maîtresse se mettent à table avec vous, font les honneurs d'un bon repas, et en partant vous payez sans marchander.° Quand on ne veut pas aller dans une auberge, on trouve des maisons de campagne où il suffit d'être bon Américain pour être reçu avec les attentions qu'on aurait en Europe pour un ami.

... Il est fort avant° dans la nuit, il fait une chaleur affreuse, et suis dévoré de moucherons° qui vous couvrent de grosses ampoules,° mais les meilleurs pays ont, comme vous voyez, leurs inconvénients.

Adieu mon coeur, adieu.

Lafayette

figurer = imaginer **obliger** = rendre service **patrie** *fatherland* **douce** *gentle* **de niveau** *at the same level* **quoiqu'il y ait** *although they are* **défie** *challenge* **la moindre** = la plus petite **bâties** *built* **propreté** *cleanliness, hygiene* **paysans** *peasants* **un bien honnête** *a property of their own* **droits** *rights* **puissant** *powerful* **marchander** *to bicker over the price* **fort avant** = très tard **moucherons** *gnats* **ampoules** *swellings*

■ **Note linguistique**

Note that La Fayette spelled Charleston as "Charlestown."

Notes culturelles

- The sentence **«La Fayette, nous voici!»** was supposedly pronounced by Colonel Stanton on July 4, 1917 as he visited the grave of La Fayette in the Picpus cemetery in Paris.
- World War I ended with the armistice signed on November 11, 1918. It was signed in **Rethondes** (France), in the dining-car of a train.
- In 1943, the first French airforce squadron armed by the U.S. took the name of **Escadrille La Fayette.**

9. *Qui a dit «La Fayette, nous voilà!» et à quelle occasion?*

On attribue cette phrase au général américain John Pershing à son arrivée en France en 1917. En rendant hommage à La Fayette, héros français de la guerre d'Indépendance, il voulait réaffirmer l'amitié et la solidarité qui unissaient le peuple français et le peuple américain. Le général Pershing était le commandant du corps expéditionnaire américain en France pendant l Première Guerre mondiale (1914-1918).

En réalité, les premiers Américains qui sor venus aider la France pendant cette guerre étaier des volontaires incorporés dans l'armée français Parmi ceux-ci, il y avait les pilotes de la fameus «Escadrille Lafayette». Il y avait aussi le ambulanciers de l'«American Field Servic Ambulance Corps». C'était des lycéens d 17 ans, des étudiants de Yale et d Harvard, ou de simples citoyens venus pa idéalisme.

Pilotes de l'Escadrille Lafayette. (Remarquez que ces pilotes américains portent des uniformes français.)

Les États-Unis sont officiellement entré en guerre aux côtés de° la France et d l'Angleterre en avril 1917. Cette année-là des centaines de milliers de soldat américains sont venus combattre sur l sol° français. Parmi ces soldats, il y avai un jeune capitaine d'artillerie venu d Missouri, Harry Truman, futur présiden des États-Unis. C'est grâce à l'interventio des troupes américaines que les Alliés on finalement pu gagner la guerre en 1918.

10. *Où se trouve Omaha Beach?*

Omaha Beach se trouve en Normandie. C'est sur cette plage et d'autres plages normandes que le plus grand débarquement° de l'histoire a eu lieu le 6 juin 1944. Ce jour-là, 100 000 soldat américains, anglais, canadiens, français, polonais ont débarqué sur le sol de France occupé pa l'Allemagne nazie. Peu après, les armée alliées commandées par le général Eisenhower ont libéré le reste de la France. Près de Omaha Beach il y a un grand cimetière où se trouvent les tombes de 9 385 soldats américains, héros de la libération de la France.

Le 6 juin 1944 les troupes alliées débarquent sur la plage d'Omaha Beach en Normandie

Un GI réconforte un enfant français

aux côtés de *on the side of* **sol** *soil* **débarquement** *landing* **polonais** *Polish*

Teaching Strategy

Divide the class into groups. Ask each group to prepare two <u>new</u> questions and answers on separate pieces of paper based on the material in the answers provided to the **dix questions** posed in this *Interlude.* (Remind students that their questions must be very different from the existing ones!) Collect all questions, shuffle them, and pass them out to the groups. Each group must answer the questions they receive and check against the "Answer Key" provided by the original groups.

Villes américaines — noms français

Un certain nombre de villes américaines portent des noms français. Ces noms rappellent quelques épisodes de la longue histoire franco-américaine.

Duluth (Minnesota)
Cette ville porte le nom d'un Français, Daniel **du Luth** (1636-1710), explorateur du Lac Supérieur et ami des Indiens de la région.

Fond du Lac (Wisconsin)
Cette ville est appelée ainsi à cause de sa position à l'extrémité sud du lac Winnebago. Au 18e siècle, c'était un centre où les Français faisaient le commerce de la fourrure avec les Indiens.

Détroit (Michigan)
Cette ville a été fondée en 1701 par un explorateur français, Antoine **de la Mothe Cadillac**, futur gouverneur de la Louisiane. À l'origine, la ville s'appelait Fort Pontchartrain du Détroit, en l'honneur du ministre français de la Marine.

Marietta (Ohio)
En 1788, d'anciens° soldats de la guerre d'Indépendance ont fondé une petite colonie qu'ils ont appelée Mariette, en l'honneur de la reine de France, **Marie-Antoinette**. Dix ans plus tôt, Marie-Antoinette avait convaincu° son mari d'envoyer ses troupes à l'aide des patriotes américains.

aramie (Wyoming)
ette ville porte le nom de Jacques **La amie**, un trappeur canadien qui est arrivé ans la région vers 1820. Il a construit une abane pour stocker ses fourrures. Plus tard, ort Laramie, bâti sur ce site, a joué un rôle nportant dans la conquête de l'ouest.

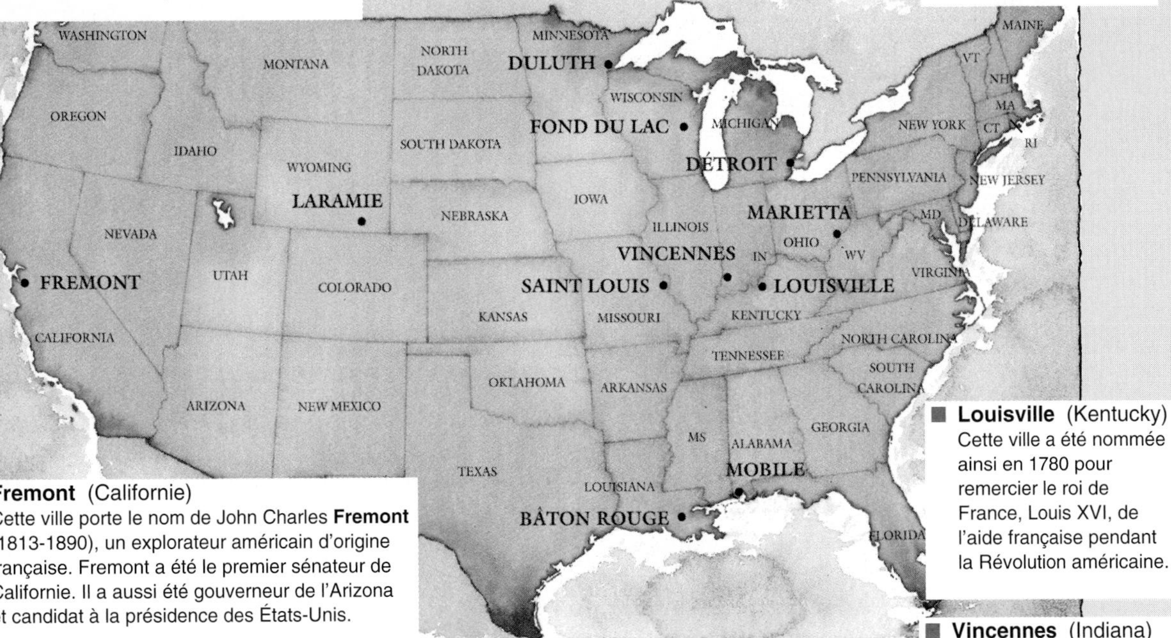

Fremont (Californie)
Cette ville porte le nom de John Charles **Fremont** (1813-1890), un explorateur américain d'origine française. Fremont a été le premier sénateur de Californie. Il a aussi été gouverneur de l'Arizona et candidat à la présidence des États-Unis.

Louisville (Kentucky)
Cette ville a été nommée ainsi en 1780 pour remercier le roi de France, Louis XVI, de l'aide française pendant la Révolution américaine.

Bâton Rouge (Louisiane)
En 1699, une expédition française découvre le site de la ville actuelle.° Les Indiens de la région appellent ce site «Istrouma» expression qui signifie «bâton° rouge». Les Français donnent ce nom au fort qu'ils construisent là quelques années plus tard.

Saint Louis (Missouri)
René Chouteau, un jeune homme de la Nouvelle-Orléans, avait seulement 15 ans quand il a fondé Saint Louis en 1764. Il a nommé la ville en l'honneur de deux rois de France: **Louis XV** et son patron, **Saint Louis**.

Mobile (Alabama)
Vers 1700, des explorateurs français sont arrivés dans la région. Ils ont construit un fort qu'ils ont appelé Fort Louis de la Mobile: Fort Louis, en l'honneur du roi de France, Louis XIV; de la Mobile, du nom de Mauvile, une tribu indienne de la région.

Vincennes (Indiana)
Cette ville porte le nom de son fondateur, l'explorateur canadien Jean-Baptiste **Vincennes** (1668-1719). Elle est restée pendant longtemps une ville française. Pendant la guerre d'Indépendance, ses habitants ont aidé les Américains contre les Anglais.

anciens *former* **convaincu** *convinced* **actuelle** *present* **bâton** *stick, pole*

Notes historiques

- **Saint Louis, le roi Louis IX** (1226–1270), was known for his integrity and strong faith. He participated in the Crusades and was responsible for the construction of the Sainte-Chapelle, in Paris.
- In 1763, the Treaty of Paris gave all the French territories *east* of the Mississippi to England. This is why Chouteau chose the *west* bank as a site for St. Louis.

Note culturelle

On appelle **le Grand Dérangement** l'exode des Acadiens qui refusèrent de prêter serment à la couronne d'Angleterre. À cette époque, des Acadiens choisirent de retourner en France. Après avoir été libres et propriétaires de leurs terres, beaucoup ne purent se réadapter à la société française. En conséquence, Louis XV mis un bateau à leur disposition pour leur permettre de retourner en Amérique, dans la colonie établie sur les bords du Mississippi.

Pour en savoir plus

The Cajun culture is known in the rest of the United States for its food and its music. See *Interlude 4*, p. 182, where **la musique cajun** and **zydéco** are presented.

Note culturelle

While the term **Cajun** is widely used throughout the United States, the French-speaking community in Louisiana more commonly uses the term **acadien**.

Les héritiers de la Louisiane française

Des gens d'origine française, venus surtout du Canada, ont été les premiers blancs à occuper la partie centrale de ce qui allait devenir les États-Unis. C'était pour la plupart des soldats, des missionnaires, des trappeurs. Ils construisirent des comptoirs° et des forts dans la vallée du Mississippi. Après la fondation de la Nouvelle-Orléans en 1718, une colonie française s'établit en Louisiane. Au cours des années qui suivirent, cette colonie s'enrichit d'éléments nouveaux: d'abord Acadiens venus du Canada, puis Créoles venus des Antilles françaises. Les descendants de ces deux groupes représentent aujourd'hui la quasi-totalité de la population de la Louisiane d'origine française.

La Mothe-Cadillac, explorateur français

Des musiciens cajuns

Les Acadiens ou «Cajuns»

Les Acadiens doivent leur nom à leur région d'origine, l'Acadie, ce territoire du Nord-Est canadien représenté aujourd'hui par les provinces du Nouveau Brunswick et de la Nouvelle Écosse.° C'est dans cette région que s'établirent des colons français dès° 1640. Devenus sujets britanniques à la suite d'°un traité° (1713) qui donnait l'Acadie à l'Angleterre, les Acadiens refusèrent de prêter serment° à leur nouveau gouvernement. Pour cet acte de rébellion, toute la population française fut expulsée d'Acadie par l'armée anglaise. Un grand nombre d'Acadiens retournèrent en France. D'autres s'éparpillèrent° dans les territoires français d'Amérique. Un premier contingent de 231 réfugiés arriva en Louisiane en 1765, suivi d'autres groupes de plusieurs milliers de personnes. Leurs descendants et leurs alliés par mariage (Espagnols, Allemands, Indiens) constituent la population «cajun» actuelle. Aujourd'hui cette population habite principalement dans la région des bayous. Les centres cajuns se reconnaissent facilement à leurs noms français: Lafayette, Abbeville, Saint Martinville, Ville Platte, Thibodaux.

Les Créoles

Il existe plusieurs définitions du terme *créole*. La définition généralement acceptée s'applique aux descendants des habitants de Saint Domingue (aujourd'hui Haïti), blancs et noirs, venus en Louisiane pendant la Révolution française (1789-1799) et, plus tard, après l'indépendance d'Haïti (1804). Ces créoles s'établirent à la Nouvelle-Orléans et dans les plantations à proximité du Mississippi et des bayous. Beaucoup de créoles de la Nouvelle-Orléans habitaient le quartier du Vieux Carré° qu'ils quittèrent vers 1910.

comptoirs *trading posts* **Nouvelle Écosse** *Nova Scotia* **dès** *beginning in* **à la suite de** *as the result of* **traité** *treaty*
prêter serment *to pledge allegiance* **s'éparpillèrent** *were scattered* **Carré** *Square*

RÉVEILLE

Réveille,° réveille! . . .
C'est les goddams qui viennent*
brûler° la récolte.°
Réveille, réveille, hommes acadiens
pour sauver le village.

Mon grand-grand-grand-grand-père
est venu de la Bretagne;
le sang de ma famille est mouillé° l'Acadie
et là les maudits viennent*
nous chasser comme des bêtes,
*détruire les saintes familles***
nous jeter° tous au vent.
Réveille, réveille! . . .

J'ai entendu parler
*de monter avec Beausoleil****
pour prendre le fusil,°
battre les sacrés° maudits.
J'ai entendu parler°
d'aller en la Louisiane
pour trouver de la bonne paix
là-bas dans la Louisiane.
Réveille, réveille! . . .

J'ai vu mon pauvre père
qui était fait prisonnier
pendant que ma mère,
ma belle mère braillait.°
J'ai vu ma belle maison
qui était mise aux flammes.
Et moi j'suis resté orphelin.°
Orphelin de l'Acadie.
Réveille, réveille! . . .

Réveille, réveille! . . .
C'est les goddams qui viennent*
voler° les enfants.
Réveille, réveille, hommes acadiens
pour sauver l'héritage.

Zachary Richard

Zachary Richard est un poète et chanteur cajun. Dans cette chanson célèbre, il évoque un événement historique important: l'attaque des Acadiens par les Anglais et leur expulsion. La sonnerie de clairon° «Réveille, réveille» alerte la population que les soldats anglais arrivent.

* **les goddams; les maudits** (*cursed ones*): Terme qui désigne les soldats anglais.
** **Les saintes familles:** Les familles acadiennes françaises étaient catholiques. Massacrées par les soldats protestants anglais, elles sont devenues martyres.
*** **Beausoleil:** Capitaine, héros de la Résistance acadienne contre les Anglais.

sonnerie de clairon *bugle call* **réveille** *wake up* **brûler** *to burn* **récolte** *crops* **mouillé** *soaked (in)* **jeter** *to throw* **fusil** *rifle* **sacrés** *«cursed»* **entendu parler** *heard about* **braillait** *was crying and screaming* **orphelin** *orphan* **voler** *to steal*

Notes culturelles

Quelques créoles célèbres

D'ORIGINE EUROPÉENNE

- **John James Audubon** (1780–1851), né à Haïti, peintre de la célèbre série *Les Oiseaux d'Amérique*.
- **P.G.T. Beauregard** (1818–1893), important général sudiste pendant la Guerre de Sécession.

D'ORIGINE AFRICAINE

- **Homer Plessy** (1862–1935) était issu d'une des nombreuses familles francophones d'origine africaine de la Nouvelle-Orléans. En 1890, il fut arrêté pour être monté dans un wagon réservé aux Blancs. Son cas fut plaidé devant la Cour Suprême des États-Unis. La décision célèbre «Plessy contre Ferguson» (1896) est à l'origine de la doctrine raciste de «séparés mais égaux».
- **Sidney Béchet** (1897–1959), était l'un des plus grands musiciens de jazz, style Nouvelle-Orléans.

Note linguistiques

- Le mot *créole* désigne également la langue parlée aux Antilles, en Louisiane et dans les îles Maurice et de la Réunion.

Standard French equivalents:

- «mon grand-grand-grand-grand-père» = mon arrière-arrière-arrière-grand-père
- «j'ai vu mon pauvre père qui était fait prisonnier» = j'ai vu que mon pauvre père était fait prisonnier

Teaching Strategy

There are many recordings of Cajun music available. You or your students may wish to play these for the class. Zachary Richard's own recordings of Réveille are powerful and moving; they may help students to appreciate the written form of the poem more easily.

Note culturelle

The **fleur de lys** was acknowledged as the symbol of the French monarchy in 1147.

Address

For more information on Louisiana, write to:

State Department of Culture, Recreation and Tourism
P.O. Box 94291
Baton Rouge, LA 10804

Additional Information

The motto of Louisiana is: **Union, Justice and Confidence.**

Le drapeau acadien

Les différents éléments du drapeau des Acadiens de Louisiane rappellent l'histoire du peuple cajun.

Les fleurs de lys sur fond bleu étaient l'emblème des rois de France. Elles représentent l'héritage français des cajuns et leur langue.

La tour jaune sur fond rouge était l'emblème des rois d'Espagne. Quand les premiers Acadiens sont arrivés en Louisiane, celle-ci était devenue espagnole. Cette partie du d peau rappelle l'hospitalité du gouver espagnol.

Le blanc était la couleur de l'ancienne Acadie. Le triangle de cette couleur rappelle l'origine canadienne des Cajuns. L'étoile jaune est un double symbole. Elle représente la dévotion des Acadiens à la Vierge Marie, leur sainte patronne. Elle symbolise aussi le patriotisme des premiers Acadiens et leur participation comme volontaires à la Guerre d'indépendance (1775-1783). À peine arrivés en Louisiane, ils se sont ralliés à la cause américaine. Organisés en milices, ils ont combattu victorieusement contre les Anglais.

NOTES CULTURELLES

- Après être restée longtemps française, la Louisiane (côté ouest du Mississippi) est devenue espagnole par le Traité de Fontainebleau de 1762.
- Les milices acadiennes furent créées par le gouverneur espagnol de la Louisiane, Bernardo de Galvez, après qui la ville de Galveston, Texas, est nommée.

Tête à tête Pair Activities

CONTENTS

■ **Teaching tip**

Have students review PHYSICAL DESCRIPTION VOCABULARY by referring them to pp. 36–37 in the textbook.

■ **Answers**

Étudiant A:

Mlle Bertin:

Mlle Bertin a le visage ovale. Elle est blonde et elle a les cheveux frisés et assez longs. Elle porte des lunettes et elle a les yeux bleus. Elle porte du rouge à lèvres. Elle a des boucles d'oreilles et un collier.

M. Moreau:

M. Moreau a le visage rectangulaire. Il est brun avec les cheveux courts et un peu frisés. Il porte des lunettes, et il a les yeux noirs. Il a aussi une moustache

Étudiant B:

Mme Dubois:

Mme Dubois a le visage ovale. Elle a les cheveux châtain clair. Elle a les cheveux courts et lisses. Elle a les yeux marron. Elle porte du rouge à lèvres. Elle a des boucles d'oreilles. Elle a un grain de beauté.

M. Mercier:

M. Mercier a le visage triangulaire. Il est blond avec les cheveux courts et en brosse. Il a les yeux noirs, et il a une cicatrice.

La rentrée — Étudiant B

Partie 1

Il y a deux nouveaux professeurs à l'école: Madame Dubois et Monsieur Mercier. Prenez une feuille de papier. Écoutez bien la description physique de ces personnes faite par votre partenaire. Dessinez leurs portraits sur la base des informations qu'il/elle vous donne.

Mlle Bertin

?

M. Moreau

Partie 2

Maintenant c'est à votre tour de faire la description de deux autres professeurs: Madame Dubois et Monsieur Mercier.

▶ Faites une description détaillée de chaque personne:

- le visage
- le nez
- les cheveux
- la bouche
- les yeux
- le(s) signe(s) particulier(s)

Votre partenaire va dessiner un portrait de ces deux personnes sur la base de vos informations.

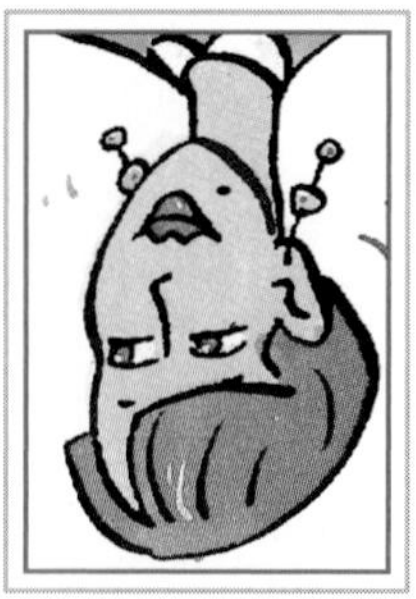

Mme Dubois

M. Mercier

La rentrée — Étudiant A

Partie 1

Il y a deux nouveaux professeurs à l'école: Mademoiselle Bertin et Monsieur Moreau.

▶ Faites une description détaillée de chaque personne:

- le visage
- le nez
- les cheveux
- la bouche
- les yeux
- le(s) signe(s) particulier(s)

Votre partenaire va dessiner un portrait de ces deux personnes sur la base de vos informations.

Mlle Bertin

M. Moreau

Partie 2

Maintenant c'est à votre tour de dessiner. Prenez une feuille de papier. Écoutez bien la description physique de deux autres professeurs, Madame Dubois et Monsieur Mercier. Dessinez leurs portraits sur la base des informations données par votre partenaire.

Mme Dubois

M. Mercier

Teaching Note

All of the **Tête à tête** activities are done in pairs as **Étudiant A** and **Étudiant B**. Quickly divide the class into **Étudiant A** and **Étudiant B** by going around the classroom and counting off: A...B...A...B. Then, have the "A" students pair up with the nearest "B" students. Instruct "B" students to turn their books upside down in order to begin the activity.

Travaux domestiques — Étudiant B

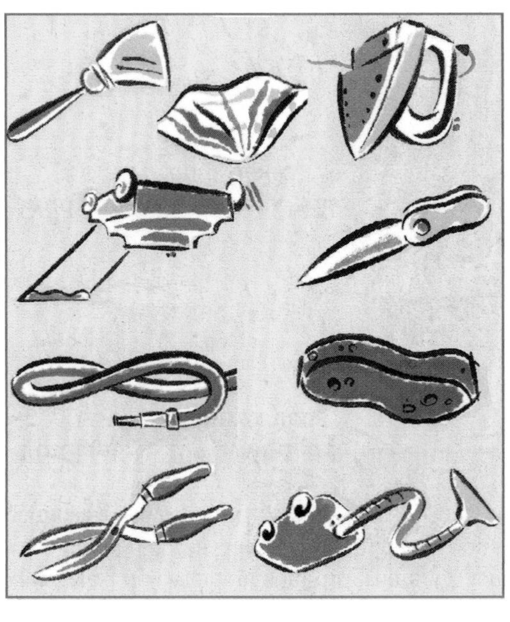

Votre partenaire vous demande de l'aider dans certains petits travaux domestiques.

▶ Acceptez et demandez-lui où est l'objet nécessaire pour accomplir chaque tâche *(task)*.

Il/elle va vous dire où trouver l'objet.

Étudiant A: Est-ce que tu peux essuyer la table?
Étudiant B: D'accord! (Volontiers!) Où est l'éponge?
Étudiant A: Je crois que l'éponge est dans la cuisine (sous l'évier, ...)

Travaux domestiques — Étudiant A

Vous travaillez à la maison et dans le jardin.

▶ Choisissez six petits travaux domestiques et demandez à votre partenaire de vous aider avec chaque tâche *(task)*.

Il/elle accepte et vous demande où trouver l'objet nécessaire à chaque tâche. Répondez-lui.

Étudiant A: Est-ce que tu peux essuyer la table?
Étudiant B: D'accord! (Volontiers!) Où est l'éponge?
Étudiant A: Je crois que l'éponge est dans la cuisine (sous l'évier, ...)

- ☐ **essuyer la table**
- ☐ **couper le pain**
- ☐ **éplucher les pommes**
- ☐ **repasser la nappe** *(tablecloth)*
- ☐ **passer l'aspirateur dans le salon**
- ☐ **laver la voiture**
- ☐ **tailler les arbustes**
- ☐ **arroser les plantes**
- ☐ **tondre la pelouse**
- ☐ **balayer le garage**
- ☐ **nettoyer la salle à manger**

TÊTE À TÊTE

■ Teaching tip

Have students review HOUSEWORK VOCABULARY by referring them to pp. 74–75, and 77 in the textbook.

■ Sample answers

A: Est-ce que tu peux ...?
B: D'accord! (Volontiers!) Où est ...?
A: Je crois ... est ...

- essuyer la table/l'éponge
- couper le pain/le couteau
- éplucher les pommes/le couteau
- repasser la nappe/le fer à repasser
- passer l'aspirateur dans le salon/l'aspirateur
- laver la voiture/le tuyau d'arrosage (l'éponge)
- tailler les arbustes/le sécateur
- arroser les plantes/le tuyau d'arrosage
- tondre la pelouse/la tondeuse
- balayer le garage/le balai
- nettoyer la salle à manger/le chiffon

■ Teaching tip

Have students review the IMPERFECT by referring them to p. 116 in the textbook.

■ Sample answers

A: Il était trois heures.
B: C'est faux! Il était presque quatre heures et demie.

B: Il y avait une vieille femme qui regardait par la fenêtre.
A: C'est faux! Il y avait un homme qui regardait par la fenêtre.

A: Il pleuvait.
B: C'est vrai.

B: La cambrioleuse sautait de la fenêtre avec l'argent.
A: C'est faux! La cambrioleuse était assise sur la moto. Elle attendait le cambrioleur qui avait l'argent.

A: La cambrioleuse avait les cheveux blonds.
B: C'est faux! La cambrioleuse était rousse.

B: Le cambrioleur portait une casque.
A: C'est faux! Le cambrioleur portait une casquette.

Cambriolage — Étudiant B

Vous avez été témoin d'un cambriolage *(burglary)* avec votre partenaire, mais vos souvenirs *(memories)* de l'accident sont différents. Chacun à son tour va décrire six (6) détails de l'événement d'après l'illustration qu'il a. Si vous n'êtes pas d'accord avec votre partenaire, rectifiez sa description.

Étudiant A: Il y avait deux voitures dans la rue.
Étudiant B: C'est vrai.
Étudiant B: La première voiture était jaune.
Étudiant A: C'est faux! Elle était bleue.

Cambriolage — Étudiant A

Vous avez été témoin d'un cambriolage *(burglary)* avec votre partenaire, mais vos souvenirs *(memories)* de l'accident sont différents. Chacun à son tour va décrire six (6) détails de l'événement d'après l'illustration qu'il a. Si vous n'êtes pas d'accord avec votre partenaire, rectifiez sa description.

Étudiant A: Il y avait deux voitures dans la rue.
Étudiant B: C'est vrai.
Étudiant B: La première voiture était jaune.
Étudiant A: C'est faux! Elle était bleue.

TÊTE À TÊTE

Les courses — Étudiant B

Cet après-midi, vous allez faire les courses dans les magasins sur votre liste des courses.

Partie 1

Dites à votre partenaire dans quels magasins vous allez aller. Pour chaque magasin, demandez-lui si vous pouvez acheter quelque chose pour lui/elle. Écoutez bien sa réponse. Puis, inscrivez sa requête dans une liste des courses comme celle à droite. (Utilisez une autre feuille de papier.)

Étudiant B: Je vais passer à la pharmacie. Qu'est-ce que je peux acheter pour toi?
Étudiant A: Achète-moi deux boîtes de coton-tiges, s'il te plaît.

Partie 2

Maintenant vérifiez votre liste.

Étudiant B: À la pharmacie je vais acheter deux boîtes de coton-tiges.
Étudiant A: Oui, c'est ça. (Non, je voulais...)

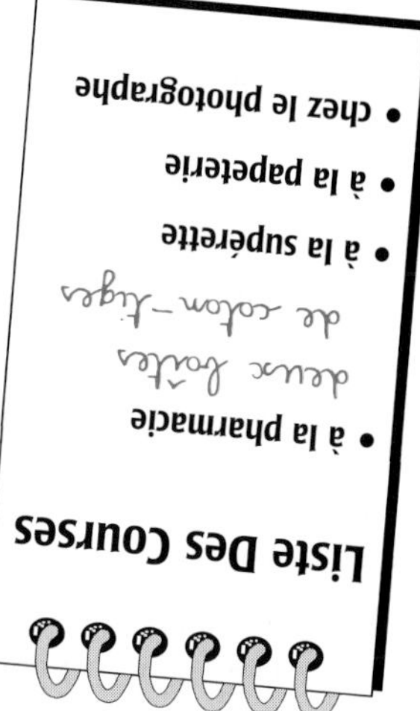

Les courses — Étudiant A

Vous avez besoin des produits suivants. Pour chaque produit, déterminez une certaine quantité (par exemple, deux boîtes de coton-tiges). Indiquez ces quantités sur une autre feuille de papier.

Partie 1

Votre partenaire va faire les courses cet après-midi et vous dit dans quels magasins il/elle va passer. Demandez-lui d'acheter les produits qui figurent sur votre liste.

Étudiant B: Je vais passer à la pharmacie. Qu'est-ce que je peux acheter pour toi?
Étudiant A: Achète-moi deux boîtes de coton-tiges, s'il te plaît.

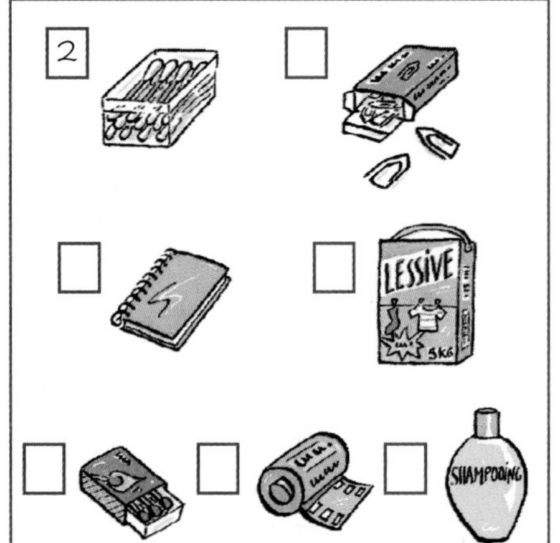

Partie 2

Maintenant votre partenaire va vérifier sa liste.

Étudiant B: À la pharmacie je vais acheter deux boîtes de coton-tiges
Étudiant A: Oui, c'est ça. (Non, je voulais...)

■ Teaching tip

Have students review SHOPPING VOCABULARY by referring them to pp. 152–153 in the textbook.

■ Sample answers

Partie 1

B: Je vais passer ... Qu'est-ce que je peux acheter pour toi?
A: Achète-moi ..., s'il te plaît.

- à la pharmacie/une bouteille de shampooing (une boîte de coton-tiges)
- à la supérette/un paquet de lessive (une boîte d'allumettes)
- à la papeterie/un carnet (une boîte de trombones)
- chez le photographe/une pellicule-couleurs

Partie 2

B: À la pharmacie (supérette/papeterie)/Chez le photographe je vais acheter ...
A: Oui, c'est ça. (Non, je voulais ...)

■ Teaching tip

Have students review TRAVEL VOCABULARY by referring them to pp. 196–198 in the textbook.

■ Answers

Partie 1

A: Combien de trains y a-t-il pour Nice?

B: Il y a trois trains pour Nice.

A: À quelle heure est le départ et l'arrivée du premier train?

B: L'heure de départ du premier train est 11h12. L'heure de l'arrivée du premier train est 17h43.

A: À quelle heure est le départ du dernier train?

B: L'heure de départ du dernier train est 22h30.

A: Quel est le train le plus rapide?

B: Le train qui part à 11h12 est le plus rapide.

Partie 2

B: Combien de trains y a-t-il pour Paris?

A: Il y a trois trains pour Paris.

B: À quelle heure est le départ et l'arrivée du premier train?

A: L'heure de départ du premier train est 9h45. L'heure de l'arrivée du premier train est 16h25.

B: À quelle heure est le départ du dernier train?

A: L'heure de départ du dernier train est 21h58.

B: Quel est le train le plus rapide?

A: Le train qui part à 9h45 est le plus rapide.

À l'agence de voyage — Étudiant B

Partie 1

Vous êtes agent de voyage. Voici l'horaire du train TGV Paris - Côte d'Azur. Répondez aux questions d'un voyageur (votre partenaire) qui veut aller de Paris à Nice.

Partie 2

Vous êtes à Nice et vous voulez aller à Paris en train TGV. Demandez les renseignements suivants à l'agent de voyage (votre partenaire).

- nombre de trains pour Paris?
- heure de départ et d'arrivée du premier train?
- heure de départ du dernier train?
- train le plus rapide?

Paris / Ile de France › Côte d'Azur

PARIS-GARE-DE-LYON	**Départ**	**11.12**	**13.49**	**22.30**
Marseille	Arrivée			
Toulon	Arrivée			5.00
Les Arcs-Draguignan	Arrivée		19.21	
ST-RAPHAEL	**Arrivée**	**16.47**	**19.39**	**5.48**
Cannes	Arrivée	17.13	20.04	6.14
Antibes	Arrivée	17.26	20.17	6.25
NICE	**Arrivée**	**17.43**	**20.33**	**6.44**

À l'agence de voyage — Étudiant A

Partie 1

Vous êtes à Paris et vous voulez aller à Nice en train TGV. Demandez les renseignements suivants à l'agent de voyage (votre partenaire).

- nombre de trains pour Nice?
- heure de départ et d'arrivée du premier train?
- heure de départ du dernier train?
- train le plus rapide?

Partie 2

Vous êtes agent de voyage. Voici l'horaire du train TGV Côte d'Azur - Paris. Répondez aux questions d'un voyageur (votre partenaire) qui veut aller de Nice à Paris.

Côte d'Azur › Paris / Ile de France

NICE	**Départ**	**8.57**	**9.45**	**12.16**	**21.58**
Antibes	Départ	9.13	10.01	12.36	22.12
Cannes	Départ	9.25	10.14	12.49	22.24
ST-RAPHAEL	**Départ**	**9.51**	**10.39**	**13.14**	**22.50**
Les Arcs-Draguignan	Départ	10.10		13.32	
Toulon	Départ	10.47			23.46
Marseille	Départ	10.40			
PARIS-GARE-DE-LYON	**Départ**		**16.25**	**19.22**	**6.46**

Vacances — Étudiant B

Partie 1

Vous êtes le/la réceptionniste à l'hôtel "Relais Soleil". Répondez à votre client(e) — votre partenaire — qui voudrait quelques renseignements.

Relais Soleil
32 chambres: de 110 € à 180 €
5 suites: de 200 € à 250 €
petit déjeuner complet: 9 €
menus: 28 € et 42 €
TV

Étudiant A: **Quel est le prix des chambres?**

Étudiant B: Les prix vont de 110 € à 180 € par jour.

Partie 2

Vous voulez passer une semaine dans un petit hôtel: "L'auberge du moulin". Avant de faire votre réservation, vous téléphonez au (à la) réceptionniste — votre partenaire — pour obtenir les renseignements *(information)* suivants.

- Nombre de chambres?
- Prix des chambres?
- Prix du petit déjeuner?
- Téléphone et télévision?
- Piscine et salle d'exercice?
- Ascenseur et air conditionné?

Vacances — Étudiant A

Partie 1

Vous voulez passer une semaine à l'hôtel de luxe "Relais Soleil". Avant de faire votre réservation, vous téléphonez au (à la) réceptionniste — votre partenaire — pour obtenir les renseignements *(information)* suivants.

- **Prix des chambres?**
- **Prix du petit déjeuner?**
- **Prix des repas?**
- **Service dans les chambres?**
- **Éléments de confort?**
- **Possibilités de faire du sport?**

Étudiant A: **Quel est le prix des chambres?**

Étudiant B: Les prix vont de 110 € à 180 € par jour.

Partie 2

Vous êtes le/la réceptionniste à "L'auberge du Moulin." Répondez à votre client(e) — votre partenaire — qui voudrait quelques renseignements.

AUBERGE DU MOULIN

12 chambres: de 50 à 100 €

petit déjeuner: 6,50 €

menus: 20 et 30 €

TÊTE À TÊTE

■ **Teaching tip**

Have students review HOTEL VOCABULARY by referring them to pp. 230–231 in the textbook.

■ **Answers**

Partie 1

A: Quel est le prix du petit déjeuner?
B: Le prix du petit déjeuner complet est 9 €.
A: Quel est le prix des repas?
B: Les menus vont de 28 à 42 €.
A: Est-ce qu'il y a le service dans les chambres?
B: Oui, il y a le service dans les chambres.
A: Quels sont les éléments de confort?
B: Il y a la climatisation, l'air conditionné, la télévision, le service dans les chambres, un ascenseur, une piscine et une salle d'exercices.
A: Est-ce qu'on peut faire du sport?
B: Oui, on peut jouer au tennis, nager (faire de la natation) et faire du vélo dans la salle d'exercices.

Partie 2

B: Combien de chambres est-ce qu'il y a?
A: Il y a 12 chambres.
B: Quel est le prix des chambres?
A: Les prix vont de 50 à 100€.
B: Quel est le prix du petit déjeuner?
A: Le prix du petit déjeuner est 6,50 €.
B: Est-ce qu'il y a le téléphone et la télévision?
A: Oui, il y a le téléphone et la télévision.
B: Est-ce qu'il y a une piscine et une salle d'exercices?
A: Il y a une piscine, mais il n'y a pas de salle d'exercices.
B: Est-ce qu'il y a un ascenseur et l'air conditionné (la climatisation)?
A: Il y a l'air conditionné (la climatisation), mais il n'y a pas d'ascenseur.

■ Teaching tip

Have students review MEDICAL VOCABULARY by referring them to pp. 264–266 in the textbook.

■ Sample answers

B: Comment allez-vous?
A: Je ne me sens pas bien.
B: Où avez-vous mal?
A: J'ai mal au dos.
B: Qu'est-ce qui s'est passé?
A: Je faisais du snowboard, quand tout à coup j'ai glissé sur la glace et je suis tombé(e).
B: Je vais vous faire une radio. En plus, prenez de l'aspirine toutes les 4 heures. Vous devez aussi vous reposer et surtout ne faites pas de snowboard!

Chez le médecin — Étudiant B

Vous êtes médecin (ou dentiste).

Vous examinez un(e) patient(e) — votre partenaire. Faites un diagnostic en complétant la conversation suivante. Puis, proposez un traitement, en vous inspirant des suggestions à droite.

- Ask how your patient feels.
- Ask where it hurts.
- Ask what happened to him/her.
- Tell him/her what you are going to do.

- **prendre la température**
- **faire une radio**
- **faire une piqûre**
- **donner des médicaments**
- **donner un antibiotique**
- **faire un pansement**
- **faire un plâtre**

****

- **faire un plombage**
- **enlever une dent**

Chez le médecin — Étudiant A

Vous allez chez le médecin (ou le dentiste). Choisissez l'un des problèmes suggérés par les illustrations. Écoutez le médecin — votre partenaire — et répondez à ses questions.

- Tell the doctor how you feel.
  Je me sens ...
  (Je ne me sens pas ...)
- Tell the doctor where it hurts.
  J'ai mal ...
- Tell the doctor what happened.
  (Use your imagination.)
  Je suis tombé(e) d'un arbre et je me suis fracturé ...

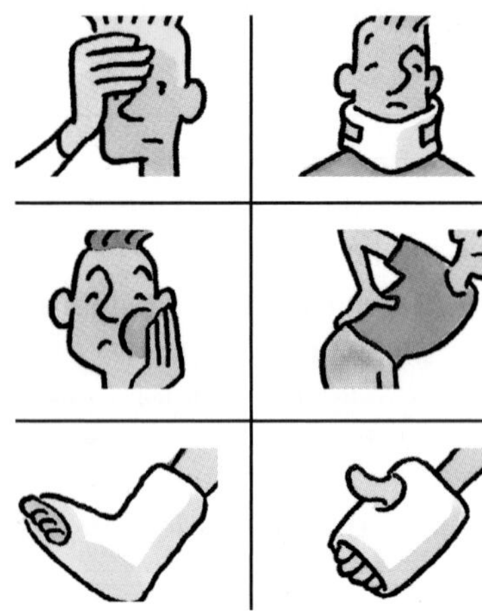

Rendez-vous parisien — Étudiant B

Vous êtes à Paris à l'hôtel d'Angleterre situé rue Jacob — "X" sur le plan *(street map)* à droite. Votre partenaire vous donne rendez-vous dans un café.

- Demandez-lui comment y aller.
- Suivez ses instructions sur le plan.

Voici le début du dialogue:

Étudiant A: Est-ce que tu veux prendre un pot avec moi dans mon café préféré?

Étudiant B: Oui, bien sûr, comment est-ce que je vais là-bas?

Étudiant A: Tu sors de l'hôtel et tu tournes à droite dans la rue Jacob.

Étudiant B: D'accord, je tourne à droite dans la rue Jacob. Et après?

Étudiant A: ...

Avez-vous trouvé le café de votre partenaire? Confirmez votre rendez-vous avec lui.

Étudiant B: Est-ce que c'est le café qui se trouve en face de (à côté de, sur) ...?

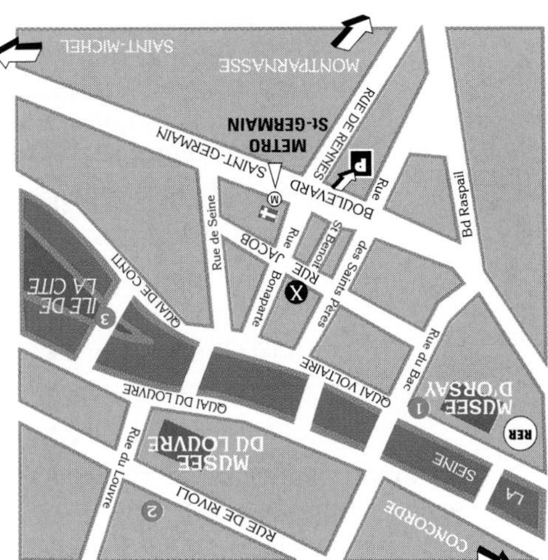

Rendez-vous parisien — Étudiant A

Votre partenaire visite Paris. Il/elle loge à l'hôtel d'Angleterre situé rue Jacob — "X" sur le plan *(street map)* à droite.

- Choisissez un des cafés marqués 1, 2 ou 3.
- Donnez-lui rendez-vous dans ce café et expliquez-lui en détail comment y aller à pied.

Voici le début du dialogue:

Étudiant A: Est-ce que tu veux prendre un pot avec moi dans mon café préféré?

Étudiant B: Oui, bien sûr, comment est-ce que je vais là-bas?

Étudiant A: Tu sors de l'hôtel et tu tournes à droite dans la rue Jacob.

Étudiant B: D'accord, je tourne à droite dans la rue Jacob. Et après?

Étudiant A: ...

À la fin, votre partenaire va confirmer votre rendez-vous.

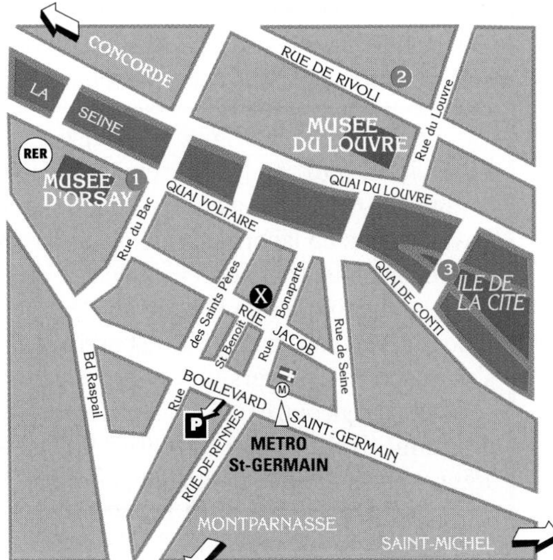

TÊTE À TÊTE

■ Teaching tip

Have students review MEETING DOWNTOWN VOCABULARY by referring them to pp. 306–307 in the textbook.

■ Sample answers

A: Est-ce que tu veux prendre un pot avec moi dans mon café préféré?
B: Oui, bien sûr, comment est-ce que je vais là-bas?
A: Tu sors de l'hôtel et tu tournes à gauche dans la rue Jacob.
B: D'accord, je tourne à gauche dans la rue Jacob. Et après?
A: Tu tournes encore à gauche dans la rue de Seine.
B: D'accord. Et après ça?
A: Tu continues dans la rue de Seine et puis tu tournes à droite sur le quai de Conti.
B: Très bien—c'est tout?
A: Non! Il faut continuer un tout petit peu sur le quai de Conti et puis tu vas tourner à gauche dans la première rue à gauche.
B: D'accord. Est-ce que c'est le café qui est situé sur l'Île de la Cité?
A: Oui, c'est ça!

Teaching Note

In preparation for this activity, model the pronunciation of the names of the places and streets on the map. Also, review vocabulary such as:

traverser (la rue, la Seine)
continuer tout droit
prendre le pont

After the conversation, have students change roles for a second conversation.

■ **Teaching tip**

Have students review PHASES OF LIFE VOCABULARY by referring them to p. 360 in the textbook.

■ **Answers**

Partie 1

B: Quelle est la nationalité d'origine de Marie Curie?

A: Marie Curie était d'origine polonaise.

B: Quand est-ce qu'elle est arrivée à Paris?

A: Elle est arrivée à Paris en 1891.

B: Comment s'appelait son mari?

A: Son mari s'appelait Pierre Curie.

B: Comment s'appelait leur fille?

A: Leur fille s'appelait Irène.

Partie 2

A: Quelles étaient les découvertes scientifiques de Marie Curie?

B: Pierre et Marie ont travaillé sur les phénomènes de la radioactivité. Ils ont découvert le polonium et le radium—deux éléments nouveaux.

A: Quelle a été sa première distinction?

B: Pierre et Marie ont reçu le Prix Nobel de Physique en 1903.

A: Quel événement tragique a eu lieu dans la vie de Marie Curie?

B: Son mari, Pierre, est mort dans un accident.

A: Quelle a été sa deuxième distinction?

B: Marie a reçu le Prix Nobel de Chimie en 1911.

A: Quand est-ce que Marie Curie est morte?

B: Marie Curie est morte en 1934.

Marie Curie — Étudiant B

Partie 1

Votre partenaire va vous lire la biographie de Marie Curie, génie scientifique du 20e siècle. Écoutez bien et prenez des notes sur les sujets suivants:

- date de naissance
- nationalité d'origine
- date de son arrivée à Paris
- nom du mari
- nom de leur fille

Si c'est nécessaire, posez des questions à votre partenaire. Puis écrivez un paragraphe basé sur vos notes.

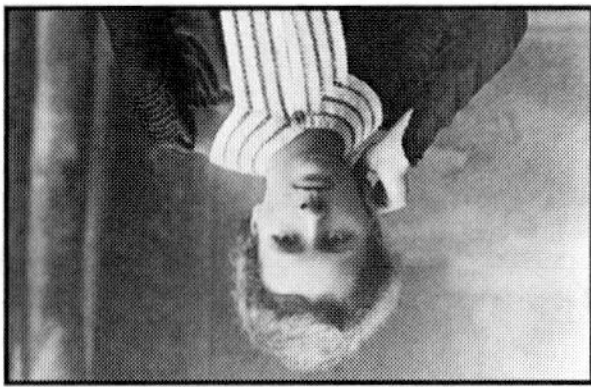

Partie 2

Voici la continuation de la biographie de Marie Curie. Lisez le texte deux fois: d'abord en silence, ensuite à haute voix pour votre partenaire.

> Dans leur laboratoire, Pierre et Marie Curie ont travaillé sur les phénomènes de la radioactivité. Dans leurs recherches, ils ont découvert deux éléments nouveaux: le polonium et le radium. Pour ces travaux, ils ont reçu le Prix Nobel de Physique en 1903. Malheureusement Pierre Curie est mort dans un accident. Marie a continué ses travaux. En 1911, elle a reçu le Prix Nobel de Chimie. Les recherches de Marie Curie sur les rayons-X ont permis les progrès de la médecine moderne. Marie Curie est morte en 1934.

Puis, répondez à ses questions.

Étudiant B: Quand est née Marie Curie?

Étudiant A: Elle est née en 1867.

Marie Curie — Étudiant A

Partie 1

Voici une courte biographie de Marie Curie, génie scientifique du 20e siècle. Lisez le texte deux fois: d'abord en silence, ensuite à haute voix pour votre partenaire.

> Marie Curie était d'origine polonaise. Elle est née à Varsovie en 1867. Au lycée, c'était une élève brillante. À l'âge de 16 ans, elle a obtenu son diplôme. Puis elle a travaillé dans un laboratoire de physique expérimentale.
>
> Après quelques années, elle a décidé de continuer ses études scientifiques en France. En 1891, elle a quitté la Pologne, son pays natal. Elle est arrivée à Paris et elle s'est inscrite à l'université.
>
> Là, elle a rencontré un jeune professeur de physique et de chimie. Il s'appelait Pierre Curie. Ils se sont mariés en 1895 et ils ont eu une petite fille, nommée Irène.

Puis, répondez à ses questions.

Étudiant B: Quand est née Marie Curie?

Étudiant A: Elle est née en 1867.

Partie 2

Maintenant votre partenaire va continuer la biographie. Écoutez bien et prenez des notes sur les sujets suivants:

- découvertes scientifiques
- première distinction
- événement tragique
- deuxième distinction
- date de la mort

Si c'est nécessaire, posez des questions à votre partenaire. Puis écrivez un paragraphe basé sur vos notes.

TÊTE À TÊTE

Choix professionnels — Étudiant B

Vous êtes conseiller(conseillère) professionnel(le).

- Votre client — votre partenaire — va vous indiquer quatre de ses préférences personnelles.
- Pour chaque option, suggérez deux (2) professions qui correspondent à cette préférence.

Étudiant A: Moi, je préfère [travailler seul(e)].
Étudiant B: Alors, vous pouvez être [écrivain ou chercheur (chercheuse).]
Étudiant A: Mais j'aime aussi ...
Étudiant B: Dans ce cas, vous pouvez devenir ...

- acteur (actrice)
- assistant(e) social(e)
- banquier (banquière)
- chercheur (chercheuse) scientifique
- chimiste
- cinéaste
- dessinateur (dessinatrice)
- diplomate
- écrivain
- fonctionnaire
- homme (femme) d'affaires
- infirmier (infirmière)
- journaliste
- médecin
- photographe
- professeur
- représentant(e) de commerce
- secrétaire
- steward (hôtesse de l'air)
- vendeur (vendeuse)

Choix professionnels — Étudiant A

Vous voulez avoir une profession qui corresponde à vos préférences personnelles.

- Choisissez une option dans quatre (4) des catégories suivantes.
- Indiquez votre première préférence à votre conseiller(conseillère) professionnel(le) — votre partenaire — et demandez-lui quelle profession vous convient.
- Il/elle vous donnera deux possibilités.
- Continuez, en lui indiquant les trois autres préférences.

D'après vous, quelle est la meilleure suggestion?

1	☐ voyager	ou	☐ rester à la maison
2	☐ gagner beaucoup d'argent	ou	☐ avoir une vie de famille
3	☐ avoir beaucoup de responsabilités	ou	☐ être indépendant(e)
4	☐ avoir une profession artistique	ou	☐ avoir une profession scientifique
5	☐ travailler beaucoup	ou	☐ avoir des vacances
6	☐ travailler seul(e)	ou	☐ travailler avec d'autres

Étudiant A: Moi, je préfère [travailler seul(e)].
Étudiant B: Alors, vous pouvez être [écrivain ou chercheur (chercheuse).]
Étudiant A: Mais j'aime aussi ...
Étudiant B: Dans ce cas, vous pouvez devenir ...

■ Teaching tip

Have students review PROFESSIONAL VOCABULARY by referring them to pp. 386–387 in the textbook.

■ Sample answers

A: Moi, je préfère avoir une profession artistique.
B: Alors, vous pouvez être photographe ou dessinatrice (dessinateur).
A: Mais j'aime aussi gagner beaucoup d'argent.
B: Dans ce cas, vous pouvez devenir femme (homme) d'affaires ou médecin.

REFERENCE SECTION

APPENDIX A: *Reprise*

1 VERBES

Révision
present tense of stem-changing verbs
Appendix C pp. R20-21

A. Le présent

Verbes réguliers

	parler	-er	finir	-ir	vendre	-re
STEM	**parl-**		**fini-**		**vend-**	
je	**parle**	**-e**	**finis**	**-is**	**vends**	**-s**
tu	**parles**	**-es**	**finis**	**-is**	**vends**	**-s**
il/elle/on	**parle**	**-e**	**finit**	**-it**	**vend**	—
nous	**parlons**	**-ons**	**finissons**	**-issons**	**vendons**	**-ons**
vous	**parlez**	**-ez**	**finissez**	**-issez**	**vendez**	**-ez**
ils/elles	**parlent**	**-ent**	**finissent**	**-issent**	**vendent**	**-ent**

NEGATIVE
je **ne parle pas**
je **ne finis pas**
je **ne vends pas**

INTERROGATIVE	
est-ce qu'il/elle **parle?**	**parle-t-**il/elle?
est-ce qu'il/elle **finit?**	**finit-**il/elle?
est-ce qu'il/elle **vend?**	**vend-**il/elle?

***Le verbe* sortir** *(to go out)*

STEM		**sor-**		**sort-**
	je	**sors**	nous	**sortons**
	tu	**sors**	vous	**sortez**
	il/elle/on	**sort**	ils/elles	**sortent**

Verbes comme **sortir**

partir	*to leave*	**je pars**	**nous partons**
dormir	*to sleep*	**je dors**	**nous dormons**
servir	*to serve*	**je sers**	**nous servons**

Les verbes* vouloir** *(want, wish),* **pouvoir** *(can, be able)* ***et **devoir** *(must, have to)*

	vouloir	pouvoir	devoir
je	**veux**	**peux**	**dois**
tu	**veux**	**peux**	**dois**
il/elle/on	**veut**	**peut**	**doit**
nous	**voulons**	**pouvons**	**devons**
vous	**voulez**	**pouvez**	**devez**
ils/elles	**veulent**	**peuvent**	**doivent**

Ils doivent travailler.

Les verbes* prendre** *(to take)* ***et **mettre** *(to put, place)*

	prendre	mettre
je	**prends**	**mets**
tu	**prends**	**mets**
il/elle/on	**prend**	**met**
nous	**prenons**	**mettons**
vous	**prenez**	**mettez**
ils/elles	**prennent**	**mettent**

Verbes comme **prendre**

apprendre	*to learn*
comprendre	*to understand*

Verbes comme **mettre**

promettre	*to promise*
permettre	*to permit, allow*

R2 Reference Section

Les verbes être, avoir, aller, faire, venir

PRESENT	**être** *(to be)*	**avoir** *(to have)*	**aller** *(to go)*	**faire** *(to do, make)*	**venir** *(to come)*
je (j')	**suis**	**ai**	**vais**	**fais**	**viens**
tu	**es**	**as**	**vas**	**fais**	**viens**
il/elle/on	**est**	**a**	**va**	**fait**	**vient**
nous	**sommes**	**avons**	**allons**	**faisons**	**venons**
vous	**êtes**	**avez**	**allez**	**faites**	**venez**
ils/elles	**sont**	**ont**	**vont**	**font**	**viennent**

Quelques expressions avec avoir

avoir chaud/froid	*to be warm, hot/cold*
avoir faim/soif	*to be hungry/thirsty*
avoir raison/tort	*to be right/wrong*
avoir sommeil	*to be sleepy*
avoir peur (de)	*to be afraid (of)*
avoir de la chance	*to be lucky*
avoir . . . ans	*to be . . . years old*
avoir mal	*to hurt*
avoir besoin de	*to need*
avoir envie de	*to feel like, to wish*

Quelques expressions avec faire

faire { **du (de l')** / **de la (de l')** / **des** } + *sport* / *subject (of study)* / *activity*

faire du ski	**faire de la natation**
faire de l'algèbre	**faire des maths**
faire du camping	**faire du théâtre**

faire attention (à)	*to pay attention (to), to be careful (with), to watch out (for)*
faire les courses	*to go shopping (for food)*
faire des achats	*to go shopping (for items other than food)*
faire la cuisine	*to cook*
faire la vaisselle	*to do the dishes*
faire ses devoirs	*to do one's homework*
faire ses valises	*to pack (one's suitcases)*
faire une promenade (à pied)	*to go for a walk*
faire une promenade (en auto, à vélo)	*to go for a ride (by car, by bicycle)*
faire un tour	*to take a walk, ride*
faire une randonnée	*to take a hike, a long drive*
faire un voyage	*to go on a trip, to take a trip*
faire un séjour	*to spend time (in a place away from home)*

Appendix A R3

B. Le passé composé

*Le passé composé avec **avoir***

PAST PARTICIPLE	parler → parlé	finir → fini	vendre → vendu
PASSÉ COMPOSÉ	j'**ai parlé** tu **as parlé** il/elle/on **a parlé** nous **avons parlé** vous **avez parlé** ils/elles **ont parlé**	j'**ai fini** tu **as fini** il/elle/on **a fini** nous **avons fini** vous **avez fini** ils/elles **ont fini**	j'**ai vendu** tu **as vendu** il/elle/on **a vendu** nous **avons vendu** vous **avez vendu** ils/elles **ont vendu**
NEGATIVE	je **n'ai pas parlé**		
INTERROGATIVE	**est-ce que** tu **as parlé**? **as**-tu **parlé**? **a-t-**il/elle **parlé**?		

PARTICIPES PASSÉS DES VERBES IRRÉGULIERS		
-é	être	j'ai **été**
-ait	faire	j'ai **fait**
-ert	ouvrir découvrir	j'ai **ouvert** j'ai **découvert**
-i	suivre dormir sentir	j'ai **suivi** j'ai **dormi** j'ai **senti**
-is	mettre prendre apprendre	j'ai **mis** j'ai **pris** j'ai **appris**
-it	dire écrire	j'ai **dit** j'ai **écrit**
-uit	conduire détruire	j'ai **conduit** j'ai **détruit**
-u	avoir boire savoir voir pouvoir devoir vouloir recevoir lire courir connaître vivre il y a il faut	j'ai **eu** j'ai **bu** j'ai **su** j'ai **vu** j'ai **pu** j'ai **dû** j'ai **voulu** j'ai **reçu** j'ai **lu** j'ai **couru** j'ai **connu** j'ai **vécu** il y a **eu** il a **fallu**

*Le passé composé avec **être***

PASSÉ COMPOSÉ	je **suis allé** tu **es allé** il/on **est allé** nous **sommes allés** vous **êtes allé(s)** ils **sont allés**	je **suis allée** tu **es allée** elle **est allée** nous **sommes allées** vous **êtes allée(s)** elles **sont allées**
NEGATIVE	je **ne suis pas allé(e)**	
INTERROGATIVE	**est-ce que** tu **es allé(e)**? **es**-tu **allé(e)**? **est**-il/elle **allé(e)**?	

VERBES CONJUGUÉS AVEC **ÊTRE**			
aller *(to go)* **venir** *(to come)*	**je suis allé(e)** **je suis venu(e)**	**passer** *(to pass)* **rester** *(to stay)* **rentrer** *(to go back)* **retourner** *(to return)* **revenir** *(to come back)*	**je suis passé(e)** **je suis resté(e)** **je suis rentré(e)** **je suis retourné(e)** **je suis revenu(e)**
arriver *(to arrive, come)* **partir** *(to leave)*	**je suis arrivé(e)** **je suis parti(e)**	**devenir** *(to become)*	**je suis devenu(e)**
entrer *(to enter, come in)* **sortir** *(to go out)*	**je suis entré(e)** **je suis sorti(e)**	**naître** *(to be born)* **mourir** *(to die)*	**je suis né(e)** **je suis mort(e)**
monter *(to go up)* **descendre** *(to go down)* **tomber** *(to fall)*	**je suis monté(e)** **je suis descendu(e)** **je suis tombé(e)**		

C. L'imparfait

The imperfect tense is formed as follows:

nous-form of the present minus **-ons** + endings

	parler	finir	vendre	faire	
(PRESENT) nous	**parl**ons	**finiss**ons	**vend**ons	**fais**ons	
IMPERFECT STEM	**parl-**	**finiss-**	**vend-**	**fais-**	**endings**
je	**parlais**	**finissais**	**vendais**	**faisais**	**-ais**
tu	**parlais**	**finissais**	**vendais**	**faisais**	**-ais**
il/elle/on	**parlait**	**finissait**	**vendait**	**faisait**	**-ait**
nous	**parlions**	**finissions**	**vendions**	**faisions**	**-ions**
vous	**parliez**	**finissiez**	**vendiez**	**faisiez**	**-iez**
ils/elles	**parlaient**	**finissaient**	**vendaient**	**faisaient**	**-aient**
NEGATIVE	je **ne parlais pas**				
INTERROGATIVE	**est-ce que** tu **parlais**? **parlais**-tu?				

IMPERFECT STEMS	
manger	je mangeais
commencer	je commençais
être	j'étais
avoir	j'avais
aller	j'allais
venir	je venais
sortir	je sortais
dormir	je dormais
mettre	je mettais
suivre	je suivais
devoir	je devais
pouvoir	je pouvais
vouloir	je voulais
savoir	je savais
connaître	je connaissais
prendre	je prenais
dire	je disais
lire	je lisais
écrire	j'écrivais
conduire	je conduisais
boire	je buvais
croire	je croyais
voir	je voyais

HIER APRÈS-MIDI, NOUS SOMMES ALLÉS EN VILLE. NOUS AVONS VU UN ACCIDENT.
PENDANT LES VACANCES, J'ALLAIS SOUVENT À LA PLAGE. IL Y AVAIT TOUJOURS BEAUCOUP DE MONDE.

D. Passé composé ou imparfait?

Use:	to describe:	
the PASSÉ COMPOSÉ	• what you did • what happened	Hier après-midi, nous **sommes allés** en ville. Nous **avons vu** un accident.
the IMPERFECT	• what you used to do • what used to be	Pendant les vacances, j'**allais** souvent à la plage. Il y **avait** toujours beaucoup de monde.
	• what you were doing • what was going on	Hier à neuf heures, je **regardais** la télé. Il y **avait** une comédie.
	• the circumstances of an event (time, weather)	Quelle heure **était**-il? Quel temps **faisait**-il?

Appendix A R5

2 LANGUE ET COMMUNICATION

A. Les articles

In French, nouns are frequently introduced by ARTICLES. The choice of article depends on the <u>context</u> in which the noun is used.

These articles . . .		introduce . . .	
DEFINITE:	**le (l')** **la (l')**	a noun used in a GENERAL or COLLECTIVE sense	J'aime **le** fromage. **La** patience est une qualité.
	les	a SPECIFIC thing (or things)	Voici **le** fromage. *(the one I bought)* **La** patience du professeur est remarquable.
INDEFINITE:	**un** **une**	one (or several) WHOLE items	J'ai acheté **un** fromage. *(a whole cheese)*
	des	one of a kind	Ce boulanger *(baker)* fait **un** pain excellent. Vous avez **une** patience extraordinaire.
PARTITIVE:	**du (de l')** **de la (de l')** **des**	SOME, ANY, a PORTION an UNSPECIFIED AMOUNT of something	Nous mangeons **du** fromage. *(just a piece)* Vous avez **de la** patience. Veux-tu **des** spaghetti?

REMARKS:

➡ In <u>negative</u> sentences, **un, une, du, de la, des → de (d').**

Marc mange **du** fromage. — Alice ne mange pas **de** fromage.
Philippe a **un** couteau. — Mélanie n'a pas **de** couteau.

➡ The DEFINITE article is generally used after the following verbs:

aimer — J'aime **le** gâteau.
préférer — Marc préfère **la** glace.

Philippe préfère le gâteau.

➡ The PARTITIVE article is often, but <u>not always</u>, used after the following:

voici	**boire**	**acheter**
voilà	**manger**	**avoir**
il y a	**prendre**	**vouloir**

It is the context that determines which article is used. Compare:

Je mange **la** pizza. *(= the pizza that I bought)*
Je mange **une** pizza. *(= a whole pizza)*
Je mange **de la** pizza. *(= a piece of pizza)*

Les boissons sont sur la table.

➡ The PARTITIVE article is <u>not</u> used to introduce a subject. Compare:

Le lait est dans le réfrigérateur. — Il y a **du lait** dans le réfrigérateur.

➡ The PARTITIVE article can be used with <u>abstract</u> as well as <u>concrete</u> nouns.

Vous avez **de l'argent.** — Moi, j'ai **du talent.**

R6 Reference Section

B. Les adjectifs irréguliers

Irregular feminine forms

MASCULINE	FEMININE		
-eux	**-euse**	**curieux**	**curieuse**
-f	**-ve**	**actif**	**active**
-en **-on** **-el**	**-enne** **-onne** **-elle**	**canadien** **mignon** **ponctuel**	**canadienne** **mignonne** **ponctuelle**
-er **-et**	**-ère** **-ète**	**régulier** **discret**	**régulière** **discrète**

Ils sont actifs!

Irregular masculine plural forms

SINGULAR	PLURAL		
-eux	**-eux**	**curieux**	**curieux**
-al	**-aux**	**loyal**	**loyaux**

Est-ce que ces belles maisons à Annecy sont nouvelles?

Les adjectifs: **beau, nouveau, vieux**

SINGULAR			PLURAL	
MASCULINE		FEMININE	MASCULINE	FEMININE
beau	**(bel)**	**belle**	**beaux**	**belles**
nouveau	**(nouvel)**	**nouvelle**	**nouveaux**	**nouvelles**
vieux	**(vieil)**	**vieille**	**vieux**	**vieilles**

REMARKS:

➡ In French, adjectives usually come after the noun.

J'aime la musique **classique**. Anne porte une jupe **rouge** et **noire**.

➡ The following adjectives usually come before the noun:

grand ≠ petit	**jeune ≠ vieux**	**joli = beau**
bon ≠ mauvais	**nouveau ≠ ancien**	

Nous avons une grande maison dans un **vieux** quartier de Tours.

NOTE: Often **des → de** before a plural adjective.

Il porte **des** sandales. Il porte **de vieilles** sandales.

Ce monsieur est-il jeune ou vieux?

C. Les noms irréguliers

SINGULAR	PLURAL		
-al	**-aux**	**un animal**	**des animaux**
-eau	**-eaux**	**un chapeau**	**des chapeaux**
-eu	**-eux**	**un cheveu**	**des cheveux**

➡ A few nouns in **-al** form their plural by adding **–s**:

un festival **des festivals**

Malice est un animal domestique.

D. Les pronoms compléments d'objet direct et indirect

FORMS AND USES

SUBJECT	DIRECT and INDIRECT
je (j')	**me (m')**
tu	**te (t')**
nous	**nous**
vous	**vous**

SUBJECT	DIRECT	INDIRECT
il	**le (l')**	**lui**
elle	**la (l')**	
ils	**les**	**leur**
elles		

A DIRECT OBJECT answers the questions:
qui? *(whom?)* or **quoi?** *(what?)*

qui?	Je vois **Pauline**.	Je **la** vois.
quoi?	Je vois **la voiture**.	Je **la** vois.

VERB + DIRECT OBJECT
(quelqu'un)

aider	**inviter**
aimer	**regarder**
chercher	**rencontrer**
connaître	**retrouver**
écouter	**voir**

An INDIRECT OBJECT answers the question:
à qui? *(to whom?)*

à qui?	Je parle **à Pauline.**	Je **lui** parle.

VERB + INDIRECT OBJECT
(à quelqu'un)

dire à
écrire à
parler à
téléphoner à
rendre visite à
rendre service à

donner à *(to give)*
emprunter à *(to borrow)*
montrer à *(to show)*
prêter à *(to lend)*
rendre à *(to return, to give back)*

E. Connaître ou savoir?

Connaître and **savoir** both mean *to know*, but they are used differently.

Connaître . . . is used with NOUNS (or pronouns) designating:

je	**connais**
tu	**connais**
il/elle/on	**connaît**
nous	**connaissons**
vous	**connaissez**
ils/elles	**connaissent**

- PEOPLE — **Je connais** Jean-Philippe.
- PLACES — **Je connais** bien Paris.
  Je connais un bon restaurant italien.
- INFORMATION — Je **ne connais pas** ton adresse.

R8 Reference Section

POSITION
Object pronouns come **before** the verb EXCEPT in affirmative commands.

	AFFIRMATIVE	NEGATIVE
Present	Je **t'**invite. Je **le** connais. Je **lui** téléphone.	Je ne **t'**invite pas. Je ne **le** connais pas. Je ne **lui** téléphone pas.
Passé composé	Je **t'**ai vu. Je **l'**ai invité. Je **leur** ai parlé.	Je ne **t'**ai pas vu. Je ne **l'**ai pas invité. Je ne **leur** ai pas parlé.
Imperative (commands)	Écris-**moi**. Invite-**les**. Rends-**leur** visite.	Ne **m'**écris pas. Ne **les** invite pas. Ne **leur** rends pas visite.
Infinitive construction	Je vais **t'**inviter. Je vais **les** voir. Je vais **leur** écrire.	Je ne vais pas **t'**inviter. Je ne vais pas **les** voir. Je ne vais pas **leur** écrire.

Savoir . . . is used (with):

je	**sais**
tu	**sais**
il/elle/on	**sait**
nous	**savons**
vous	**savez**
ils/elles	**savent**

- ALONE — **Tu sais**? Non, je ne **sais** pas.
- a CLAUSE introduced by . . .
  - **que** *(that)* — **Je sais** que tu as une nouvelle moto.
  - **si** *(if, whether)* — Est-ce que tu **sais** si Éric va venir?
  - an INTERROGATIVE expression — Je ne **sais** pas où tu habites. **Sais**-tu qui a téléphoné? Je ne **sais** pas quand je vais aller à Nice.
- an INFINITIVE — **Savez**-vous utiliser un ordinateur?
- a NOUN designating something LEARNED — Les élèves ne **savent** pas la leçon.

Appendix A R9

3 VOCABULAIRE

A. Les nombres et les dates

LES NOMBRES CARDINAUX

To count, we use CARDINAL numbers: 1, 2, 3 . . .

0 à 99

0	zéro	10	dix	20	vingt	60	soixante
1	un	11	onze	21	vingt et un	61	soixante et un
2	deux	12	douze	22	vingt-deux	70	soixante-dix
3	trois	13	treize	23	vingt-trois	71	soixante et onze
4	quatre	14	quatorze	30	trente	72	soixante-douze
5	cinq	15	quinze	31	trente et un	80	quatre-vingts
6	six	16	seize	40	quarante	81	quatre-vingt-un
7	sept	17	dix-sept	48	quarante-huit	90	quatre-vingt-dix
8	huit	18	dix-huit	49	quarante-neuf	91	quatre-vingt-onze
9	neuf	19	dix-neuf	50	cinquante	99	quatre-vingt-dix-neuf

100 à 1 000 000

100	cent	400	quatre cents	1 000	mille
101	cent un	520	cinq cent vingt	1 210	mille deux cent dix
110	cent dix	675	six cent soixante-quinze	2 000	deux mille
200	deux cents	880	huit cent quatre-vingts	15 000	quinze mille
215	deux cent quinze	900	neuf cents	100 000	cent mille
371	trois cent soixante et onze			1 000 000	un million

LES NOMBRES ORDINAUX

To rank or put in sequence, we use ORDINAL numbers: 1st, 2nd, 3rd . . .

ordinal number = cardinal number + **ième**
(minus **-e**, if any)

deux → **deuxième**
douze → **douzième**
vingt et un → **vingt et unième**
cent huit → **cent huitième**

EXCEPTIONS:
un → **premier (première)**
cinq → **cinquième**
neuf → **neuvième**

LA DATE

When giving the date in French, use cardinal numbers:

le douze octobre
le vingt juillet

However, use the ordinal number (**premier**) for the first of the month:

le premier mai

B. La nourriture et les boissons

Boulangerie Pâtisserie

le pain *bread*
un croissant
un gâteau *cake*
une tarte *pie*

Boucherie

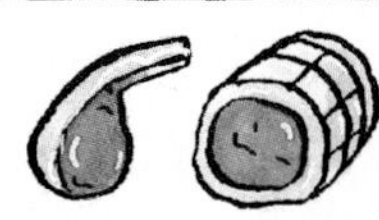

la viande *meat*
le rosbif
le jambon *ham*
le porc
le veau *veal*

Alimentation générale

le ketchup
la mayonnaise
le sel *salt*
le poivre *pepper*
le sucre *sugar*
la confiture *jam*
le riz *rice*
les spaghetti
les céréales

Produits laitiers *(Dairy products)*

le lait *milk*
le beurre *butter*
la margarine
le fromage *cheese*
la glace *ice cream*
le yaourt *yogurt*
un oeuf *egg*

Poissonnerie

le poisson *fish*
la sole
le thon *tuna*
le saumon *salmon*

Fruits

une orange
une banane
un melon
une pomme *apple*
une poire *pear*
une pamplemousse *grapefruit*
une fraise *strawberry*
une cerise *cherry*
du raisin *grapes*

Légumes

le céleri
une salade *lettuce*
une carotte
une tomate
une pomme de terre *potato*
des petits pois *peas*

Boissons

le thé
le café
l'eau *water*
l'eau minérale
le jus de fruits
le jus de pomme
le jus de raisin

Appendix A R11

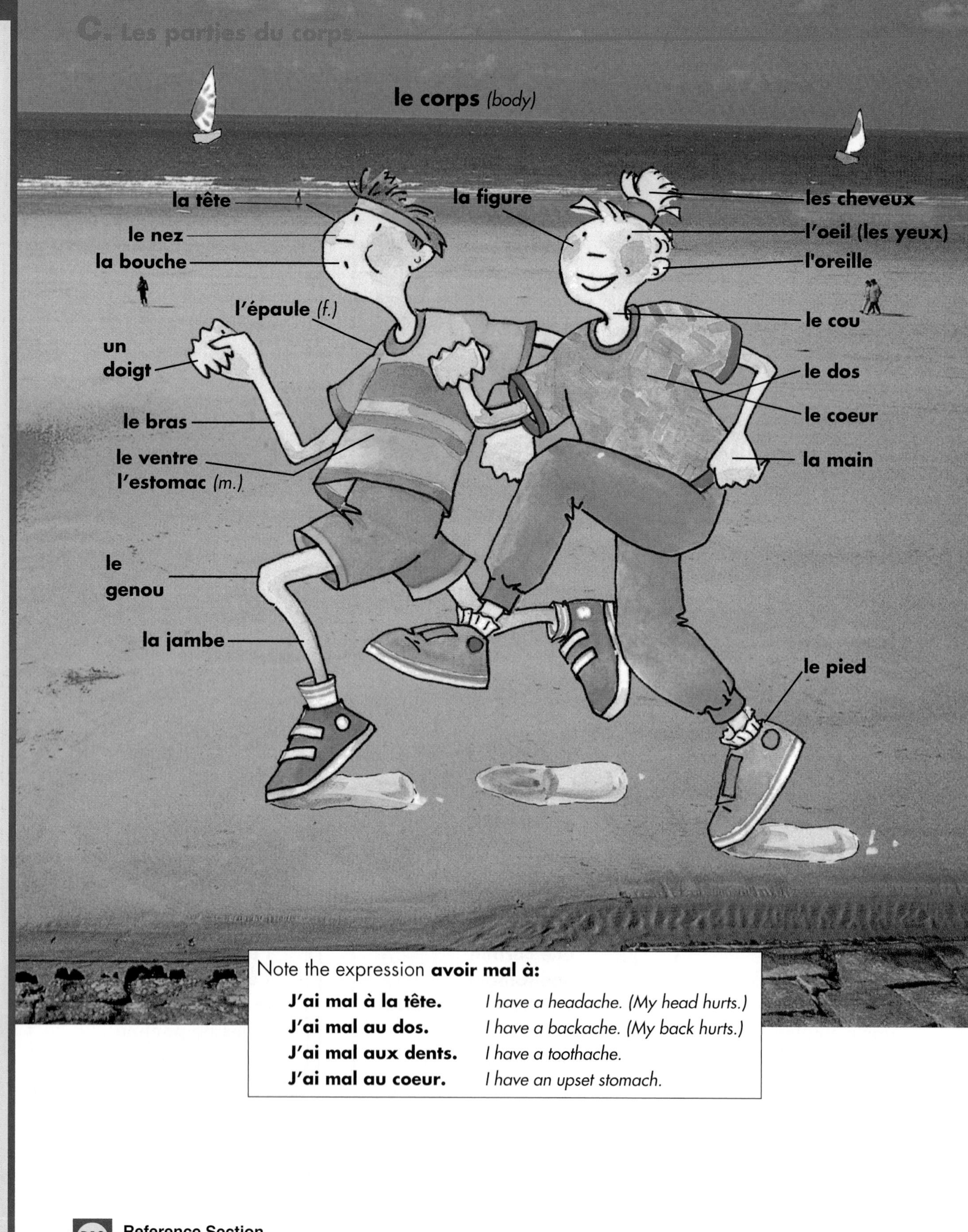

Note the expression **avoir mal à:**

J'ai mal à la tête.	*I have a headache. (My head hurts.)*
J'ai mal au dos.	*I have a backache. (My back hurts.)*
J'ai mal aux dents.	*I have a toothache.*
J'ai mal au coeur.	*I have an upset stomach.*

D. Les vêtements et les accessoires

un sweat
un tee-shirt
des sandales
un short
un maillot de bain
des chaussettes
des tennis
un blazer
un polo
une veste
une casquette
un survêtement
un pull
un blouson
un chapeau
un pantalon
une cravate
un jean
un bracelet
des boucles d'oreilles
un chemisier
une bague
des baskets
des lunettes de soleil
un tailleur
(woman's suit)
un collier
un imperméable
une ceinture
un costume
(man's suit)
une jupe
une robe
un manteau
un parapluie
des collants
un foulard
des bottes
des chaussures
un sac

Appendix A R13

E. Les pays

LES CONTINENTS ET LES PAYS DU MONDE

L' Amérique du Nord et l'Amérique du Sud
1. le Canada
2. les États-Unis
3. le Mexique
4. le Guatemala
5. le Venezuela
6. le Pérou
7. le Brésil
8. l'Argentine
9. le Chili

L' Afrique
10. le Maroc
11. l'Algérie
12. la Tunisie
13. l'Égypte
14. le Sénégal
15. la Côte d'Ivoire
16. la République démocratique du Congo
17. Madagascar

L' Europe
18. la France
19. l'Espagne
20. le Portugal
21. l'Angleterre
22. l'Irlande
23. l'Écosse
24. la Belgique
25. le Luxembourg
26. la Suisse
27. les Pays-Bas
28. l'Allemagne
29. l'Italie
30. la Grèce
31. le Danemark
32. la Norvège
33. la Suède
34. la Pologne
35. la Russie

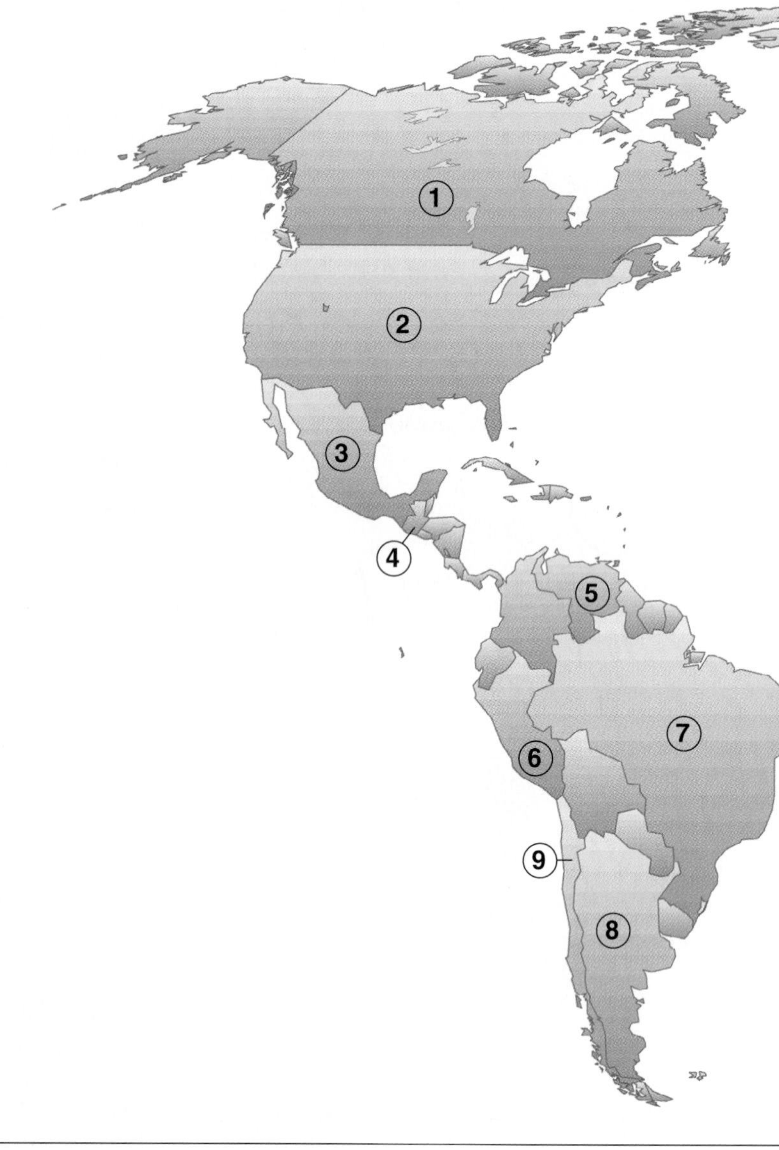

Le Moyen-Orient
36. Israël
37. le Liban
38. l'Arabie Saoudite

L' Asie et l'Océanie
39. la Chine
40. le Japon
41. la Corée
42. le Viêtnam
43. le Cambodge
44. l'Inde
45. les Philippines
46. l'Australie
47. la Nouvelle-Zélande

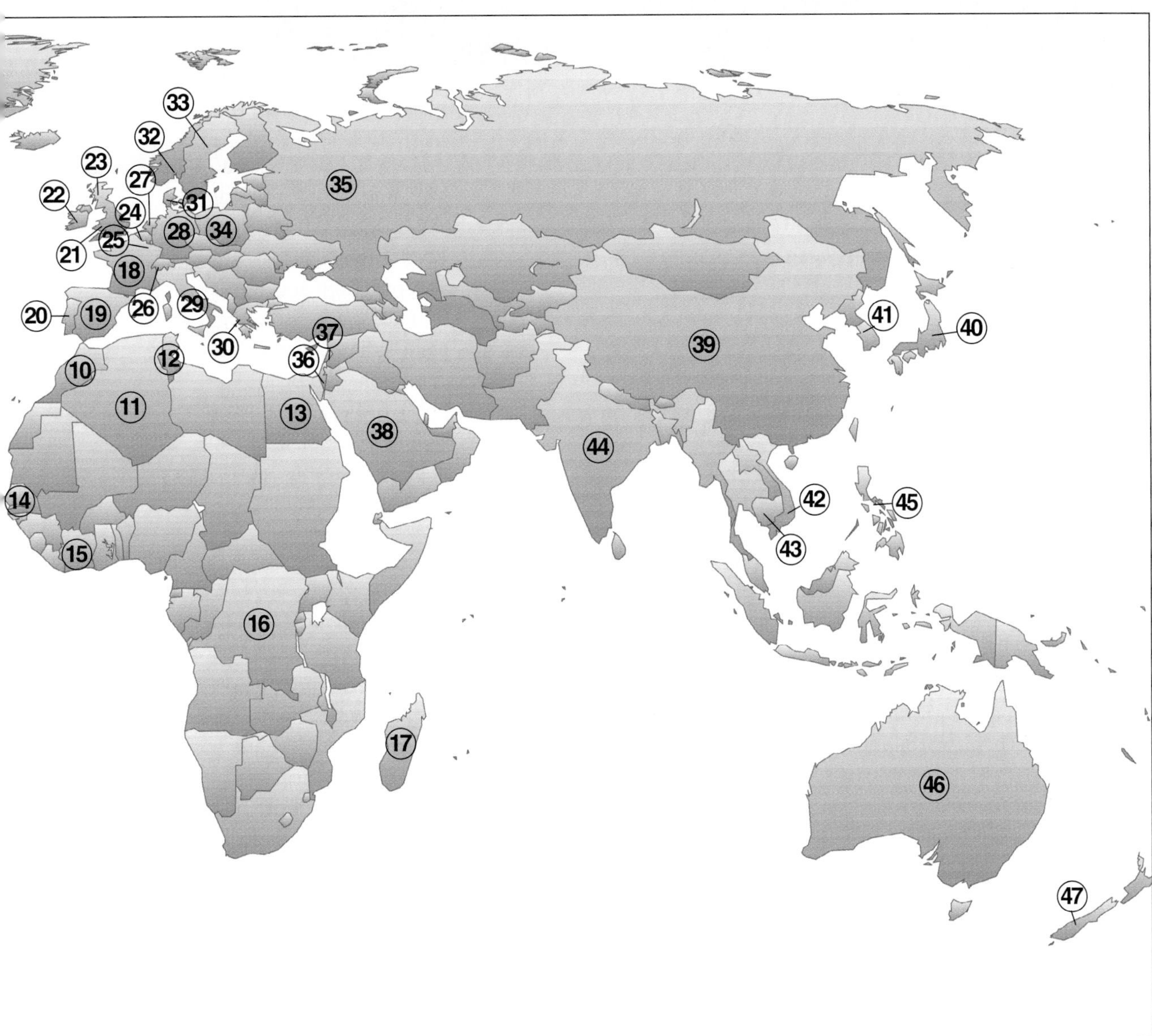

Les articles et les prépositions avec les noms de pays

	masculine country beginning with a consonant	*feminine country or masculine country beginning with a vowel*	*plural country*
Je visite . . .	**le** Canada	**la** France **l'**Iran	**les** États-Unis
Je vais . . . J'habite . . .	**au** Canada	**en** France **en** Iran	**aux** États-Unis
Je viens . . .	**du** Canada	**de** France **d'**Iran	**des** États-Unis

Appendix A R15

APPENDIX B: *Sound-Spelling Correspondence*

Vowels

SOUND	SPELLING	EXAMPLES
/a/	**a, à, â**	Madame, là-bas, théâtre
/i/	**i, î**	visite, Nice, dîne
	y (initial, final, or between consonants)	Yves, Guy, style
/u/	**ou, où, oû**	Toulouse, où, août
/y/	**u, û**	tu, Luc, sûr
/o/	**o** (final or before silent consonant)	piano, idiot, Margot
	au, eau	jaune, Claude, beau
	ô	hôtel, drôle, Côte d'Ivoire
/ɔ/	**o**	Monique, Noël, jolie
	au	Paul, restaurant, Laure
/e/	**é**	Dédé, Québec, télé
	e (before silent final **z, t, r**)	chez, et, Roger
	ai (final or before final silent consonant)	j'ai, mai, japonais
/ɛ/	**è**	Michèle, Ève, père
	ei	seize, neige, tour Eiffel
	ê	tête, être, Viêtnam
	e (before two consonants)	elle, Pierre, Annette
	e (before pronounced final consonant)	Michel, avec, cher
	ai (before pronounced final consonant)	française, aime, Maine
/ə/	**e** (final or before single consonant)	je, Denise, venir
/ø/	**eu, oeu**	deux, Mathieu, euro, oeufs
	eu (before final **se**)	nerveuse, généreuse, sérieuse
/œ/	**eu, oeu** (before final pronounced consonant except /z/)	heure, neuf, Lesieur, soeur, coeur, oeuf

Nasal vowels

SOUND	SPELLING	EXAMPLES
/ɑ̃/	**an, am**	France, quand, lampe
	en, em	Henri, pendant, décembre
/ɔ̃/	**on, om**	non, Simon, bombe
/ɛ̃/	**in, im**	Martin, invite, impossible
	yn, ym	syndicat, sympathique, Olympique
	ain, aim	Alain, américain, faim
	(o) + in	loin, moins, point
	(i) + en	bien, Julien, viens
/œ̃/	**un, um**	un, Lebrun, parfum

Semi-vowels

SOUND	SPELLING	EXAMPLES
/j/	**i, y** (before vowel sound)	bien, piano, Lyon
	-il, -ill (after vowel sound)	oeil, travaille, Marseille
/ɥ/	**u** (before vowel sound)	lui, Suisse, juillet
/w/	**ou** (before vowel sound)	oui, Louis, jouer
/wa/	**oi, oî, oy** (before vowel)	voici, Benoît, voyage

Consonants

SOUND	SPELLING	EXAMPLES
/b/	**b**	Barbara, banane, Belgique
/k/	**c** (before **a, o, u,** or consonant)	Coca-Cola, cuisine, classe
	ch(r)	Christine, Christian, Christophe
	qu, q (final)	Québec, qu'est-ce que, cinq
	k	kilo, Kiki, ketchup
/ʃ/	**ch**	Charles, blanche, chez
/d/	**d**	Didier, dans, médecin
/f/	**f**	Félix, franc, neuf
	ph	Philippe, téléphone, photo
/g/	**g** (before **a, o, u,** or consonant)	Gabriel, gorge, légumes, gris
	gu (before **e, i, y**)	vague, Guillaume, Guy
/ɲ/	**gn**	mignon, champagne, Allemagne
/ʒ/	**j**	je, Jérôme, jaune
	g (before **e, i, y**)	rouge, Gigi, gymnastique
	ge (before **a, o, u**)	orangeade, Georges, nageur
/l/	**l**	Lise, elle, cheval
/m/	**m**	Maman, moi, tomate
/n/	**n**	banane, Nancy, nous
/p/	**p**	peu, Papa, Pierre
/r/	**r**	arrive, rentre, Paris
/s/	**c** (before **e, i, y**)	ce, Cécile, Nancy
	ç (before **a, o, u**)	ça, garçon, déçu
	s (initial or before consonant)	sac, Sophie, reste
	ss (between vowels)	boisson, dessert, Suisse
	t (before **i** + vowel)	attention, Nations Unies, natation
	x	dix, six, soixante
/t/	**t**	trop, télé, Tours
	th	Thérèse, thé, Marthe
/v/	**v**	Viviane, vous, nouveau
/gz/	**x**	examen, exemple, exact
/ks/	**x**	Max, Mexique, excellent
/z/	**s** (between vowels)	désert, télévision, Louise
	z	Suzanne, zut, zéro

Appendix B R17

APPENDIX C: *Verbes*

1 REGULAR VERBS

INFINITIF	**parler** *(to talk, speak)*	**finir** *(to finish)*	**vendre** *(to sell)*	**se laver** *(to wash oneself)*
PRÉSENT	je **parle** tu **parles** il **parle** nous **parlons** vous **parlez** ils **parlent**	je **finis** tu **finis** il **finit** nous **finissons** vous **finissez** ils **finissent**	je **vends** tu **vends** il **vend** nous **vendons** vous **vendez** ils **vendent**	je **me lave** tu **te laves** il **se lave** nous **nous lavons** vous **vous lavez** ils **se lavent**
IMPÉRATIF	**parle!** **parlons!** **parlez!**	**finis!** **finissons!** **finissez!**	**vends!** **vendons!** **vendez!**	**lave-toi!** **lavons-nous!** **lavez-vous!**
PASSÉ COMPOSÉ	j'**ai parlé** tu **as parlé** il **a parlé** nous **avons parlé** vous **avez parlé** ils **ont parlé**	j'**ai fini** tu **as fini** il **a fini** nous **avons fini** vous **avez fini** ils **ont fini**	j'**ai vendu** tu **as vendu** il **a vendu** nous **avons vendu** vous **avez vendu** ils **ont vendu**	je **me suis lavé(e)** tu **t'es lavé(e)** il/elle **s'est lavé(e)** nous **nous sommes lavé(e)s** vous **vous êtes lavé(e)(s)** ils/elles **se sont lavé(e)s**
IMPARFAIT	je **parlais** tu **parlais** il **parlait** nous **parlions** vous **parliez** ils **parlaient**	je **finissais** tu **finissais** il **finissait** nous **finissions** vous **finissiez** ils **finissaient**	je **vendais** tu **vendais** il **vendait** nous **vendions** vous **vendiez** ils **vendaient**	je **me lavais** tu **te lavais** il **se lavait** nous **nous lavions** vous **vous laviez** ils **se lavaient**
PLUS-QUE-PARFAIT	j'**avais parlé** tu **avais parlé** il **avait parlé** nous **avions parlé** vous **aviez parlé** ils **avaient parlé**	j'**avais fini** tu **avais fini** il **avait fini** nous **avions fini** vous **aviez fini** ils **avaient fini**	j'**avais vendu** tu **avais vendu** il **avait vendu** nous **avions vendu** vous **aviez vendu** ils **avaient vendu**	je **m'étais lavé(e)** tu **t'étais lavé(e)** il/elle **s'était lavé(e)** nous **nous étions lavé(e)s** vous **vous étiez lavé(e)(s)** ils/elles **s'étaient lavé(e)s**
PASSÉ SIMPLE	je **parlai** tu **parlas** il **parla** nous **parlâmes** vous **parlâtes** ils **parlèrent**	je **finis** tu **finis** il **finit** nous **finîmes** vous **finîtes** ils **finirent**	je **vendis** tu **vendis** il **vendit** nous **vendîmes** vous **vendîtes** ils **vendirent**	je **me lavai** tu **te lavas** il **se lava** nous **nous lavâmes** vous **vous lavâtes** ils **se lavèrent**

R18 Reference Section

INFINITIF	**parler** *(to talk, speak)*	**finir** *(to finish)*	**vendre** *(to sell)*	**se laver** *(to wash oneself)*
FUTUR	je **parlerai** tu **parleras** il **parlera** nous **parlerons** vous **parlerez** ils **parleront**	je **finirai** tu **finiras** il **finira** nous **finirons** vous **finirez** ils **finiront**	je **vendrai** tu **vendras** il **vendra** nous **vendrons** vous **vendrez** ils **vendront**	je **me laverai** tu **te laveras** il **se lavera** nous **nous laverons** vous **vous laverez** ils **se laveront**
CONDITIONNEL	je **parlerais** tu **parlerais** il **parlerait** nous **parlerions** vous **parleriez** ils **parleraient**	je **finirais** tu **finirais** il **finirait** nous **finirions** vous **finiriez** ils **finiraient**	je **vendrais** tu **vendrais** il **vendrait** nous **vendrions** vous **vendriez** ils **vendraient**	je **me laverais** tu **te laverais** il **se laverait** nous **nous laverions** vous **vous laveriez** ils **se laveraient**
CONDITIONNEL PASSÉ	j'**aurais parlé** tu **aurais parlé** il **aurait parlé** nous **aurions parlé** vous **auriez parlé** ils **auraient parlé**	j'**aurais fini** tu **aurais fini** il **aurait fini** nous **aurions fini** vous **auriez fini** ils **auraient fini**	j'**aurais vendu** tu **aurais vendu** il **aurait vendu** nous **aurions vendu** vous **auriez vendu** ils **auraient vendu**	je **me serais lavé(e)** tu **te serais lavé(e)** il/elle **se serait lavé(e)** nous **nous serions lavé(e)s** vous **vous seriez lavé(e)(s)** ils/elles **se seraient lavé(e)s**
SUBJONCTIF	que je **parle** que tu **parles** qu'il **parle** que **nous parlions** que **vous parliez** qu'**ils parlent**	que je **finisse** que tu **finisses** qu'il **finisse** que **nous finissions** que **vous finissiez** qu'ils **finissent**	que je **vende** que tu **vendes** qu'il **vende** que nous **vendions** que vous **vendiez** qu'ils **vendent**	que je **me lave** que tu **te laves** qu'il **se lave** que nous **nous lavions** que vous **vous laviez** qu'ils **se lavent**
PASSÉ DU SUBJONCTIF	que j'**aie parlé** que tu **aies parlé** qu'il **ait parlé** que nous **ayons parlé** que vous **ayez parlé** qu'ils **aient parlé**	que j'**aie fini** que tu **aies fini** qu'il **ait fini** que nous **ayons fini** que vous **ayez fini** qu'ils **aient fini**	que j'**aie vendu** que tu **aies vendu** qu'il **ait vendu** que nous **ayons vendu** que vous **ayez vendu** qu'ils **aient vendu**	que je **me sois lavé(e)** que tu **te sois lavé(e)** qu'il/elle **se soit lavé(e)** que nous **nous soyons lavé(e)s** que vous **vous soyez lavé(e)(s)** qu'ils/elles **se soient lavé(e)s**
PARTICIPE PRÉSENT	**parlant**	**finissant**	**vendant**	**se lavant**
INFINITIF PASSÉ	**avoir parlé**	**avoir fini**	**avoir vendu**	**s'être lavé(e)**

2 VERBS WITH SPELLING CHANGES

Some **-er** verbs have spelling changes in certain tenses. These changes are highlighted in the chart below. All other forms of these verbs are similar to those of regular **-er** verbs.

The verbs listed below follow the pattern of the indicated model verbs. Note that reflexive verbs are conjugated with **être** in the compound tenses. (All others are conjugated with **avoir**.)

verbs like **acheter** *(to buy)*

amener *(to take, bring along)*
élever *(to educate, to raise)*
enlever *(to take off)*
lever *(to lift, raise)*
se lever *(to get up)*
mener *(to take, to lead)*
promener *(to walk [a dog])*
se promener *(to take a walk, take a ride)*

verbs like **appeler** *(to call)*

s'appeler *(to be named, to be called)*
empaqueter *(to bag)*
épousseter *(to dust)*
étinceler *(to twinkle)*
jeter *(to throw)*
rappeler *(to call back)*
se rappeler *(to remember)*
rejeter *(to reject)*

verbs like **préférer** *(to prefer)*

accélérer *(to accelerate)*
célébrer *(to celebrate)*
espérer *(to hope)*
s'inquiéter *(to worry)*
posséder *(to possess, to own)*
protéger *(to protect)*
répéter *(to repeat)*
sécher *(to dry)*
se sécher *(to dry oneself)*
suggérer *(to suggest)*

INFINITIF	PRÉSENT		IMPÉRATIF	PASSÉ COMPOSÉ	IMPARFAIT
acheter e → è	j'**achète** tu **achètes** il **achète**	nous **achetons** vous **achetez** ils **achètent**	**achète!** **achetons!** **achetez!**	j'**ai acheté**	j'**achetais** nous **achetions**
appeler l → ll *(double consonant)*	j'**appelle** tu **appelles** il **appelle**	nous **appelons** vous **appelez** ils **appellent**	**appelle!** **appelons!** **appelez!**	j'**ai appelé**	j'**appelais** nous **appelions**
préférer é → è	je **préfère** tu **préfères** il **préfère**	nous **préférons** vous **préférez** ils **préfèrent**	**préfère!** **préférons!** **préférez!**	j'**ai préféré**	je **préférais** nous **préférions**
payer y → i	je **paie** tu **paies** il **paie**	nous **payons** vous **payez** ils **paient**	**paie!** **payons!** **payez!**	j'**ai payé**	je **payais** nous **payions**
commencer c → ç *(before a,o)*	je **commence** tu **commences** il **commence**	nous **commençons** vous **commencez** ils **commencent**	**commence!** **commençons!** **commencez!**	j'**ai commencé**	je **commençais** nous **commencions**
manger g → ge *(before a,o)*	je **mange** tu **manges** il **mange**	nous **mangeons** vous **mangez** ils **mangent**	**mange!** **mangeons!** **mangez!**	j'**ai mangé**	je **mangeais** nous **mangions**

verbs like **payer** *(to pay, pay for)*

balayer *(to sweep)*
employer *(to use, to employ)*
s'ennuyer *(to be bored)*
essayer *(to try)*
essuyer *(to wipe, to dry)*
nettoyer *(to clean)*

verbs like **commencer** *(to begin, start)*

annoncer *(to announce, proclaim)*
divorcer *(to divorce)*
se fiancer *(to get engaged)*
menacer *(to threaten)*

verbs like **manger** *(to eat)*

arranger *(to arrange, to fix)*
changer *(to change)*
charger *(to charge)*
s'en charger *(to take charge)*
corriger *(to correct)*
dégager *(to shorten)*
déranger *(to disturb)*
diriger *(to direct, to run)*
exiger *(to demand)*
égorger *(to slit the throat)*
embaucher *(to hire)*
interroger *(to interrogate)*
juger *(to judge)*
mélanger *(to mix)*
nager *(to swim)*
négliger *(to neglect)*
neiger *(to snow)*
obliger *(to oblige)*
partager *(to share)*
plonger *(to dive)*
protéger *(to protect)*
ranger *(to pick up, to put away)*
venger *(to avenge)*
voyager *(to travel)*

PASSÉ SIMPLE	FUTUR	CONDITIONNEL	SUBJONCTIF	PARTICIPE PRÉSENT
j'**achetai** il **acheta** ils **achetèrent**	j'**achèterai**	j'**achèterais**	que j'**achète** que nous **achetions**	**achetant**
j'**appelai** il **appela** ils **appelèrent**	j'**appellerai**	j'**appellerais**	que j'**appelle** que nous **appelions**	**appelant**
je **préférai** il **préféra** ils **préférèrent**	je **préférerai**	je **préférerais**	que je **préfère** que nous **préférions**	**préférant**
je **payai** il **paya** ils **payèrent**	je **paierai**	je **paierais**	que je **paie** que nous **payions**	**payant**
je **commençai** il **commença** ils **commencèrent**	je **commencerai**	je **commencerais**	que je **commence** que nous **commencions**	**commençant**
je **mangeai** il **mangea** ils **mangèrent**	je **mangerai**	je **mangerais**	que je **mange** que nous **mangions**	**mangeant**

Appendix C R21

3 AUXILIARY FORMS

INFINITIF	PRÉSENT		IMPARFAIT		FUTUR	
avoir	j'**ai** tu **as** il **a**	nous **avons** vous **avez** ils **ont**	j'**avais** tu **avais** il **avait**	nous **avions** vous **aviez** ils **avaient**	j'**aurai** tu **auras** il **aura**	nous **aurons** vous **aurez** ils **auront**
être	je **suis** tu **es** il **est**	nous **sommes** vous **êtes** ils **sont**	j'**étais** tu **étais** il **était**	nous **étions** vous **étiez** ils **étaient**	je **serai** tu **seras** il **sera**	nous **serons** vous **serez** ils **seront**

4 IRREGULAR VERBS

For the conjugation of the irregular verbs listed below, follow the pattern of the indicated verbs. Verbs conjugated with **être** as an auxiliary verb in the compound tenses are noted with an asterisk (*). All others are conjugated with **avoir**.

accueillir	(*see* **cueillir**)	**craindre**	(*see* **peindre**)	* **s'endormir**	(*see* **dormir**)
admettre	(*see* **mettre**)	**cuire**	(*see* **conduire**)	* **s'enfuir**	(*see* **fuir**)
apercevoir	(*see* **recevoir**)	**débattre**	(*see* **battre**)	**entreprendre**	(*see* **prendre**)
apparaître	(*see* **connaître**)	**décevoir**	(*see* **recevoir**)	**entretenir**	(*see* **tenir**)
appartenir	(*see* **tenir**)	**découvrir**	(*see* **ouvrir**)	**éteindre**	(*see* **peindre**)
apprendre	(*see* **prendre**)	**décrire**	(*see* **écrire**)	* **s'étendre**	(*see* **rendre**)
atteindre	(*see* **peindre**)	* **se déplacer**	(*see* **placer**)	**inscrire**	(*see* **écrire**)
attendre	(*see* **rendre**)	**déplaire**	(*see* **plaire**)	**interdire**	(*see* **dire**)
combattre	(*see* **battre**)	**détruire**	(*see* **conduire**)	**interrompre**	(*see* **rompre**)
comprendre	(*see* **prendre**)	**descendre**	(*see* **rendre**)	**intervenir**	(*see* **venir**)
confier	(*see* **planifier**)	* **devenir**	(*see* **venir**)	**introduire**	(*see* **conduire**)
conquérir	(*see* **acquérir**)	**disparaître**	(*see* **connaître**)	**joindre**	(*see* **peindre**)
construire	(*see* **conduire**)	**effacer**	(*see* **placer**)	**lancer**	(*see* **placer**)
contenir	(*see* **tenir**)	**élire**	(*see* **lire**)	**maintenir**	(*see* **tenir**)
convaincre	(*see* **vaincre**)	**entendre**	(*see* **rendre**)	* **se marier**	(*see* **planifier**)
couvrir	(*see* **ouvrir**)	* **s'entendre**	(*see* **rendre**)	* **se méfier**	(*see* **planifier**)

INFINITIF	PRÉSENT		IMPÉRATIF	PASSÉ COMPOSÉ	IMPARFAIT
acquérir (*to acquire, get*)	j'**acquiers** tu **acquiers** il **acquiert**	nous **acquérons** vous **acquérez** ils **acquièrent**	**acquiers** **acquérons** **acquérez**	j'**ai acquis**	j'**acquérais**
aller (*to go*)	je **vais** tu **vas** il **va**	nous **allons** vous **allez** ils **vont**	**va** **allons** **allez**	je **suis allé(e)**	j'**allais**

CONDITIONNEL		SUBJONCTIF	
j'**aurais** tu **aurais** il **aurait**	nous **aurions** vous **auriez** ils **auraient**	que j'**aie** que tu **aies** qu'il **ait**	que nous **ayons** que vous **ayez** qu'ils **aient**
je **serais** tu **serais** il **serait**	nous **serions** vous **seriez** ils **seraient**	que je **sois** que tu **sois** qu'il **soit**	que nous **soyons** que vous **soyez** qu'ils **soient**

mentir	(*see* **sortir**)	**promettre**	(*see* **mettre**)	***revenir**	(*see* **venir**)
obtenir	(*see* **tenir**)	**reconnaître**	(*see* **connaître**)	**sentir**	(*see* **sortir**)
offrir	(*see* **ouvrir**)	**réconcilier**	(*see* **planifier**)	**servir**	(*see* **sortir**)
opérer	(*see* **céder**)	**reconstruire**	(*see* **conduire**)	**souffrir**	(*see* **ouvrir**)
paraître	(*see* **connaître**)	**récupérer**	(*see* **céder**)	**sourire**	(*see* **rire**)
parcourir	(*see* **courir**)	**redécouvrir**	(*see* **ouvrir**)	**soutenir**	(*see* **tenir**)
***partir**	(*see* **sortir**)	**réduire**	(*see* **conduire**)	***se souvenir**	(*see* **venir**)
parvenir	(*see* **venir**)	**remarier**	(*see* **planifier**)	**subvenir**	(*see* **venir**)
pendre	(*see* **rendre**)	**remercier**	(*see* **planifier**)	**succéder**	(*see* **céder**)
***se perdre**	(*see* **rendre**)	**remettre**	(*see* **mettre**)	**surprendre**	(*see* **prendre**)
permettre	(*see* **mettre**)	***se rendre à**	(*see* **rendre**)	**survenir**	(*see* **venir**)
peser	(*see* **acheter**)	**renoncer**	(*see* **placer**)	**survivre**	(*see* **vivre**)
plaindre	(*see* **peindre**)	**renvoyer**	(*see* **envoyer**)	**tondre**	(*see* **rendre**)
poursuivre	(*see* **suivre**)	**répandre**	(*see* **rendre**)	***se tordre**	(*see* **rendre**)
prédire	(*see* **dire**)	**répondre**	(*see* **rendre**)	**traduire**	(*see* **conduire**)
prévoir	(*see* **voir**)	**ressentir**	(*see* **sortir**)		
produire	(*see* **conduire**)	**retenir**	(*see* **tenir**)		

PASSÉ SIMPLE	FUTUR	CONDITIONNEL	SUBJONCTIF	PARTICIPE PRÉSENT
j'**acquis**	j'**acquerrai**	j'**acquerrais**	que j'**acquière** que nous **acquérions**	**acquérant**
j'**allai**	j'**irai**	j'**irais**	que j'**aille** que nous **allions**	**allant**

Appendix C R23

INFINITIF	PRÉSENT		IMPÉRATIF	PASSÉ COMPOSÉ	IMPARFAIT
appuyer *(to push)*	j'**appuie** tu **appuies** il **appuie**	nous **appuyons** vous **appuyez** ils **appuient**	**appuie!** **appuyons!** **appuyez!**	j'**ai appuyé**	j'**appuyais**
s'asseoir *(to sit down)*	je **m'assieds** tu **t'assieds** il **s'assied**	nous **nous asseyons** vous **vous asseyez** ils **s'asseyent**	**assieds-toi!** **asseyons-nous!** **asseyez-vous!**	je **me suis assis(e)**	je **m'asseyais**
avoir *(to have)*	j'**ai** tu **as** il **a**	nous **avons** vous **avez** ils **ont**	**aie!** **ayons!** **ayez!**	j'**ai eu**	j'**avais**
il y a *(there is, are)*	**il y a**		– –	**il y a eu**	**il y avait**
battre *(to beat)*	je **bats** tu **bats** il **bat**	nous **battons** vous **battez** ils **battent**	**bats!** **battons!** **battez!**	j'**ai battu**	je **battais**
boire *(to drink)*	je **bois** tu **bois** il **boit**	nous **buvons** vous **buvez** ils **boivent**	**bois!** **buvons!** **buvez!**	j'**ai bu**	je **buvais**
céder *(to cede)*	je **cède** tu **cèdes** il **cède**	nous **cédons** vous **cédez** ils **cèdent**	**cède!** **cédons!** **cédez!**	j'ai **cédé**	je **cédais**
conduire *(to drive)*	je **conduis** tu **conduis** il **conduit**	nous **conduisons** vous **conduisez** ils **conduisent**	**conduis!** **conduisons!** **conduisez!**	j'**ai conduit**	je **conduisais**
connaître *(to know)*	je **connais** tu **connais** il **connaît**	nous **connaissons** vous **connaissez** ils **connaissent**	**connais!** **connaissons!** **connaissez!**	j'**ai connu**	je **connaissais**
courir *(to run)*	je **cours** tu **cours** il **court**	nous **courons** vous **courez** ils **courent**	**cours!** **courons!** **courez!**	j'**ai couru**	je **courais**
croire *(to believe, think)*	je **crois** tu **crois** il **croit**	nous **croyons** vous **croyez** ils **croient**	**crois!** **croyons!** **croyez!**	j'**ai cru**	je **croyais**
cueillir *(to gather, pick)*	je **cueille** tu **cueilles** il **cueille**	nous **cueillons** vous **cueillez** ils **cueillent**	**cueille!** **cueillons!** **cueillez!**	j'**ai cueilli**	je **cueillais**
devoir *(must, to have to, owe)*	je **dois** tu **dois** il **doit**	nous **devons** vous **devez** ils **doivent**	**dois!** **devons!** **devez!**	j'**ai dû**	je **devais**

R24 Reference Section

PASSÉ SIMPLE	FUTUR	CONDITIONNEL	SUBJONCTIF		PARTICIPE PRÉSENT
j'**appuyai**	j'**appuierai**	j'**appuierais**	que j'**appuie** que nous **appuyions**		**appuyant**
je **m'assis**	je **m'assiérai**	je **m'assiérais**	que je **m'asseye** que nous **nous asseyions**		**s'asseyant**
j'**eus**	j'**aurai**	j'**aurais**	que j'**aie** que tu **aies** qu'il **ait**	que nous **ayons** que vous **ayez** qu'ils **aient**	**ayant**
il y eut	**il y aura**	**il y aurait**	qu'**il y ait**		--
je **battis**	je **battrai**	je **battrais**	que je **batte** que nous **battions**		**battant**
je **bus**	je **boirai**	je **boirais**	que je **boive** que nous **buvions**		**buvant**
je **cédai**	je **céderai**	je **céderais**	que je **cède** que nous **cédions**		**cédant**
je **conduisis**	je **conduirai**	je **conduirais**	que je **conduise** que nous **conduisions**		**conduisant**
je **connus**	je **connaîtrai**	je **connaîtrais**	que je **connaisse** que nous **connaissions**		**connaissant**
je **courus**	je **courrai**	je **courrais**	que je **coure** que nous **courions**		**courant**
je **crus**	je **croirai**	je **croirais**	que je **croie** que nous **croyions**		**croyant**
je **cueillis**	je **cueillerai**	je **cueillerais**	que je **cueille** que nous **cueillions**		**cueillant**
je **dus**	je **devrai**	je **devrais**	que je **doive** que nous **devions**		**devant**

Appendix C R25

INFINITIF	PRÉSENT		IMPÉRATIF	PASSÉ COMPOSÉ	IMPARFAIT
dire *(to say, tell)*	je **dis** tu **dis** il **dit**	nous **disons** vous **dites** ils **disent**	**dis!** **disons!** **dites!**	j'**ai dit**	je **disais**
dormir *(to sleep)*	je **dors** tu **dors** il **dort**	nous **dormons** vous **dormez** ils **dorment**	**dors!** **dormons!** **dormez!**	j'**ai dormi**	je **dormais**
écrire *(to write)*	j'**écris** tu **écris** il **écrit**	nous **écrivons** vous **écrivez** ils **écrivent**	**écris!** **écrivons!** **écrivez!**	j'**ai écrit**	j'**écrivais**
envoyer *(to send)*	j'**envoie** tu **envoies** il **envoie**	nous **envoyons** vous **envoyez** ils **envoient**	**envoie!** **envoyons!** **envoyez!**	j'**ai envoyé**	j'**envoyais**
être *(to be)*	je **suis** tu **es** il **est**	nous **sommes** vous **êtes** ils **sont**	**sois!** **soyons!** **soyez!**	j'**ai été**	j'**étais**
faire *(to make, do)*	je **fais** tu **fais** il **fait**	nous **faisons** vous **faites** ils **font**	**fais!** **faisons!** **faites!**	j'**ai fait**	je **faisais**
falloir *(to be necessary)*	il **faut**	– –	– –	il **a fallu**	il **fallait**
fuir *(to flee)*	je **fuis** tu **fuis** il **fuit**	nous **fuyons** vous **fuyez** ils **fuient**	**fuis!** **fuyons!** **fuyez!**	j'**ai fui**	je **fuyais**
lire *(to read)*	je **lis** tu **lis** il **lit**	nous **lisons** vous **lisez** ils **lisent**	**lis!** **lisons!** **lisez!**	j'**ai lu**	je **lisais**
mettre *(to put, place)*	je **mets** tu **mets** il **met**	nous **mettons** vous **mettez** ils **mettent**	**mets!** **mettons!** **mettez!**	j'**ai mis**	je **mettais**
mourir *(to die)*	je **meurs** tu **meurs** il **meurt**	nous **mourons** vous **mourez** ils **meurent**	**meurs!** **mourons!** **mourez!**	je **suis mort(e)**	je **mourais**

R26 Reference Section

PASSÉ SIMPLE	FUTUR	CONDITIONNEL	SUBJONCTIF	PARTICIPE PRÉSENT
je **dis**	je **dirai**	je **dirais**	que je **dise** que nous **disions**	**disant**
je **dormis**	je **dormirai**	je **dormirais**	que je **dorme** que nous **dormions**	**dormant**
j'**écrivis**	j'**écrirai**	j'**écrirais**	que j'**écrive** que nous **écrivions**	**écrivant**
j'**envoyai**	j'**enverrai**	j'**enverrais**	que j'**envoie** que nous **envoyions**	**envoyant**
je **fus**	je **serai**	je **serais**	que je **sois** que nous **soyons** que tu **sois** que vous **soyez** qu'il **soit** qu'ils **soient**	**étant**
je **fis**	je **ferai**	je **ferais**	que je **fasse** que nous **fassions**	**faisant**
il **fallut**	il **faudra**	il **faudrait**	qu'il **faille**	– –
je **fuis**	je **fuirai**	je **fuirais**	que je **fuie** que nous **fuyions**	**fuyant**
je **lus**	je **lirai**	je **lirais**	que je **lise** que nous **lisions**	**lisant**
je **mis**	je **mettrai**	je **mettrais**	que je **mette** que nous **mettions**	**mettant**
je **mourus**	je **mourrai**	je **mourrais**	que je **meure** que nous **mourions**	**mourant**

Appendix C R27

INFINITIF	PRÉSENT		IMPÉRATIF	PASSÉ COMPOSÉ	IMPARFAIT
naître *(to be born)*	je **nais** tu **nais** il **naît**	nous **naissons** vous **naissez** ils **naissent**	**nais!** **naissons!** **naissez!**	je **suis né(e)**	je **naissais**
ouvrir *(to open)*	j'**ouvre** tu **ouvres** il **ouvre**	nous **ouvrons** vous **ouvrez** ils **ouvrent**	**ouvre!** **ouvrons!** **ouvrez!**	j'**ai ouvert**	j'**ouvrais**
peindre *(to paint)*	je **peins** tu **peins** il **peint**	nous **peignons** vous **peignez** ils **peignent**	**peins!** **peignons!** **peignez!**	j'**ai peint**	je **peignais**
placer *(to place)*	je **place** tu **places** il **place**	nous **plaçons** vous **placez** ils **placent**	**place!** **plaçons!** **placez!**	j'ai **placé**	je **plaçais**
plaire *(to please)*	je **plais** tu **plais** il **plaît**	nous **plaisons** vous **plaisez** ils **plaisent**	**plais!** **plaisons!** **plaisez!**	j'**ai plu**	je **plaisais**
planifier *(to plan)*	je **planifie** tu **planifies** il **planifie**	nous **planifions** vous **planifiez** ils **planifient**	**planifie!** **planifions!** **planifiez!**	j'ai **planifié**	je **planifiais**
pleuvoir *(to rain)*	il **pleut**	--	--	il **a plu**	il **pleuvait**
pouvoir *(to be able, can)*	je **peux** tu **peux** il **peut**	nous **pouvons** vous **pouvez** ils **peuvent**	--	j'**ai pu**	je **pouvais**
prendre *(to take, have)*	je **prends** tu **prends** il **prend**	nous **prenons** vous **prenez** ils **prennent**	**prends!** **prenons!** **prenez!**	j'**ai pris**	je **prenais**
recevoir *(to receive, get, obtain)*	je **reçois** tu **reçois** il **reçoit**	nous **recevons** vous **recevez** ils **reçoivent**	**reçois!** **recevons!** **recevez!**	j'**ai reçu**	je **recevais**
rendre *(to render)*	je **rends** tu **rends** il **rend**	nous **rendons** vous **rendez** ils **rendent**	**rends!** **rendons!** **rendez!**	j'ai **rendu**	je **rendais**
résoudre *(to resolve)*	je **résous** tu **résous** il **résout**	nous **résolvons** vous **résolvez** ils **résolvent**	**résous!** **résolvons!** **résolvez!**	j'**ai résolu**	je **résolvais**
rire *(to laugh)*	je **ris** tu **ris** il **rit**	nous **rions** vous **riez** ils **rient**	**ris!** **rions!** **riez!**	j'**ai ri**	je **riais**

R28 Reference Section

PASSÉ SIMPLE	FUTUR	CONDITIONNEL	SUBJONCTIF	PARTICIPE PRÉSENT
je **naquis**	je **naîtrai**	je **naîtrais**	que je **naisse** que nous **naissions**	**naissant**
j'**ouvris**	j'**ouvrirai**	j'**ouvrirais**	que j'**ouvre** que nous **ouvrions**	**ouvrant**
je **peignis**	je **peindrai**	je **peindrais**	que je **peigne** que nous **peignions**	**peignant**
je **plaçai**	je **placerai**	je **placerais**	que je **place** que nous **placions**	**plaçant**
je **plus**	je **plairai**	je **plairais**	que je **plaise** que nous **plaisions**	**plaisant**
je **planifiai**	je **planifierai**	je **planifierais**	que je **planifie** que nous **planifiions**	**planifiant**
il **plut**	il **pleuvra**	il **pleuvrait**	qu'il **pleuve**	**pleuvant**
je **pus**	je **pourrai**	je **pourrais**	que je **puisse** que nous **puissions**	**pouvant**
je **pris**	je **prendrai**	je **prendrais**	que je **prenne** que nous **prenions**	**prenant**
je **reçus**	je **recevrai**	je **recevrais**	que je **reçoive** que nous **recevions**	**recevant**
je **rendis**	je **rendrai**	je **rendrais**	que je **rende** que nous **rendions**	**rendant**
je **résolus**	je **résoudrai**	je **résoudrais**	que je **résolve** que nous **résolvions**	**résolvant**
je **ris**	je **rirai**	je **rirais**	que je **rie** que nous **riions**	**riant**

Appendix C R29

INFINITIF	PRÉSENT		IMPÉRATIF	PASSÉ COMPOSÉ	IMPARFAIT
rompre *(to break)*	je **romps** tu **romps** il **rompt**	nous **rompons** vous **rompez** ils **rompent**	**romps!** **rompons!** **rompez!**	j'**ai rompu**	je **rompais**
savoir *(to know)*	je **sais** tu **sais** il **sait**	nous **savons** vous **savez** ils **savent**	**sache!** **sachons!** **sachez!**	j'**ai su**	je **savais**
sortir *(to go out)*	je **sors** tu **sors** il **sort**	nous **sortons** vous **sortez** ils **sortent**	**sors!** **sortons!** **sortez!**	je **suis sorti(e)**	je **sortais**
suivre *(to follow)*	je **suis** tu **suis** il **suit**	nous **suivons** vous **suivez** ils **suivent**	**suis!** **suivons!** **suivez!**	j'**ai suivi**	je **suivais**
se taire *(to be quiet)*	je **me tais** tu **te tais** il **se tait**	nous **nous taisons** vous **vous taisez** ils **se taisent**	**tais-toi!** **taisons-nous!** **taisez-vous!**	je **me suis tu(e)**	je **me taisais**
tenir *(to hold)*	je **tiens** tu **tiens** il **tient**	nous **tenons** vous **tenez** ils **tiennent**	**tiens!** **tenons!** **tenez!**	j'**ai tenu**	je **tenais**
vaincre *(to win, conquer)*	je **vaincs** tu **vaincs** il **vainc**	nous **vainquons** vous **vainquez** ils **vainquent**	**vaincs!** **vainquons!** **vainquez!**	j'**ai vaincu**	je **vainquais**
valoir *(to be worth, deserve, merit)*	je **vaux** tu **vaux** il **vaut**	nous **valons** vous **valez** ils **valent**	**vaux!** **valons!** **valez!**	j'**ai valu**	je **valais**
venir *(to come)*	je **viens** tu **viens** il **vient**	nous **venons** vous **venez** ils **viennent**	**viens!** **venons!** **venez!**	je **suis venu(e)**	je **venais**
vivre *(to live)*	je **vis** tu **vis** il **vit**	nous **vivons** vous **vivez** ils **vivent**	**vis!** **vivons!** **vivez!**	j'**ai vécu**	je **vivais**
voir *(to see)*	je **vois** tu **vois** il **voit**	nous **voyons** vous **voyez** ils **voient**	**vois!** **voyons!** **voyez!**	j'**ai vu**	je **voyais**
vouloir *(to want, wish)*	je **veux** tu **veux** il **veut**	nous **voulons** vous **voulez** ils **veulent**	**veuille!** **veuillons!** **veuillez!**	j'**ai voulu**	je **voulais**

R30 Reference Section

PASSÉ SIMPLE	FUTUR	CONDITIONNEL	SUBJONCTIF	PARTICIPE PRÉSENT
je **rompis**	je **romprai**	je **romprais**	que je **rompe** que nous **rompions**	**rompant**
je **sus**	je **saurai**	je **saurais**	que je **sache** que nous **sachions**	**sachant**
je **sortis**	je **sortirai**	je **sortirais**	que je **sorte** que nous **sortions**	**sortant**
je **suivis**	je **suivrai**	je **suivrais**	que je **suive** que nous **suivions**	**suivant**
je **me tus**	je **me tairai**	je **me tairais**	que je **me taise** que nous **nous taisions**	**se taisant**
je **tins**	je **tiendrai**	je **tiendrais**	que je **tienne** que nous **tenions**	**tenant**
je **vainquis**	je **vaincrai**	je **vaincrais**	que je **vainque** que nous **vainquions**	**vainquant**
je **valus**	je **vaudrai**	je **vaudrais**	que je **vaille** que nous **valions**	**valant**
je **vins**	je **viendrai**	je **viendrais**	que je **vienne** que nous **venions**	**venant**
je **vécus**	je **vivrai**	je **vivrais**	que je **vive** que nous **vivions**	**vivant**
je **vis**	je **verrai**	je **verrais**	que je **voie** que nous **voyions**	**voyant**
je **voulus**	je **voudrai**	je **voudrais**	que je **veuille** que nous **voulions**	**voulant**

Appendix C R31

5 PASSÉ SIMPLE

The PASSÉ SIMPLE is a past tense which is used mainly in literary French. You may encounter the passé simple in newspaper and magazine articles, in short stories and novels. The passé simple is generally not used in conversational French, nor is it used in informal notes and letters.

FORMS

The PASSÉ SIMPLE is a simple tense.
For REGULAR VERBS, this tense is formed as follows:

PASSÉ SIMPLE = INFINITIVE STEM + PASSÉ SIMPLE ENDINGS

INFINITIVE	**parler**	
STEM	parl-	ENDINGS
je	**parlai**	**-ai**
tu	**parlas**	**-as**
il/elle/on	**parla**	**-a**
nous	**parlâmes**	**-âmes**
vous	**parlâtes**	**-âtes**
ils/elles	**parlèrent**	**-èrent**
INFINITIVE	**finir**	
STEM	fin-	ENDINGS
je	**finis**	**-is**
tu	**finis**	**-is**
il/elle/on	**finit**	**-it**
nous	**finîmes**	**-îmes**
vous	**finîtes**	**-îtes**
ils/elles	**finirent**	**-irent**
INFINITIVE	**vendre**	
STEM	vend-	ENDINGS
je	**vendis**	**-is**
tu	**vendis**	**-is**
il/elle/on	**vendit**	**-it**
nous	**vendîmes**	**-îmes**
vous	**vendîtes**	**-îtes**
ils/elles	**vendirent**	**-irent**

PASSÉ SIMPLE OF SELECTED IRREGULAR VERBS *(FOR RECOGNITION)*

il alla	**aller**
il but	**boire**
il conduisit	**conduire**
il connut	**connaître**
il craignit	**craindre**
il crut	**croire**
il dit	**dire**
il dormit	**dormir**
il dut	**devoir**
il eut	**avoir**
il écrivit	**écrire**
il fallut	**il faut**
il fit	**faire**
il fut	**être**
il lut	**lire**
il mit	**mettre**
il mourut	**mourir**
il naquit	**naître**
il ouvrit	**ouvrir**
il plut	**plaire**
il plut	**il pleut**
il prit	**prendre**
il put	**pouvoir**
il reçut	**recevoir**
il rit	**rire**
il sortit	**sortir**
il suivit	**suivre**
il tint	**tenir**
il vécut	**vivre**
il vit	**voir**
il voulut	**vouloir**
il sut	**savoir**

Many IRREGULAR VERBS have irregular stems in the passé simple.
These are always given in the **je**-form in dictionaries and verb charts.

Irregular verbs fall into three groups, according to their endings:

	je-form in **-us** connaître		**je**-form in **-is** prendre		**je**-form in **-ins** venir	
je	**connus**	**-us**	**pris**	**-is**	**vins**	**-ins**
tu	**connus**	**-us**	**pris**	**-is**	**vins**	**-ins**
il/elle/on	**connut**	**-ut**	**prit**	**-it**	**vint**	**-int**
nous	**connûmes**	**-ûmes**	**prîmes**	**-îmes**	**vînmes**	**-înmes**
vous	**connûtes**	**-ûtes**	**prîtes**	**-îtes**	**vîntes**	**-întes**
ils/elles	**connurent**	**-urent**	**prirent**	**-irent**	**vinrent**	**-inrent**

➡ Note that **aller** follows the pattern of **-er** verbs: **j'allai, il alla, ils allèrent.**

USES

The passé simple corresponds to the simple past in English.

Champlain **fonda** Québec en 1608. *Champlain **founded** Quebec in 1608.*

Contrast the use of the past tenses in French:

To express:	in LITERARY French:	in CONVERSATIONAL French:
• an on-going event or action (*what was happening*)	IMPERFECT **Il neigeait.** *(It was snowing.)*	IMPERFECT **Il neigeait.** *(It was snowing.)*
• a habitual past action (*what used to happen*)	IMPERFECT **En hiver, nous faisions du ski.** *(In winter, we used to go skiing.)*	IMPERFECT **En hiver, nous faisions du ski.** *(In winter, we used to go skiing.)*
• a specific event completed at a given moment in the past *(what happened)*	PASSÉ SIMPLE **Paul tomba et se cassa le bras.** *(Paul fell and broke his arm.)*	PASSÉ COMPOSÉ **Paul est tombé et il s'est cassé le bras.** *(Paul fell and broke his arm.)*
• an action that took place in the past at an indefinite time and has consequences in the present *(what has happened)*	PASSÉ COMPOSÉ **Personne ne l'a vu depuis l'accident.** *(Nobody has seen him since the accident.)*	PASSÉ COMPOSÉ **Personne ne l'a vu depuis l'accident.** *(Nobody has seen him since the accident.)*

Appendix C R33

APPENDIX D

1 MAPS

La France

l'Angleterre
la Belgique
l'Allemagne
le Luxembourg
la Manche
Lille
NORD[2]
HAUTE-NORMANDIE
PICARDIE
Le Havre
Rouen
Caen
BASSE-NORMANDIE
Versailles
PARIS
RÉGION PARISIENNE[1]
CHAMPAGNE-ARDENNE
Seine
LORRAINE
Meuse
Nancy
LES VOSGES
Strasbourg
ALSACE
Rhin
Colmar
BRETAGNE
Rennes
PAYS DE LA LOIRE
Loire
CENTRE
Tours
Nantes
Dijon
BOURGOGNE
FRANCHE-COMTÉ
Saône
la Suisse
POITOU-CHARENTES
LIMOUSIN
Vichy
AUVERGNE
Clermont-Ferrand
Annecy
RHÔNE-ALPES
Lyon
Grenoble
LES ALPES
l'Italie
OCÉAN ATLANTIQUE
Bordeaux
Garonne
LE MASSIF CENTRAL
Rhône
AQUITAINE
MIDI-PYRÉNÉES
Albi
Nîmes
Avignon
PROVENCE CÔTE D'AZUR[3]
Nice
Monaco
Cannes
Toulouse
Montpellier
LANGUEDOC-ROUSSILLON
Marseille
Toulon
Saint-Tropez
l'Espagne
LES PYRÉNÉES
Mer Méditerranée
LA CORSE

[1]Also known as Île-de-France
[2]Also known as Nord-Pas-de-Calais
[3]Also known as Provence-Alpes-Côte d'Azur (Bottin 1989)

Paris

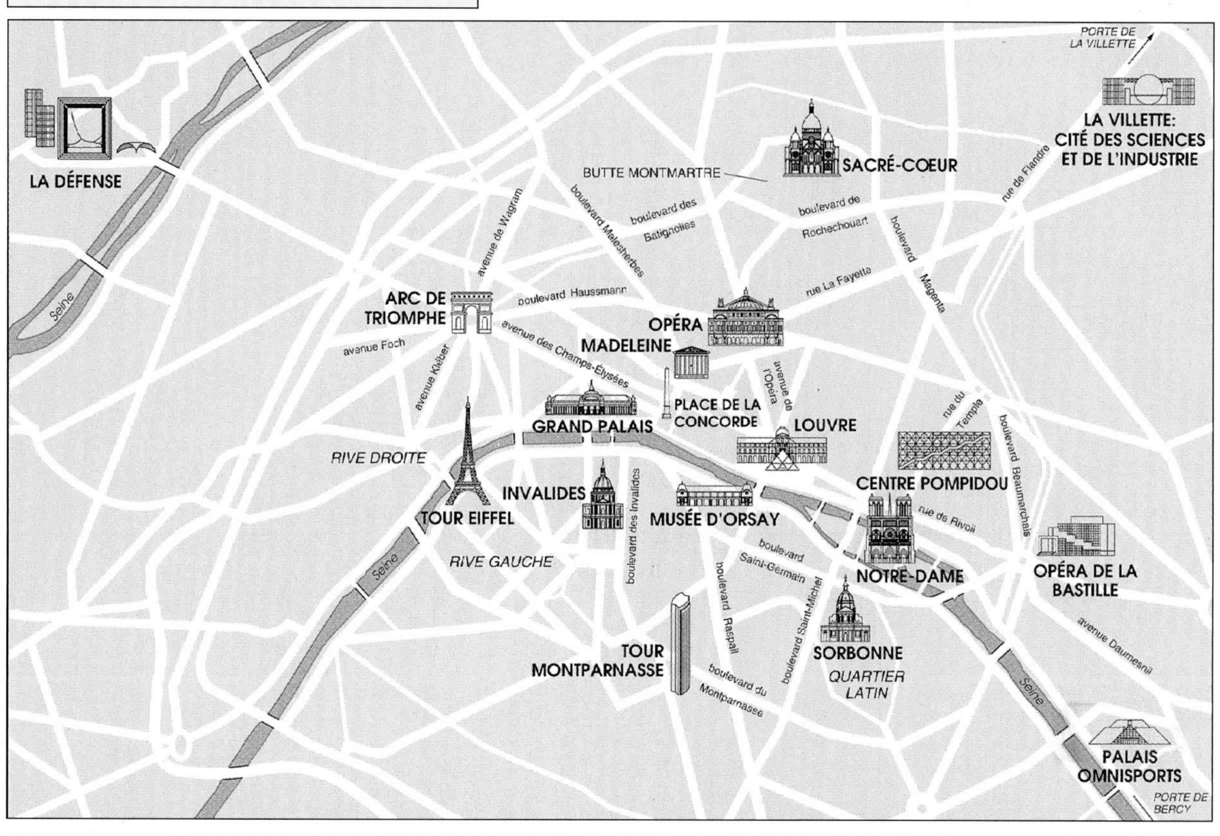

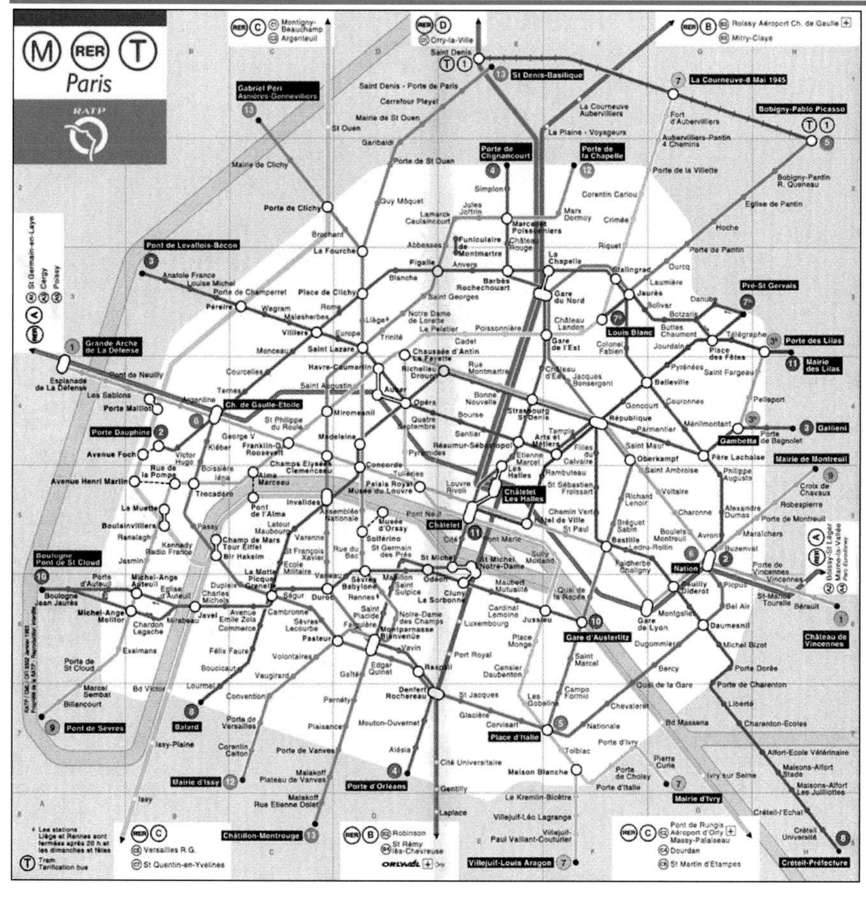

Paris Métro Map

Appendix D R35

En mai 1997, le président Laurent Kabila a changé le nom du Zaïre en République démocratique du Congo (le Congo démocratique).

Le Monde francophone

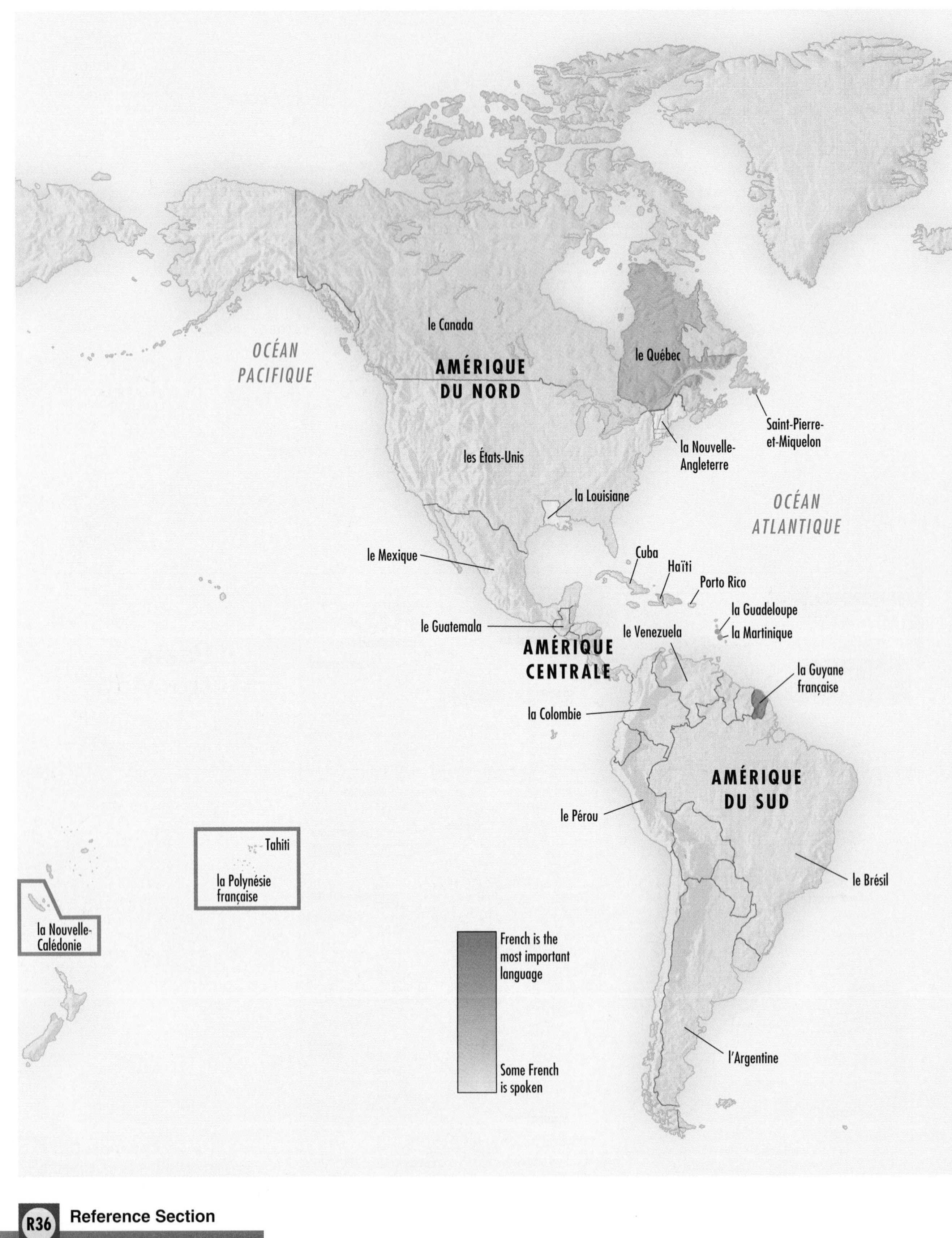

Appendix D R37

VOCABULAIRE: Français–Anglais

The French—English vocabulary contains active and passive words from the text, as well as the important words of the illustrations used within the units.

The numbers and letters following an entry indicate the first unit section in which the word or phrase is activated. The following abbreviations have been used:

R	Reprise
L	Lecture
IM	Info Magazine
IC	Interlude Culturel
FP	Français Pratique
TA	Teacher's Annotation
LC	Langue et Communication
A	Appendix

The number after the section abbreviation indicates the unit *Partie* in which the vocabulary word is introduced.

An asterisk (*) after the unit reference indicates that the word or phrase is presented in the *Mots Utiles* section of the reading.

Nouns: If the article of a noun does not indicate gender, the noun is followed by *m. (masculine)* or *f. (feminine)*. If the plural is irregular, it is given in parentheses.

Adjectives: Adjectives are listed in the masculine form. If the feminine form is irregular, it is given in parentheses. Irregular plural forms are also given in parentheses.

Verbs: Verbs are listed in the infinitive form. An asterisk (*) in front of an active verb means that it is irregular. (For forms, see the verb charts in the Appendix.) Irregular past participle *(p. p.)*, present participle *(pres. part.)*, future *(fut.)*, and subjunctive *(subj.)* forms are listed separately.

Words beginning with an **h** are preceded by a bullet (•) if the **h** is aspirate; that is, if the word is treated as if it begins with a consonant sound.

A

à to, at
à + *length of time* (length of time) from . . . **8.FP2**
à + *distance* (distance) from . . . **8.FP2**
à + *date, time until,* see you at (date, time) **8.FP1**
à + *mode of transport* by (mode of transport) . . .
abord: d'abord first, at first **3.FP2**
aborder to approach
l' **abri** *m.* shelter
abriter to shelter
un **accent** accent, tone
accès: un accès pour personnes handicapées handicap access **6.FP1**
un **accident** accident **3.FP2**
un **accord** chord
d'accord OK **2.FP2**
accorder to grant
***accueillir** to provide shelter; to welcome
acheter to *buy* **5.FP2**
s' **acheter** to buy (oneself) **1.FP3**
l' **acier** *m.* steel **2.FP3**
***acquérir** to acquire
actif: à mon actif to my credit
actuel (actuelle) current, present
actuellement currently
adieu *(pl. adieux)* farewell
un **adjoint (une adjointe)** assistant
un **adolescent (une adolescente)** teenager
l' **admiration** *f.* admiration **9.FP1**
s' **adresser à** to speak to
adroitement skillfully
l' **aéroport** *m.* airport **5.FP2**
une **affaire** business, affair
faire l'affaire to be qualified **10.FP3**
les **affaires** *f.* business **2.L***
l' **affection** *f.* affection **9.FP1**
affluent tributary
agence: une agence de voyages travel agency **5.FP2**
agent: un agent d'assurances insurance agent **10.FP1**
un agent de change stockbroker **10.FP1**
un agent de police policeman
un agent immobilier real estate agent **10.FP1**
***agir** to act
*s' **agir: il s'agit de** it is about
aider (à) to help **2.FP2**
aïe! ouch! **7.FP1**
ailleurs elsewhere **7.IM**
d'ailleurs besides **8.L***
aimer to like **2.LC2;** to love **9.FP1**

aimer bien to like **9.FP1**
l' **aîné(e)** eldest **R.L***
ainsi que as well as
l' **air** *m.* aria
l'air conditionné air conditioning **6.FP1**
aise: à l'aise comfortable
ajouté added
ajouter to add
alléché attracted, tempted
aller: un aller et retour round-trip ticket **5.FP2**
un aller simple one-way ticket **5.FP2**
***aller** to go **6.FP1**
aller à l'entretien to go on an interview **10.FP2**
aller à la pêche to go fishing **3.FP1**
aller voir to go look **1.L***
*s' **en aller** to go away **1.LC4**
une **allergie** allergy **7.FP1**
une **alliance** wedding ring
allumer to light **10.L***
allumer un feu to light a fire **2.L***
une **allumette** match **4.FP1**
une **allure** allure, impression
alors que whereas
les **Alpes** *f.* the Alps **1.LC1**
l' **alpinisme** *m.* mountain climbing
faire de l'alpinisme to go mountain climbing **3.FP1**
altier (altière) proud
l' **aluminium** *m.* aluminum **2.FP3**
amaigri very thin
une **amande** almond
un **amateur** amateur
une **ambiance** atmosphere **10.FP2**
l' **ambition** *f.* ambition **10.FP3**
l' **âme** *f.* soul
à l'âme tendre with a soft heart
aménagé equipped, developed
amer (amère) bitter
un **ami (une amie)** friend **9.FP1**
l' **amitié** *f.* friendship **9.FP1**
l' **amour** *m.* love
amoureux (amoureuse) de in love with
l' **ampleur** *f.* extent **4.L***
un **ampli** amplifier **4.FP3**
l' **ampoule** *f.* swelling
s' **amuser** to have fun **1.FP3**
ancien (ancienne) old, former **2.FP3**
un ancien élève alumnus **8.L***
l' **angine** *f.* strep throat **7.FP1**
un **animal** *(pl. animaux)* animal **2.FP1**
un **animateur (une animatrice)** counselor
l' **animosité** *f.* animosity **9.FP1**
une **annonce** notice, ad **2.IM**
annulé canceled **5.FP2**
annuler to cancel **5.FP2**
une **antenne** antenna **4.FP3**
un **antibiotique** antibiotic **7.FP1**
l' **antipathie** *f.* antipathy **9.FP1**
l' **anxiété** *f.* anxiety
s' **apaiser** to calm down
l' **appareil-photo** *m.* camera **4.FP3**
un **appareil-photo numérique** m. digital camera **4.FP3**
apercevoir** to notice **6.L
*s' **apercevoir** to notice
un **apôtre** apostle, defender
l' **apparence** *f.* appearance **2.FP3**
un **appartement** apartment **8.FP2**
appartenir à** to belong to **2.L
appeler to call **6.FP2**
s' **appeler** to be called, named **1.LC4**
un **apport** contribution
apporter to bring **6.L***
s' **approcher (de)** to approach, come closer **1.LC4**
appuyer to lean **10.L*** to push
après after, afterwards **3.FP2**
l' **après-rasage** *m.* aftershave **1.FP2**
l' **aquarium** *m.* aquarium **2.FP1**
un **arbuste** shrub **2.FP1**
l' **arc-en-ciel** *m.* rainbow
arche: l'Arche *f.* **de Saint Louis** the Arch of St. Louis **2.FP3**
l' **argent** *m.* silver **R.L***
l' **armée** *f.* the army
une **armoire** wardrobe, closet **1.L***
arraché torn away
arracher to pull out
arranger to fix **4.L***
ça s'arrangera things will be okay **9.FP1**
arrêter to arrest **5.L***
s' **arrêter** to stop (oneself) **1.FP3**
l' **arrière-garde** *f.* rear guard
arriver to happen **3.FP2**
arriver à to manage to **4.L***
il arrive it happens
il est arrivé quelque chose something happened
on y arrive one can do it
arroser to water (plants, flowers)
l' **arrosoir** *m.* watering can
un **article** item **4.FP1**
l' **ascendance** *f.* ancestry
un **ascenseur** elevator **6.FP1**
l' **aspirateur** *m.* vacuum
l' **aspirine** *f.* aspirine **4.FP1**
*s' **asseoir** to sit down **1.LC4**
assez enough **3.LC1**
l' **assistance** *f.* audience
un(e) **assistant(e) sociale** social worker **10.FP1**
assister à to be present at; to see **3.FP2**
l' **assurance** *f.* insurance
s' **assurer** to make sure **8.L***
l' **asthme** *m.* asthma **7.FP1**
astucieux (astucieuse) smart
un **atelier** studio
un atelier d'artisan craftsman workshop
athlétique athletic **1.FP1**
attacher to attach **5.FP2**
***atteindre** to reach
***attendre** to wait **5.FP2**
*s' **attendre à** to expect
attendant: en attendant in the meantime
attendrissant touching
***atterrir** to land **5.FP2**
attirant attractive, alluring
attiré attracted
attirer to attract
attraper to catch, get **3.FP1**
attraper un coup de soleil to get a sunburn **3.FP1**
une **auberge** inn **6.FP1**
une auberge de jeunesse youth hostel **6.FP1**
aucun no
aucunement not at all
augmenter to increase
l' **aumône** *f.* charity
auparavant before
auprès de with; next to
aussitôt que as soon as **5.LC2**
autant as much
d'autant plus que all the more that **9.L***
un **autel** altar
l' **autoroute** *f.* turnpike
autour de around **9.L***
autre: un autre another; another one **4.LC1**
autre chose? is there something else? **4.FP1**
autre chose à faire something else to do **2.FP2**
d'autres other(s), some other(s); other ones **4.LC1**
les autres the others
autrefois in the past

l' **Autriche** *f.* Austria
autrichien (autrichienne) Austrian
avaler to swallow **7.FP1**
une **avance** advance, progress
en avance early **5.FP2**
dix minutes d'avance ten minutes early **5.FP2**
avant: avant de before **10.LC1**
avant tout above all
l' **avant-bras** *m.* forearm
avant-hier the day before yesterday **3.FP2**
avantage: un avantage social fringe benefit **10.FP2**
l' **avenir** *m.* future
l' **aversion** *f.* aversion **9.FP1**
averti notified
un **aveu** *(pl. aveux)* admission
aveugle blind
avis: à votre avis in your opinion **RA**
un **avocat (une avocate)** lawyer **10.FP1**
***avoir** to have
avoir affaire à to have to deal with **8.FP2**
avoir beau essayer to try in vain **4.L***
avoir confiance to trust **9.FP2**
avoir de la chance to have good luck **9.FP1**
avoir de la peine to be sad, in pain **3.L***
avoir l'air décontracté to look relaxed
avoir le coup de foudre pour to fall in love with at first sight **9.FP1**
avoir le mal de mer to be seasick **3.FP1**
avoir le trac to be scared, nervous
avoir lieu to take place **2.L***
avoir mal to hurt, have pain **7.FP1**
avoir mal à l'estomac to have an upset stomach **1.L***
avoir mal à la gorge to have a sore throat **7.FP1**
avoir mal à la tête to have a headache **1.L***
avoir mal au cœur to feel nauseous **7.FP1**
avoir mal au ventre to have a stomach ache **7.FP1**
avoir peur to be scared **7.LC1**
avouer to admit, avow **2.L***

B

un **badaud** onlooker
les **bagages** *m.* baggage, luggage **5.FP1**
un bagage à main carry-on luggage **5.FP1**
une **bague** ring **R.L***
un **bahut** cupboard
se **baigner** to go swimming **3.FP1**
un **bain** bath **1.FP3**
un **baiser** kiss **7.L***
baisser to turn down, lower **6.FP2**
se **baisser** to stoop, bend down **7.L***
un **bal** dance **8.L***
un **balai** broom **2.FP1**
une **balance** scale
balayer to sweep **2.FP1**
balbutier to mumble
un **balcon** balcony **6.FP1**
une **balle** bullet
un **ballon** balloon **2.FP3**
un **banc** bench
une **bande** gang **5.L***
en bande in a group
la **banlieue** suburbs
la **banque** bank **10.FP2**
une banque d'affaires investment bank
un **banquier (une banquière)** bank teller **10.FP1**
des **bans** official announcements
une **barbe** beard **1.FP1**
barbu bearded **1.FP1**
bas (basse) low **2.FP3**
à bas down with
bâtiment: le bâtiment de l'ONU (or: de l'Organisation des Nations unies) United Nations building **2.FP3**
***bâtir** to build
un **bâton** stick, pole
la **batterie** drums
battre** to beat **7.L
*se **battre** to fight
battu beaten
bavarder to chat
beaucoup a lot; very **3.LC1**
beaucoup de mal a lot of difficulty, pain
bénéfique beneficial
bénévole voluntary
une **béquille** crutch **7.FP2**
berger: un berger allemand shepherd dog
une **bestiole** small animal
une **bête** animal **3.L***
une **bêtise** silliness, stupidity **3.L***

une **bibliothèque** library, bookcase **8.FP2**
bien well, good **1.FP4**
bien portant in good health **7.FP1**
bien serré close together **6.FP1**
bien situé well located **6.FP1**
bien sûr of course **2.FP2**
un **bien** possession; asset
un bien honnête a property of one's own
les **biens** *m.* wealth **2.L***
les biens immobiliers *m.* real estate
un **bien-aimé** beloved
le **bien-être** well-being **10.L***
un **bienfait** benefit, blessing
bientôt soon
un **bijou** *(pl. bijoux)* jewel, jewelry **9.L***
un **billet** letter; ticket **5.FP2**
la **biologie** biology **10.FP1**
le **blé** wheat
blessé injured, wounded
blesser to hurt
se **blesser** to get hurt, injure oneself **3.FP1**
bleu blue **1.FP1**
un **bloc** pad (of paper) **4.FP1**
blond blond **1.FP1**
un **bocal** glass jar **3.L***
le **bois** wood **2.FP3**
en bois wooden
un **bois** woods
une **boîte** club, nightspot; box **4.FP1**
une boîte de couleurs paintbox
le **bonheur** happiness
bon (bonne) right; good
il est bon que it is good that **2.LC2**
bonhomme good-natured
un **bonhomme** fellow, man
la **bonté** goodness
le **bord** brim; edge **3.IM**
au bord de on the edge of
un **bossu** hunchback
la **bouche** mouth **1.FP1**
bouclé curly, wavy
la **boue** mud
la **bouffe** food, grub
la **bougeotte** travelling urge
bouger to move (around)
sans bouger without moving
boule: la boule à zéro bald head **4.L***
bouleversé overwhelmed **7.L***

un **boulot** job
bourdonner to buzz
bourguignon (bourguignonne) people native to Burgundy
une **bourse** scholarship
bout: au bout de after, at the end of **8.L***
une **bouteille** bottle **2.FP3**
une **boutique** shop **4.FP1**
un **bouton** button (on camera) **4.FP3**
des boutons a rash **7.FP1**
un **bracelet** bracelet **9.L***
brailler to cry and scream
branche: une branche d'activité branch office **10.FP2**
brancher to plug in
le **bras** arm **7.FP2**
Bravo! Bravo! **9.FP1**
bref brief
les **bretelles** *f.* suspenders
le **bric-à-brac** odds-and-ends
le **bricolage** fixing and building things
un **brigand** bandit
brillant shiny **2.FP3**
briller to shine **3.FP3**
la **brique** brick **2.FP3**
brisé broken
briser to break
se **briser** to break
la **bronchite** bronchitis **7.FP1**
bronzé light brown, tan
bronzer to tan oneself **3.FP1**
brosse: une brosse à cheveux hairbrush **1.FP2**
une brosse à dents toothbrush **1.FP2**
se **brosser** to brush (one's hair, one's teeth) **1.FP2**
se brosser les dents to brush one's teeth **1.FP2**
le **brouillard** fog **3.FP3**
la **brousse** bush, undergrowth
la **broussaille** brushwood
un **bruit** noise
brûlé burned
brûler to burn
se **brûler** to burn oneself **7.FP2**
la **brume** fog **3.FP3**
brun brown **1.FP1**
bruyant noisy **6.FP1**
un **buffet** sideboard **1.L*,** food wagon
un **bureau** *(pl. bureaux)* office
un bureau de tabac tobacco shop
le **but** objective
dans ce but to this end
un **butin** booty
butte: en butte à faced with

C

ça: ça a eu lieu this happened, took place **3.FP2**
ça fait combien? how much does that come to? **4.FP1**
ça ira things will go well
ça n'a pas d'importance that doesn't matter **10.L***
ça s'est passé . . . this happened . . . **3.FP2**
ça vous fait mal? does it hurt you? **7.FP2**
une **cabine** booth
cabinet: un cabinet d'avocat lawyer's office **10.FP2**
un cabinet de médecin doctor's office
caché hidden
cacher to hide **5.L***
se **cacher** to hide (oneself)
un **cachet** tablet (medicine) **7.FP1**
un **cadeau** *(pl. cadeaux)* gift **6.L***
un **cadre** frame **10.L***
un(e) **cadre** executive
la **cage** cage **2.FP1**
la **caisse** check-out counter
calme calm **1.FP4**
un(e) **camarade** acquaintance, classmate **9.FP1**
un **cambriolage** burglary **3.FP2**
un **camion** truck
la **campagne** country (side)
le **Canada** Canada **1.LC1**
un **canapé** small sofa **1.L***
les **Canaries** *f.* Canary Islands **5.FP1**
cantonné quartered, stationed
une **carotte** carrot **2.FP1**
le **caoutchouc** rubber **2.FP3**
la **capacité** capacity, volume **2.FP3**
un **caprice** whim **8.L***
un **car** bus
une **carie** cavity **7.FP2**
un **carnet** notebook **4.FP1**
carré square **1.FP1**
carreaux: à carreaux plaid
un **carrosse** horse-drawn carriage
carte: une carte d'embarquement boarding pass **5.FP2**
une carte d'identité identification card **5.FP1**
une carte de crédit credit card **6.FP1**
une carte mémoire *f.* memory card **4.FP3**
une carte postale postcard **4.FP1**

un **carton** cardboard **2.FP3**
cas: un cas d'urgence emergency
un **cascadeur (une cascadeuse)** stuntman
caserne: une caserne de pompiers fire station **8.FP2**
une **casquette** *f.* cap
cassé broken **4.FP3**
casser to break **3.FP1**
se **casser** to break (body part) **3.FP1**
se casser la jambe to break one's leg **3.FP1**
une **casserole** pot, pan **1.L***
cause: à cause de because of **7.L***
une **caution** deposit
un **cavalier (une cavalière)** horseman (horsewoman)
ce: ce n'est pas croyable! that's not for real! **3.FP2**
ce sera prêt this will be ready **4.FP3**
c'est arrivé it happened **3.FP2**
c'est incroyable! that's unbelievable! **3.FP2**
c'est tout? that's all? **4.FP1**
c'est votre tour it's your turn **4.FP1**
c'est vous le patron (patronne)! you're the boss! **2.LC2**
céder to give up
ceinture: une ceinture de sécurité seat belt **5.FP2**
célèbre famous
célibataire single
celui (celle) this one **6.LC2**
celui-ci (celle-ci) this one **2.L***
celui-là (celle-là) that one
celui (celle) de that of, the one belonging to **6.LC2**
celui (celle) qui the one who(m), the one that **6.LC2**
la **cendre** ash(es)
centre: un centre d'apprentissage training school
un centre de loisirs recreation center **8.FP2**
un centre sportif gym, sports center **8.FP2**
le **centre-ville** town center, downtown **8.FP2**
certain(e)s some; certain ones **4.LC1**
chacun each person
une chaîne *f.* station **5.IM**

la **chair** flesh
la **chaleur** warmth
chambre: une chambre à air inner tube
une chambre d'hôte guest room
champêtre rural
un **champ** field **6.L***
sur le champ immediately
la chance luck
une **chandelle** candle **6.L***
changer: changer d'avis to change one's mind **7.L***
un **chantier** worksite
chaque each
une **charge** burden **2.L***; rank
chargé loaded; responsible
chargé de laden with; loaded with
charger to load
se **charger** to take care of
un chargeur de piles *m.* battery charger
un **chariot** shopping cart
chassé expelled
la **chasse** hunting
une chasse au trésor treasure hunt **R**
le **chat** cat **2.FP1**
châtain chestnut (hair) **1.FP1**
châtain clair gold (hair) **1.FP1**
châtain foncé brown (hair) **1.FP1**
chaud hot/warm **2.FP3**
le **chauffage** heating
une **chaussure** shoe
chauve bald **1.FP1**
chef: un chef de personnel head of personnel **10.FP1**
un **chef-d'œuvre** masterpiece
chemin: un chemin de fer railroad
la **cheminée** fireplace
une **chemise** shirt **2.FP1**
un **chenil** kennel
chèque: un chèque de voyage traveler's check **6.FP1**
par chèque (paid) by check **6.FP1**
cher (chère) precious, dear
chercher to claim (luggage) **5.FP2**
chercher à to try to **10.L***
un **chercheur (une chercheuse)** researcher **10.FP1**
chéri darling
un cheval horse
un **chevalier** knight
chevet: au chevet bedside
les **cheveux** *m.* hair **1.FP1**
les cheveux en brosse crew-cut **1.FP1**
la **cheville** ankle **7.FP2**
chez: chez des particuliers at private homes
chez soi at home
le **chien** dog **2.FP1**
un **chiffon** cloth rag **2.FP1**
chiffonné wrinkled
un **chiffonnier (une chiffonnière)** ragpicker
la **chimie** chemistry **10.FP1**
un **chirurgien (une chirurgienne)** surgeon **7.FP1**
***choisir** to choose **9.FP2**
le **chômage** unemployment
un **chômeur (une chômeuse)** unemployed person
chouette super **3.L***
la **chrétienté** Christendom
une **cicatrice** scar **1.FP1**
le **ciel** *(pl. cieux)* sky
une **cime** peak
un **cintre** hanger **6.FP2**
circulaire circular **2.FP3**
la **circulation** traffic **6.L***
les **ciseaux** *m.* scissors **1.FP2**
un **citadin** city dweller
un **citoyen (une citoyenne)** citizen
clair light; sunny **6.FP1**
classe: la classe affaires business class **5.FP2**
la classe économique tourist class **5.FP2**
la deuxième classe second class **5.FP2**
la première classe first class **5.FP2**
classer to file **10.FP3**
la **clé** key
la **climatisation** air conditioning **6.FP1**
le **climatiseur** air conditioner
le **clou** nail (metal) **2.FP3**
coalisé allied
une **cocarde** cockade
code: le code de la route traffic regulations **8.FP2**
un **coffre** safe **R.L***
coiffer to cover (head)
le **coiffeur (la coiffeuse)** hairdresser **4.FP2**
une **coiffure** hairstyle
un **coin** corner
au coin on the corner
du coin from the neighborhood, area
la **colère** anger **7.LC1**
en colère angry **1.FP4**
un **colis** package **4.FP1**
la **colle** glue **4.FP1**
coller to stick, to glue
une **colombe** dove
un **colon** settler
combien: combien de temps? how long? **6.FP1**
combien en voulez-vous? how many would you like? **4.FP1**
combien est-ce que je vous dois? how much do I owe you? **4.FP1**
comble: à son comble at its height
une **commande** order
comme since
comme convenu as agreed
comme d'habitude as usual
comme si as if **8.L***
le **commerce** business, trade **10.FP1**
un **commerce** (small) business, shop **8.FP2**
commun in common, shared
la **communication** communication **10.FP2**
une **compagnie** company **10.FP2**
une compagnie internationale international company **10.FP2**
complet (complète) complete, full (sold out) **5.FP2**
un(e) **complice** accomplice **5.L***
composer to dial
composter to punch (ticket) **5.FP2**
le **composteur** ticket-punching machine **5.FP2**
***comprendre** to include
y compris including
un **comprimé** pill (medicine) **7.FP1**
la **comptabilité** accounting **10.FP1**
un(e) **comptable** accountant **10.FP1**
compte: à son propre compte on his own account **10.FP2**
compter to count on, to plan; to count **6.FP1**
le **comptoir** trading post; counter **5.FP2**
la **comtesse** countess **7.L***
un **concours** competitive exam
la **condition** condition **2.FP3**
à condition que provided, on condition that **10.LC2**
de bonnes conditions de travail good working conditions **10.FP2**

conduire** to lead **3.L; to drive
une **confiance** trust **9.FP1**
confiant trusting
confier entrust
confirmer to confirm **5.FP2**
la **confiture** jam
confortable comfortable **6.FP1**
confus upset
une **connaissance** acquaintance **9.FP1**
  en connaissance de cause knowingly
  faire la connaissance to meet (for the first time)
  les connaissances techniques technical knowledge **10.FP3**
connu known
un **conseil** advice
conseillé recommended
la **consigne** baggage-check **5.FP2**
une **consigne** rule
la **consistance** consistency **2.FP3**
consterné dismaying
***construire** to build
un **conte** short story
***contenir** to contain
content happy **1.FP4**
conteur (le/la conteuse) storyteller
continuer to continue
un **contrebandier (une contrebandière)** smuggler
contrepartie: en contrepartie in exchange
contrôle: un contrôle de sécurité security check **5.FP2**
  un contrôle de passeports passport check **5.FP1**
***convaincre** to convince
convaincu convinced
convaincant convincing
convoiter to desire secretly
convoquer to call in (for an interview)
un **copain (une copine)** boy/girlfriend **9.FP1**
la **coqueluche** whooping cough **7.FP1**
un **cor** horn
une **corbeille** wastepaper basket, trash **2.FP1**
un **corbeau** *(pl. corbeaux)* crow
le **cordonnier** shoe repairer **4.FP3**
une **corne** horn
Cornouailles Cornwall (in southwestern England)

le **corps** body
une **correspondance** connection (plane) **5.FP2**
la **Corse** Corsica
cortège: un cortège funèbre funeral procession
costaud solid, well-built **1.FP1**
côte: la Côte d'Azur French Riviera (blue coast)
un **côte** side **4.L***
  à côté (de) besides, next to
  d'à côté next door
  de l'autre côté de on the other side of
  de leur côté as far as they are concerned
  sur les côtés on the sides **4.FP2**
un **coton-tige** cotton swab **4.FP1**
le **cou** neck **1.FP1**
couché in bed
se **coucher** to go to sleep **1.FP3;** to set (sun); to be doubled over
couler to flow
un **couloir** aisle **5.FP2;** corridor
coup: un coup de main a helping hand, help
  un coup de pinceaux brush stroke
  un coup de téléphone phone call
une **coupe** (hair) cut
  une coupe de cheveux haircut **4.FP2**
une **coupe-brushing** haircut and a blow-dry **4.FP2**
couper to cut **2.FP1**
se **couper** to cut (oneself) **1.FP2**
  se couper à la main to cut one's hand **7.FP2**
  se couper les cheveux to cut one's hair **4.FP2**
  coupez-les-moi courts cut my hair short **4.FP2**
une **cour** courtyard; court
courant fluent
courbé rounded, arched **2.FP3**
se **courber** to bend over
coureur: un coureur (une coureuse) des bois fur trapper
courir** to run **1.L
une **couronne** crown
le **courrier** mail **4.FP1**
cours: au cours (de) during, in the course of
  au cours de l'engagement during battle

la **course** water; race
court short
un **couteau** *(pl. couteaux)* knife **2.FP1**
couvert overcast **3.FP3**
une **couverture** blanket **2.L***
***couvrir** to cover
***craindre** to fear, be afraid of **7.LC1**
la **crainte** fear **7.LC1**
le **crâne** skull **4.L***
un **crayon** pencil **4.FP1**
créer: créer sa propre entreprise start one's own business **10.FP2**
crème: la crème à raser shaving cream **1.FP2**
le **crépuscule** dusk
cri: un cri de ralliement rallying cry
criard loud (color)
crier to yell, shout **1.L***
une **crise** fit
***croire** to believe **7.LC1**
un **croisement** crossing
se **croiser** to cross, meet
croissant increasing
une **croix** cross
la **croyance** belief
***cueillir** to pick (flowers)
cuisiner to cook
cuit: cuit à la vapeur steamed
le **cuivre** copper **2.FP3**
un **cultivateur (une cultivatrice)** farmer **8.L***
un **curriculum vitae** résumé **10.FP3**
cutané of the skin

D

dans: dans les approximately
  dans tous ses états very upset
dame: une dame de compagnie lady-in-waiting
un **débarquement** landing
débarquer to disembark, land **5.FP2**
débarrasser to clear **2.FP1**
  débarrasser la table to clear the table **2.FP1**
se **débarrasser** to get rid of **3.L***
se **débloquer** to unlock
débordant overflowing
debout standing
le **début** beginning
un **débutant (une débutante)** beginner
un **décès** death
des **déchets** *m.* trash

décimé killed
décoller to take off (plane) **5.FP2**
un décolleté low neckline
un découpage division
découpé cut out
découper to cut (into pieces) **8.L***
***découvrir** to discover
décrocher to pick up (phone)
déçu disappointed, deceived **1.FP4**
un défaut fault, failing
défendu forbidden **3.L***
défier to challenge
dégager to shorten (hair) **4.FP2**
des dégâts *m.* damage
dehors outside **3.FP2**
en dehors outside
déjà already, yet; ever **3.LC1**
de façon à in order to **7.IC**
délivrer to give, deliver
demander to ask, necessitate
demande: sur demande on request
se demander to wonder **8.L***
démarche: les démarches *f.* **amoureuses** steps in courtship
démissionner to resign
se démocratiser to become democratic
demoiselle: une demoiselle d'honneur bridesmaid
démontable that can be dismantled
démonter to take apart
une dent tooth **7.FP2**
une dent de sagesse wisdom tooth **7.FP2**
le dentifrice toothpaste **1.FP2**
un(e) dentiste dentist **7.FP1**
le déodorant deodorant **1.FP2**
dépaysé lost (in a strange place)
se dépêcher to hurry (oneself) **1.FP3**
dépens: aux dépens(de) at the expense (of)
se déplacer to move (around)
déplaire à to displease someone **5.IM**
déplorer to deplore **7.LC1**
déprimé depressed **7.FP1**
depuis peu recently
un député congressman
déranger to bother
la dérision mockery
dernier (dernière) last **3.FP2**
se dérouler to take place
derrière in back **4.FP2**
le derrière behind, rear end
dès as of; beginning in
dès lors from then on
dès que as soon as **5.LC2**
un désastre catastrophe **4.L***
***descendre** to get off (train) **5.FP2;** to bring down **6.FP2**
descendre: avoir + descendu to have taken or carried something down **3.LC1**
descendre: être + descendu to have gone down **3.LC1**
se déshabiller to get undressed **1.FP3**
désirer to wish **2.LC2**
désolé sorry, sad **2.FP2**
le désordre: en désordre in disorder **2.FP1**
désormais henceforth
le dessin design, art
dessus: par-dessus on
sur le dessus on top **4.FP2**
se détacher to separate, break away
détective: un détective privé private eye **5.L***
une détente relaxation
***détruire** to destroy
devant in front (of) **8.FP1**
sur le devant in front **4.FP2**
une devanture (de magasin) storefront
développer to develop (photos, personnality) **4.FP3**
***devenir** to become
deviner to guess **3.FP2**
une devise motto
***devoir** must; to owe **4.FP1**
dévoué devoted **7.L***
une diapo picture slide **4.FP1**
un dieu (une déesse; pl. dieux) god, deity **2.IC**
Dieu *m.* God **2.IC**
Mon Dieu! My goodness **3.FP2**
digne dignified **8.L***
la dimension dimension, size **2.FP3**
la diminution decrease
dîner to dine, have dinner **3.LC1**
un(e) diplomate diplomat **10.FP1**
un diplôme diploma **10.FP3**
***dire: à vrai dire** to tell the truth
direct direct (flight) **5.FP2**
un directeur (une directrice) director **10.FP1**
se diriger vers to move toward **8.L***
un discours speech
disparaître** to disappear, go away **5.L
la disparition disappearance
disposé arranged
disposer to have (at one's disposal)
une dispute argument **9.FP1**
se disputer to have an argument **9.FP1**
dissimuler to hide
***distraire** to amuse
***se distraire** to have fun
divorcer to get a divorce **9.FP2**
un docteur doctor **1.LC1**
dommage: il est dommage que it is too bad that **2.LC2**
donc therefore
donner: donner à manger à to feed **2.FP1**
donner lieu to give rise
donner rendez-vous à to make an appointment/date with **8.FP1**
donner un coup de main to give a hand **2.FP2**
donnez-m'en dix give me ten (of them) **4.FP1**
se donner rendez-vous to agree to meet **8.FP1**
dont whose
doré gilded, golden
la dorure gilt
une dot dowry
la douane customs **5.FP1**
un douanier (une douanière) customs officer
doucement gently
la douceur kindness
une douche shower **1.FP3**
doué gifted **8.L***
une douleur pain, suffering **7.FP2**
douloureux (douloureuse) painful **7.L***
se douter bien to be sure
doux (douce) soft, gentle
un drap sheet (bedding) **6.FP2**
dressé placed, prepared
une drogue drug
droit straight, upright **2.FP3;** straightforward
le droit law; right
drôlement truly **4.L***

dur hard **2.FP3;** difficult
la **durée** duration, period
durer to last **2.L***

E

eau: l'eau *f.* **de toilette** perfume **1.FP2**
ébahi open-mouthed
s' **écarter** to move aside
échapper à to escape from
échapper de peu to escape narrowly
une **écharpe** sash
un **échec** failure
une **échelle** ladder
des échelles in steps (hair), uneven **4.L***
échouer to fail
un **éclair** (flash of) lightning **3.FP3**
éclatant very loud
éclater to break out
une **écorce** bark (tree)
écossais Scottish
l' **écran** *m.* screen
un **écrivain** writer
écroulé collapsed
une **éducatrice spécialisé** special ed teacher **R**
l' **eczéma** *m.* rash (skin) **7.FP1**
effacer to erase
effrayé scared
également equally, also
égorger to slit the throat of
l' **égout** *m.* sewer
un **élastique** rubber band **4.FP1**
l' **électronique** *f.* electronics **10.FP2**
élémentaire elementary
élevé raised, high **2.FP3**
mal élevé impolite, poorly raised
élever to raise (children) **2.L***
s' **élever** to stand up
élu elected
l' **emballage** *m.* packaging
embarquer to board (plane) **5.FP2**
l' **embarras** *m.* difficulty
embaucher to hire
un **emblème** emblem, logo
s' **embêter** to get bored **1.LC4**
l' **embouteillage** *m.* traffic jam
embrasser to kiss **1.L***
une **embuscade** ambush **2.IC**
émerveillé amazed
emmener (person) to bring **3.L***

empaqueter to bag (groceries)
empêcher de to prevent, keep from (doing) **1.L***
n'empêche que nevertheless
s' **empêcher (de)** to stop, prevent oneself from **4.L***
l' **emplacement** *m.* site, location
un **emploi** employment, job **10.FP1**
un emploi à mi-temps half-time job **10.FP3**
un emploi à plein temps full-time job **10.FP3**
un emploi à temps complet a full-time job **2.IM**
un emploi à temps partiel part-time job **10.FP3**
un emploi temporaire temporary job **10.FP3**
un **employé (une employée)** employee, clerk **10.FP1**
emporter to take along; to carry off
ému moved, touched
encore still
encore lui! him again!
***encourir** to incur
*s' **endormir** to fall asleep
endroit: cet endroit précis this very spot
énervé nervous; upset, bothered **1.FP4**
s' **énerver** to get upset **1.LC4**
l' **enfance** *f.* childhood
enfiler to put on (clothes)
enfin at last **3.FP2**
***enfouir** to bury
*s' **enfuir** to run away, flee
engagé politically active; hired
un **engagé** volunteer
l' **engagement** *m.* military service
s' **engager** to enlist
enlever to take off, remove **4.FP3**
s' **ennuyer** to be bored
ennuyeux (ennuyeuse) boring
énorme enormous **2.FP3**
*s' **enquérir de** to inquire
une **enquête** survey
enregistrer to check (luggage) **5.FP2**
enseigner to teach
ensuite next **3.FP2**
entendre: entendre dire** to hear (it said) **8.L
entendre parler de to hear about
*s' **entendre** to get along with
entendu agreed **8.FP1**

enterré buried
l' **enterrement** *m.* funeral
enterrer to bury
entonner to begin to sing
entouré surrounded
s' **entraider** to help each other out
un **entraînement** training **2.IM**
suivre un entrainement to undergo a training
entre among
entre-temps meanwhile
***entreprendre** to undertake
une **entreprise** company **10.FP2**
entrer to be accepted (school)
***entretenir** to take care of
entretenu maintained
un **entretien** interview **10.FP3**
***entrevoir** to anticipate
une **entrevue** interview **10.FP3**
un **envahisseur** invader
une **enveloppe** envelope **4.FP1**
envelopper to wrap **7.L***
l' **envers** *m.* reverse
l' **envie** *f.* envy, desire
environ about, approximately
l' **environnement** *m.* environment **3.FP1**
un **envoyé** messenger
envoyer to send
épais (épaisse) thick **2.FP3**
épargne spare
s' **éparpiller** to scatter
l' **épaule** *f.* shoulder
une **épée** sword
éperdument madly
une **épine** thorn
une **épingle** pin **4.FP1**
une épingle de sûreté safety pin **4.FP1**
éplucher to peel **2.FP1**
une **éponge** sponge **2.FP1**
épouser to marry **2.L***
épouvantable ghastly
les **époux** *m.* spouses, husband and wife
épris enamored
éprouver to feel, experience
une **équipe** team
en équipe as a team **2.IM**
l' **escalade** *f.* rock climbing
faire de l'escalade to go rock climbing
une **escale** stopover, connection **5.FP2**
l' **esclavage** *m.* slavery
un(e) **esclave** slave
espèces: en espèces in cash **6.FP1**
un **espion (une espionne)** spy **5.L***

l' **espoir** *m.* hope
l' **esprit** *m.* soul, spirit; mind
un esprit d'initiative enterprising mind **10.FP3**
essayer to try
l' **essence** *f.* gasoline **6.L***
essentiel: il est essentiel que it is essential that **2.LC2**
essoufflé out of breath
essuyer to wipe **2.FP1**
s' **essuyer** to wipe (oneself) dry **1.FP2**
s'essuyer les mains to dry one's hands **1.FP2**
et and **5.LC1**
s' **établir** to settle, establish
l' **étagère** *f.* shelf
un **étang** pond
une **étape** step, stage
l' **état** *m.* condition **2.FP3**
les **États-Unis** *m.* United States **1.LC1**
***éteindre** to turn off
***s' éteindre** to go out, be extinguished
éteint out, off, extinct
un **étendard** military banner
***étendre** to extend
***s' étendre** to extend
éternuer to sneeze **7.FP1**
l' **étoffe** *f.* fabric **2.FP3**
une **étoile** star
étonnant amazing **6.LC1**
étonné astonished **7.LC1**
l' **étonnement** *m.* amazement **7.LC1**
étouffé suffocated
étranger: à l'étranger abroad **5.FP1**
***être** to be
être accueilli to be welcomed, invited
être d'accord to agree **9.FP2**
être enrhumé to have a cold **7.FP1**
être reçu to be accepted (school)
être témoin de to witness **3.FP2**
être tranquille to be alone, undisturbed **1.L***
un **être** human being
étroit narrow, tight **2.FP3**
une **étude** course of study **10.FP1**
faire des études (de) to study **9.FP3**
les études d'ingénieur engineering studies **10.FP1**
les études vétérinaires veterinary studies **10.FP1**
étudier to study **10.FP1**
s' **évader** to escape
l' **éveil** *m.* wakefulness **10.L***
éveiller to wake up **10.L***
un **événement** event **3.FP2**
un **évêque** bishop
l' **évier** *m.* kitchen sink
avoir plein l'évier to have a sink full (of pots)
éviter to avoid **3.FP1**
examiner to examine **7.FP1**
s' **excuser** to excuse oneself apologize **1.FP3**
exécuter: exécuter une ronde to dance in a circle
un **exemplaire** copy (books, magazines)
exiger to insist **2.L***
expérience: l' expérience *f.* **professionnelle** professional experience **10.FP3**
expliquer to explain **2.L***
exposer to exhibit **9.L***
exprimé expressed
exprimer to express **5.IM**
exquis exquisite **7.L***
exténué exhausted

F

fabriquer to do, make **3.L***
la fac *f.* college **R**
face: en face de opposite **6.L***, across from **8.FP1**
fâché upset **3.L***
se **fâcher** to be upset **9.FP1**
la **façon** manner
de facon à in order to **7.IC**
faible weak **1.FP1**
la **faïence** glazed pottery
la **faim** hunger
***faire** to make, do
faire appel to call; to ask
faire bouillir to boil **4.LC3**
faire carrière to have a career **10.FP2**
faire connaître to make known
faire couper les cheveux to get a haircut
faire cuire to cook **4.LC3**
faire de la planche à voile to go windsurfing **3.FP1**
faire de la plongée sous-marine to go scuba diving **3.FP1**
faire du camping to go camping **3.FP1**
faire (du) mal à to hurt **3.L***
faire frire to fry **4.LC3**
faire l'innocent to act innocent
faire la cour to court (somebody)
faire la vaisselle to wash the dishes **2.FP1**
faire le ménage to do housework **2.FP1**
faire partie to be a part of
faire rage to rage
faire réchauffer to reheat
faire taire to silence, stifle
faire un pique-nique to have a picnic **3.FP1**
faire un plâtre to make a cast (broken bone) **7.FP2**
faire une analyse de sang to take a blood sample **7.FP1**
faire une promenade en bateau to take a boat trip **3.FP1**
***se faire: se faire des amis** to make friends **9.FP2**
se faire mal to get hurt **3.FP1**
se faire nommer to name oneself
se faire tuer to have oneself killed
s'en faire** to worry **4.L
un **fait** fact **3.FP2**
un fait divers a minor news event **3.FP2**
***falloir** to be necessary
il me faut I need **4.FP1**
fané withered
fard: le fard à paupières eyeshadow **1.FP2**
fatigué tired **1.FP4**
la **faune** wildlife
un **fauve** wild beast
fécond prolific
Félicitations! Congratulations! **9.FP1**
féliciter to congratulate **9.FP1**
femme: la femme de chambre chambermaid
le **fer (metal)** iron **2.FP3**
un fer à repasser iron (for clothes) **2.FP1**
une **ferme** farm **6.L***
ferroviaire railroad
un **feu (pl. feux)** fire
une **feuille** form (paper); leaf (tree)
le **feuillage** leaves
les **fiançailles** *f.* engagement
se **fiancer** to get engaged **9.FP2**
la **ficelle** string **4.FP1**

fichu ruined
fidèle loyal, faithful
fier (fière) proud 3.L*
la fierté pride
la fièvre fever 7.FP1
la figure face 1.FP1
figurer to appear, figure; to imagine
un filet net
le filtre filter 4.FP3
fin refined
la fin end
à la fin towards the end
finalement finally 3.FP2
la finance finance 10.FP2
*finir to finish 3.LC1
une firme firm (company) 10.FP2
se fixer to settle
le flash camera flash 4.FP3
une fleur flower 2.FP1
*fleurir to bloom
un fleuve river
flexible flexible 2.FP3
la flore plant life
un flot stream, cascade; wave
une flotte fleet
le foie liver
fois: une fois once 7.FP1
à la fois at the same time
deux fois par jour twice a day 7.FP1
une folie madness, lunacy
fonction: la fonction publique civil service 10.FP2
fonctionner to function 4.FP3
un(e) fonctionnaire civil servant 10.FP1
le fond background; depth
au fond in the back; deep down
fonder to found
*fondre: fondre en larmes to break into tears
la force strength
la forêt forest 3.FP1
la formation training
la forme form 2.FP3
en forme in shape 1.FP4
formidable great, terrific
fort loud 6.L*; strong 1.FP1; tightly
fort avant very late
fou (folle) crazy 3.L*
un fou (une folle) madman/madwoman 7.L*
un fouet whip
fougueux (fougueuse) brave
fouiller to search
un foulard silk scarf 1.IM
la foule crowd
se fouler to sprain 7.FP2

le four oven 1.L*
la fourrure fur
se fracturer to fracture 7.FP2
fragile weak 2.FP3
la fraîcheur coolness
frais (fraîche) fresh, cool
frais et dispos fresh and rested
le français French (language) 1.LC1
à la française in the French manner
*franchir to cross, to bridge
frapper to knock (on door) 1.L*; to strike
les freins *m.* brakes 4.FP3
fréquenter to visit
les fringues *f.* clothing
frisé curly, frizzy 1.FP1
frissonner to shiver, shudder 9.L*
froid cold 2.FP3
la froidure cold weather
le front forehead 1.FP1
la frontière border
*fuir to flee
en fuite in flight, fleeing
*s' enfuir to flee
la fumée smoke
furieux (furieuse) furious 1.FP4
un fusil gun, rifle
fusillé shot and killed

G

gagner: gagner sa vie to earn one's living R.L*
un gaillard guy
un gamin kid
gant: un gant de toilette wash cloth 1.FP2
un garçon bellboy 6.FP2
un garçon d'honneur usher (wedding)
garde: un garde du corps bodyguard
garder to keep
la gare train station 5.FP2
gâter to spoil 7.L*
le gazon grass
gelé frozen 3.FP3
une gélinotte grouse
gênant bothersome 3.L*
une gendarmerie police station 8.FP2
un genou (pl. genoux) knee, lap 7.L*
un genre kind
gens: les gens *m.* de service servants

gentil (gentille) nice 2.FP2
le/la gérant(e) manager 6.FP2
la gestion management 10.FP1
un gilet vest
gitan gypsy
un gîte simple lodging
glacé: glacé d'effroi frozen with fear
la glace ice 3.FP3; mirror 1.FP2
glisser to slip 3.FP1
le goût taste
le goût des responsabilités the inclination for responsibility 10.FP3
une goutte drop 7.FP1
une gouvernante governess
grâce à thanks to
grain: un grain de beauté beauty mark 1.FP1
grand big 1.FP1
un grand centre commercial mall 8.FP2
un grand ensemble housing project
une grande surface shopping center
grandir to grow (in size) 3.L; to grow up 9.FP3
gratuit free
gratuitement free of charge
la Grèce Greece 5.FP1
grêle frail
le grenier attic
une grenouille frog 3.L*
grièvement seriously
la grippe flu 7.FP1
gris grey 1.FP1
grogner to grunt
gronder to scold
gros (grosse) fat, heavyset; big
la guerre war
guerrier (guerrière) warlike
un guerrier (une guerrière) warrior
le guichet ticket window 5.FP2

H

habilement skillfully
s' habiller to get dressed 1.FP3
habit: habit *m.* noir formal evening dress
habitué à accustomed to
haie: une haie d'arbustes hedge 6.L*
hardiment boldly
hasard: par hasard by chance
haut high 2.FP3
le•haut-parleur loudspeaker 4.FP3
héberger to shelter
l' herbe *f.* grass 2.FP1

Vocabulaire: Français—Anglais

Français-Anglais R47

hériter (de) to inherit 8.L*
un héritier (une héritière) heir/heiress R.L*
heure: à l'heure on time 5.FP2
heureux (heureuse) happy 1.FP4
hier yesterday 3.FP2
hier soir last night 3.FP2
l' histoire *f.* history 10.FP1
un HLM (Habitation à Loyer Modéré) low-income housing 8.IM
homme: un homme (une femme) d'affaires business man, woman 10.FP1
mi-homme half man
honteux (honteuse) ashamed
l' hôpital *m.* hospital 7.FP2
un horaire schedule 5.FP2
un hôtel hotel 6.FP1
un hôtel bon marché inexpensive hotel 6.FP1
un hôtel de luxe luxury hotel 6.FP1
hôtesse: l'hôtesse *f.* de l'air stewardess 5.FP2
l' humeur *f.* mood 4.L*
de bonne humeur in a good mood 1.FP4
de mauvaise humeur in a bad mood 1.FP4
humide humid, wet 2.FP3

I

ici: d'ici une semaine one week from now 4.FP3
il y a ago 3.FP2
il n'y a pas de quoi you're welcome 2.FP2
il n'y aura pas there won't be
s' illuminer to brighten
un immeuble apartment building
l' immobilier *m.* real estate 10.FP2
s' impatienter to get impatient 1.LC4
une impératrice emperor's wife
important important 10.FP2
l' important *m.* the important thing 8.IM
il est important que it is important that 2.LC2
n'importe quel any
n'importe qui (just) anyone
n'importe quoi anything 7.L*
imprescriptible that which cannot be legally taken away
imprimé printed
imprimer to print
improviste: à l'improviste unannounced
imprudent careless, imprudent
inattendu unexpected 8.L*
incendié burned to the ground
un incendie fire
s' incliner to bow
un inconnu (une inconnue) stranger 7.L*
un inconvénient inconvenience, drawback
l' indigestion *f.* indigestion 7.FP1
indispensable: il est indispensable que it is indispensable that 2.LC2
indisponible unavailable
l' industrie *f.* industry 10.FP2
inexpérimenté inexperienced
infirme crippled
un infirmier (une infirmière) nurse 7.FP1
un informaticien (une informaticienne) computer specialist 10.FP1
un ingénieur engineer 10.FP1
injuste unfair R.L*
inoffensif (inoffensive) harmless 8.L*
l' inondation *f.* flood
*inquiet (inquiète) worried
s' inquiéter to worry
*inscrire to enroll; to register to inscribe
insensible insensitive
insister: insister pour que to insist that 2.LC2
l' insolation *f.* sunstroke
insouciant carefree
inspecteur: un inspecteur de police police detective 5.L*
s' installer to settle 8.L*
instituer to create, institute
une institutrice (primary school) teacher
l' instruction *f.* education
insu: à l'insu de without the knowledge of
*interdire to prohibit
interdit forbidden
s' intéresser to be interested
intérieur: à l'interieur inside
intérieurement internally, inside
interrogé interviewed, asked
interroger to interrogate
*interrompre to interrupt
*intervenir to intervene
une interview interview 10.FP3
*introduire to introduce; to lead
un invité (une invitée) guest

J

la jalousie jealousy 9.FP1
jardin: un jardin public public garden 8.FP2
le jardinage gardening
jeter to throw 3.FP1
se jeter to throw oneself
le jeûne fast
job: un job d'été summer job 10.FP3
la joie joy 7.LC1
joindre to contact (someone) 9.L
un jongleur (une jongleuse) juggler
la joue cheek
jour: dans deux jours in two days' time 4.FP3
un jour de congé day off 4.L*
il fait grand jour the sun is up and shining
le journalisme journalism 10.FP1
la journée day
un(e) juge judge 10.FP1
juger to judge, think
un Juif (une Juive) Jew
jurer to swear
jusqu'à up to, until
jusqu'à quand until when 6.FP1
jusqu'alors until then
jusqu'au bout to the end 7.L*
jusqu'ici until now 4.L*
juste fair R.L*
il est juste que it is fair that 2.LC2
justement precisely at that moment 8.L*; as a matter of fact

L

laboratoire: un laboratoire de recherche research laboratory 10.FP2
lâcher to loosen, let go
laid ugly
la laine wool
laisser to leave R.L*
laisser ouvert to leave open
laisser tomber to drop
laissez-les-moi longs leave

my hair long (haircut) **4.FP3**
lancer to launch **4.L*;** to send out
lancer un défi to challenge
la **langue** tongue
une langue étrangère foreign language **10. FP1**
la langue maternelle native language
un **lapin** rabbit **2.FP1**
un **larcin** small theft
le **lard** salt pork
large wide **2.FP3**
une **larme** tear **7.L***
le **lavabo** bathroom sink **2.FP1**
laver to wash **2.FP1**
laver le linge to do laundry **2.FP1**
se **laver** to wash (oneself) **1.FP3**
se laver la figure to wash one's face **1.FP2**
léger (légère) light **2.FP3**
les **légumes** *m.* vegetables **2.FP1**
le **lendemain** the day after **6.L***
la **lenteur** slowness
la **lentille** (camera) lens **4.FP3**
les lentilles *f.* **de contact** contact lenses **1.FP1**
lequel (laquelle) which
lesquels (lesquelles) which
la **lessive** detergent **4.FP1**
une **lettre** letter **4.FP1**
une lettre de recommandation letter of recommendation **10.FP3**
levant rising
lever to raise
se **lever** to get up
libre free **2.FP2**
le **libre-échange** free trade
librement freely
la licence B. A. degree **2.IM**
lié interwoven, linked
lien: les liens *m.* **de sang** blood ties
lier: lier conversation to talk, initiate conversation
un **lieu (pl. lieux)** location
au lieu de instead of
le **linge** laundry
une **lingère** laundry woman
la **lingerie** laundry room **2.FP1**
***lire** to read
lisse straight (hair) **1.FP1;** smooth **2.FP3**
lit: à un lit with one bed **6.FP1**
faire le lit to make the bed **2.FP1**
un **litre** liter **1.LC1**
la **littérature** literature **10.FP1**

le **littoral (pl. littoraux)** coast
livraison: la livraison des bagages baggage claim **5.FP2**
une **livre** pound
se **livrer** to give oneself up
un **livret** booklet
un(e) **locataire** tenant
loger to live, lodge **2.L***
la **loi** law
loin far, far away **8.FP2**
au loin in the distance **6.L***
lointain distant
long (longue) long **1.FP1**
à la longue in the long run
le long de along
lorsque when **3.LC2**
un **lot** plot
louer to rent
une **loupe** magnifying glass **5.L***
lourd heavy
loyer: un loyer modéré low rent
une **lueur** gleam
la **lumière** light
lundi Monday **3.FP2**
la **lune** moon
une **lutte** fight, struggle
en lutte struggling
la lutte pour la vie the struggle for survival

M

mâcher to chew
machinalement unconsciously
un **magazine** magazine **2.FP1**
un **magnan** red ant
maigre skinny **1.FP1**
main: sous la main at hand, available
la **main-d'œuvre** labor, manpower
maintes many, several
le **maire** mayor
la **mairie** city hall **8.FP2**
le **maïs** corn
maison: une Maison des Jeunes youth center **8.FP2**
une maison individuelle single-family house **8.FP2**
mal bad **1.FP4,** harm
mal au foie abdominal pain
mal aux dents toothache **7.FP4**
malade sick **1.FP4**
une **maladie** sickness, disease **7.FP1**
une maladie d'enfance childhood illness **7.FP1**

maladroit clumsy
une **malédiction** curse
maléfique detrimental
un **malfaiteur (une malfaitrice)** criminal
malgré in spite of
malheureux (malheureuse) unhappy **1.FP4**
malicieux (malicieuse) inclined to tease, malicious
une **mallette** briefcase **5.L***
malpoli impolite
une **manche** sleeve
une **manifestation** demonstration
manifester to show, manifest
manquer to lack
les **maquis** guerilla troops
le **maquillage** makeup
se **maquiller** to put on makeup
se maquiller les yeux to apply eye makeup **1.FP2**
un **marchand (une marchande)** merchant **2.L***
le/la marchand(e) d'antiquités antique dealer **9.L***
marchander to bargain over the price
marche: la marche à pied walking
un **marché** deal
marcher to work, function **4.FP2**
faire marcher to operate (equipment) **4.LC3**
marcher bien to go well
marcher sur to step on **1.LC3**
les **marches** *f.* steps, stairs
marécageux (marécageuse) swampy
se **marier** to get married **9.FP2**
marin marine
un **marin** sailor
le **marketing** marketing **10.FP1**
une **marque** designer, brand name
de marque important
marrant funny
marron brown **1.FP1**
le **mascara** mascara **1.FP2**
massif (massive) massive **2.FP3**
un **massif de fleurs** flower bed
mater to put down
le **matériel (pl. matériaux)** material, equipment
les **maths** *f.* mathematics **1.LC1**
la **matière** material **2.FP3**
la matière synthétique synthetic material **2.FP3**

Français-Anglais R49

maudit darned
mauvais bad
le **matin** morning **7.FP1**
la **matinée** morning
la **méchanceté** malice
méchant mean, nasty **2.L***
une **mèche** streak, highlight (hair)
méconnu unrecognized
la **Mecque** Mecca
un **médecin** doctor **7.FP1**
la **médecine** medicine (the practice of) **10.FP1**
le **médicament** medicine, drugs
médiocre average, mediocre
se **méfier** to be distrustful
mégarde: par mégarde by accident
un mélange mix **5.IM**
mélanger to mix
mélanger les colorants to mix dyes
mêlé mixed together
même even
Mémé grandma
mener to take, lead
la **menthe** mint
***mentir: sans mentir** to tell the truth, honestly
mention: avec mention with honors
le **menton** chin **1.FP1**
menu small
merci thank you **2.FP2**
merci beaucoup thank you very much **2.FP2**
merci mille fois thanks a million **2.FP2**
la **messe** (Catholic) Mass
Messire My Lord
mesurer to measure **1.FP1**
le **métal (pl. métaux)** metal **2.FP3**
la **météo** weather forecast **3.FP3**
un **métier** trade
mètre: à 100 mètres 100 meters away **8.FP2**
metteur: le metteur en scène director
***mettre** to put, place, turn on **6.FP2**
mettre des sutures to put stitches (in a wound) **7.FP2**
mettre la table to set the table **2.FP1**
mettre le couvert to set the table (silverware) **2.FP1**
mettre le feu to set a fire **3.FP1**
mettre en garde to warn
mettre en question to question

meuble: des meubles *m.* **rustiques** rustic furniture **6.L***
le **Mexique** Mexico **5.FP1**
le **micro** microphone **4.FP3**
le **miel** honey
millénaire 1000 years old
un **milliard** one billion
millier: des milliers thousands
mince thin **1.FP1**
miné weakened
minuscule minuscule **2.FP3**
un **miroir** mirror **1.FP2**
mise: une mise en plis a set (hair) **4.FP2**
le **Mississippi** Mississippi **1.LC1**
une **mode** way
modeste modest
modique low, modest
la **moindre** the least, the smallest
un **moine** monk
moins less **6.FP1**
à moins que unless **10.LC2**
un **mois** month **3.FP2**
la **moitié** half **2.L***
moment: au moment où just as **3.LC2**
mondain social, of fashionable society
la **monnaie** change
les **monnaies** *f.* coins
la **mononucléose** mononucleosis **7.FP1**
monter to get on (train) **5.FP2;** to bring up, carry up **6.FP2**
monter une garde vigilante to keep watchful guard
monter: avoir + monté to have taken or carried something up **3.LC1**
monter: être + monté(e) to have gone up **3.LC1**
montrer: montrer du doigt to point at **8.L***
un **montreur (une montreuse)** exhibitor
se **moquer de** to make fun of
un **morceau (pl. morceaux)** piece
morfondu upset
la **mort** death
un **mot** word **6.L***
mou (molle) soft **2.FP3**
un **moucheron** gnat
un **mouchoir** handkerchief **1.L***
un mouchoir en papier paper tissue **4.FP1**
mouillé wet **2.FP3**

un **moulin** coffee grinder
***mourir** to die **9.FP2**
mourir de faim to die of hunger
la **moustache** moustache **1.FP1**
le **moyen** means
moyen (moyenne) average; average size **10.FP2**
en moyenne on the average
le **Moyen Âge** Middle Ages
au Moyen Âge in the Middle Ages
muet (muette) silent **7.L***
***mugir** to roar
multinational multinational **10.FP2**
un **mur** wall
murmurer to murmur, say in a low voice
un **musée** museum **8.FP2**
la **musique** music **10.FP1**
musulman Moslem

N

nager to swim **3.FP1**
naguère in the past
***naître** to be born **9.FP2**
la **nature** nature **3.FP1**
naturel: il est naturel que it is natural that **2.LC2**
la **nausée** nausea **7.FP1**
une **navette** shuttle train
un **navire** boat, ship
ne . . . aucun no, not any **5.LC1**
ne . . . jamais never **3.LC1**
ne . . . ni . . . ni neither . . . nor **5.LC1**
ne . . . nulle part nowhere **5.LC1**
ne . . . pas encore not yet **3.LC1**
ne . . . personne no one, nobody **RC**
ne. . . plus no longer, not anymore **1.L***
ne. . . point not (at all)
ne . . . que only
ne . . . rien nothing **RC**
la **neige** snow **3.FP3**
nerveux (nerveuse) nervous **7.FP1**
le **nettoyage** cleaning **2.FP1**
nettoyer to clean **2.FP1**
neuf (neuve) brand new **2.FP3**
un **neveu (pl. neveux)** nephew **R.L***
le **nez** nose **1.FP1**
ni . . . ni neither . . . nor

un **nid** nest
niveau: de niveau at the same level
le niveau de vie standard of living
la **noblesse** nobility
les **noces** *f.* marriage
nocif (nocive) harmful
noir black **1.FP1**
il fait noir it's dark **3.FP3**
il fait nuit noire it's pitch black
nombreux (nombreuses) numerous
se **nommer** to be called, named
normal: il est normal que it is normal that **2.LC2**
la **Norvège** Norway
notable important, notable
la **note** bill **6.FP2**
***nourrir** to feed
nouveau: de nouveau again **1.L***
les **nouvelles** news
la **Nouvelle Écosse** Nova Scotia
se **noyer** to drown **3.FP1**
nu naked, nude
un **nuage** cloud **3.FP3**
***nuire à** to ruin, damage
nul (nulle) zero. nothing

O

l' **objectif** *m.* lens (focus) **4.FP3**
obligatoire compulsory
obliger to oblige, do a favor
l' **obscurité** *f.* darkness **4.L***
obsédé obsessed
observer to observe **3.FP1**
***obtenir** to get, obtain
occasion: d'occasion second-hand, used **2.FP3**
l' **occident** *m.* Western world
occidental (occidentaux) western
occupé busy **2.FP2**
s' **occuper de** to be busy, take care of **1.LC4**
un **oculiste** ophthalmologist **7.FP1**
un **œil (pl. yeux)** eye **1.FP1**
l' **œuvre** *f.* work (of art)
***offrir** to offer, give
un **oiseau (pl. oiseaux)** bird **2.FP1**
l' **ombre** *f.* shadow
faire de l'ombre to cast a shadow
ondulé wavy **2.FP3**
un **ongle** nail **1.FP2**
opérer to work, operate
opprimé oppressed
l' **or** *m.* gold **R.L***
un **orage** storm **3.FP3**
un **orchestre** band
un **ordinateur** computer **10.FP3**
une **ordonnance** prescription **7.FP1**
les **ordures** *f.* garbage **2.FP1**
une **oreille** ear **1.FP1**
un **oreiller** pillow **6.FP2**
les **oreillons** *m.* mumps **7.FP1**
l' **orgueil** *m.* pride **7.LC1**
l' **origine** *f.* background
orner to decorate, embellish
un **orphelin (une orpheline)** orphan
oser to dare
ou or **5.LC1**
l' **ouate** *f.* cotton **4.FP1**
les **oubliés** *m.* forgotten people
un **ouragan** hurricane **3.FP3**
un **ours** bear
un **outil** tool
outre: en outre in addition
outre-mer overseas
un **ouvrier (une ouvrière)** worker **R.L***
les ouvriers working class
***ouvrir** to open
ovale oval **1.FP1**

P

un **paillasson** doormat **1.L***
la **paille** straw
une **paillote** straw hut
le **pain** bread **2.FP1**
paisible peaceful, quiet
la **paix** peace
un **palais** palace
un **pansement adhésif** bandage **4.FP1**
faire un pansement to dress a wound **7.FP2**
une **pantoufle** slipper
la **papeterie** stationery store **4.FP1**
le **papier** paper **2.FP3**
le papier à lettres stationery paper **4.FP1**
le papier hygiénique toilet paper **4.FP1**
un **paquet** package **4.FP1**
un **parachute** parachute **2.FP3**
paraître** to appear **7.L
il paraît que it seems that
le **parapente** parasailing
par contre on the other hand **R**
un **parc** park **8.FP2**
***parcourir** to travel through
parfait perfect **3.L***
le **parfum** perfume **1.FP2**
parier to bet **7.L***
parler: parler anglais to speak English **10.FP3**
parmi among
part: à part entière one hundred percent
le **partage** division
partager to share
parterre: les parterres de fleurs *m.* flower beds
un **parti** political party
***partir** to leave **5.LC2**
à partir de from
partir à (en, pour) to leave for (destination) **5.LC2**
partir de to leave from (place) **5.LC2**
partout everywhere **3.L***
un **pas** step
pas mal a lot; not bad
pas possible! impossible! **3.FP2**
un **passant (une passante)** passerby
un **passeport** passport **5.FP1**
passer to pass
passer (un vêtement) to put on
passer l'aspirateur to vacuum **2.FP1**
passer la nuit to spend the night **6.FP1**
passer par to go through **5.FP2**
passer: avoir + passé to have spent (time) **3.LC1**
passer: être + passé to have passed by **3.LC1**
se **passer** to happen **3.FP2**
un **passionné (une passionnée)** real devotee
une **pastille** tablet (medicine)
pâté: le pâté de cochon type of meatloaf
la **patrie** native land
un **patron (une patronne)** boss **10.FP1**
la **paume** palm
pauvre: Mon (Ma) pauvre! . . . My poor . . . ! **10.FP1**
un **pays** country **5.FP1**
un **paysage** landscape
un **paysan (une paysanne)** peasant, farmer
un **péage** toll (highway)
la **peau (pl. peaux)** skin
dans sa peau in one's skin

Français-Anglais R51

une **pêche** peach **8.L***
pêcher to fish **3.L***
un **pêcher** peach tree **8.L***
un **pêcheur (une pêcheuse)** fisherman
le **peigne** comb **1.FP2**
se **peigner** to comb one's hair **1.FP2**
***peindre** to paint
peiné hurt
la **peine** effort, trouble; sorrow
  à peine hardly **2.IC**
  faire de la peine to make sad, upset
la **peinture** painting
un **pèlerinage** pilgrimage
une **pèlerine** cape
une **pellicule** film **4.FP1**
  une pellicule en noir et blanc black and white film **4.FP1**
  une pellicule-couleurs color film **4.FP1**
une **pelote** ball (of string) **4.FP1**
la **pelouse** lawn **2.FP1**
pendant during **3.LC2**
  pendant que while **3.LC2**
pendre** to hang (up) **10.L
pénible painful
pension: la pension complète full room and board **6.FP1**
  la demi-pension room with breakfast and dinner **6.FP1**
un(e) **pensionnaire** boarding student
une **pépite** nugget
***perdre: perdre l'équilibre** to lose one's balance **3.FP1**
*se **perdre** to get lost **3.FP1**
perfectionner to improve
périr perish, die
une **permanente** hair perm **4.FP2**
***permettre** to allow
permis: un permis de conduire driver's license **5.FP1**
perplexe perplexed **1.FP4**
la **perruche** parakeet **2.FP1**
peser to weigh **1.FP1**
petit small, short **1.FP1**
peuplé populated
la **peur** fright
  faire peur à to scare **3.FP1**
un **phare** lighthouse
la **pharmacie** pharmacy **4.FP1;** pharmaceutics (practice of) **10.FP1**
un **pharmacien (une pharmacienne)** pharmacist **10.FP1**
le **phénix** phoenix

la **philosophie** philosophy **10.FP1**
une **photocopie** photocopy **4.FP1**
le/la **photographe** photographer **4.FP1**
la **physique** physics **10.FP1**
pièce: une pièce d'argent coin
  une pièce d'eau pool
  une pièce d'identité identity card **5.FP1**
  une pièce d'or gold coin **7.L***
pied: à pied on foot **8.FP2**
  pieds nus bare feet
une **pierre** stone **2.FP3**
pieux (pieuse) pious
une **pile** battery **4.FP1**
un **pillard** looter
un **pilote** pilot **5.FP2**
une **pilule** pill
pimenté hot, spicy
le **pinceau (pl. pinceaux)** brush
pincé pinched
piquer to sting **3.FP1**
  être piqué par les moustiques to be bitten by mosquitos **3.FP1**
piqûre: une piqûre de novocaïne shot of novocaine **7.FP2**
  faire une piqûre to give a shot, injection **7.FP1**
pire worse **7.L***
une **piscine** swimming pool **6.FP1**
pitoyable pitiful **4.L***
une **place** seat **5.FP2**
  de la place room **5.FP2**
  la place d'Armes parade ground
***plaindre** to feel sorry for **7.LC1**
*se **plaindre de** to complain about **7.LC1**
***plaire** to please
plan: un plan d'eau artificial lake
plaisanter: tu plaisantes! you're kidding! **3.FP2**
plaisir: avec plaisir! with pleasure! **2.FP2**
  faire plaisir à to please **8.L***
planifier to plan
une **plante** plant **2.FP1**
plaque: une plaque d'immatriculation license plate **5.L***
le **plastique** plastic **2.FP3**
  en plastique plastic **2.FP3**
plat flat **2.FP3**
plein full

  en plein air outdoors
  plein de a lot of
pleurer to cry **1.L***
plier to fold (up) **3.L***
le **plomb** lead **2.FP3**
un **plombage** tooth filling **7.FP2**
la plongée sous-marine deep-sea diving **R**
plonger to plunge
la **pluie** rain **3.FP3**
une **plume** (quill) pen
la **plupart** most of them, the majority **4.LC1**
  la plupart de most of **4.LC1**
plus more **6.FP1**
  en plus in addition
  de plus en plus more and more
  plus d'allure
plusieurs several **4.LC1**
un **pneu (pl. pneus)** tire
une **pneumonie** pneumonia **7.FP1**
une **poche** pocket **1.L***
le **poids** weight **1.FP1**
un **poignet** wrist **7.L***
un **poing** fist
point: sur le point de on the verge
pointu pointed **2.FP3**
poissonneux (poissonneuse) full of fish
la **poitrine** chest **8.L***
poli polished **2.FP3**
la **police** law enforcement **8.FP2**
la **Pologne** Poland
polluer to pollute **3.FP1**
la **pollution** pollution **8.FP3**
polonais Polish
une **pommade** ointment
un **pompier** firefighter
un **pont** bridge
la **porte** door; boarding gate **5.FP2**
un **portemanteau (pl. portemanteaux)** hanger **6.FP2**
un **porte-parole** spokesperson
porter: porter des lunettes to wear eyeglasses **1.FP1**
  se porter bien to be in good health **7.FP1**
un **portier (une portière)** doorman
une **portière** train door **7.L***
le **Portugal** Portugal **5.FP1**
poser to put, to place
posséder to own, possess **9.L***
possibilité: la possibilité de promotion opportunity for promotion **10.FP2**

la poste post office **4.FP1**
la poste restante general delivery **4.FP1**
un poste position (employment) **2.IM**
poste: le poste de police police station **8.FP2**
un pot jar
un pote buddy
une poubelle garbage can **1.L***
un pouce inch
la poudre powder
la poudrerie powdery snow
les poumons *m.* lungs
pour in order to **10.LC1**
pour que so that **10.LC2**
un pourboire restaurant tip
pourtant however
pousser to grow
pousser des cris to scream **3.L***
pousser un gros soupir to let out a large sigh
la poussière dust
***pouvoir** to be able to
le pouvoir power
un pratiquant (une pratiquante) practitioner (religion)
se précipiter to dash
préconiser to advocate
***prédire** to predict **3.FP3**
préférer to prefer **2.LC2**
les premiers soins *m.* first aid **2.IM**
***prendre** to take
on ne l'y prendrait plus he wouldn't be taken in again
prendre connaissance to become aware
prendre la température to take one's temperature **7.FP1**
prendre la tension to take one's blood pressure **7.FP1**
prendre le deuil to be in mourning
prendre rendez-vous to make an appointment, date **7.FP1**
prendre sa retraite to retire **9.FP2**
prendre un bain de soleil to sunbathe **3.FP1**
prendre un pot to go for a drink **8.FP1**
pris seized
préoccupé worried **1.FP4**
se préparer to get ready **1.FP3**
préposé assigned
près: de près closely, from close up **4.L***
présenter to present, show **5.FP2**
se présenter to show up
presque almost
pressé in a hurry
se presser to hurry
prêter: prêter serment to pledge allegiance
prétexte: un prétexte quelconque some pretext or other
prêt à ready to **2.IM**
un prêtre priest
la preuve proof
prévenir** to warn **3.L
***prévoir** to plan ahead for
prier to pray
je t'en prie you're welcome **2.FP2**
une prière prayer
une princesse princess **1.LC1**
la prise taking; electrical plug **4.FP3**
le prix prize
prochain next **5.FP2**
proche close
***produire** to produce
***se produire** to happen
profiter de to take advantage of **1.L***
la proie prey
le prolongement extension
promener to walk **2.FP1**
***se promener** to take a walk **1.FP3**
***promettre** to promise
promouvoir to promote **7.IC**
propre own; clean
la propreté cleanliness, hygiene
un(e) propriétaire owner **R.L***
prosterné prostrate, face to the ground
***protéger** to protect **3.FP1**
provoqué caused, provoked
la psychologie psychology **10.FP1**
la publicité advertising **10.FP1**
une puce microchip
puis then **3.FP2**
puisque since **3.L***
puissant powerful
un pupitre school desk
pur fresh

Q

le quai platform **5.FP2**
quand when **5.LC2**
quand même anyhow **3.L***
la quantité quantity **4.FP1**
qu'est-ce que. . . : qu'est-ce qu'il y a? what's wrong? **1.FP4**
qu'est-ce qu'il y a eu? What happened? **3.FP2**
qu'est-ce que tu as? what's the matter? **1.FP4**
qu'est-ce qui. . . : qu'est-ce qui a eu lieu? what happened? **3.FP2**
qu'est-ce qui est arrivé? what happened? **3.FP2**
qu'est-ce qui ne marche pas? what doesn't work? **4.FP3**
qu'est-ce qui ne va pas? what's wrong? **7.FP1**
qu'est-ce qui s'est passé? what happened? **3.FP2**
quant à as for
le quartier neighborhood, district **8.FP2**
que whom, that, which **9.LC1**
quel (quelle) what, which **4.FP1**
quel dommage! too bad! **9.FP1**
quel est le problème? what is the problem? **4.FP3**
quel genre? what kind, type? **6.FP1**
quelle bonne nouvelle! what good news! **9.FP1**
quelle malchance! what bad luck! **9.FP1**
quel que soit whatever
quelle sorte de what type of **5.FP2**
quelques some, a few **4.LC1**
quelqu'un someone, somebody **RC**
quelque chose something **RC**
quelque chose à déclarer something to declare **5.FP1**
quelque chose d'autre something else **4.FP1**
quelque part somewhere **5.LC1**
quelques-un(e)s some, a few **4.LC1**
se quereller to quarrel, have a fight **9.FP1**
question: question de because of
quête: en quête de in search of
faire la quête to pass the hat
queue: une queue de cheval ponytail **1.FP1**
qui who, that, which **9.LC1**

Français-Anglais R53

un **quiproquo** misunderstanding
quitter to leave (place/person) **5.LC2**
quoi: quoi de neuf? what's new? **3.FP2**
quoi que ce soit whatever it is
quoi qu'il arrive whatever happens
quoi qu'il lui en coûte whatever it may cost her
quoi qu'il y ait although there is (are)
quotidien (quotidienne) daily, common

R

la **racine** root
raconter to tell (what happened) **3.FP3**
une **radio** x-ray
faire une radio to x–ray **7.FP1**
une **rafale** gust of wind
raide straight
raison: la raison de vivre aim in life
ralentir** to slow down **7.L
un **ramage** song
ramasser to pick up **7.L***
une **rame** oar
ramener to bring back **3.L***
une **randonnée** long hike
une randonnée pédestre hiking
un **rang** row
rangé clean, put-away **2.FP1**
ranger to put away **2.FP1**
rappeler to remind
se **rappeler** to remember, to recall **1.LC4**
un **rapport** connection, relation **9.FP1**
bons rapports good relations **9.FP1**
mauvais rapports bad relations **9.FP1**
rapporter to equal, match, relate **3.IM**
se **raser** to shave **1.FP2**
le **rasoir** shaver **1.FP2**
rater to flunk; to miss (bus) **5.FP2**
rattrapé caught
se **rattraper** to catch up with
ravi delighted **7.LC1**
rayé striped
un **rayon** department (in store) **4.FP1**
***réagir** to react

un **réalisateur (une réalisatrice)** movie director
recensé registered
le **récepteur** receiver
la **réception** reception desk **6.FP1;** gala, party
le/la **réceptionniste** receptionist, secretary **6.FP2**
***recevoir** to get, receive
recherche: la recherche scientifique scientific research **10.FP2**
recherché sought after
rechercher to research; to look for, search for **10.FP2**
récif: le récif de corail coral reef
un **récit** story
une **récolte** crop
faire la récolte to harvest
récompenser to reward **4.L***
*se **réconcilier** to make up **9.FP1**
la **reconnaissance** gratitude
reconnu recognized
***reconstruire** to rebuild
recouvert: recouvert de covered with
récréatif (récréative) recreational
rectangulaire rectangular **1.FP1**
recueilli adopted, taken in
reculé remote
récupérer to get back, recuperate **5.L***
***redécouvrir** to rediscover
redonner to give back
redoubler to repeat a grade
une **référence** reference **10.FP3**
réfléchir to think things over; to reflect on **7.L***
un **réfrigérateur** refrigerator **2.FP3**
un **regain** renewal
un **regard** glance, look
réglé: réglé par structured according to
le **règlement** rule
le **regret** regret **7.LC1**
regretter to regret **2.FP2**
la **reine** queen **1.LC1**
les **reins** *m.* kidneys
*se **réjouir** to be happy **9.FP1**
relâché released
les **relations** *f.* relations **9.FP1**
les relations publiques public relations **10.FP2**
relié linked
un relooking makeover **1.IM**
se **remarier** to remarry **9.FP2**
remarquer to notice **2.L***

remercier to thank **2.FP2**
remettre to put back **9.L***
se **remettre** to get back (into shape), restart
une **remise** shed
remonter to put back together; to go back (in time); go up
rempli filled
remplir to fill **2.FP1**
un **renard** fox
rencontrer to meet by chance, run into (person) **8.FP1**
se **rencontrer** to meet each other **8.FP1**
un **rendez-vous** appointment, date **7.FP1**
*se **rendormir** to go back to sleep **10.L***
***rendre grâce** to give thanks
rendre service to do a favor **2.FP2**
*se **rendre** to go, to render oneself
se rendre compte to realize **2.L***
un **renfort** reinforcement
renoncer to give up
un **renseignement** information
renvoyé fired
renvoyer to send away, send back
*se **répandre** to spread
répandu spilled
réparer to fix, repair **4.FP3**
repasser to iron **2.FP1**
***répondre** to respond **10.FP3**
se **reposer** to rest **1.FP3**
repousser to grow back
repousser du pied to kick away
un(e) **représentant(e)** representative **10.FP1**
la **représentation** performance
se **représenter** to retake (the exam)
repris: un repris de justice prison inmate
une **requête** request **8.L***
une **réservation** reservation **5.FP2**
réserver to reserve **6.FP1**
une **résidence** apartment complex
***résoudre** to solve, resolve
le **respect** respect **9.FP1**
respecter to respect **3.FP1**
respirer to breathe
une **responsabilité** responsibility **10.FP2**
***ressentir** to feel (pain or emotion) **1.FP4**
le **ressort** spring (in watch) **4.FP3**

rester: il ne reste que . . . there is/are only . . . left **10.L***
il reste . . . there is/are . . . left **8.L***
il vous reste . . . you have . . . left
rester au lit to stay in bed **7.FP1**
un **resto** restaurant
retard: en retard late **5.FP2**
une heure de retard one hour late **5.FP2**
retentissant big, huge
***retentir** to resound
retirer to withdraw (money)
se **retourner** to turn around **7.L***
se **retrouver** to meet each other **8.FP1**
réuni reunited
*se **réunir** to unite, get together
une **réunion** meeting **5.IM**
un **rêve** dream
un **réveil** alarm clock
réveiller to wake (something, someone) **6.FP2**
se **réveiller** to wake (oneself) up **1.FP3**
revenir** to come back **1.L
rêver to dream
***revoir** to see again
révolu long past
un **rhume** a cold **7.FP1**
un rhume des foins hayfever **7.FP1**
ricaner to laugh
rien: de rien you're welcome **2.FP2**
rien à déclarer nothing to declare **5.FP1**
rien à voir (avec) nothing to do (with)
rien que only
rigolo amusing **3.L***
le **rimmel** mascara **1.FP2**
***rire** to laugh
une **rive** bank, shore
robe: une robe de chambre bathrobe
le **robinet** faucet
rocambolesque incredible, fantastic
le **roi** king
le Roi du Ciel King of Heaven
romantique romantic
rompre** to break **7.L
rompre (avec) to break up (with) **9.FP1**
rond round **1.FP1**
la **roue** wheel **4.FP3**
rouge red **1.LC1**
le rouge à lèvres lipstick **1.FP2**
la **rougeole** measles **7.FP1**
rougir** to blush **4.L
un **rouleau (pl. rouleaux)** roll (of paper towels) **4.FP1**
rouler to roll; to travel, drive
roux (rousse) red-headed **1.FP1**
un **royaume** kingdom
un **ruban** ribbon
la **rubéole** German measles **7.FP1**
une **rubrique** column
rude rough
rugueux (rugueuse) rough, uneven **2.FP3**
rupestre on rock walls
la **Russie** Russia **5.FP1**
rustre boorish, lacking good manners

S

le **sable** sand
un **sac** bag **5.FP1**
un sac à dos backpack
un sac à provisions shopping bag
sacré "cursed"
la **sagesse** wisdom
saigner to bleed **7.FP1**
saigner du nez to get a nosebleed **7.FP1**
sain healthy, sain
saint holy
saisi seized, taken
saisir** to seize, take **9.L
*se **saisir** to seize, take
un **salaire** salary **10.FP2**
sale dirty **2.FP1**
une **saleté** something gross, dirty
une **salle** hall
la salle d'armes fencing hall
la salle d'attente waiting room **5.FP2**
la salle d'exercices exercise gym **6.FP1**
la salle de bains bathroom **6.FP1**
un **salon** show
une **salopette** overalls
saluer to salute, greet, take one's leave of
samedi on Saturday **1.LC1**
le samedi on Saturdays **1.LC1**
le **sang** blood
sanglant blood-stained
un **sanglier** wild boar
sans (que) without **10.LC1**
sans bouger without moving
sans cesse unceasingly
sans trêve unceasingly
les **sans-abri** *m.* homeless people
la **santé** health
en bonne santé in good health **7.FP1**
le **saucisson** sausage
sauf except
sauter to jump **1.L***
sauvage wild
sauver to save **5.L***
se **sauver** to escape
savant trained
un **savant** scientist
la **saveur** taste
le **savon** soap **1.FP2**
un **scénario** script
scène: sur scène on the stage
une **scie** saw **2.FP3**
science: les sciences *f.* **économiques** economics **10.FP1**
les sciences *f.* **politiques** political science **10.FP1**
un(e) **scientifique** scientist **10.FP1**
le **scotch** scotch tape **4.FP1**
un **seau (pl. seaux)** bucket
sec (sèche) dry **2.FP3**
un **sécateur** shrub clippers **2.FP1**
se ***sécher** to dry (oneself) **1.FP2**
se sécher les cheveux to dry one's hair **1.FP2**
une **sécheresse** drought
le **séchoir** (hair) dryer **1.FP2**
secouer to shake **10.L***
***secourir** to help
secours: crier au secours to call for help
un **secrétaire** writing desk
un(e) **secrétaire** secretary **10.FP1**
section: la section fumeur smoking section **5.FP2**
la section non-fumeur non-smoking section **5.FP2**
séduisant attractive **7.L***
séduit attracted, seduced
le **seigneur** lord
un **séjour** stay
faire un séjour to go on holiday, spend some time **5.FP1**
séjourner to stay, lodge **6.FP1**
une **semaine** week **3.FP2**
sembler to seem, to appear **1.FP4**
la **semoule** semolina
le **sens** sense, direction, meaning

Vocabulaire: Français—Anglais

Français-Anglais R55

le sens des contacts humains ability to network 10.FP3
la **sensation** feeling
sensible sensitive **1.IM**
un **sentier** trail
***sentir** to smell **1.FP4**
*se **sentir** to feel
comment te sens-tu? how do you feel? **1.FP4**
se sentir chez soi to feel at home
ne pas se sentir de joie to be beside oneself with joy
se **séparer** to separate (husband & wife) **9.FP2**
un **serpent** serpent **3.FP1**
serré held tightly, close together
serrer to clutch
serrer la main de to shake hands with
service: le service en chambre room service **6.FP1**
la **serviette** towel **1.FP2;** napkin
***servir** to serve **6.FP2**
*se **servir de** to use **10.FP3**
seul alone, lonely
le seul the only
un seul only one
le **shampooing** shampoo **1.FP2**
un shampooing a shampoo (hair salon) **4.FP2**
si if **5.LC2**
un **siècle** century
un **siège** a seat **5.FP2**
siffler to whistle **3.L***
sifflet: un sifflet à roulette whistle **3.L***
un **signe** sign
la **signification** meaning
signifier to represent, signify
sillonner to travel across
un **singe** monkey
singulier (singulière) strange
situé: bien situé well located **6.FP1**
mieux situé better located **6.FP1**
une **société** society, company **10.FP2**
soigner to treat (medical) **7.FP1**
soignez-le (la)! pay careful attention to it!
se **soigner** to take care of one's health
le **soir** evening **7.FP1**
soit all right, so be it
le **sol** floor **2.FP1**
des **soldes** sale
le **soleil** sun
le soleil levant rising sun
solliciter to solicit, ask for **10.FP3**
solide solid **2.FP3**
sombre black, somber
le **sommeil** sleep
un **son** beat
sonner to ring; to blow
sonnerie: la sonnerie de clairon bugle call
le **Sopalin** paper towels (brand name) **4.FP1**
la **sorcellerie** witchcraft
un **sorcier (une sorcière)** witch doctor
le **sort** fate
la **sortie** exit **5.FP2**
***sortir** to take (something) out; to go out **2.FP1**
sortir la poubelle to take out the trash **2.FP1**
sortir: avoir + sorti to have taken something out **3.LC1**
sortir: être + sorti to have gone out **3.LC1**
un **sot (une sotte)** stupid person
souche: de souche native born
un **souci** concern, worry
souffler to blow out **10.L*;** to blow **3.FP3;** to prompt
***souffrir** to suffer
souhaiter to wish **2.LC2**
soupir: un soupir de soulagement sigh of relief
la **source** spring
sourd deaf
souriant smiling
***sourire** to smile
un **sourire** smile
une **souris** mouse
***soustraire à** to protect from
***soutenir** to support
un **souvenir** memory
en souvenir de in memory of **8.L***
souvent often **3.LC1**
*se **souvenir (de)** to remember
spacieux (spacieuse) roomy **6.FP1**
se **spécialiser en** to specialize, major in **10.FP1**
un(e) **spécialiste** specialist **7.FP1**
un(e) spécialiste de données data processor **10.FP1**
un(e) spécialiste de logiciel software specialist **10.FP1**
un(e) spécialiste de marketing marketing specialist **10.FP1**
un spectacle son et lumière sound and light show **2.IM**
spirituel (spirituelle) witty
un **square** public garden
un **stage** training session, internship
faire un stage to do an internship
un **standard** operator **6.FP2**
station: une station thermale hot springs resort
une **station-service** gas station **8.FP2**
statue: la statue de la Liberté Statue of Liberty **2.FP3**
une **stèle** stele (stone marker with an inscription) **6.L***
le **steward** steward **5.FP2**
une **strophe** verse
stylo: un stylo à bille ball point pen **4.FP1**
subit sudden
***subvenir** to meet
subvenir aux besoins to meet the needs
une **subvention** subsidiary
se **succéder** to follow one another
succomber to die, succumb
la **sueur** sweat
***suffire** to be sufficient
il suffit . . . it is sufficient . . .
il suffit d'y penser you just have to think about it
la **suite** series, sequence
à la suite de right behind; as a result of
suivant according to; next **5.FP2**
***suivre** to take (a class); to follow
une **supérette** convenience store **4.FP1**
supporter to bear, stand **2.L***
supprimé abolished
sûr safe, sure
bien sûr of course **2.FP2**
surprenant surprising
surprendre** to surprise **9.L
surpris surprised **7.LC1**
sursaut: en sursaut with a start
la **survie** survival
susceptible touchy
sympa nice, kind **2.FP2**
la **sympathie** instinctive liking **9.FP1**

syndicat: le Syndicat d'Initiative Chamber of Commerce **6.LC1**

T

la **table** table **2.FP1**
un **tableau (pl. tableaux)** painting
le tableau d'affichage billboard **5.FP2**
une **tablette** bar
un **tabouret** stool **4.L***
une **tache** spot, stain
les taches *f.* **de rousseur** freckles **1.FP1**
la **taille** height, size (person) **1.FP1**
de taille moyenne average size **1.FP1**
tailler to prune, trim **2.FP1**
un tailleur woman's suit **1.IM**
***se taire** to be quiet, shut up **1.LC4**
un **talon** heel (of shoe) **4.FP3**
talonné followed close on one's heels
le **tambour** drum
la **Tamise** Thames (River)
une **tanière** lair
tant: tant de so many; so much
tant que as long as
tant pis! too bad! **2.LC2**
un **tapis** rug **1.L***
la **tapisserie** tapestry
tard late **3.LC1**
tas: des tas tons, a lot
un **technicien (une technicienne)** technician **10.FP1**
le **teint** complexion
la **teinte** color
le **teinturerie** the cleaners **4.FP3**
le **téléobjectif** telephoto lens **4.FP3**
le **téléphone** telephone **6.FP1**
téléphoner to telephone, call **10.FP3**
la **télévision** television **6.FP1**
tel (telle) such
tel qu'on le connaît as we know him
tellement so much **4.L***
pas tellement not that much
téméraire bold
un **témoin** witness
la **température** temperature **2.FP3**
la **tempête** storm **3.FP3**
une tempête de neige snowstorm **3.FP3**
le **temps** time **2.FP2**
le beau temps nice weather **3.FP3**
le mauvais temps bad weather **3.FP3**
de temps en temps from time to time **4.L***
tendre** to hand, give **7.L
tendu tense, uptight **1.FP4;** stretched out
***tenir** to hold **3.L*,** to have; present
tenir à to hold dear, cherish **9.L***
tenir compagnie to keep company **9.L***
tenir un langage parler
qu'à cela ne tienne that won't matter
tentative: une tentative d'évasion escape attempt
tenter to tempt **9.L***
terne dull **2.FP3**
la **terre** land, earth, soil
la terre d'asile land of asylum
la terre ferme solid ground
par terre on the ground
sous terre underground
la Terre Sainte Holy Land
Terre-Neuve Newfoundland
un **testament** will
un **têtard** tadpole **3.L***
tête: tête à tête face to face
en tête leading
une **thèse** thesis, essay
tiède warm **2.FP3**
un **tiers** one-third
le **tiers-monde** third world
une **tignasse** unruly mop (of hair) **4.L***
un **timbre** stamp
tiré fired
tirer to take out; to derive
tirer au sort to choose at random
tiré de based on
le **tissu** fabric
la **toile** canvas
le **toit** roof
une **tombe** tombstone
tomber to fall **3.FP1**
tomber amoureux (amoureuse) de to fall in love with
tomber dans l'eau to fall in the water **3.FP1**
tomber malade to get sick **9.FP2**
une **tondeuse** lawn-mower **2.FP1;** clippers **4.L***
tondre** to mow, cut very short **2.FP1;** to clip very short **4.L
une tonne ton **5.IM**
le **tonnerre** thunder **3.FP3**
tonte: la tonte des moutons sheep-shearing
tort: à tort wrongly
une **tortue** turtle
tôt early **3.LC1**
toujours still
un **tour** turn; trick
faire des tours to do tricks **3.L***
faire le tour to go around
faire un tour to walk **3.FP1**
une **tour** tower, high-rise **8.FP2**
la tour Eiffel Eiffel Tower **2.FP3**
le **tournage** making (of a film)
une **tournée** tour
tourner to film
se **tourner** to turn around
tousser to cough **7.FP1**
tout any
tout à fait completely
tout à l'heure in a little while **4.FP3**
tout court directly
tout d'un coup all of a sudden
tout de même nevertheless
tout de suite immediately
tout le temps all the time, always
tous les . . . every
toutes les 4 heures every four hours **7.FP1**
tout petit very young
tout près nearby **8.FP2**
une **toux** cough
***trahir** to betray
une **trahison** betrayal
un **train** train **5.FP2**
un **trait** feature
un **traité** treaty
la **traîtrise** treachery
une **trame** plot
tranquillement safely
traqué tracked, hunted down
le **travail (pl. travaux)** work **2.FP1**
les travaux domestiques housework **2.FP1**
les travaux des champs farm work
travailler to work **9.FP2**
travers: à travers across, through **1.L***
de travers in a strange way
traverser to cross

Vocabulaire: Français—Anglais

tremblement: un tremblement de terre earthquake
trempé soaking wet
triangulaire triangular 2.FP3
tricher to cheat
tricolore blue, white, red
le tricot knitting 9.L*
triste sad 1.FP4
la tristesse sadness 7.LC1
un trombone paper clip 4.FP1
se tromper to make a mistake 1.LC4
trôner to occupy a place of honor
trop too 3.LC1
un trottoir sidewalk 9.L*
un trou hole
trousse: la trousse de toilette toiletry kit 1.FP2
trouver to find 9.FP2
se trouver to be (located); to find oneself
un tube tube 4.FP1
tuer to kill
tuméfié swollen
tuyau: le tuyau d'arrosage garden hose 2.FP1
un tuyau d'incendie fire hose 2.IM
un type guy, person

U

usagé worn 2.FP3
usé worn out, old 4.FP3
une usine factory 10.FP2
utile: il est utile que it is useful that 2.LC2
utiliser to use 10.FP3

V

la vaisselle dishes 2.FP1
la valeur value
une valise suitcase 5.FP1
*valoir to be worth 3.IC
il vaut mieux que it is better that 2.LC2
valoriser to emphasize the value of
valser to waltz
vaniteux (vaniteuse) boastful
se vanter to boast
la varicelle chicken pox 7.FP1
vase: un vase de Venise Venetian glass vase
un vassal (pl. vassaux) subject
une vedette star
la végétation vegetation 3.FP1
la veille previous day
la veilleuse low (light)
un vélodrome bicycle racetrack
velours: le velours côtelé corduroy
un vendeur (une vendeuse) salesperson 10.FP1
venger to avenge
*venir to come
faire venir to bring
un verger orchard 8.L*
le verglas sheet ice 3.FP3
véritable true
vernis: le vernis à ongles nail polish 1.FP2
un verre glass 2.FP1
les verres de Bohême Bohemian glasses
les verres de contact contact lenses 1.FP1
vers towards; at, about 1.FP3,
verser to pour 3.L*
vert green 1.FP1
le vertige dizzy spell, vertigo 7.FP1
les vêtements *m.* clothes 2.FP1
un(e) vétérinaire veterinary doctor 10.FP1
vêtu dressed
une victime victim, casualty
vide empty 2.FP3
vider to empty 2.FP1
la vie life R.V
la vie courante daily life
un vieillard elderly man
*vieillir to grow old 9.FP2
le vieillissement aging
vieux (vieille) old 2.FP3
vif (vive) bright
vif d'esprit alert
la ville the city
une ville fantôme ghost town 5.IM
vingt: vingt et un coups de canon 21-gun salute
la Virginie Virginia 1.LC1
le visage face 1.FP1
une vitamine vitamin 4.FP1
la vitesse speed
en vitesse quickly
une vitre window pane 2.FP1
la vitrine store window 9.L*
vivant living
*vivre to live
une voie way
voilà there you go 4.FP1
voile: un voile de dentelle lace veil
une voile sail
*voir to see
faire voir to show 4.LC3
la voiture car 2.FP1
voix: à mi-voix in a low voice
un vol flight 5.FP2; theft
volé stolen
voler to steal 5.L* to fly 9.C
les volets shutters 8.IC
un voleur (une voleuse) thief 5.L
la volonté will 7.LC2
volontiers! sure! with pleasure! I'd love to! 2.FP2
volumineux (volumineuse) voluminous, large in volume 2.FP3
vomir to throw up 7. FP1
*vouloir to want, to wish 2.LC2
vouloir bien to want (used to accept an offer), to accept, agree 4.FP1
vouloir dire to mean 10.L*
*voyager to travel 5.FP1
un voyage voyage, trip
vrai true
à vrai dire to tell the truth 8.L*
Vraiment? Really? Truly? 3.FP3
une vue: une belle vue a nice view 6.FP2

W

un wagon car (train) 5.FP2
un wagon-lit sleeping car (train) 5.IM
un wagon-restaurant dining car (train) 5.IM

Y

y: j'y vais there: I'm going (there) 4.LC1
les yeux *m.* (un œil) eyes 1.FP1

Z

les zébrures *f.* stripes, welts 9.IC

VOCABULAIRE: Anglais—Français

The English—French vocabulary contains active and passive words from the text, as well as words introduced in the *Mots utiles* sections of the Lectures.

The numbers and letters following an entry indicate the first unit section in which the word or phrase is activated. The following abbreviations have been used:

R Reprise
L Lecture
IM Info magazine
IC Interlude Culturel
FP Français pratique
TA Teacher's Annotation
LC Langue et communication
A Appendix

The number after the section abbreviation indicates the unit *Partie* in which the vocabulary word is introduced.

An asterisk (*) after the unit reference indicates that the word or phrase is presented in the *Mots Utiles* section of the reading.

Nouns: If the article of a noun does not indicate gender, the noun is followed by *m. (masculine)* or *f. (feminine)*. If the plural is irregular, it is given in parentheses.

Verbs: Verbs are listed in the infinitive form. An asterisk (*) in front of an active verb means that it is irregular. (For forms, see the verb charts in the Appendix.)

Words beginning with an **h** are preceded by a bullet (•) if the **h** is aspirate; that is, if the word is treated as if it begins with a consonant sound.

A

ability: ability to network le sens des contacts humains **10.FP3**
abroad à l'étranger **5.FP1**
accident un accident **3.FP2**
accomplice un(e) complice **5.L***
accountant un(e) comptable **10.FP1**
accounting la comptabilité **10.FP1**
acquaintance une connaissance, un(e) camarade **9.FP1**
across à travers **1.L***
across from en face de **8.FP1**
adhesive: adhesive bandage un pansement **4.FP1**
admiration l'admiration *f.* **9.FP1**
to **admit** avouer **2.L***
advertising la publicité **10.FP1**
affection l'affection *f.* **9.FP1**
after au bout de **8.L*;** après **3.FP2**
afterwards après **3.FP2**
aftershave l'après-rasage *m.* **1.FP2**
again de nouveau **1.L***
ago il y a **3.FP2**
to **agree** *être d'accord **9.FP2**
to agree to meet se donner rendez-vous **8.FP1**
agreed entendu **8.FP1**
air conditioning l'air *m.* conditionné **6.FP1,** la climatisation **6.FP1**
airport l'aéroport *m.* **5.FP2**
aisle un couloir **5.FP2**
all: all the more that d'autant plus que **9.L***
allergy une allergie **7.FP1**
Alps les Alpes *f.* **1.LC1**
already déjà **3.LC1**
aluminum l'aluminium *m.* **2.FP3**
alumnus un ancien élève **8.L***
amazement l'étonnement *m.* **7.LC1**
amazing étonnant **6.LC1**
ambition l'ambition *f.* **10.FP3**
amplifier un ampli **4.FP3**
amusing rigolo **3.L***
and et **5.LC1**
anger la colère **7.LC1**
angry en colère **1.FP4**
animal une bête **3.L*,** un animal (pl. animaux) **2.FP1**
animosity l'animosité *f.* **9.FP1**
ankle la cheville **7.FP2**
another, another one un autre **4.LC1**
antenna une antenne **4.FP3**
antibiotic un antibiotique **7.FP1**
antipathy l'antipathie *f.* **9.FP1**
antique: antique dealer le/la marchand(e) d'antiquités **9.L***
anyhow quand même **3.L***
anything n'importe quoi **7.L***
apartment un appartement **8.FP2**
to **appear** *paraître **7.L***
appearance l'apparence *f.* **2.FP3**
to **apply: to apply eye make up** se maquiller les yeux **1.FP2**
appointment un rendez-vous **7.FP1**
to **approach** s'approcher (de) **1.LC4**
aquarium l'aquarium *m.* **2.FP1**
arch: Arch of St. Louis l'Arche *f.* de Saint Louis **2.FP3**
argument une dispute **9.FP1**
arm le bras **7.FP2**
around autour de **9.L***
to **arrest** arrêter **5.L***
as: as if comme si **8.L***

as soon as aussitôt que, dès que **5.LC2**
aspirin l'aspirine *f.* **4.FP1**
asthma l'asthme *m.* **7.FP1**
astonished étonné **7.LC1**
at: at about vers **1.FP3**
at last enfin **3.FP2**
at the end of au bout de **8.L***
athletic athlétique **1.FP1**
atmosphere une ambiance **10.FP2**
to **attach** attacher **5.FP2**
attractive séduisant **7.L***
average: average size de taille moyenne **1.FP1,** moyen (moyenne) **10.FP2**
aversion l'aversion *f.* **9.FP1**
to **avoid** éviter **3.FP1**
to **avow** avouer **2.L***

B

B.A. degree la licence **2.IM**
bad mal **1.FP4**
bag un sac **5.FP1**
baggage les bagages *m.* **5.FP1**
baggage claim la livraison des bagages **5.FP2**
baggage-check la consigne **5.FP2**
balcony un balcon **6.FP1**
bald chauve **1.FP1**
bald head la boule à zéro **4.L***
ball (of string) une pelote (de ficelle) **4.FP1**
ball point pen un stylo à bille **4.FP1**
balloon un ballon **2.FP3**
bank la banque **10.FP2**
banker un banquier (une banquière) **10.FP1**
bath un bain **1.FP3**
bathroom la salle de bains **6.FP1**
bathroom sink le lavabo **2.FP1**
battery une pile 4.FP1
battery charger un chargeur de piles
to **be alone, undisturbed** *être tranquille **1.L***
to be bitten by mosquitos *être piqué par des moustiques **3.FP1**
to be born *naître **9.FP2**
to be busy with s'occuper de **1.LC4**
to be called, named s'appeler **1.LC4**
to be happy *se réjouir **9.FP1**
to be in good health se porter bien **7.FP1**
to be present at assister à **3.FP2**
to **be qualified** *faire l'affaire **10.FP3**
to be quiet *se taire **1.LC4**
to be sad, in pain *avoir de la peine **3.L***
to be scared *avoir peur **7.LC1**
to be seasick *avoir le mal de mer **3.FP1**
to be upset se fâcher **9.FP1**
to **bear** supporter **2.L***
beard une barbe **1.FP1**
bearded barbu **1.FP1**
to **beat** *battre **7.L***
beauty: beauty mark un grain de beauté **1.FP1**
because of à cause de **7.L***
before avant de **10.LC1**
to **begin to** *se mettre à **3.L***
to **believe** *croire **7.LC1**
bellboy le groom **6.FP2**
to **belong to** *appartenir à **2.L***
besides d'ailleurs **8.L***
to **bet** parier **7.L***
big grand **1.FP1**
bill la note **6.FP2**
billboard le tableau d'affichage **5.FP2**
biology la biologie **10.FP1**
bird un oiseau (pl. oiseaux) **2.FP1**
black noir **1.FP1**
black and white film une pellicule en noir et blanc **4.FP1**
blanket une couverture **2.L***
to **bleed** saigner **7.FP1**
blond blond **1.FP1**
to **blow** souffler **3.FP3;** (out) souffler **10.L***
blue bleu **1.FP1**
to **blush** *rougir **4.L***
to **board (plane)** embarquer **5.FP2**
boarding: boarding pass une carte d'embarquement **5.FP2**
to **boil** *faire bouillir **4.LC3**
bookcase une bibliothèque **8.FP2**
boss un patron (une patronne) **10.FP1**
bothered énervé **1.FP4**
bothersome gênant **3.L***
bottle une bouteille **2.FP3**
box une boîte **4.FP1**
boyfriend, (girlfriend) un copain (une copine) **9.FP1**
bracelet un bracelet **9.L***
brakes les freins *m.* **4.FP3**
branch: branch office une branche d'activité **10.FP2**
brand: brand new neuf (neuve) **2.FP3**
Bravo! Bravo! **9.FP1**
bread le pain **2.FP1**
to **break** casser **3.FP1,** *rompre **7.L*;** (body part) se casser **3.FP1**
to break a leg se casser la jambe **3.FP1**
to break up (with) *rompre (avec) **9.FP1**
brick une brique **2.FP3**
briefcase une mallette **5.L***
to **bring (object)** apporter **6.L*;** (person) emmener **3.L***
to bring back ramener **3.L***
to bring down *descendre **6.FP2**
to bring up, carry up monter **6.FP2**
broken cassé **4.FP3**
bronchitis la bronchite **7.FP1**
broom un balai **2.FP1**
brown brun **1.FP1,** châtain foncé (hair) **1.FP1,** marron **1.FP1**
to **brush (one's hair, one's teeth)** se brosser (les cheveux, les dents) **1.FP2**
to brush one's teeth se brosser les dents **1.FP2**
burden une charge **2.L***
burglary un cambriolage **3.FP2**
to **burn oneself** se brûler **7.FP2**
business les affaires *f.* **2.L***
business (small) un commerce **8.FP2**
business le commerce **10.FP1**
business class classe affaires **5.FP2**
businessman, woman un homme (une femme) d'affaires **10.FP1**
busy occupé **2.FP2**
button (on camera) le bouton **4.FP3**
to **buy** acheter **5.FP2**
to buy (oneself) s'acheter **1.FP3**

C

cage la cage **2.FP1**
to **call** appeler **6.FP2**
calm calme **1.FP4**
camera l'appareil-photo *m.* **4.FP3**
camera flash le flash **4.FP3**
Canada le Canada **1.LC1**
canary: Canary Islands les îles Canaries *f.* **5.FP1**
to **cancel** annuler **5.FP2**
canceled annulé **5.FP2**
candle une chandelle **6.L***
cap une casquette
capacity la capacité **2.FP3**

car une voiture **2.FP1**; (train) un wagon **5.FP2**
cardboard un carton **2.FP3**
carrot une carotte **2.FP1**
carry-on: carry-on luggage un bagage à main **5.FP1**
cat le chat **2.FP1**
catastrophe un désastre **4.L***
to **catch** attraper **3.FP1**
cavity une carie **7.FP2**
certain: certain ones certain(e)s **4.LC1**
chamber: Chamber of Commerce le Syndicat d'Initiative **6.LC1**
to **change: to change one's mind** changer d'avis **7.L***
check: (paid) by check par chèque **6.FP1**
to **check (luggage)** enregistrer **5.FP2**
chemistry la chimie **10.FP1**
chest la poitrine **8.L***
chestnut (hair) châtain **1.FP1**
chicken: chicken pox la varicelle **7.FP1**
childhood: childhood illness une maladie d'enfance **7.FP1**
chin le menton **1.FP1**
to **choose** *choisir **9.FP2**
circular circulaire **2.FP3**
city: city hall la mairie **8.FP2**
civil: civil servant un(e) fonctionnaire **10.FP1**
civil service la fonction publique **10.FP2**
to **claim (luggage)** chercher **5.FP2**
classmate un(e) camarade **9.FP1**
clean, put-away rangé **2.FP1**
to **clean** nettoyer **2.FP1**
cleaners le teinturier **4.FP3**
to **clear** débarrasser **2.FP1**
to clear the table débarrasser la table **2.FP1**
to **clip: to clip very short** *tondre **4.L***
clippers une tondeuse **4.L***
closely, from close up de près **4.L***
cloth: cloth rag un chiffon **2.FP1**
clothes les vêtements *m.* **2.FP1**
cloud un nuage **3.FP3**
cold froid **2.FP3**; un rhume **7.FP1**
college la fac
color: color film une pellicule-couleurs **4.FP1**
comb le peigne **1.FP2**
to **comb: to comb one's hair** se peigner **1.FP2**
to **come: to come back** *revenir **1.L***
to come closer s'approcher (de) **1.LC4**
comfortable confortable **6.FP1**
communication la communication **10.FP2**
company une entreprise, une compagnie **10.FP2**
to **complain about** *se plaindre de **7.LC1**
complete, full (sold out) complet (complète) **5.FP2**
computer un ordinateur **10.FP3**
computer specialist un informaticien (une informaticienne) **10.FP1**
condition l'état *m.* **2.FP3**; la condition **2.FP3**
to **confirm** confirmer **5.FP2**
to **congratulate** féliciter **9.FP1**
Congratulations! Félicitations! **9.FP1**
connection, relation un rapport **9.FP1**; (plane) une correspondance **5.FP2**
consistency la consistance **2.FP3**
contact: contact lenses les lentilles *f.* de contact, les verres *m.* de contact **1.FP1**
to **contact (someone)** *joindre **9.L***
convenience: convenience store une supérette **4.FP1**
to **cook** *faire cuire **4.LC3**
copper le cuivre **2.FP3**
cotton l'ouate *f.* **4.FP1**
cotton swab un coton-tige **4.FP1**
to **cough** tousser **7.FP1**
to **count** compter **6.FP1**
counter le comptoir **5.FP2**
countess la comtesse **7.L***
country un pays **5.FP1**
course: course of study des études **10.FP1**
crazy fou (folle) **3.L***
credit: credit card une carte de crédit **6.FP1**
crew: crew-cut les cheveux en brosse **1.FP1**
crutch une béquille **7.FP2**
to **cry** pleurer **1.L***
curly, frizzy frisé **1.FP1**
customs la douane **5.FP1**
to **cut** couper **2.FP1**; (into pieces) découper **8.L***; (oneself) se couper **1.FP2**
cut my hair short coupez-les-moi courts **4.FP2**
to cut one's hair se couper les cheveux **4.FP2**
to cut one's hand se couper à la main **7.FP2**
to cut very short *tondre **2.FP1**

D

dance un bal **8.L***
darkness l'obscurité *f.* **4.L***
data processing l'informatique *f.* **10.FP1**
data processor un(e) spécialiste de données **10.FP1**
day after le lendemain **6.L***
day before yesterday avant-hier **3.FP2**
day off un jour de congé **4.L***
date un rendez-vous **7.FP1**
delighted ravi **7.LC1**
dentist un dentiste **7.FP1**
deodorant le déodorant **1.FP2**
department (in store) un rayon **4.FP1**
to **deplore** déplorer **7.LC1**
depressed déprimé **7.FP1**
detergent la lessive **4.FP1**
to **develop (photos, personality)** développer **4.FP3**
devoted dévoué **7.L***
digital camera l'appareil-photo numérique *m.* **4.FP3**
to **die** mourir **9.FP2**
dignified digne **8.L***
dimension, size la dimension **2.FP3**
to **dine, have dinner** dîner **3.LC1**
diploma un diplôme **10.FP3**
diplomat un(e) diplomate **10.FP1**
direct (flight) direct **5.FP2**
director un directeur (une directrice) **10.FP1**
dirty sale **2.FP1**
to **disappear, go away** *disparaître **5.L***
disappointed, deceived déçu **1.FP4**
to **disembark, land** débarquer **5.FP2**
dishes la vaisselle **2.FP1**
to **displease someone** déplaire à **5.IM**
distance: distance from . . . à + distance **8.FP2**
dizzy spell, vertigo le vertige **7.FP1**
to **do, make** fabriquer **3.L***
to do a favor rendre service **2.FP2**
to do housework faire le ménage **2.FP1**

to do laundry laver le linge 2.FP1
to do tricks *faire des tours 3.L*
does it hurt you? ça vous fait mal? 7.FP2
doctor un médecin 7.FP1, un docteur 1.LC1
doctor's office un cabinet de médecin 7.FP1
dog le chien 2.FP1
door, boarding gate la porte 5.FP2
doormat un paillasson 1.L*
to dress a wound faire un pansement 7.FP2
driver's license un permis de conduire 5.FP1
drop une goutte 7.FP1
to drown se noyer 3.FP1
dry sec (sèche) 2.FP3
dryer (hair) le séchoir 1.FP2
to dry (oneself) se sécher 1.FP2
to dry one's hair se sécher les cheveux 1.FP2
to dry one's hands s'essuyer les mains 1.FP2
dull terne 2.FP3
during pendant 3.LC2

E

each (pronoun) chacun 5.IM
each (adj.) chaque 1.IM
ear une oreille 1.FP1
early tôt 3.LC1, en avance 5.FP2
to earn: to earn one's living gagner sa vie R.L*
economics les sciences *f.* économiques 10.FP1
Eiffel Tower la tour Eiffel 2.FP3
electrical plug la prise 4.FP3
electronics l'électronique *f.* 10.FP2
eldest l'aîné R.L*
elevator un ascenseur 6.FP1
employee, clerk un employé (une employée) 10.FP1
employment, job un emploi 10.FP1
empty vide 2.FP3
to empty vider 2.FP1
engineer un ingénieur 10.FP1
engineering studies les études *f.* d'ingénieur 10.FP1
enormous énorme 2.FP3
enough assez 3.LC1
envelope une enveloppe 4.FP1
evening le soir 7.FP1
event un événement 3.FP2
ever déjà 3.LC1
every: every four hours toutes les 4 heures 7.FP1
everywhere partout 3.L*
to examine examiner 7.FP1
to excuse oneself, apologize s'excuser 1.FP3
exercise gym la salle d'exercices 6.FP1
to exhibit exposer 9.L*
exit la sortie 5.FP2
to explain expliquer 2.L*
to express exprimer 5.IM
exquisite exquis 7.L*
extent l'ampleur *f.* 4.L*
eye un œil (pl. yeux) 1.FP1
eyeliner l'eye-liner *m.* 1.FP2
eyeshadow le fard à paupières 1.FP2

F

fabric l'étoffe *f.* 2.FP3
face la figure 1.FP1, le visage 1.FP1
fact un fait 3.FP2
factory une usine 10.FP2
fair juste R.L*
to fall tomber 3.FP1
to fall in love with at first sight avoir le coup de foudre pour 9.FP1
to fall in the water tomber dans l'eau 3.FP1
far, far away loin 8.FP2
farm une ferme 6.L*
farmer un cultivateur (une cultivatrice) 8.L*
fear la crainte 7.LC1
to fear, be afraid of craindre 7.LC1
to feed donner à manger à 2.FP1
to feel (pain or emotion) *ressentir 1.FP4
to feel nauseous avoir mal au cœur 7.FP1
to feel sorry for *plaindre 7.LC1
fever la fièvre 7.FP1
field un champ 6.L*
to file classer 10.FP3
to fill remplir 2.FP1
film une pellicule 4.FP1
filter le filtre 4.FP3
finally finalement 3.FP2
finance la finance 10.FP2
to find trouver 9.FP2
to finish finir 3.LC1
fire hose un tuyau d'incendie 2.IM
fire station une caserne de pompiers 8.FP2
firm (company) une firme 10.FP2
first aid les premiers soins *m* 2.IM
first, at first d'abord 3.FP2
first class la première classe 5.FP2
to fish pêcher 3.L*
to fix, repair réparer 4.FP3
to fix arranger 4.L*
flat plat 2.FP3
flexible flexible 2.FP3
floor le sol 2.FP1
flower une fleur 2.FP1
flu la grippe 7.FP1
fog la brume 3.FP3
to fold (up) plier 3.L*
forbidden défendu 3.L*
forehead le front 1.FP1
foreign languages les langues étrangères 10.FP1
forest la forêt 3.FP1
form la forme 2.FP3
to fracture se fracturer 7.FP2
frame le cadre 10.L*
freckles les taches *f.* de rousseur 1.FP1
free libre 2.FP2
French (language) le français 1.LC1
friend un ami (une amie) 9.FP1
friendship l'amitié *f.* 9.FP1
fringe benefit un avantage social 10.FP2
frog une grenouille 3.L*
from time to time de temps en temps 4.L*
frozen gelé 3.FP3
to fry faire frire 4.LC3
full room & board la pension complète 6.FP1
full-time employment un emploi à plein temps 10.FP3
to function, work fonctionner 4.FP3; marcher 4.FP3
furious furieux (furieuse) 1.FP4

G

gang une bande 5.L*
garbage les ordures *f.* 2.FP1
garbage can la poubelle 1.L*
garden hose le tuyau d'arrosage 2.FP1
gas station une station-service 8.FP2
gasoline l'essence *f.* 6.L*
general delivery la poste restante 4.FP1
German measles la rubéole 7.FP1

to get a nosebleed saigner du nez **7.FP1**
to get a sunburn attraper un coup de soleil **3.FP1**
to get angry se mettre en colère **1.LC4**
to get back, recuperate récupérer **5.L***
to get bored s'embêter **1.LC4**
to get dressed s'habiller **1.FP3**
to get engaged se fiancer **9.FP2**
to get hurt, injure oneself se faire mal **3.FP1;** se blesser **3.FP1**
to get impatient s'impatienter **1.LC4**
to get lost se perdre **3.FP1**
to get married se marier **9.FP2**
to get off (train) *descendre **5.FP2**
to get on (train) monter **5.FP2**
to get ready se préparer **1.FP3**
to get rid of se débarrasser **3.L***
to get sick tomber malade **9.FP2**
to get undressed se déshabiller **1.FP3**
to get upset s'énerver **1.LC4**
to get attraper **3.FP1**
ghost town une ville fantôme **5.IM**
give me ten (of them) donnez-m'en dix **4.FP1**
to give a hand donner un coup de main **2.FP2**
to give a shot, injection faire une piqûre **7.FP1**
gift un cadeau (pl. cadeaux) **6.L***
gifted doué **8.L***
girlfriend une copine **9.FP1**
glass un verre **2.FP1**
glass jar un bocal **3.L***
glue la colle **4.FP1**
to go aller **6.FP1**
to go away s'en aller **1.LC4**
to go back to sleep *se rendormir **10.L***
to go camping faire du camping **3.FP1**
to go fishing aller à la pêche **3.FP1**
to go for a drink prendre un pot **8.FP1**
to go look aller voir **1.L***
to go mountain climbing faire de l'alpinisme **3.FP1**
to go on a trip *faire un voyage **5.FP1**
to go on an interview aller à un entretien **10.FP3**
to go on holiday, spend some time faire un séjour **5.FP1**
to go out *sortir **2.FP1**
to go scuba diving faire de la plongée sous-marine **3.FP1**
to go swimming se baigner **3.FP1**
to go through passer par **5.FP2**
to go to bed se coucher **1.FP3**
to go windsurfing faire de la planche à voile **3.FP1**
God Dieu *m.* **2.IC**
gold l'or *m.* **R.L***
gold coin une pièce d'or **7.L***
gold (hair) châtain clair **1.FP1**
good working conditions de bonnes conditions de travail **10.FP2**
grass l'herbe *f.* **2.FP1**
Greece la Grèce **5.FP1**
green vert **1.FP1**
grey gris **1.FP1**
to grow (in size) **3.L***
to grow old *vieillir **9.FP2**
to grow up grandir **9.FP3**
to guess deviner **3.FP2**
gym, sports center un centre sportif **8.FP2**

H

hair les cheveux *m.* **1.FP1**
hair perm une permanente **4.FP2**
hairbrush une brosse à cheveux **1.FP2**
haircut une coupe de cheveux **4.FP2**
haircut and a blow-dry une coupe-brushing **4.FP2**
hairdresser le coiffeur **4.FP2**
half la moitié **2.L***
half-time employment un emploi à mi-temps **10.FP3**
to hand, give *tendre **7.L***
handicap access un accès pour personnes handicapées **6.FP1**
handkerchief un mouchoir **1.L***
to hang (up) *pendre **10.L***
hanger un portemanteau (pl. portemanteaux) **6.FP2;** un cintre **6.FP2**
to happen se passer **3.FP2;** arriver **3.FP2**
happy heureux (heureuse) **1.FP4;** content **1.FP4**
hard dur **2.FP3**
harmless inoffensif (inoffensive) **8.L***
to have pain, to hurt avoir mal **7.FP1**
to have a career faire carrière **10.FP2**
to have a cold être enrhumé **7.FP1**
to have a headache avoir mal à la tête **1.L***
to have a picnic faire un pique-nique **3.FP1**
to have a soar throat avoir mal à la gorge **7.FP1**
to have a stomach ache avoir mal au ventre **7.FP1**
to have an argument se disputer **9.FP1**
to have an upset stomach avoir mal à l'estomac **1.L***
to have good luck avoir de la chance **9.FP1**
to have fun s'amuser **1.FP3**
to have to deal with avoir affaire à **8.FP2**
hayfever un rhume des foins **7.FP1**
head of personnel un chef de personnel **10.FP1**
in good health en bonne santé **7.FP1**
to hear (it said) entendre dire **8.L***
hedge une haie d'arbustes **6.L***
heel (of shoe) un talon **4.FP3**
height, size (person) la taille **1.FP1**
heir (heiress) un héritier (une héritière) **R.L***
to help aider à **2.FP2**
to hide cacher **5.L***
high haut **2.FP3**
history l'histoire *f.* **10.FP1**
hired engagé(e) **2.IM**
to hold *tenir **3.L***
to hold dear, cherish *tenir à **9.L***
horse un cheval *m.* **2.IM**
hospital l'hôpital *m.* **7.FP2**
hot/warm chaud **2.FP3**
hotel un hôtel **6.FP1**
housework les travaux *m.* domestiques **2.FP1**
how much does that come to? ça fait combien? **4.FP1**
how do you feel? comment te sens-tu? **1.FP4**
how long? combien de temps? **6.FP1**
how many would you like? combien en voulez-vous? **4.FP1**

how much do I owe you? combien est-ce que je vous dois? **4.FP1**
humid, wet humide **2.FP3**
hurricane un ouragan **3.FP3**
to **hurry (oneself)** se dépêcher **1.FP3**
to **hurt** faire du mal **3.L***
to hurt one's head se blesser à la tête **7.FP2**

I

I need il me faut **4.FP1**
ice la glace **3.FP3**
identification card une carte d'identité **5.FP1**
if si **5.LC2**
important important **10.FP2**
impossible! pas possible! **3.FP2**
in disorder en désordre **2.FP1**
in a bad mood de mauvaise humeur **1.FP4**
in a good mood de bonne humeur **1.FP4**
in a little while tout à l'heure **4.FP3**
in back derrière **4.FP2**
in cash en espèces **6.FP1**
in front sur le devant **4.FP2,** (of) devant **8.FP1**
in good health bien portant **7.FP1**
in memory of en souvenir de **8.L***
in order to de façon à **7.IC,** pour **10.LC1**
in shape en forme **1.FP4**
in steps (hair), uneven des échelles **4.L***
in the distance au loin **6.L***
in two days' time dans deux jours **4.FP3**
in your opinion à votre avis **R.A.**
inclination for responsibility le goût des responsabilités **10.FP3**
indigestion l'indigestion *f.* **7.FP1**
industry l'industrie *f.* **10.FP2**
inexpensive hotel un hôtel bon marché **6.FP1**
to **inherit** hériter (de) **8.L***
initiative un esprit d'initiative **10.FP3**
inn une auberge **6.FP1**
to **insist** exiger **2.L***
to insist that insister pour que **2.LC2**
instinctive liking la sympathie **9.FP1**
insurance agent un agent d'assurances **10.FP1**
international company une compagnie internationale **10.FP2**
Internet access accès Internet **6.FP1**
interview un entretien **10.FP3,** une entrevue **10.FP3**
to **iron** repasser **2.FP1**
iron (for clothes) un fer à repasser **2.FP1;** (metal) le fer **2.FP3**
is there something else? autre chose? **4.FP1**
it is better that . . . il vaut mieux que . . . **2.LC2**
it is essential that il est essentiel que **2.LC2**
it is fair that il est juste que **2.LC2**
it is good that il est bon que **2.LC2**
it happened c'est arrivé **3.FP2**
it is important that il est important que **2.LC2**
it is indispensable that il est indispensable que **2.LC2**
it is natural that il est naturel que **2.LC2**
it is normal that il est normal que **2.LC2**
it is too bad that il est dommage que **2.LC2**
it is useful that . . . utile: il est utile que . . . **2.LC2**
it's dark il fait noir **3.FP3**
it's your turn c'est votre tour **4.FP1**
item un article **4.FP1**

J

jealousy la jalousie **9.FP1**
jewel, jewelry un bijou (pl. bijoux) **9.L***
journalism le journalisme **10.FP1**
joy la joie **7.LC1**
judge un(e) juge **10.FP1**
to **jump** sauter **1.L***
just as au moment où **3.LC2**

K

to **keep company** *tenir compagnie **9.L***
kiss un baiser **7.L***
to **kiss** embrasser **1.L***
knee, lap un genou (pl. genoux) **7.L***
knife un couteau (pl. couteaux) **2.FP1**
knitting le tricot **9.L***
to **knock (on door)** frapper **1.L***

L

to **land** atterrir **5.FP2**
to **last** durer **2.L***
last dernier (dernière) **3.FP2**
last night hier soir **3.FP2**
late tard **3.LC1;** en retard **5.FP2**
one hour late une heure de retard **5.FP2**
to **launch** lancer **4.L***
laundry room la lingerie **2.FP1**
law enforcement la police **8.FP2**
lawn la pelouse **2.FP1**
lawn-mower la tondeuse **2.FP1**
lawyer un avocat (une avocate) **10.FP1**
lawyer's office un cabinet d'avocat **10.FP2**
lead le plomb **2.FP3**
to **lead** *conduire **3.L***
to **lean** appuyer **10.L***
to **leave** laisser **R.L*;** partir **5.LC2**
to leave my hair long (haircut) laissez-les-moi longs **4.FP2**
to leave (place/person) quitter **5.LC2**
to leave from (place) partir de **5.LC2**
to leave for (destination) partir à (en, pour) **5.LC2**
length: length of time from . . . à + length of time **8.FP2**
lens (camera) la lentille **4.FP3**
lens (focus) l'objectif *m.* **4.FP3**
less moins **6.FP1**
letter une lettre **4.FP1**
letter of recommendation une lettre de recommandation **10.FP3**
library une bibliothèque **8.FP2**
license plate une plaque d'immatriculation **5.L***
light léger (légère) **2.FP3**
to **light** allumer **10.L***
to light a fire allumer un feu **2.L***
lightening (flash of) un éclair **3.FP3**
to **like** aimer **2.LC2**
to like aimer bien **9.FP1**
lipstick le rouge à lèvres **1.FP2**
liter le litre **1.LC1**
literature la littérature **10.FP1**
to **live, lodge** loger **2.L***
long long (longue) **1.FP1**

to look for, search for rechercher **10.FP2**
to lose one's balance perdre l'équilibre **3.FP1**
loud fort **6.L***
loudspeaker le•haut-parleur **4.FP3**
to love aimer **9.FP1**
low bas (basse) **2.FP3**
low-income housing un HLM (Habitation à Loyer Modéré) **8.FP2**
low neckline un décolleté **1.IM**
luggage les bagages *m.* **5.FP1**
luxury hotel un hôtel de luxe **6.FP1**

M

madman/woman un fou (une folle) **7.L***
magazine un magazine **2.FP1**
magnifying glass une loupe **5.L***
mail le courrier **4.FP3**
to make a cast (broken bone) faire un plâtre **7.FP2**
to make a mistake se tromper **1.LC4**
to make an appointment/date with donner rendez-vous à **8.FP1**
to make an appointment, date prendre rendez-vous **7.FP1**
to make friends se faire des amis **9.FP2**
to make sure s'assurer **8.L***
to make the bed faire le lit **2.FP1**
to make up se réconcilier **9.FP1**
makeover un relooking **1.IM**
mall un grand centre commercial **8.FP2**
to manage to arriver à **4.L***
management la gestion **10.FP1**
manager le/la gérant(e) **6.FP2**
marketing le marketing **10.FP1**
marketing specialist un(e) spécialiste de marketing **10.FP1**
to marry épouser **2.L***
mascara le mascara **1.FP2,** le rimmel **1.FP2**
massive massif (massive) **2.FP3**
match une allumette **4.FP1**
material le matériel **2.FP3**
mathematics les maths *f.* **1.LC1**
mean, nasty méchant **2.L***
to mean *vouloir dire **10.L***
measles la rougeole **7.FP1**
to measure mesurer **1.FP1**
medicine (the practice of) la médecine **10.FP1**
to meet each other se rencontrer **8.FP1**
to meet by chance, run into (person) rencontrer **8.FP1**
meeting une réunion **5.IM**
memory card une carte mémoire **4.FP3**
merchant un marchand **2.L***
metal le métal (pl. métaux) **2.FP3**
Mexico le Mexique **5.FP1**
microphone le micro **4.FP3**
minuscule minuscule **2.FP3**
minor news event un fait divers **3.FP2**
mirror un miroir **1.FP2;** la glace **1.FP2**
to miss (bus) rater **5.FP2**
Mississippi le Mississippi **1.LC1**
mix un mélange **5.IM**
Monday lundi **3.FP2**
mononucleosis la mononucléose **7.FP1**
month un mois **3.FP2**
mood l'humeur *f.* **1.FP4**
more plus **6.FP1**
morning le matin **7.FP1**
most of la plupart de **4.LC1**
most of them, the majority la plupart **4.LC1**
moustache la moustache **1.FP1**
mouth la bouche **1.FP1**
to move toward se diriger vers **8.L***
to mow *tondre **2.FP1**
multinational multinational **10.FP2**
mumps les oreillons *m.pl.* **7.FP1**
museum un musée **8.FP2**
music la musique **10.FP1**
must devoir **4.FP1**
My Goodness! Mon Dieu! **3.FP2**
My poor . . . Mon (Ma) pauvre . . . **9.FP1**

N

nail (metal) le clou **2.FP3**
nail un ongle **1.FP2**
nail polish le vernis à ongles **1.FP2**
narrow, tight étroit **2.FP3**
nature la nature **3.FP1**
nausea la nausée **7.FP1**
nearby tout près **8.FP2**
neck le cou **1.FP1**
neighborhood, district le quartier **8.FP2**
neither . . . nor ni . . . ni **5.LC1**
nephew un neveu (pl. neveux) **R.L***
nervous nerveux (nerveuse) **7.FP1**
never ne . . . jamais **3.LC1**
next suivant **5.FP2;** ensuite **3.FP2**
next prochain **5.FP2**
nice, kind sympathique **2.FP2**
no longer, not anymore ne . . . plus **1.L***
no one, nobody ne . . . personne **RC**
no, not any ne . . . aucun **5.LC1**
noisy bruyant **6.FP1**
non-smoking section la section non-fumeur **5.FP2**
nose le nez **1.FP1**
not yet ne . . . pas encore **3.LC1**
notebook un carnet **4.FP1**
nothing ne . . . rien **RC**
nothing to declare rien à déclarer **5.FP1**
to notice remarquer **2.L*;** apercevoir **6.L***
nowhere ne . . . nulle part **5.LC1**
nurse un infirmier (une infirmière) **7.FP1**

O

to observe observer **3.FP1**
of course bien sûr **2.FP2**
often souvent **3.LC1**
O.K. d'accord **2.FP2**
old vieux (vieille) **2.FP3**
former ancien (ancienne) **2.FP3**
on foot à pied **8.FP2**
on his own account à son propre compte **10.FP2**
on time à l'heure **5.FP2**
on Saturday samedi **1.LC1**
on Saturdays le samedi **1.LC1**
on the sides sur les côtés **4.FP2**
on top sur le dessus **4.FP2**
once une fois **7.FP1**
on the other hand par contre **R**
one hundred meters away à 100 mètres **8.FP2**
one week from now d'ici une semaine **4.FP3**
one-way ticket un aller simple **5.FP2**
the one who(m), the one that celui (celle) qui **6.LC2**
to operate (equipment) faire marcher **4.LC3**
operator un standard **6.FP2**

opportunity for promotion la possibilité de promotion **10.FP2**
opposite en face de **6.L***
ophthalmologist un oculiste **7.FP1**
or ou **5.LC1**
orchard un verger **8.L***
other ones d'autres **4.LC1**
ouch! aïe! **7.FP1**
outside dehors **3.FP2**
oval oval **1.FP1**
oven un four **1.L***
overcast couvert **3.FP3**
overwhelmed bouleversé **7.L***
to **owe** devoir **4.FP1**
to **own, possess** posséder **9.L***
owner un propriétaire **R.L***

P

package un paquet **4.FP1;** un colis **4.FP1**
pad: pad (of paper) un bloc **4.FP1**
pain, suffering une douleur **7.FP2**
painful douloureux (douloureuse) **7.L***
paper le papier **2.FP3**
paper clip un trombone **4.FP1**
paper tissue un mouchoir en papier **4.FP1**
paper towels (brand name) le Sopalin **4.FP1**
parachute un parachute **2.FP3**
parakeet la perruche **2.FP1**
park un parc **8.FP2**
to **pass by** passer **3.LC1**
passport un passeport **5.FP1**
passport check un contrôle des passeports **5.FP1**
peach une pêche **8.L***
peach tree un pêcher **8.L***
to **peel** éplucher **2.FP1**
pencil un crayon **4.FP1**
perfect parfait **3.L***
perfume l'eau *f.* de toilette **1.FP2;** le parfum **1.FP2**
perplexed perplexe **1.FP4**
pharmaceutics (practice of) la pharmacie **10.FP1**
pharmacy la pharmacie **4.FP1**
pharmacist un pharmacien (une pharmacienne) **10.FP1**
philosophy la philosophie **10.FP1**
photocopy une photocopie **4.FP1**
photographer le photographe **4.FP1**
physics la physique **10.FP1**
to **pick up** ramasser **7.L***
picture slide une diapo **4.FP1**
pillow un oreiller **6.FP2**
pill (medicine) un comprimé **7.FP1**
pilot le pilote **5.FP2**
pin une épingle **4.FP1**
pitiful pitoyable **4.L***
plant une plante **2.FP1**
plastic en plastique (adj.) **2.FP3;** le plastique (n.) **2.FP3**
platform le quai **5.FP2**
to **please** faire plaisir à **8.L***
pneumonia une pneumonie **7.FP1**
pocket une poche **1.L***
to **point: point at** montrer du doigt **8.L***
pointed pointu **2.FP3**
police: police detective un inspecteur de police **5.L***
police station le poste de police **8.FP2;** une gendarmerie **8.FP2**
polished poli **2.FP3**
political science les sciences *f.* politiques **10.FP1**
to **pollute** polluer **3.FP1**
ponytail une queue de cheval **1.FP1**
Portugal le Portugal **5.FP1**
position (employment) un poste **2.IM**
postcard une carte postale **4.FP1**
post office la poste **4.FP1**
pot, pan une casserole **1.L***
to **pour** verser **3.L***
precisely at that moment justement **8.L***
to **predict** prédire **3.FP3**
to **prefer** préférer **2.LC2**
prescription une ordonnance **7.FP1**
to **present, show** présenter **5.FP2**
to **prevent, keep from doing** empêcher de **1.L***
pride l'orgueil *m.* **7.LC1**
princess une princesse **1.LC1**
private eye un détective privé **5.L***
professional experience l'expérience *f.* professionnelle **10.FP3**
to **promote** promouvoir **7.IC**
proud fier (fière) **3.L***
provided, on condition that à condition que **10.LC2**
to **prune, trim** tailler **2.FP1**
psychology la psychologie **10.FP1**
public: public garden un jardin public **8.FP2**
public relations les relations *f.* publiques **10.FP2**
to **punch (ticket)** composter **5.FP2**
to **put, place, turn on** mettre **6.FP2**
to put away ranger **2.FP1**
to put back *remettre **9.L***
to put stitches (in a wound) mettre des sutures **7.FP2**

Q

quantity une quantité **4.FP1**
to **quarrel, have a fight** se quereller **9.FP1**
queen la reine **1.LC1**

R

rabbit un lapin **2.FP1**
raconter to tell (what happened) **3.FP2**
rain la pluie **3.FP3**
to **raise (children)** élever **2.L***
raised, high élevé **2.FP3**
rash (skin) l'eczéma *m.* **7.FP1;** des boutons **7.FP1**
ready to prêt à **2.IM**
real estate l'immobilier *m.* **10.FP2**
real estate agent un agent immobilier **10.FP1**
Really? Vraiment? **3.FP2**
to **realize** se rendre compte **2.L***
reception desk la réception **6.FP1**
receptionist, secretary le/la réceptionniste **6.FP2**
recreation center un centre de loisirs **8.FP2**
rectangular rectangulaire **1.FP1**
red rouge **1.LC1**
redhead roux (rousse) **1.FP1**
reference une référence **10.FP3**
to **reflect on** réfléchir **7.L***
refrigerator le réfrigérateur **2.FP3**
regret le regret **7.LC1**
to **regret** regretter **2.FP2**
relations les relations *f.* **9.FP1**
good relations bons rapports. *m.* **9.FP1**
bad relations mauvaises relations **9.FP1**
to **remarry** se remarier **9.FP2**
to **remember, recall** se rappeler **1.LC4**

representative un(e) représentant(e) **10.FP1**
request une requête **8.L***
research laboratory un laboratoire de recherche **10.FP2**
researcher un chercheur (une chercheuse) **10.FP1**
to **reserve** réserver **6.FP1**
reservation une réservation **5.FP2**
respect le respect **9.FP1**
to **respect** respecter **3.FP1**
to **respond** répondre **10.FP3**
responsibility une responsabilité **10.FP2**
to **rest** se reposer **1.FP3**
résumé un curriculum vitae **10.FP3**
to **retire** prendre sa retraite **9.FP2**
to **reward** récompenser **4.L***
ring une bague **R.L***
roll (of paper towels) un rouleau (pl. rouleaux) **4.FP1**
room de la place **5.FP2**
room service le service en chambre **6.FP1**
room with breakfast, dinner la demi-pension **6.FP1**
roomy spacieux (spacieuse) **6.FP1**
rough, uneven rugueux (rugueuse) **2.FP3**
round rond **1.FP1**
round-trip ticket un aller et retour **5.FP2**
rounded, arched courbé **2.FP3**
rubber le caoutchouc **2.FP3**
rubber band un élastique **4.FP1**
rug un tapis **1.L***
to **run** *courir **1.L***
Russia la Russie **5.FP1**
rustic furniture des meubles *m.* rustiques **6.L***

S

sad triste **1.FP4**
sadness la tristesse **7.LC1**
safe un coffre **R.L***
safety pin une épingle de sûreté **4.FP1**
salary un salaire **10.FP2**
sales person un vendeur (une vendeuse) **10.FP1**
to **save** sauver **5.L***
saw une scie **2.FP3**
scar une cicatrice **1.FP1**
to **scare** faire peur **3.FP1**
schedule un horaire **5.FP2**
scientist un(e) scientifique 10.FP1
scientific research la recherche scientifique **10.FP2**
scissors les ciseaux *m.* **1.FP2**
scotch tape le scotch **4.FP1**
to **scream** pousser des cris **3.L***
seat un siège **5.FP2;** une place **5.FP2**
seat belt une ceinture de sécurité **5.FP2**
second class la deuxième classe **5.FP2**
second-hand, used d'occasion **2.FP3**
secretary un(e) secrétaire **10.FP1**
security check un contrôle de sécurité **5.FP2**
see you (date, time) à + date, time **8.FP1**
to **see** assister à **3.FP2**
to **seem, appear** sembler **1.FP4**
to **seize, take** saisir **9.L***
sensitive sensible **1.IM**
to **separate: to separate (husband & wife)** se séparer **9.FP2**
serpent un serpent **3.FP1**
to **serve** *servir **6.FP2**
set (hair) une mise en plis **4.FP2**
to **set a fire** mettre le feu **3.FP1**
to set the table (silverware) mettre le couvert **2.FP1**
to set the table mettre la table **2.FP1**
to **settle** s'installer **8.L***
several certain(e)s, plusieurs **4.LC1**
to **shake** secouer **10.L***
shampoo le shampooing **1.FP2**
a shampoo (hair salon) un shampooing **4.FP2**
to **shave** se raser **1.FP2**
shaver le rasoir **1.FP2**
shaving cream la crème à raser **1.FP2**
sheet: sheet (bedding) un drap **6.FP2**
sheet ice le verglas **3.FP3**
to **shine** briller **3.FP3**
shiny brillant **2.FP3**
shirt une chemise **2.FP1**
to **shiver, shudder** frissonner **9.L***
shoe repairer le cordonnier **4.FP3**
shop une boutique **4.FP1;** un commerce **8.FP2**
to **shorten (hair)** dégager **4.FP2**
shot of novocaine une piqûre de novocaïne **7.FP2**
to **show** *faire voir **4.LC3**
shower une douche **1.FP3**
shrub un arbuste **2.FP1**
shrub clippers un sécateur **2.FP1**
to **shut up** *se taire **1.LC4**
sick malade **1.FP4**
sickness, disease une maladie **7.FP1**
side un côté **4.L***
sideboard un buffet **1.L***
sidewalk le trottoir **9.L***
silent muet (muette) **7.L***
silk scarf un foulard **1.IM**
silver l'argent *m.* **R.L***
since puisque **3.L***
single-family house une maison individuelle **8.FP2**
to **sit down** *s'asseoir **1.LC4**
to sit down to eat se mettre à table **1.FP3**
skinny maigre **1.FP1**
skull le crâne **4.L***
to **slip** glisser **3.FP1**
to **slow down** *ralentir **7.L***
small, short petit **1.FP1**
small sofa un canapé **1.L***
to **smell** *sentir **1.FP4**
smoking section la section fumeur **5.FP2**
smooth lisse **2.FP3**
to **sneeze** éternuer **7.FP1**
snow la neige **3.FP3**
snowstorm une tempête de neige **3.FP3**
so much tellement **4.L***
so that pour que **10.LC2**
soap le savon **1.FP2**
social worker un(e) assistant(e) social(e) **10.FP1**
soft mou (molle) **2.FP3**
software specialist un(e) spécialiste de logiciel **10.FP1**
something else to do autre chose à faire **2.FP2**
to **solicit, ask for** solliciter **10.FP3**
solid solide **2.FP3**
some, a few quelques **4.LC1;** quelques-un(e)s **4.LC1;** certain(e)s **4.LC1**
someone, somebody quelqu'un RC
something quelque chose **RC**
something else quelque chose d'autre **4.FP1**
something to declare quelque chose à déclarer **5.FP1**
somewhere quelque part **5.LC1**
very sorry, sad désolé **2.FP2**
sound and light show un spectacle son et lumière **2.IM**
to **speak English** parler anglais **10.FP3**
to **specialize, major in** se spécialiser

en **10.FP1**
specialist un(e) spécialiste **7.FP1**
to **spend (time)** passer **3.LC1**
to **spend the night** passer la nuit **6.FP1**
to **spoil** gâter **7.L***
sponge une éponge **2.FP1**
to **sprain** se fouler **7.FP2**
spring (in watch) le ressort **4.FP3**
spy un espion (une espionne) **5.L***
square carré **1.FP1**
to **stand** supporter **2.L***
to **start** *se mettre à **3.L***
to start one's own business créer sa propre entreprise **10.FP2**
station la chaîne **5.IM**
stationery store la papeterie **4.FP1**
stationery paper le papier à lettres **4.FP1**
Statue of Liberty la statue de la Liberté **2.FP3**
to **stay, lodge** séjourner **6.FP1**
to stay in bed rester au lit **7.FP1**
to **steal** voler **5.L***
steel l'acier *m.* **2.FP3**
stele (stone marker with an inscription) une stèle **6.L***
to **step on** marcher sur **1.LC3**
steward le steward **5.FP2**
stewardess l'hôtesse *f.* de l'air **5.FP2**
to **sting** piquer **3.FP1**
stockbroker un agent de change **10.FP1**
stone une pierre **2.FP3**
stool un tabouret **4.L***
to **stoop, bend down** se baisser **7.L***
to **stop, prevent oneself from** s'arrêter **1.FP3;** s'empêcher (de) **4.L***
stopover, connection une escale **5.FP2**
store window une vitrine **9.L***
storm la tempête **3.FP3;** un orage **3.FP3**
straight lisse **1.FP1**
straight, upright droit **2.FP3**
stranger un(e) inconnu(e) **7.L***
strep throat l'angine *f.* **7.FP1**
string la ficelle **4.FP1**
strong fort **1.FP1**
to **study** étudier **10.FP1,** faire des études (de) **9.FP3**
suit (woman's) un tailleur **1.IM**
suitcase une valise **5.FP1**
summer job un job d'été **10.FP3**
sunny clair **6.FP1**
to **sunbathe** prendre un bain de soleil **3.FP1**
super chouette **3.L***
surgeon un chirurgien (une chirurgienne) **7.FP1**
to **surprise** *surprendre **9.L***
surprised surpris **7.LC1**
to **swallow** avaler **7.FP1**
to **sweep** balayer **2.FP1**
to **swim** nager **3.FP1**
swimming pool une piscine **6.FP1**
synthetic material la matière synthétique **2.FP3**

T

table la table **2.FP1**
tablet (medicine) un cachet **7.FP1**
tadpole un têtard **3.L***
to **take** *prendre **5.FP2**
to take a blood sample faire une analyse de sang **7.FP1**
to take a boat trip faire une promenade en bateau **3.FP1**
to take a walk se promener **1.FP3**
to take advantage of profiter de **1.L***
to take care of s'occuper de **1.LC4**
to take off (plane) décoller **5.FP2**
to take off, remove enlever **4.FP3**
to take one's blood pressure prendre la tension **7.FP1**
to have taken or carried something up monter: avoir + monté **3.LC1**
to take out the trash sortir la poubelle **2.FP1**
to take place avoir lieu **2.L***
to **tan oneself** bronzer 3.FP1
team une équipe
as a team en équipe **2.IM**
tear une larme **7.L***
technical knowledge les connaissances *f.* techniques **10.FP3**
technician un technicien (une technicienne) **10.FP1**
telephone le téléphone **6.FP1**
to **telephone, call** téléphoner **10.FP3**
telephoto lens le téléobjectif **4.FP3**
television la télévision **6.FP1**
temperature la température **2.FP3**
temporary employment un emploi temporaire **10.FP3**
to **tempt** tenter **9.L***
ten minutes early dix minutes d'avance **5.FP2**
tense, uptight tendu **1.FP4**
to **thank** remercier **2.FP2**
thank you merci **2.FP2**
thank you very much merci beaucoup **2.FP2**
thanks a million merci mille fois **2.FP2**
that que **9.LC1**
that doesn't matter ça n'a pas d'importance **10.L***
that of, the one belonging to celui (celle) de **6.LC2**
that's all? c'est tout? **4.FP1**
that's not for real! ce n'est pas croyable! **3.FP2**
that's unbelieveable! c'est incroyable! **3.FP2**
then puis **3.FP2**
therefore donc **5.IM**
there is/are . . . left il reste . . . **8.L***
there is/are only . . . left il ne reste que . . . **10.L***
thick épais (épaisse) **2.FP3**
thief un voleur (une voleuse) **5.L***
thin mince **1.FP1**
things will be okay ça s'arrangera **9.FP1**
this happened, took place ça a eu lieu **3.FP2;** ça s'est passé . . . **3.FP2**
this one celui-ci (celle-ci) **2.L***
this one, the one celui (celle) **6.LC2**
this will be ready ce sera prêt **4.FP3**
through à travers **1.L***
to **throw** *jeter **3.FP1**
to throw up *vomir **7.FP1**
thunder le tonnerre **3.FP3**
ticket un billet **5.FP2**
ticket window le guichet **5.FP2**
ticket-punching machine le composteur **5.FP2**
time le temps **2.FP2**
full-time à temps complet
tire la roue **4.FP3**
tired fatigué **1.FP4**
to **the end** jusqu'au bout **7.L***
toilet paper le papier hygiénique **4.FP1**
toiletry bag la trousse de toilette **1.FP2**
ton une tonne **5.IM**
too trop **3.LC1**
too bad! tant pis! **2.LC2;** quel dommage! **9.FP1**

tooth une dent 7.FP2
tooth filling un plombage 7.FP2
toothache mal aux dents *m.* 7.FP4
toothbrush une brosse à dents 1.FP2
toothpaste le dentifrice 1.FP2
tourist class la classe économique 5.FP2
towel la serviette 1.FP2
tower, high-rise une tour 8.FP2
town centre, downtown le centre-ville 8.FP2
trade le commerce 10.FP1
traffic la circulation 6.L*
traffic regulations le code de la route 8.FP2
train un train 5.FP2
train door une portière 7.L*
train station la gare 5.FP2
training un entraînement 2.IM
undergo a training suivre un entrainement
travel agency une agence de voyages 5.FP2
to travel voyager 5.FP1
traveler's check un chèque de voyage 6.FP1
to treat (medical) soigner 7.FP1
triangular triangulaire 2.FP3
truly drôlement 4.L*
trust une confiance 9.FP1
to trust avoir confiance 9.FP1
to try in vain avoir beau essayer 4.L*
to try to chercher à 10.L*
tube un tube 4.FP1
to turn: to turn around se tourner 4.L*
to turn down, lower baisser 6.FP2
twice a day deux fois par jour 7.FP1

U

unexpected inattendu 8.L*
unfair injuste R.L*
unhappy malheureux (malheureuse) 1.FP4
United Nations building le bâtiment de l'ONU 2.FP3
United States les États-Unis *m.* 1.LC1
unless à moins que 10.LC2
unruly mop (of hair) la tignasse 4.L*
until now jusqu'ici 4.L*
until when jusqu'à quand 6.FP1
upset fâché 3.L*; énervé 1.FP4

to use utiliser 10.FP3; *se servir de 10.FP3

V

to vacuum passer l'aspirateur 2.FP1
vegetable un légume 2.FP3
vegetation la végétation 3.FP1
very much beaucoup 3.LC1
veterinary: veterinary doctor un(e) vétérinaire 10.FP1
veterinary studies les études *f.* vétérinaires 10.FP1
view une vue 6.FP1
Virginia la Virginie 1.LC1
vitamin une vitamine 4.FP1
volume la capacité 2.FP3
voluminous volumineux (volumineuse) 2.FP3

W

to wait attendre 5.FP2
waiting room la salle d'attente 5.FP2
to wake up (something, someone) réveiller 6.FP2
to wake (oneself) up se réveiller 1.FP3; s'éveiller 10.L*
wakefulness l'éveil *m.* 10.L*
to walk faire un tour 3.FP1; promener 2.FP1
to want *vouloir 2.LC2
wardrobe, closet une armoire 1.L*
warm tiède 2.FP3
to warn *prévenir 3.L*
to wash laver 2.FP1
to wash (oneself) se laver 1.FP3
to wash one's face se laver la figure 1.FP2
to wash the dishes faire la vaisselle 2.FP1
wash cloth un gant de toilette 1.FP2
wastepaper basket, trash la corbeille 2.FP1
wavy ondulé 2.FP3
weak faible 1.FP1; fragile 2.FP3
wealth les biens *m.* 2.L*
to wear glasses porter des lunettes 1.FP1
bad weather le mauvais temps 3.FP3
nice weather le beau temps 3.FP3
weather forecast la météo 3.FP3
week une semaine 3.FP2

to weigh peser 1.FP1
weight le poids 1.FP1
well, good bien 1.FP4
well-being le bien-être 10.L*
well-built, solid costaud 1.FP1
well located bien situé 6.FP1
wet mouillé 2.FP3
what quel (quelle) 4.FP1
what bad luck! quelle malchance! 9.FP1
what doesn't work? qu'est-ce qui ne marche pas? 4.FP2
what good news! quelle bonne nouvelle! 9.FP2
what happened? qu'est-ce qu'il y a eu? 3.FP2; qu'est-ce qui a eu lieu? 3.FP2; qu'est-ce qui est arrivé? 3.FP2; qu'est-ce qui s'est passé? 3.FP2
what is the problem? quel est le problème? 4.FP3
what kind, type? quel genre? 7.FP1
what type of quelle sorte de 5.FP2
what's new? quoi de neuf? 3.FP2
what's the matter? qu'est-ce que tu as? 1.FP4
what's wrong? qu'est-ce qu'il y a? 1.FP4; qu'est-ce qui ne va pas? 7.FP1
when lorsque 3.LC2; quand 5.LC2
which quel (quelle) 4.FP1; que 9.LC1
while pendant que 3.LC2
whim un caprice 8.L*
whistle un sifflet à roulette 3.L*
to whistle siffler 3.L*
who, that, which qui 9.LC1
whom que 9.LC1
whooping cough la coqueluche 7.FP1
wide large 2.FP3
wind le vent 3.FP3
window pane une vitre 2.FP1
to wipe essuyer 2.FP1
to wipe (oneself) dry s'essuyer 1.FP2
wisdom tooth une dent de sagesse 7.FP2
to wish souhaiter 2.LC2; désirer 2.LC2
with one bed à un lit 6.FP1
with pleasure avec plaisir 2.FP2
without sans (que) 10.LC1
to witness être témoin 3.FP2
to wonder se demander 8.L*

wood le bois **2.FP3**
word un mot **6.L***
work le travail (pl. travaux) **2.FP1**
to **work** travailler **9.FP2**
worker un ouvrier (une ouvrière) **R.L***
worn usagé **2.FP3**
worn out, old usé **4.FP3**
to **worry** s'en faire **4.L***
worried préoccupé **1.FP4**
worse pire **7.L***
to **wrap** envelopper **7.L***
wrist le poignet **7.L***

X

to **x-ray** faire une radio **7.FP1**

Y

to **yell, shout** crier **1.L***
yesterday hier **3.FP2**
you're kidding! tu plaisantes! **3.FP2**
you're the boss! c'est vous le patron (patronne)! **2.LC2**
you're welcome de rien **2.FP2;** je t'en prie **2.FP2;** il n'y a pas de quoi **2.FP2**
yet déjà **3.LC1**
youth center une Maison des Jeunes **8.FP2**
youth hostel une auberge de jeunesse **6.FP1**

INDEX

Index R71 Index

Text Credits

p. 4: source: *Bulletin Pacijou* volume 1, number 4, June 1992. **p. 56:** Eugène Ionesco, "Deuxième conte pour enfants de moins de trois ans," *Présent passé, Passé présent* © 1968 Mercure de France. **p. 67:** Robert Desnos, "La fourmi," from *Chantefables et chantefleurs* ©1944 Librairie Gründ. **p. 68:** Jacques Prévert, "Pour faire le portrait d'un oiseau" from *Paroles* © 1949 Éditions Gallimard Collections Folio. **p. 96:** "Le Partage de la couverture," in Louis Brandin, ed., *Lais et Fabliaux du Treizième siècle.* [Poèmes et récits de la vieille France, tome XV] © 1932 Boccard. **pp. 100–101:** Excerpt from *Astérix le Gaulois* © 1961 Éditions Albert René/Goscinny–Uderzo. **p. 110:** source: *Journal Français d'Amérique*, May 3, 1993. **p. 111:** source: *Journal Français d'Amérique*, May 26 1992. **p. 123:** Jacques Prévert, "Soyez polis," from *Histoires* © 1963 Gallimard. **p. 134:** Sempé/Goscinny, "King" in *Les Aventures de Petit Nicolas* © 1966 Macmillan/Glencoe Publishing. **pp. 142–145:** *Cyrano de Bergerac*, © 1989. **p. 146:** La Fontaine, "Le corbeau et le renard," from *Fables Choisies*, Livre I. **p. 170:** "Une histoire de cheveux" adapted from "Une bonne coupe," by Christian Grenier, in Michel Barbier, ed., *Onze Nouvelles Inédites*. © Hachette. **p. 183:** Lyrics to "Mon pays" by Gilles Vigneault © Musicor. **p. 256:** Paul Éluard, "Liberté," from *Oeuvres complètes* © 1968 Gallimard: Bibliothèque de la Pléiade. Illustrations by Fernand Léger © 1953 Éditions Senghers. **pp. 256–259:** *Au revoir, les enfants* © 1986. **p. 282:** Guy de Maupassant, "En voyage," *Le Gaulois*, May 10 1883. **p. 297:** source: *INSEE* 1999. **p. 301:** Lyrics to "Éthiopie" © 1985 EMI Records. **p. 326:** "Les pêches," by André Theuriet and adapted by D. C. Heath. **p. 336:** source: Interview with Aimé Césaire in *Les écrivains noirs de langue française: naissance d'une littérature*, Lilyan Kesteloot © 1964 Université de Bruxelles. **p. 337:** "Pour saluer le tiers-monde," from *Ferrements*, Aimé Cesaire © 1960 Éditions Le Seuil. **p. 339:** René Depestre, "Pour Haïti," from *Journal d'un animal marin*, © 1964 Éditions Senghers. **pp. 342–343:** *Rue Cases-nègres*, © 1983. **p. 345:** source: *Francoscopie*, 1993. **p. 359:** source: *Francoscopie*, 1993. **p. 366:** Michelle Maurois, "Le bracelet," *Contes de Michelle Maurois*, © 1966 Meiden, Boston: Houghton Mifflin. **p. 377:** Blaise Cendrars, "La gélinotte et la tortue," from *Anthologie nègre*, © 1921 Éditions la Sirène. **p. 378:** David Diop, "Afrique," from *Coups de Pilon* © 1964 Éditions Senghers. **pp. 380–381:** Bernard Dadié, "Légende baoulé," from *Légendes africaines* © 1966, 1973 Éditions Seghers. **p. 387:** source: *Francoscopie*, 1993. **p. 403:** Yves Thériault, "Le Portrait," *L'île introuvable* © 1968 Éditions du jour. **p. 415:** excerpt from LaFayette *In the Age of the American Revolution: Selected Letters and Papers, 1777–1790*, Volume 1 © 1977 Cornell University Press. **p. 419:** Lyrics to "Réveille" by Zachary Richard © 1976–1986 Les Éditions du Marais Bouleur.

Realia Credits

34 *tl & bl:* Courtesy of H&M, 2005; *br:* © Regis International Franchising Sarl 2005; **35** *l:* © MaxMara; *r:* CAUDALIE ®; **72** *l:* realia from *Astrapi* magazine July 1989; *r:* realia from *l'Ami des jardins* magazine April 1986; **109-110:** Ministère de l'environnement, France; **121:** environmental ad campaign from Monoprix stores June 1989; **123:** compilation of realia from *La Redoute*, spring summer 1990, and *Elle*, September 10, 1984; **127:** weather map from *Le Figaro* January 27, 1994; **159** *bkgd:* Le Ministère de Tourisme, Quebec; **161:** compilation of realia from Alain Zinzius, Jordi Coiffure, and Jean Louis David salons; **163:** France Telecom; **181:** Compilation of CD and tape jackets from Youssou N'Dour, The Lion, Virgin Records © 1989; Souskous Stars, Gozando, Stern's Records © 1993; Touré Kunda Dance of the Leaves (The Celluloid Recordings 1983-1987), Metrotone Records © 1993; Zap Mama Adventures in Afropea 1, Warner Bros. Records © 1993.; **190:** Mix of realia from Embassy of Switzerland, Washington, DC; Brittours; Air Canada; Swissair; International Travel Service Tunisia; **194:** Eurail, USA; **199:** Compilation of realia from Martinique Tourist Office/IGN Paris; British Airways; and Recta Folder Maps/Cartographia; **203:** Greater Quebec Area Tourism and Convention Bureau; Quebec Minister of Tourism and International Relations; **228-229:** *Le Guide Michelin Rouge* 1992 by la Manufacture des pneumatiques Michelin/Michelin et compagnie, propriétaires-éditeurs; **233:** Syndicat d'Initiative d'Amboise; **241:** compilation of realia from French Office of Tourism and l'Hôtel Saint Germain; **264-266:** mix of realia from Ministère des Communications/Communication-Québec; France Telecom; Healthwest Consultants, May 1991; Heath and Welfare, Canada; Canadian Psychiatric Association; République Rwandaise/Ministère de la santé publique et des affaires sociales; Clinique de traitement de l'asthme; Weber Vitamins; Uniprix; Jean Coutou.; **268-269:** compilation of realia from Clinic Lac-Saint-Louis, Pointe-Claire Québec; Centre de Santé, Kirkland Québec; Clinique de traitement de l'asthme; KiloControl; **277:** compilation of realia from Médecins aux pieds nus, Médecins du monde, Médecins sans frontièrs; **279:** *Marie Claire*, number 394 June; **383:** Ministère de l'éducation

Photo Credits

Interior: All photos by Tom Craig, except:
1: © Owen Franken; **2** *t:* © Pixers/TIPS Images; *m:* © Robert Fried/ robertfriedphotography.com; *b:* © Ron Krisel/Getty Images; **3** *t:* © Jean Louis Batt/Getty Images; *m:* © David Young-Wolff/PhotoEdit, Inc.; **6:** © Bilderlounge/TIPS Images; **10:** Palmer/Brilliant/© D.C. Heath; **11** *t:* © D.C. Heath; *tl & bml:* © Owen Franken; *tml:* © Richard Lucas/The Image Works; *bl:* © D. Donne Bryant/DDB Stock; *tr:* Francois Perri/Cosmos/ Woodfin Camp & Associates; *tmr:* © Robert Fried/ robertfriedphotography.com; *bmr:* © Lee Snider Photo Images/The Image Works; *br:* © Zubin Shroff/Getty Images; **12:** © D.C. Heath; **19:** © Michel GAILLARD/REA/Redux; **20, 21:** © D.C. Heath; **24** *all:* © D.C. Heath; **25** *all:* © D.C. Heath; **26:** Yves Levy/© D.C. Heath; **32:** © Owen Franken; **33** *tl, tr, tmr, & br:* © Bridgeman-Giraudon/Art Resource, NY; *tml:* © Art Resource, NY; *bml:* © Erich Lessing/Art Resource, NY; *bmr:* © Bridgeman-Giraudon/Art Resource, NY © 2007 Estate of Pablo Picasso/Artists Rights Society (ARS), New York.; **35:** © Royalty-Free/CORBIS; **36** *l:* © Spencer Grant/PhotoEdit, Inc.; *m:* © Bob Torrez/Getty Images; *r:* © Simon Marcus/CORBIS; **37:** M. Heron/© D.C. Heath; **38** *all:* © D.C. Heath; **40** *t:* © Patrick ALLARD/REA/Redux; *b:* © Wesley Hitt/TIPS Images; **41** *t:* © Daniel Allan/Getty Images; *m:* © Zubin Shroff/Getty Images; *b:* Berthold Steinhilber/Peter Arnold, Inc.; **42** *t:* © Royalty Free/CORBIS; *b:* © Jean Bernard/TIPS Images; **46, 47:** © D.C. Heath; **48:** © Jutta Klee/CORBIS; **49:** © Royalty Free/CORBIS; **51:** © AB/Photonica/Getty Images; **52:** © Tom Stewart/CORBIS; **53:** M. Heron/© D.C. Heath; **56:** © Eva Rudling/Sipa Press; **60:** © Réunion des Musées Nationaux/Art Resource, NY; **61** *tl & bl:* © Réunion des Musées Nationaux/Art Resource, NY; *tr:* Pierre-Auguste Renoir, French, 1841-1919. *Dance at Bougival*, 1883. Oil on Canvas. 181.9 x 98.1 cm (71-5/8 x 38-5/8 in.) Museum of Fine Arts, Boston. Picture Fund. 37.375; *br:* Berthe Morisot. French (1841-1895). *La Lecture (Reading)*, 1888. Oil on canvas. 29-1/4 x 36-1/2 in. Museum of Fine Arts, St. Petersburg, FL. Museum purchase in memory of Margaret Acheson Stuart 1981.2; **62** *tr:* © Réunion des Musées Nationaux/Art Resource, NY; *l:* Claude Monet, French, 1840–1926, Arrival of the Normandy Train, Gare Saint-Lazare, 1877, oil on canvas, 59.6 x 80.2 cm, Mr. and Mrs. Martin A. Ryerson Collection, 1933.1158. Reproduction, The Art Institute of Chicago.; *mr:* Musée Marmottan, Paris, France, Giraudon/Bridgeman Art Library; *br:* 1963.10.179.(1843)/PA. Monet, Claude. *Rouen Cathedral, West Façade, Sunlight*, Chester Dale Collection. Image © 2006 Board of Trustees, National Gallery of Art, Washington.; **63** *tr:* Monet Painting in His Garden at Argenteuil, 1873. Pierre-Auguste Renoir, French, 1841–1919. Oil on canvas; 1957.614. Wadsworth Atheneum Museum of Art, Hartford, CT. Bequest of Anne Parrish Titzell; *br:* © Joseph De Casseres/Photo Researchers, Inc.; *mr:* Claude Monet, 1840-1926. Waterlilies and Japanese Bridge. Oil on canvas; 90.5 x 89.7 c. Princeton University Art Museum. From the Collection of William Church Osborn, Class of 1883, Trustee of Princeton University (1914–1951), President of the Metropolitan Museum of Art (1941–1947); given by his Family. Photo Credit Bruce M. White. Y1972–15; *bl:* © Farrell Grehan/Photo Researchers, Inc. **64** *tl & bl:* Digital Image © The Museum of Modern Art/Licensed by SCALA, Art Resource, NY; *mr:* ©Erich Lessing/Art Resource, NY; **65** *tl:* © Private Collection, The Stapleton Collection/Bridgeman Art Library; *mr:* La desserte rouge: © 2007 Succession H. Matisse, Paris/Artists Rights Society (ARS), New York. Photo: © Bridgeman-Giraudon/Art Resource, NY; *ml:* Icarus: © Succession H. Matisse, Paris/Artists Rights Society (ARS), New York. Photo: © Archives Matisse, Paris; **66** *tr:* © 2007 C. Herscovici, Brussels/ARS, New York © Bridgeman-Giraudon/Art Resource, NY; *m:* Copyright Duane Michals. Courtesy Pace/MacGill Gallery, New York; *br:* 1985.64.24.PA. Magritte, René, *The Blank Signature*. Collection of Mr. and Mrs. Paul Mellon. Image © 2006 Board of Trustees, National Gallery of Art, Washington. National Gallery of Art Washington. © ARSNY; **67:** © Martinie/Roger-Viollet; **68:** © Lipnitzki/Roger-Viollet; **69** *tl:* © D.C. Heath; *tr & bl:* © D.C. Heath/© 2007 Artists Rights Society (ARS), New York/ADAGP, Paris; *br:* © Ted Russell/Polaris Images. © 2007 Artists Rights Society (ARS), New York/ADAGP, Paris; **70, 71:** © D.C. Heath; **73** *all:* D.C. Heath; **74:** M. Heron/© D.C. Heath; **77:** © Harold V. Green/Valan Photos; **82** *t:* © Bill Aron/PhotoEdit, Inc.; *m:* © Reuters/CORBIS; *b:* © D.C. Heath; **83** *t:* Royalty Free/CORBIS; *b:* © Patrick ALLARD/REA/Redux; **85** *all:* © D.C. Heath; **99** *l:* © Mary Evans Picture Library/The Image Works; *tr:* © Bibliothèque Nationale, Paris/Bridgeman Art Library; *br:* © Bridgeman-Giraudon/Art Resource, NY; **103:** © Lebrecht Music and Arts Photo Library/Alamy; **104:** © Bridgeman-Giraudon/Art Resource, NY; **106:** © Lee Snider Photo Library/The Image Works; **108:** © D.C. Heath; **109** *all:* © Francis de Richmond/The Image Works; **110** *t:* © Jacques Witt/Sipa Press; *b:* © Ginies/Sipa Press; **111** *t:* © Ty Allison/Getty Images; *b:* © Alex Farnsworth/The Image Works; **113:** © Adrian Weinbrecht/Getty Images; **115:** M. Heron/© D.C. Heath; **119:** © D.C. Heath; **120** *t:* © Bebert/SIPA; *bl:* © Bettmann/CORBIS; *br:* © Jouanneau Thomas/CORBIS Sygma; **122** *t:* © Julian Nieman/Digital Vision/Getty Images; *m:* © Nicholas Parfitt/Getty Images; **124:** © Owen Franken; **125:** M. Heron/© D.C. Heath; **127** *l:* © Michael A. Keller/zefa/CORBIS; *r:* © CWA-Dann Tardif/zefa/CORBIS; **133:** © Bettmann/CORBIS; **140** *tl:* © D.C. Heath; *tr:* © MedioImages/Getty Images; **141** *tl:* © Réunion des Musées Nationaux/Art Resource, NY; *tr:* © Bridgeman-Giraudon/Art Resource, NY; *mr & bl:* © D.C. Heath; *br:* © Laurie Platt Winfrey, Inc.; **143** *all:* © B. Barbier/CORBIS Sygma; **145** *all:* © B. Barbier/CORBIS Sygma; **147** *tl & tr:* © MedioImages/Getty Images; *tml, bml, bmr, & bl:* © Less Snider Photo Images/The Image Works; *tmr:* © Gavin Hellier/Robert Harding/Getty Images; *br:* © Owen Franken; **148:** © D.C. Heath; **151** *all:* © D.C. Heath; **152** *t:* © Owen Franken; *b:* © Tatiana Markow/CORBIS Sygma; **154:** © D.C. Heath; **155** *t:* © D.C. Heath; *b:* © David Young-Wolff/PhotoEdit, Inc.; **158:** © Tim Hall/Photodisc/Getty Images; **159** *tl & ml:* © D.C. Heath; *r:* © Ross M. Horowitz/Getty Images; **160:** © D.C. Heath; **161:** © Photodisc; **166** *t:* © Mel Curtis/Photodisc/Getty Images; *m:* © Owen Franken; *b:* Science & Society Picture Library/The Image Works; **167:** D.C. Heath; **169** *tl, tm, & br:* © D.C. Heath; *tr, bl, & br:* M. Heron/© D.C. Heath; **176** *br:* © 2007 Estate of Pablo Picasso/Artists Rights Society (ARS), New York © Bridgeman-Giraudon/Art Resource, NY; *bl:* © Musée de la Ville de Paris, Musée Carnavalet, Paris, France, Archives Charmet / Bridgeman Art Library; **177** *tl:* © Jean Guichard/SYGMA/CORBIS; *tml:* © James Andanson/Sygma/Corbis; *tmr:* © P. Varney/SYGMA/CORBIS; *tr:* © CP/ABACA/Jean-Pierre AMET; *b:* © CP/Everett; **178** *t:* © Photos12.com-Enguerand; *b:* © Bettmann/CORBIS; **179** *tl:* © Hulton Archive/Getty Images; *tr:* © Eric Fougere/VIP Images/Corbis; *bl:* © D.C. Heath; *mr:* © FOURGERE ERIC/CORBIS/SYGMA; *br:* © BEMBARON JEREMY/CORBIS SYGMA; **180** *l:* © CP/ABACA/Giancarlo Gorassini; *r:* Courtesy of Martinique Development and Promotion Bureau; **181** *t:* © ROBERT ERIC/CORBIS SYGMA; *b:* © Youri Lenquette; **182** *t:* © CP/INF/Dara Kushner; *m:* © D. Donne Bryant/DDB Stock; *b:*

© Kindra Clineff/Index Stock; **183:** © CP/Paul Chiasson; **184** *t:* © Laurie Platt Winfrey, Inc.; *b:* © Photos12.com-Oasis; **185** *b:* © Collection Roger-Viollet © 2007 Artists Rights Society (ARS), New York/ADAGP, Paris; **186:** © Yann Guichaoua/TIPS Images; **187:** © Robert Fried/robertfriedphotography.com; **189:** © Owen Franken; **191** *t:* © D.C. Heath; *b:* John Henebry/© D.C. Heath; **194:** © Raymond Stott/The Image Works; **195** *all:* © Nicolas Fievez/Sipa Press; **197** *m:* © PhotoDisc; *bl, bm, & br:* D.C. Heath; **198** *mr:* M. Heron/© D.C. Heath; *ml, bml, bl, & br:* © D.C. Heath; **200:** M. Heron/© D.C. Heath; **203** *all:* © D.C. Heath; **217** *tr & bl:* © Bridgeman-Giraudon/Art Resource, NY; *ml:* © SCALA/Art Resource, NY; **218:** © Bibliothèque Nationale, Paris, France, Archives Charmet/Bridgeman Art Library; **219** *tl:* © Photos12.com-ARJ; *tr:* © Owen Franken; *m:* © Lee Snider Photo Images/The Image Works; *bl:* © Collection Roger-Viollet; *br:* © SCALA/Art Resource, NY; **220:** John Henebry/© D.C. Heath; **221** *tm & tr:* © D.C. Heath; *mm:* © Nathan Benn/CORBIS; *ml:* © Owen Franken; *b:* © Louvre, Paris, France, / Bridgeman Art Library; **223** *t:* © British Library, London, UK / Bridgeman Art Library; *b:* © Collection Roger-Viollet; **224:** © Bridgeman-Giraudon/Art Resource, NY; **225:** © Erich Lessing/Art Resource; **226:** © John-Francis Bourke/zefa/CORBIS; **227** *tl:* © Rubberball/Getty Images; *tr & bl:* © D.C. Heath; *bm:* © Raymond Stott/The Image Works; **228:** © D.C. Heath; **230, 232:** © Owen Franken; **233, 234:** © D.C. Heath; **240:** © Owen Franken; **241:** © D.C. Heath; **245:** © RoyaltyFree/CORBIS; **252** *t:* ©Bridgeman-Giraudon/Art Resource, NY; *m:* © ND / Roger-Viollet; *b:* John Henebry/© D.C. Heath; **253** *t:* © Collection Roger-Viollet; *m:* © Hulton Archive/Getty Images; *b:* © M. Pelletier/Sygma/CORBIS; **254** *l:* © Bettmann/Corbis; *r:* © Photos12.com-Hachede; **255** *t:* © Bettmann/CORBIS; *m:* © Collection Roger-Viollet; *b:* © Roger-Viollet; **256** *tl:* © Martinie/Roger-Viollet; *tr:* © Musée d'Art ed d'Histoire, Saint-Denis, France, Archives Charmet / Bridgeman Art Library © 2007 Artists Rights Society (ARS), New York/ADAGP, Paris; *b:* © Jeanne Louise Bulliard/Sygma/CORBIS; **257:** © Laura Platt Winfrey, Inc. ©2007 Artists Rights Society (ARS), New York/ADAGP, Paris; **258** *tr:* © Fabian/Sygma/CORBIS; *bl, bm, & br:* © Jeanne Louise Bulliard/Sygma/CORBIS; **259** *all:* © Jeanne Louise Bulliard/Sygma/CORBIS; **260:** © D.C. Heath; **261** *t:* © Jose Peleaz/CORBIS; *b:* © Tom Stewart/CORBIS; **262** *all:* © D.C. Heath; **264:** © D.C. Heath; **265:** Royalty-Free/CORBIS; **267:** © Freitag/zefa/CORBIS; **269:** © Digital Vision/Getty Images; **276** *tr:* © Alois Hug/MSF; *tl:* © Stefan Pleger/MSF; *b:* © Nicolas/Sipa Press; **278:** © D.C. Heath; **279** *t:* © D.C. Heath; *b:* © Patrick Allard/REA/Redux; **281:** A. Sagalyn/© D.C. Heath; **282:** © Hulton Archive/Getty Images; **293** *tl, tr, & bl:* © D.C. Heath; *tml:* © Owen Franken; *bml:* P. Pipard © D.C. Heath; **294** *t:* © J. Cuinières/Roger-Viollet; *b:* © PELLETIER Micheline/CORBIS Sygma; **295** *t:* © Frédéric de Lafosse/Corbis; *m & b:* D.C. Heath; **296, 298:** © D.C. Heath; **299:** ©Mark Antman/The Image Works; **300** *t:* © LANGEVIN/CORBIS Sygma; *b:* © Reuters/CORBIS; **302:** © D.C. Heath; **303:** © Collection Roger-Viollet; **305, 306:** © Owen Franken; **307:** © Robert Fried/robertfriedphotography.com; **310** *tl, ml, & mr:* © Lee Snider Photo Images/The Image Works; *tr:* © Owen Franken; *bl:* © D.C. Heath; **311** *tl:* © David Sailors; *tr:* © Lee Snider Photo Images/The Image Works; *b:* © D.C. Heath; **312:** © D.C. Heath; **313:** Yves Levy/© D.C. Heath; **314** *all:* © D.C. Heath; **319:** © Daniel Joubert/REA/Redux; **321:** © Karen Preuss/The Image Works; **336** *tr:* © ND / Roger-Viollet; *bl:* © Sergio Gaudenti/Kipa/Corbis; **338:** © Hulton Archive/Getty Images; **339** *bkgd:* © Kay Shaw; **340** *l:* Courtesy of Selden Rodman. Owned by L. Clayton Willis, Palm Beach, FL; *r:* Courtesy of Selden Rodman; **341** *tl& br:* Courtesy of Selden Rodman; *tr:* Courtesy of Selden Rodman. Owned by Reynald Lally, Haiti; *bl:* Courtesy of Selden Rodman; Owned by Patricia & Maurice Thompson, Wilton, CT; **342:** © GIRAUD PHILIPPE/CORBIS Sygma; **343** *t:* © Francois Lehr/Sipa Press; *tl, tr, ml, mr, bl, & br:* © Photofest; **344:** © Larry Luxner/larry@luxner.com; **345** *all:* © D.C. Heath; **347** *all:* D.C. Heath; **348:** © D.C. Heath; **350:** © David De Lossy/Getty Images; **354** *t:* © Robert Fried/robertfriedphotography.com; *b:* © StockByte; **356:** © Royalty-Free/CORBIS; **358** *all:* Owen Franken/ © D.C. Heath; **359:** Owen Franken/ © D.C. Heath; **360:** © Julio Donoso/ CONTACT/Woodfin Camp & Associates; **361:** © Jean Bruneau/Valan Photos; **363:** © Bridgeman-Giraudon/Art Resource, NY; **364** *tl:* © Romilly Lockyer/Getty Images; *tr:* M. Heron/ © D.C. Heath; *bl:* © Jason Homa/Getty Images; *br:* © Owen Franken; **372** *t:* © Kazuyoshi Nomachi/Corbis; *b:* The Granger Collection; **373:** The Metropolitan Museum of Art, The Michael C. Rockefeller Memorial Collection, Gift of Nelson A. Rockefeller, 1965 (1978.412.309). Photograph © 1983 The Metropolitan Museum of Art; **375** *t:* © Sandro Vannini/CORBIS; *bl:* © Mary Jelliffe / ArkReligion.com; *br:* Nik Wheeler; **376** *t:* © Nic l'Anson/Eye Ubiquitous/Hutchison Pictures; *b:* © Margaret Courtney-Clarke/CORBIS; **377:** © Bettmann/CORBIS; **378** *t:* Courtesy of Presence Africaine; *b:* © Liba Taylor/Eye Ubiquitous/Hutchison; **379** *l:* © Bridgeman-Giraudon/Art Resource, NY; *ml:* 1963.10.241.(A-1710)/SC/ Modigliani, Amedeo. *Head of a Woman.* Chester Dale Collection. Image © 2006 Board of Trustees, National Gallery of Art, Washington. National Gallery of Art Washington; *mr:* © Bridgeman-Giraudon/Art Resource, NY; *r:* © 2007 Estate of Pablo Picasso/Artists Rights Society (ARS), New York. Reunion des Musees Nationaux/Art Resource, NY; **382:** © Royalty-Free/CORBIS; **383, 384:** © D.C. Heath; **385** *t:* © D.C. Heath; *b:* © Jacques Witt/Sipa Press; **386:** © Robert Holmes/CORBIS; **392:** © Sean Justice/Getty Images; **393:** © D.C. Heath; **394:** © Chabruken/Getty Images; **396:** © Owen Franken; **397** *t:* © Patrick Allard/REA/Redux; *b:* © David Young-Wolff/PhotoEdit, Inc.; **400:** © Lee Snider Photo Images/ The Image Works; **402:** CP/La Presse; **410** *t:* © A.J. Sisco/Corbis; *tr:* © Richard Pasley; *tl:* © 2006 Kevin Harkins; **411:** National Archives of Canada/Valan Photos; **412:** © Bettmann/CORBIS; **413** *tl & tm:* © Bettmann/CORBIS; *b:* © The Granger Collection; **414:** © Bridgeman-Giraudon/Art Resource, NY; **416** *all:* © Bettmann/CORBIS; **418** *l:* © Bettmann/CORBIS; *r:* © Kindra Clineff/Index Stock; **419:** © Les Riess; **420:** © Kennon Cooke/Valan Photos; **PA10:** © Boyer/Roger-Viollet; **R2:** © D.C. Heath; **R6** *all:* © D.C. Heath; **R7** *all:* D.C. Heath; **R12:** © D.C. Heath

Illustration Credits

Francis Back: 102–103, 140–141, 183, 326–332, 410, 411, 412, 419

Pierre Ballouhey: 36, 37*t*, 80, 125, 126, 140, 141, 165, 167, 325

Jean-Louis Besson: 54, 57–59, 91*t*, 129, 130, 273, 303, 317

Dave Clegg: 18*t*, 187, 192, 201

Véronique Deiss: 47, 67, 132, 149, 150, 243, 316, 322, 350*c,b*, R3

Chris Demarest: 135*t*, 136

Patrick Deubelbeiss: 27–30, 93–96, 105*b*, 216, 217

Philippe Dumas: 68, 366–370

Jacques Ferrandez: 209–215

Caroline Finadri: 42*b*, 43, 91*b*, 119, 126, 152, 154, 160, 263, 264*bl*, 270, 275, 278, 304, 318, 320–321, 359, 401, R11, R13

Michel Garneau: 5, 6, 9, 12, 13, 16–17, 22, 23, 37*c*, 38, 44, 50, 53, 71, 72, 76, 78, 81, 117, 162, 168, 188, 197, 198*t*, 205, 228*b*, 234, 236, 238–239, 244, 267, 272, 274, 346, 349, 350*t*, 351, 355, R4, R5, R9

Paul Giambarba: 15

Laurie Gilburne: 228*c*

Marsha Goldberg: 387

Tama Hochbaum: 337

Carol Inouye: 176, 335

Louise-Andrée Laliberte: 378, 380–381

Diana Maloney: 315

Mapping Specialists, Ltd.: R34, R36–R37

Winslow Pinney Pels: 402–408

Mike Reagan: 92, 104*t*, 105t, 220, 222, 282, 292, 297, 334, 373, 374*b*, 412, 417

John Rumery: 14, 195, 262

Lauren Scheuer: 170–174

Élisabeth Schlossberg: R12

Dave Shepherd: 18*b*, 42*t*, 90, 104*c*, 198*br*, 218, 219, 232*t*, 254, 335*t*, 361*b*, 392–393, 395, 420

Lorraine Silvestri: 283–290

Anna Vojtech: 98, 146, 374*t*, 377

Laura Wallace: 77

Fabrice Weiss: 106–107, 224–225, 247–250

Yayo: 34, 164, 352, 388, 390